写给癌症病人的饮食指导书

改变『癌状态』从『吃』开始

《养生堂》《健康之路》

《生活大调查》《聚健康》等栏目主讲专家

『状态疗法』创始人

李忠教授谈：

著

阶段

作者简介

李忠，著名中医肿瘤临床专家，北京中医药大学东直门医院肿瘤血液科主任医师、教授、博士研究生导师，北京中医药大学首批临床肿瘤学博士。

现任世界中医药学会联合会肿瘤外治法专业委员会常务副会长兼秘书长，中华中医药学会中青年科技创新专家委员会委员，中国医疗保健国际交流促进会保健养生专业委员会副主任委员，北京中医疑难病研究会副会长，北京中西医结合学会肿瘤专业委员会委员，北京抗癌学会中西医结合专业委员会委员，北京中医药学会肿瘤专业委员会委员，国家自然科学基金委员会函审专家，北京市食品药品监督管理局新制剂评审专家。

长期从事中医药及中西医结合治疗恶性肿瘤的临床、科研和教学工作，熟悉肿瘤中西医研究的最新动态，在采用中医药和中西医结合疗法治疗恶性肿瘤方面积累了丰富的临床经验。尤其擅长中医药治疗肺癌、肝癌、胃癌、肠癌、乳腺癌、淋巴瘤、脑瘤、白血病等多种恶性肿瘤，并在肿瘤术后预防复发、转移和癌性疼痛的治疗及肿瘤放、化疗中药增敏解毒方面有较为深入的研究。

在临床大胆实践的同时，不断汲取现代肿瘤研究成果，根据肿瘤细胞的特性及中医用药特点，首次提出了“癌”的状态论。认为“癌”是一种人与自然、人体内部五脏六腑之间失衡的状态。并根据“癌状态”论，首次提出了改变“癌状态”的“状态疗法”，该疗法突破了传统中医治癌理论的束缚，开创了中医抗癌的新理念。根据此理论，研制出系列抗癌中药内服外用配方，如芪甲扶正胶囊、三黄散结胶囊、镇痛贴、体若康胶囊等，临床取得了较好的疗效。

先后主编和参编中医肿瘤专著及其他医学专著20余部，发表学术论文60余篇。代表著作《临床中医肿瘤学》《专科专病名医诊治经验——肿瘤》《现代中医肿瘤诊疗手册》《癌，是一种状态》《李忠肿瘤验案精选》等，主持及参与多项国家部局级、大学校级科研课题的研究，并先后负责5项国家中药三类新药的临床设计与开发研究。

2018年4月17日，水利部部长鄂竟平（前排左二）在湖北武汉东湖港检查指导长江流域防汛抗旱工作（鲁梦　摄）

2018年9月6日，国务院国资委党委书记郝鹏在中国电力建设集团有限公司董事长晏志勇的陪同下参观中国电建水电七局的建设项目（曾艾林　摄）

2018年8月9日，云南省委书记陈豪到华能澜沧江水电股份有限公司小湾水电厂调研

2018年7月19日，海南省委副书记、省长沈晓明前往南方电网调峰调频发电有限公司文昌项目现场考察调研（张柳琦　摄）

2018年1月12日，由中国水力发电工程学会与国家电网公司联合主办的“2018中国水电发展论坛暨水力发电科学技术奖颁奖典礼”在北京举行，来自全国水力发电战线80多个单位的300余名新老水电工作者代表以及来自有关水电国际组织的专家出席了会议。会议对2017年评选出的45项“水力发电科学技术奖”进行了颁奖

2018年9月26日，由中国水力发电工程学会和水电水利规划设计总院联合主办的“改革开放40年中国水电纪念大会”在北京隆重召开。汪恕诚、陆佑楣、周大兵、矫勇等老领导、老专家，陈厚群、张楚汉、马洪琪、张建民等院士，以及来自政府有关部门、水电企事业单位、高校科研机构和有关行业社团组织的领导、专家和水电工作者代表230余人参加了大会

2018年11月，大渡河大岗山水电站荣获“国家优质工程金质奖”

2018年11月，江西洪屏抽水蓄能电站荣获“国家优质工程金质奖”

2018年6月3日，雅砻江锦屏一级水电站荣获“詹天佑奖”。同年9月10日，在德国柏林召开的国际咨询工程师联合会2018年年会上，锦屏一级水电站荣获“菲迪克2018年工程项目杰出成就奖”

2018年6月3日，云南糯扎渡水电站荣获“詹天佑奖”

2018年12月27日，江西省峡江水利枢纽工程荣获中国水利工程协会“2017~2018年度中国水利工程优质（大禹）奖”

2018年12月27日，右江百色水利枢纽工程荣获中国水利工程协会“2017~2018年度中国水利工程优质（大禹）奖”

2018年11月30日，金沙江白鹤滩水电站右岸大坝标段主体混凝土当月完成浇筑16.15万m^3（柴俊锋　摄）

世界最大地下厂房——白鹤滩水电站左岸地下厂房正在施工

2018年10月4日，金沙江乌东德水电站大坝上游面施工形象（许健　摄）

2018年10月30日，国内首个百万千瓦级EPC项目——杨房沟水电站大坝首仓混凝土浇筑

2018年3月，世界第一高坝——双江口水电站大坝基坑正在施工

2018年12月12日，丰满水电站旧坝拆除工程成功实施首次爆破，拆除工程进展顺利，新坝建设高质量推进

2018年6月1日，苗尾水电站4号机组72小时试运行顺利结束，4台机组全部投入生产运行

2018年6月9日，大华桥水电站首台机组投产发电（陈锐　摄）

2018年7月5日，黄登水电站首台机组投产发电（陈锐　摄）

2018年10月29日，里底水电站首台机组投产发电

2018年12月，大渡河猴子岩水电站完成枢纽工程竣工安全鉴定

2018年8月31日，大渡河沙坪二级水电站6号机组一次性并网发电成功，标志着沙坪二级水电站全部6台机组正式并网发电

2018年12月27日，南方电网调峰调频发电有限公司鲁布革电厂投产30周年（侯海琳　摄）

2018年6月15日，南方电网调峰调频发电有限公司天生桥二级水力发电有限公司成立30周年（骆允　摄）

龚嘴水电站大坝全景

吉牛水电站库区全貌

沙沱水电站雪景（赵梅　摄）

深溪沟水电站大坝

铜街子水电站大坝

枕头坝一级水电站

2018年6月15日，世界最大抽水蓄能电站——河北丰宁抽水蓄能电站机电安装工程正式开工

2018年7月6日，安徽最大抽水蓄能电站——绩溪抽水蓄能电站下水库下闸蓄水（李建龙　摄）

2018年7月30日，海南首个抽水蓄能电站——琼中抽水蓄能电站全面投产发电（张柳琦　摄）

2018年9月26日，国内首个城市内大型抽水蓄能电站——深圳抽水蓄能电站全面投产（肖茜　摄）

2018年6月17日，中国电力建设集团有限公司承建的亚洲第一长坝、柬埔寨最大的水电工程——桑河二级水电站5号机组顺利完成72小时试运行，正式投产发电（江先辉　摄）

2018年12月17日，柬埔寨首相洪森视察桑河二级水电站中控室

2018年9月10日，中国南方电网有限责任公司首个海外BOT投资项目——老挝南塔河1号水电站首台机组正式投产（刘福钦　摄）

2018年10月22日，中国企业安装的巴基斯坦塔贝拉4期水电站最后一台（15号）机组，完成全部有水调试并顺利移交业主，进入商业运行（黄海宁　摄）

2018年10月29日，中国企业承建的几内亚苏阿皮蒂水利枢纽工程10月份混凝土浇筑突破20万m^3（张虎林　摄）

2018年9月3日，中国企业承建的刚果（金）布桑加水电站大江截流成功（王冬阳　摄）

2018年12月31日5时18分，由黄河上游水电开发有限责任公司负责建设的国内最大单体85万kW莫合风电场成功并网，那仁10万kW风电场也同时并网，合计投产容量达到95万kW，这是世界上一次性并网容量最大的风电项目（李龙　摄）

2018年6月29日，中国电建贵州工程公司EPC总承包建设的首个水上渔光互补光伏项目——广东湛江鼎瑞渔光一体100MW光伏发电项目成功并网（黎光军　摄）

全国 2018 年装机容量和年发电量

项目	总量	水电	火电	核电	风电	太阳能发电
装机容量（万 kW）	190012	35259	114408	4466	18427	17433
年发电量（亿 kW·h）	69947	12321	49249	2950	3658	1769

注 1. 资料来源于中国电力企业联合会。
2. 总量数中还包括其他能源发电的装机容量、发电量。
3. 风电、太阳能发电为并网的装机容量、发电量。
4. 未含中国台湾、香港、澳门数据。

2018 年装机容量结构图

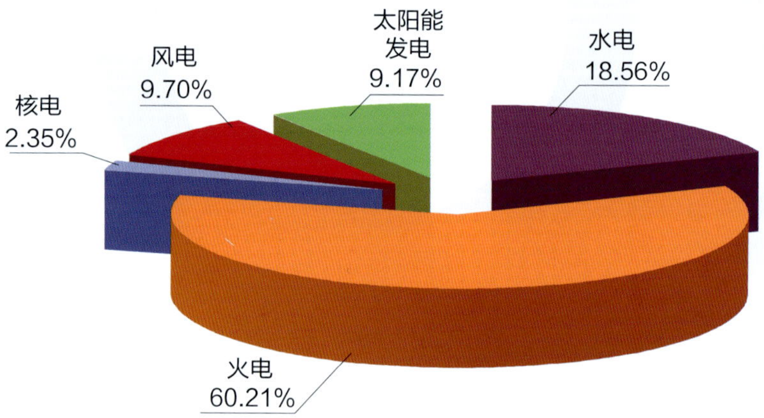

2018 年年发电量结构图

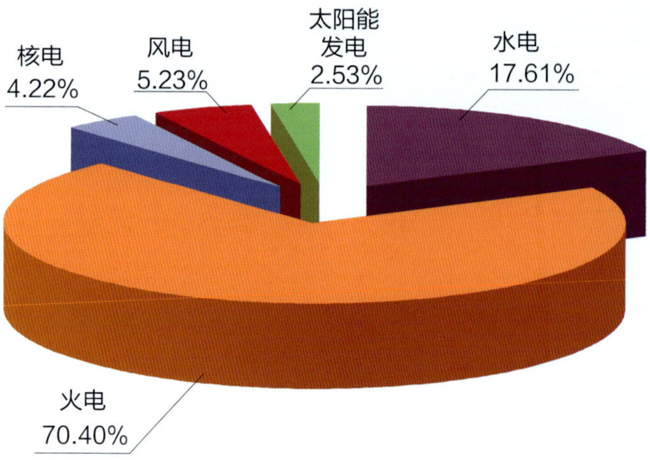

全国历年水电装机容量增长情况表

万 kW

年份	中国大陆	中国台湾	全国合计	新增装机容量	年份	中国大陆	中国台湾	全国合计	新增装机容量
1949	36.0	18.0	54		1984	2560.0	148.0	2708	148.4
1950	36.2	22.1	58	4.3	1985	2641.5	248.9	2890	182.4
1951	37.8	(24.0)	(62)	(3.5)	1986	2754.2	256.4	3011	120.2
1952	38.5	(27.0)	(66)	(3.7)	1987	3019.3	255.8	3275	264.5
1953	53.0	(30.0)	(83)	(17.5)	1988	3269.8	255.8	3526	250.5
1954	60.6	33.0	94	10.6	1989	3458.3	256.2	3715	188.9
1955	69.5	(34.0)	(104)	(9.9)	1990	3604.6	256.2	3861	146.3
1956	91.4	(36.0)	(127)	(23.9)	1991	3788.3	256.2	4045	183.7
1957	101.9	(38.0)	(140)	(12.5)	1992	4068.1	257.7	4326	281.3
1958	121.6	(40.0)	(162)	(21.7)	1993	4489.3	257.7	4747	421.2
1959	162.0	(42.0)	(204)	(42.4)	1994	4906.1	364.8	5271	523.9
1960	194.1	44.8	239	34.9	1995	5218.4	418.3	5637	365.8
1961	233.3	(47.0)	(280)	(41.4)	1996	5557.8	428.8	5987	349.9
1962	237.9	53.8	292	11.4	1997	5972.6	428.8	6401	414.8
1963	243.0	(56.0)	(299)	(7.3)	1998	6506.5	442.2	6949	547.3
1964	268.3	(59.0)	(327)	(28.3)	1999	7297.1	442.2	7739	790.6
1965	302.0	62.8	365	37.5	2000	7935.2	442.2	8377	638.1
1966	363.8	(65.0)	(429)	(64.0)	2001	8300.6	442.2	8743	365.4
1967	383.9	(67.0)	(451)	(22.1)	2002	8607.4	451.1	9059	315.7
1968	438.8	(70.0)	(509)	(57.9)	2003	9489.6	451.1	9941	882.2
1969	505.3	72.2	578	68.7	2004	10524.2	451.0	10975	1034.5
1970	623.5	90.1	714	136.1	2005	11738.8	451.0	12190	1214.6
1971	780.4	(96.0)	(876)	(162.8)	2006	13029.2	451.2	13480.4	1290.4
1972	870.0	113.1	983	106.7	2007	14823.2	452.0	15275.2	1794.6
1973	1029.9	113.2	1143	159.9	2008	17260.4	454.0	17714.4	2439.2
1974	1181.7	136.5	1318	175.2	2009	19629.0	(454.0)	20083.0	2368.6
1975	1342.8	136.5	1479	161.1	2010	21605.7	(454.0)	22059.7	1976.7
1976	1465.5	136.5	1602	122.7	2011	23298	464	23762	1702
1977	1576.5	136.5	1713	111.0	2012	24947	(464)	25411	1649
1978	1727.7	139.2	1867	153.9	2013	28044	(464)	28508	3097
1979	1911.0	139.2	2050	183.3	2014	30486	(464)	30950	2442
1980	2031.8	138.6	2170	120.2	2015	31954	(464)	32418	1468
1981	2193.3	138.7	2332	161.6	2016	33207	(464)	33671	1253
1982	2295.9	138.7	2435	102.6	2017	34359	(464)	34823	1152
1983	2416.5	143.1	2560	125.0	2018	35259	(464)	35723	900

资料来源：2017 年及以前的资料来源于《中国水力发电年鉴》第二十二卷；2018 年中国大陆资料来源于中国电力企业联合会；2018 年台湾地区数据沿用上年数据。

注：（ ）内数据表示缺当年资料，用上、下数据插补得出或沿用上年数据。

全国历年水电年发电量增长情况表

亿 kW · h

年份	中国大陆	中国台湾	全国合计	年增率(%)	年份	中国大陆	中国台湾	全国合计	年增率(%)
1949	12.0	6.0	18		1984	867.8	44.3	912	−0.2
1950	13.2	9.7	23	27.2	1985	923.7	69.3	993	8.9
1951	14.9	(10.0)	(25)	(8.7)	1986	944.8	74.2	1019	2.6
1952	18.3	(12.0)	(30)	(21.7)	1987	1002.3	71.2	1073	5.3
1953	25.5	(14.0)	(40)	(30.4)	1988	1091.8	61.5	1153	7.4
1954	32.0	15.6	48	20.5	1989	1184.5	66.8	1251	8.5
1955	34.0	(16.6)	(51)	(6.3)	1990	1263.5	81.9	1345	7.5
1956	47.1	(17.0)	(64)	(26.7)	1991	1248.4	55.1	1303	−3.1
1957	48.2	(18.0)	(66)	(3.3)	1992	1314.7	83.5	1398	7.3
1958	41.1	(19.0)	(60)	(−9.2)	1993	1516.0	67.2	1583	13.2
1959	43.6	(20.0)	(64)	(5.8)	1994	1667.9	88.9	1757	11.0
1960	74.1	20.6	95	48.9	1995	1867.7	88.8	1956	11.4
1961	74.1	(21.1)	(95)	(0.5)	1996	1869.2	90.4	1960	0.2
1962	90.4	21.6	112	17.6	1997	1945.6	95.7	2041	4.2
1963	86.9	(23.0)	(110)	(−1.9)	1998	2043.0	106.1	2149	5.3
1964	106.0	(24.0)	(130)	(18.3)	1999	2129.3	89.4	2219	3.2
1965	104.1	24.4	129	−1.2	2000	2431.3	78.5	2510	13.0
1966	126.2	(25.0)	(151)	(17.7)	2001	2611.1	82.3	2693	7.3
1967	131.4	(27.0)	(158)	(4.8)	2002	2745.7	57.9	2804	4.1
1968	115.0	(28.0)	(143)	(−9.7)	2003	2813.3	64.3	2878	2.6
1969	160.1	30.5	191	33.3	2004	3309.9	59.7	3370	17.1
1970	204.6	26.4	231	21.2	2005	3964.0	59.7	4024	19.4
1971	250.6	(30.0)	(281)	(21.5)	2006	4147.7	80.0	4227.7	5.1
1972	288.2	34.2	322	14.9	2007	4714.0	87.0	4801.0	13.6
1973	389.0	34.0	423	31.2	2008	5655.5	77.4	5732.9	19.4
1974	414.4	47.1	461	9.1	2009	5716.8	(77.4)	5794.2	1.1
1975	476.3	52.6	529	14.6	2010	6867.4	(77.4)	6944.8	19.9
1976	456.4	42.8	499	−5.6	2011	6681	(79)	6760	−2.7
1977	476.5	40.2	517	3.5	2012	8556	(79)	8635	27.7
1978	446.3	49.7	496	−4.0	2013	8921	(79)	9000	4.2
1979	501.2	45.7	547	10.3	2014	10601	(79)	10680	18.7
1980	582.1	29.3	611	11.8	2015	11127	(79)	11206	4.9
1981	655.5	47.9	703	15.1	2016	11748	(79)	11827	5.5
1982	744.0	47.8	792	12.6	2017	11931	(79)	12010	1.5
1983	863.6	49.9	913	15.4	2018	12321	(79)	12400	3.2

资料来源：2017 年及以前的资料来源于《中国水力发电年鉴》第二十二卷；2018 年中国大陆资料来源于中国电力企业联合会；2018 年台湾地区数据沿用上年数据。

注：（ ）内数据表示缺当年资料，用上、下数插补得出或沿用上年数据。

2018

中国水力发电年鉴

李鹏

第二十三卷

中国水力发电工程学会 主办
中国水力发电年鉴编辑部 编纂

中国电力出版社

二〇一九年·北京

图书在版编目（CIP）数据

中国水力发电年鉴．第二十三卷/中国水力发电工程学会主办．—北京：中国电力出版社，2019.12
ISBN 978-7-5198-4079-2

Ⅰ.①中…　Ⅱ.①中…　Ⅲ.①水利电力工业—中国—年鉴　Ⅳ.①F426.61-54

中国版本图书馆 CIP 数据核字（2019）第 282137 号

出版发行：中国电力出版社
地　　址：北京市东城区北京站西街 19 号（邮政编码 100005）
网　　址：http：//www.cepp.sgcc.com.cn
责任编辑：安小丹（010－63412367）　姜　萍　孙建英
责任校对：黄　蓓　常燕昆　朱丽芳
装帧设计：张俊霞　赵姗姗
责任印制：吴　迪

印　　刷：三河市万龙印装有限公司
版　　次：2019 年 12 月第一版
印　　次：2019 年 12 月北京第一次印刷
开　　本：787 毫米×1092 毫米　16 开本
印　　张：43.25　12 彩页
字　　数：1512 千字
定　　价：380.00 元

《中国水力发电年鉴》第二十三卷

编 纂 委 员 会

余圣刚	余卓憬	邹　君	张　芳	张敏娟
张喜英	陈天红	陈立秋	陈念水	邵增富
欧阳忠	周双超	周维娟	郑宗旺	赵英林
赵建达	姜　薇	娄　萱	祝培华	袁　帅
袁　蕊	柴晓玲	高　鹏	唐　兰	唐　勇
唐成书	唐奇志	曹　娅	曹园园	程　骏
程文辉	程志华	曾艾林	鲍玉征	甄学宝

《中国水力发电年鉴》第二十三卷

编辑出版工作人员

主　　　编　吴义航

副　主　编　程运生　陈东平

技术编辑　黄景湖　张志良　刘春宇　孙　卓

　　　　　　王立涛　殷利利　由　洋　宁传新

编　　　务　李　明　雷定演　胡丹蓉　徐海英

终　　　审　张运东

复　　　审　杨伟国

责任编辑　安小丹　孙建英　姜　萍

美术设计　张俊霞

版式设计　赵姗姗

责任校对　黄　蓓　常燕昆　朱丽芳

出版印刷　吴　迪

编 辑 说 明

（一）《中国水力发电年鉴》属专业性行业年鉴，主要面向全国水电行业从事规划、勘测、设计、施工、科研、咨询、建设管理、设备制造、生产运行、院校教育的工程技术人员、师生和各级有关领导与专家。

（二）本卷年鉴的资料时段为2018年，按序排列为第二十三卷。框架结构由篇目、栏目、条目三个层次组成，共编列17个篇目、51个栏目、483个条目。每个篇目均以隔页列出，栏目、条目名称分别用通栏、双栏并铺以不同的网底印出，以示醒目。

（三）本卷年鉴的编辑工作，在习近平新时代中国特色社会主义思想指引下，按照国家“积极发展水电，大力发展新能源”的方针，力求全面、真实地反映2018年度我国水电行业各方面所取得的成就和技术进步，努力做到“大事不漏、小事不上”，更好地服务于水电行业。

（四）本年鉴实行文责自负，各条目的内容、数据、插图等均由撰稿人核对无误并由单位有关部门审定、核实。

（五）本卷年鉴编辑实行主编负责制。主编负责总体框架结构设计、征询意见、组稿与初审等工作；各篇目的责任编辑负责稿件的征集、修改、编排、整理。

“工程勘测”篇目的责任编辑为刘春宇；“水工设计”“土建施工”篇目的责任编辑为张志良；“大中型水电工程”“机电及金属结构”“科学研究与技术创新”“水电站生产运行”“环境保护与水库移民”“机构与学术团体”篇目的责任编辑为黄景湖；“特载”“水能及新能源开发”“国际合作与技术交流”“技术标准与图书”“水电建设管理”“农村水电及电气化”“统计资料”“大事记”篇目的责任编辑为程运生。

（六）《中国水力发电年鉴》始终坚持政治的严肃性，资料的准确性，内容的全面性、科学性、实用性和连续性，对历史负责，对后人负责。编辑过程中力求资料翔实、语言规范、文字精练。但由于水平所限，不妥、疏漏甚至错误之处在所难免，敬请广大读者批评指正。

联系地址：北京市海淀区车公庄西路22号A座中国水力发电工程学会《中国水力发电年鉴》编辑部，邮编：100048。

《中国水力发电年鉴》主编

吴义航

2019.11

篇　　目

1. 特载
2. 水能及新能源开发
3. 大中型水电工程
4. 工程勘测
5. 水工设计
6. 土建施工
7. 机电及金属结构
8. 科学研究与技术创新
9. 国际合作与技术交流
10. 技术标准与图书
11. 水电建设管理
12. 水电站生产运行
13. 环境保护与水库移民
14. 农村水电及电气化
15. 机构与学术团体
16. 统计资料
17. 大事记

目　　录

编辑说明

1 特　　载

重要文件 …… 3

国务院关于修改和废止部分行政法规的决定 …… 3

国务院决定取消一批行政许可等事项 …… 3

国务院办公厅关于开展工程建设项目审批制度改革试点的通知 …… 4

国务院办公厅关于成立国家科技领导小组的通知 …… 7

中共中央办公厅、国务院办公厅印发《水利部职能配置、内设机构和人员编制规定》 …… 7

国家发展改革委发布《企业投资项目事中事后监管办法》 …… 9

国家发展改革委、国家能源局印发《关于加强和规范涉电力领域失信联合惩戒对象名单管理工作的实施意见》 …… 11

国家发展改革委、国家能源局关于提升电力系统调节能力的指导意见 …… 15

国家发展改革委关于降低一般工商业电价有关事项的通知 …… 18

国家发展改革委印发《必须招标的工程项目规定》 …… 18

国家发展改革委、工信部、财政部、人民银行等四部委联合发布《关于做好2018年降成本重点工作的通知》 …… 19

国家发展改革委关于电力行业增值税税率调整相应降低一般工商业电价的通知 …… 22

国家发展改革委印发《水电前期工作中央预算内投资专项管理办法》 …… 22

国家发展改革委、财政部、国家能源局关于2018年光伏发电有关事项的通知 …… 23

国家发展改革委决定废止两项电力规章 …… 24

国家发展改革委关于利用扩大跨省区电力交易规模等措施降低一般工商业电价有关事项的通知 …… 24

国家发展改革委关于修改《关于调整水电建设管理主要河流划分的通知》引用规范性文件的通知 …… 25

国家发展改革委关于降低一般工商业目录电价有关事项的通知 …… 25

国家发展改革委、财政部、国家能源局关于2018年光伏发电有关事项说明的通知 …… 25

国家发展改革委、国家能源局印发《清洁能源消纳行动计划（2018～2020年）》 …… 26

国家发展改革委印发《投资咨询评估管理办法》 …… 29

国家能源局印发《关于进一步加强电力建设工程质量监督管理工作意见》 …… 31

国家能源局关于印发2018年能源工作指导意见的通知 …… 33

国家能源局、国务院扶贫办印发《光伏扶贫电站管理办法》 …… 39

国家能源局关于减轻可再生能源领域企业负担有关事项的通知 …… 40

国家能源局印发《分散式风电项目开发建设暂行管理办法》 …… 42

国家能源局关于修改水电领域6件规范性文件的通知 …… 45

国家能源局发布《能源行业标准英文版翻译指南》 …… 46

国家能源局综合司关于进一步深入做好流域水电综合监测及水能利用监测工作的通知 …… 50

国家能源局综合司、国务院扶贫办综合司关于做好光伏扶贫电站验收评估工作的通知 …… 50

财政部《关于降低部分政府性基金征收标准的通知》 …… 51

水利部印发《水利建设质量工作考核办法》 …… 51

领导讲话 …… 52

水电要当生态文明建设生力军 …… 52

努力开创水电发展的新局面 ………………………… 54
改革开放　成就中国水电走向辉煌 ……………… 55
专家论坛 ……………………………………… 59
统筹优化　促进西南水电高质量发展 …………… 59
“水电妖魔化”严重制约着我国水安全保障能力提升 …………………………………… 61
水电：能源领域改革开放“先行者” ………… 65
水电在能源革命中的关键作用 ………………… 68
正确看待小水电与生态环境保护的辩证关系 …………………………………………… 71
央企工作 ……………………………………… 73
中国电力建设集团有限公司 2018 年改革发展情况 ………………………………………… 73
中国华电集团有限公司 2018 年工作情况 ………………………………………………… 75
中国三峡建设管理有限公司 2018 年经营发展情况 ………………………………… 76

2 水能及新能源开发

水能开发 ……………………………………… 81
浙江省抽水蓄能电站选点规划调整 …………… 81
安徽省抽水蓄能电站选点规划调整 …………… 82
贵州省抽水蓄能电站选点规划进展情况 ……… 83
西藏易贡藏布水电规划进展情况 ……………… 84
新能源开发 …………………………………… 85
青海省海南州特高压外送基地电源配置规划情况 ……………………………………… 85
三峡新能源庄河Ⅲ（300MW）海上风电场工程设计 ……………………………… 85
三峡新能源庄河Ⅲ（300MW）海上风电场关键技术及应用 ……………………… 87
中国水电顾问集团金塘风电厂 2018 年生产管理情况 ……………………………………… 87
高海拔山区风电场测风数据分析处理 ………… 88
高海拔山区风电场风电机组选型 ……………… 90
高海拔山区风电场电气设备选型研究分析 …… 91
高海拔山区风电场施工辅助工程技术指标研究 …………………………………………… 92
财务风险分析在 A 光伏发电企业财务管理中的应用 ……………………………………… 93
新能源高渗透率区域电网规划研究 …………… 95
2018 年国家电网清洁能源运行消纳情况 ……… 95
2018 年华北电网新能源消纳情况 ……………… 96
2018 年华东电网积极消纳清洁能源情况 ……… 97
2018 年西北电网积极消纳清洁能源情况 ……… 98
2018 年西南电网清洁能源运行消纳情况 …… 100
2018 年辽宁电网积极消纳清洁能源情况 …… 101
2018 年河南电网积极消纳清洁能源情况 …… 102
2018 年青海电网清洁能源消纳情况 ………… 103
青海共和 5 万 kW 光热电站工程 2018 年建设管理情况 ……………………………… 104
茨达、铁炉风电场工程建设情况 …………… 105

3 大中型水电工程

常规水电工程 ……………………………… 109
白鹤滩水电站工程 2018 年建设情况 ………… 109
乌东德水电站工程 2018 年建设情况 ………… 110
向家坝与溪洛渡水电站工程 2018 年建设情况 ………………………………………… 112
杨房沟水电站工程 2018 年建设进展情况 …… 113
两河口水电站工程建设情况 ………………… 114
大华桥水电站“一年四投”全部机组投产发电 ……………………………………… 115
金沙水电站工程 2018 年建设情况 ………… 116
拉哇水电站工程 2018 年建设进展情况 …… 116
苗尾水电站 4 台机组全部投产发电 ………… 117
双江口水电站工程建设情况 ………………… 118
木扎提河三级水电站工程建设进展情况 …… 119
苏洼龙水电站工程 2018 年建设进展情况 …… 119
象鼻岭水电站工程 2018 年建设情况 ………… 120
旭龙水电站工程 2018 年建设情况 ………… 120
巴塘水电站工程 2018 年建设进展情况 …… 121
高生水电站工程 2018 年建设情况 ………… 121
加查水电站工程建设情况 …………………… 122
旬阳水电站工程 2018 年建设进展情况 …… 123
杨家湾水电站工程 2018 年建设进展情况 …… 123

叶巴滩水电站工程 2018 年建设进展情况 …… 124
中国电建承建的重点常规水电工程 2018 年进展情况 …… 125
硬梁包水电站工程建设情况 …… 126
银江水电站工程 2018 年建设情况 …… 127
夏特水电站工程 2018 年建设进展情况 …… 127
中国华电集团有限公司 2018 年前期项目筹建情况 …… 128
国电大渡河流域水电开发有限公司 2018 年前期项目筹建情况 …… 128
猴子岩水电站工程通过枢纽竣工安全鉴定 …… 129
向家坝升船机投入试通航 …… 129
云南滇中引水工程 2018 年建设情况 …… 131
抽水蓄能工程 …… 132
中国电建承建的抽水蓄能工程 2018 年进展情况 …… 132
清原抽水蓄能电站工程 2018 年建设进展情况 …… 133
丰宁抽水蓄能电站工程 2018 年建设进展情况 …… 133
敦化抽水蓄能电站工程 2018 年建设进展情况 …… 134
周宁抽水蓄能电站工程 2018 年建设进展情况 …… 135
芝瑞抽水蓄能电站工程 2018 年设计进展情况 …… 135
永泰抽水蓄能电站工程 2018 年建设进展情况 …… 136
易县抽水蓄能电站工程 2018 年设计进展情况 …… 137
沂蒙抽水蓄能电站工程 2018 年建设进展情况 …… 137
文登抽水蓄能电站工程 2018 年建设进展情况 …… 138
南方电网调峰调频发电有限公司 2018 年电源建设情况 …… 139

4 工程勘测

工程地质勘察与评价 …… 143
灰色系统预测模型在锦屏一级水电站沉降观测中的应用 …… 143
赤平投影在边坡稳定性中的应用 …… 144
基于易损性理论边坡安全评价方法在三岔河水电站工程中的应用 …… 145
滇中引水工程昆呈隧洞岩溶水文地质问题研究 …… 146
工程地质问题处理 …… 147
糯扎渡水电站导流洞 F_3 断层带围岩稳定性分析及施工处理 …… 147
溧阳抽水蓄能电站下水库均质土坝淤泥质黏土基础处理研究 …… 148
蓄水后库岸堆积体边坡变形特征及稳定性分析 …… 149
象鼻岭水电站 BT2 堆积体治理设计 …… 150
苗尾水电站边坡倾倒变形机理与加固效果分析 …… 151
梨园水电站念生垦沟堆积体变形规律研究 …… 152
九龙峡水电站坝区温泉渗漏及工程处理 …… 154
红层高地应力区隧洞围岩流变特征及支护研究 …… 155
老挝南湃水电站泥质边坡处理 …… 156
勘测技术与设备 …… 157
工程岩石渗流力学关键技术及应用 …… 157
TRT 超前地质预报技术在 TBM 隧洞施工中的应用 …… 157
阵列式位移计在滑坡体深部变形监测中的应用 …… 159
提高无人机航测空三加密精度的方法研究 …… 160
光纤光栅仪器在牛栏江—滇池补水长隧洞工程监测中的应用 …… 161
埃及阿塔卡抽水蓄能电站软弱漏失地层超深孔钻探施工工艺 …… 162

5 水工设计

大坝设计 …… 167
三岔河水电站混凝土面板堆石坝设计 …… 167

明朗水库大坝塑性混凝土防渗墙设计………… 168
淋溪河水电站坝型比选研究………………… 169
向家坝水电站坝基混凝土防渗墙研究及应用…………………………………… 170
桑河二级水电站均质土坝强透水基础处理…… 170
桑河二级水电站土坝分区设计……………… 171
茨哈峡水电站工程枢纽区三维渗流分析……… 173
大桥水电站混凝土重力坝温度及温度应力分析……………………………………… 173
衢江抽水蓄能电站面板堆石坝折线型布置研究……………………………………… 174

引水发电建筑物设计 ………………………… 175

三江口水电站 2 号引水隧洞扩建关键技术研究……………………………………… 175
清远抽水蓄能电站引水隧洞高压灌浆质量控制……………………………………… 176
觉巴水电站沉沙池设计……………………… 177

泄水建筑物设计 …………………………… 178

白鹤滩水电站水力过渡过程研究……………… 178
长龙山抽水蓄能电站下水库泄水建筑物优化研究…………………………………… 179
绩溪抽水蓄能电站竖井式溢洪道优化设计…… 180
沙坪二级水电站厂房坝段防排沙优化设计…… 182
新荣水电站水力过渡过程分析研究…………… 183
鱼塘水电站溢洪道泄槽段水毁原因…………… 184
高生水电站整体水力学模型深化试验研究…… 185
水闸工程安全评价及除险加固关键技术研发……………………………………… 185

施工导流与围堰设计 ……………………… 185

拉哇水电站施工组织设计综述……………… 185
杨房沟水电站施工导流设计………………… 187
黄登水电站 2 号导流洞出口工作闸室分析…… 188
旬阳水电站一期全年围堰设计与优化………… 189
苏洼龙水电站导流隧洞设计与施工…………… 190
托口水电站导流底孔结构受力分析与坝上游面拉应力控制措施…………………………… 191

其他 ………………………………………… 192

锦屏一级水电站渗流水质及析出物分析……… 192
白鹤滩水电站右岸地下厂房岩壁吊车梁补强加固设计………………………………… 193
乌东德水电站工程几项勘测设计简介………… 194
大湾水电站厂房屋顶出线架结构设计………… 195
抽水蓄能电站发电厂房系统布置及厂房结构设计………………………………… 196
虹吸管在讨赖河流域已建水电站中的应用…… 197
卡鲁玛水电站拦污漂固定墩稳定、应力及变形特性分析………………………… 198

6 土建施工

大坝施工 ………………………………………… 203

两河口水电站大坝心墙雨季填筑施工………… 203
乌弄龙水电站大坝混凝土拌和系统工艺设计与布置优化…………………………………… 204
枕头坝一级水电站主体混凝土快速施工技术…………………………………………… 205
收缝式双向可调翻转模板在象鼻岭水电站拱坝中的应用………………………………… 206
南公 1 水电站面板堆石坝堆石料碾压参数研究…………………………………………… 207
混凝土面板滑模施工技术在安拉沟水库的应用…………………………………………… 207
混凝土面板坝面板应力分析可视化程序研发与应用………………………………………… 209
数字化智能碾压系统在丰宁抽水蓄能电站中的应用………………………………………… 210
沙沱水电站四级配碾压混凝土筑坝关键技术及工程应用……………………………………… 211
乌东德水电站围堰土工膜质量控制…………… 212
乌弄龙水电站下游围堰防冲墙布置研究……… 213
果多水电站混凝土裂缝成因分析及控制……… 214
象鼻岭水电站高拱坝无盖重固结灌浆施工技术……………………………………… 215
枕头坝一级水电站工程施工方案优化………… 216
自愈型防渗外加剂在象鼻岭水电站双曲拱坝防渗中的应用……………………………… 217

引水发电建筑物施工 ……………………… 218

丰宁抽水蓄能电站压力管道长斜井预留孔钻孔灌浆技术……………………………… 218
阜康抽水蓄能电站压力管道斜井导孔施工孔斜控制与纠偏……………………………… 219
压力管道开挖控制技术在双江口水电站的应用……………………………………… 220
悬臂式掘进机在隧洞引水工程中的应用……………………………………… 221
开敞式 TBM 洞内拆卸技术 ………………… 222

泄水建筑物施工 …… 223
白鹤滩水电站闸门槽施工开创性采用云车技术…… 223
黄登水电站尾水调压室开挖支护施工技术…… 223
白鹤滩反拱形水垫塘基础开挖与处理设计…… 224
白鹤滩水电站高流速流道镜面混凝土施工关键技术…… 225
白鹤滩水电站右岸尾水隧洞固结灌浆试验…… 226
纳米材料喷射混凝土在溧阳抽水蓄能电站中的应用…… 227
基础处理 …… 228
白鹤滩水电站右岸坝基柱状节理玄武岩开挖施工技术…… 228
苏洼龙水电站导流洞出口深覆盖层基坑渗流控制设计与施工…… 229
白河水电站反向灌浆治理渗水技术…… 231
牙扎水库帷幕灌浆第三方质量检测及评价…… 232
其他 …… 233
大古水电站工程截流施工…… 233
卡鲁玛水电站高落差大流量河道截流方案实施…… 234
桓仁水库进水口围堰水下拆除爆破技术…… 235
孤山航电枢纽工程一期全年围堰主河床截流技术…… 236
向家坝右岸坝后电站下游围堰爆破拆除设计…… 237
灰岩人工砂石粉含量对泵送混凝土性能的影响…… 238
可视化附着式振捣器控制系统研发与应用…… 239
杨房沟水电站地下长距离曲线带式输送机关键技术设计与应用…… 240
喷射混凝土机口与现场喷射大板抽样强度对比分析…… 241
碳纤维加固技术在水电工程中的应用…… 242
TBM 施工隧洞大股高压涌水处理 …… 244
苏阿皮蒂水电站辉绿岩人工骨料开采爆破技术…… 245
兰州市供水工程超长隧洞多工作面灌浆施工技术…… 246
新型骨料仓料位指示仪…… 247

7 机电及金属结构

水电机组及辅机 …… 251
白鹤滩水电站左岸电站水轮机模型验收试验 …… 251
洪屏抽水蓄能电站发电电动机设计特点与问题处理…… 252
安康水力发电厂研发出发电机上机架千斤顶剪断销更换专用工具…… 254
安谷水电站大型轴流转桨式转轮翻身采用新技术…… 255
哈尔滨电机厂有限责任公司 2018 年重点水电机组研制工程进展情况…… 256
白市水电厂机组振动区过大处理方案研究…… 257
溧阳抽水蓄能机组推力外循环系统异常振动故障分析及处理…… 259
喜河水电厂 1 号机组上端轴同轴度偏心分析处理…… 261
仙居抽水蓄能电站可逆式抽水蓄能机组底环安装新技术…… 261
电气 …… 262
向家坝水电站带状态监测和断路器合闸闭锁功能的地线管理系统开发…… 262
苗尾水电站电气一次设计…… 263
广州抽水蓄能电站自动发电控制系统的关键技术简介…… 265
向家坝水电站厂用电系统故障计算及继电保护整定计算系统开发…… 266
基于关键性能指标的水电机组振动故障智能预警研究…… 266
对五强溪水电站加装静止无功补偿装置的研究…… 267
德尔西水电站开关站出线架结构设计情况…… 269
基于水电站生产数据平台的状态分析技术与应用…… 270
金属结构 …… 271
向家坝水电站液压抓梁水下安全稳定运行研究…… 271
丰宁抽水蓄能电站弯管段钢管制作及安装方案优化…… 272
引汉济渭水利枢纽供水工程贴边斜岔管的制作…… 272
大型数控龙门镗铣床在弧形闸门面板加工的应用…… 273
大藤峡水利枢纽主坝泄水低孔弧门的制造…… 274
几内亚苏阿皮蒂水电站尾水肘管制作技术…… 275

8 科学研究与技术创新

水电科学研究…………………………………… 281
我国高土石坝抗震安全研究进展情况………… 281
超高面板堆石坝安全性及关键技术研究……… 282
面板堆石坝变形与渗流安全指标体系创建及其应用…………………………………… 284
寒冷地区抽水蓄能电站水库冰情研究………… 285
高水头下坝面土工膜缺陷演化机制与渗漏耦合效应研究………………………………… 285
分布式电源与微网并网保护方案研究及控制仿真软件开发……………………………… 286
典型环境下水工混凝土植筋系统的承载力退化机理研究………………………………… 286
沅水流域梯级水电站安全风险调查及对策措施研究…………………………………… 286
东方电气集团东方电机有限公司 2018 年水电技术进步有关情况…………………… 288
哈尔滨电机厂有限责任公司 2018 年主要科研项目情况…………………………………… 288
河海大学 2018 年科研工作情况 ……………… 290
中国电力建设集团有限公司 2018 年科技发展与创新情况………………………… 290
中国葛洲坝集团股份有限公司 2018 年科技工作情况…………………………………… 292
雅砻江流域水电开发有限公司 2018 年度科技工作情况……………………………… 294
黄河水利科学研究院 2018 年科研工作情况 … 295
中国电建集团贵阳勘测设计研究院有限公司 2018 年科技工作情况 ……………… 296
中电建水电开发集团有限公司 2018 年科技工作简要情况………………………… 298
中国水利水电第四工程局有限公司 2018 年科技工作情况……………………………… 298
中国水利水电第五工程局有限公司 2018 年科技工作情况……………………………… 299
水电技术创新…………………………………… 300
300m 级特高拱坝安全控制关键技术及工程应用研究………………………………… 300
大型地下厂房洞室群围岩稳定耗散能理论分析方法研究及应用……………………… 301
复杂地质条件下 500m 级深竖井关键技术研究…………………………………………… 302
复杂地质条件下巨型尾水调压室断面形状选择研究…………………………………… 303
土石坝长效安全运行重大关键技术研究……… 305
面板堆石坝精细化模拟与动态控制关键技术研究…………………………………… 305
荒沟抽水蓄能电站土石坝填筑料现场碾压工艺性试验研究…………………………… 306
强震区深厚覆盖层 250m 级特高土心墙堆石坝防渗系统关键技术研究与应用…………… 307
双江口水电站 300m 级心墙堆石坝可行性研究阶段筑坝关键技术研究…………… 308
向家坝水电站机组跳闸应急补水策略研究…… 310
荒沟抽水蓄能电站混凝土抗溶出型侵蚀试验研究…………………………………………… 310
强震区卸荷裂隙密集带复杂岩体边坡稳定性评价与加固关键技术…………………… 312
去学水电站 170m 级高沥青混凝土心墙堆石坝设计关键技术研究……………………… 313
向家坝升船机过机船舶吃水自动检测研究…… 314
水电水利工程地下水勘察评价及危害防治技术…………………………………………… 314
水利工程建设管理智能化关键技术研究与应用…………………………………………… 315
特硬岩地层 TBM 施工高效掘进关键技术研究…………………………………………… 316
西部复杂地质环境区水电工程重大滑坡灾变演化过程及控制关键技术……………… 316
南水北调中线工程新型聚脲基防渗体系关键技术与实践……………………………… 317
黄河水利科学研究院 2018 年科研创新平台建设情况…………………………………… 317
“水安全与水科学协同创新中心”获教育部认定批准…………………………………… 318
获奖项目简介…………………………………… 318
锦屏一级特高拱坝枢纽泄洪消能与减雾关键技术…………………………………… 318
各向异性岩石力学特性力学模型及工程应用…………………………………………… 319
景洪水力式新型升船机建设关键技术研究与应用………………………………………… 320
喜马拉雅域大埋深超长隧洞施工关键技术研究

与应用…………………………………………… 321
流域梯级水电站协同调度关键技术与应用…… 322
大型水泵水轮机稳定性与厂房减振关键技术
及工程应用………………………………………… 324
长江上游重大水利工程影响下鱼类保护关键
技术研究与应用…………………………………… 325
适应复杂环境的水工建筑物聚脲基防渗防护
体系关键技术研究与应用………………………… 325
大型水电工程建设场地地质灾害监测预警
与应急管理研究及应用…………………………… 326
特大型升船机施工安全控制关键技术………… 327
大型水电机组定子局部放电智能监测预警
关键技术研究与应用……………………………… 328
高重力坝地基深厚软弱破碎岩体处理技术
研究与应用………………………………………… 328
水电水利工程水下大孔口浮体闸门封堵技
术研究及应用……………………………………… 329
复杂多变条件下雅砻江梯级水库群精细化
调度关键技术……………………………………… 330
重大水利水电工程鱼类生境保护关键技术
与应用……………………………………………… 331
大粒径心墙砾石土填筑质量检测设备及快
速测定技术………………………………………… 332
乌东德水电站超深覆盖层超深基坑围堰施
工关键技术………………………………………… 332
强溶蚀复杂地层防渗灌浆技术研究与
应用………………………………………………… 333
金沙江下游梯级全寿命期绿色水电开发生态
保护关键技术……………………………………… 334
基于 HydroStation 平台的水电站全生命周期
管理系统…………………………………………… 335
非线性防晕材料自动检测及发电机防晕结构
多参量检测系统的研发与应用…………………… 336
大型高流速常年泄流泄洪洞耐冲磨混凝土施
工关键技术………………………………………… 336
高水头大容量冲击式水轮机组安装技术……… 337
水电行业技术标准体系课题研究……………… 338
大型梯级水电站群负荷实时智能调度技术…… 339
复杂地形多种料源高面板堆石坝变形控制
筑坝技术…………………………………………… 340
大型竖井混凝土施工成套技术研究及应用…… 340
水工结构物软硬交界区域复合土工膜力学
特性研究及工程应用……………………………… 341
45°缓倾斜井反导井开挖及复杂结构滑
模衬砌技术………………………………………… 342
水环境治理工程智能管控关键技术研发与
集成应用…………………………………………… 342
水库沥青混凝土面板智能喷淋冷却系统关键
技术研究与应用…………………………………… 343
澜沧江流域水电站群巨型分布式集控监控系
统的构建及应用…………………………………… 343
大型水电机组高灵敏继电保护技术深化研究
及应用……………………………………………… 344
水工岩体损伤状态精细识别与安全预警关键
技术………………………………………………… 345
岩石盖重固结灌浆施工工艺研究……………… 346
水电工程移民安置独立评估管理信息系统研发
与应用……………………………………………… 347
获得 2018 年度国家科学技术奖的水电科技
项目………………………………………………… 348
获得 2018 年度中国电力科学技术奖的水电
科技项目…………………………………………… 349
中国电力建设集团有限公司 2018 年重大科技
项目成果简介……………………………………… 351
中国电建集团北京勘测设计研究院有限公司
2018 年科技成果获奖情况 ……………………… 353
中国电建集团成都勘测设计研究院有限公司
2018 年科技成果获奖情况 ……………………… 354
中国电建集团贵阳勘测设计研究院有限公司
2018 年度科技成果获奖情况 …………………… 355
中国葛洲坝集团股份有限公司 2018 年科技成
果获奖情况………………………………………… 356
中国水利水电第五工程局有限公司 2018 年科技
成果获奖情况……………………………………… 358
中国水利水电第八工程局有限公司 2018 年
科技成果获奖情况………………………………… 359
黄河水利科学研究院 2018 年科技成果获奖
情况………………………………………………… 359
专利项目简介…………………………………… 360
河海大学 2018 年获得国家水利水电类专利
情况………………………………………………… 360
中国葛洲坝集团股份有限公司 2018 年
获得国家发明专利情况…………………………… 363
中国电建集团北京勘测设计研究院有限
公司 2018 年获得国家专利授权情况 ………… 365
中国电建集团成都勘测设计研究院有限公司
2018 年获得国家专利授权情况 ………………… 366
中国电建集团贵阳勘测设计研究院有限公司
2018 年获得国家专利授权情况 ………………… 369
中国水利水电第五工程局有限公司 2018 年
获得国家专利授权和软件著作权登记证书
情况………………………………………………… 372
中国水利水电第八工程局有限公司 2018 年
获得国家专利授权和软件著作权登记证书

情况…………………………………………… 377
哈尔滨电机厂有限责任公司 2018 年获得国家专利授权情况………………………………… 381
国电大渡河流域水电开发有限公司 2018 年度获国家专利授权和软件著作权登记证书情况…………………………………………… 384
黄河勘测规划设计有限公司 2018 年获得国家专利授权情况………………………………… 386
黄河水利科学研究院 2018 年获得国家专利授权和软件著作权登记证书情况……………… 388

9 国际合作与技术交流

国际技术交流………………………………… 393
高坝大库抗震安全国际学术研讨会在成都召开…………………………………………… 393
中国大坝工程学会参加国际大坝委员会第 86 届年会和第 26 届大会情况……………… 394
几内亚苏阿皮蒂水利枢纽项目业主人员培训班结业典礼在河海大学举行………………… 395
雅砻江流域水电开发有限公司 2018 年国际合作与交流情况……………………………… 396
哈尔滨电机厂有限责任公司 2018 年国际学术交流情况………………………………… 397
2018 年农村水电国际交流与合作有关情况…………………………………………… 397
黄河水利科学研究院 2018 年国际学术交流情况………………………………………… 398
对外经营与国外工程 ……………………………… 399
中国电力建设集团有限公司 2018 年国际合作与经营情况……………………………… 399
中国电力建设集团有限公司国际重大工程承包项目 2018 年进展情况 ………………… 400
中国电建集团北京勘测设计研究院有限公司 2018 年国际业务开展情况 ……………… 401
中国电力建设集团有限公司承建的海外水电工程 2018 年进展情况 …………………… 402
津巴布韦卡里巴南岸扩机工程科技创新及社会效益…………………………………… 403
印尼 Poso-1 水电站工程建设进展情况 ……… 403
巴西圣西芒水电站特许经营权转让 2018 年进展情况………………………………… 404
玻利维亚圣何塞水电站工程建设情况………… 405
科特迪瓦格西波-波波里水电站工程 2018 年建设情况 ………………………… 406
几内亚凯乐塔水利枢纽工程建设进展情况…………………………………………… 407
赞比亚下凯富峡水电站工程 2018 年建设进展情况………………………………… 408
尼日利亚 KAINJI 水电站改造项目全面竣工…………………………………………… 409

10 技术标准与图书

标准化管理工作情况 ………………………… 413
2018 年电力标准化管理工作情况 …………… 413
2018 年农村水电技术标准制修订情况 ……… 415
中国电建集团成都勘测设计研究院有限公司 2018 年标准化工作情况 ……………… 416
哈尔滨电机厂有限责任公司 2018 年标准化工作有关情况……………………………………… 416
南方电网调峰调频发电有限公司 2018 年标准化工作情况………………………………… 417
技术标准制修订情况 ………………………… 418
2018 年国家标准化管理委员会下达的电力国家标准制定或修订计划项目……………… 418
2018 年住房和城乡建设部下达的电力工程建设国家标准制定或修订计划项目………… 421
2018 年国家能源局下达的电力行业标准制定或修订计划项目…………………………… 422
2018 年国家能源局下达的电力行业标准英文版翻译计划项目…………………………… 437
2018 年由水电水利规划设计总院归口管理的技术标准制修订计划项目……………… 438
水电水利规划设计总院 2018 年标准送审稿审查项目情况…………………………… 441
中国葛洲坝集团股份有限公司 2018 年主编和参编技术标准情况……………………… 444

新颁标准 …………………………………… 445
2018 年国家标准化管理委员会发布的电力国家标准…………………………………… 445
2018 年住房和城乡建设部发布的电力工程建设国家标准…………………………………… 446
2018 年国家能源局发布的电力行业标准 …… 447
2018 年发布的由水电水利规划设计总院归口管理的技术标准…………………………… 455
2018 年大电机、水轮机新颁标准 ………… 456
2018 年发布的水利技术标准 ……………… 456
截至 2018 年已完成电力标准英文翻译 ……… 457
水电新书 …………………………………… 469
中国电力出版社 2018 年水电新书 ………… 469
《水电站典型作业危险点分析及控制措施》出版发行…………………………………… 471
《灯泡贯流式水轮发电机组运行与检修》出版发行…………………………………… 471

11 水电建设管理

工程管理 …………………………………… 475
杨房沟水电站 EPC 工程总承包管理实践 …… 475
基于 RFID 的抽水蓄能电站智慧物资管理系统研究及应用…………………………… 476
水电工程成本管理和成本控制研究………… 478
基于 BIM 的水利水电工程全生命周期管理平台建设与应用…………………………… 479
二维码技术在丰宁抽水蓄能电站施工管理中的应用…………………………………… 480
厄瓜多尔水电站总承包项目劳工管理研究…… 480
国际 EPC 项目分包商结算的精细化管理 …… 482
国际工程造价文件编制方法研究…………… 483
企业管理 …………………………………… 485
中国长江三峡集团有限公司水电工程建设创新管理情况…………………………………… 485
黄河上游水电开发有限责任公司 2018 年经营管理情况……………………………… 487
湖北清江水电开发有限责任公司 2018 年经营管理情况……………………………… 488
国网新源控股有限公司 2018 年经营管理情况…………………………………… 489
南方电网调峰调频发电有限公司 2018 年企业管理有关情况………………………… 490
华能澜沧江水电股份有限公司 2018 年经营管理情况……………………………… 491
国电大渡河流域水电开发有限公司 2018 年经营管理情况…………………………… 492

12 水电站生产运行

电力生产及管理 ………………………… 497
中国长江电力股份有限公司 2018 年生产管理情况…………………………………… 497
三峡水力发电厂 2018 年生产管理情况 ……… 498
向家坝水力发电厂 2018 年生产管理情况 …… 499
黄河上游水电开发有限责任公司所属大中型水电站 2018 年生产管理情况 …………… 500
雅砻江流域水电开发有限公司 2018 年电力生产情况…………………………………… 505
中国水电顾问集团所属的 3 个水电厂 2018 年生产管理情况…………………………… 506
五凌电力有限公司 2018 年生产管理情况 …… 508
中电建水电开发集团有限公司 2018 年电力生产管理情况…………………………………… 509
三门峡水力发电厂 2018 年生产管理情况 …… 509
黄河万家寨水利枢纽有限公司 2018 年生产管理情况……………………………… 510
国家电投集团广西长洲水电公司 2018 年生产管理情况……………………………… 511
故县水力发电厂 2018 年生产管理情况 ……… 512
技术改造 …………………………………… 512
白莲河抽水蓄能电站钢管鼓包原因分析与处理措施……………………………… 512
石泉水电厂引水管道钢衬脱空原因分析及处理…………………………………… 514
万家寨水电厂 1～4 号机组接力器锁锭漏油分析及升级改造…………………………………… 515
宝珠寺电厂水轮发电机组增设纯机械过速

保护装置 …… 517
三板溪水电厂 3 号发电机定子接地故障处理 …… 518
沙沱发电厂设置发电机集电环及碳刷热成像在线监测系统 …… 519
柘溪水力发电厂 220kV 母线保护改造的二次安全措施 …… 519
三板溪水电厂定子铁芯改造采用修复的硅钢片 …… 521
安康联营电站水轮机主轴密封水压异常波动处理 …… 521
水情预报与调度 …… 523
2018 年清江梯级水电站调度运行情况 …… 523
丰满水电站全面治理工程施工期水库调度情况 …… 524
刘家峡水库汛限水位动态控制研究 …… 525
宝珠寺电站洪水调度优化方案研究 …… 526
大坝安全管理 …… 527
2018 年度水电站大坝注册与备案进展情况 …… 527
2018 年水电站大坝安全定期检查工作情况 …… 529
2018 年水电站大坝安全应急管理概述 …… 532
国家电力投资集团有限公司大坝管理中心成立 …… 532
大坝安全监测与分析 …… 533
2018 年水电站大坝安全监控管理情况 …… 533
2018 年水电站大坝安全监测管理工作情况 …… 533
大坝安全监察信息共享平台上线运行应用 …… 534
柔性测斜仪在去学水电站高土石坝中的应用 …… 534
苗家坝水电站采用温度示踪法探测水库渗漏 …… 536
南瑞沉降环定位传感器的研制与应用 …… 538
高坝洲大坝安全监测自动化改造 …… 538
老挝南立 1-2 水电站外部变形监测网设计与实施 …… 539
柬埔寨额勒赛下游水电站初蓄期面板堆石坝监测资料分析 …… 541
折线型大坝水平位移监测 …… 541
其他 …… 542
金安桥水电站顺利完成金沙江干流“11・3”白格堰塞湖险情的应急处置 …… 542
拉哇水电站工程科学应对金沙江白格堰塞湖险情 …… 543
清江梯级水电站水毁修复项目全部完工 …… 544
万家寨水利枢纽排沙洞淤堵原因分析及疏通处理 …… 545

13 环境保护与水库移民

环境保护 …… 551
乌东德水电站工程 2018 年生态环境保护工作情况 …… 551
向家坝与溪洛渡水电站工程 2018 年环境保护工作情况 …… 551
中电建水电开发集团有限公司 2018 年环境保护工作情况 …… 551
雅砻江流域水电开发有限公司 2018 年生态环境保护工作情况 …… 552
羊曲水电站项目表土资源利用与土壤改良措施研究 …… 553
安谷水电站生态试验场建设情况 …… 555
岩泊渡水电站建设对湖南张家界大鲵国家级自然保护区的影响评价 …… 555
水库移民 …… 557
新的土地政策及产业结构下水电移民生产安置方式研究 …… 557
“同地同价同税”对水电移民征地补偿的影响分析 …… 559
城乡一体化下水库移民政策创新研究 …… 560
南方电网调峰调频发电有限公司 2018 年水库移民情况 …… 561
水电水利规划设计总院组织开展水库移民专业学术交流情况 …… 561
董箐水电站顺利完成建设征地移民安置竣工验收有关情况 …… 562
行业标准《水电工程建设征地实物指标分类编码规范》制定有关情况 …… 564
行业标准《水电工程建设征地实物指标调查规范》修订有关情况 …… 564
《云南省大中型水利水电工程移民安置方式实践与创新研究》通过验收 …… 565

14 农村水电及电气化

农村水电建设…………………………………… 569
2018年全国农村水电总体情况 ………………… 569
2018年农村小水电扶贫工程建设情况 ……… 570
2018年绿色小水电站创建情况 ……………… 570
农村水电管理…………………………………… 571
2018年农村水电行业安全监管工作情况 …… 571
2018年长江经济带小水电站清理整改工作情况……………………………………………… 571
水利部关于全面加强农村水电安全监管工作的通知………………………………………… 572
水利部、国家发展改革委、生态环境部、国家能源局关于开展长江经济带小水电清理整改工作的意见………………………………… 573
农村水电改造…………………………………… 575
2018年农村水电增效扩容改造情况 ………… 575
普定水电站增容改造工程电气一次设计……… 575
石头河坝后水电站主变压器增容更新改造…… 576
岩屋潭Ⅰ级水电站增效扩容改造工程………… 578

15 机构与学术团体

机构 …………………………………………… 583
水电建设单位情况一览表……………………… 583
水电设计单位情况一览表……………………… 584
水利设计单位情况一览表……………………… 585
水利水电施工单位情况一览表………………… 586
学术团体 ……………………………………… 588
中国水力发电工程学会2018年工作情况 …… 588
中国水力发电工程学会分支机构情况表……… 591
各省、直辖市、自治区水力发电工程学会组织情况表…………………………………… 594
中国水力发电工程学会成功举办改革开放40年中国水电系列纪念活动 ……………… 597
中国水力发电工程学会大型水电工程建设总承包论坛在北京召开………………………… 597
中国大坝工程学会2018年工作情况 ………… 598
中国水利学会2018年工作情况 ……………… 601
中国电机工程学会2018年工作情况 ………… 604
河海大学2018年举办水电学术活动情况 …… 606
黄河水利科学研究院2018年几项学术活动情况…………………………………………… 607
西藏水电发展论坛在北京召开………………… 607
风光水能互补开发研讨会在青海西宁召开…… 607

16 统计资料

2018年全国水电增长情况表 ………………… 611
2018年农村水电装机容量及发电量基本情况表…………………………………………… 612
2018年全国电源建设投资完成情况表 ……… 613
2018年大中型水电厂生产运行情况表 ……… 614
2018年全国电力统计基本数据一览表 ……… 624
2018年全国水电40MW及以上容量机组运行可靠性综合指标…………………………… 629

17 大事记

2018年大事记 ………………………………………………………………………………… 633

CONTENTS

Chapter 1 Specials

1) Important Documents

The decision of China's State Council on amending and abolishing Some Administrative Regulations

The items of canceling a batch of administrative licenses decided by China's State Council

The notice of the General Office of the State Council on the pilot reform of the examination and approval system for The construction projects

The notice of the General Office of the State Council on the establishment of the national leading group for science and technology

The provisions on function disposition, internal institutions and manning quotas of the Ministry of Water Resources issued by the General Office of the CPC Central Committee and the General Office of the State Council

The measures of on-going and ex-post supervision of enterprise investment projects issued by the National Development and Reform Commission (NDRC)

The implementation suggestions on strengthening and standardizing the management of the list of objects for the joint punishment of dishonest in power domain issued by the National Development and Reform Commission and the National Energy Administration announced.

The guidance from the National Development and Reform Commission and the National Energy Administration on improving the regulation capacity of the power system

The notice of the National Development and Reform Commission on the reduction of general industrial and commercial electricity prices

The regulations on engineering projects subject to tender announced by the National Development and Reform Commission

"The key work of cost reduction in 2018" announced jointly by the National Development and Reform Commission, the Ministry of Industry and Information Technology, the Ministry of Finance and the People's Bank of China

The adjustment of value-added tax rate of electric power industry and the corresponding reduction of general industrial and commercial electricity price noticed by the National Development and Reform Commission

"The management of the special investment within the central government budget for hydropower preliminary work" announced by the National Development and Reform Commission

"The photovoltaic power generation in 2018" announced by the National Development and Reform Commission, the Ministry of Finance and the National Energy Administration

The decision of abolishing two electricity regulations by the National Development and Reform Commission

The reduction of general industrial and commercial electricity prices by expanding the scale of electricity trading across provinces and regions announced by the National Development and Reform Commission

The quotation of normative documents and the adjustment of the division of major rivers in the management of hydropower The construction announced by the National Development and Reform Commission

The Notice of reducing the electricity price of general industrial and commercial catalogue by the National Development and Reform Commission

The photovoltaic power generation in 2018 announced by the National Development and Reform Commission, the Ministry of Finance and the National Energy Administration

The action plan on clean energy consumption (2018-2020) announced by the National Development and Reform Commission and the National Energy Administration

The Measures for the administration of the evaluation of investment consultation announced by the National Development and Reform Commission

The suggestions on further strengthening supervision and management of quality of power The construction projects announced by the National Energy Administration

The guidance of energy work in 2018 issued by the National Energy Administration on issuing

The administration of photovoltaic power stations for poverty alleviation issued by the National Energy Administration and the poverty alleviation office of the State Council

The matters related to lighten the burden on enterprises in the field of renewable energy announced by the National Energy Administration

The interim administrative measures on development and The construction of distributed wind power projects issued by the National Energy Administration

The revision of six normative documents in the field of hydropower announced by the National Energy Administration on

The guide to English translation of energy industry standards issued by the National Energy Administration

The works of further deepening the comprehensive monitoring of river basin hydropower and water energy utilization, announced by the National Energy Administration's general office

The acceptance and assessment of photovoltaic power stations for poverty alleviation announced by the National Energy Administration's general office and the general division of poverty alleviation office of the State Council

The reduction of the collection standard of some governmental funds announced by the Ministry of Finance on

Measures for quality inspection of water conservancy construction issued by the Ministry of Water Resources

2) Leader's Speech

Hydropower as a vital force in ecological progress

The efforts to creat a new prospect of hydropower development

The reform and opening up have made China's hydropower great achievements

3) Expert Forum

The coordination and optimization promote high-quality development of southwest hydropower

The demonization of hydropower seriously restricts the improvement of China's water security capability

Hydropower as the "pioneer" of reform and opening up in the field of energy

The key role of hydropower played in the energy revolution

The correct view of dialectical relationship

between small hydropower and ecological environmental protection

4) The Work of Central Enterprises

The reform and development of PowerChina Group in 2018

The Work Report of China Huadian Corporation, Ltd in 2018

The management and development of China Three Gorges Projects Development Corporation Limited in 2018

Chapter 2 Hydropower and New Energy Development

1) Hydropower Development

The pumped storage power station selection planning adjustment of Zhejiang province

The pumped storage power station selection planning adjustment of Anhui province

The pumped storage power station selection planning adjustment of Guizhou province

The Yigong River hydropower planning progress of Tibet Autonomous Region

2) New Energy Development

The power supply configuration planning of the base of UHV transmission to the outside in HaiNan District of Qinghai province

The ZhuangheⅢ (300 MW) project design of offshore wind farm by China Three Gorges New Energy

The key technology and application of ZhuangHeⅢ (300 MW) project of offshore wind farm designed by China Three Gorges New Energy

The production management of HydroChina Jintang Wind Power Plant in 2018

The wind data processing and analysis of wind farm in high altitude mountain area

The selection of wind turbines in high altitude mountain area

The research and analysis on electrical equipment selection of wind farm in high altitude mountain area

A study on aided technical indexes of wind power farm The construction in high altitude mountain area

The application of financial risk analysis in the financial management of A photovoltaic power generation enterprise

A study on regional power grid planning with high permeability of new energy

The acceptance and consumption of clean energy of State Grid in 2018

The acceptance and consumption of new energy of North China Power Grid in 2018

The acceptance and consumption of clean energy of East China Power Grid in 2018

The acceptance and consumption of clean energy of Northwest Power Grid in 2018

The acceptance and consumption of clean energy of Southwest Power Grid in 2018

The acceptance and consumption of clean energy of Liaoning Power Grid in 2018

The acceptance and consumption of clean energy of Henan Power Grid in 2018

The acceptance and consumption of clean energy of Qinghai Power Grid in 2018

The construction management of PowerChina Qinghai Gonghe 50MW photothermal power station in 2018

The construction of Cida iron furnace wind power plant project

Chapter 3 Large and Medium-sized Hydropower Project

1) Conventional Hydropower Project

The construction of Baihetan hydropower station in 2018

The construction of Wudongde hydropow-

er station in 2018
The construction of Xiangjiaba and Xiluodu hydropower station in 2018
The construction of Yangfanggou hydropower station in 2018
The construction of Lianghekou hydropower station in 2018
All four generator sets of Dahuaqiao hydropower station put into operation
The construction of Jinsha hydropower station in 2018
The construction of Lawa hydropower station in 2018
All four generator sets of Miaowen hydropower station put into operation
The construction of Shuangjiangkou hydropower station in 2018
The construction of Muzati river third-level hydropower station
The construction of Suwalong hydropower station in 2018
The construction of Xiangbiling hydropower station in 2018
The construction of Xulong hydropower station in 2018
The construction of Batang hydropower station in 2018
The construction of Gaosheng hydropower station in 2018
The construction of Jiacha hydropower station in 2018
The construction of Xunyang hydropower station in 2018
The construction of Yangjiawan hydropower station in 2018
The construction of Yebatan hydropower station in 2018
The construction of key conventional hydropower projects undertaken by PowerChina Group in 2018
The construction of Yingliangbao hydropower station in 2018
The construction of Yingjiang hydropower station in 2018
The construction of Xiate hydropower station in 2018
The construction of the early-stage project of China Huadian Corporation, Ltd in 2018
The construction of the early-stage project of PowerChina Dadu river basin hydropower development Co., Ltd in 2018
The project completion safety appraisal of Houziyan hydropower station
The ship lift put into trial navigation of Xiangjiaba hydropower station
The construction of central Yunnan province water diversion project in 2018

2) Pumped Storage Project

The construction of pumped storage projects undertaken by PowerChina Corporation in 2018
The construction of Qingyuan pumped storage projects in 2018
The construction of Fengning pumped storage projects in 2018
The construction of Dunhua pumped storage projects in 2018
The construction of Zhouning pumped storage projects in 2018
The construction of Zhirui pumped storage projects in 2018
The construction of Yongtai pumped storage projects in 2018
The construction of Yixian pumped storage projects in 2018
The construction of Yinmeng pumped storage projects in 2018
The construction of Wendeng pumped storage projects in 2018
The power supply The construction of China Southern Power Grid Peak and Frequency Modulation Power Generation Corporation, Ltd in 2018

Chapter 4 Project Investigation

1) Geological Exploration and Evaluation

The application of grey system prediction model in settlement observation of Jinping-I Hydropower Station

The application of stereographic projection in slope stability

The application of slope safety evaluation method based on vulnerability theory in the project of Sanchahe Hydropower Station

A Study on hydrogeological problems of tunnel and karst of water diversion project in central Yunnan

2) Solutions and Research of Engineering Geological Problems

The stability analysis and The construction treatment of surrounding rock of F3 fault zone of diversion tunnel in Nuozhadu Hydropower Station

A study on basic treatment of silty clay in homogeneous earth dam of lower storage resevoir in Liyang pumped storage power station

The analysis on deformation characteristics and stability of the deposit slope of bank slope after impoundment

The management design of BT2 accumulation body of Xiangbiling Hydropower Station

The analysis on toppling deformation mechanism and reinforcement effect of slope of Miaowei Hydropower Station

A Study on accumulation body deformation law of Nianshengken ditch in Liyuan Hydropower Station

The seepage engineering treatment of hot springs in the dam area of Jiulongxia Hydropower Station

A study on rheological characteristics and support of tunnel surrounding rock in red-storey high geostress zone

The Treatment of muddy slope at Nam Phay Hydropower Station of Laos

3) Exploration Technology and Equipment

The key technology and its application of seepage mechanics in engineering rock

The application of TRT advanced geological prediction technology in TBM tunnel The construction

The application of array displacement meter in deep deformation monitoring of landslide body

A method to improve aerotriangulation encryption precision of UAV aerial survey

The application of fiber grating instrument in the monitoring of Niulan River-Dianchi water filling the long tunnel project

The drilling technique for super deep hole in weak and leaky formation of Ataka pumped storage power station in Egypt

Chapter 5 Hydraulic Structure Design

1) Design of Dam

The design of concrete face rockfill dam for Sanchahe Hydropower Station

The design of plastic concrete cutoff wall for Minglang reservoir dam

The Comparison and selection of dam type for Linxi River Hydropower Station

The research and application of dam foundation concrete cutoff wall for Xiangjiaba Hydropower Station

The treatment of strong permeable foundation of homogeneous earth dam of Sanghe II hydropower station

The partition design of earth dam for Sanghe-II hydropower station

The three-dimensional seepage analysis of hub area of Cihaxia Hydropower Station project

The temperature and stress analysis of concrete gravity dam of Daqiao Hydropower Station

A study on folding line layout of face rockfill dam for Qujiang pumped storage power station

2) Design of Water Diversion and Generation System

A study on key technology of expansion of No. 2 diversion tunnel of Sanjiangkou hydropower station

The quality control of high-pressure grouting of diversion tunnel in Qingyuan pumped storage power station

The design of sand sink for Jueba Hydropower Station

3) Design of Drainage Buildings

A study on hydraulic transient process of Baihetan Hydropower Station

A study on optimization of discharge building of reservoir in Changlongshan pumped storage power station

The optimization design of shaft spillway for Jixi pumped storage power station

The optimization design of sand discharge prevention for plant monolith of Shaping-II hydropower station

The analysis and research on hydraulic transient process of Xinrong hydropower station

The reasons of water damage of discharge chute of spillway section in Yutang hydropower station

The further experimental study on overall hydraulics model of Gaosheng hydropower station

The research and development of key technologies for safety evaluation and reinforcement of sluice project

4) Design of Construction Diversion and Cofferdam

The overview of The construction organization and design of Lawa hydropower station

The design of The construction diversion for Yangfanggou hydropower station

The analysis of working chamber of No. 2 diversion tunnel exit of Huangdeng hydropower station

The design and optimization of annual cofferdam for the first-stage project of Xunyang hydropower station

The design and The construction of diversion tunnel for Suwalong hydropower station

The stress analysis of bottom hole of diversion and the control measures of tension stress on upper face of dam in Tuokou hydropower station

5) Others

The analysis of seepage water quality and precipitates in Jinping-I hydropower station

The reinforcement design of crane beam of rock wall for right bank underground powerhouse of Baihetan hydropower station

A brief introduction of investigation and design of Wudengdong hydropower station project

The structural design of wire outlet rack of the roof of powerhouse of Dawan hydropower station

The systematic layout and structural design of power plant in pumped storage power station

The application of siphon in the hydropower stations built in Taolai River basin

The analysis of stability, stress and deformation characteristics of the fixing pier of trash rack at Kaluma hydropower station

Chapter 6 Civil Engineering Construction

1) Dam Construction

The filling The construction of the core

wall of dam of Lianghekou hydropower station in rainy season
The process design and layout optimization of concrete mixing system for dam of Wulong hydropower station
The rapid The construction technology of concrete of main body for Zhentouba-I hydropower station
The application of double-direction adjustable reversible formwork with closed seam in the arch dam of Xiangbiling hydropower station
The study on parameters of rockpill material rushing of face rockfill dam of Nangong-1 hydropower station
The technology application of slip form concrete slab The construction in Anlagou reservoir
The research and application of visualization program of stress analysis of concrete face slab
The application of digital intelligent rolling system in Fengning pumped storage power station
The key technology Research and engineering application of concrete rolled-out dam The construction of the fourth level for Shatuo hydropower station
The quality control of geofilm for earth cofferdam of Wudongde hydropower station
A study on the layout of downstream cofferdam wall of Wunonglong hydropower station
The cause analysis and control of concrete crack in Guodao hydropower station
The construction technology of non-cover-weighted consolidation grouting of high arch dam for Xiangbiling hydropower station
The optimization design of the The construction scheme of Zhentouba-I hydropower station
The application of self-healing anti-seepage admixture in anti-seepage of double arch dam of Xiangbiling hydropower station

2) Construction of Water Diversion and Generation Works

The drilling and grouting technology for reserved hole of long inclined well in pressure pipeline of Fengning pumped storage power station
The hole deviation control and correction during the The construction of guide hole in inclined well of pressure pipeline in Fukang pumped storage power station
The application of excavation control technology of pressure pipe in Shuangjiangkou hydropower station
The application of cantilever excavator in tunnel water diversion project
The open TBM in-tunnel disassemble technology

3) Construction of Release Works

The cloud car technology used creatively in the The construction of sluice gate slots of Baihetan hydropower station
The excavation and support technology of tail water pressure regulating chamber in Huangdeng hydropower station
The excavation and treatment design of the foundation of Baihetan inverted arch plunge pool
The key technology of mirror concrete The construction in high velocity channel of Baihetan hydropower station
The consolidation grouting test of tailwater tunnel on the right bank of Baihetan hydropower station
The application of nanometer material shotcrete in Liyang pumped storage power station

4) Foundation Treatment

The basalt excavation technology of columnar joints structure in right bank dam foundation of Baihetan hydropower station
The seepage control design and The construction of deep overlaying foundation pit at the exit of diversion tunnel in Su-

walong hydropower station

The techonology of reverse grouting to treat seepage of Baihe hydropower station

The quality inspection and evaluation of the third party of curtain grouting in Yazha reservoir

5) Others

The river closure The construction of Daguo hydropower station

The implementation of the scheme of high-drop and large-flow river closure for Kaluma hydropower station

The underwater demolition and blasting technology for cofferdam at inlet of Huanren reservoir

The main river bed closure technology of annual cofferdam in the first phase of Gushan-I navigation junction project

The blasting demolition design of downstream cofferdam behind the right bank of Xiangjiaba dam

The influence of limestone artificial sand powder on the performance of pumping concrete

The development and application of the control system of visual attached vibrator

The key technology of design and application of the long underground curved belt conveyor in Yangfanggou hydropower station

The comparative analysis of sampling strength between shotcrete nozzle and spot shotcrete slab

The application of carbon fiber reinforcement technology in water-power engineering

The treatment of a large of high pressure water gush in The construction tunnel

The mining and blasting technology for artificial diabase aggregate in Souapiti hydropower station

The grouting The construction technology of multi-face of overlong tunnel in Lanzhou water supply project

A new type of aggregate storage bin level indicator

Chapter 7 Electrical-Mechanical and Metal Structure

1) Hydropower Units and Auxiliary Equipment

The acceptance test of hydraulic turbine model for the left bank of Baihetan hydropower station

The design characteristics and problems of generator-motor in Hongping pumped storage power station

Ankang hydropower plant researched and developed special tools to replace the break pin of jack on the upper bracket of generator

A new technology of turnover for the axial flow set turbine of Angu hydropower station

The progress of key hydropower unit development project of Harbin Electric Machinery Comany Limited in 2018

A study on oversize treatment scheme for vibration zone of hydroelectric units of Baishi hydropower plant

The analysis and treatment of abnormal vibration of thrust external circulation system of Liyang pumped storage unit

The analysis and treatment of coaxiality eccentricity of the upper shaft of unit-1 of Xihe River power plant

A new technology for bottom ring installation of reversible pumped storage unit in Xianju pumped storage power station

2) Electrical

The ground line management system of Xiangjiaba hydropower station with status monitoring and switch closing and locking functions

The primary electrical design of Miaowei

hydropower station
An introduction to key technologies of automatic power generation control system in Guangzhou Pumped Storage Power Plant
The development of electrical fault calculation system and relay protection setting calculation system of Xiangjiaba hydropower station
A Study on intelligent early warning of hydropower unit vibration fault based on key performance index
A study on static var compensator of Wuqiangxi hydropower station
The structure design of wire outlet rack of the switching station of Delxi hydropower station
The state analysis technology and application based on production data platform of hydropower station

3) Metal Structure
A study on safe and stable underwater operation of hydraulic grab beam in Xiangjiaba hydropower station
The optimization of production and installation scheme of steel pipe in bended segment of Fengning pumped storage power station
The production of flanged bifurcated pipe for water supply project of Hanjiang to Weihe River Project
The Application of large CNC plane boring and milling machine in processing of arc gate panel
The manufacture of low-hole arc gate for discharge from main dam of Datengxia water conservancy project
The production technology of draft elbow tube for Souapiti hydropower station in Guinea

Chapter 8 Scientific Research and Technological Innovation

1) Scientific Research of Hydropower
The research progress on seismic safety of high rockfill dams in China
A study on safety and key technology of super high face rockfill dam
The establishment and application of deformation and seepage safety index system for face rockfill dam
A study on reservoir ice of pumped storage power station in cold regions
A study on the mechanism of geomembrane defect evolution and the coupling effect of seepage in the lower dam face with high-head water
The research on the protection scheme of the connection between distributed power supply and micro grid and the development of control simulation software
The research on the degradation mechanism of bearing capacity of hydraulic concrete rebar fastening system under typical environment
The safety risk investigation and countermeasures of cascade hydropower station in Yuanshui river basin
The progress of hydropower technology in 2018 in Dongfang Electric Machine Co., Ltd.
The scientific research projects of Harbin Electric Machinery Comany Limited in 2018
The scientific research work of Hohai University in 2018
The development and innovation of science and technology in 2018 of PowerChina Construction Group Co., Ltd.
The works of science and technology of China Gezhouba Co., Ltd. in 2018
The works of science and technology of Yalong River Hydropower Development Co., Ltd. in 2018
The scientific research work of Yellow River Institute of Hydraulic Research in 2018

The works of science and technology of Powerchina Guiyang Engineering Co., Ltd. in 2018

An Brief introduction to works of the science and technology of PowerChina Hydropower Development Group co., Ltd. in 2018

The works of science and technology of Sinohydro Engineering Bureau 4 Co., Ltd. in 2018

The works of science and technology of Sinohydro Engineering Bureau 5 Co., Ltd. in 2018

2) Innovation of Hydropower Technology

The key technology and engineering application research on the safety control of 300 meters extra-high arch dam

The theoretical analysis method and application of stable dissipative energy in surrounding rock of large underground powerhouse

The research on key technologies of 500m deep shaft under complex geological conditions

A study on shape selection of giant tail surge tank under complex geological conditions

A study on the key technology on long - term safe operation of earth-rockfill dam

A study on the key technology of fine simulation and dynamic control of face rockfill dam

An experimental study on field rolling technology of filling material for earth-rockfill dam in Huanggou pumped storage power station

The research and application of the key technology of seepage control system of 250m extra high earth core rockfill dam in deep overlying layer in meizoseismal area

A study on key techniques of dam construction during the feasibility study of 300m core rockfill dam of Shuangjiangkou hydropower station

A study on emergency strategy for unit tripping in Xiangjiaba hydropower station

An experimental study on anti - dissolution erosion of concrete in Huanggou pumped storage power station

The key technology of slope stability evaluation and reinforcement for the complex rock mass in the unloading crack dense zone in meizoseismal area

A study on key technologies of design of 170m high asphalt concrete core rockfill dam for Quxue hydropower station

A study on automatic draft detection of ship lift passing machine of Xiangjiaba hydropower station

The survey evaluation and hazard prevention techniques of groundwater for water resources and hydropower projects

The research and application of the key technology of intelligent management of water conservancy project

A study on the key technology of efficient tunneling in TBM construction of extra-hard rock formation

The evolution process and key control technology of major landslide disaster of hydropower project in complex geological environment area of west China

The key technology and practice of new polyurea base seepage control system in the middle route of the South-to-North Water Transfer Project

The construction of scientific research innovation platform of Yellow River Institute of Hydraulic Research in 2018

The "Collaborative innovation center for water security and water science" was approved by the Ministry of Education

3) Introduction of Awarded Projects

The key technology of flood energy dissipation and fog reduction for the extra-high arch dam hub in Jinping-I

The mechanical model and engineering application of anisotropic rock mechanical

properties
The research and application of key technologies for construction of Jinghong hydraulic type ship lift
The research and application of key technologies in the construction of large-depth and super-long tunnels in Himalayan region
The key technology and application of coordinated dispatching for the cascade hydropower stations
The key technology and engineering application of stability and vibration reduction of large pump turbine and workshop
The research and application of key technology of fish conservation under the influence of major water conservancy projects in the upper reaches of the Yangtze river
The research and application of key technologies of polyurea - based seepage protection system for hydraulic structures adapted to complex environment
The study and application of geological disaster monitoring and early warning and emergency management in construction sites of large-scale hydropower projects
The key technology of construction safety control of oversized ship lift
The research and application of intelligent monitoring and early warning for stator partial discharge of large hydropower units
The research and application of treatment technology for deep weak fractured rock mass in foundation of high gravity dam
The research and application of sealing technology of large underwater orifice floating gate for water resources and hydropower projects
The key technology of fine dispatching of cascade reservoirs of Yalong river under complex and varied conditions
The key technology and application of fish habitat protection in major water conservancy and hydropower projects
The quality testing equipment and rapid measurement technology for gravel soil filling of large core wall
The key technology of cofferdam construction of super deep foundation pit for super deep overlaying layer of Wudongde hydropower station
The research and application of anti-seepage grouting technology for complex formations with strong dissolution
The key technologies for ecological protection of all-life-cycle green hydropower development in the lower reaches of Jinsha river
The full life cycle management system based on hydropower platform
The research and application of automatic detection system of nonlinear anti-halo materials and multi-parameter detection system of anti-halo structure of generator
The key technology for construction of abrasion resistant concrete of large - scale high flow perennial spillway tunnel
The installation technology of the impulse turbine unit of high head and large capacity
The subject study on technical standard system of hydropower industry
The real-time intelligent load dispatching technology for large cascade hydropower stations
The control of deformation of high face rockfill dam of varieties of material sources for complex terrain
The research and application of complete set of concrete construction technology for large shaft
The research on mechanical properties and engineering application of composite geomembrane in soft - hard interface area of hydraulic structures

The technology of reverse guide shaft excavation and sliding form lining of complex structure for 45°gently slant well
The research and integrated application of the key technology of intelligent control in water environment governance engineering
The research and application of the key technology of intelligent spray cooling system for asphalt concrete facing of reservoir
The construction and application of giant distributed centralized control and monitoring system for hydropower stations in Lancang river basin
The research and application of high sensitivity relay protection technology for large hydropower units
The key technology of fine identification and early warning of damage state of hydraulic rock mass
A study on construction technology of heavy consolidation grouting for rock cover
The research and application of independent evaluation and management information system for the migration resettlement of hydropower projects
The science and technology projects of hydropower that won the 2018 State Science and Technology Award
The science and technology projects of hydropower that won the 2018 China Electric Power Science and Technology Award
The introduction to the achievements of major science and technology projects of PowerChina Corporation Limited in 2018
The awards for scientific and technological achievements of PowerChina Beijing Engineering Corporation Limited in 2018
The awards for scientific and technological achievements of PowerChina Chengdu Engineering Corporation Limited in 2018
The awards for scientific and technological achievements of PowerChina Guiyang Engineering Corporation Limited in 2018
The awards for scientific and technological achievements of China Gezhouba Corporation in 2018
The awards for scientific and technological achievements of Sinohydro Engineering Bureau 5 Co., Ltd. in 2018
The awards for scientific and technological achievements of Sinohydro Engineering Bureau 8 Co., Ltd. in 2018
The awards for scientific and technological achievements of Yellow River Institute of Hydraulic Research in 2018
4) Introduction of Patent Project
The obtaining situation of water conservancy and hydropower of national authorized patent of Hohai university in 2018
The obtaining stuation of national authorized patent inventions of China Gezhouba Corporation in 2018
The obtaining stuation of national authorized patent of PowerChina Beijing Engineering Corporation Limited in 2018
The obtaining stuation of national authorized patent of PowerChina Chengdu Engineering Corporation Limited in 2018
The obtaining stuation of national authorized patent of PowerChina Guiyang Engineering Corporation Limited in 2018
The obtaining stuation of national authorized patent and softwave copyright register certificate of Sinohydro Engineering Bureau 5 Co., Ltd. in 2018
The obtaining stuation of national authorized patent and software copyright register certificate of Sinohydro Engineering Bureau 8 Co., Ltd. in 2018
The obtaining stuation of national authorized patent of Harbin Electric Machinery Comany Limited in 2018

The obtaining stuation of national authorized patent and software copyright register certificate of PowerChina Dadu river basin hydropower development Co., Ltd. in 2018
The obtaining stuation of patent national authorized patent of Yellow River Engineering Corporation Limited in 2018
The obtaining stuation of national authorized patent and software copyright register certificate of Yellow River Institute of Hydraulic Research in 2018

Chapter 9 International Cooperation and Technology Exchange

1) International Technology Exchange
The international symposium on seismic safety of high dam with large resevoir held in chengdu
The situation of the Chinese Dam Engineering Society attending the 86th annual conference and the 26th general conference of the International Commission on Large Dam
The graduation ceremony of the training course for owners of the Souapiti hydropower project in Guinea was held in hohai university
The international cooperation and exchange in 2018 of Yalong River Hydropower Development Co., Ltd
The international academic exchange of Harbin Electric Machinery Company Limited in 2018
The international cooperation and exchange of rural hydropower in 2018
The international academic exchange of Harbin Electric Machinery Company Limited in 2018
2) International Business and Overseas Projects
The International cooperation and operation of PowerChina Corporation Limited in 2018
The major international contracting projects of PowerChina Corporation Limited in 2018
The international business development of PowerChina Beijing Engineering Corporation Limited in 2018
The overseas hydropower projects undertaken by PowerChina Corporation Limited in 2018
The technology innovation and social benefits of Lake Kariba south bank expansion project of Zimbabwe
The construction progress of Poso-1 hydropower station in Indonesia
The progress of franchise transfer of Brazil's San Simao Hydropower Station in 2018
The construction of the San Jose Hydropower Station in Bolivia
The construction of the Gribo-Popoli Hydropower Station in Côte d'Ivoire
The construction of the Guinea Kaleta Hydropower Station
The technological achievements and social influence of Lower Kafue Gorge Hydropower Station in Zambia
The reconstruction project of Nigeria's KAINJI Hydropower Station has been completed

Chapter 10 Technical Norms and Books

1) Standardization Management
The standardization management of electric power in 2018
The technical standards formulation and revision of rural hydropower in 2018
The standardization works of PowerChina Chengdu Engineering Corporation Limited in 2018

The standardization works of Harbin Electric Machinery Company Limited in 2018
The standardization works of China Southern Power Grid Peak and Frequency Modulation Power Generation Corporation Limited in 2018
2) Technical Standards Making and Revision
The national standards formulation or revision of electric power projects issued by the Standardization Administration of China in 2018
The national standards formulation or revision of power engineering construction projects issued by the Ministry of Housing and Urban-Rural Development in 2018
The project of standards formulation or revision of power industry issued by the National Energy Administration in 2018
The English translation projects of power industry standard issued by National Energy Administration in 2018
The project of technical standard formulation and revision managed by the China Renewable Energy Engineering Institute in 2018
The project of the draft standard to investigate of the China Renewable Energy Engineering Institute in 2018
The technical standard works edited or paticipated by China Gezhouba Corporation Limited in 2018
3) New Issue Standards
The national electric power standard issued by the Standardization Administration of China in 2018
The national standard of power engineering construction projects issued by the Ministry of Housing and Urban-Rural Development in 2018
The power industry standard issued by National Energy Administration in 2018
The technical standard managed by the China Renewable Energy Engineering Institute issued in 2018
The new standards for large electrical machinery and water turbines in 2018
The technical standard for water conservancy of 2018
The English translation version of power industry standard finished in 2018
4) New Hydropower Books
The new books of hydropower published by China Electric Power Press in 2018
The publication and distribution of "the analysis and control measures of typical operational risk points in hydropower stations"
The publication and distribution of "the operation and maintenance of bulb tubular turbine generator set"

Chapter 11 Management of Hydropower Construction

1) Management of Projects
The management practice of Engineering Procurement Construction project of Yangfanggou hydropower station
The research and application of intelligent material management system for pumped storage power station based on RFID
A study of the cost management and control of hydropower projects
The construction and application of full life cycle management platform for water conservancy and hydropower projects based on BIM
The Application of two-dimensional code technology in construction management of Fengning pumped storage power station
The labor management of general contract project of the hydropower stations in Ecuador
The fine management of subcontractor settlement of international EPC project
A study on compilation method of international project cost files

2) Management of Enterprises

The innovative management of hydropower project construction of China Three Gorges Projects Development Corporation Limited

The operation and management of Yellow River Hydropower Development Co., Ltd. in 2018

The operation and management of Hubei Qingjiang River Hydropower Co., Ltd. in 2018

The operation and management of the State Grid New Energy Shareholding Co., Ltd. in 2018

The management of China Southern Power Grid Peak and Frequency Modulation Power Generation Corporation Limited

The operation and management of Huneng Lancang River Hydropower Incorporation in 2018

The operation and management of PowerChina Dadu River Hydropower Development Co., Ltd. in 2018

Chapter 12 Production and Operation of Hydropower Stations

1) Power Generation and Management

The production management of China Yangtze Power Co., Ltd. in 2018

The production management of the Three-Gorge Hydropower Plant in 2018

The production management of the Xiangjiaba Hydropower Plant in 2018

The production management of the large-medium hydropower stations of the Yellow River Hydropower Development Co., Ltd. in 2018

The power production of Yalong River Hydropower Development Co., Ltd. in 2018

The production management of three hydropower plants of Sinohydro in 2018

The production management of Wuling Power Co., Ltd. in 2018

The power production management of PowerChina Hydropower Development Co., Ltd. in 2018

The production management of Sanmenxia Hydropower Plant in 2018

The production management of Yellow River Wanjiazhai water conservancy project Co., Ltd. in 2018

The production management of SPIC Guangxi Changzhou Hydropower Development Co., Ltd. in 2018

The production management of Guxian County Hydropower Plant in 2018

2) Technical Reform

The causes analysis and treatment measures of steel tube bulging in Bailianhe pumped storage power station

The cause analysis and treatment of steel lining void of water diversion pipe in Shiquan hydropower plant

The oil leakage analysis and upgrading of relay lock spindle of No. 1-4 units in Wanjiazhai hydropower station

The pure mechanical overspeed protection device added to the water turbine set of Baozhusi hydropower plant

The treatment of stator grounding fault of No. 3 generator in Sanbanxi hydropower plant

The online monitoring system of generator collector ring and carbon brush thermal imaging of the Shatuo power plant

The secondary safety measures for 220kV bus protection transformation in Zhexi power plant

The repaired silicon steel sheet used in the stator core reconstruction of Sanbanxi hydropower plant

The treatment of abnormal fluctuation of seal water pressure on the main shaft of Ankang co-operated power station

3) Hydrologic Forecasting and Scheduling

The management and running of cascade

hydropower stations on Qingjiang river
The reservoir regulation during the comprehensive governance of construction period of Fengman hydropower station
A study on dynamic control of flood control level in Liujiaxia reservoir
The flood dispatching optimization scheme of Baozhusi hydropower station
4) Large Dam Safety Management
The registration and filing of hydropower station dams in 2018
The progress of regular safety inspection of hydropower station dams in 2018
An overview of safety emergency management of hydropower station dams in 2018
The establishment of the dam management center of the State Power Investment Corporation Limited
5) Large Dam Safety Monitoring
The safety monitoring and management of hydropower station dams in 2018
The safety monitoring and management of hydropower station dams in 2018
The on-line operation of information sharing platform of the dam safety supervision
The application of flexible inclinometer in the high earth and rockfill dam of Quxue hydropower station
The use of the temperature tracer method to detect reservoir leakage in Miaojiaba hydropower station
The development and application of the positioning sensor of the Nanrui sedimentation ring
The automatic reconstruction of the dam safety monitoring of Gaobazhou hydropower station
The design and implementation of external deformation monitoring network for Nanli 1-2 hydropower station in Laos
The data analysis of the face rockfill dam monitoring during initial impound period of Stung Russei Chrum downstream hydropower station in Cambodia
The horizontal displacement monitoring of the line type dam
6) Others
The successful emergency disposal in November 3rd of the Baige barrier lake in the Jinsha River main stream by Jinanqiao hydropower station
The completion of water damage repair of Qingjiang river cascade hydropower station
The scientific response of Laowa hydropower station to the Baige barrier lake emergency of Jinsha River
The cause analysis and treatment of the muddy sediment of desilting tunnel in Wanjiazhai water conservancy project

Chapter 13 Environment Protection and Resettlement of Reservoir Area Residents

1) Environment Protection
The ecological and environmental protection of the Wudongde hydropower station in 2018
The ecological and environmental protection of the Xiangjiaba hydropower station and Xiluodu hydropower station in 2018
The ecological and environmental protection of the PowerChina Hydropower Development Group Co., Ltd. in 2018
The ecological and environmental protection of the Yalong River Hydropower Development Co., Ltd. in 2018
The utilization of topsoil resources and the measures of soil improvement for Yangqu hydropower station project
The construction of ecological test site of Angu hydropower station
The impact of Yanpodu hydropower sta-

tion on giant salamander national nature reserve in zhangjiajie of Hunan

2) Resettlement of Residents

A study on production and resettlement mode of hydropower migration under the new land policy and industrial structure

The impact of the same price and tax on land expropriation compensation for hydropower migration

The innovation research on reservoir migration policy under the urban-rural integration

The reservoir migration of China Southern Power Grid Peak and Frequency Modulation Power Generation Corporation Limited

The academic and professional exchange on reservoir migration organized by the China Renewable Energy Engineering Institute

The successful completion and acceptance of the land acquisition resettlement of immigrants of Dongjing hydropower station

The industry standard formulation of "specification for classification and coding of physical indicators of land expropriation for hydropower project construction"

The industry standard formulation of The relevant situation of the revision of the industry standard "investigation specification of physical indicators of land expropriation for hydropower project construction"

The acceptance of "Practice and innovation of resettlement mode of large and medium-sized water conservancy and hydropower projects in Yunnan province"

Chapter 14 Rural Hydropower and Rural Electrification

1) Rural Hydropower Construction

The nationwide development of rural hydropower in 2018

The construction of poverty alleviation project of rural small hydropower in 2018

The establishment of green small hydropower station in 2018

2) Rural Hydropower Management

The safety supervision of rural hydropower industry in 2018

The cleaning and rectification of small hydropower stations in the Yangtze river Economic Zone in 2018

The comprehensive safety supervision of rural hydropower by the Ministry of Water Resources

"The cleaning and rectification of small hydropower stations in the Yangtze river Economic Zone" issued by the Ministry of Water Resources, the National Development and Reform Commission, the Ministry of Ecology and Environment and the National Energy Administration

3) Rural Hydropower Reconstruction

The Improvement of efficiency and capacity of rural hydropower in 2018

The primary electrical design for capacity expansion project of Puding hydropower station

The renovation of capacity expansion of main transformer for the hydropower station after the Stone river dam

The efficiency improvement and capacity expansion project of Yanwutan-I hydropower station

Chapter 15 People, Agencies and Academic Groups

1) Agencies

The list of hydropower construction corpo-

rations
The list of hydropower engineering corporations
The list of water conservancy engineering corporations
The list of the construction units of water conservancy and hydropower
2) Academic Groups
The works of the China Society of Hydropower Engineering in 2018
The list of the branches of the China Society of Hydropower Engineering
The list of the societies of hydropower engineering of each province, municipality and autonomous region
A series of commemorative activities to mark the 40th anniversary of reform and opening up held successfully by the China society of hydropower engineering has
The forum of the general contracting of large hydropower projects by the China society of hydropower engineering was held in Beijing
The works of the China Society of Dam Engineering in 2018
The works of the Chinese Hydraulic Engineering Society in 2018
The works of the China Society for Electrical Engineering in 2018
The hydropower academic activities held by Hohai university in 2018
Several academic activities of the Yellow River Institute of Hydraulic Research in 2018
The TIbetan Hydropower Development Forum was held in Beijing
The seminar on complementary development of the energy of wind, light and water was held in Xining, Qinghai

Chapter 16 Statistical Data

The table of nationwide hydropower growth in 2018
The table of the installed capacity and power generation of rural hydropower in 2018
The table of nationwide power source investment in 2018
The statistical table of operation and production of the nationwide large and medium-sized hydropower station in 2018
The list of the base data of electric power in China in 2018
The comprehensive index of turbin (40 MW and 40 MWplus) operational reliability in 2018

Chapter 17 Chronicle of Events

January to December

彩 色 插 页 目 录

2018 年 4 月 17 日，水利部部长鄂竟平（前排左二）在湖北武汉东湖港检查指导长江流域防汛抗旱工作（鲁梦　摄）

2018 年 9 月 6 日，国务院国资委党委书记郝鹏在中国电力建设集团有限公司董事长晏志勇的陪同下参观中国电建水电七局的建设项目（曾艾林　摄）

2018 年 8 月 9 日，云南省委书记陈豪到华能澜沧江水电股份有限公司小湾水电厂调研

2018 年 7 月 19 日，海南省委副书记、省长沈晓明前往南方电网调峰调频发电有限公司文昌项目现场考察调研（张柳琦　摄）

2018 年 1 月 12 日，由中国水力发电工程学会与国家电网公司联合主办的“2018 中国水电发展论坛暨水力发电科学技术奖颁奖典礼”在北京举行，来自全国水力发电战线 80 多个单位的 300 余名新老水电工作者代表以及来自有关水电国际组织的专家出席了会议。会议对 2017 年评选出的 45 项“水力发电科学技术奖”进行了颁奖

2018 年 9 月 26 日，有中国水力发电工程学会和水电水利规划设计总院联合主办的“改革开放 40 年中国水电纪念大会”在北京隆重召开。汪恕诚、陆佑楣、周大兵、矫勇等老领导、老专家，陈厚群、张楚汉、马洪琪、张建民等院士，以及来自政府有关部门、水电企事业单位、高校科研机构和有关行业社团组织的领导、专家和水电工作者代表 230 余人参加了大会

2018 年 11 月，大渡河大岗山水电站荣获“国家优质工程金质奖”

2018 年 11 月，江西洪屏抽水蓄能电站荣获“国家优质工程金质奖”

2018 年 6 月 3 日，雅砻江锦屏一级水电站荣获“詹天佑奖”。同年 9 月 10 日，在德国柏林召开的国际咨询工程师联合会 2018 年年会上，锦屏一级水电站荣获“菲迪克 2018 年工程项目杰出成就奖”

2018 年 6 月，云南糯扎渡水电站荣获“詹天佑奖”

2018 年 12 月 27 日，江西省峡江水利枢纽工程荣获中国水利工程学会“2017～2018 年度中国水利工程优质（大禹）奖”

2018 年 12 月 27 日，右江百色水利枢纽工程荣获中国水利工程学会“2017～2018 年度中国水利工程优质（大禹）奖”

2018 年 11 月 30 日，金沙江白鹤滩水电站右岸大坝标段主体混凝土当月完成浇筑 16.15 万 m^3（柴俊锋　摄）

世界最大地下厂房——白鹤滩水电站左岸地下厂房正在施工

2018 年 10 月 4 日，金沙江乌东德水电站大坝上游面施工形象（许健　摄）

2018 年 10 月 30 日，国内首个百万千瓦级 EPC 项目——杨房沟水电站大坝首仓混凝土浇筑

2018 年 3 月，世界第一高坝——双江口水电站大坝基坑正在施工

2018 年 12 月 12 日，丰满水电站旧坝拆除工程成功实施首次爆破，拆除工程进展顺利，新坝建设高质量推进

2018 年 6 月 1 日，苗尾水电站 4 号机组 72 小时试运行顺利结束，4 台机组全部投入生产运行

2018 年 6 月 9 日，大华桥水电站首台机组投产发电（陈锐　摄）

2018 年 7 月 5 日，黄等水电站首台机组投产发电（陈锐　摄）

2018 年 10 月 29 日，里底水电站首台机组投产发电

2018 年 12 月，大渡河猴子岩水电站完成枢纽工程竣工安全鉴定

2018 年 8 月 31 日，大渡河沙坪二级水电站 6 号机组一次性并网发电成功，标志着沙坪二级水电站全部 6 台机组正式并网发电

2018 年 12 月 27 日，南方电网调峰调频发电有限公司鲁布革电厂投产 30 周年（侯海琳　摄）

2018 年 6 月 15 日，南方电网调峰调频发电有限公司天生桥二级水力发电有限公司成立 30 周年（骆允摄）

龚嘴水电站大坝全景

吉牛水电站库区全貌

沙沱水电站雪景（赵梅　摄）

深溪沟水电站大坝

铜街子水电站大坝

枕头坝一级水电站

2018 年 6 月 15 日，世界最大抽水蓄能电站——河北丰宁抽水蓄能电站机电安装工程正式开工

2018 年 7 月 6 日，安徽最大抽水蓄能电站——绩溪抽水蓄能电站下水库下闸蓄水（李建龙　摄）

2018 年 7 月 30 日，海南首个抽水蓄能电站——琼中抽水蓄能电站全面投产发电（张柳琦　摄）

2018 年 9 月 26 日，国内首个城市内大型抽水蓄能

电站——深圳抽水蓄能电站全面投产（肖茜　摄）
2018 年 6 月 17 日，中国电力建设集团有限公司承建的亚洲第一长坝、柬埔寨最大的水电工程——桑河二级水电站 5 号机组顺利完成 72 小时试运行，正式投产发电（江先辉　摄）
2018 年 12 月 17 日，柬埔寨首相洪森视察桑河二级水电站中控室
2018 年 9 月 10 日，中国南方电网有限责任公司首个海外 BOT 项目——老挝南塔河 1 号水电站首台机组正式投产（刘福钦　摄）
2018 年 10 月 22 日，中国企业安装的巴基斯坦塔贝拉 4 期水电站最后一台（15 号）机组，完成全部有水调试并顺利移交业主，进入商业运行（黄海宁　摄）
2018 年 10 月 29 日，中国企业承建的几内亚苏阿皮蒂水利枢纽工程 10 月份混凝土浇筑突破 20 万 m^3（张虎林　摄）
2018 年 9 月 3 日，中国企业承建的刚果（金）布桑加水电站大江截流成功（王冬阳　摄）
2018 年 12 月 31 日 5 时 18 分，由黄河上游水电开发有限责任公司负责建设的国内最大单体 85 万 kW 莫合风电场成功并网，那仁 10 万 kW 风电场也同时并网，合计投产容量达到 95 万 kW，这是世界上一次性并网容量最大的风电项目（李龙　摄）
2018 年 6 月 29 日，中国电建贵州工程公司 EPC 总承包建设的首个水上渔光互补光伏项目——广东湛江鼎瑞渔光一体 100MW 光伏发电项目成功并网（黎光军　摄）
全国 2018 年装机容量和年发电量
2018 年装机容量结构图
2018 年年发电量结构图
全国历年水电装机容量增长情况表
全国历年水电年发电量增长情况表

中國水力發電年鉴

1

特　　载

重 要 文 件

国务院关于修改和废止部分行政法规的决定

国务院 2018 年 3 月 19 日发布第 698 号令《关于修改和废止部分行政法规的决定》，该“决定”全文如下。

为了依法推进简政放权、放管结合、优化服务改革，国务院对取消行政许可项目及制约新产业、新业态、新模式发展涉及的行政法规进行了清理。经过清理，国务院决定：

一、对 18 部行政法规的部分条款予以修改。（附件 1）

二、对 5 部行政法规予以废止。（附件 2）

本决定自公布之日起施行。

附件：1. 国务院决定修改的行政法规
　　　2. 国务院决定废止的行政法规

附件 1

国务院决定修改的行政法规

一、略。

二、将《中华人民共和国河道管理条例》第十五条中的“上级河道主管机关”修改为“县级以上地方人民政府河道主管机关”。

三、删去《中华人民共和国防治海岸工程建设项目污染损害海洋环境管理条例》第十一条。

第十二条改为第十一条，修改为：“海岸工程建设项目竣工验收时，建设项目的环境保护设施经验收合格后，该建设项目方可正式投入生产或者使用。”

四、将《水库大坝安全管理条例》第十六条修改为：“大坝坝顶确需兼做公路的，须经科学论证和县级以上地方人民政府大坝主管部门批准，并采取相应的安全维护措施。”

五、将《城市供水条例》第十九条修改为：“城市自来水供水企业和自建设施对外供水的企业，经工商行政管理机关登记注册后，方可从事经营活动。”

删去第三十二条第一款中的“报城市供水行政主管部门和卫生行政主管部门批准”。

六～十二、略。

十三、删去《防治海洋工程建设项目污染损害海洋环境管理条例》第十条第一款、第十三条中的“委托具有相应环境影响评价资质的单位”。

删去第十五条。

第二十九条改为第二十八条，第一款修改为：“海洋工程需要拆除或者改作他用的，应当在作业前报原核准该工程环境影响报告书的海洋主管部门备案。拆除或者改变用途后可能产生重大环境影响的，应当进行环境影响评价。”

第四十七条改为第四十六条，将第三项中的“批准”修改为“备案”。

十四～十七、略。

十八、删去《中华人民共和国招标投标法实施条例》第十一条第一款。

删去第十三条第一款中的“其资格许可和”，删去第三款。

此外，对相关行政法规中的条文序号作相应调整。

附件 2

国务院决定废止的行政法规

一、中华人民共和国私营企业暂行条例（1988 年 6 月 25 日国务院发布）

二、中华人民共和国水污染防治法实施细则（2000 年 3 月 20 日国务院发布）

三、地质勘查资质管理条例（2008 年 3 月 3 日国务院公布）

四、种畜禽管理条例（1994 年 4 月 15 日国务院发布　根据 2011 年 1 月 8 日《国务院关于废止和修改部分行政法规的决定》修订）

五、劳动教养试行办法（1982 年 1 月 21 日国务院批准）

国务院决定取消一批行政许可等事项

国务院 2018 年 7 月 28 日以国发〔2018〕28 号文

决定“取消一批行政许可等事项的决定”，该“决定”全文如下。

经研究论证，国务院决定取消11项行政许可等事项，现予公布。另有6项依据有关法律设定的行政许可事项，国务院将依照法定程序提请全国人民代表大会常务委员会修订相关法律规定。对取消的行政许可等事项，相关部门要制定完善事中事后监管细则，自本决定发布之日起20个工作日内按规定向社会公布，并加强宣传解读、确保落实到位。

附件

国务院决定取消的行政许可等事项目录
（共计11项）

序号	项目名称	审批部门	设定依据	加强事中事后监管措施
1	企业集团核准登记	市场监管总局，省级工商行政管理部门	《中华人民共和国企业法人登记管理条例》	取消审批后，市场监管总局通过以下措施加强事中事后监管：1. 尽快修订有关法规规定，明确在名称中使用“集团”字样的标准和要求。2. 强化企业母公司（集团公司）的信息公示，接受社会监督
2～7	略			
8	国内企业在境外投资开办企业（金融企业除外）核准初审	省级商务主管部门	《境外投资管理办法》（商务部令2014年第3号）	取消地方初审后，由商务部直接受理审批。商务部通过以下措施加强事中事后监管：采取重点督查和“双随机、一公开”检查等方式加强监管
9	设立分公司备案	省级及以下工商行政管理部门	《中华人民共和国公司登记管理条例》	取消该事项后，工商和市场监管部门通过以下措施加强事中事后监管：建设维护信息系统，完善规章制度，明确分公司设立信息要及时推送、及时更新、及时掌握，加强监管
10	外商投资合伙企业设立、变更、注销分支机构备案	省级及以下工商行政管理部门	《外商投资合伙企业登记管理规定》（原工商总局令2014年第63号）	取消该事项后，工商和市场监管部门通过以下措施加强事中事后监管：建设维护好信息系统，完善规章制度，明确分支机构设立、变更、注销信息要及时推送、及时更新、及时掌握，加强部门协同监管
11	营业执照作废声明	各级工商行政管理部门	《中华人民共和国公司登记管理条例》	取消该事项后，工商和市场监管部门采取以下管理措施加强事中事后监管：对营业执照遗失或损毁申请补领的，不再要求申请人委托媒体刊登作废声明，改为在审批部门官方网站免费发布公告

国务院办公厅关于开展工程建设项目审批制度改革试点的通知

国务院办公厅2018年5月14日以国办发〔2018〕33号文印发《关于开展工程建设项目审批制度改革试点的通知》，该“通知”全文如下。

为贯彻落实党中央、国务院关于深化“放管服”改革和优化营商环境的部署要求，推动政府职能转向减审批、强监管、优服务，促进市场公平竞争，国务院决定开展工程建设项目审批制度改革试点。经国务院同意，现就试点工作有关事项通知如下：

一、总体要求

（一）指导思想。全面深入贯彻党的十九大和十九届二中、三中全会精神，以习近平新时代中国特色社会主义思想为指导，按照党中央、国务院关于深化“放管服”改革和优化营商环境的部署要求，以推进政府治理体系和治理能力现代化为目标，对工程建设项目审批制度进行全流程、全覆盖改革，努力构建科学、便捷、高效的工程建设项目审批和管理体系。

（二）试点地区。北京市、天津市、上海市、重庆市、沈阳市、大连市、南京市、厦门市、武汉市、广州市、深圳市、成都市、贵阳市、渭南市、延安市和浙江省。

（三）改革内容。改革覆盖工程建设项目审批全过程（包括从立项到竣工验收和公共设施接入服务）；主要是房屋建筑和城市基础设施等工程，不包括特殊工程和交通、水利、能源等领域的重大工程；覆盖行政许可等审批事项和技术审查、中介服务、市政公用服务以及备案等其他类型事项，推动流程优化和标准化。

（四）工作目标。2018 年，试点地区建成工程建设项目审批制度框架和管理系统，按照规定的流程，审批时间压减一半以上，由目前平均 200 多个工作日压减至 120 个工作日。2019 年，总结推广试点经验，在全国范围开展工程建设项目审批制度改革，上半年将审批时间压减至 120 个工作日，试点地区审批事项和时间进一步减少；地级及以上城市建成工程建设项目审批制度框架和管理系统。2020 年，基本建成全国统一的工程建设项目审批和管理体系。

二、统一审批流程

（五）优化审批阶段。将工程建设项目审批流程主要划分为立项用地规划许可、工程建设许可、施工许可、竣工验收等四个阶段。其中，立项用地规划许可阶段主要包括项目审批核准备案、选址意见书核发、用地预审、用地规划许可等。工程建设许可阶段主要包括设计方案审查、建设工程规划许可证核发等。施工许可阶段主要包括消防、人防等设计审核确认和施工许可证核发等。竣工验收阶段主要包括规划、国土、消防、人防等验收及竣工验收备案等。其他行政许可、涉及安全的强制性评估、中介服务、市政公用服务以及备案等事项纳入相关阶段办理或与相关阶段并行推进。

（六）分类细化流程。根据工程建设项目类型、投资类别、规模大小等，分类细化审批流程，确定审批阶段和审批事项。简化社会投资的中小型工程建设项目审批，对于带方案出让土地的项目，不再对设计方案进行审核，将工程建设许可和施工许可合并为一个阶段。对于出让土地的工程建设项目，将建设用地审批纳入立项用地规划许可阶段。

（七）大力推广并联审批。每个审批阶段确定一家牵头部门，实行“一家牵头、并联审批、限时办结”，由牵头部门组织协调相关部门严格按照限定时间完成审批。

三、精简审批环节

（八）精简审批事项和条件。取消不符合上位法和不合规的审批事项。取消不合理、不必要的审批事项。对于保留的审批事项，要减少审批前置条件，公布审批事项清单。取消施工合同备案、建筑节能设计审查备案等事项。社会投资的房屋建筑工程，建设单位可以自主决定发包方式。

（九）下放审批权限。按照方便企业和群众办事的原则，对下级机关有能力承接的审批事项，下放或委托下级机关审批。相关部门要加强沟通协调，制定配套措施，完善监管制度，开展指导培训，提高审批效能。

（十）合并审批事项。由同一部门实施的管理内容相近或者属于同一办理阶段的多个审批事项，应整合为一个审批事项。推行联合勘验、联合测绘、联合审图、联合验收等。将消防设计审核、人防设计审查等技术审查并入施工图设计文件审查，相关部门不再进行技术审查。推行以政府购买服务方式开展施工图设计文件审查。将工程质量安全监督手续与施工许可证合并办理。规划、国土、消防、人防、档案、市政公用等部门和单位实行限时联合验收，统一竣工验收图纸和验收标准，统一出具验收意见。对于验收涉及的测量工作，实行“一次委托、统一测绘、成果共享”。

（十一）转变管理方式。对于能够用征求相关部门意见方式替代的审批事项，调整为政府内部协作事项。建设工程规划许可证核发时一并进行设计方案审查，由发证部门征求相关部门和单位意见，其他部门不再对设计方案进行单独审查。推行由政府统一组织对地震安全性评价、地质灾害危险性评估、环境影响评价、节能评价等事项实行区域评估。

（十二）调整审批时序。落实取消下放行政审批事项有关要求，环境影响评价、节能评价、地震安全性评价等评价事项不作为项目审批或核准条件，地震安全性评价在工程设计前完成即可，其他评价事项在施工许可前完成即可。可以将用地预审意见作为使用土地证明文件申请办理建设工程规划许可证，用地批准手续在施工许可前完成即可。将供水、供电、燃气、热力、排水、通信等市政公用基础设施报装提前到施工许可证核发后办理，在工程施工阶段完成相关设施建设，竣工验收后直接办理接入事宜。

（十三）推行告知承诺制。对通过事中事后监管能够纠正不符合审批条件的行为且不会产生严重后果的审批事项，实行告知承诺制。公布实行告知承诺制的审批事项清单及具体要求，申请人按照要求作出书面承诺的，审批部门可以直接作出审批决定。对已经实施区域评估的工程建设项目，相应的审批事项实行告知承诺制。在部分工程建设项目中推行建设工程规划许可告知承诺制。

四、完善审批体系

（十四）“一张蓝图”统筹项目实施。加快建立“多规合一”业务协同平台，统筹各类规划。以“多规合一”的“一张蓝图”为基础，统筹协调各部门提出项目建设条件，建设单位落实建设条件要求，相关部门加强监督管理和考核评估。

（十五）“一个系统”实施统一管理。在国家和地方现有信息平台基础上，整合形成“横向到边、纵向到底”的工程建设项目审批管理系统，覆盖各部门和市、县、区、乡镇（街道）各层级，实现统一受理、并联审批、实时流转、跟踪督办、信息共享。其中，涉密工程按照有关保密要求执行。审批管理系统要与“多规合一”业务协同平台、各部门审批管理系统等信息平台互联互通，做到审批过程、审批结果实时传送。通过工程建设项目审批管理系统，加强对地方工程建设项目审批工作的指导和监督管理。

（十六）“一个窗口”提供综合服务。整合各部门和各市政公用单位分散设立的服务窗口，设立工程建设项目审批综合服务窗口。建立完善“前台受理、后台审核”机制，综合服务窗口统一收件、出件，实现“一个窗口”服务和管理。

（十七）“一张表单”整合申报材料。各审批阶段均实行“一份办事指南，一张申请表单，一套申报材料，完成多项审批”的运作模式，牵头部门制定统一的办事指南和申报表格，每一个审批阶段申请人只需提交一套申报材料。不同审批阶段的审批部门应当共享申报材料，不得要求申请人重复提交。

（十八）“一套机制”规范审批运行。建立健全工程建设项目审批配套制度，明确部门职责，明晰工作规程，规范审批行为，确保审批各阶段、各环节无缝衔接。建立审批协调机制，协调解决部门意见分歧。建立督办督查制度，实时跟踪审批办理情况，对全过程实施督查。

五、强化监督管理

（十九）加强事中事后监管。建立与工程建设项目审批制度改革相适应的监管体系。全面推行“双随机、一公开”监管，加大监督检查力度，严肃查处违法违规行为。对于实行告知承诺制的审批事项，审批部门应当在规定时间内对申请人履行承诺的情况进行检查，对申请人未履行承诺的，撤销行政审批决定并追究申请人的相应责任。

（二十）加强信用体系建设。建立工程建设项目审批信用信息平台，建立黑名单制度，将企业和从业人员违法违规、不履行承诺的不良行为向社会公开，构建“一处失信、处处受限”的联合惩戒机制。

（二十一）规范中介和市政公用服务。建立健全管理制度，实行服务承诺制，明确服务标准和办事流程，规范服务收费。依托工程建设项目审批管理系统建立中介服务网上交易平台，对中介服务行为实施全过程监管。

六、统筹组织实施

（二十二）强化组织领导。住房城乡建设部要切实担负起工程建设项目审批制度改革工作的组织协调和督促指导责任，各有关部门要加强协作、密切配合。试点地区人民政府要高度重视工程建设项目审批制度改革工作，成立以主要负责同志为组长的领导小组，完善工作机制，层层压实责任。试点地区要根据本通知编制实施方案，细化分解任务，明确责任部门，制定时间表、路线图，确保试点工作有序推进，并于2018年6月15日前将实施方案报送住房城乡建设部。鼓励改革创新，改革中涉及突破相关法律法规及政策规定的，按照程序报有权机关授权。支持试点地区在立法权限范围内先行先试，依法依规推进改革工作。研究推动在农村地区因地制宜开展相关工程建设项目审批制度改革。

（二十三）建立考评机制。住房城乡建设部要会同相关部门建立工程建设项目审批制度改革考核评价机制，重点考核评价试点地区全流程、全覆盖实施改革情况，考核评价试点地区统一审批流程、精简审批环节、完善审批体系等情况，及时总结试点做法，形成可复制、可推广的经验，并将有关情况报国务院。试点地区人民政府要加大对有关部门改革工作的督查力度，跟踪督查改革任务落实情况。试点地区要定期向住房城乡建设部报送工作进展情况。对于工作推进不力、影响工程建设项目审批制度改革进程的，特别是未按时完成阶段性工作目标的，要依法依规严肃问责。

（二十四）做好宣传引导。试点地区要通过多种形式及时宣传报道相关工作措施和取得的成效，加强舆论引导，增进社会公众对试点工作的了解和支持，及时回应群众关切，为顺利推进试点工作营造良好的舆论环境。

国务院办公厅关于成立国家科技领导小组的通知

国务院办公厅 2018 年 7 月 28 日以国办发〔2018〕73 号文发布《关于成立国家科技领导小组的通知》，该“通知”全文如下。

按照深化党和国家机构改革统一部署，根据议事协调机构调整有关安排和工作需要，国务院决定将国家科技教育领导小组调整为国家科技领导小组，现将有关事项通知如下：

一、主要职责

研究、审议国家科技发展战略、规划及重大政策；讨论、审议国家重大科技任务和重大项目；协调国务院各部门之间及部门与地方之间涉及科技的重大事项。

二、组成人员

组　长：李克强　国务院总理
副组长：刘　鹤　国务院副总理
成　员：何立峰　发展改革委主任
陈宝生　教育部部长
王志刚　科技部部长
苗　圩　工业和信息化部部长
刘　昆　财政部部长
张纪南　人力资源社会保障部部长
韩长赋　农业农村部部长
易　纲　人民银行行长
肖亚庆　国资委主任
白春礼　中科院院长
李晓红　工程院院长
刘国治　中央军委科学技术委员会主任
怀进鹏　中国科协党组书记
陆俊华　国务院副秘书长（2018 年 8 月 27 日，国办函〔2018〕56 号文，任命国务院副秘书长陆俊华为国家科技领导小组成员，免去国务院机关党组成员高雨的国家科技领导小组成员职务）

国家科技领导小组办公室设在科技部，承担领导小组日常工作，办公室主任由科技部部长王志刚兼任。

中共中央办公厅、国务院办公厅印发《水利部职能配置、内设机构和人员编制规定》

中共中央办公厅、国务院办公厅 2018 年 7 月 30 日以厅字〔2018〕57 号文印发《水利部职能配置、内设机构和人员编制规定》，该“规定”全文如下。

水利部职能配置、内设机构和人员编制规定

第一条　根据党的十九届三中全会审议通过的《中共中央关于深化党和国家机构改革的决定》《深化党和国家机构改革方案》和第十三届全国人民代表大会第一次会议批准的《国务院机构改革方案》，制定本规定。

第二条　水利部是国务院组成部门，为正部级。

第三条　水利部贯彻落实党中央关于水利工作的方针政策和决策部署，在履行职责过程中坚持和加强党对水利工作的集中统一领导。主要职责是：

（一）负责保障水资源的合理开发利用。拟订水利战略规划和政策，起草有关法律法规草案，制定部门规章，组织编制全国水资源战略规划、国家确定的重要江河湖泊流域综合规划、防洪规划等重大水利规划。

（二）负责生活、生产经营和生态环境用水的统筹和保障。组织实施最严格水资源管理制度，实施水资源的统一监督管理，拟订全国和跨区域水中长期供求规划、水量分配方案并监督实施。负责重要流域、区域以及重大调水工程的水资源调度。组织实施取水许可、水资源论证和防洪论证制度，指导开展水资源有偿使用工作。指导水利行业供水和乡镇供水工作。

（三）按规定制定水利工程建设有关制度并组织实施，负责提出中央水利固定资产投资规模、方向、具体安排建议并组织指导实施，按国务院规定权限审批、核准国家规划内和年度计划规模内固定资产投资项目，提出中央水利资金安排建议并负责项目实施的监督管理。

（四）指导水资源保护工作。组织编制并实施水资源保护规划。指导饮用水水源保护有关工作，指导地下水开发利用和地下水资源管理保护。组织指导地下水超采区综合治理。

（五）负责节约用水工作。拟订节约用水政策，组织编制节约用水规划并监督实施，组织制定有关标

准。组织实施用水总量控制等管理制度，指导和推动节水型社会建设工作。

（六）指导水文工作。负责水文水资源监测、国家水文站网建设和管理。对江河湖库和地下水实施监测，发布水文水资源信息、情报预报和国家水资源公报。按规定组织开展水资源、水能资源调查评价和水资源承载能力监测预警工作。

（七）指导水利设施、水域及其岸线的管理、保护与综合利用。组织指导水利基础设施网络建设。指导重要江河湖泊及河口的治理、开发和保护。指导河湖水生态保护与修复、河湖生态流量水量管理以及河湖水系连通工作。

（八）指导监督水利工程建设与运行管理。组织实施具有控制性的和跨区域跨流域的重要水利工程建设与运行管理。组织提出并协调落实三峡工程运行、南水北调工程运行和后续工程建设的有关政策措施，指导监督工程安全运行，组织工程验收有关工作，督促指导地方配套工程建设。

（九）负责水土保持工作。拟订水土保持规划并监督实施，组织实施水土流失的综合防治、监测预报并定期公告。负责建设项目水土保持监督管理工作，指导国家重点水土保持建设项目的实施。

（十）指导农村水利工作。组织开展大中型灌排工程建设与改造。指导农村饮水安全工程建设管理工作，指导节水灌溉有关工作。协调牧区水利工作。指导农村水利改革创新和社会化服务体系建设。指导农村水能资源开发、小水电改造和水电农村电气化工作。

（十一）指导水利工程移民管理工作。拟订水利工程移民有关政策并监督实施，组织实施水利工程移民安置验收、监督评估等制度。指导监督水库移民后期扶持政策的实施，协调监督三峡工程、南水北调工程移民后期扶持工作，协调推动对口支援等工作。

（十二）负责重大涉水违法事件的查处，协调和仲裁跨省、自治区、直辖市水事纠纷，指导水政监察和水行政执法。依法负责水利行业安全生产工作，组织指导水库、水电站大坝、农村水电站的安全监管。指导水利建设市场的监督管理，组织实施水利工程建设的监督。

（十三）开展水利科技和外事工作。组织开展水利行业质量监督工作，拟订水利行业的技术标准、规程规范并监督实施。办理国际河流有关涉外事务。

（十四）负责落实综合防灾减灾规划相关要求，组织编制洪水干旱灾害防治规划和防护标准并指导实施。承担水情旱情监测预警工作。组织编制重要江河湖泊和重要水工程的防御洪水抗御旱灾调度及应急水量调度方案，按程序报批并组织实施。承担防御洪水应急抢险的技术支撑工作。承担台风防御期间重要水工程调度工作。

（十五）完成党中央、国务院交办的其他任务。

（十六）职能转变。水利部应切实加强水资源合理利用、优化配置和节约保护。坚持节水优先，从增加供给转向更加重视需求管理，严格控制用水总量和提高用水效率。坚持保护优先，加强水资源、水域和水利工程的管理保护，维护河湖健康美丽。坚持统筹兼顾，保障合理用水需求和水资源的可持续利用，为经济社会发展提供水安全保障。

第四条 水利部设下列内设机构：

（一）办公厅。负责机关日常运转工作，承担信息、安全、保密、信访、政务公开、信息化、新闻宣传等工作。

（二）规划计划司。拟订水利战略规划，组织编制重大水利综合规划、专业规划和专项规划，审核重大水利建设项目建议书、可行性研究报告和初步设计。组织指导有关防洪论证工作。指导水工程建设项目合规性审查工作。组织实施中央水利建设投资计划，承担水利统计工作。

（三）政策法规司。起草水利法律法规草案和部门规章，研究拟订水利工作的政策并监督实施。指导水利行政许可工作并监督检查。承办部行政应诉、行政复议和行政赔偿工作。组织指导水政监察和水行政执法，协调跨省、自治区、直辖市水事纠纷，组织查处重大涉水违法事件。

（四）财务司。编制部门预算并组织实施，承担财务管理和资产管理工作。组织提出中央水利财政资金安排建议，并统筹协调项目实施的监督管理和绩效评价。提出有关水利价格、税费、基金、信贷的建议。

（五）人事司。承担机关和直属单位的干部人事、机构编制、劳动工资工作，指导水利行业人才队伍建设。承担水利体制改革的有关工作。

（六）水资源管理司。承担实施最严格水资源管理制度相关工作，组织实施水资源取水许可、水资源论证等制度，指导开展水资源有偿使用工作。指导水量分配工作并监督实施，指导河湖生态流量水量管理。组织编制水资源保护规划，指导饮用水水源保护有关工作。组织开展水资源调查、评价有关工作，组织编制并发布国家水资源公报。参与编制水功能区划和指导入河排污口设置管理工作。

（七）全国节约用水办公室。拟订节约用水政策，组织编制并协调实施节约用水规划，组织指导计划用水、节约用水工作。组织实施用水总量控制、用水效率控制、计划用水和定额管理制度。指导和推动节水型社会建设工作。指导城市污水处理回用等非常规水源开发利用工作。

（八）水利工程建设司。指导水利工程建设管理，制定有关制度并组织实施。组织指导水利工程蓄水安全鉴定和验收，指导大江大河干堤、重要病险水库、重要水闸的除险加固。指导水利建设市场的监督管理和水利建设市场信用体系建设。

（九）运行管理司。指导水利设施的管理、保护和综合利用，组织编制水库运行调度规程，指导水库、水电站大坝、堤防、水闸等水利工程的运行管理与划界。

（十）河湖管理司。指导水域及其岸线的管理和保护，指导重要江河湖泊、河口的开发、治理和保护，指导河湖水生态保护与修复以及河湖水系连通工作。监督管理河道采砂工作，指导河道采砂规划和计划的编制，组织实施河道管理范围内工程建设方案审查制度。

（十一）水土保持司。承担水土流失综合防治工作，组织编制水土保持规划并监督实施，组织水土流失监测、预报并公告，审核大中型开发建设项目水土保持方案并监督实施。

（十二）农村水利水电司。组织开展大中型灌排工程建设与改造，指导农村饮水安全工程建设管理工作，指导节水灌溉有关工作。组织拟订农村水能资源开发规划，指导水电农村电气化、农村水电增效扩容改造以及小水电代燃料等农村水能资源开发工作。指导农村水利社会化服务体系建设。承担协调牧区水利工作。

（十三）水库移民司。承担水利工程移民管理和后期扶持工作，组织实施水利工程移民安置验收、监督评估等制度，审核大中型水利工程移民安置规划，组织开展新增水库移民后期扶持人口核定，协调推动对口支援工作。

（十四）监督司。督促检查水利重大政策、决策部署和重点工作的贯彻落实情况。组织实施水利工程质量和安全监督。指导水利行业安全生产工作，指导水库、水电站大坝及农村水电站的安全监管。

（十五）水旱灾害防御司。组织编制洪水干旱防治规划和防护标准、重要江河湖泊和重要水工程的防御洪水抗御旱灾调度以及应急水量调度方案并组织实施。承担水情旱情预警工作。组织协调指导蓄滞洪区安全建设、管理和运用补偿工作，承担洪泛区、蓄滞洪区和防洪保护区的洪水影响评价工作。

（十六）水文司。组织指导全国水文工作，负责水文水资源（含水位、流量、水质等要素）监测工作，负责国家水文站网建设和管理。组织实施江河湖库和地下水监测。发布水文水资源信息、情报预报。

（十七）三峡工程管理司。组织提出三峡工程运行的有关政策建议，组织指导三峡工程运行调度规程规范编制并监督实施。指导监督三峡工程运行安全。组织三峡工程验收有关工作。承担三峡后续工作规划的组织实施、综合协调和监督管理。

（十八）南水北调工程管理司。协调落实南水北调工程有关重大政策和措施。组织南水北调工程竣工财务决算、审计和工程验收有关工作。制定南水北调年度供水计划并组织调度实施。指导监督工程运行管理工作。组织开展南水北调后续工程前期和建设管理工作。督促指导地方配套工程建设。

（十九）调水管理司。承担跨区域跨流域水资源供需形势分析，指导水资源调度工作并监督实施，组织指导大型调水工程前期工作，指导监督跨区域跨流域调水工程的调度管理等工作。

（二十）国际合作与科技司。承办国际河流有关涉外事务，承办国际合作和外事工作，拟订水利行业技术标准、规程规范并监督实施，组织重大水利科学研究、技术引进和科技推广。

机关党委。负责机关和在京直属单位的党群工作。

离退休干部局。负责离退休干部工作。

第五条 水利部机关行政编制 502 名（含两委人员编制 10 名、援派机动编制 6 名、离退休干部工作人员编制 31 名）。设部长 1 名，副部长 4 名，司局级领导职数 88 名（含总工程师 1 名、总规划师 1 名、总经济师 1 名、督察专员 4 名、机关党委专职副书记 1 名、离退休干部局领导职数 3 名）。

第六条 长江水利委员会、黄河水利委员会、淮河水利委员会、海河水利委员会、珠江水利委员会、松辽水利委员会、太湖流域管理局为水利部派出的流域管理机构，在所管辖的范围内依法行使水行政管理职责。具体机构设置、职责和编制事项另行规定。

第七条 水利部所属事业单位的设置、职责和编制事项另行规定。

第八条 本规定由中央机构编制委员会办公室负责解释，其调整由中央机构编制委员会办公室按规定程序办理。

第九条 本规定自 2018 年 7 月 30 日起施行。

国家发展改革委发布《企业投资项目事中事后监管办法》

国家发展改革委 2018 年 1 月 4 日发布第 14 号令，公布《企业投资项目事中事后监管办法》，该“办法”全文如下。

企业投资项目事中事后监管办法

第一章 总 则

第一条 为加强对企业投资项目的事中事后监管，规范企业投资行为，维护公共利益和企业合法权益，依据《行政许可法》《行政处罚法》《企业投资项目核准和备案管理条例》等法律法规，制定本办法。

第二条 各级发展改革部门根据核准和备案职责，对企业在境内投资建设的固定资产项目（以下简称项目）核准和备案的事中事后监督管理，适用本办法。

第三条 项目事中事后监管是指各级发展改革部门对项目开工前是否依法取得核准批复文件或者办理备案手续，并在开工后是否按照核准批复文件或者备案内容进行建设的监督管理。

各级发展改革部门开展项目事中事后监管，应当与规划、环保、国土、建设、安全生产等主管部门的事中事后监管工作各司其职、各负其责，并加强协调配合。

第四条 各级发展改革部门对项目实施分级分类监督管理。

对已经取得核准批复文件的项目，由核准机关实施监督管理；对已经备案的项目，由备案机关实施监督管理。对项目是否依法取得核准批复文件或者办理备案手续，由项目所在地县级以上地方发展改革部门实施监督管理。

第五条 各级发展改革部门应当建立健全行政监督和监管执法程序，加强监管执法队伍建设，保障监管执法经费，依法行使监督管理职权。

对政府投资项目以及企业投资项目使用政府投资的稽察工作，按照有关规定执行。

第二章 对核准项目的监管

第六条 核准机关对本机关已核准的项目，应当对以下方面进行监督管理：

（一）是否通过全国投资项目在线审批监管平台（以下简称在线平台），如实、及时报送项目开工建设、建设进度、竣工等建设实施基本信息；

（二）需要变更已核准建设地点或者对已核准建设规模、建设内容等作较大变更的，是否按规定办理变更手续；

（三）需要延期开工建设的，是否按规定办理延期开工建设手续；

（四）是否按照核准的建设地点、建设规模、建设内容等进行建设。

第七条 核准机关应当根据行业特点、监管需要和简易、可操作的原则，制定、上线核准项目报送建设实施基本信息的格式文本，并对报送的建设实施基本信息进行在线监测。

第八条 核准机关对其核准的项目，应当在项目开工后至少开展一次现场核查。

第九条 已开工核准项目未如实、及时报送建设实施基本信息的，核准机关应当责令项目单位予以纠正；拒不纠正的，给予警告。

第十条 项目未按规定办理核准批复文件、项目变更批复文件或者批复文件失效后开工建设的，核准机关应当依法责令停止建设或者责令停产，并依法处以罚款。

第十一条 项目未按照核准的建设地点、建设规模、建设内容等进行建设的，核准机关应当依法责令停止建设或者责令停产，并依法处以罚款。

对于有关部门依法认定项目建设内容属于产业政策禁止投资建设的，核准机关应当依法责令停止建设或者责令停产并恢复原状，并依法处以罚款。

第十二条 县级以上地方发展改革部门发现本行政区域内的项目列入《政府核准的投资项目目录》，但未依法办理核准批复文件、项目变更批复文件或者批复文件失效后开工建设的，应当报告对该项目有核准权限的机关，由核准机关依法责令停止建设或者责令停产，并依法处以罚款。

第三章 对备案项目的监管

第十三条 备案机关对本机关已备案的项目，应当对以下方面进行监督管理：

（一）是否通过在线平台如实、及时报送项目开工建设、建设进度、竣工等建设实施基本信息；

（二）是否属于实行核准管理的项目；

（三）是否按照备案的建设地点、建设规模、建设内容进行建设；

（四）是否属于产业政策禁止投资建设的项目。

第十四条 备案机关应当根据行业特点、监管需要和简易、可操作的原则，制定、上线备案项目报送建设实施基本信息的格式文本，并对报送的建设实施基本信息进行在线监测。

第十五条 项目自备案后 2 年内未开工建设或者未办理任何其他手续的，项目单位如果决定继续实施该项目，应当通过在线平台作出说明；如果不再继续实施，应当撤回已备案信息。

前款项目既未作出说明，也未撤回备案信息的，备案机关应当予以提醒。经提醒后仍未作出相应处理的，备案机关应当移除已向社会公示的备案信息，项目单位获取的备案证明文件自动失效。对其中属于故意报备不真实项目、影响投资信息准确性的，备案机关可以将项目列入异常名录，并向社会公开。

第十六条　备案机关对其备案的项目，应当根据“双随机一公开”的原则，结合投资调控实际需要，定期制定现场核查计划。对列入现场核查计划的项目，应当在项目开工后至少开展一次现场核查。列入现场核查计划的项目数量比例，由备案机关根据实际确定。

第十七条　已开工备案项目未如实、及时报送建设实施基本信息的，备案机关应当责令项目单位予以纠正；拒不纠正的，给予警告。

第十八条　项目建设与备案信息不符的，备案机关应当责令限期改正；逾期不改正的，依法处以罚款并列入失信企业名单，向社会公开。

对于有关部门依法认定项目建设内容属于产业政策禁止投资建设的，备案机关应当依法责令停止建设或者责令停产并恢复原状，并依法处以罚款。

第十九条　县级以上地方发展改革部门发现本行政区域内的已开工项目应备案但未依法备案的，应当报告对该项目有备案权限的机关，由备案机关责令其限期改正；逾期不改正的，依法处以罚款并列入失信企业名单，向社会公开。

第二十条　对本行政区域内的已开工项目，经有关部门依法认定属于产业政策禁止投资建设的，县级以上发展改革部门应当依法责令停止建设或者责令停产并恢复原状，并依法处以罚款。

第四章　监管程序和方式

第二十一条　各级发展改革部门对项目的现场核查，可以自行开展，也可以发挥工程咨询单位等机构的专业优势，以委托第三方机构的方式开展。

委托第三方机构开展现场核查的，应当建立核查机构名录，制订核查工作规范，加强对核查工作的指导和监督。委托第三方机构开展现场核查的经费由委托方承担。

第二十二条　各级发展改革部门应当依托在线平台，运用大数据、互联网、移动计算等信息技术手段，加强对各类信息的分析研判，提高发现问题线索的能力。

第二十三条　各级发展改革部门应当畅通投诉举报渠道，对投诉举报反映的问题线索及时予以处理。

第二十四条　各级发展改革部门对发现的涉嫌违法问题，应当按照法定权限和程序立案查处，并作出处理决定。

对发现的涉及其他部门职权的违法违纪线索，应当及时移送。涉嫌犯罪的，应当移送司法机关追究刑事责任。

第二十五条　各级发展改革部门对项目的行政处罚信息，应当通过在线平台进行归集，并通过在线平台和“信用中国”网站向社会公开。

对在项目事中事后监管中形成的项目异常名录和失信企业名单，应当通过在线平台与全国信用信息平台共享，通过“信用中国”网站向社会公开，并实施联合惩戒。

第二十六条　各级发展改革部门应当与规划、环保、国土、建设、安全生产等主管部门建立健全协同监管和联合执法机制，参加本级人民政府开展的综合执法工作，提高监管执法效率。

第二十七条　各级发展改革部门应当建立健全项目事中事后监管责任制和责任追究制，通过约谈、挂牌督办、上收核准权限等措施，督促下级发展改革部门落实工作责任。

第五章　法律责任

第二十八条　本办法第九条、第十七条所称的警告，均指《行政处罚法》规定的行政处罚罚种，各级发展改革部门应当依照法定程序和要求实施。

第二十九条　核准机关对未按规定办理核准手续的项目，未按照核准的建设地点、建设规模、建设内容等进行建设的项目，处以罚款的情形和幅度依照《企业投资项目核准和备案管理条例》第十八条执行。

第三十条　备案机关对未依法备案的项目，建设与备案信息不符的项目，处以罚款的情形和幅度依照《企业投资项目核准和备案管理条例》第十九条执行。

第三十一条　对属于产业政策禁止投资建设的项目，处以罚款的情形和幅度依照《企业投资项目核准和备案管理条例》第二十条执行。

第三十二条　违反本办法规定，但能够积极配合调查、认真整改纠正、主动消除或者减轻危害后果的，可以在法定幅度内减轻处罚。

第六章　附　　则

第三十三条　外商投资项目事中事后监督管理另有规定的，从其规定。

第三十四条　事业单位、社会团体等非企业组织在境内投资建设的项目事中事后监督管理适用本办法，但通过预算安排的项目除外。

第三十五条　本办法由国家发展和改革委员会负责解释。

第三十六条　本办法自2018年2月4日起实施。

国家发展改革委、国家能源局印发《关于加强和规范涉电力领域失信联合惩戒对象名单管理工作的实施意见》

国家发展改革委、国家能源局2018年2月3日以发改运行规〔2018〕233号文发布《关于加强和规范涉电力领域失信联合惩戒对象名单管理工作的实施意见》，该“意见”全文如下。

为贯彻落实党的十九大精神，加强诚信体系建设，根据《中共中央 国务院关于进一步深化电力体制改革的若干意见》（中发〔2015〕9号）、《国务院关于印发社会信用体系建设规划纲要（2014～2020年）的通知》（国发〔2014〕21号）、《国务院关于建立完善守信联合激励和失信联合惩戒制度加快推进社会诚信建设的指导意见》（国发〔2016〕33号）、《国家发展改革委 人民银行关于加强和规范守信联合激励和失信联合惩戒对象名单管理工作的指导意见》（发改财金规〔2017〕1798号）的相关要求及规定，加强对涉电力领域市场主体的信用监管，建立失信联合惩戒对象名单（以下简称“黑名单”）制度，完善违法失信惩戒的联动机制，促进行业健康发展，现提出如下实施意见。

一、总体要求

（一）政府主管部门及行业监管部门对存在严重违反电力法律、法规、规章等严重失信行为的涉电力领域市场主体，依法依规列入“黑名单”，并向社会公布，实施信用约束、联合惩戒。市场主体存在违法失信行为且情节较轻的，可先纳入诚信状况重点关注对象名单（以下简称“重点关注名单”）。

（二）国家发展改革委、国家能源局负责对全国涉电力领域“黑名单”管理工作进行指导和协调，县级以上行业主管部门、相关监管部门根据职能负责本地区“黑名单”管理工作。

（三）坚持“谁认定、谁负责”的原则，认定“黑名单”的部门和单位负责“黑名单”的公布、信用修复、异议处理、退出等工作。

（四）认定为涉电力领域“黑名单”市场主体的相关信息应纳入全国信用信息共享平台，按照《关于对电力行业严重违法失信市场主体及其有关人员实施联合惩戒的合作备忘录》等有关规定，实施联合惩戒。

二、认定标准

（五）涉电力领域市场主体包括发电企业、售电企业、参与电力市场交易的电力用户、电网企业、电力建设、施工、监理、勘察、设计企业、电能服务企业、电力设备供应企业。

（六）涉电力领域市场主体存在下列情形之一的，应按照规定程序列入“黑名单”：

1. 未取得许可从事相关业务、涂改许可证、隐瞒有关情况或者以提供虚假申请材料等方式违法违规进入市场，未按要求及时变更注册信息和用户登记信息，且拒不整改；

2. 违反信用承诺且拒不整改；

3. 在其他领域因严重违法失信行为被列入相关“黑名单”；

4. 存在其他违法违规行为，受到行政处罚等法律处罚，情节严重或拒不整改。

（七）发电企业存在下列情形之一，情节严重或拒不整改的，应按照规定程序列入“黑名单”：

1. 未执行并网调度协议，未服从电力调度管理；

2. 经审核符合准入条件的企业自备电厂，未足额缴纳政府性基金及政策性交叉补贴；

3. 违反相关规定，建设电厂向用户直接供电的专用线路，以及与其参与投资的增量配电网络连接的专用线路。

（八）售电企业存在下列情形之一，情节严重或拒不整改的，应按照规定程序列入“黑名单”：

1. 超出准入条件规定的售电量范围开展售电业务；

2. 未承担保密义务，违规泄露用户信息。

（九）参与电力市场交易的电力用户存在下列情形之一，情节严重或拒不整改的，应按照规定程序列入“黑名单”：

1. 存在违约用电、窃电或者破坏电力设施行为；

2. 存在用电安全隐患等影响电力安全稳定运行或威胁人身安全的行为；

3. 以各种形式逃缴、拒缴和拖欠政府性基金或政策性交叉补贴。

（十）电网企业存在下列情形之一，情节严重或拒不整改的，应按照规定程序列入“黑名单”：

1. 未按国家有关规定和合同约定承担保底供电服务和普遍服务；

2. 未严格落实电网安全责任，供电质量未达到承诺标准；

3. 未做到对发电企业、电力用户及其他电网企业的无歧视公平接入；

4. 存在干预发电企业、售电公司、电力用户之间相互自主选择的行为。

（十一）电力建设、施工、监理、勘察、设计企业存在下列情形之一，情节严重或拒不整改的，应按照规定程序列入“黑名单”：

1. 转让、出租出借、借用挂靠、涂改、伪造许可资质（资格）证书或者以其他方式允许其他单位或者个人以本单位名义承揽工程；

2. 超越许可范围承揽工程；

3. 弄虚作假骗取中标、不正当手段承揽工程；

4. 将工程转包或者违法分包；

5. 存在重大安全、质量隐患，经督查不及时整改；

6. 未按核准文件确定的招标方式开展招标；

7. 发生因工程安全质量问题引发的较大安全责任事故；

8. 严重违反合同约定。

（十二）电能服务企业存在下列情形之一，情节严重或拒不整改的，应按照规定程序列入“黑名单”：

1. 提供的平台或产品问题给用户造成经济损失；

2. 拒不处理客户投诉；

3. 采用不正当手段竞争，扰乱市场秩序；

4. 骗取国家政府补贴。

（十三）电力设备供应企业存在下列情形之一，情节严重或拒不整改的，应按照规定程序列入“黑名单”：

1. 降低产品设计标准、偷工减料，或在生产制造过程中使用伪劣原材料、组部件以次充好；

2. 在施工（建筑、安装等）、调试或运行过程中，出现质量问题，发生安全事故或质量事故；

3. 不能安全稳定运行或技术、质量等性能指标与设计值出现重大偏差，且无法通过进一步调试和正常维护得到解决；

4. 存在商业行贿受贿行为，经营者为销售或购买商品而采用财务或其他手段贿赂对方单位或个人。

（十四）涉电力领域市场主体在电力市场交易方面存在下列情形之一，情节严重或拒不整改的，应按照规定程序列入“黑名单”：

1. 无故未履行市场交易合同或具有法律效力的交易意向；

2. 未按时进行交易结算，拖欠电费；

3. 恶意串通、操纵市场或变相操纵市场；

4. 提供虚假信息，违规发布信息，或未按规定披露、提供信息；

5. 违反电力市场交易规则开展交易。

（十五）涉电力领域市场主体在电力规划设计、政策标准执行及项目合作、建设管理方面有下列情形之一，情节严重或拒不整改的，应按照规定程序列入“黑名单”：

1. 未按照规划总量进行产能布局、重复建设、开发利用效率低下、发展失衡，违反相关优选原则；

2. 选择性执行或变相、消极、错误执行国家有关能源政策；

3. 违反电力行业标准化工作有关强制性规定或执行国家强制性标准情况不达标；

4. 新建电力项目违法违规转让开展前期工作资格或核准文件；

5. 违法违规变更新建项目投资主体；

6. 需核准的电力项目未经核准先行开工建设，或者未按核准文件规定建设；

7. 电力项目存在超容量建设、停产整顿项目继续建设、为争取国家补贴指标而虚报项目、以资源综合利用名义建设低效项目等情形。

（十六）涉电力领域市场主体在安全生产、应急管理和节能减排方面有下列情形之一，情节严重或拒不整改的，应按照规定程序列入“黑名单”：

1. 发生《生产安全事故报告和调查处理条例》所规定的重大生产安全事故，或一年内累计发生责任事故死亡 10 人（含）以上；

2. 发生《电力安全事故应急处置和调查处理条例》所规定的重大电力安全事故；

3. 重大安全生产隐患不及时整改或整改不到位；

4. 发生暴力抗法的行为，或未按时完成行政执法指令；

5. 发生事故隐瞒不报、谎报或迟报，故意破坏事故现场、毁灭有关证据；

6. 经监管执法部门认定严重威胁安全生产的其他行为；

7. 在电力、核电厂等领域未按国家要求有效落实应急管理责任；未建立电力应急指挥体系，未制定电力安全应急预案，不按规定开展应急演练；

8. 未按规定安装、运行环保设备，污染物排放不符合环保标准和规定，瞒报、伪造、篡改统计数据和相关备查资料；

9. 阻碍、抗拒依法实施的节能监管，情节严重或隐匿、拒不提供相关资料。

（十七）在许可监管中发现涉电力领域市场主体有下列情形之一，情节严重或拒不整改的，应按照规定程序列入“黑名单”：

1. 出租出借或借用挂靠许可资质；

2. 超出许可范围或者超过许可期限从事相关业务且限期未完成整改；

3. 不具备许可条件仍从事相关业务，未在规定期限内申请许可变更或注销且限期内未完成整改；

4. 未经批准，擅自停业、歇业。

（十八）市场主体具有相关失信行为，但尚未达到“黑名单”认定标准的，应按照规定程序列入重点关注名单，通过约谈、提醒、下达整改函等方式督促整改。

（十九）市场主体列入重点关注名单未能在整改期限完成整改并退出，或无明确整改期限的未能在 3 个月内完成整改并退出，或一年内 3 次或 3 次以上被列入重点关注名单，应按照规定程序列入“黑名单”。

三、认定与发布

（二十）县级以上行业主管部门、相关监管部门可按照认定标准，根据职能认定涉电力领域“黑名单”、重点关注名单。国家发展改革委、国家能源局可根据需要授权全国性行业协会商会，按照认定标准认定涉电力领域“黑名单”、重点关注名单。

（二十一）鼓励电力交易机构、行业协会商会等各类单位和公民个人积极支持和配合认定工作，向认定部门（单位）提供市场主体的失信行为信息。认定部门（单位）应积极委托大数据企业开展大数据监管，将大数据分析结果作为认定“黑名单”的重要参考依据。

（二十二）认定部门（单位）应按照以下程序认定“黑名单”：

1. 正式告知拟列入“黑名单”的市场主体列入事由和列入依据，允许其在10个工作日内提交有关申辩材料；

2. 组成相关政府部门、社会组织及行业专家参加的小组，根据各方提供的材料进行审查，提出市场主体是否列入“黑名单”的认定意见书；

3. 县级以上行业主管部门、相关监管部门认定的“黑名单”直接生效；授权的全国性行业协会商会认定的“黑名单”，需经相应信用建设牵头部门或能源监管部门审核后生效；

4. 完成认定后，认定部门（单位）应向列入“黑名单”的市场主体下达认定决定函。

（二十三）建立全国涉电力领域“黑名单”信息管理系统，各认定部门（单位）认定的“黑名单”均统一纳入信息管理系统。市场主体被列入“黑名单”后，认定部门（单位）应于列入当日将有关信息录入“黑名单”信息管理系统。录入信息主要内容包括：一是基本信息，包括法人和其他组织名称（或自然人姓名）、统一社会信用代码、全球法人机构识别编码（LEI码）（或公民身份证号码、港澳台居民的公民社会信用代码、外国籍人身份号码）、法定代表人（或单位负责人）姓名及其身份证件类型和号码等；二是列入名单的事由，包括认定违法失信行为的事实、认定部门（单位）、认定依据、认定日期、有效期等；三是市场主体受到联合奖惩、信用修复、退出名单的相关情况。

（二十四）涉电力领域“黑名单”信息管理系统应主动将相关信息共享至全国信用信息共享平台，供各级国家机关、法律法规授权具有管理公共事务职能的组织共享使用。

（二十五）认定生效的“黑名单”，由认定部门（单位）通过其门户网站、地方政府信用网站、“信用中国”网站、电力交易机构网站等向社会公众发布。对于涉及企业商业秘密和个人隐私的信息，发布前应进行必要的技术处理。

（二十六）认定部门（单位）对列入重点关注名单的市场主体，应制定有关标准和程序，录入“黑名单”信息管理系统，共享至全国信用信息共享平台。

四、名单退出与权益保护

（二十七）已被列入“黑名单”的市场主体，符合以下条件的，经认定部门（单位）确认，可以退出“黑名单”：

1. 市场主体自被列入“黑名单”之日起满3年，未再发生严重违法失信行为；

2. 市场主体被列入“黑名单”的主要事实依据被撤销；

3.“黑名单”认定标准发生改变，不符合新认定标准；

4. 按照有关规定和标准完成自主信用修复，经认定部门（单位）审核同意；

5. 经异议处理，“黑名单”认定有误。

（二十八）市场主体退出“黑名单”后，认定部门（单位）应及时通过原发布渠道发布名单退出公告，并将其列入重点关注名单。对于认定有误的“黑名单”，不列入重点关注名单。

（二十九）认定部门（单位）应建立市场主体自主信用修复机制，在下达“黑名单”认定决定函时结合失信行为的严重程度，明确市场主体能否修复信用以及修复的方式和期限。可通过履行相关义务纠正失信行为的“黑名单”市场主体，可在履行相关义务后，向认定部门（单位）提交相关材料申请退出。

（三十）认定部门（单位）应建立“黑名单”异议处理机制，明确异议受理渠道、办理流程和时限。有关单位和个人对被列入“黑名单”有异议的，可向认定部门（单位）提交异议申请并提供证明材料。认定部门（单位）应严格按时限反馈是否受理的意见，受理后要按时限反馈处理结果。当事人对反馈结果仍有异议的，可依法申请复议。

（三十一）认定部门（单位）自主发现的，或接到相关部门、单位、个人反映、投诉的名单信息不准确情况，要及时进行核实。确因认定部门（单位）工作失误导致有关单位和个人被误列入“黑名单”的，认定部门（单位）应及时更正当事人的诚信记录，向当事人书面道歉并进行澄清，恢复其名誉。导致当事人权益受损的，依法给予赔偿。

五、保障措施

（三十二）国家发展改革委、国家能源局负责指导监督全国涉电力领域“黑名单”管理工作，各认定部门（单位）按照国家统一规定开展“黑名单”认定工作。

（三十三）国家发展改革委、国家能源局负责建设和管理全国涉电力领域“黑名单”信息管理系统，建立健全并严格执行保障信息安全的规章制度并做好落实。各认定部门（单位）要严格按照规定录入、查询、维护和使用信息，确保信息真实，严防信息泄露。

（三十四）对“黑名单”认定过程中出现的违法违规行为，各认定部门（单位）应当及时予以纠正。各认定部门（单位）及其相关工作人员在“黑名单”认定相关工作过程中存在滥用职权、玩忽职守、徇私舞弊、因故意或工作失误泄露不公开信息等行为的，由所在单位或上级主管部门视情节轻重对直接责任人和其他负有责任的主管人员依法依规予以处理；对市场主体造成损失的，依法承担相应责任；构成犯罪的，移送司法机关依法追究刑事责任。

（三十五）省级行业主管部门和相关监管部门在管辖区域内可根据本实施意见，制定涉电力领域失信联合惩戒对象名单管理实施细则。经授权的全国性行业协会商会可根据本实施意见，制定本协会商会内部的管理实施细则。

（三十六）行业协会商会、电力交易机构、大数据企业等在配合政府部门开展“黑名单”管理工作中要注重加强自身信用建设，坚持公平公正、实事求是。

本文件自发布之日起试行，有效期至 2020 年 12 月 31 日。

国家发展改革委、国家能源局关于提升电力系统调节能力的指导意见

国家发展改革委、国家能源局 2018 年 2 月 28 日以发改能源〔2018〕364 号文印发《关于提升电力系统调节能力的指导意见》，该“意见”全文如下。

为贯彻落实党的十九大精神，按照 2017 年中央经济工作会议部署，以习近平新时代中国特色社会主义思想为指导，扎实推动能源生产和消费革命，推进电力供给侧结构性改革，构建高效智能的电力系统，提高电力系统的调节能力及运行效率。现提出以下指导意见：

一、重要意义

党的十九大报告指出，要推进能源生产和消费革命，构建清洁低碳、安全高效的能源体系。2017 年中央经济工作会议提出，要增加清洁电力供应，促进节能环保、清洁生产、清洁能源等绿色产业发展。当前，我国电力系统调节灵活性欠缺、电网调度运行方式较为僵化等现实造成了系统难以完全适应新形势要求，大型机组难以发挥节能高效的优势，部分地区出现了较为严重的弃风、弃光和弃水问题，区域用电用热矛盾突出。为实现我国提出的 2020 年、2030 年非化石能源消费比重分别达到 15%、20%的目标，保障电力安全供应和民生用热需求，需着力提高电力系统的调节能力及运行效率，从负荷侧、电源侧、电网侧多措并举，重点增强系统灵活性、适应性，破解新能源消纳难题，推进绿色发展。

二、加快推进电源侧调节能力提升

（一）实施火电灵活性提升工程

根据不同地区调节能力需求，科学制定各省火电灵活性提升工程实施方案。“十三五”期间，力争完成 2.2 亿 kW 火电机组灵活性改造（含燃料灵活性改造，下同），提升电力系统调节能力 4600 万 kW。优先提升 30 万 kW 级煤电机组的深度调峰能力。改造后的纯凝机组最小技术出力达到 30%～40%额定容量，热电联产机组最小技术出力达到 40%～50%额定容量；部分电厂达到国际先进水平，机组不投油稳燃时纯凝工况最小技术出力达到 20%～30%。

（二）推进各类灵活调节电源建设

加快已审批的选点规划推荐的抽水蓄能电站建设，适时开展新一轮选点规划，加快推进西南地区龙头水库电站建设。“十三五”期间，开工建设 6000 万 kW 抽水蓄能电站和金沙江中游龙头水库电站。到 2020 年，抽水蓄能电站装机规模达到 4000 万 kW（其中“三北”地区 1140 万 kW），有效提升电力系统调节能力。

在气源有保障、调峰需求突出的地区发展一定规模的燃气机组进行启停调峰，“十三五”期间，新增调峰气电规模 500 万 kW，提升电力系统调节能力 500 万 kW。

积极支持太阳能热发电，推动产业化发展和规模化应用，“十三五”期间，太阳能热发电装机力争达到 500 万 kW，提升电力系统调节能力 400 万 kW。

（三）推动新型储能技术发展及应用

加快新型储能技术研发创新，重点在大容量液流、锂离子、钠硫、铅炭电池等电化学储能电池、压缩空气储能等方面开展创新和推广，提高新型储能系统的转换效率和使用寿命。在调峰调频需求较大、弃风弃光突出的地区，结合电力系统辅助服务市场建设进度，建设一批装机容量1万kW以上的集中式新型储能电站，在“三北”地区部署5个百兆瓦级电化学储能电站示范工程。开展在风电、光伏发电项目配套建设储能设施的试点工作。鼓励分布式储能应用。到2020年，建成一批不同技术类型、不同应用场景的试点示范项目。

三、科学优化电网建设

（四）加强电源与电网协调发展

坚持市场需求为导向，在确定电源规划和年度实施方案过程中，组织相关方确定电力消纳市场、送电方向，同步制定接入电网方案，明确建设时序。根据不同发电类型和电网工程建设工期等，合理安排电源及配套电网项目的核准建设进度，确保同步规划同步实施同步投产，避免投资浪费。

（五）加强电网建设

加强新能源开发重点地区电网建设，解决送出受限问题。落实《电力发展“十三五”规划》确定的重点输电通道，“十三五”期间，跨省跨区通道新增19条，新增输电能力1.3亿kW，消纳新能源和可再生能源约7000万kW。进一步完善区域输电网主网架，促进各电压等级电网协调发展。

开展配电网建设改造，推动智能电网建设，满足分布式电源接入需要，全面构建现代配电系统。按照差异化需求，提高信息化、智能化水平，提高高压配电网“N－1”通过率，加强中压配电网线路联络率，提升配电自动化覆盖率。

（六）增强受端电网适应性

开展专项技术攻关，发展微电网等可中断负荷，解决远距离、大容量跨区直流输电闭锁故障影响受端安全稳定运行问题，提升受端电网适应能力，满足受端电网供电可靠性。

四、提升电力用户侧灵活性

（七）发展各类灵活性用电负荷

推进售电侧改革，通过价格信号引导用户错峰用电，实现快速灵活的需求侧响应。开展智能小区、智能园区等电力需求响应及用户互动工程示范。开展能效电厂试点。鼓励各类高耗能企业改善工艺和生产流程，为系统提供可中断负荷、可控负荷等辅助服务。全面推进电能替代，到2020年，电能替代电量达到4500亿kW·h，电能占终端能源消费的比重上升至27%。在新能源富集地区，重点发展热泵技术供热、蓄热式电锅炉等灵活用电负荷，鼓励可中断式电制氢、电转气等相关技术的推广和应用。

（八）提高电动汽车充电基础设施智能化水平

探索利用电动汽车储能作用，提高电动汽车充电基础设施的智能化水平和协同控制能力，加强充电基础设施与新能源、电网等技术融合，通过“互联网＋充电基础设施”，同步构建充电智能服务平台，积极推进电动汽车与智能电网间的能量和信息双向互动，提升充电服务化水平。

五、加强电网调度的灵活性

（九）提高电网调度智能水平

构建多层次智能电力系统调度体系。优化开机方式，确定合理备用率。开展风电和太阳能超短期高精度功率预测、高渗透率新能源接入电网运行控制等专题研究，提高新能源发电参与日内电力平衡比例。实施风光功率预测考核，将风电、光伏等发电机组纳入电力辅助服务管理，承担相应辅助服务费用，实现省级及以上的电力调度机构调度的发电机组全覆盖。国家能源局批复的电力辅助服务市场改革试点地区，按照批复方案推进执行。完善日内发电计划滚动调整机制，调度机构根据风光短期和超短期功率预测信息，动态调整各类调节电源的发电计划以及跨省跨区联络线输送功率。

探索电力热力联合智能调度机制，在调度机构建立热电厂电力热力负荷实时监测系统，并根据实际热力负荷需求确定机组发电曲线。研究制定储热装置、电热锅炉等灵活热源接入后的智能调度机制。

（十）发挥区域电网调节作用

建立常规电源发电计划灵活调整机制，各区域电网内共享调峰和备用资源。研究在区域电网优化开机方式，提升新能源发电空间。在新能源送出受限地区，开展动态输电容量应用专题研究。

（十一）提高跨区通道输送新能源比重

优化在运跨省跨区输电通道运行方式。调整和放缓配套火电建设的跨区输电通道，富余容量优先安排新能源外送，力争“十三五”期间，“三北地区”可再生能源跨区消纳4000万kW以上。水电和风电输电通道同时送入的受端省份，应研究水电和风电通道送电曲线协调配合方式，充分发挥风电和水电的互补效益，增加风电通道中风电占比。

六、提升电力系统调节能力关键技术水平

（十二）提高高效智能装备水平

依托基础研究和工程建设，组织推动提升电力系统调节能力关键装备的技术攻关、试验示范和推广应用。突破一批制约性或瓶颈性技术装备和零部件的技术攻关，推动一批已完成技术攻关的关键技术装备开展试验示范，进一步验证技术路线和经济性，推广一批完成试验示范的技术装备实现批量化生产和产业化应用。

（十三）升级能源装备产业体系

在电力装备领域，形成一批具有自主知识产权和较强竞争力的装备制造企业集团，形成具有比较优势的较完善产业体系和产学研用有机结合的自主创新体系，总体具有较强国际竞争力，实现引领能源装备制造业转型升级。

（十四）加强创新推动新技术应用

建立企业、研究机构、高校多方参与的提升电力系统调节能力技术创新应用体系。加强火电灵活性改造技术的研发和应用，推进能源互联网、智能微电网、电动汽车、储能等技术的应用。着力通过技术进步和规模化应用促进电力系统与信息技术的融合和电储能技术成本的降低。

七、建立健全支撑体系

（十五）完善电力辅助服务补偿（市场）机制

按照“谁受益、谁承担”的原则，探索建立发电企业和用户参与的辅助服务分担共享机制。进一步完善和深化电力辅助服务补偿（市场）机制，实现电力辅助服务补偿力度科学化，合理确定火电机组有偿调峰的调峰深度，并根据系统调节能力的变化进行动态调整，合理补偿火电机组、抽水蓄能电站和新型储能电站灵活运行的直接成本和机会成本。鼓励采用竞争方式确定电力辅助服务承担机组，鼓励自动发电控制和调峰服务按效果补偿，鼓励储能设备、需求侧资源参与提供电力辅助服务，允许第三方参与提供电力辅助服务。

（十六）鼓励社会资本参与电力系统调节能力提升工程

支持社会资本参与火电灵活性改造，以及各类调峰电源和大型储能电站建设。支持地方开展抽蓄电站投资主体多元化和运行模式探索。鼓励以合同能源管理等第三方投资模式建设、运营电厂储热、储能设施。火电厂在计量出口内建设的电供热储能设施，按照系统调峰设施进行管理并对其深度调峰贡献给予合理经济补偿，其用电参照厂用电管理但统计上不计入厂用电。

（十七）加快推进电力市场建设

加快电力市场建设，大幅度提高电力市场化交易比重，建立以市场为导向的促进新能源消纳的制度体系。逐步建立中长期市场和现货市场相结合的电力市场，通过弹性电价机制释放系统灵活性。研究利用市场机制支持储能等灵活调节电源发展的政策，充分反映调节电源的容量价值。在电力现货市场建立之前，通过峰谷电价、分时电价等价格机制，支持电力系统调节平衡。大力推进售电侧改革，鼓励售电公司制定灵活的售电电价，促进电力消费者与生产者互动。以北方地区冬季清洁取暖为重点，鼓励风电企业、供暖企业参与电力市场交易，探索网、源、荷三方受益的可持续发展机制。

（十八）建立电力系统调节能力提升标准体系

开展有关电力系统调节能力提升的标准制订和修编工作。对现有火电厂技术标准进行修编，“三北”地区新建煤电达到相应灵活运行标准，新建热电机组实现“热电解耦”技术要求。研究编制新型储能技术以及需求侧智能化管理的相关标准。借鉴国际电力系统灵活运行先进经验，促进电力系统调节能力提升技术标准的国际交流与合作。

八、按职责分工抓紧组织实施

（十九）加强组织领导

国家发展改革委、国家能源局牵头开展电力系统调节能力提升工程及监管相关工作，统筹协调解决重大问题。各省级人民政府相关主管部门因地制宜研究制定本省（自治区、直辖市）电力系统调节能力提升工程实施方案，将电力系统调节能力提升效果纳入节能减排考核体系。电力现货市场建设试点地区可结合市场设计方案，自行设计提高电力系统调节能力及运行效率的调度机制。各电网企业和发电企业是提升电力系统调节能力的实施主体，要积极制定实施计划，落实项目资金，推动项目建设。国家能源局各派出能源监管机构会同各地方能源主管部门负责电力系统调节能力提升工程的具体监管工作，国家能源局各派出能源监管机构负责组织推进当地电力辅助服务补偿（市场）工作及日常事务的协调处理。各单位要根据指导意见相关要求，统筹谋划，协作配合，科学组织实施，务实有序推进相关工作。

（二十）强化监督管理

国家能源局各派出能源监管机构会同各地方能源主管部门对电力系统调节能力提升工程开展专项监管。对于实施方案整体落实不到位的省份，将削减其新能源等电源建设指标。对已享受相关优惠政策但实际运行效果未达到的项目，将向社会公布，视情节取消相关优惠政策。对已纳入灵活性改造范围的火电机组，未按时完成改造或未达到规定调节效果的，将暂时削减其计划发电量。国家能源局将按年度对全国电

力系统调节能力提升工程的进展情况进行评价考核。

国家发展改革委关于降低一般工商业电价有关事项的通知

国家发展改革委 2018 年 3 月 28 日以发改价格〔2018〕500 号文印发《关于降低一般工商业电价有关事项的通知》，该“通知”全文如下。

为贯彻落实中央经济工作会议关于降低企业用能成本和《政府工作报告》关于降低一般工商业电价的要求，决定分两批实施降价措施，落实一般工商业电价平均下降 10%的目标要求，进一步优化营商环境。现将第一批降价措施有关事项通知如下。

一、主要措施

（一）全面落实已出台的电网清费政策。要严格按照《关于取消临时接电费和明确自备电厂有关收费政策的通知》（发改办价格〔2017〕1895 号）规定，做好电网清费工作，一是督促电网企业组织清退已向电力用户收取的临时接电费，二是减免余热、余压、余气自备电厂政策性交叉补贴和系统备用费，确保政策精准落地。

（二）推进区域电网和跨省跨区专项工程输电价格改革。根据《关于核定区域电网 2018～2019 年输电价格的通知》（发改价格〔2018〕224 号）和《关于调整宁东直流等专项工程 2018～2019 年输电价格的通知》（发改价格〔2018〕225 号）核定的区域电网和跨省跨区专项工程输电价格，将降低部分用于核减相关省份输配电价。

（三）进一步规范和降低电网环节收费。一是提高两部制电价的灵活性。完善两部制电价制度，两部制电力用户可自愿选择按变压器容量或合同最大需量缴纳电费，也可选择按实际最大需量缴纳电费。逐步实现符合变压器容量要求的一般工商业及其他用电选择执行大工业两部制电价。二是全面清理规范电网企业在输配电价之外的收费项目。重点清理规范产业园区、商业综合体等经营者向转供电用户在国家规定销售电价之外收取的各类加价。产业园区经营的园区内电网，可自愿选择移交电网企业直接供电或改制为增量配电网。商业综合体等经营者应按国家规定销售电价向租户收取电费，相关共用设施用电及损耗通过租金、物业费、服务费等方式协商解决；或者按国家规定销售电价向电网企业缴纳电费，由所有用户按各分表电量公平分摊。

（四）临时性降低输配电价。将省级电网企业已核定的规划新增输配电投资额转为用于计提折旧的比例由平均 75%降至 70%，减少本监管周期定价成本，并相应降低输配电价。

二、执行时间

第一批降价措施全部用于降低一般工商业电价，自 2018 年 4 月 1 日起执行。

三、有关要求

（一）各省（自治区、直辖市）价格主管部门要按照本通知规定，抓紧研究提出降低一般工商业电价具体方案，经同级人民政府同意并报我委（价格司）备案后实施。相应降低各省（自治区、直辖市）一般工商业输配电价水平。

（二）各省（自治区、直辖市）价格主管部门、电网企业要精心组织、周密安排，做好宣传解释工作，主动服务企业，确保电价政策平稳实施。执行中遇到的情况和问题，请及时报送我委（价格司）。

国家发展改革委印发《必须招标的工程项目规定》

国家发展改革委 2018 年 3 月 27 日以第 16 号令发布已经国务院批准的《必须招标的工程项目规定》，该“规定”全文如下。

必须招标的工程项目规定

第一条 为了确定必须招标的工程项目，规范招标投标活动，提高工作效率、降低企业成本、预防腐败，根据《中华人民共和国招标投标法》第三条的规定，制定本规定。

第二条 全部或者部分使用国有资金投资或者国家融资的项目包括：

（一）使用预算资金 200 万元人民币以上，并且该资金占投资额 10%以上的项目；

（二）使用国有企业事业单位资金，并且该资金占控股或者主导地位的项目。

第三条 使用国际组织或者外国政府贷款、援助资金的项目包括：

（一）使用世界银行、亚洲开发银行等国际组织贷款、援助资金的项目；

（二）使用外国政府及其机构贷款、援助资金的项目。

第四条 不属于本规定第二条、第三条规定情形的大型基础设施、公用事业等关系社会公共利益、公众安全的项目，必须招标的具体范围由国务院发展改革部门会同国务院有关部门按照确有必要、严格限定的原则制订，报国务院批准。

第五条 本规定第二条至第四条规定范围内的项目，其勘察、设计、施工、监理以及与工程建设有关的重要设备、材料等的采购达到下列标准之一的，必须招标：

（一）施工单项合同估算价在400万元人民币以上；

（二）重要设备、材料等货物的采购，单项合同估算价在200万元人民币以上；

（三）勘察、设计、监理等服务的采购，单项合同估算价在100万元人民币以上。

同一项目中可以合并进行的勘察、设计、施工、监理以及与工程建设有关的重要设备、材料等的采购，合同估算价合计达到前款规定标准的，必须招标。

第六条 本规定自2018年6月1日起施行。

国家发展改革委、工信部、财政部、人民银行等四部委联合发布《关于做好2018年降成本重点工作的通知》

国家发展改革委、工业和信息化部、财政部、人民银行等四部委2018年4月28日联合以发改运行〔2018〕634号文发布《关于做好2018年降成本重点工作的通知》，该“通知”全文如下。

在党中央、国务院坚强领导下，经过各方共同努力，两年来降低实体经济企业成本工作取得显著成效，年度目标任务顺利完成。党的十九大报告指出，必须坚持质量第一、效益优先，以供给侧结构性改革为主线，推动经济发展质量变革、效率变革、动力变革，提高全要素生产率。为不断增强我国经济的创新力和竞争力，切实提高供给体系质量，显著增强我国经济质量优势，按照中央经济工作会议和《降低实体经济企业成本工作方案》（国发〔2016〕48号）要求，结合近两年工作实践，降低实体经济企业成本工作部际联席会议2018年将重点组织落实好9个方面30项任务。

一、2018年降成本目标任务和总体要求

深入学习贯彻习近平新时代中国特色社会主义思想和党的十九大精神，坚持稳中求进工作总基调，深化供给侧结构性改革，持续推进降成本工作，确保完成国发〔2016〕48号文件提出的3年左右使实体经济企业综合成本合理下降，盈利能力较为明显增强的目标任务。

在降成本工作中，更加注重中长期目标确立和长效机制建设，把降成本与产业转型升级、提升持续发展能力结合起来，以提高实体经济供给体系质量为重点，持续增强我国经济质量优势。坚持统筹谋划、分类实施，坚持远近结合、标本兼治，坚持外部减负、内部挖潜，坚持上下联动、互相借鉴。在降低制度性交易成本、税费成本和要素成本上协同发力，降低企业负担。

二、持续降低税费负担

（一）通过结构性减税支持实体经济发展。统筹推进增值税改革，优化调整增值税税率，落实支持创业创新的税收优惠政策，落实对中小微企业、科技型企业的税收优惠政策，下调部分产品进口关税。

（二）提高纳税便利程度。尽快推出分行业扩大小规模纳税人自行开具增值税专用发票试点范围等具体改革措施；研究推出改进税收优惠备案方式、简并优化申报表、建立信用积分制度等具体改革措施。规范办税程序，推进纳税服务一体化。推进异地纳税便利化，实施“互联网＋税务”行动计划，推行全国统一规范的电子税务局，加快实现电子与实体服务同质化，营造良好税收环境。

（三）归并减免政府性基金和合理降低行政事业性收费。修订《行政事业性收费标准管理暂行办法》。对行政事业性收费情况进行梳理，降低偏高的收费标准。落实排污交易改革思路。

（四）进一步清理规范经营服务性收费。降低电信资费，督促基础电信企业进一步落实取消手机国内长途和漫游费等降费措施，进一步降低流量资费、中小企业专线标准资费和国际港澳台漫游资费。取消、降低部分服务性收费和相关行业协会商会收费。

（五）依法查处各类涉企违法违规收费。检查涉企收费目录清单落实情况，确保收费目录清单执行到位。重点查处电子政务平台、行政审批中介服务、行业协会等领域违规收费行为。严格落实中央和地方已印发的关于行政审批中介服务事项清理规范的文件，梳理重点部门行政审批前置中介服务及相关政策法规依据，应当由行政机关委托中介机构并付费的，督促有关部门及时整改。继续深化行业协会商会与行政机关脱钩改革，规范行业协会商会收费，着力消除利用行政影响力收费现象。

（六）深化收费目录清单制管理。建立公布《政府定价的经营服务性收费目录清单》，建立目录清单动态调整机制，根据形势发展变化及时调整。凡具备竞争条件的经营服务性收费项目一律放开，不具备放开条件的均列入收费目录清单，严格监管。

三、合理降低融资成本

（七）加强和改进对制造业的金融支持和服务。鼓励金融机构坚持区别对待、有扶有控原则，不断优化金融支持方向和结构，在风险可控、商业可持续原则下，着力加强对制造业科技创新和技术改造升级的中长期金融支持，合理安排融资利率、授信期限和还款方式。引导金融机构积极开发符合企业资金需求特点的流动资金贷款产品，鼓励有条件的依法合规开展“应收账款融资”及“年审制”等合理金融创新。

（八）发展普惠金融支持小微企业发展。落实好对普惠金融领域贷款达到一定标准的金融机构的定向降准政策，持续推进中小微企业信用体系建设，积极运用信贷政策支持再贷款、再贴现等工具，引导金融机构加大对小微企业的支持力度。积极稳妥推进村镇银行培育发展，督促村镇银行全面提升支农支小服务能力和水平。深化“银税互动”和“银税合作”，有效解决银企信息不对称难题，降低银行风险管控成本。

（九）发展融资担保支持小微企业发展。推动融资担保机构回归服务小微和“三农”本源、专注融资担保主业。尽快设立国家融资担保基金，支持地方政府性担保机构发展，改善小微企业融资环境。推动省级农业信贷担保机构向市县延伸。

（十）提升金融对实体经济的服务能力。继续推进多层次资本市场建设，提高直接融资比重。积极支持符合条件的企业通过资本市场进行股权融资。进一步简化中小企业股份转让许可，完善融资制度安排，创新融资品种和服务。继续推动债券市场创新发展，增强服务实体经济能力。进一步完善和细化全口径跨境融资宏观审慎管理政策，在有效防范外债风险的前提下，继续拓宽境内企业融资渠道。不断优化和完善人民币跨境业务政策，引导企业在对外贸易及相关投融资活动中使用人民币进行计价结算。

四、着力降低制度性交易成本

（十一）营造公平竞争市场环境。全面实施公平竞争审查制度，打破行政垄断、地区分割，维护全国统一市场。加大对公用事业、网络型行业等领域的反垄断执法力度。全面实施“双随机、一公开”监管，完善监督检查工作机制，推动跨部门联合检查。强化企业公共信用监管的作用，进一步完善企业经营异常名录和严重违法失信企业名单管理，推动部门间企业公共信用信息共享和失信联合惩戒。推进检验检测结果互认，采信第三方认证结果，提升监管效率。推动认证国际合作，推进“一审多证”，减轻企业负担。

（十二）在全国推开“证照分离”改革，全面规范“多证合一”改革。抓好“证照分离”改革提速，推动“照后减证”，着力解决准入不准营的问题，大幅缩短商标注册周期。建立国家层面统一的“多证合一”整合目录，推进全国范围内“多证合一”改革模式的规范统一。鼓励有条件的地区开展减证便民行动，全面清理各级政府机关及所属事业单位在行使行政职权和提供公共服务时要求行政相对人提供的证明材料。

（十三）进一步压缩企业开办时间。通过大力推进企业登记全程电子化和电子营业执照应用、加快企业名称登记管理改革等多项措施，着力提升企业登记注册便利度。选择北上广深作为重点地区，落实地方政府主体责任，狠抓具体部门和工作环节，大幅压缩企业开办时间，争取2018年年底前在北上广深率先实现企业开办时间（包括工商登记事项办理、刻制印章、申领发票）不超过8.5天。及时总结推广先进经验，缩小与国际先进水平的差距。研究开展取消新设企业开立基本存款账户许可事项试点。加强信息共享和业务协同，探索实践更加简化、便捷的市场准入退出机制。

（十四）持续优化营商环境。与国际营商环境先进水平进行对标，建立完善开办企业时间统计通报制度。鼓励有条件的地区开展营商环境对标提升行动，查找存在问题和差距，持续改进。

（十五）推进“互联网＋政府服务”。鼓励有条件的地区在现有省级电子政务服务平台的基础上，不断丰富完善服务事项网上办理功能，加快政府信息系统互联互通，打破信息孤岛，实现数据共享，变串联审批为并联审批；推进“最多跑一次”改革、“不见面”审批服务。

（十六）简化企业投资项目审批程序。鼓励有条件的地区对非核准类项目实施企业投资项目承诺制试点，加快项目报建手续办理；探索通过强化“区域能评、环评＋区块能耗、环境标准”机制，推动简化项目能评、环评工作内容，避免重复评价，精简审批程序。

（十七）进一步压减工业产品生产许可。除涉及安全、环保事项外，凡是技术工艺成熟、通过市场机制和事中事后监管能保证质量安全的产品，一律推动取消生产许可；对与消费者生活密切相关、通过认证能保障产品质量安全的，一律推动转为认证，加强事中事后监管。确需保留的，严格实行目录清单管理，简化审批程序。

五、延续“五险一金”缴存比例等政策降低人工成本

（十八）保持政策连续性降低人工成本。加快落实《划转部分国有资本充实社保基金实施方案》。延

长阶段性降低住房公积金缴存比例、企业职工基本养老保险单位缴费比例和失业保险费率实施期限；保持工伤保险行业基准费率不变，阶段性对符合条件省份的费率进行下调。完善城镇职工基本养老保险和城乡居民基本养老保险制度，建立企业职工基本养老保险基金中央调剂制度。修订《失业保险条例》，扩大失业保险基金支出范围。

（十九）完善残疾人就业保障金和工会会费缴纳政策。研究修改《残疾人就业条例》，调整完善残疾人就业保障金政策。研究工会经费收缴使用的科学性、合理性。

（二十）实施技能人才培训福利计划。鼓励有条件的地方通过政府购买服务等方式，支持职业院校、企业和社会培训机构开展职业技能培训。按规定落实职业培训和职业技能鉴定补贴政策，为产业转型升级、经济结构调整提供技能人才支撑。

六、有效降低用能用地成本

（二十一）合理降低用能成本。深化电力、天然气价格改革。继续开展电力市场化交易，制订完善电力市场化交易细则，推进建立有利于促进公平竞争、交易电量和交易比例大幅提升的市场结构及市场体系，更好地发挥市场在资源配置中的决定性作用。持续深入推进输配电价格改革，开展区域电网输电价格和跨省跨区专项输电工程输电价格的成本监审和价格审核。通过清理规范电网环节收费，临时性降低输配电价、扩大跨省区电力交易规模以及降低政府性基金等措施，一般工商业电价平均降低10%。支持有条件的企业自建分布式能源，支持新能源发电与用能企业就近就地进行交易。指导地方加强省内天然气管道运输和配气价格监管。

（二十二）降低企业用地综合成本。指导地方研究出台长期租赁、先租后让、租让结合等方式供应土地的实施细则，加快政策落地。对省（区、市）层面统筹推进的重大项目，优先保障用地计划，加快用地审查报批，提高用地配置效率。

（二十三）积极推进不动产登记制度改革。通过优化工作流程、增设服务窗口、增加办事人员、创新信息化服务举措等方式，进一步精简办事环节、压缩抵押登记等办理时限。健全信息互通共享机制，大力推行不动产登记、交易“一窗受理、并联办理”，提高不动产登记效率和便利化程度。

七、加快降低物流成本

（二十四）规范公路、港口和车辆检审收费。加快推进《收费公路管理条例》修订，深化收费公路制度改革，降低过路过桥费用。进一步规范公路治超执法，督促指导各地落实《关于治理车辆超载超限联合执法常态化制度化工作的实施意见（试行）》。落实货运车辆年检年审依法合并工作。推行高速公路通行费增值税电子普通发票开具工作。稳步扩大高速公路分时段差异化收费试点。加强价格行政执法，规范市场自主定价的港口经营服务性收费行为，推动港口企业调减港口作业包干费收费标准。

（二十五）通过多种途径优化运输方式。大力发展先进运输组织方式，充分发挥各种运输方式比较优势，提高运输组织效率。深化铁路改革，提升运输效率和服务水平，发展集装箱等成组化运输，发挥铁路在多式联运中的突出作用，积极提升铁路货运比例。支持无车承运人等“互联网＋”物流新业态发展，促进物流资源合理配置，降低货车空驶率，提高物流运作效率。加快修订《道路运输条例》，完善相关法规制度，推动无车承运人有序健康发展。推进物流配送网络建设，实施城乡高效配送专项行动。加大物流标准化推广力度，完善托盘、周转筐、包装、集装箱等相关物流设施设备标准。开展物流降本增效综合改革试点，进一步破除制约物流降本增效和创新发展的体制机制障碍。

（二十六）支持重要节点物流基础设施建设。加强物流规划和用地管理，将物流用地纳入土地利用总体规划、城市总体规划，并在城乡规划中综合考虑物流发展用地，统筹安排物流及配套设施用地选址和布局。充分利用存量物流用地资源，提高闲置土地资源利用效率，合理增加物流设施用地。研究开展供应链创新与应用试点，积极推进供应链平台建设工作。

八、提高资金周转效率

（二十七）继续清理规范涉企保证金。修订农民工工资保证金管理办法，落实差异化缴存措施。推广银行保函替代现金形式保证金。

九、激励企业内部挖潜

（二十八）支持引导企业降本增效。支持企业围绕智能化、绿色化等方向进行技术升级改造，瞄准国际标杆，全面提高产品技术、工艺装备、能效环保、质量效益和安全水平。鼓励有条件的地区通过事后奖补等手段，支持企业技术研发创新和升级改造。引导企业重视供应链管理和精细化物流管理，降低能源原材料采购成本。鼓励地方有关部门和行业协会总结内部挖潜、降本增效工作成效显著的典型企业做法，梳理企业提升内部管理、降低能耗物耗和各项费用等方面的有效途径，引导其他企业对标挖潜、降本增效。

十、加强长效机制建设

（二十九）深入推进降成本长效机制建设。不断完善降成本工作推进体系和工作机制，充分发挥相关领导小组、协调机制的作用，加强部门之间、部门地区之间的相互配合、信息沟通、协调会商，协同推进降成本工作。建立台账制度，将任务逐项分解落实，逐条明确相关要求。建立动态跟踪制度，加强统筹协调，密切跟踪配套政策制定情况、重点任务进展完成情况，及时解决政策推进中的困难和问题。

（三十）加强政策宣传和经验推广。充分利用各种宣传渠道和手段，加大降成本政策宣传力度，向企业传达解读各项优惠、扶持政策，为企业享受政策红利创造条件。有关部门和各地应充分听取企业意见，强化对企业反映问题的反馈和及时处置。降低实体经济企业成本工作部际联席会议将加强对各地好的经验、做法和案例的梳理，加强宣传和推广。

同时，按照国发〔2016〕48号文件要求，组织做好降成本总结评估工作，切实解决评估中发现的问题，确保降成本目标任务圆满完成。

请各单位认真做好相关重点工作。

国家发展改革委关于电力行业增值税税率调整相应降低一般工商业电价的通知

国家发展改革委2018年5月15日以发改价格〔2018〕732号文印发《关于电力行业增值税税率调整相应降低一般工商业电价的通知》，该“通知”全文如下。

为进一步贯彻落实中央经济工作会议关于降低企业用能成本和《政府工作报告》关于一般工商业电价平均下降10%的目标要求，现就电力行业增值税税率调整相应降低一般工商业电价有关事项通知如下。

一、电力行业增值税税率由17%调整到16%后，省级电网企业含税输配电价水平和政府性基金及附加标准降低、期末留抵税额一次性退返等腾出的电价空间，全部用于降低一般工商业电价。

二、以上规定自2018年5月1日起执行。

三、各省（自治区、直辖市）价格主管部门要按照本通知规定，抓紧研究提出增值税税率调整相应降低一般工商业电价具体方案，经同级人民政府同意并报我委（价格司）备案后实施。相应降低各省（自治区、直辖市）一般工商业输配电价水平。

四、各省（自治区、直辖市）价格主管部门、电网企业要精心组织、周密安排，做好宣传解释工作，确保上述电价政策平稳实施。执行中遇到的情况和问题，请及时报送我委（价格司）。

国家发展改革委印发《水电前期工作中央预算内投资专项管理办法》

国家发展改革委2018年5月25日以发改投资规〔2018〕795号文印发《水电前期工作中央预算内投资专项管理办法》，该“办法”全文如下。

水电前期工作中央预算内投资专项管理办法

第一章 总 则

第一条 为加强水电前期工作管理，建立健全水电前期工作管理机制，促进水电持续健康有序发展，提高中央预算内投资使用效益和效率，根据《中央预算内直接投资项目管理办法》（国家发展改革委第7号令）、《中央预算内投资项目日常监管实施办法（试行）》（发改稽察规〔2017〕2276号）、《中央预算内投资计划编制管理暂行办法》（发改投资〔2015〕3092号）及有关法律法规，结合水电前期工作实际，特制订本管理办法。

第二条 国家发展改革委负责管理属于政府行为的水电前期工作，主要包括：全国水力资源普查（含复查）、大中型河流（河段）水电规划及其补充规划编制（修编）、具有战略意义的部分大型水电站预可行性研究、全国或部分省份抽水蓄能电站选点规划编制（调整）等。

第三条 国家发展改革委安排中央预算内投资专项（以下简称“专项投资”）用于第二条所列水电前期工作。国家发展改革委委托中国电力建设集团有限公司所属水电水利规划设计总院（以下简称“水电规划总院”）组织项目实施。

第四条 专项投资安排和使用坚持公开公正、突出重点、统筹兼顾、有效监管的原则。

第二章 安排程序

第五条 水电规划总院科学合理提出年度水电前期工作任务并测算年度资金需求，及时将符合条件的项目（涉密项目除外）纳入全国重大建设项目库三年滚动投资计划库、年度投资计划库。通过投资计划编报库上报的投资计划数据应与通过重大项目库上报的三年滚动投资计划相关数据衔接一致。

第六条 年度投资计划申请文件由中国电力建设集团有限公司按照国家发展改革委年度投资计划申报

时限规定，按时报送国家发展改革委。中国电力建设集团有限公司按照申报规定和要求，认真审核水电规划总院提出的水电前期工作任务和资金需求，并对审查结果和申报材料的真实性、合规性负责。

第七条　年度投资计划申请文件视情况还应包括：续建项目任务进展情况、资金到位情况、新安排项目建议书等。

第八条　年度投资计划按项目安排。国家发展改革委受理年度投资计划申请文件后，重点对以下事项进行审查：

（一）符合党中央、国务院决策部署、有关规划、政策要求；

（二）符合中央预算内投资安排要求和本办法规定；

（三）申报材料齐备、有效，开展年度水电前期工作任务条件具备、科学合理，经费测算合理。国家发展改革委委托咨询评估机构对年度投资计划申请文件开展评估工作。

第九条　年度投资计划由国家发展改革委下达给中国电力建设集团有限公司，中国电力建设集团有限公司在收到投资计划下达文件后 10 个工作日内转发下达给水电规划总院。

第三章　使用管理

第十条　水电前期工作项目实施实行招标投标制和合同管理制，由水电规划总院负责组织招投标工作并与中标勘测设计单位签订合同，按合同进行全过程管理。

第十一条　项目完成后，由水电规划总院按合同组织验收，并报国家发展改革委。

第十二条　利用专项投资完成的预可行性研究项目，继续实行项目成果有偿转让制度，有偿转让收入列专户，滚动使用，根据国家发展改革委计划用于水电开发前期工作，进一步推动水电前期工作的开展。

第十三条　水电规划总院按月于每月 10 日前将项目启动情况（涉密项目除外）、资金使用情况、工作最新进展等通过重大项目建设库报送国家发展改革委。

第四章　监督检查

第十四条　水电前期工作项目单位为水电规划总院，日常监管直接责任单位为中国电力建设集团有限公司。项目日常监管直接责任单位及监管责任人对项目申报、建设管理、信息报送等履行日常监管直接责任。项目单位承担项目建设主体责任，自觉接受审计等部门的监督检查，保证中央预算内投资的合理使用和项目顺利实施。

第十五条　专项投资使用严格执行有关财务管理规定，设立专门账户，专款专用，严禁截留、转移、侵占和挪用。

第十六条　国家发展改革委接受单位、个人对水电前期工作专项资金安排、项目实施过程中违法违规行为的举报，按照有关规定办理。

第十七条　国家发展改革委按照有关规定对使用专项投资项目进行检查和考核，对发现的问题严格按照《中央预算内直接投资项目管理办法》（国家发展改革委令第 7 号）、《中央预算内投资项目日常监管实施办法（试行）》（发改稽察〔2017〕2276 号）等进行处理。

第十八条　项目出现下列情形之一，国家发展改革委责令限期整改，采取措施核减、收回或者停止拨付中央预算内投资，并可以根据情节轻重提请或移交有关机关依法追究有关责任人的行政或者法律责任。

（一）提供虚假情况，骗取中央预算内投资的；

（二）转移、侵占或者挪用中央预算内投资的；

（三）擅自变更前期工作实施任务和标准的；

（四）无正当理由未及时实施的；

（五）拒不接受依法进行的监督检查的；

（六）其他违反国家法律法规和本办法规定的行为。

第五章　附　　则

第十九条　本办法由国家发展改革委负责解释。

第二十条　本办法自公布之日起执行，有效期 5 年。2014 年印发的《国家发展改革委水电前期工作管理暂行办法（2014 年修订）》同时废止。

国家发展改革委、财政部、国家能源局关于 2018 年光伏发电有关事项的通知

国家发展改革委、财政部、国家能源局 2018 年 5 月 31 日以发改能源〔2018〕823 号文印发《关于 2018 年光伏发电有关事项的通知》，该“通知”全文如下。

近年来，随着我国光伏发电建设规模不断扩大，技术进步和成本下降速度明显加快。为促进光伏行业健康可持续发展，提高发展质量，加快补贴退坡，现将 2018 年光伏发电有关事项通知如下。

一、合理把握发展节奏，优化光伏发电新增建设规模

（一）根据行业发展实际，暂不安排 2018 年普通

光伏电站建设规模。在国家未下发文件启动普通电站建设工作前，各地不得以任何形式安排需国家补贴的普通电站建设。

（二）规范分布式光伏发展。今年安排1000万kW左右规模用于支持分布式光伏项目建设。考虑今年分布式光伏已建情况，明确各地5月31日（含）前并网的分布式光伏发电项目纳入国家认可的规模管理范围，未纳入国家认可规模管理范围的项目，由地方依法予以支持。

（三）支持光伏扶贫。落实精准扶贫、精准脱贫要求，扎实推进光伏扶贫工作，在各地落实实施条件、严格审核的前提下，及时下达“十三五”第二批光伏扶贫项目计划。

（四）有序推进光伏发电领跑基地建设。今年视光伏发电规模控制情况再行研究。

（五）鼓励各地根据各自实际出台政策支持光伏产业发展，根据接网消纳条件和相关要求自行安排各类不需要国家补贴的光伏发电项目。

二、加快光伏发电补贴退坡，降低补贴强度

完善光伏发电电价机制，加快光伏发电电价退坡。

（一）自发文之日起，新投运的光伏电站标杆上网电价每千瓦时统一降低0.05元，Ⅰ类、Ⅱ类、Ⅲ类资源区标杆上网电价分别调整为每千瓦时0.5元、0.6元、0.7元（含税）。

（二）自发文之日起，新投运的、采用“自发自用、余电上网”模式的分布式光伏发电项目，全电量度电补贴标准降低0.05元，即补贴标准调整为每千瓦时0.32元（含税）。采用“全额上网”模式的分布式光伏发电项目按所在资源区光伏电站价格执行。分布式光伏发电项目自用电量免收随电价征收的各类政府性基金及附加、系统备用容量费和其他相关并网服务费。

（三）符合国家政策的村级光伏扶贫电站（0.5MW及以下）标杆电价保持不变。

三、发挥市场配置资源决定性作用，进一步加大市场化配置项目力度

（一）所有普通光伏电站均须通过竞争性招标方式确定项目业主。招标确定的价格不得高于降价后的标杆上网电价。

（二）积极推进分布式光伏资源配置市场化，鼓励地方出台竞争性招标办法配置除户用光伏以外的分布式光伏发电项目，鼓励地方加大分布式发电市场化交易力度。

（三）各地、各项目开展竞争性配置时，要将上网电价作为重要竞争优选条件，严禁不公平竞争和限价竞争，确保充分竞争和建设质量。省级能源主管部门应及时将采取竞争方式确定的项目及上网电价或度电补贴额度抄送省级价格、财政主管部门和国家能源局派出监管机构。

国家发展改革委决定废止两项电力规章

国家发展改革委2018年6月2日发布第17号令、2018年11月11日发布第20号令分别决定废止两项电力规章，全文如下。

1. 因机构调整和工作需要，现决定废止《电力监管信息公开办法》（原国家电力监管委员会令第12号）。

2. 根据《国务院关于取消一批行政许可事项的决定》（国发〔2017〕46号），现决定废止《电工进网作业许可证管理办法》（原国家电力监管委员会令第15号）。

3. 以上两决定自公布之日起施行。

国家发展改革委关于利用扩大跨省区电力交易规模等措施降低一般工商业电价有关事项的通知

国家发展改革委2018年7月19日以发改价格〔2018〕1053号文印发《关于利用扩大跨省区电力交易规模等措施降低一般工商业电价有关事项的通知》，该“通知”全文如下。

为贯彻落实好中央经济工作会议关于降低企业用能成本和《政府工作报告》关于一般工商业电价平均下降10%的目标要求，现就利用扩大跨省区电力交易规模等措施降低一般工商业电价有关事项通知如下。

一、将扩大跨省区电力交易规模、国家重大水利工程建设基金征收标准降低25%、督促自备电厂承担政策性交叉补贴等电价空间，全部用于降低一般工商业电价。

二、以上规定自2018年7月1日起执行。

三、各省（自治区、直辖市）价格主管部门可根据当地实际，通过停征地方水库移民后期扶持资金、扩大一般工商业用户参与电力直接交易规模、从跨省跨区现货市场直接购买低价电量等方式，进一步降低一般工商业电价。

四、各省（自治区、直辖市）价格主管部门要按照本通知规定，抓紧研究提出再次降低一般工商业电价具体方案，经同级人民政府同意后，于7月底前报我委（价格司）备案后实施。

五、各省（自治区、直辖市）价格主管部门要严格按照国家要求，将今年以来国家部署的各项降价措施，全部用于降低一般工商业电价，不得挪作他用；要精心组织、周密安排，确保各项降价措施平稳实施；要认真开展降价措施落实情况自查，抓好各项措施落实，做好迎接第三方评估和国务院第五次大督查的准备。各省（自治区、直辖市）价格主管部门执行中遇到的情况和问题，请及时报送我委（价格司）。

国家发展改革委关于修改《关于调整水电建设管理主要河流划分的通知》引用规范性文件的通知

国家发展改革委2018年8月3日以发改能源规〔2018〕1144号文印发《〈关于调整水电建设管理主要河流划分的通知〉引用规范性文件的通知》，该“通知”全文如下。

为加强和完善水电建设管理工作，现决定对《国家发展改革委关于调整水电建设管理主要河流划分的通知》（发改能源〔2016〕1346号，以下简称《通知》）的部分条款予以修改。

将《通知》第二条“请各地方政府和有关单位按照《政府核准的投资项目目录（2014年本）》（国发〔2014〕53号）、《河流水电规划报告及规划环境影响报告书审查暂行办法》（发改能源〔2011〕2242号）和《国家发展改革委水电前期工作管理暂行办法（2014年修订）》（发改投资〔2014〕2377号）等要求”修改为“请各地方政府和有关单位按照《政府核准的投资项目目录》《河流水电规划报告及规划环境影响报告书审查暂行办法》（发改能源〔2011〕2242号）和《水电前期工作中央预算内投资专项管理办法》（发改投资规〔2018〕795号）等要求”。《通知》其他内容不变。

国家发展改革委关于降低一般工商业目录电价有关事项的通知

国家发展改革委2018年8月18日以发改价格〔2018〕1191号文印发《关于降低一般工商业目录电价有关事项的通知》，该“通知”全文如下。

今年以来，我委已经部署了8项降低一般工商业电价的措施，并要求各地根据实际情况，通过停征地方水库移民后期扶持资金、扩大一般工商业用户参与电力直接交易规模、从跨省跨区现货市场直接购买低价电量等方式，进一步降低一般工商业电价。为进一步加大力度，确保完成《政府工作报告》关于一般工商业电价平均降低10%的要求，现就有关事项通知如下：

一、各地要确保将已经部署的8项降低一般工商业电价的政策措施，以及结合本地实际自行采取的降低一般工商业电价的政策措施落实到位，全部用于降低一般工商业目录电价。

二、各地采取8项降价措施及挖掘本地降价潜力后，一般工商业目录电价降幅未达到10%的，可将省级电网经营区内首个监管周期平均电量增速超过预测电量增速带来的降价空间用于降低一般工商业目录电价。

三、各地使用以上降价空间后，一般工商业目录电价降幅仍未达到10%的，可将省级电网经营区内2017年1月—2018年7月间因用电量增速超过预测电量增速已经产生的超收收入用于降低一般工商业目录电价。

四、各地采取以上措施后，一般工商业目录电价降幅还未达到10%的，可由电网企业通过内部调剂的方式弥补省电力公司的资金缺口，或在下一输配电价监管周期统筹平衡，执行结果向我委报告。个别省份一般工商业目录电价难以降低10%的，要加大清理和规范转供电加价工作力度，切实降低一般工商业用户电费支出。

请相关省（自治区、直辖市）价格主管部门尽快测算降价方案，报省级人民政府审核和我委备案后抓紧实施。国家电网公司、南方电网公司要指导各省电网企业积极配合将相关政策落实到位，确保自9月1日起执行新的目录电价。

国家发展改革委、财政部、国家能源局关于2018年光伏发电有关事项说明的通知

国家发展改革委、财政部、国家能源局2018年10月9日以发改能源〔2018〕1459号文印发《关于2018年光伏发电有关事项说明的通知》，该“通知”全文如下。

5月31日，国家发展改革委、财政部、国家能源局联合印发了《关于2018年光伏发电有关事项的通知》（发改能源〔2018〕823号）。为进一步做好文件贯彻落实工作，现就实施中的有关事项说明如下。

一、今年5月31日（含）之前已备案、开工建设，且在今年6月30日（含）之前并网投运的合法合规的户用自然人分布式光伏发电项目，纳入国家认可规模管理范围，标杆上网电价和度电补贴标准保持不变。

二、已经纳入2017年及以前建设规模范围（含不限规模的省级区域）、且在今年6月30日（含）前并网投运的普通光伏电站项目，执行2017年光伏电站标杆上网电价，属竞争配置的项目，执行竞争配置时确定的上网电价。

三、请各省级能源、价格主管部门和电网公司做好政策宣介落实工作。请各派出能源监管机构加强对并网及政策执行情况的监管。

国家发展改革委、国家能源局印发《清洁能源消纳行动计划（2018～2020年）》

国家发展改革委、国家能源局2018年10月30日以发改投资规〔2018〕1575号文印发《清洁能源消纳行动计划（2018～2020年）》，该“计划”全文如下。

清洁能源消纳行动计划（2018～2020年）

清洁能源是能源转型发展的重要力量，积极消纳清洁能源是贯彻能源生产和消费革命战略，建设清洁低碳、安全高效的现代能源体系的有力抓手，也是加快生态文明建设，实现美丽中国的关键环节。

近年来，我国清洁能源产业不断发展壮大，产业规模和技术装备水平连续跃上新台阶，为缓解能源资源约束和生态环境压力作出突出贡献。但同时，清洁能源发展不平衡不充分的矛盾也日益凸显，特别是清洁能源消纳问题突出，已严重制约电力行业健康可持续发展。从现在到2020年，是我国全面建成小康社会的关键决胜期，是能源发展转型的重要战略机遇期。为贯彻落实习近平新时代中国特色社会主义思想和党的十九大精神，全面促进清洁能源消纳，制定本行动计划。

总体要求：以习近平新时代中国特色社会主义思想为指导，深入贯彻党的十九大精神，全面落实党中央、国务院决策部署，紧紧围绕“五位一体”总体布局和“四个全面”战略布局，牢固树立创新、协调、绿色、开放、共享的发展理念。立足我国国情和发展阶段，着眼经济社会发展全局，以促进能源生产和消费革命、推进能源产业结构调整、推动清洁能源消纳为核心，坚持远近结合、标本兼治、安全优先、清洁为主的原则，贯彻“清洁低碳、安全高效”方针，形成政府引导、企业实施、市场推动、公众参与的清洁能源消纳新机制，切实践行“绿水青山就是金山银山”的理念，为建设美丽中国而奋斗。

工作目标：2018年，清洁能源消纳取得显著成效；到2020年，基本解决清洁能源消纳问题。

具体指标：2018年，确保全国平均风电利用率高于88%（力争达到90%以上），弃风率低于12%（力争控制在10%以内）；光伏发电利用率高于95%，弃光率低于5%，确保弃风、弃光电量比2017年进一步下降。全国水能利用率95%以上。全国大部分核电实现安全保障性消纳。

2019年，确保全国平均风电利用率高于90%（力争达到92%左右），弃风率低于10%（力争控制在8%左右）；光伏发电利用率高于95%，弃光率低于5%。全国水能利用率95%以上。全国核电基本实现安全保障性消纳。

2020年，确保全国平均风电利用率达到国际先进水平（力争达到95%左右），弃风率控制在合理水平（力争控制在5%左右）；光伏发电利用率高于95%，弃光率低于5%。全国水能利用率95%以上。全国核电实现安全保障性消纳。（重点省份分年度目标见附件。）

一、优化电源布局，合理控制电源开发节奏

（一）科学调整清洁能源发展规划。结合能源、电力及可再生能源“十三五”规划中期评估，科学调整“十三五”发展目标，优化各类发电装机布局规模，清洁能源开发规模进一步向中东部消纳条件较好地区倾斜，优先鼓励分散式、分布式可再生能源开发。

（二）有序安排清洁能源投产进度。各地区要将落实清洁能源电力市场消纳条件作为安排本区域新增清洁能源项目规模的前提条件，严格执行风电、光伏发电投资监测预警机制，严禁违反规定建设规划外项目。存在弃风、弃光的地区原则上不得突破“十三五”规划规模。

（三）积极促进煤电有序清洁发展。发挥规划引领约束作用，发布实施年度风险预警，合理控制煤电规划建设时序，严控新增煤电产能规模。有力有序有效关停煤电落后产能，推进煤电超低排放和节能改造，促进煤电灵活性改造，提升煤电灵活调节能力和高效清洁发展水平。

二、加快电力市场化改革，发挥市场调节功能

（四）完善电力中长期交易机制。进一步扩大交易主体覆盖范围，拓展延伸交易周期向日前发展，丰富中长期交易品种，进一步促进发电权交易，促进清洁能源以与火电等电源打捆方式在较大范围内与大用户、自备电厂负荷等主体直接签订中长期交易合约。创新交易模式，鼓励合约以金融差价、发电权交易等方式灵活执行，在确保电网安全稳定运行情况下，清洁能源电力优先消纳、交易合同优先执行。

（五）扩大清洁能源跨省区市场交易。打破省间电力交易壁垒，推进跨省区发电权置换交易，确保省间清洁能源电力送电协议的执行，清洁能源电力可以超计划外送。在当前跨区域省间富余可再生能源电力现货交易试点的基础上，进一步扩大市场交易规模，推动受端省份取消外受电量规模限制，鼓励送受两端市场主体直接开展交易。各地不得干预可再生能源报价和交易。合理扩大核电消纳范围，鼓励核电参与跨省区市场交易。

（六）统筹推进电力现货市场建设。鼓励清洁能源发电参与现货市场，并向区外清洁能源主体同步开放市场。在市场模式设计中充分考虑清洁能源具有的边际成本低、出力波动等特性。电力现货市场建设试点从 2019 年起逐步投入运行。持续推动全国电力市场体系建设，促进电力现货市场融合。

（七）全面推进辅助服务补偿（市场）机制建设。进一步推进东北、山西、福建、山东、新疆、宁夏、广东、甘肃等电力辅助服务市场改革试点工作，推动华北、华东等地辅助服务市场建设，非试点地区由补偿机制逐步过渡到市场机制。实现电力辅助服务补偿项目全覆盖，补偿力度科学化，鼓励自动发电控制和调峰服务按效果补偿，按需扩大储能设备、需求侧资源等电力辅助服务提供主体，充分调动火电、储能、用户可中断负荷等各类资源提供服务的积极性。

三、加强宏观政策引导，形成有利于清洁能源消纳的体制机制

（八）研究实施可再生能源电力配额制度。由国务院能源主管部门确定各省级区域用电量中可再生能源电力消费量最低比重指标。省级能源主管部门、省级电网企业、售电公司和电力用户共同承担可再生能源电力配额工作和义务。力争在 2018 年全面启动可再生能源电力配额制度。

（九）完善非水可再生能源电价政策。进一步降低新能源开发成本，制定逐年补贴退坡计划，加快推进风电、光伏发电平价上网进程，2020 年新增陆上风电机组实现与煤电机组平价上网，新增集中式光伏发电尽早实现上网侧平价上网。合理衔接和改进清洁能源价格补贴机制。落实《可再生能源发电全额保障性收购管理办法》有关要求，鼓励非水可再生能源积极参与电力市场交易。

（十）落实清洁能源优先发电制度。地方政府相关部门在制定中长期市场交易电量规模、火电机组发电计划时，应按照《可再生能源发电全额保障性收购管理办法》《保障核电安全消纳暂行办法》要求足量预留清洁能源优先发电空间，优先消纳政府间协议水电跨省跨区输电电量和保障利用小时内的新能源电量。逐步减少燃煤电厂计划电量，计划电量减小比例应不低于中长期市场的增加比例；考虑清洁能源的出力特性，细化燃煤电厂计划电量的分解至月度，并逐步过渡至周。鼓励核电开展“优价满发”试点，充分发挥资源环境效益，合理平衡经济效益。因清洁能源发电影响的计划调整，经省级政府主管部门核定后，不纳入“三公”考核。系统内各类电力主体共同承担清洁能源消纳义务。

（十一）启动可再生能源法修订工作。随着我国可再生能源产业的快速发展，可再生能源已逐渐成为我国的主要能源品种之一，面对可再生能源规模化发展、对电力系统渗透率不断提高等新形势，应尽快启动可再生能源法修订工作，更好地促进清洁能源健康发展。

四、深挖电源侧调峰潜力，全面提升电力系统调节能力

（十二）实施火电灵活性改造。省级政府相关主管部门负责制定年度火电灵活性改造计划，国家能源局派出机构会同相关部门组织省级电网公司对改造机组进行验收。研究出台火电灵活性改造支持性措施，将各地火电灵活性改造规模与新能源规模总量挂钩。

（十三）核定火电最小技术出力率和最小开机方式。国家能源局派出机构会同相关部门，组织省级电网公司开展火电机组单机最小技术出力率和最小开机方式的核定；2018 年底前全面完成核定工作，并逐年进行更新和调整；电力调度机构严格按照核定结果调度火电机组。

（十四）通过市场和行政手段引导燃煤自备电厂调峰消纳清洁能源。进一步扩大清洁能源替代自备电厂负荷市场交易规模，研究出台自备电厂负荷调峰消纳新能源的相关政策，加强自备电厂与主网电气连接，率先实现新能源富集地区自备电厂参与调峰。督促自备电厂足额缴纳政府性基金和附加，提高清洁能源替代发电的竞争性。2018 年，清洁能源年替代自备电厂发电量力争超过 100 亿 kW・h；到 2020 年，

替代电量力争超过500亿kW·h。

（十五）提升可再生能源功率预测水平。可再生能源发电企业利用大数据、人工智能等先进技术提高风况、光照、来水的预测精度，增加功率预测偏差奖惩力度，对于偏差超过一定范围的电量进行双向考核结算，国家能源局派出机构或地方能源主管部门做好考核细则制定工作，区域和省级电网公司做好功率预测的汇总和考核工作。

五、完善电网基础设施，充分发挥电网资源配置平台作用

（十六）提升电网汇集和外送清洁能源能力。加快推进雅中、乌东德、白鹤滩、金沙江上游等水电外送通道建设；研究推进青海、内蒙古等富集地区高比例可再生能源通道建设。加强可再生能源富集区域和省份内部网架建设，重点解决甘肃、两广、新疆、河北、四川、云南等地区内部输电断面能力不足问题。

（十七）提高存量跨省区输电通道可再生能源输送比例。充分发挥送受两端煤电机组的调频和调峰能力，调度机构要充分利用可再生能源的短期和超短期功率预测结果，滚动修正送电曲线。2020年底前，主要跨省区输电通道中可再生能源电量比例力争达到平均30%以上。

（十八）实施城乡配电网建设和智能化升级。持续开展配电网和农网改造建设，推动智能电网建设，提升配电自动化覆盖率，增强电网分布式清洁能源接纳能力以及对清洁供暖等新型终端用电的保障能力。

（十九）研究探索多种能源联合调度。研究试点火电和可再生能源联合优化运行，探索可再生能源电站和火电厂组成联合调度单元，内部由火电为可再生能源电站提供调峰和调频辅助服务；联合调度单元对外视为整体参加电力市场并接受电网调度机构指令。水电为主同时有风电、光伏发电的区域，以及风电、光伏发电同时集中开发的地区，可探索试点按区域组织多种电源协调运行的联合调度单元。鼓励新建核电项目结合本地实际，配套建设抽水蓄能等调峰电源。

（二十）加强电力系统运行安全管理与风险管控。调度机构要科学合理安排运行方式，建立适应新能源大规模接入特点的电力平衡机制。加强涉网机组安全管理，增强电网对新能源远距离外送的安全适应性，完善分布式新能源接入的技术标准体系。加快建设完善新能源发电技术监督管理体系，加强新能源企业电力监控系统安全防护等网络信息安全工作，提高新能源发电设备的安全运行水平。针对新能源并网容量增加出现的安全风险，电力企业要落实电力安全生产主体责任，全面加强电网安全风险管控工作。国家能源局派出机构和省级政府能源主管部门要按照职能，切实加强电力系统运行安全管理与风险管控，定期开展监督检查工作。

六、促进源网荷储互动，积极推进电力消费方式变革

（二十一）推行优先利用清洁能源的绿色消费模式。倡导绿色电力消费理念，推动可再生能源电力配额制向消费者延伸，鼓励售电公司和电网公司制定清洁能源用电套餐、可再生能源用电套餐等，引导终端用户优先选用清洁能源电力。

（二十二）推动可再生能源就近高效利用。选择可再生能源资源丰富的地区，建设可再生能源综合消纳示范区。开展以消纳清洁能源为目的的清洁能源电力专线供电试点，加快柔性直流输电等适应波动性可再生能源的电网新技术应用。探索可再生能源富余电力转化为热能、冷能、氢能，实现可再生能源多途径就近高效利用。

（二十三）优化储能技术发展方式。充分发挥储电、储热、储气、储冷在规模、效率和成本方面的各自优势，实现多类储能的有机结合。统筹推进集中式和分布式储能电站建设，推进储能聚合、储能共享等新兴业态，最大化利用储能资源，充分发挥储能的调峰、调频和备用等多类效益。

（二十四）推进北方地区冬季清洁取暖。全面落实《北方地区冬季清洁取暖规划（2017－2021年）》要求，加快提高清洁供暖比重。加强清洁取暖总体设计与清洁能源消纳的统筹衔接，上下联动落实任务分工，明确省级清洁取暖实施方案。2019年、2021年实现北方地区清洁取暖率达到50%、70%。

（二十五）推动电力需求侧响应规模化发展。鼓励大工业负荷参加辅助服务市场，发挥电解铝、铁合金、多晶硅等电价敏感型高载能负荷的灵活用电潜力，消纳波动性可再生能源。鼓励并引导电动汽车有序充电。加快出台需求响应激励机制，培育需求侧响应聚合服务商等新兴市场主体，释放居民、商业和一般工业负荷的用电弹性，将电力需求侧资源纳入电力市场。

七、落实责任主体，提高消纳考核及监管水平

（二十六）强化清洁能源消纳目标考核。科学测算清洁能源消纳年度总体目标和分区域目标，进一步明确弃电量、弃电率的概念和界定标准。弃水、弃风、弃光情况严重和核电机组利用率低的省（自治区、直辖市），当地能源主管部门要会同国家能源局派出监管机构制定本地区解决清洁能源消纳问题的专项方案。组织具备接受外送清洁能源消纳条件的省

(自治区、直辖市)，明确本区域消纳目标。明确新能源与煤电联合外送通道中，非水可再生能源占总电量的运行比重目标，并实施年度考核。原则上，对风电、光伏发电利用率超过95%的区域，其限发电量不再计入全国限电量统计。对水能利用率超过95%的区域和主要流域（河流、河段），其限发电量不再计入全国限电量统计。

（二十七）建立清洁能源消纳信息公开和报送机制。电网企业和电力交易机构按月向国家能源主管部门提供发电计划和跨省跨区通道的送电曲线、各类电源逐小时实际出力情况和清洁能源交易情况备查。国家能源主管部门组织第三方技术机构对清洁能源消纳进行监测评估，并向社会公布。

（二十八）加强清洁能源消纳监管督查。全面梳理各地和电网企业对《解决弃水弃风弃光问题实施方案》《保障核电安全消纳暂行办法》等清洁能源消纳政策的落实情况。对实施方案和消纳目标完成情况按月监测、按季度评估、按年度考核，国家能源局派出监管机构开展清洁能源消纳专项督查和清洁能源消纳重点专项监管，对政策执行不力和达不到消纳目标的地区依法予以追责。畅通12398能源监管热线，及时分析统计涉及清洁能源消纳的投诉、举报和咨询等情况。

附件：清洁能源消纳主要目标。

附件　　清洁能源消纳主要目标

	2018年		2019年		2020年	
	利用率	弃电率	利用率	弃电率	利用率	弃电率
一、风电						
1. 新疆	75%	25%	80%	20%	85%	15%
2. 甘肃	77%	23%	80%	20%	85%	15%
3. 黑龙江	90%	10%	92%	8%	94%	6%
4. 内蒙古	88%	12%	90%	10%	92%	8%
5. 吉林	85%	15%	88%	12%	90%	10%
6. 河北	94%	6%	95%	5%	95%	5%
二、光伏						
1. 新疆	85%	15%	90%	10%	90%	10%
2. 甘肃	90%	10%	90%	10%	90%	10%
三、水电						
1. 四川	90%		92%		95%	
2. 云南	90%		92%		95%	
3. 广西	95%		95%		95%	

国家发展改革委印发《投资咨询评估管理办法》

国家发展改革委2018年11月5日以发改投资规〔2018〕1604号文印发《投资咨询评估管理办法》，该“办法”全文如下。

投资咨询评估管理办法

第一章　总　　则

第一条　为进一步完善国家发展改革委投资决策程序，提高投资决策的科学性和民主性，规范投资决策过程中的咨询评估工作，保障咨询评估质量，根据《中共中央 国务院关于深化投融资体制改革的意见》(中发〔2016〕18号)、《企业投资项目核准和备案管理条例》(国务院令第673号)、《工程咨询行业管理办法》(国家发展改革委2017年第9号令）等要求，制定本办法。

第二条　国家发展改革委在审批固定资产投资项目及其相关专项规划时，应当坚持“先评估、后决策”的原则，经相关工程咨询单位咨询评估，在充分考虑咨询评估意见的基础上作出决策决定。国家发展改革委在进行其他投资决策过程中，也要充分发挥相关工程咨询单位的作用。国家发展改革委委托相关工程咨询单位开展投资咨询评估工作，适用本办法。

第三条　国家发展改革委委托的投资咨询评估纳入投资决策程序、为投资决策服务，咨询评估范围、咨询评估机构由国家发展改革委确定，咨询评估费用由国家发展改革委支付，咨询评估质量由国家发展改革委管理。

第四条　国家发展改革委通过竞争方式择优选择投资咨询评估机构，建立“短名单”并实行动态管理。国家发展改革委根据本办法规定的咨询评估范围，委托“短名单”内机构承担投资咨询评估任务。国家发展改革委委托“短名单”内机构承担本办法规定的咨询评估范围以外任务的，工作程序、费用支出等根据业务需要执行相关规定。

第二章　咨询评估范围

第五条　国家发展改革委委托的投资咨询评估包括以下事项：

（一）投资审批咨询评估，具体包括：

1. 专项规划，指国家发展改革委审批或核报国务院审批的涉及重大建设项目和需安排政府投资的专项规划（含规划调整）；

2. 项目建议书，指国家发展改革委审批或核报国务院审批的政府投资项目建议书；

3. 可行性研究报告，指国家发展改革委审批或核报国务院审批的政府投资项目可行性研究报告；

4. 项目申请报告，指国家发展改革委核准或核报国务院核准的企业投资项目申请报告；

5. 资金申请报告，限于按具体项目安排中央预算内投资资金、确有必要对拟安排项目、资金额度进行评估的资金申请报告；

6. 党中央、国务院授权开展的项目其他前期工作审核评估。

（二）投资管理中期评估和后评价，具体包括：

1. 对本条上一款中的专项规划的中期评估和后评价；

2. 政府投资项目后评价；

3. 中央预算内投资专项实施情况的评估、专项的投资效益评价。

第六条 国家发展改革委审批政府投资项目初步设计和概算核定，原则上由国家投资项目评审中心实行专业评审。需要特殊专业技术服务的，经投资司同意后，主办司局可以委托投资咨询评估。安排中央预算内投资额度较大的地方政府投资项目资金申请报告，也可由国家投资项目评审中心实行专业评审。

第三章 咨询评估机构管理

第七条 承担具体专业投资咨询评估任务的评估机构，应当具备以下条件：

（一）通过全国投资项目在线审批监管平台备案并列入公示名录的工程咨询单位；

（二）具有所申请专业的甲级资信等级，或具有甲级综合资信等级；

（三）近3年完成所申请专业总投资3亿元以上项目可行性研究报告、项目申请报告编制，项目建议书、可行性研究报告、项目申请报告、项目资金申请报告及规划的评估业绩共不少于20项（特殊行业除外）。国家发展改革委可以确定具有相关能力的机构作为投资咨询评估机构，以备承担特殊行业或特殊复杂事项的咨询评估任务。

第八条 国家发展改革委对承担投资咨询评估任务的咨询机构实行“短名单”管理。确定“短名单”的程序是：

（一）根据各有关司局的需求，确定投资咨询评估专业；

（二）投资司根据确定的投资咨询评估专业，经过公开遴选程序，提出咨询评估机构建议名单；

（三）各专业司局对咨询评估机构建议名单研提意见；

（四）投资司根据各专业司局意见拟订“短名单”报请委领导审核；

（五）确定“短名单”并予以公告。

第九条 国家发展改革委根据投资管理需要，结合投资咨询评估机构管理情况，对“短名单”机构进行动态调整，原则上每三年调整一次。

第十条 其他部门委托国家发展改革委“短名单”机构承担咨询评估任务、发现存在服务质量问题的，可以告知国家发展改革委作出相应处理。

第四章 委内工作程序

第十一条 承担委托任务的咨询评估机构的排序和选取，按以下规则进行：

（一）分专业对评估机构进行初始随机排队；

（二）按照初始随机排队的先后顺序，确定承担评估任务的机构；

（三）评估机构接受任务后，随即排到该专业排队顺序的队尾；评估机构如果拒绝接受任务，应提交书面说明，排到排队顺序的队尾；

（四）选取咨询评估机构应当符合回避原则，承担某一事项编制任务的机构，不得承担同一事项的咨询评估任务；承担咨询评估任务的机构，与同一事项的编制单位、项目业主单位之间不得存在控股、管理关系或者负责人为同一人的重大关联关系。

第十二条 具体选取咨询评估机构，除绝密事项外，均通过委内委托评估系统办理，具体程序是：

（一）按照投资决策委内职责分工，由主办司局通过委托评估系统提出咨询评估申请，填写事项基本情况、评估要求、评估时限等，申请事项填写完毕并确认后，由委托评估系统自动生成咨询评估机构名单；

（二）主办司局对自动生成的咨询评估机构名单，按照回避原则进行核实，对符合回避原则的予以确认，完成确定咨询评估机构；

对不符合回避原则的，委托评估系统再次自动生成咨询评估机构，由主办司局核实并最终完成确定咨询评估机构；

（三）确定咨询评估机构后，委托评估申请发送投资司审核，投资司对委托评估的必要性、咨询评估范围、咨询评估机构选取等是否符合本办法规定进行审核，审核同意后，发回主办司局；

（四）主办司局根据审核后的委托评估申请，办理咨询评估委托书发文事宜。对特别重要项目或特殊事项的咨询评估任务，可以通过招标或指定方式确定评估机构。

第十三条 对国民经济和社会发展有重要影响的

专项规划和重大项目的项目申请报告、项目建议书、项目可行性研究报告，可以委托多家评估机构承担咨询评估任务。

第五章　咨询评估工作规范

第十四条　在接受评估任务后，评估机构应当确定项目负责人，成立评估小组，制定评估工作计划，定期反馈评估工作进度，在规定时限内提交评估报告。项目负责人应当是经执业登记的咨询工程师（投资）。参加评估小组的人员应当熟悉国家和行业发展有关政策法规规划、技术标准规范，评估小组应当具有一定数量的本专业高级技术职称人员。

第十五条　涉密项目的咨询评估任务应按照《保守国家秘密法》及其实施条例规定，由国家发展改革委主办司局通过与评估机构签订保密协议并监督执行的方式进行保密管理。

第十六条　评估报告的内容包括：标题及文号、目录、摘要、正文、附件。评估机构在评估工作中要求补充相关资料时，应当书面通知评估事项的项目单位。该书面通知及补充资料应当作为评估报告的附件报送国家发展改革委。评估报告应当附具项目负责人及评估小组成员名单，并加盖评估机构公章和项目负责人的咨询工程师（投资）执业专用章。

第十七条　国家发展改革委委托咨询评估的完成时限一般不超过 30 个工作日。评估机构因特殊情况确实难以在规定时限内完成的，应在规定时限到期日的 5 个工作日之前向国家发展改革委主办司局书面报告有关情况，征得委托司局书面同意后，可以延长完成时限，但延长的期限不得超过 60 个工作日。

第十八条　评估机构应不断改进内部管理机制，优化评估工作流程，完善评估专家库，保证独立、公正、客观、科学地开展评估工作，提高评估工作水平和质量。

第六章　咨询评估质量管理

第十九条　咨询评估任务完成后，国家发展改革委主办司局应当通过委托评估系统填写对评估报告质量的评价，评价情况分为较好、一般、较差。质量评价结果与服务费用、“短名单”动态管理挂钩。对评估报告首次评价为较差的咨询机构，由投资司进行约谈、警告；对累计两次评价为较差的咨询机构，由投资司暂停其“短名单”机构资格一年；对累计三次评价为较差的咨询机构，由投资司将其从“短名单”中删除。

第二十条　评估机构应于每年 1 月底前向国家发展改革委投资司报送上一年度的评估工作总结报告。评估工作总结报告内容主要包括：上一年度承接、完成国家发展改革委委托咨询评估任务情况；评估工作中遇到的问题及有关意见建议等。

第二十一条　国家发展改革委受理对评估机构的举报、投诉，并组织或委托有关机构和专家进行检查核实，对查实的问题按照规定进行相应处理。

第二十二条　除根据第十九条对咨询评估质量进行管理外，评估机构有下列情形之一的，国家发展改革委应当将其从“短名单”中删除：

（一）评估报告有重大失误；

（二）累计两次拒绝接受委托任务；

（三）未在规定时限或者经批准的延期时限内完成委托任务；

（四）违反《工程咨询行业管理办法》有关规定的。出现上述（一）所列情形的，对涉及的咨询工程师（投资），取消其执业登记。

第二十三条　咨询评估机构存在违反第二十二条规定的，将相关信用信息纳入全国信用信息共享平台；情节严重的，通过“信用中国”网站向社会公示。

第二十四条　国家发展改革委有关工作人员，在投资咨询评估管理工作过程中玩忽职守、滥用职权、徇私舞弊、索贿受贿的，对负有责任的领导人员和直接责任人员依法给予处分；构成犯罪的，依法追究刑事责任。

第七章　附　　则

第二十五条　国家发展改革委按年度根据咨询评估任务完成情况，安排中央预算内投资结算咨询评估费用。评估机构及其工作人员，不得收取所评估事项的项目单位任何费用，不得向项目单位摊支成本。

第二十六条　地方发展改革部门可以参照本办法的规定，制定有关管理办法。

第二十七条　本办法由国家发展改革委负责解释。

第二十八条　本办法自 2019 年 1 月 1 日起施行。《国家发展改革委关于印发委托投资咨询评估管理办法（2015 年修订）的通知》（发改投资〔2015〕1761 号）和《国家发展改革委办公厅关于印发委托投资咨询评估委内工作规则（2015 年修订）的通知》（发改办投资〔2015〕2032 号）同时废止。

国家能源局印发《关于进一步加强电力建设工程质量监督管理工作意见》

国家能源局 2018 年 2 月 14 日以国能发安全

〔2018〕21号文印发《关于进一步加强电力建设工程质量监督管理工作的意见》，该“意见”全文如下。

关于进一步加强电力建设工程质量监督管理工作的意见

为深入学习贯彻党的十九大精神，严格落实《建设工程质量管理条例》、《中共中央国务院关于开展质量提升行动的指导意见》（中发〔2017〕24号）、《国家发展改革委 国家能源局关于推进电力安全生产领域改革发展的实施意见》（发改能源规〔2017〕1986号）等规定，现就进一步加强电力建设工程质量监督管理工作提出如下意见。

一、国家能源局依法依规对全国电力建设工程质量实施统一监督管理。贯彻执行国家关于电力建设工程质量监督管理的法律法规和方针政策，不断完善电力建设工程质量监督管理规章制度和标准规范体系，组织、指导和协调全国电力建设工程质量监督管理工作，组织开展全国电力建设工程质量监督管理巡查督查和专项检查，监督指导地方政府电力管理等有关部门和各派出能源监管机构的电力建设工程质量监督管理工作。

国家能源局电力安全监管司归口全国电力建设工程质量监督管理工作，其他有关司和单位依其职责做好相关工作。国家能源局各派出能源监管机构按照国家能源局授权承担所辖区域内除核安全外的电力建设工程质量安全的监督管理，对电力建设工程质量监督机构（以下简称质监机构）进行业务监督指导，依法组织或参与电力事故调查处理。

二、地方各级政府电力管理等有关部门依法依规履行地方电力建设工程质量监督管理责任，按照国家能源局有关规定，继续做好可再生能源发电工程的质量监督管理，并积极配合派出能源监管机构，做好其他电力建设工程质量监督管理相关工作；对质监机构进行业务监督指导。

三、国家能源局电力可靠性管理和工程质量监督中心（以下简称可靠性和质监中心）受国家能源局委托，研究拟定电力建设工程质量监督政策措施、规章制度及监督检查大纲并组织实施相关工作，协调解决质量监督工作存在的突出问题；对质监机构进行业务监督指导；参与涉及电力建设工程质量重大争议处理、重大事故调查及相关专项检查；负责全国电力建设工程质量监督信息管理等工作。

四、电力工程质量监督总站更名为电力工程质量监督站；水电工程质量监督总站和国家可再生能源发电工程质量监督总站合并，更名为可再生能源发电工程质量监督站。

质监机构要继续按照国家能源局现行文件规定的业务范围开展工程质量监督，其中各电力建设工程质量监督中心站（以下简称中心站）可开展可再生能源发电工程质量监督。根据工作需要，各监督站、中心站可设立项目站。

质监机构要规范设置，持续加强机构建设和队伍建设，制定本机构各项工作管理制度，配备专职工作人员，配置必要的检测仪器和设备，建立与质量监督任务相适应的组织体系和保障体系；要充分发挥专家和第三方检测机构作用，严禁工程建设项目参建单位人员作为质监机构专家或工作人员参加本项目的质量监督。

质监机构对各级政府部门审批、核准、备案的电力建设工程按照职责分工同步开展质量监督，要加强对有关电力建设工程质量的法律、法规和强制性标准执行情况的监督检查；要按照依法依规、严谨务实、清正廉洁、优质高效的原则，独立、规范、公正、公开开展工作。

质监机构要认真履职，采取措施确保工作不断、秩序不乱、队伍不散、质量不降。凡因机构职能弱化、履职不力等造成工程质量事故或重大质量隐患的，将依法依规严肃追究责任。

五、质量监督不代替建设、监理、设计、施工等单位的质量管理工作。未经审批、核准、备案的电力建设工程，质监机构不得受理其质量监督注册申请。未通过质监机构监督检查的电力工程，不得投入运行。

六、质监机构要按规定将年度和阶段性质监工作计划等信息，及时向地方政府电力管理等有关部门、国家能源局电力安全监管司、各派出能源监管机构、可靠性和质监中心报送。报送信息的内容、程序及时限等要求另行发文规定。

各监督站、中心站要及时将主要负责人名单、项目站设置情况及工作联系方式报告所在地省级政府电力管理等有关部门、派出能源监管机构、可靠性和质监中心。

七、各企业要进一步健全电力建设工程质量管控体系，明确具体部门负责工程质量监督对口联系；要全面落实各参建单位的工程质量责任，特别要强化建设单位的首要责任和勘察、设计、施工单位的主体责任，并充分发挥监理单位作用；要按照国家法律法规和标准规范要求，加强施工现场管理，落实工程质量管控措施，坚决遏制重特大质量事故发生。

各企业要主动接受各级政府电力管理等有关部门、派出能源监管机构、质监机构开展的质量监督管理和专项检查等活动。

八、地方政府电力管理等有关部门和派出能源监管机构要按照国家有关规定，统筹项目核准备案、市场准入、行政执法等环节力量，进一步强化电力建设工程质量监督管理，加强对质监机构的监督指导。对发现的问题责令限期整改，对整改不到位或存在重大质量隐患的电力建设工程，依法采取停止施工、停止供电等强制措施，并给予上限经济处罚。

九、各有关单位要认真落实本意见要求，确保各项工作落实到位。国家能源局将适时对执行情况开展督查。

国家能源局关于印发2018年能源工作指导意见的通知

国家能源局2018年2月26日以国能发规划〔2018〕22号文印发《2018年能源工作指导意见》，该“意见”全文如下。

2018年能源工作指导意见

2018年是贯彻党的十九大精神的开局之年，是改革开放40周年，是决胜全面建成小康社会、实施“十三五”规划承上启下的关键一年。做好全年能源工作，对推动新时代能源转型发展，提高能源发展质量和效率，增强能源安全保障能力和水平，促进经济社会可持续发展，具有十分重要的意义。

一、指导方针和主要目标

（一）指导思想

全面贯彻党的十九大精神，以习近平新时代中国特色社会主义思想为指导，坚持稳中求进工作总基调，坚持新发展理念，遵循能源安全新战略思想，按照高质量发展的要求，以推进供给侧结构性改革为主线，推动能源发展质量变革、效率变革和动力变革，围绕解决能源发展不平衡不充分问题，着力补短板、强基础、调结构、促改革、惠民生，努力构建清洁低碳、安全高效的能源体系，为经济社会发展和人民美好生活提供坚实的能源保障。

（二）政策取向

把“清洁低碳、安全高效”的要求落实到能源发展的各领域、全过程，努力建设坚强有力的安全保障体系、清洁低碳的绿色产业体系、赶超跨越的科技创新体系、公平有序的市场运行体系、科学精准的治理调控体系、共享优质的社会服务体系、开放共赢的国际合作体系，全面推进新时代能源高质量发展。

更加注重绿色低碳发展。坚持绿色低碳的战略方向，加快优化能源结构，壮大清洁能源产业，稳步推进可再生能源规模化发展，安全高效发展核电，推进化石能源清洁高效开发利用，提高天然气供应保障能力。坚持节约优先，大力推进能源综合梯级利用，倡导绿色低碳的生产生活方式，推动形成人与自然和谐共生的能源发展新格局。

更加注重提高能源供给体系质量。坚持质量第一、效益优先，深化供给侧结构性改革，大力破除无效供给，优化存量资源配置，扩大优质增量供给。充分发挥质量、能效和环保标准等市场化措施的作用，统筹推进化解过剩产能与发展先进产能，提高有效供给能力，促进供需动态平衡。着力解决清洁能源消纳问题，提高可再生能源发展的质量和效益。

更加注重提高能源系统效率。着力补短板、强弱项，加强天然气产供储销体系和电力系统调峰能力建设，加强需求侧管理，增强需求侧响应能力。优化能源发展布局，统筹发展各类能源，推动能源生产、加工转化、输送储存及消费各个环节协同发展，加强能源系统整体优化，提升能源系统协调性和整体效率。

更加注重依靠创新驱动发展。深入实施创新驱动发展战略，加强应用基础研究，促进科技成果转化，推动互联网、大数据、人工智能与能源深度融合，培育新增长点、形成新动能。深化能源体制改革，加快能源市场体系建设，完善市场监管体制，着力构建市场机制有效、微观主体有活力、宏观调控有度的能源体制，不断增强创新力和竞争力。

更加注重保障和改善民生。坚持把人民对美好生活的向往作为奋斗目标，加快能源民生保障工程建设，深入开展脱贫攻坚，提升能源普遍服务水平，让能源改革发展成果更多更公平惠及全体人民。按照生态文明建设对能源发展的新要求，努力降低能源生产消费对生态环境的影响，满足人民日益增长的优美生态环境需要。

更加注重开放合作共赢发展。遵循共商共建共享原则，以“一带一路”建设为重点，推动能源产能合作，加强基础设施互联互通，构建全方位、深层次的能源国际合作新格局，实现开放条件下的能源安全。积极参与全球能源治理体系改革和建设，贡献中国智慧和力量。

更加注重深化能源依法治理实践。完善能源法律法规体系，深入推进依法行政。充分发挥能源法治的保障作用，将依法治理作为促进能源发展与改革的基本方式，并贯穿于能源战略规划、政策、标准的制定、实施和监督管理全过程，推进能源治理体系和治理能力现代化。

（三）主要目标

——能源消费。全国能源消费总量控制在45.5亿t标准煤左右。非化石能源消费比重提高到14.3%

左右，天然气消费比重提高到7.5%左右，煤炭消费比重下降到59%左右。

——能源供应。全国能源生产总量36.6亿t标准煤左右。煤炭产量37亿t左右，原油产量1.9亿t左右，天然气产量1600亿m^3左右，非化石能源发电装机达到7.4亿kW左右、发电量达到2万亿kW·h左右。

——能源效率。单位国内生产总值能耗同比下降4%以上。燃煤电厂平均供电煤耗同比减少1g左右。

二、加快能源绿色发展，促进人与自然和谐共生

（一）壮大清洁能源产业

统筹优化水电开发利用。坚持生态保护优先，妥善解决移民安置问题，有序推进金沙江、雅砻江、大渡河、黄河上游等水电基地建设，控制中小水电开发。加快雅砻江两河口、大渡河双江口等龙头水库电站建设，积极推进金沙江中游龙盘水电综合枢纽工程前期工作，提高流域梯级水电站调节能力。完善流域综合监测平台建设，加强水电流域综合管理。以四川、云南和周边省区为重点，实施跨流域跨区域的统筹优化调度和水电丰枯调节，有效缓解弃水问题。

稳妥推进核电发展。落实“核电安全管理提升年”专项行动要求，进一步提升核电安全管理水平，确保在运核电机组安全稳定运行，在建核电工程安全质量可控。在充分论证评估的基础上，开工建设一批沿海地区先进三代压水堆核电项目。进一步完善核电项目开发管理制度，做好核电厂址资源保护工作。继续推动解决部分地区核电限发问题，促进核电多发满发。继续实施核电科技重大专项，建设核电技术装备试验平台共享体系，加快推进小型堆重大专项立项工作，积极推动核能综合利用。

稳步发展风电和太阳能发电。强化风电、光伏发电投资监测预警机制，控制弃风、弃光严重地区新建规模，确保风电、光伏发电弃电量和弃电率实现“双降”。有序建设重点风电基地项目，推动分散式风电、低风速风电、海上风电项目建设。积极推进风电平价上网示范项目建设，研究制定风电平价上网路线图。健全市场机制，继续实施和优化完善光伏领跑者计划，启动光伏发电平价上网示范和实证平台建设工作。稳步推进太阳能热发电示范项目建设。

积极发展生物质能等新能源。因地制宜，积极推广生物质能、地热能供暖。推进城镇生活垃圾、农村林业废弃物、工业有机废水等城乡废弃物能源化利用。加强垃圾焚烧发电项目运行及污染物排放监测，定期公布监测报告。开展垃圾焚烧发电领跑者示范项目建设，推动垃圾焚烧发电清洁绿色发展。组织开展海洋能调查研究，适时启动示范项目建设。

有序推进天然气利用。推动建立天然气产供储销体系，加快国内天然气增储上产，全力推进天然气基础设施互联互通，完善天然气储备调峰体系。有序发展天然气分布式能源和天然气调峰电站。以京津冀及周边地区、长三角、珠三角、东北地区为重点，按照统筹规划、循序渐进、量力而为、以气定改的原则推进“煤改气”工程。稳步推进天然气车船发展和加气（注）站建设。加快推动天然气价格改革，推广天然气用户与气源方直接交易，消除或减少工业用户和民用用户在输配价格和终端气价上的交叉补贴，降低天然气综合使用成本，落实天然气接收和储运设施公平开放。

（二）加快传统能源清洁高效开发利用

推进煤炭绿色高效开发利用。在煤矿设计、建设、生产等环节，严格执行环保标准，因地制宜推广充填开采、保水开采、煤与瓦斯共采等绿色开采技术，大力发展煤炭洗选加工和矿区循环经济。继续安排中央预算内投资支持煤矿安全改造和重大灾害治理示范工程建设，总结推广重大灾害治理示范矿井技术成果和管理经验。强化商品煤质量监管。开展煤炭深加工产业升级示范，深入推进低阶煤分质利用技术示范。大力推广成熟先进节能减排技术应用，加快西部地区煤电机组超低排放改造，中部地区具备条件的煤电机组基本完成超低排放改造，促进煤电清洁高效发展。

持续推进油品质量升级。重点做好京津冀及周边地区“2+26”城市国六标准车用汽柴油、船用低硫燃油，以及全国硫含量不大于10ppm普通柴油的供应保障工作。研究制定深入推进成品油质量升级的指导意见，明确国六标准油品炼油装置改造方案和时间表。加快淘汰炼油行业落后产能，提高炼厂能效，研究实施炼油行业能效领跑者计划。编制实施全国生物燃料乙醇产业布局方案，扩大生物燃料乙醇生产，推广使用车用乙醇汽油，提高交通运输燃料中非化石能源比重。完善成品油市场监管体系，加大油品质量专项抽查力度，依法严厉查处违法违规行为，营造公平竞争的市场环境，确保油品质量升级取得实效。

（三）推动能源绿色消费

大力推进能源资源节约利用。深入实施能源消费总量和强度“双控”，推动重点用能单位建立健全能源管理体系，加大节能力度和考核，抑制不合理能源消费，推行“合同能源管理”、能效领跑者制度，推广先进节能技术装备，提高能源转化利用效率，完善能源计量体系，促进能源行业节能和能效水平提升。倡导绿色生活方式，从源头减少不合理能源消费，使节约用能成为全社会的自觉行动。

提升终端能源消费清洁化水平。实施煤炭终端消费减量替代，严格控制大气污染重点防治地区煤炭消费，提高清洁取暖比重，积极稳妥实施“煤改电”“煤改气”工程，提升高品质清洁油品利用率。积极开展电能替代，推进长春、吉林、四平、白城和松原等五个城市电能替代试点。统一电动汽车充电设施标准，优化电动汽车充电设施建设布局，建设适度超前、车桩相随、智能高效的充电基础设施体系。推广靠港船舶使用岸电，全面启动水运领域电能替代。

三、深化供给侧结构性改革，提高能源供给质量和效率

（一）切实化解过剩产能

继续推进化解煤炭过剩产能。用市场化和法治化办法化解煤炭过剩产能。把处置“僵尸企业”作为重要抓手，加快退出违法违规、不达标和安全风险大的煤矿，继续淘汰落后产能，引导长期亏损、资不抵债等煤矿有序退出，适当提高南方地区煤矿产能退出标准。继续按照减量置换原则有序发展优质产能，倒逼无效低质产能加快退出，提高煤炭先进产能比重，更多发挥北方地区优质先进产能作用。推进煤矿企业兼并重组和煤电、煤运、煤化工上下游产业融合，提高抵御市场风险能力。加强化解煤炭过剩产能和建设先进产能的统筹，实现煤炭供需动态平衡，保持价格稳定。

推动化解煤电过剩产能。坚持市场化手段和政府调控并举，充分发挥煤电规划建设预警机制的作用，从严控制新增规模，清理整顿违规项目，继续加快淘汰落后产能，促进煤电转型升级和结构优化。建立健全目标分解和责任落实机制，强化事中事后监管和督查问责。加强化解煤电过剩产能与电力供应保障的统筹，科学规划电源规模、布局和建设时序。加强需求侧管理，合理安排运行方式，有效化解区域性、时段性电力供应紧张矛盾，保障电力可靠供应和系统安全稳定运行，实现电力供需动态平衡。

（二）补齐能源系统短板

着力解决清洁能源消纳问题。认真落实《解决弃水弃风弃光问题实施方案》，多渠道拓展可再生能源电力消纳能力。完善可再生能源开发利用目标监测评价制度，推动实行可再生能源电力配额制，落实可再生能源优先发电制度，推进可再生能源电力参与市场化交易，建立可再生能源电力消纳激励机制，做好可再生能源消纳与节能减排、能源消费总量控制等考核政策的衔接。优化可再生能源电力发展布局，优先发展分散式风电和分布式光伏发电，鼓励可再生能源就近开发利用。完善跨省跨区可再生能源电力调度技术支持体系，优化电网调度运行，提升可再生能源电力输送水平。加强电力系统调峰能力建设，继续实施煤电机组调峰灵活性改造，加快龙头水库、抽水蓄能电站、燃气电站和先进储能技术示范项目建设，推动先进储能技术应用。做好全国抽水蓄能电站选点规划及规划调整工作。出台关于提升电力系统调节能力的指导意见，建立健全辅助服务补偿（市场）机制，切实提高电力系统调峰和消纳清洁能源的能力。

增强油气储备应急能力。加快国家石油储备项目建设，推进国家石油储备基地三期项目前期工作，加大力度推进国家储备原油收储，继续做好国家石油库存数据发布工作。加大储气调峰设施建设力度，建立多层次天然气储备体系，支持地方政府与企业合建储气服务设施，研究制定化解迎峰度冬、度夏天然气消费峰谷差矛盾的根本性措施，出台《关于加快储气设施建设和完善储气调峰辅助服务市场机制的意见》，形成通过市场解决储气调峰问题的长效机制。

（三）夯实能源供应基础

提高油气供给保障能力。坚持“盘活保有储量和加快新储量发现动用”两手抓，加强常规油气资源勘探开发，保证石油产量基本稳定，天然气产量较快增长。加大页岩气、煤层气、深水石油天然气资源的勘探开发力度。研究完善页岩气、煤层气、衰竭老油气田、煤制油、煤制气等支持政策。重点支持深层页岩气资源的勘探开发，完善页岩气安全、环保、技术等有关标准，推动页岩气产业化发展。加强煤矿瓦斯综合防治，推进煤层气（煤矿瓦斯）规模化开发利用，加快建设山西沁水盆地、鄂尔多斯盆地东缘、贵州毕水兴、新疆准噶尔盆地南缘煤层气产业化基地。充分利用好境外油气资源，增强境外油气资源供应，加强重大项目协调，巩固油气战略通道建设。

进一步完善电网结构。继续优化主网架布局和结构，深入开展全国同步电网格局论证，研究实施华中区域省间加强方案，加强区域内省间电网互济能力，推进配电网建设改造和智能电网建设，提高电网运行效率和安全可靠性。根据目标市场落实情况，加快西南水电外送通道建设，稳妥推进跨省区电力输送通道建设，推动新疆、青海、四川、陕西等地区电力外送通道前期工作。

加快推进油气管网建设。加快油气主干管网、区域性支线管网和配气管网建设，完善LNG接收站布局和配套外输管道。增强中石油、中石化、中海油等企业管网互联互通，实现应联尽联、应通尽通。

四、深入实施创新驱动战略，推动能源发展动力变革

（一）加快重点技术与装备创新

加快实施能源科技重大专项，推动陆上深层、海

洋深水和非常规油气勘探开发科技攻关，深入推进先进燃煤发电、煤炭清洁转化、高温气冷堆和模块化小型堆等安全先进核电、新能源、能源互联网、储能节能等技术的试验示范工程建设。推动能源装备创新发展，落实《中国制造 2025—能源装备实施方案》，制定能源装备自主创新工作方案，加强燃气轮机技术攻关和试验示范，推进燃气轮机关键技术装备国产化，推进核电、大容量柔性输电等智能电网、天然气长输、煤炭深加工、LNG 冷能利用、LNG 多式联运和小型 LNG 储罐高效储存等关键设备研制和示范应用。进一步完善能源科技创新体系，建立协同创新工作机制，优化国家能源研发中心管理。加强能源技术标准体系建设，以核电、可再生能源规模化、化石能源清洁化、能源系统智能化等为重点，实施一批能源行业标准化专项。围绕能源精细化管理、新能源利用等，加强能源计量关键技术和设备研发，提升重点能源行业和产业计量技术支撑能力和水平。

（二）深化实施能源体制改革

深入推进电力体制改革。持续完善中长期电力交易机制，进一步推进电力辅助服务市场建设，积极稳妥推进电力现货市场建设试点，规范电力市场交易行为，加快推进配售电改革，完善增量配电业务改革试点配套政策，加强售电侧市场规范与引导，提高电力市场化交易比重，进一步降低企业用能成本。以电力体制改革为重点，推动新疆、内蒙古等地区能源综合改革。

加快推进油气体制改革。贯彻落实《中共中央国务院关于深化石油天然气体制改革的若干意见》，研究制定相关配套政策和措施，推动油气管网运营机制改革，理顺省级管网体制，加快推动油气基础设施公平开放，完善油气储备设施投资和运营机制。推进四川、重庆、新疆、贵州、江苏、上海、河北等地方油气体制改革综合试点及专项试点。

（三）培育能源发展新动能

积极发展新兴能源产业，推动能源生产消费新模式、新业态发展壮大，实施能源系统人工智能、大数据应用等创新行动，推广智能化生产、储运和用能设施。扎实推进“互联网＋”智慧能源（能源互联网）、多能互补集成优化、新能源微电网、并网型微电网、储能技术试点等示范项目建设，在试点基础上积极推广应用。

五、加大惠民利民力度，增进能源民生福祉

（一）提高能源普遍服务水平

加强配电网、燃气管网等城乡供能基础设施建设，保障城乡居民电、热、冷、气等多样化能源需求，改善城乡居民用能条件。按照“宜管则管、宜罐则罐”的原则，综合利用管道气、撬装 LNG、CNG 等多种方式，打通天然气利用“最后一公里”，提高天然气通达能力。研究提出加强电力普遍服务的政策措施。

（二）推进贫困地区农网改造升级和能源扶贫

以贫困地区为重点，特别是“三区三州”深度贫困地区，以及国家扶贫开发工作重点县、集中连片特困地区和革命老区，深入实施农网改造升级工程。聚焦深度贫困地区，深入开展脱贫攻坚，做好能源定点扶贫和对口支援工作，实施“十三五”光伏扶贫计划，加强光伏扶贫项目管理，保障光伏扶贫工作稳妥有序开展。

（三）扎实推进北方地区冬季清洁取暖

落实《北方地区冬季清洁取暖规划（2017～2021 年）》，完善配套政策措施。“宜气则气、宜电则电”，因地制宜发展可再生能源供暖、天然气供暖、电供暖、工业余热供暖、清洁燃煤集中供暖等清洁供暖方式，严控散煤取暖，构建绿色、节能、高效、协调、适用的北方地区清洁供暖体系。坚持清洁燃煤集中供暖的主体地位，逐步提高集中供暖面积，替代低效小锅炉。加快推进县域生物质热电联产和生物质锅炉清洁供热项目建设，有效减少散煤消费。积极推动中深层地热供暖。在落实气源的前提下，有规划地推进天然气供暖。充分考虑电网承载能力和新增电网项目安排，积极推广电供暖。在风电富集地区，重点利用低谷时期富余风电供暖。积极研究推动北方地区核能供暖试点工作。

（四）加快能源领域军民融合深度发展

编制实施边境地区能源建设规划，加快电网、油气管网、清洁能源供能等基础设施建设。推进边防部队电网建设，完成第一批 226 个边防哨所通电任务，研究制定第二批边防部队电网建设实施方案，切实提高边境地区部队及边民电力保障能力。启动实施部队重要设施电网改造升级工程。推动离网地区军民融合可再生能源局域网建设，以新能源融合储能、配电网等方式，为岛屿、高原哨所等离网地区提供热电冷综合能源服务。

六、拓展能源国际合作，保障国家能源安全

（一）推进“一带一路”建设

巩固“一带一路”国际合作高峰论坛成果，落实《推动“一带一路”能源合作愿景与行动》，筹建能源合作交流平台，运营好能源国际合作信息服务平台，推进能源项目库建设。支持国内有关地区充分发挥比

较优势，参与“一带一路”能源合作。发挥好上海国际能源交易中心、上海和重庆石油天然气交易中心的作用，支持新疆建立国际油气交易中心。

（二）加强能源基础设施互联互通

加强能源资源保障能力建设，深化与相关国家的能源资源合作。加强与周边国家能源基础设施互联互通，完善东北、西北、西南和海上四大油气进口通道，维护跨境油气管线的安全稳定运营，积极落实“全球能源互联网”倡议，促进与周边国家电网互联。

（三）深化技术装备和产能合作

加强能源规划、政策、技术、装备、标准服务等领域合作。推进能源行业“走出去”，深化能源国际产能合作，围绕能源转型、技术创新和重大项目合作，携手开发第三方市场。创建能源行业“走出去”样板工程，培育“中国制造”“中国创造”国际化品牌。

（四）积极参与全球能源治理

加强与国际能源论坛、可再生能源署、国际能源署、能源宪章等国际组织的合作，制定更加开放、包容、普惠、平衡、共赢的规则，完善全球能源治理体系。积极参与现有多边框架下能源合作，包括联合国、二十国集团、APEC、金砖国家、上合组织、澜沧江—湄公河合作、大湄公河次区域、中国—东盟、东盟与中日韩以及东亚峰会等多边框架，合作构建绿色低碳的全球能源治理格局。推动成立“全球能源变革联盟”。继续开展中国—东盟清洁能源能力建设计划和中阿清洁能源培训中心建设，发挥中国—中东欧国家能源项目对话与合作中心的作用，启动“16＋1”能源合作联合研究项目。

七、加强能源行业管理，提升能源行业治理水平

（一）推进能源法治建设

成立能源法治建设领导小组，协调能源法治建设重大问题。积极推动《能源法》《电力法》《可再生能源法》《煤炭法》《石油天然气法》《石油天然气管道保护法》《国家石油储备条例》《海洋石油天然气管道保护条例》《核电管理条例》《能源监管条例》等法律法规的制定和修订工作，健全适应生态文明建设和能源转型变革要求的法律法规制度体系。清理废除妨碍统一市场和公平竞争的能源法律、法规、规章和规范性文件，加强能源改革与立法的有效衔接。加强政策文件的合法性审核、公平竞争审查，确保出台的规章规范性文件与相关法律法规、改革方向协调一致。完善能源系统普法工作机制，创新能源普法方式，提高能源领域法治意识。加强能源行业依法行政，严格规范公正文明执法，依法做好行政复议和行政应诉工作。规范能源重大事项决策机制，健全资金使用、行政处罚、资质许可等事项决策程序，进一步推进能源决策科学化、民主化、法治化。

（二）强化能源战略规划实施

研究编制2050年能源发展战略纲要，深化能源领域重大课题研究，明确2020年、2035年、2050年等重要时间节点的阶段性目标和路线。加强能源统计分析和发展形势研判，推动能源大数据平台建设，探索建立规划实施信息采集和共享机制。组织开展“十三五”能源规划实施中期评估和调整工作，建立和完善能源规划实施监测和评估机制，全面评估规划主要目标、重点任务、重大工程的落实情况，并做好规划中期调整，完善相关政策和措施，推动规划有效实施。

（三）进一步深化“放管服”改革

继续取消和下放行政审批事项，探索创新能源投资项目管理方式，推动实施能源投资项目负面清单管理机制，促进投资主体多元化。规范试点示范类项目，开展专项督查。创新能源行业监管，促进能源规划、政策、标准的落实和简政放权承接落实，确保能源项目投资规范有序。加快能源行业信用体系建设，建立守信激励和失信惩戒机制。进一步优化服务，规范行政行为、优化办事程序，推进行政许可标准化，持续开展“减证便民”行动，加快提升“互联网＋政务服务”。

（四）强化能源市场监管

坚持依法监管、精准监管、创新监管，加强电力调度交易与市场秩序、油气管网设施公平开放、电力价格成本等重点领域监管，深化供电监管，进一步落实优化供电营商环境工作方案，提高群众用电满意度。创新监管方式，实现“双随机、一公开”监管全覆盖，借助“互联网＋”、大数据等现代科技手段，不断丰富监管方式，持续完善监管标准体系，提高监管的协调性、有效性和准确性。严肃查处市场主体违法违规行为，积极化解能源市场矛盾纠纷，认真处理12398热线投诉举报事项。

（五）加强能源生产建设安全管理

贯彻落实《中共中央 国务院关于推进安全生产领域改革发展的意见》和《国家发展改革委 国家能源局关于推进电力安全生产领域改革发展的实施意见》，牢固树立安全发展理念，进一步理顺体制、厘清职责，大力提升能源安全生产整体水平。坚持问题导向，把握监管定位，压实企业安全生产主体责任，依法履行行业安全监管责任，落实地方安全生产管理责任。全面构建安全风险分级管控和隐患排查治理双重预防机制，防范大面积停电系统性风险，坚决遏制

重特大人身伤亡事故以及水电站大坝溃坝、垮坝等事故，加强油气管道保护工作，全面推行管道完整性管理。以技术进步和精细化管理实现监管手段创新，持续加大监管执法和问责力度，不断推进本质安全建设，营造良好安全文化氛围，保持安全生产形势持续稳定。

八、能源重大工程

（一）非化石能源可持续发展工程

水电。积极推进已开工水电项目建设，年内计划新增装机规模约 600 万 kW。扎实推进具备条件项目的核准建设，年内计划开工建设金沙江拉哇等水电站。

核电。积极推进已开工核电项目建设，年内计划建成三门 1 号、海阳 1 号、台山 1 号、田湾 3 号和阳江 5 号机组，合计新增核电装机约 600 万 kW。积极推进具备条件项目的核准建设，年内计划开工 6～8 台机组。扎实推进一批厂址条件成熟、公众基础好的沿海核电项目前期论证工作。

风电。稳步推进风电项目建设，年内计划安排新开工建设规模约 2500 万 kW，新增装机规模约 2000 万 kW。扎实推进部分地区风电项目前期工作，项目规模约 2000 万 kW。积极稳妥推动海上风电建设，探索推进上海深远海域海上风电示范工程建设，加快推动分散式风电发展。

太阳能。稳妥推进光伏发电项目建设，规范促进分布式光伏发电发展。有序推进太阳能热发电示范项目建设，年内计划建成中广核德令哈、首航节能敦煌等示范项目，装机容量约 20 万 kW。

生物质发电。年内计划建成生物质发电装机规模约 150 万 kW。

（二）化石能源清洁高效开发利用工程

煤炭。严格落实煤炭产能减量置换政策，积极发展先进产能，以神东、陕北、黄陇、新疆等大型煤炭基地为重点，有序核准建设一批大型现代化煤矿。

煤电。全年煤电投产规模较 2017 年更进一步减少，淘汰高污染、高能耗的煤电机组约 400 万 kW。继续深入推进煤电机组超低排放和节能改造提速扩围工作，2018 年完成中部地区具备条件煤电机组超低排放和节能改造，推进西部地区煤电机组超低排放和节能改造，促进煤电清洁高效发展。

煤炭深加工。扎实推进已开工示范项目建设，年内计划建成山西潞安高硫煤清洁利用油化电热一体化示范项目。有序推进具备条件项目的核准建设，年内计划开工建设伊泰伊犁 100 万 t/年煤制油示范项目、北控京泰 40 亿标准立方米/年煤制天然气示范项目。做好神华煤直接液化示范项目第二、三条生产线和陕西未来榆林煤间接液化一期后续项目前期工作。

（三）电力基础设施建设工程

跨省跨区输电通道。年内计划建成内蒙古上海庙—山东临沂±800kV 特高压直流、新疆准东—华东皖南±1100kV 特高压直流等输电通道，新增输电能力 2200 万 kV。扎实推进具备条件项目的核准建设，年内力争开工建设张北柔性直流试验示范工程、乌东德送电广东广西柔性直流、四川水电外送第四回直流等输电通道。扎实推进陕西、青海、新疆、陇彬、白鹤滩水电、金沙江上游水电电力外送输电通道，以及闽粤联网工程前期论证。

电网。进一步加强电网主干网架，年内计划新增 500kV 及以上变电容量（含换流容量）1.7 亿 kV·A，输电线路 2.2 万 km。

（四）电力系统补短板工程

抽水蓄能电站。积极推进已开工项目建设，年内计划建成投产广东深圳、海南琼中等抽水蓄能电站，扎实推进具备条件项目的核准建设。

储能。积极推进已开工项目建设，年内计划建成大连 100MW/400MW·h 液流电池储能调峰电站、辽宁绥中电厂 24MW/12MW·h 火电机组联合调频储能、大连 30MW/120MW·h 网源友好型风电场储能、江苏金坛压缩空气储能等项目。研究推进 100MW 压缩空气储能电站和 100MW 锂离子电池储能电站等项目前期工作。

（五）天然气产供储销体系建设工程

天然气生产。多措并举做好天然气稳供增供，全力稳定进口气源，优化国内油气企业投资安排，加快常规、非常规气上产步伐。

天然气管网。推进天然气管网互联互通，打通“南气北上”等反输和调运瓶颈，消除增量气源的入网瓶颈，加强气源间互供互保。推进中石油中缅管道与中石化广西 LNG 接收站外输气管道、舟山 LNG 外输管道与浙江管网、大鹏 LNG 外输管道与中海油广东管网、深圳 LNG 与大鹏 LNG 外输管道等管网联通。加快建设中俄东线北段、鄂安沧天然气管道、新疆煤制气外输管道南段、西气东输三线中段和闽粤支干线、天津浮式替代工程、上海 LNG 储罐扩建和输气管道复线及反输码头、深圳、舟山、温州、漳州 LNG 接收站，以及上海、唐山、江苏、山东、浙江 LNG 接收站扩建等项目。推进中俄东线中段和南段、川气东送二线、青岛—南京输气管道、蒙西煤制气外输管道、唐山 LNG 接收站应急调峰工程及外输管道复线、江苏 LNG 接收站应急调峰工程及外输管道复线、滨海 LNG 接收站等项目进展。

储气调峰能力建设。建立天然气储备制度，落实县级以上地方人民政府、供气企业、城燃企业和不可中断大用户的储气调峰责任和义务，提升储气调峰能力。加快已建储气库扩容达容。加快文23储气库、新疆油田克75井区储气库建设，2018年底前具备注气条件。

天然气供应。建立健全天然气需求侧管理和调峰机制，在供气紧张时段合理压减非民生用气，优先保障民生用气。推动供用气双方签订中长期购销合同，保障天然气市场平稳运行。

（六）能源改革创新工程

电力体制改革试点。大力推进第一批106个、第二批89个增量配电业务改革试点，启动第三批增量配电业务改革试点工作。推动南方（以广东起步）、蒙西、浙江、山西、山东、福建、四川、甘肃等8个地区电力现货市场建设试点。持续推进电力辅助服务市场专项试点工作。有序推进分布式发电市场化交易试点工作。

油气体制改革试点。推进四川、重庆、新疆、贵州、江苏、上海、河北等地方油气体制改革综合试点及专项试点。

能源新模式新业态。积极推进55个“互联网+”智慧能源（能源互联网）示范项目、23个多能互补集成优化示范工程、28个新能源微电网项目以及储能技术试点示范项目建设。加快推进浙江、四川、甘肃、宁夏等清洁能源示范省以及河南兰考等农村能源革命示范县建设。

（七）能源绿色消费及惠民利民工程

电能替代。在燃煤锅炉、窑炉、港口岸电等重点替代领域，实施一批电能替代工程，全年计划完成替代电量1000亿kW·h。

电动汽车充电设施。积极推进充电桩建设，年内计划建成充电桩60万个，其中公共充电桩10万个，私人充电桩50万个。

北方地区清洁取暖工程。因地制宜推动实施一批清洁取暖工程项目，新增清洁取暖面积10亿m^2以上。

农村能源建设工程。年内计划下达农网改造升级工程中央预算内投资120亿元；下达村级光伏扶贫电站规模约1500万kW，惠及约200万建档立卡贫困户。

各省（自治区、直辖市）能源主管部门、各能源企业，要深刻领会习近平新时代中国特色社会主义思想，全面贯彻党的十九大精神，认真落实党中央、国务院关于能源工作的决策部署，根据本指导意见要求，围绕补短板、强基础、调结构、促改革、惠民生等重点工作，全力抓好各项任务落实。国家能源局各部门，要抓紧制定工作方案，明确责任单位和进度安排，加强统筹协调和衔接配合，确保各项工作顺利开展。

国家能源局、国务院扶贫办印发《光伏扶贫电站管理办法》

国家能源局、国务院扶贫办2018年3月26日以国能发新能〔2018〕29号文印发《光伏扶贫电站管理办法》，该“办法”全文如下。

光伏扶贫电站管理办法

第一条 光伏扶贫是资产收益扶贫的有效方式，是产业扶贫的有效途径。为规范光伏扶贫电站建设运行管理，保障光伏扶贫实施效果，根据《中共中央国务院关于打赢脱贫攻坚战的决定》（中发〔2015〕34号）和《关于实施光伏发电扶贫工作的意见》（发改能源〔2016〕621号），制定本办法。

第二条 光伏扶贫电站是以扶贫为目的，在具备光伏扶贫实施条件的地区，利用政府性资金投资建设的光伏电站，其产权归村集体所有，全部收益用于扶贫。

第三条 本办法适用于国家“十三五”光伏扶贫电站项目。

第四条 光伏扶贫对象为列入国家光伏扶贫实施范围的建档立卡贫困村的建档立卡贫困户，优先扶持深度贫困地区和弱劳动能力贫困人口。

第五条 光伏扶贫电站原则上应在建档立卡贫困村按照村级电站方式建设。根据当地实际情况，确有必要并经充分论证可以联建方式建设村级电站。

第六条 光伏扶贫电站由各地根据财力可能筹措资金建设，包括各级财政资金以及东西协作、定点帮扶和社会捐赠资金。光伏扶贫电站不得负债建设，企业不得投资入股。

第七条 村级扶贫电站规模根据帮扶的贫困户数量按户均5kW左右配置，最大不超过7kW，单个电站规模原则上不超过300kW，具备就近接入和消纳条件的可放宽至500kW。村级联建电站外送线路电压等级不超过10kV，建设规模不超过6000kW。

第八条 光伏扶贫电站由县级政府按照“规划、设计、施工、验收、运维”五统一的原则实施，运用市场化方式委托专业机构负责光伏扶贫电站的建设、运行和维护。电站建设应符合国家相关规程规范和技术要求，确保质量与安全。光伏组件、逆变器等主要设备应采用国家资质检测认证机构认证的产品，鼓励采用达到“领跑者”技术指标的先进技术。鼓励采用设计施工采购（EPC）总承包方式统一开展县域内村级电站建设。

第九条　县级政府负责落实村级扶贫电站的建设场址和用地，场址土地不得属于征收土地使用税、耕地占用税的范围，不得占用基本农田，并符合《国土资源部 国务院扶贫办 国家能源局关于支持光伏扶贫和规范光伏发电产业用地的意见》（国土资规〔2017〕8号）规定。

电网公司负责建设配套接入电网工程，将光伏扶贫电站接网工程优先纳入电网改造升级计划，确保村级扶贫电站和接入电网工程同步建成投产。

第十条　省级政府能源、扶贫主管部门根据光伏扶贫政策要求组织对各县级光伏扶贫电站进行验收和评估，并将验收和评估情况形成书面报告报送国家能源局和国务院扶贫办。国家能源局会同国务院扶贫办对光伏扶贫电站验收和评估情况进行监督检查。

第十一条　电网公司保障光伏扶贫项目优先调度与全额消纳。

第十二条　光伏扶贫电站不参与竞价，执行国家制定的光伏扶贫价格政策。

第十三条　光伏扶贫电站优先纳入可再生能源补助目录，补助资金优先发放，原则上年度补助资金于次年1季度前发放到位。

第十四条　光伏扶贫电站收益分配与使用管理，按国务院扶贫办《村级光伏扶贫电站收益分配管理办法》（国开办〔2017〕61号）执行。

第十五条　光伏扶贫电站实行目录管理。国家能源局会同国务院扶贫办按建档立卡贫困村代码，对光伏扶贫电站统一编码、建立目录。纳入目录的，享受光伏扶贫电站政策。光伏扶贫电站有关信息统一纳入国家可再生能源信息管理平台。

第十六条　光伏扶贫电站项目计划下达后，对于一年内未开工建设、验收不合格且未按期整改的项目撤回计划，并给予通报。

第十七条　国家能源局、国务院扶贫办负责组织协调光伏扶贫重大问题，会同相关部门审核各省光伏扶贫实施方案，下达项目计划，对各省光伏扶贫实施工作进行指导监督。国务院扶贫办负责扶贫对象的识别认定和扶贫收益分配的管理监督。省级政府能源、扶贫主管部门负责本省光伏扶贫工作的统筹协调和管理监督，审核县级政府申报的扶贫实施方案和光伏扶贫补助目录，编制本省光伏扶贫实施方案并上报项目计划，出台本省光伏扶贫管理实施细则，组织本省光伏扶贫电站的验收和评估，保障本省光伏扶贫电站财政补助资金及时拨付和收益合理分配。县级政府负责落实光伏扶贫电站各项建设条件，编制本县光伏扶贫实施方案，申报光伏扶贫补助目录，组织实施光伏电站建设与运维，做好光伏扶贫收益分配。

第十八条　鼓励光伏企业积极履行社会责任，采取农光、牧光、渔光等复合方式，以市场化收益支持扶贫。

第十九条　本办法发布前已纳入国家光伏扶贫计划且已建成的集中式电站，按本办法执行。省级政府能源、扶贫主管部门应根据本办法制定本省光伏扶贫实施细则。

第二十条　本办法由国家能源局会同国务院扶贫办负责解释，自发布之日起施行。

国家能源局关于减轻可再生能源领域企业负担有关事项的通知

国家能源局2018年4月2日以国能发新能〔2018〕34号文印发《关于减轻可再生能源领域企业负担有关事项的通知》，该“通知”全文如下。

为深入贯彻国务院关于减轻市场主体负担的有关要求，进一步规范可再生能源行业管理，减轻可再生能源企业（含其他机构和个人投资者，以下同）投资经营负担，促进可再生能源成本下降，支持可再生能源相关实体经济健康发展，现就有关政策落实的要求和支持措施通知如下。

一、严格落实《可再生能源法》要求，切实保障可再生能源产业健康发展

（一）严格执行可再生能源发电保障性收购制度。对符合国家可再生能源开发利用规划以及在国务院能源主管部门下达的年度建设规模内，经省级能源管理部门列入年度实施方案，且符合国家可再生能源保障性收购及产业投资环境监测预警机制、市场环境监测评价机制有关政策的风电、光伏发电、生物质发电等可再生能源发电项目，电网企业要及时受理项目并网申请，明确提供并网接入方案的时限，对符合并网安全技术标准的项目，不得自行暂停、停止受理项目并网申请或拒绝已办理并网手续的项目并网运行。电网企业应与符合规划以及年度建设规模（年度实施方案）且规范办理并网手续的项目单位签订无歧视性条款的符合国家法规的并网协议，承诺按国家核定的区域最低保障性收购小时数落实保障性收购政策（国家未核定最低保障性收购小时数的区域，风电、光伏发电均按弃电率不超过5%执行），因技术条件限制暂时难以做到的，最迟应于2020年达到保障性收购要求。对于未落实保障性收购要求的地区，国务院能源

主管部门将采取暂停安排当地年度风电、光伏发电建设规模等措施控制项目开发建设节奏，有关省级能源管理部门不得将国务院能源主管部门下达的风电、光伏发电建设规模向此类地区配置。水力发电根据国家确定的上网标杆电价（或核定的电站上网电价）和设计平均利用小时数，通过落实长期购售电协议、优先安排年度发电计划和参与现货市场交易等多种形式，落实优先发电制度和保障性收购。

（二）电网企业负责投资建设接网工程。各类接入输电网的可再生能源发电项目的接网及输配电工程，全部由所在地电网企业投资建设，保障配套电网工程与项目同时投入运行。之前相关接网等输配电工程由可再生能源发电项目单位建设的，电网企业按协议或经第三方评估确认的投资额在2018年底前完成回购。电网企业投资建设可再生能源发电项目的接网及输配电工程的合理费用，在扣除可再生能源电价附加补助资金后，计入所在省级电网输配电价核定成本范围。接入配电网的分布式可再生能源发电项目，接网工程及配套电网改造工程由电网企业（含社会投资增量配电网企业，以下同）投资建设。所有可再生能源发电项目的电能计量装置和向电网企业传送信息的通讯设施均由电网企业出资安装。

（三）电力市场化交易应维护可再生能源发电企业合法权益。各电网企业和电力交易机构应遵循《可再生能源法》和电力改革关于可再生能源优先发电相关规定，按照《可再生能源发电全额保障性收购管理办法》（发改能源〔2016〕625号），对国务院能源主管部门会同经济运行主管部门核定的区域最低保障性收购小时数内的电量（国家未核定最低保障性收购小时数的区域，风电、光伏发电均按弃电率不超过5%执行），按国家价格主管部门核定或经招标、优选等竞争性方式确定的上网电价落实保障性收购。鼓励可再生能源发电企业超过最低保障性收购小时数的电量参与市场化交易。电网企业应与可再生能源发电企业签订优先发电合同，优先发电合同可以转让并按可再生能源发电企业所获经济利益不低于按国家价格主管部门核定或经招标、优选等竞争性方式确定的上网电价执行优先发电合同的原则获得相应补偿。实施可再生能源电力配额制，对各省级行政区域规定可再生能源占电力消费比重配额指标并进行考核，提高可再生能源利用水平。

二、优化投资环境，降低可再生能源开发成本

（四）减少土地成本及不合理收费。各地区能源管理部门应编制好可再生能源开发利用规划，并与相关土地利用、农牧林业、生态环保等规划衔接，优先利用未利用土地，鼓励按复合型方式用地，降低可再生能源项目土地等场址相关成本。地方能源管理部门在进行可再生能源项目布局时，应充分考虑土地类型及适用政策等因素，避免在适用城镇土地使用税和耕地占用税增加土地成本偏多的范围内规划布局集中式风电、光伏电站项目。村集体可以土地折价入股等方式参与项目投资，降低土地成本，并将所得收益用于支持村集体公益事业和增加农民收入。

（五）通过绿色金融降低企业融资成本。鼓励金融机构将可再生能源开发利用纳入绿色金融体系，加大对可再生能源项目投资企业的信贷投放，建立符合可再生能源项目的信用评级和风险管控体系，对信用良好的投资企业，在国家规定的基准利率基础上适度下浮，适当延长贷款期限并给予还贷灵活性。支持和鼓励可再生能源企业发行绿色债券和非金融企业绿色债务融资工具。鼓励地方通过专业化绿色担保机制等手段撬动更多社会资本投资于可再生能源等绿色产业领域。鼓励可再生能源投资企业与金融机构合作开展可再生能源投资项目资产证券化。完善可再生能源投资项目质量监测和风险评价体系。

（六）制止纠正乱收费等增加企业负担行为。各级地方政府有关部门不得向可再生能源投资企业收取任何形式的资源出让费等费用，不得将应由地方政府承担投资责任的社会公益事业相关投资转嫁给可再生能源投资企业或向其分摊费用，不得强行要求可再生能源企业在获取项目配置资格的同时对当地其他产业项目进行投资，不得将风电、光伏发电指标与任何无直接关系的项目捆绑安排，不得强行从可再生能源项目提取收益用于其他用途。已向风电、太阳能发电、生物质能等可再生能源项目违规收取资源出让费（或有偿配置项目，以下同）的地区，应按照“谁收取，谁退还”的原则，在本通知发布一年内完成清退。对继续强行收取资源出让费的地区，国家不在该地区布局各类可再生能源示范工程，有关省级能源管理部门不得将国务院能源主管部门下达的风电、光伏发电建设规模向此类地区配置。

三、完善政府放管服等公共服务，激发市场活力

（七）创新可再生能源项目开发机制，切实做好可再生能源政府服务。鼓励地方能源管理部门组织可再生能源项目前期工作，在落实项目建设外部条件后，采取招标方式选择项目投资主体。地方负责前期工作且采取招标方式组织的项目建设过程中，由地方能源管理部门会同有关部门负责落实各种审批手续。鼓励按照“谁审批，谁负责”的原则，建立能源管理部门牵头，相关部门协同配合的项目核准、备案等

"一站式"服务。

（八）加强政策落实和监管。国家建立可再生能源开发利用法规政策执行监测评价机制，将相关法规政策执行和优化政府服务列入可再生能源项目投资预警机制的监测评价范围。国务院能源主管部门派出机构要加强对可再生能源项目年度建设规模、项目优选、项目接网情况、优先上网及保障性收购情况的监管，加强对各地区落实可再生能源产业政策情况的监督。各省级能源管理部门应将可再生能源开发利用规划、项目配置办法等进行公示。电网企业应按月向所在地区的能源监管机构报送可再生能源发电项目接网、优先上网、保障性收购相关信息。各省级能源管理部门在编制项目建设年度实施方案或组织项目配置时，应要求市（县）级有关部门对项目涉及土地类型、税费等作出说明或承诺。对监测评价不合格的地方，停止在该地区安排国家组织开展的示范工程或支持的新的可再生能源开发利用项目。

（九）减少可再生能源项目物流成本。鼓励各地区公路管理机构要强化风机超大部件运输管理服务能力建设，提升大件运输行政许可服务水平。鼓励各地区对秸秆储存给予政策支持。

四、完善行业管理，减少投资和经营负担

（十）规范技术标准及其应用。电网企业应按照有关标准对可再生能源发电项目并网运行进行审查，确保电网安全高效运行。电网企业应根据电网安全以及网络与信息安全需要合理选择技术标准，避免可再生能源项目不必要的设备配置。区分接入电压等级、规格设定适宜的技术条件，对分布式发电功率因数等考核要考虑自发自用利用方式影响，在分布式电源满足接网安全技术及质量标准的前提下，能够在电网系统采取措施改善电能质量，不向分布式发电用户提出不合理的技术要求或进行不合理的考核收费。对风电、光伏发电等项目功率预报考核要公平合理。

（十一）转变风电设备质量风险控制方式。鼓励发挥保险的风险转移作用，促进风电设备质量保险发展，创新风电设备质量保险服务模式，丰富质量保险产品，加强风电设备质量监测评价和信用体系建设，鼓励以风电设备质量保险替代风电设备质量保证金。

（十二）规范各类检查和收费。电网企业对可再生能源发电项目进行并网及运行安全检查不收取费用，并网检测技术机构对项目采用已检测过的产品不重复检测，仅当检查或运行中发现项目所用涉网设备不符合并网标准，且项目单位完成技术整改后，才进行复查检测并按国家核定标准收费。各类检查均不得将应由本单位负担的公务费用向可再生能源项目单位转嫁。减少各种检查工作的随意性和对项目生产经营的干扰。

本通知自印发之日起执行。

国家能源局印发《分散式风电项目开发建设暂行管理办法》

国家能源局 2018 年 4 月 3 日以国能发新能〔2018〕30 号文印发《分散式风电项目开发建设暂行管理办法》，该"办法"全文如下。

分散式风电项目开发建设暂行管理办法

第一章 总 则

第一条 为推进分散式风电发展，规范分散式风电项目建设管理，根据《中华人民共和国可再生能源法》《中华人民共和国电力法》《中华人民共和国行政许可法》《中华人民共和国土地管理法》以及《分布式发电管理暂行办法》，制定本办法。

第二条 分散式风电项目是指所产生电力可自用，也可上网且在配电系统平衡调节的风电项目。项目建设应满足以下技术要求：

（一）接入电压等级应为 110kV 及以下，并在 110kV 及以下电压等级内消纳，不向 110kV 的上一级电压等级电网反送电。

（二）35kV 及以下电压等级接入的分散式风电项目，应充分利用电网现有变电站和配电系统设施，优先以 T 或者 π 接的方式接入电网。

（三）110kV（东北地区 66kV）电压等级接入的分散式风电项目只能有 1 个并网点，且总容量不应超过 50MW。

（四）在一个并网点接入的风电容量上限以不影响电网安全运行为前提，统筹考虑各电压等级的接入总容量。

国家关于分布式发电的政策和管理规定均适用于分散式风电项目；110kV（东北地区 66kV）电压等级接入的分散式风电项目，接入系统设计和管理按照集中式风电场执行。

第三条 鼓励各类企业及个人作为项目单位，在符合土地利用总体规划的前提下，投资、建设和经营分散式风电项目。鼓励开展商业模式创新，吸引社会资本参与分散式风电项目开发，充分激发市场活力。

第四条 各省级能源主管部门在国务院能源主管部门的组织和指导下，负责本地区分散式风电项目的开发规划、建设管理以及质量和安全监督管理职责。

第二章 规划指导

第五条 地方各级能源主管部门会同国土、环保、规划等部门和相关企业，依据当地土地利用总体规划和风能资源、电网接入、清洁能源消纳能力等开发建设条件，制订当地分散式风电开发建设规划，并依法开展环境影响评价工作，编制规划环境影响报告书，同时结合实际情况及时对规划进行滚动修编。分散式风电开发建设规划应做好与《风电发展“十三五”规划》的衔接，在落实消纳条件和分散式风电技术要求的条件下，严格按照《国家能源局关于可再生能源发展“十三五”规划实施的指导意见》对风电建设规模的相关要求以及我局关于风电预警管理的相关规定编制，不得随意扩大建设规模。

规划编制可按以下流程开展：1. 能源主管部门根据土地、资源等提出规模及布点方案；2. 电网企业据此方案，基于电网、负荷，按照电网接入条件约束进行容量和布点的优化；3. 能源主管部门公开发布分散式风电规划报告并进行滚动修编。

第六条 全面拓宽应用领域。鼓励分散式风电项目与太阳能、天然气、生物质能、地热能、海洋能等各类能源形式综合开发，提高区域可再生能源利用水平；与生态旅游、美丽乡村、特色小镇等民生改善工程深入结合，促进县域经济发展；与智慧城市、智慧园区、智慧社区等有效融合，为构建未来城市（社区）形态提供能源支撑；与海岛资源开发利用充分结合，促进发展海洋经济、拓宽发展空间。

第七条 各级电网企业应积极配合分散式风电开发建设规划制订工作，提供本地区电网建设规划、潮流、新能源消纳等相关信息，并明确各并网点及其潜在接入容量等数据。鼓励分散式风电等分布式发电建设条件好的市（县）及地区电网企业编制分布式新能源电网接入和消纳的专项规划。

第八条 分散式风电项目开发建设规划应与土地利用、生态保护、乡村发展、电网建设等相关规划有效衔接，并符合城乡规划，避免分散式风电开发建设规划与其他规划冲突。

第三章 项目建设和管理

第九条 各地方要简化分散式风电项目核准流程，建立简便高效规范的核准管理工作机制，鼓励试行项目核准承诺制。地方能源主管部门制订完善的分散式风电项目核准管理工作细则，建立简便高效规范的工作流程，明确项目核准的申报材料、办理流程和办理时限等，并向社会公布。对于试行项目核准承诺制的地区，地方能源主管部门不再审查前置要件，审查方式转变为企业提交相关材料并作出信用承诺，地方能源主管部门审核通过后，即对项目予以核准。

第十条 鼓励各地方政府设立以能源主管部门牵头的“一站式”管理服务窗口，建立国土、环保等多部门高效协调的管理工作机制，并与电网企业有效衔接，建立与电网接入申请、并网调试、电费结算和补贴发放等相结合的分散式风电项目核准等“一站式”服务体系。

第十一条 分散式风电项目开发企业在项目取得土地、规划、环保等职能部门的支持性文件后，按照地方政府有关规定，向相应的项目核准机关报送项目申请报告。各地相关部门要针对分散式风电项目的特点简化工作流程，降低项目前期成本。

第十二条 开发企业应按照核准文件的要求进行建设。项目核准后两年内不开工建设的，按照《企业投资项目核准和备案管理办法》（国家发展和改革委员会令第 2 号）处理。项目开工以第一台风电机组基础浇筑为标志。

第十三条 在满足国家环保、安全生产等相关要求的前提下，开发企业可使用本单位自有建设用地（如园区土地），也可租用其他单位建设用地开发分散式风电项目。

分散式风电项目不得占用永久基本农田。对于占用其他类型土地的，应依法办理建设用地审批手续；在原土地所有权人、使用权人同意的情况下，可通过协议等途径取得建设用地使用权。

第十四条 分散式风电项目申请核准时可选择“自发自用、余电上网”或“全额上网”中的一种模式。自发自用部分电量不享受国家可再生能源发展基金补贴，上网电量由电网企业按照当地风电标杆上网电价收购，其中电网企业承担燃煤机组标杆上网电价部分，当地风电标杆上网电价与燃煤机组标杆上网电价差额部分由可再生能源发展基金补贴。对未严格按照技术要求建设的分散式风电项目，国家不予补贴。

第十五条 鼓励开发企业将位于同一县域内的多个电网接入点的风电机组打捆成一个项目统一开展前期工作，办理相关支持性文件，进行项目前期工作和开发建设。

第四章 电网接入

第十六条 通过 110kV（东北地区 66kV）电压

等级接入的分散式风电项目，应满足国家标准 GB/T 19963《风电场接入电力系统技术规定》及其他国家/行业相关标准的技术要求；通过 35kV 及以下电压等级接入的分散式风电项目，应满足国家标准 GB/T 33593《分布式电源并网技术要求》及其他国家/行业相关标准的技术要求。

第十七条 电网企业应为纳入专项规划的 35kV 及以下电压等级的分散式风电项目接入电网提供便利条件，为接入系统工程建设开辟绿色通道。接入公共电网的分散式风电项目，接入系统工程以及接入引起的公共电网改造部分由电网企业投资建设。接入用户侧的分散式风电项目，在用户范围内的接入系统工程由项目业主投资建设，接入引起的公共电网改造部分由电网企业投资建设。

第十八条 电网企业应完善 35kV 以下电压等级接入分散式风电项目接网和并网运行服务。由地市或县级电网企业设立分散式风电项目“一站式”并网服务窗口，按照简化程序办理电网接入，提供相应并网服务，并及时向社会公布配电网可接入容量信息。

第十九条 35kV 及以下电压等级接入分散式风电项目办理并网手续的工作流程、办理时限，参照以下要求执行：

（一）地市或县级电网企业客户服务中心为分散式风电项目业主提供并网申请受理服务，向项目业主填写并网申请表提供咨询指导，接受相关支持性文件，不得以政府核准文件、客户有效身份证明之外的材料缺失为由拒绝并网申请。

（二）电网企业为分散式风电项目业主提供接入系统方案制订和咨询服务，并在受理并网申请后 20 个工作日内，由客户服务中心将接入系统方案送达项目业主，经项目业主确认后实施。

（三）分散式风电项目主体工程和接入系统工程竣工后，客户服务中心受理项目业主并网调试申请，接收相关材料。

（四）电网企业在受理并网调试申请后，10 个工作日内完成关口电能计量装置安装服务，并与项目业主（或电力用户）签署购售电合同和并网调度协议。合同和协议内容参照有关部门制订的示范文本内容。

（五）电网企业在关口电能计量装置安装完成后，10 个工作日内组织并网调试，调试通过后直接转入并网运行。

（六）电网企业在并网申请受理、接入系统方案制订、合同和协议签署、并网调试全过程服务中，不收取任何费用。

第二十条 电网企业应按规定的并网点及时完成应承担的接网工程，在符合电网运行安全以及网络与信息安全技术要求的前提下，尽可能在用户侧以较低电压等级接入，允许内部多点接入配电系统，避免安装不必要的升压设备。

第二十一条 电网企业应根据分散式风电接入方式、电量使用范围，本着安全、简便、及时、高效的原则做好并网管理，提供相关服务。

第二十二条 分散式风电与电网的产权分界点为风电机组集电线路最靠近电网的最后一台风电机组处，电量计量点原则上尽可能接近产权分界点，在技术条件复杂时可由开发企业与当地电网企业协商确定。电网企业提供的电能计量表应可明确区分项目总发电量、“自发自用”电量和上网电量。

第二十三条 完善分散式风电项目电费结算和补贴拨付。

（一）电网企业按月（或双方约定）与分散式风电项目单位（含个人）结算电费和转付国家补贴资金，按分散式风电项目优先原则做好补贴资金使用预算和计划，保障国家补贴资金及时足额转付到位。

（二）电网企业应按照有关规定配合当地税务部门处理好购买自然人（个人）分散式风电项目电力产品发票开具和税款征收问题。

（三）电网企业应做好项目电费结算和补贴发放情况的统计，并按要求向国务院能源主管部门及其派出机构、省级能源主管部门报送相关信息。

（四）分散式风电项目并网调试完成，并具备正式结算条件后，由电网企业按季度按流程向财政部、国家发展改革委、国家能源局申报纳入可再生能源发电补贴目录。

第二十四条 对于接入 10kV 及以上电压等级电力系统的分散式风电项目，开发企业应确保其安装的风电机组型号通过了相关国家标准、行业标准所规定的测试，并网运行时电能质量和所在公共电网的接入点电压合格。分散式风电应充分利用自身无功电压调节能力，补偿分散式风电接入带来的无功和电能质量控制需求。电网企业根据当地电网运行需要，统一建立覆盖本地区的功率预测预报体系。

第二十五条 分散式风电项目根据其所用的风电机组技术特性运行，在确保电力系统网络与信息安全的前提下，向地市或县级电网调度部门上传运行信息。

第五章　运行管理

第二十六条 分散式风电项目运营主体应当遵守电力业务许可制度，依法开展发电相关业务，并接受国务院能源主管部门及其派出机构的监管。

第二十七条 加强分散式风电项目监测和评价。

电网企业应与分散式风电项目建立沟通协调机制，及时掌握分散式风电运行情况。在电网和分散式风电项目检修期间，做好接入点隔离措施。

第二十八条 完善产业技术服务体系。通过市场机制培育分散式风电项目规划设计、工程建设、评估认证、运行维护等环节的专业化服务能力，满足分散式风电项目多元化参与主体的技术需求。

第二十九条 探索新型专业化的运维商业模式。鼓励分散式风电项目应用智能化运行管理技术，实现无人值守的运行模式；鼓励开发企业委托第三方专业机构提供运维服务。

第三十条 完善分散式风电项目机组退役管理。制订风电机组剩余寿命评估标准，在风电机组并网运行达到设计寿命前1～2年内，对机组状况、运行条件及剩余寿命等进行综合评估，按照标准要求对机组采取延期服役或拆除处理。

第六章 金融和投资开发模式创新

第三十一条 创新投融资机制。鼓励各类企业、社会机构、农村集体经济组织和个人参与投资分散式风电项目，实现投资主体多元化。

（一）鼓励项目所在地政府建立分散式风电项目融资服务平台，与银行、保险公司等金融机构合作开展金融服务创新，如设立公共担保基金、风险补偿基金等。鼓励项目所在地政府结合民生项目对分散式风电项目提供贷款贴息。

（二）鼓励银行等金融机构，在有效防控风险的前提下，综合考虑社会效益和商业可持续性，积极为分散式风电项目提供金融服务，探索以项目售电收费权和项目资产为质押的贷款机制。

（三）在确保不增加地方政府隐性债务的前提下，鼓励合法合规地采用融资租赁方式为分散式风电项目提供一体化融资租赁服务；鼓励各类基金、保险、信托等与产业资本结合，探索建立分散式风电项目投资基金；鼓励担保机构对中小企业和个人提供建设分散式风电项目的信用担保，支持分散式风电入户、入社区（乡村和工业园区等）。

第三十二条 积极开展商业模式创新。在农民自愿的前提下，可以将征地补偿费和租用农用地费作为资产入股项目，形成集体股权，并量化给农村集体经济组织成员，建立公平、公正、公开的项目收益分配制度，以组、村、乡镇不同层级农村集体经济组织为股权持有者，其成员为集体股权受益主体，推动实现共享发展。鼓励社会资本采取混合所有制、设立基金、组建联合体等多种方式，以PPP合作模式参与地方政府主导的分散式风电项目投资建设。

第三十三条 鼓励项目所在地开展分散式风电电力市场化交易试点，允许分散式风电项目向配电网内就近电力用户直接售电，市场化交易范围、交易方式、交易电价、输配电价、交易各主体权利和义务等按照分布式发电市场化交易相关规定执行。

第七章 附 则

第三十四条 本办法自颁布之日起实施，有效期5年。

第三十五条 本办法由国家能源局负责解释。

国家能源局关于修改水电领域6件规范性文件的通知

国家能源局2018年5月16日以国能发新能〔2018〕45号文印发《关于修改水电领域6件规范性文件的通知》，该“通知”全文如下。

为进一步落实国务院“放管服”改革有关要求，现决定对《国家能源局关于加强水电建设管理的通知》（国能新能〔2011〕156号）等6件规范性文件的部分条款予以修改。

一、国家能源局关于加强水电建设管理的通知（国能新能〔2011〕156号）

删去第一条第（三）项中的“要充分发挥工程咨询的重要指导作用，提高前期设计工作质量；要进一步加强和改进设计审查，并对审查结论负责；要对大坝防震抗震、移民安置规划大纲和报告、工程建设方案等重要技术问题加强指导、严格审查，对工作内容和深度达不到规范要求的，不予安排审查”。

二、国家能源局关于印发水电工程勘察设计管理办法和水电工程设计变更管理办法的通知（国能新能〔2011〕361号）

（一）《水电工程勘察设计管理办法》中删去以下内容：

1. 第四章全文；
2. 第三十三条中“报原审查单位审查”。

（二）《水电工程设计变更管理办法》中删去以下内容：

1. 第五条中“水电工程概算调整管理办法另行制定”；
2. 第六条中“报原审查单位审查”；
3. 第十条和第十一条全文。

三、国家能源局关于做好水电建设前期工作有关要求的通知（国能新能〔2012〕77号）

删去第二条中的“未经主管部门许可，任何单位和个人不得擅自开展水电项目前期工作，包括项目勘测设计招标及项目预可行性、可行性研究工作。主要河流上的项目前期工作由国家能源主管部门管理，其他河流上的项目前期工作由省级能源主管部门管理。对于同意开展前期工作的项目”。

删去第四条中的“要建立健全管理制度，加强水电建设前期工作管理，水电水利规划设计总院等单位要严格设计审查管理，对于无开发规划、未经同意擅自开展前期工作以及其他不符合建设管理程序和要求的项目，不得进行技术咨询和设计审查”。

四、国家能源局关于澜沧江等流域水电开发有关事项的通知（国能新能〔2012〕257号）

删去第三条中的“水电水利规划总院在发挥技术管理优势，把好前期勘测设计工作技术质量关的同时，要按照国家基本建设程序和行业管理要求，严格设计审查管理，对于国家未明确开发主体的项目，不得进行技术咨询和设计审查；今后，除预可行性研究报告、可行性研究报告、移民安置等重大专项及设计变更技术审查，需报经我局委托外，凡国家未出具前期工作函的项目，其技术审查均需获得我局授权委托，或经我局同意”。

五、国家能源局关于金沙江上游等流域水电开发有关事项的通知（国能新能〔2013〕10号）

删去第二条中的“对于国家未出具前期工作函的项目，待条件成熟后，要按规定履行同意开展项目前期工作程序，确保有序推进项目核准和筹建相关工作”。

删去第三条中的“水电水利规划设计总院在发挥技术管理优势，把好前期勘测设计工作技术质量关的同时，要按照国家基本建设程序和行业管理要求，严格设计审查管理，对于国家未明确开发主体的项目，不得进行技术咨询和设计审查。今后，不仅预可行性研究报告、可行性研究报告、移民安置等重大专项及设计变更技术审查，需报经我局委托，而且凡国家未出具前期工作函的项目，其技术审查也均需获得我局授权委托，或经我局同意”。

六、国家能源局关于促进水电健康有序发展有关要求的通知（国能新能〔2013〕155号）

删去第五条中的“技术审查单位要严格把关，从严管理设计及其变更”。

国家能源局发布《能源行业标准英文版翻译指南》

国家能源局2018年10月12日以2018年11号公告发布《能源行业标准英文版翻译指南》，该“指南”全文如下。

能源行业标准英文版翻译指南

一、前言

编制《能源行业标准英文版翻译指南》的目的是：

1. 对能源行业标准英文版翻译中需要统一的格式进行规范；

2. 对能源行业标准英文版翻译中需要统一的语句和用词进行规范。

本指南适用于将能源行业标准（NB编号）翻译成英文文本，能源领域其他行业标准英文版翻译可参照使用。除本指南外，按照GB/T 1.1《标准化工作导则第1部分：标准的结构和编写》给出的规则编制的行业标准英文版翻译还应符合GB/T 20000.10《标准化工作指南第10部分：国家标准的英文译本翻译通则》、GB/T 20000.11《标准化工作指南第11部分：国家标准的英文译本通用表述》的相关要求。按照《工程建设标准编制规定》（建标〔2008〕182号）给出的规则编制的行业标准英文版翻译还应符合住房城乡建设部发布的《工程建设标准英文版翻译细则（试行）》（建标标函〔2008〕79号）相关要求，与本指南要求不一致之处，以后者为准。

二、用词和用语

（一）封面用语的英文表述

1. 中华人民共和国能源行业标准 Energy Sector Standard of the People’s Republic of China

2. 国家能源局发布 issued by National Energy Administration

3. 发布日期 issue date

4. 实施日期 implementation date

5. 备案号 record number

6. 代替 replace (s)

7. 封面格式 封面格式见附录，除第三行

"Energy Sector Standard of the People's Republic China" 以外，其他字体及排版要求可参照 GB/T 20000.10—2016 附录 B 的相关要求。

（二）目次用语的英文表述

1. 目次 table of contents

2. 附录×（规范性附录）annex×（normative）

3. 附录×（资料性附录）annex×（informative）

4. 参考文献 bibliography

5. 索引 index（es）

6. 图 figure（s）

7. 表 table（s）

（三）前言部分用语的英文表述

1. 前言 foreword

2. 本标准附录×为规范性附录 Annex/Annexes ×of this standard is/are normative

3. 本标准附录×为资料性附录 Annex/Annexes ×of this standard is/are informative

4. 本标准是对××××进行修订。除编辑性修改外，与上一版标准的主要技术变化如下：This standard is a revision to××××. In addition to a number of editorial changes, the following technical deviations have been made with respect to its previous edition:

5. 本标准从实施日期起代替×××× This standard replaces×××× from the implementation date.

6. 本标准由×××× 提出 This standard was proposed by××××

7. 本标准由×××× 归口 This standard was prepared by××××

8. 本标准由×××× 负责具体内容解释 ×××× is responsible for the explanation of specific contents

9. 本标准英文版翻译单位××××（可选项）The main translation organizations of the English version of this standard are ××××

10. 本标准英文版主要翻译人员××××（可选项）The main translators of the English version of this standard are××××

11. 本标准英文版主要审查人员××××（可选项）The main examiners of the English version of this standard are××××

12. 本标准首次发布时间××××，本次是第×次修订。This standard was issued in××××as first edition. This is the×revised edition.

13. 本标准历次版本发布情况为：××××The previous editions of this standard are as follow（s）: ××××

（四）引言部分用语的英文表述

引言 introduction

（五）范围部分用语的英文表述

1. 本标准规定……的方法 This standard specifies a method/ methods of ……

2. 本标准规定……的性能 This standard specifies the characteristics of ……

3. 本标准规定……的系统 This standard establishes a system for ……

4. 本标准规定……的基本原理 This standard establishes general principles for……

5. 本标准适用于…… This standard is applicable to ……

6. 本标准不适用于…… This standard is not applicable to ……

（六）规范性引用文件的英文表述

1. 规范性引用文件 normative references

2. 下列文件对于本文件的应用是必不可少的。凡是注日期的引用文件，仅注日期的版本适用于本文件。凡是不注日期的引用文件，其最新版本（包括所有的修改单）适用于本文件。The following referenced documents are indispensable for the application of this standard. For dated references, only the edition cited applies. For undated references, the latest edition of the referenced document (including any amendments) applies.

（七）术语和定义的英文表述

以下及××××给出的术语和定义适用于本标准 For the purposes of this standard, the terms and definitions given in××××and the following apply.

（八）常用术语的英文表述

1. 标准化及标准文件

1.1 标准化 standardization

1.2 标准文件 normative document

1.3 国际标准 international standard

1.4 区域标准 regional standard

1.5 国家标准 national standard

1.6 行业标准 sector standard

1.7 地方标准 local standard

1.8 团体标准 association standard

1.9 企业标准 enterprise standard

1.10 导则 directive

1.11 指南 guide
1.12 规范 specification
1.13 通用规范 general specification
1.14 技术规范 technical specification
1.15 规程 code
1.16 规则（规定）rule
1.17 手册 handbook
1.18 技术报告 technical report
1.19 强制性标准 mandatory standard
1.20 推荐性标准 voluntary standard
1.21 指导性技术文件 technical guide
1.22 法规 regulation
1.23 技术法规 technical regulation

2. 标准化组织及标准机构

2.1 国际标准化组织 International Organization for standardization（ISO）
2.2 国际电工委员会 International Electrotechnical Commission（IEC）
2.3 国际电信联盟 International Telecommunication Union（ITU）
2.4 国家能源局 National Energy Administration
2.5 能源行业××××标准化技术委员会 energy sector standardization technical committee on ××

3. 标准文件的结构

3.1 封面 title page
3.2 标准名称 title
3.3 范围 scope
3.4 规范性引用文件 normative reference（s）
3.5 术语和定义 terms and definitions
3.6 符号 symbol
3.7 图形符号 graphical symbol
3.8 文字符号 letter symbol
3.9 缩略语 abbreviation
3.10 抽样 sampling
3.11 计数抽样 sampling by attributes
3.12 测试 testing
3.13 试验 test
3.14 试验方法 test method
3.15 试验报告 test report
3.16 检测实验室 testing laboratory
3.17 校准实验室 calibration laboratory
3.18 实验室能力验证 laboratory proficiency testing
3.19 实验室间比对试验 inter-laboratory test comparisons
3.20 分类 classification
3.21 标志 sign
3.22 标签 label（s）
3.23 包装 packaging
3.24 运输 transport
3.25 贮存 storage
3.26 注 note
3.27 脚注 footnote
3.28 技术制图 technical drawing
3.29 电路图 circuit diagram

4. 标准文件的层次划分

4.1 部分 part（s）
4.2 篇 section
4.3 章 clause
4.4 条 subclause
4.5 段 paragraph

5. 标准文件的内容

5.1 正文 text
5.2 条文 provision
5.3 方法性条文 deemed-to-satisfy provision
5.4 说明性条文 descriptive provision
5.5 性能条文 performance provision
5.6 陈述 statement
5.7 指示 instruction
5.8 推荐 recommendation
5.9 要求 requirement
5.10 必达要求 exclusive requirement
5.11 可选要求 optional requirement
5.12 通用要求（一般要求）general requirement
5.13 特殊要求 particular/ special requirement
5.14 安全要求 safety requirement

6. 标准文件的制定

6.1 标准计划 program of standards development
6.2 标准项目 project of standard development
6.3 标准草案 draft standard
6.4 标准征求意见稿 draft standard for comment
6.5 标准送审稿 draft standard for examination
6.6 标准报批稿 draft standard for approval
6.7 有效期限 period of validity
6.8 发布日期 issue date
6.9 实施日期 implementation date
6.10 审查 examination
6.11 函审 examination by correspondence
6.12 会审 examination by joint meeting
6.13 审核 examination & verification

6.14 审批 examination & approval
6.15 复审 review
6.16 勘误 corrigenda
6.17 增补 supplement
6.18 修改 amendment
6.19 修订 revision
6.20 重印 reprint
6.21 新版 new edition
7. 与质量有关的术语
7.1 合格/符合 conformity
7.2 检验 Inspection
7.3 自检 self-inspection
7.4 认证 certification
7.5 认可 accreditation
7.6 客观证据 objective evidence
7.7 极限值 limit (s)
7.8 不确定度 uncertainty
7.9 鉴定 qualification
7.10 鉴定合格 qualified
7.11 质量管理 quality management
7.12 质量控制 quality control
7.13 质量保证 quality assurance
7.14 质量改进 quality improvement
7.15 质量评价 quality evaluation
7.16 质量监督 quality surveillance
7.17 质量审核 quality audit

附录 封面格式

IOS XXXXX
XXX
Reoord Number:XXXX

NB

Energy Sector Standard of the People's Republic China

NB/T XXXXX-XXXX

Replace NB/T XXXXX-XXXX

能源行业标准名称（英文）
能源行业标准名称（中文）

(English Translation)

Issue date:XXXX-XX-XX Implementation date:XXXX-XX-XX

Issued by National Energy Administration of the People's Republic of China

国家能源局综合司关于进一步深入做好流域水电综合监测及水能利用监测工作的通知

国家能源局综合司2018年2月27日以国能综通新能〔2018〕29号文印发《关于进一步深入做好流域水电综合监测及水能利用监测工作的通知》，该“通知”全文如下。

为贯彻落实党的十九大精神，以习近平新时代中国特色社会主义思想为指导，认真落实生态文明建设和绿色发展有关要求，进一步加强流域水电综合管理，推进流域水电综合监测和水能利用监测体系建设，在已开展的长江、金沙江、大渡河、雅砻江、乌江等流域水电综合监测试点工作基础上，深入做好流域水电综合监测和水能利用监测工作。现将有关要求通知如下。

一、进一步完善流域水电综合监测体系，提升监测平台覆盖范围，对主要河流、大中型水电站系统开展流域水电综合监测工作。

二、请各有关单位按照《国家能源局关于印发〈水能利用率计算导则〉〈水能利用监测与发布管理办法〉和〈流域梯级工程特性及运行情况资料报表（试行）〉的通知》（国能发新能〔2017〕4号）有关要求，协助做好流域水电综合监测及水能利用监测工作，提升水电站信息化管理水平，落实数据交换技术基础工作，会同国家可再生能源信息管理中心研究落实安全、可行的数据对接方案，积极推动监测平台对接和数据报送工作。

三、请国家可再生能源信息管理中心加强监测平台建设，认真落实生态文明建设和绿色发展有关要求，持续推进流域水电开发运行涉及的生态环境影响、水能资源利用、流域风险因素、移民安置和库区经济社会发展等监测工作；提升监测平台运行水平，协助加强数据安全管理和数据分析能力建设；完善流域水电信息共享平台，提高信息资源的利用效率。

四、请各省、自治区、直辖市及新疆生产建设兵团能源主管部门梳理本地区在运、在建的大中型水电站（单站总装机容量5万kW及以上）情况，并请于3月15日前将有关情况反馈我局（新能源和可再生能源司）。

联系方式：任爱武 68555033/5037（传真）

附件：大中型水电站情况统计表

________省（自治区、直辖市）大中型水电站情况统计表

序号	电站名称	所在流域（河流）	装机容量（万kW）	电站状态（在运/在建）	项目业主单位	联系方式

国家能源局综合司、国务院扶贫办综合司关于做好光伏扶贫电站验收评估工作的通知

国家能源局综合司、国务院扶贫办综合司2018年12月19日以国能综通新能〔2018〕198号文印发《关于做好光伏扶贫电站验收评估工作的通知》，该“通知”全文如下。

为贯彻落实《中共中央 国务院关于打赢脱贫攻坚战的决定》和《中共中央 国务院关于打赢脱贫攻坚战三年行动的指导意见》，扎实有序推进光伏扶贫，保障光伏扶贫实施效果，请你们按照《光伏扶贫电站管理办法》等要求，认真组织开展本省（自治区、直辖市）光伏扶贫电站的验收、评估工作。现将有关事项通知如下。

一、请各省级能源、扶贫主管部门高度重视，制定光伏扶贫电站验收评估工作方案，建立验收评估工作机制，以县为单元对已建成且纳入国家光伏扶贫目录的光伏扶贫电站开展验收、评估。验收、评估应包括电站建设质量、建设资金、运行维护、收益分配等内容。

二、请各省级能源、扶贫主管部门落实职责分工、加强协调配合。省（自治区、直辖市）发改委（能源局）牵头组织集中式光伏扶贫电站的验收、评估，省（自治区、直辖市）扶贫办（局）牵头组织村级电站（含户用）的验收、评估，对验收、评估过程中发现的相关问题要明确责任单位和人员，及时督促整改。

三、请各省级能源、扶贫主管部门于1月底前将本省（自治区、直辖市）已开展的验收、评估工作情况及下步工作安排报送国家能源局和国务院扶贫办。国家能源局、国务院扶贫办将邀请纪检监察部门、审计署适时对各省（自治区、直辖市）相关工作开展情况进行抽查检查。

联系电话：国家能源局　010-68555894

国务院扶贫办　010-84419684

财政部《关于降低部分政府性基金征收标准的通知》

财政部2018年4月13日以财税〔2018〕39号文印发《关于降低部分政府性基金征收标准的通知》，该“通知”全文如下。

为进一步减轻社会负担，支持实体经济发展，现就降低部分政府性基金征收标准有关政策通知如下：

一、自2018年4月1日起，将残疾人就业保障金征收标准上限，由当地社会平均工资的3倍降低至2倍。其中，用人单位在职职工平均工资未超过当地社会平均工资2倍（含）的，按用人单位在职职工年平均工资计征残疾人就业保障金；超过当地社会平均工资2倍的，按当地社会平均工资2倍计征残疾人就业保障金。

二、自2018年7月1日起，将国家重大水利工程建设基金征收标准，在按照《财政部关于降低国家重大水利工程建设基金和大中型水库移民后期扶持基金征收标准的通知》（财税〔2017〕51号）降低25%的基础上，再统一降低25%。调整后的征收标准=按照《财政部 国家发展改革委 水利部关于印发〈国家重大水利工程建设基金征收使用管理暂行办法〉的通知》（财综〔2009〕90号）规定的征收标准×(1－25%)×(1－25%)。

征收标准降低后南水北调、三峡后续规划等中央支出缺口，在适度压减支出、统筹现有资金渠道予以支持的基础上，由中央财政通过其他方式予以适当弥补。地方支出缺口，由地方财政统筹解决。

三、各地区、各有关部门和单位应当按照本通知规定，及时制定出台相关配套措施，确保上述政策落实到位。

水利部印发《水利建设质量工作考核办法》

水利部2018年5月24日以水建管〔2018〕102号文印发《水利建设质量工作考核办法》，该“办法”全文如下。

水利建设质量工作考核办法

第一条　为加强水利建设质量工作，落实质量责任，提高水利建设质量水平，根据《中共中央国务院关于开展质量提升行动的指导意见》《国务院关于印发质量发展纲要（2011～2020年）的通知》《国务院办公厅关于印发质量工作考核办法的通知》和《国务院办公厅关于促进建筑业持续健康发展的意见》等规定，结合水利建设实际，制定本办法。

第二条　考核工作坚持客观公正、科学管理、突出重点、统筹兼顾、因地制宜的原则。

第三条　考核对象为各省、自治区、直辖市水利（水务）厅（局），新疆生产建设兵团水利局（以下简称“省级水行政主管部门”）。每年7月1日至次年6月30日为一个考核年度。

第四条　考核工作由水利部建设与管理司牵头，有关司局、单位和流域管理机构配合，水利部建设管理与质量安全中心承担有关具体工作。

第五条　考核内容包括水利建设质量工作总体考核和项目考核两部分。考核评分细则在年度质量考核工作中另行制定。

第六条　考核采用评分和排名相结合的综合评定法，满分为100分，其中总体考核得分占考核总分的60%，项目考核得分占考核总分的40%。考核结果分4个等级，分别为：A级（考核排名前10名，且得分90分及以上的）、B级（A级以后，且得分80分及以上的）、C级（B级以后，且得分在60及分以上的）、D级（得分60分以下或发生重、特大质量事故的）。

第七条　考核采取以下步骤：

（一）发布细则。水利部于每年年初发布年度水利建设质量工作考核评分细则。

（二）自我评价。各省级水行政主管部门按照本办法和年度评分细则，结合本地区质量工作的目标、任务和特点进行自我评价，并于每年8月10日前将上一考核年度的质量工作情况自评报告及相关材料、考核年度内在建项目清单、考核年度内开展的监督检查情况等报水利部。

（三）集中核查。组织总体考核工作组，依据各省级水行政主管部门上报的自评报告等，集中开展总体考核。同时根据各省级水行政主管部门上报的在建工程项目清单，按照工程类型、规模选取一定数量的项目作考核抽查对象（具体数量及要求在年度考核评分细则中规定）。

（四）实地核查。组织现场考核工作组，对所选项目进行实地核查，同时核查总体考核中的有关问题。

（五）综合评价。统计汇总总体考核和项目考核情况，提出各省份考核得分及考核等级建议，形成考核报告。

（六）结果认定。考核结果经水利部审定后，报送全国质量工作考核部际联席会议办公室，并向社会公告。

（七）整改工作。考核结果通报各省级水行政主管部门，抄送各省、自治区、直辖市人民政府，同时提出整改建议，限期整改。

第八条 考核结果作为项目和资金安排的一个重要参考因素。对考核结果为D级的，省级水行政主管部门应在考核结果通报后一个月内向水利部作出书面报告，提出限期整改措施。

第九条 对在质量工作考核中瞒报、谎报情况的，予以通报批评；对直接责任人员依法依规追究责任。

第十条 各省级水行政主管部门可根据本办法，结合当地实际，对本行政区域内水利建设质量工作进行考核。

第十一条 本办法由水利部负责解释。

第十二条 本办法自印发之日起施行。

领 导 讲 话

水电要当生态文明建设生力军

水利部原副部长、中国大坝工程学会理事长
矫勇

［编者按：此文为水利部原副部长、中国大坝工程学会理事长矫勇接受中国能源报记者采访的报道。］

水电是全国最早推进改革开放的行业之一，不仅在电力领域处于领先位置，在能源领域甚至是整个基础建设领域，其改革开放步伐也是最快的。40年来，我国水电装机规模由小到大，从改革开放初期的2000万kW，快速增至2017年的3.4亿kW，增幅达到16倍；行业由弱到强，从规划勘测设计、施工组织、建设管理、技术装备的多方位落后，发展到如今的全产业链全球领先，取得了“世界水电看中国”的巨大成就。期间，水电在带动经济发展、改善民生、节能减排等方面发挥了重要作用。但同时，行业发展也暴露出一系列新问题，未来发展也面临着不少全新挑战。

回顾改革开放40年，中国水电发生了哪些显著变化？与人民美好生活需要的差距在哪里？在经济由高速度发展向高质量发展中会发挥什么作用？未来发展空间如何？带着这些问题，中国能源报记者专访了水利部原副部长、中国大坝工程学会理事长矫勇。

中国能源报：您怎么评价水电行业改革开放的进程、成就？

矫勇：我本人是干水利工作的，但水利和水电关系密切，对水电发展多少有一些了解。总体来看，水利水电在过去40年改革开放中都有巨大发展，但从改革角度看，水电比水利的市场化改革更充分、更彻底。虽然电力也具有公益性，但经济回报是显著的，相比之下水利的公益性更强。所以大中型水电建设和运行均走向了市场，由市场调节，但公益性或以公益性为主的水利事业，如防洪、灌溉、乡村供水、水土保持等，还是由政府主导。

中国能源报：如果简单将改革开放40年以来的水电事业发展分成几个阶段，您会怎么划分？

矫勇：水电行业对水电事业发展阶段的划分比较一致，从体制机制改革的角度讲，大致可分为三个阶段。

第一阶段是解放初期到1979年，这一阶段电力行业的特点是以计划经济的方式由国家统一办电，从建设到运营，国家统管起来。第二阶段从1979年到本世纪初，水电建设管理体制经历了适应市场经济基本规律的摸索阶段。这一时期国家在电力行业推行集资办电，形成了国家和地方办电相结合、内资与外资办电相结合的多元化水电投资格局。建设管理体制上水电行业经历了“鲁布革冲击波”，逐步形成了项目法人责任制、招标投标制、建设监理制、合同管理制等市场化的水电建设管理体制，水电建设步伐明显加快，效益显著提高。第三阶段是2002年以后，电力体制改革进一步明确了市场化改革方向。当时，为打破电力行业垄断，形成了国网南网两大电网、五大发电公司及四大副业集团等，在电力市场上形成了多家市场主体的竞争格局。这一阶段是我国水电技术全面引进消化、自主创新、大力发展的阶段，也是水电技术赶超世界先进水平的阶段。

中国能源报：是的，2002年以来，我国水电发展非常迅速。

矫勇：对。我梳理了一组数据：水电装机从建国初期的16万kW，经过30年发展，增长到了1980年的2032万kW；1981～1990年10间增加了1573万kW；1991～2000年间增加了4330万kW；2001～2010年间增加了1.3亿kW；2011～2017年间增加了1.25亿kW。如果画出一条装机规模增长曲线，那么这条曲线每10年就会有一个向上的拐点，表明了每一个阶段水电体制内部改革和外部环境变化共同促进了水电的发展。

一、国内外因素共同促成跨越发展

中国能源报：哪些因素促成了水电的大发展？

矫勇：一方面是改革开放、西部大开发战略的推动。改革开放促进了水电行业市场化竞争，调动了电力企业的积极性。西部大开发在政策层面上创造了良好的水电建设环境，使水电建设重点西移，突破了高海拔、高地震烈度、高边坡、深厚覆盖层等一系列高坝和超高坝建设中的技术难题，发展进一步加快。另一方面是国际社会关于应对全球气候变化的倡议。2000年前后，国际上有一股反坝风潮。反对者认为大水电不是清洁能源。这源于非洲、南美洲等地的一些大型水电站，库容特别大，当地没有能力清库，水库淹没的大量热带雨林在水中腐烂后释放了温室气体甲烷，成为国际上反坝者的证据。实际上从全球的角度讲这不具有普遍性，比如我国的水库均实行清库，不存在树木在水中浸泡腐烂问题。

我曾作为我国谈判组成员参加了2002年南非约翰内斯堡“世界可持续发展首脑会议”。会议提出2015年全球各国非化石能源占比需达到15%，但特别标注了“非化石能源不包括大水电”。这对我们是很不利的。中国和其他发展中国家与代表反坝派的国家交锋了十多天，“吵”得异常激烈。直到各国领导人到会后各方才达成共识，把“非化石能源不包括大水电”改为“包括大水电”，在国际上统一了大型水电是清洁能源的共识。“正名”之后，我国水电也开始了一个新的发展阶段。

中国能源报：移民也是水电发展的大难题。像三峡移民接近130万，即约每1000个中国人中，就有一个三峡移民。现在移民安置费用在水电投资中的占比也越来越高。怎么看待、解决水电移民问题？

矫勇：改革开放40年来，水电移民政策、移民管理体系都得到了完善，从单一的大农业安置方式逐渐向多元化安置、更注重后续发展转变。

实事求是地讲，受2004年四川瀑布沟水电站移民事件的影响，水库移民问题的社会敏感性越来越高。所以，国务院修订了《大中型水利水电工程建设征地补偿和移民安置条例》，把征地补偿标准提高了16倍；并对全部水库移民实行了统一的后期扶持政策，即不分水利水电水库移民、新老水库移民、中央水库和地方水库移民，均按照每人每年600元的标准发放扶持资金，连续扶持20年。

其实国家对于水库移民问题始终是高度重视的。铁路、公路、机场、港口等工程建设涉及的群众搬迁都叫拆迁，只有水库搬迁叫移民。为什么？因为水库建设导致被搬迁群众原有的生产力遭到全面破坏，生产关系均被打乱，土地淹没、村庄消失，搬迁后需要在资源、环境、社会和经济关系等多方面重新调整和重建，所以对水库包括水电站移民实行前期补偿和后期扶持相结合的政策。即便现在水利水电工程的征地补偿和其他基础设施建设的征地补偿标准完全一致，都是执行地方政府公布的土地片区地价，仍然保持了水库的移民后扶政策。

水利水电移民政策调整，推动了我国水电移民工作。虽然增加了水电站建设成本，但做到了潘家铮院士所期盼的“建设一座电站、带动一方经济、改善一片环境、造福一批移民”。如今新建水库和水电站移民工作已经基本能做到“移得出、稳得住、能致富”。

所以，总体来讲，市场化改革、西部大开发、应对气候变化、完善移民政策等因素，都为水电发展提供了动力。

二、新定位：助力生态文明建设

中国能源报：回看40年，我国水电最大变化是什么？

矫勇：经过40年发展，我国水电装机已居世界首位。最主要的变化有三个方面：

一是水电企业体制机制发生了根本变化。企业完全按市场经济规律办事，真正做到了产权清晰、责权明确、政企分开、自主经营、自负盈亏，市场在资源配置中的决定性作用在电力市场得到了很好的展现。

二是科技和建设管理创新已经走在世界前列。当前我国水电建设已经引领世界潮流，世界上77座200m级以上的超高坝，我国占了20座。在宏大的水电建设实践中，通过引进、消化、再创新，探索产学研紧密结合的联合创新，我们破解了一系列水电建设方面的世界级技术难题，例如大体积混凝土浇筑温控技术、700MW以上水轮机组建造技术、600m级以上的高边坡稳定处理技术、深厚覆盖层基础处理技术、高水头大流量消能技术、超大型地下厂房和洞室群施工技术等，为建成三峡水利枢纽工程，建成锦屏一级、小湾、溪洛渡水电站等一批300m级左右的高坝奠定了扎实的基础。还有正在施工的乌东德、白鹤滩、两河口等大型水电站，都是世界级的巨大水电工程，如果没有科技创新的支撑，建设这些工程是无法想象的。

三是水电建设运营的理念发生了深刻变化，更加注重生态环境保护。比如，由于气候变暖导致的海平面上升，加之频繁的河道采沙，珠江三角洲前些年咸潮现象凸出，不仅是生态问题，也严重影响到澳门、珠海等地的饮用水安全。为解决珠江三角洲咸潮倒灌和澳门等地的饮水安全问题，珠江流域的水电企业主动承担起生态调度的任务。从 2005 年起，每年冬季从远离珠江三角洲 1500km 的天安桥水电站开始，通过流域梯级水电站向下游实施“压咸补淡”，抵御珠江三角洲的咸潮上溯。再如，黄河小浪底枢纽工程装机 180 万 kW，也是大型水电站，为治理黄河下游河床萎缩问题，从 2000 年开始调沙调水，使黄河下游河道生态得到根本性好转。还有三峡、糯扎渡等水利水电工程积极开展水库生态调度，扩大河道枯水期生态流量，创造适于鱼类产卵的流量环境，等等。这些事例说明水电央企的理念发生了变化，开始自觉贯彻绿色发展、生态优先，把维护和再造有坝河流的良好生态作为企业的使命。

中国能源报：那么在新时代经济社会发展中，水电将担当什么角色？

矫勇：全国生态环境保护大会刚刚闭幕，党中央国务院又出台了《关于全面加强生态环境保护坚决打好污染防治攻坚战的意见》，形成了新时代习近平生态文明思想。总书记特别强调人与自然和谐共生、绿水青山就是金山银山、良好生态环境就是最普惠的民生福祉、山水林田湖草是生命共同体等生态文明理念，特别强调要打赢蓝天保卫战，打好碧水保卫战。我觉得水电在促进经济增长、保障国家能源安全和改善民生中已经做出了重要贡献，今后更要在生态文明建设中做出重要贡献。比如我国目前一年要消耗相当于 27 亿 t 标准煤的原煤，而美国消耗大约 5 亿 t 标准煤，日本仅消耗 1.7 亿 t 标准煤，所以我国的煤炭燃烧排放是大气污染的主要来源。打赢蓝天保卫战关键在减煤，调整工业结构和能源结构，水电可以大有作为。我国水能资源世界排名第一，理论蕴藏量为 6.9 亿 kW，技术可开发量 5.4 亿 kW，目前开发了 3.4 亿 kW，其中包括了抽水蓄能电站。如果我国常规水电开发达到技术可开发量的 80%，每年可减少约 8 亿 t 原煤，将对我国大气污染防治、促进高质量发展做出重要贡献。当然，水电开发过程中要始终坚持绿色发展、生态优先，统筹解决好生态流量、鱼类增殖、河流生态系统稳定等问题，维系有坝河流的良好生态。

我到中国大坝工程学会工作快两年了，接触了许多水电央企，感到水电央企过去是水电事业发展的引领者、水电科技创新和技术进步的推动者，今后更要做河流生态文明的建设者。

努力开创水电发展的新局面

国家能源局监管总监 李冶

［此文为国家能源局监管总监李冶 2018 年 1 月 12 日在 2018 中国水电发展论坛暨水力发电科学技术奖颁奖典礼上的讲话，题目是编者加的。］

刚刚过去的 2017 年，党的十九大胜利召开，国家“十三五”规划稳步推进。在以习近平同志为核心的党中央坚强领导下，我国能源行业统筹推进稳增长、促改革、调结构、惠民生、保安全、防风险等各项工作，能源供给质量进一步提升，能源消费结构进一步优化，能源国际影响力持续增强，“一带一路”国际能源合作深入推进。水电作为我国能源结构的重要组成和非化石能源的主力，继续保持着较好的发展势头。初步统计，全国水电装机容量达到 3.4 亿 kW 左右，新核准开工金沙江白鹤滩、巴塘，澜沧江托巴等 3 个大型水电项目，总装机容量 1815 万 kW。同时白鹤滩百万千瓦水轮机组成功自主研发，标志着中国的电力装备在继百万千瓦火电等技术实现了国产化的基础上，全面进入了自主创新的百万时代。加快推进抽水蓄能电站建设，2017 年新核准开工浙江宁海、缙云，河南大鱼沟，湖南平江，内蒙古芝瑞，河北易县等 6 个抽水蓄能电站，总装机容量 840 万 kW。此外，国家“西电东送”战略骨干项目乌东德水电工程稳步推进。已建水电工程积极发挥出在防洪、抗旱、供水、航运、旅游、促进库区经济发展等综合社会功能；国家发展改革委印发《关于促进西南地区水电消纳的通知》和《解决弃水弃风弃光问题实施方案》，有力推进缓解了弃水弃风弃光状况。水电已经成为国家优化能源结构、实现节能减排、改善生态环境、主动应对全球气候变化的重要举措，水电的科学有序发展为促进经济社会可持续发展做出了积极贡献。水电战线一系列成绩的取得，得益于广大水电干部职工的艰辛努力和拼搏奉献，也是广大水电工作者开拓创新、锐意进取的结果。

多年来，水电学会在各届理事会正确带领及广大会员积极参与下，始终坚持围绕水电科技进步与国民经济社会发展需求，积极主动在学术交流、科学普及、科技奖励、人才培养、决策咨询和社会服务等方面开展了卓有成效的工作，取得了突出的成绩。学会举办了世界水电大会等大量的国内外学术交流活动，行业影响力不断提升；依托“水力发电科学技术奖”和“潘家铮奖”，发现和培养了大量科技人才，促进了大批优秀科技成果不断涌现；完成了弃水研究和建言等多项决策咨询及多个行业标准制定，行业专家群体优势和智囊团作用得到充分体现；管理运作的潘家铮水电科技基金，有力支撑多项水电科技公益活动的持续开展，等等。学会已发展成为引领我国水电事业创新发展的重要社团组织，成为党和政府联系团结广大水电科技工作者的牢固桥梁和纽带。

当前，我国正处在工业化城镇化发展过程和全面建成小康社会的决胜阶段，随着能源环境问题的日益凸显，能源在经济社会发展中既扮演着提供保障和支撑的重要作用，也逐渐成为发展的重要制约。从全球范围看，随着国际社会对保障能源安全、保护大气环境、应对气候变化等问题的日益重视，推动实现化石能源体系向清洁低碳能源体系转变为特征的能源转型成为世界各国普遍共识，开发利用可再生能源越来越受到各方重视。水电是可再生的清洁能源，虽然经过多年发展，我国水电开发规模已多年稳居世界第一，开发程度持续上升，按发电量计算达到了40%左右，但与丰富的水能资源量相比，还有开发潜力，水电在非化石能源和能源中仍将扮演重要角色，在保护好生态环境、妥善安置移民的前提下，积极稳妥发展水电仍是今后一段时期水电发展的主题。

党的十九大对能源发展作出了一系列重大决策部署，进一步指明了新时代能源发展的方向，提出了新的更高要求。水电在我国能源发展战略中具有不可或缺的重要作用，水电行业要坚持以习近平新时代中国特色社会主义思想为指导，全面贯彻党的基本理论、基本路线、基本方略，着眼“两个一百年”的战略安排和部署，落实创新、协调、绿色、开放、共享的发展理念，把发展水电作为能源供给侧结构性改革、确保能源安全、促进贫困地区发展和生态文明建设的重要战略举措。力争通过各方努力，实现“十三五”新开工常规水电和抽水蓄能电站各6000万kW左右，新增投产水电6000万kW，2020年水电总装机容量达到3.8亿kW，其中常规水电3.4亿kW，抽水蓄能4000万kW，年发电量1.25万亿kW·h，折合标煤约3.75亿t，在非化石能源消费中的比重保持在50%以上。

2018年是全面贯彻十九大精神的开局之年，是改革开放40周年的纪念之年，是决胜全面建设小康社会的关键之年，也是实施国家能源“十三五”规划的承上启下之年，做好能源工作意义重大。水电行业要主动适应发展的新形势、新要求，一是要更加重视生态保护工作，牢固树立和深入践行“绿水青山就是金山银山”的理念，坚持生态优先，推进绿色发展，落实科学有序开发大型水电、严格控制中小水电、支持水电扶贫的要求；二是要更加重视移民安置和库区发展，不断完善移民安置政策和水电开发政策，研究建立水电开发利益共享机制，共同打响精准扶贫攻坚战；三是要更加重视水电发展的协调性，统筹水电开发、电网建设和电力市场，加快调节性水库电站和抽水蓄能电站建设，优化电源建设结构；四是要更加重视水电管理，加快推进体制机制创新，完善水电开发和建设管理体制，提升流域综合管理水平。坚持问题导向，进一步推进解决水电弃水问题和安全管理薄弱环节；五是要更加重视水电“走出去”，坚持开放发展，加强国际合作，以“一带一路”建设为统领，推动水电装备、技术、标准和工程服务对外合作。

同志们，水电行业的持续健康发展离不开大家的共同努力，希望大家通过这次论坛交流信息、沟通情况，共商水电发展大计，推动行业创新发展，为2018年和“十三五”共同做好水电领域各项工作奠定良好基础。希望水力发电工程学会进一步发挥行业引领作用，做好大家沟通的桥梁和平台，服务行业发展。我局将和大家一道，努力开创水电发展的新局面。

改革开放　成就中国水电走向辉煌

中国水力发电工程学会理事长　张野

[编者按：此文为国务院南水北调工程建设委员会办公室原副主任，中国水力发电工程学会理事长张野2018年9月26日在“改革开放40年中国水电”纪念大会上的主旨发言。]

40年前，党的十一届三中全会胜利召开，改革开放的春风吹遍了神州大地，全国上下各行各业掀起了一场解放和发展生产力的新的伟大革命。在国家改革开放总的方针路线指引下，我国水电行业与其他领域改革一样发生了深刻变革，有力推动了中国水电从小到大、从弱到强、从学习跟跑并跑到领跑直至全面超越，装机容量和年发电量均位居世界第一。改革开放之初，中国水电装机容量和发电量仅为1727万kW和446亿kW·h，至2017年底分别为3.41亿kW和1.19万亿kW·h、增长了近20倍和26倍。中国水电在规划设计、施工安装、设备制造、运行管理、投资融资等全产业链的综合技术和管理水平迈入了世界先进行列。

中国水电的长足发展成就斐然，得益于中国共产党的坚强领导，得益于坚定走改革开放的道路，得益于几代中国水电工作者的锐意改革、敢于创新、勇于实践、艰苦奋斗和精诚奉献。

一、改革开放是中国水电事业健康快速发展动力之源

改革开放40年来，中国水电工作者以自我革命的勇气和魄力，努力实践水电建设体制机制的改革，勇于直面改革开放所带来的巨大冲击和挑战，悉心探索推进水电健康快速发展之路。

1978年，中国开始了改革开放的伟大历史征程。在党中央、国务院的正确路线、方针和能源政策指引下，中国水电的改革也从此拉开序幕。1980年中国水力发电工程学会在新安江水电站成立，从此我国水电有了团结凝聚科技力量服务行业创新发展的重要纽带和平台；1982年，在葛洲坝水电站首台机组投产发电之后，水电总局在红石和太平湾水电站推行工程概算“总承包”试点，成为推动水电建设内部改革，打破“大锅饭”调动水电施工企业积极性的转折；1984年鲁布革水电站获世界银行贷款并进行国际招标，外方企业以远低于标底的价格中标，提前工期和高质量地完成项目，形成的“鲁布革冲击”促进了水电改革，也为全国建筑业管理体制改革提供了借鉴，对我国建筑行业改革发展产生了深远影响；1985年开始鼓励“集资办电”，国家和地方办电相结合、内资与外资办电相结合的多元化水电投资格局逐步形成。对外开放进一步扩大，不仅补充了水电投资，而且引进了国际先进技术和管理，进一步推动了我国水电的改革和发展。以五强溪、隔河岩、岩滩、水口、漫湾老“五朵金花”和广蓄、二滩、天荒坪、李家峡、棉花滩新“五朵金花”以及小浪底为代表的大型水电水利项目，以在工期、质量、造价等方面的良好成绩推动了水电体制改革深化发展，为“优质、高速、低耗”建设大型水电站提供了十分宝贵的经验；1994年国家颁布《公司法》，水电建设全面实施以项目法人责任制为中心的现代企业制度改革，多家流域开发公司的组建或改制，迈出了“产权清晰、政企分开、权责分明、管理科学”的重要一步；1996年国务院提出水电开发“流域、梯级、滚动、综合”八字方针，成为国家水电建设的开发指引；1997年国家电力公司成立，中央水电投资主体形成，推动了多项大型巨型水电工程和流域梯级电站建设。以三峡工程为代表的一批大中型水电项目，积极践行和不断完善业主负责制、招标承包制、合同管理制和建设监理制的建设管理模式，探索和开辟了具有中国特色的水电建设新路子。

进入21世纪，以全国水力资源复查为依据，确立了十三大水电基地的开发蓝图。国家西部大开发战略实施，“西电东送”工程全面启动，西部水电开发翻开了新篇章，中国水电也全面步入流域梯级开发的新阶段。2002年国务院颁布《电力体制改革方案》，在国家层面建立了多元化的水电开发市场主体，五大电力公司和四个辅业公司等相继成立，加快了我国水电开发的进程。三峡工程建成在即，以龙滩、景洪、瀑布沟、拉西瓦等为代表的一批在国家西部大开发战略和“西电东送”战略实施之后开工的大型水电站先后投产发电，中国水电进入了高速发展时期；2004年电价体制由“新电新价”向“标杆电价”改革，确立了水电项目投融资的市场化评价标准，同时国家推动金融创新为水电开发提供了资金保障。这些市场化改革和竞争机制的确立，有力促进了水电事业快速向前发展。2012年党的十八大以来，遵循习近平总书记提出的“节水优先、空间均衡、系统治理、两手发力”新时期治水思路，水电建设在快速发展的同时，着力安全发展和高质量发展，为构建国家水安全保障体系发挥了重要作用；2016年国家发布《关于进一步推进工程总承包发展的若干意见》，以百万千瓦级的杨房沟水电工程总承包项目为标志，我国大型水电工程建设管理模式进入改革发展新阶段，工程总承包制的大力推广必将对促进水电行业健康可持续发展产生深远的影响。

40年改革开放，40年沐雨栉风。中国水电在改革开放大潮中乘风破浪、砥砺前行，不仅为国家经济社会发展提供了源源不断的清洁电能，同时为保障国家能源安全和改善民生、大江大河束水安澜、宝贵淡水资源充分综合利用，以及推进全球节能减排、应对气候变化做出了巨大贡献。中国水电人以国家富强、民族振兴为己任，坚韧不拔、坚持立足国情探索改革发展道路，以海纳百川的胸怀锐意进取、真抓实干，成就了中国水电综合实力领先世界的历史辉煌。

二、科技创新引领中国水电发展攀登高峰

40年来，改革开放大潮中的中国水电秉承科学技术是第一生产力的发展理念，以科技创新为引领，以电力建设为主战场，以国家重大工程为依托，从变革体制机制入手，虚心学习借鉴世界先进技术和发展经验，大力推进原始创新、集成创新和引进消化吸收再创新，积极推动科技成果转化和工程应用，科学技术实力和管理水平不断提升，在解决了体制机制和资金的制约之后，是科技创新有力支撑了水电事业高质量快速发展。

水电体制机制改革释放出巨大的科技创新活力，中国水电人以精湛的技术和精细的管理，建成了举世瞩目的长江三峡水电站和溪洛渡、向家坝、小湾、水布垭、糯扎渡、构皮滩、锦屏等一批世界级大型水电

工程，白鹤滩、乌东德等一批具有国际领先水平的巨型水电工程正在推进建设之中。科技创新促进坝工技术不断取得新跨越，已建的锦屏一级305m双曲拱坝、水布垭233m混凝土面板堆石坝、龙滩216m碾压混凝土坝、深厚覆盖层上长河坝240m堆石坝和在建的双江口312m堆石坝均为世界第一，而与高坝工程密切相关的高边坡稳定、大体积混凝土浇筑温控、地下工程施工、深厚覆盖层基础处理、长隧洞施工、泄洪消能、高坝抗震等一系列世界级高新技术均处于国际领先。

一系列大型工程实践推动水电装备水平不断迈向新高度。通过三峡等工程“技术转让、消化吸收、自主创新”的实践，我国仅用7年时间便实现大型水电装备的自主设计、制造和安装，如今不仅世界上单机70万kW以上的水轮发电机组绝大部分都安装在中国，而且拥有自主知识产权的单机容量达到80万kW和100万kW的水轮发电机组也为中国仅有。

据不完全统计，2000年以来，获得国家和省部级奖励的水电科技成果有1308项，其中，获得国家科技进步奖或技术发明奖的项目共88项。科技进步和不断创新推动了水电科学技术的发展，推动着我国从水电大国走向水电强国。

40年来中国水电改革创新发展的伟大实践，铸造了雄厚的综合科技实力，中国水电已成为名副其实的中国创造和国之重器。

三、推动实施国家战略水电发展奉献社会

改革开放40年，中国水电不仅是国家发展电力事业的主力军，同时也是国家“西电东送”“西部大开发”和“打赢精准脱贫攻坚战”等宏伟蓝图战略实施的有力推动者，特别是在帮助贫困地区群众脱贫致富中发挥了重要作用。

“西电东送”作为我国重要的能源发展战略，水电在其中扮演了十分重要的角色。20世纪九十年代，建设天生桥水电站送电广东，开启了西电东送的序幕。2010年，小湾和向家坝水电站送电广东和上海，推动了我国±800kV直流特高压输变电线路的建设。水电建设对助力西部大开发战略实施起到了重要的作用，并初步形成了“西电东送、南北互供、全国联网、水火互济”的电力发展格局。目前依托“西电东送”骨干水电工程已建成了5条特高压直流输电线路，输送水电容量5000多万kW，年送电量2000多亿kW·h，相当于替代原煤1亿t、减排二氧化碳2亿t。

“西部大开发”是国家重要的区域发展战略，开发水电是推进西部大开发战略的重要支撑。我国水电资源80%集中在西部地区，经过长期努力已开发约2亿kW，占我国已建常规水电的65%。多年来西部水电开发从投资拉动、区域发展、清洁能源供应等方面有力促进了西部地区经济社会的发展。

我国水电工程大多地处深山峡谷、老少边穷地区，涉及移民多为贫困群众，通过库区移民安置实现脱贫致富是水电工程建设的重要内容。40年来，中国水电建设始终把高度重视水库移民安置作为重点，并在项目实施过程中加以认真落实，努力实现开发与移民致富的共赢，得到了社会各界的广泛认同。

水电开发性移民工作在不断完善中前进，移民政策和举措也在不断调整，体制机制逐步健全，补偿标准稳步提高，安置效果越来越好，走出了一条具有中国特色的水电移民安置和支持后续发展之路，创新出富有区域特点和地方特色的移民后期扶持政策，帮助移民群众走上勤劳致富的道路，推动电站所在区域的经济社会发展，移民“移得出、稳得住、逐步能致富”的目标得以实现。党的十八大以来，党和国家事业发生了历史性变革，推动中国特色社会主义进入新时代。我国水能资源开发的重心已逐步向贫困人口集中的西南地区转移，广大水电企业和水电工作者要积极履行社会责任，在承担公共服务、提供智力支持、实施项目帮扶、协助科学决策等方面主动作为，努力在打赢脱贫攻坚战中做出更大的贡献。

四、“一带一路”引领中国水电走向国际造福人类

改革开放40年，深刻改变了中国，也深刻影响了世界。中国水电取得了“世界水电看中国”的伟大成就，成为“一带一路”建设、推动构建人类命运共同体的践行者。

放眼国际大舞台，中国水电是国内最早“走出去”的行业之一。在习近平总书记提出“一带一路”建设重要思想后，中国水电企业把“走出去”深度融合到“一带一路”之中，积极促进国际合作，努力实现政策沟通、设施联通、贸易畅通、资金融通、民心相通，打造国际合作新平台，增添共同发展新动力。经过多年的海外经营和发展，成功占领了水电工程国际工程承包、国际投资和国际贸易三大业务制高点，具备了先进的水电开发、运营管理、金融服务和资本运作能力以及包括设计、施工、重大装备制造在内的完整产业链整合能力。与100多个国家和地区建立了水电开发多形式的合作关系，承接了60多个国家的电力和河流规划，业务覆盖全球140多个国家，拥有海外权益装机超过1000万kW，在建项目合同总额超过1500亿美元，国际项目签约额名列我国“走出去”的行业前茅，累计带动数万亿美元国产装备和材

料出口。在“一带一路”沿线国家建立起了多个“三峡工程”，如马来西亚巴贡水电站、苏丹麦洛维水电站、几内亚乐塔水电站等等。中国水电人的身影闪现在中巴经济走廊和东南亚，在广袤的非洲大地，在南美洲崇山峻岭之中，足迹遍布世界各地。

经过40年的顽强拼搏和锐意改革，中国水电已经成为我国在全球综合技术和管理水平领先的重要产业，是国际上一张靓丽的“中国名片”，更是中华文明传播的重要载体。澜沧江的水电开发，成功应对了2016年湄公河全流域的干旱灾害，使下游五国受益，成为构建人类命运共同体的典范事例。

构建人类命运共同体是中国共产党人站在中华民族伟大复兴和人类发展进步相结合的高度，旨在重构中国与世界关系而提出的重大战略思想。“一带一路”是构建人类命运共同体的幸福之路，也是引领中国水电走向国际、造福人类的发展之路。

五、生态文明指引中国水电可持续发展道路

党的十八大提出把生态文明建设放在突出位置，融入经济建设、政治建设、文化建设、社会建设各方面和全过程，努力建设美丽中国。推进生态文明建设成为时代主题，构建清洁低碳、安全高效的能源体系，成为水电在新时期的重要使命。新时代赋予水电新的任务，水电应当在能源生产和消费革命、建设生态文明等方面发挥更加突出的作用。

水电是技术成熟且可大规模开发的清洁可再生能源，世界上很多国家都把水电开发放在能源发展的优先位置。我国水电资源蕴藏量居世界首位，积极发展水电是实现国家非化石能源发展目标的必由之路，是有效降低温室气体排放的重要途径，是增加清洁能源供应、保障能源安全、应对气候变化、推进节能减排、实现可持续发展的重要举措。水电作为全国最早推进改革开放的行业之一，改革开放40年来在国家发展战略指引下，广大水电工作者在建造起一座座工程丰碑的同时，始终不断强化提升环境保护意识，积极践行绿色发展。

绿水青山就是金山银山，维护绿水青山、再造秀美山川，中国水电功不可没。在水电开发过程中，同步规划、设计、建设生态环境保护设施，不断开展生态流量、鱼类保护、低温水缓减等关键技术科研攻关和技术创新，把生态环境保护落实于规划设计、建设施工和后期的施工撤场、发电运营等全过程，取得了丰硕的成果。可持续发展理念不断深化，逐步形成了生态保护与修复技术体系，努力维护好河流生态系统健康和独特的人文自然景观，实现人与自然和谐共生。如今，全国星罗棋布的水电站几乎都是旅游休闲胜地，成为当地生态良好的典范，如新安江水电站库区形成了闻名遐迩的“千岛湖”，二滩水电站将原本植被稀疏的干热河谷变成了国家级森林公园等等。不仅如此，水电开发还对维护河流生命健康发挥了重要作用。三峡、天生桥、龙滩、糯扎渡水电站建成后，通过实施生态调度，增加枯水期生态流量，分别对长江、珠江、湄公河三角洲区“压咸补淡”发挥了不可替代的作用。

经过多年的建设发展，中国水电的节能减排生态环保效益十分显著。40年来水电累计发电量超过14万亿kW·h，约相当于替代标煤43亿t、减排二氧化碳113亿t、二氧化硫0.37亿t、氮氧化物0.32亿t，为打赢蓝天碧水保卫战做出了重要贡献。

同志们！回顾过去是为了更好地面向未来。40年沧海桑田，中国经济飞速发展，国家面貌日新月异。党的十九大以来，以习近平新时代中国特色社会主义思想为指引，中国经济开始由高速增长向高质量增长转型，我国社会已进入新时代开启新征程。新时代对能源供给提出了新要求，清洁能源是经济社会高质量发展的必然选择，也必将为经济社会可持续发展提供新动能。水电作为全球公认并为世界各国所大力发展使用的清洁能源，目前是我国非化石能源的绝对主力，在新时代承担着无可替代的历史使命，在未来能源体系中水电与风电太阳能等新能源必将发挥越来越重要的作用。中国水电要在坚持节约资源和保护环境的基本国策，着力推进绿色发展、循环发展、低碳发展的方针指引下，在工程建设中更加注重统筹考虑和正确处理好生态环境保护、移民安置、地方经济发展等方面关系，真正使水电成为清洁高效能源体系的主力军、生态文明建设的重要力量。坚持以人民为中心的发展理念，让改革发展成果更多更好地惠及全体人民，努力使流域沿线的人民群众都能因为水电开发而享受到改革发展带来的成果，实现水电的可持续发展。

满眼生机转化钧，天工人巧日争新。今年是我国改革开放40周年，是贯彻落实党的十九大精神开局之年。党的十九大描绘了把我国建成社会主义现代化强国的宏伟蓝图，开启了实现中华民族伟大复兴的新征程。认真总结改革开放40年来水电发展的成功经验，使水电发展在新时代更好地服务于中国特色社会主义建设大局，为建设美丽中国做出更大贡献，是每一位水电人义不容辞的责任。我们要通过总结和回顾改革开放40年来我国水电发展取得的辉煌业绩和成就，传承和弘扬中国水电的改革精神和奋斗精神，积极开展学习宣传在改革发展过程中涌现出的先进人物和事迹，使勇于改革、敢于创新的科学精神成为广大水电工作者共同推崇的价值追求，不断提高我国水电

的科技实力和创新能力，共同促进中国水电和新能源事业迈向更好更高质量的发展。

同志们！改革开放天地宽，砥砺奋进正当时。水电事业是光明的事业、伟大的事业！让我们在习近平新时代中国特色社会主义思想指引下，坚持走中国特色自主创新道路，坚持抓创新就是抓发展、谋创新就是谋未来，坚持以深化改革激发创新活力，把科技进步、社会进步和生态文明建设有机结合起来，在新的起点上承前启后、继往开来，为实现建成社会主义现代化强国的伟大目标、实现中华民族伟大复兴的中国梦而不懈奋斗！

专 家 论 坛

统筹优化　促进西南水电高质量发展

中国电力企业联合会常务副理事长　杨昆

［编者按：此文为中国电力企业联合会常务副理事长杨昆发表在《中国电力企业管理》2018 年第 1 期上的文章。］

习近平总书记在十九大报告中要求："推进能源生产和消费革命，构建清洁低碳、安全高效的能源体系""优化区域开放布局，加大西部开放力度""强化举措推进西部大开发形成新格局"。

而加快西南水电建设，是撬动西部大开发形成新格局的重要支点，对于加快电力转型、实现能源电力高质量发展、促进民族团结和社会稳定、点燃西部经济发展"引擎"、建设美丽中国具有重要意义。

一是促进藏区加快发展。西藏 1.74 亿 kW 水电持续开发，对于改善西藏生产生活水平、促进民族团结和社会稳定、推动西藏跨越式发展具有十分重要的意义。四川阿坝、甘孜未开发水电合计 3700 万 kW，加快开发可显著增强四川藏区的自我发展能力。

二是促进我国能源结构优化。预计 2030 年西南水电装机容量将达到 2.6 亿 kW、年发电量 1 万亿 kW·h，折合标煤约 3 亿 t。水电的持续发展已成为我国实现 2030 年非化石能源消费比重达到 20%目标的重要影响因素。

三是改善东中部地区环境质量。2030 年西南水电外送规模将达到 1.2 亿 kW，每年可向东中部地区输送清洁电力超过 5000 亿 kW·h，可替代原煤 2.2 亿 t，减排二氧化碳 4.1 亿 t、二氧化硫 20 万 t、氮氧化物 18 万 t。

四是拉动经济增长。2016—2030 年西南水电开发和电网建设投资约 2.87 万亿元，将持续拉动机械制造、土建、水泥、钢材等相关产业投资大幅增加。

五是推进与周边国家开发合作，服务一带一路建设。雅鲁藏布江、澜沧江、怒江、红河、伊洛瓦底江等河流，均为跨越印度、孟加拉、缅甸、泰国、柬埔寨、越南、老挝等多国的国际河流。通过合理开发利用国际河流，共享资源，共同受益，对维护我国在国际河流的正当权益、促进睦邻友好、服务"一带一路"建设具有重大意义。

一、潜力巨大待字闺中

我国水能资源蕴藏量居世界第一，水电发展取得了举世瞩目的成就，装机容量突破 3 亿 kW，年发电量突破 1 万亿 kW·h，均居世界首位。

水电工程技术居世界领先水平，拥有三峡、溪洛渡等一批超级水电工程，具有全产业链整合能力。但与发达国家相比，我国水能资源开发程度仍有较大差距，剩余待开发水电集中在西南地区。

四川、云南、西藏三省（自治区）是我国水资源最丰富的地区，理论蕴藏量占全国总量的三分之二，技术可开发量 4.25 亿 kW，占全国总量的 71%。截至 2016 年底，西南三省（自治区）水电装机容量 1.35 亿 kW，开发程度仅为 31.7%（按装机计算），相比发达国家较高的水电开发度，如瑞士 92%、法国 88%、意大利 86%、德国 74%、日本 73%、美国 67%，我国西南水电开发潜力巨大。

西南水电资源主要集中在金沙江、雅砻江、澜沧江、怒江、雅鲁藏布江、大渡河等"五江一河"流域，各流域干流规划总装机容量约 3.8 亿 kW，目前已建成项目装机容量 7869 万 kW，在建项目装机容量 4660 万 kW，尚有 2.55 亿 kW 水电未开发，待开发水电占比超过 67%。

在国家"积极开发水电"方针的指引下，近年来，电力企业加大水电前期勘察和研究论证工作力度，已完成预可研、可研的水电项目达到 6000 万 kW 以上，预计 2017～2030 年西南水电新增投产 1.2

亿 kW，届时西南水电装机容量可达到 2.6 亿 kW。

不可否认，西南水电开发条件较为复杂，生态环境保护压力大，移民安置难度高，经济负担和建设成本持续上升。因而，需要充分认识西南水电开发过程中的“不平衡不充”问题，统筹研究，促进西南水电高质量发展。

二、抽丝剥茧困难重重

弃水问题较为突出。据统计，2016 年国家四大水电基地——大渡河、雅砻江、金沙江、澜沧江 20 多座大型水电站有效水量利用率、有效水能利用率均不到 80%，有的电站甚至不到 60%。四川调峰弃水电量 140 亿 kW·h，云南装机弃水电量 314 亿 kW·h。2017 年前三季度，全国弃水局面有所好转，弃水电量同比减少 35 亿 kW·h，西南水电水能利用率同比提高约 2 个百分点，弃水问题仍然十分突出。

弃水的原因，主要有：一是用电增幅下滑，市场消纳总量不足，“十二五”期间，四川电网新投产电源 4449 万 kW，而最大负荷五年仅增长约 1000 万 kW。二是水电装机比重大，自身调节能力差，四川具有季、年调节能力的水库电站装机仅占水电总装机的 36%，丰枯期出力比例达到 7∶3。三是跨区输电通道能力不足，“十二五”期间，四川水电需要新增外送能力近 3000 万 kW，而实际仅增加 1520 万 kW。四是市场消纳机制不完善，部分地方电力市场交易规则明显保护当地电源，省间壁垒进一步强化。

流域统筹规划和管理薄弱。一是龙头电站造价高，梯级补偿机制缺位，导致龙头电站建设滞后，影响全流域梯级水电利用效率。二是流域统筹开发和优化调度机制不健全，全流域各电站水雨情测报、防洪、蓄水、发电计划编制、运行调度实施缺乏制度性的沟通，影响流域梯级水电站群整体经济效益。三是流域环境管理工作统筹不够，相关环境管理工作各项目单位分散组织实施，产权归属、管理责任不明晰，造成部分设施重复投入、项目批复迟缓、验收滞后等问题。

移民安置主体责任落实不到位，规划约束性不强。一是移民安置实施的主体责任不强，缺少约束、考核、监督机制，导致移民管理工作成效低，工程推进困难。二是移民安置规划缺乏严肃性，移民安置方案调整、设计变更较为普遍，出现人为扩大规模、提高标准等情况。以溪洛渡、向家坝水电站建设为例，移民安置实际投资超出概算 470 亿元。三是移民安置资金筹措渠道单一，水电企业现金流难以覆盖还本付息、运营成本、移民补偿费用。

税费政策和管理制度不尽合理。一是水电企业承担的税负过高，国家对水电即征即退的优惠政策到期后，水电行业增值税实际税负将恢复到 16.5%左右，远高于风电、光伏发电 8%左右的水平。二是水电项目未享受国家可再生能源优惠政策，作为优质的可再生能源，水电未被纳入可再生能源电力配额制和绿色证书交易机制。三是各地电力市场交易规则中，未考虑水电企业公益性、政策性收费等刚性成本，水电与煤电同等参与市场竞争，部分水电企业亏损程度加大。

后续水电开发成本提高，水电建设步伐明显放缓。一是随着后续水电开发难度的不断加大，水电建设成本大幅提高，加之电站公益性、政策性成本不断攀升，水电竞争力逐步下降。澜沧江上游梯级电站平均电价达到 0.386 元/kW·h 时，送到广东后基本没有竞争力。二是现行政策难以保障水电的合理收益，企业开发建设水电的积极性受到较大影响，水电建设步伐明显放缓。“十三五”期间，我国水电年均增速不到 3%。三是部分流域电站未列入国家能源发展规划，项目前期工作难以推进。

三、张弛有度方得始终

西南水电发展存在的问题，已经引起国家有关部门高度重视。近期，国家发展改革委、国家能源局相继出台《关于促进西南地区水电消纳的通知》《解决弃水弃风弃光问题实施方案》，对促进西南水电科学发展作出了一系列部署。在此基础上，各级政府、企业和行业仍需艰苦奋斗、卓越前行。

加强统一规划和统筹协调，实现水电在更大范围内消纳。西南三省（自治区）普遍存在水电开发规模大、自身用电负荷小的问题，需要统筹考虑就地消纳和电力外送，在满足本地区用电需求基础上，实施“西电东送”，在更大范围内消纳。

东中部地区是我国用电负荷中心，用电需求仍有较大增长空间，预计 2017～2030 年增加的市场空间将达到 2.91 亿 kW，西南水电新增外送规模仅占 24%，统筹考虑东中部地区新增的核电、新能源发电以及“热电联产”项目，东中部地区具备接纳西南水电新增外送规模的能力。

四川“十三五”期间将建设雅中特高压直流工程，送电 1000 万 kW，“十四五”初期建成白鹤滩特高压直流工程，送电 1600 万 kW，2030 年外送规模将超过 5000 万 kW；云南“十三五”期间将建设滇西北特高压直流工程，送电 500 万 kW，建设乌东德电站直流工程，送电 800 万 kW，2030 年外送规模近 4000 万 kW；2030 年前，藏东南水电开发 3000 万 kW，可全部外送。2030 年后，重点开发雅鲁藏布江“大拐弯”的大型水电，部分送电东中部，部分作为四川、云南和贵州西电东送接续电源。西南水电消纳空间充裕，但需要科学规划，有序送出。

一是加强统一规划，做好各类电源、电源与电网发展的合理衔接，确保水电开发与外送通道同步规划；尽快核准建设水电基地外送通道。二是加强电网互联互通和水火互济输电通道规划和建设，优化同步电网格局，加强西南、西北电网联网；大力推进与东南亚电网互联互通项目。三是完善市场交易协调机制，按照全国电力统一优化配置原则，采取“计划+市场”的交易模式，落实西南水电消纳市场；理顺电价形成机制，加大执行丰枯、峰谷分时电价、两部制电价力度，提高各类电源综合利用效率。

加强水电流域统筹规划建设，提高流域整体效益。一是建立水电站调节补偿机制，通过增配发电量指标或提取水库调节基金等方式，补贴龙头水库电站，鼓励龙头电站建设，优化流域梯级电站蓄放水次序，推动水电高效利用。二是整合流域各企业，组建流域公司或进行资产置换，实现流域电站统一管理，组织制定水利、电力联合优化调度运行规程和技术标准，实现流域优化调度。三是立足流域或区域生态保护，进行统筹规划，明确水库产权归属，强化流域环境管理。

强化移民管理，切实落实水电移民安置。一是制定移民安置条例实施细则，进一步明确各方责权利，建立移民工作国家跟进审计机制，制定移民工作目标责任考核办法。二是制定库区和移民安置发展规划，强化规划实施的刚性和权威性。三是创新管理模式，探索水电移民与水电资源捆绑建设的新模式，研究跨省区移民外迁安置方式，建立移民保障性机制，多渠道解决移民安置。

完善水电税费政策，促进水电企业健康发展。一是水电行业增值税超过8%的部分，继续采用“即征即返”的优惠政策，作为国家支持水电开发的长期性政策。二是对水电站免收水资源费，减轻企业经营成本。三是将水电纳入可再生能源电力配额制和绿证交易范畴。

加大金融政策支持力度，加快西南水电建设。一是给予藏区水电金融政策支持，西藏、川藏、滇藏段各流域梯级电站，建议参照西藏内需项目政策，列入中央预算内投资补助范畴。二是借鉴三峡基金经验，调剂部分基金用于西南贫困地区、少数民族地区水电开发。三是抓住当前电力供需缓和的有利时机，开工建设一批大中型水电站。四是将怒江流域开发纳入能源电力发展规划，与其他流域电站统筹推进。

党的十九大指出，我国社会主要矛盾已经转化为人民日益增长的美好生活需要和不平衡不充分的发展之间的矛盾。西南水电开发的问题，是能源电力领域发展不平衡不充分问题的一个突出表现，需要有关各方从经济社会发展全局高度，加强政策支持，加强统筹协调，处理好中央与地方之间、水电的送端与受端省份之间、政府与企业之间、发电企业与电力用户之间的关系，加快电力市场机制和输送通道建设，促进西南水电更大范围消纳，实现可持续发展。

“水电妖魔化”严重制约着我国水安全保障能力提升

国务院发展研究中心研究员　王亦楠

［编者按：本文国务院发展研究中心研究员王亦楠发表于《中国经济周刊》2018年第25期的文章。］

水是基础性自然资源和战略性经济资源，是生态环境的控制性要素，是人类和一切生物赖以生存的基本物质条件。早在1977年，联合国就向全世界发出严重警告：水资源短缺不久将成为一个比石油危机更可怕的社会危机，因为水资源没有任何物质可以替代。

中国是世界上人口最多的发展中国家，与美国、加拿大、澳大利亚等国家“水资源占世界比重远远大于人口所占比重”的充沛条件相反，中国要用仅占世界6%的水资源养活世界20%的人口，人均水资源量（涵盖着一个国家从工业到农业到刷牙洗脸的全部用水量）仅为世界平均水平的28%。按目前实行的“最严格水资源管理制度”，我国2020年、2030年“用水总量控制目标”必须控制在人均大约500m³/年，按照国际标准属于“严重缺水”状态。那么，在如此严苛的水资源约束下，如何保障粮食安全、完成工业化并实现经济社会可持续发展，对中国乃至世界都是前所未有的挑战。

英国《金融时报》2014年就曾报道“唯一能阻止中国奇迹的就是水”，2018年3月则进一步报道：“中国缺水危机迫在眉睫，可能产生比人口结构变化、债务问题和去杠杆严重得多的经济、社会后果。你可以印钞票，但印不出水。”同时提出很大困惑，“为什么缺水在中国不是经济前景研究的一个核心议题？不被认为是对经济增长、进而对中国实力的一个制约因素？”

我国正处于“决胜全面小康社会、建设社会主义现代化强国、实现中华民族伟大复兴”的关键阶段，比历史上任何时候都更需要清醒地认识自身的国情和水情，尤其需要看到：严重缺水的危机已经离我们如此之近；没有水，经济发展、粮食安全、生态保护都将“皮之不存，毛将焉附”，从根本上尽快解决水资源短缺的严重制约已是生态文明建设、维护国家安全的当务之急。

一、亟须高度重视我国异常严峻的水资源短缺形势

1. 我国人均水资源量很少且水资源的时空分布严重不均

虽然我国每年地表径流水资源总量位居世界第六，但人均水资源量只有 2063m³，仅为世界平均水平的 28%，是美国的 20%、巴西的 8%、加拿大的 2%（见表 1）。

表 1 世界主要国家每年地表径流和人均水资源量对比

国别	地表径流资源（万亿 m³）	人均水资源量（m³）
巴西	5.2	26897
俄罗斯	4.8	32896
加拿大	3.1	94320
美国	3.0	9489
印度尼西亚	2.8	13887
中国	2.8	2063
印度	1.8	1526
全世界	47	7833

来源：《国外资源、能源和环境统计资料汇编—2013》
编辑制表：《中国经济周刊》采制中心。

除了人均占有量严重不足外，我国水资源的时空分布也极不均衡。

一是水资源的空间分布与土地、人口和生产力布局严重错位。长江以北的耕地面积占全国 64%、人口占 46%、GDP 占 44%，而拥有的水资源却仅占 19%；长江以南耕地占全国 36%、人口占 54%，而水资源占有却高达 81%。“人地水”不平衡的矛盾在京津冀和西南诸河地区表现得最为明显：京津冀地区水资源仅占全国 1%，却承载着全国 2%的耕地、8%的人口和 11%的经济总量，而西南诸河地区耕地仅占全国 1.8%，人口仅占 1.5%，却拥有全国 21.6%的水资源。

二是水资源量年际差别大，年内分配则相差更为悬殊，致使洪旱灾害的威胁特别严重。地表径流在时间上的集中程度反映了水资源的优劣。我国每年汛期（5～8 月）的地表径流量占全年 70%左右（海河、黄河部分地区超过 80%，西北诸河地区高达 90%），使本来就严重不足的水资源量中，2/3 以上都是威胁人们生命财产的洪水径流量，而冬春季节的枯水又导致农业干旱。我国自古以来洪旱灾害频发，尤以长江、黄河流域严重。

2. 水资源短缺造成严重的生态问题并威胁着国家安全

一是生产、生活和生态用水之争日益尖锐，粮食安全受到严峻挑战。按目前的正常需要且不超采地下水的情况下，正常年份全国缺水量达每年 500 亿 m³，全国 600 多座城市中 2/3 供水不足，严重缺水城市 110 座。北方“严重缺水”和“缺水”的 12 个省份，占全国农业产出的 38%、发电量的 50%、工业产值的 46%，实际是长期靠牺牲生态环境用水，来维持经济社会发展用水需求。京津冀人均水资源量大大低于国际“严重缺水”的警戒线，70%用水依靠地下水超采，平均生态用水赤字高达 90 亿 m³。

尤其需要关注的是粮食安全问题。十九大报告特别强调“确保国家粮食安全，把中国人的饭碗牢牢端在自己手中”。我国 50%的耕地处于干旱半干旱地区，水资源保障对粮食安全举足轻重，目前农业抵御洪旱灾害的能力远远不够。据统计，1970 年以来每年都有干旱、洪灾发生，严重时受旱面积超过全国耕地 1/3，最小年也接近 1 亿亩，每年平均减产粮食 200 亿 kg，黄河流域的粮食减产尤为突出。近 30 年来全国总供水量的增加重点保障工业和城市需要，农业用水所占比重从 1980 年代的 85%降至 2016 年的 62%，但农业节省出来的水资源依然无法满足工业化和城市化的发展速度。黄河分水协议早就面临配额指标远远不够的压力，生产着中国 56%的小麦、25%的玉米的冀鲁豫三省，必须靠超采地下水才能维持粮食生产，山东东营稻农已被迫改养羊或种棉花。粮食安全面临严峻挑战。

二是深层地下水已严重超采，华北平原已成全世界最大的漏斗区。深层地下水很难更新、循环迟缓，因此在国际上并不属于可利用的水资源范畴，我国地下水公报公布的也是浅层地下水开采情况。然而，中国科学院测量与地球物理研究所利用重力卫星的最新观测发现：华北平原地下水超采已高达每年 60 亿～80 亿 t，80%以上是难以恢复的深层地下水，超采面积高达 7 万多 km²，全国地下水超采已扩大到 30 多万 km²。

地下水超采不像黑臭水体、空气污染能马上感觉到，但其后果却非常严重：河道断流、湖泊干涸、湿地萎缩、地面沉降、海水倒灌，进而导致地下水水质持续恶化。目前全国已有 50 多个城市发生地面沉降和地裂缝灾害，沉降面积高达 9.4 万 km²；沿海地区频频发生海水倒灌，造成群众引水困难、土地盐渍化、农田减产或绝收，其中环渤海地区发展最为迅速，海水倒灌面积高达 2457km²，比 20 世纪 80 年代末增加了 62%。

二、“水电妖魔化”严重制约着我国水安全保障能力提升

有研究表明：按照十九大确定的“2020年全面建成小康社会、2035年基本实现社会主义现代化、2050年建成社会主义现代化强国”的宏伟目标，我国2020年经济总量将比2010年翻一番，2050年将比2020年翻两番。按照目前的耗水量，2020年将需要11500亿 m^3 的水。根据《全国水资源综合规划（2010～2030）》，在保证河湖生态流量情况下，我国水资源可利用量仅为8140亿 m^3。虽然“最严格水资源管理制度”已将2020年、2030年总用水量分别限制在6700亿 m^3 和7000亿 m^3，但在当前人均用水量已低至“严重缺水”的情况下，靠“节水”来解决未来供需缺口注定是步履维艰，甚至是难以实现的（因为物理效率上的节水潜力并没那么大），除非放弃“粮食自主”等政策。

纵观历史，任何一个发达国家，若没有特殊的气候地理环境形成天然水资源的充足保证，几乎无一例外都必须依靠水库大坝蓄水、跨流域调水来解决水资源的供应问题，即把丰水年/丰水期造成灾害的洪水蓄存起来，变成枯水年/枯水期的宝贵水资源。目前除了修建水库大坝，人类还没有其他手段解决天然水资源的时空分布不均矛盾。要从根本上解决我国的水资源短缺危机，当务之急不仅仅是“节流”——建设节水型社会，更重要的是“开源”，即尽快建设一批大型调蓄水库、提升我国水资源调控能力，从而大大增加我国可利用的水资源总量。

1. 水资源比我国充沛得多的发达国家，都建立了远高于我国的调控能力

2007年联合国的调查结果显示：除极个别特例以外，一个国家和地区的水库蓄水能力和水电开发程度越高，经济社会越发达，生态环境越好。目前世界人均库容水平为580m^3，发达国家平均高达3200m^3，而发展中国家平均不足540m^3；世界水电开发程度为35%，发达国家平均在70%以上（日本、法国、英国等水电开发程度高达90%以上），非洲地区水电开发程度不足8%，我国和印度分别为39%和20%。以人均库容和水电开发程度为标志的水资源调控能力，在国际上不仅不存在什么“警戒线”，反而是越高越好！我国与部分典型国家的人均库容对比如图1所示。

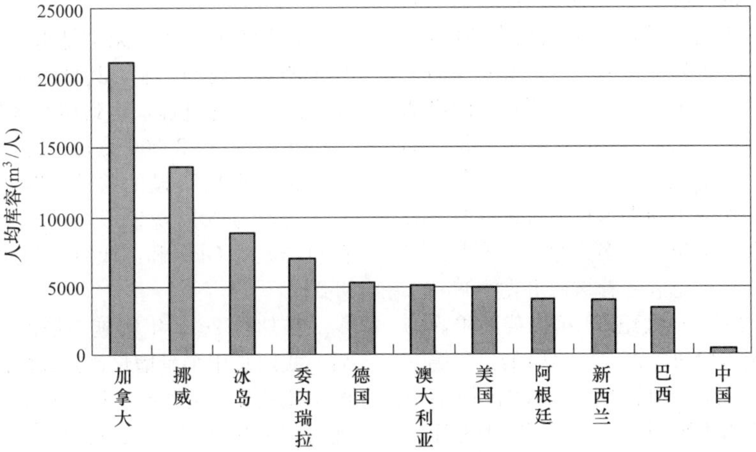

图1 典型国家的人均库容水平对比

编辑制图：《中国经济周刊》采制中心。

尽管我国目前拥有的水库数量位居世界第一，但99%是水资源调控能力不高的中小型水库，所以人均库容还很低，仅为发达国家平均水平的22%。

尤其值得关注的是国土面积、地表径流总量相差不多的中美两国在水资源调控能力上的巨大差距：中国9.8万座水库的总蓄水量仅为9000亿 m^3，而美国8.3万座水库的总蓄水量高达14000亿 m^3；中国大型水库只有756座（数量仅占1%），美国大型水库高达8724座（数量占10.5%），是我们的12倍；美国先天的人均水资源量是中国5倍，但后天建设的人均库容水平则是中国7倍！

河流径流的“调控能力”（即梯级水电开发所获得的调节库容与河流年径流量之比），是衡量水资源管理水平的最典型指标。从表2可见，人均水资源量远高于我国的美国、加拿大，主要河流的调控能力基本都在50%以上，美国密苏里河和科罗拉多河、加拿大马尼夸根河和拉格朗德河的调节库容甚至高达河流年径流量的102%～217%，河流水资源利用完全

可以做到水旱由人、不必再听天由命。

表 2　我国与美国、加拿大典型河流的调控能力对比

国家	河流名称	年平均径流量（亿 m^3）	梯级有效总库容（亿 m^3）	调控能力（%）
美国	科罗拉多河	219	519	237.0
	密苏里河	662	673	101.7
	田纳西河	254	136	53.5
加拿大	拉格朗德河	928	990	107.0
	马尼夸根河	324	414	127.8
	乌塔尔德河	125	114	91.2
中国	黄河	580	299	50.7
	澜沧江	680	234	34.4
	红水河	1328	200	15.1
	长江	9960	1304	13.1

编辑制表：《中国经济周刊》采制中心。

水库库容足够大，洪水就是资源和财富，反之就是危险和灾害。欧美发达国家不仅从未进入过所谓的“拆坝时代”，反而正因为有了充足的水库库容、建立了强大的水资源调控能力，所以能吸纳更大的洪水、抵御更严重的干旱。美国科罗拉多河水资源开发的关键工程——胡佛大坝基本不泄洪，而我国长江因汛期水量过于集中而调节库容远远不够，三峡大坝每年都要泄洪多次，上游每年高达 4500 亿 m^3 的宝贵水资源，近千亿立方米是作为汛期洪水被迫排进大海，对水资源严重不足的我国来说，是多么惊人的浪费。

2. “水电妖魔化”舆论有着特殊的历史背景

“水电妖魔化”本是 20 世纪 60 年代美苏争霸的产物。当时埃及嫌美国要价太高，将当时的世界第一大坝——阿斯旺大坝转给苏联建造。为攻击政治对手，美国发动全世界诋毁阿斯旺大坝，国际上充斥着大量反水库大坝建设的“科研成果”。好在美国等西方发达国家已基本完成本国大型水电开发，“水电妖魔化”并未伤及自身，但是对江河急需治理、水资源开发程度还很低的发展中国家却造成了严重影响。20 世纪八九十年代，大坝防洪、供水、灌溉等正面效益完全被熟视无睹，而以偏概全、本末倒置地强调“水电破坏生态之罪”却成了时髦。

进入 21 世纪，面对全球 20 亿人缺电、10 亿人缺饮用水的难题，水库大坝对人类社会不可替代的重大作用重新为人们所重视。自 2004 年起，联合国、世界银行等国际权威机构就不断呼吁“投资储水设施就是投资绿色经济”，“发达国家已拥有很多基础设施及大坝，在应对极端天气灾害、保障水安全方面已有良好基础；而发展中国家限于资金、技术、人力等因素，水库大坝基础设施还远远不足以提供所需的能源及水资源、支撑经济发展，建设新坝仍是当务之急”。

值得注意的是，当国际社会对水电发展的重大意义已经正本清源并纠正“水电妖魔化”误导的情况下，反水库大坝建设的极端环保组织却在我国异常活跃起来。“十一五”期间，在我国经济快速发展急需电力支撑，而我国水电开发程度连发达国家平均水平一半都不到的情况下，“中国水电开发已严重过度、水电破坏生态”等各种欺骗性宣传就在社会上甚嚣尘上，导致水电建设成了众矢之的、完全停滞长达 4 年，每年相当于 10 亿 t 煤炭的清洁水能白白付诸东流，而煤炭消费却以每年增加 2 亿～3 亿 t 的速度激增，长江流域数十座核电站密集布阵、蓄势待发。“水电妖魔化”舆论严重误导了社会公众、干扰了政府决策，导致一些事关国家长治久安和生态环境保护的重大水电水利工程搁浅至今。

三、政策建议：如何实现经济社会可持续发展，尽早解除水资源的严重制约

1. 将解决水资源短缺问题的迫切性提到国家安全高度

国际经验表明：无论是水资源较为丰富的国家，还是相对缺乏的国家，其总用水量均经历了“库兹涅茨曲线”变化过程，达到用水峰值时的人均 GDP 基本处于 15000～20000 美元（按购买力平价计），且产业结构呈现出明显的共性，即农业比重降为 5%左右，工业为 30%～40%，第三产业在 60%以上。我国目前人均 GDP 和产业结构与此相比还有相当大的差距。

虽然自 2012 年实施“最严格水资源管理制度”后，我国总用水量增长比较缓慢甚至还略有下降，但绝不能就此认为“我国用水总量的增长态势已得到全面遏制和扭转”，也不能轻率地认为“实现 2020 年 6700 亿 m^3、2030 年 7000 亿 m^3 的用水总量控制目标几乎毫无悬念”，亟须清醒地认识到：我国用水需求的峰值并未到来，目前的增长缓慢是建立在“生产生活严重受限、生态用水出现严重赤字”基础之上，未来 10～20 年经济社会发展与用水总量之间的矛盾仍将十分尖锐。保障我国水安全，当务之急不仅要整治黑臭水体、打好水污染防治攻坚战，还要充分估计、及早应对我国已经异常严峻的水资源短缺形势。

2. 尽早启动、部署事关国家安全的大型水电水利工程

按照目前可利用的水资源总量，我国“实现全面小康和社会主义现代化”只能在国际标准“严重缺

水”情况下艰难前行。事实上我们并非别无选择，因为目前的“总量控制目标”是在还有大量可调蓄的水资源白白流失情况下确定的。我国水资源调控能力与发达国家差距甚大，尽快建设一批骨干水源工程和江河连通工程，提高水资源调控水平和供水保障能力，是维护我国水资源安全迫切需要补齐的短板。

国际形势复杂多变，我国要抓住宝贵的战略机遇期，要谨防“水电妖魔化”舆论再次误导政府决策。无论是制定“水资源开发利用红线”，还是“生态保护控制红线”，当前亟需澄清一个重要问题：“生态红线”的划定不能以牺牲“国家安全底线”和“人民的生存发展底线”为代价，不能把“水资源开发”与“水资源使用或消耗”混为一谈、把“水库大坝的存在”与“保持河道生态流量”截然对立起来。

水库大坝的本质是水资源开发（蓄丰补枯、解决天然水资源时空分布不均的矛盾），目的是储备水资源，而非消耗和使用（水力发电只是利用水流的落差发电、并未消耗一立方米水）。河道断流、湖泊干涸的根本原因不是大水库太多、截断了河流，恰恰是大水库太少、蓄水能力太低导致水资源严重供不应求。三峡建设前我国长江枯水期最低流量不足 $4000m^3/s$，有了三峡水库才使得最低流量不低于 $6000m^3/s$，正如联合国报告所指出的“有了足够的蓄水能力，才能实施生态调度，维护河流的健康生命”。

3. 尽快完善有利于我国水资源开发的管理体制和机制

大型水库是现代社会不可缺少的重要基础设施，水力发电只是水库建设的副产品，和水资源调控是密不可分的整体。正因为水电开发具有防洪、供水、灌溉、航运等任何其他能源都无法替代的巨大经济社会效益，所以在高度推崇市场化的美国、法国，大型水电开发全部由国家主导，不允许私人资本进入，以避免市场化下的恶性竞争、利益博弈阻碍水电开发，影响国家的水资源调控。

当前，我国水电开发“全部推向市场”导致国家整体利益和长远利益被局部利益、眼前利益的复杂博弈所取代，恶性竞争已经让国有水电企业不堪重负。跨省区河流开发的不同地方政府之间的利益冲突、各涉水管理部门对水电工程综合利用功能的不同诉求、地方政府诉求和企业承受能力之间的矛盾、电力市场消纳的省际壁垒等诸多矛盾交织在一起。水电开发企业不仅无法协调各种矛盾，反而陷入了“为尽社会责任出的钱越多、矛盾越大”的怪圈。水电新项目开发的社会成本越来越高，在运水电站的电力消纳又无法保证，企业投资积极性已严重挫伤，水电建设已明显降速。

水电开发直接关系着我国的水安全，当前亟须从国家层面明确水电开发对维护国家安全、建设生态文明不可替代的重大战略意义，纠正水电开发“过度市场化”的体制机制弊端，理顺“政府与市场的关系”，使我国经济社会可持续发展尽早摆脱水资源短缺的严重制约。

水电：能源领域改革开放“先行者”

中国水力发电工程学会副秘书长　陈东平

［编者按：此文为中国水力发电工程学会陈东平副秘书长 2018 年 9 月 26 日在“改革开放 40 年中国水电”纪念大会上的专题发言。］

改革开放以来，水电在全国建筑业领域率先探索和推动了由计划经济迈向市场经济的建设管理体制改革。期间，水电伴随着改革的步伐取得了长足发展，也经历了很多的坎坷与矛盾。

新中国成立以来，我国水电建设管理体制总体上经历了计划经济模式、计划向市场过渡模式和市场经济模式三部曲。

一、计划经济时期·1979 年以前

1979 年之前，我国电力管理体制的基本形态表现为：水电部＋水电总局。水电部包括电力（电网与火电）、水利和水电等三大部分的政府与行业管理职能，其中水电部分的业务由直属的水电总局全权负责管理。

期间，我国水电建设的体制特征为：全国 15 大水电工程局按照国家计划并代表国家实行自营建设体制；同时，实行建管分离的管理模式，水电工程局负责建设电站，建成后移交电力局运行。水电工程局随着工程走，实行“大兵团作战模式”，一切按国家计划调遣和执行，国家对水电开发负无限责任。

二、计划向市场过渡时期·1979～1997 年

1978 年党的十一届三中全会确立了国家实施以经济建设为中心的发展方针，揭开了国家改革开放的序幕。我国水电伴随着国家改革开放步伐，逐步推进了建设管理体制由计划经济模式向市场经济模式的改革，主要经历了工程概算总承包责任制、项目业主责任制和项目法人责任制三个阶段。

第一个阶段改革的代表性工程为东北的红石和太平湾水电站。20 世纪 80 年代初在水电部水电总局的领导下，工程实行概算总承包制度，以不突破工程概算为目标，强化企业内部管理，首次在水电施工领域

打破“大锅饭”体制，有效控制了工程造价，在生产力层面显著提高了水电工程局的整体管理水平，为后来的深化改革打下了良好的基础。

第二个阶段改革的代表性工程为鲁布革水电站。随着我国经济体制改革的不断深化，国家开放利用外资市场，鲁布革水电站于1982年在全国建筑业率先引用世界银行贷款，工程建设按照国际惯例实行招标投标制，首次在水电建筑业内引入竞争机制，开始打破长期以来的自营建设体制。

1984年，“鲁布革冲击波”全面揭开了水电建设体制在生产关系层面向市场化改革的序幕，水电建设的三项制度，业主责任制、建设监理制和招标承包制随之应运而生。此后，随着国家拨改贷政策的实行，以及随着当时代表国家全权行使水电建设行政管理职能的水电部水电总局职能的转变，其所属的各大水电工程局几乎一夜之间断绝“皇粮”，我国水电建筑业从此迅速进入市场，水电建设管理体制开始发生了根本性的变化。

水电建设在计划向市场过渡期间，不断完善着市场发展机制，有效推动了水电事业的发展。这一时期改革的代表作是被誉为“五朵金花”的5座百万千瓦级的大型水电站（水口、岩滩、五强溪、隔河岩、漫湾）。这一阶段的体制特征为指定业主责任制，由水电站所属地区的省电力局作为项目业主单位，并组建项目建设管理局，具体负责水电站的建设与运行管理。在计划的自营“大锅饭”体制基础上已经向市场化改革大大迈进了一步。

第三阶段的改革实际上是伴随着党的十四大以来建立社会主义市场经济体制的方针以及《公司法》的出台而展开的。对于水电建设来讲，就是对老项目实施公司化改制，对新项目按照《公司法》成立有限责任公司等规范化运作，推进现代企业制度建设，体制特征为项目法人责任制。这与第二阶段的业主责任制有着本质的区别，项目业主是出资方组成的董事会，换句话说，项目法人责任制是真正意义上的业主责任制。在这一阶段，清江、二滩、五凌、桂冠等公司率先进行公司化改造，之后所有水电项目全部按照《公司法》实施现代企业管理制度。新的机制保证了水电的健康发展，期间广蓄、三峡等相继建设。

水电建设管理体制通过以上三个阶段的改革，实现了由计划经济向市场经济的成功转轨。

随后，水电经历了1997年和2002年两次电力体制根本性改革，电力行业也全面进入了市场经济发展模式。

三、1997年·以政企分开为基本原则的改革

1997年以前，尽管我国电力管理的体制形式发生了多次变化，从1982年的电力部到水电部、1988年的能源部、1993年的电力部等，但这些都是电力管理体制的结构性调整，并非体制改革。真正意义上的第一次电力体制改革发生在1997年，以撤消电力部、电力政府职能划归国家经贸委、组建国家电力公司，行使中央电力资产的企业管理职能为标志，实现了电力政企职能分开的改革。

这次改革对于水电开发来说，客观上形成了中央水电投资主体，通过与地方电力建设投资主体联动，在发展机制上形成了中央和地方两个积极性。在国家电力公司存续期间，充分调动和发挥办电各方积极性，成功推动和形成了以“五大一小”（龙滩、小湾、公伯峡、三板溪、洪家渡和杂谷脑）为代表工程的流域性水电开发格局，水电开发迈上了一个新台阶。可以肯定地说，1997年电力体制改革形成了水电发展的良性机制，有力推动了水电生产力的健康发展。

表1　　40年水电改革发展时间表

时间	事件	标志性意义（代表性工程）
1978年（计划体制）	十一届三中全会召开	开启以经济建设为中心的改革开放
1982年	概算总承包试点	打破大锅饭体制，首批试点工程：红石、太平湾
1984年	第一次引进外资建设，鲁布革冲击	建立水电建设三项制度（业主、监理、招投）：鲁布革，漫湾、水口、隔河岩、五强溪、岩滩（五朵金花）
1988年	第一次投资体制改革	成立能源部、国家能源投资公司、启动中央与地方集资办电政策；广蓄、二滩
1993年	十四届三中全会召开	《中共中央关于建立社会主义市场经济体制若干问题的决定》
1994年（市场体制）	第一部《公司法》颁布	全面启动现代企业制度建设：清江、五陵等公司率先改制，推动水电全面进行现代企业制度改制。三峡开始建设
1995年	第一次投融资体制改革	成立国家开发银行，组建国家开发投资公司
1996年	电力建设两分钱政策	《电力建设资金基金征收管理办法》，推动了地方投资公司的组建

续表

时间	事件	标志性意义（代表性工程）
1997 年	第一次电改，政企分开	建立中央电力投资主体。开工建设：龙滩、小湾、公伯峡、三板溪、洪家渡和杂谷脑红叶二级等“五大一小”项目
2002 年	第二次电改，网厂分开	打破电力行政体系，成立两大电网和五大电力集团全面推进电力建设
2013 年	“一带一路”倡议	“走出去”的改革开放
2017 年	改革成果	全国总装机容量：17.7 亿 kW，水电总装机容量：3.4 亿 kW

四、2002 年·以厂网分开为基本原则的改革

2002 年的电力体制改革是根本性的，以打破电力垄断为突破口，以网厂分开为原则，在我国第一次打破电力行政体系，改革撤消了国家电力公司，组建了两大电网公司和五大电力公司，加上原有中央电力投资企业，形成了中央电力投资主体的多元化格局，宏观上对加快电力市场化进程具有积极的推动意义。

这次改革以打破垄断，引入竞争为主题展开，改革的目的和初衷是良好的，即通过竞争，加快电力发展、保证电力供应、降低电力价格、惠及百姓与社会。但是在缺乏科学统筹发展理念和与之配套的法制建设条件下，其建立的新型电力体制在发展机制上出现了种种不协调的矛盾。这次改革在理念上有几点问题值得大家认真思考：

1. 改革对象的性质定位。这次改革实质上是通过拆分国家电力公司，重新组建若干电网与发电公司来实现的。但是这里存在一个对国家电力公司基础性质的认识问题，实事求是地说，改革是建立在对国家电力公司性质错误定位的基础上进行的。国家电力公司的性质不是发电公司，是中央电力资产的管理公司和中央电力的投资公司。这就意味着拆分国家电力公司如同拆分一个投资公司，引入的不是电价竞争，而是“资源”与“地盘”的竞争。这也是各大电力集团不断“跑马圈地”的现象所在。

2. 改革对象的市场定位。国家电力公司在市场中的定位应该是以创造社会效益为主的国有公司。由于国有电力公司所拥有资产的特殊性，决定了它无需通过竞争解决基本生存问题，市场化改革对电力公司不会形成生存压力，这与施工企业进入市场完全不同。因此，在缺失配套法制建设的前提下，简单地将市场经济规则引入国有大型电力投资公司的改革是形而上学的，如同“乘坐航空母舰下海”，是没有风险的自由航行，实践证明改革引入更多的是资源无序竞争，公司体量盲目攀比。改革放松了统筹规划与法制管理，改革成本难控。

3. 改革形成的竞争局面。改革在发电市场领域形成多元化电力投资主体，市场机制极大激发了企业资源占有与开发竞赛的热情。同时，由于竞争需要，企业会相互“保密”其发展规划，公开上报能源主管部门的建设规模会小于实际规模，必然使建立在不实规划数据条件下的国家宏观调控措施难以奏效。缺乏统筹的无序竞争形成后来全国电力结构性矛盾的突出，东部火电利用小时严重下降，西部水电大量弃水，发电与电网缺乏统筹规划，系统经济性低下，建立在资源极大浪费条件下的电力繁荣是不可持续的，电力体制改革任重道远。

改革没有回头路，没有矛盾就没有发展。2002 年电改实施以来，电力行业破除了独家办电的体制束缚，形成了电力市场主体多元化竞争格局，改革毫无悬念地推动了电力的高速发展，极大促进和提高了电力企业管理科学化水平，有效拉动了地方经济，满足了经济社会发展对电力的巨大需求。期间，水电装机实现历史性的快速增长，到 2017 年全国水电总装机容量已经达到 3.4 亿 kW，较 2002 年的 8600 万 kW，净增 3 倍。

2015 年 3 月，新一轮电力改革启动。新电改主要还是对 2002 年电力体制改革既定方案的完善与深化，属于生产力层面的调整性改革，而非 1997 年和 2002 年两次生产关系层面的根本性改革。期望新电改能够建立电力的科学良性发展机制，努力化解电力发展的结构性矛盾，进一步完善电力的法规建设，助力国家电力事业健康持续发展。

小湾水电站——中国水电装机容量突破两亿千瓦标志性工程。电站装设 6 台 70 万 kW 机组，总装机容量为 420 万 kW。2002 年开工，2008 年首台机组发电，2010 年全部机组投产。小湾电站大坝最大坝高 294.5m。

龙滩水电站——世界最高的碾压混凝土大坝，拥有世界最大的地下厂房。一期工程装设 7 台 70 万 kW 机组，装机总容量 490 万 kW。2001 年开工，2007 年首台机组发电，2009 年全部机组投产。电站最大坝高 216.5m。

溪洛渡水电站——总装机容量1386万kW，世界第三、中国第二大水电站。装设18台单机容量77万kW水电机。2005年开工，混凝土浇筑开工，2013年首台机组发电，2014年全部机组投产。

白鹤滩水电站——全球第二大、在建最大水电站。总装机容量1600万kW，创下地下洞室群规模、单机容量100万kW等多项世界第一。装设16台100万kW机组。2017年工程全面开工，计划2021年首批机组发电，2022年全部机组投产。

藏木水电站——世界海拔最高的大型水电站。装设6台8.5万kW机组，总装机容量51万kW。电站是雅鲁藏布江干流上的第一座水电站、第一座百米高坝。2014年首台机组发电，2015年全部机组投产。

五、未来水电发展的建议

回顾改革开放以来水电改革历程，水电行业发展成就显著，问题也层出不穷，改革就是在不断解决新矛盾的过程中得以不断深化，发展方向也愈加明确。

未来水电的可持续发展，首先应认识到“西电东送与电源开发协调发展的重要性”。我国的社会发展与资源分布决定了水电与火电发展的地域不平衡性，西电东送不仅能解决资源与经济的平衡，也是电力结构调整的需要。但是受制于体制形成的电网与电源相对独立的发展格局，网与厂的发展规划不易统筹，易形成发展的相互制约与不平衡性。同时，市场条件下的企业利益机制也一定程度上阻碍了西部区域内水火互补的系统性经济优化进程。随着社会进步和水电向纵深发展，与水电相关的经济与结构性矛盾将会越来越突出。显而易见，仅仅依靠电网与发电企业难以协调这些矛盾，需要站在国家大局层面，从电力与社会发展的总体利益出发，理性思考和统筹研究西电东送与电源开发的协调问题。这样才有可能突破瓶颈，推动水电可持续发展。

另外，应意识到“宏观政策研究的重要性”。水电政策研究包括移民、环保、经济等多方面，核心是以价格代表的经济问题。我国目前实行的是以市场为基础的政策性电价体系，主要体现在电站开发成本和地区发展水平上，不同电站和地区的电力价格水平不尽相同。

随着水电开发向西部发展，水电建设和输电成本将不断提高，例如西藏电力上网电价在无补贴条件下应该在6毛钱以上，如果在现行电价形成机制下远距离东送显然没有任何竞争力。因此，针对西电东送的电价政策应从战略高度扩展考虑到其环境价值、使用价值、长期价值，以及战略价值，设法找到时间上的经济平衡点。需要在国家层面通过税收、融资以及建立在宏观利益机制下的价格优惠政策，突破西部水电短期发展瓶颈，获取水电长远运行的社会经济价值与国家利益。

水电建设管理体制的改革始终伴随着国家改革开放的步伐，1979年的改革是引入市场机制，打开窗户的改革，当前中央“一带一路”倡议可以认为是打开大门，走出去的改革，具有改革的里程碑意义。水电从鲁布革开始，必将在国家“一带一路”倡议为核心的改革道路上不断与时俱进，进一步完善水电建设从规划设计开始的全过程市场化改革，提升中国水电在国际市场上的竞争力，助推水电与清洁能源安全、环保与理性发展。

水电在能源革命中的关键作用

中国水力发电工程学会副秘书长 张博庭

［编者按：本文为张博庭2018年11月30日在武汉2018水利水电科技创新高端论坛上的发言。文章分六部分，即：能源的进化与革命、联合国的减排目标以及巴黎协定、应对减排，国内的几种电力转型路线图 、对于巴黎协定的态度，我国上下出现了较严重的错位、如何满足《巴黎协定》的减排要求和结束语。这里节选第五部分与大家分享。］

（一）100%的用非化石能源发电是“净零排放”的前提

国内外的研究机构普遍认为，要想实现巴黎协定所提出的争取把温升控制在1.5℃，在本世纪下半叶就实现净零排放的要求，那么2050年的能源结构中，非化石的比重至少要占80%以上。相应的在电力构成中，应该达到100%的非化石能源。

最近，10月8日，IPCC又发布了《IPCC全球升温1.5℃特别报告》再次强调要在2050年实现净零排放的重要性。

所谓实现“净零”排放，虽然还不是说，完全不再使用化石能源，但是，起码在发电领域内，必须要满足不再使用化石能源的要求。因为，我们人类用可再生能源替代化石能源的主要手段，就是通过可再生能源发电。同时再通过提高整个社会电能替代的比例，从而尽可能实现替代化石能源的净零排放。

然而，由于电能的替代，几乎很难达到100%，所以，即使我们发电用的能源，已经是100%的非化石了，但还是免不了在一些领域，还必须要使用一些化石能源。也就是说，“净零”排放的前提，首先就是发电能源100%来自非化石能源。除此之外，我们还要对一些暂时不能实现电能替代的领域内所使用的少量的化石能源，想办法创造出相等的“碳汇”以平衡碳排放。

可见，百分之百的非化石能源发电，可以说是兑现巴黎协定“净零排放”的前提。

（二）2050年百分之百的非化石能源发电的可行性

对于《巴黎协定》的力争控制在1.5℃内，本世纪下半叶就实现净零排放的要求，某些国际研究机构（如：芬兰和德国学者发表最新研究成果、美国电气与电子工程师协会（IEEE）旗下《光谱》杂志、斯坦福大学气候与能源项目主任马克·雅各布森）认为：根据现有的技术水平，到2050年全球实现百分之百的由可再生能源供电，无论是技术上还是经济上都是可行的。

例如：文章《专家：世界2050年前有望全部使用可再生能源》（2017年4月13日经济日报 ）认为，在2050年在全球实现百分之百的由可再生能源供电，是完全可行的。而且该文章还进一步认为，这不仅技术上可行，而且经济上还能比发展传统的化石能源更有优势。

那么，这个结论在中国是否能成立呢？客观的说，根据目前的有关新闻报道来看，我国的电力企业界包括工程院和国家的能源研究智库机构，都没有给出可行的答案。但是，笔者认为，这个问题可以由我国的水电工作者来回答。尽管我们仅仅是专门搞水电的，可能不是特别了解其他种类能源的具体情况，似乎应该没有权威性。但是，我们完全可以借用一些综合性的研究专家已经给出的研究结论，并且针对其中我们所了解、所熟悉的水电部分，做一些更深入的研究，把我国水电的潜力进一步挖掘出来。这样我们就可以通过这种在别人研究成果上进一步挖潜的捷径，来解决这个问题。

（三）如何在现有研究成果中挖掘我国水电资源的潜力

我们看最近的这篇《专家判断：未来我国中东部能源自给为主“西电东送”将成为辅助》文章曾提到：中国工程院某副院长（下称：企业界）披露“2017年，我国非化石电力占比30.2%，到2020年，占比将达到35%，2030年达到48%，到2050年，达到78%。”

而国家发展改革委能源研究所某副所长披露（下称：智库）认为，“2050年，全社会用电量中，风电占比50%，太阳能占到23%，水电占到12%，核电和火电各占到6%。”

计算一下不难发现智库的预测是：2050的非化石占比要高达94%。

显然，一个企业界的减排目标是78%，而另一个智库的目标却是94%。可见，这篇文章中，同样反映出我们前面章节所提到的问题，即：我国企业界和智库研究界的减排路线图，还是有巨大差距的。

首先，我们应该承认智库（能源研究所）的研究结论是可行的。在此基础上，我们发现能源研究所对我国水电的减排作用，挖掘、体现的还不够十分充分。

根据我们专业人士对中国水电的了解，我们认为：水电在未来的我国发电总量中的比重，决不应该仅占12%，而是要大大高于目前的18%，最终应该可以达到20%以上。显然，如果我们能证明中国水电在未来发电能源中的比重，可以达到20%，那么能源研究所已有的结论，是不是就可以修正为：到2050年我国的“风电占比50%，太阳能占到23%，水电占到20%，核电4%和火电0%”了呢？

火电发电0%，也就是说，我国2050年可以实现百分之百的用非化石能源发电。相应的也说明了，我国已经具备了落实巴黎协定承诺的客观条件。

（四）水电在未来电力中的比重可达到20%的依据

我们搞水电的人士，为何坚信2050年水电仍能够提供20%的电力能源呢？根据2016年才公布的“水电发展十三五规划”以及最新的一些研究成果，我国目前可开发的水能资源总量，是每年3.07万亿kW·h（理论资源量6万多亿）。

需要说明一下，这个可开发的资源量，还仅仅是截止到目前的勘测所得到的结果，今后随着水电资源勘测工作的细化、深入，还会有所上升。

两年前才颁布的水电发展十三五规划中，我国水电的资源量还是3万亿kW·h/年。现在仅仅过了2年，新的勘测研究就已经又增加了700亿kW·h（接近增加了一个三峡），可见，未来我国水电可开发资源量的增长，仍有可能相当可观。

这一点非常重要，目前社会上很多人（包括一些研究能源问题的专家）都认为我国水电可开发潜力已经所剩无几了。这是因为，直到世纪之交，我国所公布的水电可开发资源量也不过只有1.7万亿kW·h/年。2006年新的水电资源普查之后，更正后公布的数字为2.47万亿kW·h。几年之后，2016年的十三五规划就上升到了3万亿kW·h。

很多人不知道，或者说没注意到，准确的水电资源勘测的复杂性、困难性，使得可开发的资源量上升的空间往往会很大。目前，我国很多能源研究课题的结论，之所以不够准确，几乎都是由于使用了以往颁布的水电资源量作为分析问题的基础。

现在，即便我们以“十三五”规划正式颁布的比较保守的3万亿kW·h/年来计算，我国而目前（截至2017年底）所开发利用的水电资源还不到40%。

我们至少还有一半以上的开发潜力。如果我们能达到目前发达国家水电开发的（大约80%的）平均水平的话，那么未来我国的水电，至少每年应该提供2.4万亿kW·h的电能。

这个电量对我国能源的作用有多大？我们不妨给大家简单的算一算。

假设我国的用电达到峰值的时候，按照14亿人口，每人每年8000kW·h电的需求，大约也就是每年11.2万亿kW·h。（据了解我国各种用电峰值的研究预测，最高的也不过就是12万亿kW·h）。

也就是说我国的水电（2.4万亿kW·h的年发电量）将可以在未来我国用电最高峰的电力构成中，至少应该能提供20%以上的电能，远高于目前的18%。也就是说，我国的资源禀赋显示：未来我国水电的作用，不仅不会比目前减少，而且还要有所增加。

（五）水电开发程度达到80%的可能性和必要性

发达国家的水电开发程度，为何普遍都在70%到90%多，平均也有80%以上呢？

其实，发达国家他们当年在开发水电的时候，国际上还没有什么碳减排的要求。然而，他们的水电，之所以都要开发到较高的程度的根本原因，主要在于社会现代化文明的发展，特别需要通过水电的开发来解决调控水资源的问题。

例如，美国著名的胡佛大坝、田纳西流域梯级水电开发的主要原动力，其实都是社会发展需要有效的调控水资源。所以，这些国家在满足了水资源的调控需求之后，往往就不再去进一步开发其他水电资源了。

而另外，像一些想靠开发水电解决能源问题的国家的水电开发程度，则普遍会更高些。例如：法国、瑞士等国的水电开发程度都超过了95%。总之，无论是哪种情况，国际社会的普遍经验说明，如果一个国家水电开发程度低于70%的话，那么这个国家的水资源调控问题，很难解决好。

因为，一个国家的水电开发程度往往都与水资源的开发程度成正比。所以，水电开发如果不能达到一定的程度，这个国家的水资源问题肯定也解决不好。目前，由于我们国家水电开发程度还不足40%，因此，我们国家的水资源调控的矛盾也就十分突出。

这方面的详细资料，建议参考国务院发展研究中心王亦楠研究员今年3月的文章《“水电妖魔化”严重制约着我国水安全保障能力提升》（《中国经济周刊》2018年第25期）。

我国的国土面积和水资源总量都与美国差不多，但是，我国目前的水库蓄水总量只有9千多亿立方米，而美国是13.5万亿m^3。我们大约还需要增加50%的水库总库容，才能达到美国那样的水资源调控水平。然而，美国的人口还只是我国的1/5左右。也就是说，如果我们不能超过美国的水电开发程度的话，我国的水资源调控矛盾，绝对是无法解决好的。

总之，我们也可以这样说，即使我们国家不再需要用水电提供能源，但为了调控水资源我们也必须要把我国的水电开发程度提高到80%以上才行。否则，水资源的调控矛盾解决不好，我们建成小康社会的目标将难以实现。

（六）2050年我国百分之百由可再生能源供电的分析

以上是我们根据能源研究所的研究结论，并依据我国资源禀赋的实际，把我国水电的作用充分反映出来之后，所作的一些宏观分析。

如果想再细致一些，我们可以具体的看看能源研究所和国家可再生能源中心的《我国2050高比例可再生能源发展情景暨路经研究》课题中，曾明确标明：到2050年我国风电和太阳能发电的装机容量分别可达到24亿kW和27亿kW。

如果按照可能的年运行小时（风电2000多小时，太阳能1000多小时）估算。届时我国的风电大约每年可提供5万亿kW·h电能，太阳能也能提供接近4万亿kW·h。有了这些电能，再加上水电的2.4万亿kW·h，就已经超过了我国用电最高峰时的峰值11.2万亿kW·h。更何况我们还要有2亿多千瓦的生物质能可以发挥作用。

总之，我国到2050年实现完全由可再生能源供电，无论从宏观上（百分比），还是微观上（具体数值上）分析，都应该是可行的。

（七）关于高比例可再生能源发电的调峰问题

除了可再生的电力总量能满足用电需要之外，风、光等可再生能源发电的随机性、间歇性等调峰的矛盾也必须要考虑解决。

笔者认为，用类比的方式，我们可以发现这个问题，基本上不必担心。因为，能源研究所的减排路线图是“风电占比50%，太阳能占到23%”，而我们的风电、太阳能的发电比重，都和研究所的结论一样，“只是用更多的水电取代了全部的火电和部分的核电”。

众所周知，水电的可调节性肯定要比火电、核电都要好得多。所以，如果研究所的减排路线图可行，不存在解决不了的调峰矛盾，我们的方案当然就更不会有问题了。

此外，我们还应该注意到：目前，尽管化学储能的技术无论从技术上还是成本上，确实都还难以满足商业化的要求，但是国内外的研究机构，为什么都还敢断言说2050年全球就实现100%的由可再生能源供电，无论在技术上还是经济上都是可行的呢？

笔者认为，其最重要的原因之一，就在于可再生能源家族中含有功能特殊的水电。水电是最优质的可再生能源，可以为风、光等可再生能源的大量入网，提供重要的保障作用。目前，世界各国所有能够实现百分之百由可再生能源公供电的国家，基本上都离不开水电的有效调节。

大家知道，挪威因为水能资源丰富，一直都依靠水电保障全国99%以上的用电需求。今年年初，葡萄牙也完成了一个多月完全由可再生能源供电的成功尝试。其原因也是由于葡萄牙的水电比重高达52%。就连退出了巴黎协定的美国的总统特朗普，在考察挪威，发现了水电的重要作用之后，也曾经表示过，他有可能会通过开发美国水电的潜力，重新考虑加入巴黎协定。这其实就是水电在未来的高比例可再生能源体系中，具有特殊的重要作用的一种体现。

当然，我们也必须承认，世界上的水能资源本身（总量有限）确实不能满足人类的电力需求，但是，由于科学开发的水电有很好的调节型，可以为大量的风、光等可再生能源的入网提供保障。这样一来，水、风、光互补发电，情况就大不一样了。

在现实中，风、光发电的间歇性与水电的季节性之间，通常有很强的互补关系。例如，我国四川省的凉山州，通过水、风、光互补，2016年凉山州除了满足自己的用电需求之外，给我国东部地区的送电超过1300亿kW·h（这大约相当于当年上海市用电量的70%）。如果，将来的送电通道建设能有保障，他们预计2020年外送电量可达2000亿kW·h。也就是说通过水、风、光的互补发电，凉山州一个州所产生的可再生能源，除了自己的需要之外，还可以满足一个像上海这样大城市的全部用电需求。

事实上，目前欧洲很多国家的用电，之所以能达到较高比例的使用可再生能源，也就是因为欧洲的水电开发程度已经比较高。而我们国家，目前之所以还不得不以煤炭发电为主的根本原因之一，也是由于我们国家的水电开发程度还不够高。

此外，在化学储能技术没有出现重大突破之前，我们水电家族中的抽水蓄能电站的作用也不能忽视。我们知道，为了给电网调峰，日本的抽水蓄能规模，早就超过常规水电。

我们也不妨设想一下，如果到2050年我们化学储能的技术，仍然还不能出现重大的突破，我们大不了需要多建一些抽水蓄能就是了。

总之，正是由于自然界中有了水电这种资源和它所具有的某些优质特性，我们国内外的专家才敢预言说在2050年实现百分之百的由可再生能源供电，无论在技术上还是经济上都是可行的。

（本年鉴编辑部）

正确看待小水电与生态环境保护的辩证关系

贵州省民营水电行业商会会长　叶行地

目前，我国国家领导人非常重视生态环境的保护，而小水电无论在国内还是国外，无论在过去或者将来都是高效清洁绿色的可再生能源，是保护生态环境忠实践行者，至于小水电存在的一些问题和不足，完全可以通过经济的、技术的和制度的措施降到理想的程度。习总书记考察长江经济带建设时指出：“正确把握生态环境保护和经济发展的关系”“推动长江经济带绿色发展，关键是要处理好绿水青山和金山银山的关系。要坚持在发展中保护、在保护中发展，不能把生态环境保护和经济发展割裂开来，更不能对立起来”。

一、我国小水电在国际上的地位及国际社会对小水电的重视程度

第一，我国小水电在国际上有极高的地位。中国的小水电开发利用，是全世界公认的成功典范。因此，联合国的小水电中心也设在了中国，由中国培训各国的小水电专家。联合国支持开发小水电主要是两个作用，减贫和减碳。小水电开发对中国的减贫和减碳作出了重大贡献。

“中国水电”“中国小水电”已成为一张响亮的中国名片，带动中国技术、中国标准、中国制造和中国文化“走出去”，是中国“一带一路”倡议中重要的角色扮演者和承载者。

第二，欧美发达国家很重视小水电开发。美国施行了《水电监管效率法案》和《垦务局小水电发展和农村就业法案》，简化和加快小水电开发监管审批的程序，积极发展小水电和微型水电站。欧盟为实现到2020年可再生能源占总能源比例达到20%的强制目标，在水电开发程度较高的情况下，仍计划通过改扩建或新建小水电工程，使2020年水电装机在2010年基础上增加6.2%。奥地利为促进小水电建设，自2010年开始，对装机容量在1万kW以下的小水电新建或改造项目进行投资补贴，每千瓦投资补助400～1500欧元。

第三，世行等国际组织持续加大对小水电项目建设的支持力度。2009年世界银行发布《水电发展方向》，认为水电对能源安全有非常重要的作用，有助于区域发展和消除贫困，有助于应对气候变化，同时作为水利基础设施能帮助调节洪旱灾害，提高水资源

配置效率。近年来，世行加大水电行业贷款，2002～2014年间超过88亿美元用于新建改建水电站，其中装机容量小于3万kW的水电站占一半左右。2015年世界水电大会上，亚行东亚部总裁兼能源委员会主席布噶瓦强调，亚太水电开发重要性毋庸置疑，水电是清洁能源，亚洲开发银行坚定支持清洁能源发展，在过去二十几年里，已为亚太地区的水电累计投资了数十亿美元。

第四，国际社会积极探索推进水电可持续发展。联合国等国际机构一再呼吁"水电开发对世界可持续发展有不可替代作用"。近年来，国际先后开展了绿色水电认证、低影响水电认证和水电可持续性评估。

二、国外的经验表明，水电和水资源开发程度越高，经济越发达，生态环境也越好

欧美发达国家的多瑙河、莱茵河、哥伦比亚河、密西西比河等著名大江大河，都进行了梯级水电的充分开发，江河生态环境不仅未因被截断成"一节节香肠"而破坏，反而是世界公认的风景胜地。在瑞士，不论河流大小和落差高低都被千方百计地加以利用。在美国，大江大河的水电早在二战后就基本开发完毕，目前对小河流发电特别重视。

目前，世界水电开发程度平均为35%，发达国家平均在70%以上（日本、法国、英国、瑞士、意大利、挪威等水电开发程度高达90%以上，美国达80%以上），而非洲地区水电开发程度还不足8%，我国和印度分别为39%和20%，实际证明，外国的生态文明程度与水电的开发程度成正比的关系。

三、发展小水电与生态环境保护是完全一致的

截至目前，全国已建成小水电装机容量近1亿kW，年发电量3000多亿千瓦时。"十二五"期间，农村小水电累计发电量超过1万亿kW·h，相当于节约3.2亿t标准煤，减排二氧化碳8亿t。减少了大量大气污染排放，节约了大量的煤炭资源，避免了大量薪柴林木的乱砍滥伐。因此，我国已建小水电不仅在解决无电缺电地区人口用电和促进江河治理、生态改善、环境保护、地方经济社会发展等方面做出了重要贡献；同时，也为我国边远农村的交通、就业、旅游和脱贫致富作出了重要贡献。因此，小水电就是绿水青山，是习总书记描绘的"绿水青山就是金山银山"真实写照和忠实践行者，发展小水电与保护生态环境是完全一致的。

四、小水电的缺陷和不足都可以很好地克服

由于小水电存在的历史已经很长，因此产生了许多历史原因及时代和技术的局限性，使小水电存在一些缺陷和不足，这些缺陷与不足主要表现在：一是一些当时政府并没有要求的手续，或者是当时没有严格要求的手续，现在政府已经严格要求了。二是有一些小水电站存在河段减脱水现象。三是一些特殊河流上的电站可能对洄游性鱼类的洄游路线有一定的影响。

第一，小水电在当时也是严格按照核准条件进入的，只因历史的原因才造成现在有部分小水电手续不足的问题，目前国家正在进行"放宽准入，加强事中和事后监管"的行政效能改革，在已经放宽准入的政策的条件下，只要加强了事中和或者事后监管，这样就完全能在事中事后监管中很好解决小水电这些历史遗留问题。

第二，由于大部分小水电是集雨面积较小的山溪河流，在枯水季节本身就会断流，加之一些早期建设的引水式电站受当时经济技术条件限制，因而没有设计、建造最小流量泄放设施，现在国家对此严格要求了，完全可以采取工程的、经济的和制度的手段加以解决。

在工程技术上，采用设置生态泄水管、增设生态机组、新建雍水坝和开展梯级联合调度等工程措施保证生态流量能够合理下放。

在经济手段上，国家给予生态补偿电价，提高企业泄放生态流量的积极性和动力。

在制度上，制订严格制度，对已经给予生态补偿电价的，而又违规不泄放生态流量的给予重罚，甚至送司法机关处理。

财政部和水利部已推行的增效扩容的改造项目在"十二五"期间，改造了老旧电站4400多座，近2000条中小河流生态环境得到修复，已经产生非常好的效果。"十三五"期间又印发了《财政部 水利部关于继续实施农村水电增效扩容改造的通知》和《农村小水电扶贫工程试点实施方案》等文件，大力扶持贫困地区小水电开发，加快推进绿色水电建设，严格落实生态环保要求的同时，更是对贫困山区农户精准扶贫的一道切实有力保障。

第三，关于鱼类保护。大部分小水电处于十分陡峭山溪性河流，枯水季节容易断流，鱼类生存机会很少，而存在洄游性鱼类的河流就更少了，因此，对有洄游性鱼类的特殊性的河流或河段，会造成一定负面影响，同时也会使喜静水生活的种类在库区成为优势种群的正面作用。对于负面影响，大都可以通过工程和技术措施予以解决，如果确有对于涉及国家和地方

重点保护、珍稀濒危或特有水生生物存在较大影响的，工程措施又不能解决的，可以按照法律程序给予补偿，合理合法退出。

五、正确合理对待已建合法企业（小水电）

第一，对于按照规定泄放生态流量的小水电，是完全优于风能和太阳能的绿色清洁可再生能源，理应给予生态补偿电价，使上网电价不低于风电上网电价，并给予风能和太阳能同等的可再生能源待遇和政策。

第二，对于确实涉及国家和地方重点保护、珍稀濒危或特有水生生物生存和安全影响很大的，确需退出的，要按照《物权法》《水法》《环保法》《可再生能源法》等法律法规，按法律程序给予补偿后，合理退出。

第三，对于自然保护区内的小水电站，应按不同部门的法律，不同的建设时期，不同的影响程度，区别对待。《自然保护区条例》的法律地位远低于《物权法》《水法》《公司法》和《可再生能源法》等法律，因此，不能根据《自然保护区条例》以行政的手段来关闭或者炸毁符合《物权法》《水法》《公司法》和《可再生能源法》的电站和大坝（我们认为部门行政权力只能暂停企业生产，而无权判取企业死刑），而是应该严格按照法律程序，按照有关法律规范和市场经济规律来处理。

总之，在我国经济发展与环境保护中，特别是在长江经济带的发展中，我们要认真、严格、全面领会习近平总书记讲话精神，正确理解小水电与生态环境的辩证关系，正确把握生态环境保护和经济发展的关系，让小水电能够克服自身的不足，在我国生态环境保护和经济发展中发挥重要的作用，而不是将小水电与生态环境保护对立起来。

（原标题：小水电就是绿水青山——正确看待小水电与生态环境保护的辩证关系）

［中国水力发电信息（2018 年报）］

央 企 工 作

中国电力建设集团有限公司 2018 年改革发展情况

2018 年，中国电力建设集团有限公司（以下简称公司）完成营业收入同比增长 11.2%；实现利润总额同比增长 9.2%；实现经济增加值 52.5 亿元；资产总额同比增长 24.7%；资产负债率为 78.22%；设备总利用率达到 78.6%。在《财富》世界 500 强企业排名上升至第 182 位，在中国企业 500 强排名上升至第 41 位；在 ENR 全球工程设计企业 150 强中排名第 2 位、全球工程承包商 250 强中排名第 6 名；荣获中国证券金紫荆“最佳上市公司”称号。

（一）业务结构不断优化，转型升级效果明显

一是营销体系进一步完善。统筹推进战略营销、区域营销和项目营销，与政府、部队和产业链相关企业建立战略合作关系。强化京津冀一体化、雄安新区、川藏铁路等重点战略区域营销布局。积极融入长江经济带、粤港澳大湾区、关中平原等国家级城市群规划和沪杭甬大湾区都市圈建设，主动服务海南自由贸易试验区战略、长江大保护战略、军民融合发展战略，中标承建了一批高难度、示范性重大区域项目，彰显公司在地下工程、能源电力、高端装备制造等方面的核心能力和比较优势。

二是能源电力业务巩固发展。大力推动流域规划、抽水蓄能调整规划审批，推动四川、云南、贵州、陕西和雄安等区域水利水电及抽水蓄能电站前期工作，充分发挥公司全产业链一体化优势，推行联营合作，2018 年新签国内外水利能源电力业务合同达 3250 亿元。

三是水资源与环境业务快速增长。“流域规划、系统治理”理念、“懂水熟电”的独特优势和行业领先的规划设计、专业技术及管理能力得到国家有关部委、多地政府高度认可。2018 年，公司水资源与环境业务实现新签合同 484 亿元，同比增长 58.6%。

四是基础设施业务持续扩大。坚持市场竞争和投资拉动双轮驱动，2018 年新签国内非投融资业务合同 3200 亿元，同比增长 30.4%。严格履行项目审批制度，从源头筑牢 PPP 业务风险防控防线，中标 PPP 项目质量有了明显提高，PPP 业务发展总体规范有序。

五是投资业务不断优化。全年完成投资 1249 亿元，拉动工程总承包业务合同 1020 亿元。固定资产及经营性投资完成营业收入 427 亿元，同比增长 10.9%；实现利润 25.35 亿元，同比增长 22.7%。

西北售电公司累计签订直购和销售电量超过2.2亿kW·h,推动火电外送价格同比提升6.68分/(kW·h)。电建地产公司全年累计签约销售合同314亿元，实现营业收入202亿元、利润总额17亿元；累计去化面积24万m^2，去化率达到87%，行业综合实力排名跃升至第53位，在“2018中国房地产开发企业运营效率10强”排名第9位。

（二）大力开拓国际市场，全球化发展再上新台阶

一是国际经营实现稳步增长。公司国际业务完成营业收入同比增长11.4%，占集团营业收入总额的24.1%；实现利润占集团利润总额的37.5%；实现新签国际业务合同占集团新签合同总额的34.1%。新开拓吉布提、南非等7个新国别，贡献合同金额134.14亿元；新进入地热、海工、炼油、援外4个行业领域，贡献合同额356.35亿。海外能源电力投资成效持续凸显，已投产电站年总发电量突破100亿kW·h。截至2018年末，巴基斯坦卡西姆港燃煤电站累计发电75.59亿kW·h，约占巴基斯坦全国总发电量的10%。

二是属地化经营取得丰硕成果。国际业务属地化发展扎实推进，区域总部凝聚、统筹区域内子企业打造立体营销体系。东南非区域通过小比例投资带动的津巴布韦旺吉燃煤电站7号、8号机组项目顺利开工；中西非区域在加纳新签一揽子项目合同27亿美元；中东北非区域成功签约沙特萨拉曼国王国际综合港务设施项目；欧亚区域实现中亚俄罗斯市场历史性突破；亚太区域中标越南16个光伏项目，超过该国别年度光伏市场份额60%；在阿根廷、墨西哥、古巴等国实现新能源类项目签约装机106.6万kW。目前公司已在全球70个国别和地区市场实现联合营销。部分子企业与当地企业联营或根据国别特点成立当地企业，先后在巴西、智利成功中标实施多个输变电项目。

三是参与“一带一路”建设取得新成效。公司着力参与“一带一路”沿线国家市场开发，全年在沿线39个国家新签对外承包工程项目合同371份；在沿线65个重点国家中的46个执行在建项目。推动巴基斯坦南北燃气管线项目进入“中巴经济走廊”能源项目清单，签署了越南油汀42万kW光伏电站EPC项目、公司签约布隆迪胡济巴济水电站项目等。筑牢了公司服务“一带一路”建设领头企业的战略定位。

四是国际履约经营合规能力进一步提升。公司进一步加强国际工程履约监管，成立项目履约监管中心。以履约为核心的子企业国际经营能力评价体系不断健全，根据评价结果对国际业务市场布局进行适应性调整，形成优胜劣汰良性机制。公司海外履约水平有所提升，中老铁路、雅万铁路建设项目施工建设顺利开展，卡鲁玛水电站项目成功化解项目工期及调差风险，塔吉克斯坦格拉夫纳亚水电站首台机组提前发电，赞比亚下凯富峡水电站等13个项目获评“海外杰出营地”和“海外优秀营地”。

（三）继续夯实基础管理，经营管理水平不断提升

一是全面深化改革不断向纵深推进。电建建筑公司、水电十四局、中南院3家企业进入国务院国资委国企改革“双百行动”企业名单，全面启动科技型企业股权分红激励改革试点工作。“处僵治困”工作稳步推进，在满足生产经营需要基础上不断压减法人机构存量。加快内部资源优化重组。不断深化医疗机构改革，减轻子企业办社会负担，改革完成率高于中央企业平均水平20个百分点。积极推进教育机构改革，组建公司职业教育学院，加强技能人才建设。幼教机构改革方案妥善制定，稳步推进。企业管理层级和法人数量压减工作成效显著，提前半年完成三年压减工作任务目标。厂办大集体改革、清理规范关联企业和自然人持股工作进入尾声，“三供一业”分离移交工作稳步推进。

二是财资管理不断深化。“三下两上”预算编制体系不断完善，预算管控力度得到加强。公司降杠杆减负债工作方案和“两金”管控方案，年内实现市场化债转股85亿元。通过金融手段实现30亿元应收账款和可再生能源补贴应收款资产证券化。参与央企结构调整ETF基金认购，直接增加企业权益超过18亿元。电建财务公司各项指标达到行业领先，资金使用效率进一步提升；直接融资取得新成效，多家子企业在境外成功发债；金融资产集约化配置优势得到较好体现。公司境外资金集中管理平台上线运行，电建租赁公司、电建基金公司服务能力大幅提升，电建保理公司业务、公司金融业务体系初步开展和形成。

三是集中采购管理能力不断提升。持续推进国务院国资委“采购管理对标”工作，公司2018年设备物资集中采购额达1307亿元，集中采购率达到94.8%，上网采购率达到82%，节资率超8%，相关指标较2017年均实现大幅提升，支撑生产、服务经营和降本增效作用有力发挥，对提质增效的贡献度日益增加。

四是法治与风险内控管理不断加强。全面落实法治建设第一责任人职责，重大决策、经济合同、规章制度的法律审核率达到100%。内部审计围绕“两金”压减、债务防控和亏损潜亏等重点领域着力开展；马其顿MS公路、柬埔寨公路改善工程等项目工期风险得到有效化解，马里塔乌萨水电站、越南松邦

4 水电站、摩洛哥拉巴特绕城高速公路等项目实现风险关闭。

五是项目信息化管理不断加强。项目管理信息化 PRP 系统在施工业务板块新开工项目覆盖率达到 99.39%。研究开发了水电工程勘测设计施工一体化信息化平台、基于 BIM 的火电工程 EPC 项目管理平台，完成了全球可再生能源规划平台、风电规划和光伏电站规划系统开发及应用并在行业大力推广。实现国际项目履约管理可视化，提升国际项目履约质量。

（四）着力推动技术进步，产品和服务质量不断提高

一是技术创新能力不断增强。全年新增国家级研发平台 2 个；新增省部级研发平台 5 个；高新技术子企业增至 86 家，14 家子企业通过省、市级创新型企业认定或试点。4 项科技成果获得国家科技进步二等奖、国家技术发明二等奖。目前，公司拥有有效专利 12136 项，其中发明专利 1890 项。《堰塞坝险情处置与开发利用保障技术与装备研发》国家重点研发计划顺利获批，实现了国家科技计划项目级任务突破。

二是产品服务质量不断提升。公司不断加强标准化体系建设，全年制修订国家与行业标准 415 项，其中新制订 134 项，完成发布 159 项；获得行业和省部级工法 340 项。全年有 28 个重大工程项目获得国家级优质工程奖荣誉，项目履约质量得到广泛认可。

三是创新成果加快转化应用。启动了“中国电建—德国科技创新中心”建设前期工作，广泛开展政产学研用协同创新。压静力植桩机系统成功研制第二代样机，两栖消防船具备市场投放条件。军民融合领域技术创新取得重大成果，中标了我国最大低速风洞装备项目。上海装备公司 2018 年共获得国内外 146 台套船用脱硫装置合同。

（五）高度重视安全环保，积极承担央企责任

一是安全环保形势持续稳定向好。公司强化安全责任落实，杜绝了较大及以上生产安全事故，未发生重大违规的职业健康、环境保护、节能减排事件，安全生产标准化、应急能力建设工作得到国家能源局及相关政府主管部门的肯定。

二是积极履行社会责任取得丰硕成果。公司高度重视社会责任建设，海外志愿者服务行动荣获全国大赛中央企业唯一金奖。2018 年，公司位列中国企业 300 强社会责任发展指数第 15 位、国有企业 100 强社会责任发展指数第 12 位，获得“中国社会责任海外履责奖”“海外履责典范企业金牛奖”等荣誉。

（中国电力建设集团有限公司）

中国华电集团有限公司 2018 年工作情况

2018 年，中国华电集团有限公司（以下简称华电集团）超额完成年度生产经营目标任务，核准电源项目 440 万 kW，开工 479 万 kW，投产 275 万 kW。发电装机总规模 1.48 亿 kW。其中可再生能源装机占 29.5%。完成发电量 5559 亿 kW·h，同比增长 8.5%。资产负债率近 10 年来首次降低到 80%以下。清洁能源装机占比达 39.7%，同比增长 0.7 个百分点，发电量、营业收入、煤炭产量、供热量均同比有较大幅度增长。

（一）提质增效成绩显著

认真落实国资委工作部署，早启动、强督导、抓短板、压责任，常态化推进提质增效，公司超额完成年度利润目标。四大产业均实现盈利，年发电量首次突破 5500 亿 kW·h，煤炭产量首次突破 5000 万 t。积极争取市场交易电量 2252 亿 kW·h，同比增加 452 亿 kW·h。设备利用小时同比增长 230h，增幅在同类型发电企业中位居前列。弃水电量同比减少 73 亿 kW·h，弃风、弃光率同比分别减少 5.6% 和 6.8%。

（二）服务国家战略主动担当

自觉服从服务国家工作大局，深入贯彻国家“四个革命、一个合作”的能源安全新战略，印发关于推动高质量发展建设具有全球竞争力的世界一流能源企业的一号文件，制订中长期发展规划纲要（2018～2035 年）。准确把握“五个坚持”，持续推进“三个转变”，努力实现“六个一流”。

（三）转型升级扎实推进

不断提升清洁能源尤其是非化石能源发展比重，非化石能源装机比重同比提高 0.25%。完成金中公司 23%股权收购，取得绝对控股权，有利于推动后续水电项目开发和资本运作。广东阳江 50 万 kW 海上风电项目获得核准。淘汰落后煤电 186 万 kW。新增供热装机 733 万 kW，供热装机占火电比重 71%，在同类型发电企业中居首位。宁夏银川“东热西送”供热项目作为全国首个长距离、穿黄河、西北最大集中供热项目顺利投运，创下多项全国纪录。

（四）科工产业实力得到增强

科工产业实现“两金”总额和系统外“两金”双下降。核心业务进一步加强，华电科工承接的大丰海上风电工程，创下了同等规模海上风电工程建设工期最短的“世界之最”；承担的国家首个生物质气化耦合发电项目混合气化试验在襄阳电厂取得成功。

（五）风险防范效果突出

建立涵盖业务职能部门、风险管理职能部门、审计和监察部门的风险管理“三道防线”工作机制，筑牢不发生重大风险底线。围绕 2020 年负债率降到 70%以下的目标，从提效益、控投资、扩权益三方面发力，对负债率在 70%以上的发电、煤炭、科工企业，依据负债水平分别进行特别监管、重点监控和重点关注，推动资产负债率有效下降。

（六）扶贫攻坚步伐坚定

聚焦定点扶贫，以深度贫困地区为重点，打出了产业扶贫、就业扶贫、消费扶贫、教育援助、干部支持等系列扶贫攻坚组合拳，实现了“输血、造血、扶智”一体化，直接投入扶贫资金 9339 万元，派驻 89 名扶贫干部和驻村队员对口精准帮扶。全面超额完成《中国华电定点扶贫责任书》（2018 年度）各承诺事项。探索以定向招生、定向培养、定点安置为主要内容的精准扶贫“三定培养”模式，在深度贫困地区定向招收 45 名学员。认真开展扶贫领域作风问题专项治理，提升了扶贫工作水平。

（七）海外发展步伐加快

以“一带一路”沿线国家为重点，扎实推进“走出去”工作。公司获得了三大评级机构的高级别国际信用评级，成立了香港财资中心。全年国际业务收入创历史新高。携手高校共建华电“一带一路”能源学院，为“一带一路”建设提供智力支持。

（八）污染防治力度加大

全面部署蓝天、碧水、净土、生态修复四大领域生态环境保护工作，制定生态环境保护责任清单，落实各级人员环保主体责任。中东部地区燃煤机组基本完成超低排放改造，超低排放机组占比达到 86.5%。单位电能烟尘、二氧化硫、氮氧化物排放量同比分别降低 32%、11%、11%。单位电能化石能源消耗同比下降 1.63g，比“十二五”末下降 7.94g。举办电力系统首届环保监督技能大赛，培训 5 万余人次。

（九）科技创新取得成效

成立科技创新委员会，构建“1＋3＋N”科技创新制度体系，建立重点项目和资金配置统筹协调机制，明确前沿技术跟踪研究、重大课题研究等十大重点任务。推进科研体制改革，完成华电电科院和科研总院整合，形成了统一研发平台。制定印发数字华电规划及 2018—2020 年建设方案，全面启动“数字华电”工作。编制公司 2019—2023 年重点研发项目五年计划。14 个项目在国家部委、行业协会组织的评奖中获奖，取得历史最好成绩。新授权专利 1045 项，同比增长 17.2%，其中发明专利 137 项。

（十）安全生产保持平稳运行

坚决贯彻中央安全生产系列部署，落实安全生产主体责任，持续深化专项排查治理，深入推进本质安全型企业建设。践行“零非停”管理理念，加大设备综合治理力度，设备可靠性持续提升。火电机组台均非停次数从 2012 年的 1.04 次下降至 2018 年的 0.436 次，下降幅度达 58.08%，为安全生产、提质增效奠定了基础。圆满完成了全国两会、上合峰会、首届进口博览会等重要时段电热安全保障和空气质量保障任务。所属国家会展中心（上海）能源站为进博会“核心区”提供高品质、无间断能源服务。在上级部门和地方政府的统一指挥下，靠前协调，迅速响应，两次成功处置金沙江堰塞湖突发自然灾害事件，保护了人民生命财产安全。西藏公司水电项目成功抵御了 50 年一遇的洪水袭击。夯实煤矿基础管理，全力提升煤矿安全生产标准化水平，克服地质构造复杂等困难，精心组织生产，在确保安全的前提下，生产经营指标创历史最好水平。落实网络安全责任制，作为参加公安部“护网—2018”演习的唯一发电集团，荣获关键信息基础设施攻防优秀单位称号。

（中国华电集团有限公司）

中国三峡建设管理有限公司 2018 年经营发展情况

中国三峡建设管理有限公司（简称建设管理公司或公司）是中国长江三峡集团有限公司（简称集团公司）的二级子企业，为国有独资公司，注册资本金 20 亿元。截至 2018 年底，公司在岗职工共 1256 人，本科及以上学历占 96.48%，高级职称占 76.21%。公司是集团公司大型水电工程开发建设的实施主体，全面承揽集团公司国内、国际水电工程开发建设业务。近年来，开发建设的国内外水电工程有：乌东德、白鹤滩、溪洛渡、向家坝、长龙山、科哈拉、卡洛特等，公司积极跟进金沙江上游及国内大型水电开发项目，努力打造中国水电“走出去”升级版。

（一）经营管理

2018 年，公司实现营业收入 17.91 亿元，合并利润总额 8.52 亿元，扣除长江电力分红 5.98 亿元后，超额完成 2 亿元利润考核目标。截至年末，公司合并资产总额 212.74 亿元，合并负债总额 58.90 亿元，资产负债率为 27.69%。①修订完善公司章程、“三重一大”决策制度等，及时调整班子分工，全年组织召开董事会会议 4 次、总经理办公会 32 次，研究决策各类议题 271 项。下属单位、子企业“三重一大”等制度逐步制定完善。②组织制定 8 大类共 36 项规章制度，累计印发各项规章制度 123 项；编制抽水蓄能项目标准化管理制度 60 项；编制内部控制手册、17项单元手册，规范138项业务管理流程，通过年度“三标一体”管理体系认证，公司内部控制体系逐步完善。③识别、分析、评估公司重大风险并制定管控措施，定期督促检查。加强法律顾问队伍建设，促进公司依法治理、改制重组、“处僵治困”、国际化经营管理能力。④建立健全公司全员安全生产责任制，组织开展境内外各类安全生产检查20余次。逐步试行年度综合检查、专项检查及突击检查相结合的质量监管模式，进一步完善违约惩戒体系，强化作业监控体系。

（二）工程建设

2018年全年累计完成建安投资88.96亿元，完成土石方开挖填筑1450.63万m^3、混凝土浇筑658.15万m^3、钢筋20.8万t、锚杆34.4万根。

（1）金沙江下游二期水电工程。紧紧围绕乌东德水电站2020年7月首批机组发电、白鹤滩水电站2021年7月首批机组发电目标，工程总体进度、投资等全面受控，圆满完成年度生产任务，实现质量安全“双零”目标，为实现按期蓄水发电目标打下良好基础。①精心组织乌东德水电站大坝混凝土施工，应用无盖重固结灌浆工艺，开展智能建造项目系统研发和应用，单坝段年度最大上升121m，浇筑混凝土101.6万m^3，顺利实现大坝浇筑“双百”目标，坝段高差、混凝土温控等指标均满足设计要求。地下电站首批5号、6号、7号机顺利完成土建向机电交面，8号机基本具备交面条件，高质量完成800MPa级高强钢蜗壳和压力钢管安装，进水塔浇筑到顶；泄洪洞工程持续大规模混凝土施工，大型金结机电及闸门安装启动，进水塔浇筑到顶；河门口大桥顺利完成合龙。成功应对山体裂缝险情、“7.12”最大洪峰、“7.31”特大暴雨。②白鹤滩水电站实现大规模开挖向混凝土浇筑顺利转序，精细控制地下洞室围岩稳定风险，安全实施泄洪洞出口高陡边坡开挖。大坝浇筑优质高效过导流底孔，高质量浇筑混凝土220.9万m^3，单坝段年度最大上升87m，累计上升高度130.5m（最大坝高289m）；左岸进水塔浇筑到顶，地下电站开挖支护基本完成，成功应对右岸厂房小桩号洞段围岩变形，巨型地下洞室群围岩总体稳定，全面转入机组肘管、锥管混凝土浇筑，首批四台机组座环吊装完成；泄洪洞工程进水塔浇筑到顶，上平段混凝土衬砌达到“镜面”效果，龙落尾段开挖支护完成，研制龙落尾段钢模台车成功开展常态混凝土边墙浇筑，填补国内行业技术空白。实施技术、管理、工艺创新，持续稳定提升工程质量。施工区安全形势平稳受控，生态环境优良，坝区和谐稳定。③乌东德、白鹤滩水电站控制性移民代建项目进度可控。皎平渡大桥及接线工程质量、安全、投资、环保总体受控，S212省道复建工程筹建工作有序推进。

（2）向家坝、溪洛渡水电站收尾工程。两电站竣工验收关键问题取得突破。两电站顺利通过水保验收，枢纽工程专项验收申请已报送川滇两省能源主管部门，重大设计变更仅余1项未完成技术审查，溪洛渡谷幅变形机理、对大坝安全影响及其后续趋势研究结论基本明确。向家坝升船机完成试通航前验收并转入试通航；横江大桥建设完成；南北干渠工程稳步推进。溪洛渡水垫塘检修完成，2号排水洞洞身混凝土浇筑完成。对外专用公路移交检测评估工作基本完成。“六路三桥”移民代建项目基本完工，遗留经济问题基本处理完成，项目验收移交积极协调推进。

（3）长龙山抽蓄电站工程。深刻吸取7号隧道弄虚作假事件教训，强化落实现场施工组织改进措施。上下库连接公路贯通，上下库坝体启动填筑，长斜井开挖施工关键难题取得突破，引水上斜井1号洞进入全断面扩挖，下斜井1号洞导井反拉完成90m，地下厂房开始向机电安装标交面。

（4）卡洛特、科哈拉水电站工程。①巴基斯坦卡洛特水电站提前实现工程截流目标，大坝河床高程410m以上全部、溢洪道控制段开挖支护完成；顺利向混凝土浇筑转序；厂房大面开挖基本完成，机组一期混凝土开始浇筑。②巴基斯坦科哈拉水电站。配合项目业主协调解决销售税及征地问题，稳步推进现场筹备。关键线路A2、A3支洞具备进洞条件、R10道路毛路全线贯通，内部制度建设、体系建设有序开展。

（三）工程综合安全监测

水文气象系统运行正常，水情预测预报准确率保持在90%以上，有效应对金沙江下游“7.16”洪水、乌东德“7.31”特大暴雨险情、金沙江白格堰塞湖险情。乌东德、白鹤滩水库地震监测台网建成运行并通过验收，台网运行率在96%以上。白鹤滩大坝安全监测信息系统投入使用，向家坝、溪洛渡水电站监测自动化项目稳步推动。水文泥沙监测为水库调度、电站发电运行提供有力保障。

（四）在建在役项目工程检测

为在建在役工程项目提供工程试验、测量、设备检测、监造等技术支持，监造乌东德、白鹤滩工程混凝土外加剂1.3万t、粉煤灰17万t，完成乌东德、白鹤滩、长龙山工程控制网建设、年度复测和科哈拉测量规划，组织实施乌东德、白鹤滩工程库区移民安置工程测量和金沙江下游地理信息系统运行管理，努力打造质量内控平台。

（五）工程信息化建设

智能建造实现大坝混凝土浇筑一条龙和温控全过

程、全方位、一体化、精细化管控，运行效果良好，各项指标控制均满足设计标准要求，荣获第六届中国管理科学学会管理科学奖（实践类）大奖，入选2017年度中国“互联网＋”优秀案例。智能灌浆系统全面应用，灌浆质量可控在控，荣获中国大坝工程学会2018年度技术发明奖一等奖和中国质量协会2018年度质量技术奖二等奖。结合公司工程建设管理经验，以“知识资产化、场景化、智能化”为目标，打造公司知识管理系统。

（六）科技创新

积极践行创新发展理念，持续提升行业核心竞争力。组织实施科研项目97项，其中国家重大科研项目5项，投入科研资金1.6亿元，牵头和参与编制行业标准21项、三峡标准38项，年内申报知识产权96项，取得国家科学技术二等奖1项，省部级、行业学会、协会各类科技创新类奖励19项。取得了良好的经济和社会效益，工程质量安全、管理效能等得到有效提升。

（七）公司改革

①组织编制公司“十三五”发展规划和改革发展方案，统筹研究三峡发展“十三五”发展规划、工程检测中心改革发展方案，完成集团公司工程建设管理体制建设、建设板块融合发展及大水电开发平台等专项研究报告，为公司改革发展提供坚实基础。②整合华水公司资质和三峡发展监理能力，积极承接长江大保护项目，成功中标兴山县城镇污水处理及基础设施工程项目，跟踪秭归县茅坪河流域综合治理项目，为九江、芜湖等试点项目提供专业咨询和技术支持。持续跟踪国网新源抽水蓄能项目；与中水电公司达成智利鲁凯威水电站项目合作意向。③积极参与集团海上风电监理项目投标。全年参与集团内外公开和非公开招标项目90个，确定中标项目66个。全年共签订新能源业务监理合同13个，合同金额1580.21万元。④坚持面向基层，面向一线的选人用人导向；研究提出建立项目经理序列和“首席师”制度、打造多元化人才成长发展通道；举办首期青年员工基础能力培训；建立职称管理和评审体系，强化薪酬社保福利保障和激励，健全完善境外薪酬管理制度；积极探索市场化项目的奖励兑现方式，强化绩效考核促提升，加强服务保障。

（八）履行社会责任

2018年，公司扶贫项目达到23个，资金1906.64万元，截至2018年底，有9个项目已经实施完成。此外，公司各单位分两次集中购买凉山州的李子和脐橙，开展消费扶贫活动，累计消费近16万元。同时，积极主动与三峡e购等电子商务平台联系，争取早日开通电商消费扶贫。2018年，通过完善制度建设、加强项目管理等各措施的落实，项目实施取得了预期效果。着力解决一线职工“四难”问题，切实缓解就医难和入学难问题。

（中国三峡建设管理有限公司）

2

水能及新能源开发

水 能 开 发

浙江省抽水蓄能电站选点规划调整

为做好浙江省抽水蓄能电站规划建设工作，更好地适应浙江省及华东电网电力系统安全经济运行和核电、新能源快速发展需要，推动抽水蓄能电站科学有序建设，受浙江省发展改革委委托中国电建集团华东勘测设计研究院有限公司开展了浙江省抽水蓄能电站选点规划调整工作，规划水平年为2025年。该省抽水蓄能电站选点规划始于20世纪70年代。截至2017年底，已建抽水蓄能电站容量458万kW，分别为天荒坪180万kW、桐柏120万kW、溪口8万kW、仙居150万kW，在建抽水蓄能电站容量530万kW，包括长龙山210万kW、宁海140万kW、缙云180万kW。

（一）合理规模

浙江电网是华东电网的重要组成部分，2016年底，浙江电网已通过安吉—芜湖2回、安吉—练塘2回、莲都—榕城共6回1000kV特高压交流线路，分别与安徽省、上海市、福建电网相连，通过汾湖—南桥2回、瓶窑—武南2回、瓶窑—敬亭1回、富阳—河沥2回、双龙—福州共9回500kV线路，分别与上海市、江苏省、安徽省、福建省电网相连。截至2016年底，考虑华东直属机组分电和区外送入电力后，浙江电网可用总装机容量10431.7万kW，其中常规水电600.8万kW，占5.8%；抽水蓄能电站243万kW，占2.3%；火电6773.1万kW，占64.9%；核电523.2万kW，占5.0%；风电及光伏457.6万kW，占4.4%；接受区外电力1834万kW，占17.6%。2016年该省全社会用电量3873亿kW·h，年均增速9.0%；全社会最高负荷7010万kW，年均增速11.4%。统调最大峰谷差2231.2万kW，年均增速0.7%。预测该省2025年最高负荷10300万kW，增长率3.5%；需电量5250亿kW·h，增长率3.0%；2030年最高负荷11100万kW，增长率1.5%；用电量5560亿kW·h，增长率1.2%。

浙江省抽水蓄能电站除满足本省需求外，还需支援华东电网内的江苏和上海。经电力系统电源结构优化研究分析，2025水平年浙江省抽水蓄能电站需求规模为1500万～1600万kW左右（满足省内需求900万～1000万kW左右，支援省外规模600万kW），在已建、在建抽水蓄能电站容量988万kW基础上，浙江省2025年前还需新增抽水蓄能容量500～600万kW左右。展望2030水平年，该省抽水蓄能电站需要规模为1800～1900万kW左右（满足省内需求1100～1200万kW左右，支援省外规模700万kW左右）。此外，为适应浙江省和江苏省、上海市能源结构调整和新能源快速发展的新形势，电网调峰需求存在一定不确定性，浙江省抽水蓄能电站需求规模有可能进一步增加。

（二）站点资源及规划比选站点

浙江省抽水蓄能资源丰富，可开发站点多、水头高、装机容量大，且各地分布较为均匀，调整后全省具有开发价值的抽水蓄能站点共48处，可开发装机容量6030万kW。已经国家能源局批复的浙江省2020年5个新建的抽水蓄能电站推荐站点中，截至2017年底，除长龙山、宁海、缙云3座电站已经核准开工建设外，衢江、磐安电站已经完成或正在开展可行性研究阶段的勘测设计工作；而泰顺、天台、建德和桐庐4个站点作为2020年的储备站点均已开展预可研设计。根据本次该省选点规划调整成果，该省内并未发现更好的资源点。考虑规划的延续性，根据该省抽水蓄能电站合理规模和外送需求、合理布局分散布置要求、站点建设条件、地理位置和上网条件，国家能源局关于规划调整工作的复函意见，省发展改革委、能源局指导意见，结合远景发展需要，将衢江、磐安、泰顺、天台、建德、桐庐等6个站点作为2025年该省抽水蓄能电站选点规划调整的比选站点。

（三）选点规划工作结论

各比选站点建设条件总体较好，工程建设技术可行，建设征地不存在制约因素，基本满足布局需要。经本次复核，上次选点规划推荐的衢江、磐安站点不存在环境制约因素，并已完成或基本完成可行性研究阶段勘测设计工作，工程方案等基本落实；泰顺、天台站点不存在环境制约因素，经济指标较好；同意衢江（120万kW）、磐安（120万kW）、泰顺（120万kW）、天台（170万kW）站点作为推荐规划站点。

建德、桐庐站点的地理位置和工程建设条件较好，技术经济指标较优，其涉及的相关环境问题正在协调解决。为适应浙江省和江苏省、上海市能源结构调整和新能源快速发展新的形势任务，考虑到电网需求与其他调峰能力建设存在一定不确定性，浙江省抽水蓄能电站需求规模可能进一步增加，同时为了保护抽水蓄能站点资源，推荐建德（240 万 kW）和桐庐（120 万 kW）站点作为推荐规划站点。

2018 年 1 月，水电水利规划设计总院、浙江省能源局、国家电网公司华东分部在北京联合组织召开并审查通过浙江省抽水蓄能电站选点规划调整报告并下发审查意见。

2018 年 9 月，国家能源局以《国家能源局关于浙江抽水蓄能电站选点规划调整有关事项的复函》（国能函新能〔2018〕116 号文）予以批复，“同意在初选衢江、磐安、泰顺、天台、建德、桐庐作为比选站点的基础上，确定衢江（120 万 kW）、磐安（120 万 kW）、泰顺（120 万 kW）、天台（170 万 kW）站点为浙江 2025 水平年抽水蓄能选点规划调整推荐站点。考虑电网需求与其他调峰能力建设存在一定不确定性，原则同意建德（240 万 kW）和桐庐（120 万 kW）站点作为推荐站点，两站点应在相关环境问题协调落实后，根据华东电网电力系统发展需要适时开发建设”。

（中国电建集团华东勘测设计研究院
有限公司　钟娜　徐玲君）

安徽省抽水蓄能电站选点规划调整

为更好适应安徽省及华东电网电力系统安全经济运行和新能源快速发展需要，推动抽水蓄能电站科学有序建设，受安徽省能源局委托中国电建集团华东勘测设计研究院有限公司开展了安徽省抽水蓄能电站选点规划调整工作，规划水平年为 2025 年。该省自 1976 年起就开展抽水蓄能电站选点查勘工作，截至目前，已建抽水蓄能电站总规模 168 万 kW，分别为琅琊山（60 万 kW）、响水涧（100 万 kW）和响洪甸（8 万 kW）共 3 座；在建抽水蓄能电站总规模 300 万 kW，分别为金寨（120 万 kW）和绩溪（180 万 kW）2 座。

（一）合理规模

安徽电网是华东电网的重要组成部分，位于华东电网西部，与华东其他省网联系紧密。截至 2016 年底，安徽省电源总装机容量 5732.7 万 kW，其中：常规水电 127.3 万 kW，占比 2.2%；抽水蓄能 168 万 kW，占比 2.9%；火电 4915.5 万 kW，占比 85.7%；风电 176.7 万 kW，占比 3.1%；太阳能及其他 345.2 万 kW，占比 6.0%；安徽还接受区外来电三峡分电，规模 92 万 kW。未来安徽电网新增电源除煤电外，将以风电、太阳能等清洁能源为主，同时积极消纳区外来电。

2016 年安徽省全社会用电量 1795 亿 kW·h，年均增速 9.5%；全社会最高负荷 3513 万 kW，年均增速 11.5%；统调最大峰谷差 1009.7 万 kW，年均增速 13.6%。“十三五”期间，预测安徽省 2025 年最高负荷 6640 万 kW，增长率 4.8%；需电量 3108 亿 kW·h，增长率 4.7%。2030 年最高负荷 7880 万 kW，增长率 3.5%；用电量 3685 亿 kW·h，增长率 3.5%。

经电力系统电源结构优化研究分析，2025 水平年安徽省抽水蓄能电站需求规模约 880 万～980 万 kW（其中满足省内需求规模 500 万～600 万 kW，支援省外规模 380 万 kW）。在省内已、在建 468 万 kW 和浙江天荒坪送入 20 万 kW 抽水蓄能规模基础上，2025 年前安徽省还需新增抽水蓄能电站规模约 392～492 万 kW。

展望 2030 年，安徽省抽水蓄能电站需求规模约 1060 万～1160 万 kW（其中，满足省内需求规模 600 万～700 万 kW，支援省外规模 460 万 kW）。

（二）站点资源及规划比选站点

安徽省抽水蓄能电站资源较好，可开发站点多、水头高、装机容量大，安徽省抽水蓄能电站资源多分布于皖中、皖南山区，全省具有开发价值的抽水蓄能站点共 28 处，合计可开发装机容量 2820 万 kW。

根据安徽省抽水蓄能电站的布局要求，皖北地区为安徽省北电南送、皖电东送的能源基地，但地势相对平缓，缺乏建设抽水蓄能电站的有利条件；皖中、皖南地区多山地，具备修建抽水蓄能电站的优势，可接受皖北地区输入基荷甚至低谷电力，提高安徽电网经济运行水平，故 2025 水平年新推荐的抽水蓄能电站宜首先考虑在皖中、皖南地区布局。参照国内外抽水蓄能电站的选点经验，结合安徽省抽水蓄能电站资源较好的实际情况，按照距负荷中心和枢纽变电站较近、送受电条件较好、距高比较小、水源条件可满足要求、地形地质、工程布置、施工交通条件较好等选点原则，选择皖中地区的桐城、岳西、毛尖山、霍山、清潭沟和皖南地区的宁国、石台共计 7 个站点作为规划比选站点。并对各规划比选站点，按选点规划阶段深度要求，开展相应的勘察设计工作。

（三）选点规划工作结论

考虑本规划以满足2025水平年安徽省内、外抽水蓄能电站建设需求为基本目标、从站点地理位置及上网条件、地形条件、地质条件、水源条件及综合利用、枢纽布置、施工条件、建设征地及移民安置、环境影响、工程投资及经济指标等技术、经济综合比较，在各比选站点没有环境制约因素的前提下，根据华东电网（上海、江苏）对抽水蓄能电站的需求、省内布局、站点分布、特高压落点和西部地区电力支撑要求，结合前期工作开展情况和《安徽省抽水蓄能电站选点规划报告》（2010年）的延续性，并考虑有利于保护抽水蓄能站点资源，本规划报告选择桐城、宁国、岳西、石台、霍山站点作为安徽省2025水平年抽水蓄能电站推荐规划站点，根据电力市场需求择机开发建设。上述推荐规划站点总规模600万kW，加上已在建抽水蓄能电站规模468万kW，2025年安徽省抽水蓄能电站规模可达到1068万kW，满足2025年安徽电网及支援华东的上海、江苏电网抽水蓄能电站容量需求。

2018年3月，水电水利规划设计总院、安徽省能源局、国家电网公司华东分部在合肥联合组织召开了安徽省抽水蓄能电站选点规划调整报告审查会议。对《安徽省抽水蓄能电站选点规划调整报告》进行审查，审查意见认为："江苏省原规划的竹海站点（拟装机容量180万kW）涉及生态红线、环境敏感因素较多，不具实施开发条件，安徽省可适当增加支援江苏的抽水蓄能电站规模，并考虑有利于保护抽水蓄能站点资源，经综合比较，同意桐城（拟装机容量120万kW）、宁国（120万kW）、岳西（120万kW）、石台（120万kW）、霍山（120万kW）作为安徽省2025水平年抽水蓄能规划调整推荐站点。"

2018年8月，国家能源局以《国家能源局关于安徽抽水蓄能电站选点规划调整有关事项的复函》（国能函新能〔2018〕99号文）予以批复，"同意在初选桐城、宁国、岳西、毛尖山、霍山、清潭沟、石台作为比选站点的基础上，确定桐城（拟装机容量120万kW）、宁国（120万kW）、岳西（120万kW）、石台（120万kW）、霍山（120万kW）站点为安徽电网2025水平年抽水蓄能规划调整推荐站点"。

（中国电建集团华东勘测设计研究院有限公司　徐玲君　钟娜）

贵州省抽水蓄能电站选点规划进展情况

随着光伏、风电的快速发展，在充分发挥水电调节能力的情况下，贵州省内调峰及新能源消纳能力不足问题日益显现，随着新能源规模的进一步扩大，电网运行的可靠性、经济性问题将更加突出。基于上述原因，为保障以光伏发电、风电、水电为主的可再生能源大规模外送及其电网系统安全稳定运行，以及光伏发电、风电电量合理利用，开展贵州省抽水蓄能电站前期选点规划工作势在必行。

贵州省抽水蓄能选点规划是我国光伏发电、风电大规模开发，以及绿色发展的新形势下，针对新能源发展中带来的随机性、间歇性、波动性等问题，发展带来的弃风弃光问题，以及绿色能源电力远距离外送等新问题，开展的新举措，对我国风电、光伏发电、水电等可再生能源多能互补电力系统安全问题运行，新能源弃电的消纳问题，可再生能源打捆外送问题等，起到非常重要的意义。

贵州省抽水蓄能电站选点规划主要里程：

（1）贵州省抽水蓄能电站普查和选点工作始于2002年，到2010年底，中国电建集团贵阳勘测设计研究院有限公司（简称贵阳院）相继开展了贵州乌江流域水电开发综合利用辅助电源——抽水蓄能电站普查选点、贵州省"十一五"乌江流域抽水蓄能专项规划、贵州乌江流域抽水蓄能电站选点规划、贵州珠江流域抽水蓄能电站选点规划等项工作。

（2）2011年2月，贵州省发展与改革委员会委托贵阳院开展贵州省抽水蓄能电站选点规划，《贵州省抽水蓄能电站选点规划报告（初稿）》于2016年2月完成。

（3）2016年3月，水电水利规划设计总院会同贵州省发展与改革委员会、贵州省能源局在北京主持召开了贵州省抽水蓄能电站选点规划工作协调会，根据会议精神，由中国电建集团中南勘测设计研究院有限公司牵头联合贵阳院在已有成果基础上共同开展贵州省抽水蓄能电站选点规划工作，对建设必要性和需求规模进行联合研究、对贵州电网负荷中心贵阳市周边进行补充普查和联合踏勘筛选，选择修文石厂坝、福泉坪上、息烽南极顶、贵定黄丝、修文大树子、都匀楠木山6个站点作为规划比选站点，进行站点方案设计和比较，选择出规划站点，贵州省抽水蓄能电站选点规划报告于2018年5月提出。

(4) 2018年5月26～27日，水电水利规划设计总院联合贵州省发展和改革委员会、贵州省能源局、中国南方电网有限责任公司在贵阳主持召开审查会，对《贵州省抽水蓄能电站选点规划报告》进行审查。审查会认为，从贵州电网对调峰电源需求、合理布局、站点建设条件、环境影响、技术经济等方面综合分析，同意《贵州省抽水蓄能电站选点规划报告》在初选修文石厂坝、福泉坪上、息烽南极顶、贵定黄丝、修文大树子、都匀楠木山6个站点作为比选站点的基础上，确定贵阳（修文石厂坝、初拟装机容量120万kW）、黔南（贵定黄丝、初拟装机容量120万kW）站点为贵州电网2025年新建抽水蓄能电站推荐站点，并报国家能源局批准。

（中国电建集团贵阳勘测设计研究院有限公司　龚兰强）

西藏易贡藏布水电规划进展情况

易贡藏布位于西藏自治区东部，涉及那曲市嘉黎县和林芝市波密县，是帕隆藏布右岸一级支流，雅鲁藏布江的二级支流，于波密县通麦镇附近汇入帕隆藏布。河流干流全长286km，天然落差3070m，流域面积13559km^2，河口多年平均流量500m^3/s，水力资源理论蕴藏量433亿kW·h（平均功率494.6万kW）。

开发易贡藏布水电资源，既是保障西藏电网安全稳定发展的需要，也是发挥西藏地区能源资源优势、壮大能源产业的必然选择；是落实中央第六次西藏工作座谈会精神，促进西藏经济社会快速发展的需要；符合国家能源发展战略，构建现代能源体系的要求；也是节能减排、生态环境保护的需要，对促进西藏自治区经济社会发展，保障和维护民族团结具有重要意义。

按照2005年西藏电力前期工作会议精神和原中国水电顾问集团公司工作安排，中国电建集团西北勘测设计研究院有限公司（简称西北院）于2005年4月开始对帕隆藏布流域（含易贡藏布、拉月曲）进行水电规划前期工作。2011年西藏自治区发展和改革委正式批复同意立项开展帕隆藏布、易贡藏布水电规划，水电水利规划设计总院为技术咨询及审查单位，西北院承担该项水电规划。易贡藏布水电规划梯级距离西藏负荷中心相对较近，且有年调节能力的忠玉龙头水库，对流域下游梯级调节补偿作用显著，可较好适应西藏电力需求。西藏易贡藏布水电规划主要历程：

(1) 2005年开始易贡藏布现场踏勘，到2017年4月，由中国水利水电建设工程咨询有限公司对西藏易贡藏布水电规划报告进行咨询，并形成了咨询意见。12年间，设计规划及相关单位进行了扎实细致的工作。

(2) 2018年5月，西藏自治区环境保护厅在成都组织召开了西藏易贡藏布水电规划环境影响报告书审查会，审查意见认为，环境影响报告书基础资料较丰富，分析内容全面，评价指标体系设置与评价方法选择较为合理，提出的规划优化调整建议和减缓不良环境影响的对策措施总体可行，评价结论基本可信。环境影响报告书经完善后，可作为水电规划报告优化调整和决策实施的依据。

(3) 2018年9月，水电水利规划设计总院在西安组织召开了西藏易贡藏布水电规划报告审查会，审查意见认为，规划报告满足流域水电规划工作内容和深度的要求，基础资料翔实，分析论证充分，规划思路基本正确，规划原则基本合理，主要结论基本合适，基本同意规划报告。

根据《西藏易贡藏布水电规划报告（审定稿）》，推荐以忠玉为控制性水库的“一库八级”开发方案，各梯级为：龙眼（3954m/26万kW）、金桥（3425m/6.6万kW）、忠玉（年调节、3220m/80万kW）、亚龙（2996m/53万kW）、日卡（2845m/26万kW）、八盖（2770m/14万kW）、朗采（2728m/80万kW）、夏曲（2480m/94万kW）等，总装机容量379.6万kW，总保证出力57.67万kW，年发电量160.68亿kW·h。

(4) 2018年12月，西藏自治区人民政府印发了《西藏自治区人民政府关于西藏自治区易贡藏布水电规划报告的批复》（藏政函〔2018〕134号），忠玉水电站作为控制性调节水库，对满足西藏电网用电需求具有重要作用，技术经济可行，是《西藏自治区“十三五”时期综合能源发展规划》的重点开工项目，要加快推进项目前期工作，力争早日开工建设。亚龙、朗采、夏曲电站要根据电力市场需求和前期工作情况适时开发。龙眼、日卡、八盖电站尚需进一步研究论证开发的必要性和开发时机。

（中国电建集团西北勘测设计研究院有限公司　王进学　姬生才）

新能源开发

青海省海南州特高压外送基地电源配置规划情况

青海省清洁、可再生能源资源丰富，且具有较好的大规模、集中开发条件。为贯彻习总书记十九大提出的构建清洁低碳、安全高效的能源体系讲话精神和视察青海时做出的重要指示，落实国家能源发展战略，青海省立足能源资源优势，加快推进清洁能源示范省建设。在立足水光互补、能源资源等优势基础上，发挥黄河水电调节作用，以创建全国清洁能源示范省为牵引，稳步建设海南州、海西州两个“千万kW级”可再生能源基地，统筹规划建设特高压外送通道的能源发展战略。

为推进海南州“千万kW级”可再生能源基地建设，科学组织青海海南—河南驻马店直流特高压外送配套电源，保障送电稳定性和经济性，根据青海省能源局的安排，开展《青海省海南州特高压外送基地电源配置规划》，工作主要历程：

(1) 2017年11月6日，根据青海省能源局工作部署，黄河水电公司组织相关单位在西安召开了《青海省海南州特高压外送特电源配置规划》协调会，初步确定由西北勘测设计研究院作为总体技术负责单位，统筹开展规划研究工作。

(2) 2017年11月10日，青海省能源局印发以青能新能〔2017〕11号正式下发《青海省能源局关于开展〈青海省海南州特高压外送基地电源配置规划〉编制工作的通知》。

(3) 2017年12月底，参编单位共同完成了《青海省海南州特高压外送基地电源配置规划》(初稿)的编制工作。

(4) 2018年1月12日，青海省能源局在西宁组织召开《青海省海南州特高压外送基地电源配置规划(初稿)》审查会，委托水电水利规划设计总院对报告进行审查。

(5) 2018年3月，参编单位根据审查意见对规划报告完成了修改和完善，形成《青海省海南州特高压外送基地电源配置规划(审定稿)》。

(6) 2018年3月底，青海省能源局以《关于〈青海省海南州特高压外送基地电源配置规划〉》(青发改能源〔2018〕196号)文正式向国家能源局报送规划报告。

(7) 2018年9月25日，按照国家能源局工作安排，青海省能源局在西宁组织召开青海省海南州特高压外送基地电源配置规划协调会，会后，参编单位根据意见对规划报告进行再次修编。

根据2018年9月修编的《青海省海南州特高压外送基地电源配置规划》，2020年海南州特高压外送基地外送电源总规模696万kW，其中水电规模146万kW、风电规模300万kW、光伏规模200万kW、光热50万kW；2020年送出电量206亿kW·h，输电年利用小时数约5150h。2022年海南州特高压外送基地外送电源总规模1686万kW，其中水电规模486万kW、风电规模400万kW、光伏规模500万kW、光热规模300万kW，2022年送出电量412亿kW·h，输电年利用小时数约5150h。后续将根据各方意见对规划报告作进一步修改完善。

(中国电建集团西北勘测设计研究院有限公司　胡小丽)

三峡新能源庄河Ⅲ(300MW)海上风电场工程设计

三峡新能源大连庄河Ⅲ海上风电场位于辽宁省大连市庄河海域，规划庄河Ⅰ海上风电场南侧，庄河Ⅱ海上风电场东侧，北侧距离航道约1km以上，西侧距离航道2km以上。南北长8.6km，东西7.7km，场址中心距离岸线约22.2km，面积约47.7km^2。

工程分两期建设，首期装机容量为20万kW，包含2台0.3万kW、48台0.33万kW和6台0.645万kW机组。二期装机容量10万kW，包含15台0.645万kW和1台0.33万kW机组。风电场主机选用金风科技，总装机容量30.33万kW。风机间行距为1200m，列距为650m，220kV海上升压站位于整个风场中北部28号风机东侧约650m，场内采用12回35kV海缆接入220kV海上升压站，海上升压站出2回220kV海缆，长度为26.9km，登陆后接1.6km长架空线路接入陆上集控中心，再以一回220kV架空线路接入500kV黄海变电站。

该项目是我国东北海域建设的第一座海上风电场，自然环境条件十分复杂：高纬度寒区海域，属于当年结冰海区，需考虑海冰对结构的不利影响；地质构造复杂，岩层中下伏溶洞，覆盖层变化幅度大，一部分风机基础需要解决大直径嵌岩桩的设计和施工问题等。

（一）工程设计

1. 风能资源　该场址区域代表年85m、90m、100m高度年平均风速分别为6.85m/s、6.88m/s和6.97m/s，对应的年平均风功率密度分别为365.56W/m²、370.40W/m²和384.28W/m²。代表年85m、90m、100m高度主风向和主风能均为N、NNW方向，且风电场主风能比较集中，有利于风机布置。风电场属IECIII类，湍流等级为C类。湍流强度很小，可减少风电机组运行、维护成本。

2. 海洋水文　工程海域潮汐属规则半日潮，潮流运动形式以旋转流为主，潮波均呈现明显的前进波特性。最大潮差6.38m。该海域场址$P=2\%$设计极端高潮位4.04m，极端最低潮位−3.94m。场址处高潮累积频率10%设计高潮位为3.04m，低潮累积频率90%设计低潮位为−2.44m。最大可能表层流速为0.81m/s。工程区50年一遇有义波高为5.16m。

一般（常）冰年黄海北部冰情特点是结冰范围在15～25海里之间，冰厚一般在20～30cm之间，最大可达50cm；重冰年黄海北部冰情特点是结冰范围大于30海里，冰厚一般大于40cm，最大可达80cm。

3. 工程地质　风场区为对建筑抗震的一般场地，工程区海床面平缓，无冲沟深槽分布，不存在导致崩塌、滑移等不良地质作用条件，下部基岩中灰岩发育串珠状溶洞，但总体上溶洞规模不大，大都有冲填，通过采取不同基础型式及合适的基础埋深等针对性工程措施可予以避免或解决上述溶洞对工程的影响，场地发生地质灾害危险性小，综合上述因素场地为基本稳定场地。场地岩土种类较多，基岩起伏较大，灰岩中有溶洞发育，但采取工程措施可以避免或解决岩溶发育对风机基岩的影响，场地可进行风机基础建设。

4. 风电机组选型、布置　该风电场风电机组，第一批次采用金风GW121/3000kW机组2台、GW140/3300kW机组48台、GW171/6450kW机组6台；第二批次采用金风GW171/6450kW机组15台、GW140/3300kW机组1台；机组布置按照当地主风向（NNW、N和S）排布，并充分利用场址面积，考虑周边规划场址对本风场的影响，最终按照垂直于主风向布置。一期区域风机行距为1200m、列距为650m，二期区域北部区域布置一行，南部区域布置为两行，行距为2250m、列距为750m。

5. 工程电气　该工程采用12回35kV海底电缆接至220kV海上升压站35kV开关柜，由2台220kV容量为240MVA双分裂绕组变压器升压后，以2回220kV线路接入陆上集控中心，再以1回220kV架空线路接入电网，该工程为目前世界上最长的单根无接头220kV交联聚乙烯三芯海缆，并在国内海上风电工程中首次实现近岸礁石段220kV三芯海缆敷设。

该工程监控系统设备配置和功能要求按照陆上“无人值班（少人值守）”和海上“无人驻守”运行管理方式设计，风电场机电设备分风电机组监控系统和220kV升压站监控系统两个局域网进行监控。两个局域网结构上相对独立，均采用全计算机监控系统、分层分布式结构，两局域网通过OPC通信服务器进行信息交换，组成全场计算机监控系统。

6. 土建工程　按照《风电场工程等级划分及设计安全标准》（试行，FD002－2007）：确定工程等别为Ⅰ等，工程规模为大（1）型；风电机组地基基础设计级别为1级，其潮水设计标准为重现期50年。根据《风电机组地基基础设计规定》（FD003－2007），风电机组基础结构安全等级为1级。海上升压站建筑物级别取与风机基础相同为1级，结构安全等级为一级。陆上集控中心建筑物级别为2级，结构安全等级为二级。根据《风电场工程等级划分及设计安全标准》（试行，FD002－2007）：确定风电场风机基础、海上升压站、陆上集控中心结构抗震设防类别为丙类。

（1）风机基础。该工程海域开阔，海底地形条件复杂，风电场在设计高水位下水深约20.3～28.3m。风场风机基础设置方式如下：2台0.3万kW风机基础采用单桩型式。49台0.33万kW风机基础采用单桩非嵌岩和单桩嵌岩两种型式，其中非嵌岩基础44台，嵌岩基础5台。21台0.645万kW风机基础均采用高桩承台。

（2）海上升压站。海上升压站主要包括上部组块与下部结构。上部组块结构采用框架—支撑体系。下部结构采用导管架嵌套桩结构，4根导管架竖管间采用横撑、斜撑相互连接组成空间桁架，上下部结构连接后形成多层空间整体桁架。其升压站平台底层甲板顶高程为14.0m，总高度（至主屋面）约16m，分四层。底层平为海上进入平台的过渡层兼作电缆层，另布置事故油罐、细水喷雾泵房；一层含主变室压器、35kV开关柜室、应急配电屏室、备品备件室、接地变压器-接地电阻成套装置、站用配电屏室；二层布置主变压器散热器、220kV GIS 室、继保室、通风机房、柴油发电机房、应急生活间、通风机房；顶层布置吊机，主变压器室屋盖可开启，局部区域布置暖通设备、其他辅助设施等。

（3）陆上集控中心。陆上集控中心场内布置控制楼、辅房、油品库、配电装置楼、变电楼等建（构）筑物。控制楼布置于场地中央，油品库位于西北角，辅房位于东北角，变电楼位于西南角，场配电装置楼位于东南角。控制楼西侧设有停车位。场地北侧中间设主入口，西侧中间设次入口，大门宽度分别为 8m 和 6m。站内道路宽 4.5m，呈环形布置，转弯半径 9m，消防车可直达站内各建筑物。

（上海勘测设计研究院有限公司）

三峡新能源庄河Ⅲ（300MW）海上风电场关键技术及应用

三峡新能源大连庄河Ⅲ海上风电场项目于 2016 年 12 月 28 日获得核准批复，2017 年 3 月 30 日举行开工仪式，2017 年 5 月开始试桩工程，2017 年 11 月 25 日首台风机吊装成功，2018 年 10 月 22 日海上升压站整体吊装成功，项目计划 2019 年 1 月并网发电，到时将标志着我国北方地区首个海上风电项目规模化投入商业运行。

（一）率先采用抗冰锥结构风机基础

为确保设计质量，成立专门攻关技术团队攻坚克难，在缺乏现场冰情资料情况下，积极与外部单位联合完善冰情参数，以揭示场址区冰情。利用天津大学冰工程重点试验室抗冰锥物理模型试验成果，以及大连理工大学对风机基础分别有无冰锥方案进行数值分析，借鉴海洋石油平台建设经验，经过反复分析论证，最终采用单桩设置抗冰锥，高桩不设抗冰锥设计方案。目前已经完成首两台 0.3 万 kW 风机基础施工和风机吊装。我国首个抗冰锥结构被首次成功推广应用到海上风场抗冰结构设计中。目前，单桩抗冰锥结构发明专利已经申报，并已纳入三峡集团技术标准。

（二）大直径嵌岩单桩首次应用

目前，国内嵌岩桩尚受制于嵌岩设备及施工工艺限制，直径基本在 4m 以内，工程首期 20 万 kW 有 5 台大直径单桩嵌岩基础，实现了单根嵌岩桩直径达 5.4m 的突破，也是全国首例正式在工程上应用的大直径嵌岩单桩基础。利用可靠、专业的大直径钻机解决国内多桩嵌岩风机基础嵌岩工效慢、造价高、风险大难题。

为解决大直径打入和嵌岩施工问题，设计过程中针对嵌岩段钢筋笼尺寸、桩长进行桩—土—基础有限元优化设计，确保嵌岩变截面段应力满足规范要求的同时，为施工提供便利。此外，参建各方尤其是业主协同设计院与施工单位，针对施工钻机设备的选择及其施工特点进行深入研究，规避嵌岩风险、寻求最佳解决方案，进而控制工程进度风险。

（三）海上升压站取得多项优化成果

风场配备 220kV 海上升压站功能区域布局，在国内同规模升压站中具有布局优，体量最小，重量最轻，消防及逃救生系统安全性高，设备运维便利，同时也是三峡集团已建成的容量最大的海上升压站。具体特点如下：①空间布局优化、平台重量降低。与其他同等规模海上升压站相比，重量大幅降低，经济性更好，主要包括：平台造价降低；由于平台重量减轻，可供选择的吊装船资源多，吊装费用降低。②通风系统设计优化。主变压器进风设盐雾过滤器，微正压通风系统不进主变压器室，提高消防安全性，减少了平台通风量，简化了微正压通风系统，降低投资和运行费用。③被动防火系统设计优化。对可能暴露在空气中，一旦垮塌断裂使火灾危险性升级的结构，如主变压器散热器与主变压器室之间的梁柱、电缆室梁柱等采用防火涂料进行防护。④疏散系统设计优化。完善海上升压平台疏散方案：合理布置室内走廊、室外走道和梯道，并且设有两个尽可能远离的便于到达登艇甲板的脱险通道，使工作人员能明确且轻松地到达安全撤离区域，避免出现因平台安全疏散方面存在安全隐患造成人员伤害事故。⑤注重平台设备运维性。通过合理布置各层吊装平台位置和船舶靠泊位置，合理确定悬臂吊臂长及起吊重量，保证平台设备维修维护的便利性。

（上海勘测设计研究院有限公司）

中国水电顾问集团金塘风电厂 2018 年生产管理情况

中国水电顾问集团金塘风电厂（简称金塘电厂）升压站于 2018 年 4 月 1 日完成倒送电，4 月 2 日实现首批机组并网，11 月 28 日，随着 22 号风机并网成功，金塘电厂顺利完成 25 台风机并网工作，投产容量 5 万 kW。

（一）精心筹划，生产准备工作有条不紊

金塘电厂自运营团队组建完成，便有计划、有步骤地开展各项生产准备工作。按照《中国水电工程顾问集团有限公司电力生产准备管理办法》要求完成《金塘电厂生产准备工作大纲》编制，先后完成《中国水电顾问集团金塘风电场安全生产管理制度》《中国水电顾问集团金塘风电场运行规程》等建章立制工作，完成安全工器具、仪器仪表、维护工具、易耗品等采购工作，完成各类运行台账准备工作，完成各厂家培训并针对生产运行开展员工“两票三制”培训，统一运行台账填写和缺陷管理流程，完成《并网调度协议》和《购售电合同》签订工作，并在投产前根据调度指令，拟写操作票，根据电厂人员分工实际编排运行值班表。在此期间，电厂全体员工还全力配合建设单位加强现场施工监管，全程跟进设备安装和调试，完成所有设备交接试验和卫生清扫，并每日跟进检查设备消缺进度，确保设备各项性能参数满足投产要求。

（二）狠抓安全，全力为生产运行工作保驾护航

金塘电厂高度重视全体员工安全教育和安全意识、习惯的培养，2018 年，电厂多次对员工进行安全生产规章制度和法律法规、规范规程的宣贯，有针对性、有计划性地开展安全生产相关工作。建立健全安全生产规章制度和安全工作规程。采购合格的安全工器具和劳动防护用品，做好各类人员的安全教育培训，确保生产人员与特种作业人员 100%持证上岗，并提前报相关部门备案。工程建设期，电厂便主动收集风机、箱式变压器、继保室屏柜、高压开关柜钥匙和操作器具，加强施工监管，确保设备双重编号规范，防雷接地合格，各柜体和外壳均有明显接地点，安全设施、安全色、安全标志、道路交通标志、安全警示线及二次安全防护等均符合相关要求。生产运行期间，按时召开月度、季度、年中、年末运行及安全生产总结分析会，严格落实“两票三制”，加强设备缺陷管理和隐患排查力度，确保备品备件满足生产需求，定期开展定值核对工作，不定期开展应急预案突击演练，针对南方极端天气频繁的现状，加强应急预案演练，提前做好相关物资准备，加强雨雪、雷电、冰冻天气特殊巡视，做到早发现、早预防。加强厂家人员监管，将风机厂家作业人员纳入电厂管理，定期组织和内部人员一起参加安全培训，养成良好的作业习惯，做到工完、料尽、场地清。对外来人员、外来施工队伍、外委单位进入升压站，均按有关要求做好安全培训、安全技术交底或告知，并安排安全监护，针对临时用电，坚决杜绝私拉乱接电线，必要时签署安全用电协议。定期检查安全台账更新情况，监督全体运维人员养成良好的安全习惯。避免物的不安全状态，杜绝人的不安全行为。大力推进安全生产标准化、流程化建设。自投产以来，风电场未出现任何形式的安全生产事故，安全生产形势总体良好。截至 2018 年底，累计安全生产 275 天。

（三）精心运维，在精细化管理中度电必争

自升压站倒送电开始，该风电厂便不遗余力地推进运行维护制度化、标准化、流程化、定置化管理与建设，完善运行维护台账并按档案管理要求统一格式，制定各报表填写说明，确定巡视路线和巡视项目，统一大小交接班注意事项，坚持每日班前例会制度，实行大交接班例会制度，每月定期召开月度运行分析会和设备故障分析会，做好元器件跟换和易耗品使用统计工作，与系统内及地区内风电厂开展对标管理，建立各风机、箱式变压器及设备的运行记录台账，形成设备历史档案。加强缺陷管理，特别是大型定检（叶片、塔筒、润滑系统、风机定检等）、技改、批量消缺、专项巡视与更换（灭火器巡视与更换、箱式变压器巡视等）等工作，悬挂于中控室公示栏，及时填写工作开展情况和完成情况，并要求责任人签字，便于统计和消缺。在物资采购和库房管理工作中，物资（包括易耗品、备品备件、仪器仪表、维护工器具）均按需采购，按需领用，按需分配，避免采购型号、质量等不合格产品和重复采购，杜绝闲置工器具及仪器仪表的采购，并对已有物资做好保管维护工作。养成随手关灯的习惯，能不开的暖（冷）气尽量不开，杜绝长明灯、长流水，倡导节能降耗，降本增效，做到度电必争。2018 年，在风资源不理想的情况下，完成发电量 2693.52 万 kW·h，上网电量 2539.57 万 kW·h，年度上网计划完成率 84.53%。

（四）加强培训，倾力打造电厂生产运维团队

金塘电厂高度重视队伍建设，加强班组各类培训，利用每次大交接班机会，定好排班表，安排主讲人，确定培训主题，将技术问答、事故预想、日常班后会培训有机结合起来，将班组培训做活、做细、做扎实，鼓励员工多参加集团内外各类培训、执业资格考试、业务提升学习，扩大视野，提升个人业务能力和技术水平。

（中国水电顾问集团金塘风电厂）

高海拔山区风电场测风数据分析处理

对于高海拔山区风电场，原有气象观测站的代表性不够，与风电场内的测风资料相关性一般，用这种方法处理的测风资料可靠性不足。该研究结合云南省

某典型高海拔山区风电场的测风资料的具体分析，提出评估时段选取的基本原则，并以典型测风塔为例，说明评估时段选取的基本步骤。

（一）评估时段选取

1. 选取原则　现行规程规范要求评估时段至少为连续一年，但未提出一年以上时段的选取原则。本研究提出超过一年测风资料的选取原则：①各测风塔观测时间的同步性；②考虑数据的完整、有效率；③尽可能避开极端气候影响时段；④考虑到测风仪器的使用年限，测风塔数据宜选用测验初期的数据；若测风时段较长，则应通过与周边参考点（如测风塔、气象站、再分析参考点）的对比，初步判断测风数据的一致性和有效性；⑤若上述条件均满足，则宜选择完整自然年为起始。若观测时间有两年及以上，仍然可按照以上述原则，选取多年（应为整年）作为评估时段。选取的时段越长，数据越具代表性。

2. 实例分析　以云南省某风电场A测风塔为例。A测风塔有2007年10月～2010年12月3年多的测风资料，其东面约7.1km有B测风塔，有2006年12月～2012年6月5年多的测风资料，A、B测风塔基本情况见表1。①缺测情况。A测风塔缺测主要集中在2008年、2009年，缺测率分别为5.1%、5.4%，2010年缺测率仅1.9%，2007年10月～12月无缺测，整体缺测率为3.8%。总体来看，A测风塔缺测条数不多。②无效情况。根据相关判别标准，A测风塔实测气温、气压均为有效值；风速、风向短时间受冰冻影响出现连续，该部分数据无效；风向数据受仪器故障影响存在较多无效数据。无效数据主要受低温冰冻以及仪器故障影响。③有效数据完整率。总体来看，2007年（仅3个月）、2008年、2009年的有效数据完整率较高。④评估时段选取。由A测风塔有效数据完整率统计成果可知，2008年、2009年的有效数据完整率均较高，且2009年年平均风速与多年平均风速更为接近。因此，选择2009年作为评估时段。

表1　测风塔基本情况

项目	A测风塔	B测风塔
海拔（m）	2195	2245
风速测验高度（m）	70/50/30/10	50/30/10
风向测验高度（m）	70/10	50/10
气温、气压测验高度（m）	7	7
测验时段	2007.10～2010.12	2006.12～2012.6

（二）测风数据处理

通常仅对风速、风向的缺测及无效数据进行处理。分析仍以A测风塔为例，对A测风塔2009年的缺测及无效数据进行处理。

1. 选取参证站　参证站通常有以下几种：①周边测风塔。有同期测验资料的同一个风电场内的其他测风塔或周边风电场的测风塔。②周边气象站点。尽量选取具有近似气候背景、具有长时段及与测风塔同期观测资料、观测场地受周边影响较小的站点。③再分析数据参考点。对于A测风塔，其周边有B测风塔（具有5年以上的测风资料）、Q气象站以及测风塔点位处的再分析数据参考点可以作为参考。从相关图及相关系数来看，综合考虑与A测风塔的相对位置、相关性、海拔差异以及数据可靠性，选取B测风塔作为A测风塔数据验证、订正的依据站。

2. 风速处理　风速插补分以下几种情况：①若同一个塔仅部分高度层的数据无效，可通过以下两种方式进行插补：a. 建立各层之间的风速相关。b. 风切变法，采用风速相关的方式。②若需插补的塔各层均同时无效，可根据相关方程进行某层插补，其余测风层根据本塔各层间的相关进行插补。③若无法采用方法①、②进行插补，通常取小时或日平均风速系列建立相关，若相关程度不高，可考虑采用月平均风速系列。④若无法采用以上三种方法，则选取邻近场址的再分析气象参考点，建立两个位置的同期风速相关，分析小时、日、月平均风速的相关性。需要注意的是，若计算机自动生成的相关趋势线在某些风速段不理想，此时需进行人工调整，必要时，可根据相关点群分布的情况，分段选取相关方程，相关方程尽量兼顾全部风速段。若连续无效数据出现的时间较短，则插补可简化，直接采用前后段数据替换即可。

3. 风向处理　本研究中A测风塔评估年2009年风速、风向序列的处理方式为：由于A测风塔各层风速基本同时出现了缺测及无效的情况，因此无法根据各层间的风速相关插补得到某层完整风速序列，因此，通过与B测风塔（50m）的日平均风速相关（此相关较好），插补得到A测风塔70m高度的风速；再通过A测风塔70m高度与其他高度的10分钟风速相关，插补得到其他各层的风速序列。对于A测风塔的风向，10m的风向有效数据完整率低，70m的风向数据有效完整率较高，因此可先将10m无效风向用70m有效风向代替，70m、10m均无效的风向，则用B测风塔50m的风向代替。

（中国电建集团昆明勘测设计研究院有限公司 甘启娣 邱良）

高海拔山区风电场风电机组选型

采用《风力发电机组 设计要求》（GB/T 18451.1—2012/IEC 61400—1：2005）（简称《设计要求》）标准条件设计的风力发电机组不一定能较好的适应高海拔山区风电场，在高海拔山区风电场风机选型时，需根据高海拔山区风电场的特点对其进行复核和改进。

（一）高海拔山区风电场风况及对风电机组的影响

1. 风速分布 通过对分布于云南省山区高程在1671～3566m之间100多座测风塔1年实测资料统计分析表明，总体上看，采用瑞利分布对高海拔山区风电场风速分布进行拟合得到的成果与实测风速分布仍有较大差别。所以在风机选型时仍需根据实测风况对风机荷载和安全性进行复核。同时，在估算高海拔山区发电量时，也应尽量采用实测数据。

2. 五十年一遇最大风速 100多座测风塔1年实测资料统计分析表明，从年最大风速与平均风速的比值看，绝大部分小于4，也小于《设计要求》中的假定值5。根据《设计要求》，50年一遇最大风速也是影响风机载荷和安全的重要因素。因此，在高海拔山区风电场风机选型时，仍需收集更多资料，采取更多的技术手段分析研究风电场50年一遇最大风速，确定风机安全等级，并进一步对风机安全性进行复核。

3. 风切变 100多座测风塔1年实测资料统计分析表明，从垂直风切变规律看，高海拔山区风场的风切变也是基本符合$V(z)=V_{\text{hub}}(z/z_{\text{hub}})^{\alpha}$关系，且绝大多数测风塔的风切变为正切变，仅极少数测风塔风切变为负切变。绝大部分高海拔山区风场风轮扫琼面积上的风切变指数α小于0.2。根据《设计要求》，假定幂律指数α为0.2。可见，对于高海拔山区风场，风切变对高海拔山区风电场风电机组选型的影响不大。

（二）高海拔山区环境条件及对风电机组的影响

1. 气温 根据对云南省山区共计84座测风塔月平均气温统计，及省内36个气象站长期气温观测资料分析，高海拔山区年平均气温比《电工产品不同海拔的气候环境条件（GB/T 14597—2010）》（简称气候条件）提出的相应海拔年平均气温低2～4℃，极端最高气温不高，但极端最低气温较低，按海拔每上升1000m气温降低6.5℃估算，海拔在2050～3250m之间的地区，累年极端最低气温在－6.5～－23.5℃之间。根据《设计要求》，标准等级风力发电机组应考虑的正常环境温度范围为－10～＋40℃，极端温度范围至少应为－20～＋50℃。标准等级风力发电机组设计假定的温度范围基本可以适应高海拔山区风场，温度对风电机组的影响不大。

2. 气压 根据对云南省山区共计82座测风塔月平均气压统计，结合省内34个气象站长期气压观测资料分析，海拔在2000m时年平均气压约80kPa，海拔在3000m时年平均气压约71kPa。年平均气压与高程基本成线性关系，实测风场年平均气压与《气候环境条件》提出的相应海拔年平均气压基本一致。山区风电场海拔大多在2000m以上，气压较低，电气元件绝缘强度降低，器件温升增加，使以空气为灭弧介质的开关电气产品灭弧能力降低，通断能力下降，高海拔山区风场风电机组应根据低气压环境进行相应改进和复核。

3. 空气密度 高海拔山区风电场海拔大多在2000m以上，空气密度仅为标准空气密度1.225kg/m^{3}的78%，3000m以上地区空气密度仅为标准空气密度的71%，空气密度较低。根据《设计要求》，标准等级风力发电机组应考虑正常空气密度为1.225kg/m^3。高海拔山区风电场海拔大多在2000m以上，空气密度较低，导致风机出力降低，发电效率降低，高海拔山区风场风电机组应根据低空气密度环境进行相应改进。

4. 太阳辐射强度 该研究选取云南省太阳能辐射较强地区7个辐射观测站连续1年数据分析，太阳辐射强度超过标准风机设计标准1000W/m^{2}的仍有一定时间，且不同场址最大辐射强度以及辐射强度超过1000W/m^{2}的时间也有所不同。鉴于高海拔山区太阳能辐射强度实测数据不多，高海拔山区风电场太阳能辐射强度建议参照《气候条件》中“不同海拔高度的最大太阳直接辐射强度”。因此，高海拔山区风场风电机组应根据太阳辐射强度进行相应的改进和加强。

5. 雷暴 根据对云南省37个气象站长期观测资料，年雷暴日数在46.6～96.6天之间，平均约63.9天。这些气象站海拔在1050～2250m之间，而大部分高海拔山区风电场海拔均在2000m以上，海拔更高，雷暴日数将更多。按照风力发电机组雷电保护设计，根据高海拔山区雷暴频繁特点，对风电机组雷电保护设计进行复核和加强。

6. 湿度　高海拔山区测风塔湿度观测数据较少，以云南省高海拔山区有湿度观测的 10 座测风塔湿度观测资料初步统计分析，湿度大于 95%的时间与全年时间的占比最大为 30.8%，最小为 8.9%，平均为 18.8%。可见，风机选型时需结合项目本身的湿度情况，采取相应的防渗和除湿措施，以保证风机在高湿环境下安全稳定运行。

7. 冰冻　高海拔地区气温较低，湿度较大，两者同时发生将会发生冰冻情况。该研究选择了 7 个气温和湿度观测较为完整的测风塔观测数据分析，其持续时间从几天到十几天不等，对风机运行和安全将造成影响。建议在高海拔山区进行风能资源观测时增加湿度观测，以对风场进行冰冻情况分析，在风机选型时根据冰冻情况对风机载荷进行复核和加强，并优化风机运行控制策略，以保证风机安全稳定高效运行。

（中国电建集团昆明勘测设计研究院有限公司　张箭）

高海拔山区风电场电气设备选型研究分析

高海拔山区风电场有着明显不同于平原地区的较强太阳紫外线辐射与热辐射强度、较大空气湿度、较低空气密度、较高的年平均风速、干湿季节分明等气候特征，该文针对海拔 1000～4000m 地区、220kV 及以下电压等级风电场电气设备选型作一些研究。

（一）电气设备选型原则

1. 配电装置选择　①配电装置选型原则。110kV 和 220kV 电压等级的配电装置采用屋外中型配电装置或屋外半高型配电装置，对于地震烈度为 9 度及以上地区宜采用 GIS 配电装置，35kV 电压等级的配电装置采用成套高压开关配置型式（交流金属封闭开关柜）。②交流金属封闭开关柜选择。从节约用地及安全可靠性的角度考虑，35kV 以下配电装置选择开关柜形式，当海拔高于 2000m 时选用固定式开关柜，当海拔低于 3000m 时选用空气绝缘开关柜，当海拔高于 3000m 时选用介质绝缘开关柜。当环境温度高于 40℃时，开关柜内的电气设备应按有关要求降容使用，并验算母线的允许电流。③GIS 设备选择。GIS 设备的内绝缘与海拔高度无关，设备外绝缘和安全净距校验按有关要求内容。④户外敞开式设备选择。常见户外敞开式装置包括电流互感器、电压互感器、断路器、隔离开关、避雷器，设备的外绝缘及安全距离校验按有关要求内容。

2. 主变压器的选择　①温升限值。对于空气冷却方式变压器及水冷却方式变压器有不同的温升限制要求，超过温升限值时按以下修正：a. 空气冷却方式变压器。按《特殊运行环境下推荐的温升限值修正值》修正。b. 水冷却方式变压器。安装场所的水冷却的最高温度/年平均温度超过正常冷却条件时，所有规定的温升限值均应按照超出的数值予以降低，并应修正到最接近的整数值。②主变压器容量。当标准型变压器使用在高海拔地区时，其容量的降低值，用相应冷却条件及额定条件下的温升限值计算。③绝缘配合及安全净距。对安装在不同海拔条件下的主变压器，设备的内绝缘与海拔高低没有关系，设备外绝缘和安全净距校验按相关部分要求。

3. 站用变压器系统选择　①温升限值。设计中需要考虑设备的温升限制，安装地点的海拔超过 1000m 的部分，以每 500m 为一级进行相应降低使用。自冷变压器每一级为 2.5%，风冷变压器每一级为 5%。②绝缘配合及安全净距。干式变压器设备绝缘配合和安全净距校验按相关部分要求。

4. SVG 装置的选择　①绝缘配合及安全净距。SVG 主要由变压器、电抗器、控制屏、IGBT 功率设备、隔离开关、避雷器、断路器等设备组成，外绝缘配合和安全净距校验按相关部分要求。②SVG 装置容量。无功补偿 IGBT 功率元件要求海拔 3000m 以下不降容使用，在 3000m 以上地区使用时需要与制造商确认使用的功率曲线、容量配置。

5. 接地装置的选择　①消弧线圈。当风电场系统单相接地故障电容电流较大时，采用消弧线圈装置。②小电阻成套装置。对于电缆线路构成的风力发电场系统，当单相接地故障电容电流较大时，宜采用小电阻接地装置。③绝缘配合及安全净距。消弧线圈及小电阻成套装置外绝缘配合和安全净距校验按相关部分要求。

6. 箱式变压器的选择　箱变柜内主要设备为油浸式变压器，需要根据相关要求进行设备选择。箱变柜内隔离刀闸、断路器、负荷开关等设备，需要根据相关要求进行选择。

（二）电气设备选型设计

1. 电气设备额定工作电流及温升　电气设备正常使用环境条件为周围空气温度不高于 40℃，海拔不超过 1000m。当环境条件发生变化时，进行相应的校验：①当环境温度高于 40℃低于 60℃时，设备允许工作电流：$I^1=I\times[1-1.8\%(T-40)]$；②当环境温度低于 40℃时，设备允许工作电流：$I^1=I\times[1+0.5\%(40-T)]\leqslant 1.2I$；③海拔大于 1000m 小于 4000m 时，设备允许温升：$T^1=T\times\left(1-\dfrac{H-1000}{100}\times 0.3\%\right)$。式中：$I$ 为标准环境下的额定电流；I^1 为周围环境温度下，设备允许工作电流；T 为实际环境温度允许温升；T^1 为超过 1000m 但低于 4000m，且最高周围空气温度为 40℃时，设备允许的温升；H 为实际海拔高度，m。

2. 电气设备绝缘配合　对于正常环境条件下，设备的额定绝缘水平从《220kV 及以下电压等级设备的标准绝缘水平》《220kV 及以下电压等级各类设备雷电冲击耐受电压》《220kV 及以下电压等级各类设备短时（1min）工频耐受电压（有效值）》等表选择。

上表中的操作和雷电冲击电压数据适用于标准参考大气条件下设备外绝缘的要求。对于海拔高于 1000m，但不超过 4000m 设备外绝缘强度应该进行相应的海拔修正，修正系数为 $k_a = e^{q\left(\frac{H-1000}{8150}\right)}$，式中：$H$ 为设备安装点海拔高度；q 为指数，详见 GB 311.1—2012《绝缘配合 第 1 部分：定义、原则和规则》中"各级污秽等级下的爬电比距"相关要求。

3. 高压配电装置设备安全净距　电气设备安全净距按照《室外配电装置的安全净距离》《室内配电装置的安全净距离》要求进行选择。对于海拔超过 1000m 时，数值应该进行修改，修正数值参见 DL/T 5352—2006《高压配电装置设计技术规程》中附录 B。

（中国电建集团昆明勘测设计研究院有限公司　张晶　刘伟　陈冰　王绎）

高海拔山区风电场施工辅助工程技术指标研究

云南省风电累计核准容量 939 万 kW，累计并网容量 412 万 kW，累计在建容量 527 万 kW。由于山区地势起伏较大，风电场施工辅助工程成为影响高海拔山区风电场安全、进度、造价的关键因素。该研究结合云南高海拔山区风电场的一些建设经验，总结了风电场施工辅助工程的一些特点，提出了道路、风机安装平台等施工辅助工程的技术指标。

（一）叶片运输

随着风机功率逐渐增大，叶片长度越来越长，即使 1500kW 风机，叶片长度也在 43m 左右。因风机机位一般位于山顶部位。为此，叶片运输需采用特种叶片扬举车进行叶片二次倒运。该装置由液压控制可以使风叶 360°旋转，运输途中使叶片产生扬起、摆动、自身旋转动作，躲避途中树木、山体、电线等障碍，从而减少道路改造工程量及场内道路新修工程量，缩短工期。

（二）道路工程

风电场道路仅在建设期间担负材料及重大件运输，在风电场建成投运后，仅需保留道路中间 4.5m 部分作为检修道路。目前设计大多以《厂矿道路设计规范》（GBJ22—1987）中的露天矿山三级道路的技术指标为设计依据。由于风电场道路单位公里投资相对较小，但却要承担大尺寸风机设备运输，因此须根据其功能、特点进行合理优化。

1. 道路分级　因风机机位布置在一个或多个山脊上，支线较多且短，长度从几十米到几公里不等，采用较高设计标准来满足其安全性是很不经济的。因此，根据道路运输功能区分，将交通流量较大、通往升压站或风机安装平台的共有线路定义为主线道路；而从主线连接各风机安装平台、施工临时设施的道路定义为支线道路。同时本着"安全可靠、经济合理"的设计理念及"主支分离、因地制宜"的设计方针，开展道路设计及优化工作。

2. 平面线性设计　风电场重大件运输过程中，最宽件一般为风机塔筒，最长件为风机叶片，最重件一般为机舱。故风机叶片长度作为平曲线半径的控制性参数。叶片运输一般采用 1＋3 轴平板挂车，叶片末端悬挑一般 10～25m 左右。因此在平曲线转弯加宽时，应根据转弯处是否有扫空障碍采取不同的加宽值。特别是在道路沿山势盘旋展线时，宜结合运输车辆及重大件参数采用车辆仿真软件进行仿真模拟，结合现场地形地质情况，因地制宜进行转弯段加宽设计。

3. 纵断面设计　风电场道路最大纵坡取决重大件参数、运输车辆性能及运输方法。为降低工程造价及避免因大挖大填而破坏生态环境，在地形受限情况下，部分支线道路最大纵坡可达到 20%。道路竖曲线设计应特别注意凹竖曲线所带来的拖尾现象，应根据运输车辆及货物情况采用作图法进行计算；凸竖曲线半径主要需满足塔筒运输车辆要求，避免出现前后轴车轮架空现象，一般应大于 300m。

4. 路面设计　风电场道路设备运输主要集中在建设阶段。为尽可能降低道路建设成本，路面材料应尽量使用当地材料，路面结构应根据路基地质条件进行设计，若现场路基开挖后为地质条件良好的石质路基，路面结构可省去路面基层；若现场路基开挖后为土基，应根据土基回弹模量来确定路面结构。

5. 标准横断面优化　根据施工期间、运维阶段风电场道路特点，可在道路开挖及大件运输阶段，取消排水边沟以减小宽度，待大件运输完毕，再在路肩进行排水边沟施工。

6. 特殊路段处理　针对山区地面起伏变化大的情况，道路建设应根据转弯段道路左右侧允许扫空的条件及大件运输车辆的轨迹进行设计，即采用 Autoturn 软件进行车辆仿真模拟，结合现场地形，对转弯半径、加宽值及加宽范围进行调整，适当采用天然休止角较大的砾石土、石块进行回填。

（三）风机安装平台

根据国内常用的0.2万kW风机所需的安装平台最小尺寸为40m×50m的要求，受山区地形影响，有些平台会出现巨大的开挖工程量。因此须根据其功能、特点及一些施工技术措施进行合理优化。

1. 综合考虑平台功能　吊装平台越小，修筑所需的工程量就越小，但是太小的吊装平台对吊装工期不利。如果吊装平台大到能存放所有风力发电机组组件及施工机械，势必造成场地浪费。因此在具体布置时，应根据地形地质条件、道路设计方案、运输方案、吊装方案设计、工期要求进行综合分析，以确定风机安装平台的尺寸大小。

2. 小平台风机吊装　受山区地形影响，采用车板吊和象腿工装两种施工技术完成风机吊装。车板吊，就是设备不卸车、在运输车辆上直接起吊。可以将常规平台尺寸减少至30m×35m。象腿工装技术是一种利用风机基础预埋锚固件构造辅助拼装支座来降低风机安装平台面积的方法。与传统叶片组装方法不同，该方法几乎可以省去叶片拼装所需用地，将风机常规安装平台面积减少到38m×22m。

（中国电建集团昆明勘测设计研究院有限公司　袁龙　罗绎昌　张云杰）

财务风险分析在A光伏发电企业财务管理中的应用

2012年，在国家政策和产业前景感召下，光伏发电A企业在新疆哈密注册成立，作为资金密集型新兴产业，经历了诸多财务风险考验，目前并网光伏电站装机容量达9万kW，5万kW风电项目尚在建设中。

（一）财务风险分析

目前光伏产业处于改革发展期，供求关系逐渐由原来的卖方市场转为买方市场，因此A企业不仅面临光伏发电行业共有风险，还面临企业自身风险。主要有：①融资风险；②盈利风险；③营运风险；④现金流风险；⑤宏观政策性风险。根据存在风险进行量化评估。

1. 因子分析法财务风险评估　根据因子分析法优势，这里构造光伏发电行业财务风险评估模型。①财务风险指标选取。根据光伏发电行业特征，从偿债能力、盈利能力、发展能力、营运能力及现金流量能力5个方面选取指标构建财务风险评价体系。②财务风险评价模型构建。该评估采用SPSS19.0分析软件。财务数据选用发电行业60家上市公司，2016年度15组财务数据，借此比较分析光伏发电行业财务风险状况。通过数据检验表明所提取公因子对15个原始变量的解释能力和代表性较强。利用方差最大正交旋转方法计算得到因子载荷矩阵：a. 资产报酬率、销售净利率、总资产净利率净、资产收益率在第一主成分$W1$上具有较大载荷系数，可以定义为反映企业盈利能力的因子；b. 营业收入现金比率、全部资产现金回收率、总资产增长率在第二主成分$W2$上具有较大载荷系数，可以定义为反映企业现金流能力的因子；c. 流动比率、资产负债率、现金比率在第三主成分$W3$上具有较大载荷系数，可以定义为反映企业偿债能力的因子；d. 固定资产周转率、流动资产周转率、总资产周转率在第四主成分$W4$上具有较大载荷系数，可以定义为反映企业营运能力的因子；e. 净利润增长率、营业利润增长率在第五主成分$W5$上具有较大载荷系数，可以定义为反映企业成长能力的因子。由表1数据得到发电行业财务风险综合评价公式：$W=0.28W1+0.21W2+0.21W3+0.17W4+0.13W5$。其中，$W$值越大表示企业的财务风险越小，财务危机发生的概率越小，财务状况越好，反之W值越小则企业不良财务风险越大。根据以上因子分析法得出的发电行业财务指标各公因子计算方法和综合评价公式，将2016年8家光伏发电企业财务风险指标体系进行具体计算，结果列入表2。从综合角度分析，光伏发电行业财务风险综合指标W值偏小，财务经营状况比较紧张，需要警惕各种财务危机可能性。③A企业财务风险行业比较。将A企业各项财务指标单独分析，对识别其财务风险作用比较有限，而根据所构建的行业财务风险评价综合指标，与同行业做横向比较分析研究发现，与其他企业相比，A企业财务管理问题比较严重，不良财务风险较大。具体来看，盈利能力$W1$和营运能力$W4$均排名第7，偿债能力$W3$排名第6，均处于行业末游，表明A企业在获取利润、资金周转方面存在较多问题，且其资本结构中负债比例过高容易造成债务危机。现金流能力$W2$排名最好，居于行业第一，但这并不代表A企业在现金流能力方面不存在问题，注意到A企业2016年主要现金流来源于以前年度项目获得的国家电价补贴，但后续展开项目要获得这项补贴就比较困难，因此现金流能力风险依旧需要警惕。成长性指标$W5$排名第3，居于中上游，表明A企业有较好的发展前景和增值空间，因此需注意给足后劲支持其快速发展。

表 1 因子权重计算表

公因子	W1	W2	W3	W4	W5
因子含义	盈利能力	现金流能力	偿债能力	运营能力	成长能力
方差贡献率	22.038	16.629	16.553	13.729	10.613
因子权重	0.277	0.209009	0.208054	0.172559	0.133395

表 2 光伏发电企业财务风险指标计算表

项目	W1	W2	W3	W4	W5	W
A 企业	−0.10207	0.380021	−0.06734	0.023105	0.20965	0.068267
太阳能	−0.02607	0.062683	0.372868	0.219975	0.4321	0.177736
银星能源	−0.19368	0.285042	0.761778	0.255216	−1.1109	0.064571
东方能源	−0.05329	0.190023	0.055543	0.899471	−0.41036	0.136212
上海电力	−0.04252	0.166739	−0.1342	0.714751	−0.274	0.080815
天富能源	−0.07236	0.08339	0.215277	0.420465	−0.02249	0.111013
乐山电力	−0.02861	0.19495	−0.24785	1.877685	1.028824	0.433834
川投能源	0.882229	−0.08143	−0.03201	−0.40411	0.160629	0.175385

2. 稳健性检验　为确保因子分析法研究结果的科学稳健性，用 Z-Score 财务预警模型和 F 分值模型分别作稳健型检验。①Z-Score 模型评估。A 企业属于非上市非制造企业，适用 Z-Score B 模型：$Z=6.56X1+3.26X2+X3+6.72X4$，根据模型判别标准，A 企业 2014～2016 年 3 年间 Z 分值均处于 1.23～2.99 的灰色区域，其中 2015 年财务状况较好，Z 值（2.8616）接近良好的临界值 2.99；2016 年情况最差，靠近破产临界值，表明财务风险较大，若不加以改善，存在破产危机。具体来看，企业盈利能力较弱，尤其是 2016 年由于限电政策，企业营业收入较少，出现亏损，导致代表企业累计获利能力的 $X2$ 为负值，当期利用总资产获利能力的 $X3$ 锐减，与此同时，企业的资本结构有失合理性，负债比率过高，至 2016 年账面价值与负债比率只有 16.76%，偿债压力增大，和因子分析法实证结论相吻合。②F 评分模型评估。F 评分模型相比 Z-Score 模型，考虑了现金流量变动，预测准确率有所提高，根据 F 分数模型：$F=-0.1774+1.1091X1+0.1074X2+1.9271X3+0.0302X4+0.4961X5$ 对 A 企业财务风险进行评估。根据 F 评分模型破产临界值 0.0274，A 企业在 2014～2015 年破产风险较小，而 2016 年 F 分值只有 −0.0725，远小于临界值，财务危机较大。具体来看，除了 Z-score 模型中已经检验过的 2016 年企业盈利能力弱、资本结构不合理外，现金流能力也表现出较大风险，$X3$ 代表取得的全部现金流量用于偿还负债能力，2016 年骤减，同时衡量企业总资产创造现金流能力的 $X5$ 也较前两年降低幅度较大。总体来看，A 企业 2014～2015 年破产风险较小，而 2016 年财务危机增大，需要从盈利能力、财务杠杆、现金流能力等多方面采取防范措施，再次验证了前述的分析结果。

（二）识别结果评价

基于以上对 A 企业财务风险分析，A 企业存在较大不良财务风险，①融资结构风险，资本结构不合理，债务比率偏高，容易给企业带来较大偿债压力和陷入偿债危机；②盈利能力风险，盈利能力在行业内处于劣势，息税前利润呈下降趋势；③营运能力风险，资金周转较慢，坏账风险较高；④现金流风险，现金流能力短期表现不错，但过度依赖国家政策补贴，未来长期现金流能力不足。

（三）风险防控措施

根据研究提出改善建议：①A 企业应构建财务风险预警体系，有效规避风险；完善内部治理机制，提升运营效率；适度调整融资结构，实现杠杆收益；提高自身现金流能力，降低政府补贴依赖；鼓励技术创新，推动盈利能力增长。②政府应打破地方保护壁垒，改善企业融资环境；减少政府性费用，增加企业利润空间；创新融资渠道，实现多样化融资。

（中国电建集团西北勘测设计研究院有限公司　程昕）

新能源高渗透率区域电网规划研究

受扬州供电公司委托，河海大学开展了《新能源高渗透率区域电网规划研究》，该项目调研电网现状，分析电网存在的问题，同时根据新能源发展情况，尤其是新能源并网存在的问题，对区域电网电力需求进行预测，最后考虑新能源高渗透率对区域电网进行规划。研究的主要内容如下：

（1）区域电网现状调研对扬州电网、宝应电网和高邮电网现状进行调研分析，得到电网目前所存在的问题。

（2）新能源发展分析主要包括新能源电厂现状，新能源电网运行情况。据此分析新能源的发展对电网的影响，最后对其中的问题进行总结分析。

（3）电力需求预测技术首先对电力需求历史数据进行分析，基于分析结果，利用GDP单耗法、时间序列外推法对全社会用电量进行预测，并利用电力弹性系数法进行校核。同时，通过最大负荷利用小时数法、空间负荷密度法、时间趋势法进行全社会最大负荷预测。

（4）新能源高渗透率下区域电网规划 首先研究新能源渗透率对电网的影响，包括对潮流、静态安全、静态电网稳定和区域电网网损的影响。然后确定不同新能源渗透率对电网的影响，最后实现对区域电网的规划。

（河海大学）

2018年国家电网清洁能源运行消纳情况

（一）清洁能源装机容量概况

2018年，国家电网公司经营区清洁能源装机仍然保持快速增长态势。年内新增清洁能源装机容量5743.96万kW，占新增总装机容量62.9%，累计装机容量达5.26亿kW，同比增长12.27%；清洁能源在总装机容量中占比达35.8%，比年初增加1.8个百分点。年内风电、光伏、水电分别新增装机容量1722.63万kW、3776.61万kW、224.72万kW，同比增加26.59%、增加65.32%、增加2.17%。新能源新增装机容量向中东部地区转移，水电新增装机容量主要集中在西南地区。华北、华东、华中地区新增新能源装机容量3921.92万kW，同比增长31.83%，占全网71.32%；三个地区风电和光伏新增装机容量占全网比例分别为72.28%和70.88%。

2018年公司经营区域内水电累计装机容量达到2.27亿kW，同比增长1.09%，占全网总装机容量15.41%。其中，华中、西南地区水电装机容量14969.56万kW，同比增长1.16%，占全部水电装机容量的66.07%。

2018年风电累计装机容量达到1.46亿kW，同比增长13.36%，占全网总装机容量9.94%。华北、东北、西北（简称三北）地区风电装机容量11305.81万kW，同比增长8.72%，占全部风电装机容量的77.37%。其中，“三北”地区风电装机容量分别为3650.40万kW、2874.55万kW和4780.86万kW，同比分别增加15.47%、4.26%和6.71%。风电装机容量占总装机容量比例超过20%的省级电网有冀北、蒙东、甘肃、宁夏和新疆。目前，有新疆、甘肃、冀北、宁夏、蒙东、山西、辽宁、黑龙江和吉林省级电网风电成为其第二大装机电源。

2018年光伏累计装机容量1.53亿kW，同比增长32.82%，占全网总装机容量8.35%。其中，“三北”地区光伏装机容量6779.02万kW，同比增长29.92%，占全部光伏装机容量57.63%。目前，光伏成为第二大装机电源的省份（地区）分别为江苏、安徽、青海、河南、冀南、陕西、西藏、天津、山东和上海。

（二）清洁能源运行与消纳

1. 清洁能源消纳成效显著　2018年公司清洁能源发电量1.22万亿kW·h，同比增加1202.80亿kW·h、增长10.90%；占总发电量比达到22.84%。水电3481h，同比减少20h；风电2068h，同比增加173h；光伏1145h，同比增加32h。水电总消纳量7843亿kW·h，同比增长1.9%，全网消纳水电占用电量比约15%。全部27个省（区）新能源消纳电量均为正增长。新疆、甘肃、山东、河南、江苏等17个省（区）消纳均超100亿；河南、浙江消纳同比增长超60%。新疆、甘肃、蒙东、宁夏、青海等5省（区）消纳占用电量比超20%，冀北、蒙西、甘肃、吉林、黑龙江等5个省（区）消纳占用电量比超10%。

2. 弃电情况得到有效缓解　2018年，调峰弃水损失电量173.2亿kW·h，同比增加2.78亿kW·h，弃水率与2017年持平。弃水主要发生的四川省，全年弃水电量136.9亿kW·h，占全网弃水电量八成，较2017年减少22.2亿kW·h，同比减少13.9%，弃电率为3.8%，同比下降0.8个百分点。

2018年，弃风弃光电量268.5亿kW·h，同比减少143.9亿kW·h，弃电率5.8%，同比降低5.2个百分点，实现新能源弃电量和弃电率“双下降”。

弃风弃光同比减少34.9%。弃风电量216.6亿kW·h，同比减少37.2%；弃光电量51.9亿kW·h，虽然光伏装机容量大幅增长33%，弃光电量仍同比减少23.0%。风电“止升转降”、水电持续下降。弃风率7.1%，同比下降5.8个百分点；弃光率3.2%，同比下降3.0个百分点。新能源装机容量严重过剩的甘肃、新疆2省弃电率超过15%；吉林、蒙东、冀北弃电率超过5%、低于15%；其余均低于5%。除冀北、山西和山东外的中东部地区均不弃电。

（三）促进清洁能源发展与消纳相关措施

2018年，国调中心加强清洁能源调度运行管理，促进清洁能源发展与消纳。在清洁能源全年依然保持快速发展态势下，实现了新能源发电量及占比“双升”，弃电量和弃电率“双降”；西南地区实现了调峰弃水电量和弃电率“双降”。

1. 保障清洁能源安全运行。①推进《风电场接入电力系统技术规定》修订；组织各省公司等单位参加标准技术研讨会和风电机组高电压穿越改造协调会，获得各方理解和支持。②开展部分地区风电高电压穿越先行改造。东北鲁固直流送端风电机组完成改造容量841万kW，占需改造容量的69%；西北祁韶、天中、灵韶等直流送端改造容量1411万kW，占需改造容量的49%；项目共提升改造地区新能源跨省跨区外送能力超过400万kW，弃风弃光问题有效缓解。③发挥三峡、溪洛渡、锦西等水库防洪作用，保证度汛安全。根据电网需求加强汛前消落和汛末蓄水过程控制，尽最大可能减少整体弃水损失。④督促做好丰满大坝重建期间水库调度，确保施工期间度汛安全；按照老坝拆除进度需要，从10月起分阶段控制丰满水位，为安全施工创造条件。

2. 促进清洁能源消纳。①根据清洁能源资源状况和发电特点确定检修窗口期，优化停电检修，尽力减少因停电检修造成的弃电损失。②加强国、网、省三级电网水库群联合调度与协调，充分利用大电网优势提高全梯级、全流域水能利用水平。③充分华中、西北等电网“电量库”开展外送清洁能源“中途”调蓄，月内滚平，有效解决部分外送通道安全约束与清洁能源外送需求之间的矛盾。④开展新能源消纳能力测算，明确消纳控制目标。形成能力测算分析报告。⑤强化平衡能力建设。深化新能源场站理论功率、可发功率和功率预测等信息接入研究，为新能源参与现货交易提供数据支撑。⑥加强新能源功率预测管理。西北将评价指标纳入“两个细则”考核，短期、超短期预测准确率分别提升5个和2个百分点，准确率均达到95%以上；浙江、江苏等省开展分布式电源预测工作，预测准确率均达到85%以上。⑦加强新能源场站基础数据管理工作。完成了5年风光资源收资订正和对标考核，数据质量提升明显。⑧加强新能源优先调度工作。冀北等地编制光伏扶贫电站优先调度细则；西北开展分层分区新能源受阻在线评估，构建基于72h新能源预测快速响应机制，指导新能源优先调度。

3. 相关技术及应用研究。主要开展了①风电/光伏发电功率预测技术及应用研究。②分布式光伏发电广域监测分析与全局出力估计关键技术研究。③新能源消纳大数据平台研发与数据挖掘应用。④储能对电网发展及运行影响和信息接入研究。⑤充分挖掘供热系统热惯性和运行灵活性研究，提升供热期新能源消纳水平；启动新一代主动支撑技术示范风电场建设；开展风电防冰抗冰技术研究，提升电网迎峰度冬期间整体供电能力。

（国家电网公司国家电力调度控制中心
周才期）

2018年华北电网新能源消纳情况

（一）新能源发展情况

1. 分布总体情况　华北电网新能源资源丰富，其中京津唐、山西、山东及蒙西电网分布较多。京津唐电网风光资源主要在张家口、承德地区。河北南网风光资源主要在石家庄、保定、邯郸、沧州地区。山西电网新能源主要在大同和忻朔地区。山东电网风光资源主要在东部、北部沿海地区和潍坊、泰安、济宁、菏泽地区。蒙西电网新能源主要在巴彦淖尔、鄂尔多斯、包头、呼和浩特、乌兰察布及锡林郭勒地区。

2. 新能源装机容量情况　截至2018年底，华北电网新能源装机容量突破8000万kW，达到8379万kW，同比增长18.8%。其中，风电装机容量5529万kW，同比增长16.1%；光伏装机容量2849万kW，同比增长24.4%。各省电网装机容量情况：京津唐1967万kW，河北南网537万kW，山西1621万kW，山东1791万kW，蒙西2462万kW。

（二）新能源发电情况

1. 最大电力情况　2018年，华北电网风电最大电力3227.9万kW，光伏最大电力1881.8万kW。各省网风电最大电力：京津唐780.3万kW、河北南网154.7万kW、山西741.0万kW、山东863.7万kW、蒙西1218.0万kW。光伏最大电力：京津唐389.9万kW、河北352.8万kW、山西442.7万kW、山东461.5万kW、蒙西470.5万kW。上述均创历史新高。

2. 发电电量情况　2018年，新能源发电量1456.55亿kW·h，同比增长21.2%；风电发电量1116.35亿kW·h，同比增长17.3%；光伏发电量340.21亿kW·h，同比增长35.7%。各省网新能源发电量情况见表1。

表1　2018年华北电网新能源发电量情况统计表

电网	华北	京津唐	河北	山西	山东	蒙西	备注
新能源发电量	1456.55	341.51	67.45	283.32	287.69	476.58	表中单位：亿kW·h
风电发电量	1116.35	276.09	30.53	212.11	211.04	386.57	
光伏发电量	340.21	65.41	36.93	71.21	76.65	90.01	

2018年，华北电网内京津唐、山西、山东电网新能源弃电量25.38亿kW·h，同比减少2.08亿kW·h；弃电率2.52%，同比减少0.86%，实现“双降”。新能源弃电以网架约束为主。新能源弃电量中网架原因弃电占比94.4%，调峰原因弃电占比5.6%，调峰弃电集中发生在春节期间的特殊时段。其中，京津唐电网网架弃电占比达到99.89%。

3. 外受电情况　2018年，华北网通过多条跨区联络线消纳区域外部清洁能源291.82亿kW·h，同比增长21.3%，认真落实国家电网“全国一盘棋”消纳新能源工作部署。

（三）促进消纳主要措施

1. 强化火电机组统一调度　按照国网规定要求，华北网对网内362台30万kW以上机组实施许可调度。由华北各省向分中心上报次日开停机方式、电力平衡及新能源消纳。通过组织各省会商，优化调整各省开机方式，对开机容量过大省网提出减少备用容量和停机要求，腾出调峰空间消纳其他省网新能源。日内根据实际情况督导各省网安排深度调峰。

2. 实施京津冀一体化消纳　根据河北省发展改革委有关要求，华北调控分中心2018年2月起实施京津冀一体化可再生能源消纳工作。河北省调向华北调控分中心上报负荷预测、开停机方案预安排。华北调控分中心依据京津唐、河北南网电力平衡和新能源消纳需要，统一安排京津冀开机方式，提出调整建议，在满足电力平衡情况下，腾出调峰空间消纳京津冀地区新能源，提高京津冀电网消纳空间200万kW以上。

3. 建设辅助服务市场　建立涵盖日前、日内、实时不同时间周期华北调峰辅助服务市场。理论联系实际，充分考虑电网安全运行和新能源消纳需求，以火电机组平均负荷率为动态标尺，充分释放价格信号，实现全华北统一边际价格出清。在全国率先实现每15分钟实时出清、自动安全校核、闭环执行功能。华北电网参与申报的机组共计692台，容量共计2.41亿kW。在新能源消纳方面起到了重要作用。

4. 功率预测纳入电力平衡　华北调控分中心研究并应用了新能源功率带预测方法，分析富风期和枯风期不同出力范围下新能源预测的正、负偏差，形成新能源功率预测上下带宽，并在日前电力平衡安排时，按下带宽安排负荷高峰正备用，按上带宽安排负荷低谷负备用，确保高峰电网安全和低谷消纳空间。京津唐电网富风期风电预测600万kW以上时，将91.3%的风电功率预测值纳入电力平衡，实现功率预测结果高比例纳入日前出力平衡。

5. 开展新能源功率分区预测　在京津唐电网中沽源、万全、张南、康保尚义、金山岭和御道口等6个新能源重点汇集地区开展分区预测，形成精细化汇集区新能源短期和超短期预测，并根据汇集区断面约束进行预测结果安全校核，将安全校核后的新能源功率预测纳入电力平衡，提高新能源纳入电力平衡精准度。

6. 科学风电送出线路检修　华北电网充分利用6～9月小风期间，合理安排影响新能源消纳输变电设备计划检修。紧凑排布工期，提前发布检修信息，与新能源发电企业做好沟通，尽量安排风电企业与电网输变电设备同步检修。施工中，密切跟踪设备检修进度，及时了解施工进展。检修完工之前预先准备送电操作票，完工后尽快送电，将输变电检修原因引起的限风减至最低。

7. 充分发挥调峰互济优势　华北电网充分发挥大电网资源配置优势，利用不同地区间用电负荷、风电发电错时特性，安排负荷低谷等重要时段省间联络线互济。2018年，组织开展省间联络线支援239次，有力促进了华北区域各省新能源消纳工作。华北电网在深入分析风电等新能源在华北区域范围内波动平缓、预测准确率高等特点，研究京、津、冀、鲁统一平衡问题，统筹实现新能源更大范围消纳。

（国家电网公司华北电力调控分中心　杨健）

2018年华东电网积极消纳清洁能源情况

（一）华东清洁能源消纳概况

1. 装机容量情况　截至2018年底，华东全网调度口径装机容量 36419 万 kW，区外直流总容量约 6500 万 kW（华东侧），区外直流容量占所有电源容量（含直流）15%，已成为仅次于燃煤机组的第二大类电源，风电、光伏等新能源机组继续快速增长，分别同比增长 19%和 26%，两者合计装机容量接近所有电源容量（含直流）10%。

2. 发电情况　2018 年因来水减少，华东电网区内常规水电累计发电量 440.74 亿 kW・h，同比减少 13.03%。风电累计发电量 329.6 亿 kW・h，同比增长 25.27%，光伏累计发电量 233.06 亿 kW・h，同比增长 136.95%。风光累计发电量占全网用电量的 3.5%。华东网内新能源最大出力 2215 万 kW（8 月 23 日），风电最大电力 1167 万 kW（12 月 7 日）、光伏最大出力 1607 万 kW（10 月 1 日）。2018 年，华东网内无弃风弃光电量，实现全额消纳。

3. 区外来电消纳情况　2018 年华东电网接入跨区直流达到 11 回，年度最大区外来电电力 3800.9 万 kW（7 月 27 日），占当日华东最高用电负荷的 14.13%，累计消纳电量 1936.72 亿 kW・h，同比增长 17.01%。全年累计组织跨区域富余可再生能源现货交易 3057 笔，合计消纳电量 16.8 亿 kW・h。

（二）清洁能源消纳工作措施

1. 积极推动调峰辅助市场建设　2018 年，华东分部积极推动调峰辅助市场建设，实现以市场机制引导调峰资源优化配置，为电网安全运行和清洁能源大规模消纳保驾护航。

2018 年 9 月 6 日，国家能源局下发《国家能源局关于同意华北、华东电力辅助服务市场试点工作的复函》。9 月 13 日，国家能源局华东监管局下发通知，明确华东电力调峰辅助服务市场于 2018 年 9 月底开展模拟运行。华东电力调峰辅助服务市场通过市场化机制实现了省间调峰互济，建立了华东分中心与省市调协调的跨省调峰辅助服务市场“需求申报—分省交易组织—全网统一出清—两级安全校核”的调峰辅助服务市场运行机制，通过市场化手段调动发电企业参与跨省调峰的积极性，缓解了华东电网调峰困难局面。华东电力调峰辅助服务市场更创新性地提出了一种根据发电企业因自身调峰不足而多发电量确定发电企业调峰电量分摊比例，进而根据调峰电量分摊比例确定发电企业调峰辅助服务分摊费用的方法，从而公平、公正、合理地解决了调峰费用分摊问题。

2. 加大抽蓄利用力度　华东调控分中心还适应区外清洁能源送电规模不断扩大和区内新能源快速发展趋势，积极研究上海和安徽电网负荷特性和用电平衡形势，挖掘潜力充分利用现有抽蓄电站调峰资源形成“琅琊山和响水涧抽蓄电站电力优化分配方案”。2018 年 5 月 30 日，华东分部组织召开了“国网上海市、安徽省电力公司 2018 年琅琊山和响水涧抽蓄电站电力优化分配框架协议签字仪式”。华东分中心即根据优化方案开展月度和日前的优化曲线安排工作。最大为上海电网夜间低谷和安徽电网腰荷分别增加 88 万 kW 和 176 万 kW 的负备用支撑能力，为上海电网和安徽电网高峰用电分别增加 80 万 kW 和 160 万 kW 的正备用支撑能力，有效缓解安徽电网腰荷调峰压力，有序减少华东网内调组停机台次并减小机组调节幅度，切实提升新能源消纳水平。此外，根据需要加大抽蓄利用力度，特别是 2018 年福建电网半岭抽蓄电站综合利用小时数高达 4624h，同比增加 25.19%。电站单台机组日均启动次数为 2.7 次，年均发电运行时长 2683h，均列全国第一，为最大化消纳清洁能源作出了积极贡献。

3. 大力开展储能技术应用　2018 年，江苏电力公司大力开展储能技术创新示范工作。年底建成电网侧储能电站一座，容量 10.1 万 kW/20.2 万 kW 时；用户侧储能电站 57 座，容量 9.499 万 kW /68.441 万 kW 时，在建用户侧储能电站 21 座，容量 6.110 万 kW /48.150 万 kW 时。江苏电网侧储能电站是目前全球容量最大、功能最全、首套实现毫秒级源网荷储响应的储能系统。储能电站采用“两充两放”或“一充一放”的日前调度计划运行模式参与早、晚用电高峰调节。10 月起，优化储能调控策略，参与大电网实时调节，采用 AGC（自动发电控制）模式，以计划值为基点功率，参与江苏电网区域控制偏差调整，并实现源网荷储、一次调频、AGC 的响应优先级。在国庆负荷低谷期间，采用新能源跟踪模式，平抑光伏反调峰特性，促进新能源消纳。

4. 加强分布式光伏信息采集管理　适应光伏扶贫政策的实施，协调安徽电网积极开展分布式电源调度管理工作。为满足安徽大量 380V/220V 低压分布式电源（共 99043 处，容量 271 万 kW）的信息采集需要，通过在地市调度主站建设无线安全接入区，其中部分地调还建设了北斗通信主站，调度管辖范围内分布式光伏信息接入率达到 100%。户用低压分布式光伏通过智能电表 HPLC 模块，实现全天 96 点运行信息的准实时采集，为开展低压分布式管理和群控群调提供了基础支撑。

（国家电网华东电力调控分中心　陆建宇）

2018 年西北电网积极消纳清洁能源情况

（一）西北电网清洁能源运行概况

截至 2018 年底，西北电网统调口径水电装机

4527台，装机容量3138.6万kW，占全网统调总装机容量的12.44%；风电场445座，装机容量4891.4万kW，占全网统调总装机容量的19.38%；光伏电站1202座，装机容量4050.7万kW，占全网总装机容量的16.05%。西北电网清洁能源发展呈现以下特点：

1. 水电发电量增长明显　2018年新增调度口径水电机组22台，总装机容量41.2万kW，装机以小水电为主，主要集中在甘肃、新疆、陕西区域。2018年黄河上游来水代表站（唐乃亥水文站）断面径流量288.93亿m^3，同比偏多56.84%，比常年偏多44.71%，属丰水年。全网水电发电量1278亿kW·h，同比增长32.71%。其中龙羊峡、拉西瓦、李家峡、公伯峡、积石峡、刘家峡水电站，实际完成发电量466.11亿kW·h，同比增长76%。

2. 新能源装机高速增长　2009年以来，西北新能源装机容量年均增速51.16%，2018年达到8942万kW，超过全网最大用电负荷，较年初新增1036万kW，占各类型电源总装机容量的35.43%，其中风电4891万kW，光伏4051万kW。分省来看，甘肃、青海、宁夏和新疆的新能源穿透率（新能源装机/用电负荷）均已超过100%（最大的新疆为157.46%）。

3. 新能源发电量逐年提升　2009年以来，西北新能源发电量年均增速50.47%，2018年发电量1352.01亿kW·h，同比增长22.50%，占全网总发电量的17.60%，其中风电870.16亿kW·h，同比增长22.42%，光伏481.85亿kW·h，同比增长22.65%。2018年以来西北新能源单日发电量创新高达8次。从全国来看，西北新能源年发电量及占总发电量比例在“三北”地区（华北不含蒙西）均为最高，从国内外来看，甘肃、青海新能源年发电量占总发电量的比例均超过20%。

4. 新能源高占比成为常态　2018年，西北新能源最大出力达到3725万kW，占当时全网用电负荷的45.25%；新能源单日最大发电量5.93亿kW·h，占当日全网用电量的31.95%，以上指标在“三北”（华北不含蒙西）地区均为最高。公司系统中，新能源出力占用电负荷最大比例超过80%的省级电网共4个，其中3个在西北（甘86.16%、青99.91%、宁91.11%），新能源占比越大，电网运行的不确定因素越多，工作难度越大，而西北新能源高占比运行已经成为常态。

5. 新能源受阻情况稳步改善　2018年西北新能源受阻电量215.51亿kW·h，同比降低27.71%，受阻率为13.75%，同比降低7.52个百分点；其中风电受阻电量为168.37亿kW·h，同比降低28.05%，弃风率为16.21%，同比降低8.56个百分点；光伏受阻电量为47.14亿kW·h，同比降低26.48%，弃光率为8.91%，同比降低5.12个百分点；分省来看，陕西、青海和宁夏新能源受阻率已在5%以内，甘肃新能源受阻率降至16.77%，同比降低13.04个百分点，新疆新能源受阻率降至21.33%，同比降低6.58个百分点。

（二）西北电网保证清洁能源消纳措施

1. 水电方面　①加强每日“水”“电”运行特性分析，有效减少水库闸门调节次数。针对水库泄水闸门不能频繁连续调节、且泄水和发电流量高度耦合的特点，逐日优化制定水库泄水闸门运行方式。同时完善弃水、发电流量监视控制功能，精益化控制不同时段的发电出库流量。②建立直调电源调频辅助控制区，满足电网调频和减弃增发双要求。为减少水电调峰和弃水，创新将西北电网东部地区直调火电纳入控制区进行调节，“智能”调用全网直调火电跟踪水电调频裕度，有效降低水电机组预留的调频备用容量最低至70万kW，实现了水电发电总电量的“提升”；“智能”跟踪送出通道功率并进行自动调节，每秒钟刷新一次调节指令，水电大发时送出通道断面负载率稳定在97%左右，调节频率和精度明显改善，实现了水电送出通道利用率的“提升”。③积极组织各方交易，跨省跨区消纳水电。加大协调力度，组织黄河水电通过中长期跨区跨省交易送出。充分利用大电网资源配置能力，积极开展日前、实时交易及置换，组织富余水电跨省消纳。汛期累计开展各类短期交易523笔，减少青海弃水电量16.35亿kW·h。

2. 新能源方面　①首创大电网备用统筹新模式。借助大数据分析提炼新能源保证出力，并科学纳入备用，降低火电开机方式；利用新能源的“时空差异”，充分发挥电网的资源平台作用，通过省间互济，保证电能平衡和新能源消纳。2018年通过“全网负备用”，累计增发新能源128亿kW·h。②创新管理机制。国内首次建立“新能源发电快速响应及柔性调度机制”，形成了“精准预测—提前预控—实时调度—后评估”的科学管理体系。该机制成功入选国家电网有限公司管理创新类项目，并荣获2018年国家电网有限公司职工创新“双越之星”劳动竞赛银奖。③积极推进调度技术升级。创建“区域电网智能协调控制系统”，并在陕北成功试点，陕北外送断面在新能源大发期间利用率由90%提升至98%，降低新能源弃电率1.5个百分点，占总弃电率的三分之一。④创新电力市场建设。国内首创“虚拟储能＋水电丰枯双向参与＋深调电量替代”的区域省间调峰辅助服务市场运营模式，2018年市场试运行34天，增发新能源1.93亿kW·h。指导甘肃、宁夏、新疆开展省内调峰辅助服务市场试运行，累计增发新能源 6.90 亿 kW·h。⑤精心调控，大力开展各类交易促消纳。密切跟踪负荷、新能源变化，从日前、实时两个层面，加大跨省跨区交易组织力度，2018 年累计组织各类交易 21837 笔，增发新能源 221.39 亿 kW·h。⑥持续提升电网输送能力。加快建设系统保护，提升跨区及区内新能源送出关键断面输送能力约 800 万 kW。首创利用直流频率控制提升祁韶直流近区风电输送能力 60 万 kW，基本解决了近区新能源消纳受限。

（三）清洁能源消纳成效

2018 年，西北电网圆满完成新能源“双升双降”目标和公司新能源弃电控制要求，新能源受阻电量继 2017 年首次出现下降拐点后继续保持较大幅度降低。西北分部在做好本区域新能源消纳的同时，积极接纳四川和西藏地区的清洁能源，2018 年累计消纳四川水电 84.37 亿 kW·h，同比增长 22.82%，消纳西藏清洁能源 6.46 亿 kW·h。

（国家电网西北电力调控分中心　赵鑫 万筱钟）

2018 年西南电网清洁能源运行消纳情况

（一）西南电网清洁能源运行概况

截至 2018 年底，西南电网统调口径水电装机容量 7451.3 万 kW，占全网统调总装机容量的 69.7%；风电装机容量 302.5 万 kW，占全网统调总装机容量的 2.8%；光伏统调装机容量 289.0 万 kW，占全网总装机容量的 2.7%。水电装机增速放缓，同比增长 1.17%；新能源持续快速发展，同比增长 30.8%。

西南电网水电站数目多，装机容量大，近一半水电装机无调节性能。统调水电站总计 321 座（四川 279 座、重庆 29 座，西藏 13 座）。其中年及多年调节水电站共 23 座，装机容量 783.9 万 kW，占比 10.5%；不完全年及季调节水电站共 28 座，装机容量 2947.0 万 kW，占比 39.6%；径流式（含日周调节）水电站共 270 座，装机容量 3720.3 万 kW，占比 49.9%。新能源装机容量较小，风光资源主要集中在川西及西藏地区。

2018 年，西南电网统调口径清洁能源发电量 3105.3 亿 kW·h，同比增加 133.1 亿 kW·h，增幅 4.5%。其中水电发电量 3001.5 亿 kW·h，同比增加 103.8 亿 kW·h，增幅 3.6%；新能源发电量 94.1 亿 kW·h，同比增加 29.3 亿 kW·h，增幅 45.1%。

（二）藏中联网清洁能源调度管理

2018 年 12 月藏中联网工程顺利投运，将西藏电网调度权正式由西北电网移交至西南电网。联网后加强调度管理，采取有效措施促进清洁能源消纳：

1. 整编西藏水电及新能源基础资料　加强西藏网内水电厂基础参数信息、径流序列、水库特征曲线、机组振动区等基础信息收资管理，开展运行数据和重要参数整编修订工作；开展新能源基础数据整治工作，逐一核查接入数据准确性，提升电厂侧接入数据质量水平，保障上传数据准确可靠。

2. 完善水电及新能源技术支撑系统　指导西藏完成水调自动化系统建设工作，并结合清洁能源运行消纳实际，推动技术支持系统升级完善，全面提升运行监视、统计分析、资源预测、优化调度等支撑能力，实现西藏重要水电厂信息全覆盖；推动弃水统计分析模块、光伏弃电计算分析模块开发建设，为清洁能源消纳“日分析、旬总结、月汇报”提供数据支撑。

3. 全面细致做好清洁能源消纳　滚动开展水电及新能源消纳分析测算工作，为清洁能源优化运行调度提供决策支撑；开展提高西藏光伏接纳能力技术方案研究，加快光伏电厂低穿策略优化改造，采用新投常规电源、启用柴拉直流 FC、增加储能设备、新投调相机等增加电网频率调节能力的措施，提升电网频率稳定能力，进一步提高清洁能源消纳能力；充分发挥现有通道能力，增加日前和实时交易，按照西藏电网电力电量富余能力安排外送，进一步优化柴拉直流功率曲线，降低西藏电网清洁能源弃电量。

（三）促进西南清洁能源消纳措施

2018 年，西南电网全面落实国家清洁能源消纳各项政策，发挥大电网优势，开辟水电外送新途径，创新交易模式，顺利完成调峰弃水电量“双降”目标。

1. 加强水库优化调度　跟踪来水及天气变化，做好电厂及全网来水预测工作，提高水情预测精度。动态优化调整水库控制运用方案，充分发挥水库调蓄作用，开展水库汛限水位动态控制，做好枯水期水库消落及汛末水库蓄水工作，提高水能利用效率。强化《西南电网减弃措施响应管理办法》执行力度，进一步规范和优化减少弃水处置流程，严控弃水发生风险，提高水电减弃工作响应效率。加强与长江防总、能监部门、贵州电网、乌江水电公司的沟通联系，探索建立跨网、跨省、跨流域水电优化协调机制。

2. 开辟水电外送新途径　创新实施重庆电量库，充分利用西南全网调峰资源，将区内各类电能资源在电量库中统筹优化，通过跨区跨省互济实现资源共享，增开重庆火电提高川渝、渝鄂输电通道利用水平，极大地增加低谷时段富余四川水电外送，又实现了重庆电网跨时空余缺互济，解决重庆电网 10 月上旬负荷轻且水电富余、下旬负荷重且电煤消耗过快的问题，缓解了度冬高峰来临前存煤目标压力较大的难题，还累计净增四川水电外送 1.04 亿 kW·h。

3. 加强跨省跨区电力互剂　积极落实电力合作互济框架协议精神，协同华东、华中、西北分部积极开展跨区水火风光电能互济、水电应急交易，利用区域负荷峰谷特性差异开展错峰调度，采取四川水电经德宝、灵绍、银东以及祁韶等直流再转送“三华”电网灵活的输电路径，累计消纳富余水电约 5 亿 kW·h。

4. 积极组织跨区外送交易　创新开展试点交易，首次组织西南水电送华中抽蓄增量交易，达成交易电量 1.04 亿 kW·h；全面启动西南—华东电网跨区水火发电权交易，达成交易电量 9.4 亿 kW·h。积极组织短期交易，5～10 月累计实现跨区现货电量 5.52 亿 kW·h，二类交易电量 1.86 亿 kW·h，一类交易电量 1.39 亿 kW·h。

通过上述措施，在保证新能源全额消纳的基础上，2018 年西南电网调峰弃水电量 138.8 亿 kW·h，同比减少 22.1 亿 kW·h，降幅 13.7%，调峰弃水弃电率 4%，同比减少 0.8%，实现水电调峰弃水“双降”目标。

（国家电网西南电力调控分中心　赵羽西）

2018 年辽宁电网积极消纳清洁能源情况

（一）辽宁电网清洁能源发展情况

截至 2018 年底，辽宁电网清洁能源新增装机容量 133.72 万 kW，占全年新增装机容量的 41.30%；合计装机容量 1809.53 万 kW，占全网总装机容量 34.85%，同比提高 0.43 个百分点，其中：核电装机容量 447.52 万 kW，占全网总装机容量 8.62%；风电装机容量 760.74 万 kW，占全网总装机容量 14.65%；光伏装机容量 302.01 万 kW，占全网总装机容量 5.81%；水电装机容量 299.26 万 kW，占全网总装机容量 5.76%。电源结构不断向清洁低碳发展。

2018 年该电网清洁能源合计发电量 544.73 亿 kW·h，同比增加 23.11%；占全网总发电量的 28.29%，同比提高 3.59 个百分点，设备平均利用小时数 3134h，同比提高 279h。其中：核电发电量 301.57 亿 kW·h，设备平均利用小时数 6739h，同比提高 1466h；风电发电量 165.09 亿 kW·h，设备平均利用小时数 2264h，同比提高 123h；光伏发电量 31.91 亿 kW·h，设备平均利用小时数 1207h，同比提高 151h；水电发电量 46.16 亿 kW·h，设备平均利用小时数 1556h，同比提高 13h。

2018 年该电网弃风电量 1.61 亿 kW·h，同比减少 11.61 亿 kW·h，同比降低 87.89%；弃风率 0.97%，同比降低 7.1 个百分点。2018 年辽宁电网未发生弃光情况。提前 2 年完成国家《清洁能源消纳行动计划（2018～2020 年）》中风电利用率达 95%的行动目标。

（二）促进清洁能源消纳主要举措

1. 加强电网承载力建设　①加快电网工程投运。500kV 宽邦、阜新输变电工程投运，新能源输电能力和供电可靠性大幅提升；多级联动，136 天内安排各电压等级线路配合停电 204 条次，推进 500kV 红南二线建设。②推进安控系统建设。深入分析潮流分布不均限制核电全方式运行成因，全力将装置试运时间缩减至 10 天以内，安控投运后每年可释放核电发电能力约 30 亿 kW·h；努力推进新能源集中地区安控系统建设，每年多消纳新能源电量约 2.85 亿kW·h。③厂网配合确保鲁固直流作用发挥。按期建成鲁固直流系统保护一期工程，6 座火电、2 座水电高频切机装置正式投运运行；完成原水电外送稳控装置改造，为直调梯级水电站可靠运行提供坚实保障。④科学安排电网运行方式。结合新能源发电预测，滚动调整 66kV 及以上输电线路停电 23 次，多消纳新能源电量约 9100 万 kW·h。

2. 打造“透明调度”模式　①开展“三公开”。即全面公开电网实时运行信息，合规公开电力调峰市场运营信息，主动公开发电企业集中关注的关键过程信息，切实提升“三公”调度水平。②转变调度管理理念。主动服务优化营商环境工作大局，发布新能源电站并网“一站式服务”“两个工作日办结”等承诺制度。并网流程平均处理时间由 7 天降为 2 天，相关各方对电网企业认同度明显提升。③提升服务能力。实现全网 4721 台风机轴瓦温度、机舱温度等关键信息全接入，集中开展风机全状态监测和大数据分析。

3. 提升清洁能源发电水平　①发挥大电网联络线动态互济优势。2018 年公司在 7 天预测支撑前提下深化备用共享机制，在风电大发时，积极协调国调东北分中心给予联络线支援，通过日内联络线临时调整接纳风电 14.4 亿 kW·h，充分发挥了辽宁作为东北电网负荷中心的资源调配作用。发挥特高压鲁固直流、高岭直流跨区输电能力，实现省内过剩清洁能源跨区消纳，2018 年合计送华北电量 37.72 亿 kW·h。②实现各类清洁能源统筹最优。按照“风电少弃与核电多发兼顾”原则，在风电多弃 1 亿 kW·h 情况下，以较小弃风代价，实现红沿河年发电量同比增长 27.80%，清洁能源消纳实现统筹最优。③统筹水电调度运行。2018 年，浑江流域经历了主汛期干旱枯水、汛末两次台风带来的集中强降雨过程，通过兼顾水电运行和民生用水需求，动态调整水库运行策略，将汛末桓仁水库控制在300.48m，既实现了桓仁水库高水位蓄水，又避免了不完全年调节的桓仁电站弃水，同时，在桓仁转满发后，及时与省防沟通，提前启动大伙房引水工作，减少下游弃水1.3亿m^3，折合发电量2900万kW·h，实现水电高效综合利用。

4. 推进火电机组灵活性改造　积极推动火电灵活性改造，电网调峰能力提升显著。①改造方式灵活多样。各电厂结合本厂实际，采取电蓄热锅炉、锅炉旁路系统改造、高背压改造、切低压缸等多种形式，增加调峰能力。②改造范围大、调峰效果好。截至2018年底，完成22台火电机组灵活性改造，容量762万kW，增加调峰能力209万kW，占国家电网有限公司经营区改造容量的一半以上。

5. 深入辽宁调峰市场运营　辽宁深调电量全网占比和调峰收益增速均连续多年超过50%，跨省调峰支援电量全网占比接近60%。①清洁能源消纳受益明显。2018年辽宁火电企业超过最小运行方式增加调峰电量68.44亿kW·h（有偿调峰电量20.96亿kW·h），同比增长37.10%，增量空间全部用于接纳清洁能源发电。②跨省调峰支撑作用巨大。2018年辽宁火电企业向北两省一区提供低谷调峰支援电量16.62亿kW·h（含无偿支援），跨省收益4.25亿元。

（国家电网辽宁省电力有限公司　孙明一）

2018年河南电网积极消纳清洁能源情况

2018年，河南电网积极落实国家电网公司促进清洁能源消纳各项工作部署，通过采取强化新能源并网运行管理、完善新能源消纳管理体系、持续加大外电入豫力度、优化储能电站全网统一调度等措施，积极吸纳外省清洁能源的同时，实现了省内清洁能源快速发展中的全额消纳。

（一）清洁能源运行消纳成效

1. 省内风光新能源装机快速增长　经过近三年快速发展，风光新能源装机容量增长近10倍。风光新能源装机容量占全网各类电源装机容量比例由2015年的2%增长至2018年的17%。2018年全年新增风光新能源装机规模522万kW，新增规模居全国第三。截至2018年底，全省风光新能源总装机容量已达1459万kW（含集中式光伏电站600万kW、集中式风电场463万kW、分布式光伏391万kW、分散式风电5万kW），位列全国第9位。

2. 大力吸收外省清洁能源　2018年公司发挥特高压互联电网优势，通过优化电网运行方式和开机方式，利用跨区特高压交直流通道，大力吸纳外省清洁能源电力，提高外来电力在河南电力消费结构中占比，减少省内燃煤电厂污染物排放。全年购入省外清洁能源电量260.8亿kW·h（其中水电112.2亿kW·h、风电127.7亿kW·h、光伏20.9亿kW·h），占外购总电量60.1%，折合减少电费消耗1201.3万t。其中购入西北电网风电、光伏电量148.6亿kW·h，在国家电网系统购电省份中位居前列。全年跨区域可再生能源现货市场吸收西北弃风弃光电力16.5亿kW·h，交易电量居全国首位。

3. 确保省内清洁能源全额消纳　通过加强新能源并网运行管理、强化新能源运行承载力分析、创新促进清洁能源消纳新技术应用、深化新能源发电功率预测与结果应用等，实现了省内清洁能源快速发展中的全额消纳。2018年全额消纳省内风光水清洁能源电力284.7亿kW·h，同比增长110.4亿kW·h，同比增长63.4%。

（二）保障新能源消纳采取的措施

1. 新能源考核管理系统建设　为保障电网安全稳定运行，落实国家可再生能源政策，规范新能源场站并网调度运行管理，积极促请河南能监办制定《河南风电场及光伏电站并网运行管理实施细则》，成为首家由国家能源局正式批复印发的省级细则，并率先建成国内功能较为完善的河南电网新能源并网运行管理系统，成为新能源大规模接入形势下保障电网安全稳定运行的有力抓手。

2. 完善新能源消纳管理体系　协同公司发展、营销、交易等部门，建立促进河南电网新能源消纳组织机构和会商机制，明确职责分工。在国内省级电网公司中率先组织地市公司滚动开展新能源运行承载能力分析工作，密切跟踪政府新能源规划及核准或分配指标的风电和光伏项目进展情况，针对存在消纳风险的区域及时发布风险预警，并积极与政府对接反映情况，推动有序接入，服务新能源持续健康发展。

3. 持续加大外电入豫力度　通过优化电网运行方式和开机方式，充分发挥抽蓄机组、燃气机组等调峰能力，留足电网吸纳空间，确保具备跨区直流全天满功率接纳能力。依托全国统一电力市场资源大范围优化配置优势，主动加强与新疆、甘肃、四川等清洁能源资源丰富省份联系沟通，最大限度购入西北地区弃风、弃光电量。充分利用跨区跨省通道输电空间，灵活采用多种交易方式，在保障电网安全运行前提下，最大限度提高清洁能源消纳规模。

4. 储能电站优化运行研究　优化分布式储能电站调度，实施省内分布式储能电站统一调度，充分发挥储能电站削峰填谷、调峰调频作用，开展储能电站与水电、燃气机组联合 AGC 快速控制研究，发挥储能装置响应快速优点，减小新能源波动对电网运行影响，提高电网安全稳定运行水平。强化创新成果培育，高质量开展电化学储能电站并网运行与控制国家标准制定。

5. 提升新能源功率预测精度　以功率预测准确率考核为抓手，加大数据上报率考核力度，促进新能源功率预测建模及方法技术进步。深度挖掘规律性问题，重点关注天气变化情况下新能源功率预测模型描述，有针对性地优化计算模型算法，提高预测算法灵敏度水平。结合国网指南科研项目《考虑云、浮尘等复杂因素的光伏出力特性多时空尺度变化规律研究与应用》实施，开展省调侧考虑云、浮沉等复杂因素区域新能源功率预测，改变现有仅将各场站数据求和作为全省预测结果的状况，通过在主站进行考虑相应因素修正后进行发布，从而在本质上提升省网新能源功率预测准确性。

（国家电网河南电力调度控制中心　柴旭铮）

2018 年青海电网清洁能源消纳情况

（一）清洁能源消纳情况

2018 年，青海电网新能源发电量 168 亿 kW·h，同比增加 48.7%，弃电量 7.13 亿 kW·h，同比减少 0.37 亿 kW·h，弃电率 4.1%，圆满完成“双降"指标。龙羊峡水库年初水位高，受连续降雨影响，黄河上游流域来水持续偏丰，水电全年发电量 510.4 亿 kW·h，同比增加 55.9%，7～10 月出现弃水，调峰弃水电量 31.09 亿 kW·h。截至 2018 年底，青海新能源装机容量 1415.5 万 kW，水电装机容量 1193.3 万 kW，其中新能源装机年增长率达到 43.21%，为近五年来最高。新能源装机容量占总装机容量 47.38%，是全省第一大装机容量，在全国各省（区）排名第一。

（二）促进清洁能源消纳

1. 拓展清洁能源消纳空间　组织相关部门定期会商，统筹安排清洁能源就地消纳及跨省外送。促成省内清洁能源与大用户开展直接交易，其中新能源交易电量 57.89 亿 kW，水电交易电量 80.5 亿 kW，稳定了省内消纳市场。2018 年青海公司跨区跨省清洁能源外送首次突破 100 亿 kW 大关，完成清洁能源外送 100.65 亿 kW·h，省间清洁能源消纳同比增长近 1.4 倍，标志着公司清洁能源消纳迈入新的阶段。

2. 深度开发调峰能力　①通过省内多能协调控制，根据水电发电和负荷变化，午间光伏大发时段水电机组参与深度调峰，进一步优化调整北部火电最小开机，提升新能源消纳空间。②积极参与跨省跨区实时和现货交易，开展实时交易送出新能源 1.42 亿 kW·h，开展现货交易累计送出新能源 2.77 亿 kW·h。③开展陕青调峰互济 101 笔，减少光伏调峰限电 4.35 亿 kW·h。2018 年 11 月，西北区域电力辅助服务市场启动试运行，调峰实行市场化。

3. 推进新能源网架建设　2018 年 12 月，750kV 月海柴串补工程建成投运，新疆一西北联网二通道电气距离缩短，青海海西地区电压稳定水平得到较大提升，日间海西新能源外送断面提升 80 万 kW，海西地区新能源受限问题得到有效缓解。

4. 最大减少新能源弃电　统筹安排新能源电站与电网检修同期进行，通过实施新能源受限风险预警机制，减少新能源弃电 1.5 亿 kW·h。

（三）重视清洁能源供电实践

在充分总结 2017 年“绿电 7 日”经验基础上，开展了以“保安全、全清洁、市场化”促进新能源最大化消纳为目标的“绿电 9 日”全清洁能源供电新实践。成功引入实施“两个机制”；深化应用“两项技术”；突出市场化“两种交易”。

1. 引入实施“两个机制”　①实施调峰补偿机制，对“绿电 9 日”期间并网机组实施调峰补偿，火电机组进行深度调峰，出力最低降至 25.5 万 kW。“绿电 9 日”期间，火电机组出力最多降低了 35 万 kW，平均降低 30 万 kW，火电机组电量累计减发 3722.9 万 kW·h，日均减发 413.7 万 kW·h，提升光伏消纳电量 4%。②实施负荷参与调峰机制，组织受限新能源（直购除外）与铁合金增量（直购除外）企业开展省内现货交易。“绿电 9 日”期间新型制造业在 8：00－20：00 负荷电量累计增加 1548.1 万 kW·h，日均增加 172 万 kW·h，提升光伏消纳电量 3%。

2. 深化应用“两项技术”　①深化应用多能互补协调控制技术。利用青海光伏、风电和水电自然、多尺度多能互补优化运行特性，以新能源和负荷短期、超短期功率预测为基础，实施省内风、光、水、火多能协调控制。新能源大发期间，根据电网运行状态实时调节各个新能源电站有功出力，AGC 按最小出力自动下调省内水、火电机组出力，使电网在同时满足多级嵌套断面安全限值以及网调调频机组旋备基础上，实现全网新能源优先消纳以及新能源厂站之间发电能力转移。②深化应用大数据技术。通过整合新能源全产业链资源优势，在国内首次开发建设针对新能源企业集中监控、功率预测、设备健康管理、共享储能、备件联储等 21 项大数据业务创新平台，推动新能源发展。

3. 突出市场化“两种交易”　①开展发电权交易，“绿电9日”期间，通过市场化手段组织停备火电机组与新能源企业开展发电权交易，达成1.99亿kW·h交易电量，停机火电企业增加收益597万元，新能源增发电量收益1.3亿元以上。②组织新能源企业与三江源地区电能替代项目直接交易，采用“价差平移”方式，使三江源地区居民真正享受到“绿电9日”带来的实惠。6月成交电量340.57万kW·h，新能源企业让利3分钱，三江源清洁能源供暖项目通过平移资金减少用电成本10.22万元。

4. 电量及节能减排情况　“绿电9日”期间，全省发电量20.95亿kW·h，清洁能源发电量占96.9%。其中水电发电量占76.9%、风电占4.6%、太阳能占15.4%、火电占3.1%。火电发电量全部以市场化手段外送，省内用电全部由清洁能源提供。“绿电9日”期间，清洁能源累计供电量17.6亿kW·h，相当于减少燃煤80万t，减排二氧化碳144万t，企业用电实现零排放，对培育工业经济发展新动能具有重要推动作用。

（国家电网青海省电力公司　李延和）

青海共和5万kW光热电站工程2018年建设管理情况

中国电建青海共和5万kW光热发电项目位于青海省海南州共和县海南生态太阳能发电园区内，距县城约12km，平均海拔2880m，占地面积约2.1km²。项目设计总装机规模为5万kW，站区设计呈直径为1632m的圆形，吸热塔位于站区镜场接近圆心位置，单台定日镜的面积为20m²，由4片5m²的子镜面组成，共30016面定日镜，镜场总采光面积约为60万m²，采用塔式聚光太阳能热发电直接空冷机组，配套汽轮机形式为超高压、一次中间再热、8级抽汽直接空冷，汽轮机容量为5万kW。并配套建设保证汽轮发电机组额定功率满发约6h的熔盐储热系统，以发电机—变压器—线路单元接线方式接入自建的110kV升压站送出，通过一回110kV架空线路接入共塔330kV升压汇集站，送出线路长度约11km。电站建成后运行期内年均设计发电量为15692.4万kW·h，年利用小时数3138h。

为推动我国太阳能热发电技术产业化发展，2015年9月国家能源局发布《关于组织太阳能热发电示范项目建设的通知》，2016年9月，国家能源局选定了20家首批光热发电示范项目，总装机容量134.9万kW，分布在青海省、甘肃省、河北省、内蒙古自治区、新疆维吾尔自治区，水电顾问青海共和5万kW光热发电项目是国家首批光热示范项目之一。项目由中国水电工程顾问集团有限公司和中电建西北勘测设计研究院有限公司共同投资建设。

（一）工程建设进展

2018年5月6日工程正式开工，截至2018年底，建设进度如下：办公宿舍楼主体及室内装修已完成，基本具备入住条件；吸热塔于2018年9月18日顺利封顶，11月22日193m顶层平台浇筑完成，主体结构完成；塔顶吸热器管屏完成吊装27片（总32片）；低温罐焊接制作完成；高温储罐正在进行焊接制作；换热区结构钢框架安装基本完成，正在进行储换热设备及熔盐管道安装工作；常规岛土建施工已基本完成，发电机定子、中低压缸、除氧器、低温加热器、GIS、主变压器、高压厂用变压器、启动备用变压器、6kV盘柜、控制电源盘柜等设备已安装就位；空冷岛混凝土框架完成；定日镜完成安装29845套（总30016套），组镜箱、行镜箱等已安装完成，镜组箱接线完成121套；10kV送出线路工程场内主电缆沟已全部完成，塔基基础浇筑及铁塔安装完成28基；35kV厂用线路的塔基及杆塔组立、架线、电缆敷设已完成。

（二）工程建设管理

共和光热项目是中国电建集团首个自主投资、设计和建设的光热项目，作为国家光热示范性项目，共和光热项目工艺技术复杂、技术集成度高，涉及设备繁多，工期紧迫，无成熟经验可循，工程建设有很大难度和风险，项目管理千头万绪。如何管理好该项目的工程建设，对缺乏各类专业人员和技术支撑、新组建的项目公司是一个严峻的考验和挑战。根据工程现场实际，主要开展了以下工作：①务实管理工程进度、扎实稳妥推进工程建设。公司及时组织召开各类专题会议，认真梳理工程进度情况，加强工程建设进度管理。本着认真务实，积极、扎实、稳妥的原则，坚决杜绝忽视安全和质量的盲目赶工。②完善工程建设管理体系，强化现场施工质量管理。依据相关标准、制度，结合项目实际，编制完成工程建设质量、进度、档案等十余项管理制度，建立健全了质量管理、档案管理等责任体系。在工程施工管理中，严格建设过程中质量、计划、安全管理，并从外部聘请专家对工程建设质量加强管理。对存在问题积极面对，组织各参建方和专家，认真分析及时有效解决。项目建设质量在2018年青海省电力质监站组织的两次质量监督检查中，得到了充分肯定。③扎实深入项目建设各环节工作，补充、完善和优化设计，及时发现协调解决出现的各类问题。面对光热项目国内相关设计规范、标准等目前仍大多处于空白状态；设计各方都缺乏经验；整体工艺以及熔盐储罐等关键技术，依靠国外设计团队，设计周期长等问题。在工程管理过程中，一方面督促总承包单位和监理单位做好图纸审查和设计交底工作，另一方面，直接同设计方加强沟通，协调设计环节，完善技术方案，加快设计进度。④抓好设备监造和供货环节，协调设备供应和设备消缺工作。对于工程进度有重大影响的设备供货，结合设备监造、对设备供应商的排产计划和制造进度进行重点督查，多次到关键设备制造厂家进行调研和催货。⑤规范项目文件资料管理。在工程建设管理过程中，高度重视档案管理工作，组织档案专家对工程资料进行专项检查和档案管理人员专项培训，编制并下发执行《项目建设文件收集与档案整理实施细则》《工程常用表式管理规定》等文件，力求项目建设中，项目资料文件的完整、准确、系统、规范。

（三）安全文明施工管理

针对光热电站的特殊性，在项目建设管理中，①认真落实安全施工管理措施，确保安全生产目标。根据水电顾问总体要求，与总承包单位、监理单位签订了《安全生产责任书》，建立完善“四个责任”体系，编制完善了相关安全管理制度，定期召开安全会议、例会，及时传达贯彻上级安全生产文件精神。对危险、有害因素加强辨识和管控，对吸热塔浇筑等危险性较大分部分项工程，要求施工单位编制专项方案，并要求总监和总承包方加强评审，并按方案要求严格执行。②切实抓好文明施工管理，创建安全文明施工样板。编制《安全文明施工策划方案》，要求施工总平面模块化、现场设施标准化、工程施工程序化、文明区域责任化、作业行为规范化、环境卫生经常化，做到施工有序、环境清洁，创建安全文明施工样板。2018 年项目建设现场，无人身及重大设备安全事故发生，安全生产局面总体可控，安全生产工作总体良好。

（四）生产准备管理

根据项目建设整体情况，提前布局生产准备工作，进行人员培训、生产规程编制等其他生产准备相关工作。组织生产管理人员、运行人员提前入场，参与项目建设管理工作，介入质检和验收工作，认真熟悉设备、系统，研究设计资料，从安全和经济运行角度提出优化设计方案，跟踪隐蔽部位和地下管道系统的布置与安装，为生产运维打好基础。

（中国电建共和西北水电光热发电有限公司）

茨达、铁炉风电场工程建设情况

茨达、铁炉风电场是四川省发展改革委核准的四川省重点工程，也是德昌县第一批山地风电场开发建设项目，由德昌风电开发有限公司投资开发。项目位于四川省德昌县西南大陆槽乡、热河镇。茨达风电场总装机容量 10.75 万 kW，共安装 43 台 0.25 万 kW 风电机组，年发电量 21317 万 kW·h，年利用小时数为 1983h，项目总投资 94963.36 万元。铁炉风电场总装机容量 10 万 kW，共安装 40 台 0.25 万 kW 风电机组，年发电量 20863.8 万 kW·h，年利用小时数为 2086h，项目总投资为 88674.9 万元。茨达、铁炉风电场共用一座升压站，由茨达风电场 220kV 升压站汇集后，由一条 220kV 输电线路接入米易县合力 220kV 变电站，线路长约 32km。项目于 2016 年 12 月核准，2018 年 4 月开工建设。

（一）工程特点

（1）海拔高、森林植被丰富。茨达、铁炉风电场项目地处凉山州德昌县，当地气候属亚热带高原季风气候，项目均位于海拔 3100m 左右的山脊，最高机位海拔 3360m，地势险峻，风电场建设环境复杂，施工难度大，对设计、工艺、人员等要求较高。同时，茨达、铁炉风电场所在区域森林植被较为丰富，风电场永久与临时占林地面积大，林地手续审核极其困难，在项目核准后，经过 1 年多的努力完成林地手续办理，顺利实现工程开工。

（2）接入系统跨市、州，协调难度大。由于接入系统涉及凉山州、攀枝花市，林地、环保、水保等专项手续办理复杂，协调难度大，极大制约了送出工程开工建设，通过与成都院的共同努力，克服各种困难，多方协调，取得核准和林地手续两大制约性因素的批复，实现开工建设。

（3）道路运输环境复杂。茨达、铁炉风电场大件运输较多，工程建设有近 2000 辆车次大件运输车辆通行。风电场距离德昌县约 60km，包含约 35km 县道，25km 乡道，一座铁路桥。其中乡道与铁路桥均不满足运输条件，道路运输环境极其复杂。从茨达镇到风电场约 25km 为乡道，宽度仅能满足单车通行，路基、路面、转弯半径等均不满足大件运输。通过与总承包的共同努力，协调德昌县开展了乡道的修建工作，加上开工后对铁路桥及乡道的改造，场外道路满足了运输条件。

（4）水保、环保要求高。近年来国家及地方政府对环境保护要求日益严苛，水保、环保工作要求高。机位、场内道路及集电线路均处于林区，设计、施工受到极大限制，水保、环保措施投入高。

（二）工程建设情况

（1）工程形象面貌。茨达风电场升压站已全部投产运行，正开展机位复垦等尾工工作。铁炉风电场目前已吊装 27 台，风力发电机组基础，场内道路、升压站设备等已完成施工，预计2019年12月20日全部机组并网。

（2）安全管理及三项业务工作开展情况。茨达、铁炉项目工程开工伊始，公司对项目安全及三项业务管理工作统筹安排，统一部署，明确了以董事长为第一责任人的安全领导体系，同时，明确了公司“四个责任体系”第一责任人及其职责，明确了安委会工作职责及工作制度，建立了纵向到底、横向到边，不留死角的安全管理网络。为细化项目安全及三项业务管理工作，使各项管理工作稳固推进，公司牵头成立了以公司总经理为组长的项目安全生产领导小组、项目三项业务领导小组、质量管理领导小组，并讨论通过了《茨达、铁炉风电场项目安全管理处罚规定》，让项目安全及三项业务管理工作有章可循、有据可查。针对在建项目地理位置特殊情况，公司成立了以公司总经理为组长的森林防火领导小组、防汛工作领导小组，召开专题会，将森林防火、防汛工作管理制度、应急措施传达到各个工作面，工作合理安排，有条不紊。并与总承包单位、与监理单位分别签订了安全生产协议书和森林防火责任书。公司总经理与部门负责人，部门负责人与员工层层签订了安全责任书，明确了控制目标、管控措施及考核办法，形成责任一级压一级，安全目标一级保一级的态势。

为切实落实项目三项业务管理工作，推动茨达、铁炉风电场环境保护、水土保持工作规范化、常态化开展，经公司审核同意，由总承包单位委托专业公司进行项目环保、水保监测工作，同时委托监理单位进行监督，确保各项工作落实到位，减轻工程建设对环境、生态造成的不利影响，杜绝重大及以上环境污染和生态破坏事件。项目安健环与节能减排工作由总承包单位统一策划实施。

（3）质量工作开展情况。①质量目标。项目（工程）建设质量管理目标：不发生重大及以上质量事故；单位工程优良品率：安装工程>90%；建筑工程>80%；分项工程（单元工程）合格率100%，一次验收合格率≥95%。争创行业及以上优质工程。②质量管理工作开展情况。茨达、铁炉风电场由监理单位全程现场监督工程施工质量，并由可再生能源发电工程质量监督站四川分站开展质量监督工作。在工程建设中，公司联合各参建方成立项目质量管理领导小组，由工程建设部依据《德昌风电开发有限公司工程建设质量管理办法》开展质量管理工作。对工程建设标准强制性条文执行情况进行检查，对重大方案履行审批程序。根据《风力发电场项目建设工程验收规程》的验收划分原则，分风力发电机组安装工程、场内电力线路工程、升压站设备安装调试工程、升压站建筑工程、场内交通工程5大类，并往下分若干分部、分项及检验批，综合统计本工程单位工程47个，分部工程328个，分项工程1435个。截至目前，已完成各单位工程、分部分项工作等，质量评定合格率100%。同时，公司不定期对质量体系的运行情况进行分析，并不断补充和完善，达到持续改进。通过进一步加强对原材料，土建工程质量，设备安装、调试，第三方质量检测管理，确保工程质量可控。

（德昌风电开发有限公司）

中國水力發電年鑒

3

大中型水电工程

常规水电工程

白鹤滩水电站工程 2018 年建设情况

白鹤滩水电站是目前世界在建的最大水电站，电站主要特性指标均位居世界水电工程前列，综合技术水平在世界坝工史上名列前茅。白鹤滩工程具有多项世界之最：地下洞室群规模世界第一、单机容量 100 万 kW 世界第一、300m 级高坝抗震参数世界第一、圆筒式尾水调压井规模世界第一、无压泄洪洞规模世界第一、300m 级高坝全坝使用低热水泥混凝土世界第一、装机容量 1600 万 kW 世界第二、拱坝总水推力 1650 万 t 世界第二、拱坝坝高 289m 世界第三、枢纽泄洪功率世界第三、工程综合技术难度名列世界前茅。

工程于 2017 年 7 月核准开工，计划于 2021 年 5 月水库开始蓄水，2021 年 7 月首批机组投产发电，2022 年 12 月工程完工。

2018 年是白鹤滩工程建设的关键之年，中国三峡建设管理有限公司白鹤滩工程建设部扎实推进工程建设，圆满完成年度任务，连续两年实现安全质量“双零”目标，创建世界一流精品工程措施有效落实，施工区“大党建”全面融入工程建设。全年共有央视舆论场、央视朝闻天下、人民日报、经济日报等专访报道白鹤滩工程及党建工作 6 次。

（一）工程进展情况

全年完成建筑安装工程投资 41.7 亿元，占年度投资计划的 106.30%。工程形象满足发电节点目标及考核要求，大坝工程优质高效过底孔，实现整体快速均衡连续上升，最高坝段浇筑至高程 676m，最高上升高度 124.5m，接缝灌浆至高程 601m，年度浇筑混凝土 220.9 万 m^3；水垫塘及二道坝实现高强度连续施工，坝基帷幕灌浆全面启动；引水发电系统开挖支护基本完成，巨型地下洞室群围岩总体稳定，右岸地下厂房小桩号洞段补强支护施工完成，实现向混凝土浇筑、金属结构制作安装转序，提前完成首批交面机组的锥管混凝土浇筑；泄洪洞工程龙落尾进入混凝土浇筑阶段；骨料品质优良，混凝土“一条龙”供应管理有序。

（二）质量安全情况

切实将安全生产放在首位，树立“红线意识”和“底线思维”，工程质量安全实现“双零”目标。推广使用多媒体培训工具箱，组织引进、建成安全体验馆 6 个，研究应用大型提升门机系统、地下工程通排风系统、液压自升式爬模等一系列本质安全技术；扎实推进质量攻关，大坝整体、均衡、连续上升，混凝土质量优良；引水发电工程应用液压钢模台车及液压滑模浇筑混凝土，体型精准、外观优良；自动化养护有效解决尾水洞衬砌表面龟裂及干热河谷大风条件下混凝土施工缝面开裂，泄洪洞高流速过流面平整光滑、无裂缝。全年验收单元工程 9837 个均合格，优良率 96%。9 项质量控制成果被评为水利工程协会、水利电力行业质量协会一等奖、二等奖。

（三）科技攻关情况

深入研究低热水泥特性，混凝土温控成效明显，大坝未发现温度裂缝；谷幅变形已建立工作基站，取得基础数据并跟踪监测；巨型地下洞室群围岩稳定控制技术，成功应对大规模开挖风险；地下厂房混凝土与埋件快速高效安全施工技术，优化工期提前实现节点目标；800MPa 级高强度钢焊接技术，保证压力钢管焊接性能优良；泄洪洞龙落尾变断面常态混凝土浇筑系统，成功填补国内行业技术空白；大风条件下缆机群安全运行与防碰撞系统研究，确保缆机运行更加安全可靠；组织研究确定导流洞封堵技术方案、地下厂房装修和坝顶建筑结构技术方案、旱谷地料场地质复勘和开采方案优化，为后续施工提供科学指导依据。

（四）工程保障情况

组织主标合同人工费调差、按期发电工程措施费用、春节连续施工措施费研究，组织超前研判合同变更，加快变更审核，强化工程建设资金保障，促进工程建设推进。优化资源配置，超前储存备料，保障高强度施工物资供应；及时完善混凝土配合比技术储备，保障现场混凝土浇筑；通过成立胎带机、布料机技术支持小组，增设缆机副司机室、缆机防碰撞系统、司机室防疲劳监视系统等措施，保证大型施工设备安全高效运行。健全综治维稳工作机制，施工区征地移民遗留问题基本得到解决，施工区和谐稳定，有效保障了工程建设。

（五）“五大工程”建设情况

（1）精品工程建设取得新进展。打造精品廊道、零缺陷横缝，应用智能化温控措施，大坝未出现一条温度裂缝；厂房机坑及尾水调压室下部贯通区域精细化开挖支护，围岩稳定、安全受控；大型埋件全面推行整体化安装，工艺精良，达到精品标准；泄洪洞洞身高流速过流面混凝土达到“镜面”效果，混凝土浇筑块对接达到金属结构安装水平；毛料开采精细化，成品骨料优质稳定；推广应用智能灌浆系统，实现“隐蔽工程、阳光作业”。

（2）创新工程建设收获新成果。大坝导流底孔研究应用门槽一期直埋技术，实现快速优质安全过孔口；采用真空喷雾加湿器，廊道养护效果良好；地下厂房500m级深大竖井研究应用混凝土滑模平台姿态监控系统，实现精准控制体型；泄洪洞研究应用混凝土温控防裂技术和智能养护系统，实现混凝土无裂缝；深化应用安全隐患排查微信系统，推进全员参与安全管理；研发应用施工期安全监测自动化，实现数据自动采集分析和及时预警；智能建造全面推进、成效初显，提升建设管理水平，在行业内起到了引领和示范效应。共开展科研项目35项，主持编制2项爆破行业规范，获得2部国家部级工法、1项部级样板工程、4件授权专利、3项中国爆破协会科学技术一、二等奖、1项中国大坝工程学会一等奖，获得10项省部级（行业级）科技成果奖、8项集团级科技创新成果奖，3个项目团队被评为集团公司“优秀创新团队”。

（3）绿色工程创造新业绩。骨料运输全面采用LNG车辆，推动施工区厕所革命，实施混凝土罐车冲洗废水循环利用系统建设运行、施工区骨料生产混凝土系统废水处理系统实现废水零排放；各项环境保护和水土保持措施有效落实，全年无环保和水土流失责任事件发生，施工区生态环境质量良好，总生态恢复面积达292公顷，美丽白鹤滩初见成效。

（4）民生工程建设展现新作为。依托大党建平台，构建企地共识，全年施工区综合维稳工作机制不断完善，施工区和谐稳定，阻工事件同比下降81%；建筑市场“七统一”管理成效显著，农民工工资专户监督管理到位；为属地提供3100多个就业岗位，为当地脱贫攻坚贡献力量。

（5）廉洁工程建设拓展新思路。狠抓“两个责任”落实，层层签订《党风廉政建设责任书》，推动反腐倡廉责任下沉；制定规范施工区廉洁行为规定，剑指“六大”廉洁从业风险；推进廉洁文化进工地、进班子、进岗位、进家庭系列活动，营造崇廉尚洁氛围；组织《灌浆者之歌》歌词评选、灌浆者党员廉洁诚信宣誓，构建灌浆工程廉洁诚信体系；整合地方和参建单位监督力量，巩固“大监督”工作格局，为工程高质量发展保驾护航。

（六）施工区大党建

坚持“围绕中心抓党建，融入管理促工程”，将党的政治优势转化为推动工程发展优势。组织学习贯彻十九大精神工地培训班、知识竞赛，在全工区掀起“学思践悟”十九大精神的热潮；党员“红旗岗、先锋号、攻关小组”活动全面铺开，122个创建项目促进党建工作与工程建设深度融合；全力推动“建功新时代”施工区劳动竞赛，开展“十大工匠”“十大科技创新人才”评选，组织电焊工、电工、混凝土工、爆破工职业技能比武，通过“比学赶帮超”和“典型引路”，提升劳动者技能素养。

（中国三峡建设管理有限公司）

乌东德水电站工程2018年建设情况

2018年是乌东德水电站主体工程建设的攻坚之年。全年紧紧围绕2020年7月首批机组投产发电目标，全力推进“五大工程”建设，大坝工程顺利实现“双百”目标，地下电站首批4台机组完成土建向机电安装交面，泄洪洞、左右岸地下电站进水塔浇筑到顶，工程造价、质量、安全、进度、环保管理受控，施工区综合管理进一步提升。

（一）工程进展情况

2018年，乌东德水电站工程建设综合计划完成投资29.35亿元（不含征地移民、贷款利息与所有分摊费的固定资产部分），占年初年度计划投资29.64亿元的99.02%，其中枢纽工程23.42亿元，其他费用5.93亿元（含独立费用与差价）。全年完成土石方开挖144.81万m^3（其中洞挖3.69万m^3）、混凝土浇筑218.27万m^3、钢筋6.64万t、锚杆4.82万根、固结灌浆18.06万m、帷幕灌浆4.96万延米。

大坝共开浇11个坝段（2～13号坝段），全年共浇筑混凝土101.6万m^3，单坝段最大浇筑上升高度121m，全坝段高差、相邻坝段高差、混凝土内部最高温度和降温速率等指标控制均满足设计标准要求，坝体质量优良，实现2018年度大坝浇筑“双百”目标。接缝灌浆至高程835m，水垫塘衬砌至高程790m，二道坝浇筑至高程795m。5～8号4台机组由土建向机电交面。泄洪洞1～3号进水塔全部浇筑到顶，左岸地下电站1～6号进水塔全部浇筑到顶，右岸地下电站7、9号进水塔浇筑到顶。完成了1～4号、6号中孔钢衬安装，单孔钢衬安装最短工期18天，远低于国内同类工程施工工期。

高质量完成 800MPa 级高强钢蜗壳和压力钢管焊接，实现 12 条压力钢管和 12 台水轮机蜗壳安装焊接质量优良，焊缝一次合格率高达 99%。

开展导流洞封堵全过程优化创新设计，提出了低水头封堵闸门结合临时堵头的下闸封堵程序和可保证结构安全的柱形堵头结构形式，基本消除了右岸 3、4 号导流隧洞进口结构安全风险和永久堵头楔形扩挖风险。

（二）质量管理情况

乌东德工程 2018 年实现了“不发生一般及以上质量事故，不出现年度绩效考核扣分项”的总体目标。全年共评定主要项目单元工程 4986 个，合格 4986 个，单元工程合格率 100%；优良 4749 个，优良率 95.2%。

构建疏密有致的“五个层级”质量控制网，预控与过程并重。一是实现政府质量监督检查的常态化和制度化；二是主动接受集团公司和建设管理公司层面的专项检查或随机抽查；三是深化乌东德工程建设部层面的质量综合检查机制；四是聘请专业总监实施日常化监督与技术咨询；五是全面实施第三方质量检验检测。

开办质量大讲堂，全年共举办 8 期，累计 690 人次参加。修订了《施工质量考核实施细则》，形成“激励与约束”并举的质量齐抓共管氛围。深入开展样板工程创建活动，2018 年共评选出 31 个样板工程，带动和促进基层一线质量管理水平的全面提升。持续深入开展质量控制小组活动，2018 年各参建单位先后成立 10 个质量控制小组，100 余人次参与质量控制小组活动，成功解决“降低大坝浇筑仓面混凝土泌水率”“提高人工砂成品合格率”“提高底板反弧段混凝土外观质量”“提高 800MPa 级高强钢压力钢管焊缝一次检测合格率”等数 10 项质量技术难题，有效促进了质量管理“末梢循环”的血液畅通，推动了工程质量稳步提升，锻炼了一批基层质量管理工作者，有力推进了基层质量管理工作向科学化、规范化、标准化方向发展。

（三）安全管理情况

一是构建横向倒边、纵向到底的责任体系，中国三峡建设管理有限公司乌东德工程建设部与 15 家参建单位签订了《2018 年安全生产目标管理责任书》，建设部内部层层签订安全生产责任书；二是对全工区管理责任划分情况进行再排查、再梳理，界定施工区所有管理区域的责任单位和责任人，形成空间、时间、职责和措施的全覆盖；三是制度建设不断进行完善，全年印发《乌东德工程建设部内设部门及各级人员安全生产职责》等文件 141 份。

强化风险管控和隐患排查治理双重预防机制。2018 年，开展月度安全生产综合大检查 12 次，通报隐患 1205 条，整改率 100%。

加大安全教育培训力度。2018 年，乌东德工程建设部通过举办安全管理知识讲座、竞赛，体验区培训等方式，共培训 4645 人次（体验区培训 3516），较 2017 年累计培训人次增加 3.2 倍；各参建单位共开展各类安全培训 1739 期，累计培训 45316 人次，较 2017 年培训期数增加 12%，培训人次增加 23.1%。

创建本质安全活动，印发了《乌东德工程本质安全班组创建活动实施方案》，参建各方通过逐级开展专项培训，从根本上实现“要我安全”向“我要安全”转变。

创新安全工作思路，2018 年 6 月，乌东德工程建设部组织 38 名党员，在大坝仓面、水垫塘及二道坝施工现场开展隐患排查活动，指正隐患 41 条，并举行“乌东德工程大党建安全隐患排查党员突击队”授旗仪式，将大党建工作与施工现场安全管理深度结合，强化党员在隐患排查中的先锋模范带头作用。10 月，乌东德工程大党建隐患排查突击队针对左右岸厂房进水口、大坝等高风险部位开展专项隐患排查，通报隐患 35 条，并督促施工单位及时整改。

切实抓好防汛防灾工作，成功应对最险地灾、最大洪峰、特大暴雨。一是 7 月 12～16 日洪峰（15900m^3/s、自 2013 年以来最大洪峰）过境的考验，参建各方按照应急预案要求，确保工程和人员安全；二是 7 月 31 日凌晨，经受住了特大暴雨（雨强 90.8mm/h）的考验，确保人员安全；三是白格堰塞湖期间，执行 24 小时防汛防灾值班制度，扎实做好水文气象加密监测和滚动预报工作，确保洪峰顺利过境。

（四）科研工作

2018 年，组织实施的科研项目共 32 项，其中在研科研项目 27 项，含国家科研项目 1 项、外委科研项目 25 项（智能建造项目 12 项）、员工科研项目 1 项。验收科研项目 3 项，新增科研项目 2 项。

“水泥灌浆智能控制关键技术和成套设备”获中国大坝工程学会 2018 年度技术发明奖一等奖，“大型水电工程水泥灌浆智能控制关键技术的创新和应用”获中国质量协会 2018 年度质量技术奖二等奖，“大型水电工程建设场地地质灾害监测预警与应急管理研究及应用”获水力发电科学技术奖二等奖，“乌东德水电站特高拱坝边坡及建基面开挖工程”获中国爆破行业协会 2018 年部级样板工程奖励，“基于质量控制小组活动的全面质量管理”荣获集团首届管理创新成果二等奖；大型水电工程定位技术研发与应用团队荣获中国三峡集团 2018 年度创新团队优秀奖。

2018年，完成发明专利申请30余件、实用新型专利申请30余件、外观专利3件，获得授权实用新型专利18件、外观专利2件；取得软件著作权登记证书10项，论文发表29篇。

（五）地质勘测工作

（1）2018年库岸及库区移民勘察工作：主要包括近坝库岸三台危岩体工程治理招标设计工作、早谷田危岩体稳定性研究专题工作、移民安置点及配套设施施工图阶段勘察等工作。主要完成各种比例地质测绘约11km²、实测剖面144km、钻孔32854.15m等。

（2）2018年坝址区现场服务及专项勘察、专题研究工作：专项勘察主要包括K25岩溶斜井专项补充勘察、库管码头专项勘察、电厂宿舍楼专项勘察等。专题研究开展了2号导流洞堵头段混凝土与岩体接触情况工程地质专题研究、导流洞堵头段顶拱及边墙中上部混凝土与岩体接触情况工程地质专题研究、施期料场碳质薄膜对混凝土影响专题研究、枢纽区灌浆工程三维可视化诊断系统研究与开发等工作。施工地质现场服务主要针对高位自然边坡、二道坝、坝后水垫塘、引水洞进口及左岸泄洪洞出口等工程边坡，泄洪洞及K25岩溶斜井等地下工程，灌浆平洞等渗控工程，以及金坪子滑坡治理及施期料场开挖工程等开展，进行了地质编录、巡视、专项勘察、现场验收和协调、施工地质简报编制等工作。主要完成1∶500补充地质测绘7.5km²、钻孔2038.6m、隧洞地质编录及验收24858.76m²/1894.25m、边坡地质编录及验收28899.9m²、施工地质简报编写2.2万字/3期、地质报告及各类报告地质篇编写217.5万字/23本等。

二道坝坝基于2018年1月开挖完成，开挖揭露坝基岩体质量、地层分布、基覆界面形态等地质条件与前期勘察成果高度一致，误差在米级以内，前期勘察成果得到了验证。

［中国三峡建设管理有限公司　孟友瑞　李华
长江三峡勘测研究院有限公司（武汉）　许琦］

向家坝与溪洛渡水电站工程 2018年建设情况

（一）向家坝水电站

2018年1月21～27日完成了升船机第一阶段实船试航工作，试验工况为电站发电，不泄洪，下泄流量范围为1600～4600m³/s。5月11日，向家坝升船机试通航前验收委员会在向家坝召开了向家坝升船机试通航前验收会议，通过了试通航前验收；5月26日，向家坝升船机正式投入试通航运行。9月20～22日，完成了升船机第二阶段实船试验工作，试验工况为电站发电和泄洪，下泄流量范围为6000～8000m³/s。

北干渠全年完成衬砌4030m，完成年度目标值4000m的100.7%；北干渠隧洞取水口事故闸门及液压启闭机安装完成。南干渠隧洞已完成所有混凝土衬砌，除S2支洞上游崩塌堆积体宽大裂隙洞段和S1支洞工作面新增灌浆外，其余隧洞回填灌浆和固结灌浆全部完成。除北干隧洞N2支洞和出口渣场顶部绿化未实施外，已完成其他南北总干隧洞渣场防护及边坡绿化。

2018年，升船机下游引航道口门区整治工程，1月完成左岸凸咀部位切除，6月完成主河槽开挖。横江大桥工程，完成水富岸引道施工，9月11日整个大桥通过合同验收。永久供电改造，电缆沟完成约3.5km，剩余1.5km；完成3座变电站灯具更换。尾工完善改造项目，完成左岸300m马道及上坝公路一线的综合整治，完成左岸坝后回填区框架柱及顶板浇筑。水保验收项目，完成草皮铺设、草籽撒播合计约113万m²，完成各类苗木种植约20万株。

劳动安全与工业卫生专项验收按计划启动，年内完成了安全设施竣工验收评价项目招标采购及合同签订工作，完成了夏季作业环境检测和安全验收评价第一次现场检查，完成了向家坝水电站工程安全验收评价项目工作大纲审查。

关于工程档案预验收，2018年6月14日，中国三峡建设管理有限公司向家坝与溪洛渡工程建设部会同集团公司办公厅就向、溪两电站档案专项验收事宜向国家档案局进行了专题汇报，考虑向家坝水电站右岸坝后电站报审方式和验收组织方式未确定，该项目档案是否纳入档案专项验收范围有待商榷，因此国家档案局明确在2018年4季度开展一次专项检查，不做预验收安排。2018年12月2～4日，国家档案局一行5人，对向家坝水电站工程档案工作进行了现场检查。专家组通过查看项目现场，听取建设单位档案工作情况汇报，查验有关佐证材料并抽查项目档案，对向家坝水电站工程档案工作进行了系统的“把脉”和“诊断”。专家组还对《金沙江向家坝水电站工程档案验收工作大纲》进行了讨论修改。此次活动是档案专项验收前的一次专项检查指导活动，为后续工程档案专项验收奠定了基础。

（二）溪洛渡水电站

2018年，水垫塘内检修工程于6月20日全部完成，具备度汛条件；廊道内渗控系统完善处理项目已经完成85%；溪洛渡沟新增2号排水洞工程于5月16日完成洞身最后一仓混凝土浇筑，满足度汛过流条件，合同内项目全部完成；2号交通洞安全度汛补充设施工程于6月底前完成。

2017年8月上旬，向家坝与溪洛渡工程建设部以川云公司名义按程序向川、滇两省能源主管部门报送了枢纽工程专项验收申请。2017年12月1日，国家能源局在北京主持召开金沙江相关电站验收工作协调会议，明确由云南省能源局作为溪洛渡水电站竣工验收的牵头组织单位。经多次协调沟通，验收申请于2018年3月报送至两省能源局。2018年5月15日，向家坝与溪洛渡工程建设部就溪洛渡竣工验收工作向云南省能源局相关处室进行了汇报，云南省能源局明确表态：枢纽工程专项验收可在重大设计变更行政审批和谷幅变形技术评审两项工作有阶段性成果后立即启动。

劳动安全与工业卫生专项验收按计划启动，完成了安全设施竣工验收评价项目招标采购与合同签订工作，完成了夏季作业环境检测和安全验收评价第一次现场检查。

（三）质量管理

向家坝重点检查北干渠衬砌施工、南干渠灌浆施工，永久供电系统改造等工程项目；溪洛渡不定期对新增2号排水洞混凝土工程、导流洞封堵工程、二道坝补充帷幕灌浆工程等隐蔽工序进行突击检查，对安全监测数据录入、校核质量和光纤电缆等线材质量开展专项检查；组织参建各方严格落实质量三检制度、关键工序监理旁站制度和项目管理人员巡查制度，确保工程建设质量。

截至2018年11月底，两电站相关重点项目共评定单元工程723个，一次验收合格单元723个，一次验收合格率100%，其中溪洛渡水电站共评定单元工程310个，向家坝共评定单元工程413个，质量管理体系运行有效，施工质量全面受控，全年未发生施工质量事故和质量缺陷，质量管理目标顺利实现。

（四）安全管理

组织开展2018年度危险源辨识和风险评价工作。加强高风险项目过程管理，主要围绕南北干渠、升船机下游口门区治理工程、太平料场及长皮带沿线、新田湾、龙坡嘴等渣场治理工程、水垫塘检修施工、溪洛渡沟新增2号排水洞施工、下游新增取水泵站施工、3号和4号导流洞出口封堵、雾化区边坡及下游河道治理等现场重点工程项目开展工作，严格落实各项安全保障措施。扎实做好防洪度汛、汛末蓄水和地质灾害防范工作，开展防汛应急演练，做好应急联动协调和各类汛情信息沟通传递，加强汛末蓄水阶段协调和涉水施工项目管控，加强近坝库岸地灾监测与防护，圆满完成2018年防洪度汛工作。

从3月开始，组织各参建单位开展“电力安全隐患排查治理深化年”、电力建设施工安全专项治理、“安全生产月”、“安全生产大检查”等专项活动，进一步落实安全生产责任，有效防范人身伤亡事故。2018年，管理区域内各项重大安全风险体受控，没有发生较大及以上生产安全责任事故、承担主要责任的人身死亡安全事故、电力安全事故，没有发生社会影响大、影响集团公司声誉的安全事件，没有发生安全事故瞒报、谎报、迟报事件；工程建筑安装投资安全事故死亡率为0.00人/亿元。

（中国三峡建设管理有限公司
中国电建集团中南勘测设计研究院
有限公司　张永涛）

杨房沟水电站工程2018年建设进展情况

2018年是杨房沟水电站设计施工总承包（EPC）管理新模式下主体工程施工的关键年，也是主体工程由开挖支护施工转向混凝土浇筑的转序年。全年工程未发生安全事故、质量事故、环境污染和生态破坏事故，全面实现安全、质量、环保水保控制目标和工作目标。截至2018年底，主要工程进展如下：

1. 大坝及泄洪系统工程　左右岸坝肩边坡开挖支护全部完成，并通过雅砻江流域水电开发有限公司组织的坝基验收。大坝首仓混凝土于2018年10月30日顺利开始浇筑，至2018年底，大坝混凝土累计浇筑14仓、1.8万m^3，最高坝段（10号坝段）浇筑至1959m高程。水垫塘、二道坝开挖基本完成，并启动水垫塘底板清基及混凝土浇筑施工。

2. 引水发电系统工程　厂房4台机组肘管全部安装完成并通过验收，其中1号机肘管二期混凝土浇筑完成，2号机肘管二期混凝土浇筑2仓（共6仓），3、4号机肘管一期混凝土浇筑完成；1号机压力钢管全部安装就位；主变压器室底板及沟槽混凝土浇筑完成75%；尾水调压室底板混凝土浇筑完成，1号井边墙混凝土浇筑至1968m高程，2号井边墙混凝土浇筑至1959m高程；母线洞边顶拱衬砌完成；出线竖井衬砌完成32m（共148m），出线上平洞边顶拱衬砌完成228m（共412m）；尾水隧洞底板混凝土完成1018m（共1187m），边顶拱衬砌完成170m（共1187m）；进水口2号塔浇筑至2064m高程，3、4号塔底板浇筑至2059m高程；开关站边坡Ⅰ区开挖至2131m高程，Ⅱ区开挖至2115m高程，Ⅲ区开挖至2102m高程；尾水出口边坡开挖全部完成，支护基本完成。

3. 其他工程

（1）金波料场：开挖至2270m高程。

（2）旦波崩坡积体：上游侧开挖至2315m高程，支护至2330m高程；下游侧开挖至2290m高程，支护至2315m高程。

（3）卡杨公路环保水保尾工项目：项目土建、绿化施工项目全部完成。

（4）二回线路工程：持续开展塔机基坑开挖和浇筑工作，累计开挖完成95基，浇筑完成68基。

（雅砻江流域水电开发有限公司　杨田）

两河口水电站工程建设情况

（一）概况

两河口水电站为雅砻江中、下游的“龙头”水库电站，开发任务以发电为主，兼顾防洪。坝址位于雅砻江干流与支流鲜水河的汇合口下游约2km河段，下距雅江县城约25km；控制流域面积为6.57万km^2，多年平均流量$666m^3/s$。电站采用坝式开发，水库正常蓄水位为2865m，总库容为107.67亿m^3，消落深度为80m，调节库容65.6亿m^3，具有多年调节能力。电站装机容量3000MW，多年平均年发电量110亿kW·h。

两河口水电站为一等大（1）型工程，采用“拦河大坝+左岸泄洪系统+右岸引水发电系统+左、右岸导流洞”枢纽建筑物总体布置格局。拦河大坝为土心墙堆石坝，最大坝高295m，为已建和在建的同类坝型中最高坝之一，建设难度大；左岸泄洪系统主要由溢洪道、深孔泄洪洞、漩流竖井泄洪洞、放空洞等组成，总泄量约为$8200m^3/s$，最大水头约250m，总泄洪功率约为21000MW，最大泄水流速大于50m/s；右岸引水发电系统主要由进水塔、压力管道、发电厂房及副厂房、升压变电系统、尾水系统、附属洞室等组成，为赋存于高地应力复杂地质环境中的大型地下洞室群结构，发电厂房最大开挖跨度28.4m，开挖高度66.80m。左岸共布置3条导流洞，其中1条后期改建为放空洞，1条与漩流竖井泄洪洞结合；右岸共布置2条导流洞，后期分别与发电尾水洞结合。

两河口水电站可行性研究报告于2013年修编完成并通过审查，按2012年4季度价格水平，工程静态总投资为478.25亿元。单位千瓦投资15942元/kW，单位电度投资4.35元/（kW·h）。

（二）勘测设计有关情况

1965年完成的《雅砻江流域水利资源及其利用》报告首次提出了中游河段的两河口水电站。2003年10月国家发展改革委以“发改办能源〔2003〕1052号”文下达了《雅砻江水能资源梯级开发主体的复函》，明确雅砻江流域水电开发有限公司（简称雅砻江公司）负责实施雅砻江水能资源的开发。雅砻江公司根据国家发展改革委“发改办能源〔2012〕2252号”文《关于同意四川省雅砻江两河口和杨房沟水电站开展前期工作的函》，开展了雅砻江两河口水电站前期工作。

2003年1月，《两河口水电站开发方式研究报告》经水电水利规划设计总院和四川省计委审查通过。2006年9月，水电水利规划设计总院以《关于印送〈四川雅砻江中游（两河口至卡拉河段）水电规划报告审查意见〉的函》（水电规规〔2006〕0072号）将审查意见印送四川省发展改革委。2008年12月，四川省人民政府以《关于〈四川雅砻江中游（两河口至卡拉河段）水电规划〉的批复》（川府函〔2008〕368号）批复了该规划。

2005年6月，中国电建集团成都勘测设计研究院有限公司（简称成都院）提出了《两河口水电站预可行性研究报告》，同年9月水电水利规划设计总院进行审查、并以水电规规〔2005〕0110号文予以批复。

2013年3月，成都院编制完成了《四川雅砻江两河口水电站可行性研究报告（送审稿）》，于2013年8月提交了审定稿。复审认为报告达到了可行性研究阶段勘测设计工作内容和深度的要求，基本同意该报告。2013年10月，水电水利规划设计总院以水电规水工〔2013〕号84文予以批复。

2014年9月，两河口水电站经国家发展改革委正式核准开工建设。计划第一批机组于2021年12月发电，2023年12月工程完工。

（三）项目总体进展情况

初期导流工程于2009年开工，2012年3月具备分流条件；2015年11月实现大江截流。三大主标（大坝工程、泄水建筑物系统工程、引水发电系统工程）于2015年全面开工，2016年11月1日大坝心墙开始填筑，2016年12月泄水系统洞室群第Ⅰ层全线贯通，2017年12月地下厂房开挖贯通。

两河口水电站2018年各项工程建设任务均按计划有序推进，完成固定资产投资49.97亿元，累计完成固定资产投资305.21亿元，占设计概算总投资664.57亿元的45.93%。2018年5月31日，大坝全断面填筑至2680m高程，进入坝体挡水度汛阶段。

（四）2018年枢纽工程进展情况

1. 大坝工程标

（1）大坝填筑：心墙填筑至2710m高程，累计填筑131m、203.7万m^3；堆石区最高填筑至2737.2m高程。2018年完成大坝填筑1350万m^3（其中心墙108万m^3），开工以来累计填筑2108万m^3（其中心墙202万m^3），约占总方量4233万m^3

的 49.80%。

（2）灌浆工程：2760m 高程以下固结灌浆全部完成；2730m 高程以下三角区帷幕灌浆全部完成。2018 年完成帷幕灌浆 11.2 万 m，开工以来累计完成 17.8 万 m；2018 年完成固结灌浆 3.1 万 m，开工以来累计完成 9.1 万 m。

（3）土石料场开采：两河口石料场累计开采有用料 1244 万 m^3，累计剥离 850 万 m^3；瓦支沟石料场，累计开采有用料 309.4 万 m^3，累计剥离 262 万 m^3。亚中土料场累计开采一类土 63 万 m^3；西地土料场累计开采接触黏土 12.4 万 m^3、一类土 19.9 万 m^3；普巴绒土料场累计开采一类土 55.9 万 m^3。

2. 引水发电系统工程标

（1）三大洞室：2018 年 1 月主厂房开挖完成，10 月三大洞室开挖全部结束并全面转入混凝土浇筑。12 月首台（6 号）机组锥管混凝土浇筑完成，移交机电标开始座环及蜗壳安装；5 号机组肘管安装及混凝土浇筑完成；4 号机组肘管安装完成。

（2）引水系统：电站进水口塔体高度 115m，顶部高程 2875.00m，混凝土设计总方量为 53.8 万 m^3（包含回填混凝土量）；2018 年主要进行塔体混凝土浇筑工作，平均浇筑至 2837m 高程（平均剩余 38m），1、2、3、4、5、6 号塔体分别浇筑至 2832、2824、2832、2844、2836、2852m 高程。引水竖井，2、3、4、6 号井全断面开挖完成；1 号井全断面开挖至 2687m 高程，余 87m；5 号井全断面开挖至 2657m 高程，余 51m。

（3）尾水系统：全部开挖完成。

3. 泄水系统工程标

（1）深孔泄洪洞：总长 1499m，开挖全部完成；洞身衬砌 360m，余 1139m；进口闸室完成 1.5m 底板浇筑（总高 70m）。

（2）放空洞：总长 1344m，开挖全部完成；洞身衬砌 456m，余 888m；进口闸室浇筑完成 43m（总高 136m）。

（3）竖井泄洪洞：上平段总长 119m，开挖全部完成；下平段总长 996.16m，开挖全部完成；洞身衬砌 402m，余 594.16m。进口闸室完成 4m 底板浇筑（总高 39m）。

（4）5 号导流洞：总长 1095.5m，开挖全部完成；洞身衬砌 517m，余 578.5m；进口闸室浇筑完成 69.8m（总高 134m）。

（5）3 号导流洞：总长 213.83m，开挖全部完成；进口闸室浇筑完成 19m（总高 55m）。

（6）洞式溢洪道：总长 403.5m，开挖全部完成。

4. 消能雾化工程标　左岸 962 根、12291m 长旋挖桩全部完成；18.2 万 m^3 边坡开挖全部完成；完成混凝土浇筑 1.2 万 m^3（占设计总量 3.53 万 m^3 的 34%）。右岸旋挖桩完成 4789m；边坡开挖全部完成（44.7 万 m^3）。

5. 机电安装标　主厂房 2 台 550t 桥式起重机负荷试验、消缺及取证完成。6 号机组于 12 月 12 日完成座环吊装；5 号机组完成锥管吊装及座环组装；4、3、2、1 号机组完成锥管拼装焊接。安装间下部配电室机电埋管埋件安装完成，其余部位管路预埋随土建进度进行。完成施工用电电缆敷设。

（五）2018 年库区移民代建工程进展情况

1. 复建县道 XV02 线密贵沟至瓦日乡段　明线路基毛路开挖完成 78km，累计完成 97.5%。隧道开挖支护完成 10km，累计完成 97.3%，混凝土衬砌完成 6.2km。下拖特大桥 6、7 号主墩箱梁完成 3 个节段。哈格达沟特大桥 2、3 号主墩箱梁浇筑分别完成 4、6 个节段。扎拖特大桥 4、5 号主墩箱梁完成 8 个节段，长征沟大桥 4、5 号主墩箱梁完成 2 个节段。

2. 库周交通恢复工程　木绒特大桥 3 号主墩墩身浇筑完成 143.25m，4 号主墩墩身浇筑完成 119.5m。红顶特大桥 1、2 号主墩 0 号块第一仓混凝土浇筑完成。洛古大桥 2、3 号主墩箱梁浇筑分别完成 9、8 个节段。阿宗村至绒坝大桥汽车便道明线路基开挖完成 35km（约 98.6%），挡墙完成 50%。

（雅砻江流域水电开发有限公司　李宏壁
中国电建集团成都勘测设计研究院有限公司
朱先文　金伟）

大华桥水电站“一年四投”全部机组投产发电

2018 年 6 月 9 日，大华桥水电站首台机组顺利通过 72 小时试运行，投入商业运行。6 月 25 日，2 号机组一次性通过 72 小时试运行投产发电；3 号机组于 7 月 12 日完成 72 小时试运行正式发电，4 号机组于 12 月 31 日 24 时完成 72 小时试运行，圆满实现了“一年四投”的既定目标。

大华桥水电站位于云南省怒江州兰坪县兔峨乡境内的澜沧江干流上，是澜沧江上游河段规划推荐开发方案的第 6 级电站，上、下游梯级分别为黄登和苗尾水电站；电站为堤坝式开发，坝址距昆明市公路里程约 588km、距兰坪县城 77km。控制流域面积 9.26 万 km^2，多年平均流量 925m^3/s。

该电站以水力发电为主，为二等大（2）型工程。水库总库容 2.93 亿 m^3，电站额定水头为 62.5m，安装 4 台单机容量为 230MW 的混流式水轮发电机组，多年平均年发电量 44.409 亿 kW·h，年发电利用小时数4501h。

电站枢纽主要建筑物由挡水建筑物、泄洪消能建筑物和引水发电建筑物等组成。其中挡水建筑物为碾压混凝土重力坝，顶顶高程1481m，最大坝高103m,，坝顶全长231.5m；从右至左分12个坝段，1～3号为右岸非溢流坝段，4～8号坝段为表孔坝段，9号为底孔坝段，10～12号坝段为左岸非溢流坝段。泄洪消能建筑物由坝身5个溢流表孔、1个泄洪排沙底孔组成。表孔消能采用宽尾墩台阶溢流面＋戽式消力池消能工，泄洪底孔消能采用异型鼻坎挑流消能工。引水发电建筑物由岸塔式进水口，压力管道、地下厂房、尾水调压室、尾水隧洞以及尾水出口组成，引水系统平面上采用一管一机布置，尾水系统采用两机一洞布置。1号输水系统总长1045m，2号输水系统总长1082m。

地下厂房、主变压器室、尾水调压室平行布置，地下厂房开挖尺寸为196m×27.8m×68.5m（长×宽×高），主变压器洞开挖尺寸为130.4m×17.5m×19.5m，尾水调压室开挖尺寸为160m×22m×58.4m。

电站施工导流采用断流围堰一次拦断河流，枯水期围堰挡水、导流隧洞泄流，汛期基坑和导流隧洞联合泄流，基坑内枯水期施工的导流方式。

大华桥水电站2007年底开始可行性研究设计工作，可行性研究报告于2013年12月中旬通过了水电水利规划设计总院审查，2014年5月取得审查批复。项目于2014年12月获得核准。2014年11月初，大江截流成功。2015年4月11日完成大坝基坑开挖，4月27日大坝垫层混凝土开始浇筑，5月28日开始进行碾压混凝土浇筑；2015年9月30日地下厂房第一仓混凝土浇筑。工程于2018年2月初实现导流洞下闸挡水，水库开始蓄水；2018年6月9日，首台机组投产发电；之后，2～4号机组分别于6月25日、7月12日、12月31日投产发电，圆满实现了“一年四投”的既定目标。

（中国电建集团北京勘测设计研究院
有限公司 黄海锋）

金沙水电站工程2018年建设情况

金沙水电站位于金沙江干流中游末端的攀枝花河段上，上距观音岩水电站坝址28.9km，下距攀枝花中心城区10.3km，是一座以发电为主，同时兼有供水、改善城市水域景观和取水条件、对观音岩进行反调节等任务的中型水电站。

该电站工程2013年动工开建，2018年主要进行了左岸厂坝边坡开挖与支护、狮子石强卸荷区处理、溢流坝及厂房地基开挖、厂坝导墙地基开挖、鱼道边坡及地基开挖、大坝防渗帷幕施工，以及溢流坝段、厂房坝段、安装场坝段、厂坝导墙等混凝土浇筑。

1号机组于2018年3月31日具备肘管安装条件，4月1日开始肘管安装；11月底，厂房各机组进口段混凝土平均浇筑至990m高程，右岸三孔溢流坝混凝土平均浇筑至1021m高程；12月底，厂房坝段平均浇筑至994m高程，溢流坝段平均浇筑至1023m高程，其中10号坝段达到设计高程1027m。2018年度，累积浇筑混凝土62.4万m^3。

[长江三峡勘测研究院
有限公司（武汉） 刘培培]

拉哇水电站工程2018年建设进展情况

拉哇水电站位于金沙江上游河段四川省和西藏自治区的界河上，右岸为西藏昌都地区芒康县，左岸为四川甘孜藏族自治州巴塘县；是金沙江上游川藏河段规划13级开发方案中的第8级，上游为叶巴滩水电站，下游为巴塘水电站。水库正常蓄水位为2702m，死水位2672m，总库容24.67亿m^3；电站装机总容量2000MW，多年平均年发电量82.24亿kW·h。该电站为一等大（1）型工程，总投资309.69亿元；计划2021年11月大江截流，2028年首台机组发电。

电站于2017年3月工程开始筹建。2018年主要施工项目为场内交通工程、沟水治理工程、施工辅助工程等。工程质量满足国家相关规程规范、设计、合同要求，工程质量获得质量监督总站的一致肯定。主要工程形象进度如下：

（1）金沙江大桥及左岸连接道路工程：1号道路隧洞开挖完成800m，路面基层全幅施工527m，明线段边坡支护全部完成。金沙江大桥1、2号拱座竖桩和斜桩开挖、浇筑完成，3号桥台桩基浇筑完成，拱箱预制35片。

（2）筹建期右岸工程：2号道路隧洞开挖累计完成288m，4号道路隧洞开挖累计完成1376m，8号道路隧洞开挖累计完成453m，12号道路隧洞开挖累计完成604m，曲引朗沟排水洞开挖累计完成740m。

（3）筹建期左岸工程：1号道路隧洞开挖累计完成1538m，3号道路隧洞开挖累计完成1055m，7号道路隧洞（主线）开挖累计完成357m，拉哇沟排水洞开挖累计完成759m，必英沟排水洞开挖累计完成175m，加多登业主营地主体结构施工完成，施工水厂土石方开挖及边坡支护全部完成。

(4)“10·11”“11·03”白格堰塞湖对电站的影响：堰塞湖溃决洪水经过拉哇水电站坝址的洪峰流量分别为 8264、22000m^3/s。“10·11”堰塞湖洪水造成一定损失，对工程建设造成一定影响，总体可控。“11·03”堰塞湖洪水通过后，左右岸低高程公路、临江施工辅助设施、上游索道桥基本冲毁，渣场挡护设施损毁严重，部分场内公路隧洞进水、淤积严重。

[华电金沙江上游水电开发有限公司巴塘（拉哇）分公司　田应辉]

苗尾水电站4台机组全部投产发电

2018年6月1日，苗尾水电站最后一台机组（4号机）完成72小时试运行，进入商业运行。至此，该电站4台机组全部投产发电。此前，1、2号和3号机组分别于2017年10月14日、11月18日和12月31日顺利完成72小时试运行，并投入商业运行。

苗尾水电站位于云南省大理州云龙县旧州镇境内，为澜沧江上游河段“一库七级”开发的第7级电站，是国家能源“十二五”规划重点建设项目，是滇西北至广东特高压直流输电重点依托电源之一。工程以发电为主，兼顾灌溉供水，并促进地方经济社会发展、移民群众脱贫致富和库区生态环境保护。电站装机容量 1400MW，水库正常蓄水位 1408.00m，相应库容 6.86 亿 m^3，调节库容 1.65 亿 m^3。

苗尾水电站顺利建成，工程设计获2018年水电行业优秀设计一等奖，主要工程设计亮点简述如下：

(1) 苗尾水电站坝址区河谷较狭窄，为妥善解决复杂工程地质条件下各项技术难题，枢纽采用十分紧凑布置，使左岸倾倒变形高边坡规模和回石山梁内大断面引水隧洞布置间距压缩到了极致，成功实现了复杂地形地质条件下大型水电工程枢纽紧凑型布置规划。

(2) 苗尾水电站是澜沧江流域地质条件最为复杂的工程，坝址区两岸岩体倾倒变形强烈，其发育范围和程度在国内外水电工程中属罕见。与常规结构状态的岩体不同，倾倒变形岩体的工程地质特性复杂，有其特殊性。倾倒变形岩体带来的坝基处理、高边坡稳定分析与治理、大断面地下洞室稳定开挖与支护设计以及陡倾顺河向砂板岩复杂地质条件下的坝基渗控等关键技术难题。通过深入的勘察、设计与研究，并与科研机构广泛合作，成功解决了倾倒变形岩体复杂地质条件下高边坡、大断面地下洞室以及复杂坝基渗控等关键技术，形成了层状结构倾倒变形岩体工程地质特性研究、倾倒变形岩体坝基利用与处理、层状结构倾倒变形岩体高边坡治理、倾倒变形岩体小间距大断面洞室开挖稳定控制、陡倾顺河向砂板岩复杂坝基渗控等创新性的技术体系。其中，层状结构岩质边坡倾倒变形机理研究与工程应用获2018年中国大坝工程学会科技进步一等奖。

(3) 苗尾水电站砾质土心墙堆石坝受料源条件影响，坝料复杂。通过现场碾压试验、原位检测、数值模拟与反馈分析等大量科研工作，成功解决了高含水率、高含砾量宽级配砾质心墙土料，低黏粒含量接触性黏土料，扁平针片状软硬相间砂板岩堆石料等复杂坝料条件下筑坝技术难题，成功实现心墙土料与堆石料开挖直接上坝，形成了高砾质土心墙堆石坝复杂坝料筑坝关键技术，取得了十分显著的经济和环境效益。

(4) 苗尾水电站溢洪道具有基岩条件差、高水头、大流量、高流速、高频率泄洪的特点，通过大量研究与试验，在溢洪道水力学设计、结构设计、基础处理、抗冲磨混凝土、泄洪雾化影响区防护等方面取得了大量的设计优化成果。2017年工程蓄水以来，已持续不间歇泄洪100多天，连续泄洪天数在国内岸坡式溢洪道工程中属罕见，并已成功通过了超10年一遇洪水安全泄洪的考验，泄洪历时与流量均位于国内同等规模溢洪道前列。

(5) 苗尾水电站创建了澜沧江流域地面厂房的标杆工程。针对大面积混凝土连续墙结构，通过厂房结构体型优化、三维协同设计、混凝土配合比优化、模板设计优化、新材料和创新工艺应用等，成功实现利用普通混凝土达到免装修混凝土的效果，是澜沧江流域首座采用免装修混凝土的地面发电厂房。

(6) 苗尾水电站三维设计贯穿工程始终。在国内水电站中，率先取消了电缆埋管敷设方式，电缆均采用明敷方式，以方便运行维护；实施了管路、桥架、电缆敷设二次工艺设计以及标准化施工；电站枢纽接地一次性达标，一次性通过消防主管部门主持的电站整体消防移交验收；并首次在澜沧江流域电站内设置了送出线路融冰短接装置和500kV母线高压并联电抗器。

(7) 苗尾水电站工程施工总布置规划践行“建设绿色生态型水电站”的理念，紧扣“与地方集镇规划紧密结合”和“节约用地和土地再造”两个主题进行设计，与国内外类似水电站工程施工总布置规划相比，本施工总布置规划体现了“与地方集镇规划紧密结合”“渣场与坝体相结合”“土地再造和返还地方政府”“重视生态环境保护”“注重节能降耗”等诸多技术创新亮点，特别是承包商营地采用“永临结合”处理方式，后期作为地方集镇学校，得到了业主、地方政府及国内知名专家等各界的广泛认可。

(8) 在国家“生态文明建设”的引导下，苗尾水电站坚持在开发中保护，在保护中开发的绿色发展理念。建立了鱼类增殖站人工增殖放流澜沧江珍稀鱼类，建设了基独河珍稀鱼类栖息地保护区，实现了73万m^2植被恢复与绿化，同时在枢纽核心区的回石山梁顶部和坝后厂区布置大面积绿色主题景观公园，创建了“景观园林水电工程”。

（中国电建集团华东勘测设计研究院有限公司 郑惠峰 危贤光 黄泰仁 吴关叶）

双江口水电站工程建设情况

（一）工程概况

双江口水电站是大渡河流域水电规划“3库22级”开发方案的第5级，位于四川省阿坝州马尔康市、金川县境内，是大渡河干流上游控制性龙头水库电站；坝址控制流域面积39330km^2，占全流域的51%左右；坝址处多年平均流量502m^3/s，千年一遇洪水流量6900m^3/s，可能最大洪水（PMF）洪峰流量为8630m^3/s。

双江口水电站采用坝式开发，开发任务以发电为主，参与长江中下游防洪，并促进地方经济社会发展。水库正常蓄水位2500.00m，死水位2420.00m，设计洪水位2501.44m，校核洪水位为2504.42m；总库容为28.97亿m^3，调节库容19.17亿m^3，具有年调节能力；每年7月水库预留最大防洪库容6.63亿m^3。电站装机容量200万kW，多年平均年发电量约77.07亿kW·h。水库调蓄可增加下游大渡河17个梯级电站枯水年枯期平均出力175.8万kW、枯期电量约66亿kW·h。

工程区地震烈度为Ⅶ度。坝址区两岸山体雄厚，河谷深切，谷坡陡峻；出露地层岩性主要为似斑状黑云钾长花岗岩和二云二长花岗岩。河床覆盖层一般厚48～57m，最大厚度达67.8m。基本地质条件好，经相应工程处理后具备修建300m级高坝的地形地质条件。

双江口水电站工程为一等大（1）型工程。枢纽工程由拦河大坝、泄洪建筑物、引水发电系统等组成。拦河土质心墙堆石坝，最大坝高315m，坝顶高程2510.00m。枢纽泄洪最大水头约250m，最大下泄流量约8200m^3/s。泄水建筑物包括洞式溢洪道、直坡泄洪洞、竖井泄洪洞和放空洞，其中洞式溢洪道、直坡泄洪洞及利用2号导流洞改建的放空洞位于右岸，利用3号导流洞改建的竖井泄洪洞位于左岸。引水发电系统布置于左岸，发电厂房采用地下式，厂内安装4台容量50万kW的立轴混流式水轮发电机组，采用“单机单管供水”及“两机一室一洞”的布置格局。

（二）勘测设计过程

受国电大渡河流域水电开发有限公司委托，中国电建集团成都勘测设计研究院有限公司于2003年初开始开展双江口水电站预可行性研究阶段勘测设计工作，2005年3月提出了《双江口水电站预可行性研究报告》，于2005年5月通过审查。

2005年7月启动可行性研究设计。2007年10月完成了可行性研究报告（咨询稿）并经咨询，之后可行性研究报告进入补充完善期，移民、环保等重要专题报告逐步完成并经审查。2011年8月，启动“先移民，后工程”相关移民安置点的建设工作。2012年8月全面完成可行性研究报告并通过审查。

2013年8月，完成了《双江口水电站项目申请报告》。中国国际工程咨询公司分别于2013年8月、2014年12月组织在成都对该申请报告进行了评估。2015年4月9日，双江口水电站项目获得国家发展改革委核准。核准概算总投资约366.14亿元。

（三）2018年工程建设进展情况

双江口水电站工程于2015年7月13日工程正式开工，2016年10月，大坝、引水发电系统、泄洪系统、土料供应、施工辅助等枢纽主体工程全面进场施工。截至2018年底，主要施工项目形象面貌如下：

1. 大坝工程 2018年11月16日，大坝基坑覆盖层开挖至基岩；12月25日，围堰防渗墙高标准通过合同完工验收。飞水岩石料场剥离开采道路启动建设，反滤料加工系统完成基础场平并启动系统基础埋件施工。土料标完成4～6号胶带系统洞挖施工，启动基础混凝土浇筑施工；自动掺合系统完成系统场平，启动基础预埋件施工；启动当卡土料标料源复勘。完成沐足渡场平填筑施工；完成英戈洛2400m高程以下坡面防护施工；完成两岸坝肩2750m高程以下危岩体治理。

2. 引水发电工程 进水口、压力管道上平段、出线场、25号路、尾水调压室交通洞、进厂交通洞、主变压器室第一层中导洞开挖支护完成，尾水调压室第一层扩挖完成。主副厂房第一层扩挖于2018年9月1日启动，至年底完成80%。

3. 泄洪消能工程 洞式溢洪道洞身段第一层于2018年7月17日开挖完成（已贯通）；深孔泄洪洞第一层于2018年7月18日开挖完成（已贯通）；放

空洞洞身非结合段开挖支护完成 492.6m；竖井泄洪洞下平段全长 1023.082m，开挖支护完成 460m。

（中国电建集团成都勘测设计研究院有限公司　王观琪　李永红
国电大渡河流域水电开发有限公司）

木扎提河三级水电站工程建设进展情况

木扎提河三级水电站位于新疆维吾尔自治区阿克苏市拜城县境内，是木扎提河干流上游段水电规划中的第 3 个梯级电站，距拜城县、阿克苏市分别为 129、132km。电站以发电为主，装机容量 160MW，多年平均发电量 5.424 亿kW·h。电站为引水式开发，枢纽由渠首、引水系统、岸边厂房及尾水建筑物等组成。渠首建筑物包括进水闸、引水明渠、泄洪冲沙闸、泄水明渠和侧堰，总长 298.6m。引水系统布置在河床左岸，由分水渠、进水口、引水暗涵、漏斗式冲砂池、压力前池、引水隧洞、调压室、压力管道等建筑物组成，全长约 15.8km（沿 4 号机）。厂房采用岸边式地面厂房，主机间尺寸 57.5m×21.5m×40.3m（长×宽×高），安装 4 台（2 台单机容量 70MW、2 台单机容量 10MW）立轴混流式水轮发电机组。

2015 年 10 月电站进入主体工程施工期，目前处于施工高峰期，计划 2019 年 12 月首台机组发电。

该工程关键技术主要如下：

（1）河流泥沙问题突出，在工程布置上需要采取综合性工程措施，保证工程的正常引水发电。

（2）工程地质条件复杂，首部枢纽建筑物、部分引水工程及电站厂房，均修建在深厚覆盖层上，需采取复杂的工程技术措施，保证建筑物安全。

（3）该工程处于环境保护敏感地区，对泄放生态水量及水生生物保护要求高，需采取生态泄放措施、过鱼设施及鱼类生殖站等措施满足环境保护要求。

（4）引水系统上布置国内外工程规模最大、水力和运行条件复杂的超大型排沙漏斗，目前正在开展智能化监测设计专题研究工作。

（5）岸边式地面厂房建筑物基础座落在第四系冲积砂卵砾石的深厚覆盖层上，在厂房基础处理中采用了桩基复合基础设计。

至 2018 年底，首部枢纽左岸引水闸系统基本完成，正在进行启闭机室等上部结构施工；排沙漏斗已完成底板和部分挡墙浇筑，预计 2019 年 6 月完成主体结构浇筑；压力前池已做好浇筑准备，预计 2019 年 6 月完成；引水隧洞已开挖完成约 80%；调压井已开挖支护完成，压力管道正在进行钢管安装。厂房已完成主体结构混凝土浇筑，内部正在进行机电安装。

（中国电建集团北京勘测设计研究院有限公司　王敬武　杨健关　李海）

苏洼龙水电站工程 2018 年建设进展情况

苏洼龙水电站是川藏河段第一个开工建设的大型电站，位于金沙江上游河段四川巴塘县和西藏芒康县的界河上，为金沙江上游水电规划 13 个梯级电站的第 10 级；坝址位于四川甘孜州巴塘县苏洼龙乡境内，上游为巴塘水电站，下游为昌波水电站。拦河坝为深厚覆盖层上的沥青混凝土心墙堆石坝，最大坝高 112m。水库正常蓄水位 2475m，库容 6.74 亿 m^3；电站总装机容量 1200MW，多年平均发电量为 54.26 亿 kW·h（联合）。该电站为一等大（1）型工程，总投资为 178.9 亿元，采用隧洞导流、全年基坑施工，计划 2021 年首台机组发电。

该电站项目于 2015 年 11 月获得国家发展改革委核准。2017 年 11 月实现大江截流。2018 年主要工程形象进度如下：

（1）拦河坝工程：2018 年 5 月底，围堰具备挡水条件，大坝基坑进入开挖和基础处理，实现安全度汛；10 月初，大坝基坑大部分开挖完成，基础振冲碎石桩完成 1373 根（22296m），坝基防渗墙累计成槽 3284m^2；坝肩覆盖层及基槽开挖基本完成。

（2）引水发电系统工程：电站进水口边坡高程 2480m 以上开挖完成，高程 2500m 以上系统支护全部完成，累计完成土石方开挖 84.8 万 m^3。引水隧洞设计开挖量 32.8 万 m^3，累计完成 9 万 m^3，完成率 27%。厂房开挖基本完成，2018 年 10 月浇筑厂房首仓混凝土。

（3）溢洪道工程：溢洪道二期开挖于 2018 年 10 月 1 日开工，累计完成 23.9 万 m^3。

2018 年 10 月 11 日凌晨，西藏江达县波罗乡白格村境内金沙江右岸山体发生大面积垮塌，导致金沙江主河道断流形成堰塞湖。10 月 12 日傍晚堰塞湖溃决。10 月 13 日 18 点 30 分，苏洼龙水电站迎来 7800m^3/s 的洪峰流量，超过 20 年一遇的导流标准。本次溃决洪水来临前，参建各方对洪水过程和苏洼龙水电站导流洞、泄洪洞泄流能力进行了演算，并对上游围堰采取加高、加固等防护措施，确保了洪水安全顺利的通过苏洼龙水电站。这次堰塞湖洪水造成一定损失，对工程建设造成一定影响，但总体可控。

2018年11月3日17：00左右，“白格”滑坡体位置再次发生山体滑坡，再次造成金沙江干流堵塞，形成的堰塞湖规模远超第一次。通过对堰塞体高度、库容、溃决时间、洪峰及洪峰过程的研判，为降低堰塞湖溃决洪水对苏洼龙水电站及下游的影响，按照相关指示和部署，苏洼龙水电站采取了主动破拆上、下游围堰，腾出天然泄洪通道的措施。溃决洪水于11月14日1时25分抵达苏洼龙水电站坝址，2时25分，堰前水位达到最高值2417.6m，3时50分，洪峰流量达到19800m³/s，远大于电站校核洪水标准PMF（可能最大洪水）12500m³/s。本次洪水过后，苏洼龙水电站水毁严重，上、下游围堰基本冲毁，拦河坝和厂房基坑基本淤为平地，引水系统下平段进水，洞内淤积严重；沥青混凝土砂石加工与拌和系统等施工辅助设施基本损毁；上、下游索桥桥台边坡受损，左右岸交通基本中断。

洪水过后，项目业主立即组织开展损失评估、两岸交通抢通工作。2018年12月初，开始了围堰防渗墙修复和基坑排水清淤工作；12月下旬，上、下游围堰开始恢复施工。

受此洪灾影响造成工期滞后。经过分析研究，在参建各方的共同努力下，苏洼龙首台机发电目标由2020年12月底调整为2021年7月底，力争将白格堰塞湖溃堰洪水造成的损失降低到最小。

（华电金沙江上游水电开发有限公司
苏洼龙分公司　唐明武
中国电建集团北京勘测设计研究院
有限公司　龙文）

象鼻岭水电站工程2018年建设情况

象鼻岭水电站位于贵州省威宁县与云南省会泽县交界处的金沙江右岸一级支流——牛栏江上，工程主要任务为发电，为二等大（2）型工程。水库正常蓄水位为1405m，总库容2.63亿m³，属不完全年调节水库。电站装机两台，总装机容量为240MW，保证出力为47.42MW，多年平均发电量为9.30亿kW·h，年利用小时为3875h。同时，依托水轮发电机组的快速调节能力和水电站水库的调节能力，在贵州省首个实现“水光互补”发电，达到平滑、稳定的发电曲线，使光伏发电成为与水电相媲美的优质电能。

枢纽建筑物由碾压混凝土拱坝、右岸引水系统和地下厂房等组成。碾压混凝土拱坝最大坝高141.5m，坝顶弧长459.21m。项目结合工程特点，开展150m级宽河谷高碾压混凝土拱坝筑坝技术研究，克服了工程区干热河谷气候、高昼夜温差、玄武岩筑坝材料特性对拱坝温控及碾压层间结合的不利影响问题，采用立体窄缝式消能工解决下游河道消能空间狭窄问题，采用50m高基础垫座解决坝肩地质缺陷等难题。

2006年8月和2010年5月，贵阳院编制的象鼻岭水电站预可行性研究和可行性研究报告分别通过审查。2011年4月，项目通过贵州和云南两省发展改革委的核准。2011年6月16日，象鼻岭水电站工程正式开工兴建；2014年12月，工程截流；2015年4月15日，大坝首仓碾压混凝土浇筑；2017年4月26日，导流洞下闸蓄水；2017年7月23日，首台机组并网发电，2017年8月18日，两台机组全面投产发电，标志着贵州省最后一个200MW以上装机的水电工程由建设期转入商业运行。2018年9月28日，水库蓄至正常蓄水位1405m。

（中国电建集团贵阳勘测设计研究院
有限公司　罗洪波）

旭龙水电站工程2018年建设情况

旭龙水电站是金沙江上游河段规划“一库13级”开发方案的第12级，其上游与昌波电站相衔接，距昌波梯级取水坝约75.5km，下游为奔子栏水电站。水库正常蓄水位2302m，死水位2297m，总库容8.29亿m³，调节库容0.8亿m³；电站装机容量240万kW，多年平均发电量98.72亿kW·h。该电站为一等大（1）型工程，主要由高213m的混凝土双曲拱坝、泄洪消能建筑物、引水发电建筑物等组成。

旭龙水电站勘测工作开始于2004年10月。2017年底，电站可行性研究阶段外业勘测工作基本完成，累计完成小口径钻孔2万余米，平洞9000余米，室内岩石物理力学500余组，原位岩体力学试验、地应力测试等70余组。开展了坝址高边坡、大坝建基可利用岩面及岩体力学特性、拱座岩体抗滑稳定、地下洞围岩稳定、施工区泥石流沟等专题研究。

在地形测量、高边坡调查、岩性与构造的空间关系、坝基岩体质量、隧洞围岩稳定分析等方面大量运用了可视化勘探技术、无人机技术、三维地质建模技术等勘察新技术，提高了勘测工作效率，保证了勘测成果的准确、可靠。

在2017年通过了预可行性研究报告审查及坝址比选、正常蓄水位、坝型坝线与枢纽布置格局、施工总布置、水库影响区等专题审查的基础上，2018年继续进行了可行性研究工作，全年补充完成勘探平洞600余米、钻孔约980余米。并相继通过了导截流、拱坝设计、天然建材料源比选等专题的咨询。

［长江三峡勘测研究院有限公司（武汉） 谭朝爽］

巴塘水电站工程2018年建设进展情况

巴塘水电站位于金沙江上游河段四川省和西藏自治区的界河上，右岸为西藏昌都地区芒康县，左岸为四川甘孜藏族自治州巴塘县；是金沙江上游水电规划的13个梯级电站中第9级电站，上游为拉哇水电站，下游为苏洼龙水电站。水库正常蓄水位2545m，库容1.28亿m^3；电站装机容量750MW，多年平均发电量为33.75亿kW·h。该水电站为二等大（2）型工程，总投资102.63亿元；计划2020年11月大江截流，2023年首台机组发电。

电站于2016年8月工程开始筹建，2017年10月获得国家核准。2018年主要施工项目为左岸开挖工程、左岸场内交通工程和右岸场内交通工程。工程质量满足国家相关规程规范、设计、合同要求，获得质量监督总站的肯定。主要工程形象进度如下：

（1）左岸开挖工程：累计完成土石方开挖约280万m^3，尾水边坡开挖至2515m高程，进水口边坡开挖至2669m高程，支护完成约50%。

（2）左岸场内交通工程：1、3、5、7号道路，巴楚河大桥及左岸交通洞施工完成。

（3）右岸场内交通工程：10号道路和达通沟桥施工完成，4号道路施工完成约90%，6号道路施工完成约75%。

（4）“10·11”“11·03”白格堰塞湖对电站的影响：堰塞湖溃决洪水经过巴塘水电站坝址的洪峰流量分别为7380、21200m^3/s。“10·11”堰塞湖洪水造成一定损失，对工程建设造成一定影响，总体可控。“11·03”堰塞湖洪水通过后，左右岸低线公路、临江施工辅助设施、索道桥基本冲毁，渣场挡护设施损毁严重，左右岸交通完全中断。

［华电金沙江上游水电开发有限公司巴塘（拉哇）分公司 田应辉］

高生水电站工程2018年建设情况

（一）工程概况

高生水电站位于贵州省务川县乌江支流洪渡河干流上，是洪渡河规划的第7级梯级电站，上游为石垭子水电站。电站距贵阳市公路里程402km，工程开发任务是发电。坝址控制流域面积3126km^2，多年平均流量69.8m^3/s。水库正常蓄水位420m，相应库容1.003亿m^3；校核洪水位426.55m，总库容1.270亿m^3；死水位416m，调节库容0.158亿m^3，具有日调节性能。电站装机容量106MW，安装2台单机容量为53MW的水轮发电机组；保证出力18.9MW，年利用小时3583h，多年平均发电量3.798亿kW·h。

该电站属二等大（2）型工程，由碾压混凝土重力坝、坝身开敞式溢流表孔、右岸引水发电系统和地下厂房等主要建筑物组成。

碾压混凝土重力坝坝顶高程427.5m，最大坝高122.5m，坝顶长126.35m，坝顶宽8～12m，最大坝底宽96.90m。河床坝段布置3孔开敞式溢流表孔。表孔尺寸为13m×20.5m（宽×高），堰顶高程399.50m，设计最大下泄流量为11179m^3/s；采用窄缝挑流的消能方式。

引水系统布置于右岸山体，由岸塔式进水塔、引水隧洞、压力管道、岔管、尾水隧洞、尾水闸门室、尾水出口等组成。引水隧洞采用一洞二机供水方式，尾水采用一机一洞出水。

厂区枢纽主要由厂房洞室、排水廊道、出线竖井、排风洞、进厂交通洞等地下洞室和出线窑洞组成。地下厂房采用一洞室布置格局，总长100m，宽19.9m，主厂房左右两侧分别布置副厂房和主变压器室，主变压器室上部布置GIS室。主厂房尺寸69.50m×19.9m×47.70m（长×宽×高），水轮机安装高程332.40m。

施工导流采用枯期隧洞导流，布置于右岸共1条，在枢纽上下游河床布置过水土石围堰进行截流。导流洞长612m，断面为8m×10m城门洞形。

（二）工程进展

截至2018年12月31日，主要工程进展如下：

1. 大坝　非溢流坝段（1、2、5、6号坝段）浇筑至427.3m高程，3、4号坝段（溢流坝段）浇筑至394m高程；3号溢流表孔混凝土浇筑完成，1、2号溢流表孔龟背混凝土浇筑完成。大坝溢流坝段1～4号闸墩已浇筑至427.3m高程。大坝护坦及护坡混凝土浇筑完成，预留冲坑开挖完成，河床清理完成。

2. 灌浆廊道　大坝右岸中层灌浆廊道完成混凝土衬砌794m（浇筑完成）。大坝底层、中层灌浆全部完成；顶层近坝区0＋0～0＋230m范围以内、溶洞段范围内的帷幕灌浆施工完成，累计完成约7万m。

3. 进水口　进水口闸墩混凝土浇筑至427.5m高程，启闭机排架浇筑完成，启闭机安装、调试完成；拦污栅安装完成；引水隧洞混凝土浇筑完成，灌浆完成。

4. 主厂房　1、2号机组343.5m高程（发电机层）以下混凝土浇筑完成，1号机主机、电气及辅助设备安装完成。主变压器室混凝土浇筑完成，主变压器安装完成。

5. 尾水隧洞及尾水闸室　1号尾水隧洞，总长192m，混凝土浇筑完成；2号尾水隧洞，总长212m，混凝土浇筑完成；1、2号尾水闸室混凝土浇筑至372m高程，尾水检修闸门及启闭机安装调试完成。

6. 引水隧洞　竖井开挖、混凝土浇筑完成；压力管道安装完成，回填混凝土及灌浆施工完成。

7. 库区复建工程　发科大桥及引道路基，全部施工完成，具备通车条件。乐居大桥及引道路基，钻孔灌注桩完成，框格梁防护1098m²（3号墩位置），桥墩混凝土浇筑1459.6m³，全部完成。长脚大桥及引道路基，钻孔灌注桩全部完成，路基土石方完成70%；桥墩混凝土浇筑完成，承台混凝土浇筑1150m³，浆砌石挡土墙2100m³。

高生水电站2018年12月通过了下闸蓄水验收，择机进行下闸蓄水。

（中国电建集团贵阳勘测设计研究院有限公司　阮祥明）

加查水电站工程建设情况

（一）工程概况

加查水电站是雅鲁藏布江干流中游桑日至加查峡谷段规划5级电站的第5级，位于西藏自治区山南地区加查县境内；枢纽工程主要建筑物由岸边挡水坝段、厂房挡水坝段、冲砂底孔坝段、混凝土溢流坝段及坝后式地面厂房等建筑物组成。电站正常蓄水位3246.00m，拦河坝坝顶高程3249.00m，最低建基高程3164.5.00m，最大坝高84.5m，总装机容量360MW，多年平均年发电量17.045亿kW·h。工程等别为二等，规模为大（2）型。

加查水电站拦河大坝总长624.84m，共分24个坝段，其中1～8号为左岸挡水坝段，长177m；9～10号为厂房安装坝段，长50m；11～13号为厂房挡水坝段，长106.35m；14号坝段为冲砂底孔坝段，长27m；15～19号为溢流坝段，长103m；20～21号坝段为导流明渠改建坝段，长度50.245m，其中20号坝段后期改建为右岸挡水坝段，21号坝段后期改建为生态泄放表孔坝段；22～24号为右岸挡水坝段，长72.245m；24号坝段右侧布置有39m长的混凝土截水墙。

大坝工程是本工程控制施工进度的关键项目，是整个主体工程施工的重点和难点所在，不仅有土石开挖工程、土石方填筑工程、基础处理工程（包含混凝土防渗墙、帷幕灌浆等），还有混凝土工程、灌浆工程（包含接缝灌浆和固结灌浆）等。加查水电站坝址区发育一条古河床，古河床既宽且深，基岩顶面沟壑相间，起伏差大，地质条件较复杂；坝址左岸为一宽缓的Ⅱ～Ⅲ级阶地台地，宽度大于1km，阶地覆盖层平均厚度大于50m，绕坝渗漏问题较突出。该电站地处高原，昼夜温差大，气候恶劣，不利于大坝混凝土的温控处理。

加查水电站可行性研究报告于2014年修编完成并通过审查，按2014年4季度价格水平，工程静态总投资为79.14亿元。单位千瓦投资15518元，单位电度投资3.226元。

（二）勘测设计与项目进展有关情况

2008年4月，完成了雅鲁藏布江中游河段水电规划报告。2012年9月，国家发展改革委以“发改办能源〔2012〕2546号”文同意加查水电站开展前期工作。2012年12月完成预可行性研究报告审查。2014年完成可行性研究报告审查。

2015年12月完成大江截流，工程开始主体施工。2016年12月大坝基础全部开挖至设计高程，建基面通过验收。2017年3月开始大坝主体浇筑，计划2019年6月大坝混凝土浇筑到顶。

工程计划2019年11月完成导流明渠三期截流，2020年5月导流明渠改建完成；2020年7月首台机组发电。

（三）2018年工程进展情况

加查水电工程混凝土总量约240万m³，其中主体工程混凝土约183万m³。2018年共完成混凝土浇筑70万m³，完成主体工程浇筑量的38%。

1. 大坝土建及金属结构安装工程　2018年大坝标累计浇筑混凝土34万m³。3～8号左岸挡水坝段最低浇筑至3242.0m高程、最高浇筑3247.0m高程；14号冲砂底孔坝段上游侧浇筑至3225.00m高程；15～19号溢流坝段浇筑至溢流顶面3225.00m高程，闸墩浇筑至3240.00m高程；22～24号右岸挡水坝段最低浇筑至3233.5m高程、最高浇筑至3247.0m高程；消力池底板浇筑完成率约70%；左导墙浇筑完成率约80%。

2. 厂房土建及金属结构安装工程　2018年厂房标累计浇筑混凝土36万m³。9～10号安装间坝段最低浇筑至3211.6m高程、最高浇筑至3236.0m高程；11～13号主机间坝段坝体混凝土最低浇筑至3193.6m高程（主机间）、最高浇筑至3227.0m高程（挡水结构）。

3. 机电安装工程　安装间轨道及工位基础埋件安装完成；1、2、3号机肘管及1、2号机锥管安装完成，机组蜗壳安装完成率约40%；桥机轨道完成率约30%。

4. 帷幕灌浆工程　2018年完成全部坝段先导孔的施工。完成14～19号坝段的帷幕灌浆施工，合计完成基岩造孔及灌浆8657.6m，帷幕灌浆完成率约35%。

5. 鱼道工程　加查鱼道布置在河床左岸，主要由进口、尾水渠段、岸坡段、过坝段、出口明渠段、出口和鱼道观测研究室等部分组成，全长2597.42m。2018年9月开始鱼道施工，截至2018年底完成鱼道基础处理约750m。

（四）其他有关情况

（1）加查水电站上游围堰处流量，2018年8月6日达到7270m³/s，洪水超过5年一遇标准；8月27日达到7430m³/s，洪水接近10年一遇标准；8月29日达到8820m³/s，洪水接近20年一遇标准，汛情红色预警Ⅰ级启动。2018年8月31日根据国家水文基本站雅鲁藏布江羊村水文站测报信息，羊村站实测洪峰流量9510m³/s，接近50年一遇洪水标准流量9620m³/s，为新中国成立以来的实测最大洪水。

（2）加查水电站的业主为华能西藏雅鲁藏布江水电开发投资有限公司加查分公司，设计单位为中国电建集团成都勘测设计研究院有限公司，主要施工单位有中国水利水电第五工程局有限公司（大坝标）、中国葛洲坝集团有限公司（厂房土建及机电安装标）。

（中国电建集团成都勘测设计研究院有限公司　田雄　黄煌）

旬阳水电站工程2018年建设进展情况

旬阳水电站是汉江上游干流陕西境段第五个梯级电站，位于陕西省旬阳县城南2km，上距安康水电站65km，下距蜀河水电站57km；其开发任务以发电为主，兼顾航运，并促进地方经济社会发展，为二等大（2）型工程；水库正常蓄水位241m，死水位239m，总库容3.25亿m³；装机容量320MW，保证出力36.7MW，多年平均发电量8.4亿kW·h（引汉济渭调水10亿m³）。

枢纽建筑物由混凝土闸坝及河床式厂房组成。大坝为混凝土闸坝，坝顶高程247m，最大坝高58m，坝轴线长462m；共分成19个坝段，从左至右依次为安装间、主机间、左导墙、左五孔冲砂泄洪闸、右导墙、右七孔冲砂泄洪闸、右非坝段。

施工导流采用分期导流、两期施工。一期导流围左岸厂房、左右导墙坝段和左五孔冲砂泄洪闸坝段，水流由右岸河床下泄。二期导流枯水期江水由已建成的左五孔冲砂泄洪闸下泄，汛期由二期过水基坑和左五孔冲砂泄洪闸联合宣泄洪水。工程总工期54个月。

2015年8月，电站可行性研究报告通过水电水利规划设计总院审查，项目获得陕西省发展改革委核准；2016年11月，工程正式开工建设；计划2020年12月底，首批机组发电，2021年6月底工程完工。

截至2018年底，工程正在进行一期基坑内厂房坝段、左导墙坝段、右导墙坝段和左五孔冲砂泄洪闸施工。右导墙坝段最高浇筑至220m高程，固结灌浆420m。左导墙坝段最高浇筑至209.5m高程，固结灌浆300m。左五孔冲砂泄洪闸坝段最高浇筑至216m高程，消力池浇筑完成35块。厂房1、2号机组坝段，上游部分浇筑至203m高程，下游尾水管中墩、边墩浇筑至204.5m高程，肘管安装坑浇筑至190.5m高程，肘管安装完成7节，最高至199.76m高程；基础固结灌浆全部完成。厂房3号机组坝段，上游部分浇筑至194.9m高程，下游尾水管底板浇筑完成，肘管安装坑浇筑至190.5m高程。厂房4号机组坝段，上游部分浇筑至200m高程，下游尾水管底板浇筑完成，肘管安装坑浇筑至190.5m高程；机组和尾水管底板基础固结灌浆完成70%。安装间坝段浇筑至193m高程。尾水渠底板浇筑完成50%。

（中国电建集团北京勘测设计研究院有限公司　李贺林）

杨家湾水电站工程2018年建设进展情况

杨家湾水电站为小金川支流抚边河水电梯级规划中第4级电站，上游为木坡水电站，下游为已建的猛固桥水电站。电站为闸坝引水式开发，主要由首部枢纽、引水建筑物和厂区建筑物等组成。工程开发任务主要为发电，兼顾下游生态环境用水要求。水库正常蓄水位2574m，总库容96.1万m³，调节库容20.9万m³，具有日调节性能。通过左岸长11366m的引水隧洞引水至耿大地沟下游约800m处建地下厂房发电。电站额定引用流量53.4m³/s，装机3台，单机容量20MW，总装机容量60MW，保证出力5.5MW，年发电量25752万kW·h，年利用小时数4292h。

（一）枢纽布置

枢纽建筑物主要由首部枢纽、引水建筑物和厂区建筑物等组成。

(1) 首部枢纽由挡、泄水建筑物和取水建筑物组成。坝顶高程 2575.3m，坝顶全长为 113.06m。挡水建筑物沿坝轴线呈一直线布置，从左至右布置冲沙闸段、泄洪闸段、非溢流坝段。取水口位于左岸冲沙闸的上游侧。枢纽各建筑物均为混凝土结构，闸坝基础基岩段采用帷幕灌浆防止绕坝渗漏。

(2) 引水隧洞布置于抚边河左岸，全长约 11370m，断面采用马蹄形，顶拱内半径 2.22m，洞高 4.44m，进口底板高程 2562.0m，至调压室处底板高程降为 2528.4m，纵坡 $i=0.296\%$。

(3) 调压室为阻抗式，为了降低最高涌浪水位，利用顶部交通洞作为上室。内径 10～11.6m，底板高程 2528.4m，交通洞底板高程 2605m，高 76.6m。井身采用钢筋混凝土衬砌，最大衬厚 1.8m，四周进行固结灌浆和锚杆加固处理。调压井下游设置检修蝶阀室，内设 $D=3.6$m 的检修蝶阀。

(4) 压力管道采用埋藏式，采用一管三机方式，由上平段、竖井段、下平段组成，主管总长 199.4m，内径 3.6m，支管内径 2.25m。

(5) 厂房位于耿大地沟下游约 800m 处左岸山体内，主要建筑物有主厂房、副厂房、尾水建筑物、GIS 楼、进厂交通等。厂房纵轴线在平面上与抚边河流向约 29°夹角，从左至右依次布置安装间、主厂房及副厂房。

(二) 建设进展情况

(1) 首部枢纽工程：于 2017 年全部完成，并具备蓄水条件。2018 年 6 月 20 日，坝顶公路混凝土浇筑全部完成；6 月 29 日，坝顶照明设施完成；7 月 20 日，通过蓄水验收；7 月 21 日，开始蓄水。

(2) 引水系统工程：2018 年 3 月 21 日，完成引水隧洞衬砌混凝土浇筑；4 月 18 日，完成引水隧洞衬砌灌浆；4 月 25 日，完成支洞封堵，引水隧洞具备充水条件；5 月 31 日，输水系统通过安全鉴定。

调压井工程于 2017 年全部施工完成；压力管道于 2018 年 3 月 23 日完成金属结构安装及回填混凝土浇筑，4 月 20 日完成压力管道灌浆。

(3) 机电安装与试验：1、2、3 号机组，分别于 2018 年 3 月 22 日、5 月 5 日、5 月 12 日安装完成；1、2 号主变压器，分别于 2018 年 4 月 9 日、5 月 18 日完成强制性试验；出线场于 2018 年 5 月 8 日完成“π”接线路施工。2018 年 8 月 8 日，完成 1、2、3 号机组启动验收；8 月 24 日，1、3 号机组进入 72 小时试运行；9 月 20 日，2 号机组进入 72 小时试运行；机组试运行期间在各种工况下运行稳定，机组轴瓦温度及振摆监测数据均在规程规范限值以内，达到设计要求。2018 年 9 月 23 日，随着 2 号机组正式并入四川电网运行，三台机组全部投产发电。

（四川小金川水电开发有限公司）

叶巴滩水电站工程 2018 年建设进展情况

叶巴滩水电站位于金沙江上游河段四川省和西藏自治区的界河上，右岸为西藏昌都地区贡觉县，左岸为四川甘孜藏族自治州白玉县；是金沙江上游 13 个梯级水电站的第 7 级，上游为波罗水电站，下游为拉哇水电站。水库正常蓄水位 2889.00m，库容 10.80 亿 m^3；电站总装机容量为 2240MW，单独运行时，多年平均年发电量 91.6 亿 kW·h，和上游岗托水库联合运行时，多年平均年发电量 102.05 亿 kW·h。该电站为一等大（1）型工程，总投资 333.6 亿元；计划 2025 年 7 月首台机组投产发电。

2016 年 11 月，项目获得国家发展改革委核准。2017 年 6 月 27 日，叶巴滩水电站与甘孜州其他基础设施工程一起举行了启动仪式。2018 年主要施工项目为导流洞工程、左岸高线公路工程、右岸高线公路工程、施工辅助工程等施工。工程质量满足国家相关规程规范、设计、合同要求，获得质量监督总站的肯定。主要工程形象进度如下：

(1) 导流洞工程：左岸导流洞长 1002m，开挖支护完成、底板混凝土浇筑完成，边顶拱衬砌完成 908m，回填灌浆完成 51%，固结灌浆完成 41%。右岸导流洞工程长 896m，开挖支护完成，底板混凝土完成，边顶拱衬砌完成 874m，进水塔浇筑至 2740m 高程，回填灌浆完成 87%，固结灌浆完成 61%，进口明渠浇筑完成 50%。

(2) 场内交通：两岸 1、2 号低线公路于 2017 年底全面完成。2018 年初，4、6 号跨江临时桥实现通车；9 月底，下游永久大桥基础形成，钢拱架形成。左岸高线公路，5 号隧道总长 9878m，开挖支护完成 7148m，边顶拱衬砌完成 970m；7 号隧道总长 1608m，开挖支护完成 1250m。右岸高线公路，4 号隧道总长度为 3812m，开挖完成 807m；6 号隧道总长 2318m，开挖完成 1216m；8 号隧道总长 1370m，开挖支护完成 1060m。

(3) 施工辅助工程：业主营地工程、施工供电工程、炸药库、施工油库、1 号砂石系统建设建成。

(4) 沟水治理工程：在 2017 年降曲河排水洞施工完成实现过流，降曲河渣场正式启用后，2018 年 6 月，俄德西沟排水洞施工完成，实现过流，俄德西沟渣场具备启用条件。

2018 年 10 月及 11 月，金沙江上游白格滑坡连续两次跨塌堵江形成堰塞湖。堰塞湖溃决洪水经过叶巴滩水电站坝址的洪峰流量分别为 7770.0、28300m^3/s，前者达 300 年一遇洪峰流量。

“10·11”堰塞湖洪水造成较严重损失，左、右岸导流洞均进水、淤积严重，洞内部分施工设备、材料被淹；沿江低线临时施工营地被冲毁；低线公路 4 号索道桥桥台发生沉降变形，桥墩基础淘脚脱空，6 号索道桥桥墩基础局部脱空；截流材料大石取料区 3 号堆积体塌滑；永久桥桥面拱架变形；沿江施工辅助设施多处损毁。

“11·03”堰塞湖洪水通过后，叶巴滩水电站遭受严重损失。左右岸导流洞洞内被动过水、淤积严重，洞内钢模台车、钢筋台车等设施全部损毁；低线公路路基、路面和挡护设施全部损毁；江沿线供电、供风、照明、水情测报系统以及施工辅助设施全部损毁；4、6 号索桥基本损毁。

受“10·11”“11·03”白格堰塞湖的影响，叶巴滩水电站截流目标被迫推迟。

（华电金沙江上游水电开发有限公司
叶巴滩分公司　赵凯
中国电建集团成都勘测设计研究院
有限公司　张冲　邓兴富）

中国电建承建的重点常规水电工程 2018 年进展情况

（一）白鹤滩水电站工程

白鹤滩水电站位于金沙江下游四川省宁南县和云南省巧家县境内，左、右岸地下厂房各布置 8 台单机容量为 100 万 kW 的水轮发电机组。

白鹤滩水电站以其高坝大库、百万机组、复杂的地质条件和工程技术成为全球瞩目的焦点，堪称“目前中国乃至世界技术难度最高的水电工程”。中国电建集团华东勘测设计研究院有限公司（简称华东院）承担了该电站的设计，中国电建所属的中国水利水电第四、五、七、八、十四工程局有限公司（简称水电四、五、七、八、十四局）等子企业承担了该电站的施工任务。2018 年，各在建项目进展顺利，履约良好；电站引水发电系统工程施工全面进入混凝土浇筑高峰期，截至 12 月底，尾水调压室开挖支护、尾水隧洞底板混凝土施工已经进入收尾阶段，尾水隧洞边顶拱混凝土正处于浇筑高峰期；全年完成土石方明挖 224.9 万 m^3，混凝土浇筑 27.74 万 m^3，锚杆 1.63 万根，固结灌浆 5.67 万 m，回填灌浆 2.77 万 m^2，钢筋制作安装 2.64 万 t；进水塔混凝土施工整体封顶。

（二）乌东德水电站工程

乌东德水电站是金沙江下游四个梯级水电站的最上一级，左右岸各布置 6 台 85 万 kW 发电机组。

中国电建所属成都院数字工程分公司承接中国三峡建设管理有限公司“I-WB1 基于仓面混凝土质量控制驱动的大坝混凝土全过程高效施工智能控制系统”项目。中国电建所属水电七局主要承担乌东德电站砂石及混凝土供应，水电八局承担右岸电站 6 台 85 万 kW 水轮发电机组和公用辅助设备安装与调试。中国电建集团贵州电力设计研究院有限公司设计贵州境内 156km 高压直流线路。

2018 年，工程各方面建设取得重大进展，其中“大坝混凝土全过程高效安全施工智能控制系统—监控系统”正式上线运行；乌东德水电站工程大坝建设实现“双百”目标，大坝平均浇筑至高程 882.3m，单坝段最大上升 121m，浇筑混凝土 101.6 万 m^3；左右岸地下电站首批机组顺利实现土建向机电交面，国内首次大规模成功应用 800MPa 级高强钢，蜗壳和压力钢管焊接高质量完成；泄洪洞进水塔、左岸地下电站进水塔、右岸地下电站进水塔（7、9 号）等“三塔”浇筑到顶；全面研发应用智能灌浆系统，革新国内外灌浆工程管理；7 号机定子机座组装等工程。完成贵州义龙试验区至罗甸县，途径贵州省义龙试验区、安龙县、贞丰县、望谟县、罗甸县 156km 高压直流线路设计任务。

（三）两河口水电站项目

两河口水电站是藏区综合规模最大、雅砻江干流中游规划建设的 7 座梯级电站中装机规模最大的水电站工程。电站由中国电建所属的成都院设计，中国电建所属的水电十四局、水电十六局、水电十二局、水电五局等子企业承担了该电站的施工任务。水电十四局作为两河口电站主要参建单位之一，与水电十六局组成联合体共同担负引水发电系统工程，并单独承担机电设备安装工程。2018 年是两河口水电站引水发电系统工程开挖向混凝土浇筑转序的关键年，竖井开挖进入攻坚阶段，金属结构安装全面启动。电站进水塔浇筑平稳上升，6 号塔浇筑至 2852m 高程，完成 2018 年保蓄水发电目标节点要求；三大洞室顺利实现从开挖向混凝土施工转序，厂房 5、6 号机组按期向机电标交面；安全标准化保持一级达标；施工质量得到水电工程质量监督总站巡视组肯定；联合体荣获四川省总工会授予的“五一劳动奖状”及管理局“诚信履约优秀项目部”等多项表彰。

（四）黄登水电站工程

黄登水电站装机容量 190 万 kW，被业界誉为“澜沧江流域施工难度最大电站”。

该工程由中国电建所属的昆明院设计，中国电建所属的水电四局、十四局、水电基础局、西北院等承担施工任务。2018年，黄登水电站主坝混凝土浇筑至全线达到1625m设计高程；7月，首台机组投产发电。

（五）杨房沟水电站项目

杨房沟水电站安装4台37.5万kW的混流式水轮发电机组，是全国首个百万千万级EPC水电工程项目，由中国电建所属的水电七局和华东院组成雅砻江杨房沟水电站设计施工总承包项目部承建。

2018年6月30日，地下厂房开挖支护全部完成；10月30日，大坝浇筑首仓混凝土，电站主体工程施工成功转序。

（六）大藤峡水利枢纽工程

大藤峡水利枢纽工程坝址区在广西桂平市，是一座以防洪、航运、发电、补水压咸、灌溉等综合利用的流域关键性工程；总库容34.79亿m^3，总装机容量160万kW。中国电建所属的水电八局主要承建一期左岸泄水闸、左岸厂房左岸泄水坝段工程、纵向围堰坝段工程、左岸厂房发电系统工程。

2018年2月3日，泄水闸工作门二期首仓混凝土开浇；4月6日，泄水闸第一根钢梁吊装；6月6日，泄水闸23号坝段一区到顶；6月17日，厂房8号机组座环开始吊装。

（七）大古水电站工程

大古水电站位于西藏自治区山南地区雅鲁藏布江干流藏木峡谷河段之上，工程区距桑日县城公路里程约43km，距山南市泽当镇约78km，距拉萨市约263km。该电站为二等大（2）型工程，开发任务以发电为主；水库正常蓄水位3447m，相应库容0.5528亿m^3；装机容量为66万kW，多年平均发电量32亿kW·h。电站枢纽建筑物由挡水建筑物、泄洪消能建筑物、引水发电系统及升压站等组成。拦河坝为碾压混凝土重力坝，坝顶高程3451.00m，最大坝高118.0m，坝顶长389.0m。发电厂房采用坝后式布置，主要由主厂房、副厂房、变电站等组成，安装4台单机容量为16.5万kW的混流式水轮发电机组。2018年8月开工建设，10月在6号坝段基础层完成大坝首仓混凝土浇筑，11月坝基开挖完成，12月大坝垫层混凝土浇筑完成，进入固结灌浆施工。

（八）瓦托水电站工程

瓦托水电站是金河水电规划中的第5个梯级，位于西藏自治区昌都市卡若镇列巴村金河下游约2.5km处，是一座以发电为主的中型水电枢纽工程。共3台机组，总装机容量5万kW，年发电量2.10亿kW·h。大坝为混凝土重力坝，最大坝高70.0m。中国电建所属的水电七局主要承建电站土建施工及发电系统、机电设备安装、导流洞、坝身进水口及厂房等施工。2018年12月31号，首台3号机组投产发电。

（九）里底水电站工程

里底水电站安装3台单机容量为14万kW的轴流转桨式机组。中国电建所属的水电十四局以施工总承包形式中标里底水电站土建、金属结构及机电安装工程。2018年5月三期施工完成，9月15日下闸蓄水，10月29日首台机组发电，12月31日第二台机组正式投产发电。

（中国电力建设集团有限公司）

硬梁包水电站工程建设情况

（一）工程概况

硬梁包水电站位于四川省甘孜藏族自治州泸定县冷碛镇境内的大渡河干流上，为四川省大渡河干流最新规划28级方案的第14级电站，上游为泸定水电站，下游梯级衔接大岗山水电站；采用引水式开发，闸址处流域面积59516km^2，多年平均流量为897m^3/s。水库正常蓄水位1246m，相应库容2075.4万m^3，调节库容826万m^3，具有日调节性能。电站总装机容量111.6万kW，与上游双江口水库联合运行多年平均年发电量51.42亿kW·h，枯水期电量10.66亿kW·h，枯水年枯期平均出力24.7万kW。电站建成后供电四川电网，参与川电外送。

该电站为二等大（2）型工程，采用混凝土闸和面板堆石坝＋左岸引水系统＋地下厂房的枢纽总布置方案。闸址处安装3.6万kW生态机组，以满足134.7m^3/s的最小生态流量下泄要求。主电站额定引用流量1261.2m^3/s，通过2条长约14.4km引水隧洞在下游花石包地下厂房安装4台单机容量为27万kW的水轮发电机组发电。

硬梁包水电站工程规模较大，特别是两条引水隧洞规模居国际前列；工程地质条件复杂，地震烈度较高；工程设计及施工技术难度大；工程为引水式开发，且紧临贡嘎山风景名胜区，环境保护要求高。工程技术难点及重点主要包括首部枢纽基础处理设计、引水隧洞开挖施工及支护设计、地下厂房洞室群施工期围岩稳定分析及支护设计、过鱼设施设计等。

（二）项目进展情况

2009年1月水电水利规划设计总院会同四川省发展改革委在四川省成都市共同主持并审查通过了《四川省大渡河硬梁包水电站开发方式研究报告》（水电规规〔2009〕8号）。同意本河段的开发任务为发电，同意硬梁包水电站采用一级低闸（坝）长引水开发方式。

2010年3月12～14日，水电水利规划设计总院会同四川省发展改革委在四川省成都市共同主持并审查通过了《四川省大渡河硬梁包水电站预可行性研究报告》。

2015年3月28～30日，水电水利规划设计总院会同四川省发展改革委、能源局在成都召开会议，审查通过了《四川省大渡河硬梁包水电站可行性研究报告》。

2016年2月25日，项目业主——四川华能泸定水电有限公司获得《四川省发展和改革委员会关于大渡河硬梁包水电站项目核准的批复》（川发能源〔2016〕65号）。

2016年5月23日，2016年四川省重大招商引资项目集中开工仪式暨华能硬梁包水电站开工仪式在泸定大渡河畔举行，硬梁包水电站开工建设。

自2016年5月以来，硬梁包项目已陆续完成了中心炸药库、35kV和10kV施工供电线路、专用油库、场内外交通（包括省道S211改线和5座跨河交通桥）、承包商管理营地等工程，施工辅助项目全面完成。2018年7月开始，引水隧洞1～7号施工支洞，调压室交通洞，地下厂房进厂交通洞、进风洞、出线兼排风洞，开关站，尾水隧洞上支洞等相继开工，预计将于2019年8～12月陆续完工，届时，硬梁包水电站项目具备主体工程全面开工条件。

另外，2018年9月，《硬梁包水电站工程设计优化初步研究报告》完成；12月30日，《硬梁包水电站工程设计优化研究报告（送审稿）》按时完成并提交业主。

（中国电建集团成都勘测设计研究院
有限公司 王锋 尹建辉）

银江水电站工程2018年建设情况

银江水电站位于金沙江中游攀枝花河段末端——金沙江和雅砻江汇合口上游约3.6km，上游衔接梯级为金沙水电站，两梯级相距21.4km；坝址控制流域面积25.89万km^2，多年平均流量1870m^3/s，年径流量590亿m^3。水库正常蓄水位998.5m，死水位998.0m，校核洪水位为1004.99m，相应总库容为0.6亿m^3；大坝为混凝土重力坝，坝顶高程1008m，最大坝高73m，采取“左厂右泄”的枢纽布置格局；电站装机容量390MW，多年平均年发电量18.34亿kW·h（龙盘建成后），为二等大（2）型工程。

2018年1月，受四川省发展改革委的委托，中国国际工程咨询有限公司组织专家召开了金沙江银江水电站项目申请报告评估会议。2018年4月金沙江银江水电站获四川省发展改革委的项目核准批复。

［长江三峡勘测研究院
有限公司（武汉） 刘培培］

夏特水电站工程2018年建设进展情况

夏特水电站位于新疆克孜勒苏柯尔克孜自治州乌恰县克孜河中游，为克孜河流域规划2库6级开发方案中的第3个梯级，从上游已建成的塔日勒嘎水电站尾水取水，经长约20km的隧洞引水至发电厂房；电站安装4台单机容量为6.2万kW的混流式水轮发电机组，总装机容量24.8万kW。该电站的业主为克州新隆能源开发有限公司（简称克州新隆公司），项目2016年1月10日取得新疆维吾尔自治区发展改革委核准的批复文件，2017年7月15日主体工程开工，计划工期48个月。

2018年克州新隆公司克服种种不利因素，工程建设进度、质量、安全、投资、环保水保处于在控受控状态，全面完成了年度计划任务。电站建设主要进展情况如下：

（1）2017年底～2018年5月，南疆地区防恐维稳形势严峻，公安机关进一步加强了火工材料管控，对夏特水电站工程施工进度造成影响，出现停工、窝工。这种情况下，克州新隆公司通过与自治区、州、县政府和边防、公安多次协调、反复沟通，经过近5个月的不懈努力，最终解决了火工材料使用、签证、运输、管理等问题。通过优化施工工艺、加大资源投入，确保施工进度按计划推进。2018年已完成主洞开挖支护进尺10869m，年计划完成率达到138%，其中2号下至3号上控制段提前实现了贯通目标。

（2）2018年工程优化设计变更涉及的环保、土地预审、移民安置规划等专题通过了审查批复。为了取得引水线路埋涵段穿越基本农田变更批复，克州新隆公司多次与县、州、自治区国土部门沟通，州国土局召开了土地复垦报告审查会，区国土资源厅组织州县国土资源局对涉及650m基本农田段进行了实地踏勘，论证后按程序进行批复。

（3）针对夏特水电站高水头、多泥沙、高地震特点，组织开展了水轮机抗磨蚀试验研究及隧洞衬砌优化工作，引水隧洞衬砌、抗硫水泥使用、调压井竖井开挖、压力钢管材质等优化工作取得明显效果；高水头水电站多泥沙处理科研项目通过验收专家组的鉴定验收，水轮机抗磨蚀试验研究及隧洞衬砌优化工作取得阶段性成果。

（4）制定了夏特水电站争创“省部级优质工程”（天山杯、电建股份优质工程、中国安装之星）策划书，推进夏特水电站工程“创优”工作；通过修订完善了质量管理制度体系，加强质量管控等手段，保证工程建设质量，验收土建单元工程652个（包括临时工程），合格率100%，优良率93.7%。

（5）圆满的完成了机电设备调研与设备选型、机电项目技术审查、设计联络、技术交流、监造管理以及水轮发电机组、球阀等主要设备招标等相关工作。

（6）落实安全生产责任制，实现“零”事故目标。开展安全生产一级达标创建、应急能力建设评估、防恐维稳等工作，实现了“零”责任事故管理目标；安全管理“四个责任体系”健全，安全管理制度体系满足安全管理需要，具有较强的针对性、适用性和全面性；全面完成年度安全生产责任目标。

（克州新隆能源开发有限公司）

中国华电集团有限公司 2018年前期项目筹建情况

（一）龙盘水电综合枢纽工程

龙盘水电综合枢纽工程为金沙江中游“一库八级”的龙盘水电站与两家人水电站，位于迪庆州与丽江市的金沙江界河段。

龙盘水电站正常蓄水位2010m，总库容386亿m^3，调节库容215.2亿m^3，具备多年调节能力；电站装机容量420万kW（6×70万kW），保证出力214万kW，年发电量175亿kW·h。两家人水电站位于龙盘水电站下游2km，完全接龙盘下泄流量发电，在规划中，与龙盘作为同一组电源点同步运行；水库正常蓄水位1781m，电站装机容量300万kW（6×50万kW），多年平均发电量122.8亿kW·h（与龙盘联合运行时发电量140亿kW·h）；电站为引水式开发，4条引水隧洞平均长约12km。

在2017年12月水电水利规划设计总院组织召开虎跳峡河段开发方案深入研究论证报告评审会的工作基础上，2018年4月取得了国家发展改革委关于龙头水库比选的批复文件（发改办能源〔2018〕474号）。该文件同意推荐的龙盘坝址方案，中国电建集团中南勘测设计研究院有限公司完成了龙盘工程预可行性研究报告编制和汇报材料准备，具备预可行性研究报告审查条件。

（二）波罗水电站

波罗水电站位于四川白玉县与西藏江达县境内的金沙江干流上，坝址区位于西藏自治区江达县藏曲河口以上约3km河段上，为规划金沙江上游川藏段13个梯级电站中的第6级，上游为岗托水电站，下游与叶巴滩水电站衔接。预可行性研究阶段推荐枢纽布置方案为混凝土双曲拱坝＋右岸引水发电系统，电站正常蓄水位为2989m，总库容为8.52亿m^3，最大坝高138m。

截至2018年底，预可行性研究报告已通过审查，可行性研究设计工作在有序推进。

（三）岗托水电站

岗托水电站位于四川德格县与西藏江达县境内的金沙江干流上，坝址区位于四川德格县色曲河口以上约9km河段上，为规划金沙江上游川藏段13个梯级电站中的第4级，上游为果通水电站，下游与岩比水电站衔接。岗托水电站为金沙江上游规划河段控制性龙头水库，预可行性研究阶段推荐枢纽布置方案为面板堆石坝＋右岸泄洪＋左岸引水发电系统，电站正常蓄水位为3215m，总库容为55.42亿m^3，最大坝高223m。

截至2018年底，预可研报告已通过审查，可行性研究设计工作在有序推进。

（四）昌波水电站

昌波水电站位于四川巴塘县与西藏芒康县境内的金沙江干流上，坝址区位于苏洼龙至昌波（麦曲河）河段上，为规划金沙江上游川藏段13个梯级电站中的第11级，上游为苏洼龙水电站，下游与旭龙水电站衔接。预可行性研究阶段推荐枢纽布置方案为混凝土闸坝＋左岸引水发电系统，电站正常蓄水位为2387m，总库容为0.167亿m^3，最大坝高45m。

截至2018年底，预可行性研究报告已通过审查，可行性研究设计工作在有序推进。

（华电云南发电有限公司　刘文斌
华电金沙江上游水电开发有限公司
波罗电站筹备处　王远龙
华电金沙江上游水电开发有限公司　申宏波
华电金沙江上游水电开发有限公司
苏洼龙分公司　唐明武）

国电大渡河流域水电开发有限公司 2018年前期项目筹建情况

（一）金川水电站

金川水电站坝址位于四川省阿坝州金川县境内，电站正常蓄水位2253m，库容4.88亿m^3，选定装机容量86万kW。2018年12月4日，四川省发展和改革委员会以川发改能源〔2018〕544号文对大渡河金川水电站项目核准进行了批复，同意金川水电站建设。

（二）安宁、巴底水电站

安宁、巴底两个梯级水电站坝址相邻，均位于大渡河上游阿坝州境内，规划总装机容量 110 万 kW，两个水电站均已完成预可研设计，可研设计正有序推进。2018 年度安宁、巴底水电站主要工作为继续深入设计优化。巴底水电站在前期优化成果的基础上，开展了对库区重要指标复核和对区域移民安置补偿政策及同流域相邻电站补偿标准的调查研究。先后完成了《巴底水电站建设征地移民安置补偿费用估算复核修改报告》《巴底水电站设计优化投资概算及投资效益分析报告》。安宁水电站开展了梯级开发方案分析、坝址方案及枢纽布置方案对比和厂房型式比选复核，完成了两级闸坝与单级开发方案的经济分析对比工作。

（三）丹巴水电站

丹巴水电站坝址位于大渡河上游甘孜州境内，规划装机容量 119.66 万 kW。可研阶段施工总布置和正常蓄水位专题报告已通过审查。2018 年继续开展设计优化工作，一是在前期设计优化成果的基础上，对隧洞减糙、引水隧洞洞渣料和天然砂石料利用等进行更深入的分析研究；二是继续开展了引水式电站减水河段生态及流量等环保专题研究。

（四）枕头坝二级、沙坪一级水电站

枕头坝二级水电站坝址位于四川省乐山市金口河区，电站装机容量 32.6 万 kW，多年平均发电量为 15.4 亿 kW·h。沙坪一级水电站坝址位于金口河区和峨边彝族自治县境内的大渡河下游河段，电站装机容量 34 万 kW，多年平均发电量为 15.94 亿 kW·h。2018 年 2 月 12 日，国电大渡河流域水电开发有限公司与乐山市人民政府签订《合作备忘录》，加快枕头坝二级、沙坪一级水电站前期工作。2018 年 9 月 12 日，国家能源集团文件批复成立国电大渡河流域水电开发有限公司枕沙水电建设管理分公司（简称枕沙建设分公司），2018 年 12 月 18 日，枕沙建设分公司正式挂牌运营。有序推进枕头坝二级、沙坪一级水电站预可研收口工作。

（五）老鹰岩水电站

老鹰岩水电站坝址位于大渡河中游雅安市石棉县境内，分两级开发，规划总装机容量 67 万 kW。2018 年，老鹰岩一、二级电站启动预可行性研究工作，设计单位于 2018 年 4 月底完成现场地勘工作，12 月底完成老鹰岩一、二级水电站预可行性研究报告初稿。

（六）帕隆藏布流域

2018 年 4 月水电水利规划设计总院组织专家对帕隆藏布流域资源规划开展了中间检查。专家组现场考察了规划河段自然地理、社会经济、生态环境、地形地质条件等基本情况。于 2018 年 6 月，在西安召开了西藏帕隆藏布水电规划报告及规划环评咨询会议，咨询意见认为报告提出的规划成果基本合适，即梯级电站按“一库九级”总装机容量 1143 万 kW，年平均利用小时 4500h 左右，年发电量 517.94 亿 kW·h，专家建议进一步完善规划设计成果及规划报告。同时，西藏自治区能源局委托了水电水利规划设计总院组织划定西藏水电生态保护红线工作，位于雅鲁藏布大峡谷自然保护区的帕隆藏布流域汇合口以下的重点梯级（通灯、新玉、帕隆）在 2018 年划出了生态红线范围，同年 11 月通过西藏自治区层面审查并上报国家林业与草原局。

（国家能源集团国电大渡河流域水电开发有限公司）

猴子岩水电站工程通过枢纽竣工安全鉴定

猴子岩水电站位于四川省甘孜藏族自治州康定县境内，是大渡河干流水电规划调整“3 库 22 级”的第 9 个梯级电站。电站采用堤坝式开发，水库正常蓄水位 1842.00m，相应库容 6.62 亿 m^3，总库容 7.06 亿 m^3，死水位 1802.00m，调节库容 3.87 亿 m^3，具有季调节性能。电站安装 4 台 425MW 的混流式水轮发电机组，总装机容量 1700MW，单独运行多年平均发电量 70.15kW·h，上游双江口水库建成后多年平均发电量 73.64 亿 kW·h。

猴子岩水电站工程为一等大（1）型工程。枢纽建筑物由拦河坝，两岸泄洪及放空建筑物、右岸地下引水发电系统等组成。拦河坝为混凝土面板堆石坝，最大坝高 223.5m，右岸布置 1 条溢洪洞和 1 条泄洪放空洞，左岸布置 1 条深孔泄洪洞和 1 条非常泄洪洞。

猴子岩水电站于 2017 年 4 台机组全部投产。2018 年 1 月，该电站工程完成竣工质量监督；11 月 25 日，完成达标投产复验；12 月 22 日，完成枢纽工程竣工安全鉴定。

（国电大渡河流域水电开发有限公司）

向家坝升船机投入试通航

2018 年 5 月 26 日上午，随着“宇航 69 号”散货船缓缓驶出向家坝升船机承船厢驶入上游向家坝库区，向家坝升船机正式投入试通航。向家坝升船机本着“安全第一、以试为主、逐步完善”的原则开展试通航，时间暂定为1年，运行计划拟分为三个阶段实施。第一阶段时间暂定为2018年5～6月底（向家坝水库泄流量接近机组满发流量止、不泄洪）。第二阶段2018年7～8月，向家坝升船机暂停试通航，开展汛期大流量实船试航工作，组织对相关试航报告进行评审，明确升船机下游最高通航水位及对应流量；并择机对升船机试通航前验收相关问题建议及第一阶段试通航过程中发现的问题进行整改完善。第三阶段2018年9月～2019年5月，进一步检验升船机设备设施运行性能，优化相关运行工艺流程，发现问题及时整改；进一步掌握过机船舶在各种通航流量级下的航行特性。试通航期间，升船机运行时间为每日8时～18时。

2018年6月29日，随着电站表孔开启泄洪，向家坝升船机停航。至此，向家坝升船机试通航第一阶段安全、顺利完成。试通航期间升船机设备设施性能良好，过机船舶安检、调度有序进行，整体安全、平稳、有序。截至6月28日，向家坝升船机共运行196厢次（含空驶厢次），通过船舶153艘次，通过货运量44352t，上行货物主要是硫磺，下行货物主要是化肥、河沙、煤炭等。

向家坝升船机为一级全平衡垂直升船机，布置在大坝左岸，包括上游引航道、上闸首（包括挡水坝段和渡槽段）、船厢室段、下闸首和下游引航道（含辅助闸室和辅助闸首）等5部分，全长约1530m。升船机按Ⅳ级航道标准设计，设计代表船型为2×500t级一顶二驳船队；2009年进行优化和扩能，以满足1000t级单船过坝的要求，承船厢的水深由2.5m增加到3.0m（船厢总长125m）。升船机最大提升高度114.20m，为世界之最。

2011年5月，向家坝升船机开始筒体及挡水结构混凝土施工，2013年10月塔柱封顶；2014年4月，船厢分段结构进场安装；2015年11月，船厢首次试验性充水；随后开展了安全机构载荷试验、驱动系统和安全制动系统调试、安全机构与驱动系统液气弹簧联动、安全机构与对接锁定装置联动、船厢全行程升降运行、船厢与闸首对接、流程调试等各项试验和调试。

2017年9月8日，升船机进行了首次过船联合调试。9月12日，升船机采用集控方式按自动流程完成了不间断往返三次过船试验，试验结果表明，升船机各机构运行正常、各系统功能正常、运行控制流程合理，满足设计要求和船舶安全通行的条件。2018年1月11～14日，水电水利规划设计总院组织开展了向家坝升船机试通航前验收现场检查工作。1月21～27日，三峡集团组织开展了向家坝升船机第一阶段实船试航，包括辅助闸室投用与不投用两种工况下空载货船、重载货船、客船过机试验，船舶超设计吃水试验，船舶夜航试验，防撞装置撞击等试验。经实船试航验证，在1600～5180m^3/s的流量条件下，上下游引航道及口门区水流平缓，通航条件良好；向家坝升船机整体运行平稳，升船机及助导航设备设施性能良好，升船机协调组织管理机构运作正常沟通顺畅、船舶通过性较好。2018年5月11日，向家坝升船机试通航前验收委员会在向家坝召开了向家坝升船机试通航前验收会议，通过了试通航前验收。5月26日，向家坝升船机投入试通航运行。

向家坝升船机为齿轮齿条爬升、短螺杆长螺母柱保安式全平衡垂直升船机，单程提升高度居世界前列（比三峡工程升船机高1.2m），其结构尺寸和承船厢带水体总重量虽比三峡升船机要小，但场地地震设计加速度比三峡要大，升船机主体结构和设备的抗震要求更高；升船机位于河道主流，周边受力条件复杂；下游引航道和河道水流坡降较大，水位波动较明显，水流条件较差。因而，向家坝升船机综合技术难度与三峡升船机基本相当，均属世界最高水平。

向家坝升船机设计和施工的难题主要有：

（1）混凝土塔柱结构与船厢设备精度控制问题。船厢室段塔柱为超高混凝土薄壁结构，布置大量高精度要求的一、二期金属结构埋件，对混凝土施工精度控制非常严格。船厢在工厂分块制造，现场拼装成整体，拼装后的长度误差正负不超过10mm，宽度误差正负不超过7mm；齿条高度达到122.4m，安装后每节齿条高度标记至最底节齿条高度标记的高度偏差正负1mm；螺母柱公称直径为1.05m，安装高度达到121.5m，安装成整体后的主要精度指标误差不超过5mm；安全机构横梁中心线距螺母柱横向中心线尺寸偏差在正负2mm以内；驱动机构横梁横向中心线距齿条中心线尺寸偏差在正负2mm以内。

（2）船厢驱动系统、安全保障系统及联动结构安全可靠性问题。升船机运行过程中，当遭遇全平衡系统破坏时（包括船厢水漏空、对接状态水满厢、对接状态沉船等事故工况），船厢需按程序进行锁死，避免发生倾覆危险。因而对船厢驱动系统、安全保障系统以及联动机构的可靠性要求特别高。

（3）非恒定流造成下游水位变率大的问题。升船机下游引航位于金沙江主河道，又临近枢纽泄洪建筑物消能区下方，口门区和航道水流条件十分复杂。尤其在泄洪或电站机组开停机工况下，非恒定流造成的下游水位变率和波浪问题十分突出。

（4）混凝土塔柱结构和船厢设备地震耦合载荷和抗震安全问题。向家坝升船机船厢加水总重约8150t，主体结构和设备规模巨大，遭遇地震工况时，将发生挤压变形或脱空事故。由于坝区场地地震设防烈度较高，升船机主体结构和设备在地震工况下耦合载荷大，抗震和防震问题十分突出。

向家坝升船机建设关键技术突破主要有：

(1) 在非恒定流通航水力学和应对措施研究方面，针对性提出了口门区和下游航道疏浚与整治方案，改善了航道条件；在船厢室下游设置了辅助闸室，保证了升船机在下游较大水位变率情况下能够连续安全运行。

(2) 研发了高精度复杂塔柱筒体结构施工技术，如研制了高精度复杂结构塔柱群液压自升式模板，采用了大跨度悬空渡槽施工技术等。

(3) 研发了高精度超大型金属结构及设备安装技术，如编制了向家坝升船机齿条、螺母柱设备安装等10多个质量检测及评定标准，为高精度安装提供了技术保障。

(4) 采取了船厢及其设备与塔柱结构变形协调技术。在设计阶段，重点研究各类结构和设备能够适应船厢与塔柱之间在各个方向的相对变位或设备制造、安装误差的措施；施工前，开展了塔柱结构施工期仿真计算，确定了合理的施工程序和施工工艺；施工时，及时进行跟踪反馈分析，指导现场土建施工和设备安装。此外，进行了全平衡齿轮齿条爬升式升船机驱动机构和安全机构适应塔柱变形的工作原理研究、事故安全机构短螺杆与螺母柱间隙需考虑的塔柱和船厢变形等因素分析、同步轴系统适应船厢结构变形的原理和要求研究，最终确定了塔柱结构和船厢结构的变形控制指标。在施工程序安排上，较高高程的螺母柱是在塔柱承重结构加载（平衡重加船厢总重，载荷约16000t）状态下，才进行安装，减少了塔柱承载后变形对螺母柱垂直度的不利影响。

(5) 升船机土建结构和设备抗震技术方面，在船厢上设置了适应地震工况的纵向、横向导向机构，安装了合理参数的阻尼器，可保证在极端地震条件下船厢与塔柱不发生机构性破坏，船厢不倾斜和坠落事故。

（中国三峡建设管理有限公司）

云南滇中引水工程 2018年建设情况

滇中引水工程是国务院确定的172项节水供水重大水利工程中的标志性工程。2018年1月，《滇中引水工程初步设计报告》（简称初设报告）通过了水利部水利水电规划设计总院技术审查（水总设〔2018〕116号）；2018年3月，初设报告取得水利部行政许可批复（水许可决〔2018〕20号）；至此，滇中引水工程全面进入招标技施阶段。

滇中引水工程勘察设计工作由长江勘测规划设计研究有限责任公司（简称长江设计公司）联合中国电建集团昆明勘测设计研究院有限公司（简称昆明院）、云南省水利水电勘测设计研究院（简称云南省院）共同承担。长江设计公司为技术总牵头并承担石鼓水源工程和输水工程大理Ⅰ段勘察设计工作，其中勘察工作由长江三峡勘测研究院有限公司（武汉）（简称三峡院）承担；昆明院承担输水工程楚雄段和昆明段勘察设计工作，云南省院承担输水工程大理Ⅱ段、玉溪和红河段勘察设计工作。

（一）技术牵头与招标设计勘察工作

2018年度，三峡院牵头完成滇中引水工程输水工程主体标招标设计阶段勘察设计工作大纲、滇中引水工程输水工程主体标技施设计阶段勘察设计工作大纲以及石鼓水源和大理Ⅰ段招标、技施工作大纲，滇中引水工程招标设计报告技术咨询及报告修编工作。

本年度开展的勘察工作主要完成石鼓水源工程跨渠桥勘探、泵站区勘探平洞试验支洞及倒车点扩洞开挖、物探测试（长勘所）及原位力学试验（长江科学院）等工作；重点完成大理Ⅰ段芹河古泥石流堆积体隧洞下穿段线路优化勘察工作以及芹河隧洞地下水监测专题QHJCZK3孔勘探工作；针对香炉山隧洞退水通道、海东退水通道、海东隧洞0号支洞排水泵站、大理州35kV施工变电站及部分塔基（邓川湿地）等部位实施了补充勘察；完成庆鑫料场替代料源北营料场的详查工作等。

完成滇中引水工程大理Ⅰ段施工1标、施工2标、施工3标及打锣箐砂石系统标的招标设计报告及施工招标文件技术条款地质章节编制工作；完成输水总干渠隧洞超前地质预报、地下水环境监测两个专项招标设计报告及招标文件技术条款、工程量清单及相关图件和附表；完成滇中引水工程大理Ⅰ段总干渠下穿芹河古泥石流堆积体洞段线路优化比选专题、滇中引水工程大理Ⅰ段下河坝暗涵输水方式比选专题、滇中引水工程大理Ⅱ段海东分（退）水工程设计专题、滇中引水工程大理Ⅰ段与大丽铁路交叉（伴行）专题等地质工作。此外，承担和参与的《香炉山隧洞穿越活动断裂工程活动性深化研究》专题正与中山大学合作顺利推进；参与的《隧洞超前地质预报系统2.0》研发初步完成了三维可视化平台建设（包括综合展示、数据采集、查询和实时更新、施工进度、诊断会商等模块），实现了三维模型文件导入和更新、隧洞施工进度动态展示、洞内外交互漫游查询和搜索等功能。

（二）施工地质及补充勘察工作

2018 年度同步开展滇中引水工程勘察试验性工程（香炉山隧洞 1、2、5 号施工支洞），大理Ⅰ段施工 2 标、施工 3 标包含的香炉山隧洞 3、3-1、4、7、8 号施工支洞，香炉山隧洞—上果园隧洞段施工支洞进场道路和沿线弃渣场，以及 35kV 施工供电项目（丽江段）等前期施工配套工程及其附属工程现场施工地质工作。

此外，针对香炉山隧洞 7 号施工支洞跨中缅天然气管道桥、波罗弃渣场等部位实施了施工地质补充勘察工作。

2018 年度，滇中引水工程各项勘察工作进展顺利，质量符合相关规程规范要求，为工程招标与技施阶段的设计和施工提供可靠技术支撑。

［长江三峡勘测研究院有限公司（武汉） 王旺盛］

抽水蓄能工程

中国电建承建的抽水蓄能工程 2018 年进展情况

（一）文登抽水蓄能电站工程

文登抽水蓄能电站安装 6 台单机容量为 30 万 kW 的单级混流可逆式抽水蓄能机组；在国内水电工程中首次大规模采用全强风化料作为混凝土面板堆石坝的坝料（占整个坝体的填筑量约 37%），以及在国内抽水蓄能电站工程中首次在地下洞室采用 TBM 掘进技术。

该电站由中国电建所属的北京院设计，土建主体工程由葛洲坝二公司、中铁十四局承担，筹建期工程由中国电建所属的水电一局、水电三局、水电七局等企业承担施工任务。截至 2018 年 12 月底，电站筹建期工程已基本完成，引水发电系统工程施工全面进入洞室开挖高峰期。

（二）沂蒙抽水蓄能电站工程

沂蒙抽水蓄能电站安装 4 台单机容量为 30 万 kW 的单级混流可逆式水泵水轮机—发电电动机机组，其主要技术难点和特点包括：上水库沥青混凝土面板堆石坝坝高坡陡，下水库混凝土面板坝折线型布置面板受力条件复杂，输水系统高压竖井一次开挖成型施工难度大，地下厂房系统采用多专业 BIM 协同设计。

该电站由中国电建所属的北京院设计，水电一局、水电二局、水电四局、水电十四局、水电十六局等子企业承担施工任务。

截至 2018 年 12 月底工程进度形象如下：供水、供电、通风兼安全洞和进厂交通洞已施工完成；场内道路基本完成。上水库库盆累计完成土石方开挖 695 万 m^3，占总开挖量的 77%；大坝填筑 390 万 m^3，占总填筑量的 63%。高压管道上平段、上弯段及下平段开挖支护均已完成；高压管道竖井正在开挖；尾水隧洞主洞正在开挖，已完成总开挖量的 83%。地下厂房开挖至蜗壳层、排风竖井开挖支护完成；主变压器室第三层开挖支护完成；地面开关站土石方开挖完成。下水库大坝已经填筑到顶；库区开挖基本完成；泄洪放空洞闸门井开挖支护完成，洞身无压段衬砌完成，有压段正在进行衬砌施工。

（三）敦化抽水蓄能电站工程

敦化抽水蓄能电站安装 4 台单机容量 35 万 kW 的单级混流可逆式抽水蓄能机组，地处严寒地区，为在建项目水头最高的抽水蓄能电站，采用沥青混凝土心墙堆石坝。

该电站由中国电建所属的北京院设计，中电建建筑集团和中国电建所属的水电六局、水电七局、水电十一局、水电十四局、水电十六局等子企业承担施工任务。截至 2018 年 12 月底，下水库大坝填筑至坝顶，泄水建筑物施工完成，具备蓄水安全鉴定的条件；引水系统贯通，地下厂房开挖支护完成，1 号机组蜗壳层浇筑完成。

（四）琼中抽水蓄能电站

由中国电建所属的中南院勘测设计，水电十二局、水电十四局、水电七局施工的海南琼中抽水蓄能电站，位于南渡江南源黎田河上游，装设 3 台单机容量 20 万 kW 的可逆式抽水蓄能机组。该电站是昌江核电站的配套工程，主要承担海南电网调峰、填谷、调频、调相、紧急事故备用和黑启动等任务，是中国首个海岛绿色抽水蓄能电站，是海南省的首个抽水蓄能电站。2018 年 2 月 6 日，随着 2 号机组成功并网发电，海南琼中抽水蓄能电站 3 台机组全部投产发电。

（中国电力建设集团有限公司）

清原抽水蓄能电站工程 2018 年建设进展情况

清原抽水蓄能电站位于辽宁省抚顺市清原满族自治县北三家镇境内，下水库坝址经北三家镇至抚顺市公路里程 117km，经抚顺市至沈阳市公路里程 176km；电站额定水头 390m，安装 6 台单机容量 300MW 的可逆式抽水蓄能机组，总装机容量为 1800MW；设计年发电量 30.11 亿 kW·h，年发电利用小时数 1673h；年抽水用电量 40.15 亿 kW·h，年抽水利用小时数为 2231h；综合循环效率为 75%。

枢纽工程主要由上水库、下水库、输水系统、地下厂房系统和地面开关站等建筑物组成。上水库混凝土面板堆石坝最大坝高为 89.2m，正常蓄水位 725m，死水位 695m，调节库容 1214 万 m^3。下水库混凝土面板堆石坝最大坝高为 49m，正常蓄水位为 319m，死水位为 298m，调节库容 1443 万 m^3。

工程项目于 2016 年 10 月 18 日获得辽宁省发展改革委核准，总投资为 109 亿元；工程建设总工期 84 个月，其中准备期 10 个月，主体工程施工期 56 个月，完建期 18 个月。

该电站采用设计牵头的 EPC 总承包模式进行工程建设，EPC 总承包联合体由中国电建集团北京勘测设计研究院有限公司、中国水利水电第六工程局有限公司、中国水利水电第八工程局有限公司组成。工程于 2017 年 5 月开工建设。

2018 年主要进行通风兼安全洞、进厂交通洞、下水库泄洪放空兼导流洞、场内道路、桶子沟渣场等部位的施工。截至 2018 年年底，通风兼安全洞（总长 1360.00m）完成洞挖 1036.50m，进厂交通洞（总长 1556.75m）完成洞挖 187.00m，下水库泄洪放空兼导流洞出口段完成洞挖 36.00m；桶子沟渣场排水洞（总长 807.00m）进口段完成洞挖 380.00m，出口段完成洞挖 286.00m。

（中国电建集团北京勘测设计研究院有限公司　张建富）

丰宁抽水蓄能电站工程 2018 年建设进展情况

丰宁抽水蓄能电站一期工程于 2013 年 5 月 29 日开工建设；二期工程 2015 年 7 月通过河北省发展改革委核准，9 月 23 日开工。截至 2018 年底，上水库大坝面板混凝土浇筑完成，下水库拦河坝填筑和拦沙坝坝顶防浪墙施工完成；一、二期工程主厂房开挖至第五层，主变压器洞Ⅱ、Ⅲ层开挖支护完成；引水系统部分下斜井未完成扩挖工作，其他部位正在进行混凝土浇筑和钢管安装工作。具体工程形象如下：

1. 上、下水库土建及金属结构安装工程（一、二期）　上水库的堆石坝面板混凝土浇筑完成；一、二期上水库进/出水口明挖支护完成，平洞和竖井开挖支护完成，明渠底板衬砌混凝土完成 40%；灌浆平洞开挖支护完成；环库路路基开挖基本完成。

下水库一、二期进/出口明挖支护完成，平洞（预留 10m 岩塞）和竖井开挖支护完成，平洞底板和防涡梁混凝土浇筑完成 70%；拦河坝坝体填筑完成，溢洪道混凝土完成 95%；拦沙库溢洪道混凝土、拦沙坝坝顶防浪墙和导沙明渠施工完成。

2. 引水系统土建及金属结构安装工程（一期）　1～3 号引水隧洞衬砌分别完成 828.1、828.1、673.4m，尚余 74.1、56.1、192.4m；1～3 号引水调压室竖井及上室衬砌完成，高压管道上平段钢管安装回填和一期施工支洞封堵完成，高压管道上斜井钢管安装回填完成，中平段（支洞上游侧）钢管安装、回填及灌浆完成；1 号高压管道下斜井扩挖支护和钢管安装轨道完成；2 号高压管道下斜井扩挖支护完成；3 号高压管道下斜井扩挖至斜直 35m。

3. 地下厂房及尾水系统土建及金属结构安装工程（一期）　地面开关站开挖支护完成；排风上平洞开挖支护完成，底板混凝土完成浇筑 90m，井口开挖 10m，锁口混凝土浇筑 7m；尾水调压室上室开挖支护完成，边顶拱混凝土浇筑 141.6m；尾闸洞岩锚梁混凝土浇筑完成；主变压器洞Ⅱ、Ⅲ层和一期主厂房洞Ⅴ层开挖支护完成；一期主厂房岩锚梁和主厂房吊顶支座梁混凝土浇筑完成；1 号尾水隧洞进尺 194m，一层开挖完成，二层开挖完成 200m；2 号尾水隧洞进尺 301m，一层开挖完成，二层开挖完成 225m；3 号尾水隧洞进尺 367m，一层开挖完成，二层开挖完成 520m。

4. 机电安装工程（一、二期）　由中国水利水电第三工程局有限公司与中国水利水电第七工程局有限公司组成联合体运营模式共同承担，前者主要承担二期工程与公用部分及部分一期工程，后者主要承担一期工程。2018 年 6 月 15 日，机电安装工程正式开工。截至 2018 年底，主厂房岩锚梁桥机轨道安装完成；主厂房 1 号 320t 主桥机及 1、2 号 32t 施工桥机大梁吊装完成；母线洞厂房侧 8m 段衬砌混凝土施工完成；鞭子沟封闭库及棚库施工完成，封闭库内 10t 龙门吊安装完成。

5. 引水系统土建及金属结构安装工程（二期）　4～6 号引水隧洞洞挖支护完成，衬砌分别完成

154.7、427.7、254.8m；4～6号引水调压室扩挖支护完成，各调压室底部隧洞上下游、阻抗孔均衬砌完成，4号竖井滑模完成72m；4～6号高压管道上斜井扩挖支护完成，4号上斜井钢管安装回填完成下弯段、斜直段80m，6号高压管道上斜井下弯段钢管安装完成；4～6号中平段（支洞上游侧）钢管安装、回填完成；钢管加工7574.6t。

6. 地下厂房及尾水系统土建及金属结构安装工程（二期） 主厂房岩壁吊车梁、吊顶支座梁及下部构造柱混凝土施工完成，主厂房Ⅴ层（高程975m以上）开挖支护完成；主变压器洞Ⅲ层（高程982.5m以上）开挖支护完成；尾水调压室上室开挖支护完成，底板混凝土完成9仓浇筑；尾闸洞Ⅱ层开挖支护完成，岩壁吊车梁结构锚杆完成90%；4号尾水隧洞上层开挖支护完成，下层完成140m；5号尾水隧洞上层开挖支护完成，下层完成35m；6号尾水隧洞上层开挖支护完成，下层完成215m；2号通风洞出口开挖支护705m，进口开挖支护740m，尚余323m；出线竖井开挖支护完成71m；2号出线下平洞（含1、2号岔洞）开挖支护完成186m。

（中国电建集团北京勘测设计研究院
有限公司　何敏
中国水利水电第三工程局
有限公司　周若愚）

敦化抽水蓄能电站工程2018年建设进展情况

敦化抽水蓄能电站于2013年7月开工建设。2018年主要进行上、下水库土建及金属结构安装工程标、引水发电系统土建及金属结构安装工程标、地下厂房及尾水系统土建及金属结构安装工程标、机电设备安装及厂房混凝土工程标等施工。截至2018年底，工程完成形象如下：

1. 上、下水库土建及金属结构安装工程标

（1）上水库进/出水口开挖完成，开始混凝土浇筑。

（2）上水库沥青混凝土心墙堆石坝开始坝体填筑、沥青混凝土施工。

（3）下水库沥青混凝土心墙堆石坝填筑完成，剩余坝顶结构施工。

（4）泄洪放空洞投入使用。

（5）溢洪道混凝土浇筑完成。

（6）下水库进/出水口混凝土浇筑基本完成。

2. 输水发电系统土建及金属结构安装工程标

（1）1、2号引水调压井混凝土衬砌完成。

（2）1、2号引水隧洞除岩塞部位外，隧洞上部已开挖支护完成。1号引水隧洞衬砌累计完成260m，约占总量的34%；2号引水隧洞衬砌累计完成200m，约占总量的25%。引水调压室后引水隧洞混凝土衬砌完成60%。

（3）1号高压管道上斜井总长381m，开挖支护完成；下斜井总长426m，开挖支护完成。

（4）2号高压管道上斜井总长381m，开挖支护完成；下斜井总长426m，开挖支护完成。

（5）高压管道上层排水洞及下层排水洞开挖支护完成。

（6）1号高压管道中平段钢管安装完成639m，约占总量的61%；2号高压管道中平段钢管安装完成537m，约占总量的61%。

（7）1～4号高压支管段钢管安装已完成，回填混凝土基本完成；高压岔管安装及回填完成。

3. 地下厂房及尾水系统土建及金属结构安装工程标

（1）主副厂房及安装间、主变压器洞工程开挖支护已完成，并移交机电设备安装及厂房混凝土工程标。

（2）尾水事故闸门洞工程开挖支护已完成；岩壁吊车梁施工完成。

（3）1、2号尾水调压室开挖支护完成。

（4）尾水隧洞工程开挖支护完成；1号尾水隧洞衬砌完成808m，占总长的62.8%；2号尾水隧洞衬砌完成651.3m，占总长的51.5%。

（5）厂房上层、中层、下层排水廊道开挖支护完成。

4. 机电设备安装及厂房混凝土工程标

2017年5月，机电安装标进场开工。

（1）生产辅助区房屋建筑工程的恒温恒湿库、封闭仓库、中控楼、开关站GIS楼主体结构、砌体完成；消防站基础混凝土浇筑完成。

（2）主变压器运输洞衬砌混凝土浇筑完成。

（3）主变压器副厂房高程622.95m以下混凝土浇筑完成。

（4）主变压器洞高程610m以下混凝土浇筑完成。

（5）主厂房桥机安装完成，并通过验收。

（6）1号机组蜗壳层混凝土浇筑完成，正进行水轮层以上混凝土浇筑；2号机组进行蜗壳外包混凝土施工；3、4号机组进行蜗壳层混凝土浇筑。

（7）主副厂房第七层（高程626.95m以下）混

凝土浇筑完成。

(8) 母线洞底板混凝土浇筑完成，边顶拱混凝土基本完成，正进行剩余边墙及顶拱混凝土衬砌施工。

(中国电建集团北京勘测设计研究院有限公司　王兆辉)

周宁抽水蓄能电站工程 2018年建设进展情况

周宁抽水蓄能电站位于宁德市周宁县七步镇境内，与宁德市、福州市的直线距离分别为50、110km，为日调节纯抽水蓄能电站，安装4台单机容量为300MW的可逆式抽水蓄能机组，年发电量12亿kW·h，年抽水电量16亿kW·h。该电站承担福建电网的调峰、填谷、调频、调相及备用等任务，是国家能源局批复的福建电网2020年新建抽水蓄能电站三个推荐站点之一，也是福建省继仙游抽水蓄能电站投产后第二个动工建设的抽水蓄能项目。

电站枢纽主要由上水库、下水库、输水系统、地下厂房及开关站等建筑物组成。上水库正常蓄水位716.0m，总库容1073万m^3，调节库容815万m^3；下水库正常蓄水位299.0m，总库容1248万m^3，调节库容799万m^3。输水系统总长1724.34m，距高比3.23。地下厂房由主副厂房洞、主变压器洞、母线洞、500kV出线洞、进厂交通洞、通风兼安全洞等洞室群组成，工程概算总投资66.93亿元。

工程于2016年5月5日获得福建省发展改革委核准，2017年3月1日主体工程开工建设。

2018年，工程年度累计完成投资4.98亿元，主要工程进展形象如下：

(1) 上水库工程：坝后排水箱涵基本浇筑完成；导流洞开挖支护基本完成。

(2) 输水下水库工程：地下厂房开挖已基本结束。

(3) 下水库工程：2018年4月20日成功截流；年底已完成下水库大坝边坡开挖支护任务。

全年单元工程质量合格率为100%，优良率达92.75%。工程质量可控在控，顺利通过了2018年度2次质量监督检查和1次达标投产检查，得到了专家组一致肯定。

(华电福新周宁抽水蓄能电站有限公司　周顺田)

芝瑞抽水蓄能电站工程 2018年设计进展情况

内蒙古芝瑞抽水蓄能电站招标及施工图阶段勘察设计合同于2018年3月15日签订，截至2018年底，编制完成《工程分标设计报告》《用电系统及施工用电设计专题报告》《工程总平面布置设计》《业主营地景观设计方案》《表层土在水土保持上的利用设计专题报告》《土石方平衡设计专题报告》《工程场内道路设计报告》《"筹建期洞室及道路工程"招标文件（技术部分)》《业主营地工程招标文件（技术部分)》《施工组织设计报告》《环保设计标准与方案设计专题报告》《用水系统及施工用水设计专题报告》《渣场设计专题报告》《场内排水系统设计专题报告》《生态环境规划专题报告》《污水处理标招标文件（技术部分)》《招标设计报告》。

2018年主要的专题报告编制工作和招标文件编制工作情况如下：

4月4日，《用电系统及施工用电设计专题报告》通过内蒙古赤峰抽水蓄能有限公司组织的专家评审。

5月23日，《工程总平面布置设计报告》通过内蒙古赤峰抽水蓄能有限公司组织的专家评审。

7月19日，《表层土在水土保持上的利用设计专题报告》《土石方平衡设计专题报告》通过内蒙古赤峰抽水蓄能有限公司组织的专家评审。

9月4日，《工程场内道路设计报告》通过内蒙古赤峰抽水蓄能有限公司组织的专家评审。

9月6日，《环保设计标准与方案设计专题报告》通过内蒙古赤峰抽水蓄能有限公司组织的专家评审。

9月29日，《业主营地工程招标文件（技术部分)》通过内蒙古赤峰抽水蓄能有限公司组织的专家评审。

10月29日，《工程分标设计报告》《施工组织设计报告》《渣场设计专题报告》通过国网新源控股有限公司组织的专家评审。

10月30日，《场内排水系统设计专题报告》通过国网新源控股有限公司组织的专家评审。

11月28日，《"筹建期洞室及道路工程"招标文件（技术部分)》通过内蒙古赤峰抽水蓄能有限公司组织的专家评审。

12月10日，《"污水处理标"招标文件（技术部分)》通过内蒙古赤峰抽水蓄能有限公司组织的专家评审。

12月31日，编制完成了《招标设计报告》。

(中国电建集团北京勘测设计研究院有限公司　蒋逵超)

永泰抽水蓄能电站工程 2018 年建设进展情况

2018 年 11 月，永泰抽水蓄能电站主体工程开工建设。该电站位于福建省永泰县白云乡，与福州市的直线距离为 37km；为日调节纯抽水蓄能电站，安装 4 台单机容量为 300MW 的可逆式抽水蓄能机组。工程开发任务为承担福建电网调峰、填谷、调频、调相及紧急事故备用等。电站设计年平均发电量 12 亿 kW·h，年发电利用小时数 1000h；年平均抽水电量 16 亿 kW·h，年抽水利用小时数 1333h，综合效率 75%。

（一）工程枢纽布置

永泰抽水蓄能电站枢纽建筑主要包括上水库、下水库、输水系统、地下厂房等，为一等大（1）型工程。上水库大坝、下水库大坝及泄洪设施、地下厂房及输水建筑物等主要永久性建筑物的洪水标准按 200 年一遇洪水设计，1000 年一遇洪水校核。上水库西副坝外侧排水系统和下水库消能防冲建筑物按 100 年一遇洪水设计。工程场地地震基本烈度为Ⅵ度。

1. 上水库及下水库　上水库主要建筑物有主坝、四座副坝、西副坝外侧抽排水系统等。主副坝均采用分区土石坝，主坝最大坝高 34m，坝顶长度 230m。上水库集雨面积 1.1km^2，水库正常蓄水位 657m，相应库容为 847 万 m^3，其中调节库容 766 万 m^3。

下水库主要建筑物有常态混凝土重力坝、库岸防护等，最大坝高 55.2m，坝顶总长 179.0m。溢流坝段采用 2 表孔+1 底孔联合泄洪的方式，表孔总净宽 14m，堰顶高程 217.0m；泄洪底孔布置在中闸墩内，出口控制断面尺寸为 4.0m×4.0m，底孔底板高程为 190.0m。下水库集雨面积 60.5km^2，水库正常蓄水位 225m，相应库容为 924 万 m^3，其中调节库容 775 万 m^3。

2. 输水系统　上、下水库进/出水口之间输水系统总长约 2041.1m（沿 4 号机输水系统长度，下同），其中引水系统长约 1120.8m，尾水系统长约 920.3m。输水隧洞采用两洞四机布置，自上平洞末端至发电厂房采用钢板衬砌，其余段采用钢筋混凝土衬砌，钢衬段总长度为 862.7m。引水上平洞洞径 7.0m，上斜井、中平洞和下斜井洞径 6.0m，下平洞洞径 5.0m，钢岔管主管直径为 5.0m，支管直径为 3.5m，靠近厂房上游侧的钢管内径渐变为 2.3m 与厂房球阀连接。尾水支管洞径为 5.2m，尾水管出口位置至尾水闸门洞中心线下游 21.5m 段采用钢板衬砌。距厂房轴线下游约 159.6m 设置钢筋混凝土衬砌岔管，衬砌厚 0.8m。阻抗式尾水调压室设置在尾水岔管下游 20.0m 处。尾水隧洞长 670.1m，内径 7.4m。

3. 地下厂房洞室群　主要由主副厂房洞、主变压器洞、尾水闸门洞三大洞室组成，此外还布置有进厂交通洞、通风兼安全洞、母线洞、500kV 出线洞、排水廊道等辅助洞室。厂区三大洞室从上游往下游依次平行布置，主副厂房洞与主变压器洞的净间距为 40.0m，主变压器洞与尾水闸门洞的净间距为 30.0m。主副厂房洞开挖尺寸 170.0m×24.5m×54.7m（长×宽×高），主变压器洞开挖尺寸 169.7m×19m×22.3m（长×宽×高）。进厂交通洞进口布置在下水库大坝下游约 275m 的右岸山脊处，通风兼安全洞进口布置在下水库进/出水口上游约 390m 处，进厂交通洞和通风兼安全洞均通过进场公路与对外公路衔接。地下厂房周围布置 3 层排水廊道。地面开关站位于下水库进/出水口上游约 55m 处，紧邻进场公路，开关站场地高程 233.0m，场地尺寸为 110m×56m（长×宽），布置有 GIS 室、继保楼以及地面出线场。

（二）工程机电设计

1. 电气主接线　该电站以 2 回 500kV 出线，就近开断莆田—水口线路接入，形成永泰抽水蓄能电站—水口、永泰抽水蓄能电站—莆田的接线，线路长度分别约 52、89km。

该电站发电电动机与主变压器的组合方式采用联合单元接线。电站 500kV 侧接线方式为四角形接线。

2. 主要机电设备

（1）主机及附属设备：水泵水轮机，水轮机工况工作水头为 399.8～453.8m，水泵工况扬程为 418.0～462.0m，额定水头 416m，额定转速为 428.6 r/min，转轮高压侧直径 4.24m，水轮机额定出力 306.1MW，安装高程 136.0m，机组拆卸型式为上拆；发电电动机，为三相、立轴、半伞、可逆式同步、空气冷却型，额定容量发电机工况为 300MW/333.33MVA、电动机工况不小于 325MW；进水球阀，公称直径为 2.3m；4 套具有 PID 调节规律的可编程微机调速器及其油压装置。

（2）500kV 设备：4 台主变压器为三相双绕组、强迫油循环水冷、无载调压变压器，额定容量 360MVA，额定电压 525±2×2.5%/15.75kV。采用 2 回 500kV XLPE 电缆作为地下与地面 GIS 连接回路，额定电压（U_0/U）：290/500kV，最高工作电压（U_m）：550kV，每回电缆最大持续工作电流为 832A。GIS 装置额定电压为 550kV，GIS 额定电流为 4000A，额定短时耐受电流及持续时间为 63kA/2s。

（3）计算机监控系统：按“无人值班（少人值守）”方式设计，采用计算机为基础的全厂集中控制方式。计算机监控系统采用开放的分层分布式结构，分电站控制级和单元控制级，通过冗余光纤环网连接。

发电电动机组、主变压器和500kV短引线的继电保护按双重化原则配置（主变压器本体保护除外），采用微机型保护装置。

（三）工程主要建设情况

2009年8月，在福建省历次抽水蓄能电站普查成果和前述选点规划工作的基础上，根据抽水蓄能电站布局要求和资源特点，择优选取了周宁、福州、永泰、厦门、长泰、漳平抽水蓄能电站作为规划站点开展新一轮选点规划工作，规划水平年为2020年。2010年10月，永泰抽水蓄能电站预可行性研究报告通过审查；2011年5月国家发展改革委批准开展前期工作。2016年4月，可行性研究报告通过审查；8月，项目获得福建省发展改革委核准；12月，前期工程开工建设。2018年11月，主体工程开工建设，计划2022年8月第一台机组发电，2023年6月全部4台机组正式投运。

（中国电建集团华东勘测设计研究院有限公司 熊燕梅）

易县抽水蓄能电站工程 2018年设计进展情况

河北易县抽水蓄能电站招标及施工图阶段勘察设计合同于2018年3月14日签订，截至2018年底，编制完成了项目分标规划、总平面设计、施工用电设计、场内道路初步设计、施工组织设计等专题报告，并编制完成项目招标阶段设计报告；配合业主编制完成项目爆破安全监理、爆破安全评估、环境监理、水土保持监测、环境保护监测、第三方土建试验室、物探试验室、施工供电以及筹建期洞室及道路工程、施工供电等招标文件。具体专题及招标文件配合工作进展如下：

1. 2018年完成的专题报告及外部审查情况

（1）《工程分标设计规划报告》于4月30日完成，12月4日通过国网新源控股有限公司基建部组织的审查。

（2）《工程总平面设计》于5月31日完成，保定易县抽水蓄能电站有限公司及国网新源控股有限公司基建部等进行了多轮讨论，目前尚未组织评审。

（3）《资源综合利用规划专题报告》于5月31日完成，7月13日通过保定易县抽水蓄能电站有限公司组织的专家审查。

（4）《引水发电系统布置优化设计专题报告》于6月30日完成，8月17日通过水电水利规划设计总院的审查。

（5）《用电系统及施工用电的设计专题报告》于9月30日完成，10月24日通过保定易县抽水蓄能电站有限公司组织的专家审查；后因地方推翻接入站点方案，目前报告尚在调整中。

（6）《工程招标设计阶段施工组织设计报告》《场内道路初步设计报告》于10月30日完成，12月4日通过国网新源控股有限公司基建部组织的审查。

（7）12月15日完成项目招标设计报告初稿。

2. 2018年招标文件配合 5月底前配合甲方完成爆破安全监理、爆破安全评估、环境监理、水土保持监测、环境保护监测等招标文件；7月底配合甲方完成第三方土建试验室、物探试验室；9月底完成施工用电招标设计文件，10月24日通过保定易县抽水蓄能电站有限公司组织的专家审查；后因地方推翻接入站点方案，目前尚在调整中。10月底配合甲方筹建期洞室及道路工程标书，后项目业主多次组织相关讨论，12月4日通过国网新源控股有限公司基建部组织的审查。

（中国电建集团北京勘测设计研究院有限公司 王春生）

沂蒙抽水蓄能电站工程 2018年建设进展情况

沂蒙抽水蓄能电站于2015年6月12日召开开工动员大会，之后下水库标、上水库标、输水发电土建及金属结构安装标等10个标段陆续开工建设。截至2018年底，工程建设形象进度如下：

1. 场内道路工程 1、2号路路基、路面、涵洞、桥梁、挡墙及附属设施已施工完成。鲁峪沟隧道开挖、支护、衬砌、路面、电缆沟、排水沟、洞内照明设施线路施工完成。2号渣场垫层排水带、挡渣坝、420m高程平台及以下左侧排水渠混凝土施工完成。3号渣场施工完成。

2. 引水系统准备工程 排风上平洞工程、引水上平洞工程已完工并移交地下厂房标。4号路一期工程边坡开挖支护及路面工程已完工。

3. 永久补水及施工供水工程 一级至五级泵站管线、水泵正常运行，可满足各单位供水需求。

4. 施工供电工程 施工供电系统完工投运。

5. 业主营地工程 业主营地工程施工完成，已通过验收。

6. 施工期污水处理标 地下排水处理站土建装修及水电设备安装、砂石废水处理站土建装修及水电设备安装已施工完成。

7. 进厂交通洞和通风兼安全洞工程　通风兼安全洞和进厂交通洞已施工完成并移交工作面。

8. 上水库工程　库岸库盆工程累计完成土石方开挖 695.54 万 m^3，剩余石方开挖 204.66 万 m^3。大坝上下游堆石区填筑至高程 563.6m，共填筑 390.77 万 m^3，剩余 224.63 万 m^3。库盆右岸边坡高程 609.4m 以上开挖边坡锚喷支护部分完成。进/出水口 1、2 号竖井下弯段开挖支护完成，2 号竖井导孔反拉完成，且锁口边坡已成型，锁口置换混凝土浇筑至高程 552.7m，初步具备扩挖条件。1 号渣场排水渠浇筑完成右侧排水渠约 200m，正进行剩余排水渠的基础开挖。

9. 输水发电系统工程

（1）引水系统：1、2 号高压管道上平段、上弯段及下平段开挖支护已完成；1～4 号引水支管开挖支护完成；1 号高压管道竖井 ϕ2.4m 导井反拉完成 366m，剩余 14m；1 号引水事故闸门井 ϕ10.2m 开挖至高程 579m，2 号引水事故闸门井 ϕ20m 直径上室开挖至高程 594m。

（2）地下厂房系统：厂房第一至七层、1～4 号机蜗开挖完成；主变压器室第一至三层、1、4 号母线洞、排风竖井开挖支护施工完成；厂房安装间具备使用条件；出线竖井 ϕ2m 导井反拉施工完成，目前正进行导井扩挖；地面开关站土石方开挖完成。

（3）尾水系统：下水库进/出水口土石方开挖完成；1 号尾水检修闸门井导井反拉施工至高程 183m；尾水事故闸门室正进行岩壁梁岩台锚杆施工，排架垫层浇筑完成；1 号尾水隧洞主洞总长 1808m，累计开挖完成 1506m，剩余 302m；2 号尾水隧洞总长 1893m，累计开挖完成 1564m，剩余 329m；尾水调压室第三层开挖支护完成。

10. 下水库工程　库区土方开挖已基本完成，石方开挖正在进行，库盆开口线基本成型；大坝填筑及上游侧翻模固坡施工完成，目前坝体正在进行沉降，趾板混凝土浇筑及其帷幕灌浆施工完成，左岸平台帷幕灌浆正在施工；泄洪放空洞闸门井开挖支护施工完成，洞身无压段全断面衬砌完成，有压段正进行衬砌施工；4 号渣场 173m 高程平台修整完成，渣场排水带填筑完成，1 号挡渣坝混凝土浇筑完成，渣场排水渠尚未开始施工；巡视便道全长 920m，路基已开挖到位，具备通车条件；仓储区综合楼、宿舍楼、排水渠及场地硬化施工完成。

（中国电建集团北京勘测设计研究院有限公司　杨子强）

文登抽水蓄能电站工程 2018 年建设进展情况

文登抽水蓄能电站于 2015 年 12 月 15 日开工建设，2017 年 7 月土建主体工程开工建设。截至 2018 年底，工程完成形象如下：

1. 上、下水库土建及金属结构安装工程标　上水库进/出水口平台 628.6m 以上边坡开挖完成，A4、A6 趾板及坝基开挖完成。下水库进/出水口平台 142m 以上边坡开挖完成，B4、B5、B6 段趾板及坝基开挖完成。

2. 输水发电系统土建及金属结构安装工程标

（1）高压管道：1 号引水总长 1078m，平段全部开挖完成 455.9m（上平 40.9m，中平段 272m，下平段 143m）；2 号引水总长 1080m，平段全部开挖完成 320.9m（上平段 40.9m，中平段 275m，下平段 5m）；3 号引水总长 1056m，开挖完成 202.9m（上平段 40.9m，中平段 147m，下平段 15m）。

（2）地下厂房系统：通风洞总长 1938m，交通洞总长 1557m，已开挖完成。1 号通风机室（总长 18m）、2 号通风机室（总长 27.18m）、安装场第一层、主机间和副厂房第一层（75.5～65m）开挖完成。主厂房自第二层开始，采用切割开挖技术，开挖至高程 64.5m。上层排水廊道总长 1005m，开挖完成 456.55m（1 号廊道 184m，2 号廊道 142m，3 号廊道 28.55m，4 号廊道 102m）；中层排水廊道总长 895m，开挖完成 20m（5、8 号廊道各 10m）。尾水调压室交通洞总长 955m，开挖完成 251m；主变压器室中导洞开挖完成 15m；主变压器通风支洞总长 49m，开挖 21.8m；主变压器交通支洞总长 156.8m 开挖完成。

（3）尾水隧洞：1 号尾水隧洞总长 1354m，开挖完成 214m；2 号尾水隧洞总长 1350m，开挖完成 152m；3 号尾水隧洞总长 1344m，开挖完成 345m。

（4）施工支洞：1 号施工支洞总长 389.703m，2 号施工支洞总长 762.768m，3 号施工支洞总长 334.01m，6 号施工支洞总长 697.748m，交通洞通风洞之间的联通洞总长 201m，排风洞总长 95m，已全部开挖完成；5 号施工支洞总长 351.72m，开挖完成 52.5m。

3. 场区道路标

（1）1 号公路总长 9578m，完成 5200m 路段土石方开挖、3810m 路段边坡支护、屋脊顶隧道（K7＋819～K8＋040）洞身开挖与支护完成。

（2）2 号公路总长 1079m，全部施工完成。2 号公路支线总长 277m，完成 270m 路段土石方开挖、

100m 路段边坡支护。

（3）3 号公路总长 1767m，完成 430m 路段土石方开挖、80m 路段边坡支护、昆嵛山 1 号隧道(K0＋200～K0＋330）洞身开挖支护完成。

（4）复建路总长 348m，完成 200m 路段土石方开挖。

4. 筹建期洞室标　通风洞、交通洞开挖完成，泄洪放空洞开挖完成 293.7m，混凝土衬砌完成 230.2m。

5. 施工供水标　完成一至五级泵站，上、下水库高位水池土建工程；上、下水库高位水池、一级泵站设备安装，管道总长 13454m，安装完成 11280m。

6. 施工供电标　35kV 施工变电站已投运；蓄能Ⅰ、Ⅱ回线塔基、挂线全部完成；厂内 10kV 线路，上水库线完成 8 塔基（共 12 个），下水库线完成 11 塔基（共 12 个）。

7. 砂石骨料加工系统标　钢结构制作安装基本完成，完成边坡防护及绿化。

8. 业主营地场平标　场平工作全部完成。

9. 业主营地房建标　业主营地房建工作基本完成。

10. 业主营地绿化工程标　办公区、生活区、水域区整体铺装施工完成；主要小品、土建节点施工基本完成；植物种植基本完成。

（中国电建集团北京勘测设计研究院有限公司　吕典帅）

南方电网调峰调频发电有限公司 2018 年电源建设情况

2018 年，南方电网调峰调频发电有限公司电源建设主要情况如下：

1. 惠州抽水蓄能电站　2018 年 10 月，受广东省发展和改革委员会《关于委托开展惠州抽水蓄能电站竣工验收工作的函》（粤发改能电函〔2017〕6700 号）的委托，水电水利规划设计总院组织成立了广东惠州抽水蓄能电站工程竣工验收委员会，并印发《广东惠州蓄能电站竣工验收工作大纲》。10 月 26 日，验收委员会组织召开竣工验收会议，通过电站工程竣工验收。

2. 深圳抽水蓄能电站　2018 年 9 月 25 日，深圳抽水蓄能电站全面建成投产。主、副厂房装修工程，交通洞沿线、交通洞洞口门楼建筑装修及深蓄电站厂区复绿工程全部完成。

3. 海南琼中抽水蓄能电站　海南琼中抽水蓄能电站已全部投入运行，整体工程进度完成 100%。2018 年 4 月 1 日，2 号机组于投入商业运行；7 月 29 日，3 号机组于投入商业运行。

4. 梅州抽水蓄能电站　梅州抽水蓄能电站前期工程基本完工，主体工程于 2018 年 6 月 27 日开工建设，厂房第Ⅱ层开挖完成，主变压器洞第Ⅰ层开挖支护完成；上水库工程 9 月 25 日开工，12 月导流洞开挖完成；上水库主坝开挖完成 15 万 m^3（36%）；下水库工程 2018 年 10 月 1 日正式开工，导流洞开挖完成，副坝及单薄分水岭开挖完成 20 万 m^3（37%），主坝开挖完成 3 万 m^3（17%）。

5. 阳江抽水蓄能电站　阳江抽水蓄能电站前期工程基本完工，主体工程进度稳步推进，厂房Ⅲ层开挖完成，岩锚梁混凝土浇筑完成 65%，主变压器洞第Ⅱ层开挖支护完成，尾闸室第Ⅱ层开挖支护完成；上水库大坝坝基土石方开挖完成约 76 万 m^3（80%）。

6. 海南文昌气电项目　文昌气电项目于 2018 年 5 月 24 日取得海南省发改委投资项目备案证明；6 月 27 日项目场平工程开工；9 月 18 日机组设备第一次设计联络会完成；11 月 7 日初步设计审查完成；11 月 16 日签订主体建筑安装标合同；12 月 12 日主体工程开工。

（南方电网调峰调频发电有限公司　曹娅）

中國水力發電年鉴

4

工　程　勘　测

工程地质勘察与评价

灰色系统预测模型在锦屏一级水电站沉降观测中的应用

现有的变形预测方法如多元回归法、神经网络法等都建立在大样本量的数据基础上，对短期或有残缺的资料无能为力。根据左岸缆机平台短期沉降观测的数据资料，建立灰色系统预测模型，对其沉降变形趋势进行预测，并与实测的变形量进行对比，结果表明灰色系统预测模型沉降观测预报是可行、有效的。

（一）灰色系统介绍

1982年，我国学者邓聚龙教授首次在荷兰的国际性杂志上发表了灰色理论，它是用来解决信息不完备系统的数学方法。传统的系统理论，对一些信息比较贫乏的系统，利用黑箱的方法，也取得了较为成功的经验，对一些内部信息部分确知、部分信息不确知的系统，却研究得很不充分。在客观世界中，大量存在的不是白色系统（信息完全明确）也不是黑色系统（信息完全不明确），而是灰色系统，因此灰色系统理论以这种大量存在的灰色系统为研究而获得进一步发展。而灰色理论的一个重要的应用领域就是趋势预测，灰色理论利用连续的灰色微分方程模型，对系统的发展变化进行全面的观察分析，并能做出长期预测，其预测精度之高是其他预测方法所无法比拟的。按研究的对象分，灰色预测可分为数列预测、灾变预测、季节突变预测、拓扑预测、系统综合预测，而且采用灰色理论为基础建立的灰色系统预测模型是一种外推型模型，属连续型预报方法，是用来处理动态观测数据的一种有效工具。目前，灰色系统预测模型（GM）在工程、社会、经济、生物等范围内已经得到了一定的应用。

而用灰色系统模型进行预测要求原始时间序列的时间间隔具有周期性，否则需要将其转换成具有周期性时间间隔的时间序列，然后再对其进行建模建立微分方程。目前常用GM（1，N）、GM（1，1）模型，其中GM（1，N）模型适合于建立系统的状态模型，为高阶系统提供基础，不适合预测用，预测模型应选用单个变量的模型，即预测量本身数据模型［GM（1，1）模型］。GM（1，1）模型是最基础的一种只包含单变量的一阶微分方程模型，通过使用某点前 t 时刻的观测值，完成 $t+1$ 状态量的预报工作。

生成GM(1，1）预测模型的算法如下：

（1）累加生成。灰色系统理论把随机量看作是在一定范围内变化的灰色量，尽管存在着不确定因素的干扰成分，但是经过一定的技术处理总能发现它的规律性。累加生成可使上下波动的时间序列变成单调升，并带有线性或指数规律的序列。

（2）灰色系统建模。由一阶累加生成序列 $x^{(1)}$ 构成的微分方程，可得预测模型GM(1，1）为：

$$x^{(1)}(k+1)=\left[x^{(0)}(1)-\frac{\beta}{\alpha}\right]e^{-ak}+\frac{\beta}{\alpha}$$

（3）累减生成。经过累加生成算法得到的时间序列已经失去了其原来的意义，所以经过方程求解的结果必须还原到原序列，即通过累减生成算法得到原序列。

（4）模型精度。以后验差比值和小误差概率两项精度检验标准来评定模型的精度。

（二）灰色系统预测模型应用实例

1. 沉降观测项目简介　锦屏一级水电站工程左岸缆机平台位于左岸EL.1959.63m高程，EL.1959.63m高程以上边坡开挖支护目前已经完成，缆机已进入运行状态。缆机平台的平台内侧和缆机轨道梁上共布设20个水准测点，其中EM01～EM10测点位于平台内侧，EM11～EM20测点位于缆机轨道梁上。观测按一等水准精度要求进行施测，双程往返观测，闭合至校核基点。有关限差执行《国家一、二等水准测量规范》要求。水准校核基点为LS01－LL，埋设于洞内稳定基岩，设定高程为0.0000m。通过对缆机平台水准测点的沉降变形观测及分析，可对缆机平台在缆机频繁作业情况下的稳定性进行评估。

2. 灰色系统预测模型实例　沉降观测中包含有确知的信息与不确知的信息，其中沉降观测数据是确知信息，而沉降原因是不确知的信息，属于灰色系统理论的范畴。在某水电站工程左岸缆机平台沉降观测中，一共观测了20个水准点。选用EM01和EM05两点的五期数据来进行研究分析。其中，前四期观测成果用来构造灰色系统预测模型，并评定模型精度等级，而采用第五期观测的累计沉降量进行检核。每期数据间隔为15天，五期数据历时两个月。

鉴于Matlab软件在计算矩阵时的优越性，用

Matlab软件编写了灰色系统预测模型GM(1，1)用于处理沉降观测数据的程序，得出EM01、EM05两点的累计沉降量的GM(1，1)预测模型，计算出第五期的预测值，与两点的第五期EM01、EM05的实测值对比，可以看出，预测的结果是比较准确的。

利用前面所述的统计检验方法，计算出后验差比值和小误差概率等指标，可以得出两个模型的预测精度等级为好，说明预测模型用于该水电站工程左岸缆机平台沉降监测的预测是可以取得相当高的精度和很好的预测效果。

（中国电建集团昆明勘测设计研究院
有限公司　罗中权 王川 张学良）

赤平投影在边坡稳定性中的应用

（一）赤平投影基本原理

赤平投影是分析岩质边坡的常用方法之一，其基本原理是：假想一个参考球（投影球），通过球心的面和线，延伸后与球面相交，其在球面上显示为圆和点，以球顶为中心，形成一个赤平面，将空间内任意产状的线和面在球面上显示出的点或圆投影到该赤平面上，赤平投影法可以在赤平面上唯一地确定空间内某一线或面的空间参数。在岩质边坡的稳定性分析中，通过边坡中的结构面的空间位置与边坡的空间位置的相互关系，讨论不利结构面与开挖边坡之间的空间关系，简单实用，易于初步定性判断不稳定体。

（二）工程概况

观音岩水电站位于云南省丽江地区华坪县与四川省攀枝花市的界河塘坝河口附近，工程以发电为主，兼顾防洪、灌溉、旅游等综合利用。水电站最大坝高159m，坝顶高程1139m，正常蓄水位1134m，总库容约20.72亿m^3，装机规模为3000MW。水库库长约100km，属峡谷型水库。

（三）边坡稳定分析

(1) 左岸坝段开挖边坡。边坡走向N35°W，坡倾向北东，低坝段设计坡比为1∶0.75，高坝段设计坡比为1∶2，开挖基岩垂直深度在35～39m之间。

左岸坝肩存在高约50～100m的开挖边坡，边坡岩体为J2s2-2岩层，以坚硬的砂岩为主，坡顶有强风化带在10m左右，下部开挖边坡位于弱风化岩体中。大平坝背斜轴部及北西翼总体为缓倾的逆向坡，边坡主要结构面为层节理和层间挤压面，其产状为N30°W，SW∠20°，与边坡方向交角较小，对边坡稳定不起控制作用，边坡总体稳定，但反倾节理（产状：N15°～40°W，NE∠65°）及沿此节理发育的卸荷裂隙对边有控制作用，卸荷带内裂隙多张开充填泥质，结构面参数明显下降，边坡产生局部倾倒破坏或掉块的可能，需采取边坡加固的措施。

左岸非溢流坝段坝基位于大平坝背斜南东翼，高程1050m以下段坝基开挖边坡较缓，为层面与坝轴线斜交，层面产状陡倾（N41°E，SE∠62)，坝基边坡稳定；高程1050m以上坝基，岩层产状由缓渐变陡，以平洞PD106结构面统计分析边坡稳定性，层面与边坡构成斜顺向坡，控制边坡稳定主要是层面，接近背斜核部发育横节理和纵张节理，层面与顺坡横节理组合会产生局部楔形失稳，因此，该段坝基需采取加固支护措施。

左岸坝基上、下游侧开挖边坡高约40～50m，边坡岩体为J2s2-1、J2s2-2坚硬岩体，上部约15～20m为强风化岩体，其下为弱风化岩体，岩层产状N35°～50°E，SE∠35°～65°，上游侧边坡为逆向坡，边坡总体稳定，局部产生倾倒破坏或掉块；下游侧边坡为顺向坡，边坡将会沿层间挤压错动面或层节理产生平面型滑移破坏，必须对边坡进行支护，以确保下游开挖边坡的稳定。

(2) 厂房坝段开挖边坡。厂房坝段左、右岸基岩边坡高约65m，设计坡比1∶0.5～1∶0.4，岩层为J2s1-3至J2s3-1，以弱微风化的砂岩、砾岩为主，岩层陡倾。左边坡为斜顺向坡，岩层倾角大于坡角，边坡总体是稳定的，但边坡纵向上将切断层面延伸，会沿层面产生岩体松弛，影响边坡的稳定，再加岩层层面产状会有所起伏，建议坡比不陡于1∶0.5，并且采取必要的支护措施。右边坡为斜逆向坡，岩层陡倾，边坡稳定，反倾节理对边坡稳定不利，但弱微风化岩体中其连通率低，结构面多闭合，不会导致边坡的整体失稳，边坡有产生局部失稳或掉块的可能，需采取必要的支护措施。

(3) 右岸坝段开挖边坡。导流明渠左边墙按设计要求保留岩埂，作为纵向围堰的基础，边墙岩埂高度20m，岩层为J2s2-1至J2s3-5，以弱微风化岩体为主，岩层产状以N30°～45°E，SE∠50°～65°为主，左边墙为斜顺向坡，不利于边墙的稳定，沿层面可产生顺层滑移，层面与横节理的交线陡于1∶0.3边坡，对边坡起控制用是层面产状，因此，建议开挖边坡比1∶0.5，对边坡进行系统喷混凝土，对不稳定段块及时用锚杆、预应力锚索加固。

岸边溢洪道方案右边墙与溢洪道相邻，岩层为J2s2-1至J2s3-5，溢洪道开挖后，泄水消能段形成40～20m高的永久边坡，以弱微风化岩体为主；溢流坝段上游引渠段边墙上部为冲积混坡积层（Qal+dl)，厚度在10.0～30.0m，下覆基岩以弱微风化为主。上部冲积混坡积层和局部全强风化层应按松散层边坡考虑，坡比应小于1∶1，并进行坡面防护。右边墙基岩层面产状与左边墙基本一致，为斜逆向坡，但与反倾节理和横节理结构面组合存在不稳定的潜在因素，主要以掉块或局部崩滑为主，需采取必要的支护措施。

(4) 右岸堆石坝心墙开挖边坡。边坡走向N15°E，坝基地段设计开挖坡比为1∶3和1∶5，坝肩设计开挖坡比为1∶1，开挖基岩深度在20～30m之间。开挖边坡岩体为J2s3-6和J2s3中J2s3-5为主的岩层，J2s3-6以泥质粉砂岩软岩为主，J2s3-5以坚硬砂岩为主，心墙基础置于弱风化上部，开挖边坡高在25m左右，以强弱风化岩层为主。心墙轴线方向为顺向坡，但地形坡度20°～25°，岩层倾角大于坡角（产状：N50°E，NW∠41°），右坡坝肩边坡局部将切层开挖，应注意边坡及时支护；上、下游侧边坡与岩层产状近垂直相交，对边坡稳定有利，但边坡岩体为强风化和弱风化上带，边坡开挖应按Ⅳ类和Ⅴ类岩体实施，边坡不高、此类边坡岩体不易采取支护措施，需设计合理的坡比是关键。

（中国电建集团昆明勘测设计研究院有限公司　张来飞　赵云）

基于易损性理论边坡安全评价方法在三岔河水电站工程中的应用

边坡系统的稳定性问题一直是边坡研究的核心问题，在边坡安全评价研究方面现阶段还存在很多缺陷和难点，基于Geostudio软件和结构易损性理论，利用随机法，根据边坡不同易损等级评价边坡安全性，当现场边坡监测出现异常状况时，该法可以与相关监测资料结合起来，对滑坡体进行综合性评价提供技术支持。

（一）边坡安全评价方法

1. 易损性定义　结构的地震易损性是指在各种不同等级的地震作用下，结构出现不同破坏极限状态的概率，在宏观上从概率的角度给出了建筑物结构的抗震能力。通过查看易损性曲线可以获取结构在不同地震作用下反应超过相应破坏等级的变形能力的条件概率，一般可以通过经验法和理论解析法得到易损性曲线。经验易损性曲线通过经验法绘制，适用于有震害资料的地区，通过人为主观根据调查总结得出的破坏概率矩阵，然后曲线拟合破坏矩阵给出的概率值，得到的曲线为经验易损性曲线；而结合理论分析法通过计算分析结构的地震反应而得到的曲线为结构理论易损性曲线，适用于缺乏震害资料的地区。

2. 结构易损性数学描述　失效函数可以表示相应的破坏模式，失效函数的自变量由在地震荷载中的地震危险性变量和结构随机变量构成，结构失效的状态可以定义为在地震作用下达到某一相应失效函数所描述的曲面时破损发生。失效函数可以表示为：$g=g(x_1, x_2, \cdots, x_n, y_1, y_2, \cdots, y_n)$，式中，$x_1$，$x_2$，…，$x_n$表示地震危险性变量，$y_1$，$y_2$，…，$y_n$表示结构的随机性变量。为此，结合失效函数曲面可以把随机变量空间分为两个域，即安全域（$g\leqslant 0$）和不安全域（$g>0$），这一假设认为失效度量达到某一g值时发生失效。易损性概率分布的选择，应遵循熵最大原理。由下式给出的Edgeworth-Kapteyn分布能使熵最大，并且符合正态分布：

$$f(x)=\frac{1}{\sqrt{2\pi\sigma}}\exp\{-[\frac{y(x)-\mu}{\sigma}]^2\}\left|\frac{\mathrm{d}y}{\mathrm{d}x}\right| \quad (1)$$

其中，函数$y(x)$的形式取决于引入的附加信息。

在地震易损性分析中，x一般为地震动峰值加速度，符合正态分布。

3. 各等级下易损性计算　结构的易损性是指结构在给定地震加速度作用下发生某种破损状态的条件概率。在易损性概念的数学描述中，失效函数g是随机变量，易损性曲线定义了失效变量g可能的概率，假定g服从正态分布，某一破坏等级下的平均值为μ，标准差为σ，则破损曲线定义为：$F_r=\phi\left(\frac{X-\mu}{\sigma}\right)$，可以绘制此等级下的易损性曲线。

4. 边坡安全评价流程　边坡稳定分析时，首先利用软件GOESTUDIO软件极限平衡法计算静力工况，通过稳定安全系数判断边坡是否失稳，若边坡没有失稳，则进行边坡非常运用条件下安全评价。其次，结合蒙特卡洛法对边坡进行可靠度分析，可以选择的随机参数如咬合力C和摩擦角φ，并根据可靠度分析结果和相关工程经验得到边坡破损等级。最后利用拟静力法计算不同地震荷载对应失效概率，得到不同等级易损性曲线，根据易损性曲线得到的易损性概率函数对边坡进行安全评价。

（二）工程实例运用

(1) 工程背景。三岔河水电站位于保山地区腾冲县猴桥镇，为槟榔江梯级的龙头水库，枢纽布置主要由混凝土面板堆石坝、右岸溢洪道、左岸泄洪放空隧洞、左岸引水发电系统和左岸导流隧洞组成。电站进水口布置在上游左岸的凹岸处，靠近泄洪（导流）隧洞。

(2) 边坡安全评价。①模型建立。利用GOESTUDIO软件建立三岔河水电站进水口边坡模型。②静力工况计算。利用极限平衡法计算静力工况，通过稳定安全系数判断边坡是否失稳，若边坡没有失稳，则进行边坡非常运用条件下安全评价。结合进水口边坡，计算得到稳定安全系数为2.15，大于规范值，进行非常工况下边坡安全评价。③破损等级确定。基于蒙特卡洛法进行边坡可靠性分析，根据分析结果并结合规范确定破损等级。④计算不同地震荷载下边坡失效概率。通过拟静力法计算不同地震荷载下边坡稳定安全系数均值和方差，通过数理统计得到边坡失效概率。⑤边坡安全综合评价。根据易损曲线公式，计算不同破损等级下地震加速度易损曲线，拟合得到其易损性概率函数，并依据易损性概率函数对边坡安全进行综合评价。

（中国电建集团昆明勘测设计研究院有限公司 冯燕明 张礼兵 杨姗姗）

滇中引水工程昆呈隧洞岩溶水文地质问题研究

昆呈隧洞处于滇中引水工程输水总干渠昆明段，基本沿昆明盆地东侧布置，隧洞沿线岩溶发育程度为中等～强，洞身处于各岩溶水系统强径流区水平径流带中，故引水隧洞穿越可溶岩地层所引起的涌水、突水和突泥问题较为突出。

（一）岩溶水文地质条件概述

1. 岩溶发育规律 昆呈隧洞沿线岩溶受岩性、构造和地形条件等影响，岩溶发育的地带性特征明显。区内可溶岩层位从新到老依次为：二叠系下统栖霞＋茅口组灰岩、中统威宁组和下统大塘组上司段灰岩、泥盆系上统宰格组白云岩和龙王庙组白云岩。区域构造发育较为复杂，两条主要断裂相交，各走向中小型断层发育。工程区位于金沙江和南盘江两大水系之分水岭地带，地下水主要接受大气降水补给，最低排泄基准面为滇池，地下水主要沿宝象河、白沙河等次级水系向滇池径流。隧洞沿线岩溶现象十分发育，地表岩溶现象包括洼地、漏斗、落水洞、溶蚀槽谷和石芽坡地等，地下岩溶包括溶洞、地下暗河和溶孔溶隙。从分水岭至河流谷盆，岩溶发育形态由开敞式～隐蔽式～覆盖式呈有规律的过渡。

2. 岩溶地下水系统的补给、径流、排泄 昆呈隧洞工程区岩溶地下水补给主要来自三个方面，一是大气降水直接入渗补给地下水；二是非可溶岩区的地表水进入可溶岩区入渗补给；三是非可溶岩中的地下水直接越流补给可溶岩地下水；另外，覆盖层孔隙水的下渗和地下水沿构造通道也能补给岩溶地下水。地下水径流主要受排泄基准面、地形地貌、构造、岩性展布特征等因素控制，各岩溶水系统径流条件不尽相同，最后向东河、螳螂川和滇池水系统排泄。地下水在径流过程中遇河流切割、阻水地层或断层错移时多以泉和暗河形式排泄，当岩溶介质较为均匀时地下水也可能通过线状排泄方式进入河流。

3. 岩溶管道系统发育下限研究 昆呈隧洞沿滇池盆地东侧的低山、丘陵地貌区布置，地形起伏不大，地面高程在1890～2230m之间，主要出露石林期Ⅳ和Ⅲ级剥夷面岩溶形态。Ⅲ级剥夷面（2250～2150m）表现为洼地、落水洞、漏斗等岩溶负地形，且十分发育，为区内地下水的主要补给区，Ⅳ级剥夷面（2000～1900m）为地下水的主要排泄区，集中出露岩溶泉和暗河出口等地下水排泄点。隧洞布置于盆地边缘，高程在1882～1900m范围内，而滇池为本区最低排泄基准面高程约在1886m附近，洞身正好处于各岩溶水系统强径流区水平径流带中，这个部位溶蚀一般强烈，多为水平岩溶形态，可能发育较多的地下溶洞。

（二）工程区主要岩溶水文地质问题

1. 工程区岩溶地质灾害类型 岩溶对昆呈隧洞的危害主要分为以下四种类型：①隧洞中涌水、突水灾害；②溶洞、溶蚀空腔充填碎屑物质，隧洞开挖时引起突泥、流砂灾害；③岩溶塌陷类灾害，即隧洞施工引发的岩溶塌陷；④隧洞揭露隐伏溶洞灾害。

2. 处理措施建议

（1）岩溶涌突水灾害处理。为减少岩溶水对环境及隧洞的不利影响，昆呈隧洞对岩溶水主要采用封堵为主、堵排结合的处理原则进行综合防治。对通过前方水量小、不影响围岩稳定、水力联系弱的可溶岩含水层，且施工排水环境影响不明显的洞段，可采用超前排水钻孔放水后再掘进的处理措施。对通过前方水量大、影响围岩稳定、水力联系强的可溶岩含水层，采用地质钻机沿开挖轮廓周圈钻设伞状灌浆孔进行隧洞周圈帷幕封水，掘进水压大的还需进行径向高压帷幕灌浆。对其中岩溶管道发育、水压大的区域，需进行高压灌浆堵水及混凝土封堵管道以提高围岩承载能力，防止地表水疏干及围岩坍塌。对水力联系强、水源补给丰富的高压涌水带，还需配合在掌子面范围进行同步超前灌浆，防止水从掌子面涌出。在预估有大量含水溶洞或松软物填充溶洞时，缩短掘进进尺，精细控制掘进参数，加强渣量监测及渣料分析，提前采取措施。

隧洞沿线上方和穿越岩溶水系统上游汇水区大气降雨入渗条件良好，地下水径流通畅，尽量安排在枯水期施工，可以降低涌、突水灾害的危险级别。

（2）岩溶突泥、地下泥石流灾害处理。昆呈隧洞通过的可溶岩中，有多处洞段穿越断层、强烈溶蚀风化带和充填型岩溶洞穴，这些部位容易发生突泥灾害，围岩稳定性差，在地下水位较高隧洞地下水头较大的部位具备发生地下泥石流的条件。可采取以下措施进行处理：①超前预注浆：固结松散破碎体、胶结细微颗粒，阻断涌水路径，控制涌水量。②管排引流：沿轮廓线径向布置过滤管引流地下水。③固结灌浆：控制隧洞变形。

（3）岩溶洞穴灾害防治。根据超前地质预报成果，对隧洞前方存在溶洞应根据空间交叉关系在有条件的情况下进行绕洞避让，如不能避让，需根据溶洞形态、规模、充水、物质充填情况的不同采取围岩和地基加固措施以保证隧洞通过。常见的工程处理措施主要有：①洞底回填或换填跨越法。②超前锚杆（管棚）钢支撑喷混凝土法。③混凝土拱帽施工法。④钢支撑挑梁法：在溶洞口 1.5～2.0m 范围内架立钢支撑、打锚杆，在钢支撑上向溶洞内顶入工字钢形成挑梁，将挑梁和钢支撑整体浇入混凝土拱中。⑤顶管法：用钢管代替钢支撑挑梁法的工字钢顶入溶洞。

（中国电建集团昆明勘测设计研究院有限公司　孙文超　刘皓　闫斌　廖存刚）

工程地质问题处理

糯扎渡水电站导流洞 F_3 断层带围岩稳定性分析及施工处理

（一）F_3 断层工程地质特性

糯扎渡水电站位于云南省思茅市和澜沧县交界的澜沧江上，F_3 断层是坝址区规模较大的断层之一，规模大、延伸长、性状差，对洞室围岩稳定性影响甚大。

（1）F_3 断层空间分布特征和性状。F_3 断层主要分布于坝址左岸，并沿 SW 方向延伸至右岸。断层总体产状为 N15°～50°E，NW∠80°～90°，呈舒缓波状延伸，长度大于 1000m；断层带宽度一般为 2～6m，局部达 20m 左右，主要由角砾岩、碎裂岩及糜棱岩、断层泥等组成，略潮湿，胶结差。

（2）F_3 断层的开挖揭露特征。根据导流洞开挖揭露情况，F_3 断层在 1、2、3、4 号导流洞中均已揭露。1、2 号导流洞揭露 F_3 断层产状为 N25°～30°E，NW∠70°～80°，破碎带宽度一般为 10m 左右，主要由碎块岩、碎裂岩、糜棱岩及灰白色断层泥组成，其中糜棱岩和断层泥主要沿两侧主裂面连续分布，靠上盘主裂面断层泥厚度约 1m，靠下盘主裂面断层泥厚度约 2m，糜棱岩有明显的高岭土化、绿泥石化现象，局部破碎带有炭化现象，蚀变明显；断层上盘有明显界面，断层下盘界面模糊，有宽约 5m 的影响带，影响带有渗水、滴水现象。3、4 号导流洞尾段揭露 F_3，断层产状为 N15°～20°E，NW∠80°～90°，破碎带宽度一般为 4～6m，主要由角砾岩、碎裂岩、糜棱岩和断层泥组成，其中糜棱岩和断层泥沿上游裂面连续分布，厚度约为 1m；断层无明显的上下界面，影响带较宽，可达 14～30m。

（二）F_3 断层带围岩稳定性

F_3 断层与 1、2 号导流洞轴线夹角在 40°～60°之间，与 3、4 号导流洞轴线夹角约为 80°，由于断层宽度较大，对导流洞特别是 1、2 号导流洞围岩稳定性有较大影响。F_3 断层带组成物质破碎，有较厚的断层泥和糜棱岩沿断层带连续分布，且胶结差；影响带宽度较宽，岩体破碎，岩体切割块度较小，断层带与影响带多为散体结构和碎裂结构，岩体完整性差，并伴随有局部集中性渗水、滴水现象，断层带与影响带岩体质量差，为Ⅴ类围岩，稳定性很差。开挖掘进过程中遇到 F_3 断层时掌子面上的断层泥即出现坍塌现象和塑性变形，小规模塌方、掉块时有发生，断层带围岩不能自稳，需要进行超前支护才能向前掘进。

（三）F_3 断层带的处理措施

（1）施工思路及原理。导流洞衬砌断面为方圆（城门洞）形，最大高度 21m，宽度 16m。施工采用新奥法施工理论为指导：“短进尺，弱爆破，少扰动，紧封闭，勤量测。”1、2、3 号导流洞开挖方案采用Ⅲ层开挖，Ⅰ层开挖方案采用 8m×7m 小导洞超前、后续扩挖的形式，4 号导流洞采用全断面开挖方式。其中 1 号导流洞在地质预报遇到 F_3 断层之前约 5m 进行 2m×2m 小导洞穿越断层开挖。施工关键点：①及时对周边围岩及掌子面实施 3～5cm 的素混凝土封闭，形成初期简单的柔性支护环。②素喷后要及时打设系统锚杆，尽早发挥其悬吊及支承拱作用；同时快速进行工字钢拱架的安装，系统喷混凝土跟进。

（2）Ⅰ层施工程序。Ⅰ层顶拱及边墙采用锚管超前支护→Ⅰ层全断面（4 号导流洞全断面）开挖进尺 0.5～1m→初喷 5cm 钢纤维混凝土支护，掌子面周边 2m 范围素喷 5cm 厚 C20 混凝土封闭→初期支护锚杆及钢拱架固定锚杆施工→安装钢拱架→分层喷钢纤维混凝土至设计厚度→剩余系统锚杆支护。

（3）Ⅱ、Ⅲ层施工程序。Ⅱ层开挖分为两小层并分半施工，Ⅲ层开挖分半施工，半幅开挖支护完毕后再开挖另一半。施工程序为：边墙超前锚杆→水平钻进2m→素喷5cm钢纤维混凝土封闭→部分系统锚杆及锁脚锚杆打设→钢拱架接腿→分层复喷到位→剩余系统锚杆适时打设。开挖采用凿岩台车水平钻进，周边密孔小药量光爆，排炮进尺1m，每排炮后及时喷护5cm钢纤维混凝土封闭岩面，开挖3～5m后进行一次系统支护。

（4）主要支护参数及施工方法。①超前支护。主断层带顶拱超前支护采用ϕ42自进式中空注浆锚杆，长4.5m，环向间距0.5m，外插角5°～15°，排距2m；断层影响带顶拱超前支护使用ϕ25砂浆锚杆。边墙超前支护采用ϕ32砂浆锚杆，长4.5m，主断层带间距1m，断层影响带间距2m，外插角25°～30°，排距3m。②系统支护。采用I20a工字钢拱架，主断层带间距为50cm，断层影响带间距为80cm。系统锚杆主要采用6m长、ϕ32的砂浆锚杆；间排距主断层带为1m×1m，断层影响带为1.5m×1.5m；主断层带造孔困难部分采用ϕ32自进式锚杆。断层范围内边顶拱均喷25cm厚C25钢纤维混凝土。③永久支护。一次支护基础上采用1.5m厚双层钢筋混凝土衬砌和围岩灌浆。④施工方法。超前支护钻孔主要采用三臂凿岩台车、自进式锚杆灌浆采用注浆机；开挖主要采用三臂台车（手风钻）钻孔；支护以多臂凿岩台车造孔为主、混凝土喷射台车湿喷工艺进行喷锚施工；工字钢拱架制作采用液压型钢弯曲机。

（四）监测反馈

断层带每5m设置一个监测断面，后期监测资料表明：导流隧洞F_3断层带围岩变形观测测值呈收敛状态，没有突变现象发生；锚杆应力受力较好，观测结果稳定；声波测试表明，爆破参数控制较好，对围岩松弛圈影响范围较小，经过支护后的F_3断层带变形曲线平缓，变形量较小，断层带目前处于基本稳定状态。

（中国电建集团昆明勘测设计研究院
有限公司　蒋正伟）

溧阳抽水蓄能电站下水库均质土坝淤泥质黏土基础处理研究

（一）下水库地质条件

溧阳抽水蓄能电站下水库位于天目湖库尾西侧，开挖形成库盆，在临近天目湖一侧修建一座均质土坝与之隔开。下水库均质土坝为2级建筑物，坝顶高程24.4m，地面高程为16～20m，库底高程－2.0m，正常蓄水位高程19.0m。下水库地质条件复杂，经现场开挖揭露后，发现上部粉质黏土厚2.0～5.0m，淤泥质黏土厚0～8.0m，砂卵砾石层厚2.20～5.50m。淤泥质黏土分布高程7.0～15.0m，位于库水位以下，均质土坝靠北侧约350m长左右一带淤泥质黏土较厚，为3～8m，往南则淤泥质黏土变薄或缺失。淤泥质黏土为软塑状，少量甚至呈流塑状，含少量碎石或砾石，稳定性极差，是影响坝（岸）坡稳定及基础沉陷的主要因素。下水库水位频繁变幅，陡涨陡落，坝基淤泥质黏土的存在给均质土坝上游坝坡的稳定带来了不利的影响。采用GEOSLOPE软件进行原始地质条件下坝坡稳定的理论计算，得到最不利工况（水位骤降＋地震）下坝坡安全系数0.773，小于规范允许安全系数1.15。运行期边坡将失稳，必须进行处理。

（二）坝基处理设计方案比选

根据下水库坝基设计要求，提出挖除置换、挤密碎石桩、重力式挡墙、高压旋喷桩等4种处理方案：① 挖除置换方案。在土坝上游侧高程18.6～9.5m范围之间，向下游20m范围内挖除淤泥质黏土，以堆石料换填，堆石料下设80cm厚碎石垫层及反滤土工布。② 挤密碎石桩方案。采用振动、冲击或水冲等方式在地基中成孔后，再将碎石挤压入已成的孔中，形成碎石所构成的密实桩体，并和原桩周覆盖层组成复合地基。③ 重力式挡墙方案。在土坝上游坝趾处设置重力式挡墙，以维持土坝坝坡稳定。挡墙的基础需坐落在基岩上，挡墙顶宽1.5m，最大底宽8m，上游坡比1：0.4，下游直立。④ 高压旋喷桩方案。在上游坝基范围内共设置9排高压旋喷桩，呈梅花形布置，第一排距坝轴线10.0m处，桩距2.0m，深度伸至基岩分界线内，高压旋喷灌浆完毕后，要求桩体有效直径不小于1.0m，抗压强度不得小于1.8MPa。对上述方案从坝坡稳定、工期、施工难度以及造价等方面进行了综合比较，确定高压旋喷桩方案较优。

（三）振冲高压旋喷钢管桩及加固框架结构方案

在高压旋喷桩施工试验过程中发现：① 岸坡加固采用的9排高压旋喷桩方案，投资较高；② 高压旋喷桩单桩抗剪强度理论值仅为70kPa，桩体抗剪能力较低，坝坡稳定储备不高。为解决上述问题，采取振冲高压旋喷钢管桩工艺，在水泥初凝前将钢管沉入旋喷桩内形成联合受力体，让钢管与高压旋喷体有效黏结成整体，并将钢管伸入基岩，形成稳定性高的桩体结构。具体布置为：在上游岸坡范围内共设置4排桩，呈梅花形布置，第一排距坝轴线18.0m，桩距2.0m，深度伸至基岩分界线以下，每个桩体内布设一根钢管。将高压旋喷钢管桩与边坡锁口梁、网格梁组合连接在一起，形成加固框架结构。

（四）现场实施

（1）钢管参数选取。采用普通碳素钢 Q235 焊接钢管，外径 110mm，有效壁厚 5.25mm，此钢管抗剪强度 125MPa，大于反演分析中坝坡稳定要求的 70MPa。

（2）旋喷灌浆参数试验。根据规范要求及现场试验情况，最终确定灌浆参数如下：孔距 2m，排距 2m，孔斜率≤1%，孔位偏差±5cm，孔深至基岩分界线，浆压 30MPa，浆量 75L/min，浆液比重 1.4～1.5g/cm³，返浆比重≥1.3g/cm³，风压 0.4～0.5MPa，风量 0.6～1m³/min，提升速度 15cm/min，旋转速度 15r/min，旋转角度 360°，高压旋喷灌浆顶高程高于岸坡开挖面 0.3m，高喷底高程以实际施工时振动器反弹情况经验为准。

（3）振冲高压旋喷钢管桩施工方法。①钢管底端加工成鸭嘴形使其能顺利振冲下沉；②利用变径连接管，将钢管与高喷灌浆机的振管轴心对接，保证钢管在沉入过程中受到能无偏心振冲挤；③ 利用高喷灌浆机喷射水泥浆成桩；④在水泥浆体初凝前，将钢管振冲沉入高压旋喷桩体内；⑤ 将钢管打入基岩 0.2m 提高桩体的稳定性。

（4）软基加固框架结构设计及施工。将坝坡的混凝土网格梁布置成矩形，间排距 3.0m×2.15m，网格梁尺寸为 0.5m 宽×0.5m 高。将高压旋喷钢管桩与边坡锁口梁、网格梁组合连接在一起，形成加固框架结构。

（5）施工工艺流程。工艺流程如下：施工准备→孔位放样→移机就位→调整喷管垂度→地面试喷→振动成孔→喷射成桩→提出喷管→沉入钢管→与网格梁组合搭接形成框架结构→进入下一流程循环。

（五）试验检测

对试验区高压旋喷钢管桩进行开挖及桩体取样做抗压强度试验以确认成桩效果。

（1）桩体开挖检查。在单桩试验处，通过对三天龄期高喷桩进行开挖，开挖最大深度为 4.5m。开挖揭露表明，桩径均能达到设计要求的有效直径不小于 1.0m，并且表观效果较好。

（2）抗压强度检测。用手动水钻在已开挖的桩体中的淤泥质黏土层（1.1～2.1m）、粉质黏土层（3.5～4.5m）、砂砾石层（2.1～3.0m）中分别取样做单轴抗压强度试验，24 天龄期抗压强度分别为 2.2、1.8、6.3MPa，大于设计强度 1.8MPa。

（六）处理成果

采用 GEOSLOPE 软件对振冲高压旋喷钢管桩及框架结构加固方案进行模拟计算，以水位骤降＋地震最不利工况进行验算，坝坡安全系数为 1.635，规范允许安全系数为 1.15，满足坝坡稳定要求。目前下水库已蓄水三年，大坝运行安全稳定。

（中国电建集团中南勘测设计研究院有限公司 刘昊 宁永升 熊文清 王小平）

蓄水后库岸堆积体边坡变形特征及稳定性分析

东岭信库岸边堆积体位于三板溪水电站上游剑河县境内，距离下游大坝坝址 80km，距离上游剑河县柳川镇直线距离仅 0.8km，库岸主要由滑坡堆积体组成，为一古滑坡体，方量约 2000×10⁴ m³。2006 年 1 月，三板溪水电站开始下闸蓄水，至 2007 年 7 月，东岭信河段库水位由蓄水前的 428.00m 高程蓄至 472.00m 高程。7 月下旬，巡查发现东岭信边坡坡面和坡顶后缘出现多条张拉裂缝，坡体出现变形，并有不断发展的趋势。

（一）堆积体边坡结构特征

（1）滑体。东岭信堆积体前缘至河床高程 420m，后缘坡顶高程 700m，水平顺河流向长度 520m，变形体方量约 2000×10⁴ m³。滑坡堆积体地表大部分为粉质黏土夹碎、块石等覆盖，前期在边坡前缘因开挖公路，揭露出堆积体表部主要为松动破碎岩体，出露岩石多呈强风化。钻孔及排水洞开挖揭露显示，堆积体岩性主要为变余凝灰质砂岩、变余层凝灰岩、条带状凝灰质粉砂质板岩，其整体性、连续性相对较好，岩体弱等至强风化，基本保留原层面形态和结构特征，岩层产状与堆积体周边基岩产状相差较大。

（2）滑带。滑坡堆积体滑带位于滑坡堆积体底部滑面以上，以灰褐色、灰黄色、黄色、灰色含砾粉质黏土为主，堆积体前缘该层内含部分碎石，含砾粉质黏土一般呈可塑状，厚度 0.5～3m 不等。

（3）滑床。滑床基岩主要为板溪群清水江组浅灰色厚层块状变余凝灰质砂岩、条带状凝灰质粉砂质板岩和灰色中厚层状变余层凝灰岩，岩石坚硬，属硬质岩类。层面产状 20°∠16°，总体倾向坡外偏上游。

（4）地下水。根据勘探资料，边坡堆积体内地下水主要为孔隙潜水，局部存在上层滞水。排水洞开挖显示，部分洞段揭穿含水层时，局部出现洞顶坍塌，水流携带泥夹块、碎石塌落，涌水量达 30～40L/min。排水洞完成后，经过多年运行，部分排水孔流量依然较大，部分排水孔出水量可达 10～20L/min，雨季时明显增大。

（二）水库蓄水后的边坡变形特征

（1）地表变形特征。监测初期堆积体边坡变形速率较大，测得的水平向变形最大速率 0.07mm/d。2011 年底，排水洞及洞内排水孔施工基本完成，边坡的变形速率降至 0.01～0.04mm/d。排水洞及排水孔的施工有效降低了坡体内地下水位，对遏制边坡变形有积极作用。根据观测资料，边坡变形仍处于缓慢发展阶段，部分测点趋于收敛。

（2）地表裂缝。地表裂缝主要出现在东岭信边坡的后缘，最早发现于 2007 年 7 月底（即蓄水结束阶段），为张拉裂缝，裂缝最大张裂宽度 75mm 左右。各条裂缝目前均处于收敛状态，未见明显的增大趋势。

（3）深部位移。根据变形监测成果，在距离边坡地表垂直深度约 60～70m 左右，曲线出现明显的拐点，该深度处于边坡的滑动面 Q^4 附近，滑动方向垂直河水流向，与地表位移观测方位一致。深部位移监测数据显示，监测初期孔口段的变形速率较大，为 0.05mm/d，截至 2016 年底，孔口段的变形速率大幅减少，达到 0.008mm/d，表明该部位的变形呈现逐年减缓趋势，趋于收敛。

（4）地下水位及排水洞流量变化。堆积体内地下水位的波动随季节变化明显：每年雨季时（5～9 月）地下水位显著升高，其余季节呈小幅波动。雨季时，洞内流量明显增大，其余季节流量显著回落。地下水位和排水洞流量观测结果均表明，边坡地下水位升高与雨季时的降雨具有明显的相关性。

（三）堆积体的形成及变形机制探讨

（1）堆积体的成因。东岭信堆积体边坡三面环山，东侧临水，南侧和北侧均被冲沟切割，下伏基岩为缓倾顺层向结构。经现场查勘及变形特征分析，堆积体为来自山体后缘的古滑坡体，后缘山体的岩体滑动至当前部位，覆盖住原来的地表，形成目前的、看似杂乱的结构形态，但堆积体内部仍保留原层面形态和结构特征。

（2）堆积体变形机制探讨。①2007 年 5 月底～7 月底，东岭信河段水位由蓄水前的 428.00m 高程上升至 472.00m 高程，上升幅度达到 44m。蓄水前，边坡前缘的堆积体位于水面以上，不受河水位影响；蓄水后，受河水位影响的堆积体方量剧增。处于前缘阻滑段的堆积体浸水软化、抗剪强度降低，加之库水位上升时间短，幅度大，从而激活了古滑坡体，导致边坡开始出现缓慢变形。②排水洞及排水孔施工后，有效降低了坡体内的地下水位，大幅减缓了边坡的变形速率，部分测点变形出现收敛趋势。

（四）蓄水前后边坡离散元计算与分析

本次计算采用二维离散元程序 UDEC 建立计算模型，考虑蓄水前、蓄水后的水位情况，通过调整岩体结构面物理力学参数模拟地下水位以下岩土体的浸水软化，分析边坡岩土体力学特征和稳定性。计算结果可知：① 蓄水前，边坡滑体与基岩交界处的滑动面出现多处塑性区，但在边坡后缘、滑动面的中部和滑坡前缘，尚未出现完全贯通的塑性区。此时的稳定性系数为 1.04，安全余度较小，处于欠稳定状态；② 蓄水结束时，边坡坡体内塑性区迅速增大，主要出现在堆积体滑面前部和后缘。（与蓄水前相比，塑性区面积增加了 77%），此时，除了滑坡前缘，滑动面的塑性区已经大部分处于贯通状态。计算得到的边坡稳定性系数为 0.98，表明边坡处于临界稳定状态。根据计算结果，总体上边坡的滑动面近似于圆弧状，从边坡后缘拉裂，在边坡前缘剪出，与监测资料基本一致，滑动面位于 Q^4 层。

（中国电建集团中南勘测设计研究院
有限公司　唐军峰　杨军　李学政）

象鼻岭水电站 BT2 堆积体治理设计

象鼻岭水电站 BT2 堆积体天然状态整体稳定，213 国道改线段通过堆积体前缘，挖除了堆积体部分坡脚，2011 年 10 月上旬，BT2 堆积体产生变形，后缘拉裂、下游侧剪出现象，不及时治理将影响施工期安全及运行发电进水口建筑物的安全。

（一）BT2 堆积体地质条件

BT2 堆积体位于坝址右岸上游，其下游侧距进水口开挖边坡约 50m，堆积体分布高程 1410～1520m，顺河向最大宽度约 250m，面积约 $3.8\times10^4m^2$，厚 18～48m，体积约 $115\times10^4m^3$，其后缘为玄武岩陡壁。BT2 堆积体为牛栏江四级阶地后缘山体在长期地质应力作用下风化、蚀变，逐步卸荷、松弛、崩塌，堆积于阶地斜坡上，其主要由底部的原始残坡积层、中部崩塌堆积层及顶部残坡积层组成。残坡积层主要分布于堆积体顶部，主要为黏土夹碎石，厚 2.5～6.3m，碎石含量约占 20%；崩坡积层分布于堆积体表层，主要为黏土夹碎、块石，厚 2.3～16.6m，黏土含量约占 60%，偶见块石随机分布，结构松散；崩塌堆积层分布于堆积体中、下部，主要为块、碎石，厚 6.8～30.5m，结构松散，未见架空现象，中间局部见一层或多层碎石夹黏土层。堆积体为单向斜坡地形，其上下游侧均有冲沟。

（二）BT2 堆积体滑动模式分析

堆积体破坏模式主要为两种：① 堆积体与基岩接触带参数较低，堆积体沿接触带滑动失稳；② 沿堆积体内部圆弧滑动。从堆积体参数来看，堆积体与基岩接触带参数较低，堆积体沿接触带滑动失稳的可能性较大，经初步计算，BT2 崩塌堆积体内部圆弧滑动安全系数均满足规范要求，主要计算堆积体沿接触带滑移模式。

（三）BT2崩塌堆积体稳定分析

（1）边坡等级。由于复建213国道通过BT2堆积体前缘，BT2堆积体即属于公路边坡，又属于水库边坡。综合公路路堑边坡与水电水利工程边坡，BT2崩塌堆积体边坡按水电水利工程边坡B类Ⅱ级边坡进行边坡稳定设计，稳定设计安全系数取持久工况为1.15，短暂工况为1.10，偶然工况为1.05。

（2）计算方法及工况。采用中国水利水电科学研究院编制的土质边坡稳定分析程序STAB2005对BT2崩塌堆积体进行分析计算。由于风化岩体碎裂，采用土质边坡稳定计算，采用Spencer法。考虑地震作用，根据运行期及施工期可能出现的情况，库岸边坡计算工况为蓄水后持久工况，短暂工况（暴雨或久雨），偶然工况（地震）。

（3）计算剖面。BT2崩塌堆积体从上游至下游的1-1′～5-5′共5个剖面进行计算。

（4）计算成果。进行213公路复建后BT2崩塌堆积体稳定计算，根据成果可知，2-2′～4-4′剖面各工况下安全系数均小于1，1-1′和5-5′剖面安全系数大于1。BT2堆积体处于不稳定状态，计算与实际状态一致。

（四）治理方案设计

根据堆积体破坏模式及稳定分析成果，研究采取了上部挖除、中部削坡减载＋坡脚抗滑桩锚索支挡和中上部削坡减载＋抗滑桩支挡两种方案，方案一削坡减载效果明显，坡脚采用小断面抗滑桩和锚索方案，施工简易方便；方案二采用少量削坡减载，坡脚采用大断面抗滑桩支挡，抗滑桩深度达40～50m，工程量大、施工难度大，经比较采用上部挖除、中部削坡减载＋抗滑桩锚索支挡方案。各部位设计详述如下：

（1）上部挖除、中部削坡减载治理设计。高程1470m以上全部挖除减载；1470～1405m按1∶2坡比削坡减载，在1430、1440m分别设置马道，且1440～1470m之间原布设一条施工道路，马道宽约2～3m，施工道路宽5m。

（2）坡脚支挡。在堆积体3-3′剖面约50m范围内坡脚复建213国道内路肩内侧设置一排锚拉抗滑桩，平均桩长为22m，桩为直径2m的圆截面桩，桩间距5m，桩身嵌入基岩约为1/3桩长。在每根桩距桩顶1m的位置设置一根2000kN级锚索，锚索伸入基岩，入射角20°，锚索平均长度40m，锚索预加应力为1000kN。

（3）坡面防护设计。削坡减载后出露基岩面采用锚喷、挂网、排水孔和随机锚杆措施。基岩面采用直径28mm，$L=9$m的锚杆与直径25mm，$L=4.5$m的锚杆间隔布置，间距4m×4m；设置排水孔，排水孔间距3m×3m，排水孔长度$L=5$m，水平仰角10°，梅花形布置。喷C20混凝土厚度10cm，挂网钢筋直径6.5mm，间距0.2m×0.2m。削坡减载后覆盖层边坡坡面采用草皮护坡，并且设置排水孔，排水孔间距3m×3m，排水孔长度$L=5$m，水平仰角10°，梅花形布置。

（4）排水系统。堆积体边坡开口线周边布设截水沟、马道内侧布置截排水沟，与坡面的排水孔组成边坡排水系统。

（五）安全监测设计及监测成果分析

在BT2堆积体设置2个主监测断面，每个监测断面布置2套4点式多点位移计，3个表面观测墩和2个测斜孔；设置2个辅助监测断面，各布置3个表面观测墩。监测数据显示，锚杆测力计、钢筋计累计应力整体不大，变化过程相对较平稳，暂无异常变化情况，蓄水前后累计应力变化不大，蓄水影响较小；多点位移计累计位移整体较小，变化过程较平稳，蓄水前后累计位移变化不大，蓄水影响较小；测斜孔累计位移整体不大。由此，BT2堆积体总体处于稳定状态。

（中国电建集团贵阳勘测设计研究院有限公司　张海超 陈毅峰 刘杰）

苗尾水电站边坡倾倒变形机理与加固效果分析

苗尾水电站位于云南省大理州云龙县旧州镇境内的澜沧江上，砾质土心墙堆石坝最大坝高131.30m，电站装机容量1400MW。2013年坝基开挖过程中，右坝基上游侧边坡产生较大范围倾倒拉裂变形，对工程安全构成严重威胁，现场立即暂停施工，进行边坡抢险加固处理。

（一）右坝基边坡基本地质条件

右岸边坡高程地形较陡，坡度50°～60°，局部形成陡崖。岸坡为中侏罗系花开左组上段第三、第四亚岩组（J_2h^{2-3}、J_2h^{2-4}）地层，岩性主要为变质石英砂岩与绿泥绢云板岩，其中坡脚处以板岩为主。总体上为陡倾坡内层状结构斜坡，正常岩层产状为N5°～20°W，NEE或SWW75°～90°，边坡坡向总体与岩层走向一致。边坡结构面较为发育，受构造作用影响，岸坡岩体风化卸荷强烈。坝址区两岸发育典型的倾倒变形现象，右坝基边坡极强倾倒岩体水平深度0～15m，强倾倒上段岩体水平深度为29～67m，强倾倒下段岩体水平深度为64～101m。

（二）右坝基边坡倾倒拉裂变形特征

右坝基开挖过程中，上游侧边坡于2013年4月

16日在开口线部位及坡面出现拉裂缝。2013年5月27日1384～1366m高程发生局部表层坍塌，方量250～300m³。随后进行的坡面及PD20平洞内裂缝调查表明，边坡倾倒拉裂变形区主要位于坝轴线上游至小溜槽沟的山脊，宽度约100m，高度范围为1290～1490m高程，近200m高，水平深度约30m，变形发生在强倾倒上段岩体内。

现场调查坡面裂缝有16条，主要分布于1390～1410m高程和1450～1490m高程附近。裂缝走向以N60°W为主，总体表现为追踪近EW节理和NWW向反倾节理发育。裂缝断续分布，单条长度不大于6m，一般为1～2m，宽度多小于2cm，最大宽度15cm。裂缝总体上以拉张变形为主，未发生明显剪切滑移或错落。

（三）边坡倾倒变形机理分析

2013年4月15日，现场巡视时发现苗尾右坝基边坡混凝土喷层存在裂缝，5月25日喷层裂缝扩大，5月27日即发生浅表局部坍塌。滑塌后坡面调查时1470～1480m高程裂缝细小，不仔细分辨很难发现，而至6月1日已很明显，PD20平洞内为新产生的裂缝。从边坡地质条件分析，右坝基上游侧基础开挖边坡坡向与岩层走向近平行，该部位堆石区基础开挖，使得边坡底部局部切脚，支撑倾倒变形的下部岩体厚度减薄，而边坡下部岩性相对较软的板岩，在上部岩体重力的作用下发生压缩变形，同时由于岩层产状不利，下部卸荷松弛为上部倾倒岩体的变形提供了空间，导致PD20平洞附近的倾倒变形岩体变形加剧，发生了新的倾倒——拉裂变形。1384m高程滑坡的发生进一步削弱了下部岩体的强度，使得倾倒变形向高高程和深部发展，导致了1460～1480m高程岩体变形拉裂和PD20平洞洞内20m以后的变形。

倾倒变形演化为滑坡的过程中，变形可分为四个阶段：①倾倒变形初期阶段。②强烈倾倒变形阶段。③蠕滑变形阶段。④滑动破坏阶段。结合右坝基边坡倾倒拉裂变形过程，可以认为边坡处于强烈倾倒变形阶段，岩体倾倒变形加剧，形成断续潜在折断面，变形体出现反向台坎。但若不及时采取加固处理，变形极有可能进一步加剧，并导致滑坡失稳。

（四）右坝基边坡加固措施

根据边坡倾倒拉裂变形机理，结合地质条件，抢险加固采取“以预应力锚固固脚锁腰为主和加强边坡排水”的综合处理措施。①边坡压脚增稳。边坡坍塌部位下方进行堆渣压坡镇脚，堆渣体由1290m至1330m高程，平台顶宽15m。表观监测表明边坡变形速率有所减小。②分区锚固支护。1460～1350m高程范围边坡以变质石英砂岩为主，对倾倒拉裂变形采用预应力锚索结合混凝土框格梁进行加固；1350m高程以下边坡以绢云板岩为主，且处于边坡下部应力集中区，该部位采取预应力锚索结合混凝土锚拉板进行加固。③加强边坡排水。右坝基边坡分为正常蓄水以上永久边坡、正常蓄水位至死水位间水位变幅区边坡和施工期边坡三个区域，坡面排水孔布置以长短结合为原则，排水孔长度8～30m。④固结灌浆处理。针对右坝基边坡坡脚1368m高程以下以绢云板岩为主，切脚开挖作用产生向坡外的卸荷回弹，导致板岩可能出现层面开裂，岩体完整性变差，强度降低，且考虑到蓄水后板岩遇水易软化将造成边坡稳定性有所降低，对右坝基坡脚部位进行固结灌浆加固处理。固结灌浆深度为20m。

（五）加固效果评价

（1）二维离散元分析。采用二维离散元法对右坝基边坡加固处理条件下的稳定性和加固效果进行分析，锚固条件下边坡整体稳定安全系数为1.24，坝体填筑完成后由于堆石体的压坡作用，边坡整体稳定安全系数为1.38，水库蓄水至正常蓄水位1408m高程时整体安全系数为1.28。

（2）监测成果分析。据1466m高程表面变形测点监测数据，2013年12月～2014年3月，向坡外变位速率平均为0.1mm/d，沉降速率平均为0.014mm/d。据同一时期1408m高程多点位移计监测成果，坡表部位平均变位速率为0.011mm/d，表明边坡内部和外部变形均已收敛。据同一时期1412m高程锚索测力计监测成果，锚索荷载变化为－8.8～9.9kN/d，锚索受力平稳。综合分析表明：经加固处理后，苗尾水电站右坝基边坡整体处于稳定状态，加固措施有效。

（中国电建集团华东勘测设计研究院有限公司　郑惠峰　吴关叶　黄泰仁）

梨园水电站念生垦沟堆积体变形规律研究

（一）堆积体概况

梨园水电站位于丽江市玉龙县与迪庆州香格里拉县交界的金沙江上，念生垦沟堆积体位于梨园水电站坝址前的右岸沟谷中，总体积约2000×10⁴m³，属于特大型堆积体。

（1）地形地貌。念生垦沟堆积体分布于坝址上游右岸，从江边高程1500m至高程1700m，临江部位堆积物沿河宽度约460m，靠后缘宽度约200m，横河方向长度约1000m，总体上堆积体两侧及后缘薄，中间部分堆积相对较厚，厚度一般30～60m。高程1700m以上分左、右耳，左耳分布高程至1800m，右耳分布高程至1850m。堆积体分布地段总体上呈上、下游均由山脊夹持的宽谷地貌，堆积体平面形态呈前宽后窄的长“喇叭”型。

（2）水文地质条件。堆积体的松散岩类孔隙水除接受大气降水补给外，尚接受周围坡体内基岩裂隙水的补给。念生垦沟上游山坡为顺向坡，岩体的流层面有利于后侧及上游侧的坡体内充裕的基岩裂隙水向堆积体排出，造成念生垦沟地下水位相对较高，且在枯水期、丰水期的地下水位变幅相对较小。

（3）堆积体物理力学特性。堆积体普遍含碎石或砾石，底部残积层的砾、碎石含量相对较低，其物理力学性状相对较差，且堆积体无成层的黏土、粉土层或软弱岩（土）条带。念生垦沟堆积体表面部分的堆积物相对松散，以细颗粒为主，主要由粉土、粉细砂夹碎块石或部分卵、砾石构成，而往深处则密实程度逐渐增加。

（二）念生垦沟堆积体安全监测的成果分析

2008年7～10月的雨季，念生垦沟堆积体内导流洞进口明渠开挖、临时道路施工及堆渣等，期间连续降雨，致使地表排水不畅、地下水位升高，从2008年9月起，念生垦沟堆积体从上部1700m高程至下部1500m高程发现了大小不一的变形以及滑动，自2009年4月～2010年10月，通过应急处理和实施压脚、边坡卸载，增加排水洞、抗滑桩、锚索等治理措施后，整体变形已得到有效控制，堆积体逐步趋于稳定状态。

（1）外部变形监测。堆积体左耳位移主要发生在雨季中，雨季位移量占总位移量的70%以上，雨季过后以及开挖完成后，位移速率明显趋缓。堆积体右耳在雨季有小量变形，治理措施完成后逐步趋于稳定状态。堆积体下部绝大部分位移发生2010年3月之前，随着支挡等治理措施的不断完善，位移速率迅速降低。

（2）深部变形监测。已发生滑面的测斜孔最大孔口位移251.72mm，滑面处相对位移达97.89mm。所测滑面深度在11.5～50.5m之间，位于残积层至强风化层一带。IN-09测孔和IN-15测孔在导流进口明渠开挖完成前发生了较大的错动变形，7月雨季期间位移变化不大。

（3）排水洞流量监测。2010年7月上旬前量水堰测值都比较稳定，7月中旬进入雨季后，排水洞实测流量逐渐增加，其中3号排水洞最大流量曾达330.6L/min，雨季后期流量逐步减小至244.9L/min。

（4）地下水位监测。雨季各水位孔中的水位均有所增加，其中1600m高程以下水位增加尤为明显。地下水位的增加，导致外部变形与深层变形的再次加速并持续增加。

（5）锚索应力监测。①受明渠进口继续开挖影响，2010年1月初～3月底，1600m高程的锚索测力计读数迅速增加，随着支档措施的实施，荷载增速降至0.98kN，支档措施抗滑效果明显。②导流明渠进口继续下挖，导致念生垦沟1520～1530m高程的锚索测力计荷载迅速增加，随着治理措施的不断完善，变形得到有效控制，雨季中荷载也未见明显变化。

（6）钢筋应力监测。2010年1月中旬拉应力增长速率最大，2月初导流明渠开挖完成后应力变化趋于收敛，7月中旬进入雨季后应力无明显变化。

（三）念生垦沟堆积体变形规律研究

利用FLAC-3D软件，对堆积体变形进行模拟计算，并与实测成果进行对比，总结变形规律，评价治理措施效果。

（1）资料收集及地质分析。根据已有地质资料，确认念生垦沟滑坡体地层分布以及发育状况等要素特征；结合监测资料界定危险区域边界条件，确定其滑动范围和滑面位置。

（2）计算模型及参数。①模型建立，选取符合主滑动方向的剖面进行分析，剖面单元划分以四边形单元为主。模型底界采用固定约束，左右两侧采用铰支约束水平向位移。②采用M-C本构模型，使用锚索单元、实体单元分别模拟锚索、抗滑桩。计算工况为自然工况，考虑了天然地形、开挖地形及开挖完毕三种不同时期。

（3）变形规律研究。分析不同开挖时期及工程措施实施阶段堆积体变形规律及稳定性，评价工程措施实施后堆积体变形及稳定性。①明渠开挖后，堆积体前缘变形明显，坡体前缘成牵引变形趋势，坡体前缘失稳后可能会引起堆积体的整体破坏。由监测变形曲线可知，堆积体开挖后前缘变形大发生早，后段堆积体变形小。②工程处理措施设置完毕后，堆积体开挖至1510m高程后，堆积体前缘变形明显，从变形趋势可以看出，上部变形较未设置抗滑桩及锚索时有一定减小。由监测位移变化曲线可知，堆积体内部变形量较小，坡表变形较大，设置了相应的抗滑支挡措施后堆积体变形趋缓，并趋于稳定。

由此，堆积体是一个整体滑动模式，局部伴随有堆积体的浅表层滑动，属于推移式滑坡，并有局部的前缘失稳。同时可知，模型计算结果与监测数据成果一致性较好。

（中国电建集团昆明勘测设计研究院
有限公司　罗中权　赵世明）

九龙峡水电站坝区温泉渗漏及工程处理

九龙峡水电站位于甘肃省迭部县境内麻牙村上游白龙江干流上的九龙峡峡谷，该峡谷全长约7km，两（两河口）—朗（朗木寺）公路从峡谷左岸通过，交通便利。该电站以发电为主，装机容量81MW，为中型Ⅲ等工程。电站正常蓄水位1962.0m，最大坝高68m，总库容1220万m^3，调节库容294万m^3。工程枢纽主要由挡水坝、泄洪建筑物、引水建筑物、发电厂房、地面开关站等建筑物组成。坝型为混凝土重力坝，最大坝高68m。泄洪建筑物由溢流坝和底孔组成，引水建筑物位于右岸，由进水口、引水隧洞、调压井及高压管道等组成，电站厂房位于大坝下游6.3km的白龙江右岸。

（一）施工前温泉的出露情况

（1）出露位置。2006年6月，对九龙峡水电站工程库坝区进行了地质调查，发现有三处温泉出露点，分别位于坝轴线上游约327m左岸河水边、坝轴线下游54m左岸河水边、坝轴线下游54m右岸河水边。

（2）地质说明。温泉出露位置岩性主要为灰色中厚层、薄层灰白色结晶灰岩及大理岩，岩石坚硬，多呈灰白色、灰黑色，层状结构。在坝轴线下游54m左右岸温泉出露点都是沿断层F_{14}溢出，F_{14}产状为NW290°～310°NE∠30°～43°，宽约30～50cm，充填碎裂岩、糜棱岩，局部有砖红色泥砂，面较弯曲粗糙，延伸较长，贯穿两岸。

在坝轴线下游54m左右岸温泉出露点都取了水样进行了水质分析，表明：温泉水为HCO_3^-—Ca^{2+}型水，对混凝土具有分解类一般酸性型弱腐蚀性。

（二）施工中温泉出露情况及处理措施

（1）出露情况。导流洞开挖过程中发现，洞身桩号导0+23.0～导0+30.0m洞有温泉水出露、河床坝基左岸2号坝段下游端开挖至1908.0m高程附近有温泉水出露、消力池位于3、4号坝段下游侧开挖至1908.0m高程时有温泉水出露。这三处温泉水量相对较大，水温明显高于河水，具有明显的硫磺味。

（2）地质分析。根据开挖后的地质编录成果分析，这几处出露高程和F_{14}、导流洞的T_{14}的温泉水溢出点是连通的，为同一温泉带。

（3）处理措施。由于温泉水来自地层深处，且具有一定的压力，难以通过灌浆等措施完全封堵（封堵后往往从其他位置出露），同时可采用的灌浆等技术措施可封堵处理的深度有限，所以采取了引流和封堵相结合的处理方案。

首先在浇筑混凝土时，在温泉水出露较集中的位置预埋钢管，将温泉水引至下游消力池中，同时在消力池底板设置盲沟，引至下游集中抽排出基坑，待混凝土浇筑完成后，再通过预留孔口浇筑混凝土，封堵盲沟。

其次对基础进行固结灌浆。在防渗帷幕线部位加强灌浆，尽可能截断沿F_{14}断层可能存在的渗漏通道。具体处理措施如下：①导流洞出露点处理。导流洞下闸后，在导流洞温泉水出露部位，对洞壁实施混凝土衬砌，进行固结灌浆，以封堵导流洞内库水的渗漏通道。②防渗帷幕线部位处理。在防渗帷幕线部位，通过加深灌浆深度，穿过F_{14}断层，截断渗漏通道，为保证灌浆效果，该段帷幕采用两排钻孔。③坝基固结灌浆。对F_{14}断层通过的2号坝段基础加强固结灌浆，将原设计的8.0m深灌浆范围调整为12.0～18.0m。

（三）水库蓄水后温泉渗漏和处理措施

导流洞下闸后，洞内温泉水出露处发生了管涌现象，库水通过温泉出水带渗漏，首先在原出水点处出露，后进一步向下游延伸，原定的在导流洞内进行固结灌浆和封闭温泉出水点的方案无法实施，最终根据现场实际情况，采取了相应的处理方案，完成了导流洞封堵等工作。

（1）渗漏水情况。2016年4月17日下午5时左右，库水位约为1932.0m时，发现导流洞出口水量增加，水质变浑。4月18日下午，发现导流洞原有温泉出水点处的出水量增加很大，且有大量的岩屑涌出，沉积在导流洞中。

（2）地质分析。结合坝轴线上游326m左岸河边、导流洞0＋32.70m处出露的温泉点发育的断层F_{14}（T14）进行推测分析，表明两温泉点处在断层F_{14}空间延伸部位，断层F_{14}为泉水通道。因此说明大坝蓄水后导流洞温泉出露点渗水量增大是库水通过温泉水通道（断层F_{14}）渗漏到导流洞中入洞。

（3）处理措施。①采取了库区铺盖防渗（包括防渗土料填筑和土工防渗布）措施后，对坝前至导流洞进口明渠上游测部位作了防渗处理，有效的降低和减少了导流洞中渗水压力和流量；②在导流洞中设置临时挡水围堰和导水钢管的情况下，完成了导流洞的封堵，同时对钢管出口处的阀门段浇筑的混凝土，彻底封闭了导水钢管。另外对导流洞封堵段的洞壁进行了回填灌浆和固结灌浆，尽量封堵了洞壁围岩的渗水。③对导流洞后部出现的漏水洞段，采取了回填混凝土并预留排水廊道的措施，保证了导流洞洞壁的安全和稳定，同时通过排水措施，降低了洞壁山体的渗流压力。

（4）水库运行温泉渗漏变化。截至2017年7月，水库已正常运行一年多时间，导流洞有少量渗水，但水质保持清澈，左岸岸坡山体上未发现异常现象，表明温泉渗漏处理取得良好效果。

（中国电建集团西北勘测设计研究院有限公司　马军）

红层高地应力区隧洞围岩流变特征及支护研究

红层是地质学上对红色地层的简称，以砂岩、粉砂岩和黏土岩（泥岩）为主，软硬相间，以软岩为主且软弱结构面发育。在建的向家坝灌区工程北干渠取水隧洞即处于J_{1-2z}和J_{2s}红层中，地应力测试显示围岩最大水平向地应力超过20MPa，现场监测资料显示围岩具有明显的流变特征。

（一）工程概况及基本地质条件

向家坝灌区工程北干渠取水隧洞位于金沙江下游向家坝水电站左岸，出口位于宜宾县境内的埝溪河右岸的圆包山，隧洞总长10.1km，隧洞开挖洞形为马蹄形，衬砌后为圆形，内径8.2m，衬砌厚度0.4～0.6m不等，纵比降1/3000。

取水隧洞直线布置，洞轴线走向N22°E，沿线未发现较大规模的断层。隧洞上游段围岩岩性以粉砂岩为主，夹有少量泥质岩，该段长度近3km；隧洞中、下游近7km洞段以泥质粉砂岩和粉砂质泥岩为主，夹部分粉砂岩和砂岩，少量泥岩。取芯及室内试验可知，泥岩强度最低，仅为9.30MPa，属于软岩；粉砂质泥岩和泥质粉砂岩强度均低于30MPa，工程上分类为较软岩。采用浅孔孔壁应变法进行现场地应力测试，成果表明，地应力的大小与隧洞岩性关系密切：$\sigma_{粉砂岩}>\sigma_{泥质粉砂岩}>\sigma_{粉砂质泥岩}$。隧洞围岩以水平向地应力为主，最大水平向地应力达到21.68MPa。

（二）隧洞围岩流变现象

1. 钢拱架扭曲及拱顶喷混凝土掉块　施工过程中，多次出现初期支护（立钢拱架、挂网、喷混凝土）后，洞顶附近钢拱架变形和大范围喷混凝土掉块的现象，并具有明显的时间效应：喷混凝土施工完后的几个月，甚至1年多时间未见开裂和掉块现象，但某段时间后，拱顶、拱肩部位会突然出现喷层开裂、掉块，块体散落在底板混凝土表面的现象。

2. 收敛变形监测曲线　取水隧洞布置多个收敛监测断面，根据监测结果：开挖初期位移变形速率较大，施工后期随着开挖掌子面的推进，位移的变形速率变缓，表现为曲线平缓。但随着时间的推移，大部分变形没有得到明显的收敛，表现出一定程度的流变现象：① 曲线在近似水平方向稳定一段时间后，变形又开始增大，呈现一种“阶梯形”的变化趋势；② 围岩在很长一段时间，甚至是2～3年后，变形并没有表现出明显的收敛，大多数断面的变形持续增长；③ 曲线的突变多出现在某一稳定期之后，并没有明显的时间规律。

3. 多点位移计监测曲线　根据布置的多点位移计监测断面监测结果可知，边墙和拱顶的曲线具有共同的特点：① 围岩变形曲线呈“阶梯形”变化趋势，曲线连续变形至一定时段后，再稳定一段时间，然后再次出现变形增大，再稳定……，即表现出阶段性稳定。② 未见明显稳定迹象。

（三）围岩变形与支护的数值分析

1. 建模及建模参数　采用$FLAC^{3D}$模拟隧洞的开挖与支护过程。根据时间施工过程，模拟的开挖支护分两阶段进行，初期开挖后即进行喷混凝土、打设锚杆和钢拱架；二期采用衬砌混凝土支护。钢拱架的施工在初期支护中埋置于喷混凝土中，故将其简化成喷混凝土层一并模拟。

2. 数值计算结果　计算得到隧洞开挖后，不支护、初期支护（喷混凝土＋锚杆＋钢拱架）和衬砌支护后的位移云图，可知：① 不支护工况下，隧洞围岩变形量较大，较大变形主要出现在拱顶、两侧边墙和底板；② 初期支护后，围岩变形分布趋于均匀，较大变形主要出现在两侧边墙一定深度范围内；③ 进行二次支护（混凝土衬砌）后，衬砌结构没有明显的变形现象。

最大剪应变增量云图计算结果显示，较大的剪应变出现在喷混凝土层与衬砌混凝土层之间的拱顶和两侧边墙。后期需要加强处理，如采用回填灌浆和固结灌浆等工程措施。

（四）变形机制与支护对策

1. 变形机制分析　① 隧洞开挖后围岩应力重分布，使得洞壁附近径向应力释放，切向应力急剧增大。在高水平向地应力作用下，拱顶附近岩体产生应力集中和挤压变形。② 隧洞开挖后，拱顶围岩应力（能量）消散历经了“集中—释放—再集中—再释放……”这一周而复始的过程，历时漫长，从而表现出明显的时间效应，说明岩体具有一定的流变特性。③ 由于水平向地应力较大，加上围岩岩性相对软弱，开挖后的隧洞侧墙变形主要为向临空面方向发展，隧洞两侧壁空间缩小。收敛变形监测曲线和数值计算结果给出了同样的结论。

2. 支护对策　现场变形现象和监测资料均显示，原有的支护设计不能满足隧洞围岩稳定性要求，数值计算分析结果也表明，隧洞拱顶以及两侧的边墙中部是易发生大变形的部位，因此对支护设计进行针对性补充和调整：① 开挖爆破前，在掌子面布置一排9根 $\phi25$ 超前锚杆，长度4.5m，仰角30°，间排距1.5m；② 调整系统锚杆，尺寸由 $\phi22$ 调整为 $\phi25$，长度从3m调整为4.5m，垂直临空面，间排距1.5m；③ 钢拱架从I16号工字钢调整为I20号工字钢，间距调整至1.0m，Ⅴ类围岩段间距0.8m；④ 挂钢筋网 $\phi8$@200×200调整为钢筋网 $\phi8$@150×150；⑤ 隧洞爆破清撬后即先喷50mm混凝土，待系统锚杆、挂网和钢拱架施工完后补喷混凝土10mm；⑥ 衬砌混凝土强度由C25调整为C30，二期衬砌完成后，进行回填灌浆和压力固结灌浆。调整隧洞支护方案以后，围岩变形得到有效控制，二期衬砌施工进展顺利，表明所采用的支护方案合理有效。

（中国电建集团中南勘测设计研究院有限公司 唐军峰 杨军 李学政 李佳武）

老挝南湃水电站泥质边坡处理

（一）边坡概况及地形、地质条件

该电站为跨流域引水式电站，电站厂房位于一山梁坡脚，边坡最大坡高101m，开挖坡比1∶1.2～1.6。厂房后边坡地形为一山梁，边坡呈下陡上缓，山梁上游侧坡较陡，自然坡度45°～55°，局部为65°；下游侧坡较缓，自然坡度25°～35°，局部临冲沟段为55°。山梁两侧发育有冲沟，上游侧冲沟规模较大。坡体地层分为三层结构，第一层为连续分布的紫红色砂质黏土类，松散无胶结；第二层为泥质胶结的崩坡积碎石土，虽然密实，但遇水后易软化，且不连续；第三层为黄色、黑色、白色、紫色等四色泥岩。

（二）边坡病害特征

厂房后边坡开挖过程中陆续出现以下病害：

（1）软化变形。厂房后边坡右侧存在一条天然冲沟，冲沟常年有水，厂房边坡开挖后地下水沿坡面出露，在右侧边坡形成若干个出水点，出水量不大但很分散。坡面长期受水的软化作用后局部出现大的变形，局部最大变形达1～2m。

（2）拉裂缝。随着边坡开挖下切，厂房后边坡出现拉裂缝，随着下切的加深，拉裂缝宽度逐渐加宽，裂缝逐渐增多，拉裂缝平均宽度25mm左右，主要集中在右侧边坡，左侧边坡基本未发现拉裂缝。

（3）崩塌。镇墩基础下切坡脚导致局部拉裂缝加宽加多，裂缝发展到一定程度后整个坡面出现泥岩崩解坍塌。

（4）雨水冲沟。工程期雨季降雨集中且降雨量大，泥岩坡面抗冲能力差，降雨在坡面形成多处冲沟，最深达80cm左右，宽度1～2m。

（5）坡面松动喷混凝土失稳。雨季期间用于保护开挖面的挂网喷混凝土面整体与坡面脱离掉落。

（三）破坏机理分析

该电站厂房后边坡出现以上现象主要与地质构造、岩性和水的作用密不可分。从规律看，左侧边坡好于右侧边坡，上部好于下部，这种规律与地下水活动规律一致。

边坡右侧存在一条常年有水的冲沟，地下水沿冲沟向山体内渗透，在左侧边坡地下水出漏，坡面出现多个出水点。泥岩强度低，易崩解，吸水膨胀，失水收缩开裂。这些岩石特征和丰富的地下水导致边坡坡脚泥岩软化、引起地表开裂，诱发厂房后边坡产生向基坑方向的变形。镇墩基础切脚开挖，加剧后边坡局部开裂变形，坡体“下部变形量大，上部变形量小”，属典型“牵引式”变形特征。当变形发展到一定程度后出现失稳崩塌破坏。坡面变形和拉裂缝的出现导致雨水进入将喷混凝土和边坡结合面细颗粒带走掏空，引起喷凝土面失去支撑而脱离滑落。

（四）处理措施

（1）加快厂房基坑混凝土浇筑尽早回填场坪压脚。现场调整施工计划，首先施工厂房四周一期混凝土封闭厂房基坑并提前对上游场坪进行回填处理，既降低边坡高度又为边坡坡脚提供了压载。

（2）边坡回填。施工期厂房边坡形成大量的拉裂缝，分布范围较广，且裂缝较宽。另外在边坡高处局部形成坍塌和松动体。这些部位不进行处理不但影响边坡运行安全，也不满足环境美化的要求。在边坡已经形成的条件下，机械很难再去对边坡进行处理。针对现场实际情况确定在满足厂房上游交通和变压器布置的前提下，对厂房后边坡进行回填处理。回填体坡面坡度为1∶2，回填高度为边坡高度的三分之一。回填体采用碎石土回填，分层碾压，压实系数不小于0.92。坡面采用斜坡碾碾压或采用超填削坡。回填体范围内的松动边坡，必须把松动体分层挖出并回填碾压至密实。回填体内布置四层排水盲沟，排水盲沟出口要与横向或纵向排水沟相接。

（3）坡面防护＋系统排水。对回填体以上未出现拉裂缝的边坡采用框格梁＋植草的方式进行防护。其他边坡直接植草护面，草皮表面用钢丝网固定。整个坡面布置系统排水，各级马道坡脚和回填体坡面均布置横向排水沟和纵向排水沟。在地下水丰富的部位布置排水花管（反滤土工布包裹），花管排距5m，深4m，直径10cm，仰角10°，外露10cm。

（4）布置监测点。边坡处理完成后在整个边坡布置了永久观测点，用于对边坡的运行状态进行监测。

采取以上措施后，经过一年的运行，监测数据显示边坡未发生大的变形，边坡整体稳定安全。

（五）结语

（1）对于泥岩边坡治水是关键。泥岩遇水软化特性决定治理泥岩边坡必先治水。泥质边坡勘察中要重视对地下水的勘探，边坡开挖前要制定完善的水处理措施，利用排水花管等方式将地下水提前引出并排走，泥岩的性质确定其出漏的地下水很分散，往往以出水点或者整个面出水方式向外排水，在坡面收集的难度很大。

（2）加宽马道比放缓边坡更有效。泥岩边坡在没有水作用的情况下边坡整体稳定性较好，施工过程中往往经过太阳暴晒、雨水浸泡等自然作用往往出现浅层的病害。留有足够宽的马道不但可以提高边坡的稳定性，而且一旦边坡出现病害方便机械进入进行处理。

（3）重视边坡表面防护，宜早不宜晚，宜柔性。泥岩边坡抗冲刷能力弱且易变形，开挖过程中要及时支护，采用柔性防护措施有更好的适应变形的能力，不易发生因为边坡的变形而引起支护结构的破坏，对于降雨强烈的地区种植草皮是一种非常有效的方式。

（中国电建集团西北勘测设计研究院有限公司　康晓娟　许战军）

勘测技术与设备

工程岩石渗流力学关键技术及应用

研究成果是十余年围绕工程岩石渗流力学关键技术研究的成果，依托国家973项目、国家科技支撑计划、国家自然科学基金以及多项重大工程科技项目开展研究。主要研究内容如下：

（1）研发了基于惰性气体的岩石渗透测试新技术，发明了基于气体脉冲压力法和气体流量法的测试原理与方法，实现了不同围压、孔压和循环加卸载状态下岩石渗透率、孔隙度以及应变的力学特性精确测试，解决了目前岩石及极低渗透材料渗透性难以测取的难点。

（2）针对不同层级渗透率的工程岩石，开展了不同围压、渗压、循环加卸载以及不同饱和度条件下的气体渗透特性测试试验，得到了不同围压、渗压以及饱和度对岩石渗透率演化规律，建立了反映岩石渗透特性的渗透率以及相对渗透率演化模型。

（3）开展了300组以上渗透及低渗透岩石气体渗流滑脱效应试验研究，揭示和论证了气体在低渗透岩石渗流过程中普遍存在滑脱效应以及非线性渗流特性，建立了滑脱因子与渗透率函数关系，为工程岩石渗透率的准确预测提供了重要科学依据。

（4）基于热力学理论和有效应力原理，提出了岩石黏弹塑性损伤时效渗流力学模型，基于岩石在渗流—应力耦合作用下流变过程中的渗透演化规律及损伤力学理论，提出了渗流—应力—流变—损伤耦合本构模型，研发了渗流流变损伤力学数值计算方法，以及岩石多尺度多场耦合数值分析方法和程序。

（5）开展了国家首个大型地下水封洞库低渗透岩石工程应用研究，解决了低渗透围岩渗透测试问题，形成了地下水封洞库低渗透岩石渗流应力耦合流变强度与长期变形参数确定方法，提出了工程运行中的长期安全性评估技术。

（6）开展了重大水电工程大坝坝基和库岸边坡岩体的渗流力学分析和工程安全评价研究。建立了工程渗流安全评价技术，在工程中得到应用。

研究成果已在国家重大水电工程高坝大库、首个大型地下水封洞库建设、防灾减灾实践中得到成功应用，并推广应用到交通工程等领域，社会经济效益及环境效益显著。在国家重大水电工程、石油战略储备、防灾减灾等领域具有广阔的推广应用前景。

（河海大学
中国电建集团中南勘测设计研究院有限公司
中国电建集团昆明勘测设计研究院有限公司）

TRT超前地质预报技术在TBM隧洞施工中的应用

TBM施工具有“掘进速度快、施工扰动小、成洞质量高、综合经济效益高”等优势，但是TBM对不良地质条件适应性较差，在断层、破碎带、软弱的夹层带、挤压性的围岩、高地应力等不良地质条件下掘进时，易出现TBM卡机、卡盾现象。利用TRT超前地质预报技术，结合相关地质分析资料综合判断出掌子面前方地质情况，从而指导隧洞施工。

（一）TRT超前地质预报技术

（1）仪器介绍。TRT（true reflection tomography）超前地质预报系统是专门用于隧洞进行超前地质预报的设备，该系统硬件主要由主机、基站、无线模块、传感器、触发装置五个部分组成。

（2）系统原理。TRT采用的是地震波超前预报法，其技术原理在于当地震波遇到声学阻抗差异界面时，一部分信号被反射回来，一部分信号透射进入前方介质。声学阻抗的变化通常发生在地质岩层界面或岩体内不连续界面。反射的地震信号被高灵敏地震信号传感器接收，通过分析，用来了解隧道工作面前方地质体的性质（软弱带、破碎带、断层、含水等）、位置及规模。反射体的尺寸越大，声学阻抗差别越大，回波就越明显，越容易探测到。TRT采用层析扫描成像技术，形成立体、直观的三维立体图，立体图中的反射边界每一点离散图像是由空间叠加所有地震波形计算得来。

（3）震源点和传感器点布置。震源点选择应靠近工作面的左、右边墙上，直接布置在稳定围岩上或者初期支护完全凝固成型的位置，震源点一般不少于12个，两侧各布置两组，每组沿竖向（高程方向）布置3个震源点。传感器点布置在左、右边墙各4个，拱顶处布置2个，呈三维空间分布，用以接收震源激发的弹性波信号。传感器与隧道洞壁之间用耦合剂黏连，必须等待耦合剂完全凝固，黏合紧密后才能进行超前预报地震波数据采集工作。所有布置的震源点及传感器点的三维坐标均要测量，测量误差少于5cm。

（4）数据采集。TRT使用重锤锤击震源点产生地震波，使用“带有无线模块的传感器组”接收在围岩中传播的地震波振动信号，传感器通过“无线传感器基站”把信号存储到计算机中。

（5）数据处理。将获得的地震波数据导入专业数据处理软件进行数据处理。

（二）应用实例

1. 辽西北供水工程T3隧洞

（1）地质特点。隧洞所处早元古代侵入巨斑状花岗岩岩层，主要节理走向NE50°～60°，倾向NW或SE，倾角40°～60°，节理面多呈起伏光滑状或平直粗糙状，微张～闭合，无充填或泥质充填。

（2）桩号76＋401～76＋296预报结果。采用TRT6000超前地质预报系统进行预报：桩号76＋401～76＋368段无明显的阻抗变化，推测该段岩体岩性变化不大，岩体较完整，节理裂隙不发育；桩号76＋368～76＋296段出现明显的阻抗变化，推测在掌子面前方大约33m处开始出现破碎带，长度约72m，该段岩体较破碎，完整性差，节理裂隙发育。

（3）开挖后地质编录情况。桩号76＋390～76＋358段岩性为元古代巨斑状花岗岩，岩石为中硬岩，微风化，节理发育，局部节理极发育，围岩稳定性差。开挖至桩号76＋370时，在护盾尾部揭露出呈条带状的构造片岩，宽度在2.0～3.0m之间，受此影响围岩开挖过后产生塌落现象，岩体较破碎，围岩不能自稳；开挖至桩号76＋358处时受构造影响，原结构、构造破坏，强度较低，局部岩体手可破碎，前护盾顶部塌落掉块严重，尾部为构造片岩带，向右侧延伸，泥化较强，无自稳能力，围岩极不稳定，局部渗水。桩号76＋358～76＋294段岩石为中硬岩，微风化，节理较发育，局部节理发育，围岩稳定性差；开挖至76＋343.7处断层压碎岩消失，但岩体仍破碎，岩石强度较低，节理发育，且节理夹泥现象严重，围岩不能自稳，开挖至76＋335处时围岩转好，岩体完整性有所提高，但节理面仍存在夹泥现象，并且局部可见方解石岩脉侵入，定向排列，成组出现。

（4）预报结果与地质素描对比结果。通过现场实际开挖情况对预报结果进行验证，证明本次预报准确的判断出断层的区间位置分布情况。

2. 辽西北供水工程T4隧洞

（1）地质资料。ygf425断层桩号为51＋710～51＋360，长度350m，其中主断层长度150m，围岩类别判定为Ⅴ类，两侧影响带长度200m，上、下游长度分别100m，围岩类别判定为Ⅳ类。ygf425断层，呈压扭性，产状NE30°NW∠80°。

（2）桩号51＋631～51＋510预报结果。采用TRT6000超前地质预报系统进行预报：桩号51＋631～51＋591段，推测该段岩体弱风化，岩质较硬，岩体较完整；在桩号51＋591～51＋510段，推测该段岩体风化相对较强，裂隙发育，岩质软硬结合，整体岩体破碎，呈块石、碎石状结构；其中51＋591～51＋571段岩体为较破碎，结合设计推测该段进入ygf425断层。

（3）开挖后地质编录情况。桩号51＋631～51＋591段，该段开挖一天进尺约30多米，传送带出渣为碎块状。从开挖后暴露的侧壁判断，弱风化，岩体较完整，发育少量X型交叉节理。无渗水。桩号51＋591～51＋510，该段开挖进尺变慢，51＋565左右开始安装钢拱架，该段传送带出渣为接近粉末状，岩石硬度和完整性变差。从开挖后暴露的侧壁判断，受构造挤压作用节理裂隙增多，弱风化～强风化，岩体较破碎，局部破碎，现场采用钢筋网固定碎裂岩掉块。

（4）预报结果与地质素描对比结果。通过现场实际开挖情况对预报结果进行验证，证明本次预报准确的判断出断层的区间位置分布情况。

（中国水利水电第三工程局有限公司
勘测设计研究院　董栋 张飞）

阵列式位移计在滑坡体深部变形监测中的应用

目前监测滑坡深部变形的仪器主要有测斜仪、光纤光栅深部位移计等，这些仪器存在人为因素影响大、难以准确地判别滑动方向、技术难度高、量程小、监测频率低等缺点。阵列式位移计有高精度、高稳定性、大变形适应能力强，安装简单、免调试，自动测量、数据上云等多种优点，易于实现自动化实时监测，节省人工成本，能够及时有效地发出滑坡地质灾害信息。

（一）阵列式位移计简介

阵列式位移计是一种新型的变形监测仪器，内部由三轴微电子机械系统（MEMS）加速度计组成，采用微机电感应方式和阵列式计算原理，可实时获取连续变形曲线。阵列式位移计每 8 节组成一个基本单元（分阵列）。每节有加速度计和微处理器，每个分阵列有一个温度传感器和一个震动模块。阵列式位移计使用 MEMS 加速度计测定单节相对于重力方向的倾斜。通过监测加速度计在重力场的变化，可以精确计算出每节阵列式位移计的变形 ΔX，ΔY，ΔZ，进而得到整个阵列式位移计的三维坐标。一旦任何位置发生变化，阵列式位移计的三维坐标也随即发生改变，两次坐标变化值就为对应关节的变化量。数据采集软件通过视频监控网络连接到采集器，将传感器数据取回，然后自动启动数据转换模块将传感器数据转换为坐标。坐标转换完成之后，运用阵列式位移计数据处理软件计算变形量、变形速率等，然后自动将数据上传到数据管理平台。

（二）阵列式位移计实例运用

1. 工程背景　沧江桥滑坡体位于沧江桥左岸，距离下坝址 24km，其后缘以上为营盘堆积体。沧江桥滑坡体地貌形态明显，呈圈椅状，后缘较宽，有数米高的陡壁，高程 1590m；前缘直到江边，相对较窄，高程 1445m，高差在 110m 以上。滑坡体自然地形坡度较缓，一般在 10°～25°，顺河向最宽约 1.2km，纵向最长约 900m，体积约 500×10^4 m^3。滑坡体上部为营盘堆积体，其分布高程为 1590～1750m，体积约 1000×10^4 m^3，其上为营盘镇所在地。

滑坡体组成物质主要为碎石质黏土、粉土夹少量块石、破碎的板岩、砂岩岩块与岩屑，夹杂第四系崩坡积的黏土。碎块石的含量不同的地方变化较大，陡坡处碎块石的含量较高，斜坡下部台地，堆积体的前缘，碎块石含量较小。钻孔岩芯一般呈土柱状，钻进过程中未出现孔壁垮塌现象，较密实，与基岩接触带未见明显的滑动面。根据地质测绘及钻孔资料，滑坡堆积体厚度后缘一般为 50～60m，中部一般为 20～40m，前缘一般为 30～50m，最厚达 58m；上游侧厚度一般为 20～50m。上游侧滑坡堆积体厚度较大，下游侧滑坡堆积体厚度较小；前后缘厚度比中部厚度稍大，符合滑坡堆积体的一般特征。下伏地层为侏罗系中统花开左组上段及白垩系上统景星组下段，大村断裂分支断裂在滑坡体中下部通过，产状：SN 倾 W ∠70°，断层带宽度 5～10m。

2. 监测方案　选取沧江桥滑坡体的 1－1 断面和 2－2 断面来分析，其中 1－1 监测剖面布置有 3 个测斜孔和 1 套阵列式位移计，2－2 监测剖面布置有 2 个测斜孔和 1 套阵列式位移计。

3. 监测结果分析　①由 1-1 断面各观测点的孔深水平合位移分布曲线可知，滑坡体上部的 IN1-1 和 IN1-2 测斜孔、下部阵列式位移计 1-1、IN1-3 均出现滑动面。由各孔滑动面的位置和孔口及滑面位移变化过程曲线可见，营盘公路以上出现局部滑动面，营盘镇以上表现为浅表层滑动（深度 10m 以内），营盘镇以下（西营村）局部出现深层滑动面（深度 42m），是否有连续贯通的滑动面还需继续观测和分析。②由 2－2 监测剖面各观测点的孔深位移分布曲线可知，2-2 监测剖面变形基本稳定。

4. 数据可靠性分析

（1）与测斜仪监测结果对比。对于 1-1 断面：阵列式位移计 1-1 与测斜孔 IN1-1、IN1-2、IN1-3 监测结果一致，均出现滑动面，且阵列式位移计 1-1 与测斜孔 IN1-1 监测结果最接近，也符合监测仪器的空间位置分布。对于 2-2 断面：阵列式位移计 2-1 与测斜孔 IN2-1、IN2-2 监测结果一致，均未出现滑动面。从以上两个断面来看，阵列式位移计监测成果与测斜孔监测成果一致，从一定程度上说明了阵列式位移计监测数据的可靠性。

（2）与钻孔取样结果对比。由地质钻孔的取芯情况：阵列式位移计钻孔 28m 深度处为红色强风化岩层，这个位置在地质上存在一个分界面，说明阵列式位移计的观测数据与地质分析结论基本吻合。

5. 数据稳定性分析

根据阵列式位移计 1-1 孔口及滑动面水平合位移

变化过程曲线可知，滑移面处的位移是缓慢增长的，并未出现突变与异常点，符合滑坡体的变形规律，证明阵列式位移计监测数据的稳定性较好。

（中国电建集团昆明勘测设计研究院有限公司 李剑萍 冯燕明 聂成良）

提高无人机航测空三加密精度的方法研究

（一）引言

无人机影像与传统航摄影像相比，具有成本低廉、时效性强等优点，近年来被广泛应用到地形图绘制和三维建模等项目。但是无人机影像也具有明显的缺点：① 姿态稳定性差；② 影像畸变大；③ 基高比小、模型切换频繁，高程精度低。

空三加密，指利用少量控制点的像方和物方坐标，解求出未知点的坐标，使得每个模型中的已知点都增加四个以上，然后利用这些已知点解求所有影像的外方位元素。空三加密精度不够，会导致航测外业的像控点量测甚至航飞环节的返工，并引起航测内业后续工序无法开展。目前市场上还没有无人机空三加密的软件能完全解决这些问题，精度很难满足传统航测规范要求。

（二）改进方法

无人机影像一般是由非量测相机获取的，必须经过畸变差校正后才能进行空三加密，这一环节需要严密的相机检校参数，否则严重影响影像匹配的精度。而自动匹配与光束法平差环节受软件性能制约，如果有匹配算法不合适与平差参数不合理的情况，导致空三加密自动化程度过低，需要大量人工干预，会降低空三加密的效率和精度，加大内外业工作量，甚至导致空三失败。

1. 优化相机检校方法，得出准确的相机参数

为达到较好的航测精度，就必须对使用的非量测相机进行检校，而且考虑到非量测相机的畸变差参数的不稳定性，就必须隔段时间就对非量测相机进行检校。简单快捷的相机标定方法及软件就显得尤为重要和迫切，比较以下三种方法来确定相机检校的实施方案。

（1）相机自检校。自检校方法是利用定焦相机的镜头光学结构不随主距变化而变化的特点，通过预检校获取内方位元素的变化规律，以此来减少检校未知数的个数，达到简化自检校模型的目的。在不需要建立检校场的情况下，只利用目标周围的影像和影像之间的对应关系对相机进行检校，此种方法造价低，操作简单，仅依靠一些影像和软件即可完成，但经过项目实验发现，此种方法的缺点是稳健性较差，对空三加密精度的提高有限，适用于相机参数本身比较准确的影像，而对相机参数已发生较大变化的影像来说，改善效果并不明显。

（2）物理检校。物理检校需要将相机送往专业的研究机构进行检校。实验表明，该方法得到的相机参数较为准确，用此相机检校参数能较大幅度的提高空三加密的高程精度。其缺点在于：① 费用较高，一台非量测相机一年的费用约为 3～5 万元；② 必须将相机送往专业的实验室，检校周期较长。

（3）自主建立室内检校场进行检校。结合无人机非量测型相机标定的需求，提出基于卡片式标定板的便携、免控制的相机标定解决方案。① 场地选择。拍摄像机标定影像，需要一个较开阔的拍摄场地。场地要求如下：a. 拍摄场地需要光线充足；b. 场地面积不能小于 3m×2m；c. 拍摄者站立位置与墙壁距离不能小于 3m；d. 背景最好为白色的墙壁；e. 墙壁平整，确保四周没有遮挡。② 摆放标定板。确定场地及摆放位置后，即可开始摆放标定板。a. 材料准备：准备泡沫板、双面胶带、大头针等材料；b. 摆放标定板时先利用双面胶带将泡沫板固定在墙上，再利用大头针将标定板固定在泡沫板上。布设标定场时，标定板之间需要有一定的高差，主要目的是模拟出地形起伏。按照标定要求在规定的三个拍摄位置：标定板正前方，标定板右前方以及标定板左前方，拍摄 45 张以上的影像，应用相应软件进行一键标定，计算出相机参数。

以贝壳梁风电场的研究对象，比对两种相机检校方法的效果，分析得到，室内检校场方法比物理检校方法的精度略低，但室内检校场可以多次利用，大幅度降低成本。

2. 针对测区特点优化软件配置组合，提高无人机航测空三加密精度

（1）Pixelgrid 软件的特点。Pixelgrid 是国产空三软件的领先者，空三加密的精度可靠，质量可控，被广泛应用于航测内业数据处理中。该软件处理无人机航测数据，步骤划分较细，优点是程序稳定，对无人机飞行姿态要求不高，每一环节都能进行人工干预和质量控制，缺点是自动化程度不够高，处理速度较慢，满足不了项目工期需要。

（2）Inpho 软件的特点。Inpho 是世界领先的航测数据处理系统，最显著的优点是自动化程度与全自动匹配精度较高，但软件对无人机飞行姿态、pos 精度、地物纹理的要求较高，如遇到条件不理想的测区，匹配错误较多，而该软件的人工干预量较少，对于困难区域无法保证空三加密精度。

（3）联合空三加密方法成果。以往采用的单一软件的空三加密，由于各软件本身的缺陷，存在较多点

位中误差超限和返工现象。将两种优势明显的软件联合使用，在充分利用 inpho 快速自动处理海量无人机数据能力的同时，能结合 Pixelgrid 过程控制的优势，实现优化资源配置，提高生产效率。

对贝壳梁风电场影像数据，采用室内检校参数，并使用 pixelgrid 与 inpho 联合空三加密方法后，结果已满足规范要求。选取了其他几个航测成图项目，利用联合空三加密得到的基本定向点中误差已满足规范要求。在此后的 1∶1000 地形图的谷梁风电场、哈密抽水蓄能等项目也得到了验证，空三加密精度完全满足国家 1∶1000 空三加密的规范要求。

（中国电建集团西北勘测设计研究院有限公司　黄文钰）

光纤光栅仪器在牛栏江—滇池补水长隧洞工程监测中的应用

安全监测是长隧洞施工期和运行期安全必不可少的组成部分，光纤光栅仪器采用光纤传输，能适应长距离的牵引，完全能满足长隧洞监测的需要。终端设置光纤光栅解调仪能实现半自动化监测，可减少人工监测工作量，降低监测误差，提高监测成果的准确性和可靠性。

（一）工程概况

牛栏江—滇池补水工程由德泽水库水源枢纽工程、德泽干河提水泵站工程及德泽干河提水泵站至昆明（盘龙江）的输水线路工程组成。输水线路布置在牛栏江左岸，自德泽干河泵站出水池到昆明，总长度约为 115.85km，其中隧洞有 10 条，长 104.52km，占线路总长的 90.23%，最长的为大五山隧洞，长度为 36.22km，开挖为 5.3m×5.75m（宽×高）的城门洞型断面，衬砌后为马蹄型过水断面。输水线路工程于 2008 年 12 月正式开工，2013 年 6 月全线贯通。

（二）监测布置及技术要求

1. 监测布置　监测布置在满足相关规程规范的前提下，以能对重点部位实施监控为原则，综合考虑隧洞的开挖断面尺寸、地形地质条件及相关计算成果，监测断面一般设置在地质条件较差、埋深较浅或计算成果安全系数较小的洞段。大五山隧洞共设置了 8 个监测断面，每个监测断面均设置围岩深部变形、锚杆应力、接缝开合度、渗水压力和衬砌钢筋应力等监测项目。

为便于隧洞后期的维护和检修，改造了 5 条永久检修支洞，监测仪器电缆或光纤采取就近原则往这 5 条检修支洞和隧洞进出口部位集中牵引。8 个监测断面中有 4 个为光纤光栅仪器监测断面（2-2、3-3、4-4、7-7），剩余的 4 个为传统的差动电阻式和振弦式等仪器监测断面（1-1、5-5、6-6、8-8），两种监测断面设置的监测项目相同。每个监测断面的光纤光栅仪器除渗压计并联外，其余各种仪器均采取先串联后并联的方式，通过一条多芯主光缆分两端引至就近的检修支洞或隧洞进出口部位集中，其中一端设置解调仪进行监测，另外一端备用，提高了仪器完好的保障率。

2. 监测技术要求

（1）监测仪器设备的检验、率定和检定。①监测仪器在安装埋设前必须进行检验与率定，通过检验和率定获取仪器设备的参数，并与相关出厂参数进行对比，判断仪器的可靠性及稳定性、仪器在搬运中是否损坏等。②所有光学、电子测量仪器、二次仪表、用于检验和率定计量设备的仪表，包括用于仪器率定的标准器具，均应按检定周期，送国家计量行政主管部门授权的计量检定机构进行检定或校验。③尚未有标准设备进行率定和检定的监测设备，应至少每年一次采用精度至少高一级的非标准设备对仪器参数进行标定。

（2）监测仪器的安装埋设。①监测仪器在安装埋设前应作好相关准备工作，准备好相应监测仪器的零配件及安装埋设所需的辅助材料，做好监测仪器的组装、光缆的熔接、仪器和光缆的编号工作等。②光纤光栅仪器的安装埋设方法与传统监测仪器的安装埋设方法相同，应严格按相关规程规范、设计要求及厂家相关要求执行。③监测仪器安装埋设后应做好仪器及光缆的相关保护工作。

（3）施工期监测。①施工期监测应按规定的监测项目、测次和时间进行。②每次监测时应收集监测仪器附近区域的相关资料，如开挖、支护、混凝土浇筑和降水等。③施工期巡视检查频次按 1～2 次/周，变形监测、接缝监测、渗流监测、应力应变及温度监测频次均按 1 次/周执行。④特殊情况下，如暴雨、洪水及周围的运行环境或受力状况发生明显变化、监测仪器周边进行开挖爆破、灌浆等施工时，应适当加密监测频次，并加强巡视检查。

（三）监测成果简述

大五山隧洞共设置了 8 个监测断面，其监测成果简述如下：①从多点位移计监测成果来看，隧洞变形量较小，最大仅为 19.55mm（出现在 2-2 断面），其余各断面的变形均在 10mm 以内。变形主要发生在施工期，施工结束后各监测断面变形基本无变化。②从锚杆应力计监测成果来看，各断面的锚杆应力较小，最大拉应力为 66.53MPa（出现在 1-1 断面），最大压应力为－76.47MPa（出现在 4-4 断面），其余各断面锚杆应力均在±30MPa 以内。锚杆应力主要受开挖爆破施工的影响，施工结束后各监测断面锚杆应力基本无变化。③从测缝计监测成果来看，衬砌混凝土和围岩接缝变化主要发生在钢筋混凝土衬砌施工期间，最大开合度为7.25mm（出现在1-1断面），其余各断面的接缝开合度均较小，且混凝土衬砌施工结束后，各测缝计测值长期无变化。④从渗压计监测成果来看，渗水压力主要受季节和地下水的影响，渗压水头一直较小，最大仅为23.25m，出现在7-7断面的雨季（2016年6月底），其余各断面的渗压水头长期较小，绝大多数在15m以内，对隧洞稳定无明显影响。⑤从钢筋计监测成果看，钢筋应力总体较小，最大拉应力为93.81MPa（出现在2-2断面），最大压应力为−85.31MPa（出现在3-3断面），其余各断面钢筋应力基本在±30MPa以内。随着混凝土温度稳定和衬砌施工结束，各断面钢筋应力长期无明显变化。

总体而言，隧洞的变形、锚杆应力、接缝开合度和衬砌钢筋应力量值较小，变化主要发生在施工期，施工结束后及2014～2016年三年运行期间，各种监测仪器的测值均无明显变化，表明隧洞长期处于稳定状态，运行状况良好。

（中国电建集团昆明勘测设计研究院
有限公司　刘伟　温丽丽）

埃及阿塔卡抽水蓄能电站软弱漏失地层超深孔钻探施工工艺

（一）地质概况

阿塔卡抽水蓄能电站位于埃及北部苏伊士省境内，初拟电站装机容量240万kW，额定水头600m。该区域地层上部以白垩质灰岩和白云岩为主，中等坚硬，溶蚀、裂隙发育；下部多为砂岩、泥质灰岩以及泥岩、页岩互层，为软岩～极软岩，岩层近水平。工程区地下水位极低，且岩石溶蚀、破碎，钻孔基本不返浆。由于地层软弱破碎、地下水位低，钻探施工困难，在地下厂房区域钻孔最大孔深226m。为查明地下厂房部位工程地质条件，在地表布置钻孔ZK04，设计钻孔深度760m，孔口高程848m。钻孔于2018年5月23日开始施工，2018年8月4日完成。

（二）钻探设备、材料选择

根据地层特点、钻孔深度、现场情况等综合考虑，选用XY-44T钻机，配备BW-250泥浆泵，柴油机直接驱动。配备ϕ168厚壁套管35m、PW套管107m、PQ钻杆360m、JS98钻杆650m、S75A钻杆900m。其中PQ钻杆和JS98钻杆完成钻进后更换跟管钻头，下入孔内可做套管使用（护壁）。

（三）钻探施工工艺

1. 绳索取芯钻进　绳索取芯钻进在软弱破碎、漏失深钻孔ZK04钻进中充分发挥了其优越性。一方面，绳索取芯钻杆在孔内对孔壁起到保护作用，避免起下钻具对孔壁的破坏，防止坍塌掉块，减少卡钻事故；另一方面，绳索取芯钻进减少了升降钻具的辅助时间，提高钻探效率，减少了工人的劳动强度。

（1）安全脱卡装置。绳索取芯安全脱卡装置由打捞器上的安全销和脱卡管组成。内管总成到位后，投下脱卡管，罩住打捞钩尾部，使打捞钩端部张开，释放捞矛头，从而使打捞器与内管总成脱离；当捞取岩芯遇阻时，可通过绳索绞车提拉钢丝绳，把安全销拉断，使打捞器上半部分与下部分完全脱离。ZK04钻孔因孔内无冲洗液，只有把脱卡管装在打捞器上，使用打捞钩挂住捞矛头，向下送内管总成，当到达外管中时，打捞钩的头部张开，而其尾部向内收缩，被脱卡管罩信，使打捞钩脱卡，然后提升打捞器，以免撞击损坏钻具和钻头。操作过程中，注意控制钢丝绳下降深度，快到钻具外管位置时，减缓下放速度，避免撞击损坏钻具和钻头。

（2）润滑、降温措施。ZK04钻孔钻进过程中基本不返浆，漏失严重，多数时间冲洗液仅能湿润钻头，无法使用堵漏措施有效堵漏，只能顶漏钻进。用计量准确并且有数显的流量计替代水表控制冲洗液用量，防止钻头烧钻。为润滑钻杆、减少钻杆阻力、减少钻杆摩擦孔壁发热，经常从孔口沿钻杆外壁注入聚丙烯酰胺和切削膏混合液，起到了良好的润滑、降温效果。

（3）充分利用套管、各级配钻杆。为减少钻孔下部钻进难度，增加钻孔安全系数，钻进过程中充分利用各级套管、钻杆，直至钻具钻进困难，才允许变径。ZK04钻孔孔内各级套管深度为：ϕ168厚壁套管30m，PW套管99m，PQ钻杆（钻进后用作套管）306m，JS98钻杆（钻进后用作套管）600m。S75A钻杆钻进至终孔760m。

2. 护壁措施

（1）冲洗液护壁。ZK04钻孔采用绳索取芯钻具钻进，钻具环状间隙较小，要求尽量使用无固相或低固相冲洗液。钻孔全孔漏失严重，必须采用顶漏钻进，并用流量计准确控制浆量。开钻后要准确计算好时间，把浆液送到孔底再开钻，做到既不浪费浆液，又保证浆液质量优良且充足。

灰岩、白云岩、砂岩地层采用1600万分子量聚丙烯酰胺（PHP）作为无固相浆液的主体，能絮凝岩屑，起到保护孔壁的作用，又有很好润滑性能。加入适量的切削膏或皂化油提高润滑性能，减少钻进阻力，加入高黏纤维素尽量减少漏失。

泥岩、页岩地层选用了植物胶、泥页岩抑制剂、C型润滑剂作为钻进冲洗液。植物胶、C型润滑剂起到絮凝、润滑作用，泥页岩抑制剂用来抑制泥页岩中所含黏土矿物的水化、膨胀、分解作用，能更好地保护泥岩、页岩地层，减少钻孔缩径，从而保护孔壁。

（2）套管护壁和水泥封孔护壁。套管护壁可靠保护钻孔孔壁，减少钻孔上部孔段漏失，增加钻进安全系数，充分利用各级套管显得尤为重要。绳索取芯钻杆钻进达到或接近材料极限深度，钻进阻力较大、钻进困难时，提出绳索取芯钻头换上跟管钻头，放入孔底进行护壁，用下一级绳索取芯钻杆继续钻进。必要时尝试同步跟管钻进，但不强制跟管，避免造成套管（钻杆）断裂发生孔内事故。

因钻孔孔径和深度限制套管护壁时，遇严重掉块、塌孔而无法正常钻进时，采用水泥封孔护壁。沿钻杆内壁倾倒足够多的混合好的水泥浆液，然后提出钻杆和钻具外管并清洗。利用水泥良好的胶结性能，使水泥浆液与孔壁凝结成较高强度的结石，从而使孔壁的坚固性提高。本次采用2段水泥封孔护壁，孔深分别为299～306m、733～748m。封孔护壁效果良好，但封孔、待凝及扫孔需要时间较长，分别为6d、7d。

（中国电建集团北京勘测设计研究院
有限公司　黄小军）

5

水 工 设 计

大 坝 设 计

三岔河水电站混凝土面板堆石坝设计

三岔河水电站位于云南省保山市腾冲县，为槟榔江梯级龙头水库，二等大（2）型工程，电站装机容量3×24MW。大坝为混凝土面板堆石坝，最大坝高94m，坝顶高程1900m，坝顶长331m，坝顶宽8m，上游坡1∶1.4。下游高程1870m马道以上坝坡1∶1.6，以下1∶1.4。总填筑量160万m^3。

（一）坝体结构设计

混凝土面板自顶部向底部逐渐增厚，顶部厚0.3m，底部厚0.62m。面板垂直缝间距为12m，共有面板25块。

（1）面板混凝土强度等级C25，抗渗不低于W12，抗冻不低于F100，二级配混凝土，水灰比不大于0.5，坍落度3～7cm，水泥采用硅酸盐水泥、普通硅酸盐水泥，掺15%～25%Ⅰ级粉煤灰和聚丙烯纤维0.9kg/m^3。

（2）混凝土面板采用双层双向配筋，每向配筋率0.4%。为增强地震抗裂性能，在0.7～0.85倍坝高范围内顺坡向钢筋含筋率增至0.55%。

（3）面板分两期施工，分期浇筑的水平施工缝凿毛、铺M30水泥砂浆并设膨胀止水条，上下层顺坡向设ϕ16@200mm、长1.2m加强筋。

（4）混凝土面板设25条垂直缝，其中大坝中部11条压性缝，缝间距均为12m，大坝右侧8条、左侧6条张性缝，缝间距均为12m。

（5）两种趾板型式，A型宽6m，厚0.6m，B型宽8m，厚0.8m。表面配筋为单层双向配筋，每向配筋率0.4%。二级配混凝土，混凝土强度等级、抗渗和抗冻等级、使用的水泥均同面板，掺15%～25%Ⅰ级粉煤灰。

（6）坝顶宽8m。防浪墙总高4.2m，墙底与面板间接缝按变形缝设计，设PVC止水及铜片止水各一道，填塞无孔泡沫板。

（二）坝体分区设计

主料场在坝址下游1.5km清水河石料场，次料场为溢洪道开挖区内的坝下石料场，可利用溢洪道开挖可用料直接上坝。坝料为粗粒花岗岩、细粒花岗岩。

坝体材料分区从上游至下游依次为垫层区（2A）、过渡区（3A）、上游堆石料区（3B）、下游堆石料区（3C）和下游排水堆石料区（3D）。

（1）垫层料采用石料场开采微风化以下岩石轧制而成，最大粒径40～80mm，小于5mm颗粒含量35%～55%，小于0.1mm颗粒含量小于等于5%。

（2）过渡料设在垫层料与上游堆石料间，料源为石料场弱风化以下岩石。过渡料最大粒径300mm，小于5mm颗粒含量5%～20%，小于0.1mm颗粒含量小于5%，且级配连续。

（3）堆石料最大粒径800mm，小于25mm颗粒含量小于40%，小于5mm颗粒含量小于等于20%，上游和下游排水堆石料小于0.1mm颗粒含量小于5%，下游堆石料小于0.1mm颗粒含量小于8%。

（4）坝前覆盖堵缝料（粉煤灰）和保护料（开挖任意料）。

（三）坝体填筑标准

坝料参数根据室内试验及现场碾压试验，参考已建工程确定（见表1）。

表1 坝料填筑设计参数

坝料种类	设计干密度（g/cm^3）	孔隙率（%）	最大粒径（mm）	渗透系数（cm/s）	铺料厚度（mm）	最少碾压遍数
垫层料（2A）	>2.18	≤18	100	1×10^{-2}～1×10^{-4}	400	6
特殊垫层区料（2B）	>2.18	≤18	40	1×10^{-2}～1×10^{-4}	200	6
过渡料（3A）	>2.13	≤20	300	$>1\times10^{-2}$	400	6
上游堆石区（3B）	>2.10	≤21	800	$>1\times10^{-1}$	800	6
下游堆石区（3C）	>2.08	≤21	800	$>1\times10^{-3}$	800	6
下游排水堆石区（3D）	>2.08	≤22	800	$>1\times10^{-1}$	800	6

（四）坝基处理

河床冲积层厚度1.5～3m，下部弱风化基岩。河床冲积层全部清除，趾板基础开挖至弱风化基岩，两岸坝基开挖清除坡积层。

趾板固结灌浆孔排距2m，A型趾板孔深8m，B型孔深10m，灌浆压力0.3～0.5MPa。沿趾板中部布置1排帷幕灌浆孔，孔距1.5m，深入岩体3Lu线以下5m。坝顶高程两岸帷幕与水库蓄水前地下水位线连接，灌浆深度28～52m，灌浆最大压力1.5MPa。

（五）监测成果

下闸蓄水前河床最大坝高监测断面沉降位移最大值756.6mm。总体上坝体沉降变形中间部位大于坝体上下游。水平位移均向下游，实测最大位移处于坝最前端。最大坝高断面1825m高程最大累计位移217mm。水库蓄水后两年，正常蓄水位下量水堰实测最大渗流量11.2L/s，库水位下降渗流量相应减少。

（中国电建集团昆明勘测设计研究院有限公司　杨旭）

明朗水库大坝塑性混凝土防渗墙设计

明朗水库位于昆明市西山区中部，属金沙江流域螳螂川水系沙河源头段水库工程。原明朗水库建于1957年，后经多次加固，水库仍存在不同程度病险。本工程在原坝址扩建加高，水库正常蓄水位从1995.5m调整至1999m，总库容936万m^3，属Ⅳ等小（1）型工程。枢纽主要建筑物包括拦河坝、输水隧洞和溢洪道，地震设防烈度为Ⅷ度。

（一）大坝存在的主要问题

明朗水库座落在石灰岩破碎发育地区，大坝建设时未进行详细勘测设计和地质钻探；施工时清基不彻底，留下7～11m厚冲积透水层；施工只追求进度，忽视质量，上坝土料辗压不实，留下了水平空洞和草根等杂物。1959年水库蓄水未达正常设计水位时，发现下游坝坡出现9条裂缝、落洞18个，虽抢修后脱险，但未彻底根治。1965年3月初，大坝裂缝逐步扩大，越过坝顶，长67m，裂口最宽处4.9cm，并向库内呈弧状发展，险情加大。后在库内抛石1057m^3，抛装土麻袋1300多个，填补了水下漏洞6个、裂缝3条。1966年、1967年8月～1970年8月水库进行帷幕防渗灌浆及补漏处理。

大坝运行至今，现坝顶面较平整，无坡面坍滑。中部坝顶高程为1999.74m，右岸坝顶2000.48m，左岸坝顶2000.33m，坝顶高差59～74cm。坝顶宽度变化不大，平均宽10m。坝坡较完整，上游坝坡有混凝土预制板护坡，坡面较完好，起伏很小，个别地段混凝土板开裂、起伏不平；下游坝坡平顺度较上游差些，凸凹起伏较明显，最大凹陷达0.47m。

据勘查，坝基渗漏主要发生在坝基河床冲积层（强透水）和浅部破碎强风化基岩（中等透水～强透水）中，在坝体与坝基接触面一带渗出。大坝下游坡脚中部与地基接触带可见相对集中渗漏点，偶测流量1.0～1.5L/s。另在下游坡脚左岸靠近输水涵管一带可见分散渗水点，流量很小。原坝后坡脚排水棱体已失效（或未建），坝体排水不畅。

（二）大坝加固措施

大坝为4级建筑物，坝顶高程2001.50m，最大坝高39.35m，坝顶宽10m，长265m。大坝加固扩建在原均质土坝上进行，从原坝体下游填筑石渣料进行加固加高，坝顶自高程1997m往上加高。坝轴线上游3m处设0.6m宽塑性混凝土防渗墙，其底部设间距2m帷幕灌浆，帷幕底线至10lu线。下游坝脚处设高6.5m梯形排水棱体。加高部分上游坝坡1991.3m以上坡度1∶2.1、1991.3m以下坡度1∶3.3，下游坝坡坡度1∶2.5，在坝坡1985m设宽2m马道。上游坝坡用混凝土预制块护坡，下游坡用植草护坡。坝顶结构进行重建。

（三）塑性混凝土防渗墙设计

坝体防渗采用塑性混凝土防渗墙，防渗墙分二序施工，标准槽段长6m，搭接0.6m，墙厚0.6m，布置于坝轴线上游3m处。防渗墙深入坝基强风化岩体1m，1997m以下防渗墙深度16～35m，1997m以上采用现浇混凝土。防渗墙下接单排帷幕灌浆，帷幕深入10Lu不透水线，灌浆孔间距2m，帷幕总长360m，分三序施工，最大帷幕灌浆压力0.2～0.3MPa。

防渗墙墙体为C10塑性混凝土，一级配，采用P.O42.5普通硅酸盐水泥，28天抗压强度1.5～5MPa，抗渗W6，弹模500～1000MPa，渗透系数小于1×10^{-7}cm/s。

（四）大坝渗流稳定计算

1. 渗流计算　选取大坝坝体最大断面进行平面渗流计算，适当简化大坝剖面和基础，进行单元划分，并确定了坝体及基岩等材料的各项计算参数，以及两种计算工况。

计算结果：在正常水位1999m、稳定渗流时，坝体单宽流量$2.68\times10^{-5}m^3/(s\cdot m)$，平均坝长为130m，日渗流量301$m^3$，年渗漏量109871.4$m^3$，占总库容1.17%。由于大坝下游坝脚增设了排水棱体，排水棱体前已按反滤要求设置反滤层，故未进行渗透稳定计算。

2. 坝坡稳定计算 坝坡稳定计算考虑四种工况（含八个部位），并确定了坝体及基岩等材料各项计算参数。计算方法为刚体极限平衡法，采用土石坝坝坡稳定程序计算。

从计算成果看，各计算工况下，坝坡抗滑安全系数均大于规范允许的安全系数，说明上下游坝坡是稳定的。

（中国电建集团昆明勘测设计研究院有限公司 郑红）

淋溪河水电站坝型比选研究

（一）水文和地质条件简述

淋溪河坝址控制流域面积 $2286km^2$，上游梯级电站坝址至淋溪河水电站坝址间面积 $146km^2$。坝址处多年平均降水量 1684.5mm，多年平均气温 15.4℃，多年平均径流量 $86.5m^3/s$。

坝址位于百步蹬峡谷下段，河道长约 800m，“V”形斜向谷，水面宽 40m，平面呈向上游稍开敞的喇叭口，谷底狭窄。河谷两岸基岩裸露，260m 以下峭壁直立，260m 以上地形坡角 45°～65°。地层为中硬灰岩和生物碎屑岩，以及中硬泥灰岩。

（二）坝型选择

根据坝址地形地貌和地质条件，以及附近料源情况，拟选择常态混凝土拱坝、碾压混凝土拱坝、碾压混凝土重力坝、混凝土面板堆石坝四种坝型作比较。

1. 常态混凝土拱坝（方案 1） 枢纽由挡水建筑物、泄水消能建筑物、输水建筑物及发电厂房等组成。双曲拱坝的中心线与河流流向基本平行，平面为抛物线型，拱冠梁上下游均为三次曲线。坝顶高程 297.5m，最大坝高 88m，拱冠梁顶部厚 6m，底部厚 22m。

坝体不设纵缝，9 道横缝将大坝分成 10 个坝段，坝段横缝上游坝面弧长间距 20～25m，其中④～⑦坝段为溢流坝段，布置 3 孔溢流表孔和 2 孔泄洪深孔，其余坝段为非溢流坝段。

坝身 3 孔开敞式溢流表孔尺寸均为 12.5m×13.0m（宽×高）。溢流堰为 WES 型实用堰，堰顶高程 280m。左、右泄洪深孔对称布置于拱坝中心线两侧的⑤、⑥坝段，闸孔孔口尺寸 6m×9m（宽×高），进口底板高程 250m。下游为窄缝式挑流消能。拱坝下游设水垫塘。

输水建筑物由进水口、输水隧洞（引水隧洞、尾水隧洞）组成。岸塔式进水口，底板高程 275m。两条有压圆形引水隧洞平行布置，总长分为 218、202m，洞径 6.8m。

发电厂房由地下洞群和地面建筑物组成。地下洞群由主厂房、主变压器洞、母线洞、交通洞、出线洞兼排风洞、排水廊道组成，主厂房洞室 107.8m×18.2m×49.3m（长×宽×高），2 台单机容量 85MW 和 1 台单机容量 5.2MW 水轮发电机组，小机组并排在②机组右侧。

汛期采用预留坝体缺口和导流洞联合泄洪的方式导流。

2. 碾压混凝土拱坝（方案 2） 枢纽由碾压混凝土拱坝、泄水建筑物、左岸输水建筑物、左岸地下厂房组成。除坝体材料分区和分缝、泄水建筑物布置与方案 1 不同外，坝体断面型式、结构尺寸及输水发电系统和施工导流均与方案 1 相同。为加大坝体碾压混凝土的比例，减小坝身泄水建筑物对坝体碾压混凝土施工的干扰，方案 2 泄水建筑物全部采用坝身泄洪表孔（5 孔），并布置在河床中部，孔口尺寸均为 13m×12m（宽×高）。

3. 碾压混凝土重力坝（方案 3） 枢纽由碾压混凝土重力坝、坝身溢流表孔、消力池、左岸输水建筑物、左岸地下厂房组成。输水建筑物和地下厂房布置与方案 1 完全一致。重力坝坝顶高程 297.5m，最大坝高 102.5m，坝顶宽 6m。坝顶轴线长 1820m，从右岸至左岸依次为①、②右非溢流坝段，③、④河床溢流坝段，⑤、⑥左非溢流坝段。大坝混凝土总量 38.8 万 m^3，其中碾压混凝土 29.94 万 m^3。泄水建筑物为 3 孔 12.5m×18.0m（宽×高）开敞式溢流表孔，设于③、④坝段。溢流堰为 WES 型实用堰，堰顶高程 275m。

4. 混凝土面板堆石坝（方案 4） 枢纽由混凝土面板堆石坝、右岸溢洪道、放空洞、左岸输水建筑物、左岸地下厂房组成。输水建筑物和地下厂房布置与方案 1 一致。堆石坝坝顶高程 298m，最大坝高 86m，坝顶总长 162m，坝顶宽 8m，上、下游坝坡均为 1∶1.35。溢洪道紧靠右坝肩布置，由进水渠、闸室、泄槽及挑坎组成，溢流堰为 WES 型低实用堰，堰顶高程 275m。放空洞利用导流隧洞封堵堵头埋设放空钢管改建而成。

5. 坝型比较 从地形地质条件看，三种坝型有较好适应性。混凝土坝没有高边坡问题，对地形地质条件适应性更好，优于堆石坝。重力坝有抗滑稳定问题，需采取工程措施。

从工程布置看，四种方案枢纽布置格局基本一致，相对紧凑独立。方案 4 需单独布置岸边溢洪道，故不如其他方案。方案 1 坝身泄洪、左岸输水建筑物及左岸地下厂房布置紧凑合理且相对独立，施工干扰小，运行条件好。洪水峰高量大要求泄洪建筑物规模较大，使方案 2 中常态混凝土占比大，碾压混凝土坝优势不能充分体现。为便于碾压混凝土连续、快速施工，需集中布置5个泄洪表孔，但河谷狭窄，比较困难，故方案1优于方案2。方案3单纯表孔泄流，方案1表孔+深孔联合泄流，运行灵活，水库检修等特殊情况可将水库放空至较低水位，故方案1略优于方案3。

从施工条件看，方案1、2、3施工导流与度汛基本相当。方案1温控费用比方案2、3高，但方案2、3碾压混凝土占比小，且需增设1套碾压混凝土施工设备，临建工程费用高，施工干扰大。方案4尽管可利用溢洪道开挖料筑坝，但需要较大转料场地，弃渣量大，弃渣场布置困难。故方案1、2、3各有优缺点，方案1施工干扰较小，方案4最差。

从工程投资看，方案4比方案1多9986万元，是因溢洪道石方开挖量为坝体填筑量2.3倍，且150m高边坡支护难度及工程量大；方案3比方案1多8704万元，是因坝高比方案1高14.5m，混凝土工程量比方案1多18.54万m^3，钢筋等其余工程量均要多，就固结灌浆少6729m；碾压混凝土可降低水泥和模板用量，故方案2比方案1少1968万元。

从地形地质条件、建筑物布置、工程投资等方面考虑，推荐采用常态混凝土拱坝坝型。

（中国电建集团中南勘测设计研究院有限公司 程波）

向家坝水电站坝基混凝土防渗墙研究及应用

向家坝水电站坝基采用“扩大坝基+坝踵齿槽+深孔固结灌浆”综合处理方案，但河床泄水坝段坝踵部位仍有约60m厚Ⅳ～Ⅴ类挠曲核部破碎带岩体，其强度较低、遇水泥化。对该岩体试验研究的结果表明，破碎带可灌性差，水泥灌浆难以满足要求，化学灌浆工艺复杂、耗浆量大，难以取得明显效果。防渗墙能满足坝基渗透稳定要求，故采用防渗墙处理方案。

（一）防渗墙的设计

1. 防渗墙设置范围　泄④～泄⑧坝基挠曲核部破碎带防渗处理采用混凝土防渗墙方案。坝基防渗墙长88m，墙厚1.2m，顶部高程210m，底部高程148m，墙底进入Ⅲ类岩体至少2m，共3432m^2。防渗墙与基岩接触面及以下岩体采用防渗帷幕防渗。

2. 防渗墙设计主要指标　按照渗流分析成果防渗墙墙体承担110m水头计，确定墙厚为1.2m，相应抗渗比降92。墙厚的确定也考虑当前国内造孔机械的现状和施工难度，以加快防渗墙的建造速度，否则将会增加工程造价。

根据本工程特点，并类比其他工程，拟定防渗墙抗压强度3～5MPa、模强比500、渗透系数不大于10^{-8}cm/s。

3. 防渗墙细部设计

（1）防渗墙与大坝衔接。根据有限元分析成果，结合工程类比，防渗墙顶部伸入坝体导槽1.3m，接头顶部和上、下游侧与坝体间均设有铜片止水，并设闭孔泡沫板，作为弹性变形空间。防渗墙接头顶部、上游侧、下游侧闭孔泡沫板厚分别为10、3、5cm。

（2）防渗墙与帷幕衔接。按坝基渗控系统总体布置，防渗帷幕采用3排同深孔，排距1.5m，孔距2m，孔底高程为90m。在泄④～泄⑥坝段防渗帷幕穿过Ⅳ～Ⅴ类挠曲核部破碎带部位采用塑性混凝土防渗墙代替第二排帷幕灌浆，防渗墙厚1.2m，墙底进入$Ⅲ_2$类岩体至少2m。第二排帷幕孔在防渗墙内埋管施工，第一排和第三排帷幕孔对防渗墙上下游经冲击扰动的Ⅳ～Ⅴ类挠曲核部破碎带及以下岩体进行灌浆。泄⑦～泄⑩坝段坝基高程210m隧洞以下防渗墙和灌浆布置同泄④～泄⑥坝段，防渗墙隧洞顶拱以上Ⅱ～$Ⅲ_1$类岩体帷幕灌浆待坝基高程210m隧洞回填混凝土后，在坝体高程245m帷幕廊道施工。

（二）防渗墙运行效果分析

向家坝水电站2012年10月下闸蓄水，坝基防渗系统经历了工程蓄水及初期运行的实践检验。为了监测坝基防渗墙的运行情况及防渗效果，在基础防渗墙部位共埋设安装渗压计31支。

首次蓄水354m期间，防渗墙渗压计折算水位随库水位上升呈增大趋势，防渗墙上游侧渗压计的折算水位比防渗墙后的折算水位高出约50m水头，说明防渗墙起到了一定防渗作用。蓄水370m后，防渗墙渗压水位随着库水位上升而升高，蓄水结束后，防渗墙上游渗压水位上升近9m，下游侧渗压水位上升近5m，防渗墙基础渗流趋缓。蓄水380m后，防渗墙上游渗压水位最大上升4.46m，下游侧渗压水位最大上升3.57m。

2013年底至今，防渗墙上游测点测值比下游测点测值高约40～70m水头，防渗墙部位渗压基本稳定。初期蓄水至今，防渗墙已在设计运行条件下正常工作4年多，充分说明了软弱破碎岩体中防渗墙具有良好的防渗效果。

（中国电建集团中南勘测设计研究院有限公司
刘要来 周红波 邹阳生 张永涛）

桑河二级水电站均质土坝强透水基础处理

（一）概述

柬埔寨桑河二级水电站大坝为均质土坝，坝顶高程81.5m，最大坝高35m，坝顶宽8m，上游坝坡

1∶2.75，下游坝坡1∶2.0，坝体筑坝材料为全风化土或全强风化土混合料，采用竖式排水接褥垫式水平排水形式。坝基无深厚覆盖层，可满足沉降和抗滑稳定要求，坝基重点是渗流控制。

部分坝基座落在中等透水强风化岩上，或座落在表层弱透水黏土质砾和全风化层上、下层中等透水层（强风化岩）双层地基上。为了解坝基渗流量和渗透稳定情况，对坝基进行敏感性计算。从计算结果看，坝基若存在贯穿性的强透水层，渗透系数大于5×10^{-4}cm/s，坝基渗透比降大于允许渗透比降，则基础在不处理情况下易发生渗透破坏。经几种处理方案比选，决定采用坝基截水槽截渗处理坝基。采用截水槽对坝基渗透稳定非常有利，配合下游排水降压措施，能进一步降低褥垫式排水前端附近的渗透比降。

（二）坝基处理工程措施

土坝坝基采用“上截下排”处理措施，在坝上0+020.00m位置设置截水槽，截水槽底宽5m，截水槽底部设20cm混凝土板，截水槽的后部设置50cm的反滤层。在下游侧坝下0+030.00m位置设置减压井，减压井底宽3m。处理措施见图1和图2。

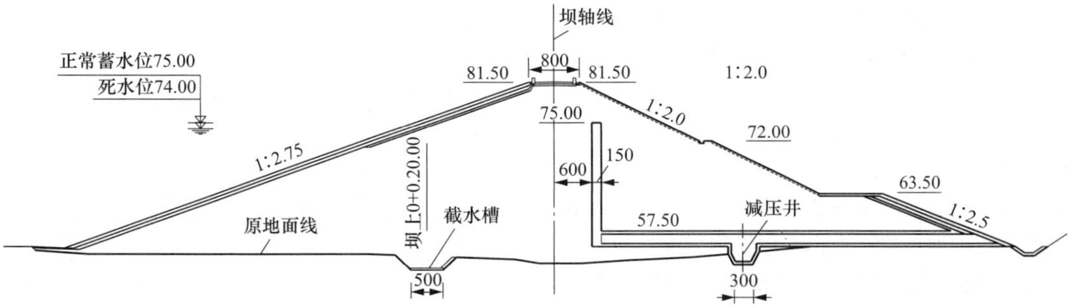

图1　坝基处理典型剖面图

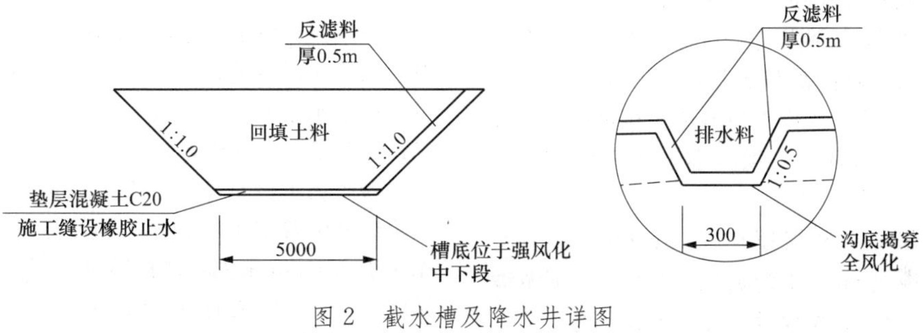

图2　截水槽及降水井详图

（三）监测反馈

土坝坝后设置量水堰对土坝的渗流量进行监测。右岸量水堰监测范围为600m，现场实测量水堰流量$2.8\sim4.1\times10^{-3}m^3/s$之间，平均值$3.45\times10^{-3}m^3/s$（$300m^3/d$）。计算得到的渗流量为0.47L/min/m，换算得到的渗流量为$406m^3/d$，计算值比实测值大，考虑到坝体基础的不均匀性，实测值较计算值偏小的结果是可靠的。

（中国电建集团华东勘测设计研究院有限公司
罗书靖　徐辉　李强）

桑河二级水电站土坝分区设计

桑河二级水电站枢纽主要建筑物包括左右岸土坝、混凝土泄洪闸坝、河床式发电厂房、混凝土重力坝和侧墙式接头等，混凝土坝最大坝高56.50m，两岸均质土坝最大坝高35.0m，土坝全长6036m，根据现场土料储备实际，左岸采用分区土坝设计，右岸采用均质土料设计，坝体内采用不同排水形式。成功地解决了坝基渗漏及渗透稳定问题。

（一）土坝基础特点

由于工程地处平原地区，坝基所在区域地形平缓，表层分布的岩土层主要为残坡积土层（含砾黏性土）或全风化基岩（含碎石粉质黏土），在坝基部分区域存在中等透水基础，主要特点如下：①大部分坝基范围残坡积土层、全风化基岩厚度一般1.5～4.5m，天然状态下渗透系数为$10^{-5}\sim10^{-6}$cm/s，为微透水，可以直接作为土坝基础。②坝基部分区域存在冲沟，局部坝段有效铺盖厚度偏薄，渗透系数为

10^{-3}cm/s，不能直接作为土坝基础，需采取工程措施。③坝基部分区域全风化层上部存在黏土质砾层，厚度1～3m不等，渗透系数为2×10^{-3}cm/s，属于中等透水，需进行相应的工程措施。

（二）分区土坝设计

电站建设地点偏远，建设材料供应难度大，尤其是水泥、钢筋等主要原材料需从国外购运入，同时，作为国际水电工程，落实项目经济性和环保要求尤为重要。必须充分利用当地材料，按照分区土坝设计。考虑到上游土层较薄，土性均匀性差，结合土料场的分布、料源储量、运距等情况，左岸土坝按照上游采用粉质黏土料、下游采用全强风化混合料的分区坝设计；右岸土坝则全断面采用全强风化混合料，形成均质土坝。

1. *左岸土坝* 左岸坝顶高程81.50m，最大坝高35.0m，坝顶宽8m，大坝上游坡比1∶2.75，下游坡比1∶2.0，在72.0m高程设一级2m宽马道，上下游坡面均采取护坡措施；根据土坝筑坝料源不同，左岸土坝在坝体内部分两个区，上游侧采用粉质黏土料，下游侧以及顶部采用全强风化料。上游粉质黏土料分区顶高程77.5m，顶宽4.25m，下游坡比1∶0.75，倾上游；在粉质黏土料与全强风化料之间会存在施工层面缝，导致坝体局部渗透性偏大。在坝高为20～35m段，坝内除设置褥垫式排水外，在坝轴线下游6m处设置竖式排水与褥垫式排水相接，以有效降低坝体内的浸润线。坝高小于20m时坝内排水仅采用褥垫式排水。

2. *右岸土坝* 右岸坝顶高程81.50m，最大坝高35.0m，坝顶宽8m，上游坡比1∶2.75，下游坡比1∶2.0，在72.0m高程设一级2m宽马道，上下游坡面均采取护坡措施。右岸土料场有用料为全强风化土，储量满足设计需求，因此，右岸土坝全部以全强风化混合料填筑。在坝高大于18m段，坝体下游63.5m高程处设一宽10m的平台，以提高下游坝坡稳定性。该段坝体竖式排水体上游面距坝轴线6.0m，水平宽1.5m。右岸土坝在坝高低于18m段采用褥垫式排水形式，褥垫式排水体上游端距坝轴线12.0m，下部设一层0.5m厚的反滤料，中部排水料厚1.5m，上部设一层0.5m厚的反滤料，总厚2.5m。

3. *坝料设计和填筑标准* 坝体填筑料主体由粉质黏土料和全强风化料组成。对粉质黏土料的坝料要求及填筑标准如下：渗透系数$K\leqslant1\times10^{-5}$cm/s，碾压后粒径大于5mm的颗粒含量不宜超过50%，最大粒径不大于150mm，0.075mm以下颗粒含量不应小于15%；填筑压实度不小于98%，施工含水量控制在土料最优含水率−2%～3%范围内。对全强风化料其小于0.075mm的细粒含量在10%～50%之间，最大干密度范围为1.72～1.97g/cm³，最优含水率范围为9.2%～17.7%。全强风化料的坝料要求及填筑标准如下：渗透系数$K\leqslant1\times10^{-4}$cm/s，碾压后粒径大于5mm的颗粒含量不宜超过50%，最大粒径不大于150mm，0.075mm以下颗粒含量不应小于15%；填筑压实度不小于98%，施工含水量控制在土料最优含水率−2%～3%范围内。由于坝内排水体均在全强风化料内，故反滤层主要针对全强风化料进行设计，同时兼顾对粉质黏土料的保护（上游护坡）和对全风化土坝基的保护。采用全强风化料的上包线和粉质黏土料的下包线作为反滤料的级配包络线，特征粒径如表1所示。

表1 反滤料级配包络线特征粒径表

特征粒径		D5	D10	D15	D60	D90	D100
百分比（%）		5	10	15	60	90	100
粒径（mm）	max	0.38	0.6	0.7	3.5	20	40
	min	0.075	0.15	0.18	0.9	5	10

全强风化料级配变化大，能否与上游的粉质黏土料之间形成反滤关系，也是一个关键问题。由于粉质黏土料中小于0.075mm的含量在85%以下，根据反滤设计要求，全强风化料的D15小于0.7mm即可满足对粉质黏土料的滤土要求。设计对全强风化料上坝填筑标准中要求细粒含量不应小于15%，这个要求相对于0.7mm来说要严格得多，因此全强风化料与粉质黏土料之间能满足反滤关系。

（三）基础处理

现场揭露的坝基地质问题主要包括坝基稳定问题和坝基渗漏问题。对于坝基稳定问题，主要出现在坝基局部揭露强风化破碎岩体部位及含黏土质砾层基础部位。通过计算分析，上游铺盖需与其他排渗减压措施配套使用。在坝基上游侧设置截水槽，以配合坝体内部竖向排水与褥垫排水，减少渗压。截水槽布置在距离坝轴线（1/2～1/3）B（B为坝基长度）的上游。在坝基下游侧设置减压井，进一步降低褥垫式排水前端附近的渗透比降。减压井布置在距离坝轴线（1/2～1/3）B（B为坝基长度）下游，且与坝内褥垫排水体相连接。采用截水槽和下游排水降压措施综合处理后，进一步降低坝基的渗透比降，满足全风化土的允许渗透比降。

（中国电建集团华东勘测设计研究院有限公司
唐杰 罗书靖 徐辉 吴宏荣）

茨哈峡水电站工程枢纽区三维渗流分析

根据茨哈峡水电站面板堆石坝工程实际情况和计算分析任务书要求，通过对大石峡水电站地形和地貌资料的分析和三维渗流有限元计算分析，得出主要结论和建议。

（1）天然模型下地下水面位置与所给地址资料和地下水资料，两者基本吻合。因此三维模型较好地模拟了自然地下水分布的情况，所截取范围的地下水符合实际情况，计算模型可用于运行期枢纽区渗流计算分析研究。

（2）研究了防渗帷幕布置方案对枢纽区渗流场的影响，明确了设计基本方案可以满足枢纽区防渗要求，其设计在技术上是合理的。

（3）研究了防渗帷幕和垫层料的渗透系数对枢纽区渗流场的影响，确定了垫层渗透系数的变化对坝体和坝基渗流场影响微小。

（4）研究了止水系统破损失效对大坝渗流性态的影响，相较于止水系统完好的情况，面板缝、周边缝止水失效情况下，坝体浸润面均有升高，渗流量也增大。面板缝止水失效时，缝宽越大、失效缝长越长、失效位置越低，则坝体浸润面位置越高。

（5）地下洞室在防渗帷幕和排水孔幕的联合作用下，厂房上游处自由面下降明显，主副厂房、主变室等地下洞室上部浸润面下降，压力水头减小。单靠防渗帷幕或是排水孔幕并不能明显起到延长渗透水流渗径，降低坝基围岩渗透压力并防止围岩变形的作用，防渗帷幕必须在幕后排水孔幕的协助下才能起到良好的渗控效果。故建议施工时确保帷幕施工质量，同时保持排水孔排水通畅，保证排水系统正常工作。

（河海大学
中国水电顾问集团西北勘测设计研究院有限公司）

大桥水电站混凝土重力坝温度及温度应力分析

（一）概述

大桥水电站位于云南省红河哈尼族彝族自治州南盘江上，为三等中型工程。选取挡水坝段进行坝体施工期变温度场和应力场有限元仿真计算分析，主要是溢流坝段平面有限元分析。仿真分析中，对坝体碾压混凝土的施工工序、分块厚度、混凝土入仓温度、混凝土温升，浇筑块温度边界条件、相邻浇筑块间歇时间等均进行了仿真模拟。通过无温控方案计算，对坝体混凝土施工工序的合理性进行评价，并对坝体混凝土施工中是否需要温度控制提出了建议。

混凝土施工时，按分层分块浇筑的原则，安排混凝土浇筑进度。碾压层厚 30cm，初凝时间 12h，每个浇筑块厚 3m，一、二期浇筑块层间间歇时间 15 天。通仓浇筑，不分块。混凝土表面与空气的对流系数按常规计算。

（二）计算模型及参数

1. 材料参数　混凝土的绝热温升公式选用双曲线函数：$\theta(\tau)=\dfrac{\theta_0\tau}{n+\tau}$。

混凝土随龄期变化的弹性模量的表达式采用三参数双指数形式：$E(\tau)=E_0(1-e^{-\alpha\tau^\beta})$。

根据已有的坝体混凝土的热学和物理力学参数，利用公式可进行相关计算。

根据《混凝土重力坝设计规范》（DL 5108—1999）的要求，坝体混凝土的最大拉应力应满足以下要求：$\gamma_0[\sigma]\leqslant\varepsilon_p E_c/\gamma_{d3}$。

经计算，常态混凝土和碾压混凝土的允许最大拉应力［σ］值分别为 1.7MPa、1.2MPa，弹性模量分别为 30GPa、24GPa。

热工计算采用中热水泥的最终水化热 $Q_0=$ 88.40kcal/kg（1kcal＝4.1858518kJ）。

2. 温差控制标准　根据《混凝土拱坝设计规范》（SL 282—2003）规定，通仓长块浇筑的混凝土基础约束区容许温差，在 0～0.2L（强约束区，L 为浇筑块长边尺寸）范围内为 16～14℃，0.2～0.4L（弱约束区）范围内 19～17℃。拱坝设计规范建议上下层温差控制在 15～20℃。还应控制坝体内最高温度与年平均气温（20.6℃）之差不大于 20℃。

3. 二维有限元模型　大桥水电站混凝土重力坝有限元模拟范围：顺河向以坝轴线为界上下游各取 62m，均为 1.5 倍坝高，铅直向取 62m，约 1.5 倍坝高。结构离散中坝体混凝土及坝基岩体用 4 结点四边形等参单元（含少量退化单元），方案中，整个计算域共剖分为 9384 个单元，9583 个结点。计算坐标系 X 轴上游指向下游为正，Y 轴铅直向上为正。

4. 温度应力计算边界条件与荷载组合　位移边界条件：上下游均为法向零位移约束，底部边界为固端约束，上部边界为自由边界。荷载组合只考虑温度荷载，不计自重与水荷载。温度采用年平均气温 20.6℃。坝体施工期无温控措施温度场和应力场进行仿真计算。

（三）温度与应力计算结果分析

计算了 13 个浇筑块的最大温度和最大拉应力，计算结果表明：浇筑块最大温度发生在四期最后浇筑混凝土块（第十三块）内，混凝土内最高温度37.5℃与年平均气温（20.6℃）之差16.9℃，小于20℃，满足规范要求内外温差限值。大坝通仓浇筑长度L为57m，基础强约束区高0～0.2L，即0～11.4m高度范围内，容许温差16～14℃，满足要求，0.2～0.4L范围内19～17℃，满足要求。

最大拉应力主要集中于坝体表面，特别是上下游坝面。后期温度逐渐降低后，最大拉应力位置变化不大，仍位于上下游坝面，最大拉应力值都满足规范要求。

仿真模拟中未考虑施工中采用冷却等温控措施，与实际施工比，浇筑时分层厚度相对较大，每次所加混凝土体积较大，所产生的水化热量较大。故计算所得温度和拉应力可能与实际情况有一定出入，需进一步细化模拟过程，使其更加接近实际情况。

（中国电建集团昆明勘测设计研究院有限公司　胡杰华）
（中水北方勘测设计研究有限责任公司　李浩东　计海力）

衢江抽水蓄能电站面板堆石坝折线型布置研究

（一）概述

衢江抽水蓄能电站装机容量1200MW，一等大（1）型工程。电站上水库为混凝土面板堆石坝，由于天然库盆条件较差，为有效控制水位变幅、降低坝顶高程，大坝轴线为凸向下游的折线，转折角度42°，是目前我国百米级混凝土面板堆石坝轴线转折角度最大的工程。

大坝轴线转折点位于左岸高程约628m岸坡，坝轴线全长565m，由左岸和河床两段组成。左岸坝段利用一条相对低矮单薄山脊布置以减小坝体填筑量，该段坝轴线长243.5m。河床坝段轴线与沟底的走向呈65°夹角，长321.5m。坝顶高程694.5m，最大坝高114.5m（趾板处）。拟定坝体上游面坡比1∶1.4，表面为C30钢筋混凝土面板，转折处设C30混凝土连接板，通过周边缝与两侧面板连接。下游坝坡坡度1∶1.3，每隔25m高差设一级马道，马道宽3m。大坝填筑料为库内开挖凝灰岩，筑坝料饱和单轴抗压强度除少量次堆石外，均在50MPa以上，属硬岩筑坝。坝体填筑料自上游向下游为垫层区、过渡区、上游堆石区和下游堆石区。

（二）计算方案及参数

1. 计算方法和计算模型　计算采用“土石坝静、动力流固耦合可视化分析软件”三维有限元计算程序。坝体堆石料采用Duncan E-B非线性弹性模型。混凝土面板采用线弹性模型。面板混凝土与垫层料采用无厚度Goodman接触面单元模拟。混凝土面板周边缝与垂直缝接缝材料采用缝单元模拟。

2. 计算参数　通过试验确定坝体填筑料的模型参数。面板、趾板、防浪墙的混凝土材料的物理及力学参数根据设计指标按规范取值，面板与垫层料间接触面模型计算参数参照天生桥一级面板坝接触面试验结果确定为：$K=4800$，$n=0.56$，$R_f=0.74$，$\delta=36.6°$。

（三）计算成果分析及评价

1. 坝体应力与变形　竣工期大、小主应力最大值分别为1.85MPa、0.78MPa，蓄水后分别为1.96MPa、0.84MPa。大、小主应力最大值均位于最大坝高处建基面附近。坝体内总体应力水平较低，竣工时最大应力水平为0.77MPa，蓄水后受水压力挤压，最大应力水平降至0.69MPa。

竣工期，坝体最大沉降62.63m，在坝体填筑最深处约1/2坝高部位靠下游侧；顺河向（垂直右坝段坝轴）位移分布以坝轴线向上游5m左右为分界线上游侧指向上游、下游侧指向下游，往下游侧最大29.76cm，往上游侧最大15.28cm。蓄水后，坝体最大沉降较竣工期有所增加，最大值63.84cm；顺河向位移除上游坡脚部位外整体指向下游，往下游侧最大位移37.88cm，往上游侧仅3.11cm。大坝蓄水前后最大沉降约占最大坝高0.55%～0.56%，与百米级硬岩筑坝其他工程基本相当。

2. 面板应力和变形及其评价　根据计算成果，面板竖向受力除坝顶局部外，均为压应力，最大压应力位于河床部位，达8.12MPa，在C30混凝土抗压承载力范围内。面板挠度最大值为27.6cm，扰度曲率1.4‰，扰度变形在一般工程经验范围之内。因此，从面板竖向应力和扰度变形看，是满足面板安全运行要求的。

面板坝轴向应力在面板在与河床接触部位出现局部压应力，但整体水平较低，最大值仅2.41MPa，远低于C30混凝土抗拉强度设计值。整个面板受拉趋势较明显，最大拉应力位于连接板底部600～620m高程间，最大值1.67MPa。拉应力虽较大，但低于C30混凝土抗拉强度的设计值，面板受拉整体安全。

3. 结构缝变形规律　水库蓄水后，连接板以左的面板垂直缝拉压变形表现为张开，最大张拉缝5.1mm，右岸面板垂直缝在连接板接缝附近和右岸周边缝附近为张开缝，张开量总体比左岸小，其余靠近河床中间部位大部分为受压。

面板与趾板间的周边缝均为张拉缝，最大24.1mm，位于连接板右侧坝高约1/2处；右岸面板周边缝张开量大于左岸；两岸周边缝剪切位移均指向河谷，最大剪切位移11.9mm，位于右岸靠近河谷部位；周边缝沉陷量相对较小，最大10.6mm，在右岸面板约2/3高程处。

连接板两侧周边缝变形以张开为主，其次为剪切。最大张开变形8.9mm，最大剪切位移5.7mm，最大值均出现在中低高程。从连接板两侧分布规律看，张开值总体上左侧大于右侧，剪切值总体上右侧大于左侧。

各结构缝变形的最大值均出现在面板与趾板周边缝上，变形值未超出目前百米级混凝土面板堆石坝结构缝变形量值的范围，故大坝的防渗结构可靠性是能够得到保证的。

（四）结语

（1）计算成果表明，大坝典型断面应力变形与直线型混凝土面板堆石坝基本一致，面板应力水平和结构缝变形在允许范围内，故凸向下游折线型混凝土面板堆石坝技术可行。

（2）折线型与直线型混凝土面板堆石坝相比，面板拉应力分布范围较大，连接板周边缝及两侧面板结构缝均表现张性缝。故折线型对面板抗拉性能、结构缝拉伸变形能力要求更高。虽计算成果与结构材料参数和已建工程实测值对比，均满足规范要求，但考虑到实际情况复杂性，在详细设计和施工中，还要进一步提高面板抗拉性能、优化结构缝设计。

（3）结构缝变形最为复杂、量值最大处均为右岸趾板周边缝，这与地形条件有关，故有必要在趾板下游局部存在倾向下游陡坎部位设置一定的增模区，控制周边缝变形。

（中国电建集团华东勘测设计研究院有限公司 朱安龙
浙江衢江抽水蓄能有限公司 郑树青）

引水发电建筑物设计

三江口水电站2号引水隧洞扩建关键技术研究

（一）工程概述

三江口水电站是云南保山苏帕河“一库五级”开发的最后一级，原水电站装机容量2×1.5万kW，1993年4月建成发电。随上游各梯级水电站相继建成，特别上一梯级阿鸠田水电站建成发电，为扩建创造了有利条件。扩建新增2台16MW机组，扩建后总装机容量6.2万kW。

原水电站首部枢纽由溢流坝、非溢流坝、冲砂闸、取水闸、上游铺盖、下游护坦、海漫等组成。引水系统布置在苏帕河左岸，由暗渠、隧洞及沉沙池等组成，为无压引水。厂区由压力前池、泄水道、压力钢管、主副厂房、升压站、尾水建筑物及附属建筑物组成。

水电站扩建以引阿鸠田水电站尾水为主，保留原水电站各建筑物及其功能。在阿鸠田水电站尾水出口，把尾水引入扩建的引水系统。扩建主体工程于2005年7月1日开工，2006年8月1日扩建引水系统完成，2009年3月27日，三江口水电站扩建工程通过竣工验收。

（二）引水系统扩建要求

三江口水电站扩建工程，直接引取阿鸠田尾水，经倒虹吸管穿过河底，至左岸新建无压隧洞，再与原引水系统相接；暗渠和沉沙池外边墙加高，2号引水隧洞扩底，压力前池局部改造，降低部分前池底板，新建中隔墙便于冲沙防淤；前池原进水口右侧23m处，新建扩建机组进水口和钢管道，新建主厂房、尾水渠和尾水池；升压站改扩建。

2号引水隧洞埋藏深洞线长，无法布置施工支洞。隧洞扩建需解决的关键技术：扩挖方案，扩建后结构计算模型，新旧混凝土接触处缝面设计，底板深挖安全施工的可行性。

（三）扩挖前2号引水隧洞基本情况

2号引水隧洞为无压洞，城门洞型，直线布置，长3186.455m，进口高程862.139m，出口高程855.766m。按围岩情况分8种衬砌形式（A～H），直墙净高2.35～2.85m，矢高0.97m，净宽3.35m。排水孔距底板2.3m。衬砌厚40～60cm。喷混凝土段占隧洞总长85%。

隧洞断面衬砌内力、配筋计算按圆拱直墙无底板衬砌型式，采用隧洞衬砌静力计算通用程序A=3衬砌型式的程序计算内力、配筋。底板衬砌最后施工，且与边墙间留有变形缝。隧洞衬砌只需按构造配筋，为节省钢筋，采用按内力图分区配筋。

（四）2号引水隧洞扩建设计

1. 扩建方案　经比选无压改有压、顶部扩挖、底板深挖等，最后采用底板深挖方案。

2. 底板下挖深度　前池按正常、最高两种水位工况计算水面线，经计算均为A1型壅水曲线，水面线在3m附近。前池水工模型试验报告要求，为了与前池底板衔接，隧洞出口高程与前池底板高程相同，经测算隧洞出口下挖1.166m。扩建后隧洞出口净空面积$S_1=2.671m^2$，断面面积$S_2=15.736m^2$，$S_1/S_2=16.974\%$，大于规范要求的15%。

3. 底板深挖设计分析　扩建隧洞考虑衬砌自重、内外水压力、山岩压力等荷载。内水压力以衬砌类型在隧洞不同位置，按其对应水面线水深取大值计。外水压力以断面直墙高度＋底板厚度为外水水深。

经分析比较，在完建工况、正常运行工况和检修工况中，选择检修工况为控制工况。计算模型及假定：底板向下深挖时，衬砌不承担上部衬砌的传力；向下深挖的底板、边墙，假设成“凹”结构，底板按弹性地基梁计，边墙按悬臂梁计，下挖边墙深度为悬臂梁梁长。

按此模型和假定计算内力，配筋时考虑原衬砌的钢筋粗细、间距，使扩挖边墙的钢筋间距与原衬砌钢筋间距相同，以便新旧钢筋间焊接和传力。

经计算扩挖衬砌配筋：A、B、D断面外层钢筋ϕ18@250，内层钢筋ϕ14@250，分布筋ϕ10@200。E、F断面外层钢筋ϕ18@200，内层钢筋ϕ14@200，分布筋ϕ10@200。

4. 新旧混凝土缝面设计　结合处缝面应防止内水外渗，且新旧混凝土协同工作。

防内水外渗措施：下挖边墙用膨胀混凝土；缝面适当位置设遇水膨胀止水条；利用水压差防止内水外渗。新旧混凝土协同：使用膨胀混凝土浇筑扩挖边墙混凝土，使新浇混凝土与原混凝土融为一体，协同工作。施工时按斜向下45°拆除原边墙，凿除边墙内侧钢筋处的混凝土。这样延长了渗径，保证下挖边墙混凝土浇筑振捣密实，最大限度保留原衬砌。

把扩挖部分的钢筋与原衬砌里的钢筋单面焊接，边墙受力时，原有钢筋就可把力传给扩挖部分的钢筋，边墙底端外侧受拉由扩挖后配置钢筋承担，这就是共同受力。

5. 底板下挖施工　底板下挖中，为避免顶拱、边墙下滑，在下挖前锚固边墙，下挖后及时用工字钢临时支撑原边墙下方临空面。隧洞衬砌段每边各设上下两排ϕ25锚杆，第一排距原底板0.6m，每根长2m；第二排距原底板1.6m，每根长3m。锚杆间距A型3m，B、D型2.5m，C、E型2m，F型1.5m。喷锚段G、H型只设第一排，距原底板0.6m，每根2m，间距2m。锚杆下倾与水平面成10°倾角。下挖工序：边墙锚杆→下挖中央底板→挖边墙脚下部分→临时工字钢支撑→浇筑底板混凝土→浇筑边墙混凝土。

浅孔小药量松动爆破开挖，分排毫秒起爆。缩短边墙悬空时间，并严密监测变形。

扩建工程自2006年8月投入运行近12年，隧洞各工况运行正常。

（中国电力建设集团昆明勘测设计研究院有限公司　高春涛
云南大学建筑与规划学院　肖梅玲　韩豫萍
广州华南师大附中国际部　喻鑫森）

清远抽水蓄能电站引水隧洞高压灌浆质量控制

清远抽水蓄能电站水道全长2779m。其中，引水道长1765m，由上库进出水口、引水隧洞（上平洞、竖井、中平洞、斜井、下平洞）、引水岔管、引水支管、施工支洞堵头等组成。引水隧洞和岔管采用钢筋混凝土衬砌，前者衬砌厚0.6m，后者厚0.8m。

（一）引水系统灌浆的内容

引水系统灌浆包括固结灌浆、回填灌浆和化学灌浆。引水隧洞的上平洞及竖井上弯段进行固结灌浆和回填灌浆，竖井直段进行固结灌浆，竖井下弯段进行固结灌浆和回填灌浆，中平洞进行固结灌浆和回填灌浆，斜井上弯段进行固结灌浆、回填灌浆和化学灌浆，斜井直段进行固结灌浆和化学灌浆，斜井下弯段进行固结灌浆、回填灌浆和化学灌浆，下平洞进行固结灌浆、回填灌浆和化学灌浆，高压岔口进行固结灌浆、回填灌浆和化学灌浆。

（二）固结灌浆质量控制要点

高压引水隧洞固结灌浆施工前，要编写作业指导书。固结灌浆质量控制要点如下。

（1）做好衬砌混凝土抬动控制及变形监测，在隧洞、岔管、钢衬支管和岔支管相交处，安设变形监测装置，监测灌浆中的变形和裂缝，发现异常，立即降低压力。

（2）埋设好用于灌浆钻孔的黑铁管，其直径大于灌浆孔孔径，并与结构钢筋焊接牢固，确保完好无损。衬砌混凝土浇筑前，灌浆孔的孔位、孔向严格按设计要求布置。

（3）检查钻孔的孔深、孔数、孔向，及钻孔记录。在断层位置增加灌浆孔时，钻孔中发生掉钻、坍孔、钻速变化、回水变色、涌水等异常情况，应做好详细记录。

（4）检查和控制灌浆数据记录，采用自动记录仪记录，压力表、流量计、密度计等应定期校验或率定。各项记录现场检查确认，资料要及时准确、真实齐全。

（5）通过试验确定灌浆参数和方法。采用循环式单孔灌浆、由浅入深、分段灌注。第一段栓塞置于灌浆段衬砌体中，逐级加压，以较低压力结束灌浆；第二段或第三段钻进长度为设计孔深，栓塞置于围岩中，逐级加压，以设计压力结束灌浆。

（6）高压固结灌浆若无外漏、串浆，应严格控制灌浆流量与压力的关系，控制灌浆压力×灌浆流量值（PQ）在设计允许范围，耗浆量较大时，及时采取相应的处理措施。

（7）高压灌浆结束时，先关闭回浆阀，然后停机，待孔口压力表压力降至零，或已经达到浆液终凝时间，再拆除环管及孔口器，确保灌浆封堵质量。

（8）对水道系统前期的勘探孔必须做好封堵和灌浆。对衬砌混凝土浇筑时在围岩中临时埋设的渗漏水引排钢管，在灌浆过程中在钢管上开孔，并用水泥灌浆予以封堵。

（9）对封堵后仍有渗漏冒白浆的灌浆孔，必须扫孔重新灌浆和重新封堵。灌浆后衬砌混凝土表面仍然浸湿严重或渗漏严重的区域，应查明地质原因，补充钻灌。

（10）不良地质洞段不仅进行压水检查，还钻孔取芯和做声波测试检测。

（11）高度重视堵头段高压固结灌浆，按设计要求完成交叉口固结灌浆、回填灌浆和化学灌浆，通过调整灌浆孔孔位、孔向、孔深，有针对性加强灌浆，确保灌浆质量。

（12）按“先洞内后洞外，先水泥后化灌，先浅孔后深孔”，做好灌浆动态设计。

（三）固结灌浆主要效果

固结灌浆灌后压水检查段数占总孔数5.69%，灌前压水透水率与灌后比有明显下降，其透水率均达到了设计水泥灌浆防渗标准。输水系统灌浆自2014年3月16日开始施工，于2015年6月25日完成，共灌注56802.8m，总耗量835227.32kg，平均耗灰量19.83kg/m。

（四）引水道充水过程及其效应

引水道充水从2015年7月21日开始，历时15天。7月30日18时水位到达竖井473.26m开始保压，保压时长24h，7月31日18时保压结束后继续充水，8月2日11时水位到达设计充水高程592.7m，开始第二阶段保压，保压时长48h。

在厂房周围上、中、下层排水廊道、堵头部位和施工支洞与中层排水廊道交叉口等处，共设12座量水堰。充水过程最大增幅仅0.86L/s，最小变化为零。高压水道部位布设钢筋计、四点位移计、测缝计等。除1支钢筋计损坏外，其他测值最大增幅77.03MPa；探洞和排水廊道渗压计最大增幅17.67m；堵头的测缝计、变位计、渗压计等，测值平稳，充水前后错动位移基本无变化，渗压计在蓄水初期呈缓慢增长趋势，后期随水力梯度增长测值增加明显。充水至设计高程稳压后，所有监测仪器测值逐渐趋于平稳和收敛。4台机组进水球阀密封良好，上、下游密封无渗漏，与水道相通的水机管路及阀门无任何渗漏。

（中国水利水电建设工程咨询中南有限公司　张养锋）

觉巴水电站沉沙池设计

西藏觉巴水电站位于澜沧江右岸一级支流登曲中下游河段，为引水式电站，装机容量3万kW。枢纽主要建筑物由首部枢纽建筑物及引水发电建筑物组成，前者由挡水建筑物、泄水消能建筑物和变压式沉沙池组成，后者包括引水建筑物和发电建筑物。变压式沉沙池设在拦河坝左后侧。

（一）沉沙池布置

沉沙池采用变压式，其顶部3221m处设1m厚钢筋混凝土平板封盖，并与边墙和中隔墩整体连接。库水位低于3221m时沉沙池为明流，高于3221m时为有压流。沉沙池包括取水口、渐变段、工作段、尾部溢流堰和冲沙孔。取水口在左岸取水坝段，底高程3218m，设宽4m、高3m平板工作门。工作门前设拦污栅和胸墙。渐变段长28.8m，宽4～11.6m，底高程由3218m到3215m。工作段净尺寸长150m、宽10m，顺水流向正中间设1.6m厚隔墙，将其分为两厢，顶板面高程3222m，进口净高6m，前100m底坡1%，后50m底坡3%。沉沙池每厢进口设宽2.5m、高6m平板闸门。沉沙池尾部设溢流堰，堰顶高程3218m，堰顶设宽5m、高3.1m平板闸门。溢流堰底部各沉沙室内设宽3m、高1.5m排沙孔，其底高程3210.5m。溢流堰后接引水隧洞，直接与沉沙池相接，引水隧洞进口底板高程3213m。

沉沙池的运行将是明满流交替，为在流态改变时给沉沙池补气或排气，在工作段每箱顶板中部每隔20m设1根ϕ300mm通气钢管。通气管顶高程与坝顶高程（3230m）相同，通气管外露部分均包裹保温材料。

（二）沉沙池水力计算

1. 宽度计算　目前无适合觉巴水电站沉沙池的设计规范。登曲河水流含沙量0.787kg/m^3、输沙率

4.46kg/s，水电站最大水头 603m，参照《水电水利工程沉沙池设计规范》（DL/T 5107），推荐觉巴水电站设计最小沉降粒径 0.1mm，大于等于此粒径泥沙沉降率为 80%～85%。

沉沙池工作段底坡均大于临界底坡，满足上述规范要求。根据经验，沉沙池进口水深不宜小于 4m，池底高程结合周边地形设计。沉沙池运行水位 3220～3230m，池内平均水深 6.25～7.25m。按规范要求及设计条件，最小沉沙粒径 0.1mm，设计流量 6.15m^3/s，淤积深按 25% 考虑，沉沙池净宽 10m。经计算，沉沙池平均流速 0.113～0.131m/s，在 0.05～0.15m/s 之间，满足规范的要求。

2. 长度计算　根据实测和有关泥沙资料，确定泥沙级配曲线，将泥沙分 6 组。登曲河泥沙含量沿程变化表现为指数型关系，可采用超饱和输沙法简化后的一维公式计算。根据各粒径组质量百分比和沉降率计算得到总沉降率为 23.3%，大于 0.1mm 的沉降率为 95.6%，满足规范要求，最终确定沉沙池工作段长度 150m。

3. 冲沙周期确定　采用定期冲洗方式。根据《水电水利工程沉沙池设计规范》（DL/T 5107）中相关公式，计算得冲洗周期为 26.4 天。

（三）沉沙池模型试验

沉沙池进行了整体水工模型试验，模型比尺 1∶35，模型试验主要结论如下。

（1）一次洪水历时 96h，来水含沙浓度分别为 1.578kg/m^3、2.367kg/m^3 时，泥沙有害粒径 $D_p \geqslant$ 0.1mm 的沉降百分数为 90.77%～98.42%，满足规范要求。

（2）死水位 3220m 时，沉沙池降水冲沙效果较好。左厢 41min 左右可将池内淤沙基本冲干净，右厢约冲 1h 可冲干净。降水冲沙时冲沙道保持明流，进口闸门局开 0.42～0.63m，冲沙流量 7.54～10.50m^3/s。

（3）正常蓄水位 3228m 冲沙时，左右厢进口闸门局开小于 1.7m 时，沉沙池水面和水翅不会砸顶部。

（4）冲沙试验表明，沉沙池及冲沙设施体型合理，能使池中淤沙全部冲走。在明流及满流情况下流态都很好。

（5）一厢发电，一厢冲沙时，过水厢流态较好，冲沙厢水位和冲沙流量容易控制，池内淤沙可全部冲走。可满足一厢冲沙，一厢发电要求。

（四）结构设计

计算工况①一厢发电一厢冲沙，工况②两厢同时过流发电。断面选工作段尾部最大断面。在此条件下，确定已有结构尺寸和水力参数，及结构混凝土基本参数，用有限元程序 ANSYS 计算不同工况下典型断面轴力、剪力及弯矩后，再根据《水工混凝土结构设计规范》（SL 191）计算结构配筋：工作段边墙、底板、顶板及中隔墙内外层环向受力筋均配 ϕ18@100（三级筋），分布筋均采用 ϕ16@200（三级筋）。

觉巴水电站于 2016 年 1 月首台机组正式投入商业运行，从外观检查及停机后内部检查情况来看，沉沙池结构稳定，冲沙效果较好，工作状况良好。

（中国电建集团昆明勘测设计研究院有限公司　孔伟）

泄水建筑物设计

白鹤滩水电站水力过渡过程研究

白鹤滩水电站总装机容量 1600 万 kW，左右岸各设 4 个水力单元，16 台单机容量 100 万 kW 混流式水轮发电机组，左右岸机组额定转速分别为 107.1r/min、111.1r/min。引水隧洞 1 洞 1 机布置、尾水隧洞 2 机 1 洞布置。尾水隧洞较长，左右岸各设 4 座尾水阻抗式调压室。

（一）设计前期阶段过渡过程研究

该阶段过渡过程计算要确定整体布置方案，建筑物的体形、尺寸及初选机组参数。

1. 洞机组合比选　考虑地下洞室与地质构造、地应力夹角等，经比选初步确定两种尾水隧洞布置形式：①3 台机组（3 洞方案）共用 1 个尾调室和 1 条尾水隧洞；②两台机组（4 洞方案）共用 1 个尾调室和 1 条尾水隧洞。经计算两方案大波动各控制参数数值相当，小波动均能较快稳定，调节品质相当，方案②水力干扰程度略优于方案①，差别很小，均满足要求；水力条件不构成控制性因素。综合考虑结构、围岩稳定等因素，选定方案②。

2. 局部建筑物优化　即调压室阻抗孔面积、右 2 和右 3 调压室上室底板高程比选。

按规范要求选取5个阻抗孔直径（6.8m、7.2m、7.6m、8.0m、8.4m）进行计算。结果表明：各方案尾水管进口最小压力计算结果相同，均为−1.75m，满足设计要求。当阻抗孔直径小于7.2m时，尾水管检修闸门井涌波出现降低趋势，继续减小阻抗孔面积将会加大尾水管检修闸门室漏空风险，不利于机组安全运行。综合考虑减小尾水管压力、尾水调压室及尾水管检修闸门室涌波幅度要求，该阶段按适当留有余地原则，阻抗孔直径确定为7.6m。

右2和右3调压室受层间错动带影响大，为改善其顶拱围岩稳定性，考虑通过设上室降低顶拱高程，上室兼做通气洞。研究表明，2号调压室上室底板高程低于624m时，其最高涌波受底板高程影响较小。从水力学角度考虑，底板高程624m较优。同时考虑上室需兼顾通气洞布置要求，故确定底部高程628m。3号调压室上室底板高程低于625m时，其最高涌波受底板高程影响较小，且能兼顾相关布置要求，故确定3号上室底板高程625m。

左岸3条、右岸2条尾水隧洞结合导流洞布置，水位较低时，结合段会出现明满流交替现象。模型试验和数值计算结果表明，尾水隧洞出口设逆坡堰可缩短明满流范围，削弱尾水波动对输水系统影响。衔接段坡度15%时，可逼明满流进入缓坡段，水头损失较小，且便于施工。此外，衔接段末端设通气孔，可有效减小明满流引起压力波动，改善其流态。

3. 整体模型试验验证　优选输水系统方案做了整体模型试验。在稳定运行状态下测量输水系统各部位水头损失、压力水头及沿程流态。过渡过程状态下，研究输水系统各部位压力极值、闸门室及尾水调压室内水位波动特性及相互影响、尾水调压室底部岔管流态及尾水隧洞明满流段水力特性。对比分析试验和数值模拟结果，总体评价认为白鹤滩引水发电系统的流道体型合理，输水系统各建筑物水力特性满足规范要求，且有一定裕度。

4. 机组参数优选

（1）机组转动惯量敏感性分析：以厂家提供的机组转动惯量为基准值，选5组值（83.33%、88.89%、94.44%、100%、105.56%）进行过渡过程计算。结果表明，转动惯量对蜗壳和尾水管进口压力影响不大，机组最大转速上升率随转动惯量增加而减小，厂家的转动惯量参数、调保参数均满足控制要求且有一定裕度，机组转动惯量设计取值合理。

（2）转轮特性敏感性分析：采用107.1r/min、111.1r/min两档转速代表性模型转轮进行计算。结果表明，对常规混流式机组，由于单位流量随开度呈线性变化，在相同关闭规律条件下，两档转速方案蜗壳和尾水管压力总体相当，而机组转速上升率由于机组惯性时间常数不同略有差异，说明两种水轮机模型转轮特性对水力过渡过程影响不大。

（3）导叶关闭规律优化：设计前期阶段原则上采用一段直线关闭规律，同时对两段折线关闭规律进行初步分析，为下阶段机组参数优化提供参考。一段直线关闭规律分析表明，为满足机组转速最大上升率和蜗壳进口最大压力控制要求，该阶段两种机组型号统一采用12s一段直线关闭规律。两段折线关闭规律分析表明，以总关闭时间12 s为基础，折点相对开度取50%，随第一段关闭时间的缩短，相应机组最大转速上升率可降低至40.92%，可见采用两段折线关闭规律可有效控制机组最大转速上升率。

（二）施工阶段过渡过程复核

施工阶段对设计前期阶段优化后的发电输水系统，进行水力过渡过程复核计算分析。

1. 大波动水力特性　根据初步成果，先选择控制性水力单元对各大波动计算工况进行系统计算分析，再复核计算其他水力单元的控制性工况，从而得到所有水力单元大波动控制性特征参数，包括蜗壳进口最大压力、尾水管进口最小压力等11项参数。结果表明，各大波动计算成果均满足过渡过程控制标准要求，且有一定安全裕度。

2. 水力干扰计算结果　在功率调节、并理想大电网频率调节和孤网频率调节三种模式下，计算受扰机组最大出力与额定出力比值为1.043～1.081，比值均没有超过1.1，满足控制要求。孤网频率模式下，受扰机组调节品质较差，部分工况机组转速进入±0.4%带宽时间较长，机组转速偏差较大，振荡次数较多，但系统稳定。

3. 小波动计算结果　选择右1和右4水力单元小波动过渡过程计算。结果表明，在控制工况下，两台机组同时减5%额定负荷，2种额定转速机组在各工况下最大转速偏差最大3.5%，振荡次数不超过1.5次，进入±0.4%频率带宽调节时间不超过37s。两台机组同时减10%额定负荷，2种额定转速机组在各工况下最大转速偏差最大6.2%，振荡次数不超过1.5次，进入±0.4%频率带宽调节时间不超过35s。两种转速方案机组的小波动均稳定。

（中国电建集团华东勘测设计研究院有限公司
吴关叶　陈顺义　李高会　孙洪亮　吕慷　陈益民）
（中国长江三峡集团公司机电工程局　戴江）

长龙山抽水蓄能电站下水库泄水建筑物优化研究

长龙山抽水蓄能电站在浙江省安吉县天荒坪镇境

内，电站装机容量 210 万 kW。枢纽由上水库、下水库、输水系统、地下厂房及开关站组成。下水库位于山河港中下游河段，挡水坝为钢筋混凝土面板堆石坝，最大坝高 95.5m。

（一）泄洪建筑物方案拟定

1. 溢洪道调节方式比较　在可行性研究阶段，下水库泄洪设施包括左岸开敞式溢洪道和右岸泄放洞，选定了其相应规模，并按 100 年一遇洪电站正常发电标准选择溢洪道设闸门方案。招标阶段对下水库岸边设表孔溢洪道进行研究。

溢洪道设闸门时，为确保总下泄流量不大于坝址入库洪水流量，闸门控制随库水位和泄放洞泄流变化而变化，风险较大。洪水泄量小于入库洪水时，可能致库水位抬高，危及电站安全；大于入库洪水时，可能影响下游潘村水库行洪安全。不设闸门时，库水位低于正常蓄水位，只需控制泄放洞闸门排放洪水；超过正常蓄水位，泄放洞和溢洪道联合排放洪水，溢洪道自由溢流，泄放洞控制下泄流量，溢洪道无须操作管理，运行可靠。此外，设与不设闸门投资差别不大。

2. 泄放洞设置必要性　经下水库调洪计算，按各频率洪水位不超过可研审定水位为原则，下水库不设泄放洞情况下，洪水期电站发电受极大限制。从电网需求看，抽水蓄能电站洪水期宜满足日平均装机利用小时 3h 要求，下水库不设泄放洞，洪水期日平均装机利用小时不能满足电网需求，故设置泄放洞是必要的。为此，下水库泄洪建筑物改为右岸泄放洞+左岸开敞自流式侧堰溢洪道方案。

（二）泄洪建筑物规模比选

根据调洪计算，20 年一遇洪水时泄放洞全开，堰长 60m 下库水位与可研阶段审定洪水位接近，故选用 60m，堰顶高程 243m。选 3 个泄放洞最大泄流量（$200m^3/s$、$150m^3/s$、$100m^3/s$）方案比较，且以发电保证率基本相当为前提。

1. 调洪成果　方案 1、方案 2，20 年一遇洪水时，电站发电基本不受影响，满发时间 5.72h，且水位不超审定洪水位；方案 3，20 年一遇洪水时，满发时间降至 5.62h，且水位超审定洪水位 0.2m，即使不发电，亦超过审定洪水位 0.18m。

2. 模型试验结果　①泄放洞出口下游消能防冲都可行，无河床冲刷；②泄放洞泄洪下游呈射流状，水流未冲击对岸岸坡；③泄放洞出口与大坝坝脚间有弱回流，流速 0.9～0.7m/s，出口左侧边坡回流流速 3.8～1.6m/s，出口对岸边坡回流流速 2.9～2m/s；④出水渠尾坎顶流速 3.7～1.7m/s，尾坎后有跌流。

3. 工程投资　3 个方案基本相当，投资额度与泄流量呈正相关。

综上所述，3 个方案中，方案 1、方案 2 洪水期发电标准基本相当，均高于方案 3；从下游消能和工程长期运行安全考虑，方案 2 比方案 1 有利，且其投资略小。故推荐方案 2，即导流泄放洞泄流规模约 $150m^3/s$ 方案。

（三）泄水建筑物布置

1. 溢流道　溢洪道沿左岸坝头布置，泄槽轴线与坝轴线夹角 68°，由侧堰、侧槽、控制段、泄槽、挑流鼻坎和出水渠组成，全长 467.18m。侧堰长 60m，堰顶高程 243m（同正常蓄水位），堰面为 WES 曲线。侧槽为近似梯形泄槽，首端高程 232.98m，宽 7m，末端高程 230m，宽 14m，槽长 59.6m，纵坡 0.05。控制段是侧槽与泄槽间连接段，长 36m，底宽 14m，底板高程 230m，断面由梯形渐变为矩形，后段为 $R=16m$ 圆弧与泄槽连接。泄槽断面矩形，底宽 14m，长 164.05m，纵坡 1∶2.44，底板钢筋混凝土厚 0.6m，泄槽段布置 2 个掺气槽。挑流鼻坎为斜切式连续挑坎，反弧半径 25m，左右侧出口挑角分别为 30°、15°。鼻坎后设长 11.5m 厚 1m 护坦，下游与出水渠底相接。出水渠预挖冲坑段长 149.99m，渠底高程 141m，末端设混凝土尾坎，顶高程 150m。

2. 泄放洞　布置在下水库右岸，由进口段、有压隧洞段、出口工作门段、出口消能工段组成。进口高程 175m，引水渠长 35m，进水渠底高程 174.5m。有压隧洞断面为圆形，内径 5m，检修闸门在隧洞首部，隧洞自进口渐变段后底坡 4.223%。隧洞上覆围岩厚度不够，采用钢板衬砌，内径渐变 D3.2m 圆形。隧洞末端有弧形工作门，孔口尺寸 1.8m×2.4m（宽×高），弧门底坎高程 154.5m。出口消能工为近似底流与面流混合消能，工作弧门后设消力池，两侧为混凝土护坡，渐扩布置，底板为 1∶3 斜坡，底板宽度由 3m 渐变为 12m，高程由 153.5m 降至 142m。

（四）水工模型试验验证

水工模型试验表明，选定的方案溢洪道、泄放洞结构设计合理，泄流能力满足设计要求，溢洪道和泄洪洞单独及联合开启时，下游消能效果良好。

（中国电建集团华东勘测设计研究院有限公司
符晓　郎玲芳　徐建伟　陈晓江）

绩溪抽水蓄能电站竖井式溢洪道优化设计

（一）竖井式溢洪道结构布置

绩溪抽水蓄能电站开敞式竖井溢洪道，设在下水库大坝右库岸，由进口段、竖井、退水隧洞、泄槽段、消力池、护坦、出水渠组成。溢流堰初步设计采用实用堰，上游接圆弧，圆弧半径 1m；溢流堰为扇形，堰顶处半径 7m，堰顶高程同正常蓄水位 340m，溢流净宽 15.87m，堰顶不设闸门，两侧设防涡导墙。竖井为内径 6m 等径圆形竖井，为防止水流冲击其底板，在底部设深 6m 消能井。消能井后接压坡段，长 6.8m，顶部压坡坡度 1∶6。压坡段后接无压退水隧洞，坡降 5.5%，长 74.3m，城门洞形，4m×5m（宽×高）。退水隧洞出口接护坦、消力池及出水渠，护坦长 1m，消力池长 27m、深 3m。泄槽沿下游冲沟地形布置，长 225m，底坡 1∶9，梯形断面，底宽 8m，高 3m，两侧坡比 1∶1。

经优化后溢洪道布置如下：进口溢流堰为环形薄壁堰，堰顶不设闸门。堰顶内径 9m，堰宽 1.5m，堰顶高程同正常蓄水位 340m，堰高 14m。堰底部接竖井，竖井为内径 5m 圆形竖井，深 17.5m。压坡段后接退水隧洞，长 88m，底坡 1∶16，城门洞形，3.5m×5.3m（宽×高）。退水隧洞出口接泄槽段，长 214.5m，底坡 1∶9，梯形断面，底宽 8m，高 4m，两侧坡比 1∶0.75。消力池在泄槽段末端，长 38m，梯形断面，底宽 8m，池深 3m，两侧坡比 1∶0.75。消力池后设 20m 长的护坦。

（二）溢洪道溢流堰体型优化

模型试验结果表明，原溢流堰设计泄流能力虽满足要求，但受进口侧收缩影响，溢流堰后水流表面存在明显水翅，导致水流冲击竖井边壁，故进口体型需适当修改。

修改中采用 3 个环形进流方案。试验结果表明，3 个方案均满足泄流能力要求，水流没有冲击竖井边壁。方案 1 在不同泄量下，各孔水舌底部存在水翅，水舌形态不稳定。方案 2 进口流速小，水流虽沿竖井壁下泄，未能形成旋转水流流态。在消能井内水流不断旋转，间歇性出现水内漩涡，将对竖井边壁产生不利影响。方案 3 在不同工况下，水流流态良好，6 孔水舌正向对撞合并后沿竖井中心下落，水流没有冲击竖井边壁，水舌底部不存在水翅，形态稳定。故最终选定方案 3（见图 1）。

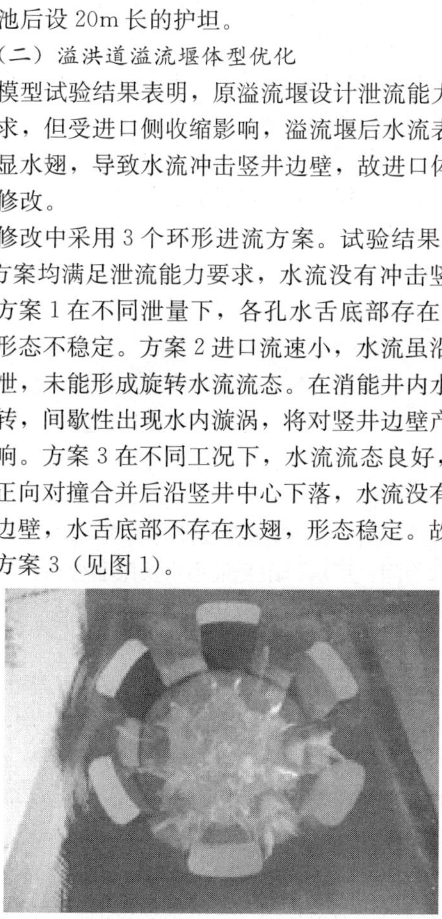

图 1 环形进流方案 3

（三）溢洪道消能方式优化

试验结果发现：退水洞进口压板处水流脱空，压板体型需修改。退水洞段明流段内水面最高达直墙顶，直墙高度需加高。消力池水流流态差，体积偏小，水流外溢明显。

针对进口压板处水流脱空现象，进行了 3 个方案的修改试验，把压板末端孔口高度分别减小为 2.0m、1.8m、1.6m。通过试验确定退水洞宽度 4m，压板末端孔口高度 1.8～2.0m 较合适，相应的明流段直墙加高 1.0～1.5m。

原方案中竖井和消力池设在溢洪道上半部分，消力池后有 21m 落差无配置消能设施。且退水洞出口之后设消力池，需相当大体积，才能达到理想消能效果。经试验，采用“竖井、台阶式泄槽和下游消力池联合消能”优化方案。在 5 个不同泄洪工况下，观测退水洞出口断面和下游消力池出口断面的水深和平均流速，并计算得出，优化方案的消能率达到 98.3%～93.9%，达到了理想的消能效果。

（四）溢洪道泄槽结构优化

试验中泄槽尾部平面转弯段因弯道半径不足、转角偏大，在惯性作用下，水流在弯道中部沿右侧边坡直接冲出边墙。结合消能方式的优化，退水隧洞出口接泄槽段，沿下游冲沟地形布置，取消出口转弯段，出口布置消力池。泄槽段长 214.5m，渠底坡坡比 1∶9，梯形断面，底宽 8m，高 4m，两侧坡比 1∶0.75，渠底及两侧采用 0.5m 厚 C25 混凝土衬砌。泄槽段底板沿程设台阶消能，台阶尺寸 4.5m×0.5m（宽×高）。

（五）溢洪道支护措施优化

（1）竖井、退水隧洞支护：根据计算成果，竖井、退水隧洞支护由原来 CF40 钢纤维硅粉混凝土衬砌，改为 $C_{90}50$ 硅粉混凝土衬砌，退水隧洞拱顶改为 C30 混凝土衬砌。

（2）泄槽段开挖边坡：为避免泄槽—护坦段开挖中顺坡面剥皮开挖，将该段混凝土贴坡区开挖坡比由原设计 1∶1，改为 1∶0.75，边坡开挖由原设计 10m 一级马道，调整为 15～18m 一级马道。

同时，为进一步降低退水隧洞出口高边坡，本阶段考虑退水隧洞加长 18m，提前进洞。根据退水隧洞围岩类别，经洞室围岩稳定计算，对退水隧洞进出口段进行了施工期强支护，以确保退水隧洞进、出口段洞室稳定和施工安全。

（中国电建集团华东勘测设计研究院有限公司
邵卿 符晓 郎玲芳）

沙坪二级水电站厂房坝段防排沙优化设计

（一）工程概况

沙坪二级水电站位于四川省峨边彝族自治县境内大渡河干流上。枢纽由河床式厂房、泄洪闸、鱼道组成。河床式厂房布置在左岸台地上，厂内有6台单机容量为58MW灯泡贯流式机组，水电站总装机容量348MW。

坝址处天然情况下多年平均含沙量0.854kg/m³。考虑上游瀑布沟、深溪沟建成后水库拦沙作用，坝址多年平均含沙量0.207kg/m³，多年平均悬移质输沙量902万t，推移质年输沙量1万t。为避免推移质、减少悬移质通过机组流道，降低泥沙对水轮发电机组造成磨蚀，预可研设计阶段，参考深溪沟和枕头坝一级、下游龚嘴水电站排沙设计，沙坪二级水电站设3个冲沙孔。厂房结构为两机一缝布置，结合灯泡贯流式机组结构特点，冲沙孔布置两机间的中墩内，冲沙孔断面4.5m×5.0m（宽×高）。

可研阶段勘探揭示出枢纽区左岸进水口前缘边坡分布有较大范围的崩坡积体，崩坡积体的稳定为工程制约因素之一。如设计取消冲沙孔布置，可缩短厂房长度，避免对崩坡积体坡脚开挖的扰动影响、降低边坡开挖支护难度，对边坡稳定有利。取消冲沙孔也可减少厂房土建工程量，缩短电站施工工期，降低工程投资。考虑到深溪沟、枕头坝、龚嘴等水电站均设厂房冲沙孔，沙坪二级水电站是否取消厂房冲沙孔布置，须慎重分析论证。

（二）取消厂房冲沙孔的可行性论证

取消厂房冲沙孔后，枢纽坝段长度缩短13.5m，减少了左岸山体的开挖，避免对崩坡积体的扰动。综合已建水电站资料，在厂房坝段布置冲沙孔的水电站中，冲沙孔运行时有的有振动问题。尤其灯泡贯流式厂房空腔比大，自重相对较轻，厂房振动问题需引起重视。如取消冲沙孔，可避免冲沙过程中引起厂房的振动，有利于尾水平台上GIS等设施安全运行。

1. 上游梯级水电站拦蓄作用及防排沙条件　沙坪二级投产发电时序晚于上游瀑布沟、深溪沟、枕头坝一级，考虑诸水电站的拦蓄作用，坝址处多年平均含沙量降低为0.207kg/m³。

沙坪二级水电站枢纽主要由泄洪闸、河床式发电厂房组成，前者布置在主河道、后者布置在左岸台地。厂房进水口为侧向进水，进水渠前缘基本未侵占天然主河道，进水口位置有利厂房引水防沙。泄洪建筑物设在原主河道，有利水电站泄洪排沙。厂房进水渠底板高于泄洪闸底板，泄洪过程中，闸前推移质泥沙将沿主河槽排入下游河道，不会对进水口造成较大影响。经泥沙淤积计算，淤积平衡后，坝前泥沙淤积高程低于厂房进水渠底板高程。

2. 水电站水库运行条件　沙坪二级水电站水库库容较小，水库正常蓄水位554m。当入库流量大于3000m³/s时，库水位降至550m运行。随泄洪流量增大，下游水位逐渐抬高，发电水头逐渐减小。下泄流量大于6200m³/s，上下游水头差已低于机组发电最小水头，此时机组停止发电。汛期大流量机组停止发电有利于避开泥沙高峰，减轻泥沙对机组的磨蚀。

受灯泡贯流式厂房结构特点制约，厂房流道进口底板与冲沙孔进口底板间高差一般不太大。预可研阶段，厂房流道进口底高程520m，冲沙孔进口底高程513.2m，高差6.8m。设冲沙孔的灯泡贯流式厂房有沙坡头和百龙滩电站，流道与冲沙孔高差，沙坡头为5.05m，百龙滩2.5m。由于流道与冲沙孔高差不大，且机组流道断面（16.2m×14.7m）较冲沙孔断面大很多，发电运行期间开启冲沙孔对降低过机泥沙效果有限，冲沙孔作用不大。

陈上群等分析国内外一些水电站资料后，提出了水轮机磨损问题的判别式：$HS_d>7$（式中H为电站水头，S_d为粒径大于0.05mm的平均含沙量），认为HS_d大于7时泥沙对水轮机磨损严重。沙坪二级水电站设计水头14.3m，粒径大于0.05mm平均含沙量0.052kg/m³，则HS_d为0.74，远小于7，水轮机磨损问题不会突出。

3. 拦排沙建筑物设计　沙坪二级水电站泄洪闸布置在原主河道，厂房进水口布置在左岸，位于微弯河道（凹岸）偏下游位置，采用侧向进水方式引水，进水渠前缘基本未侵占天然主河道。厂房进水渠口门位置设顺原河岸方向的拦沙坎，拦沙坎顶高程高出泄洪闸底板7m，进水口布置设计对厂房引水防沙有利。大洪水期间，厂房机组受最小水头限制停机运行，河道推移质泥沙将沿主河槽从泄洪闸排入下游河道，泥沙淤积不会对厂房进水口造成较大影响。

为防止泄洪闸下泄泥沙在下游向左侧厂房尾水渠扩散淤积，在厂房尾水渠设置一道尾水拦沙坎，拦沙坎与厂坝间尾水导墙相连。尾水拦沙坎设置以不抬高正常的发电尾水为原则，经计算比选，拦沙坎高度为5m，坎顶低于一台机发电尾水位2m。

4. 水工模型试验验证　为验证电站泥沙淤积状况，检验泄洪时对厂房进水口前泥沙的拦沙效果，在水工泥沙模型试验中进行了进水口推移质沙带模拟试验。试验分别采用 5 年、50 年一遇洪水流量进行。试验结果表明，推移质基本上没有翻过拦沙坎进入厂房进水口区域；即使在假设拦沙坎前堆满推移质泥沙的情况下，泄洪闸敞泄后也会将坎前泥沙冲走。水工模型试验同时表明，在汛期厂房停机时段，会有少量的细颗粒泥沙通过悬浮形式越过拦沙坎，落淤在厂房进水口前，但当电站开始引水发电后，落淤在进水口的泥沙会迅速被水流冲走。

（中国电建集团华东勘测设计研究院有限公司
田建海　刘加进　郭德昌）

新荣水电站水力过渡过程分析研究

（一）概述

新荣水电站在西藏昌都地区洛隆县，装机容量 5000kW（4×1250kW），压力钢管采用“一管四机”“卜”形明敷布置，主管内径 4.5m，未设调压井，地面式厂房。水电站出线电压等级为 35kV、10kV。3 台机组（①～③号机组）与 1 台主变压器组成扩大单元接线，升压至 35kV 电压等级以一回长 26.4km 线路接入宗扎措水电站；另 1 台机组（④号机组）与 1 台主变压器组成单元接线，升压至 10kV 电压等级以一回线路至达龙乡，另一回线路至新荣乡。

机组基本参数：水轮机为立轴混流式，型号为 HLA551c-LJ-120，额定出力 1330kW，转轮直径 1.2m，机组安装高程 3248m，吸出高度 0.00m，单台机组额定流量 $7.56m^3/s$，发电机单机容量 1250kW，额定转速 300r/min，飞逸转速 550r/min，机组转动惯量 $25.48t \cdot m^2$，调速器为高油压蓄能罐组合式微机调速器，进水阀为高压蓄能液控双平板蝶阀。

（二）调节保证计算控制值

调节保证计算的目的是根据电站压力输水系统特性和机组转动惯量，选定导水机构的合理关闭时间，保证在选定关闭时间内，压力和转速变化不超过允许值。本电站额定水头 19m。《小型水力发电站设计规范》（GB 50071）规定，额定水头在 40m 以下，蜗壳最大允许压力上升率不得大于 70%，机组额定出力甩全负荷时，最大转速上升率不宜大于 50%～60%。

电站调节保证计算控制值如下：① 机组甩负荷时最大转速升高率不超过 50%（电站占系统容量 56%）；②蜗壳末端最大压力上升率不得大于 70%；③尾水管进口断面最大真空保证值经修正不大于 4.4m；④引水系统管道顶部压力水头都不小于 2m。

（三）计算工况

1. 大波动过渡过程　根据电站引水系统的特点，大波动过渡过程的计算工况如下。

（1）设计工况 D1：上游正常蓄水位 3269.2m，额定水头 19m，4 台机组同时甩全负荷；D2：下游最低尾水位 3248.00m，机组最大水头 21.47m，4 台机组同时甩额定负荷；D3：上游死水位 3267.10m，下游正常尾水位 3248.80m，4 台机组运行，1 台机组增负荷。

（2）校核工况 D4：上游正常蓄水位 $H_{上}$ 为 3269.2m，下游正常尾水位 $H_{下尾}$ 为 3248.8m，4 台机组同时甩额定负荷，其中①号机组导叶拒动；D5：$H_{上}$ 为 3269.2m，$H_{下尾}$ 为 3248.8m，4 台机组同时甩额定负荷，其中④号机组导叶拒动；D6：$H_{上}$ 为 3269.20m，$H_{下尾}$ 为 3248.8m，3 台机组同时甩全负荷后，另 1 台机组（④号机组）甩全负荷；D7：$H_{上}$ 为 3269.20m，$H_{下尾}$ 为 3248.80m，1 台机组（④号机组）甩全负荷后，另 3 台机组同时甩全负荷。

2. 小波动过渡过程　计算目的是为了整定调速器参数，研究在负荷阶跃条件下，机组转速、导叶开度、机组出力变化规律，以保证机组稳定运行、良好调节品质和供电质量。

小波动过渡过程的计算工况 X1：$H_{上}$ 为 3269.2m，额定水头 19m，4 台机组额定出力时，同时突减 10%负荷；X2：$H_{上}$ 为 3269.20m，额定水头 19m，4 台机组 80%额定出力时，同时突减 10%负荷；X3：$H_{上}$ 为 3269.20m，$H_{下尾}$ 为 3248.80m，4 台机组 80%额定出力时，同时突减 10%负荷；

3. 水力干扰　电站机组联入有限电网，其能力将影响电网的供电质量，数值计算的目的就是研究运行机组在受扰动情况下的调节品质。

计算中采用小波动过渡过程整定的调速器参数，对参与调频条件下机组出力变化和机组调节品质进行如下 3 种工况的水力干扰过渡过程计算。即 GR1：上游正常蓄水位 3269.2m，额定水头 19m，①～③号机组额定出力正常运行，④号机组甩额定负荷；GR2：上游正常蓄水位 3269.2m，额定水头 19m，①～③号机组额定出力正常运行，④号机组从空载增至额定负荷；GR3：上游正常蓄水位 3269.2m，额定水头 19m，④号机组额定出力正常运行，①～③号机组同甩额定负荷。

（四）过渡过程计算结果

采用武汉大学水电站过渡过程可视化软件 TOPsys-TP 计算。计算前绘制从进水口到机组的计算简图，确定对应引水发电系统计算参数。系统计算参数包括机组管段的长度、当量直径、波速、糙率、发电局部水头损失、发电岔管水头损失等。

1. 大波动过渡过程计算结果　经过计算，对其结果进行数据分析，表明蜗壳末端最大动水压力、尾水管进口真空度、转速上升率等均满足调保控制值要求，说明采用导叶直线有效关闭时间为5.55s的关闭规律是合理的。

2. 小波动过渡过程计算结果　在小波动稳定性分析过程中，着重分析各工况机组转速动态过程，即调节品质分析。计算结果表明，对于3种小波动工况下的各台机组转速（发电频率）均能在60s内进入±0.2%带宽，调节稳定性都较好，满足小波动设计要求。

3. 水力干扰过渡过程计算结果　在运行机组调速器参与调节条件下进行水力干扰计算。结果表明3种正常运行机组受水力干扰后的出力摆动幅度不超过20%，振荡次数最多3次，机组稳定性较好，波动总趋势收敛，理论上不会造成事故扩大，使运行机组甩负荷。

新荣水电站4台机组已于2017年4月15日投入运行，情况良好，洛隆县电网供电品质得到了极大的提升，过渡过程分析研究为机组及电网的稳定运行提供有力的保证。

（中国电建集团中南勘测设计研究院有限公司　龙良民）

鱼塘水电站溢洪道泄槽段水毁原因

（一）工程概况

鱼塘水电站位于贵州省遵义市道真仡佬族苗族自治县境内，水电站以发电为主，兼顾灌溉、养殖等要求，装机2台，总装机容量75MW，二等大（2）型工程。枢纽由混凝土面板堆石坝、左岸开敞式岸边溢洪道、右岸引水隧洞、地面厂房及升压站等组成。工程于2003年动工兴建，2007年完成竣工安全鉴定。

溢洪道泄槽段地面高程421.8～446.0m，地形坡角35°，基岩裸露，出露地层为灰岩，岩层倾向与坡向相同，倾角与地形坡角基本一致，走向与泄槽纵轴线夹角近于垂直。沿线地质构造简单，岩体强、弱风化带下限埋深分别为4～7m和10～12m。

开敞式溢洪道紧靠左岸坝肩布置，由进水渠、闸室段、泄槽段、消力池组成。开敞式闸室有3孔，单孔孔口闸门尺寸14.5m×16.0m（宽×高）。溢流堰为WES曲线型低实用堰，闸室长33.4m。泄槽段为等宽矩形断面，槽宽51.5m，3孔共用1槽。泄槽为分离式底板，底板厚1～2m。底流消能，池长122.372m，净宽51.5m，底板厚2m。尾部设连续式尾槛。

（二）泄槽底板水毁情况及原因分析

2014年7月18日，在泄洪后发现溢洪道泄槽2～3段部分底板出现损坏，主要集中在左侧，损毁面积662m^2。

从泄槽第1段板1-2和板1-3缝间残留止水片情况看，损毁的主要原因是由于板1与板2间横向止水片下游翼板与混凝土黏接不紧密，高速水流从止水片与混凝土间缝隙窜入泄槽底板下，引起其抬动，并撕裂两侧止水片，从而掀翻泄槽底板。

（三）修复方案

为确保汛期泄洪安全，防止水毁进一步加剧和扩大，特别是防止泄洪时对右侧挡墙基础的淘刷，先临时用C40素混凝土回填水毁区至原溢洪道结构面，周边缝不做止水处理，缝面填充沥青油毡作为隔缝材料。此后，做了永久性修复。

1. 修复设计原则　芙蓉江在5月进入汛期，5月上旬常有大洪水发生，溢洪道在每年汛期都必须泄洪，故必须在2015年2月底前完成泄槽底板全部修复施工。底板修复原则上按原设计恢复，包括体型、止排水、基础处理等，修复设计应加强底板的混凝土强度、厚度、锚筋、止排水及基础处理等。

2. 修复方案细部设计　泄槽体型仍按照原设计进行恢复。修复范围为桩号溢0+039～溢0+069段泄槽全部分离式底板，即板2－1～板2－4、板3－1～板3－4，共8块底板重新浇筑。细部设计如下。

（1）底板拆除范围：临时抢险方案实施完成后，混凝土已回填至溢洪道底板原结构溢流面。全部拆除抢险回填的C40混凝土，未冲毁但已松动的底板拆除至原结构基础。

（2）底板修复设计：原冲坑区域清基处理后用C20混凝土回填至底板基础高程。按原结构设计恢复拆除后的底板，底板为原设计厚1m，并与上、下游原结构底板平顺连接。

（3）止水设计：修复底板采用一道“W”形铜片止水，其厚度为1mm，翼宽为40cm，埋设深度30cm。修复部位的底板与原结构缝面相接时，对老混凝土进行刻槽，刻槽最小深度50cm，宽度200cm，重新埋设止水，浇筑C30微膨胀混凝土。修复底板的铜止水应与老混凝土中的橡胶止水良好搭接，确保形成封闭系统。

（4）底板锚筋设计：为加强修复部位底板整体稳定，确保底板有效地锚固，加强了锚筋的设置。锚筋间距由原3m×3m调整为1.5m×1.5m，直径由原来ϕ28加大到ϕ32，锚筋顶部与底板面层钢筋有效焊接，锚孔灌注M30砂浆。底板基础锚筋入岩深度为7.7m。

(5) 基础排水设计：修复底板下的基础排水沟采用岩面刻槽方式，排水管用透水软管，沟内回填级配小石。在排水沟内设 ϕ76mm 排水孔，孔距4m，孔深入基岩5m。

(四) 修复效果

鱼塘水电站溢洪道修复至今，已经顺利通过两个汛期的考验，溢洪道运行正常，修复设计工作是安全可靠的。

(中国电建集团中南勘测设计研究院有限公司 于海龙)

高生水电站整体水力学模型深化试验研究

贵州高生水电站装机容量106MW，属二等大(2)型工程，枢纽方案由碾压混凝土重力坝、坝身开敞式溢流表孔和右岸引水发电系统地下厂房等主要建筑物组成。最大坝高121m，河床坝段布置3孔开敞式溢流表孔，表孔尺寸13.0m × 20.5m (宽×高)，设计最大下泄流量为11166m³/s，采用挑流消能方式。高生水电站工程具有泄洪单宽流量大、水头高、过流断面流速大、下游水深较浅及基岩抗冲能力不强等特点，故要求泄洪、消能建筑物应有足够的泄洪能力和消能防冲能力，以满足大坝枢纽安全泄洪的要求。同时，泄水、消能防冲建筑物的布置，应使下泄水流能够顺畅地进入下游主河道。

高生水电站水力学模型试验研究，通过1/80比尺的整体水工模型试验，在前期研究的基础上，专题进行水电站泄水建筑物泄流能力等水力特性、泄洪消能方案和水库泄洪闸门运行方式等的深化研究，验证泄水建筑物设计方案和结构体型的合理性，提出满足工程设计、施工和运行要求的结构体型优化的成果报告。对初始设计方案和比较方案进行了物理模型试验研究，主要内容包括表孔流量(流量系数)和水位关系、表孔底部和侧墙等时均动水压力分布、水流流态、表孔水面线、下游河床水面线和河床流速分布和动床冲刷地形等。根据模型试验研究结果，修改方案Ⅴ作为高生水电站表孔体型的推荐方案。研究同时分析了基岩面升高及预开挖措施对河床冲坑及下游堆丘的影响，提出了河床预开挖建议方案。

(河海大学
中国电建集团贵阳勘测设计研究院有限公司)

水闸工程安全评价及除险加固关键技术研发

项目现场调研水闸混凝土结构在不同工况下的病害特征及劣化规律，选取典型工程实例，采用有限元方法分析荷载、变形等因素作用下的劣化机制，定量分析各因素对水闸结构性能的影响。基于结构安全、正常使用和耐久性指标，建立基于可靠度的水闸混凝土结构的寿命预测模型。研究混凝土病害发展机理，提出土石接合部渗漏、脱空以及止水带老化失效等问题的数值模拟方法，建立基于模糊系统可靠度理论的水闸安全评价体系，包括单指标(渗流、强度或稳定)模糊可靠度和考虑时效影响的系统模糊可靠度分析方法，开发相应的分析软件。

项目创新点包括：

(1) 研究水闸混凝土结构在荷载、变形等多因素作用下的病害特征及劣化机理，分析各因素对结构性能的定量影响效应。

(2) 建立基于可靠度的水闸混凝土结构的安全评价方法和寿命预测模型。

(河海大学
黄河水利科学研究院)

施工导流与围堰设计

拉哇水电站施工组织设计综述

拉哇水电站位于金沙江上游，是金沙江上游13级开发的第8级，一等大(1)型工程，枢纽由混凝土面板堆石坝，及右岸的溢洪洞、泄洪放空洞、输水发电系统组成，装机容量2000MW。

(一) 施工条件

对外交通通过国道可通向四川、云南、西藏等省

(自治区)。物资在四川、云南等地采购。川藏联网的巴塘变电站已投入运行。主要工程量：土石方明挖1487万m^3，石方洞挖729.36万m^3，土石方填筑1971.68万m^3，混凝土350.96万m^3，金属结构安装1.85万t。

(二) 施工导流

工程施工采用围堰一次性拦断河床隧洞导流方式，分三期导流。根据地形地质条件，2条导流洞推荐布置在右岸。上游土石围堰堰顶高程2597m，最大堰高60m。下游围堰堰顶高程2557m，最大堰高21.5m。围堰均采用塑性混凝土防渗墙及复合土工膜防渗。

(三) 料源规划

拉哇水电站工程区内的大理岩成石率83.9%，成砂率66.8%，石粉含量19.3%。角闪片岩成石率89%，成砂率76%，石粉含量15.2%。前期混凝土骨料利用交通洞及排水洞洞挖料加工，主体及导流工程混凝土粗骨料及垫层料，由料场开采，细骨料全部利用开挖料。大坝填筑料料源为开挖料及必英沟开采料。大坝上游铺盖利用坝基开挖低液限黏土料作为防渗土料。

(四) 主体工程施工

1. 坝基开挖　左右岸坝肩自上而下分层开挖，高300多米，工期2年。左坝肩规划4层开挖道路，右岸布置5层开挖道路。坝基覆盖层采用常规开挖运输方式。堰塞湖沉积黏土层，先分层降水固结后开挖，自卸车运输。高峰月平均强度46.17万m^3，工期18个月。

2. 坝体填筑及面板施工　填筑石料从必英沟料场开采及曲引朗沟回采，下游上坝。坝体分9期填筑，规划8层道路，工期45个月，高峰月强度58.83万m^3。面板最大斜长分3期浇筑。堆石料铺料厚0.8m，4m^3挖掘机配32t自卸车上坝，混合卸料，235kW推土机铺平，洒水量按堆石体积15%控制，非增模区用32t自行式振动碾碾压8～10遍；底部和岸坡增模区12遍，25t冲击碾补碾12遍；顶部增模区碾压10～12遍，25t冲击碾补碾10～12遍。面板混凝土水平运输采用混凝土搅拌运输车，无轨滑模跳仓浇筑，溜槽输送入仓。

3. 右岸地下建筑物施工　包括交通洞、导流洞、溢洪洞、泄洪放空洞、输水洞、主副厂房、主变室等68条洞室，总长39km。以高线上坝②道路、中线沿江④道路为依托，布置施工支洞24条，长5.2km。钻爆法开挖洞室、压入式通风，自卸车出渣。主副厂房(长187m、宽28m、高73.45m)分9层开挖。隧洞衬砌采用针梁钢模台车，泵送混凝土入仓。

4. 压力钢管安装　安装总量2636t，内径7.9～9.0m，采用洞内智能组焊安装工艺。钢管瓦片卷制防腐后在支洞内智能组焊加工，成品钢管分节运至下平段，再完成节间焊接。

(五) 施工交通运输

1. 对外交通　物资运输总量224.57万t，高峰年运输量39.75万t。大宗物资采用公路、铁路转公路运输方式。重大件运输采用公路、铁路转公路及水运转公路运输方案。

2. 场内交通　在沿江低线和上坝道路基础上，以大坝开挖和填筑，泄洪和输水发电系统出渣，混凝土和开采料运输为交通主线，骨料加工运输及工厂与主体工程衔接为辅线，布置场内施工道路，根据需要再布置支线。主干道路总长30.82km，其中隧道22.12km，占比71.8%。一级道路宽9.5m，限高4.5m。工程共布置2座临时索桥、1座永久大桥。

(六) 施工工厂

筹建期在曲引朗沟口下游阶地布置砂石加工和混凝土生产系统。主体工程开工后在必英沟、曲引朗沟口布置砂石加工系统，在拉哇沟、格茸沟下游布置混凝土系统，生产能力280m^3/h。按7个区供气，总供气量1200m^3/min。供水以曲引朗沟水和必英沟水为水源。左岸水厂(处理规模9700m^3/d)供应营地生活用水。生产用水直接配入各区。高峰期用电负荷20550kW，设1座110kV变电站，进线110kV，35kV出线1回、10kV线路8回。

(七) 施工总布置

料场区、主体工程施工区、生产生活区的占地面积37.80万m^2。必英沟料场区设石料场、弃渣场、碎石加工系统、施工营地及施工场地等。主体工程施工区布置混凝土系统等。生产生活区布置生活营地、混凝土系统、曲引朗沟弃渣场及中转料场、变电站、加油站、施工水厂等。总征地面积539.14万m^2，含永久征收220.77万m^2，临时征用318.37万m^2。

(八) 施工总进度

筹建期3年，施工总工期9年。第1年1月开工导流洞及岸坡开挖施工。第2年10月底导流洞具备通水条件。第2年11月大江截流。第3年3月底上下游围堰防渗墙工程完工，基坑完成抽水，当年4月河床覆盖层开挖。第4年9月底坝基开挖完成，当年10月河床趾板及大坝基础垫层浇筑、下游堆石体填筑。第8年6月底完成坝体填筑，当年11月，导流洞下闸封堵，次年5月封堵完成。第9年3月完成三期面板浇筑，当年6月底首台机组投产发电，12月底工程完工。河床覆盖层开挖总工期18个月，坝体填筑总工期45个月，混凝土高峰月浇筑强度5.75万m^3。工程施工高峰人数6200人。

（中国电建集团中南勘测设计研究院有限公司
吴文洪）

杨房沟水电站施工导流设计

（一）导流方式、标准和程序

杨房沟水电站坝址河谷狭窄，呈“V”形。枯水期水位1983～1985m时水面宽56～102m，正常蓄水位2094m时水面宽150m，两岸岸坡陡，考虑水文、地形地质条件、大坝和厂房布置型式，拟采用围堰一次断流，隧洞过流导流方式。导流标准和程序见表1。

表1 导流标准和程序

导流阶段	时段	导流标准		导流建筑物		上游水位（m）	下游水位（m）	导流洞	
		频率	流量（m^3/s）	挡水建筑物	泄水建筑物			流量（m^3/s）	流速（m/s）
截流	2016年11月，旬平均	10%	713	戗堤	两条导流洞	1991.77	1984.51	/	
初期导流	2016年11月～2020年10月	5%	6460	围堰	两条导流洞	2023.87	1994.87	6218	16.0
中期导流	2020年11月～2021年10月	全年1%	7930	坝体	两导流洞＋4泄洪中孔	2034.75	1996.22	7669	19.8
后期导流	2021年11月～2022年3月	11至次年3月，5%	1620	坝体	永久泄洪建筑物	2088.00	1986.93	/	/
导流洞蓄水	2022年11月上旬	旬平均10%	892	坝体	两条导流洞＋生态泄放孔	1996.87	1985.07	/	/
导流洞封堵	2022年11月～2023年3月	5%	1220	坝体	永久泄洪建筑物	2088.00	1985.96	/	/

（二）导流建筑物布置与设计

杨房沟水电站采用全年导流方案。

1. 导流隧洞　导流隧洞为4级临时建筑物。地下厂房布置左岸，确定2条导流洞设在右岸。导流洞呈单弯、平行布置，洞轴线间距45m，进、出口高程分别为1985m、1981m城门洞型，全断面钢筋混凝土结构衬砌，净过流断面13m×16m（宽×高）。1号洞靠江，2号洞靠山，分别长716m、833m。导流洞出口高速水流对下游对岸直接冲刷，对进厂公路和低线混凝土场地安全造成不利影响，为此要求公路挡墙采用混凝土挡墙并坐落在基岩上，并将导流洞出口底高程降低2m至1981m，避免波状水跃对公路挡墙的不利影响。

2条导流洞同一个进水渠，进口采用岸塔式，进口段设封堵闸门，长16m，顶面为喇叭形，进口设中墩，厚4m，将其分成2个宽6.5m孔口，两侧边墙厚3.5m，底板厚3.5m，前部设齿槽，进水口总体高度41.5m。导流洞出口岩壁陡峭，出口不用明渠段，洞内预留岩梗加混凝土围堰作为导流洞出口围堰，在完成洞内衬砌等，将其爆破拆除，导流洞过水。

导流洞进口围堰采用土石围堰，高喷灌浆防渗，进口围堰在过水前爆破拆除。

2. 围堰　上下游围堰堰均为土石围堰，采用混凝土防渗墙＋土工膜防渗。

上游围堰堰顶高程2027m，最大堰高47m，堰顶宽10m，轴线长228.38m。上游边坡2003.5m高程以上为1∶1.8，2003.5m以下1∶1.5；下游边坡1996m以上为1∶1.7，1996m以下1∶1.5。堰体1996m高程以上为土工膜心墙防渗，防渗体高30m，土工膜两侧设垫层及过渡层。堰体1996m高程以下堰体及基础采用塑性混凝土防渗墙防渗，墙厚1m，最大墙深37m，施工平台高程1996m。截流戗堤在堰体内，上、下戗堤顶宽20m，上戗堤轴线在围堰轴线上游50m，下戗堤轴线在围堰轴线下游40m。

3. 导流洞封堵闸门　进口段被中墩分隔成两孔，每孔设1扇封堵闸门，按水库正常蓄水位2094m加适当超高设计。挡水设计水头110m，总水压力111330kN，平面滑动钢闸门，Ⅱ型门槽。卷扬机容量10000kN，扬程30m。闸门分节制造，现场拼装焊接成整体。闸门止水布置在下游侧。闸门主轨为

Q345B 厚钢板和 1Cr18Ni9 轨头焊接组合结构，止水座面为不锈钢 1Cr18Ni9，其余为型钢和 Q345B 钢板焊接结构。

4. 永久封堵堵头　导流隧洞堵头为 1 级永久挡水建筑物，堵头按 500 年一遇洪水设计，最大设计水头约 119m，单条导流隧洞堵头总水推力约 28403t。为保证大坝坝基防渗帷幕的连续性，在导流隧洞穿过大坝坝基防渗帷幕线位置布置永久堵头。

导流隧洞堵头长 40m，为方便堵头施工，缩短堵头段施工工期，降低造价，采用预留体形方案，即施工时在堵头位置隧洞断面按堵头外形尺寸开挖、衬砌。堵头混凝土回填在闸门保护下施工，堵头和闸门间设排水措施；堵头段进行帷幕、固结、回填和接触灌浆。帷幕灌浆为大坝帷幕灌浆的一部分，施工提前进行。固结灌浆改善堵头段围岩物理力学性能和防渗性能。回填和接缝灌浆使堵头与围岩结合良好。考虑施工进度和温控要求，堵头分两段施工。堵头内设灌浆廊道，廊道长 30m，城门洞形，2.5m×3.0m（宽×高）。

永久堵头段前期防渗帷幕采用两排灌浆孔，导流隧洞全断面帷幕灌浆入岩孔深 15m，两排帷幕灌浆孔的排距 2m，孔距 2m，间错布置。帷幕灌浆压力 1～4 MPa，混凝土与岩基接触段的透水率 100%不大于设计值 1Lu，其余各段的合格率不小于 90%，不合格试段透水率不超过设计规定 100%，且不集中，灌浆质量可认为合格。

（中国电建集团华东勘测设计研究院有限公司
江金章）

黄登水电站 2 号导流洞出口工作闸室分析

（一）概述

黄登水电站采用围堰一次断流、右岸两条导流隧洞泄流的全年导流方式。1 号、2 号导流洞均为城门洞形，断面分别为 16m×20m、8m×12m，洞身长分别为 1121.959m、1298.138m。1 号、2 号导流洞已分别于 2017 年 11 月 10 日、2017 年 11 月 28 日安全下闸封堵。

为满足下闸期间向下游供生态流量及下游水电站最小发电流量 280m³/s 的需要，1 号导流洞下闸封堵后，2 号导流洞控泄向下游供水。这种状况下，2 号导流洞出口工作弧门承受高水头，出口工作闸室应力、变形及其抗滑稳定是否满足要求是弧门安全运行的关键。

（二）计算模型、参数及工况

2 号导流洞出口工作闸室长 30m，宽 15m，高 23m，墩墙厚 3.2m，顶高程 1492m。工作弧门孔口尺寸 7m×9m（宽×高），孔口上游压坡 1∶12.808。1492m 平台上设启闭排架。2 号导流洞出口工作闸室基础置于弱风化板岩上，岩体呈薄层状结构，局部为层状碎裂结构。

1. 计算模型　2 号导流洞出口工作闸室应力变形分析，利用 Inventor 软件建立闸室三维模型，然后导入到 ANSYS，在 ANSYS 前处理中对模型进行有限元划分，形成有限元模型。X 轴为顺水流方向，下游向为正，Y 轴为铅直向，向上为正，Z 轴按右手螺旋法则确定，垂直水流方向。计算模型采用 Solid 185 六面体单元，共划分 16415 个单元，19991 个节点。闸室底部采用全约束，顺水流方向，左右两侧采用法相约束，前后两侧无约束。

2. 计算参数　2 号导流洞出口工作闸室混凝土为 C40，混凝土与基岩有关参数见表 1。

3. 计算工况及荷载　根据下闸进度安排，1 号导流洞下闸封堵后，2 号导流洞控泄向下游供水，2 号导流洞竖井封堵闸门下闸前，出口弧形工作闸门挡水水头达 74.5m。本次计算针对该工况进行三维有限元计算，荷载组合为结构自重＋水压力＋弧门推力。

表 1　　　　混凝土及基岩物理力学参数

弹性模量（GPa）	泊松比	容重（kN/m³）	混凝土/基岩抗剪断摩擦系数	混凝土/基岩抗剪断凝聚力（MPa）	混凝土轴心抗拉强度设计值（MPa）	混凝土轴心抗压强度设计值（MPa）
32.5	0.167	25	0.8	0.6	1.71	19.1

（三）计算结果与分析

1. 应力变形分析　当出口弧形工作闸门下闸挡水时，水压力通过弧形工作闸门传递到大梁上，因此，需要了解大梁的应力分布及顺水流向位移。

从大梁的主应力图可知，大梁的第一主应力在靠近两个支铰处最大，最大值为 5.3MPa；超过 C40 混凝土抗拉强度设计值 1.71MPa 的范围，也主要集中在两个支铰附近，范围不大，可通过配筋解决；水压力通过弧形工作门传递到大梁上，在两支铰处出现最大压应力，最大压应力为 15.62MPa，未超过 C40 混凝土最大抗压强度设计值 19.1MPa。从大梁顺水流方向位移可知，在水压力作用下，大梁顺水流向最大位移为1.55mm，变形较小。

2. 整体稳定分析 根据《水工混凝土结构设计规范》(DL/T 5057—2009)，结构构件应验算承载能力极限状态，其表达式：

$$\gamma_0 \psi \gamma_Q S_{Qk} \leqslant \frac{1}{\gamma_d} R(f_d, a_k)$$

极限状态相关计算参数见表2。

表2 承载能力极限状态计算参数

结构重要性系数 γ_0	设计状况系数 ψ	水压力分项系数 γ_Q	结构系数 γ_d	抗剪断摩擦系数分项系数	抗剪断凝聚力分项系数
0.9	0.95	1.2	1.2	1.7	2.0

将各参数代入下面计算式中，求得：

作用效应： $\gamma_0 \psi \gamma_Q S_{Qk} = 0.9 \times 0.95 \times 1.2 \times 2 \times 45262 = 92877.62\text{kN}$

抗力效应：

$$\frac{1}{\gamma_d} R(f_d, a_k) = \frac{1}{1.2} \times \left\{\frac{0.8}{1.7} \times [8021 \times 25 + 10 \times (74.5 \times 7.594 \times 7 - 65.5 \times 2.176 \times 7) - 0.5 \times 10 \times 74.5 \times 15 \times 30] + \frac{0.6}{2.0} \times 1000 \times 30 \times 15\right\} = 137019.90\text{kN}$$

因此，$\gamma_0 \psi \gamma_Q S_{Qk} = 92877.62\text{kN} < \frac{1}{\gamma_d} R(f_d, a_k) = 137019.90\text{kN}$，黄登水电站2号导流洞出口工作闸室整体抗滑稳定满足要求。

（中国电建集团昆明勘测设计研究院有限公司 华栋 林陶枫 曹永雷）

旬阳水电站一期全年围堰设计与优化

陕西旬阳水电站根据地形地质条件、汉江洪水特性、枢纽布置及工程特点，施工导流采用两期导流方式。一期围左岸厂房和右导墙左侧的五孔泄洪冲砂闸坝段，江水由右岸拓宽后的导流明渠泄流，一期基坑在上、下游全年围堰和右导墙围护下全年施工。待厂房坝段具备挡水条件且左五孔泄洪冲沙闸具备泄流条件后，二期截流，二期枯水期江水由泄洪冲沙闸下泄，汛期由二期过水基坑和泄洪冲砂闸联合泄洪。

（一）设计标准及堰顶高程

一期上下游全年围堰为4级建筑物，挡水标准全年20年一遇洪水，坝址处河道洪峰流量21600m³/s。考虑上游安康水库调控作用，导流度汛20年一遇洪峰流量为19500m³/s。

一期导流右岸导流明渠泄流，明渠宽142m，渠底高程214m，经水力学计算并结合模型试验成果，上下游围堰挡水水位分别为237.5m、234.65m，堰顶高程分别为238m、236m。

（二）堰型选择

混凝土围堰比土石围堰投资大，且将增加一期枯水期混凝土浇筑强度，故选土石围堰。

堰体和堰基黏土心墙防渗施工工艺简单、快捷，防渗质量易保证，但增加了基础覆盖层开挖工程量，投资略大。堰体复合土工膜心墙+堰基高喷墙防渗和堰体黏土心墙+堰基高喷墙防渗无需开挖基础覆盖层，但高喷墙施工相对复杂、施工较慢，质量不易保证。考虑堰基和一期基坑需开采覆盖层砂砾石料供混凝土骨料使用，故选用土石围堰防渗型式。

（三）围堰料源

一期全年围堰堰壳填筑料主要利用左岸坝肩千枚岩开挖料。千枚岩强度低，抗风化和抗变形能力差，水稳定性较差，其颗粒会随碾压过程、裸露时间及含水量情况而变化。一期基坑内覆盖层砂卵砾石开挖料为混凝土骨料源，不满足要求的弃料也可为围堰填筑料。

坝址区汉江两岸分布丰富的土料，料场在坝址左岸烂木滩沟右侧山坡上，与坝线相距50m左右，土料各项技术指标均符合围堰防渗土料质量要求。

（四）围堰布置、断面设计及优化

一期上、下游全年围堰轴线与坝轴线交角分别为17°、9°，左堰肩与基岩裸露的左岸坡衔接，右堰肩与右导墙上、下游延伸段衔接，轴线长分别为249m、240m。

上下游围堰堰顶宽10m，最大堰高分别为41m、37m，迎水侧坡比1∶2，背水侧坡比1∶1.7。堰基覆盖层砂卵砾石全部挖除，座落在基岩上。堰体黏土心墙防渗，心墙顶高程分别为238.25m、235.25m，顶宽2m，两侧坡比均为1∶0.2，心墙上、下游侧分为2m厚反滤料，反滤料外侧为石渣填筑区。围堰迎水面右堰肩采用50cm厚钢筋混凝土面板防护（围堰与右导墙上延段交界处向左50m）。

围堰填筑料现场检测成果表明，石渣颗粒偏细，粒径≤5mm的平均含量达48.6%，粒径≤0.075mm的达30.6%，粉黏粒含量偏高。为确保围堰稳定并满足坡面抗冲刷要求，对围堰体型结构作了优化：围堰迎水面 15m/10m 宽（上部/下部）采用基坑天然砂砾石料填筑；背水面 2m 宽采用砂砾石料防护；背水坡底部设砂卵砾石排水棱体，棱体顶宽 3m，最小高度 5m；取消石渣料与防渗心墙土料间反滤料，采用开挖石渣料填筑。

（五）围堰抗滑稳定计算

一期上、下游全年围堰规模大且堰体采用千枚岩软岩石渣料填筑，需进行围堰渗流及堰坡稳定计算。计算工况包括围堰设计洪水位、堰前水位降落和施工期 3 种工况。采用毕肖普法计算土石围堰堰坡稳定，4 级建筑物的最小安全系数为 1.15。

渗流计算结果表明围堰堰体、高喷灌浆防渗墙、黏土心墙和堰基覆盖层渗透坡降均在允许范围内，不会发生渗透破坏。

从表 1 可见在各工况下的堰坡满足稳定要求。上、下游堰坡滑弧类型均为浅层滑动，在堰体内最大深度为 2m。

表 1　围堰堰坡稳定计算成果表

计算工况	稳定系数			
	一期上游全年围堰		一期下游全年围堰	
	迎水堰坡	背水堰坡	迎水堰坡	背水堰坡
施工期	1.51	1.28	1.51	1.28
设计洪水位	1.38	1.16	1.38	1.24
堰前水位降落	1.15	1.25	1.23	1.28

（六）围堰运行情况

自 2018 年 7 月一期上、下游全年土石围堰竣工后，已经历汛期考验，汛后检查围堰完好无损。至今围堰堰体和堰基未见明显渗漏，堰坡无滑塌、裂缝等异常现象。

（中国电建集团北京勘测设计研究院有限公司
何竹叶　卢军民　薛宝臣）

苏洼龙水电站导流隧洞设计与施工

（一）概述

苏洼龙水电站位于金沙江上游河段四川巴塘县和西藏芒康县的界河上，为金沙江上游水电规划 13 个梯级水电站的第 10 级。枢纽建筑物主要由沥青混凝土心墙坝、右岸溢洪道和泄洪放空洞、左岸引水系统和地面厂房等组成。沥青混凝土心墙坝最大坝高 112m，总库容 6.38 亿 m^3，装机容量 1200MW，为一等大（1）型工程。

拦河坝采用断流围堰一次拦断河流、隧洞泄流（枯水期导流隧洞泄流，汛期导流隧洞与泄洪放空洞联合泄流）的全年施工导流方式。

（二）导流隧洞设计及特点

导流隧洞为 4 级建筑物，设计洪水标准采用全年 20 年一遇，对应洪峰流量 6180m^3/s。

导流隧洞位于坝址右岸，地形陡峭，大部分基岩裸露，地面高程 2425～2680m，为高原-高山峡谷地貌。基岩岩性主要为花岗岩、石英片岩及少量大理岩。其中花岗岩约占总长度的 81.9%，以微新岩体为主。

进口设置岸塔式进水塔，长 22m，宽 30m，高 61m，设一道中墩，两个孔口尺寸均为矩形 7.5m×19m（宽×高），分别设置一扇平板闸门。洞身采用城门洞型，净断面尺寸 15m × 19m。洞身长 896.53m，其中明洞段长 10.68m，洞进口底板高程 2379m，出口底板高程 2376m，洞身纵坡 3.53‰。平面设一弯段，转弯半径 100m，转角 60°。出口明渠内布置异型反台阶消力池，设 5 级台阶，台阶高程分别为 2370m、2374m、2378m、2382m、2386m。

导流隧洞设计有三大技术创新应用。

（1）解决了偏压、浅埋、大断面导流隧洞进口开挖支护稳定难题。进口渐变段为Ⅳ类围岩，最大开挖断面 27m×27.2m，规模大且渐变段左侧发育冲沟，岩体最小覆盖厚度约 18m。采用洞顶及左侧悬吊锚筋桩＋洞口锁口锚索＋洞内钢支撑复合支护型式，确保了洞口开挖施工的安全。

（2）发明并应用了异型反台阶整流消能方法及消力池。该消能工适用于低水头、大单宽流量（大于 300m^2/s）、弗劳德数低（小于 2）、深厚覆盖层条件下的岸边泄洪消能。

（3）结合导流隧洞地质条件，对洞身衬砌进行优化。国内首次在土石坝、单条导流隧洞条件下，取消了堵头段及堵头段后Ⅱ类、Ⅲ类围岩洞段顶拱衬砌，确保了截流目标的实现。

（三）导流隧洞施工及运行情况

导流隧洞于 2015 年 11 月 25 日开工，2017 年 11 月 18 日过流。

截至 2018 年 12 月底，导流隧洞先后经历了 2018 年汛期洪水、“10.11”和“11.03”两次白格堰塞湖溃决洪水的考验。2018 年洪水流量超过 4000m^3/s 的两次，最大洪峰流量分别为 4160m^3/s（7 月 13 日）和 4380m^3/s（9 月 14 日）。“10.11”和“11.03”白格堰塞湖溃决洪水在苏洼龙电站坝址洪峰流量分别为 7800m^3/s、19800m^3/s，远超设计洪水标准。其中“10.11”白格堰塞湖溃决洪水由上游围堰挡水，堰前最高水位 2426.34m，导流隧洞最大下泄流量 4955m^3/s。“11.03”白格堰塞湖溃决洪水由于上游围堰采取破口措施，堰前最高水位 2416.79m，导流隧洞最大下泄流量 4200m^3/s。导流隧洞成功过流，运行情况良好。

（中国电建集团北京勘测设计研究院有限公司
王剑涛）

托口水电站导流底孔结构受力分析与坝上游面拉应力控制措施

托口水电站工程在左岸布置 4 个 8.0m×12.5m（宽×高）导流底孔，底孔断面为有倒角的矩形，底板高程 188m，底孔长 73m。导流底孔进水口为整体浇筑，与孔身段（坝内）间分缝施工。

（一）计算模型

建立左岸导流底孔边孔坝段的有限元计算模型。根据经验和计算结果分析，基岩深度（Y 向）取 60m（1 倍坝高），上、下游方向（Z 方向）基岩各按坝体底宽 1 倍考虑，取 59.15m。基岩左右两侧、上下游端面及底部均采用法向位移约束。大坝两侧分缝为自由边界。

计算模型中混凝土与基岩均采用 8 节点等参单元（SOLID45）模拟。在结构分缝位置，则采用面-面接触单元（targe170、conta174）模拟。混凝土与基岩材料均为线弹性材料。

（二）封堵期结构受力与变形分析

封堵期计算工况为，导流底孔下闸，表孔不溢流，底孔未回填，上游洪水位 250m，下游无水，坝基防渗系统已形成。导流底孔结构所受荷载有结构自重、土压力和水荷载等。水荷载包括：坝上游面静水压力、大坝两侧缝内静水压力、底孔内壁测压管水头对应的静水压力、坝基扬压力、底孔闸门水推力和表孔弧形闸门水推力等。

封堵期，在上述荷载作用下，大坝主要发生向下游变形和向底孔右侧横河向变形，坝顶横河向（X 方向）位移最大达 1.6mm。在底孔孔口闸门槽位置横河向拉应力最大达 2.634MPa，坝体横河向应力数值为－0.46～1.38MPa。

计算结果表明，在坝上游面出现较大范围拉应力区，主要出现在底孔底板高程之上部位，表现为横河向拉应力，拉应力值为 0.03～0.85MPa。对 203.5m 高程断面，拉应力（横河向）值为 0.01～0.44MPa，靠近坝上游面最大，往下游拉应力逐渐减小。

重力坝在水压力作用下，因泊松比效应，除坝踵部位外坝上游面一般以压应力为主。但因存在导流底孔，计算中坝上游面出现横河向拉应力，范围较大，最大 0.85MPa。如考虑温度应力等，大坝上游面混凝土抗裂安全度明显不足，可能产生裂缝，不利于大坝安全。

（三）坝上游面出现拉应力的原因

坝上游承担的荷载分为坝体自重和土压力，及水荷载两类。水荷载较复杂。

（1）在自重和土压力荷载共同作用下，因边孔坝段导流底孔结构不对称性，大坝有向孔口右侧倾斜趋势（横河向倾斜趋势），横河向最大位移 1.44mm。底孔顶板高程之下坝面表现为压应力，底孔顶板以上坝上游面为拉应力区，拉应力值 0.03～0.27MPa。203.5m 高程断面，拉应力值 0.01～0.2MPa，上游侧拉应力最大达 0.27MPa，往下游逐渐减小。

（2）在坝上游面静水压力、大坝两侧缝内静水压力和闸门上游底孔内壁测压管水头对应的静水压力荷载作用下，孔口有向右岸变形趋势，横河向最大位移 1.55mm。孔口底板高程之上的上游坝面出现较大横河向拉应力，为 0.04～0.91MPa，超过了所有荷载作用下坝上游面拉应力 0.85MPa。对 203.5m 高程断面，拉应力值为 0.025～0.75MPa，上游侧拉应力最大为 0.85MPa，往下游逐渐减小。

（3）在弧门和底孔闸门水推力、弧门前侧向压力、闸墩头静水压力等荷载共同作用下，底孔闸门槽位置出现较大横河向拉应力，最大值为 1.62MPa，但坝上游面仅在孔口中下部产生 0.006～0.15MPa 拉应力。对 203.5m 高程断面，拉应力值 0.04～0.19MPa，与自重作用下坝面应力值差不多。

分析 3 种荷载情况下典型高程断面的应力值可见，自重和静水压力（尤其是导流底孔坝外孔身段外表面水压力的水平分量）是产生坝上游面拉应力的主要原因。其中自重引起孔口顶板高程之上坝上游面拉应力，随高程增加，拉应力占比例越显著。例如 203.5m、205.5m、210m 高程，自重产生的拉应力分别为 0.21MPa、0.18MPa、0.15MPa，分别占总拉应力的 26%、42%和 94%。静水压力引起孔口顶板高程四周的坝上游面产生拉应力，例如 203.5m 静水压力产生的拉应力值为 0.64MPa，占总拉应力 80%；199.5m 静水压力产生的拉应力值 0.69MPa。

（四）减小坝上游面拉应力的措施

针对坝上游面产生拉应力的原因，采取以下措施：①在满足施工布置要求的同时，将底孔进水口与孔身段分缝位置移至坝上游面平齐位置；②考虑大坝两侧缝内填缝材料作用。大坝两侧缝内填缝材料对大坝两侧横河向变形有一定约束作用。

采取措施①分缝位置移至坝上游面平齐位置时，坝上游面拉应力值为 0.01～0.5MPa，减少了 42%，此措施减小拉应力可行。

对措施②，计算设填缝材料（不同弹性模量）时的坝面拉应力。计算结果表明：坝段分缝间的填缝材料弹模越大，对减小坝上游面拉应力的效果越显著。例如 203.5m 高程，坝段分缝间不设填缝材料方案中拉应力为 0.8MPa，在填缝材料弹模为 2、3、4MPa 时，坝上游面拉应力分别为 0.22MPa、0.12MPa、0.06MPa，减小了 72.5%、85%和 92.5%。

（水能资源利用关键技术湖南省重点实验室 程宵
中国电建集团中南勘测设计研究院有限公司
魏春林 杨庆妮）

其 他

锦屏一级水电站渗流水质及析出物分析

利用两岸坝基帷幕灌浆平洞、坝基排水平洞和抗力体排水洞分层布置绕坝渗流测点。帷幕后布置 1 个断面，从 6 层帷幕灌浆平洞钻孔安装渗压计；排水幕线上布置 1 个断面，从 6 层坝基排水平洞钻孔安装渗压计；5 层抗力体排水洞各布置 3～4 个断面，从抗力体排水洞钻孔安装测压管。绕坝渗流测点间距 50～100m。

（一）现场水质取样

锦屏一级水电站运行期，在枯水期和丰水期水质分析各取水样 30 组（库区 3 组，下游河道 1 组，坝基帷幕洞、坝基排水洞、抗力体排水洞和地下厂房排水洞等 26 组），洞室水样从渗水点采样；枯水期和丰水期析出物分析样品均 15 组，分别在坝基帷幕洞和排水洞、抗力体排水洞和地下厂房排水洞等采取渗水处的析出物。2014～2017 年共 3 轮取样和分析。

（二）水质分析

渗流水质分析按相关规范进行，水样对混凝土腐蚀性评价依据有关规范进行。

1. 水质分析成果 通过锦屏一级水电站库水和尾水水样试验结果对比分析，可知：

(1) 16 号、17 号、18 号 3 个库水水样试验结果基本一致，水样对混凝土无腐蚀。

(2) 水垫塘下游河道的 19 号水样对混凝土无腐蚀。

(3) 锦屏一级水电站 26 个工程内部渗流水取样点中 19 个水样（3～9 号、11 号、14 号、15 号、20～25 号、27～29 号）对混凝土无腐蚀；1 个取样点（30 号）枯水期时水样对混凝土有重碳酸型弱腐蚀，丰水期时水样转为对混凝土无腐蚀；6 个取样点水样（1 号、2 号、10 号、12 号、13 号、26 号）对混凝土有重碳酸型中等腐蚀。

2. 环境水对混凝土具有腐蚀性的反应机理分析

环境水腐蚀性分为一般酸性型、碳酸型、重碳酸型、镁离子型、硫酸盐型五类。它们分别按 pH 值、侵蚀性 CO_2 含量、HCO_3^- 含量、Mg^{2+} 含量、SO_4^{2-} 含量加以判别，一旦指标超出规定范围将对混凝土产生腐蚀性。

3. 不同取样时间水样对混凝土的腐蚀性 对不同时期各取样点水样对混凝土腐蚀性进行比较，结果表明，2013 年至今锦屏一级水电站各个取样点中，有 4 处水样（3 号、4 号、8 号、30 号）对混凝土腐蚀性已消除；有 6 处（1 号、2 号、10 号、12 号、13 号、26 号）对混凝土仍具重碳酸型中等腐蚀，其他水样对混凝土均无腐蚀性。

（三）析出物化学分析成果

析出物化学分析按有关试验规程进行。从析出物化学成分分析成果可知，15 个取样点采集样品的化学成分分析成果基本一致。15 个样品的烧失量为 40.22%～43.86%、氧化钙为 46.78%～53.95%。

根据析出物化学成分分析成果确定，工程内部 15 个采样点采集的不同颜色的粉末、颗粒状析出物样品中的主要成分为碳酸钙。

（四）渗流水水源分析

通过三个方面分析渗流水来源：一是将各取样点渗流水水质分析成果与库水水质分析成果比较；二是通过分析，了解外部水流经新建工程混凝土内部时可能发生某些成分的变化；三是参考电站设代处提供的大坝建成前水质分析资料。

通过比较分析，初步推断工程内 26 个取样点渗流水、下游河道水的水源主要为库水，其中某些位置渗流水可能是山体渗水和绕渗库水的混合水。其理由如下。

(1) 与库水相比，编号为 1 号、2 号、10 号、12 号、13 号 5 组渗流水样 pH 值和 CO_3^{2-} 浓度升高、无 HCO_3^-，3 号、5～8 号、22 号、26 号、30 号 8 组渗流水样 pH 值和 CO_3^{2-} 浓度升高、HCO_3^- 浓度

降低，其他检测项目测定值均在一定范围内波动。这是因为水流经混凝土过程中，水中 HCO_3^- 与混凝土内水泥水化物 $Ca(OH)_2$ 发生化学反应，导致水中 HCO_3^- 浓度降低，pH 值升高，CO_3^{2-} 因化学反应生成的 $CaCO_3$ 微量溶解而导致水中 CO_3^{2-} 浓度升高。

(2) 与库水相比，编号为 4 号、9 号、11 号、14 号、15 号、20～25 号、27～29 号 13 组渗流水 HCO_3^- 浓度升高，其他检测项目测定值均在一定范围内波动。这是因为空气中二氧化碳溶入渗流水中与混凝土中析出碳酸盐发生溶蚀反应，生成可溶性 $Ca(HCO_3)_2$，$Ca(HCO_3)_2$ 溶于水后发生电解反应产生 HCO_3^-，导致水中 HCO_3^- 浓度升高。

综上所述，锦屏一级水电站大坝帷幕防渗性能良好、工作正常，帷幕和大坝混凝土被溶蚀程度不高。

（中国电建集团中南勘测设计研究院有限公司
周绿　陈丽琴　史武详
雅砻江流域水电开发有限公司　冯艺）

白鹤滩水电站右岸地下厂房岩壁吊车梁补强加固设计

白鹤滩水电站右岸地下厂房开挖尺寸 438m×88.7m×34.0m（31m）（长×高×宽），起重设备选用 2 台 1300/125t 桥式起重机，最大起吊重量 23500kN，单个最大轮压 1100kN。吊车梁为岩壁吊车梁，因地应力高，地质条件复杂，岩壁吊车梁结构稳定是工程的重点。

（一）岩壁吊车梁结构基本参数

右岸地下厂房岩壁吊车梁梁体采用 C30 混凝土，高 3.30m，宽 2.85m，岩壁角 35°。上部 2 排受拉锚杆采用热轧带肋 4 级钢筋 HRB500，直径 40mm，长 12m，间距 0.7m；下部 1 排受压锚杆采用热轧带肋 3 级钢筋 HRB400，直径 32mm，长度 9m，间距 0.7m。岩壁吊车梁结构基本参数见图 1。

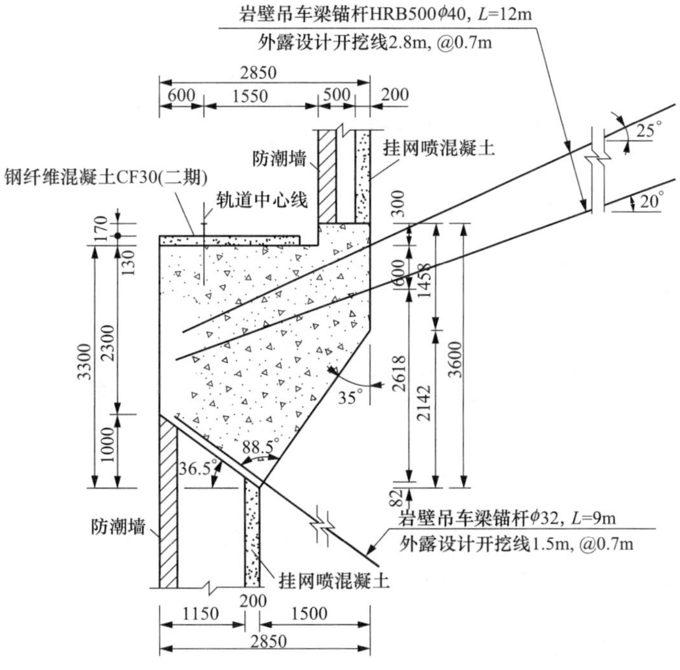

图 1　岩壁吊车梁结构基本参数（单位：mm）

（二）主要工程地质问题

右岸地下厂房水平埋深 420～800m，垂直埋深 420～540m。岩壁吊车梁岩性为玄武岩、角砾熔岩和少量凝灰岩。地质构造较发育，主要发育层间和层内错动带、陡缓倾角裂隙、倾角裂隙，对岩壁吊车梁成型影响较大，或易在岩壁吊车梁形成潜在不稳定块体。此外，右岸地下厂房岩石局部存在应力集中现象，厂区总体上属高地应力区。

在开挖中下游侧岩壁梁产生大范围破裂现象，影响深度 30～50cm，局部 80～150cm，应力调整产生的裂缝一般张开 3～5mm，局部达 1～2cm，导致下游侧岩壁梁开挖成型完整率低，岩台完全缺失比例超 60%。

（三）补强加固设计

1. 补强加固措施　采取的补强加固措施主要有

A、B、C 三种型式。

(1) A型：岩壁梁能成型，超挖小，超挖部分回填混凝土，岩壁梁下部设80cm厚附壁墙，设2排预应力锚索和1排预应力锚杆压住附壁墙，岩壁梁及附壁墙范围内固结灌浆。

(2) B型：岩壁梁部位超挖大，斜壁座呈70°，超挖部位用附壁墙修补，附壁墙凸出原设计开挖线40cm，设3排预应力锚索和1排预应力锚杆压住附壁墙，同样范围固结灌浆。

(3) C型：岩壁梁部位超挖很大，斜壁座呈8°，超挖部位用附壁墙修补，附壁墙凸出原设计开挖线40cm，设3排预应力锚索和2排预应力锚杆压住附壁墙，岩壁梁及附壁墙范围内固结灌浆。先浇筑补强结构，待加固措施完成后再浇筑岩壁梁混凝土，二期混凝土之间凿毛。

2. 结构稳定分析　岩壁梁加固后结构稳定分析采用有限元法和刚体平衡法。

(1) 有限元法：选用大型通用有限元软件ANSYS对A、B、C型加固进行有限元计算。计算中结合实际情况，设定了一些条件，根据有关设计规范，采用应力积分法计算岩壁梁安全系数。对比A、B、C型计算结果，随岩壁梁的超挖程度加大，岩壁梁抗滑稳定性和受拉锚杆安全系数逐渐减小，但受拉锚杆和结合面抗滑稳定安全系数均较大，满足规范要求。

(2) 刚体平衡法：规范规定，岩壁吊车梁结构设计采用概率理论为基础的极限状态设计方法。但加固后的岩壁梁结构体型、承载机理与一般岩壁梁相差较大。在考虑补强加固后岩壁梁结构变化情况下，采用刚体平衡法验算加固段结构抗滑稳定性，选取单宽结构，根据岩壁结合面下滑力 S 与阻抗力的比值计算抗滑稳定安全系数 K_j，即 $K_j=R/S$。计算的结合面 K_j 均大于1.815（由结构重要性系数、设计状况系数、抗滑稳定结构系数相乘所得）。计算结果表明，B、C型补强加固后的结合面抗滑稳定安全系数满足规范要求。

综合有限元法和刚体平衡法的计算结果，下游侧岩壁吊车梁在现状基础上补强加固后，受拉锚杆和结合面抗滑稳定的安全系数均满足规范要求。

（中国电建集团华东勘测设计研究院有限公司
钱军　邵兵　万祥兵　江亚丽
陈建林　陆健健　陈鹏　李良权）

乌东德水电站工程几项勘测设计简介

乌东德水电站勘测设计由长江勘测规划设计研究有限责任公司承担，项目设计人员以精准勘察、精心设计、精细服务为宗旨，充分发挥技术优势，开展多项重大技术研究，均一次性通过外部评审，设计成果质量得到高度评价。现将2018年进行的几项工作简介如下：

（一）导流隧洞下闸封堵优化

乌东德水电站布置5条导流隧洞，其中4号导流隧洞进口部位左侧隔墩岩体较薄，导流隧洞封堵期设计挡水水头达108.88m，存在一定的安全风险。另外，封堵段围岩未进行预扩挖施工，若考虑传统楔形堵头设计，对围岩扩挖将破坏岩体及大坝主帷幕，影响工期。

针对上述问题，通过研究导流隧洞群下闸封堵程序、对比不同型式堵头受力分析、临时堵头布置方案、直柱形堵头结构等，形成了“低水头封堵闸门结合临时堵头的导流隧洞群新型下闸封堵方法”研究成果。

采用该新型封堵方法，可将右岸3号、4号导流隧洞设计挡水水头由108.88m降低至33m，基本消除隔墩结构安全风险，并为进口金属结构系统大幅简化奠定基础，显著节省工程投资。首次采用直柱形堵头应用于乌东德水电站大型导流隧洞群，并提出保证安全性的相关措施，替代传统楔形堵头，取消扩挖，大幅降低施工安全风险，缩短施工工期。

（二）蓄水发电条件专题研究

开展乌东德水电站蓄水发电相关的6个专题研究，并形成综合研究报告。专题研究以提高主体建筑物结构安全、工程度汛安全为前提，不压缩大坝施工、机组安装等关键项目直线工期，通过优化工序、微调施工组织，优化资源配置，辅以相应的配套措施和资源投入，优化和完善乌东德水电站蓄水发电进度，提出8+4装机方案以及各主要项目的进度节点目标和进度计划安排意见。

三峡集团机电公司已调整两岸机组安装进度，与推荐方案基本一致，机组全投产时间将提前6个月，并有效利用2021年汛期来水，预计多获电量约20亿kW·h。

（三）危岩体治理设计

乌东德水电站库区内滑坡、大型堆积体及危岩体发育。其中，早古田危岩体体积达亿方级，规模巨大，且所处金沙江河道狭窄，若危岩体滑动入江，将影响水库正常运行，而且可能造成较大的灾难；三台危岩体总体积110万m^3，距坝址约1.7km，若发生失稳，可能影响工程运行安全。

通过多次地质勘探与深入分析评价，危岩体整体基本稳定。早古田危岩体局部可能产生部分崩塌破坏和块体稳定，正进行补充地质勘探和监测工作。三台危岩体采用地表设置截排水、系统锚索、抗剪洞、勘探平硐回填和安全监测的综合治理方案。

（长江勘测规划设计研究有限责任公司　陈东斌）

大湾水电站厂房屋顶出线架结构设计

大湾水电站位于楚雄彝族自治州双柏县的礼社江上，厂房为岸边式，电站装机容量 49.8MW（2×24.9MW），主厂房包括主机间和安装间，电气副厂房布置在主机间左侧，主变压器布置于副厂房，开关设备为户内 GIS 方式布置。

（一）出线架布置

大湾水电站 110kV 出线场位于左端电气副厂房屋顶层，高程 711.6m。为架空高压线需设计出线杆塔及出线横梁，两者均采用钢结构。

导线出线高度及避雷线高度根据电气设备布置与安全距离要求确定，导线距屋顶高度为 10m，构架钢梁为 3 相挂点，跨度 9m，地线柱高 3m。导线共 1 组，分 A、B、C 三相，各相导线间距 4m。设 2 个出线杆塔架立于框架柱顶，与框架柱固接，一根横梁架于出线杆架间，与杆塔单跨简支连接。导线挂在出线横梁底部，避雷线挂在出线杆塔上。根据布置要求，杆塔最大间距 9m，总高度 13m，横梁跨度 9m。

（二）出线架结构设计

大湾水电站厂房屋顶出线架采用钢结构。

1. 变电构架的特点　变电构架受力以水平荷载为主，主要是导线及地线的张力，其次是风力。导线张力大小与导线的档距、弧垂、自重、覆冰厚度、引下线重量和安装导线检修上人有关。导线弧垂随温度变化而变化。不同气象条件下导线张力不同。根据电气要求，不同电压等级要求带电导线对地面和其他构筑物保持一定距离，因此构架特点是柱高而断面细小，属于大柔度结构。

2. 变电构架的荷载及其组合　作用在构架上荷载有：导线和避雷线的张力（运行、安装及检修）A_1，导线、避雷器、引下线、绝缘子串和金属器具、覆冰重量等 A_2，构架自重 A_3，风载（包括构架及导线、避雷器、引下线、绝缘子串上的风压）A_4，安装检修时人及工具重（一般 1.5～2kN）A_5，地震荷载 A_6。

不同工况下的荷载组合如下。

运行工况：取最大风速、覆冰或最低气温时，对构架及基础的最不利荷载，即 $A_1+A_2+A_3+A_4$。

安装工况：考虑构架独立、导线紧线及紧线时作用在梁上的人及工具重，即 $A_1+A_2+A_3+A_4+A_5$。

检修工况：高度大于 10m 的构架，考虑单项带电检修作用在导线的人及工具重。三相同时停电检修时，作用在每相导线上人和工具重不少于 1kN。对未上人那一相导线，按安装情况时的导线张力；导线中部无引下线时不考虑导线上人。对出线构架线路一侧只考虑单相带电检修时导线上人的荷载，即 $A_1+A_2+A_3+A_4+A_5$。

特殊工况：当考虑地震荷载时，取最大风速、覆冰或最低气温时荷载及地震力，对构架及基础的最不利荷载，即 $A_1+A_2+A_3+A_4+A_6$。

3. 变电构架内力计算及截面设计　本次计算采用最不利荷载组合即特殊工况，钢管塔和横梁采用钢结构计算软件 3D3S 10.0 进行空间计算，使之更符合实际受力性能，整体建模时将梁简化为 1 根杆件，整体模型主要用来计算构架柱内力和基础反力，构架梁可以单独计算。

（1）计算模型：A 型柱、横梁及端撑均采用无缝焊接钢管，横梁采用热轧等肢角钢，梁柱间按刚性连接计算，端撑与柱顶间用销子，按铰接连接计算，端撑与 A 型柱间的中间杆采用无缝钢管，与主钢管为搭接，按铰接连接计算。参考以往设计经验，初步选定规格，然后计算分析校核，视需要作必要调整，以求经济合理。

（2）荷载信息：出线架计算荷载类型见表 1。

荷载组合系数：结构体形系数取 1，风振系数取 1，可变荷载及永久荷载分项系数分别取 1.4 及 1.3、1.2 及 1.3。

表 1　荷　载　类　型

荷载类型	导线张力（kN/相）	地线张力（kN/相）	基本风压（kN/m^2）	地震烈度	最高温度（℃）	最低温度（℃）
数值	26.2	23	0.4	7 度（0.15g）	35	−30

（3）计算结果：横梁上、下弦杆采用 $\phi114\times8$，腹杆用∠80×8；构架 A 字柱及端撑用 $\phi299\times10$，联系杆用 $\phi203\times10$，材料为 Q235 钢。计算中节点位移值、图形显示、内力、允许位移、应力、设计强度、长细比等结果均满足《钢结构设计规范》（GB 50017）中钢结构的各项设计指标。

（中国电建集团昆明勘测设计研究院有限公司　伏瑞　刘唯）

抽水蓄能电站发电厂房系统布置及厂房结构设计

抽水蓄能电站常采用地下式厂房，发电厂房内安装可逆式水轮发电机组。本文主要阐述地下发电厂房系统布置。

（一）厂区布置

1. 主洞室布置 主副厂房洞由安装场、机组段、副厂房组成，一般按“一”字形布置，中间机组段，安装场和副厂分置于机组段的两端。主变压器设在地下洞室。水泵水轮机组与主变压器设在一个洞室（一洞式布置)，适用于机组台数少电站。二洞式是水泵水轮机组和主变压器各独立布置在主副厂房洞和主变洞内，大中型电站多采用二洞式布置。尾水系统单机单洞布置，尾水洞较短时，一般将事故闸门与尾水检修闸门一并布置在下库进出水口处。尾水洞较长时，需在尾水洞适当位置布置尾水事故闸门（多机一洞布置时，尾水事故闸门设在岔管前尾水支洞上)，它可设在单独设置的尾水事故闸门洞内，也可与尾调室、主变洞等合并布置，国内此类电站通常在主变洞下游布置专门尾水事故闸门洞。

2. 主洞室间距 主副厂房洞和主变压器洞独立平行布置时，两洞间距以工程经验及工程类比为主，辅以数值分析补充论证。其控制因素是母线洞内电气设备布置和围岩稳定要求，大中型抽水蓄能电站两洞净距与相邻两洞室平均跨度之比为1.5～2.0，净距30～40m。随机组国产化及容量增加，大型抽水蓄能电站的母线洞长度有加长趋势，一般为35～45m。

3. 开关站布置 开关设备有敞开式和GIS组合式。敞开式布置在地面，投资较少，但占地多，可靠性差，国内近几年已很少采用。GIS式占用空间远小于敞开式，且运行可靠，可在地面或在地下。地面开关站运行条件好，可减少洞挖量，地形平缓时，常采用地面户内GIS。边坡较陡或无合适场地布置地面GIS时，可将其设在地下主变压器洞主变压器室上层。

（二）厂房内部布置

抽水蓄能电站主厂房内有水轮发电机组及其辅助设备，满足发电运行及安装检修作业需要，主机段设发电机层、水轮机层、蜗壳和尾水管层。厂房内、蜗壳进口前设进水球阀。

机组采用单级混流可逆式机组。水泵水轮机的转轮检修拆卸方式有上拆、中拆和下拆三种。机组拆卸方式的不同对厂房内部结构及通道布置有一定影响。

主变压器洞除布置主变压器、主变运输道、厂用变、地下GIS外，为满足机组水泵工况电动机起动要求，还布置启动母线及静态变频启动装置（即SFC系统)。启动母线与SFC系统相连，一般设在主变洞上游专门的启动母线廊道内。SFC系统通常布置在主变洞一端。

（三）厂房结构设计

抽水蓄能电站地下厂房主要结构的设计与常规电站地下厂房基本相同，但厂房结构刚度和振动控制要求较高，楼板、机墩风罩、蜗壳外围混凝土、尾水管等结构设计有所不同。

1. 楼板结构 有板梁结构和厚板结构两种，板梁结构刚度和抗振性能好于厚板结构。楼板结构边界约束越强，结构抗振性能越好。一般在与围岩接触的板梁及支撑柱、墙体范围内增设锚筋，在主要孔洞周围布置较大断面的梁系结构，同时尽量减少框架柱长细比。如天荒坪采取上下游柱与围岩用锚筋联结，并增加楼板上下游梁的断面尺寸。采取以上措施后，1阶振型的自振频率由10.02提高到34.14，使厂房结构的动力特性得到优化。

2. 机墩及风罩结构 机墩结构的厚度一般3m左右。转轮上拆的机组，上下游均可布置通道，机墩形状选用圆筒或多边形。中拆机组，机墩上需开一个较大搬运道，机墩结构的刚度削弱较大，要采取工程措施加以弥补。天荒坪蓄能电站为中拆方式，机墩上开一个5.9m×2.44m转轮顶盖搬运道。为提高机墩整体刚度，将机墩紧贴下游岩壁布置，内部开一廊道，用以布置电缆、水管、风管等，运行通道布置在机墩上游。

风罩墙为圆筒或多边形，厚0.8～1m。墙上开2个孔，即进人孔和主母线引出孔，有些工程还开有中性点设备引出孔。风罩下部固定在机墩上，顶部同发电机层楼板整体浇筑。

3. 蜗壳外围混凝土结构 抽水蓄能电站均采用金属蜗壳，可承担全部内水压力，蜗壳外围混凝土结构可按限裂设计。其作为上部结构基础，尺寸满足结构受力和机组运行稳定的要求。已建电站的经验，厚度一般不小于1.5m，局部最小不小于0.5倍蜗壳直径。外围混凝土结构一侧宜紧靠围岩，天荒坪、泰安、桐柏、宜兴、宝泉电站均采用该布置型式。

抽水蓄能电站机组转速高，运行工况转换频繁，使机组产生较大振动。为此，蜗壳外围混凝土与金属蜗壳采用联合受力方式。在蜗壳充水保持一定压力情况下，浇筑外围混凝土。通过调整蜗壳保压值控制运行期外围混凝土与蜗壳分担内水压力的比例，在保证外围混凝土结构安全条件下，使其与蜗壳联合承担内水压力，提高蜗壳结构整体刚度。抽水蓄能电站与常规电站相比，蜗壳尺寸较小，同时在厂房内布置有进水阀，故厂房内也具有设置保压闷头空间。

4. 尾水管结构　其结构有3个特点：水头较高，尾水管尺寸相对较小；因是双向运行，尾水管在水泵工况兼作进水管；机组安装高程低，尾水管内水压力远大于常规电站。

尾水管内侧均设钢衬，可单独承受全部内水压力。钢衬与外围混凝土间为锚筋连接。

尾水管常兼作厂房下层开挖施工通道，尾水管钢衬外包混凝土厚度由厂房施工及钢衬安装需要确定。为保证钢衬与外围混凝土紧密结合，尾水管钢衬底板应预留接触灌浆孔。

（中国电建集团华东勘测设计研究院有限公司
鲍利发　江亚丽　吴喜艳）

虹吸管在讨赖河流域已建水电站中的应用

讨赖河流域的镜铁山、东水峡、冰沟等引水式水电站建设中，被引水河段的部分河段断流。为解决此问题，需增设生态流量放水孔。获取生态流量可在水电站拦河大坝适当位置凿孔铺设涵管向下游输水，也可在水电站拦河大坝泄洪或排沙系统相应的挡水闸门上开孔向下游输水，或利用水电站拦河大坝原有布置，在大坝适当位置铺设虹吸管道引水至下游。对镜铁山、东水峡、冰沟等坝高较低的小型水电站，用虹吸管输水代替坝体打孔铺设涵管输水，造价低，工期短，使用灵活，管理、维护方便。

（一）电站概况

自上而下依次建成的镜铁山、东水峡、冰沟水电站，其概况如下。

1. 镜铁山　主要建筑物有拦河坝、引水发电系统、泄洪排沙系统、发电厂房，Ⅳ等小（1）型工程。电站装机容量36MW，设计水头64m。大坝为浆砌块石外包混凝土的重力坝，坝顶高程2948m，最大坝高56m，坝顶宽7m，坝顶长94m。上游坝面边坡高程2920m以上为铅直，以下为1∶0.35边坡，下游坝面边坡1∶0.75。泄水建筑物由溢流坝与导流泄洪排砂洞组成。溢流坝段45m，在河床中部，坝顶自由溢流，堰顶高程2940m，前沿宽42m。设计最大泄水量525m^3/s，校核最大泄水量1180m^3/s。

2. 东水峡　枢纽为闸坝结合“一”字形集中布置，建筑物主要包括进水闸、排砂闸、泄冲闸及左右岸连接建筑物，Ⅲ等中型工程。电站装机容量52.8MW，设计水头189m。工程水库为日调节水库，闸坝顶高程2570m，闸底2559.5m，正常蓄水位2568m，最大坝高10.5m。

3. 冰沟　主要建筑物有浆砌块石外包混凝土重力坝、引水发电系统、泄洪排沙系统、发电厂房，Ⅳ等小（1）型工程。电站装机容量21MW。工程水库为日调节水库，坝顶高程2021.5m，闸底2000m，正常蓄水位2020m，最大坝高21.5m，坝顶宽12.3m。

（二）虹吸管路的设计布置

镜铁山等的虹吸管布置原则是，在不破坏原有建筑物及设备条件下，尽量缩短虹吸管路径，减少虹吸道转弯次数，当库区水位在死水位时确保向下游输水的最小流量不变。

1. 镜铁山　依据电站坝形布置，经现场踏勘确定在泄水建筑物溢流坝坝顶铺设虹吸管向下游输水，以满足向下游河道输送生态流量。虹吸管进口高程2937m，穿越坝顶管道中心线高程2939.5m，虹吸管出口高程2933m。

2. 东水峡　枢纽建筑物自左向右依次布置1孔进水闸、1孔排砂闸、3孔泄洪闸及左右岸连接建筑物。3孔8.5m×8.84m（宽×高）泄洪闸布置在坝体中部靠主河一侧，且为表孔弧形工作闸门。经现场踏勘确定在3孔表孔弧形工作闸门上铺设虹吸管向下游输水，既不破坏原有弧形工作闸门，又可满足向下游输送生态流量。进口高程2566m，垂直上升越过闸门顶部的虹吸管中心线安装高程2568.825m，再顺着闸门内侧向下，出口高程2561m。

3. 冰沟　电站大坝为浆砌石重力坝，外包混凝土厚0.5～1.5m。自左向右依次为1孔进水闸、1孔冲砂闸、2孔泄洪闸及左右岸副坝连接建筑。经现场踏勘确定在冲砂闸检修闸门下游侧与工作闸门上游胸墙间的空间距离（0.7m）布置虹吸管进口段。进口高程2018m，垂直上升越过闸门顶部的水平虹吸管中心线高程2021.2m，再垂直向下，出口高程2013.5m。

（三）虹吸管设计

虹吸管水力计算主要是确定虹吸管的流量及其顶部最大允许安装高程。讨赖河流域均属高原气候，计算时虹吸管最大真空度取7m，按短管进行水力计算，依据计算公式求得出水流量、虹吸管安装高程和进口最小淹没深度。

（四）虹吸管设计中注意问题

虹吸管运行的核心问题是防止虹吸管内进入空气，其要点如下：

（1）虹吸管设计布置一定要满足虹吸管最小淹没深度，在满足淹没深度的条件下，虹吸管进口方向朝下布置。

（2）虹吸管尽量选择优质无缝钢管，减少焊缝数量，控制好每道焊缝质量，确保虹吸管的密封性。

（3）防止在虹吸管进口处吸入杂物，影响虹吸管性能，进口处设拦污栅。

(4) 虹吸管出口优选密封性能好的球阀，以减少管内进入空气。

(中国电建集团西北勘测设计研究院有限公司 任国良)

卡鲁玛水电站拦污漂固定墩稳定、应力及变形特性分析

乌干达卡鲁玛（Karuma）水电站位于基奥嘉尼罗河（River Kyoga Nile）上。电站总装机容量 6×100MW，低坝＋长引水＋地下厂房开发。拦河坝由两岸挡水坝、溢流坝段、冲沙底孔坝段、生态流量泄放坝段和鱼道等 21 个坝段组成，长 314.43m。进水口在河流左岸，与左一1 坝段相邻，前缘与坝轴线成 111.7°夹角，闸坝为“正向泄洪冲沙，侧向取水”布置。进水口为岸塔式结构，6 个单元“一”字排开。进水口单元包括拦污栅段、喇叭口和闸门塔，单元间设结构缝。单个进水口宽 24m，总宽度 144m，塔高 20.5m，沿水流方向长 29.4m。

(一) 拦污漂结构布置

据电站坝址及库区调查，漂浮物量大、季节性不强。拦污漂轴线拟与溢洪道主流向接近，漂浮物可顺流从排漂闸排走。为缩短每段拦污漂长度，设置 5 个进水口拦污漂固定墩。

固定墩初拟断面以圆内接五边形截面为主（见图 1），五边形角度考虑拦污漂连接角度。固定墩为基岩上悬臂钢筋混凝土偏心受压构件，结构独特，相关规范无详细设计要求，故参考陆军工程师兵团重力坝设计规范，采用三维有限元法进行结构稳定计算和配筋设计。

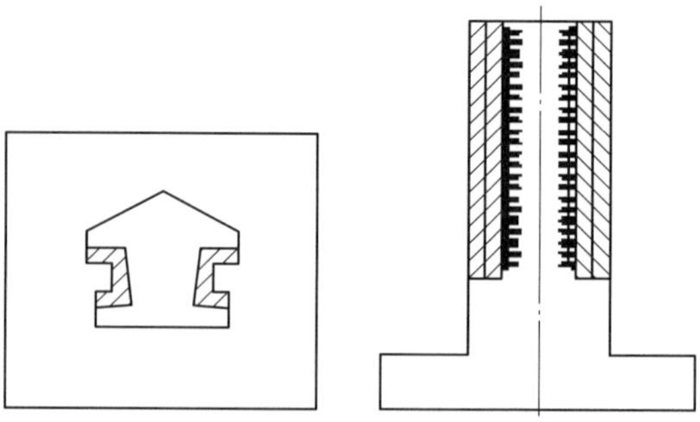

图 1 拦污漂固定墩典型断面示意图

(二) 拦污漂固定墩稳定分析

固定墩在进水口前缘 50～60m 处，基础底高程 1018m，结构顶高程 1032m，总高度 14m。

计算荷载有自重、浮托力、水压力、拦污漂拉力和地震作用力。在正常、非常和极端荷载条件下，在Ⅰ正常蓄水工况、Ⅱ洪水工况、Ⅲ正常蓄水＋OBE 地震工况和Ⅳ正常蓄水＋MDE 地震工况下，采用抗滑稳定安全系数计算公式进行计算。抗滑稳定计算结果见表 1。

表 1 拦污漂固定墩抗滑稳定安全系数及基底应力计算成果

计算工况	合力位置（m）		抗滑稳定安全系数 *FS*		基底前缘应力（kPa）		基底后缘应力（kPa）	
	计算值	标准值	计算值	标准值	计算值	标准值	计算值	标准值
Ⅰ	4.26	3.33～6.67	202.40	2.0	95.71	7590	37.10	7590
Ⅱ	3.32	2.5～7.5	88.59	1.7	133.36	12650	－0.56	－984
Ⅲ	3.92	0～10	37.49	1.3	71.57	22770	－14.27	－2460
Ⅳ	3.56	0～10	20.02	1.3	200.33	22770	－67.53	－2460

由表 1 可知，拦污漂固定墩抗滑稳定安全系数和基底作用位置满足规范要求，基底压应力和拉应力满足规范要求，且裕度较大。

(三) 拦污漂固定墩结构计算

计算选取河中固定墩建立三维模型，计算模型网格共 10292 个节点，9200 个单元。X 向垂直于固定墩一侧拦污漂滑槽轨道，Z 向竖直向下。固定墩基础底面完全固定，其他表面为自由面。计算荷载、计算工况同稳定分析，在既定的荷载组合下进行计算。

位移计算结果表明：在洪水工况下，拦污漂固定墩位移值最大，X 向最大位移为 1.07mm，出现在固定墩顶部下游侧；Z 向最大位移为－0.32mm，出现在固定墩顶部上游侧。在各种工况下，拦污漂固定墩的位移值都非常小。

竖向应力计算结果表明：拦污漂固定墩竖向主要处于受压状态，但各工况下，在受力另一侧拦污漂滑槽底部出现拉应力；洪水工况下，拉应力最大值 1.45MPa，超过混凝土抗拉强度（1.27MPa），需设计配筋。

X 向应力计算结果表明：拦污漂固定墩 X 向主要处于受压状态，但各工况下，固定墩柱体顶部和基础底板上表面局部出现拉应力，拉应力值很小，远小于混凝土抗拉强度。故拦污漂固定墩沿水平方向仅需配置构造钢筋。

（四）拦污漂固定墩有限元配筋

根据上述应力计算分析结果，计算拦污漂固定墩配筋。固定墩配筋结果见表2、表3。

表2　拦污漂固定墩竖直方向配筋

工况	实际配筋
Ⅱ洪水工况	一层 ϕ28@20cm
Ⅲ正常蓄水＋OBE地震工况	一层 ϕ28@20cm
Ⅳ正常蓄水＋MDE地震工况	一层 ϕ28@20cm

表3　拦污漂固定墩水平方向配筋

工况	实际配筋
Ⅲ正常蓄水＋OBE地震工况	ϕ22@17.5cm
Ⅳ正常蓄水＋MDE地震工况	ϕ22@17.5cm

根据计算，竖向钢筋采用1层 ϕ28@20cm，水平向钢筋采用1层 ϕ22@17.5cm，可满足受力要求。

（中国电建集团华东勘测设计研究院有限公司
石亚远　刘晓宇　王晓鹏）

中國水力發電年鑒

6

土建施工

大 坝 施 工

两河口水电站大坝心墙雨季填筑施工

（一）工程区气象条件

两河口地区多年平均降水量 746.1mm，雨季（5～10 月）降水量，占全年 93%。降雨突然、历时短、瞬时雨强大。两河口专用气象站 2010～2014 年实测资料显示，多年平均降水量 721.7mm，雨季（5～10 月）降水量占全年 89%，月平均降雨量约 150mm。实际施工中，3～11 月均不同程度降雨。2017 年3 月～11 月降雨量 799.3mm、降雨 139 天。不良气象条件可能影响心墙正常填筑及填筑质量。

（二）问题及难点

（1）两河口水电站心墙土料小于 0.075mm 和小于 0.005mm 颗粒含量均比糯扎渡、长河坝等同类工程高，心墙土料填筑对降雨的敏感性更强，在坝址区干燥气候条件下，土层表面水分蒸发较快，降雨引起土层表面含水率变化大。

（2）2017 年两河口雨季周期长、降水量增多，雨情超出预期，实际有效施工 169 天，比投标时有效施工 214 天明显减少，给如期完成心墙填筑增加了难度。

（3）2017 年 11 月降雨量 0.4mm，停工 14h。2017 年 3 月 26～27 日，坝区当日最大雨强 0.2mm/min，日累计降雨量 3.4mm，小于 5mm，现场停工 21.3h。《水电工程施工组织设计规范》（DL/T 5397—2007）中给出的“砾石土（掺合土），日降雨量＜5mm 照常施工；5～10mm 雨日停工”的规定不适用于两河口水电站。

（三）主要应对措施

结合两河口工程的气象条件及土料特性，采取对应的雨季施工措施如下。

1. 心墙填筑面施工措施

（1）填筑面形成中间高上下游低的“龟背”状，坡比控制在 2%内，利于排水。

（2）填筑面采用 1/4 仓面快速轮换施工。

（3）左右岸接触性黏土用塑料薄膜覆盖，施工时揭开、完成后及时覆盖，并与两岸盖板混凝土紧贴，确保雨水沿塑料薄膜流下，再从“龟背”流至上下游。

（4）在降雨来临前 30min，在填筑面形成“龟背”状及接触性黏土覆盖的基础上，用 18t 平碾对砾石土料进行光面处理，将土料压实，利于排水。

（5）降雨后及时利用光面斜坡将雨水引排至反滤区以，反滤料 1 和 2 挖槽铺塑料薄膜引排，积水较多处用人工或小型抽水泵清除，受雨水污染的接触性黏土局部挖除换填。

（6）雨后复工对填筑面进行含水率及压实度检测。

2. 天气预报　采用 ACCU 天气预报软件预报气象，利用甘孜州气象雷达进行现场实时天气观测及预报，指导心墙填筑施工。施工区域天气预判准确率由前期 50%提高至 93%。

3. 辅助工程施工措施　土料开采、掺拌及各心墙料运输均在晴天进行，汛前提前备存 10 万 m^3 砾石土成品料，并用防雨布覆盖保护。

（1）汛期土料场采用小范围剥离、鉴定和开采的方式。

（2）土料制备中，各备料仓底部设 4%左右的坡度，各互层备料表面也有 4%左右坡度，最后一层土料备料完成后用 18t 平碾碾压光面。降雨前，掺拌过程中的砾石土料及成品砾石土料料堆，先用反铲拍平，再用防雨布覆盖。汛期砾石土料掺拌均用正铲集中进行。

（3）土料及成品砾石土料运输过程中，须用防雨布全方位覆盖。砾石土料上坝前须进行含水率、级配试验检测，各项指标检测合格后方可上坝填筑。

（4）接触性黏土汛期不开采，均在汛前开采备料。黏土备料仓面中间高四周低，备存的黏土等成品料均用防雨布覆盖。汛期反滤料提前生产堆存在雨棚料仓内脱水，填筑时优先使用雨棚内反滤料。做好反滤料的生产、脱水及上坝仓的循环作业。

（四）雨季施工效果检查

1. 施工质量　雨季施工期间心墙砾石土填筑最大铺料层厚（松铺）30cm，最小层厚（松铺）21cm，平均层厚（松铺）27.9cm，满足虚铺厚度不大于 30cm 的设计要求。压实层厚最大 28.9cm，最小 18cm，平均 25.9cm，满足设计要求。

将正常施工时段及雨后复工时段的砾石土料试验检测数据成果进行分析，除部分雨后复工检测含水率较大外（含水率偏上限，但满足要求），其余检测结果均100%满足要求（即P5含量为30%～50%、小于20mm压实度≥100%）。

雨季期间做了3组砾石土和6组黏土室内渗透试验，以及3组砾石土和1组黏土现场原位渗透试验，检测结果均满足设计要求，合格率100%。

总之，虽2017年雨季降雨持续时间长，雨强高，但通过有序组织并采取相应措施，确保降雨和非降雨时段心墙土料填筑质量的一致性，心墙填筑采取的措施十分有效。

2. 施工进度　结合历年气象情况及投标文件对比分析，虽实际有效施工天数比投标有效施工天数减少45天，但实际心墙填筑上升高度却比投标时高出5.5m，并提前36天完成了2017年年度目标。

（中国水利水电建设工程咨询西北有限公司
武波　魏雄　杨晓鹏）

乌弄龙水电站大坝混凝土拌和系统工艺设计与布置优化

乌弄龙水电站大坝混凝土拌和系统距下游砂石加工系统7.5km，该系统生产混凝土总量约116万m^3，高峰月浇筑强度7.25万m^3，预冷混凝土设计生产能力218m^3/h。

（一）系统工艺及布置

1. 系统组成　由拌和楼，骨料、胶凝材料和外加剂储运，压缩空气，制冷、二次筛分车间，供排水及废水处理，电气等子系统组成，布置在高程1830、1837、1857m平台。

（1）两座HL320-2S4500L强制式拌和楼，单台产量320m^3/h，预冷混凝土240m^3/h。

（2）骨料进料有3个受料坑，储存于3个直径16m、高20m粗骨料罐，2个直径16m、高20m细骨料罐，每个罐4000m^3，钢筋混凝土结构。一次风冷料仓6个，分别储存大中小石，单个料仓断面4m×6m。冷却区高4m，冷却层储量140m^3。22条胶带机运送骨料上楼。

（3）水泥、掺合料（粉煤灰）储量保证混凝土连续浇筑所需用量。有3座1500t水泥罐和3座1000t掺合料罐，满足10d储量要求。罐体为铝卷板筒仓结构，钢结构柱支撑。

（4）空气压缩机车间面积20m×8m，设3台40m^3/min和1台20m^3/min空气压缩机，利用管路输送至拌和楼等用风部位，满足系统用风需要。

（5）外加剂车间面积20m×8m，建有钢筋混凝土结构池6个，满足3种外加剂一配一用切换使用，再利用管路输送至拌和楼上。

（6）制冷系统装机容量600×104kcal/h（1kcal=4186.8J），其中一次风冷350×104kcal/h，二次200×104kcal/h；制冷水50×104kcal/h（均标准工况）。冷水生产能力40m^3/h，提供5～2℃低温水。设一次和二次风冷车间，建筑面积分为22m×14m和20m×14m。根据混凝土特点和降温幅度，采取一次、二次风冷粗骨料为主、加低温水拌和方案。骨料地面一次风冷＋搅拌楼料仓风冷＋低温水拌和，满足常态混凝土出机口温度12℃、碾压混凝土13℃要求。

（7）二次筛分设备在骨料罐与一次风冷车间之间。骨料经装车、运输、卸料储存后有破碎、裹粉，利用二次筛分再次分级、脱水、去粉，保证进入一次风冷料仓的骨料级配合格、清洁。配置2座3YKR3060圆振动筛，筛子底部设2台FC-15洗砂机。

按骨料二次筛分冲洗用水量，计入损耗，确定废水处理规模为160m^3/h。骨料冲洗脱水后带走的水量约10t/h，产生废水约150t/h，用“机械处理＋辐流沉淀池＋压滤”工艺处理废水。骨料分级、冲洗产生的废水，进入筛子下方的螺旋分级机，将其中粗颗粒回收，通过胶带机送至钢结构弃渣仓堆存，自卸汽车装运至渣场。螺旋分级机中的废水加药后自流至辐流沉淀池，沉淀后的清水进入回收水池回收利用，用于骨料冲洗。辐流沉淀池底部泥浆经渣浆泵抽至压滤车间压滤，压滤后的弃渣运至指定渣场。

2. 系统工艺流程　骨料从砂石加工系统装车称量后，运至拌和系统成品骨料受料仓，经胶带机运至各骨料罐。生产时，细骨料由胶带机运至拌和楼储存和使用。粗骨料通过骨料罐下部廊道，经给料机送至胶带机，再运至二次筛分车间冲洗、分级、脱水。重新分级后的各级配粗骨料经胶带机运至制冷系统一次风冷料仓降温后，胶带机运至拌和楼顶部骨料仓堆存，拌和楼上冷风机对粗骨料再次风冷。制冷车间为拌和楼生产提供3℃拌和冷水。

外加剂储运系统由外加剂车间及相应管路构成，可同时制备储存和输送3种外加剂至拌和楼。胶凝材料储运系统由3个1500t水泥罐、3个1000t掺合料罐及相关风、灰管路构成。高压空气由压缩空气系统提供。拌和系统生产产生的废水处理后全部回用。

3. 系统布置　1857m平台用于骨料运输车辆倒车、卸料和受料。受料平台有3个受料仓。1837m平台布置混凝土骨料罐、二次筛分车间、配电房、一次风冷车间、一次风冷料仓、废水处理系统压滤车间、辐流沉淀池、回收水池、泵房、实验室。1830m平台布置2座拌和楼、空气压缩机车间、二次风冷车间、6个胶凝材料罐、外加剂车间、沉淀池及地磅等。

（二）系统优化及其效果

优化方案在原方案基础上，主要作了以下调整。

（1）保证拌和系统生产能力情况下，利用现有闲置设备，拌和楼改为2座旧2×6m^{3}强制式搅拌楼，型号HL360-2S6000L，铭牌生产能力360m^3/h，温控混凝土生产能力270m^3/h。

（2）三组钢筋混凝土结构的受料坑改为两组。

（3）将施工难度大的骨料罐改为成品料场。粗骨料一次风冷，细骨料直接上楼，两者分开设置。料场堆高15m，大中小石、常态砂、碾压砂堆长分别为25、30、40m，中间挡墙隔离。粗骨料仓3个，1个料仓活容积约3000m^3，满足高峰期2天使用。细骨料仓2个，常态砂活容积3000m^3，碾压砂4100m^3，可满足高峰期3天使用。

（4）原骨料上料用两条胶带机，优化后粗细骨料分别采用单胶带机上楼。

（5）胶凝材料储存改为金属结构罐，直径10m、高14.57m（带锥体部分高20.66m）。

（6）将一、二次风冷车间合并布置在高程1837m平台，制冷车间采用砖混结构，建筑面积30m×18m。优化后使高程1830m平台比较宽敞。

（7）在业主同意下，取消二次筛分冲洗，采用干筛。配套废水处理系统也随之取消。

通过对系统的调整优化，减少了系统设备的投入、土建工程量、运行费用。该系统于2016年9月投产运行，截至2018年6月累计生产混凝土108万m^3，完成合同工程量的93%。

（中国水利水电第七工程局有限公司 袁强强）

枕头坝一级水电站主体混凝土快速施工技术

（一）工程概况

枕头坝一级水电站枢纽建筑物由混凝土重力坝、发电厂房、5孔泄洪闸及消力池、1孔排污闸、安装间等组成。大坝坝顶高程626.5m，最大坝高86.5m，坝顶长317.55m，自左至右依次为左岸1～3号非溢流坝段，4～7号厂房坝段，8号2孔泄洪闸坝段、9号1孔排污闸坝段、10号3孔泄洪闸坝段和11号右岸非溢流坝段。大坝及发电厂房混凝土总量121万m^3，其中常态混凝土111万m^3，碾压混凝土10万m^3，钢筋总量4.33万t。

电站前期施工工期滞后114天，为实现2015年8月电站发电目标，采用了混凝土快速施工技术。从2012年8月10日首仓浇筑至当年12月31日共完成大坝及发电厂房混凝土浇筑30万m^3，月最高浇筑混凝土达10.4万m^3，超过了施工组织设计的9.6万m^3。

（二）混凝土施工布置

1. 拌和系统　混凝土拌和系统布置在大坝右岸下游约1.5km处，混凝土生产及制冷系统按月浇筑强度9.6万m^3/月设计，配置2座HL240-2S3000L型拌和楼，常温混凝土生产能力为360m^3/h，预冷混凝土（出机口温度15℃）生产能力为261m^3/h。

2. 施工机械布置　大坝及发电厂房混凝土垂直运输主要用门塔机。共布置10台门塔机：2台门机和1台塔机布置在大坝及发电厂房上游，3台门机布置在大坝及发电厂房下游，1台门机布置在纵向混凝土围堰，1台门机布置在右非坝顶，1台门机布置在左非1号坝段坝顶，1台门机布置在消力池底板，完全覆盖大坝及发电厂房施工全部范围。

（三）主体混凝土施工赶工措施

1. 优化混凝土种类　电站主体工程混凝土总量121万m^3，其中大坝及厂房基础下部回填混凝土约20万m^3，原设计为常态混凝土。结合现场条件，将左非坝段、厂房坝段下部和泄洪闸下部等11.48万m^{3}常态混凝土，优化为碾压混凝土。这样简化了混凝土温度控制，且碾压混凝土用自卸汽车直接入仓，提高了入仓强度，明显加快了进度。厂房坝段提前15天，1、2号泄洪闸坝段提前30天，左非2、3号坝段提前53天到达坝顶高程。

2. 改变混凝土入仓方案　左非坝段混凝土原采用门塔机入仓浇筑，优化后调整为碾压混凝土，不再用门塔机入仓。根据现场条件，在左非1号坝段（已施工到顶）顶部626.5m高程设一条负压溜槽至左非2、3号坝段仓面，仓内汽车转料入仓。溜槽入仓每班300～400m^3，2012年12月左非坝段混凝土创下1.9万m^{3}施工强度。再利用1台门机和1台塔机配合入仓，使左非2、3号坝段比合同工期提前53天到达坝顶高程。

3. 基础下部常态混凝土用长臂反铲入仓　长臂反铲入仓强度高、机动灵活、投入快，适用于大坝及发电厂房坝段下部基础混凝土施工。在门塔机投产前用6台长臂反铲浇筑厂房下部、消力池底板、导墙基础等部位混凝土。从2012年8～12月共浇筑该部位混凝土30万m^3，其中约20万m^{3}用长臂反铲入仓，有效地保证了混凝土施工强度。

4. 采用预制构件　主要预制构件包括帷幕灌浆廊道151块、检修排水廊道88块、尾水扩散段顶板倒“T型”预制梁264根、尾水闸墩联系梁24根、进水口闸墩联系梁36根、GIS室桥机梁、闸室顶部双向门机大梁、交通桥、工作桥等。

5. 常态混凝土改为泵送混凝土　进水口胸墙、

主机间蜗壳及泄洪闸胸墙等部位混凝土改为泵送混凝土，电站共浇筑泵送混凝土18.6万m^3。其中厂房进水口胸墙以上增加泵送混凝土入仓，厂房进水口上游引水渠左右侧及4号机进水口胸墙下游左侧安装间，共增设4台混凝土泵入仓。泵送混凝土使用低热水泥、铺设冷却水管，解决温控问题。增加混凝土入仓手段后，腾出门塔机吊装钢筋、模板，用于门轨安装。使进水口胸墙混凝土每层施工由14～18天，缩短到8～12天，加快进度赶回已滞后近2个月工期。

6. 混凝土蜗壳调整为蜗壳钢衬　混凝土蜗壳运行期间气蚀对其损伤严重，检修周期比钢衬蜗壳长，后期维护成本高。为此将原混凝土蜗壳优化为蜗壳钢衬，C35钢纤维混凝土内衬调整为C25常态混凝土。改钢衬蜗壳虽增加钢衬工程量，但也减少大量钢纤维和高标号混凝土工程量，总的减少投资1717.13万元。蜗壳钢衬加快了主机间混凝土施工进度。

7. 减小固结灌浆与混凝土施工互相干扰　大坝及厂房基础均有大量盖重固结灌浆。盖重混凝土厚度达到设计要求后，方可在混凝土上钻孔进行固结灌浆。在盖重混凝土上预埋钢管，可减少混凝土中钻孔量，也避免直接钻到钢筋，加快了固灌进度，保证了质量。

为满足固结灌浆的盖重要求，岸坡坝段固结灌浆是随坝体混凝土施工同步进行，因此固结灌浆将影响混凝土的施工进度。为减小影响，在混凝土连续上升2～3层后，集中进行一次固结灌浆。虽钻孔量有增加，但减少了固结灌浆施工准备时间及清理灌浆对仓号污染的时间，加快了混凝土施工进度。

8. 上游引水渠铺盖混凝土体型优化　大坝进水口上游引水渠设计为回填砂卵砾石分层平整碾压后浇筑1m厚铺盖混凝土。因施工道路需要，须等引水渠内布置的门塔机拆除后，才能开始引水渠铺盖混凝土施工。为此，对引水渠铺盖结构体型进行调整，对引水渠铺盖混凝土结合已形成的施工道路修改体型。这样在引水渠混凝土施工时，引水渠各工作面施工道路不会阻断，使布置在进水口上游的塔机拆除前，可提前施工引水渠铺盖混凝土，从而缩短了施工总工期。

（中国水利水电第三工程局有限公司　王伟）

收缝式双向可调翻转模板在象鼻岭水电站拱坝中的应用

象鼻岭水电站位于贵州省威宁县与云南省会泽县交界处的牛栏江上，系牛栏江流域中下游河段规划梯级的第三级水电站。工程以发电为主，水库正常蓄水位为1405m，电站装机两台，装机容量24万kW。枢纽建筑物由碾压混凝土拱坝、右岸引水系统和地下厂房等组成，泄水建筑物由3溢流表孔和2中孔组成，坝顶高程1409.50m，最大坝高141.5m，坝顶长459.21m，坝顶宽8m。大坝上下游面最大倒悬度分别为0.148和0.51，最大中心角97.433°，混凝土总量约68.9万m^3，其中碾压混凝土58.9万m^3。

（一）研究背景

在碾压混凝土双曲拱坝施工中，传统的翻转模板水平方向相邻两块模板搭接处存在明显折角，不利于拱坝水平方向上的体型控制。若满足该要求，需在相邻模板搭接处采用木板镶嵌处理或待混凝土施工完成后，用角磨机对棱角作磨光处理。这将加大体型控制难度，也增加工程量和成本。因此，翻转模板需改造。

（二）技术方案选择

新型翻转模板应结构简单、制安方便，能通过自身调节，以满足水平向带弧度大体积碾压混凝土施工需求。通过对大坝体形参数分析和不同模板计算机三维模拟比较，结合象鼻岭拱坝的体形特征，最终将模板设计成“面板双向可调、上下套模板可相对移动、可连续上升的收缝式翻转模板”。主要调整方案如下：

（1）将传统翻转模板整个主面板的普通刚性面材，调整为普通刚性面材与柔性面材镶嵌组合。

（2）将传统翻转模板主板面背面均布的加强筋板，调整为主板面柔性背面不设加强筋板，其余部位维持不变。

（3）将已改造完成的新型翻转模板主面板背部安装上操作平台等附属系统，再将水平调节系统（一端连接于新型面板背部水平方向两侧“普通刚性材料段”边缘位置、另一端连接在紧贴于模板背部的“主梁桁架”上）安装于模板背部附属系统与主板面背部间。一块模板配套4套水平调节系统。

（4）水平调节系统为简单的螺旋结构，主要由中间可旋转主杆（两端带旋转丝扣）和两端连接套筒（套筒内壁带丝扣与可旋转主杆两端丝扣配套）组成。当中间可旋转主杆顺时针旋转时，可旋转主杆两端深入套筒，整个杆件变短，起紧拉作用；逆时针旋转时，可旋转主杆两端逐渐退出套筒，整个杆件变长，起紧撑作用。紧拉与紧撑使主板面柔性段弯曲变形，从而形成弧度。

（三）新型翻转模板工艺原理

单块模板通过操作水平调节系统，使新型翻转模板主板面柔性板材段产生向内或向外小幅度弯曲，从而在水平方向上具有一定弧度，通过多块带弧度的模板水平相连后，在总体上满足双曲拱坝水平方向上的体型（弧度）要求。

（中国水利水电第三工程局有限公司　安芳科）

南公1水电站面板堆石坝堆石料碾压参数研究

南公1水电站位于老挝南部的阿速坡省内的南公河上，为老挝、越南、柬埔寨三个国家的交界区域。工程等别为二等大（2）型，主要任务是发电。工程由首部枢纽及引水发电系统组成。首部枢纽包括面板堆石坝、左岸溢洪道、左岸导流隧洞和右岸电站进水口。引水发电系统由电站进水口、引水隧洞、上游调压井、竖井、压力管道及地下厂房洞室群、尾水支洞、尾水隧洞、尾水出口等组成。挡水建筑物为混凝土面板堆石坝，坝顶长400m，坝顶宽8.8m，坝顶高程325m，最大坝高90m。坝体上游坝坡1∶1.4，下游坝坡1∶1.35。坝体填筑总量$184.7\times10^4m^3$。

（一）材料要求

堆石料料源主要为溢洪道料场、石料场、建筑物枢纽弱风化及以下流纹岩。材料要求：堆石料碾压后应有良好级配，级配范围应符合设计要求；填筑堆石料的最大粒径800mm，初定最少碾压遍数8遍，含泥量不大于5%，孔隙率小于22%，干密度大于$2.12g/cm^3$。

（二）试验流程

坝料碾压试验场地设在1号渣场，场地用推土机推平，碾压至坚实不再下沉，再用弱风化流纹岩进行基础硬化，振动碾碾压到设计标准，消除基础面对碾压试验的影响。在地基上铺一层试验料，表面不平整度不超过10cm。试验场地尺寸为30m×60m，面积$1800m^2$，每条试验带有效面积为6m×15m。试验流程如下：

（1）用全站仪测量布点位置，测量碾压前高程。

（2）采用进占法卸料。

（3）铺料整平后，振动碾静碾两遍，用全站仪测量测点的松铺厚度。

（4）采用进退错距碾压，两碾之间搭接不小于20cm。

（5）振动碾行进速度2.5km/h左右，振动频率25Hz左右，振幅在1.3～1.4mm左右，激振力不低于320～410kN。

（6）碾压完毕后，用全站仪找出方位点，并放出各点位置，测量碾后高程，确定压实厚度和沉降量。

（7）人工挖坑取样，坑径为最大粒径的2～3倍，灌水法检测干密度，灌水用塑料薄膜厚度为0.08mm。

（8）设计不同铺料厚度、不同碾压遍数，确定碾压机具对应的最佳碾压遍数、铺料厚度等技术参数。

（三）碾压试验及成果分析

堆石料试验项目包括压实干密度、颗粒分析、含水率及孔隙率。干密度测定用灌水法，含水率测定用烘干法，颗粒级配筛分是对试坑内测定干密度用的全料分级筛分。根据试验测定成果，绘制颗粒级配曲线图。

从试验成果分析，堆石料铺料厚度90、100、110cm，碾压6遍、8遍、12遍，随碾压遍数增加，干密度值增大，铺料厚度增加干密度降低，符合基本规律。铺料厚度90cm，碾压6遍、8遍；铺料厚度100cm，碾压8遍、10遍；铺料厚度110cm，碾压10遍；平均干密度与孔隙率均能满足设计要求。铺料厚度110cm，碾压8遍时，孔隙率满足设计要求，平均干密度不满足设计要求。

通过以上分析，施工中选用相对经济且施工强度相对较高的堆石料铺料厚度为110cm，进占法卸料，加水10%，32t振动碾进退错距碾压，行车速度2.5km/h，重叠宽度不小于20cm，静碾2遍，动碾10遍，满足设计干密度与孔隙率要求。

（中国水利水电第三工程局有限公司
刘永年　韩婷）

混凝土面板滑模施工技术在安拉沟水库的应用

哈密市安拉沟水库大坝为混凝土面板砂砾石坝，分主、副坝。主坝长287m，坝顶宽5m，坝高50.5m，坝坡1∶1.6。面板为整体式钢筋混凝土面板，板宽12m，厚0.4m，最大斜长88m。主坝面板共25块，首尾各一块为三角形。副坝长397m，坝高22.7m，采用分离式无筋混凝土面板，板厚0.3m，分块尺寸6m×4m。主、副坝面板浇筑均采用滑模技术。面板施工时，对传统滑模技术进行了改进。

（一）模板设计制作

传统无轨滑模侧模是钢木定型模板，滑模是角钢桁架结构，与混凝土接触面板为5mm厚钢板，分节加工现场组装。模板周转使用后易变形破损，故需对传统滑模技术作改进。

1. 侧模设计制作　将钢木结构侧模改为全钢结构定型尺寸，现场组装。设计混凝土面板厚度0.4m，选用［40槽钢，按3m模数切割下料。每块侧模其槽钢无腿面作为混凝土接触面，槽口面为支撑固定面。端部槽口内0.5m处各焊接1个活动固定支架（见图1）。

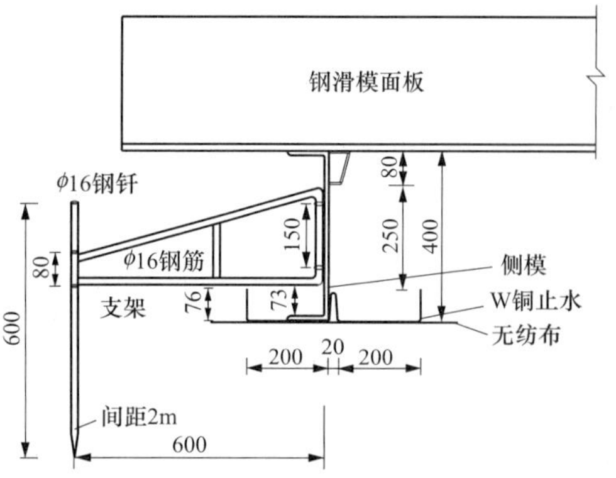

图 1　滑模断面示意图（尺寸单位：mm）

侧模安装时将支架以槽钢内的钢管为转轴与槽钢形成 90°角，用 $\phi16$ 钢钎插入支架中钢管法向打入坝体，使侧模安装与加固一次性完成。活动支架可收入槽钢内，不占空间。侧模端部用 8mm 厚钢板封堵，并在其上钻孔配螺栓用以侧模间纵向连接，侧模随每块面板的长度安装并加固。在侧模滑行面槽钢腿上钻 2 孔，间距 1m，作为钢钎插销孔眼，在滑模运行中停靠的保险装置之一。面板间的伸缩缝上口设有弹性聚氨酯填缝预留梯形槽，在侧模槽钢与混凝土接触面上部用角钢或扁钢焊接固定成直角梯形断面，混凝土浇筑脱模后就形成半个嵌缝槽口。补仓时用胶合板做成嵌缝口形状倒梯形放入，形成完整的伸缩缝口。

2. 滑模设计制作　滑模宽度和长度及结构根据大坝面板的宽度、坝面坡度及混凝土凝结速度等确定。滑模由底部钢面板、上部型钢桁架及操作平台、抹面平台组成。底部钢面板为厚 16mm 钢板，长 13.5m、宽 1.5m，用槽钢焊成一体。先在钢板上焊接与面板等长的 3 根［30 槽钢作为纵肋，槽钢一侧腿按滑模面宽上中下位置焊在钢板上（分段间隔焊）。再在滑模纵断面设 9 道人字结构，两头距滑模端 750mm，中间按 1500mm 间距均分（见图 2）。

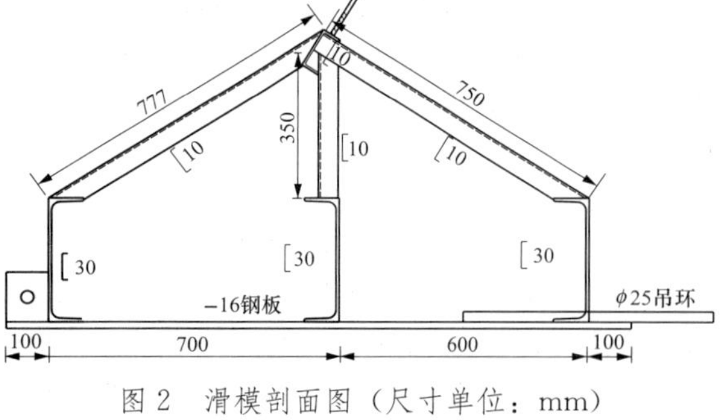

图 2　滑模剖面图（尺寸单位：mm）

在中间两跨人字坡的两面分别设置焊接两个斜向支撑，如平面投影的剪刀撑。滑模上口距端部 2m 处各焊一个 $\phi25$ 牵引吊环，再向内各 2.8m 再焊 2 个吊运及保险吊环。滑模剖面各部位尺寸按坝坡 1∶1.6 设计。安设在侧模上后，铺上木板即可形成 1 个 750mm 宽可铺料和振捣的操作平台，再安装栏杆、密目网作为安全防护设施。滑模尾部焊接 9 个插销式连接口，形成易装拆的一、二级修整收面平台。

3. 滑模的自重、配重及牵引力计算　滑模重量应大于等于浇筑混凝土时对滑模产生的上浮力。经计算，混凝土上浮力 50kN，滑模自重 43kN，配重 17kN，施工荷载 12kN，因此，滑模重量取 72kN。

经计算，滑模牵引力为 160kN。

因上浮力计算结果出入较大，而滑模重量可通过加配重来调整，故计算的滑模重量仅作参考。加配重以混凝土振捣不“浮模”为原则，现场增减。配重袋装砂砾石料，加在侧模与牵引钢丝绳之间的上方。滑模上设防滑安全保护装置，在滑模中部的 2 个吊环上各增设手动葫芦 1 台，挂在面板钢筋网上，用钢丝绳拉紧，随模板滑升而收短，使其始终处于受力状态。

（二）滑模的安装运行

滑模用 2 台 100kN 卷扬机牵引，卷扬机用地锚固定牢固。跳仓浇筑的面板两侧安装侧模，补仓利用已浇面板作支撑。侧模就位前，按设计要求调整固定好无纺布和铜止水。

滑模与卷扬机钢丝绳连接溜放至仓面起始点就位，经检查滑模与侧模安全无误后及时加配重，试滑二、三次，调整卷筒钢丝绳与坝坡面角度一致。滑模滑升前，清除坡面超浇混凝土。滑模连续滑升，每次行程 25～30cm，间隔时间不超过 30min，最大滑升速度不超过 2m/h。滑升时两端提升平稳、匀速、同步。每仓面板浇筑完成后，滑模吊出仓外检查，若有变形或脱焊，及时修补，并将表面混凝土及杂物清干净。

主坝使用的两套滑模，在主面板完成 80%后，其中一套一分为二作为副坝面板滑模，降低了成本，提高了效益。

（三）面板施工质量

浇筑完成的面板混凝土，外观抹面均匀，表面平整，无高低起伏、无鼓胀。接缝侧各 1m 内的混凝土表面，检查平整度均在 5mm 内。混凝土试件试验结果表明：龄期 28 天抗压强度平均值 34.8MPa，强度保证率 97%，离差系数 0.10。面板混凝土完成初期未出现宽度大于 0.2mm 的裂缝，有水平向短浅表面裂缝 11 条及一些不规则裂缝。跨越一个冬季后面板出现宽度大于 0.2mm 的裂缝 25 条。对裂缝进行化灌水溶性聚氨酯材料处理，表面用聚氨酯防水黏结涂料涂刷封闭。水库蓄水运行 3 年，运行情况良好。

（新疆绿翔建筑安装工程有限责任公司　夏元清）

混凝土面板坝面板应力分析可视化程序研发与应用

混凝土面板堆石坝的面板在运行中长时间挡水，随库水位的升降，面板在垫层坡面上随堆石体的变形而产生位移与挠曲变形。如坝体沉降变形较大，及面板与堆石体变形不协调，面板内部会形成极复杂的应力状态，从而引发面板局部挤压破坏和面板结构性裂缝。进一步研究中高面板堆石坝面板的应力问题，加强面板应力监测与分析，对改进设计方法和面板渗漏查找修复具有重要的工程意义。

（一）面板应力监测数据分析

对于大坝面板应力监测，通常选取河谷最长面板条块及其左右岸坡各一面板条块。对高度超过 100m 的 1 级坝，宜在可能产生挤压破坏的面板条块增设 1 个监测断面。测点设在面板条块中心线上，钢筋计布置顺坡和水平两向。高坝及形态特殊的大坝面板，要专门研究应力监测方案，增加监测点数量。一般说，大坝面板的监测仪器数量多，各支仪器从埋设后开始采集数据，在持续数年的施工期，会积累庞大的监测数据，分析工作量较重。

面板应力监测数据分析的主要困难在于，监测点数量众多、空间分布不同，且在施工期数据处于不断变化中。对某一关键时刻面板整体应力分布规律，可通过逐一查看此时各测点的应力值，能获得一个宏观的认识。但想获得面板整体应力分布随时间动态变化趋势则工作量骤增。常规的面板应力监测数据分析，先绘制各测点应力变化过程曲线，通过分别查看各测点的过程曲线来了解大坝面板的整体情况。其缺点是获得的监测数据相对独立，无法将所有测点的历史数据形成一个随时间同步推进同步展示的整体进行分析，因而对不同时刻的整个面板全部测点综合应力分布规律难以掌握。为此，开发了一款对全局数据进行同步推移同步展示的辅助程序，用来辅助面板应力监测数据的分析。

（二）程序简介

1. 编程工具　采用可视化程序语言 Visual Basic（以下简称 VB），该编程工具是结构化、模块化、面向对象、包含协助开发环境的事件驱动为机制的可视化程序设计语言。

2. 基础数据　需要的基础数据包括，所有测点应力数据表 1 份（xls 格式）和大坝面板应力监测点分布图（jpeg 格式）1 张。

3. 程序界面　程序包含两个窗口。先是数据输入窗口，在该窗口可以通过按钮“输入应力值”，从测点应力数据表（xls 格式）选取应力，输入的监测数据显示在本窗口内。此后会自动启动“应力动态分布图”窗口（见图 1），展示的面板体型为事先导入的“大坝面板应力监测点分布图”；底部为滑动条控件，用于控制窗口中显示的数据值时刻；左下角为图例及大坝面板的相关参数。

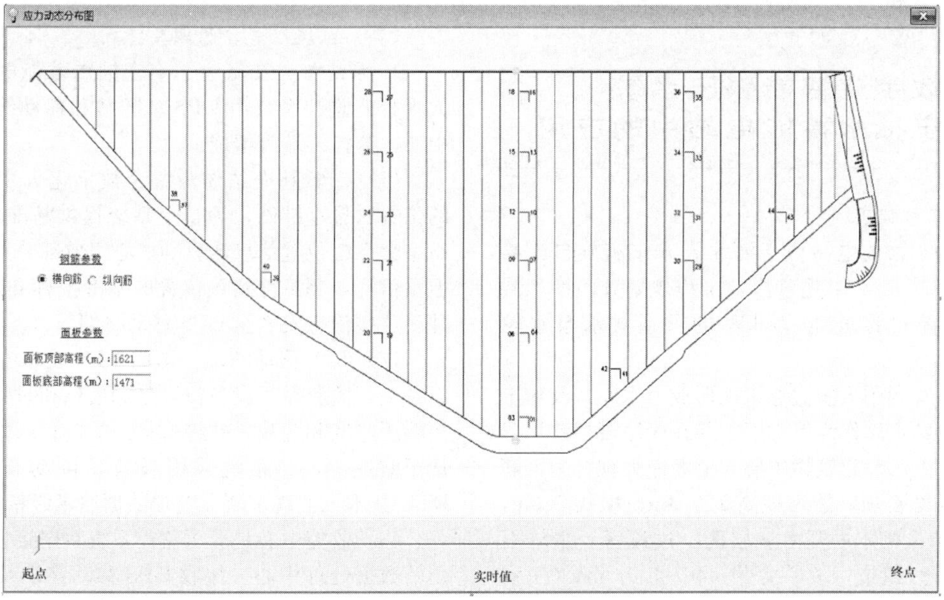

图 1　应力动态分布图界面

4. 功能简介

(1) 用户可手动拖动滑动条的滑块，使其指向任意想要查看的时刻。

(2) 应力动态分布图窗口中显示出滑块所指日期各监测点应力值分布总图。压应力用蓝色表示，拉应力红色表示。横向钢筋计应力用水平短线表示，纵向钢筋计应力用竖直短线表示。

(3) 如果滑块所指示时刻水库已蓄水，应力动态分布图窗口中会显示指示时刻的库水在大坝面板上的淹没线，并标注当前库水位高程。

(4) 本程序设置了动态预警分析功能，用户可手动输入面板应力警戒限值，当某监测点应力超限时，会在应力动态分布图窗口中突出显示。

(三) 应用演示

梨园水电站高面板堆石坝面板应力监测资料，采用 VB 程序对面板整体应力演变过程进行分析，时间跨度从监测仪器安装埋设至水库蓄水运行。图 2 为 2015 年 3 月 13 日蓄水至正常蓄水位时面板钢筋计应力分布图。

(中国电建集团西北勘测设计研究院有限公司 袁秋霜 管强
西安航天基地配套工程服务有限公司 韩庆)

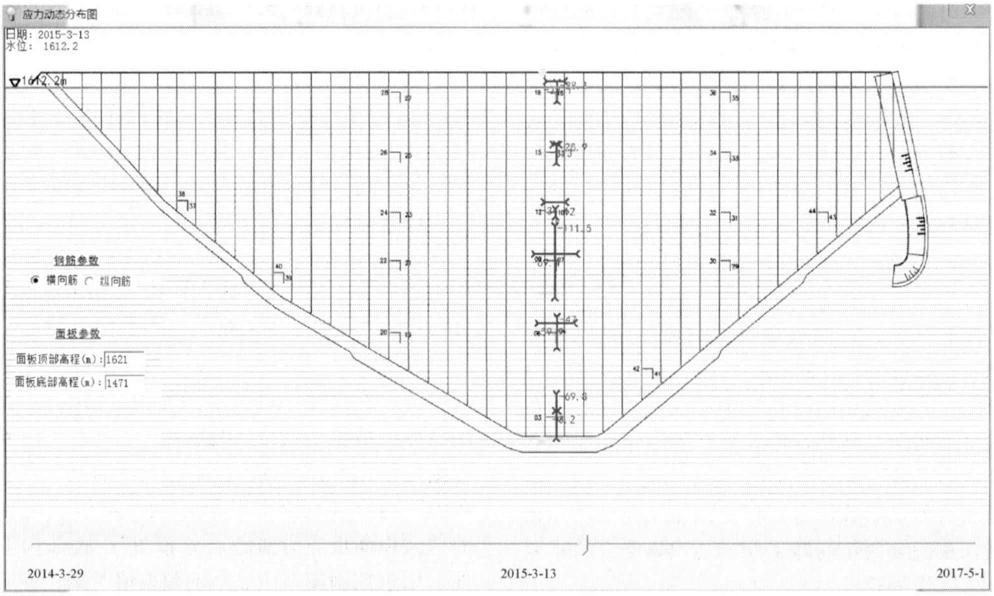

图 2 面板钢筋计应力分布图（正常蓄水位）

数字化智能碾压系统在丰宁抽水蓄能电站中的应用

(一) 工程概况

丰宁抽水蓄能电站位于河北省丰宁满族自治县境内，为一等大（1）型规模。工程规划分两期，共安装 12 台单机容量 30 万 kW 的可逆式水泵水轮机组。

枢纽布置利用天然盆地筑坝形成上水库，改建丰宁一级水电站水库作为下水库，并在库尾设拦沙坝形成拦沙库。上水库建筑物主要为上水库大坝，为钢筋混凝土面板堆石坝，最大坝高 120.3m，坝长 556m，坝顶宽 10m。坝体主要由垫层区、过渡区、主堆石区、次堆石区组成，填筑方量 446.95 万 m^3（压实方）。

(二) 系统组成、原理及特点

1. 系统组成及原理　丰宁抽水蓄能电站数字化大坝智能监控系统由 GPS 基准站和移动终端、监控中心、监控终端等组成。

(1) GPS 基准站作为整个数字化大坝监控系统的位置测量基准站，为整个系统提供基准位置信息，是整套系统位置信息测算的核心组成部分。通过接收卫星信号，测算得到该位置的基准坐标和时间信息，并将这些信息发送至 GPS 移动终端。

(2) GPS 移动终端，即将 GPS 设备安装在碾压设备上，监测碾压设备位置坐标信息和时间信息，监控碾压厚度和遍数，并将采集到的信息以数据形式发送至监控中心。系统采用载波相位动态实时差分 RTK 技术，实现了碾压监控数据厘米级精度的要求。

(3) 监控中心是碾压监控系统数据接收及数据输出的数据处理中心。接收 GPS 移动终端及其他配套传感器测量信息，并进行分析计算，汇总后得到相应施工过程中间结果和最终结果报告，实现了对施工质量的实时监控，并作为判断施工质量合格与否的标准。

（4）监控系统设置外接端口，可方便参建各方实时查看大坝碾压情况。碾压机械上安装的工业平板可接收监控中心的实时碾压信息，操作手可及时了解碾压情况，接受指令。

2. 系统特点

（1）智能化程度高，基本不需人工操作。调试正常后，即可实现自动对碾压设备的速度、碾压区域、厚度等进行连续、实时监控。其他终端也可同步看到完全一样的内容。

（2）灵活性好，可根据现场情况确定仓面面积及形状，实现一层多个分区、不同层不同区的同时施工。仓面信息可在碾压施工前后采集，都不影响对碾压过程的监控。

（3）机动性强，碾压设备工作时，各方人员均可了解碾压情况，便于与操作手沟通，并做出调整和安排。作业面有干扰时，操作手可调至其他区域碾压，提高机械使用效率。

（4）稳定性好，施工中断电时，配套 UPS 设备确保系统稳定运行。网络信号不佳影响数据传输时，系统启用数据离线储存，在网络信号恢复正常后自动上传离线数据。

（三）系统辅助质量控制应用

1. 系统试验　在次堆石区随机选取 15m×15m 区域进行碾压施工，在专人现场旁站同时，开启碾压监控系统监控。碾压完毕后，旁站人员记录结果均为动碾 10 遍，且相邻碾压面间搭接紧密，基本没有漏碾。碾压监控系统显示，动碾 10 遍，振动碾（强振）遍数 10 遍及以上占比 98.35%。两者结果可认为一致，系统能准确监控碾压施工参数。

用全站仪对该区域测量，区域尺寸 14.5m×14.8m，平均高程 1430.76m。碾压监控系统显示尺寸 14.5m×14.8m，平均高程 1430.77m。系统测量精度满足设计和施工要求

结合现场情况，需将大坝碾压工艺从错距碾调整为搭接碾。将第 92 层次堆石区的四个仓，分别做错距碾和搭接碾试验。结果表明，不同碾压工艺，平均压实厚度小于设计要求的 80cm，动碾 10 遍及以上占比大于 95%时，挖坑取样检验的孔隙率均＜23%（设计要求），干密度均≥2.048t/m^3（设计要求）。

2. 系统运行　取 1457～1463m 高程第 111～118 层 104 个仓面冬季施工数据，按主次堆石区碾压情况及挖坑取样结果进行分析。结果表明，平均压实厚度小于 60cm（冬季施工要求），动碾 10 遍及以上占比大于 95%时，按碾压参数控制，主堆石区试坑取样结果孔隙率均＜21%，干密度≥2.101t/m^3，次堆石区试坑取样结果孔隙率均＜23%，干密度≥2.048t/m^3，均满足大坝碾压质量要求。

3. 系统运行效果　截至 2017 年 5 月 31 日，上水库大坝填筑高程 1470.20m，至坝顶 1510m 还有 50 层，经测算，填筑工期为 200d。比工期目标 2017 年 9 月 30 日延长 2 个月零 20d，且临近冬季，施工难度大，质量难以保证。为此，以数字化大坝碾压监控系统监控结果为主导，安排施工。将次、主堆石区分别按左右岸、上下游划分 4 个小区域，当每个小区域碾压监控结果显示合格，即可铺填下一层，流水作业，挖坑试验可随机在 4 个小区域中选一块进行验证。

经工序调整，大坝铺填、碾压一层平均为 3 天，且数字化大坝碾压结果合格，对应挖坑检测也符合设计要求，实际工期提前至 2017 年 10 月 22 日，提前了两个月。

（国网新源河北丰宁抽水蓄能有限公司
马雨峰　李斌
北京木联能软件股份有限公司
韩彦宝　关凯）

沙沱水电站四级配碾压混凝土筑坝关键技术及工程应用

沙沱水电站位于贵州省沿河县境内乌江干流河段，是乌江干流梯级第九级电站、乌江干流贵州境内最后一级梯级电站。装机容量 112 万 kW，多年平均发电量 45.52 亿 kW·h。

（一）四级配碾压混凝土筑坝关键技术简介

四级配碾压混凝土技术是将三级配碾压混凝土中的骨料最大粒径由 80mm 增加到 120mm 的筑坝技术。国内外在四级配碾压混凝土材料性能、试验方法、配合比、施工工艺及质量控制等的研究几乎空白。贵州省科技厅组织的科技成果鉴定认为："该研究成果达到国际领先水平，同意通过科技成果鉴定。建议进一步加快该成果的推广应用"。

（二）主要创新性成果

1. 材料性能　四级配碾压混凝土与传统三级配碾压混凝土材料性能的差异如下：①拌和物材料中，用水量降低 8～10kg/m^3，胶凝材料降低 16～20kg/m^3；②强度方面，抗压强度无明显差异，劈拉强度降低约 10%，抗拉强度满足百米级重力坝承载要求；③变形性能方面，干缩率低 15%～25%，极限拉伸值低 15%，抗压弹模大 1%～3%，泊松比接近，自生体积变形略小；④热学性能，水化热温升降低 2.2～2.5℃，导温系数接近，导热系数和比热略小；⑤耐

久性能方面，抗渗性能略低，但满足设计要求，抗冻融循环能力相当，经100次冻融循环后质量损失率及相对动弹性模量差别不大；⑥抗裂性能方面，胶凝材料用量和水化热温升降低，干缩值、自生体积变形值下降，抗裂综合性能有所提高。

2. 结构设计关键技术　①坝体上游面采用三级配变态混凝土与三级配碾压混凝土相结合的自身防渗结构，并与内部四级配碾压混凝土同步上升，实现了全断面碾压；②四级配与三级配碾压混凝土坝结构设计总体相同，要重视骨料粒径增大后引起的细部设计调整，如材料分区、冷却水管布置、坝体分缝及止水设计、层间结合处理；③四级配与三级配碾压混凝土坝上游防渗区厚度相当；④四级配碾压混凝土绝热温升比三级配碾压混凝土低2～3℃，冷却水管间距由1.5m优化为3m，温控防裂措施可适当简化；⑤采用适当层间处理措施，四级配碾压混凝土大坝基础及层间抗滑稳定满足要求，且差别不大，但层间结合仍为关键控制性环节。

3. 工艺控制标准　①用水量71kg/m³、*VC*值3～5s时，拌和物大骨料表面砂浆包裹充分，具有较好抗分离性，表面液化泛浆情况好，可碾性强；②与三级配相比，四级配碾压混凝土拌和物大骨料含量高、摊铺厚度高，其屈服应力增大、塑性黏度系数减小，易密性和相对压实度略低，需提高激振力、降低振动碾行走速度；③相对压实度不低于98%的工艺参数为，碾压层厚0.5m时2遍无振＋8遍有振＋2遍无振碾压，层厚0.4m时2遍无振＋6遍有振＋2遍无振碾压，振动碾激振力395kN，行走速度1.0～1.2km/h；④与三级配相比，高温环境下四级配碾压混凝土*VC*值损失较快，施工中应根据现场情况，通过原材料质量控制、*VC*值动态控制、骨料分离综合处理、斜层浇筑仓面面积动态控制、保证振动碾行走速度及碾压遍数等，确保施工质量；⑤采用层面间隔2h不处理、层间间隔24h冲毛铺砂浆两种层面处理措施，层面结合抗剪断性能均满足设计指标要求。

4. 施工工艺关键技术　①动态控制拌和物*VC*值，低温、阴天、小雨，*VC*值3～5s；高温、大风，*VC*值1～3s，喷雾保湿。同步上升的三级配碾压混凝土*VC*控制值较四级配碾压混凝土高0.5～1s；②小反铲或平仓机配合人工分散大骨料，动态控制铺厚、平仓面，确保碾压质量；③及时碾压，保证碾压速度、遍数及条带搭接；④变态混凝土加浆静置、浆液流入拌和物底部后，再充分振捣；⑤加大切缝机刀片深度和功率。

5. 质量控制　要点如下：①碾压层厚50cm时，采用双管核子密度仪现场检测压实容重；②坝体四级配碾压混凝土及上游三级配碾压混凝土相对压实度均大于设计要求的98.5%，碾压层面处理及抗剪断参数满足设计要求；③压水试验结果表明，坝体上游防渗区三级配碾压混凝土透水率小于0.5Lu，内部四级配碾压混凝土透水率小于1Lu，均满足设计要求；④蓄水以来，四级配碾压混凝土层面无渗水，大坝运行正常，处于安全状态。

（三）四级配碾压混凝土在沙沱大坝中的应用

四级配碾压混凝土筑坝技术首次应用于沙沱大坝左岸1～4号、右岸13～16号坝段，累计浇筑18万m³。坝体内部采用C_{90}15四级配碾压混凝土，上游面采用C_{90}20三级配碾压混凝土及C_{90}20三级配变态混凝土防渗，坝体下游侧50cm范围内采用C_{90}15四级配变态混凝土，坝体上游三级配、内部四级配碾压混凝土同步上升。施工中，碾压层厚0.5m，无振2遍＋有振碾压8遍＋无振碾压2遍，激振力395kN，振动碾行走速度1.0～1.2km/h。同时采用自卸车多点交叉卸料，辅以人工分散防止大骨料分离。各项检测指标满足设计要求。

采用该技术减少混凝土胶凝材料用量16～20kg/m³，降低水化热温升2.2～2.5℃，取消了骨料预冷，节约工程投资约15%；减少骨料生产中的粉尘和噪声，促进了工程环保，节约生产用电1.2kW·h/m³；碾压层厚由30cm增至50cm，经济效益2亿多元，工期提前45天。

2014年达正常蓄水位365m，蓄水过程及运行期间，大坝安全监测指标均在设计范围内，坝体运行状况良好。

（沙沱发电厂　赵梅）

乌东德水电站围堰土工膜质量控制

乌东德水电站河床围堰为3级挡水建筑物。上、下游围堰为土石结构，堰体防渗采用“复合土工膜＋塑性混凝土防渗墙＋墙下帷幕灌浆”。围堰复合土工膜采用“二布一膜”，膜材为高密度聚乙烯土工膜（HDPE）。

（一）事前质量控制

1. 原材料控制

（1）土工膜性能指标：抗拉强度（经、纬向）≥20kN/m；上游围堰主膜厚度≥1.2mm，土工布500g/m³；渗透系数$i\times10^{-11}\sim i\times10^{-12}$cm/s；伸长率>30%；耐静水压>0.5MPa。

（2）土工膜进场查验发货清单、检测报告、合格证。同批产品小于等于50卷批次最少取样2卷，大于50卷批次最少取3卷，检测11项均符合要求。铺设前每卷土工膜检查外观，不允许出现重缺陷，轻缺陷每 200m² 不超过 5 个，禁用外观质量不符合要求土工膜。

2. 施工工艺控制　做好岗前培训，掌握工艺特点。编制专项技术方案及作业指导书。绘制土工膜铺设顺序和区块图，土工膜焊缝编号。土工膜作业范围周边做好安全防护围挡。

（二）事中质量控制

1. 土工膜存储与运输　设立符合要求的堆放仓库，并由专人管理。采用人工配合汽车吊装卸土工膜，吊绳采用尼龙编织带等柔性绳带。

2. 焊接工艺试验　包括热熔焊接和挤压焊接，工艺试验不代替试焊。通过试验确定土工膜焊接施工的焊接温度、预热温度、焊接速度等参数。

3. 土工膜施工

（1）施工要求：铺设开始后，严禁在可能危害土工膜安全的范围内开挖、放炮、凿洞、电焊、运输等作业；严禁吸烟或使用各种火源；进入现场人员必须穿软底鞋或棉袜；已完成铺设范围禁止车辆和机械入内，除检测人员外，其他人员均不许入内；实行三检制。

（2）施工程序：支持层清尖→放样→铺设→裁剪→试焊→焊件检验→焊接→取样检验→临时压固→验收。注意事项：清除支持层上各种尖棱杂物；测量放样精确定位各膜块位置；展开的膜卷不得超过当天焊接范围，恶劣天气时减少展开膜卷数；按实际尺寸在平坦场地裁剪，编号记录；边坡铺设大块或整卷土工膜时，不能自由滑落展开；注明已铺土工膜顺序号、卷码和日期；预留伸缩量，避开夏季高温铺设；外露土工膜边缘用砂袋压覆。

（3）焊接及取样检测要求：土工膜以热熔焊接为主，挤压焊接用于修复和热熔焊机达不到处；搭接长度热熔焊接 100±25mm，挤压焊接 75±20mm；每个焊接试验取 3 个样品，焊缝两端及中间各取 1 个，样品宽 25.4mm，长度满足拉力机检测要求；各项检测符合要求。

4. 修补要求　在土工膜上标明施工缺陷，做好记录。合格后在膜表面记录修补情况。

土工膜缺陷修补的主要形式如下：

（1）补片修补：补片适用于修补撕裂、破洞和穿过土工膜的针孔破洞，还用于覆盖不均匀的树脂和汽油等污染部位。补片为圆形，平整完好，须超出缺陷范围 200mm。补片和缺陷处无污物、水分、杂质。补焊前用热风焊枪将补片临时粘在土工膜表面，补片周边打磨出粗糙面，接缝处形成斜面。热风焊枪和打磨不得引起土工膜过度熔解、磨损或穿洞。

尽量减少补片数量。相邻缺陷一块大补片修补，补片过多处用整块补片或土工膜修补。

（2）挤压接缝帽（盖帽）：挤压接缝帽适合修补不合格搭接焊缝。修补前用角磨机将接缝表面和接缝周边磨毛，在挤压焊接处形成一个粗糙面、接缝处形成一个斜面。打磨在修补焊接前 1h 内完成，且不能引起膜过度磨损或穿孔，不能明显超出挤压焊接范围。

（3）打磨焊接：打磨挤压焊接适用于修补长度小于 300mm 小型接缝缺陷、表面小损伤和未穿透整个膜厚的局部缺陷。焊接前 1h 内在修补处打磨成粗糙面。

5. 施工干扰　土工膜施工遵循"上层施工、下层停工"的原则，避免上下交叉作业。无法避免时，或已完土工膜上部有其他施工时，土工膜表面堆放沙袋做好防护。

6. 雨季施工措施

（1）用干净纱布擦净、擦干待焊接的两幅防渗膜接缝，必要时可用热风器烘干接缝。

（2）下雨无法施工时，用防水塑料布把焊机包好，放于干燥处。

（3）雨后施工时，须调整焊接参数，试焊检测合格后方可施工。

（4）已铺好的膜应及时焊接，避免因雨水造成场底湿滑泥泞无法施工。

（三）事后质量控制

主要是对土工膜焊接质量的检测。

1. 非破坏性检测　焊接完成 4h 后，对每条焊缝进行非破坏性检测。热熔焊接用气压检测，合格率 100%；挤压焊接根据焊缝条件做真空检测或电火花测试，合格率 100%。

2. 破坏性检测　初期在已铺设焊接土工膜上，按 1000m² 取 1 个 1000mm×350mm 样品做焊缝破坏性检测。随后每 5000～10000m² 取 1 个样品。强度测试要求合格率 100%。

3. 检测要求及成果　每个试样裁取 10 个 25.4mm 宽标准试件，分别做 5 个剪切和 5 个剥离试验。每种试验 5 个试样的测试结果中至少有 4 个符合要求，且平均值应达到标准值要求、最低值不得低于标准值 80%，则判定通过强度测试。如未通过测试，则在不合格处沿焊缝两端各 6m 范围内重新取样测试，直至合格为止。有怀疑部位用挤压焊接补强。

（中国水利水电建设工程咨询西北有限公司
杨俊峰　兰肃）

乌弄龙水电站下游围堰防冲墙布置研究

（一）概况

乌弄龙水电站下游围堰导流标准选用 20 年重现

期洪水，相应洪水流量 5900m³/s（全年）。下游围堰堰顶高程 1828m，顶宽 10m，迎水侧和背水侧坡比均为 1∶1.75，围堰最大高度 21m。堰体水下采用 C20 混凝土 80cm 厚防渗墙防渗，水上采用复合土工膜直心墙。围堰水上部分堰体由碾压石渣料、过渡料Ⅰ、过渡料Ⅱ和干砌块石护坡、钢筋笼等组成，围堰堰体迎水面用大块石和钢筋石笼（水平厚度 5m）保护。

受该工程短导流洞方案制约，下游围堰迎水面坡脚距导流洞出口导墙边线不足 20m。导流模型试验表明，20 年一遇流量 5900m³/s 时，导流洞出口冲坑深 10.9m，冲坑地表直径 45m，地面 1807m 等高线距下游围堰堰脚 8m。根据经验，模型试验中的导流洞出口明渠末端冲坑位置大致可以固定。但试验数据往往与实际会有差异，如导明渠末端冲坑底部扩大到河床基岩顶板线，则冲坑地表直径增至 60m；冲坑中心距下游围堰堰脚 60m 不变，则冲坑上缘（1805m 等高线）抵近下游围堰堰脚，1807m 等高线距下游围堰堰脚约－5m（即冲坑已到下游围堰堰脚里侧 5m），水流冲刷已影响到下游围堰堰脚稳定，需设下游围堰防冲墙。

（二）下游围堰防冲墙设置研究

假定导流洞出口冲坑扩大到下游围堰堰脚里侧约 5m，按工况 1（围堰设计水位 1825.94m 计，基坑无水）和工况 2（挡水边坡水位骤降，高程 1825.94～1807m，基坑无水）分别进行不设防冲墙和设置防冲墙的下游围堰稳定验算。

1. 不设防冲墙稳定验算　下游围堰边坡稳定模型计算结果表明，当遇设计标准洪水、围堰计算工况 1 时，围堰下游边坡的抗滑稳定安全系数为 0.948，小于控制标准 1.2；当遇设计标准洪水、围堰计算工况 2 时，围堰下游边坡的抗滑稳定安全系数为 0.932，小于控制标准 1.1。故下游围堰边坡不满足稳定要求。也就是说，当导流洞出口明渠末端冲坑直径达 60m 时，即冲坑假定扩大到下游围堰堰脚里侧 5m 时，下游围堰下游坡稳定不满足要求，须设防冲墙保护。

2. 设防冲墙后的稳定验算　模型计算（计算模型同上）结果表明，当遇设计标准洪水、围堰计算工况 1 时，围堰下游边坡的抗滑稳定安全系数为 1.477，大于控制标准 1.2；当遇设计标准洪水、围堰计算工况 2 时，围堰下游边坡的抗滑稳定安全系数为 1.162，大于控制标准 1.1，故下游围堰边坡满足稳定要求。

通过稳定验算得知，导流洞出口明渠末端冲坑直径即使达到 60m，在下游围堰迎水侧边坡设防冲墙后，围堰迎水侧边坡保持稳定。

（三）下游围堰防冲墙设计

1. 防冲墙布置　结合下游围堰结构特性及计算模型，乌弄龙水电站下游围堰防冲墙布置于距防渗墙下游 28m 处，钢筋混凝土结构，其右端头与堰基防渗墙混凝土相接，左端头与导流洞出口右导墙相接，顶高程 1819m，并穿过堰体和覆盖层深入基岩 1m，厚度 80cm。

2. 防冲墙稳定验算　假定防冲墙后堰体冲毁，防冲墙存在侧向稳定问题。钢筋混凝土防冲墙设在下游围堰轴线下游，深约 28m，厚 80cm，入岩 1m，深入覆盖层 22m，露出覆盖层 9m。防冲墙按固定在覆盖层内悬臂梁计算，并假定下游侧面凌空。

计算结果表明，最大剪力 83.03kN、最大弯矩 362.57kN·m，大于素混凝土抗力要求，在配单宽 5 根、直径 20mm 的受力钢筋后可满足防冲墙强度要求。

（中国水利水电第七工程局有限公司
万明栋　吴俊丽
华能澜沧江水电股份有限公司　崔景涛）

果多水电站混凝土裂缝成因分析及控制

（一）工程概况

果多水电站位于西藏自治区昌都县境内，为扎曲水电规划“两库五级”中第二个梯级电站，电站装机容量 16 万 kW（4×4 万 kW），三等中型工程。枢纽建筑物包括：碾压混凝土重力坝，泄洪冲沙系统，左岸引水系统和坝后地面厂房。

施工区平均海拔 3400m 左右，极端最低气温－20.7℃，极端最高气温 33.4℃，多年平均气温 5.6℃，最大月平均日温差达 18.8℃，年平均日温差 16℃。扎曲河段地处澜沧江上游，平均气温较同纬度其它地区低，日照时间长，多年平均降水量 499.5mm。降雨集中在 5～9 月，占全年降雨量的 83%。冬季寒冷，水边有结冰，河面有时封冻，3 月气候转暖。

（二）混凝土裂缝产生的主要原因

（1）水泥品种选择不当、水泥受潮变质，粗细骨料级配不合理、含泥量超标。

（2）在西藏水工混凝土易受自然条件的影响。

（3）混凝土浇筑时下料高度过高，分层厚度偏大，骨料分离无法到达预期效果。混凝土漏振或过振，密实度不足。

（4）提前脱模、养护时间不足，混凝土在温度或收缩应力影响下开裂。

(5) 西藏地区昼夜温差大，白天日照强，混凝土温升阶段内外温差大。

(三) 混凝土裂缝控制措施

1. 材料　选用发热量低的中热硅酸盐水泥或低热矿渣硅酸盐水泥，不得将不同品种或标号的水泥混合使用；采用非碱活性骨料，严控粗细骨料的粒径和细度模数、含泥量，级配连续且良好；掺加适量粉煤灰；采用具有减水、缓凝、早强特性的高效减水剂；拌和用水根据浇筑气温选用水的温度，严禁使用碱性水。

2. 拌和　尽量采用常态混凝土，改善级配设计，采用低流态混凝土；减少水泥用量，降低混凝土水化热；粗骨料高温季节遮阳、低温季节保温，堆高大于6m，高温季节不高于月平均气温，低温季节骨料不冻结、料堆中下部温度不低于3℃；细骨料常年采取遮雨措施，低温季节保温；高温季节骨料采用风冷加以预冷，加片冰、制冷水拌和，低温季节，加热水拌和，热水温度不高于60℃。

3. 混凝土浇筑一般要求　尽量避开高温、曝晒、多风、骤然降温天气；控制浇筑层最大高度和浇筑间歇时间，做好温控工作；按设计要求分层浇筑，大坝基础约束区和老混凝土约束部位浇筑层高不大于1.5m，脱离基础约束区浇筑厚度不大于3m，廊道等处根据结构适当调整，当上、下浇筑层间歇时间超过28天时，下层混凝土按照老混凝土处理。

4. 高温季节混凝土施工　运输、入仓设备外包保温材料；大体积混凝土均预埋冷却水管并通冷水；用喷雾机喷雾在仓面上形成雾状隔热层；振捣完成后，表面覆盖保温被；施工完成后，仓面花管流水养护。

5. 低温季节混凝土施工

(1) 低温季节前，运输设备及混凝土外露面均固定保温材料。坝体温度降至要求温度。保护好已浇底板、护坦、闸墩、孔洞部位的表面，并将空腔封闭。

(2) 越冬时，坝顶先后铺设1层厚0.6mm塑料薄膜、3层2cm厚聚乙烯保温被、1层三防帆布；大坝侧面先后依次铺设1层厚0.6mm塑料薄膜、4cm厚XPS板、1层三防帆布。

(3) 浇筑中及时在模板外覆盖保温被，并配电热毯、暖风机等提高浇筑仓面温度。

(4) 每层混凝土浇筑结束后，其上表面覆盖一层土工膜和5cm厚聚苯乙烯保温卷材；永久外露侧面粘贴5cm厚保温板、临时外露侧面粘贴5cm厚保温卷材封闭保温。

(5) 根据混凝土强度、混凝土内外温差确定拆模时间，避免夜间或气温骤降时拆模。

(四) 裂缝处理技术

果多水电站裂缝修补有表面封闭法、压力灌浆法及填堵法。

1. 表面封闭法　对宽度小于0.3mm的裂缝，可将聚合物水泥膏、弹性密封胶或渗透性防水剂涂刷于裂缝表面。该法仅适用于浅裂缝。其施工流程：表面刷毛并冲洗→嵌补表面缺损（用环氧胶泥或乳胶水泥）→选材涂覆。需要注意：涂层较薄，应选用黏结力强且不宜老化的材料；对活动裂缝，应采用延伸率较大的弹性材料；涂覆均匀，不得有气泡。

2. 灌浆法　宽度大于0.3mm且深度较大的裂缝，采用灌浆方法将聚氨酯、环氧树脂或水泥浆液注入裂缝深处。其施工流程：凿槽→埋设浆嘴→封缝→密封检查→配制浆液→灌浆→封孔→质量检查。施工要点：①材料用黏结力强、可灌性好的环氧树脂；②宽度大于2mm特大裂缝用水泥类材料，活动性裂缝采用稀释的环氧树脂或聚氨酯；③水泥灌浆压力0.4～0.8MPa，化灌压力0.2～0.4MPa；④待浆液初凝不外渗时可拆下灌浆嘴（盒、管）。

3. 填堵法　对大于0.5mm宽大裂缝或钢筋锈蚀裂缝，沿裂缝将混凝土凿成“U”型或“V”型槽，再嵌填修补材料。施工流程：凿槽→混凝土去污、钢筋除锈→涂刷结合剂（环氧树脂浆液）→嵌填修补材料→面层处理。根据情况嵌填材料选用环氧树脂、环氧砂浆、聚合物水泥砂浆、聚氯乙烯胶泥或沥青油膏；对锈蚀裂缝，先对钢筋除锈，再涂防锈涂料。

（中国水利水电第七工程局有限公司
万明栋　黄艳梅）

象鼻岭水电站高拱坝无盖重固结灌浆施工技术

1. 概述　象鼻岭水电站位于贵州省威宁县与云南省会泽县交界处的牛栏江上，系牛栏江流域中下游河段规划梯级的第三级水电站，上游为大岩洞水电站，下游为小岩头水电站。电站装机两台，总装机容量24万kW。电站大坝为碾压混凝土拱坝，最大坝高141.50m，坝顶长449.87m。高程1409.5m以下坝基均需固结灌浆，高程1280m以下为有盖重固结灌浆，盖重不小于3m；1280m以上为建基面1m以下无盖重固结灌浆加1m范围内引管灌浆。

碾压混凝土成本低，施工速度快、工期短，但对坝基固结灌浆施工工期要求高，如先浇筑混凝土后固结灌浆，则因混凝土龄期、固结灌浆施工和检查孔等待龄期等因素，会影响混凝土浇筑工期，且钻孔时容易破坏埋设的冷却管路和其他埋件。

2. 无盖重固结灌浆技术的特点 固结灌浆是大坝施工关键线路项目，制约着大坝浇筑进度和电站蓄水发电的目标。原设计方案为有盖重固结灌浆，即在碾压混凝土浇筑、等强后，进行该部位固结灌浆施工，并在质量检查后再进行大坝混凝土浇筑。施工中混凝土浇筑和固结灌浆相互影响、相互制约，影响了总的施工进度。无盖重固结灌浆将避免交叉作业，加快施工进度，缩短工期，并能解决钻孔破坏埋件等问题，具有确保工期和灌浆质量的双重优势。

所谓无盖重就是在碾压混凝土浇筑前进行固结灌浆，然后在1m范围内预埋灌浆管，再在混凝土浇筑完成后，进行浅层埋管灌浆。无盖重固结灌浆，既保证混凝土浇筑的速度，又确保了灌浆施工质量，有效地解决了碾压混凝土施工和固结灌浆施工互相影响的矛盾。

3. 无盖重固结灌浆取得的效果

（1）在工期方面，使固结灌浆开工日期大大提前，根本上缩短了施工工期。在施工中减少了坝基固结灌浆与大坝混凝土浇筑之间的相互干扰，确保了大坝浇筑的工期。

（2）在技术方面，通过生产性试验，对施工工艺和参数进行合理优化。实践表明技术可行，效果良好，质量符合设计要求，且避免了钻孔对坝体混凝土整体性破坏，保证铺设的冷却管路、埋设的观测仪器和其他埋件完好无损。

（3）在经济方面，节约了固结灌浆钻孔、埋管的费用；工期缩短，减少了人员、设备的投入，提高了经济效益。

（中国水利水电第三工程局有限公司
路丙辉 曹弌）

枕头坝一级水电站工程施工方案优化

（一）大坝下部大体积混凝土优化

枕头坝一级水电站左岸2、3号非溢流坝段、发电厂房坝段540～560m高程、泄洪闸552.9～582m高程为大体积常态混凝土。考虑现场施工条件，在施工组织设计中建议将左岸2、3号非溢流坝段、发电厂房、泄洪闸下部基础大体积混凝土，由常态混凝土调整为碾压混凝土，碾压混凝土由自卸汽车直接入仓浇筑。这样水泥用量有所减少，粉煤灰用量增加，使混凝土水化热温升降低，最高温度得到有效控制，对混凝土温控极为有利，也利于实现计划工期目标，节省工程投资。

最终设计单位确定，将11.48万m^3常态混凝土优化为碾压混凝土，明显加快下部混凝土施工进度，其中厂房坝段提前工期15天，1、2号泄洪闸坝段提前工期30天，左非2、3号坝段比合同工期提前53天到达坝顶高程。减少了水泥用量，节约工程投资553.85万元。

（二）钢纤维混凝土蜗壳优化

混凝土蜗壳在电站运行期间空蚀对其损伤严重，其检修周期比钢衬蜗壳长，影响电站正常运行，后期维护成本较高。结合公司在向家坝水电站蜗壳混凝土的经验，建议将枕头坝电站投标阶段机组混凝土蜗壳内衬优化为蜗壳钢衬，得到了设计单位的认可。

实施中，将原设计机组蜗壳内衬由强度等级C35钢纤维混凝土结构，调整为C25常态混凝土钢衬。这一改变，虽增加了钢衬工程量，但也减少了钢纤维和高强度混凝土的工程量，比原方案减少工程投资1717.13万元。另外，设置钢衬蜗壳可避免电站运行期间造成混凝土损伤、漏水，减少检修周期，增加发电效益；节约蜗壳混凝土施工中的曲面异型模板安拆时间，简化施工工艺和施工成本，节约工期约15天。

（三）取消卡子岗料场开采

根据厂坝标招标文件中料场规划，江沟料场可加工骨料135.75万m^3，与所需混凝土骨料总量173.2万m^3相比缺口较大，需在卡子岗天然砂砾料场补采50万m^3。卡子岗料场枯期开采（11月6日～5月25日），考虑水下开采5m，终了高程575m，规划采量50万m^3。开采结束后要用石渣回填，恢复原地形，渣料从江沟渣场回采。卡子岗料场主要工程量：大块石抛填护坡21838m^3，石渣回填678343m^3，浆砌石挡墙6966m^3，征地212.94亩（1亩=666.67m^2）。

2012年10月，二期基坑开挖基本结束，对江沟渣场用料场堆存区域详勘测量，确认堆存区开采料总量176万m^3，其中砂卵砾石约122.5万m^3，玄武岩料约53.5万m^3。回采率按砂卵砾石75%、玄武岩80%计算，可生产骨料134.67万m^3。

在建设过程中，提出了取消卡子岗料场开采，得到参建各方同意。其主要措施是：

1. 高峰期外购骨料 2012年11～12月为混凝土施工高峰期，利用当地资源外购成品砂石骨料10.714万t。

2. 提高回采利用率

（1）在5号路起点江沟下游桥处主供水管线上，破口增设1条DN200供水管引至筛分车间，加强冲洗；另从高线接引一条水管，解决骨料含泥量大的问题。

（2）用破碎锤对超径石破碎再利用。

（3）在排放尾水末端增加设备回收弃沙，使砂卵砾石回采率达85%，玄武岩回采率达到92%。

3. 利用当地资源补充骨料需求　尾水左岸下游护坡浇筑碳铬铁合金渣混凝土8539.14m^3。将四川乐山鑫河公司生产的铬渣筛选破碎后变废为宝，有效提高铬铁废渣资源利用率，也防止大量废渣对生态环境造成污染。

在不开采卡子岗料场的情况下，采取相应的措施，满足了厂坝标和鱼道标的混凝土125万m^3生产任务。取消卡子岗料场开采后，节约工程投资2244.80万元。

（中国水利水电第三工程局有限公司　王伟）

自愈型防渗外加剂在象鼻岭水电站双曲拱坝防渗中的应用

象鼻岭水电站大坝为双曲拱坝，坝体上游面C_{90}20二级配碾压混凝土浇筑区域掺加水泥基渗透结晶型自愈型防渗外加剂，以达到良好的防渗效果。

（一）现场室内试验

采用C_{90}20W8F100（二级配）变态混凝土施工配合比为基准配合比，外掺自愈型防渗外加剂，开展混凝土各项指标性能试验。

1. 掺加工艺的选定　有两种掺加工艺。

第一种：将自愈型防渗外加剂掺入变态浆液中，搅拌均匀，再掺入混凝土中进行拌制。试验结果表明，自愈型防渗外加剂掺入变态浆液后，其密度明显变大（掺加前1750kg/m^3变为2200kg/m^3），将浆液洒入碾压混凝土中渗入较慢，5min渗入深度约三分之一（模拟现场铺料厚度，将拌和物堆高25cm，观察变态浆液渗入情况）。

混凝土拌制时搅拌方式分两种，一是拌和机搅拌混凝土3min，置于钢板上，再将掺有防渗剂的变态浆液，洒到混凝土面上，人工翻拌3～4次，拌合物坍落度18mm，含气量3.1%；二是拌和机搅拌混凝土2min，再将掺有防渗剂的变态浆液，加入拌和机中搅拌1.5min，拌和物坍落度23mm，含气量4.7%。后一种搅拌方式的混凝土状态，优于人工翻拌的混凝土，含气量也明显增大，混凝土均匀性好，且泛浆效果明显。

第二种：将自愈型防渗外加剂直接掺入混凝土中进行拌制。将粗骨料、自愈型防渗外加剂、胶凝材料和细骨料依次加入搅拌机中，搅拌1min，再将减水剂、引气剂、水加入搅拌3min。试验成果：引气剂掺量分别为0.2%、0.25%，拌和物坍落度分别为14、25mm，含气量分别为3.0%、4.9%。

为验证变态浆液在碾压混凝土中的渗入效果，在此种拌制方式情况下，在掺有防渗剂的混凝土出机后，将变态浆液洒入碾压混凝土中，5min后能够渗透至底部，渗入效果较好。

2. 掺量试验　通过不同自愈型防渗外加剂掺量（4%、6%和8%）试验，以确定外加剂的最优掺量。不同外加剂掺量试验成果见表1。

（二）在变态混凝土中掺加自愈型防渗外加剂

在象鼻岭水电站坝体上游1m厚变态混凝土中应用。在碾压混凝土单盘称量中，将防渗外加剂投入到中石秤中，进行混凝土拌制。

1. 施工控制措施　为区分和摊铺不同种类碾压混凝土，采取如下措施：①拌和系统严格按用量掺加防渗剂，运输车辆上设标牌，区分不同碾压混凝土；②先铺普通碾压混凝土，并预留试验区，平仓机推料，人工辅助，至填满试验区域；③现场试验人员检查无混料现象后，进行下一步工序；④掺加有防渗剂的碾压变态混凝土，所加浆液与其他部位相同，均集中制浆；⑤1h内完成振捣，并按要求取样及做好记录；⑥变态混凝土与碾压混凝土结合部位，专门碾压密实，随碾压混凝土逐层浇筑。

2. 质量控制检测　现场取样成型，养护至设计龄期进行试验。在应用和非应用自愈型防渗剂区域各设2个取芯孔，芯样直径130mm，长1m。

（1）掺加和未掺加防渗外加剂混凝土的试验成果分别见表2、表3。

（2）掺加与未掺加防渗外加剂混凝土钻孔取芯的试验成果分别见表4和表5。

表1　不同外加剂掺量试验成果

设计要求	出机性能		强度性能		变形性能		耐久性能	掺量（%）
	坍落度（mm）	含气量（%）	抗压强度（MPa）	劈裂抗拉强度（MPa）	极限拉伸值（$\varepsilon\times10^{-4}$）	弹性模量（GPa）	抗渗等级	
试验结果	25	4.9	30.5	2.27	0.86	32.4	W8	基准
	15	4.5	27.9	2.41	0.83	31.6	W8	4.0
	23	4.1	32.8	2.32	0.91	34.2	W8	6.0
	10	3.0	28.2	2.53	0.88	30.5	W8	8.0

表 2 掺加防渗外加剂混凝土试验成果

试验项目	出机性能		强度性能		变形性能		耐久性能	
	坍落度（mm）	含气量（%）	抗压强度（MPa）	劈裂抗拉强度（MPa）	极限拉伸值（ε×10⁻⁴）	弹性模量（GPa）	渗水高度（mm）	抗渗等级
试验结果	33	2.9	26.7	2.28	0.78	28.8	25	W8
	39	3.4	22.1	2.23	0.81	30.3	28	W8
	36	3.7	24.3	2.25	0.84	32.6	27	W8
	35	3.3	26.3	2.50	0.79	29.9	24	W8

表 3 未掺加防渗外加剂混凝土试验成果

试验项目	出机性能		强度性能		变形性能		耐久性能	
	坍落度（mm）	含气量（%）	抗压强度（MPa）	劈裂抗拉强度（MPa）	极限拉伸值（ε×10⁻⁴）	弹性模量（GPa）	渗水高度（mm）	抗渗等级
试验结果	46	3.9	22.5	2.25	0.78	27.4	41	W8
	45	3.4	25.3	2.28	0.81	30.6	50	W8
	49	3.7	26.3	2.35	0.86	32.3	51	W8
	52	3.9	24.8	2.24	0.79	28.5	51	W8

表 4 掺加防渗外加剂混凝土钻孔取芯试验成果

试验项目	强度性能			耐久性能	
	破坏荷载（kN）	单块强度（MPa）	平均值（MPa）	渗水高度（mm）	抗渗等级
试验结果	208	25.4	28.1	34	W8
	241	29.4			
	243	29.6			

表 5 未掺加防渗外加剂混凝土钻孔取芯试验成果

试验项目	强度性能			耐久性能	
	破坏荷载（kN）	单块强度（MPa）	平均值（MPa）	渗水高度（mm）	抗渗等级
试验结果	201	24.5	25.4	44	W8
	200	24.5			
	223	27.1			

（中国水利水电第三工程局有限公司 米淑琴 刘兆飞）

引水发电建筑物施工

丰宁抽水蓄能电站压力管道长斜井预留孔钻孔灌浆技术

河北丰宁抽水蓄能电站引水系统基础处理工程，包括引水隧洞，高压管道上平段、上斜段、中平段、下斜段、下平段、支管，引水洞调压室，高压管道中平段排水廊道等部位的钻孔灌浆，其项目有固结灌浆、帷幕灌浆、回填灌浆、接触灌浆。其中高压管道大倾角长斜井的垂直高度较大。围岩灌浆施工技术已有非常成熟的施工方法，但压力管道长斜井灌浆施工的资料很少，尤其是压力管道预留孔灌浆施工。因此，进行压力管道长斜井预留孔灌浆施工技术研究很必要。

（一）技术要点

（1）用卷扬机牵引钻灌台车的方式进行施工，提高了灌浆施工的安全性。

（2）搭设排架先施工上斜井下弯管段、利用卷扬提升系统施工斜直段、借助卷扬机牵引钻灌平台使钻灌台车移动至上弯管段适宜位置，使台车顶部平台呈水平状态，然后以钻灌台车顶部平台为基础搭设排架施工上弯管段，避免了上下交叉作业。

（3）采用“环间不分序，环内加密”的原则，减少了台车上下移动的频率，加快了施工进度。

（4）采用 HS-XB8B 型灌浆泵（灌浆时压力平稳），确保压力管道的成品保护。

（二）工艺原理

高压管道上斜井钻孔和灌浆均在斜井钻灌台车上进行，钻灌台车采用卷扬机牵引的方式上下运行，采用输浆泵通过输浆管将浆液送至工作面自制的可移动式钻灌平台上进行灌浆。斜井钻灌台车在上斜井下弯管和上弯管有不同形式，上斜井下弯管在搭设简易排架上作业；上弯管段待上斜井斜直段灌浆完成后，拆除钻灌台车上的钻灌设备，将台车移至上弯管段适宜位置，然后以呈水平状态的台车顶部平台为基础搭设排架在排架上作业，排架主框架、支撑及斜拉支撑均为 ϕ48.3 钢管组成，外围设安全防护网。

压力管道上斜井钻灌平台以槽钢为主，整体焊接成双层钻灌台车。斜井段施工人员通行，采用槽钢焊接的单层运输台车。钻灌平台及运输台车分别采用 1 台 JM10 电动卷扬机、2 台 JM5 电动卷扬机进行牵引并独立运行，台车上时刻配有安全绳，供现场施工人员使用。

上斜井斜直段钻灌台车及运输台车与该部位的倾角互余，使之形成水平作业平台，以方便人员站立及材料和设备摆放。钻灌平台面板采用 3mm 花纹钢板，护栏底部设 20cm 高花纹钢板围挡。所有焊缝高度不小于 8mm，吊耳焊缝焊角不小于 16mm。台车底部设橡胶轮，避免台车行走对钢管内壁造成伤害。为确保灌浆泵、搅拌槽在台车移动过程中不出现移动、倾覆，设备放置到钻灌台车上后利用拉筋将钻灌设备焊接在钻灌台车上。为确保安全，台车在运行至施工部位时，及时利用短钢丝绳将台车与钢管内壁吊耳连接。

（三）取得的成果

该钻灌施工技术成果在河北丰宁抽水蓄能电站成功实践，既缩短施工工期，又保证施工安全，更有利于文明施工，各种资源能较好地利用，取得了较好的经济效益，解决了压力管道内壁不允许焊接、成品保护等难题，为今后有效解决压力管道长斜井预留孔灌浆，提供一种新的思路和方法。

（中国水利水电第三工程局有限公司　曹弋　洪敏浩）

阜康抽水蓄能电站压力管道斜井导孔施工孔斜控制与纠偏

阜康抽水蓄能电站引水系统有 2 条平行布置的压力管道，洞轴线间距 43.72m。立面上采用双斜井布置，设有上平段、上斜段、中平段、下斜段和下平段，上、下斜井角度为 60°。1、2 号压力管道的上斜井斜直段分别为 175.51、175.81m，上斜井上弯段夹角分别为 57.03° 和 57.05°，下斜井斜直段均为 263.85m，下斜井上弯段夹角均为 60°。压力管道下斜井反井钻导井施工长度达 300m（含上、下弯管段），施工中极有可能造成导孔不能穿越下部隧洞而增加施工成本，延长工期或由于导孔偏斜较大而形成后期较大的超挖、超填。为此，需研究反井钻施工中对长斜井导孔孔斜的控制与纠偏。

（一）孔斜控制与纠偏技术的特点

将反井钻机钻具改为组合钻具（纠偏螺杆钻具＋牙轮钻头），通过对光纤陀螺测斜仪加装纠偏引鞋工具，以测量纠偏螺杆钻具工作面角，实现长斜井高精度导井施工。此技术可有效解决由于孔道弯曲造成扩孔交边扭矩大、钻杆断裂等问题。

（二）工艺原理

通过测量仪器放样下钻点位置，将反井钻机安装在斜井井口已浇混凝土基础上。反井钻机钻具连接牙轮钻头直接钻成 ϕ280m 导孔，清水或泥浆作循环钻井液排渣。在牙轮钻头部位钻具加工纠偏工具键对应其外圆上的一条母线，该母线须与 1.5°弯曲螺杆钻具弯角母线重合（或存在一定角度须准确记录），以便把测斜仪器下放到钻具工具处，钻具纠偏工具键会落入到引鞋定位槽内，即可进行测试点工具方位角和工具垂向角的测量。然后把 1.5°弯曲螺杆钻具弯角转到需纠偏的位置，通过钻井液为螺杆钻具提供动力，把液体压力能换为机械能。当泥浆泵泵出的泥浆流经旁通阀进入马达，在马达的进、出口形成一定的压力差，推动转子绕定子的轴线旋转，并将转速和扭矩通过万向轴和传动轴传递给钻头，从而实现导孔偏斜处纠偏定位。使得导孔轨迹沿设计轨迹钻孔施工，直至导孔与下部支洞贯通后，拆掉导孔牙轮钻头，连接直径为 2500mm 反导孔扩孔钻头由下向上扩孔。钻屑从刀盘接触面自由下落到下水平巷道，由装运设备将岩渣从下部支洞运出，当扩孔钻头从上井口透出后，整个导井扩孔施工完成。

（三）取得的成效

孔斜控制与纠偏技术既能缩短施工工期，减少定向钻机设备的重复投入，又能够避免采用定向钻机造孔形成的孔道弯曲造成扩孔交边扭矩大、钻杆断裂等现象。该技术操作简单、运行平稳可靠、效率高，便于精确测控；安装运输简便，机械化连续作业，成井速度快、质量好，为后期施工创造了良好的条件，综合效益显著。该技术也降低了安全风险、减少了职业健康危害，为施工提供良好作业环境。反井钻开挖斜井导井已取代以往阿里马克爬罐开挖斜井导井，可达到扩挖溜渣的预期，为有效解决反井钻施工长斜井导孔，提供一种新的方法。

（中国水利水电第三工程局有限公司　马超群）

压力管道开挖控制技术在双江口水电站的应用

（一）工程概述

双江口水电站大坝为砾石土心墙堆石坝，最大坝高 312m。引水发电系统布置于左岸，地下式发电厂房内安装 4 台发电机组，单机单管供水，两机一室一洞。压力管道平行布置，设计开挖断面为平均直径 10.3m 的圆形断面，衬砌成型后管径 8.3m。

1. 地质条件　压力管道岩性为灰白色似斑状黑云钾长花岗岩，局部伟晶岩脉较发育，岩体新鲜，洞壁大多干燥～潮湿，岩石坚硬，岩体完整，多呈块状～整体状结构，岩体中地应力高，考虑高应力折减后，围岩以Ⅲa 类为主，成洞条件较好。

压力管道处于高地应力区，强度应力比小于 4。

2. 施工重点难点　压力管道地应力方向与管轴线交角大，对围岩稳定不利，施工中可能出现岩爆，安全风险大。管道渐变段存在集中松弛裂缝（宽 4～10cm），并有结构面切割，岩体较破碎，Ⅳ类围岩，成洞条件差，开挖成型难。压力管道空间弯管段为空间三维螺旋形结构，施工体型须跟进洞轴线在空间三维方向持续扭转变形，施工控制难度大。

（二）施工程序和方法

1. 施工程序　压力管道上平段开挖支护总体遵循 4、2 号与 1、3 号交错开挖顺序。施工程序：施工准备→洞口锁口→洞口段开挖支护→空间转弯段开挖支护→直线段开挖支护→上弯段开挖支护（部分）→洞内下层石方反方向开挖（循环）。

2. 施工方法

（1）渐变段开挖：渐变段长 17.604m，由 11.6m×11.6m 方形渐变成直径 11.6m 的圆形，分上、下两层开挖。上层高 8.9m，下层高 2.7m。洞口部位开挖采取先导洞后周边光爆成型。然后短进尺爆破循环开挖，循环进尺不超过 2m。

（2）压坡段开挖：均采用上、下分层断面开挖，下层预留厚度 2m。上层由外向里掘进，先中部掏槽，周边光爆控制轮廓；上层开挖后由里往外开挖下层，水平光爆开挖成型。开挖时上层钻孔用自制风钻台车 YT28 汽腿钻；2 号岩石乳化炸药，人工装药、联网，非电毫秒雷管簇联分段微差控制爆破；压力管道上平洞段开挖中，适时跟进系统喷锚支护，不良地质段超前支护。

（3）空间转弯段开挖：均采用上、下分层断面开挖，下层预留厚度 2m。上层由外向里掘进，先中部掏槽，周边光爆控制轮廓；上平段全部上层开挖后由里往外开挖下层，水平光爆成型。

每个空间转弯段开挖分 22 个循环开挖，钻孔前先测量计算偏移角度与钻孔深度。循环进尺 1.5m，标准循环段左侧最大钻进约 1.7m，右侧边墙钻孔深 1.3m，以实现空间转弯。爆破设计参数和钻爆参数见表 1、表 2。

表 1　爆破设计主要参数

开挖断面（m^2）	钻孔总数	爆破方量（m^3）	总装药量（kg）	炸药单耗（kg/m^3）	预期进尺（m）
65.86	121	98.8	95.7	0.97	1.5

表 2　钻爆参数初设值表

炮孔名称	钻孔直径（m）	平均孔深（cm）	孔距（cm）	孔数	药卷直径（mm）	单孔药量（kg）	总装药量（kg）	线装药密度（kg/m）	雷管段别
掏槽孔	42	165	50	16	32	1.5	24		Ms1
崩落孔	42	155	70	22	32	1.2	26.4		Ms3
缓冲孔	42	150	70	27	32	0.9	24.3		Ms5
周边孔	42	150	50	42	25	0.3	12.6	0.2	Ms7
底孔	42	155	60	14	32	0.6	8.4		Ms9
合计				121			95.7		

开挖方法：上层钻爆作业同压坡段；开挖中需控制每循环进尺角度和各部位钻孔深度，参数见表2。开挖中，适时进行系统喷锚支护，不良地质段超前支护。

（4）上弯段开挖。上弯段需扩挖，以满足反井作业空间需要，扩挖区为弯段顶部24.37m×9.9m三角部分。在其顶拱设天锚，以满足卷扬系统工作需要。

（三）开挖质量

1. 质量控制要点　每个循环爆破钻孔前根据施工图测量放样，并检查上一循环超欠挖情况；钻孔作业定人、定机、定位；光爆孔、预裂孔药卷按爆破设计装药结构要求捆绑于竹片上，不耦和装药系数应大于1.5；爆破开挖质量按每排炮进行检查和评定；空间转弯段钻孔前由测量计算偏移角度与孔深，循环进尺控制在1.5m内；开挖后及时支护，遇断层及不利结构面及时采取有效措施。

2. 质量控制效果　围岩松动控制在20～120cm；检测189个断面，947个超欠挖点，无欠挖，平均超挖12.4cm；检测189个断面，3255个不平整度点，最大值16.5cm，均值14.5cm，合格率93.4%，1133个半孔率点，半孔率92.2%。

（国电大渡河双江口工程建设管理分公司
林开盛　段斌　余俊良
四川农业大学　张杰）

悬臂式掘进机在隧洞引水工程中的应用

四川省蓬溪船山灌区为武都引水第二期工程的发展灌区，是一项综合性大型水利工程。灌区的文吉分干渠25.88km渠线项目中，隧洞长20.038km，占77.4%。隧洞为城门洞型，开挖尺寸2.3m×2.4m～3.1m×3.35m（宽×高），全断面混凝土衬砌，衬砌平均厚30cm。渠线出露地层岩性为鲜红色泥岩、泥质粉砂岩、粉砂质泥岩、砂岩，为Ⅳ、Ⅴ类围岩。新鲜粉砂质泥岩和弱风化砂岩饱和湿抗压强度2.9～3.4MPa，为极软岩类；新鲜泥质粉砂岩饱和湿抗压强度25.5MPa，为较软岩类。渠线隧洞选择悬臂式掘进机开挖。

（一）隧洞开挖方法选择

1. 钻爆法　最常见、应用最广的隧洞开挖方法，适用于各类条件。但周围扰动大，超挖量大。

2. TBM全断面法　适用于圆形断面洞室，开挖直径3～12m，掘进长度不小于10km，岩石物理力学指标及构造较均匀，岩石单轴饱和抗压强度小于200MPa。可连续开挖无爆破震动，减少超挖，节约支护和衬砌费用。

3. 悬臂式掘进机开挖　最先用于煤矿巷道开采，不同功率设备适用不同强度岩石及隧洞断面，适宜岩石强度小于50MPa。可减少超挖，节约支护及衬砌费用。小巧灵活，投资少，施工准备时间短，再利用率高。

渠线隧洞共27条，城门洞型，隧洞间由明渠或渡槽连接，故TBM全断面法不适用。开挖断面为特小或小断面，平均衬砌厚30cm，衬砌混凝土量小，钻爆法超挖导致超填混凝土量占比结构混凝土量极大，而此工程量不予计量，故经济风险较大。最终选用悬臂式掘进机开挖。

（二）悬臂式掘进机施工

1. 施工准备　根据BBZ120型掘进机功率，选定ZGS11-Z-10/1.2-500型变压器，10kV转1.14kV，容量500kVA。掘进机由刀头和机身组成，现场组装，具有自行功能，移动和工作均使用自身电机。

2. 掘进施工　洞脸开挖支护完成后开挖隧洞。掘进机驶入隧道一头，在掌子面切削掘进。切削渣土由第一运输机输送至掘进机后方的第二运输机，第二运输机传送至后方自卸车出渣。掘进完成后将初支台车运至掌子面进行初期支护，掘进机则后退至不影响后续施工的位置等待下一循环掘进。

3. 粉尘控制　掘进机切割头设有内、外喷雾控制阀，开始掘进时打开水阀（水量可控），使切割头内外喷雾用以降低粉尘。

4. 底板预留保护层　掘进机行走为履带式，自身重量达35余吨，开挖中会碾压底部软岩，故预留30cm保护层，以免导致超挖。

（三）效果对比

悬臂式掘进机在文吉分干渠项目获得成功，其效果如下。

1. 进度　人工钻爆平均进尺3～4m/天，火工材料供应、通风排烟、支护及出渣等影响其效率。掘进机平均进尺为5～7m/天，支护及出渣影响其效率。掘进机效率是钻爆法1.6～1.7倍，可减少各类资源投入。

2. 成本　经测算，特小或小断面的隧洞洞挖，人工钻爆综合成本220元/m^3，掘进机综合成本140元/m^3，前者是后者的1.5倍。

3. 质量　渠线岩石发育层状结构、且为Ⅳ、Ⅴ类围岩，悬臂式掘进机以磨岩为主，对岩石振动扰动小，能较好控制超挖，减少钻爆法施工必需的15～20cm超挖量，也减少了超填混凝土量。实测悬臂式掘进机平均径向超挖3～5cm，钻爆法平均径向超挖

20～30cm。

4. 安全　采用掘进机人工钻爆的工作面数量可减少很多，避免劳动密集带来的安全风险，且大幅减少了火工材料的使用，有利安全管理及控制。

（中国水利水电第三工程局有限公司　高文甫）

开敞式 TBM 洞内拆卸技术

辽西北供水桓集引水隧洞工程采用 TBM 和钻爆法施工，共投入 8 台 TBM 开挖。TBM 运行中，经常要从洞内移到洞外检修，也涉及到拆卸技术。

（一）拆卸前的准备工作

1. 土建工程　为确保 TBM 顺利拆卸并从支洞运出，掘进贯通前提前完成 TBM 扩大洞室施工。拆卸洞室长 80m，开挖高 17m，底部净宽 12.5m，C30 混凝土底板厚 30cm。

2. 吊机吊件　拆卸洞室布置 100＋100＋25t 和 20t 桥式起重机，使用前要做好检查。

3. 拆卸工具　按紧固力矩量程由小到大排列，可使用的工具包括各种扳手和气推油式液压张紧成套工具。工器具提前运至拆卸现场。

（二）拆卸

1. 拆卸程序　TBM 掘进段贯通后，依靠步进机构步进至主机拆卸洞预定位置。按主机→连接桥→后配套顺序拆卸。主机拆卸完成后，后配套用装载机逐节牵引至桥机覆盖区，拆卸后运至洞外储存场地。主机和后配套台车拆卸同时，拆除连续皮带系统、TBM 通风、高压电缆供电系统。

2. 主机拆卸　拆卸由刀盘开始，再拆除钻机、拱架安装器及平台，然后从后支撑至机头架依次拆卸。装车区在刀盘后部，为顺利运出部件，顶护盾最后拆除，便于装车。

（1）刀盘拆卸：停机前将刀盘转正，用碳弧气刨刨开边块焊缝，在刀盘两侧焊接吊耳，桥吊将钢丝绳收紧，桥机操作室显示起重重量 20t，刀盘下侧用钢凳垫稳，气刨刀盘正面的边块与中心块间焊缝；拆开刀盘与机头架连接螺栓，拔出所有双头螺栓和定位销后，缓缓起吊刀盘至离地 50cm 处，桥机大车向隧洞上游方向行走 3m 后，缓缓降落刀盘，刀盘正面（已气刨焊缝）向下；气刨刀盘背面和两侧挡渣条焊缝，拆除挡渣条；拆除刀盘边块与中心块间连接螺栓；对称拆除刀盘边块。

（2）侧护盾和顶护盾拆卸：将两侧护盾伸出，确保顶护盾有空间吊出；将侧护盾在外侧临时支撑固定；拆除顶侧护盾的销子、顶侧护盾、油缸与机头架连接销子，并直接装车运至洞外；拆除侧护盾油缸，将侧护盾吊好，固定好楔块油缸，拆除连接销，整体吊出。

（3）钻机拆卸：将左侧钻机驱动行走到钻机齿圈拱顶，拆除凿岩机及其行走托架上的油管，并给所有油管接头安装堵头；通过行吊、倒链和吊带将钻机推进大臂固定，拆除大臂；通过行吊、倒链固定行走托架并拆除；用相同方法拆除右侧钻机；通过行吊、倒链、吊带及焊接辅助支撑将齿圈固定，拆除连接螺栓，拆除左右齿圈组成部分及行走轮。

（4）后支腿拆卸：将后支腿撑起，在主梁尾段和连接桥做好临时支撑，再将其落下，收回油缸；拆除主机与连接桥连接机构。将后支腿吊好，拆除其与主梁尾段连接螺栓。

（5）鞍架及主梁拆卸：拆除 4 根推进油缸；随后拆除撑靴，吊至刀盘前部，放平；拆除底部和顶部撑靴油缸；在主梁前段安装临时支撑；拆除连接螺栓，整体吊下主梁中段及鞍架，直接放在地面；在地面将主梁中段及鞍架分开。

（6）主驱动拆卸：拆除连接螺栓，由上至下依次拆除主驱动，再用盖子封堵安装孔。

（7）机头架拆卸：机头架顶部连接法兰处设 4 个专用吊耳，按要求上扭矩。为防止机头架前倾无法拆除连接螺栓，也确保安全，调整好吊具将机头架吊平，再拆除连接螺栓。

3. 连接桥拆卸　连接桥按从后到前、先附属后主要部件顺序拆卸。拆除流程：拆风水电连接→拆附属设备→拆工作平台→拆后段支撑→拆后段和尾轮→拆段支撑→拆门架拖拉机构→拆前段→运到洞外。

4. 后配套拆卸　从后至前拆卸后配套。先拆除各节后配套间连接销，用钢丝绳将装载机与一节后配套连接牵引至拆卸洞，到位后拆除，再拆卸下一节。后配套台车的拆卸先局部，后整体结构件，自上至下，尽量保持构件完整。

（三）运输

运输平板车进入拆卸洞内，可在其中转弯，然后倒行驶入拆卸洞。拆卸洞拆下的 TBM 各部件吊放在平板车上，并固定好，经支洞运出洞外存放场地。

（四）效果

截至 2017 年 3 月 15 日，采用此技术已安全、快速完成了 5 台 ϕ8.5 级开敞式 TBM 的拆卸，最短用时 35 天，刷新了国内同级 TBM 拆卸记录，为类似项目 TBM 拆卸提供了经验。

（中国水利水电第三工程局有限公司
李光前　焦吉坤　左立富）

泄水建筑物施工

白鹤滩水电站闸门槽施工开创性采用云车技术

（一）闸门门槽一期直埋云车技术应用背景

对于安装高度大的高拱坝泄水孔门槽施工，传统施工工艺是大坝主体提前上升，后浇筑门槽二期混凝土。该技术较成熟，且应用广泛。但存在如下弊端：门槽安装及二期混凝土浇筑与坝体混凝土浇筑存在交叉作业，且交叉作业时间长，干扰大；二期混凝土施工工序多、工期长，存在非关键工期转变成关键工期的风险，甚至占用关键工期；与大坝下闸蓄水矛盾显著；一、二期混凝土结合不好。为解决这些问题，迫切需要研究应用门槽一期直埋云车技术。通过应用云车技术，个性化设计，实现门槽台车悬挂施工和自爬升，释放台车下部空间，有效促进施工进度，保证施工质量，满足施工精度等要求。

（二）闸门门槽一期直埋云车技术的特点

水电工程特高拱坝施工工期长，进度紧，质量要求精细，安全风险高，需要深入研究门槽一期直埋云车技术在高拱坝应用。新工艺门槽一期直埋施工工艺特点：①减少工程制约，优化高坝施工工期，避免传统技术导致门槽坝段滞后，综合发挥技术潜力；②优化施工组织设计；③缩短单位工程关键工期；④解决立体交叉施工存在的安全隐患，节约施工资源；⑤及时完成闸门启闭机安装，保障下闸节点目标及防洪度汛。

（三）闸门门槽一期直埋云车技术应用

白鹤滩大坝为椭圆线型混凝土双曲拱坝，最大坝高 289m，坝身布置 6 个导流底孔，门槽依托云车开创性采取一期直埋施工工艺一次性施工。即取消门槽二期施工，门槽埋件在一期混凝土浇筑前完成调整安装，直接埋进一期混凝土中。

平板闸门门槽云车是在门槽空间内布置一套嵌固型的悬臂钢桁架门槽台车，上下游面采用螺杆调整装置实现云车紧固和反轨的精确定位，并设置专门的液压提升装置，可在门槽安装空间内随主体混凝土上升实现悬挂和自爬升，从而实现门槽与坝体混凝土一体化浇筑，取消门槽二期混凝土。

（四）闸门门槽一期直埋云车技术应用成效

门槽一期直埋云车技术在白鹤滩特高拱坝中的成功应用，确保门槽下闸节点工期；规避了混凝土与门槽埋件结合问题，高精度、高标准完成了门槽埋件安装；消除了上下交叉作业，减少脚手架搭设，规避在狭小空间作业，取得了好的效果。

（四川二滩国际工程咨询有限责任公司　李世伟）

黄登水电站尾水调压室开挖支护施工技术

黄登水电站尾水调压室，由 2 个调压室组成。高程 1455m 以上为圆筒式调压井，以下为调压室与尾水隧洞（洞顶 1456.70m）、尾水支洞（洞顶 1456.70m）相交部分。1455m 处调压井由大断面突变为小断面。调压井开挖直径 32.4～36m，底部开挖高程 1437m，顶部 1514.538m，高 77.538m，两室中心距 70m。调压井 1505.154m 以上为球形穹顶，球形半径 18.675m。两调压室间在 1488.20m 设连通上室，断面 13.9m×16.9m（宽×高），城门洞型。

（一）地质条件

尾水调压室段岩性为角砾岩、细砾岩夹变质凝灰岩，微风化～新鲜岩体。围岩受两条相互交叉Ⅲ级断层影响：F230-1 横穿 1 号尾水调压室，F230-2 从左向右分别穿过 1 号尾水调压室下游井壁等处。1 号调压室开挖揭露Ⅳ级结构面 19 条（断层 7 条，挤压面 12 条）。

（二）尾调室主要施工方法

1. 施工分区和施工通道　2 个尾调室自上而下分为Ⅰ、Ⅱ、Ⅲ、Ⅳ、Ⅴ五个区施工。调压室下部与尾水隧洞和 2 条尾水支洞相处形成“四岔口”。调压室顶部设 5-1、5-2、5-3 施工支洞，均为调压室上部施工通道。每条尾调室底部与 1 条尾水隧洞和 2 条尾水支洞相贯，井筒出渣通过溜渣井到尾水洞，再经施工支洞运出洞。

2. 1 号尾调室Ⅰ区　先锋槽开挖起始断面 7m×5m（高×宽），5-3 作通道，顶部沿设计边线造孔开挖至穹顶中心部位，下部 20％坡度升坡。槽段开挖每次进尺不大于 1.2m，出渣后及时支护。先锋槽完成后，先开挖设计边线处 A 区，及时跟进支护，进尺 1m。再开挖中间剩余区域 B 区，B 区延迟 A 区 4 排炮施工，进尺 2m。最后穹顶以下 1503～1501

部位。

3. 2号尾调室Ⅰ区　先锋槽起始开挖高7m，宽5m，5-1作通道，水平开挖至穹顶设计边线，再大断面开挖槽段。顶部沿设计边线开挖至穹顶中心，下部回填石渣，坡度为20%。施工方法同1号尾调室。先锋槽完成后，自中心向两侧开挖。断面较宽，自中心向外分为A、B、C施工，B、C开挖滞后A两排炮，进尺不大于1m，系统支护后方可开挖下一段。

4. 尾调室Ⅱ区、Ⅲ区　Ⅱ区开挖底部高程1498m，5-1进入2号尾调室，降坡10.8%开挖至连通上室Ⅰ层底部1498m，向右开挖，完成1号尾调室Ⅱ区施工后，从右向左推进，完成连通上室Ⅰ层剩余工程、2号尾调室Ⅱ区施工，回填施工道路至5-3作为施工通道。

Ⅱ区施工高度3m，YT-28手风钻造孔爆破，先掏槽至调压室中心，再两侧扩挖。扩挖时周边预留2m保护层，随下一次扩爆。YT-28造竖直孔，周边光爆，开挖后及时支护；连通上室Ⅰ层用钻架台车配手风钻造水平孔，周边光爆。

连通上室Ⅱ层及尾调室Ⅲ区从5-2向两侧开挖，开挖方法同上。

5. 尾调室Ⅳ区　先开挖导井，再扩挖溜渣井，最后分层二次扩挖。开挖前，先通过尾水隧洞打设中导洞至尾调室底部。导井用LM200反井钻机开挖，自上至下用反井钻机打ϕ216mm先导孔与下部中导洞（8m×9m）贯通，再用反井钻机从下反向扩挖成ϕ1.4m导井。溜渣井自上而下利用吊笼，YT-28手风钻造孔，爆破高2m，扩挖至ϕ4m。溜渣井成型后，再自上而下分层（3m）扩挖。扩挖清渣完成后，用ϕ5m井盖将溜渣井封闭，在上面掏槽（2m×2m）开挖，手风钻造孔，分段爆破，进尺不大于4m，开挖至设计线。

6. 尾调室Ⅴ区（“四岔口”）　“四岔口”开挖以水平向为主分5层开挖支护，垂向分Ⅰ～Ⅲ区。第2层为前期已开挖导洞，第5层为保护层。每层完成一区开挖支护后，再进行另一区施工，每层全部完成后再进行下一层开挖。

“四岔口”采用平洞开挖方法，尾调井随尾水隧洞及尾水支洞逐层向下开挖。在调压室开挖至1464m高程时，开挖石渣暂不出渣，底部垫渣扩挖1464～1456.7m高程，距1456.7m高程上部约5m时，造竖直孔分两区光面爆破。待1456.7m高程以上全部开挖支护结束后，再将除施工通道垫渣外的多余石渣运至洞外。此前在调压井开挖中已将尾水隧洞导洞贯通，调压室下挖至下部隧洞洞顶后即开挖“四岔口”。“四岔口”开挖以尾水隧洞为通道，先调压室1456.7m高程预应力锁口锚杆，再对尾水支洞及尾水隧洞导洞扩挖至设计边线，并施工尾水隧洞、尾水支洞预应力锁口锚杆，然后分层下挖。

第二层导洞两侧预留岩体开挖采用光面爆破，第三、四层每区开挖时，先边墙预裂，再手风钻造水平孔开挖，底部保护层厚2.7m，采用水平光爆开挖。边墙预裂用手风钻造ϕ42mm竖直孔，孔深4.2m，间隔装药，磁电雷管起爆。岩柱开挖根据分层高度，用手风钻ϕ42mm水平孔开挖，孔深3m，连续装药，磁电雷管起爆。

尾水隧洞和尾水支洞与尾调室相交突变部位开挖时，从尾水隧洞（尾水支洞）将尾水隧洞（尾水支洞）前期开挖的中导洞按尾水隧洞（尾水支洞）开挖宽度扩挖至调压室底部，再从上至下爆破拆除“四岔口”预留岩体。剩余边角部位从调压室底部往尾水隧洞造孔，另一边从尾水支洞突变部位钻孔，两侧同时爆破挖除。

（三）浅表层变形及掉块处理措施

尾调室开挖中多次出现掉块、喷锚剥落，除增加锚杆、锚筋桩、预应力锚索外，在掉块及喷锚剥落部位大面积增加GPS2主动防护网。其结构为：ϕ16纵横向支撑钢绳，钢格栅网（ϕ2.2mm，网孔50mm×50mm），钢丝绳网（菱形网，ϕ8mm，网孔300mm×300mm），ϕ10缝合钢绳，用钢绳卡连接。

（中国水利水电第十四工程局有限公司
张永岗　黄金凤）

白鹤滩反拱形水垫塘基础开挖与处理设计

（一）水垫塘地形地质条件

拱坝下游消能区自坝轴线下游50～500m间河道较顺直，河谷呈不对称阶梯状V形，右岸地形陡峻，平均坡度65°，左岸地形较缓，坡度30°～35°。河床地面高程576～581m，枯水期水面高程590m，水面宽50～90m。

河床砂（卵）砾石覆盖层厚5～25m，右岸较厚，基岩顶面高程560m。水垫塘基岩主要为柱状节理玄武岩、角砾熔岩、隐晶质玄武岩，岩体以弱风化下段为主，强卸荷不明显。左岸边坡为斜顺向坡，层内错动带顺层或小角度切层发育，有数条宽1～3m断层带，风化强烈，局部受错动带控制，卸荷强烈。右岸边坡为逆向坡，错动带为反倾坡内，无大规模断层，岩体风化、卸荷不强烈，无强卸荷岩体。

总体上水垫塘基础左缓右陡，河床覆盖层厚薄不一，岩体质量不均，局部破碎且缓倾角错动带发育，以$Ⅲ_2$类为主，局部Ⅳ类，抗冲能力差，需衬砌混凝土。

（二）水垫塘布置与结构设计

白鹤滩大坝采用 6 表孔和 7 深孔坝身泄洪方式，坝身承担枢纽约 70%泄洪量，最大泄量 30098m^3/s，最大泄洪功率 60000MW。为满足消能需求，水垫塘末端设二道坝。将二道坝设在深孔出口下游 400m 处，水垫塘长 360m。由于地形不对称，为避免水舌冲击左岸岸坡，水垫塘底板中心线与泄洪孔口溢流中心线平行且向右岸偏移 7m，与拱坝中心线成 5°夹角。水垫塘底板需满足水垫深度要求，结合河床条件，尽量减小开挖，经比较确定水垫塘底板最低高程 560m。

由于泄洪功率高，脉动压力大，水垫塘底板采用稳定性好的反拱形。适应地形条件，减少开挖，采用左缓右陡不对称结构。反拱圆弧形半径 107.02m，底板弧底顶面高程 560m，拱端高程 582m，矢高 22m。两岸拱端处设拱座，其基底高程 578.82m，此高程以上左岸边坡坡度 1∶1.0，右岸边坡坡度 1∶0.4，高程 606m 设宽 5m 马道，水垫塘顶宽 210m。考虑塘内最高运行水位及安全超高确定水垫塘顶高程 635m。水垫塘反拱底板混凝土衬砌厚 4m，左、右岸边坡混凝土衬砌厚 3m。

（三）水垫塘基础开挖与设计

水垫塘左岸边坡 1∶1 坡比，右岸边坡 1∶0.4，均常规梯级预裂爆破开挖。根据底板体型，底板圆弧采用梯段和水平开挖相结合。两侧高程 559～578.82m 较陡处梯段开挖，利用分段斜线拟合圆弧线，梯段间高差 3.5～6.8m，高程低，高差小。梯段间设 1.5m 宽马道，分段后基础开挖线与理论圆弧开挖线最大超深 0.78m。底部高程 559～556m 坡度最缓部位水平开挖，水平开挖厚度 3m。

底板基岩质量差，故河床及左岸反弧段底板基础采取预留岩石保护层爆破，分两次开挖，保护层厚 3～6m；右岸反弧段底板基础，岩石开挖厚度薄，所以右岸高程 559m 以上底板基础一次性爆破完成开挖。

（四）基础缺陷处理

水垫塘建基面岩体多为Ⅲ$_2$ 类岩体，总体能满足强度及变形要求。但一些部位存在易卸荷松弛和强卸荷岩体、断层及层内错动带、深坑，这些缺陷需处理。

（1）挖除河床深坑内覆盖层，回填置换混凝土。

（2）断层及错动带局部挖槽并回填置换混凝土及固结灌浆处理。错动带宽超过 0.5m，槽挖深度按 1.5 倍带宽且不小于 1m；断层带宽超过 0.5m，槽挖深度按 1.5 倍带宽且不大于 2m；小于 0.5m 断层及错动带不做处理，只做建基面清理。

（3）受断层错动带切割组合边坡，可能失稳岩体采用预应力锚索支护。

（4）水垫塘底板、拱座及左岸边坡进行固结灌浆处理。

（五）基础固结灌浆设计

水垫塘左岸边坡岩体，灌浆孔 2m 间排距，孔深 5m，强卸荷深厚区 7m。底板及拱座，在中段水流强冲击区，间排距 2m，孔深 7m；在上游非冲击区，间排距 2m，孔深 5m；下游非冲击区，间排距 3m，孔深 5m；规模较大构造带加密灌浆孔。

两序灌浆，分序加密。孔深 5m，全孔一次灌浆，Ⅰ序孔灌浆压力 0.5MPa，Ⅱ序孔 0.5～0.8MPa。孔深 7m，自上而下分段灌浆，Ⅰ序孔灌浆压力 0.5～0.8MPa，Ⅱ序孔 0.5～1.0MPa。

质量检查以声波测试为主，压水试验为辅。质量合格标准：①反拱底板及拱座部位单孔平均波速不小于 4400m/s，波速值小于下限值 3900m/s 比例不超过 10%，且不集中；左岸高程 591m 以上边坡单孔平均波速不小于 4000m/s，波速值小于下限值 3200m/s 比例不超过 10%，且不集中；②压水试验中 85%以上检查孔透水率不大于 3Lu，不合格孔段透水率不大于 4.5Lu，且不集中。

（中国电建集团华东勘测设计研究院有限公司
薛阳　彭育　何明　陶俊佳）

白鹤滩水电站高流速流道镜面混凝土施工关键技术

白鹤滩水电站泄洪洞工程，由 3 条泄洪洞组成，单洞洞长 2.3km，过流断面 15m×18m，设计单洞过流量 4200m^3/s，最大流速 47m/s，结构复杂，过流面混凝土施工质量要求高。施工中重点研究了镜面混凝土的配合比、施工工艺、技术参数、质量控制及外观质量等关键技术，最终获取了镜面混凝土施工工艺和质量控制标准，形成了水工高流速流道镜面混凝土成套施工技术。

（1）针对高流速流道混凝土体型精准、平整光滑、耐磨防裂的高标准要求，提出了过流面镜面混凝土的施工理念，确定了镜面混凝土施工质量技术标准。

（2）针对不同结构和部位特点，进行了流道异形模板、平段多循环重型衬砌台车、斜坡段变断面液压自行衬砌钢模台车的设计和制作，以及相关设备的选择和现场工艺试验；进行了大跨度三滚轴整平装置的设计和制作，研究形成高流速流道收面工艺和施工缝控制措施；研发了垂直橡胶止水带保护装置。通过采用平面大模板、WISA模板、悬臂模板、定型组合钢模板和定型圆弧模板，以及大断面整体钢模台车，形成了镜面混凝土模板的设计、制作、安装技术和质量控制标准。

（3）研究了低水化热、低坍落度、抗磨蚀镜面混凝土配合比，研制了有限空间5～7cm坍落度混凝土连续输送入仓系统，优化了振捣器具及工艺，保证了混凝土质量。

（4）完成了混凝土智能保湿养护系统的设计和制作，以及相关设备的选择及现场工艺试验。研发了镜面混凝土智能化养护控制系统，实现了主控数据的实时采集和反馈分析，智能控制喷淋养护，提高了混凝土保湿养护质量。

通过实践与研究，项目获发明专利1项，实用新型专利6项，省部级工法6项，在白鹤滩泄洪洞工程中首次实现了5～7cm低坍落度混凝土的衬砌施工，全面推广采用低热水泥，在保证混凝土外观质量的同时，有效地控制了大体积、高标号混凝土温度裂缝的产生，打破了水利水电工程中无洞不裂的规律，为泄洪洞高流速运行提供了安全保障。

（中国水利水电第五工程局有限公司
袁幸朝　陈敏）

白鹤滩水电站右岸尾水隧洞固结灌浆试验

白鹤滩水电站尾水隧洞地质条件差，存在不利地质构造，故在相应部位布置固结灌浆。

（一）固结灌浆生产性试验

1. 试验区基本情况　右岸尾水隧洞固结灌浆段大部分在柱状节理玄武岩洞段，选择右⑧尾水隧洞柱状节理玄武岩区域进行固结灌浆生产性试验，桩号（RW⑧0＋765m）～（RW⑧0＋795.5m），$Ⅲ_1$类围岩，存在顺洞向陡倾角小断层，宽3～5cm，顺层向缓倾角裂隙。

2. 灌浆方法及参数　灌浆孔孔径50mm，孔深入岩6m，间排距2.5m，共12排，单数排8孔，双数排7孔，共90孔，灌浆压力0.5～1.5MPa。采用环间不分序环内加密、环间分序环内加密方法。纯压式自上而下分段灌浆（2、4m）及全孔一段灌浆（6m）两种方式。

3. 灌浆工序　灌浆工序流程：环间不分序环内加密（两序），测放孔位→预埋导向管→施工准备→Ⅰ序孔钻孔灌浆→Ⅱ序孔钻孔灌浆→灌浆质量检查；环间分序环内加密（四序），测放孔位→预埋导向管安装→施工准备→Ⅰ序环Ⅰ序孔钻孔灌浆→Ⅰ序环Ⅱ序孔钻孔灌浆→Ⅱ序环Ⅰ序孔钻孔灌浆→Ⅱ序环Ⅱ序孔钻孔灌浆→灌浆质量检查。

4. 灌浆技术要求　①灌浆预埋管为ϕ60mm普通焊管，上端距底板混凝土表面2cm，下端至少穿过混凝土底层钢筋；②抬动观测孔孔径75mm，入岩8m；③钻孔结束后冲洗钻孔，直到回水澄清，冲洗压力是灌浆压力80%，且大于1MPa，冲洗时间大于20min；④灌前简易压水试验压力为灌浆压力80%，且大于1MPa；⑤采用42.5普通硅酸盐水泥浆液，水灰比3∶1、2∶1、1∶1、0.8∶1、0.5∶1五个比级（重量比）；开灌水灰比2∶1及3∶1；⑥灌浆压力保持不变，注入率持续降低，或注入率不变而压力持续升高时，不改变水灰比；某级浆液注入量达300L以上，或灌注时间30min，灌浆压力和注入率均无改变或改变不显著，改浓一级水灰比，注入率＞30L/min根据情况越级变浓；⑦设计压力下注入率≤1L/min后，继续灌30min可结束；⑧灌浆结束后用0.5∶1纯水泥浆封孔，压力0.5MPa，持续30min，孔内浆液凝固后，对钻孔空余部位使用水泥砂浆封填密实、孔口压抹齐平。

5. 抬动观测　设4个抬动观测孔，每10min记录一次。抬动大于0.1mm，即停止灌浆。

6. 质量检查　检查采用单点压水试验，检查孔不少于灌浆孔5%，检查结束后进行灌浆和封孔。合格标准：85%以上检查孔透水率≤3Lu，其余透水率≤4.5Lu，且分布不集中。

（二）生产性试验成果分析

试验段灌前平均透水率62.9Lu，其中Ⅰ序孔105Lu，Ⅱ序孔15Lu，Ⅱ序较Ⅰ序减少85.7%，透水率随孔序增加而递减，符合规律。灌浆平均单耗79.01kg/m，Ⅰ序120.11kg/m，Ⅱ序32.03kg/m，Ⅱ序单耗较Ⅰ序减少73.3%，单耗随孔序增加而递减，符合灌浆规律。

1. 灌浆分序对比　将不同洞段的环间不分序环内加密及环间分序环内加密灌浆进行对比（见表1）。两者均为全孔一段灌浆，开灌水灰比均为3∶1。表中“单耗/透水率”比值在一定程度上反映洞段自身差异加权后的灌浆效果。

由表1可知，环间不分序环内加密（方式①）“单耗/透水率”为1.06，环间分序环内加密（方式②）“单耗/透水率”为7.86，后者是前者7倍多，一定程度上说明方式②效果较好。但方式②实际上分四序施工，对施工组织要求更高，对施工进度有影响。

2. 灌浆分段对比　试验进行了两段灌浆与全孔一段灌浆对比（见表2）。

由表2可知，两段灌浆方式Ⅰ序孔灌完后，Ⅱ序单耗及透水率均明显低于一段灌浆，说明前者效果更优。两段灌浆孔口入岩 2m 段灌浆压力较低（0.5MPa），下部 4m 段灌浆压力 1.5 MPa；一段灌浆Ⅰ序灌浆压力 0.5～0.8MPa，Ⅱ序为 1.5MPa，孔口段最大压力 1.5MPa，易引起混凝土抬动。此外，质量检查时，两段灌浆区均合格，一段灌浆区有 1 个检查孔不合格，经两次补灌方合格。一段灌浆平均单孔耗时 223min，两段灌浆平均单孔耗时 313min。

3. 开灌水灰比对比　2∶1 与 3∶1 开灌水灰比灌浆在不同洞段，前者对应环间分序环内加密，后者 3∶1 对应环间不分序环内加密（见表 3），均为两段灌浆。

表 1　灌浆分序试验成果统计表

分序方式	孔序	单耗(kg/m)	灌前平均透水率（Lu）	所有序孔平均单耗（kg/m）	所有序孔平均透水率（Lu）	单耗/透水率[kg/(m·Lu)]
①环间不分序	Ⅰ	104.6	123.83	83.19	78.75	1.06
	Ⅱ	58.72	27.24			
②环间分序	Ⅰ	46.6	5.94	33.01	4.20	7.86
	Ⅱ	17.47	2.21			

表 2　不同灌浆分段方式单耗成果统计表

灌浆分段	段长(m)	单耗（kg·m⁻¹）					灌前平均透水率（Lu）				
		Ⅰ序孔	Ⅱ序孔	Ⅰ序孔	Ⅱ序孔	小计	Ⅰ序孔	Ⅱ序孔	Ⅰ序孔	Ⅱ序孔	小计
两段灌	2	198.18	1.24	135.61	5.35	74.82	228.63	2.99	90.81	2.62	49.66
	4	104.33	7.40				21.91	2.44			
一段灌	6	104.60	58.72	104.60	58.72	83.19	119.09	27.11	119.09	27.11	76.17

表 3　不同开灌水灰比试验成果统计表

分序方式	孔序	开灌水灰比	单耗(kg/m)	平均透水率（Lu）	所有序孔平均单耗（kg/m）	所有序孔平均透水率（Lu）	单耗/透水率[kg/(m·Lu)]
环间分序	Ⅰ	2∶1	135.61	125.27	74.82	68.18	1.10
	Ⅱ		5.35	2.93			
环间不分序	Ⅰ	3∶1	31.1	7.2	18.84	7.00	2.69
	Ⅱ		4.82	6.78			

由表 3 可知，开灌水灰比 2∶1 的“单耗/透水率”低于开灌水灰比 3∶1，2∶1 灌浆效果较差。第一类柱状节理洞段虽柱面节理及微裂隙发育，但开挖后及时封闭条件下，柱面及微裂隙闭合，裂隙较细小，采用高水灰比更易灌入，故不能认为 2∶1 一定劣于 3∶1。

（中国电建集团华东勘测设计研究院有限公司
王恒乐　陈益民　杨飞　倪绍虎　李治平）

纳米材料喷射混凝土在溧阳抽水蓄能电站中的应用

溧阳抽水蓄能电站尾水主洞洞室开挖后，顶拱部位围岩稳定性差，尤其在渗漏水作用下，围岩呈泥状，极易塌方。为此，在普通喷射混凝土中掺加无机纳米及仿钢纤维、钢纤维等材料，快速喷射混凝土封闭围岩，比喷射常规混凝土的效果好。

（一）纳米材料喷射混凝土的特点

纳米钢纤维及纳钢纤维喷射混凝土不仅能显著提高混凝土的抗压强度、抗渗性、抗折性、抗冲击性、抗磨损性及韧性等指标，与普通喷射混凝土比有如下特点：①渗水、掉块部位能快速封闭围岩；②一次喷厚 40cm，不必多次复喷；③回弹率较小（顶拱回弹率小于 8%，边墙回弹率小于 5%）；④起强快，初凝 4min，终凝 10min，终凝后抗压强度大幅提高。

（二）纳米喷混凝土配合比设计

在原普通 C25 喷混凝土配合比的基础上，外掺 10%纳米材料代替减水剂及 5kg/m³ 仿钢纤维或 10%钢纤维。现场进行生产性试验，根据喷射效果及试样强度调整和确定配合比。

1. 原材料检测

（1）水泥采用 P.O42.5R 水泥。水泥的各项指标检测结果均符合要求。

(2) 细骨料和粗骨料均为骨料加工系统加工的人工骨料。骨料的各项指标检测结果均符合要求。

(3) 速凝剂采用无碱液态速凝剂 RCMG-10C 型。速凝剂各项指标检测结果均符合要求。

(4) 纳米材料是一种经充分研磨、材料颗粒直径达纳米级的高性能混凝土外加剂。钢纤维规格为 CW04-30-1000/直径 0.55mm，各项指标检测结果均符合要求。仿钢纤维采用 concrete power3000 纤维，是一种替代钢纤维的高分子聚合物纤维。仿钢纤维的各项指标检测结果均符合要求。

2. 配合比　经室内配合比试验和现场生产性试验，确定每方 CF25 纳米钢纤维喷射混凝土材料用量：水泥 362kg，水 159kg，砂 1115kg，米石 683kg，纳米 (10%) 45kg，速凝剂 (7%) 25.34kg，钢纤维 (10%) 45kg；纳米仿钢纤维喷射混凝土材料用量：水泥 451kg，水 159kg，砂 1028kg，米石 686kg，纳米 (10%) 45kg，速凝剂 (7%) 31.57kg，仿钢纤维 5kg。

(三) 喷射混凝土施工

1. 混凝土的拌和及运输　混凝土在拌和站拌制，纳米、钢纤维和仿钢纤维按配合比采用人工添加送入拌和机。在加纤维前按正常时间 (90s) 搅拌混凝土，混凝土搅拌完毕后，在搅拌机中投入纤维材料，再搅拌 30s。混凝土拌制后，用搅拌运输车运至施工现场。

2. 喷射混凝土施工　选定 1 号尾水主洞 0+721.8 及 0+978.2 局部渗水段试验，在 1 号尾水主洞 0+769.3 与 2 号尾水主洞桩号 0+408.9 两个渗水和塌方洞段实际应用。

喷射纳米钢纤维混凝土采用混凝土湿喷机械手施工。作业时喷嘴距喷射部位保持在 1.0～1.5m，尽量与喷射部位保持垂直。在预喷射部位从一边向另一边间隙 3～5min 循环喷射，每次喷厚 20cm 左右。在塌方部位，喷嘴对准塌方部位摆动扫射，随时观察掉落情况，围岩稳定后停止喷射，并支立拱架及副拱加固。施工现场进行大板取样。

(四) 喷射混凝土实施效果

1. 回弹率　喷射前将作业面整平，铺设彩条布收集回弹料。喷射结束后，对回弹量进行计量。经测定，洞室顶拱喷射混凝土回弹率为 7%，边墙部位回弹率为 3.5%。

2. 凝结时间　喷混凝土试验时，测定混凝土初凝时间 4min，终凝时间 10min。

3. 混凝土试块强度　现场取大板试样进行强度检测，检测结果见表 1。

表 1　　纳米钢纤维和纳米仿钢纤维混凝土强度检测结果

检测项目		1 天	3 天	7 天	28 天
纳米钢纤维混凝土	抗压强度 (MPa)	3.6	14.7	19.2	30.4
	抗折强度 (MPa)	—	2.39	2.93	4.80
纳米仿钢纤维混凝土	抗压强度 (MPa)	3.7	14.1	18.4	29.1
	抗折强度 (MPa)	—	2.82	3.46	5.13

4. 现场喷射效果　纳米钢纤维及纳米仿钢纤维喷射混凝土的终凝时间较短，强度增长快，在富水区能及时封闭围岩，达到止水效果，避免洞室坍塌；在渗水、断层塌方洞段，喷混凝土 40cm 以上后，能达到快速封堵的效果，有效地抑制了塌方的蔓延。喷射纳米钢纤维及纳米仿钢纤维喷射混凝土技术在溧阳抽水蓄能电站尾水主洞得到成功应用。

(中国水利水电第六工程局有限公司　何金星)

基　础　处　理

白鹤滩水电站右岸坝基柱状节理玄武岩开挖施工技术

(一) 坝址地质条件及岩体特性

白鹤滩水电站右岸坝基高程 590～545m 出露岩体为 $P_2\beta^3$ 岩流层中第一类柱状节理玄武岩 $P_2\beta_3{}^3$。岩体以微新为主，局部断层发育部位弱风化下段，无卸荷。柱状节理玄武岩为柱状镶嵌结构，整体性差。在原生状态未受扰动时力学参数较高，坝基开挖后应力状态改变，岩体向临空面卸荷松弛，松弛厚度 2～3m，松弛后岩体声波波速 3500～4000m/s。开挖揭露初期卸荷松弛较快，随时间延长，松弛岩体波速略有下降；

末松弛岩体声波波速 4750～5100m/s。若存在顺向层内错动带或软弱夹层，还可能出现卸荷剪切变形。

（二）坝基开挖流程和方案

1. 开挖流程　为增加坝基柱状节理玄武岩力学性能及岩体完整性，尽量减弱爆破开挖对玄武岩建基面扰动，控制坝基开挖后卸荷松弛。按设计要求，右岸大坝高程 590m 以下坝基采用双保护层方式开挖，预留保护层厚 5m。保护层表面按大坝建基面要求实施预裂爆破技术开挖，然后利用保护层作为岩石盖重进行坝基固结灌浆，并在灌浆孔下设锚筋桩对保留岩体预锚。同时，根据右岸大坝高程 590m 以下坝基上陡下缓结构特点，对其上部陡坡段，用常规预裂爆破技术开挖，下部缓坡段和水平段用复合消能爆破技术开挖。

建基面开挖流程：施工准备→前缘梯段开挖→保护层顶面开挖→保护层盖重固结灌浆质量检查→灌后封孔扫孔→安装锚筋桩→保护层开挖至建基面。

2. 开挖方案　为确保实现右岸坝基快速开挖，坝基固结灌浆和开挖作业同步实施。即坝基保护层顶面自上而下开挖至 565m 后，上部坝基固结灌浆开始施工，固结灌浆自上而下到 555m 后，开始坝基预留保护层开挖。坝基开挖和固结灌浆间的安全距离不小于 30m。

右岸坝基固结灌浆及锚筋桩完成后，全面展开柱状节理玄武岩保护层开挖。右岸坝基上陡下缓，保护层开挖分陡坡段、缓坡段和水平段。时间上分两个时段，坝基 563m 以上固结灌浆结束后，即启动陡坡段（590～570m）开挖，按“自上而下、分层梯段开挖”实施；缓坡段和水平段固结灌浆完成后，在缓坡段坡脚进行水平段抽槽开挖，形成爆破临空面后，同步开挖缓坡段和水平段保护层。最终提前 19 天完成坝基保护层开挖。

（三）坝基开挖施工方法

1. 保护层顶面开挖　为避免保护层顶面开挖直接影响柱状节理玄武岩建基面，开挖时预留 5m 厚保护层对建基面表层保护。据设计要求，保护层顶面开挖按坝基建基面质量标准控制；顶面开挖时距爆破梯段顶面 10m 处振速不大于 10cm/s，爆后第一次测试坝基岩体距孔口 1m 处声波波速值衰减率不得大于 10%。为此，在地质条件相近部位进行多次试验。当预裂孔孔径 76mm，孔距 60cm，线状药密度 220g/m，最大段单响药量控制 15kg（4 个预裂孔一响），主爆孔最大单响药量控制 30kg 时，可满足爆破振动速度和声波损伤设计要求。开挖中监测每个梯段爆破振动和声波损伤，据此优化下一梯段爆破参数。

2. 岩石盖重固结灌浆　保护层顶面开挖结束后，利用预留 5m 岩体作为岩石盖重进行固结灌浆。固结灌浆孔深 25～30m，孔排距均 2m，采用循环灌浆法，分排序加密，按Ⅰ、Ⅱ、Ⅲ次序依次施工。如灌浆部位存在临空面，则先周边灌浆。Ⅰ、Ⅱ序孔自上而下分段灌浆，Ⅲ序孔采用综合灌浆法。灌浆分级加压逐步达到设计值，预留 5m 保护层部位压力 0.5MPa，建基面以下第一段灌浆压力 0.8～1.0MPa，最大灌浆压力 3MPa。单孔灌注，如串孔且设备满足施工要求，则并联灌注（孔数不得多于 3 个）。串通孔灌浆或多孔并联灌浆时，严格控制压力，加强抬动监测，防止抬动破坏。保护层段岩体采用低压灌浆优先灌注。

3. 锚筋桩锚固　固结灌浆完成后，将灌浆孔扫孔，下设长 9～12m 锚筋桩并注浆，深度控制在建基面以下 10cm。下设过程中孔内居中放置对中环，确保注浆管和排气管畅通。

4. 保护层开挖技术　右岸坝基保护层顶面和高程 590～555m 保护层开挖，采用预裂爆破技术，开挖梯段高度陡坡段 5m，缓坡段 2～3m。

坝基 555m 以下缓坡段和水平段保护层采用垂直密炮孔复合消能爆破技术一次开挖。该技术利用孔底设置的铁球进行反射消能（见图 1），炮孔垂直建基面，孔径 90mm，孔深 5m，孔排距均 1.5m。药卷直径 70/32mm，单孔药量小于 6kg，最大段单响药量小于 13kg。

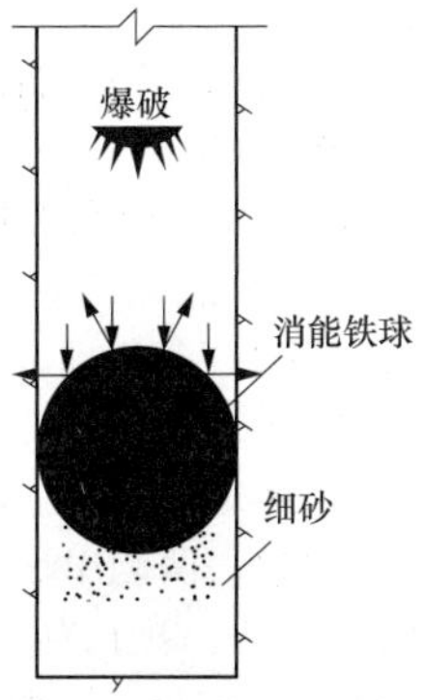

图 1　铁球消能示意图

对坝基保护层预裂爆破及复合消能爆破进行监测，前者最大振动速度为 4.76～5.12cm/s，后者为 7.32～8.2cm/s，均满足小于 10cm/s 的设计要求。爆后检测复合消能爆破岩体损伤深度 0.68～0.79m，预裂爆破为 0.86～0.87m，均满足不大于 1m 的设计要求。

（中国水利水电第八工程局有限公司
刘建程　陈勇）

苏洼龙水电站导流洞出口深覆盖层基坑渗流控制设计与施工

苏洼龙水电站为金沙江上游 13 个梯级电站的第

10级，一等大（1）型工程。枢纽建筑物由沥青混凝土心墙堆石坝、右岸溢洪道和泄洪放空洞、左岸引水系统和地面厂房等组成。导流洞及泄洪放空洞出口围堰的堰基，大部分位于右岸一级堆积阶地上，覆盖层30～50m，由崩塌块碎石、低液限黏土和冰积块碎石组成。

（一）围堰设计

结合地质条件、防渗效果、工期投资等因素，在比较高喷灌浆、防渗墙、帷幕灌浆等方案后，最终选定高喷灌浆接复合土工膜作为导流洞及泄洪放空洞出口围堰的防渗形式，

1. 轴线布置 尽可能在导流洞及泄洪防空洞出口结构线外，堰体不占压出口明渠体型，并满足两洞出口明渠开挖出渣和混凝土浇筑运输，避免过多侵占汛期河床行洪断面。

2. 堰顶高程 导流洞及泄洪放空洞出口围堰设计标准采用全年10年一遇重现期洪水，相应流量5510m^3/s，对应厂址水位2393.6m。出口围堰位于厂址下游150m左右，考虑一定的安全超高，出口围堰堰顶高程取2395m。

3. 断面结构及填料设计 考虑围堰开挖现状，结合高喷灌浆设备钻孔能力、基岩及围堰内侧开挖的最低高程等，围堰开挖至2385m高程作为施工平台。2385m以下预留土坎，2385m以上填筑土石方。堰顶宽8m，轴线长265.36m，迎水面边坡和背水面边坡均为1∶1.5，底部最大宽度53m。迎水面用1m厚大块石护面，其坡脚用2层钢筋石笼保护。

4. 防渗设计 2385m高程以下采用高喷灌浆，孔距1m，伸入基岩0.5m；无法入岩处，底部至2362m，构成悬挂高喷墙；两侧岸坡根据情况，延伸高喷灌浆形成封闭。2385m以上为复合土工膜心墙，土工膜与高喷墙用混凝土连接。围堰右堰肩为导流洞出口右护岸开挖边坡，左堰肩为泄洪洞出口上游侧原始边坡，两者均开挖至岩面，用混凝土固定土工膜。

5. 防冲措施 汛期围堰迎水面流速较大，需用1m厚大块石护面和钢筋石笼护底。

（二）围堰抗滑稳定计算

导流洞及泄洪放空洞出口围堰规模较大，最大高度15m，轴线长265.36m。围堰岩埂层内错动带发育，围堰稳定受其控制。选择岩层内错动带滑动面做抗滑稳定分析，用抗剪公式计算，未考虑扬压力折减，在各工况下安全稳定系数均大于1.05，满足抗滑稳定要求。

（三）围堰施工

1. 高喷墙 河床冲积砂卵石夹块、漂石层厚度大，用钻机跟管钻孔，孔径133mm，孔内下设133mm钢套管。钻至设计孔深后，在钢套管内下设110mm PVC花管护壁至孔底，再拔出钢套管。在花管防护下，自下而上高喷灌浆，采用双管法旋喷套接施工工艺。

高喷灌浆分两序，浆液水灰比1.37～1.5，压力0.6～0.8MPa。提升速度8～12cm/min，孔口不返浆时不得提升，返浆量小时速度2～5cm/min。孔口返浆量大时，压力不变，适当加快提升速度；孔口返浆量小或不返浆时，适当提高压力并减速或不提升。因拆卸喷管复喷长度不少于0.2m，喷嘴堵塞中断复喷长度不少于0.5m。停机超过3h对泵体输浆管路清洗后方可继续施工，复喷长度不少于0.5m。

2. 围堰填筑 填筑料用边坡及洞挖料，石渣料用弱风化～微风化或新鲜岩石，粒径小于80cm，级配良好。用20t自卸汽车运输，进占卸料，推土机铺平，摊铺厚90cm，20t振动碾碾压，静碾2遍，动碾8遍。土工膜墙保护料采用河床砂砾石，与相邻石渣同时碾压，碾压参数同石渣，靠近土工膜部位用小型振动夯夯实。

3. 土工膜施工 复合土工膜为两布一膜，为短纤针刺非织造HDPE复合土工膜，单幅宽4m，土工膜与土工布一次热压成型，接处留20cm光膜不热塑，即膜与布脱开。现场堆放期间需覆盖防护，清除铺设面上树根、杂草和尖石，确保平整并碾压密实。土工膜与保护料结合面吻合平整，不留空隙。土工膜与防渗墙相接位置设伸缩节，并预留伸缩量。接头在现场双面焊接，搭接长10cm，焊接程序：铺膜→缝底层布→焊膜翻面→缝上层布。

4. 土工膜锚固 土工膜与高喷墙间采取混凝土锚固连接。高喷墙施工完成后，沿墙顶开挖锚固槽，露出完整、平整的高喷墙体后，直接浇筑混凝土进行土工膜锚固。

（四）围堰拆除

围堰拆除分区：水上部分为Ⅰ区、内侧削薄部分（防渗轴线内侧）为Ⅱ区、水下部分（防渗轴线外侧）Ⅲ区，水下部分（防渗轴线区域）为Ⅳ区。出渣道路可通行后，由下游向上游开始拆除。先除围堰水上部分，厚度10m，分3层拆除。同时拆除Ⅱ区和Ⅲ区，厚5m，一次到底。Ⅱ区完成后，拆除Ⅳ区，厚6m，一次到底。最后拆除围堰上游端头部分。

（五）基坑抽排水设计与施工

基坑排水量包括围堰渗流、地基渗流及降雨汇水三部分。经计算围堰渗流为82m^3/h，地基渗流为1150m^3/h，降雨汇水20m^3/h，基坑经常性排水按1252m^3/h配置设备。

考虑抽排效率（85%）、较大渗水强排等因素，要适当加大抽排水量。在导流洞及泄洪放空洞出口围堰坡脚设泵坑，分散布置7台300m^3/h潜水排污泵，

泵坑尺寸 20m×5m，深 2m。用潜水泵从开挖最低处 2364m 高程泵坑中，抽至 2385m 集中泵坑，再用 3 台 790m³/h 离心清水泵排出围堰外侧。

（中国水利水电第三工程局有限公司　罗奋强）

白河水电站反向灌浆治理渗水技术

白河水电站工程的全年土石围堰和纵向混凝土围堰，将泄洪闸和厂房与汉江水分隔在基坑内外。基坑开挖中，厂房和泄洪闸结合段出现 F_{10}、F_9、F_8 三条断层。开挖至高程 166m 后，基坑渗水，随开挖深度下降渗水通道也下移，沿 F_8 和 F_9 方向分布，至 155m 出现集中渗水通道，渗流量高达 2400m³/h。基坑开挖后，在锚杆钻孔完成时，渗水从锚杆孔内流出，流量和压力均较大。在枯水期治理渗水，此时段河床水位 174m，渗水点最低 150m，且 150～166m 渗水点多达 40 处，水平和垂直向均有分布。

（一）渗水原因及治理方案

渗水坝段岩性为含石英结晶灰岩夹钙质千枚岩，岩体多呈碎片状，局部泥化、见光面，少见结晶灰岩碎块，泥质胶结欠密实。沿断层面铁质侵染，风化呈褐黄色。断层走向与岩层走向近于一致，微切层，属张性（正）断层。断层影响带岩体完整性相对较差。经多次试验，认为渗水为江水通过断层裂隙渗流淘刷，形成集中渗水通道。

在枯水期分两阶段采用有盖重封闭灌浆治理渗水。第一阶段为垂直面封堵，第二阶段为水平面封堵。

（二）渗水治理实施

2018 年枯水期河床水位较低，泄洪闸坝段混凝土浇筑至高程 165m 以上，混凝土浇筑完成 7 天进行反向灌浆。施工前，测量所有渗水预埋管涌水流量及压力，再对 1 号泄洪闸坝段渗水点进行憋水试验。试验完成后，进行 1 号泄洪闸坝段反灌。按“先低后高”、再“自下游向上游”顺序，选择 2、3 个大渗水引排管反灌，其余串通孔出浓浆后封孔，不再进行串通孔灌浆。2、3 号泄洪闸坝段的非串通孔按从右岸到左岸，再自下游向上游顺序进行。1～3 号泄洪闸坝段反向灌浆结束后，再施工 168.23m 平台剩余固结灌浆。

1. 渗水点引排　1～3 号泄洪闸坝段陡坡渗水点用风钻钻孔，孔深按实际情况确定，尽可能深入渗水点。钻孔完成后塌孔点预埋 ϕ300mm 回填灌浆钢管，一般渗水点预埋 ϕ90mm 或 ϕ25mm PE 管。预埋管周围及其他渗漏点用棉絮、棉纱、堵漏宝封堵密实。出水量较大 2 个渗水点分别预埋 ϕ165mm 和 ϕ108mm 钢管，再回填 C20 混凝土封闭。

预埋的 PE 管及钢管上安装变径接头、蝶阀。压水、灌浆过程采用灌浆塞或通过蝶阀变径直接与预埋管连接进行灌浆。

2. 抬动孔　1 号泄洪闸坝段的边墙和导墙分别布置 2 个和 1 个抬动孔。2、3 号坝段的抬动孔为已有固结灌浆抬动观测孔。抬动孔入岩 6m，抬动变形允许值不大于 200μm。

3. 憋水试验　灌浆前做憋水试验，试验在 1 号泄洪闸坝段陡坡渗水点高程较低、涌水流量最大的一根管实施，试验前将其他管路全部封闭，并测量该涌水孔的压力及流量。

憋水试验开始压水压力为 0.1MPa，逐级提升压力，每级压水试验按简易压水试验进行。压水升压过程中观察 5 个抬动孔，若压力达到一定数值后，未发生抬动破坏，且满足压水流量 15L/min 以上，最大流量不超过 30L/min，则该压水压力的 80%数值确定为该涌水孔最终灌浆压力。其他反向灌浆管根据涌水情况，且满足设计要求，适当调整灌浆压力。

4. 反向灌浆　1～2 号泄洪闸混凝土浇筑至高程 165m 后，对原预留回填灌浆钢管及 PE 管按程序逐管进行纯水泥浆液灌浆。首次反灌注入水泥总量控制在 250t，且确保一次性完成灌浆施工。首灌孔灌浆中，1～3 号泄洪闸坝段其余串通孔出浆后，不再进行串通孔灌浆。对串通孔用消防带绑扎，保留细小缝隙，起泌水保浆作用，避免引排管涌水流量过大稀释浆液。灌浆要求如下。

（1）反向灌浆水泥浆液采用 0.8：1、0.6：1、0.5：1（重量比）三个比级。泄洪闸坝段渗水点引排管涌水孔及串通孔，采用 0.6：1 或 0.5：1 浓浆直接灌注，2、3 号泄洪闸非串通孔采用单孔逐孔灌注，水灰比 0.8：1、0.5：1，开灌水灰比采用 0.8：1，可灌性较好时（流量 20～30L/min 以上），直接浓浆灌注。灌浆压力 0.2MPa，可根据情况适当调整。

（2）灌浆结束标准按最终吸浆量较小且能达到 0.2MPa 左右灌浆压力确定；若吸浆量仍较大，则总量控制需上调；若江水出现返浆现象，继续灌注 5～10min 可结束灌浆。

（3）灌浆中，发现地表及其他通道漏冒浆按常规灌浆处理；如发现其他引排管串浆，即用木楔直接从孔口钉牢，周围用适宜材料封闭处理，不能采用间歇灌浆或中断灌浆作业。

灌浆中，在未灌完规定的注入总量前已停止吸浆，可改在其他管路灌注。

首灌结束 48h 后打开引排管，若依然涌水，需再反向灌浆。反灌注入水泥量可视情况按大于 5t 加以控制，直至达到管口无漏水。

灌浆中，产生抬动时限流、降压，如无效果停止灌浆，按监理工程师要求处理。

(4) 灌注结束后，封闭管口 48h 后缓慢打开。无出水时割除灌浆管，封孔磨平管口。

（三）灌后效果评定

反向灌浆质量检查在保证所有引排管管头无漏水情况下，结合补充固结灌浆质量检查进行综合评定。按有关规范进行固结灌浆的质量检查和评定。经渗水引排、混凝土施工封闭及枯水期两个阶段的反向灌浆技术的实施，成功地解决了工程渗水治理的难题。

（中国水利水电第三工程局有限公司
苏飞标　曹六八）

牙扎水库帷幕灌浆第三方质量检测及评价

青海牙扎水库帷幕灌浆施工自检质量全部合格后，建设单位引入第三方检测帷幕的质量，并解决了问题，突显了第三方检测的重要性。

（一）工程概况

1. 设计概况　青海牙扎水库工程是一项集调蓄、水源涵养、灌溉为一体的拦蓄式综合性水利工程，坝高 57.3m，兴利库容 $200.2\times10^4m^3$，工程等级为四等小（Ⅰ），大坝坝型为壤土心墙砂壳坝。

大坝填筑前对坝基进行固结灌浆及帷幕灌浆做防渗处理。固结灌浆孔设双排，孔排距 3m，孔深 8m，灌浆压力 0.3MPa。帷幕灌浆采用双排灌浆孔，孔距 1.5m，排距 1m，设计帷幕透水率按 5Lu 以内控制，采用自上而下，孔口封闭灌浆法，按 2、3、5、5、5m 分段灌浆，对应灌浆压力为 0.3、0.5、0.7、1.0MPa。

2. 工程地质条件　坝基岩体左岸为白垩系砂岩、砂砾岩，右岸为加里东期安山岩。砂岩、砂砾岩属中硬岩，岩体内陡倾角裂隙中等发育，层厚 10～20cm。安山岩属中硬岩，微裂隙极发育，裂隙多闭合，岩体破碎，薄层状结构。砂砾岩与安山岩呈角度不整合接触，接触带风化较强烈，岩体质量差。

（二）第三方质量检测

1. 检测孔　第三方质量检测帷幕长度 285m。检测孔孔位由建设、监理根据灌浆情况确定，设在两排灌浆孔中间；数量为灌浆孔总数 1%～3%；深度比灌浆深度少 0.5m。

2. 检测设备　①XY-150 型立轴回转钻机、孔径 75mm 金刚石“双管单动”钻头，提高岩芯获得率；②灌浆自动记录仪，气压式止水栓塞封孔，提高压水试验质量；③孔内高清全景彩色数字成像系统，观察水泥灌浆充填情况；④孔内智能声波检测仪，检测声波在岩体内穿透情况。通过这些手段综合评价帷幕灌浆质量。

3. 检测试验段长和压力　压水试验检测试验段长与帷幕灌浆段长度一致，第一段 2m，第二段 3m，以下各段为 5m。水库坝高 57m，根据《水工建筑物水泥灌浆施工技术规范》（SL 62—2014），除特殊情况外，灌浆工程各部位进行试验压力为设计灌浆压力的 80%。

（三）检测结果分析与评价

1. 一期检测　坝基最初布置 10 个检测孔，钻孔 305m，压水试验 59 段。其中透水率大于 5Lu 试验段 14 段，占比达 23.7%，不合格段主要集中在前 1～3 段试验段。为进一步验证不合格范围边界，在不合格相对集中部位增加两个检测孔，每个检测孔深均为 16m，共做 10 段压水试验，检测结果表明＞5Lu 段依然集中在帷幕深度 15m 范围内。

据统计，一期检测孔岩芯获得率 60%～94%，*RQD* 值均低于 68%，其中 *RQD* 值低于 10% 占比达 80%。一期检测孔仅在 6 个孔里发现 9 处水泥结石，岩芯破碎，安山岩岩芯以碎块状、散体颗粒状为主。

通过孔内摄像及声波测试，透水率大于 5Lu 试验段岩体质量差、灌浆痕迹不明显。检测孔 ZK04 前三段（0.5～15.6m）压水试验透水率分别为 34.61、12.89、13.57Lu，ZK05 前两段（0.6～11m）压水试验透水率分别为 33.42、14.1Lu。孔内声波测试显示，在透水率较大试验段内均有波速较低点。根据波速统计，平均波速为 3500m/s，不合格段波速 1900～2900m/s。

ZK08 检测孔岩性为安山岩，1.2～8.5m 孔内摄像岩体破碎，灌浆痕迹不明显。其中第一段（1.2～6.5m）压水试验透水率 26.10Lu，获得率 68%，*RQD* 值均为 0；第二段（6.4～11.7m）压水试验透水率 13.38Lu，获得率 53%，*RQD* 值均为 0；以下各段透水率均＜5Lu，岩芯获得率有所提高，*RQD* 值依然较低，但孔内摄像显示岩体质量有变好趋势。孔口渗水较严重，通过简易测试，渗水量达 1L/min，渗水来源于帷幕破碎带。

选取有代表性检测孔 ZK04 及 ZK05，对各种检测手段数据分析得到如下特征：随钻孔深度增加，波速曲线逐渐升高并趋于稳定；岩芯获得率与 *RQD* 值逐渐升高，但安山岩受岩性影响，*RQD* 值均较低；压水试验透水率在表部 15m 范围值较大，不满足设计要求。

透水率线型与孔深呈负相关关系，声波、获得率及 *RQD* 值线型与孔深均呈正相关。

2. 二期检测　针对以上检测结果综合对比分析，帷幕灌浆质量问题集中在河床浅表部15m范围及岩性接触带部位。河床浅表部岩体风化强烈、裂隙发育，帷幕灌浆压力偏小等原因使孔间浆液扩散半径未形成有效搭接。灌浆处理后，虽各项指标与原勘探结果比有很大改善，但帷幕质量仍不能满足设计要求。经各方讨论决定对不合格段补强灌浆，在原设计两排灌浆孔中间增加一排灌浆孔。补强灌浆完成后，增加检测孔进行二期质量检测。

二期帷幕检测共布置9个检测孔，计160m，38段压水试验。试验结果显示：仅ZK16第二段（2.8～5.8m）、第三段（5.8～10.8m）压水试验透水率分别为41.48、5.39Lu，其余试验段透水率均小于5Lu。分析认为，ZK16位置为岩性不整合接触带，受风化影响岩体质量差，灌浆效果不佳。故再布置14个灌浆孔补强处理，随后布置检测孔，透水率均小于5Lu，孔内摄像揭示，补强灌浆后灌浆饱满度较一期检测明显增多。补强灌浆后，ZK08渗水现象消失。说明二期检测均满足设计要求，帷幕灌浆质量评价为合格。

（中国电建集团西北勘测设计研究院有限公司
王立志　马军　司富生　杨发军）

其　他

大古水电站工程截流施工

（一）围堰地质地形和水文气象条件

1. 上游围堰　大古水电站上游围堰左、右岸基岩裸露，河床冲洪积层厚4.5～38.9m，基岩为花岗闪长岩，清除覆盖层及不稳定块体后，可利用基岩作为堰基。上游围堰防渗墙左岸基岩裸露，右岸为江边滩地，河床冲洪积层厚4.4～38.9m，稍密～中密，中～强透水层，基岩面起伏大，大孤石含量较高、分布不均，表层透水率大于5Lu。

2. 下游围堰　左岸为覆盖层，右岸为基岩，河床冲洪积层厚15～27m，基岩为花岗闪长岩。左岸及河床覆盖层稍密～中密，满足围堰对岩基变形及强度要求，左岸河滩及河床覆盖层透水性强。堰基覆盖层大孤石含量高，基岩面起伏较大。基岩段表层透水率大于5Lu。

3. 水文气象条件　坝址控制集水面积157407km^2，多年平均流量1010m^3/s。洪水由暴雨形成，洪枯流量相差悬殊，6～10月为汛期，11月～次年5月为枯水期。上下游水文站年最大洪峰流量分别发生在7～9月和6～9月，最大洪峰流量分别为8870m^3/s和13100m^3/s。

（二）戗堤位置调整

原方案1、2号洞过流，戗堤按设计位置布置。戗堤轴线与围堰轴线平行，距上游围堰轴线上游42.5m处，轴线长121m，顶高程3376m。调整后把戗堤上移至1号导流洞下游侧，双洞导流，截流施工。戗堤轴线与围堰轴线平行，距上游围堰轴线上游140m处，轴线长93m，顶高程3376m。这有利于水力学参数的改善和防渗墙施工进度。

（三）施工期导流过程和截流特点

1. 导流过程　河床截流开始，至大坝浇筑高程超出上游围堰堰顶高程并具备临时挡水条件止，为初期导流。此阶段上、下游围堰挡水，导流隧洞泄流。2016年12月底至次年3月底，2条隧洞导流，设计标准12月至次年3月10年一遇洪水，流量601m^3/s，上游水位3375.51m；2017年4月至当年5月底，2条隧洞导流，设计标准4月至5月10年一遇洪水，流量907m^3/s，上游水位3377.31m，6月至大坝浇筑高程超出上游围堰堰顶高程期间，设计标准为全年20年一遇洪水，流量8840m^3/s，上游水位3416.79m。

大坝浇筑高程超出上游围堰堰顶高程并具备临时挡水条件开始，至导流隧洞下闸封堵止，为中后期导流。此阶段由坝体临时度汛断面挡水，导流隧洞结合泄洪冲沙底孔泄流，坝体临时度汛标准为全年50年一遇洪水，流量10300m^3/s，上游水位3422.97m。

2. 截流特点和难点　龙口最大平均流速4.86m/s；河床深厚砂卵石覆盖层，试验冲深3～4m，不利于截流戗堤稳定；小粒径抛投料难以稳定，存在安全隐患；抛投料运输困难；截流块石仅3000m^3，严重不足。

（四）截流方案设计

采取上游单戗单向立堵截流，龙口设在河床右侧。戗堤按梯形断面设计，顶宽35m，上下游坡比1∶1.4，端头坡比1∶1.2。龙口靠近右岸。左岸场地开阔，宜于车辆暂停和卸料，故左岸向右岸进占。

根据本工程河床覆盖层特性，暂不考虑河床护底及右岸裹头保护。

戗堤分预进占段（长61m）和龙口段（长60m）。龙口段分Ⅰ、Ⅱ、Ⅲ区。

（五）截流材料规划

龙口段采用石渣料、块石料、特大石和钢筋石笼，备料46507m^3；非龙口段备料11872m^3；另备应急需要1000m^3块石串。大块石、特大石料来自坝肩标坝址附近集渣平台，不足部分在坝区收集。中块石、石渣料、钢筋石笼来自2号渣场。

（六）截流施工

1. 施工强度　预进占段抛投7天，日平均抛投强度3376m^3，日最大抛投强度5064m^3，小时最大抛投强度253m^3（每天20h）。龙口段截流合龙用48h，平均抛投强度550m^3/h，最大抛投强度825m^3/h。堤头最大抛投强度1200m^3/h。4个卸料点满足戗堤抛投施工要求。

2. 设备配置　大石选2m^3液压反铲或16t汽车式起重机挖装，特大石、中块石及石渣料用2m^3液压反铲和1.6m^3液压挖掘机挖装，钢筋石笼、块石串用25t/16t汽车式起重机吊装。运输设备为25t自卸汽车。共用25t自卸车53辆，推土机3台、挖装设备7台、汽车式起重机5辆。

3. 预进占段施工　施工程序：测量放样→非龙口段预进占→戗堤裹头保护，预留龙口宽60m。该段抛投总量约26700m^3，历时7天，平均强度3814m^3/天。戗堤用25t自卸汽车抛填进占。堤头用大功率推土机推料。期间根据情况决定是否抛填钢筋石笼等特殊料物。

4. 龙口段施工　抛投总量约26413m^3，施工历时48h，平均强度约550m^3/h，高峰强度825m^3/h。全断面推进和凸出上游挑角进占，堤头直接、集中推运和卸料冲砸抛投。

龙口Ⅰ区从左岸单向进占，宽度60～40m，流速4.76～4.86m/s，泄流量404～283m^3/s。进占物料总量15568m^3。在宽度接近40m时，另需单独抛填1000m^3块石串。

龙口Ⅱ区从左岸单向进占，宽度40～20m，流速3.37～4.86m/s，泄流量283～53.8m^3/s。进占物料总量8570m^3。

龙口Ⅲ区从左岸进占，宽度由20m进占至合龙，流速3.37～0m/s，泄流量53.8～0m^3/s。进占物料总量约2275m^3。

（中国水利水电第七工程局有限公司
张伯夷　李东福　翁锐）

卡鲁玛水电站高落差大流量河道截流方案实施

（一）工程概况

卡鲁玛水电站位于基奥加尼罗河上，河道上设拦河闸坝，基本不抬高河道水位，然后将部分河水引入地下管道，利用地下厂房发电，电能经输电线路输出，水流经管道排回原河床。电站为全埋式引水发电，总装机容量60万kW，拦河闸坝为径流式，闸坝前正常蓄水位1030m。按中国行业标准该电站为二等大（2）型工程。拦河坝由非溢流坝、泄水闸、冲沙底孔等组成，长314.43m。坝顶高程1032m，顶宽6m，最大坝高14m。

工程区域大部分是热带气候，从3～5月、9～11月为雨季，平均年降雨量900～2000mm。由坝址上游8.3km处水文站资料分析得多年平均流量为995m^3/s，

坝区河谷开阔，断面呈U形。坝顶高程处河谷宽270m。河床高程1021～1023m。大坝左岸分布大片基岩孤岛，右岸为河流冲刷形成的跌坎。坝轴线附近河水流速较大，河床覆盖层厚度0.5～2m，其下伏为弱风化花岗片麻岩。

（二）闸坝和进水口施工导流方式

闸坝处河水常年流量大，水流湍急，同时两岸基岩埋置较深和河床宽度有限，不宜采用隧洞或分期导流方式。根据闸坝和进水口布置方式，只能选择在右岸开挖明渠导流，同时考虑到工程进度要求和河流的水流特征，选择围堰全年挡水施工。

（三）原设计截流方案

1. 导流明渠设计　导流明渠底宽40m，进口底板高程1021m，出口底板1019m，长404.11m，纵坡0.5%。明渠进口布置喇叭口，其控制段长142.6m，前沿控制高程为1025m，后为1021m。

2. 截流时段和标准　计划6月中旬截流，截流流量为5年一遇月平均流量1480m^3/s。根据确定的截流标准，可计算出围堰前上游水位为1028.886m。

3. 围堰和龙口布置　截流选择在上游围堰上进行。上游围堰为土石围堰，挡水标准为全年25年一遇洪水，洪峰流量2500m^3/s，堰顶高程1032.50m，顶宽10m。龙口靠右岸布置，预留龙口宽度60m。根据截流标准，戗堤顶部高程为1029.0m；为保证3辆20t自卸汽车同时抛投，截流戗堤顶宽为15m。

4. 截流难度分析　龙口靠近下游深槽，对截流材料稳定不利。此外，从龙口水力学参数看，最大落差大于7.56m，高于三峡明渠4.11m和溪洛渡

4.49m；龙口单宽功率最大达114t/s，大于三峡明渠上戗83.61t/s，小于溪洛渡292.34t.m/s.m。根据龙口单宽功率判断，原设计截流方案需高度重视，精心准备截流才能成功。

（四）截流方案改进

原设计截流方案落差大，单宽功率大，截流难度相当大。且在国外很难专门为截流施工调动大量设备，因故对原截流方案进行了改进。改进措施如下。

1. 截流标准改进　改进的截流标准为截流时段月平均流量，即6月份月平均流量1010m^3/s，相应截流时上游围堰前最高水位1027.28m，截流合龙时最高水位降低1.6m。

2. 围堰和龙口布置　截流时龙口下游水位与下游河床高程和龙口泄水量有关。在不改原围堰断面设计的前提下，将龙口布置在1025高程线与左岸间，可利用中间小岛作为截流戗堤的裹头，还可以抬高约2m龙口下游河床高程，进一步降低落差。

3. 修正后的龙口水力学参数　根据明渠过流能力，考虑河床水位变化，计算得截流最大落差为3.28m，龙口最大单宽功率为20.26t/s，最大平均流速为2.35m/s。

4. 修正截流方案分析　龙口远离明渠进口，水流进入明渠可能产生附加落差。截流最大落差已经降至3.28m，虽仍大于3m，但已远低于三峡明渠和溪洛渡截流落差。龙口最大单宽功率已经降至20.26t/s，远低于三峡明渠和溪洛渡数值。龙口单宽功率不大，修改后截流作业较简单，但地质条件和流量的不确定性，仍需精心准备才能使截流顺利进行。

（五）方案实施与偏差分析

2015年6月10日截流准备就绪，开始截流，并对水力参数进行观测和记录。下午2点开始，晚8点遇暴雨停工3h，次日凌晨3点顺利合龙，净耗时10h。截流施工中没有投入大型推土机和重型自卸汽车，只有1台D80推土机和30辆20t公路型自卸汽车。

1个单宽功率达100t/s的截流，没有投入大量设备，也没有抛入较大石笼，且在推进的关键时期遇强降雨，只用10h就顺利完成截流，这归功于修改后的截流方案。但实际截流与设计方案的水力参数有较大差异。经过分析，造成差异的主要原因是：

（1）设计时没有注意裹头岛1025m高程线向左岸突出部分是礁石，当龙口推进至礁石部位时，龙口泄流受阻，下游水位被壅高，龙口的净落差减少。

（2）水流进入明渠前在上游河道1025m平台形成水跃，实测上游水位1028.86m与设计1027.28m相差1.6m，主要消耗在水跃和明渠进口跌水上，明渠过流能力计算有误差。

截流施工时，对未受截流壅水影响的河道水位进行连续观测，发现原河道水位没有变化，维持在月平均流量水平。因此，选择月平均流量作为截流标准是可行的。

（中国水利水电第八工程局有限公司
彭运河　徐盛剑　刘豫）

桓仁水库进水口围堰水下拆除爆破技术

桓仁水库进水口围堰轴线位置沟底宽约70m，沟底地面高程255～282m，枯水期轴线位置水深约28m，水底基本无松散堆积物，基岩裸露。围堰设计长81.70m，堰顶填筑宽度13～15m，由钻爆法洞挖石渣料填筑而成。根据水库地形条件和水工建筑物布置特点，施工防洪度汛标准为50年一遇，相应设计库水位为307.11m。

（一）围堰拆除内容

围堰拆除的一期工程为围堰水下部分防渗体爆破及渣土清除，二期工程为围堰水下岩坎爆破开挖及渣土清除。在围堰交通洞出口靠山体一侧修建临时道路和码头、系缆地锚等设施，供交通船系泊停靠，人员、火工器材等物资进出水上作业平台。

（二）围堰水下拆除爆破参数

1. 水下防渗体拆除爆破参数　主爆区基岩爆破孔为竖直孔，垂直钻孔，矩形布置。孔距2.8m，抵抗线1m，排距1.8m。依据炮孔所在位置至开挖底部高度确定钻孔深度，另需钻孔超深1.5m。

根据经验，爆破孔为竖直孔时，堵塞2m。水下松动爆破，炸药单耗1.12kg/m^3。装药前核对每个炮孔装药量，且根据震动监测数据、爆破试验调整。计算单孔最大装药量58kg，孔内分段装药，每段药量20、15、15、8kg。

经爆破震动验算，最近的新建闸室水工构筑物，抗震速度5cm/s，距离40m，质点振动速度1.18m/s，能够满足安全防震要求。

2. 水下岩坎拆除爆破参数　主爆区基岩爆破孔为竖直孔，钻孔孔径120mm，装ϕ90mm乳化炸药。

经计算水下爆破参数为：单耗1.48kg/m^3，炮孔深度11.5m（其中超钻2m），延米装药量7.63kg/m，水下堵塞段长度1m。

炮孔采用不连续装药，进行安全校核，结合试爆监测数据进行推算，爆破振动速度超过控制标准时，爆破时应采用孔内微差方法。

单孔最大装药量71kg，不连续装药，分为4段，自下至上分别为20、20、16、15kg。施工中根据试爆效果、爆破震动监测数据和基岩面实际高度，及时调整各参数。爆破实施过程中每排孔均需进行安全药量计算，确保建筑物安全。

据各部位最大允许起爆药量要求，在距离建筑物较近时采用孔间、孔内微差方式进行，即以毫秒级时差顺序起爆各个药包，把爆破总能量分割为多数较小的能量，将最大药包产生的地震波变成一长串小幅值的地震波，从而降低地震破坏效应，把爆破振动控制在允许值以下。该工程孔内微差间隔为100ms，孔外延时间隔为42ms。

（三）围堰水下爆破拆除安全

1. 爆破飞石　该工程为水下爆破，水深大于5m，出现飞石的可能性较小。从安全角度考虑，陆上警戒距离设为200m。

2. 水中冲击波的安全距离控制　在水深不大于30m水域内水下爆破，水下采用钻孔装药时，水中冲击波的最小安全允许距离可根据一次爆破药量大小确定。本工程单次爆破最大药量控制1000kg以内，航道中无其他水下人员作业，仅考虑船舶的安全。水上安全警戒距离按一次爆破药量大于1000kg时确定，即最小安全允许距离500m可保证施工安全。

3. 爆破震动控制　本工程进水口启闭机室距爆源距离最小，且允许振速较小，因此在爆破过程中，单响起爆最大炸药量以不超过78kg。考虑到最多3孔同时点火，孔内分段的单段最大药量不能大于25kg。

4. 微差爆破控制　微差爆破就是通过毫秒级时差顺序完成起爆操作，其效果是将大量药包产生的地震波转变为一串小幅地震波，各药包产生的地震波相互干涉而降低地震效应，将爆破振动控制在允许值范围之内。

5. 爆破安全防护　防渗体、岩坎爆破开挖时采取的安全防护措施如下。

爆破时控制好爆破方向，当被爆体水深小于5m爆破时，水面以上混凝土结构需覆盖木板或竹夹板加以防护，防止飞石砸坏混凝土表面。

爆破前，在进水口每孔闸门前，设三组气泡帷幕发生器，每一组间距0.5m，每组气泡帷幕主要通过一根气泡帷幕发射管组合而成。而两组气泡帷幕发射管主要通过两端实现进气，另外一组则通过中间进气，确保气泡数量处于均匀的状态。水下爆破进行起爆操作前5min，打开所有空压机，将空气直接注入发射管，利用发射管的小孔组成相对密集的气泡群。气泡质量较轻，密集气泡会逐步有发射管上升扩大，组成三道气泡帷幕。

（中国水利水电第三工程局有限公司
王立成　刘文贤）

孤山航电枢纽工程一期全年围堰主河床截流技术

（一）概况

孤山航电枢纽主要任务是发电、航运。水库正常蓄水位177.23m，正常蓄水位以下库容1.09亿m^3，水库总库容2.12亿m^3，电站装机容量18万kW（4×4.5万kW），多年平均发电量5.90亿kW·h，规划航道等级为Ⅳ级。

根据1951～2013年系列统计，孤山坝址天然多年平均径流量为247亿m^3，平均流量783m^3/s，年径流量409mm。孤山坝址11～4月的径流量50.2亿m^3，占年水量的20.3%。考虑本流域洪水季节特点及施工组织需要，主河床截流施工期确定为11月1日～5月20日。

（二）截流方式

采用单戗双向立堵法截流，以左岸进占为主，右岸为辅，左、右岸向中间单戗双向进占截流。预进占时戗堤上、下游高程167m，合龙时流量为11月坝址枯水期流量1000m^3/s。

截流戗堤为上游围堰堰体组成部分，戗堤轴线布置在上游围堰轴线下游侧27.2m处。戗堤顶长346m，堤顶高程167m，戗堤顶宽15m，梯形断面，迎水和背水面坡比为1：1.5。截流龙口布置在右侧主河道上，经水力学计算，预留龙口宽度80m时，流速1.08m/s，其中龙口30～50m为龙口合龙困难区，最大流速1.98m/s，发生在龙口顶口宽30m时。

（三）截流水力学计算

1. 截流合龙水力学计算　预进占完成以后，龙口宽度为80m时，为保证水流壅高不大，需校核龙口泄水能力是否满足设计泄洪要求。在截流流量为1000m^3/s，对应戗堤前最高水位165.23m，龙口底部高程156.4m条件下，立堵截流预留龙口泄水能力按龙口梯形或三角形断面的宽顶堰计算其泄水能力。

2. 龙门抛石稳定分析　根据计算水力学参数分析，龙口宽度逐渐减小时，龙口流速由1.08m/s逐渐增至1.98m/s，在30～50m合龙时，其流速及单宽功率较大，抛填最困难。

3. 抛石冲距计算　截流料是在动水条件下抛填，在抛填中块石在河底稳定后距抛投点的距离与水流参数和河床粗糙度有关。根据经验公式，可计算不同龙口宽度抛投石料抛石冲距。

（四）龙口分区和抛投料

根据截流时流速变化对抛填料粒径大小的要求，将龙口分Ⅰ、Ⅱ、Ⅲ区进行抛填施工。

龙口从80m缩减至50m范围为Ⅰ区，抛填粒径为60cm以下混合料，并抛投少量块石，备料考虑30%的流失量。

龙口由50m缩减至20m范围为Ⅱ区，随着不断向龙口进占，龙口流速由1.08m/s增大至截流最大流速1.98m/s。此阶段截流最困难，抛投料流失较严重，除了抛投20～40cm石渣外，还抛投40～60cm块石及部分块石钢筋笼。备料考虑35%的流失量。

Ⅲ区为龙口宽度20m进占至合龙，进占长度20m，龙口流速由0.82m/s逐渐减小至0m/s，龙口形状为三角形。此时龙口流量已经很小，截流进入合拢阶段，抛投粒径20～40cm石渣及少量块石，并将戗堤顶高程填筑到167m高程。备料考虑30%的流失量。

（五）截流施工

1. 截流程序　主要程序为：左右岸施工道路及江心道路填筑→上游围堰预进占→左右岸戗堤预进占至龙口部位→裹头防护→在平台上堆放块石、钢筋笼等→备料→左侧河道疏浚及江心道路挖除→龙口Ⅰ、Ⅱ、Ⅲ区抛填→龙口合龙→下游围堰截流。

2. 截流戗堤施工　戗堤填筑分三个阶段：①纵向临时围堰填筑及左侧河道疏浚分流；②上游围堰左、右岸戗堤段预进占，直至设计龙口位置，再裹头防护；③龙口合龙区施工。

截流石渣料、块石料临时堆放在围堰附近空地，钢筋笼运至上游围堰堆料平台上。

左岸向右岸进占龙口端头形成堆料平台，并在左岸戗堤进占至龙口部位时用钢筋笼对龙口裹头防护。同时右岸戗堤进占，在端头形成堆料平台，并用钢筋笼对龙口裹头防护。

截流龙口段采用全断面推进施工，用大石料、钢筋石笼等抛在堤头上游角迎水侧抗冲稳角，石渣料、中大石料、特大石料和钢筋石笼齐头并进，全断面进占。在满足抛投强度、堤头稳定情况下，尽量采用自卸汽车直接抛填。在容易坍塌抛填区段采用堤头赶料抛投。当戗堤龙口合龙，流速过大导致合龙进展缓慢时，将大块石用自卸车抛投至龙口，加强龙口稳定，促使戗堤顺利合龙。

3. 施工强度与机械设备配置　截流设计标准流量$1000m^3/s$情况下，龙口段预计抛投总量约3.7万m^3，龙口合龙时间为72h，平均抛投强度$513m^3/h$，最大抛投能力$668m^3/h$。

根据进占强度$1636m^3/h$配置挖装运设备，主要选用液压反铲（斗容1.2～$1.6m^3$）9台，推土机2台，装载机3台，以及20t自卸汽车38辆，可满足进占强度要求。

（中国水利水电第三工程局有限公司　王秀红）

向家坝右岸坝后电站下游围堰爆破拆除设计

（一）工程概况

向家坝右岸坝后电站下游横向围堰设在电站尾水渠末端，其左右端分别与消力池右导墙末端和排沙洞泄槽相接，轴线长131.675m。围堰为碾压混凝土（C15）重力式结构。堰顶高程282.2～291.5m，堰顶宽12m，下游迎水面铅直，上游侧高程278.6m以上铅直，以下为坡度1∶0.75的台阶状边坡，最大堰高31.5m。

围堰爆破拆除长度101m，总拆除工程量3.7万m^3。拆除范围：围堰（下横0+000m）～(坝右0+277.350m）拆除至283.2m高程；（坝右0+277.350m)～(下横0+126.0m）拆除至260m高程；围堰（下横0+126.0m）～（下横0+131.675m）拆除至267m高程。围堰拆除时尾水渠内未完项目多。

（二）工程特点和难点

1. 拆除环境复杂　围堰左右端分别与消力池右导墙和排沙洞泄槽相接。围堰上游100m是电站尾水平台及挡水闸门、平台顶部尾水门机、电站厂房；右岸方向有8号公路；与左端头出厂线垂直距离仅40m。尾水渠底板等工程尚未完成。拆除前围堰Ⅴ区仍将继续挡水。

2. 钻孔要求高　钻孔总量约2.3万m，其中预裂孔钻孔精度要求很高。

3. 安全防护难度大　围堰紧邻电站建筑物，拆除爆破振动必须控制在允许范围内。爆破前需对尾水渠底板新浇筑混凝土等多个建筑物和设备加以防护，且爆破不产生飞石。

4. 爆破网络复杂　爆破拆除需一次成功，爆后粒径要满足挖装要求；必须严控单响起爆药量；主爆孔必须逐孔起爆。爆破网路连接极复杂，雷管多，地表网路联结工作量大。

（三）爆破设计

1. 爆破方案　采用分区拆除，钻孔爆破方案。分区之间垂直面布置预裂孔，在围堰底部高程260m处布置一排水平预裂孔。Ⅰ～Ⅳ区为水上爆破，Ⅴ区为水下爆破。各区根据尾水一线施工进度及汛期需求爆破拆除。

2. 网孔参数

（1）孔排距：孔深小于5m炮孔用手风钻造孔，孔径42mm，其他孔采用快速钻造孔，孔径76mm。手风钻孔孔距0.8m，排距0.65m；快速钻孔孔距1.5m，排距1.2～1.3m；预裂孔孔距0.75m；缓冲孔孔距 0.65～1.5m。主爆孔采用菱形布置。

（2）孔深：爆破孔根据孔口高程与分区高程计算孔深，水平预裂孔孔深按结构轮廓线控制，垂直预裂孔孔深按孔底或边界轮廓线控制，水平预裂孔与垂直预裂孔孔底错位布置。孔深控制在允许误差范围内。

（3）堵塞：炮孔堵塞长度 0.45～1.99m，根据炮孔深度和直径、装药结构确定。

3. 装药量　考虑拆除结构为碾压混凝土，根据炮孔装药结构，预裂孔线装药密度取 0.3～0.4kg/m；主爆孔炸药单耗取值范围 0.50～0.60kg/m^3；缓冲孔炸药单耗取主爆孔炸药单耗 70%左右，约 0.3～0.4kg/m^3。

4. 装药结构　主爆孔装药采用 ϕ32mm 和 ϕ50mm 药卷，间隔 0.3～0.6m 装药，双股导爆索连接，双发 600ms 雷管起爆；缓冲孔装药采用 ϕ32mm 药卷，间隔 0.15～0.2m 装药，双股导爆索连接，深孔在底部和中部各安装 1 发 600ms 雷管；预裂孔装药采用 ϕ32mm 药卷，底部连续装药，装药量 0.4～2kg，中间正常装药段间隔 0.5m 装药，上部减弱装药段间隔 0.6m 装药。

5. 爆破危害控制　根据向家坝二期纵向围堰拆除爆破经验，爆破最大单响药量小于 31kg。爆破振动控制标准。在厂房、右导墙等处布置爆破安全振速测点。对Ⅴ区水下爆破，根据经验公式计算得水中冲击波为 0.11MPa，小于闸门允许水中冲击波 0.6MPa。对爆破飞石，经计算飞散距离 76～91.2m，覆盖防护后，飞石距离可控制在 50m 范围内，以拆除建筑物为中心设置 300m 警戒范围。

6. 爆破网络　围堰拆除爆破需严控爆破单段药量、段间时差，不允许出重段、跳段。爆破网路用非电导爆管网路，用高精度毫秒延期雷管，采用孔间、排间微差起爆法。采用双干线网路，排间设多点搭接，地表低段接力传爆，孔内高段延时起爆。孔内药包爆炸前，网路地表雷管已大部分传爆完毕。爆区从中部起爆，自起爆点向左右两侧传爆，将爆区分为左右两个片区，自临空面向后分排顺序起爆。传爆导爆管采用双发传爆，孔内双发起爆。

7. 安全防护　堰体爆区为主动防护。左端 500kV 高压线下用保温被、砂袋、钢丝网、胶皮带、水袋多重覆盖防护。其余部位建筑物为被动防护，用挂保温被、挡渣栏等保护。

（四）爆破效果

Ⅱ区拆除量小，距左岸 500kV 输电线距离近，用液压破碎锤拆除。Ⅰ、Ⅲ、Ⅳ、Ⅴ区分 4 次拆除，使用炸药 21.3t，高精度雷管 7938 发，导爆索 54000m，最大单段药量 28kg。

Ⅰ、Ⅲ区爆破飞石全部落在基坑内，控制在 50m 内，爆破块径约 20cm。围堰顶部无向上飞石，水袋降尘明显。Ⅳ、Ⅴ区由下游中部起爆，向左右两端分排起爆，碎块落入江中。

爆破质点振动监测 36 点次未超标，合格率 100%。振动最大值在Ⅰ区爆破时距爆源 15m，排沙槽下游端头顶部 1 号测试仪的垂直向，测值 8.741cm/s，主振频率不大于 63.477Hz。保护范围未发现爆破造成损坏。

（中国葛洲坝集团三峡建设工程有限公司　陈靖敏）

灰岩人工砂石粉含量对泵送混凝土性能的影响

乌东德水电站建设中进行了灰岩人工砂石粉含量对泵送混凝土拌和物与硬化物性能影响的试验，通过试验建议灰岩人工砂石粉含量控制范围为 12%～16%。

（一）混凝土原材料

1. 试验用人工砂　石粉含量对泵送混凝土性能影响的试验用砂为人工砂，8 种人工砂的石粉含量为 7.1%、9.6%、11.2%、13.3%、15.1%、18.8%、20.6%、23.8%。经检验得到各种石粉含量人工砂的细度模数、表观密度和堆积密度。

2. 其他原材料　包括华新 42.5 中热硅酸盐水泥、曲靖 F 类Ⅰ级粉煤灰、苏博特 PCA-Ⅰ缓凝型聚羧酸高性能减水剂、苏博特 GYQ 引气剂、灰岩人工碎石、水。这些原材料品质检验的结果均符合相应规范的技术要求。

（二）泵送混凝土配合比

泵送混凝土为二级配，其中石∶小石级配比为 40∶60。经试拌并做最优砂率及用水量试验，确定配合比中石粉含量 15.1%，水胶比 0.45，掺 20%粉煤灰、0.7%PCA-1 减水剂、0.5/万 GYQ 引气剂，设计坍落度 160～180mm，含气量 4%～5%的基准混凝土，最优砂率为 42%。基准泵送混凝土每方材料用量为：水 139kg，水泥 247kg，粉煤灰 62kg，砂 834kg，小石 693kg，中石 462kg，PCA-12.162kg，GYQ0.015kg。

其他石粉含量泵送混凝土配合比的水胶比、砂率、粉煤灰掺量、减水剂掺量与基准混凝土配合比相同，坍落度按 160～180mm、含气量按 4%～5%控制，由试拌确定。

（三）石粉含量对泵送混凝土拌和物性能的影响

1. 对坍落度的影响　泵送混凝土拌和物机口坍落度、含气量基本保持相同，混凝土水胶比、砂率、减水剂掺量不变，人工砂石粉含量范围7%～24%，试验结果分析如下。

（1）泵送混凝土用水量与石粉含量呈近似线性关系，正相关。用水量随石粉含量增减而增减，石粉含量每增大2～3个百分点，用水量增加2～3kg/m³。说明用水量不变情况下，坍落度随石粉含量增大而减小，石粉含量越大，混凝土拌和物坍落度越小。

（2）各种石粉含量泵送混凝土拌和物坍落度均随时间损失。拌和物搁置30min，坍落度损失率均小于10%，基本不受石粉含量影响。搁置60min，坍落度损失率与石粉含量呈近似二次多项关系，正相关，损失率随石粉含量增减而增减，含量小于17%，损失率小于15%，含量影响较小，含量大于17%，随含量增加，坍落度损失率有所加大，含量影响相对较大。搁置90min，坍落度损失率与石粉含量呈近似三次多项关系，含量11%～15%，损失率较小（小于45%），含量大于17%，随含量增加，损失率以较快速度加大，对坍落度影响亦较快加大。

（3）各种石粉含量的泵送混凝土拌和物扩散度均随时间损失，搁置时间，石粉含量对混凝土扩散度损失的影响不明显。

（4）石粉含量小于11%，混凝土拌和物性能较差，黏聚性不好，且泌水、骨料分离。

2. 对含气量的影响　泵送混凝土拌和物机口坍落度基本保持相同，混凝土水胶比、砂率、减水剂掺量不变，如维持混凝土含气量基本相同，人工砂石粉含量在7%～24%范围，引气剂掺量与石粉含量呈近似指数关系，正相关。引气剂掺量随石粉含量增减而增减，石粉含量小于17%，其含量每增大2个百分点，引气剂掺量增加0.05个万分点；石粉含量大于17%，其含量每增大1个百分点，引气剂掺量增加0.05个万分点。也就是说，在引气剂掺量不变时，泵送混凝土含气量随石粉含量增加而减少，石粉含量小于17%，对含气量的影响相对较小，石粉含量大于17%，对含气量的影响则相对较大。

（四）石粉含量对泵送混凝土硬化物性能的影响

1. 对强度及力学变形性能的影响　泵送混凝土拌和物机口坍落度、含气量基本保持相同，混凝土水胶比、砂率、减水剂掺量不变，人工砂石粉含量7%～24%，试验结果表明：

（1）各龄期混凝土抗压强度与石粉含量呈二次多项关系。石粉含量18%时，混凝土抗压强度最高，含量大于或小于18%，混凝土抗压强度随石粉含量增减均呈降低趋势。

（2）各龄期混凝土抗压强度与胶材总量亦呈二次多项关系。石粉含量15%时，胶材强度发挥最佳，含量小于15%，混凝土抗压强度随胶材总量增加而上升，含量大于15%，虽胶材总量增加，但混凝土抗压强度则下降，含量越高，石粉对胶材强度的抑制作用越大。

（3）石粉含量10%以上，含量对混凝土劈裂抗拉强度、极限拉伸值、轴拉强度无明显影响。

2. 对干缩性能的影响　试验结果表明，在泵送混凝土拌和物坍落度、含气量基本保持相同条件下，石粉含量11.2%～18.8%时，混凝土各龄期干缩值相近，石粉含量对混凝土干缩影响不明显。含量小于11.2%或大于18.8%，泵送混凝土各龄期干缩呈增大趋势。

3. 对耐久性能的影响　试验结果表明，在混凝土含气量基本保持相同条件下，石粉含量11.2%～23.8%，对泵送混凝土的抗冻性能、抗渗性能无明显影响。

（中国水利水电第三工程局有限公司　余跃雄）

可视化附着式振捣器控制系统研发与应用

中电建成都混凝土制品有限公司新津管片厂，自主研发了一种可视化附着式振捣器控制系统，实现了振捣频率、时间、振幅和气动压力的远程监测和程序化控制。

（一）控制系统原理

可视化附着式振捣器控制系统通过调节气压调节阀精确控制气动压力，通过调节电磁阀开度大小精确控制振捣频率，通过PLC中央处理单元精确控制振捣时间。控制系统上位机采用工业组态软件进行画面组态，通过PROFINET通讯协议与PLC中央处理单元连接，从而在上位机上实现振捣频率、时间、振幅和气动压力等参数的远程监测和程序化控制。

（二）控制系统动作流程

附着式振捣器控制系统启动后，上位机将预设的气动压力、振捣时间、振捣频率等参数，通过通讯模块传输至PLC中央处理单元，PLC通过输出模块D/A转换驱动气压调节和电磁阀动作，附着式振捣器开始工作，并按振捣程序预设优先进入弱振阶段。弱振结束后进入强振阶段。振捣过程中，压力、频率和位移传感器将检测到的气动压力、振捣频率、振幅等，通过输入模块A/D转换传输至PLC，PLC将各实时监测参数通过通讯模块传输至上位机显示，并将各参数预设值和实际值进行比较运算。若气动压力实测值与预设值有偏差，则通过气压调节阀调整气动压力；若振捣频率实测值与预设值有偏差，则调节电磁阀开度大小调整通气量，从而控制振捣频率。当弱振时间计时达到预设值，则进入强振阶段，当强振时间计时达到预设值强振结束，整个控制系统工作完成。系统动作流程如下：

步骤1：系统通电后，配电柜开始为PLC中央处理单元等系统各部件供电。切换按钮“自动/手动”，若为“自动”状态，则系统进入自动模式，反之进入手动操作模式。

步骤2：系统进入自动模式后，上位机设置气动压力、振捣频率、振捣时间等参数预设值，并将参数传输至PLC。

步骤3：点击“启动”按钮，系统进入运行模式。

步骤4：空压机先启动运行，产生的气体经压力罐压缩后通过管路进入气压调节阀，再进入分气缸，并分入各支路，经管路传至电磁阀，进入附着式振捣器，驱动振捣器振捣。

步骤5：系统进入弱振阶段，“弱振指示灯”亮，弱振开始计时。弱振时间达到预设值，弱振结束，“弱振指示灯”熄灭。系统依次进入强振阶段，“强振指示灯”亮，强振开始计时。强振时间达到预设值，强振结束，“强振指示灯”熄灭，“振捣完成指示灯”亮。

步骤6：振捣中，位移传感器、频率传感器、压力传感器将实时检测的数据经输入模块传输至PLC。上位机通过Profinet通信协议与PLC连接，实时监控振捣频率、振幅、气动压力、振捣时间等参数，以实现人机间的数据交互。

步骤7：振捣中，频率传感器将实时检测的振捣频率经输入模块传输至PLC，PLC对检测频率进行处理。若频率检测值等于预设值，则保持电磁阀开度大小稳定不变；若频率检测值大于预设值，则调小电磁阀开度，以降低振捣频率；若频率检测值小于预设值，则调大电磁阀开度，以提高振捣频率。

步骤8：振捣中，压力传感器将实测气动压力经输入模块传输至PLC，PLC对检测的气动压力进行处理。若气动压力检测值等于预设值，则保持气压调节阀开度大小稳定不变；若实际压力检测值大于预设值，则调小气压调节阀开度，以降低气动压力；若实际压力检测值小于预设值，则调大气压调节阀开度，以提高气动压力。

步骤9：振捣中，若点击“停止”按钮，则系统停止振捣。振捣时若遇到紧急情况，点击“紧急停止”按钮，控制系统立即停止运转，振捣瞬间停止，以确保人员设备安全。

步骤10：振捣过程自动结束。

（三）工程实例

中电建成都混凝土制品有限公司新津管片厂设有两条生产线，2＋5管片生产线及其控制系统由厂家设计完成，另一条2＋4管片生产线机械部分由厂家提供，生产线电气及控制系统由新津管片厂自主研发，并将可视化附着式振捣器控制系统嵌入其中。运行实践证明，厂家设计的2＋5管片生产线2条作业线同时施工生产节拍为6min，自主设计的2＋4管片生产线采用弹性可调节可视化智能控制系统，优化了生产流程、振捣与养护参数，在2条作业线同时投入使用、交替作业时，生产节拍可控制在5min，较厂家生产线节拍少1min，月产能多生产管片约134环管片，在每月满负荷生产情况下，理论上年度可多生产管片1608环，生产效率提高16.6%。按3万元/单环计算，每年可产生经济效益约4824万元。

（中国水利水电第七工程局有限公司　王鹏）

杨房沟水电站地下长距离曲线带式输送机关键技术设计与应用

杨房沟水电站在四川省凉山彝族自治州木里县境内，工程地形条件复杂，料场与砂石加工系统距离较远，砂石系统加工所需半成品料和生产的成品料均采用带式输送机运输。

（一）线路选择及布置

杨房沟工程长距离带式输送系统布置时，利用现场地形特点，多次优化方案。半成品输送由3条输送机组成，总长3.95km。A1胶带机设在料场竖井底部粗碎车间卸料端，为短距离胶带机，能满足卸料段出现故障时紧急停机，减小对长距离胶带机运行的影响，同时调整角度，增大A2长距离胶带机曲率半径。A2胶带机采用空间曲线布置，全线在隧洞内，在杨房沟附近设曲线转弯，转弯半径5500m。为避让杨房沟、滴水崖沟对输送线路的影响，在满足隧洞排水坡度要求前提下，全程小角度上运或下运。隧洞断面选型兼顾土建施工费用和胶带机后期运行维护需求，采取经济合理断面。A2隧洞有两种断面：Ⅰ型4.5m(宽)×4m(高)，长2.56km，布置半成品料输送机；Ⅱ型6.5m(宽)×4m(高)，长1.2km，平行布置半成品料A2输送机和成品料输送机。

为适应地形、避免供料线对卡杨专用公路的影响和避让周边建筑，半成品输送线采用全隧洞布置。布设时尽量远离沿江边山坡，选择隧洞围岩相对均匀、稳定处，减少隧洞支护工程量，确保施工进度；为方便管理，节省费用，成品料与半成品输送线共用隧洞；利用半成品、成品输送线转料环节局部扩挖集中布置电控驱动站；半成品输送线空间曲线胶带机布置，满足了空间转角和系统排水要求，优化了半成品输送线运行工况。

（二）驱动方式选择

设计时，对长度在 3km 以内输送机，一般采用头部集中驱动；长度 5km 以上，采用头尾驱动；单机长度超过 10km，一般考虑中间转载驱动。

杨房沟工程长距离带式输送系统采用变频软启动，其运行效果满足大型带式输送机软启动及调速性能要求。变频驱动优点是：变频器加、减速曲线可在宽广范围内设定，能满足控制带式输送机加速度和减速度要求，变频调速系统机械特性基本与电动机的固有特性相同，使用开环系统控制输送机的驱动可满足技术要求。变频调速的精度高，易实现启、制动速度曲线的自动跟踪，能提供可控、理想的启、制动性能，适于长距离、线路复杂的带式输送机，可控制输送机按设定的“S”曲线启动和制动，以满足整机动态稳定性及可靠性要求。当用多台变频调速电动机驱动一台带式输送机时，通过变频器调整各电动机特性使之尽量接近，减小各电动机间负载功率差异；能实现软启动，电机起动对电网冲击小，能减少供配电系统设备的投入。

变频驱动方案总体减少了驱动装置的尺寸和重量，节约场地空间，软起、制动的加减速度可控制在 $\alpha \leqslant 0.05 m/s^2$，将电机起动电流和输送带起动张力控制在允许范围内，保证系统平稳启动、停机和运行。可实时根据运量情况调节带速，节能运行，解决工程对系统运行要求存在生产能力不平衡的问题，起到保护输送机系统、延长输送机系统寿命的作用。

（三）曲线胶带的纠偏

长距离胶带机一般会根据现场地形设置曲线转弯段，转弯半径根据计算确定。只要现场条件允许，转弯半径应尽量大些。与直线胶带机不同，转弯胶带机曲线段在胶带张力 S 作用下产生一个向心合力 F，使胶带有向曲线内侧滑移的趋势。平面转弯胶带机的转弯结构设计的关键是产生向曲线外侧的导向力来抵消 F。当胶带偏移量达带宽 5%时，必须纠偏。跑偏量过大会造成胶带磨损、撒料，严重时会使胶带刮破、撕裂，影响安全生产，带来经济损失。据统计输送带损坏 30%以上是因跑偏磨损而报废。

杨房沟工程长距离带式输送系统曲线段采取的纠偏措施：上下托辊内曲线适当抬高；托辊设置前倾；加大槽角，胶带机曲线段上托辊采用 45°托辊；曲线内侧面设置挡辊和带面设置压带辊。

（四）多站电气自动化控制设计

杨房沟工程带式输送系统共设 6 个控制站，其中 2 号站为控制主站，其他 5 个站为控制分站。每个控制站由 PLC 和工业光纤以太网、现场总线组成控制网络，完成系统内设备、保护装置全程监控、监测，构成完善监控系统。电气设备控制装置就近分散布置在各控制站内，每控制站配置有相应设备的电气控制装置、通信装置，系统人机自动化控制操作界面。系统控制采用 PLC＋变频软启动控制技术，系统各操作站和现场设备通过现场总线、光纤通信技术，组建可靠、快速通信网络将各控制站整合为一体，并采用人机操作界面实现系统自动化控制。

（中国水利水电第七工程局有限公司
郭子晗　李松）

喷射混凝土机口与现场喷射大板抽样强度对比分析

对湿喷混凝土机口与现场喷大板混凝土强度进行统计和分析，将有利于完善喷射混凝土配合比的设计方法。

（一）混凝土原材料及配合比

原材料采用葛洲坝水泥厂 42.5 普通水泥，下岸溪生产人工砂及粒径 5～15mm 瓜米石，上海 Rheoplus26R 羧酸高效减水剂及 SA160 无碱速凝剂，上海佳密克斯钢纤维，掺量 $40 kg/m^3$。

现场使用的混凝土配合比见表 1（表中 CF—钢纤维喷射混凝土，C—喷射混凝土）。

表 1　喷射混凝土现场用配合比

搅拌站	设计等级	水灰比	砂率（%）	Rheoplus26R 减水剂掺量（%）	SA160 速凝剂掺量（%）	钢纤维（kg/m^3）	材料用量（kg/m^3）水	水泥	砂	石
A	C25	0.45	59	0.8	6.0	/	189	420	1028	715
	C25	0.42	58				189	450	996	721
B	CF30	0.45	70	0.8	6.0	40	225	500	1054	451
	C25	0.50	70			/	225	450	1088	467

（二）混凝土试件的制作

喷射混凝土抗压强度的检测试件制作过程如下。

（1）喷射混凝土作业时，按实际施工条件向垂直放置的长 450mm、宽 350mm、高 120mm 的开敞式大板木模内，沿水平方向移动喷射混凝土，在施工现场养护 1 昼夜后脱模。

（2）将混凝土大板移至试验室，在标准养护条件下养护 7 天，用切割机去掉周边和上表面（底面可不切割），加工成边长为 100mm 立方体试件。立方体试件的允许偏差为：边长不超过±1mm，直角不超过±2°。

（3）继续在标准条件下养护至 28 天龄期，进行抗压和劈拉强度试验。

（三）试验结果

三峡右岸地下电站施工以来，在 2005 年 8 月 1 日～2007 年 3 月 22 日，从 A、B 搅拌站机口分别取混凝土试样 30 组和 40 组，在仓面分别取大板试件 30 块和 41 块。试验结果如下。

1. 抗压强度　A 搅拌站生产的喷射混凝土为 C25 素喷混凝土，B 搅拌站生产的喷射混凝土为 CF30 钢纤维混凝土及 C25 素喷混凝土。机口和仓面大板抗压强度试验结果表明：

（1）各强度等级喷射混凝土仓面大板取样的抗压强度满足设计要求，CF30 钢纤维混凝土仓面大板试样拉压比达 7.2%，其他拉压比为 6.1%～6.5%，CF30 钢纤维混凝土仓面大板试样拉压比高于 C25 素喷混凝土 0.7%。

（2）TGPS·T32—2005 规范要求，现场抽检试件 28 天抗压强度离差系数 $Cv \leqslant 0.25$。右岸地下电站 C25 素喷混凝土、C30 钢纤维喷射混凝土的机口和仓面大板离差系数 Cv 值为 0.13～0.14，均小于规范规定值，说明喷射混凝土的质量均匀性较好。

（3）从喷射混凝土机口和仓面离差系数的对比看，数值趋于相同。仓面喷射混凝土和混凝土出机口的质量匀质性，相对稳定且抗压强度较富余，更有利于施工质量的控制。

2. 机口与仓面大板强度对比　取机口强度与仓面大板混凝土强度对比试验 70 组。对比结果分析如下。

（1）喷射混凝土机口强度与大板强度差有一定的直线相关性，且是密切的。

（2）喷射混凝土仓面大板抗压强度普遍低于机口取样的抗压强度，28 天 CF30 和 C25 平均强度下降分别为 14.8、16.9MPa，即平均降低 23.3%、29.1%。

（3）大板比机口强度低的原因：首先，喷混凝土的密实度不如标准条件成型试件，标准试件可通过插捣、振动使其密实，而大板密实度与喷射工艺有关，受作业人员、喷射角度和距离的影响大，加之喷射会带入混凝土中一定气泡。其次，大板试件加工成试件，加工过程、试件尺寸和形状都会给试验结果带来负误差。再者，大板混凝土掺入速凝剂后凝结快，其水泥水化产物结构较粗大，强度受到一定影响。

（4）钢纤维喷射混凝土劈拉强度的降低百分率低于素喷混凝土，即大板劈拉强度平均值降低百分率，钢纤维喷射混凝土为 10.3%，而素喷混凝土为 24.9%。

（四）试验误差

试验误差是指重复取样误差，即在一次试验中同时取得 3 个或 2 个试件间的强度差异。此值衡量试验系统的试验水平，它与试件成型特别是大板试件的加工过程、尺寸和形状，试验机的运行状况等有关。喷射混凝土机口和仓面抗压强度试验误差统计计算结果见表 2。

表 2　　喷射混凝土抗压强度试验误差统计表

搅拌站	取样地点	组数	平均值（MPa）	试验误差（%）
A	机口	24	56.1	4.5
	仓面	22	40.6	5.4
B	机口	40	62.6	4.2
	仓面	36	45.9	4.9

由表 2 可见，A、B 搅拌站机口试验误差分别是 4.5%、4.2%，试验水平良好，仓面大板取样试验误差 A 搅拌站是 5.4%属一般水平，B 搅拌站是 4.9%虽属良好，接近一般水平。

此外，仓面大板取样试验误差大于机口取样的试验误差，特别是 A 搅拌站混凝土存在小型喷射机及人工手喷因素，表明试验结果受速凝剂掺量、湿喷台车性能（或小型喷射机）及操作者水平、混凝土试件加工制作等因素的影响较大。

（中国水利水电第三工程局有限公司　余跃雄）

碳纤维加固技术在水电工程中的应用

碳纤维复合材料是一种采用高强度的连续纤维按

一定规律排列，经用胶黏剂浸渍、黏结、固化后形成的具有纤维增强复合效应的复合材料。钢筋混凝土梁、板、柱、壳结构，表面粘贴碳纤维复合材料后，结构承载力较原结构有大幅度的提高。

（一）碳纤维复合材料加固原理及特性

碳纤维片材属于轻质高强材料，其单位强度高但直径极小，与环氧树脂结合成一体后在纤维方向上具有高抗拉强度。碳纤维强度虽然很高（约为钢筋的十倍，见表1），而其弹性系数却与钢筋差不多，碳纤维用于加固钢筋混凝土不会有搭配问题，可弥补钢筋混凝土内钢筋的抗拉不足。碳纤维借助胶黏剂与混凝土结合，胶黏剂涂抹于平整的混凝土表面。其黏度较低，易于渗入混凝土内与混凝土结合成类似树脂混凝土，可加强其强度，并与碳纤维密切结合，有效传递剪力，达到补强加固的目的。

表1　混凝土、钢筋和碳纤维主要性能比较

项目	混凝土	钢筋	碳纤维
弹性系数（GPa）	25	200	230
抗拉强度（MPa）	20	300～400	3000～3500
延展性（%）	0.2～0.3	0.2～0.3	0.9～1.5

碳纤维复合材料及其加固技术的特点如下。

（1）碳纤维复合材料的单位面积质量仅200～300g/m^2，片材厚度仅0.1～0.2mm，故在加固工程结构时，几乎不增加结构截面尺寸与重量。

（2）厚度小，便于交叉重叠。可弯曲成型，对各类曲面、壳体、异形构件及复杂节点的加固优势更为明显 。

（3）质地柔软，可自由剪裁，适用于各种形状构件加固。

（4）具有良好的耐久性、耐磨性，耐腐蚀性强，耐酸、碱、盐与大气的环境腐蚀。

（5）能有效阻止有害介质浸渗，对内部结构起保护作用，达到双重加固的目的。

（6）无湿作业和明火施工，占用场地小，不用大型施工机具，施工方便，工效高。

（7）用于桥梁、隧道、大坝、闸墩、混凝土钢管等多种结构面的补强加固。

（二）适用范围

适用于钢筋混凝土受弯、轴心受压、大偏心受压及手拉构件的加固。被加固构件的实测混凝土强度等级不应低于C15，不适用于加固素混凝土构件，包括纵向受力钢筋一侧配筋率小于0.2%的构件。

（三）粘贴碳纤维复合材料的配套材料

碳纤维复合材料用于工程加固时，需使用专业厂家生产的碳纤维布和配套专用胶黏剂材料，方能满足施工质量的要求。

1. 碳纤维片材　其抗拉强度、受拉弹性模量、伸长率等安全性能指标，应符合设计规范中相应指标的要求。

2. 粘贴碳纤维的配套胶　用碳纤维片材对混凝土结构加固时，应采用与其配套的底胶、修补胶和具有良好浸渍、黏结能力强的结构胶黏剂，配套胶性能指标应符合相关要求。

（1）底胶具有把作用在混凝土表面上的荷载传递到碳纤维片上的力学性能。

（2）浸渍胶是能完好地渗透到碳纤维片内部的浸渗黏着树脂，固化后形成一体。与底胶、修补胶一样，必须具有把作用在混凝土面上的应变传递到碳纤维片上的功能。

（四）工程应用实例

下面主要是小浪底水利枢纽排沙洞锚具槽渗油（水）的处理。

1. 概况　小浪底排砂洞采用无黏结预应力混凝土衬砌，自1999年投入使用以来，经过多年运行后发现部分锚具槽施工缝处有油脂和水渗出。分析认为这些油脂来自预应力环锚钢绞线内的保护油脂。由于排砂洞长期处于高水位下运行，锚具槽长期渗油和渗水将直接影响钢绞线的耐久性，并危及到排砂洞的安全运用。

2. 处理方案　采用施工缝内化学灌浆，表面粘贴碳纤维补强防渗的综合处理方案。

3. 碳纤维补强施工工艺

（1）基面处理：磨光机打磨施工面，用吹风机清理干净。

（2）基面找平：对表面凹坑不平处刮涂环氧胶泥直至平顺。

（3）涂底胶：找平材料充分固化且有一定强度时，根据所贴碳纤维布的尺寸将底胶均匀涂刷在基面上。

（4）裁剪碳纤维布：按要求尺寸及数量裁剪碳纤维布，搭接长度不得小于20cm。

（5）粘贴碳纤维布、涂浸渍胶：用滚筒反复滚压，去除气泡，使浸渍胶充分浸透碳纤维布。

4. 处理结果　共处理排沙洞锚具槽1254块，粘贴碳纤维片约2000m^2，锚具槽内部化学灌浆，根治了锚具槽漏油、漏水的问题。碳纤维表面的补强加固，有效地解决了锚具槽一期和二期混凝土不能联合受力的缺陷，处理后已经过多年过流考验，情况良好。

（中国水利水电第三工程局有限公司　曹珂）

TBM施工隧洞大股高压涌水处理

新疆引额供水二期工程引水隧洞总长283.393km，隧洞共采用十多台TBM及钻爆法施工。该标段包括23.34km主洞，主洞两个施工段采用1台直径7m的敞开式TBM施工。

（一）涌水情况及其处理

TBM掘进至临库区转弯段桩号3+887时，隧洞左侧腰线上方发现一条长约4m裂隙，并有两股涌水。

1. 实际出露情况　涌水点桩号3+887，该段岩性为凝灰质砂岩，呈青灰色，岩质较硬，围岩完整、稳定性好，围岩填充少量石英脉，为Ⅱ类围岩。洞壁左侧有1条裂隙，长4m，与洞轴线略有夹角，裂隙面光滑，张开度2～5cm，填充土黄色泥质膏状物。沿裂隙有两处大股涌水，喷射状流出。据统计涌水量280m^3/h。洞壁右侧有3～5条裂隙，有线状流水。

2. 涌水处理　经两次处理后，最终采取"水泥+水玻璃"灌浆方案，并成功封堵涌水。

（二）初次处理方案试验

初次处理方案实施步骤：简易封挡→泄压分流→化学灌浆封堵。

1. 强行简易封挡　为防止涌水喷射到TBM电动机设备上，对洞壁左侧两处涌水点分别用80cm×50cm、60cm×50cm两块6mm厚钢板覆盖封挡，四角用M14膨胀螺栓锚固，同时利用拱架连接筋调整位置并加固，必要时相邻拱架间焊接[12加固。

2. 泄压分流　围绕出水点1～4m直径范围内打设水平钻孔"泄压分流"，梅花型布置，共20个，孔径50mm，孔深2.9～5m。成孔后孔口安装"铁打塞"形成可控排水，安设灌浆管装置。

3. 化学灌浆封堵　待出水点水流量减小，水压力降低后，灌注化学浆材聚氨酯A、B组分，组分配合比1∶1。先在出水点最外围灌浆，形成止水帷幕，浆液填充该处裂隙加固围岩。再由远到近、由外向里，缩小渗水区域。

4. 实施结果　涌水区域距水库近涌水量大，洞壁完整岩石距离渗水裂隙面最薄处不足2m，渗径短，故涌水点周围钻孔难以"泄压分流"。试验表明A、B组分材料不适用大流量涌水堵漏。

（三）二次处理方案试验

第一阶段无法有效堵水，为此用Q235C材质10mm钢板贴壁锚固，对涌水点强压加固。

1. 加固钢板制作　钢板面积能覆盖涌水点，钢板弯弧尽可能贴合洞壁，四边打ϕ22孔，顶部焊接吊耳，并预留100mm泄水孔，焊接L型排水管，连接配套球阀。靠近洞壁侧铺垫防渗反滤材料。

2. 洞壁清理　钢板安装前凿除涌水点附近混凝土，凿除范围稍大于钢板。用高效堵漏剂填平涌水点周边未出水缝隙，使钢板安装尽可能与洞壁贴合。

3. 钢板安装加固　钢板安装后用ϕ22、长50cm锚杆锚固。为防止钢板鼓起，在其两侧相邻拱架间焊接槽钢，并与钢板紧固，钢板四周渗水用棉纱塞填+高效堵漏剂封堵。

4. 闭水实验　灌浆作业前在距涌水点较远"泄压孔"进行注水试验，压力1.5～2MPa，持续10min以上。注水中逐个关闭泄压孔孔口球阀，最后关闭钢板泄水球阀。如钢板四边、泄压孔孔口渗水，钢板"鼓包"，则终止试验，需继续加固钢板至试验通过方可灌浆。

5. 化学灌浆　第二阶段利用第一阶段预留排水减压孔逐孔进行纯压式化灌注浆。先灌距主要涌水点较远较深的孔，后灌较近较浅的孔。灌浆改用遇水快速固化膨胀的聚氨酯，用油溶性聚氨酯灌注较大流量裂隙，待涌水量显著减小后，改换水溶性聚氨酯继续灌注。

6. 试验结果　钢板直接贴岩壁进行封堵涌水点，堵水封浆效果不佳，无法承受灌浆压力，导致浆液大量流失。

（四）最终处理方案

经重新调整后的方案如下。

（1）涌水点在原封堵钢板上覆盖30cm厚混凝土挡墙，在挡墙与洞壁接触面增设止浆槽、止浆片，并进行化学接触灌浆。挡墙外侧设井字型钢，作为挡墙和灌浆段洞壁的支撑。浇筑挡墙混凝土后，灌浆前关闭涌水点球阀检验挡墙密封性。

（2）在距涌水点约8m处洞壁新增1个灌浆孔，孔径75mm，最大孔深25m，孔向与洞壁成一定角度。该孔能达到推断的渗水通道区，且与涌水点有一定距离。通过延长浆液渗透路径，减少浆液对挡墙的压力，给浆液足够的凝结时间。

（3）改用"水泥浆+水玻璃"双液灌注。采用水泥净浆∶水玻璃（体积比）=1∶1，净浆水灰比0.5，水玻璃浓度35%。试验表明，在实验室初凝时间50s，终凝时间约180s，灌浆压力1.5MPa（水压力+0.5MPa）。

灌浆浆液与试验配合比相同，在持续灌注约2h后，周边泄压孔及涌水点球阀孔均流出浓浆。逐一关闭孔口球阀，继续灌注1.5h后，涌水点出水已有效封堵。再灌注约1h，达设计压力后，持续灌注约30min、吸浆量小于1L/min后停止灌浆。灌浆量约50t，用时约4h。浆液初凝后，凿除挡墙混凝土，观察到涌水点已完全被封堵，满足设计堵水要求。

（中国水利水电第三工程局有限公司
刘文贤　王东）

苏阿皮蒂水电站辉绿岩人工骨料开采爆破技术

（一）工程概况

几内亚苏阿皮蒂水电站位于非洲几内亚孔库雷河中游，规模为大（1）型，总装机容量45万kW，混凝土350万m^3。需砂石骨料378万m^3，全部为人工骨料，料源在大坝下游2.4km左岸辉绿岩料场，开采高程155～217m。岩体微风化或新鲜，呈深灰、青灰色，块状结构，水平构造。矿物成分为辉石、斜长石，致密坚硬。料场月高峰期开采强度26万m^3，爆破粒径不大于80cm。

（二）初期开采存在的问题及解决思路

前期料场爆破孔径120mm，台阶高10m。为消除根底，超深2m，孔深12m。单耗药量为0.45kg/m^3，间距4m，排距3m，封堵3m，耦合间隔2m装药，有效装药长度7m，毫秒雷管分段起爆，最大单响药量600kg。爆破存在的问题：单次爆破规模小，采量无法满足骨料加工需要；炮孔利用率低，仅58%；爆破后大块率高，约35%；爆破后冲破坏明显，保留岩体节理、裂隙和水平层面张开，对下一循环爆破影响较大。

解决问题的思路：优化爆破网络，在控制最大单响药量的条件下，增大单次爆破规模；采用小直径爆破孔，耦合连续装药，提高炮孔利用率；优化火工材料、钻孔方向、炮孔间排距、微差起爆、单耗药量等，降低大块率；控制后排爆破减少爆破后冲破坏。

（三）爆破优化

1. 钻孔　优化方案如下。

（1）减小孔径：辉绿岩坚硬，抗压强度达170MPa，可钻性差，120mm大直径钻进速度慢。且需分段间隔装药，药量集中，工序多，孔口封堵段长，炮孔利用率低，速度慢，孔口和间隔处易出现大块。经试验，爆孔钻进用阿特拉斯D7液压钻机，钻头直径78mm，扩孔系数1.15，成孔直径90mm。可加快钻孔速度，并能解决前述爆破工序中问题。

（2）调整孔向：辉绿岩岩层接近水平，钻工水平不高，钻孔方向选垂直向下。垂直孔精度易控，偏差小，钻进快，爆破能量不会顺水平层面损失，能提高岩体破碎效果。

（3）孔深：垂直孔孔深为台阶高加超深，台阶高度考虑岩性、钻机和挖装机械性能等选为10m，超深2m，钻孔深12m。

（4）钻孔间排距：间距为4m，排距2m。大孔距、小排距可增大爆破漏斗角，形成弧形自由面，为岩石拉伸破坏创造条件。能防止爆炸气体从相邻炮孔间裂隙散逸，提高爆破能量利用率，减弱炮孔间应力叠加作用，提高岩石破碎率。

2. 火工材料　初期用国产火工材料为散装2号岩石硝铵炸药和乳化炸药。保质期1年，采购运输6个月，到工地后仅6个月保质期，造成超过保质期后多次拒爆。后选西班牙和法国火工材料，价格同国产材料，但炸药保质期2年，采购运输3个月。选用卷状水胶炸药，装药简便迅速。毫秒导爆管雷管与导爆索连接为卡扣式，联网迅速，比国产绑扎速度提高2倍以上。

3. 装药　据初期爆破参数和相关资料，料场开采单耗药量调整为0.64kg/m^3，单孔药量51.2kg。使用ϕ70mm水胶炸药，单节长50cm，密度1.25g/cm^3，药重2.4kg/节。孔底1m范围装5节划开HDPE包装膜的炸药，耦合装药，装药8kg/m。上部9m连续装18节包装完整的ϕ70mm水胶炸药，孔口封堵长2m。

4. 爆破网路　采用微差爆破。前排孔爆破时产生的短裂隙有利于后排孔爆破时对孔间岩石破碎，以提高破碎质量。孔内炸药用导爆索至孔底起爆，保证孔内炸药完全起爆。爆破网络用高段位MS22（延时900ms）孔内延时，用100ms连接块排间延时。为确保最大单响药量不超过600kg，同排间爆破孔用42ms连接块延时间隔，控制最大单响药量，一次起爆孔数不超过11个。起爆规模可根据需要，加大单次起爆孔数。

5. 采区宽度　单次爆破选择合理的采区宽度，能保证爆破质量，提高石渣挖运速度，可为下一循环爆破创造良好的临空面。参照初期爆破和相关资料，采区宽度选择0.8～1.2倍梯段高度效果较好，实际爆破选10m。

6. 后排控制　初期开采爆破经验说明，最后一排孔需采取控制措施，降低后冲作用。采区内最后一排孔排距2m，孔距2m，不耦合连续装药，孔底2m范围加强2倍装药，药卷为ϕ40mm水胶炸药，不耦合系数2.25，单孔药量25kg/孔。料场开挖轮廓线处采用光面爆破，孔距1.2m，底部加强装药，药卷为ϕ32mm水胶炸药，间隔装药，线装药密度450g/m。

（四）爆破效果

近6个月的爆破开采，有用料累计开挖80万m^3，爆破参数通过优化调整效果明显。

（1）降低了钻孔难度，炮孔利用率由初期58%

提高至83%，节约钻孔时间30%以上。

（2）简化火工材料采购和雷管分发操作，加快了爆破网路连接速度，提高了爆破作业效率和毛料开采速度。单次起爆规模达2万m^3/次，毛料供应量达21万m^3/月。

（3）爆破岩体大块率（粒径≥80cm）从初期40%降至5%。

（4）爆破后底板平整，无明显残留埂坎。后冲破坏得到有效控制，保留岩体基本完整，临空面处大块石明显减少。

（中国水利水电第三工程局有限公司 李刚 李玉凡）

兰州市供水工程超长隧洞多工作面灌浆施工技术

（一）概述

兰州水源地建设工程以刘家峡水库作为引水水源，向兰州市供水。工程包括取水口、输水隧洞主洞、分水井、调流调压站和水厂等。工程取水口位于临夏回族自治州东乡县境内，输水隧洞末端设置分水井。隧洞主洞长31.29km，其中TBM2施工段长13.46km。隧洞施工以双护盾TBM为主，开挖洞径5.49m，管片衬砌，内径4.6m。管片厚0.3m，环宽1.5m，管片与围岩间用豆砾石充填并进行回填灌浆。在TBM掘进贯通后，进行接触、固结灌浆，固结灌浆10.50万m，接触灌浆12.14万m^2。

国内超长距离大洞径引水隧洞一般采用大型钻灌台车同步进行灌浆施工，施工空间充足，不占直线工期。但兰州市供水工程输水隧洞洞径小，洞内施工人员和设备材料等都需通过小火车运输，钻孔台车最大施工空间仅1.8m，灌浆平台宽仅1.1m。常规集中推进式灌浆不能满足工期要求，最终采用15个工作面同时灌浆的方案。

（二）方案的选择

1. 确定工作面布置　从作业面台车结构，变压器类型，洞内灌浆站位置及浆液中转方式等，对集中推进式和全线平均分布式作业对比分析（见表1），确定后者为布置方式。

表1　两种作业方式对比

项目	集中推进式	全线平均分布	备注
对工期影响	互相影响大，对工期影响大	互相独立，影响不大，对工期有利	
变压器数量	5台500kVA变压器，置于小火车平板上，随作业面移动，安全隐患大	15台250kVA变压器，固定在管片壁，电缆多，成本高，安全隐患小	洞内用电最大功率2100kW
钻灌平台	用工字钢有资质厂家生产，成本高，人员设备在车上隐患大	用方钢、角铁、钢管自行加工，成本少4/5，移动方便，人员设备不在车上隐患小	
制浆站	洞内用袋装水泥制浆，粉尘大，无需浆液中转	洞外集中制浆，洞内粉尘很少，需多级中转	实际在13～15号工作面为洞内制浆

2. 洞内通信　有3种方式：一是利用TBM掘进期间的系统通信，用于小火车间及各工作面的对外联系；二是各工作面之间短距离采用对讲机通信；三是浆液中转时，各工作面间及与洞外制浆站通过程控电话联系。

3. 钻灌平台及变压器平台布置　根据洞内围岩类别和工程量计算出每个工作面覆盖的施工区域，合理布置各种平台。钻灌平台需精确设计及安全计算，确保安全有效运行。

4. 浆液中转站　洞外设2套自动制浆系统，洞内通过接力中转为11km区域供浆，最多中转4次，每次中转距离650～900m。洞内浮动道岔设简易袋装水泥制浆站（喷雾降尘）为洞内2.4km范围供浆。由此解决了长距离输浆难题，减少了洞内水泥运量和交通压力，提高了作业区安全，加快了施工进度。

5. 洞内环境监测　制定洞内监测流程，用手持式粉尘含量测定仪、气体含量测定仪等，对洞内气体进行有效监测并制定措施，保证施工安全。

（三）多工作面灌浆技术的效果

在施工中，合理布置40台钻灌设备、15台20/0.4kV变压器和浆液中转站，采用3种通信方式，降低小火车通行与运送灌浆设施和人员的小火车相互干扰，确保洞内氧气含量、粉尘、噪声和废气含量符合标准。多工作面灌浆施工取得了好的效果。

（1）灌浆施工达到了高安全性、高效率，低成本水平，有效地解决了小断面超长隧洞灌浆的难题。

（2）在实施本方案后，关键线路上的接触灌浆和固结灌浆，均提前完成了工期目标，节约了成本。节约工期18天，创经济效益约73万元，达到了预期灌浆效果。

（中国水利水电第三工程局有限公司 般银蕊）

新型骨料仓料位指示仪

拌和楼骨料仓分大、中、小、特大、砂1、砂2等6个料仓。料仓内的料位指示选用两种传感器分：一是模拟量信号传感器，如超声波、雷达、电容等料位器；一种是开关量信号传感器，如限位开关料位器。前者造价高，误判断频率高；后者工作稳定性较差。目前拌和系统已基本实行自动控制，但运行时料位观察还是基本靠人工观察。要实现料仓骨料自动补给，准确、及时地反馈料仓内料位情况显得尤为重要。

（一）传统骨料仓料位仪的弊端

拌和楼骨料仓设料位仪的作用是，判断料位情况及控制骨料输送系统自动上料运行。这样，模拟量料位器最大优势，即判断骨料仓料位的功能就显得没有必要，且其造价过高，对工作环境要求较高，而料仓内环境恶劣导致经常出现误判甚至不工作。由此在生产过程中即使料仓内装有模拟量料位器，也很少能正常使用。开关量料位仪采用机械式触点，这类料位仪价格便宜，其功能已能满足拌和楼骨料仓料位指示要求。但它在骨料仓恶劣环境下稳定性太差，生产中也几乎弃之不用，基本还靠人工观察料位情况。简单重复的劳动不仅增加了工人的劳动强度，也加大了生产成本。

新型骨料仓料位指示仪（发明专利号：ZL2008100455995）克服了传统骨料仓料位指示仪的不足，是一种可靠性高，能适应料仓恶劣环境的料位指示仪。

（二）新型料位指示仪技术方案

新型料位指示仪包括仓浅料位和仓满料位指示仪。在仓浅部位采用受压薄板承受骨料的压力，在骨料仓壁与受压薄板间产生压力差，利用这个压力差通过压力开关并发出仓浅信号。在仓满部位则采用光电开关所处环境的改变而发出仓满信号。

与现有技术相比，此发明专利的优点是：大大提高了料位指示的可靠性，完全能适应骨料仓恶劣环境，且不需人工观察料仓内料位情况，降低了劳动强度，节约成本。

（三）工作原理及结构

仓浅料位，主要是压力开关料位，包括支承底座，缓冲块，压力开关，受压薄板，定位螺栓，压力调节螺栓，仓浅信号灯等，安装在骨料仓下部。仓满料位，包括透明材料外壳，光电开关，缓冲块，外照光源，仓满信号灯等，安装在骨料仓上部。仓内骨料上升到仓浅位置时，由于料仓仓壁与受压薄板厚度不同，在骨料对仓壁的侧压力下造成变形不同从而产生压力差，利用这个压力差压通过压力开关并发出仓浅信号。当料位上升到仓满位置时骨料挡住外照光源，使仓满料位的光电开关接通，发出仓满信号，实现料位指示功能。

（四）实施方式

新型料位指示仪结构如图1所示。

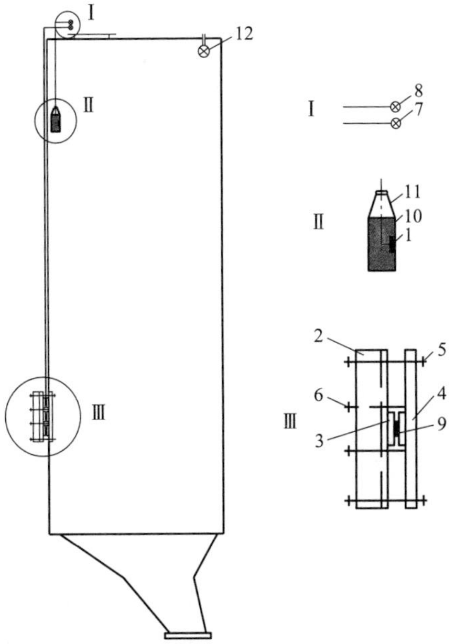

图1　料仓结构及料位仪示意图

1—光电开关；2—支承角铁；3—缓冲橡胶；4—1.5mm受压薄板；5—定位螺栓；6—压力调节螺栓；7—仓浅信号灯；8—仓满信号灯；9—压力开关；10—缓冲海绵；11—透明材料外壳；12—外接光源

仓浅料位的安设：将缓冲橡胶固定在∠75×5mm支承角铁上，支承角铁两头开ϕ14孔并安装2个ϕ12螺栓，作为压力开关位置调节和固定用，中间开两个ϕ12孔安装2个ϕ10的螺栓用作调节压力开关最大受压压力。将压力开关固定在缓冲橡胶上，同时在压力开关上再固定一层缓冲橡胶，形成仓浅料位仪。料仓底部2m处开1个300mm×300mm孔，将400mm×400mm受压薄板固定在已开300mm×300mm孔上，再将支承角铁与仓壁、薄板连接在一起。骨料上升到薄板时，通过压力开关动作发出仓浅信号，提示供料系统及时补料。

仓满料位的安设：将光电开关放在透明容器中，在容器空余位置填充缓冲海绵。把透明容器固定ϕ50mm，2.2m长的镀锌管上，导线从镀锌管中穿出，再将镀锌管安放在料仓不易受冲击的部位，外接电源放在料仓观察孔中。当骨料上升到透明容器的位置挡住外接电源光线时，光电开关导通，发出仓满信号提示。

（中国水利水电第七工程局有限公司　王鹏）

7

机电及金属结构

水电机组及辅机

白鹤滩水电站左岸电站水轮机模型验收试验

白鹤滩水电站共装设 16 台（左、右岸各 8 台）单机容量为 1000MW 的立轴混流式水轮发电机组，最大水头 243.1m，最小水头 163.9m，额定水头 202m。左岸电站 8 台机组由东方电气集团东方电机有限公司（以下简称东电）供货。2015 年 9 月，东电委托中国水利水电科学研究院（以下简称水科院）在其水力机械实验室 TP1 试验台进行白鹤滩左岸电站水轮机模型验收试验，中国长江三峡集团有限公司（以下简称三峡公司）组织相关单位组成验收组参加本次验收试验。现将验收试验情况简介如下。

（一）模型主要参数

转轮进口直径为 417.65mm，出口直径为 351.29mm，喉口直径为 350mm，转轮叶片数 15，活动导叶数 24，固定导叶数 23。原型水轮机转轮出口直径为 7124.21mm，模型与原型的比尺为 1∶20.28。

（二）试验装置及其标定

TP1 试验台的主要性能参数为：试验最高水头 150m、试验模型转轮直径范围 250～500mm、试验流量范围 0～1.5m^3/s、测功电机功率 540kW、测功电机转速 0～2600r/min。对电磁流量计、水头差压传感器、尾水绝压传感器、主轴力矩传感器、摩擦力矩传感器、蜗壳差压传感器、压力脉动传感器、轴向水推力传感器和导叶水力矩传感器等测量设备进行了标定检查或现场标定和测量数据验证。经误差分析试验台模型效率综合误差为±0.146%，满足合同不超出±0.25%的要求；模型效率重复测试误差不超出±0.10%，满足验收试验各参数测量精度的要求；试验过程中水温不超过 35℃。

（三）各项目试验情况

1. 水轮机效率试验　最优效率点试验在能量工况（高空化系数）下进行，其他效率试验在电站空化系数下进行，空化系数计算参考面为导叶中心线。原型水轮机效率根据模型试验效率按两步法进行修正。固定雷诺数，按合同文件要求为 5.5×10^6。

（1）最优效率试验：选择在最优效率点附近的 4 个导叶开度 19°、19.5°、20°、20.88°下进行，为更好验证试验台的重复性，每天开始各项试验前均先进行最优效率点试验。验收试验成果：n_{10}＝53.05r/min，Q_{10}＝0.587m^3/s，模型水轮机最优效率 95.07%，大于合同保证值 95.02%；相应原型水轮机的最优效率工况点为水头 222.86m，功率 936.09MW，原型最优效率为 96.69%，大于合同保证值 96.67%。

（2）加权平均效率试验：对合同中有加权因子的每个工况点进行验收见证试验，得到模型加权平均效率为 94.29%，高于合同保证值 94.16%；相应原型水轮机的加权平均效率为 95.92%，高于合同保证值 95.81%。

2. 功率试验　选择 8 个水头进行试验，得到各水头下的最大功率，满足合同要求，并确定能发水轮机额定功率 1015MW 的最小水头为 194.96m（合同保证值为 195m）。白鹤滩水电站机组投产时的发电初期极限最小运行水头范围为 159～163.9m。为验证在此水头范围内的运行稳定性，验收试验补充了此水头区域试验内容。试验结果表明机组在此水头范围内运行稳定，水头 159m 的最大功率为 714.93MW，162m 的最大功率为 740.18MW。

3. 空化试验　试验水头 30m，参考基准面为导叶中心线。试验前、后均测量水中的空气含量，得到水的空气含量体积比为 0.737%，满足“在标准大气压下，水温 20℃时水中空气含量不低于 0.2%的水容积”的要求。

（1）空化观测：验收试验表明，在合同规定的各特征工况点 σ_p/σ_i 均大于 1.1。在水轮机运行范围内转轮出口无可见卡门涡。叶道涡初生和发展试验结果中虽有部分水头下的试验值略超过合同保证值，但叶道涡初生线及发展线均未进入合同规定的水轮机长期连续安全稳定运行范围。

（2）空化外特性：选择 H_p＝163.9、175、185、195、202、210、220、230、243.1m 及极限最小水头 159m 共 10 个水头，各水头分别在 11 个工况点进行空化试验。试验结果显示个别工况点的临界空化系数略大于合同保证值，但在合同规定的各特征工况点满足 σ_p/σ_1 均大于 1.6 的合同要求。

4. 压力脉动试验　在不补气条件下，对 10 个水头进行了压力脉动测量。合同规定的各测点压力脉动试验值满足合同要求。试验中，整个运行范围内未发现高部分负荷高频压力脉动带，无异常脉动区域。

变空化压力脉动试验表明，在各水头可能出现的尾水位变幅范围内，空化系数的变化对各测点压力脉动无明显影响。

5. 轴向水推力试验　合同要求“轴向水推力是在最不利的运行工况下及转轮密封2倍设计间隙时的水轮机最大轴向水推力”。因在水科院无法进行部件的加工，验收试验只做了设计间隙下的轴向水推力测试，得到的最大轴向水推力为13070kN；这与东电初步试验得到的设计间隙下最大轴向水推力为9107kN存在一定差异，但均满足合同保证值（14260kN）要求。东电在验收试验后，加工2倍设计间隙下的装置，并完成试验，结果满足合同要求。

6. 飞逸特性试验　在能量工况下进行，试验水头大于10m。将试验结果绘制成飞逸特性曲线，换算出原型飞逸转速。验收试验在最大水头、最大导叶开度下的最大飞逸转速为201.4r/min，略小于合同保证值202r/min。

7. 蜗壳差压测流试验　在水头为243.1、220、202、163.9m下，测量蜗壳测流断面上两测压孔之间的压差，据此建立蜗壳压差与流量之间的关系函数，得出：$Q_M = 0.2206P_M^{0.4952}$。

8. 导叶水力矩试验　进行了同步下导叶水力矩试验和非同步下导叶水力矩试验。试验表明：导叶开度从4°～28°之间导叶具有自关闭趋势，满足合同要求。

9. 补气试验　表1列出试验结果。试验表明：在部分负荷工况下，补气对降低尾水管的压力脉动幅值效果明显，对其他测点的压力脉动幅值影响较小。

表1　尾水管与导叶后转轮前区域压力脉动混频峰峰值补气试验结果

水头（m）	功率（MW）	尾水管 $\Delta H/H$（%）				导叶后转轮前区域 $\Delta H/H$（%）			
		不补气	补气量 $0.2\%Q_r$	补气量 $0.3\%Q_r$	补气量 $0.37\%Q_r$	不补气	补气量 $0.2\%Q_r$	补气量 $0.3\%Q_r$	补气量 $0.37\%Q_r$
220	471	3.19	0.88	0.67	0.70	1.78	1.64	1.60	1.54
202	456	3.35	0.74	0.61	0.58	2.56	1.80	1.62	1.60
185	412	3.72	0.96	0.82	0.61	2.60	1.60	1.58	1.40
	929	1.68	2.36	1.93	1.49	2.55	3.01	2.86	2.67
163.9	351	3.31	2.58	2.25	1.76	1.62	1.86	2.00	1.81

10. 尺寸检查　对水轮机模型的转轮出口直径、下止漏环间隙、活动导叶高度、蜗壳进口测压断面直径、尾水锥管进/出口直径、尾水管出口高度和宽度、尾水管高度及长度等尺寸进行检查，几何尺寸符合标准规定。

（四）其他说明

验收试验完成后，东电根据一些已投运电站机组固定导叶出现裂纹的情况，在白鹤滩座环强度详细计算时发现固定导叶尾部局部应力较高，提出对固定导叶进行加强。加强的方法为保持原固定导叶叶型，对固定导叶按比例适当放大，并保持固定导叶布置和安放角不变，保持固定导叶的进出口水流角。2016年2月三峡公司组织专题会进行研究，同意东电对白鹤滩机组固定导叶进行加强，并制造新的模型座环，对水轮机主要性能重新进行验收试验。2016年7月，在东电DF-80试验台进行固定导叶改型后的验收试验，试验项目包括主要测量设备标定检查、效率试验、压力脉动试验、模型尺寸检查等。验收试验表明，除原型水轮机最优效率、蜗壳进口压力脉动个别工况点略超合同保证值外，其他性能满足合同要求。

（中国电建集团华东勘测设计研究院有限公司　方晓红　曹春建）

洪屏抽水蓄能电站发电电动机设计特点与问题处理

洪屏抽水蓄能电站一期安装4台单机容量为300MW的可逆式抽水蓄能机组。其发电电动机型号为1DH6661-3WE06-Z，额定容量333.3MVA/325MW（发电/电动），额定电压18kV，额定转速500r/min，飞逸转速725r/min。

（一）设计特点

洪屏抽水蓄能电站发电电动机由上海福伊特水电设备有限公司设计、制造，无论是电磁方案的确定，还是详细结构的设计，都引入了较先进的设计技术。这些先进设计技术主要有：①为削弱谐波分量，保证电势波形质量，转子磁极冲片极靴形状设计成三段圆弧；②上机架将推力轴承和上导轴承分置组合设计，既分散了轴承发热点又便利了检查检修；③为便于用户检修并顾及推力轴承、上导轴承的安全性，供推力轴承油冷却用的冷却器布置在坑外，并配制一套油压装置专向两轴承油槽输油，以实现轴承冷却油自循环；④定、转子的冷却采用机座外装设空气冷却器，空气冷却后经双回路径轴混合自循环通风系统；⑤为使刷架、制动器产生的尘埃不对定、转子造成污染，提高发电电动机运行的可靠性并延长使用寿命，采用挡风装置把风路与制动器、刷架完全隔开方式，并特地为刷架和制动器各自设计了特殊的独立的吸尘装置；⑥为防止电机轴承油槽内的油雾逸出，污染电机及环境，设计了一套特殊的油雾密封及排出、过滤装置。主要部件的设计特点如下：

1. 定子　机座分两瓣，运至工地后，把合复位、整调检测，把合缝处两合缝板焊接成整体。机座与定子基础板之间的连接采用径向滑板轴向圆柱销定位、螺栓把合结构，铁芯与机座能适应热膨胀位移。铁芯由单位损耗小于 1.1W/kg 的 0.5 厚的优质冷轧硅钢片叠成，靠鸽尾筋定位；高度 3414mm，分四次预紧，用拉紧螺杆、螺母、垫圈及碟形弹簧压紧。下齿压条用装焊模具定位、点焊在定子下环板上；上齿压条在制造厂就已经焊接为一个整体，便于铁芯现场叠装。定子绕组线棒绝缘采用公司最先进的优质结构，线棒槽楔压紧比常规多用了弹性充填导电胶，以防止在一段时间热机械运动后槽中线棒松动、绝缘损坏。

2. 转子　转轴与水机轴同钻铰联轴孔，校核摆度。转子支架立筋加工有键槽，键槽内安装有弹性键，待磁轭拼装参数调整完毕，以安装凸形键替换安装定位键后，拧紧弹性键背侧的调整螺栓，对磁轭径向数据作最后调整。磁轭键不用传统的热打键，而用电加热设备加热磁轭后直接放入。磁极装配时要根据磁极外圆直径调整内侧垫片或磁极键的厚度。上导轴承滑转子与套筒经热套后加工，两者之间有环氧玻璃坯布包压成的绝缘层，能有效、永久地防止电机轴电流的产生。

3. 上机架及上导轴承　集上导轴承和推力轴承于一体，分上下两个各自独立油槽，推力轴承置上油槽，上导轴承置下油槽，发热点分置，有利散热。两油槽共配制一个抽油雾装置和一个外循环油装置。六条支腿端部装有德国福伊特专利弹性支撑装置，以利柔性减震。拆卸两轴承油盆盖即可对推力瓦和上导瓦进行检查、装拆方便。

4. 推力轴承　由推力头（推力头下平面即镜板），推力瓦组（推力瓦、橡胶弹性垫、定位框架、可撕调整垫片、支撑垫板），轴承座环，压力油腔，挡油装置等组成。推力头与轴用键及卡环定位，其间夹绝缘层的设计与上导滑转子的一样。均布 12 块巴氏合金推力瓦，每个推力瓦的厚度尺寸都在制造厂经严格检测，装配后推力瓦组的水平面最大允许高差为 0.05mm。每块可撕调整垫片总厚度为 2mm，由厚度为 0.05mm 薄片压制而成的，推力瓦水平面高差就是以增减可撕调整垫片来实现的。设计每块瓦下垫 18 个橡胶弹性垫，每个厚度 10mm，平均刚度 32kN/mm，容许负荷下最大变形量 2mm，本机额定负荷下最大变形压缩量 1.24mm，推力瓦水平受力就靠它们的变形量自调节达到。每块推力瓦装配两个 RTD（热电阻），一个测发电工况温度，一个测泵工况温度。推力轴承润滑油设计为强迫外循环。

5. 下机架及下导轴承　下机架合缝腿不拆而仅拆中心体就能从定子铁芯内孔吊出，从而减少检修工作量。

（二）安装中发现的问题及处理

洪屏抽水蓄能电站机电安装自 2014 年 1 月开始，至 2016 年 12 月底，4 台机组先后投入商业运营。安装历经三年，也出现过很多相关技术难题，主要有推力轴承温度偏高、盘车上导摆度过大、定子切向受力不够等问题。

1. 推力轴承温度偏高　2016 年 6 月，1 号机组开机运转仅半小时推力瓦温度就高达到 80℃，企稳时达 86℃。在设备生产厂家的指导下，通过增减橡胶弹性垫数量、修刮进油边等措施进行处理，可以在 84℃状态下稳定运行。后安装的 2、3、4 号机组推力轴承温度有不同程度的降低，尤以 4 号机推力轴承温度最低，稳定运行最高温度为 74℃。但与厂家设计推力轴承温度 65℃仍有很大差异。因此，制造厂同意进行推力轴承设计改造。

改造方案为：①增大推力头镜板和推力瓦径向尺寸，比原设计直径大 110mm；②将弹性橡胶簧垫支撑更改为金属蝶形弹簧簇支撑，推力轴承瓦组由推力瓦、蝶形弹簧、定位框架、可撕垫片等组成，每块推力瓦由 47 个蝶形弹簧簇支撑，每个蝶形弹簧可承受 11.2kN 的工作负载，其特性比橡胶簧垫更软，刚度更低，变形更具线性。

改造后，推力轴承运行温度最高 68℃，比改造前低了 16℃，基本满足了机组安全运行要求。

2. 轴线调整上导摆度过大　2016 年 3 月中旬，2 号机组进行轴线调整，经过多日反复盘车，其镜板水平、下导水导摆度均符合技术要求，唯上导摆度达 0.18mm。虽多方努力仍不得其解，一度使技术人员陷入困境。后转换思维，从不被怀疑的地方入手，提出在上导滑转子同一方位三个不同高度位置架设百分表，以检验其倾斜度。结果中心线处百分表的读数在 0.03mm 以内，上下端部百分表读数绝对值相等方向相反。这就说明上导滑转子存在倾斜值，是厂家在热套时操作精度不够造成的。处理方案：在上导滑转子上端部高点架一千斤顶和一只百分表，再将上导滑转子加温至 150～200℃，操作千斤顶将上导滑转子下压至计算数值校正，待冷却后撤出操作工具。处理后盘车，结果完全符合技术要求。

3. 定子基础结构刚度不够　因为设计对定子极端瞬时工况正反切向力稍欠考虑，基础板仅靠背面筋板与混凝土结合，没有传统的螺栓锁固点。定子机座安装就位后发现基础固定结构强度不够，只得采取补救加固。方案为：在基础板外缘补焊钢板，打孔用锚筋固定；另外，在基础板两侧200mm厚二期混凝表面上用钢板锚筋固定压实。

（三）结语

洪屏抽水蓄能电站4台发电电动机，在主体设计制造上采用了先进技术和较新颖的结构，除推力轴承和定子基础出现设计缺陷外，发电电动机本身达到了设计要求。自2016年12月初全部投入商业运营以来，发电、抽水工况运行稳定。

［编者按：本文作者张伯超系洪屏抽水蓄能电站机组安装质检专家］

（湖北正源电力有限公司天堂抽水蓄能分公司
张伯超　熊永俊）

安康水力发电厂研发出发电机上机架千斤顶剪断销更换专用工具

安康水力发电厂发电机组型号为SF200-56/12800，上机架是安置上导轴承的支撑部件，其支臂外端设置承受径向力的千斤顶。该千斤顶如图1所示，安装位置上部0.5m有盖板覆盖，下部悬空3m。

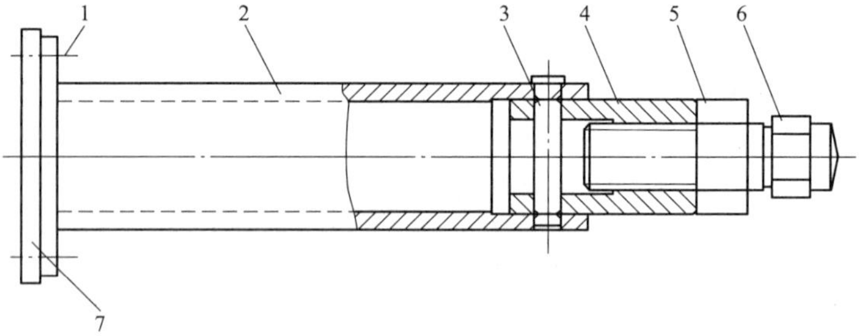

图1　上机架千斤顶结构图

1—连接螺栓；2—顶座；3—剪断销；4—套筒；5—锁紧螺母；6—顶丝；7—垫板

机组运行，会出现上机架千斤顶因承受径向力过大剪断销被剪断情况。这就需要更换剪断销。由于被剪断的剪断销与套筒一起挤压到千斤顶座内孔里，常用工具无法在千斤顶安装位置将剪断销与套筒一起移动，需要先拆除发电机上机架盖板，再拆下千斤顶并吊运到安装间，固定在安装间的地锚上，利用桥式起重机吊钩拉拔套筒，使残余剪断销与安装孔对正再用工具冲出。千斤顶上没有专用吊点，桥式起重机拉力有冲击，存在钢丝绳松脱崩断等不安全隐患，参与工作人员也较多（8人左右），整个工作费力费时。

为了解决上机架千斤顶剪断销更换难这个问题，安康水力发电厂决定研制一套千斤顶不需从安装位置拆下吊出而在原位将剪断销与套筒一起移动的专用工具。经过广泛查阅资料，与检修人员一起集思广益，经过多次探讨，借用扩张器原理，研发出了一套专用工具。它主要由两副顶板和两台液压薄型液压千斤顶组成（参见图2），并配一台手动液压泵。

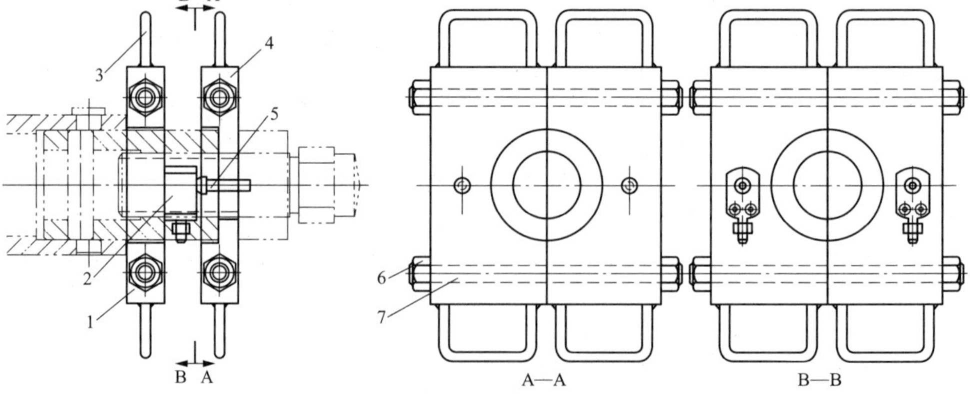

图2　专用工具结构图

1—顶板Ⅰ；2—薄型液压千斤顶；3—扶手；4—顶板Ⅱ；5—调节螺栓；6—螺母；7—销钉螺栓

顶板Ⅰ与顶板Ⅱ都为分瓣结构用销钉螺栓组装连接，便于拆装。为保证分瓣顶板组合后平整并承力良好，销钉螺栓选择 40cr 钢制造；中部销钉段长 70mm、直径 30mm，与孔的配合公差控制在 0.05～0.1mm；销钉段两侧各有 20mm 长的锥形过渡段，便于装入；螺栓为 M27，有足够紧力。顶板Ⅰ装有两薄型液压千斤顶，安装在千斤顶套筒上，靠紧顶座，工作时不动。顶板Ⅱ安装在千斤顶锁紧螺母从锁紧位置退开的顶丝上，通过调整调节螺栓（该螺栓与薄型液压千斤顶接触面为球面）使其顶紧锁紧螺母并均匀受力；工作时被薄型液压千斤顶推动，带动顶丝、套筒外移，将剪断销孔对齐。手压泵用来给两台薄型液压千斤顶同时供油。薄型液压千斤顶原选用 5t 顶力的，后发现操作力不足，改用 10t 的。

该专用工具采用液压操作将套筒外移，待剪断销孔对齐就可以用冲子将损坏的剪断销退出，省力、安全；上机架千斤顶不需拆卸、外运，工序简化，可节省大量人力及检修时间。

该专用工具已经在实际中运用多次，效果理想。如安康水电厂 4 号机组大修时，需要更换 2 个上机架千斤顶剪断销，就在上机架千斤顶工作位置采用该专用工具，只用了 4 个人，半个小时就顺利的将一个剪断销取出；拆除第二个剪断销，只用 3 个工作人员就可胜任。

（安康水力发电厂　李军）

安谷水电站大型轴流转桨式转轮翻身采用新技术

安谷水电站轴流转桨式水轮机转轮为五叶片结构，在厂房安装间进行组装。其组装工艺流程，先将转轮轮毂体倒置装配活塞杆、连杆拐臂、枢轴、活塞缸等桨叶操作机构，安装活塞缸盖和进行压力试验合格后将转轮翻身，再装配桨叶及操作油管。通常情况下转轮翻身利用双桥式起重机、或桥式起重机主副钩、或桥式起重机在汽车式起重机辅佐下进行，即先用一个吊钩吊起要翻身的转轮轮，另一个吊钩起到扶正翻转作用，当转轮轮翻转一定角度时，两钩作用互换。此方法操作难度大，安全系数低。安谷水电站大机转轮组装后重量达 240t，在未安装桨叶时转轮轮毂带桨叶操作机构翻身重量（含吊具）为 180t，而厂房虽配置了两台桥式起重机，但小桥式起重机主钩最大起吊重量仅为 100t，不能满足翻身工作。且由于受安装场面积和房顶高度限制，利用大型汽车吊辅助进行翻身在技术上难以实现。因此，研发应用了采用主桥式起重机单钩在特制翻身装置配合下进行转轮轮翻身的新技术。

转轮翻身专用装置由两个回转轴吊耳、一个半圆形轴套座以及轴套座基础构成。半圆形轴套座装置如图 1 所示，回转轴吊耳装置如图 2 所示。

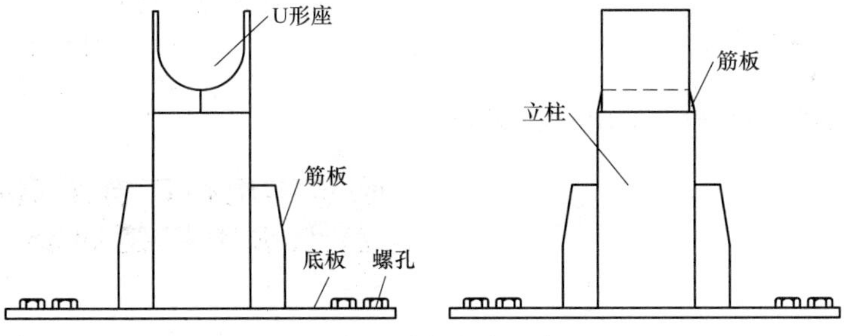

图 1　半圆形轴套座示意图

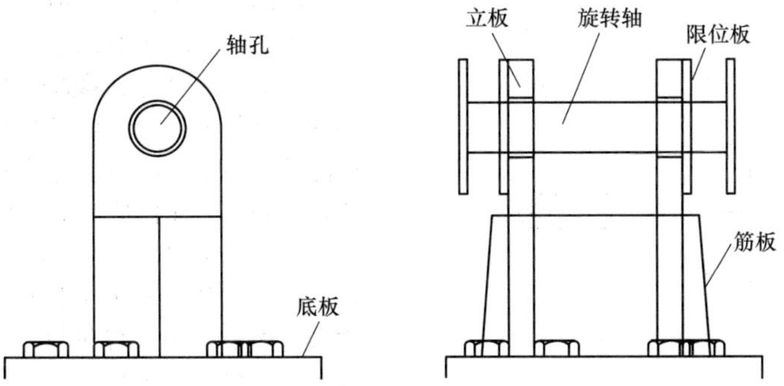

图 2　回转轴吊耳示意图

在进行转轮组装基础埋设时，预埋轴套座基础在混凝土中，半圆形轴套座利用螺栓把和在轴套座基础上。回转轴吊耳则安装在转轮轮毂体使用。

转轮翻身实施方法如下：

（1）将回转轴吊耳Ⅰ安装在轮毂体上，钢丝绳挂在回转轴吊耳立板外侧的旋转轴上，利用主桥式起重机缓慢将转轮吊离装配支座；再将回转轴吊耳Ⅱ置于半圆形轴套座上，吊耳立板中间的旋转轴涂抹黄油与半圆形轴套座接触，临时支撑稳当后将转轮吊上与之连接；吊钩缓慢移动及下落，将转轮平放，利用枕木、千斤顶临时固定，如图3所示。

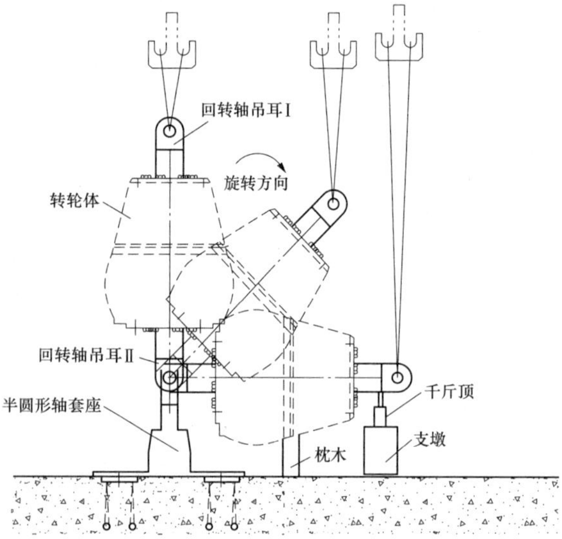

图3 转轮翻身平放布置图

（2）挂装回转轴吊耳Ⅱ钢丝绳，利用桥机将转轮水平移动，如图4所示。

图4 转轮平吊布置图

（3）将吊耳Ⅰ置于半圆形轴套座上，并拆除回转轴吊耳Ⅰ钢丝绳上。吊钩缓慢移动及上升，回转轴吊耳Ⅰ围绕半圆形轴套座缓慢旋转，完成转轮整体翻身；待转轮翻正后拆除回转轴吊耳Ⅰ，如图5所示。

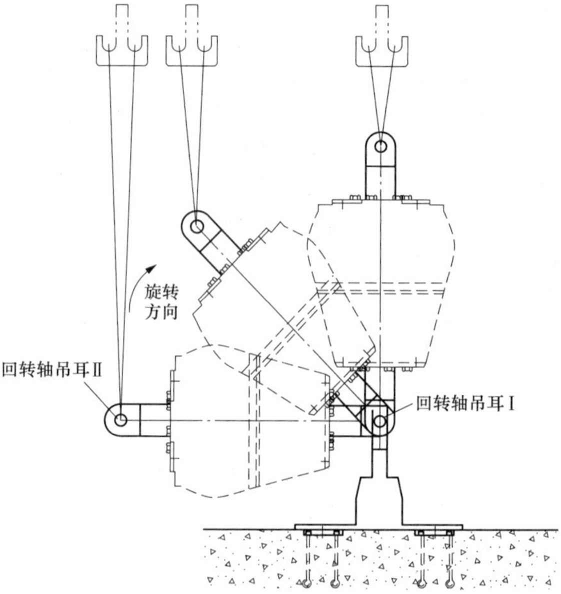

图5 转轮完成翻身旋转布置图

采用该技术进行转轮翻身，只需一名司机操作，操作难度小，钢丝绳受力更均匀，不会发生钢丝绳间交叉、憋劲、滑移。

该技术研究已获1项实用专利、2项外观专利。

（中国水利水电第五工程局有限公司
张龙 张志新 蒋佳驰 王开柱 吴霞）

哈尔滨电机厂有限责任公司2018年重点水电机组研制工程进展情况

（一）苏丹上阿特巴拉项目80MW机组

苏丹上阿特巴拉大坝枢纽工程是苏丹在建的第二大水电站枢纽工程，大坝总长13km，建成后将形成一个约30亿m^3库容的水库，灌溉面积达50万hm^2，可为700万人口解决灌溉用水问题，为300万人口提供饮用水保障，为上百万人提供电力供应，重要的是还能够减轻尼罗河两岸的洪水威胁和洪涝灾害，给当地百姓安居乐业创造一个坚实的臂膀。

苏丹当地时间2018年6月11日9时30分，哈电集团所属的哈尔滨电机厂有限责任公司（以下简称哈电电机公司）提供机组设备的苏丹上阿特巴拉水电项目最后一台机组——1号机组成功并网发电，并顺利完成额定负荷80MW运行，各项技术指标均达到合同要求。至此，哈电电机公司为该项目提供的4台机组全部投产发电。这极大缓解苏丹电力短缺问题，全国三分之一的人口将直接受益，并为即将在中国举办的中非合作论坛北京峰会献上了一份大礼。

该项目已经投运的4台机组运行情况良好，赢得了苏丹业主及德国监理工程师的认可和好评，为公司进一步开拓非洲水电市场奠定了坚实基础。

（二）黄登475MW混流式机组研制

黄登水电站位于云南省怒江州兰坪县境内，为澜沧江上游河段规划中的第5个梯级，其上游与托巴水电站衔接，下游梯级为大华桥水电站。电站机组单机容量为475MW，共4台。

2018年7月5日晚8点、7月12日下午5点，黄登水电站1、2号机组分别完成72小时试运行，振动、摆度、瓦温等各项指标优良，均顺利投入商业运行。从2017年4月初起，经过定子机座组装、定子装配整体耐压试验、转子吊装、机组有水调试等一系列工作，黄登水电站1、2号机顺利投入运行，得到了业主的高度认可。同时，2号机组是华能澜沧江水电装机容量突破20000MW的标志性机组。

（三）白鹤滩1000MW水轮发电机组研制

白鹤滩水电站是中国长江三峡集团有限公司开发的金沙江下游河段梯级的第二级电站，共安装16台混流式水轮发电机组，机组单机容量为1000MW，总装机容量达到16000MW，电站建成后，将仅次于三峡水电站，成为中国第二大水电站。哈电电机公司承制其中8台机组。

白鹤滩水电站机组为中高水头、中低转速、巨型混流式水轮发电机组。机组不仅运行水头高、变幅范围广，而且结构外形尺寸巨大。哈电电机公司从机组安全高效运行角度出发，重点针对巨型机组稳定性、水力开发、电磁、结构、绝缘技术、疲劳破坏和过渡过程、通风冷却试验及测试方法等方面进行科研攻关，攻克了多项世界性技术壁垒，推动着我国巨型水轮发电机组制造技术进一步走向成熟。2018年10月27日，白鹤滩世界首台百万水电机组导水机构验收仪式在哈电电机公司举行。该导水机构由7300个零部件组装而成，装配完成后高近8m，最大外圆直径13m，总重量达830t。为了将白鹤滩项目打造成精品工程，哈电机在吸收三峡、溪洛渡、向家坝等巨型机组导水机构的研制经验基础上，充分考虑改善机组高水头运行的稳定性，同时兼顾低水头出力发电的要求，重点以水轮机结构型式、重大部件结构创新为课题，进行了科研攻关，取得了导水机构顶盖、底环、导叶等关键部件的加工制造以及整体装配等多项世界性技术突破。2018年12月21日，哈电电机公司研制的白鹤滩电站右岸首台百万机组座环在地下厂房机坑内顺利整体吊装成功。该座环外径14.5m，最大长度（含大舌板）17.2m，高约4m，总重超过500t，是白鹤滩水轮机所有结构组件中单体重量最大的部件，也是水轮机结构组件中运输尺寸最大的部件。该座环的成功组焊并顺利吊装，为白鹤滩后续机组及项目的执行积累了宝贵的经验，也标志着白鹤滩水电站埋件安装进入了崭新的阶段。自白鹤滩项目执行以来，哈电电机公司始终秉承“严、细、实”的工作态度，以三峡集团“七个零”工作要求为标准，精细过程、精品结果，通过开展技术复查、合理配备资源、加强质量管控、统抓生产进度等措施，确保精品工程的实现。

（四）厄瓜多尔美纳斯水电站90MW冲击式水轮发电机组

美纳斯水电站位于厄瓜多尔阿苏艾省，安装3台单机容量为90MW的冲击式水轮发电机组。哈电电机公司负责提供3台水轮发电机组，以及调速器系统、励磁系统、机组自动化等，同时提供机组在线监测服务。

厄瓜多尔当地时间2018年4月27日，美纳斯水电站首台机组（厂内3号机组）一次性启动成功，机组振动、摆度等数据优良，满足ISO标准和合同规定要求。当地时间2018年10月24日，美纳斯水电项目3台机组全部并网发电。根据监测数据表明，机组摆度、振动数据良好，轴承瓦温满足技术规范要求，均达到优良标准。

厄瓜多尔美纳斯水电项目是哈电集团响应国家“一带一路”倡议以及高端装备制造产业加快“走出去”步伐的重点项目，是哈电集团进入南美市场的首个水电总承包项目，对于全面开拓南美市场具有重要的战略意义。主要发电设备水轮发电机组、励磁及调速器等系统均由哈电集团设计、制造、供货，其他辅助系统设备也均由中国制造厂商制造提供。

美纳斯水电项目3台机组顺利并网发电以及机组良好运行参数，不但验证了哈电集团优秀的产品设计能力和过硬的设备制造质量，也充分展现了总承包能力和卓越的海外项目工程管理水平。

（哈尔滨电机厂有限责任公司　刘保生）

白市水电厂机组振动区过大处理方案研究

白市水电厂安装3台单机容量为140MW的水轮发电机组。2015年1月9日至2月4日，电厂组织国网湖南省电力公司科学研究院分别在上游水位300、298、296m进行了机组稳定性测试。试验结果为在各个水头下，机组下导摆度、水导摆度在各个工况点均合格，但机组顶盖垂直振动在各个水头下、较大负荷区间内均存在超标现象，最大达到171μm（顶盖垂直振动国标限值为110μm，厂家规定的上限为150μm），机组在100～110MW负荷下运行时出现了机组、厂房楼板的间歇性振动，振动周期为0.8～1.1s，其中49.9m水头时机组、厂房间歇性振动最为明显。为确保机组安全运行，电厂向网调报备的机组振动区在25～85MW、100～110MW，经网调批复，单机负荷按照30MW、110～140MW控制，负荷调整时按照AGC/AVC避振策略尽快穿越机组振动区达到设定负荷。白市电厂为华中网调直调电厂，机组振动区过宽将直接影响网调有功功率调节，机组长期穿越振动区运行及厂房间歇性振动现象，存在很大安全风险。因此，寻求改善机组、厂房的减振措施并进行有效处理，从而优化机组振动区、减小厂房间歇性振动便显得非常必要和迫切。

为了查明机组振动区过宽的原因，电厂组织国网湖南省电力公司科学研究院、五凌电力科技有限公司等相关单位开展了不同水头下的稳定性复核试验、大轴补气阀拆装试验等一系列试验研究，对机组振动问题进行了前期的探索和分析。2017年6月16日、2017年8月22日两次组织中国电建中南勘测设计研究院有限公司、湖南省电力科学研究院、浙江富春江水电设备有限公司、哈尔滨电机厂有限责任公司、武汉大学等多家单位的专家召开了“关于白市水电厂机组及厂房振动专家咨询会”，通过对试验数据的论证、分析，明确了引起水轮机顶盖垂直振动超标、厂房振动的主要振源是水力因素，并就如何改善机组振动区及厂房间歇性振动提出了处理方案和建议。

（一）主要研究内容

项目的主要研究内容为：①顶盖真空破坏阀强迫补气对机组振动的影响分析；②顶盖无叶区强迫补气对机组振动的影响分析；③大轴补气阀拆除后对机组振动的影响分析；④改变转轮泄压通道、顶盖补强的可行性研究论证；⑤固定导叶修形的可行性论证研究。

为了排查振动原因，决定在2号机组开展以下三项试验：

（1）顶盖真空破坏阀处强迫补气对机组、厂房减振效果验证试验。在顶盖真空破坏阀自然补气和在真空破坏阀位置强迫补气两种条件下，测试机组、厂房振动情况，确认通过顶盖真空破坏阀强迫补气对降低机组、厂房振动位移幅值的可行性。

（2）顶盖无叶区强迫补气对机组、厂房减振效果验证试验。在机组正常状态运行、通过在顶盖无叶区钻孔强迫补气两种条件下，测试机组、厂房振动情况，确认通过顶盖无叶区钻孔强迫补气对降低机组、厂房振动位移幅值的可行性。

（3）机组大轴补气阀对机组、厂房振动影响验证试验。在机组大轴补气阀正常运行、拆除大轴补气阀两种条件下，测试机组、厂房振动情况，确认大轴补气阀对机组、厂房振动的影响。

上述三项试验可分解为6小项，其中顶盖真空破坏阀自然补气、顶盖无叶区无补气状态、大轴补气阀自然补气3小项试验条件相同，可同时进行。

试验测点布置了蜗壳进口、无叶区、尾水管进口水压脉动，顶盖下水压，储气罐气压，下导X、Y摆度，水导X、Y摆度，上机架、下机架、定子机座、顶盖径向水平振动（振幅），下机架、顶盖垂直振动（振幅），下机架径向水平振动（加速度），下机架垂直振动（加速度），顶盖径向水平振动（加速度），顶盖垂直水平振动（加速度），顶盖把合螺栓处振动（加速度），发电机层振动噪声声压，水车室振动噪声声强，发电机层GCB处竖直向振动（振幅），发电机层吊物孔处竖直向振动（振幅），机组有功率等25个；其中，振动有采用振幅和加速度测量两种方法。

为增强试验对比性，进行各项试验时，上游水位、下游水位尽可能保持一致，机组段水头偏差控制在1m范围内。

2号机组在完成测点布置、试验条件满足要求后开机并网，在20、30、40、50、60、70、80、90、100、110、120、130、140MW工况点附近稳定2～3min，记录各测点数据。

（二）试验结果及数据分析

（1）顶盖真空破坏阀处强迫补气试验结果表明：机组负荷在50MW及以下时，顶盖真空破坏阀强迫补气对顶盖水平/垂直振动、吊物孔垂直振动、GCB楼板垂直振动以及蜗壳进口、尾水进口压力脉动均有较大改善；机组负荷在60～100MW时补气对水导摆度、顶盖垂直振动、GCB楼板垂直振动有劣化；机组负荷在50MW及以上时补气对顶盖水平/垂直振动稍有改善，对其他测点影响不明显。

（2）顶盖无叶区强迫补气试验结果表明：顶盖无叶区强迫补气在全负荷段内对顶盖水平/垂直振动、吊物孔垂直振动、GCB楼板垂直振动以及蜗壳进口压力脉动均有较大改善，对尾水进口水压脉动、无叶区水压脉动影响较小。同时，顶盖无叶区强迫补气对80～100MW工况下的厂房振动改善明显，特别对降低25～45Hz的中高频振动降幅明显。

（3）大轴补气阀拆除后试验结果表明：大轴补气阀拆除对机组整体振动影响不大，顶盖垂直振动在80～100MW 工况降低 10～20 μm；厂房振动在80MW 以下负荷时稍有降低，在 80MW 以上负荷时有所增加；机组下导摆度在 90MW 以上负荷工况有所降低，降幅较小，机组水导摆度在 60MW 以上时有大幅降低，降幅基本在 30μm 以上；尾水进口压力脉动、无叶区水压脉动整体看有降幅，蜗壳进口压力脉动变化不明显。

（三）处理情况

通过以上试验，发现采用顶盖无叶区强迫补气对改善机组振动较好，但实施难度大。最后通过机组有限元分析，决定在 2 号机组顶盖内进行顶盖筋板加固处理。顶盖筋板材料为 Q235B，加强筋板用 t16 Q235B 钢板，与顶盖现有筋板进行焊接。

顶盖筋板加固处理后进行相应试验，试验结果如下：

（1）顶盖刚度得到提升，振动明显改善，水平、垂直振动（振幅）最大幅值降幅分别达 20.8%、55.7%，水平、垂直振动（加速度）最大幅值降幅分别达 61.3%、41.1%。

（2）顶盖加强后，对水导轴承的支撑作用得到提升，水导摆度明显改善，X、Y 摆度最大幅值降幅分别达 26.6%、30.8%。

（3）上机架径向水平、定子机座径向水平、下机架垂直、发电机层 GCB 处竖直向、发电机层吊物孔处竖直向振动（振幅）也下降，其最大值降幅分别为 7.8%、12.8%、32.5%、12.8%、18.4%，这可能与原泄压孔恢复有关系。

（4）在当前水头下，全负荷范围内顶盖垂直及水平振动，均满足国家标准要求。

（五凌电力白市水电厂
曾平　安元　汤鸿　罗世材）

溧阳抽水蓄能机组推力外循环系统异常振动故障分析及处理

溧阳抽水蓄能电站安装 6 台单机容量为 250MW 的抽水蓄能机组。机组为哈尔滨电机厂有限责任公司生产，推力轴承油冷却采用外循环。外循环油泵为三螺杆泵，型号为 LPQ140N1IRYP，工作转速 1495r/min，最大差压 1.6MPa（16bar）。机组调试期间出现推力外循环系统异常振动故障，油泵和管道振动大，并伴有撞击声，噪声超标，管道出口手动阀手轮脱落，严重影响机组安全运行。

为寻找振动故障原因，2017 年 3 月 24 日，现场对 4 号机组 2 号推力外循环油泵及其管道的振动和噪声进行测试试验。在机组处于停机热备工况，油泵正常启动，在额定转速 1490r/min 下运行稳定，振动较小。机组转速由零升速至额定，油泵振动、管道振动不断增大，并伴随撞击声。机组升速到额定转速 300r/min 时泵的轴向振动 4.8mm/s、水平振动 7.4mm/s，管道振动 25.3mm/s，噪声也由 91.3dB 增大到 103.6dB。

机组停机后推力外循环油泵采用变频启动，油泵设定初始转速为 800r/min，油流量为 260m³/h，满足设计要求。分别在机组停机和机组运行两个工况下以 50r/min 为间隔逐渐提高油泵转速至额定值。两个工况下油泵变频升速过程中各测点振动变化趋势如图 1 和图 2 所示，试验数据如表 1 所示。可以看出机组停机状态下，随着油泵转速的升高油泵振动和管道振动增大，但增大幅度很小；机组运行状态下，随着油泵转速的升高油泵振动和管道振动大幅增大，并且管道振动增大较大；管道振动在转速 1200r/min 存在一个峰值，其振动频谱，1 倍频分量很小，以 8 倍频分量为主。

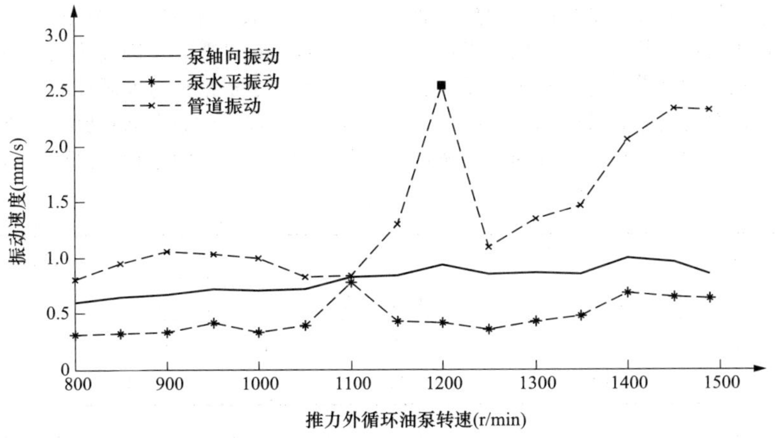

图 1　机组停机工况下油泵升速过程中各测点振动变化趋势

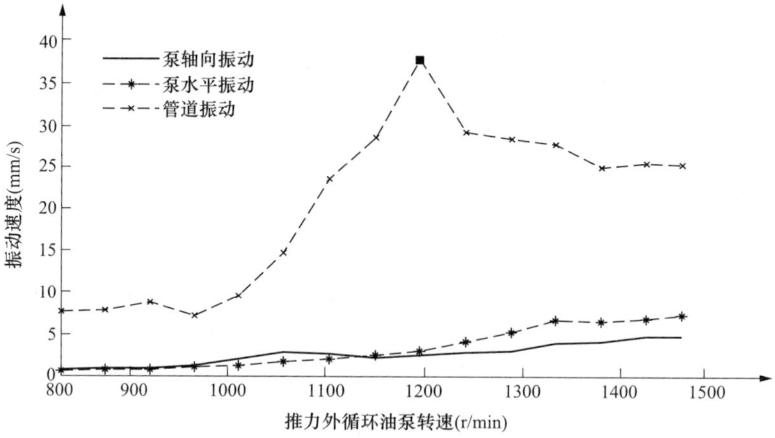

图2　机组运行时油泵升速过程中各测点振动变化趋势

表1　泵以额定频率运行时振动和噪声数据

机组工况	油泵转速 (r/min)	轴向振动 (mm/s)	水平振动 (mm/s)	管道振动 (mm/s)	噪声（dB）
停机	800	0.6	0.3	0.8	85.2
	1490	0.9	0.6	2.3	91.3
机组运行	800	0.8	0.6	7.7	87.5
	1490	4.8	7.4	25.3	103.6

机组运行状态下，油泵水平振动达7.4mm/s，管道振动达25.37.4mm/s，油泵在工频运行振动较大，管道振动幅值远大于油泵振动。据振动频谱分析，管道与油泵的振动频谱分布一致，1倍频分量较小，主要是以4X、8X和12X等倍频分量为主。由此分析，油泵和管道振动主要是由于泵内部流体力造成。

液体在泵内流动时，在一定条件下会出现空化现象。为了避免螺杆泵空化现象的发生，泵的安装应在距离油箱液面一定高度范围之内，否则易造成泵的空化，并导致泵及管路系统的振动和噪声。

溧阳抽水蓄能电站推力外循环油泵高压力降，液流在泵和管道中易产生气液两相的空化现象。机组运行时，推力头及镜板在油中旋转，搅起泡沫，导致油内挟附的气体较多；油泵运行时，其吸油腔内产生一定负压，油进入后随着压力的降低，油中的空气被释放并作为微气泡出现；当油流通过运行中的螺杆泵的螺杆啮合区进入油泵压油腔时，这些微气泡突然暴露于较高的压力中，受到周围液体的压缩，其中一些迅速溃灭，此时，产生极大的压强。当这个过程发生在固体边界附近时，边界面就受到强烈的冲击作用，产生振动和噪声。

机组外循环系统的管道振动与油泵振动频谱一致，管道振动远大于油泵本身振动是由于管道刚度不足，可以通过增大刚度和减小激振力方法解决。油泵在900r/min转速下变频运行，降低了激振力，油泵和管道振动降低，有利于安全运行。经测试，油泵在900r/min转速下油泵油流量为260m^3/h，能够满足机组运行设计要求，因此进行了油泵变频运行改造。表2给出了机组推力外循环油泵改造前后下导瓦和推力瓦瓦温稳定试验数据对比。改造后，瓦温稳定，符合要求。油泵变频运行能保证机组安全稳定运行。

表2　机组瓦温数据

工况	下导瓦最高瓦温（℃）		推力瓦最高瓦温（℃）	
	发电工况	抽水工况	发电工况	抽水工况
工频运行	62.77	69.05	61.75	61.80
变频运行	63.12	69.55	62.6	62.4

机组推力外循环油泵进行变频改造后不仅解决了油泵及管道振动大、噪声大的问题，而且能耗大大降

低，油泵功率由原来的 120kW 降低至 51kW。每台机组按年运行 7000h、0.36 元/(kW·h) 计算，年总节电效益达 17 万元，效益明显。

（江苏方天电力技术有限公司
马运翔　彭辉　吴建标　曹扬　殷翔）

喜河水电厂 1 号机组上端轴同轴度偏心分析处理

喜河水电厂安装 3 台单机容量为 60MW 的轴流转桨式机组。机组由东方电气集团东方电机有限公司生产制造。该机组发电机为具有上导轴承的半伞型结构，其上端轴下端连接在转子上端面上、中部有热套安装的轴领，轴领的下部为上导轴承滑转子。1 号机投产后运行，上导轴承运行摆度偏大、温度偏高、油槽甩油。经加装接油槽和下降油位等措施，甩油现象有所减小，但随着机组运行摆度及振动的变化，仍有少量甩油现象。

2016 年 1 月，该机组进行 A 级检修，盘车检查调整轴线，包括上导轴承在内各测点摆度都严格控制，都达到规范要求；但机组启动试运行发现，监测装置的上导轴承运行摆度超出标准要求。鉴于上导轴承运行摆度监测位置与盘车时摆度测量的位置不同，前者在轴领上端加工面，后者在轴领下段工作面即滑转子上，因此，打开上导轴承盖，分别在上导轴领上端加工面和滑转子的上、中、下部架设百分表（见图 1)，同时在上端轴顶端处架设百分表，在机组低转速情况下测量摆度。各点摆度如表 1 所示，轴领上端加工面处的摆度明显偏大。

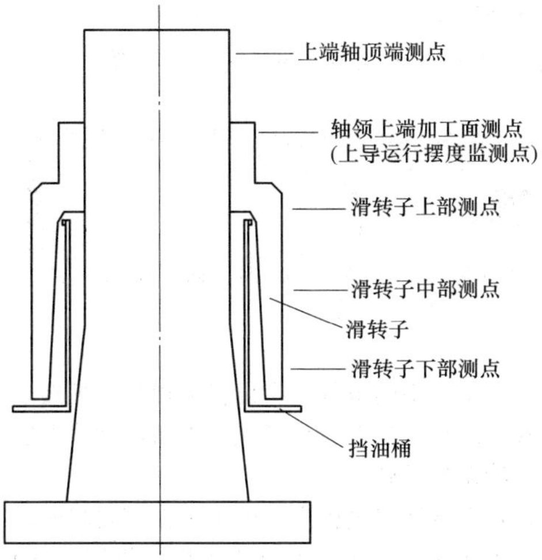

图 1　上端轴结构及测点布置图

表 1　低转速下上端轴各部位摆度

测量部位	X 方向	Y 方向	备注
上端轴顶端	0.11mm	0.12mm	
轴领上端加工面	0.51mm	0.58mm	轴号 3 点摆度最大，说明中心向轴号 7 点偏
滑转子上部	0.07mm	0.08mm	
滑转子中部	0.06mm	0.05mm	
滑转子下部	0.05mm	0.05mm	

对上导轴领肩部宽度进行测量，轴号 1～8 处分别为 114.20、114.20、114.30、114.20、114.22、114.16、114.14、114.18，最大偏差处轴号 3 点为 114.30mm，7 点为 114.14mm，从数据的趋势上也可判断轴线中心偏向了轴号 7 点。

初步确认上导轴领存在偏心问题后，又在机组变转速和稳定性试验时对上导摆度进行对比监测，上导轴领上端加工面及上端轴顶端分别用监测摆度探头，滑转子设百分表。监测显示结果，与低转速测得的摆度情况基本一致，上端轴顶端摆度和滑转子摆度分别在 0.23mm 和 0.10mm 左右，都较小，而轴领上端加工面摆度达 0.50～0.80mm，明显偏大。另外，实测挡油桶底部和主轴间隙存在 1mm 偏心。

由此可见，上端轴上导轴领的确存在同轴度偏心问题，决定返厂处理。

上端轴返厂进行复测，确定上导轴领滑转子直径加工余量为 1.5mm。通过复核计算，滑转子外径缩小后，对瓦承载能力及温度无不良影响，但原有调整块不可用，需重新加工一套。

1 号机组在 A 修时，处理了上端轴同轴度偏心，并为了消除甩油现象，在挡油桶上部端面加焊了宽度为 3mm 内部挡油环板。A 修后，该机组在不同工况下进行了稳定性状况测试，振动和摆度都合格，上导轴承在变转速、变励磁、变负荷时，X、Y 的最大摆度为 116、112μm，不再偏大超标；同时，机组油槽甩油现象也消除。此次上端轴同轴度偏心处理达到故障消除效果。

（陕西汉江投资开发有限公司喜河水力
发电厂　田峰）

仙居抽水蓄能电站可逆式抽水蓄能机组底环安装新技术

通常，可逆式抽水蓄能机组水泵水轮机的机坑里衬上管口直径比底环外径小，而底环安装必须在座环机加工合格后方可吊入机坑进行。这存在蜗壳混凝土浇筑后，上部工作需在座环机加工结束并完成底环吊装后才能进行，从而影响机坑里衬上部的安装和混凝土浇筑进度问题。浙江仙居抽水蓄能电站，坑里衬上管口直径5100mm，底环外径6524mm，其座环直径达6500mm，机加工一般需要30天左右。因总体机电安装工期偏紧，承担该电站机组安装的中国水利水电第五工程局有限公司研制了一套可逆式抽水蓄能机组水泵水轮机底环安装新技术，形成了新工法并成功实施，实现了底环提前吊入机坑，座环机加工工作与机坑里衬上部土建混凝土浇筑施工并行作业，从而缩短了工期，提高了效益。

该技术工艺流程为：施工准备→现场制作及安装临时支撑平台→水泵水轮机底环吊入机坑悬置固定→水泵水轮机座环机加工、水机预埋件施工及土建混凝土浇筑。主要创新点：

（1）首次研究可逆式抽水蓄能电站水泵水轮机底环设备安装施工新工艺，研发并设计相应的专用施工平台，并成功应用于工程实践。

（2）优化了抽水蓄能电站水泵水轮机底环安装工艺，改变底环吊装、座环机加工、机坑里衬渐变段之间的安装流程，实现土建浇筑施工与座环机加工及底环安装并行作业。

（3）采用自主研发设计的机组底环支撑平台，将底环提前吊入机坑固定，提高机组设备安装施工的效率，节约施工成本，效果显著。

研发的底环临时支撑平台，见图1，安装在机坑里衬圆周方向上，由8个单元斜支撑组成，选择I25b和I16b工字钢为制作支撑材料，上铺ϕ25钢筋。

仙居抽水蓄能电站4台机组成功应用该技术，节约工期30～40天。研究成果获得实用新型专利1项，填补了国内同行业的技术空白。

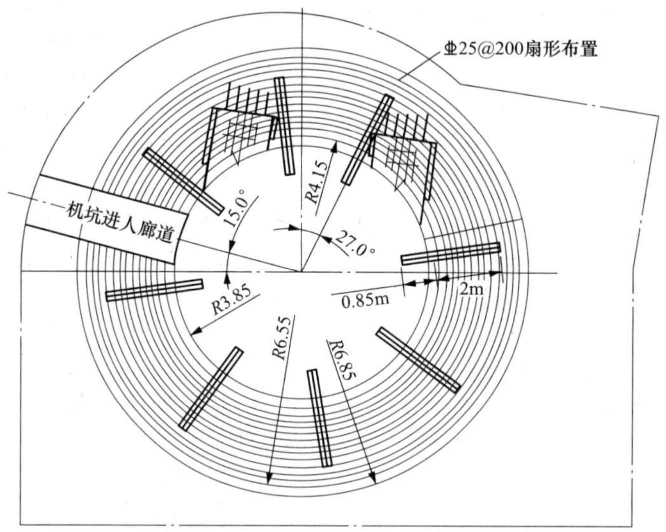

图1　底环支撑平台安装俯视图

（中国水利水电第五工程局有限公司　姜如洋　袁幸朝）

电　气

向家坝水电站带状态监测和断路器合闸闭锁功能的地线管理系统开发

电气一次设备停电检修时，正确挂接地线是一项非常重要的安全技术保障措施，但目前存在如下问题：

（1）检修中的电气一次设备装设的接地线远方无法监视，运行人员对装设了地线设备和地线的状态无法直观清楚的了解。

（2）设备检修过程中，由于工作需要临时取下接地线，工作完成后却由于疏忽而忘记将接地线挂回，中控室人员也无法第一时间获知地线的挂接情况而未提前提醒，可能会对在该线路上进行其他作业的人员造成伤害。

(3) 恢复送电过程中，如果因人为疏忽未完全拆除地线，而10kV断路器无闭锁功能可能造成带地线合闸等电气设备安全事故。

向家坝电厂全厂生产区域共有22个供电点，每个供电点每年度均需常规检修一次，停电做安全措施和拆除临时安全设施恢复运行的操作量很大，如果全靠人员自身的作业行为进行控制，存在潜在的误操作安全风险。因此，向家坝水力发电厂开展了本项目，通过自主研发带挂接信号反馈的新型三相接地线和全厂地线管理平台，以实现远程实时监视厂用电系统检修时地线挂接情况，同时利用现地布置的PLC输出对应10kV断路器的合闸闭锁触点，从根本上杜绝发生厂用电检修转运行时带地线合闸的严重安全生产事故。

(一) 主要成果及技术创新点

(1) 自主设计制作地线专用接地桩和新型接地线。接地线钳子本体静触头内侧上设置有弹簧微动开关，接地桩敷设位置反馈信号线，当接地线挂接后，接地线静触头处的微动开关动作，送出地线挂接信号。

(2) 一个400V供电点布置一套现地PLC，采用西门子S7-200-226CN，用于采集400V母线和10kV干式变（高、低压侧）三相接地线挂接信号。现地PLC实时上送地线挂接的装拆变位信号，同时当任意一相地线挂接到位后现地PLC驱动开出继电器送出闭锁触点至相应10kV馈线开关合闸回路，达到防止带地线合闸的目的。

(3) 自主设计全厂地线管理系统，与现地PLC通过以太网通信，实时采集地线挂接信号，用于远方监视。当地线挂接或者取下时，系统均发出语音报警和事件记录，提醒运行人员立即检查并及时恢复。

(二) 实施效果及应用推广情况

该系统和专用接地线在现场使用过程中，地线管理系统实现了远方直观实时监视厂用电设备停电检修时地线挂接情况，在地线挂接或取下时能发出语音报警和事件记录，同时现地布置的PLC输出闭锁触点送至对应10kV断路器合闸闭锁回路，达到了闭锁10kV断路器带地线合闸的目的，从根本上杜绝发生带地线合闸的严重安全生产事故。

该研发成果可推广用于电力行业内所有需要进行挂接地线进行检修的单位，实现全厂地线的实时显示，有效防止带地线合闸，杜绝人身伤害事故发生。

（向家坝水力发电厂　陈保臻）

苗尾水电站电气一次设计

(一) 工程概况

苗尾水电站装机4×350MW，多年平均发电量59.99亿kW·h。电站送出线路路径方案因需穿越三江并流自然保护区，技施阶段重新调整，由500kV出线1回至大华桥电站、预留3个500kV出线间隔，调整为500kV出线3回，1回至大华桥电站（线路长度为56km、导线截面面积4×400mm³），2回接入滇西北至广东±800kV特高压直流输电新松换流站（线路长度为105km、导线截面面积4×400mm³），并预留1个500kV出线间隔场地。

(二) 电气主接线

采用发电机—变压器单元接线，发电机出口均装设断路器。500kV侧高压配电装置采用GIS，接线方案采用3串3/2断路器、1串双断路器和1个母线高压并联电抗器回路的混合接线方式，共12个断路器间隔。该期出线三回，另一回为备用500kV出线，500kV侧设置一组150Mvar（3×50 Mvar）母线高压并联电抗器。

(三) 主要电气设备简介

1. 发电机　为立轴半伞式，型号为SF350-56/14000，额定容量389MVA/350MW，额定电压18kV，额定电流12477A，额定功率因数0.9，飞轮力矩100480t·m²，全空冷，直轴同步电抗不饱和值为1.009、饱和值为0.865，直轴瞬变电抗X'_{du}=0.308、X'_{ds}=0.289，直轴超瞬变电抗X''_{du}=0.224、X''_{ds}=0.206，交轴同步电抗X_{qu}/X''_{qu}=0.697/0.232，绝缘等级为F级，绕组支路数/连接方式为4支路/Y。

2. 主变压器及高压并联电抗器　采用单相变压器，共设置13台（1台备用）型式为户外、铜芯双绕组、强迫油循环水冷却、无励磁调压升压电力变压器，采用组合分配式泡沫喷雾灭火系统。主变压器型号DSP-13000/550；额定容量130MVA；额定电压$550/\sqrt{3}$-2×2.5%/18kV；短路阻抗14%；联结组标号为单相I、I_0三相组YN，d11；中性点直接接地。

高压并联电抗器为单相油浸式自然冷却并联电抗器，采用组合分配式泡沫喷雾灭火系统。其额定容量为50Mvar；额定电压，高压侧$550/\sqrt{3}$ kV，中性点侧126kV；额定频率50Hz；联结组标号为单相I三相Y_0；调压方式为无励磁调压；中性点直接接地；冷却方式为油浸自冷（ONAN）。

3. 500kV气体绝缘金属封闭开关设备（GIS）　额定电压550kV，额定电流5000A，额定短路开断电流及持续时间为 63kA/3s，额定峰值耐受电流为171kA，额定短路时间为3s，SF_6 气体年漏气率不大于0.5%，外壳防护等级为IP5X，断路器型式为 SF_6 气体绝缘，断路器操作机构为液压弹簧，母线导体材料为铝合金，断路器隔室 SF_6 气体压力 0.5MPa。

4. 发电机出口电压设备　离相封闭母线额定电压为20kV，主母线额定电流为16000A，分支母线额定电流为4000A，电制动回路母线及变压器△连接回路额定电流为10000A，导体材料为铝，1min工频耐受电压为50kA（湿试）/68kA（干试），额定短时耐受电流（有效值）/时间为125kA/2s，额定峰值耐受电流为315kA。

发电机断路器型号为FKG1F，额定电压24kV，额定电流13500A，额定短路开断电流（系统源）为100kA（直流分量≥65%），额定短路开断电流（发电机源）为80kA（直流分量≥110%），额定短路关合电流（峰值）为274kA。

（四）主要电气设备布置

发电厂房引水式地面厂房。主厂房安装4台350MW立式半伞式水轮发电机及其附属设备，机组间距30m；发电机主引线从中间层+Y轴偏+X 25°引出，中性点设备柜布置在第三象限，从－Y轴偏－X轴40°引出。发电机电压设备布置在上游副厂房各层。

13台500kV主变压器均布置在上游副厂房1324.30m高程户外平台上，相邻单相变压器间设置防火隔墙。变压器低压侧与封闭母线相连，高压侧与GIS管道母线相连。变压器中性点设备布置在相邻变压器隔墙上，用铝管母线相连；中性点采用铝绞线与铝管母线连接成“Y”形，并经电流互感器接地。单相主变压器间隔长度为10m，深度为8.5m。

550kV GIS开关站布置于上游副厂房地面第二层1332.30m高程室内，GIS室高15.7m、宽19.18m、长156m，布置GIS本体及汇控柜。550kV出线场设备布置在GIS开关站屋顶1348.0m高程。

500kV并联电抗器及其附属设备均布置在上游副厂房1324.30m高程户外平台上，相邻电抗器间设置防火隔墙。并联电抗器高压侧采用油/SF_6 套管通过GIS分支母线与GIS设备连接，中性点采用铝绞线与铝管母线连接成“Y”形，并经电流互感器直接接地。

10kV高压厂用电设备安装在上游副厂房1324.30m高程；0.4kV上游、下游公用电设备分别布置在上游及下游副厂房1315.60m高程；0.4kV自用电设备及0.4kV检修变布置在下游副厂房1315.60m高程，检修母线槽布置在主厂房中间层1310.00m高程下游侧；0.4kV照明用电设备布置在上游副厂房1315.60m高程。

电站值守楼布置端副厂房内，端副厂房电缆通道经安装场段电缆廊道与上游副厂房电缆层连接。

（五）厂用电系统

电站厂用电采用10kV和0.4kV二级电压供电。

10kV供电系统分为四段母线，从1、2、3号发电机各引接一组高压厂用变压器，分别接至厂用电工作母线Ⅰ、Ⅱ、Ⅲ段上，三段工作母线之间装设联络断路器并设置备自投装置；另从拟永久保留的施工变电所引接1回10kV进线和柴油发电机组（经升压至10kV后）接入母线Ⅳ段，从Ⅳ段母线上出线3回分别与Ⅰ、Ⅱ、Ⅲ段母线联络，作为此三段厂用电工作母线的备用电源及保安电源。

0.4kV低压厂用电系统共设置了机组自用电、上游公用电、下游公用电、照明用电、检修用电及坝区用电系统。除检修用电0.4kV母线为单母线接线，采用插接式母线槽外，其余0.4kV母线均分为A、B两段，每段电源均分别取自10kV工作母线，经10/0.4kV配电变接入，A、B两段设置备自投装置。

坝区厂用变压器高压侧设置两组进线柜，每组两面10kV开关柜，分别为真空断路器柜、避雷器及电压互感器柜。坝区用电系统共设置2台变压器，电源分别引自10kV厂用电Ⅰ、Ⅲ段工作母线，另将坝区柴油发电机组接入0.4kV B段母线，作为备用及保安电源。

另在灌溉取水管交通洞洞口设置2台箱式变电站，电源分别引自10kV厂用电Ⅱ、Ⅲ段工作母线。

（六）接地设计

电站500kV系统中性点为直接接地，属大电流接地系统，最大接地故障不对称电流有效值为10.3kA，接地电阻设计要求值为0.47Ω。

由于接地网地位升大于2000V，按规范要求重点做好电站均压和电位隔离措施，厂房区域接地体采用导电性能好、耐腐蚀强的铜包钢绞线、镀铜圆钢，500kV电气设备区域接地体采用铜排。

全电站由坝前水库水下接地网、坝后接地网、溢洪道接地网、厂房接地网、尾水渠接地网、厂前区接地网组成。同时在坝前水库末端左右岸边、尾水右岸末端、尾水渠左端部水下分别设置了3、1、3个垂直深井接地极（采用底孔爆裂并压力灌注物理型降阻剂）。

经云南电力试验研究院现场测试，苗尾水电站接地电阻测量值为0.4241Ω，跨步电位差最大值为2.14V，接触电位差最大值为0.447V，满足设计及规范要求。

（中国电建集团华东勘测设计研究院有限公司
郑珊珊　任洪涛）

广州抽水蓄能电站自动发电控制系统的关键技术简介

广州抽水蓄能电站（以下简称广蓄）B厂上位机监控系统于2016年初完成改造，其AVC系统同步投入运行。新AVC系统经过长时间的静态和动态试验，并结合调度侧要求和机组运行特性，遵循最优制的原则设计出合理的控制策略、分配策略和安全策略。经过一年多的运行实践，新系统的AVC在稳定性、响应时间、人机交互等方面都有很大地提高。现将其关键技术简介如下。

1. AVC系统配置结构　电厂监控系统AVC子站接收来自调度侧AVC主站系统/电站侧下发的全厂控制目标（电厂高压母线电压、全厂总无功等），并按照控制策略、分配原则和安全策略等将无功/电压调节指令分配给每台机组，机组向其发电机的励磁系统发送增减磁信号以调节其发电机无功出力，使电厂变高侧母线电压或者各机组无功出力向目标值逼进，形成电厂侧AVC子站系统与调度主站系统的闭环控制，实现全厂多机组电压/无功的自动控制。

2. AVC系统控制策略

（1）恒无功控制：根据调度层/电站层给定的全厂总无功直接控制参与AVC机组的无功目标值。具体的公式为$Q_{AVC}=Q_{SET}-Q_{\overline{AVC}}$，式中$Q_{SET}$为全厂无功设定值，$Q_{\overline{AVC}}$为不参加AVC机组所发无功之和，$Q_{AVC}$为全厂无功AVC分配值。

（2）母线电压控制和电压曲线控制：根据调度层/电站层设置的母线电压目标值或当前时段的电压曲线值，与实发电压值作比较，如果差值超过死区，则通过“电压调差系数”计算出需要调节的无功值，进而设定可调机组的无功功率，使其维持母线电压在“死区限值”范围内。具体的公式为$Q_{AVC}=Q_{ACT}+\Delta V\cdot K_{VNOR}-Q_{\overline{AVC}}$，式中$Q_{ACT}$为全厂无功实发值，$\Delta V$为实际母线电压与给定电压值偏差/母线电压增量，$K_{VNOR}$为母线电压在正常电压值范围内的调压系数。

当母线电压值出现突变或异常时，按紧急调压系数进行调节。具体的公式为$Q_{AVC}=Q_{ACT}+\Delta V\cdot K_{VEMG}-Q_{\overline{AVC}}$，式中$K_{VEMG}$为母线电压在正常电压值范围外的调压系数。

广蓄B厂，根据调度侧控制方式的要求和机组的实际情况采用了母线电压控制为主，恒无功控制为辅的控制方式。

3. AVC系统分配策略　蓄能机组在发电、抽水、发电调相、抽水调相四种工况均可以发出/吸收无功来调节电压。但各工况的机组运行特性不同，其无功调节能力也不同，所以AVC分配时应充分考虑机组P-Q（有功-无功）曲线限制。

针对多机组、多工况运行状态，将全厂无功AVC分配值在满足机组P-Q限制的情况下合理分配各机组，可采用的分配算法有等功率因数原则、无功功率等比例原则、相似调整裕度、动态优化原则等，具体的分配逻辑如下：

（1）等功率因数原则：$Q_{iAVC}=Q_{AVC}\cdot\dfrac{P_i}{\sum_{i=1}^{n}P_i}$　（$i=1, 2, \cdots, n$），式中n为参加AVC的机组数；P_i为参加AVC的第i台机组的当前有功实发值；$\sum_{i=1}^{n}P_i$为参加AVC机组当前有功实发值之和，Q_{iAVC}为AVC分配到第i台参加AVC机组的无功。

（2）无功功率等比例原则：$Q_{iAVC}=Q_{AVC}\cdot\dfrac{Q_{iMax}}{\sum_{i=1}^{n}Q_{iMax}}$　（$i=1, 2, \cdots, n$），式中Q_{iMax}为参加AVC的第i台机组的最大无功容量，$\sum_{i-1}^{n}Q_{iMax}$为参加AVC机组的最大无功容量之和。

（3）相似调整裕度原则：$Q_{iAVC}=Q_{AVC}\cdot\dfrac{Q_{iMax}-Q_i}{\sum_{i=1}^{n}(Q_{iMax}-Q_i)}$　（$i=1, 2, \cdots, n$），式中Q_{iMax}为参加AVC的第i台机组的无功调整裕度，$\sum_{i=1}^{n}Q_{iMax}$为参加AVC机组当前无功调整裕度之和。

（4）动态优化原则：$Q_{iAVC}=Q_{AVC}\cdot\dfrac{F_i}{\sum_{i=1}^{n}F_i}$　（$i=1, 2, \cdots, n$），式中F_i为参加AVC的第i台机组的当前优化系数，$\sum_{i=1}^{n}F_i$为参加AVC机组的当前优化系数之和。

这四种分配方式都是经过多年运行检验的成熟的、可行的、可靠的分配原则，可根据电厂需求选用任一项。广蓄电厂根据机组的性能和对响应速度的要求，采用的是无功功率等比例分配原则。

4. AVC系统安全策略

（1）AVC输出闭锁策略：当AVC子站检测到主站下发的命令非法时［如主站下发的目标值越限（上下限、最多调节量）或控制方向与实际不符］，AVC系统应能闭锁AVC输出并保持原设定值。

（2）AVC增磁、减磁闭锁策略：当高压母线电压、厂用母线电压、机组有功/无功功率越闭锁限值，定子电流/电压、转子电流越最大限值时，AVC系统应能相应地闭锁增磁/减磁控制。

(3) AVC自动退出策略：当无机组参加AVC、母线电压测量值异常、系统电压振荡等情况时全站AVC自动退出，并给出告警信号；当机组无功不可调、机组LCU故障、机组励磁装置故障、机组无功测量品质坏等情况时机组AVC自动退出，并给出告警信号。

(广州蓄能水电厂　梁彦　冯凌云)

向家坝水电站厂用电系统故障计算及继电保护整定计算系统开发

继电保护定值的正确性是装置能够正常发挥作用和保证电力系统安全运行的前提。传统的做法是借助PSASP等软件的仿真故障计算结果手动计算整定值，该方式工作量大，耗时长、难以避免人为错误。现有的某些电厂的厂用电继电保护整定计算软件存在功能单一、用户界面不友好、不能适应系统设备变化和整定原则变化、计算速度慢等问题。

向家坝水力发电厂与华中科技大学合作，成功开发了“向家坝电站厂用电系统故障计算及继电保护整定计算系统”。该系统是一个基于网络数据库实现全图形化操作的继电保护高级应用软件，主要用于10kV及400V厂用电系统的故障分析、继电保护定值的整定和管理，实现了接线图管理、参数管理、供电方式管理、故障分析、保护装置整定计算、定值单和计算报告生成、定值单审批等功能。在设备参数和供电方式配置完成后，全站1700多套保护装置和脱扣器仅需半小时即可完成整定计算。

(一) 技术创新点

(1) 实现了接线图管理、整定计算等全部功能的图形化操作，实现了厂用电系统故障计算和继电保护整定计算的全过程、快速、自动化计算。

(2) 提出了基于自定义脚本语言的厂用电继电保护装置定值整定计算方法，能够适应系统结构、一次设备和继电保护装置的变化以及继电保护整定原则的变化，具有较好的通用性、可扩展性和可移植性。

(3) 采用用户权限审核、数据修改历史全面记录、定值计算结果校验等安全策略，具有较高的数据安全性。

(4) 预留与其他电厂或调度部门整定计算软件数据连接的接口，具有较好的可扩展性。

(二) 实施效果及应用推广情况

该研究成果改进了传统的整定计算工作方式，提升了故障及整定计算的自动化水平，避免通过人工核算定值过程中出现的人为错误，提升继电保护设备运行安全水平。依靠该系统，用户可以自主完成所辖厂用电设备的整定值复算校核工作，每年可节省数十万元的委托计算费用。该成果解决了传统整定计算软件不能灵活适应厂用电系统结构和保护装置变化的问题，实现了较好的通用性和可扩展性，推进了发电厂厂用电系统故障计算及继电保护整定计算的技术发展，在行业内具有广阔的推广应用前景。

(向家坝水力发电厂　陈保臻)

基于关键性能指标的水电机组振动故障智能预警研究

常规的水电机组振动故障诊断由专业的系统提供机组振动监测的波形数据、状态数据，而后由资深专家以数据为基础，结合知识进行人工交互式诊断，需人工的大量参与，距离自动、智能故障诊断尚存在一定距离。鉴于此，五强溪水电厂与湖南五凌电力科技有限公司合作开展了基于关键性能指标（Key Performance Index，KPI）的水电机组振动故障智能预警研究。

(一) 预警系统设计思路

目前水电厂均装设的机组振摆在线监测系统，主要记录机组振动摆度波形数据及运行工况背景量参数。为实现基于KPI预警系统指标建设，安装一台数据服务器，建立故障机理模型；开发软件，读取水电厂机组振摆在线监测系统历史数据及实时数据；布置数据平台，在算法平台上配置各种指标的计算程序，运用大数据技术实现量化指标的智能计算；开发用户应用平台，向专业人员展示KPI计算结果。

(二) 智能预警KPI计算

水电机组振动故障智能预警KPI计算，关键在于振动监测波形数据特征参量的提取。机组在运行中，监测波形数据偏离了正常状态就可能出现故障，表征它的特征向量也会变化。只要故障存在，这种故障信息就会通过特征参数表现出来。因此，以信息量作为出现故障的量度，就可以对机组状态进行诊断。某种故障类型发生所能引起变化的物理参数很多，但是可用作故障特征的参量有限，选取故障特征参量应遵循以下原则：①灵敏性，要对机组运行状态变化有敏感的反应；②高可靠性，通常通过特征参数的稳定性来表征；③可实现性，可以有相应的仪器将之检测出来或在故障诊断计算中可以被实现。

以发电机轴心指标计算为例，测值过大会造成上导摆度超标，在轴瓦温度不超标的前提下，通过减小轴瓦间隙或对转子进行配重，可以使该指标达到合适值，减小上导摆度。此指标计算需要用到上导、推力、水导的X、Y向摆度测点的波形数据，将计算的发电机轴心指标值与设置的报警阈值进行比较判断机组健康状态。该指标具体计算过程如下：①在中间量算法中，使用空间轴线算法模板，计算出上导轴承处的摆度影响量；②将第一步计算出来的摆度影响量作为三维的Z轴，用水头和导叶开度作为X、Y轴，进入三维模型算法中进行收敛计算；③将三维模型中收敛出来的摆度影响量进行圈点，选择额定水头附近、开度60%以上的特征信号进行提取，作为特征值输出；④对从三维模型中提取出来的特征信号进行报警判定后形成指标。此指标值超过报警值对应的故障缺陷有三种可能：①上导轴承瓦间隙过大；②转子质量不平衡；③转子磁拉力不平衡。

通过对水电机组振动机理的研究，目前共进行了发电机轴心、主轴弯曲、上导动态盘车、水导动态盘车、大轴窜动、转子离心力、定子叠片松动、定子线棒松动、上导支撑松动、镜板不垂直、推力机架垂直振动、水导支撑松动、转轮离心力、水轮机开口不匀等14个KPI指标设计、计算。

（三）工程应用

该系统已成功在五强溪水电厂投入运行，以下列举两个典型诊断案例。

（1）5号机组质量不平衡故障指标验证：针对5号机组在2014年间存在质量不平衡缺陷，利用开发的预警系统通过对2014年至2015年历史数据进行算法验证。计算结果是：2014年10月至2015年2月底，转子离心力指标达18.7，上机架水平振动指标达76；电厂2015年2月对机组动平衡试验进行了转子配重后，指标值明显下降，转子离心力只有8.5，上机架水平振动降至36。因此从三维模型中提取的转子离心力、上机架水平振动特征信号能够反应出发电机转子是否存在质量不平衡情况。

（2）3号机组瓦间隙偏大故障指标验证：五强溪3号机组在2016年间存在轴瓦间隙偏大缺陷，利用开发的预警系统通过对2016年历史数据进行算法验证。由算法计算的健康指标变化趋势可以看出，2016年机组上导摆度指标值为240～230、水导摆度指标值为230；2017年1月对机组瓦间隙进行调整后，机组上导、水导摆度值明显下降，指标值分别约为210、220。因此，从三维模型中提取的上导摆度、水导摆度特征信号能够反应出机组轴瓦间隙缺陷情况。

（四）结语

针对水电机组故障特点，利用大数据算法工具，通过理论分析建立故障的机理模型，对水轮机组振摆在线监测的大量历史数据进行频谱分析，深入挖掘提取特征信号，建立水电机组振动故障智能预警KPI，可以根据指标值变化情况，提前发现潜在故障，指导机组安全稳定运行。但要建立完善的水轮机组状态在线预警系统，尚有大量工作要做。

（五强溪水电厂　肖丰明
湖南五凌电力科技有限公司　张培　李汉臻）

对五强溪水电站加装静止无功补偿装置的研究

水电厂调节无功和电压的手段，一般是利用发电机进相运行或者在母线高压侧装设并联电抗器。但机组轻载进相运行调压不够经济，且机组的振动、摆度常成倍增加甚至超标，带来安全隐患；同时，进相运行使定子端部漏磁场增大，铁损加大，铁芯端部发热。而电抗器不能根据目标电压值自动调节其感性无功输出，需要运行人员根据系统电压情况手动投切；用机械开关投切电抗器容易产生截流过电压，影响安全运行。目前在动态无功补偿领域技术较先进、应用最为成熟的就是静止无功补偿装置（Static Var Compensator，SVC），其中晶闸管控制电抗器（Thyristor Controlled Reactor，TCR）提供可调的感性无功功率，滤波器为系统滤波并提供容性无功补偿。因此，针对枯水期电网负荷轻时，线路充电无功过剩，使处于线路末端的水电厂存在母线电压偏高的问题，国家电力投资集团有限公司立项，开展基于SVC技术的水电站低谷调压设计及仿真研究。现将五强溪水电站加装SVC的系统的设计及仿真分析情况简介如下。

（一）系统设计

五强溪水电站现有5台单机容量为260MW的水轮发电机组，发电机—变压器组采用单元接线方式。加装SVC的补偿目标侧电压等级为500kV侧，但采用TCR型SVC直挂电压等级目前技术较成熟的不超过66kV，必须加装升压变压器。在保障安全的情况下，节省投资的做法是利用机组现有300MVA主变压器，将SVC安装在两台主变压器低压侧。由以往运行经验可知，当两套机组输出200Mvar无功时，夜间能将系统母线电压降低到合理范围。采用TCR进行无功补偿，则其输出容量应不低于200Mvar。故五强溪水电站加装的SVC，设计采用两套容量为100Mvar（感性）的TCR，分别接于两台300MVA主变压器低压侧。

由于TCR型SVC运行时，含有谐波电流，需要配套一定容量的滤波器吸收谐波。单套SVC的动态无功输出容量范围是－30Mvar（容性）～100Mvar（感性），两套SVC的动态无功输出容量范围是－60Mvar（容性）～200Mvar（感性）。因此，TCR

容量采用130Mvar，滤波器容量30Mvar。

五强溪水电站加装SVC的电气主接线如图1所示。

其中：相控电抗器主要参数见表1，滤波器参数见表2。

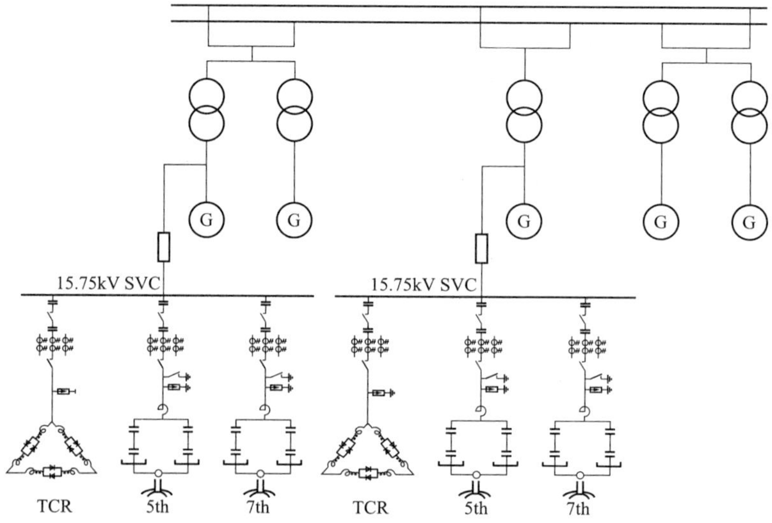

图1 五强溪水电站加装SVC的电气主接线图

表1 相控电抗器主要参数

三相额定容量（Mvar）	额定电压（kV）	频率（Hz）	触发角（°）	额定电流（A）	额定电感（mH）
130	15.75	50	110	2752	2×5.22

表2 滤波器参数

调谐次数	额定相电压（kV）	Q_{cn1}（kvar）	连接方式（并）	连接方式（串）	单台容量（kvar）	X_C（Ω）	X_1（Ω）	额定电流（A）
5	10.5	21000	7	2	500	15.75	0.63	666.67
7	10	15000	5	2	500	20.00	0.41	500.0

（二）仿真分析

1. 电压调节　基于PSCAD搭建仿真分析模型，对各种工况的仿真结果汇总如下：

夜间空载电压541.1kV，投入2台机组，每台无功输出为80Mvar，进相运行，向母线注入感性无功功率160Mvar，母线电压为537.6kV，电压下降幅度3.5kV。

采用TCR补偿方案时，当母线电压升高时，TCR触发角度下降达到最小值时，SVC的感性无功功率达到最大，低压侧感性无功94.74Mvar，高压侧感性无功105.3Mvar（考虑主变压器无功后），两套SVC总的无功功率达到210.6Mvar。母线电压为536.5kV，电压下降幅度4.6kV。

由此可见，采用TCR可以替代双机进相运行，将母线电压调节到合理的范围。

单独投入两组TCR、退出滤波支路时，无功出力更高，低压侧感性无功116.5Mvar，高压侧感性无功128.8Mvar（考虑主变压器无功后），两套TCR总的无功功率达到261Mvar。母线电压为535.3kV，电压下降幅度5.8kV。

2. 谐波特性分析　TCR装置产生的3次和3次倍数的谐波电流不会注入系统，其特征谐波电流含量为5次、7次、11次、13次，由于11次、13次及以后的高次谐波电流含量较小，因此，仅对5次和7次谐波电流含量进行分析。

TCR装置谐波电流含量随触发角变化而变化，5，7次谐波电流较大，最大幅值可达基波电流的0.95，随触发角的增大，谐波电流将大幅减小。

由此，对比滤波支路滤波器投入前后，单套装置注入500kV母线的5次谐波电流、7次谐波电流见表3。

表3　滤波支路滤波器投入前后谐波潮流

工况	谐波	单套	两套
滤波支路未投入	5次谐波电流（A）	10.62	21.22
	7次谐波电流（A）	3.93	7.88
滤波支路投入	5次谐波电流（A）	1.41	2.82
	7次谐波电流（A）	0.40	0.80

对比波形可知，滤波投入前，谐波含量较高，电压电流波形畸变较为严重，投入后，谐波含量大大降低，波形畸变小。

（三）结语

根据仿真结果，设计的SVC系统能够很好的在低负荷时段母线电压过高的情况下，吸收系统剩余无功，将电压调节至合理的范围；相对于静态电抗器，动态响应速度快，对系统冲击小，运行维护更方便；相对于机组进相运行，由于没有旋转机械安全性更高，损耗较低，还可以抑制低频振荡，动态跟随系统电压进行补偿，提高电压稳定效果，并且能避免机组进相运行带来定子端部发热，振摆超标等安全隐患，经济上可以降低用电损耗和发电耗水率。

（长沙理工大学　胡蝶　粟时平
五强溪水电厂　肖丰明　蔡军）

德尔西水电站开关站出线架结构设计情况

德尔西水电站位于厄瓜多尔Zamora Chinchipe省Zamora河上，为引水式，额定水头495m，安装3台冲击式水轮发电机组，总装机容量180MW，多年平均发电量12.18亿kW·h。

该电站开关站采用户外布置方式，在厂区右侧，地面高程965.0m，面积为37m×73m；其出线架为钢桁架结构，由四跨组成，相邻跨间距12m，高20m，要求采用美国钢结构规范（AISC-Load And Resistance Factor Design Specification For Structural Steel Buildings，以下简称“AISC-LRFD”）设计。

德尔西水电站设计由中国电建集团西北勘测设计研究院有限公司承担，现将开关站出线架结构设计有关情况简介如下。

（一）结构设计基本参数

根据《水电站压力钢管设计规范》(DL/T 5141—2001）及《110kV～750kV架空输电线路设计标准》（GB 50545—2010)，出线架钢材选用Q345，其抗拉、抗压和抗弯强度为295 N/mm²，屈服强度为345 N/mm²；设计计算工况分正常运行、检修期和正常运行十地震三种，荷载组合都有自重、出线荷载、风荷载，工况3增加地震力；最大出线荷载，导线的水平拉力、竖直荷载、侧向力分别为21、4.8、3.6kN。

（二）结构分析

建立开关站出线架三维分析模型，经计算，各杆件控制内力见表1。

表1　出线架各杆件控制内力表

杆件	轴力（kN）	弯矩（kN·m）
立柱	265.81	10.711
横梁	47.387	3.292
水平杆	43.938	0.997
斜杆	31.003	0.734

（三）结构稳定性评价

1. 中国规范　根据中国规范《架空送电线路杆塔结构设计技术规定》（DL/T 5154—2012）及《钢结构设计规范》(GB 50017—2003)，计算公式如下：

（1）轴心受力构件：

$$\sigma = \frac{N}{A_n} \leqslant mf$$

式中　σ——正应力；

N——轴心拉力或轴心压力设计值；

A_n——构件净截面面积；

m——构件强度折减系数，依据规范取值；

f——钢材的强度设计值。

（2）压弯构件：

$$\frac{N}{\phi m_N A} + \frac{M}{W\left(1 - 0.8\dfrac{N}{N_{EX}}\right)} \leqslant f$$

式中　M——弯矩设计值；

N——轴心压力设计值；

A——构件毛截面面积；

W——截面抵抗矩；

ϕ——轴心受压构件稳定系数，依据规范取值；

f——钢材的强度设计值。

采用中国规范进行稳定分析，开关站出线架各杆件的断面选择见表2。

2. 美国规范　根据美国规范《AISC-LRFD》，计算公式如下：

（1）受拉构件，设计强度 $\phi_t P_n$，取毛截面屈服强度和净截面抗拉强度两种计算结果的较小值。其中毛截面：

$$\phi_t = 0.9$$

$$P_n = F_y A_g$$

净截面：

$$\phi_t = 0.75$$

$$P_n = F_u A_e$$

式中 F_y——钢材屈服强度；

F_u——钢材抗拉强度；

A_g——构件毛截面面积；

A_e——构件净截面面积。

（2）受压构件，设计强度 $\phi_c P_n$，其中：

$$\phi_c = 0.85$$

$$P_n = A_g F_{cr}$$

当 $\lambda_c \leqslant 1.5$ 时 $F_{cr} = (0.658^{\lambda_c^2}) F_y$

当 $\lambda_c > 1.5$ 时 $F_{cr} = \frac{0.877}{\lambda_c^2} F_y$

式中 A_g——构件毛截面面积；

F_y——钢材屈服强度。

（3）受弯构件：对于T形截面和角钢，抗弯设计强度为 $\phi_b M_n$，其中：

$$\phi_b = 0.9$$

$$M_n = M_{cr} = \frac{\pi \sqrt{EI_y GJ}}{L_b}(B + \sqrt{1+B^2})$$

$$B = \pm 2.3(d/L_b)\sqrt{\frac{I_y}{J}}$$

式中 E——钢材的弹性模量；

I_y——绕y轴的截面惯性矩；

G——钢材的剪切模量；

J——截面的极惯性矩。

$M_n \leqslant 1.5 M_y$ 时为拉杆，B 取正值；$M_n \leqslant 1.0 M_y$ 时为压杆，B 取负值。

采用美国规范进行稳定分析，开关站出线架各杆件的断面选择见表2。

表2 断面选择表

杆件名称	断面（mm×mm）	
	中国规范	美国规范
立柱	∠160×16	∠160×14
横梁	∠100×12	∠100×10
水平杆	∠75×8	∠75×8
斜杆	∠75×8	∠75×8

3. 差异性分析

（1）受拉构件，美国规范《AISC-LRFD》取毛截面屈服强度和净截面抗拉强度两种计算结果的较小值；而中国规范DL/T 5154—2012则按净截面屈服强度进行计算，中国规范计算结果偏于安全。

（2）压弯构件，中国规范主要是依据边缘纤维屈服准则并考虑压弯构件二阶效应，即以截面应力最大的边缘开始屈服的临界荷载作为压弯构件的稳定承载力；而美国规范采用含折减系数的实用公式进行验算。

（中国电建集团西北勘测设计研究院有限公司 黄佳 尹小刚 许战军）

基于水电站生产数据平台的状态分析技术与应用

水电站生产数据平台是指基于现有的自动化系统建设的用于进一步数据分析的全厂性数据平台。作为设备状态分析的数据源，数据质量是关键，水电站生产数据平台的数据应进行一系列处理才能保证其质量。国网电力科学研究院因此开展了基于水电站生产数据平台的状态分析技术研究，主要研究内容及成果简介如下。

（一）数据处理关键技术

（1）数据的整合和初筛。保证数据的唯一性和全面性，尤其是机组功率、定子电流等重要数据只能有一个数据源；在获取数据测值的同时，必须同时获取数据的品质，品质坏的数据直接剔除，测值明显异常的数据直接剔除。

（2）误差的判断与剔除。粗大误差对测量结果的影响最大，其判别与剔除方法中，有四种比较常用的准则，依次是拉伊达准则、格拉布斯准则、肖维勒准则和狄克逊准则，最常用的为拉伊达准则。

（3）机组状态监测特征数据的处理。关键数据包括有效值、平均值、峰峰值等，其中机组振摆峰峰值反映了机组振摆幅度大小，直观体现了机组的实时稳定性状态。目前振摆峰峰值的计算方法主要有四种：置信度（Conf）、单周峰—峰值平均法、平均时段法、RMS等效峰—峰值（RMPpp）。建议采用的是置信度（conf97）融合平均时段法。

（4）数据的录入和补召。水电站试验数据、巡检数据、缺陷数据等常常无法实现在线监测，应支持这些离线数据的录入功能。某些已记录的数据不正确或者因通信故障造成的数据错误和数据不完整，应支持历史数据的补录、重录功能；还应支持数据补召功能，当通信恢复后，自动向对端补召通信故障期间的数据。

（二）基于水电站生产数据平台的设备状态分析

1. 机组工况标定 根据机组工况的特征参数，应准确判断机组所处工况及起止时间，并记录工况及相关参数信息。根据机组的运行特性，将整个运行范围分成若干个合适的区间，可认为处于一个区间内的工况是同一工况，将这些工况用不同的标号表示，同一工况下的参数可进行互相比较。生产数据平台采集到的每一组数据都附带机组工况的标号，并根据机组工况标号进行后续处理。

2. 数据分级存储　数据入库保存通常采用两种方式。一是按照给定时间间隔保存数据，另一种方式是分段间隔的数据库入库方案。直接采用定时间间隔入库或者分段间隔入库，可能丢失有用数据，应采用入库频度自适应方法，其原则：①如果工况和相关参数基本不变，入库频度降低；②工况变化过程中的参数自动入库；③虽然工况未变，但被测参数发生变化，则数据入库频度增加；④机组运行在特殊工况下，则入库频度增加。

3. 多维度监测预警

（1）设定分工况高报和低报阈值。水电机组的工况经常变动，不同工况下机组的特征是不同的，因此对于不同运行工况应该设定不同报警阈值。

（2）设定最少报警次数令牌。为避免信号采集或者传输发生异常而导致误报警，系统采取在一段时间内，同一报警至少连续出现若干次数才触发报警，这里引入报警令牌来限制误报。

（3）关联通道报警。考虑到报警发生时，有时关联的通道也会同时出现报警，因此可采取组合报警策略进行关联，必须所关联的通道同时报警才触发报警。

4. 趋势预测　可能影响机组正常运行的参量属于渐变量，一般不会发生突变。很多设备事故或故障发生之前都是有征兆的。对于渐变量来说，分析的一个重要方法是趋势预测法，包括水平趋势预测法、逐步回归预测法、灰色理论预测法。在趋势预测前，数学模拟模块将根据时间序列数据拟合精度和是否有时间函数关系式来决定采用哪一种预测方法进行预测。预测结果可以用正向预测和反向预测两种形式来展现。

（三）设备状态分析技术应用

1. 设备状态统计和分析　通过统计油泵、水泵等设备的启停次数及运行时间，并进行直观的展示，或者在数据库中设置阈值（例如技术供水水泵 1 小时内运行时间太长是不正常的）进行报警，及时发现设备存在的问题。

实际测量中得到的状态监测信号一般都是时域信号，采用时域分析方法主要可以对与幅值相关的一些统计量进行分析计算，如最小值、最大值、峰峰值、平均值、有效峰峰值、中间值等。

2. 设备状态趋势分析　针对设备运行的关键参数，例如油压装置的油压、机组三部轴承温度，进行关键参数的趋势分析，在信号异常时，及早地发现异常，并迅速预警。

3. 设备状态对比分析　对比分析有多种方式，包括不同机组之间的设备状态对比分析，同机组的同类型的设备进行对比分析。另外，还可以通过统计关键参数的最大值、最小值、平均值来分析设备状态。

4. 数据挖掘分析　可以分析相同出力或同一水头下各台机组油温和瓦温的趋势，可以分析相同出力时各台机组的振动、摆度的趋势。

（国网电力科学研究院　李东风　张红芳）

金　属　结　构

向家坝水电站液压抓梁水下安全稳定运行研究

向家坝水电站门机取物装置为液压抓梁，在闸门的提落工作中，液压抓梁经常在水下进行穿销、退销工作，它的运行情况直接关系到闸门启闭成功与否。为更好地运行管理好液压自动抓梁，向家坝水力发电厂组织项目组，通过对抓梁各种常见的故障缺陷进行原因分析，对水下密封形式、电缆连接方式等调研，并对穿销、退销作业中的薄弱环节进行辨识，制订有效对策，使液压抓梁在运行过程中更加安全稳定，降低门机液压自动抓梁穿销故障率，保障液压抓梁水下安全稳定运行。

（一）技术创新点

（1）重新设计水下密封盒结构，优化主电缆插头（插座）、密封盒接线形式及电缆插头（座）结构形式，提高密封盒的可靠性。

（2）增设水下摄像头，实现液压抓梁水下穿销过程可视化，传感器及信号反馈系统更加立体化。

（3）提高主随行电缆的抗拉能力，优化随行电缆的收放控制方式；通过计算，编写速度转换程序，加入到 PLC 控制程序中，同时对变频器运行方式进行设置，保证抓梁电缆给定速度与抓梁实际速度相匹配，从而避免电缆受力过大被拉断或电缆堆积问题的出现。

（二）实施效果及应用推广情况

深水密封盒的结构形式、电缆及摄像头的选择参数以及电缆的控制方式在试验中均得到了有效的验证，平均每百小时故障数从之前的 5.6 次，降到了现在的0次，极大的提高了液压抓梁工作的可靠性，可在相关行业和领域进行推广使用。

（向家坝水力发电厂 陈保臻）

丰宁抽水蓄能电站弯管段钢管制作及安装方案优化

丰宁抽水蓄能电站为目前世界最大规模的抽水蓄能电站，一、二期压力钢管制作安装总工程量约4.5万t，其中弯管段工程量约3759t、合计534节弯管。按施工组织安排，钢管制作完成后通过40t牵引式半挂汽车运输到鞭子沟渣场暂且临时停放，待钢管安装时再运输至施工隧洞内。因此，从钢管制作完成至钢管安装完成过程中所进行的钢管运输工作量比较大。

由于洞内施工作业空间狭窄，钢管安装进行管节对接和焊缝焊接十分不便，施工进度比较慢，需要投入的人员多。丰宁抽水蓄能电站引水隧洞上斜井和下斜井角度均为53°左右，洞内钢管安装安全风险等级达4级，安全风险系数高，不利于钢管焊缝焊接质量的控制。承担压力钢管制作安装的中国水利水电第三工程局有限公司经研究，决定将原设计的在钢管厂将2节弯管组装为一个单元的方案优化为将3节弯管组装为一个单元的方案，尽可能将洞内进行的弯管对接和环缝焊接工作调至条件良好的钢管厂内完成。由此，原设计534节弯管、267个单元改进优化至534节弯管、178个单元进行制作安装，这不但可以提高钢管对接和焊接质量，还可以减少弯管运输89个单元，降低施工成本。

3节弯管为一个单元最大重量23.422t，钢管厂内配备了2台50t龙门式起重机，满足吊装要求；采用40t牵引式半挂汽车，能够满足增加摞节后的运输要求；而斜井段安装均采用35t双滚筒卷扬机，运输最大钢管管重约29t，也满足3节弯管为一个单元的溜放条件。

该项目于2017～2018年成功实施，使89条洞内安装环缝调至钢管厂内进行制作完成，减少弯管运输89次，节省工期约178天，创造经济效益约47万元。

弯管在钢管厂内进行制作，由于施工作业环境优越，吊装、对接和焊接更为方便，减少了施工风险，安全效益明显；质量便于控制，环缝焊接一次合格率均达到99.8%以上，质量效益也显著。

（中国水利水电第三工程局有限公司
杨联东 屈刚 杨建军）

引汉济渭水利枢纽供水工程贴边斜岔管的制作

陕西省引汉济渭工程为一等大（1）型工程。三河口水利枢纽为引汉济渭工程的两个水源工程之一，水库总库容为7.1亿m^3，调节库容6.5亿m^3，主要由大坝、坝身泄洪放空系统、坝后引水系统组成；其地面厂房临河侧设有6个贴边斜岔管。这种岔管共分3种规格：①接可逆机组支管的2个，主管内径4500mm，支管内径1600mm；②接常规机组支管的2个，主管内径3800mm，支管内径2600mm；③接供水阀支管的2个，主管内径3000mm，支管内径2000mm。6个岔管均采用内外贴边，承受内水头（含水击压力）160m（1.6MPa），最大岔管的HD值为720m·m。以可逆机组岔管为例，主、支管钢板均为Q345C、δ32mm，内、外贴边加强板均为Q345C、δ28mm，分岔角60°，该贴边斜岔管体型结构布置及参数如图1所示。

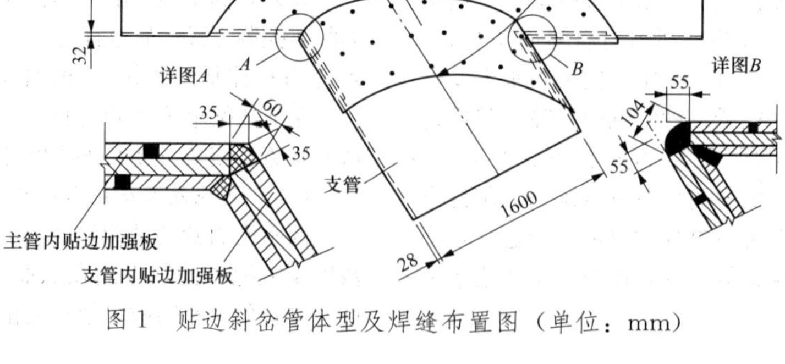

图1 贴边斜岔管体型及焊缝布置图（单位：mm）

贴边斜岔管制作的难点，一是岔管相贯线处焊缝过于集中，最大宽度达 104mm，焊接应力大，其内部质量和焊接变形控制，直接影响岔管制作的整体质量；二是岔管主、支管的纵缝、环缝，以及内、外贴边加强板的纵缝、对接缝、塞焊等焊缝集中，按规范要求错开一定距离（即俗称的错缝）布置，设计有些难度。经研究，制作工艺要点如下：

1. 放样　采用 Auto CAD 与 Auto POL for Windows 相结合的方式对岔管进行展开放样。首先用 Auto CAD 软件根据图纸按 1∶1 比例做出岔管及其内、外贴边的三维图形，检查无误后，按需将构件以钢板中性层的三维图导入 Auto POL for Windows 放样软件中，输入相关参数后进行平面展开。由于岔管外形尺寸超过了公路运输限制，主、支管及其贴边加强板需采取满足公路运输的分节设计，这就要求分节、错缝工艺设计相互兼顾。另外，主、支管与水压试验用闷头焊接处应预留 150mm 修割余量。

2. 切割下料　所有单元节钢板均采用数控切割机下料。由于支管、贴边加强板展开放样后均为异形，为便于卷板时操作和卷板受力均匀，在下料时有意先用数控切割机进行曲线划线而不切割，等待卷板后再进行切割。为避免转入卷板工序时出现错误，在下料后一定要根据工艺图纸划出瓦片的轴线，并标记内、外弧面及水流方向，避免卷制方向错误。

3. 单元件卷制成型　由于卷板机最大卷板宽度不能超过 3.0m，贴边加固板工艺设计时按照图 2“切角补边法”进行下料（切下阴影三角形，移对边拼焊上），以便于卷板。这样既提高了材料的利用率，又使贴边加固板在卷制时不易出现失圆，更好地保证其与管壁的贴合度。

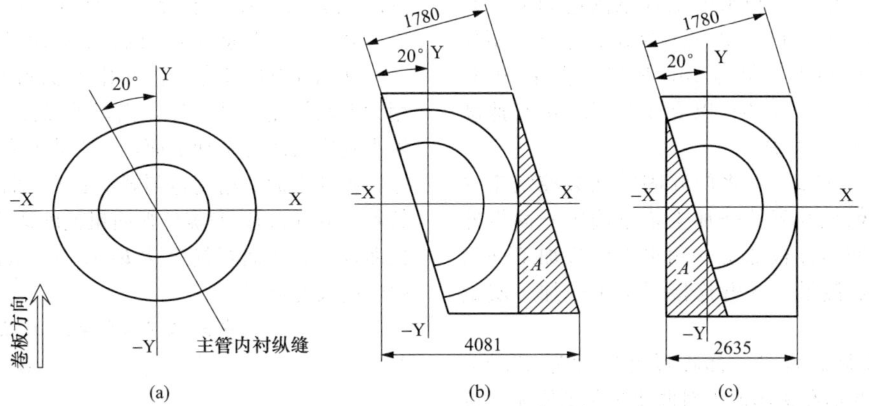

图 2　岔管内、外贴边单元件卷制

（a）贴边加固板；（b）贴边加固板下料 1；（c）贴边加固板下料 2

4. 组拼　为保证岔管在工地组拼顺利，在制造厂需按照工地正式拼装一样的工序进行预拼装。预拼装时，需注意的事项如下：

（1）Auto POL for Windows 软件在输入板厚后，按照板厚中心不发生近似变化的原理对个单元件进行平面展开，不能全面考虑到岔管各相邻单元件对接存在一定的角度，导致对接处因壁厚存在空隙和误差（参见图 1 中的详图 A 和详图 B），因此在预拼装时需进行坡口修切，使之满足坡口尺寸要求，便于工地焊接。

（2）预拼装验收合格后应安装定位板，以方便工地快速组拼和几何尺寸到位。同时对单元件采用型钢进行加固，以防止运输和组拼是变形。

5. 焊接　为减少焊接应力，按照焊接工艺评定和焊接规程执行，严格控制焊接线能量。在主、支管及其相贯线处的焊缝焊接完成后，进行高频振动消除应力后进行无损检测，合格后方可组拼贴边加强板并进行焊接。

（中国水利水电第三工程局有限公司
刘锐　邹振忠　刘乾坤）

大型数控龙门镗铣床在弧形闸门面板加工的应用

高水头弧形闸门设计时往往要求对其门叶面板外弧面整体机加工，以保证其曲率半径尺寸和粗糙度满足设计要求。传统的门叶面板外弧面整体机加工，大多采用自行设计制作的专用工装，其加工耗时长、精度不高（弧形为折线而非圆弧线）、通用性不强（针对不同外形尺寸、曲率半径需要不同专用工装）。随着机加工设备与技术的进步，应用大型数控龙门铣床对弧形闸门门叶面板外弧面和节间进行铣削加工，精度高、无需制作任何加工工装、节省工期。中国水利水电第三工程局有限公司在几内亚苏阿皮蒂水利枢纽底孔高水头弧形闸门制造中，成功应用这一技术。现将有关情况简介如下。

1. 弧形闸门简况　几内亚苏阿皮蒂水利枢纽底孔弧门孔口宽5m、高6m，面板曲率半径11.0m，每套重144t；单节加工最大外形尺寸为弧长7488mm、宽2443mm、面板平放时高1841mm，招标文件规定的曲率半径允许加工偏差为±1.0mm。

2. 机加工设备　加工选用由中捷合资生产的CMC40120mr3数控龙门移动式加工中心（以下简称数控铣床），其工作台尺寸4000mm×12000mm，两立柱间距5180mm，满足加工需求。

3. 整体退火　为保证门叶外形几何尺寸满足机加工要求，进入退火炉前将门叶用型钢固定在退火炉移动台车上，并用水准仪进行扭曲测量，其扭曲不超过±3.0mm。根据《水利水电工程钢闸门制造安装验收规范》（GB/T 14173—2008）规定，退火控制最高温度为580～600℃，保温2h；加热速度在300℃以下不大于220℃/h，300℃以上50℃/h；冷却速度80℃/h，300℃以下出炉。

4. 门叶机加工工序　将门叶固定在数控铣床移动台车上→几何尺寸复核→加工余量确定→面板外弧面加工→节间连接板加工→侧水封座板加工→门叶翻身、固定、测量→支臂连接板加工→加工质量验收。

5. 加工余量的确定　面板设计厚度为28mm，考虑弧门焊接变形和整体退火对曲率半径的影响，按照经验工艺机加工余量预留12.0mm，即面板用材板厚为40mm。节间连接板、侧水封座板设计厚度均为25mm，考虑到弧门在宽度方向的焊接收缩量，工艺机加工余量预留5mm，即节间连接板、侧水封座板用材厚度均达到30mm。门叶焊接校正完成及退火后检测门叶的曲率半径及扭曲、与支臂连接的4个连接板的角度和扭曲，计算出最优机加工组合尺寸，确定面板外弧面平均加工量为8.0mm，节间连接板、侧水封座板平均加工量为5.0mm。

6. 面板外弧面加工

（1）将门叶牢固压紧，完全无滑动、无晃动；找正门叶4个角上的点，检查弧顶高度。

（2）将曲率半径、圆点坐标、加工精度控制数据输入数控龙门铣PLC程序中，空车运行一次，检查激光点轨迹，应满足弧面加工要求。

（3）主轴装夹ϕ160R10刀盘，先空试车走运行轨迹，再开始粗加工弧面。加工工序每刀行走宽度为150mm、进刀量为4.0mm；加工方向设定为对角线方向交叉进行。

（4）粗加工弧面过程结束后，根据图纸尺寸和要求检查工件弧面加工余量和粗糙度，然后编制程序，进行半精铣加工弧面。加工工序每刀行走宽度为20mm、进刀量为3.0mm。

（5）半精铣加工弧面过程结束后，根据图纸尺寸和要求检查工件弧面加工精铣加工余量，然后编制程序，进行精铣加工弧面。加工工序每刀行走宽度为5mm、进刀量为1.0mm。

（6）整体弧面加工程序完成，去毛倒刺，清理铁屑，开始检验工序。采用表面光洁度表对照，检验表面光洁度是否达到图纸要求；用激光跟踪仪整平面检测弧度尺寸，确保偏差在标准规定的允许范围内。

7. 节间连接板和侧水封座板加工　铣刀换为端面的镗刀。以加工后的外弧面为基准，对节间连接板和侧水封座板进行加工，保证与面板外弧面垂直。加工步骤同面板外弧面加工。由于CMC40120mr3数控龙门铣加工中心Z轴行程是800mm，节间连接板立向1500mm，需通过接刀的方法来加工。

几内亚苏阿皮蒂泄洪底孔弧形闸门机加工成功应用大型数控龙门镗铣床，面板外弧面、节间连接板、侧水封座板的三个加工面，一次装夹完成所有加工工序，各加工面的精度达到规定要求，曲率半径的加工偏差为0.5mm，面板外弧面粗糙度达*Ra*25，节间连接面及水封座面粗糙度达*Ra*12.5，从而保证了闸门整体的装配质量。

（中国水利水电第三工程局有限公司
吕华　邹振忠）

大藤峡水利枢纽主坝泄水低孔弧门的制造

大藤峡水利枢纽主坝泄水低孔工作弧门是目前我国水电站中弧形闸门曲率半径最大的弧门，其主框架的结构型式采用双主纵梁焊接结构，三直支臂支撑；弧门孔口尺寸为9m×18m（宽×高），曲率半径为33m；面板弧长22.16m，采用Q345B，表面机加工后要求粗糙度*Ra*＝12.5；门叶结构纵向分为3节，单节重达97t；单片支臂重约165t。支承钢梁整体制作，单件重约为230t。

该弧门外形尺寸超大，门叶纵主梁及支臂主要材料为30mm厚钢板；面板采用低合金材料，板材厚度达38mm；弧门孔口数量多，工作时调节频繁且有局部开启要求，运行安全及可靠性要求高；制造精度高、难度大，据文献资料查询，目前还未搜索到类似此弧门的有关技术文献，故应是国内外首创。中国水利水电夹江水工机械有限公司承担了该工程11套工作弧门的制作，为满足制造要求，认真分析了制造难点，研究了制造工艺，应用了智能化和数控化技术。现将主要成果简介如下。

1. 变形控制

（1）优化面板对接坡口。门叶面板外形尺寸为38mm×9050mm×22180mm。通常对接坡口均为K型45°，焊接时先焊接内侧焊缝，外侧背缝在对焊缝进行清根后再焊接，但因清根较深，焊接量大，造成面板变形较大，修校很困难。经研究，将面板对接坡口改为不对称K型，内侧深23mm、25°，外侧深13mm、30°、2mm钝边。通过焊接试验，对接处的平面度为2mm左右，不需修校即可满足技术要求。

（2）优化小纵梁小拼。门叶小纵梁为T型结构，腹板高745mm、翼板宽300mm，为细长构件，焊接变形不均衡易产生正向弯曲，对面板弧度影响大。经研究，在小纵梁腹板下料编程时采取反变形处理。实践效果较好，减少了构件焊后修校工作量。

（3）优化焊接工艺。采取小规范、小电流焊接；只允许2名焊工同时作业，采用对称跳跃焊接，先立焊、再平焊，先横向焊接、再纵向焊接的焊接顺序；加强变形监控，穿插进行修校。

（4）采取残余应力消减措施。门叶完成拼焊后进行了振动时效消应处理。

通过以上控制优化措施，有效地控制了弧门的焊接变形，使各项焊后数据检测满足要求。

2. 门叶结构加工工艺　最终确定的门叶制造工艺流程为：门叶拼焊→振动时效→复拼划线→面板加工→大拼→后翼板加工→大拼→验收合格后编号拆解门叶，点焊加固侧水封压板→钻孔→防腐。

门叶加工分两步，第一步：加工门叶面板及侧水封座板、侧轮座板。第二步：加工门叶主梁后翼板及吊耳孔，配冲主梁后翼板螺栓孔。

（1）门叶面板加工工艺：选用数控镗床进行加工，工件在工作平台上侧卧装夹（与构件划线状态一致），加工步骤如下：①数控编程走刀，虚拟加工校核构件所划面板加工线半径（$R=33$m）是否准确，待其无误后，根据该线虚拟走刀，对整体面板横、纵向进行走刀，检查各处余量是否足够（数值差标注在未加工的面板上），最终检查无误后方可进行后续加工；②编程加工基准边，加工后检查面板厚度并与虚拟加工理论数值进行对照，确认各处板厚度不小于名义尺寸（即>25mm）、半径$R=33$m无误后整体加工面板；③面板加工完成后在工件不动的状态下（同基准）加工下段底缘，按构件加工线加工底缘。

（2）门叶后主梁翼板的加工：①校正构件划线，使主梁后翼板面对主轴，按构件所冲孔位加工主梁后翼板上的孔；②钻孔后按构件划线加工主梁后翼板。

3. 铰座、铰链的制造

（1）铸造。铰座、铰链各22件，材料为ZG35CrMo，单件重量为20t，其在水工行业已属于超大铸钢件，在国内无几家厂家可铸造。对于批量如此大的铸件，根据预计的技术难题，技术人员积极与铸造专家进行技术研讨，研究生产过程中联合开炉和浇铸工艺，加强过程控制，制订科学合理的操作控制规程，解决了大型铸件的浇铸难题。

（2）机加工。铰座加工时，控制单件铰座两轴承孔与底面的相对高度为0.1mm，控制两铰座的相对高度为1mm。加工时先加工内孔，再在镗床上以内孔为基准进行校正，加工底面。铰链采用同样的加工方法控制两端面轴孔中心线与底面的相对距离。

大藤峡水利枢纽主坝泄水低孔工作弧门的成功制造，满足了工程建设的需要，丰富了我国闸门制造产品的种类。

（中国水利水电夹江水工机械有限公司　闫军）

几内亚苏阿皮蒂水电站尾水肘管制作技术

几内亚苏阿皮蒂水利枢纽由中国水利水电第三工程局有限公司（简称公司）承建。其电站4套尾水肘管，每套重52.855t、由12个单元节组成，采用δ20mm、Q235B材料；肘管上口内径5191.0mm，出口内壁宽11463.4mm、高2664.4mm，整体高度6363.2mm、上口圆中心到下口矩形边缘总长度6497.9mm。这种规模的尾水肘管的下料设计，采用传统方法约需45天。公司曾委托外单位开发肘管的下料设计软件，但使用效果不理想。因此，公司组织人员研究，成功开发了利用自动计算机辅助设计软件（Auto CAD）三维建模，转换到钣金展开软件（Auto POL for Windows）进行平面展开放样的技术，使该尾水肘管的下料设计只用约4天的时间就完成，提高了工作效率，也保证了质量。现将该技术的要点简介如下。

1. Auto CAD三维建模　根据设计图纸提供的肘管各单元节坐标表，画出肘管单线图（见图1左侧图）；再根据设计图纸提供的各单元节断面平面图，与肘管单线图合成如图1右侧所示的三维模型框线图。

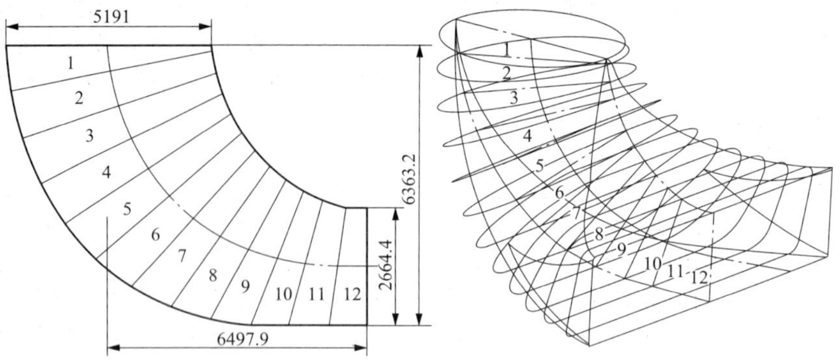

图1 肘管单线和三维模型线框图（单位：mm）

2. Auto CAD三维模型中各单元节的提取

（1）先在已形成的肘管三维模型框线图中逐步将各单元节提取出来（本例为第3单元节，见图2左侧），并将需要展开放样的图形单独提取，在命令行输入“loft”命令，光标选取弧形线并回车，然后在命令栏输入“导向（G）”，光标选取两弧形的连接线并回车，得到三维线框图，并通过点击“视图”→“视觉样式”→“概念”，得到如图2右侧所示的肘管单元节效果图。

（2）将肘管单元节效果图单击Auto CAD“输出”→选择“其他格式”→保存为“.sat”格式→点击“保存”。

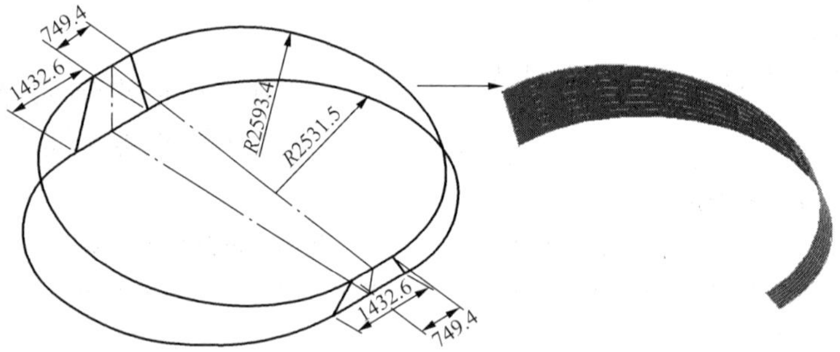

图2 肘管第3单元节提取（单位：mm）

3. Auto POL中单元节展开　打开Auto POL for Windows软件，导入保存的“.sat”格式的单元节，点击“展开”按钮，在“厚度”一栏输入钢板厚度，点击“展开”按钮，得到展开平面图，导出为“.DXF”格式保存，方便在Auto CAD中导入和编辑。

按照上述步骤获得肘管各单元节的展开平面图形，在Auto CAD中进行综合布料（需考虑节间和接板的焊缝错位），并将布料结果形成工艺文件交由材料采购、数控切割下料等工序。

4. 节间环缝坡口的设计

（1）Auto POL for Windows软件默认钢板厚度中心层不发生变化原理，对单元节曲面进行平面展开，不考虑肘管各相邻单元节环缝对接时存在角度，而使对接处因钢板厚度存在误差，因此需要根据肘管各相邻单元节的环缝对接角度情况进行坡口设计。

（2）目前大多数制造加工厂的数控切割机只能按照固定的角度切割坡口，其结果是肘管相邻单元节环缝对接时的坡口宽度与图纸要求不符，从而影响其环缝焊接质量。在工艺设计阶段可按照如下两种方案进行。方案一：在Auto CAD中按照钢板厚度进行三维实体建模，应用“实体编辑”中的“差集”命令，可以得到相邻单元节环缝的完美吻合；利用“打断”功能将内壁、外壁的曲面分别提出保存并展开放样，将放样的平面展开图叠加在一起，得到如图3内外壁坡口切割图。方案二：在单元节下料阶段不考虑坡口设计，在Auto POL for Windows“厚度”一栏输入钢板厚度，得到钢板中心层展开平面图，直接输入数控切割机程序中进行下料切割，单元节卷圆组拼时根据实际情况，用划针按照设计的坡口宽度进行划线和手工切割。

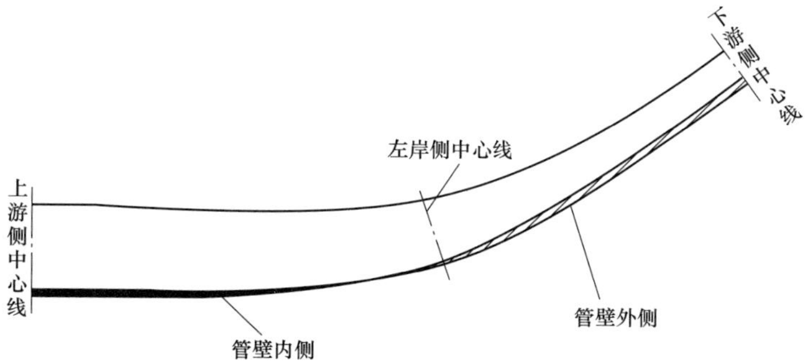

图 3　单元节内外壁切割示意图

实践表明：方案一因动态切割轨迹中的角度不断变化，无法采用数控切割机切割坡口；采用手工切割时，没有直观的参照对象而导致坡口切割质量较差，切割工时较长。方案二卷制成型后相邻单元节组拼时，虽然因角度变化存在组拼偏差，但可以互为参考，便于划线和切割。对比结果是方案二要比方案一提高 1/3 的工效，因此采用方案二比较经济实用。

值得注意的是肘管必须进行整体安装状态总拼装和加固。只有总拼装才能发现配合质量缺陷，并加以修正；检测空间几何尺寸满足设计值要求后，安装定位板并标识各单元节安装中心参考线，以保证缩短工地安装调整时间和提高安装精度。

（中国水利水电第三工程局有限公司　邹振忠
西安比亚迪汽车有限公司　邹明琦）

8

科学研究与技术创新

水电科学研究

我国高土石坝抗震安全研究进展情况

我国尚需在西部地区建设一批高坝大库工程，其中有不少挡水建筑物为高土石坝。这些工程有不少建设于高地震烈度区，其抗震安全性一直是社会以及水利水电行业关注的重点问题。由于地震动作用、土石材料的复杂性，高土石坝的抗震安全也一直是科学研究的热点。我国通过大量科学研究和工程实践，在这方面取得了大量研究成果，现简介如下。

（一）高土石坝抗震设防标准

国外一些国家主要采用不同重现期地震参数进行抗震设防，比如，智利地震活动性强烈，重现期800年的地震峰值加速度（PGA）大于0.5g；意大利重现期2500年的PGA为0.6g；英国地震活动性较弱，重现期3000年的PGA为0.375g；瑞士重现期10000年的PGA约为0.5g。我国多数高坝所在的西南地区，重现期5000年的PGA一般为0.3～0.4g，重现期10000年可达0.4～0.5g，有的甚至超过0.6g。

我国大坝抗震设防水准确定的基本原则与国外的基本一致，但甲类设防的重要高坝的抗震设防水准和性能目标要求则更为严格。

（二）高土石坝抗震安全评价准则及分析方法

高土石坝抗震安全需重点关注的震害现象为：①滑动失稳，主要是坝坡整体或局部失稳滑动；②地震永久变形，即沉降与水平位移；③地震裂缝，即产生的纵向、横向或其他形状的裂缝，应重点关注滑动裂缝（滑裂面）、贯穿土质防渗体或混凝土面板的裂缝等；④坝基土层地震液化及其引起的滑动、坍塌等；⑤防渗体系功能的损坏。我国采用的安全评价准则及计算分析方法如下：

1. 坝坡稳定分析方法及安全判断标准　拟静力法坝坡稳定分析是现行抗震规范规定的基本方法，但对于高地震烈度区的高土石坝，在进行拟静力法计算的同时应进行动力计算。坝坡动力稳定分析，安全评价标准为：$(F_s)_{min}>[F_s]$，其中$[F_s]$为安全系数的允许值，安全系数极小值$(F_s)_{min}$可利用数学规划法来求解。Newmark滑块分析法可用于计算土石坝在地震作用下产生的永久滑动位移，据此评价坝坡的动力稳定性。数值分析方法包括有限元法、差分法和离散单元法等，其中最为常用是有限元法。此外，地震作用下坝坡稳定分析还可采用地震滑动危险度法和临界滑动面法。

2. 坝体变形评价准则及分析方法　在地震作用下，除坝顶一定区域的坝坡表面出现鼓胀、松动现象外，高土石坝宏观上呈现“震缩”现象，即整体上产生震陷。对于采用重型碾压机械压实的现代土石坝和堆石坝，允许震陷率一般不应超过1%～2%，坝高100m以下可以取高限，坝高100m以上的高土石坝一般取低限值1%。

常用的土石坝动力反应分析方法主要有：简化分析方法（剪切楔法）、集中质量法和数值分析方法（以有限元、有限差分为主），其中数值分析方法最为常用。根据计算中对动荷载的处理方式，土石坝地震反应分析可分为拟静力分析和动力反应分析；根据动力本构模型不同，可分为基于等价黏弹性模型的等效线性分析方法和基于弹塑性模型的真非线性分析方法等。从是否考虑孔隙水压力的角度可分为总应力法和有效应力法，而有效应力法又可分为排水有效应力法和不排水有效应力法。

3. 液化破坏标准及分析方法

（1）动孔隙水压力判别法：根据地震产生的动孔隙水压力（u）与该部位的上覆压力（rh）比值，即孔隙压力水平$D_l=u/rh$进行判断，一般认为，$D_l\geqslant0.9$为液化区，$0.5<D_l<0.9$为可能液化区，其中，r为上覆土层的平均重度。

（2）抗液化剪应力比判别法：将地基土的抗液化剪应力比与该部位地震引起的最大动剪应力比的比值，定义为抗液化安全系数，若抗液化安全系数大于1，则该部位不会液化，反之则发生液化。

（3）动抗剪强度判别法：定义抗震液化安全系数F_e是材料动强度τ_f与地震时潜在破坏面上总剪应力τ的比值，若$F_e>1.0$，则该部位不会发生动力失效或地震液化。

4. 防渗体断裂判断方法　可采用应力判断和变形判断。应力判断时分别采用压应力和拉应力进行评价，包括拉裂与压裂两种破坏模式。采用变形判断时，则根据永久变形计算结果并采用“倾度法”等经验方法分析产生裂缝的可能，多用于土质心墙堆石坝中。

5. 高土石坝极限抗震能力分析　目前，高土石坝极限抗震能力尚未形成统一的评价标准。一般认为，可针对上述几种破坏模式进行以下分析评价：

（1）坝坡稳定抗震极限分析：采用拟静力法时如果坝坡整体稳定安全系数 $F_s<1.0$，则可认为坝坡失稳；采用有限元时程分析法时，地震过程中如果 $F_s<1.0$ 时间累加起来超过一定时间，比如 2s，则坝坡失稳。

（2）坝基砂层液化：可采用上述孔压法、抗液化剪应力比判别法等来评价坝基覆盖层液化土层判断的液化可能性，并分析土层液化是否导致坝坡整体失稳。

（3）坝体震陷率：取震陷率破坏标准为不大于1%基本合适，但该标准尚需进一步研究。

（三）高土石坝抗震工程措施

1. 高土石坝抗震薄弱部位与薄弱环节　高土石坝的地震薄弱部位通常是指坝基地质缺陷部位、坝坡以及大坝坝顶建筑物。研究表明，大坝震后永久变形相对较大，与主震历时长、等效振次高以及距震中较近密切相关；堆石体震缩产生的永久变形导致混凝土面板的顶部出现脱空现象，混凝土面板横缝、水平缝发生挤压、拉伸和剪切破坏。

2. 坝体抗震工程措施

（1）适当放缓大坝上部坝坡。对于强震区高土石坝工程，一般宜在顶部约 1/4～1/5 坝高区域适当放缓坝坡，必要时设置马道。

（2）坝料及压实度。由于“鞭梢”效应，强震时高土石坝的坝顶区动力响应较大。良好的压实质量是提高其抗震稳定的重要措施。此外，在坝顶区和坝坡表面采用大粒径填筑料，可增强颗粒间的嵌固作用、提高坝料的抗剪强度，有助于提高坝顶区抗震性能。我国高土石坝的坝坡通常采用干砌或浆砌块石进行护坡。

（3）适当加大坝顶宽度。地震时，坝顶加速度往往有所放大，坝顶区域有发生坡面滑动的可能，为不危及整个坝顶区抗震安全，坝顶应具有足够宽度，且强震区应适当加宽。糯扎渡水电站心墙堆石坝和在建的 300m 级双江口水电站、两河口水电站心墙堆石坝坝顶宽度分别为 18、16、16m，均在规范规定的10～15m 基础上适当加宽。

（4）抗震加筋措施。我国高土石坝建设中，主要坝坡抗震加筋措施包括埋设土工格栅、铺设钢筋网等。冶勒水电站沥青混凝土心墙堆石坝在约 3/4 坝高以上的部位采用土工格栅进行了加固，其后泸定、长河坝、猴子岩、毛尔盖等多座水电站高土石坝也采用了该加固措施。糯扎渡水电站心墙堆石坝在坝顶约 1/5 坝高区域的上、下游坝壳堆石中埋入顺河向不锈钢锚筋 $\phi20@2.0m\times2.5m$，$L=18.0m$；并在相应区域上、下游坝面铺设扁钢网与埋入坝壳内的不锈钢锚筋焊接。

（5）抗震钢筋混凝土框格梁。抗震梁可有效增加坝顶区域坝体的整体性，对坝顶区域坝坡稳定有利。泸定水电站心墙堆石坝就在坝体和坝坡设置了抗震钢筋混凝土梁。

3. 覆盖层坝基抗震处理措施　深厚覆盖层坝基是高土石坝施工建设常常面临的挑战，近年来我国在深厚覆盖层上建设了大量高土石坝工程。目前已在深厚覆盖层坝基处理上取得了大量经验。对判定为可能液化的坝基砂层，应采取挖除置换法。在挖除比较困难或很不经济时，可采取人工加密措施。对浅层宜用表面振动压密法，对深层宜用置换振冲、强夯等方法加密，还可结合振冲处理设置砂石桩，加强坝基排水以及采取盖重等防护措施。

比如，瀑布沟水电站心墙堆石坝在下游坝脚处增设了 60m 长的弃渣压重，以提高坝基中砂层透镜体的抗液化安全性；长河坝水电站心墙堆石坝将坝基埋深 4～30m 范围内厚度 0.75～12.5m 的可能液化砂层全部挖除；狮子坪水电站心墙堆石坝对心墙与下游堆石下部的含碎砾石粉砂层进行了 8～15m 深的振冲加固处理；龙头石水电站心墙堆石坝对坝基砂层采取了振冲碎石桩处理措施；黄金坪水电站沥青混凝土心墙堆石坝对坝基可能液化砂层采取了基本挖除及设置下游坝坡压重等处理措施。

由于地震动作用和土石材料的复杂性，高土石坝计算分析和抗震安全评价中仍需大量借助经验判断，如何合理提出定量的评价指标仍是研究难点。比如，目前坝体震动变形安全评价仍主要采用经验的震陷率；大坝地震永久变形分析仍主要采用等效线性分析加经验公式的方法。因此，进一步研究合理实用的本构模型、永久变形计算模式、接触面模拟方法、地震动输入、库水—坝体—地基等的动力相互作用和耦合效应，发展实用的非线性动力分析方法，分析高土石坝地震破坏模式及机理，进而提出定量指标，仍是未来高土石坝抗震安全的研究重点。

（中国电力建设集团有限公司　周建平
水电水利规划设计总院　王富强　刘超　杨泽艳）

超高面板堆石坝安全性及关键技术研究

面板堆石坝因其适应性、安全性和经济性良好而得到广泛应用。但是，由于近年建设的几座 200m 级高面板堆石坝，部分工程出现坝体变形比预计的偏大、面板出现挤压破损、坝体渗漏量较大等问题，一些专家对能否安全建成200～300m级高面板堆石坝表示担忧和质疑。面板堆石坝正面临从200m级坝高向超坝高发展的技术挑战。

为研究解答超高面板堆石坝建设可靠性问题，由马洪琪院士领导的、具有广泛代表性的科研团队依托古水、茨哈峡、马吉和如美等4座坝高250～300m级、正在进行可行性研究的水电站工程，开展了超高面板堆石坝安全性及关键技术研究，取得一系列新的认识和重要成果。

（一）主要研究成果

1. 超高面板堆石坝安全评价

（1）200m级以上超高面板堆石坝属超级工程，要求有更高的洪水设计标准和抗震设计标准。超高大坝应满足抗滑稳定、渗透稳定和变形稳定的要求。据此，研究制定相应的大坝设计、施工和运行监测控制指标。

（2）研究证实，超高坝坝坡抗滑稳定目标可靠指标正常运用工况下宜取4.45～4.7，相应抗滑稳定安全系数为1.6～1.7。经复核典型大坝，正常情况下坝体渗透稳定可靠度指标大于9，变形可靠指标竣工期和蓄水期分别可达2.2和2.0，蓄水期面板挠度可靠度指标可达1.8，稳定安全有保证。

（3）坝体最大沉降控制在最大坝高的1%～1.5%，面板挠度与面板长度之比宜小于25%，周边缝张拉和沉降位移宜小于80mm、剪切位移宜小于60mm。面板水力梯度宜小于200，垫层料水力梯度宜不超过50。面板浇筑前下部坝体预沉降时间宜大于5个月，坝体沉降速率宜不超过5mm/月。

2. 筑坝材料及坝体断面分区

（1）作为超高坝，上下游坝坡宜适当放缓。古水、茨哈峡、马吉、如美等四个工程推荐坝坡范围为1∶1.4～1∶1.7，上下堆石分区坡比不小于1∶0.5。

（2）四个工程面板堆石坝拟采用级配良好、中硬岩（或砂砾石）材料，堆石孔隙率控制在17%～19%，砂砾石料相对密度控制标准大于0.90，取0.92～0.95，上下游堆石区模量差不大于30%。中国猴子岩坝（高223.5m）、江坪河坝（高219m）的工程实践表明，这些控制指标是能达到的。

3. 堆石料缩尺效应

（1）高围压条件下，颗粒破碎是导致缩尺效应的原因之一，围压越大，缩尺效应越明显。随最大粒径的增加，体变模量明显减小，杨氏模量系数变化相对较小。应力路径对堆石料强度的影响不大，但是堆石料的流变量和流变趋稳时间均有所增加。

（2）堆石料的颗粒破碎存在两种与尺寸有关的细观机制：一是大颗粒易于破碎，导致大试件材料参数低于小试件；二是大颗粒的咬合作用强于小颗粒，导致大试件材料参数高于小试件。从监测数据分析，即表现为高坝的实际变形值大于计算预测值，大坝堆石的变形模量参数低于室内三轴试验值。

（3）试验结果表明，砂砾石料的K值高于块石料；减小孔隙率和提高模量，可显著抑制坝体变形；小于5mm的颗粒含量越少，破碎率越高，在高围压条件，颗粒粒径越大，颗粒破碎越明显。

4. 堆石本构模型及精细化数值模拟　改进了反映堆石颗粒破碎特性的堆石本构模型、反映堆石材料的流变特性及相应的数值分析模型、反映堆石材料时效变化规律及其相应的数值模拟方法；堆石与混凝土材料的非线性接触特性及相关模拟方法考虑颗粒破碎的剪胀方程；提出精细化建模及大规模数值计算的并行计算方法。

5. 超高面板堆石坝应力变形规律

（1）当混凝土面板坝坝高达到300m量级时，坝体和面板的总体应力变形规律与200m级坝高的混凝土面板坝基本相当，但堆石体的位移和混凝土面板的应力均有较为明显的增大。

（2）计算揭示150、200、250、300m高坝之间的变形大于坝高的线性关系、小于坝高平方的抛物线关系，这种关系介于线性和平方关系之间，与材料试验的缩尺效应的规律基本吻合。

6. 面板压损破坏机理　通过大规模精细化数值分析，揭示了高坝面板挤压破损的原因是过大的堆石体变形、面板横缝处转动挤压、位移挤压和剪切挤压的共同作用。混凝土面板纵缝非均匀受力，尤其是应力集中，更容易导致混凝土的局部破损。

以往，面板纵缝简单地分为压性缝和张性缝，可能是不恰当的。实质上，面板受力机理极其复杂，同一纵缝既可能表现为张拉，又可能表现为剪切挤压。

为避免混凝土面板挤压破损，需要控制坝体堆石的变形、优化面板结构和压性纵缝间设置柔性填充物等。

7. 抗震安全及工程措施

（1）改进和发展了筑坝堆石料的广义塑性本构模型、真非线性模型、循环本构模型和三维弹塑性接触面本构模型；提出了高面板坝波动分析方法和波函数组合法的非一致地震输入、面板塑性损伤分析、非线性库水与大坝耦合及涌浪的精细化分析方法，集成了高效、大规模三维静动力分析软件。

（2）建立了基于稳定分析、变形分析、面板防渗体系的高面板坝抗震安全性评价方法、评价标准以及极限抗震能力分析方法；结合古水工程，论证了坝顶下游坝坡加钢筋网、面板上部设置永久性水平缝、面板中部压性竖缝内间隔填充复合橡胶板等抗震工程措施的有效性。

8. 安全监测关键技术

（1）调查发现，现有监测仪器和设备已不能完全适应300m高面板堆石坝建设要求。

（2）研发了管道机器人、柔性测斜仪、1000m级超长管路沉降仪、坝内廊道等内部变形监测仪器和监测技术，通过实验表明，精度满足高土石坝监测要求。同时深入研究了SAR数据的特征以及各类SAR数据的特性，建立相应的处理流程，形成了高分辨率雷达卫星数据InSAR与D-InSAR处理技术，实验结果表明精度在2cm以内，可满足高面板堆石坝外部变形监测要求。

（二）成果应用

研究成果已在古水、茨哈峡、马吉、如美、拉哇和大石峡等水电站坝型选择和工程设计中应用。古水、茨哈峡、拉哇和大石峡等工程已确定采用面板堆石坝坝型。未来还需结合各个工程的具体条件，进一步深入研究筑坝材料特性、坝体结构和坝料分区，预测大坝应力应变规律，细化施工工艺和质量控制措施。

（中国电力建设集团有限公司　周建平
水电水利规划设计总院　杨泽艳　王富强　刘超）

面板堆石坝变形与渗流安全指标体系创建及其应用

"面板堆石坝变形与渗流安全指标体系创建及其应用"是中国华电集团有限公司的科技项目，目标是建立一套集混凝土面板堆石坝变形、渗流数据的检测、监测、数据分析、指标判别至建立面板堆石坝变形和渗流安全指标体系。该项目由华电宁德电力开发有限公司承担，2017年12月完成。该项目获2018年度福建省科学技术进步奖二等奖。

（一）主要研究内容

（1）综合应用实测资料和面板堆石坝三维有限元分析模型，研究混凝土面板堆石坝运行期变形的变化规律和主要影响因素，提出堆石体本构模型和流变参数反演分析方法，揭示了运行期混凝土面板堆石坝面板、垫层、堆石体的变形演变规律，建立堆石坝面板应力的时变分析模型。

（2）提取影响混凝土面板温度应力变化的最不利气温过程，分析了最不利荷载组合对面板应力场的影响，揭示气温变化过程对面板应力的影响规律。

（3）从环境荷载和堆石体变形以及施工和运行等方面，解释堆石坝混凝土面板裂缝成因，并应用断裂力学理论，提出堆石坝面板裂缝的稳定性和发展趋势判别指标。

（4）建立混凝土面板堆石坝渗流三维有限元分析模型，分析坝后量水堰测值对大坝防渗体系演变的敏感性，提出面板堆石坝渗流量监控方法。

（5）运用裂隙渗流分析理论，建立含接（裂）缝混凝土面板渗流分析模型，研究不同程度裂缝对坝后渗流量的影响，建立混凝土堆石坝坝后渗流量监控模型，提出面板堆石坝坝后渗流量安全指标。

（6）应用最大熵理论、置信区间法和数模分析法等，确定混凝土面板堆石坝变形和渗流量安全指标，建立面板堆石坝变形和渗流安全指标体系。

（7）建立芹山大坝三维动态可视化模型，通过监测数据库的实时连接，实现芹山大坝实测变形的场景模拟与体验，动态展示变形和渗流量变化过程及其安全指标。

（8）将以上研究成果进行推广应用，建立万安溪和洪家渡混凝土面板堆石坝的变形和渗流安全指标体系。

（9）针对水下面板状态检测难点，提出面板堆石坝水下面板塌陷和裂缝渗漏检测方法。

（二）技术经济指标

提出混凝土面板堆石坝材料参数反演分析方法，揭示运行期混凝土面板堆石坝面板、垫层、堆石体的变形演变规律，提出了混凝土面板缝成因和发展趋势判别方法，建立了面板堆石坝变形和渗流安全指标体系，申请11件技术专利，获授权9件。发表论文23篇，其中SCI检索8篇。项目应用每年新增利润3200多万元，经济效益、防洪及环保等社会效益显著。

（三）对促进行业科技进步的作用和意义

运行期混凝土面板堆石坝安全直接取决于上游面板的工作状态。面板工作状态目前主要依据面板挠度变形、结构接缝的测缝计和面板的钢筋计以及坝后渗压和渗漏观测量进行判断。随着运行期延长，面板的面板挠度变形、测缝计、钢筋计和渗压计常较多失效，面板新出现的裂缝一般难以安装测缝计（除可降水位以上），工作状态也难以保证。因此，直接通过堆石体内外变形和坝后渗漏量判断大坝面板工作性态是必然选择。项目研究成果为依据面板堆石坝堆石体内外变形（尤其外部变形）和坝后渗漏量判断面板工作状态，监控大坝安全提供了新的技术和方法，对确保面板堆石坝长期运行安全有重要意义，为面板坝变形与渗流安全指标的国家标准创建提供技术支撑。

（四）应用推广情况

成果已在福建芹山大坝进行应用，并推广应用于贵州洪家渡、福建万安溪和周宁混凝土面板堆石坝等工程，并通过合作单位的优势，将成果进一步推广至全国相关行业以及国外相关合作工程。

（华电宁德电力开发有限公司　郑志太 吴金荣）

寒冷地区抽水蓄能电站水库冰情研究

“寒冷地区抽水蓄能电站水库冰情研究”是2012年12月中国水电工程顾问集团公司委托北京勘测设计研究院开展的项目，2013年1月正式启动，2018年7月完成。

（一）项目背景

冰情对寒冷及严寒地区抽水蓄能电站的施工、运行和防洪影响较大。寒冷地区抽水蓄能电站在运行中可能出现的冰情包括：

（1）水库水位涨落幅度大，若出现水面短暂冰封，随着水位迅速下降，可能发生冰盖/岸冰破裂，出现破碎冰带的现象。冰盖/岸冰在破裂过程中，会对接触到的水工建筑物产生作用，可能损坏相关建筑物，如库岸护坡、防渗结构和拦污栅等。

（2）在水面不能完全冰封的情况下，水体与大气直接接触进行热交换，水体中会产生冰花，冰花一般具有较强的粘附性，容易黏附在水工建筑物上，如进/出水口拦污栅，影响过流面积。

（3）非正常运行条件下，水库水位长时间静止，库水表面可能会全部封冻，形成冰盖，对电站抽水或发电可能会产生不利影响。

因此在抽水蓄能电站设计和运行中，需要考虑电站冰冻情况及消长过程，结冰对电站运行的影响，以及结冰量对水库有效库容的侵占情况，系统研究寒冷及严寒气候条件下抽水蓄能电站水库冰冻情况，以及抽水蓄能电站水库冰的形成、发展和消融过程。项目选取我国寒冷及严寒地区建成的十三陵、张河湾、西龙池、蒲石河、呼和浩特5个典型抽水蓄能电站为研究对象开展研究工作。

（二）研究内容

（1）通过对寒冷地区典型抽水蓄能电站进行原型监测、现场调查与资料收集等方式，获取电站冰情资料，分析其形成及长消过程，为电站防治冰害提供依据。分析抽水蓄能电站气温、风速和风向、辐射等气象因子的特性及其对抽水蓄能电站冰情的影响。

（2）总结电站冰情和电站抽水/发电次数、抽水/发电时间、上下库水位变幅、水温等运行因子的特性，分析抽水蓄能电站水库冰情与运行方式之间的相互关系。

（3）分析寒冷地区抽水蓄能电站冰厚的影响因素，提出电站最大冰厚的计算方法与冰冻库容的确定方法，为寒冷地区抽水蓄能电站冰冻库容设计提供技术支撑。

（4）对寒冷地区抽水蓄能电站水库冬季结冰过程进行数值模拟，为电站防治冰害提供参考依据。

（5）总结抽水蓄能电站冰情对水工建筑物影响的一般类型，分析汇总抽水蓄能电站冰情对水工建筑物的影响规律，提出电站水工建筑物防治冰害应注意的问题。

（三）主要成果和创新点

（1）首次对我国北方寒冷和严寒地区抽水蓄能电站水库冰情开展了系统的原型监测，分析了水库冰情的影响因素及其影响特征，总结了抽水蓄能电站水库冰层的形成及其消长规律。

（2）首次建立了反映上、下水库水体混掺作用的抽水蓄能电站水库冰情数学模型，模拟结果与实测结果比较接近，该模型提供了一种抽水蓄能电站冰情预报工具，完善了冰情研究方法。

（3）提出了抽水蓄能电站最大冰厚和冰冻库容计算经验公式，并改进了水电站下游最小不封冻距离计算公式。

（4）提出了冰情对水工建筑物的影响类型，分析研究了抽水蓄能电站冻融循环次数，为抽水蓄能电站防冰害材料设计和措施选择提供了参考依据。

（5）提出了寒冷与严寒地区抽水蓄能电站冬季防冰害运行方式。

项目经鉴定为整体达到国际先进水平，在抽水蓄能电站水库冰情数值模拟及冰冻库容计算方法方面达到国际领先水平。项目发表论文3篇，目前获2项发明专利申请受理通知书。

（四）成果应用

该项目提出的冬季防冰运行方式在呼和浩特、张河湾和西龙池等抽水蓄能电站进行了两个冬季的应用，采用建议的方式运行，电站运行均几乎不受冰情的影响，具有良好的经济效益。同时，该课题提出的冰冻库容计算方法已在红石、蛟河、清原、尚义和浑源抽水蓄能电站的工程设计中应用，降低了水库坝高，节约了工程投资。

（中国电建集团北京勘测设计研究院有限公司　赵海镜）

高水头下坝面土工膜缺陷演化机制与渗漏耦合效应研究

“高水头下坝面土工膜缺陷演化机制与渗漏耦合效应研究”为江苏省自然科学基金项目，由河海大学承担并于2018年9月完成。

该项目着重对土工膜缺陷相关的力学特性和渗流（渗漏）特性开展相关的试验研究、理论分析和数值模拟，并借助典型土工膜防渗土石坝，开展一定的工程应用研究，获得一些定性和定量的研究成果。具体研究内容主要包括以下几个方面：

（1）阐述和评价工程界关注的土工膜缺陷属性及缺陷引起的渗漏问题的国内外研究现状和研究成果。

（2）利用图像数字相关技术，通过拉伸试验对土工膜缺陷演化过程进行全程测试分析。

（3）利用改装的大型剪切仪，对土工膜与砂砾石开展剪切试验，获得土工膜接触面循环剪切劲度和阻尼比变化规律，供土工膜稳定分析之用。

（4）对典型的土工膜防渗土石坝开展土工膜不同缺陷条件（缺陷大小、缺陷位置、单个或随机多个）大坝三维渗流场数值计算，分析和评价缺陷渗漏对大坝防渗安全性的影响程度，提出土工膜缺陷渗漏工程控制措施。

（5）对坝面土工膜缺陷条件下土工膜的局部稳定性开展了计算分析，考虑了不同的缺陷属性（大小、位置、数量）的影响，同时对库水降落速度和垫层透水性等进行定量分析，为运行期坝面土工膜抗滑稳定设计提供理论指导。

（6）在探讨土工膜渗透机理及缺陷渗漏特性的基础上，采用水气二相非饱和渗流理论对坝面防渗土工膜有、无缺陷条件下的土石坝开展库水降落过程时的大坝非恒定渗流场分析，考虑土工膜缺陷渗漏的耦合效应，按照非饱和土强度理论计算库水降落过程中上游坝坡的抗滑稳定安全系数和失效概率的变化规律，同时分析了基质吸力和气相对大坝上游坝坡稳定性的影响程度。

（河海大学）

分布式电源与微网并网保护方案研究及控制仿真软件开发

“分布式电源与微网并网保护方案研究及控制仿真软件开发”为企事业单位委托科技项目，由河海大学与南京四方亿能电力自动化有限公司合作，于2018年12月完成。

该项目针对目前我国分布式发电高速发展，研究了分布式电源接入电网的一系列问题。主要研究成果如下：

（1）提出新的逆变器电源控制方式（自适应控制）以及逆变器电源故障后控制方式（变频控制）。

（2）提出分布式电源接入配电网的分层控制方案，将有分布式电源接入的配电网分为配网层，并网层，微网层，采用不同的策略分别进行保护。

（3）在并网层面，提出基于逆变器电源自适应控制的反孤岛保护方案，即利用逆变器电源的控制特性，使得处于孤岛运行的逆变器电源更具明显的孤岛特征。

（4）在微网层面，提出变频式继电保护方法，即通过逆变器电源将故障点信息调制到频率中去，保护装置能够通过解调获得虚拟短路电流，该电流等价于旋转发电机的短路电流，同时可以恢复出相应的虚拟电压。

（河海大学）

典型环境下水工混凝土植筋系统的承载力退化机理研究

“典型环境下水工混凝土植筋系统的承载力退化机理研究”为江苏省自然科学基金项目，由河海大学承担并于2018年3月完成。

该项目从混凝土基材的劣化到典型环境下胶混黏结界面的劣化等多方面入手，通过大量的单筋拉拔试验，研究了典型环境下化学植筋承载力的短期劣化性能；通过内聚力模型和ABAQUS有限元软件，研究了胶混黏结界面的模拟方法及其劣化本构关系的构建方法，建立了基于混凝土损伤与胶混黏结界面劣化的化学植筋劣化模型。

项目创新地将内聚力模型引入到化学植筋承载力数值模拟计算中，推导了黏结界面内聚力模型中关键参数的理论公式，建立了化学植筋受力系统劣化模型。项目发表论文7篇，其中SCI/EI收录论文3篇；申请发明专利3项，已授权发明专利2项；项目培养研究生2名。项目的推广应用前景广阔。

（河海大学）

沅水流域梯级水电站安全风险调查及对策措施研究

“沅水流域梯级水电站安全风险调查及对策措施研究”是原国家安全生产监督管理总局2015年安全生产重大事故防治关键技术科技项目“流域梯级水电站安全与应急研究”课题的组成部分，由中国电建集团中南勘测设计研究院有限公司承担，现将研究成果简介如下。

（一）沅水流域安全风险现状分析

1. 工程安全风险

（1）流域地震灾害风险：沅水流域位于华南地震区的雪峰—武夷地震带及华中地震区的汉水地震带，

根据地震历史记录，自公元1509年以来，沅水流域除下游常德曾发生过6.5级地震外，流域内及其附近地区所发生的历史地震相当于或小于6级。沅水流域大部分地区地震动峰值加速度为0.05g，相应地震基本烈度为6度；下游桃源地震动峰值加速度为0.10g，常德地震动峰值加速度为0.15g，相应地震基本烈度为7度。沅水流域梯级各水电站工程区附近均无大的活动断裂存在，库区大型滑坡堆积体、蠕动变形岩体均距离枢纽工程区较远。地震可能会造成近坝库岸和部分堆积体崩塌，引发地质灾害，但以局部小规模的崩塌、小型滑坡灾害为主。因此，地震灾害对流域各水电站的工程影响较小。

（2）流域地质灾害风险：调查发现，沅水流域主要地质灾害隐患有：东岭信滑坡堆积体、岩洞湾滑坡、乃寿老渡口岸坡、展依变形岸坡、南埃大寨变形岸坡、南包变形岸坡、红土坡滑坡体、麻阳蠕变体、菜溪蠕变体、三门溪蠕变体和坌处蠕变体等；大型滑坡堆积体、蠕动变形岩体一般距离枢纽工程区较远，近坝库岸变形体一般规模相对较小，一般处于稳定或基本稳定状态。工程区潜在的不稳定边坡等地质灾害隐患已采取了有效的工程措施进行治理，并布设了安全监测系统。沅水流域地质灾害总体可控，对工程影响较小。

（3）超标洪水及溃坝风险：近年来，极端天气出现频率有逐渐增加的趋势，各流域内因高强度、长历时暴雨导致的超标洪水也偶有出现。2014年7月11～18日，沅水中下游的部分干支流发生了超历史的特大洪水。其中武水河溪站和桃源水库入库洪峰流量频率达到50年一遇。调研发现，沅水流域河道内乱挖乱采现象已导致水电站坝前水位壅高，使得实际坝前水位和流量关系曲线与计算采用的曲线产生偏差。这极大影响了电站的防汛调度，梯级水库群面临溃坝的风险也大幅提高，尤其是对于无调节能力的径流式电站。

（4）调度事故风险：沅水流域梯级水电站为多业主单位开发，水情信息未实现共享。各电站对上下游水情信息的获取主要通过水情信息公众号、电话、微信群等方式，但这些方式存在时效性差、信息不对等、信息不透明等问题，直接影响各电站对闸门的调度。目前，沅水流域各电站的防洪调度由地方防汛办负责，并未实现全流域的统筹调度和水情信息共享。调研过程中，各电站均表达了对实现流域统一、联合调度的强烈诉求。

2. 公共安全风险

（1）近坝库区风险：沅水流域各水电站库区内河道采砂、水产养殖、电鱼捕鱼等现象十分普遍，各类船只、养殖网箱在近坝区域分布较多。偶发性洪水或汛期上游泄洪时段，船只容易失控成为僵尸船，冲向大坝，极大影响闸门安全运行，甚至威胁大坝安全。2017年7月3日，清水塘水电站库区一艘采砂船失控，漂至坝前阻塞闸门，给正常运行带来严重影响，处理耗费了大量的人力和精力。

（2）坝顶公路交通风险：沅水流域多个电站的坝顶被用作社会公路，来往车辆普遍存在超载、超限现象，且无人监管，极大影响了大坝的结构安全。此外，危化品车辆一旦在坝顶公路上发生爆炸或倾覆，将威胁整个电站的安全。现场调研发现，清水塘水电站在坝顶公路设置了限宽、限高设施和标志，但过往车辆因不遵从规定，超限现象普遍。

（3）通航风险：沅水流域各水电站都具有通航功能，船只过闸时若发生火灾、倾覆等事故，将极大影响电站的安全运行，引发不良的社会影响。目前，部分水电站船闸超负荷运行，给电站安全运行带来风险。现场调研发现，桃源水电站在通航过程中出现过船只因超载超限而搁浅，从而导致通航船只人员与电站发生纠纷；甚至有船只不遵从通航的规定和规范要求，在闸室过夜，给电站通航管理带来巨大风险。

（4）战争及恐怖袭击事件风险：据不完全统计，2001～2017年，国外共发生了25起大型水利水电设施严重受袭事件，并有逐步增加的趋势，严重威胁了大坝的运行安全，造成了极大的社会影响。沅水流域多个水电站坝顶被用作社会公路，且无人监管，不法分子或恐怖分子极易在坝顶制造恐怖袭击事件，潜在的风险巨大。

（二）风险防范对策措施研究

（1）健全水库大坝安全管理法规。《水库大坝安全管理条例》有关大坝业主和政府监管部门在大坝安全方面的责任与现行上位法的相关规定不符，对各级政府和各行业主管部门的职责划分不清晰，对不履行主体责任的大坝运行单位和不履行监管责任的政府监管机构的处罚过轻、过于笼统，甚至没有规定。因此加快修订《水库大坝安全管理条例》，并尽快出台，加强执法力度，可从根源上解决目前存在的库区乱采乱挖和养鱼电鱼、坝顶用作社会公路、通航超载超限等现象。

（2）充分利用河长制的制度优势。2017年推行河长制以来，沅水流域河长制工作稳步推进，已建立省、市、县、乡、村五级河长体系，深入开展僵尸船、排污口整治、网箱养鱼、坝前垃圾清理等专项行动，取得了较好的工作成效。沅水流域各梯级水电站应充分利用河长制的制度优势，积极配合依托河长制开展的僵尸船、网箱养鱼、采砂整治等专项行动，解决僵尸船、网箱养鱼、库区采砂等问题，减少因此带来的安全风险。

（3）建设沅水流域安全与应急综合信息平台。通过该平台建设，可以实现流域水情信息的共享；实现流域防汛的统一、联合调度；实现流域地质、大坝、库区数据的统一监测和预警，以及出现较大事故时全流域的应急资源统一调配、灾情预警及应急联动。

（4）加强流域水电站反恐怖防范体系建设。当前，沅水流域大部分水电站已建立反恐怖防范体系。但现场调研发现，部分水电站尚未建立反恐怖防范组织机构，反恐怖防范重要目标分类结果也未报地方人民政府反恐怖主管部门审核、备案。因此，应坚持“突出重点、预防为主、属地负责、分级管理”的原则，按照国家现行《电力行业反恐怖防范标准（试行）（水电工程部分）》和《电力设施治安风险等级和安全防范要求》的有关要求，结合各电站实际，加强反恐怖防范体系建设，提高流域水电站反恐怖能力。

（中国电建集团中南勘测设计研究院有限公司　袁东成　戴陈梦子　潘建）

东方电气集团东方电机有限公司 2018年水电技术进步有关情况

2018年，东方电气集团东方电机有限公司（简称东方电机）按照公司“十三五”科技发展规划的总体部署，主动适应经济发展新常态，开展了白鹤滩百万水电机组、长龙山高水头抽水蓄能机组等一批高端水电新产品的开发，推进了产品技术向高性能、高质量、高可靠方向发展，积极打造水电差异化产业技术竞争优势，持续提升了自主创新能力。在水电主导产品研制、关键核心技术攻关等方面均取得了突出成绩。

（一）1000MW混流式水电精品工程扎实推进

围绕打造白鹤滩1000MW水电机组精品工程，东方电机立足于自主创新，以研究和试验为基础，开展了一系列新技术研究以确保白鹤滩巨型机组的设计合理，确保机组的长期连续安全稳定高效运行。

2018年，东方电机白鹤滩1000MW水轮发电机主要部件施工设计及水轮机全套施工图纸、技术资料的设计和编制全部提前完工。

2018年，东方电机白鹤滩首台精品座环和转轮均顺利通过了业主的验收，各项指标全面满足精品制造要求，精品工程扎实推进。

（二）长龙山350MW抽水蓄能机组等研制取得突破

2018年，东方电机以长龙山350MW抽水蓄能机组开发项目为依托，以研制成功750m水头段350MW级抽水蓄能机组为目标，开展了机组的总体设计、水力开发、电磁设计、高效全空冷技术、推力轴承技术、定子绝缘技术、转轮动应力测试、材料研究、关键部件制造技术等重大专题科研攻关。长龙山模型转轮通过了用户验收，发电机主要部件设计、机组全部施工图纸、技术资料的编制及生产用工艺文件的编制全部完成。

东方电机还持续开展了丰宁二期等高水头、大容量抽水蓄能机组的技术开发，使得机组的效率、稳定性和可靠性等指标再上新台阶；可变速抽水蓄能机组关键技术研究也取得了阶段性成果。

（三）水电机组降本取得实效

为提升水电机组的市场竞争力，东方电机从设计改进、结构优化、智能制造、工装工具通用化等方面持续推进水电机组的降本工作，并取得实效。

（四）水电机组设计和开发管理体系不断完善

东方电机持续推进了水电机组设计和开发管理体系的完善工作。重点梳理了设计和开发流程、接口，结合ISO9001体系新要求，于2018年修订了设计开发控制管理制度，保证了水电机组设计和开发有序、高效、保质开展，防范了水电机组设计和开发风险。

（五）冲击式水力试验台建设稳步推进

作为水力开发当中最为重要的手段和工具，模型试验台承担着验证水力设计、预测真机性能、开展基础研究、执行验收试验等功能。为拓展市场空间，加快冲击式水电机组的自主开发进程，东方电机于2018年完成了冲击式水力试验台设备的安装调试，2019年将正式投入使用。

（东方电气集团东方电机有限公司　余小波）

哈尔滨电机厂有限责任公司 2018年主要科研项目情况

2018年，哈尔滨电机厂有限责任公司（简称哈电电机公司）主要科研项目进展情况如下：

1. 海水抽水蓄能电站可变速机组关键技术研究

对可变速抽水蓄能机组设计、制造及海水抽水蓄能机组过流部件防污、防腐关键技术进行了深入研究和分析。在交流励磁发电电动机绝缘方案设计、结构设计，可变速水泵水轮机参数选择、转轮设计、防腐结构分析等方面均取得阶段性成果。针对可变速抽水蓄能交流励磁发电电动机特点，自主开发了一套可变速抽水蓄能交流励磁发电电动机电磁设计软件，并进行了10MW可变速交流励磁发电电动机进行电磁设计。海水抽水蓄能电站防污、防腐、防渗关键技术研究方面，针对海水抽蓄机组的结构特点，分析了外加电流阴极保护及电解海水防污技术的应用可行性，对机组技术管路、蝶阀等部件的防污方案进行了设计研究。

2. 水力发电设备智能远程运维新模式　该项目在已开发的水力发电设备智能远程运维系统 V1.0 的基础上，全面开展智能远程运维新模式建设。充分整合机组相关运行数据，对机组的运行状态进行全面诊断；采用多维全信息智能诊断技术，提取出科学的控制指标，实现对发电设备的运行状态测评；运用 FTA 故障诊断分析工具，面向机组的故障现象，形成机组故障诊断的专家知识库。使电站机组由“状态监测”提升至“智能化运维”，构建以水电云服务平台为中心，集故障智能诊断、产品维护、售后服务、备品管理及产品优化为一体的水力发电设备智能远程运维新模式。

3. 新型并列转子结构无刷混合励磁同步发电机研究　对新型并列转子结构无刷混合励磁同步发电机研究进行了深入研究和分析。提出的端部铁芯磁极结构，可使电机定子铁芯长度降低 7.6%，进一步提高了功率密度。提出基于谐波相抵的转子磁极匹配方法，改善了输出电压波形质量。采用 3D 有限元法进行了仿真计算，并试制了 2 台样机进行试验验证，样机的仿真及试验结果基本一致。

4. 基于 PEEK 复合材料的低损耗高速重载推力轴承研究　此项目以基于聚醚醚酮（polyetheretherketone PEEK）复合材料的低损耗高速重载推力轴承为研究对象，利用研制的试验台，完成了 3 种 PEEK 复合材料模型轴承的 1200 次启停磨损试验，考核 PEEK 复合材料的模型特性，筛选出耐磨性最优的 PEEK 复合材料。通过有限元编程计算雷诺方程、能量方程等其他方程、公式，最终开发出了不考虑界面滑移效应的轴承热弹流润滑理论计算程序。下一步将对 PEEK 复合材料的耐磨机理进行研究，并在高速推力轴承试验台上完成复合材料轴承的试验。

5. 大中型电机定子线棒高导热主绝缘材料基础研究　此项目以大中型电机定子线棒高导热主绝缘材料为研究对象，于 2018 年 8 月荣获黑龙江省自然科学基金重点项目支持。高导热胶黏剂导热性能优化分为小颗粒直径、小颗粒添加量、直径 10μm 大颗粒添加量三个因素，开展大量试验工作，初步摸索出了 BN 填料颗粒直径、BN 填料小颗粒填充量、BN 填料大颗粒填充对复合材料导热性能的影响，并结合试验结果试制出高导热云母带，测试并对比导热系数，并用高导热云母带压制试验线棒，完成介质损耗、击穿电压等电气试验，后续将开展电老化试验。

6. 超高水头单级水泵水轮机水力性能研究　此项目以阳江抽水蓄能为依托。该电站单机容量 400MW、转速 500r/min，是目前国内单机容量最大的超高水头抽水蓄能电站。项目针对超高水头水泵水轮机空化初生、压力脉动、效率等问题开展了深入研究，进行了水泵水轮机全流到数值模拟，经过多次的试验验证，在水轮机效率、水泵效率、水泵驼峰区安全裕度和水轮机“S”区安全裕度等性能上均取得了优异成果，使我国水泵水轮机关键性能已达到或接近世界同类机组水平，超高水头、超大容量水泵水轮机水力研发达到世界一流的水平。

7. 低水头混流式水轮机水力性能开发研究　此项目以五强溪为依托，针对低水头混流式水轮机的特点，从水力通道和转轮优化、叶片翼型的优化设计、尾水管形状优化等方面展开研究，建立了尾水管涡带和压力脉动之间的关系，设计合理的面积变化规律和压力分布规律，不但有利于水轮机水力效率的提高，而且对于减弱尾水管涡带压力脉动强度也十分有益。该项目在中国水利水电科学研究院进行的水轮机同台对比试验表明，其模型转轮性能与之前在该院复核试验的结果基本一致，其中复核试验结果水轮机真机加权效率高达 92.59%，达到了同水头段世界先进水平。

8. 单吸多级离心泵的水力研发　我国对于多级泵的叶轮技术经验比较匮乏，在叶轮开发和级间导叶开发方面存在难点。此项目基于小浪底引黄项目，以现有的性能良好的单级单吸大泵的叶轮以及抽水蓄能水轮机的转轮为基础，选取参数相近的基础叶轮，结合设计要求，通过 CFD 优化设计并结合模型试验，根据实际工程情况，对流道和叶轮进行反复优化，开发参数合适、性能良好并满足要求的单吸多级泵。水力设计方面，已经完成了单吸双级泵的各部件的水力通道设计工作；模型装置设计方面，针对多级泵有两个叶轮的特点，初步完成了模型装置的结构设计工作。

9. 高水头大容量抽蓄机组顶盖、蜗壳座环联合受力计算模型确定　抽水蓄能机组逐步向高水头、大容量和高转速化方向发展，机组结构尺寸增大，刚强度水平受到严峻考验。该项目对高水头大容量抽蓄机组顶盖、蜗壳座环非线性联合受力方式进行分析研究，确定了联合受力力学模型，规范了非线性分析接触参数的选择原则，并和独立计算结果进行比较，以满足实际工程的需要。

10. 绝缘技术研究　此项目致力于材料研发、工艺优化、技术创新等方面工作，在新型高场强主绝缘材料研制基础上，全面开展高压电机定子线棒主绝缘厚度减薄工作，已取得阶段性成果。该项目的成功攻关将为最大限度的减少电机材料用量，提高电机产品容量提供强有力的支持，目前该项目正在进行中。

11. 水电机组关键材料疲劳及断裂性能研究　此

项目主要研究用于蜗壳制造的几种高强钢板的异种焊接接头金相组织及力学性能及其影响因素，参考B780CF钢板与B610CF钢板以及B610CF钢板与S500Q钢板常规焊接工艺，综合分析论证，采用盲孔法残余应力测试钢板焊接后的热处理效果，对高强钢板焊接接头裂纹扩展速率及门槛值进行研究，对高强钢板焊接接头断裂韧性研究，确定合适的消除残余应力热处理工艺参数，保证焊缝及热影响区的力学性能，对于保证大型水电机组安全运行具有重要意义。

12. 重点技术引进、技术合作项目情况　2017年底，与美国GE公司签订了W86燃气轮发电机技术引进项目；2018年初，收到GE提供的典型机资料，图纸、规范共1200多份，在年底完成所有资料的翻译转化。2017年6月，与瑞士洛桑水力机械试验室签订灯泡式水轮机开发模型试验技术引进项目；2018年9月顺利完成模型试验，各项指标符合要求；同时，瑞方向哈电电机公司提供了全部图纸和资料，这标志着哈电电机公司6叶片贯流式水轮机技术水平登上了更高的台阶。

（哈尔滨电机厂有限责任公司　刘保生）

河海大学 2018年科研工作情况

2018年，河海大学在科研经费、科技奖励、科技成果及基地等方面的情况如下：

在科研经费方面，全年新增科技经费总量9.61亿元，其中科技合同经费6.53亿元，到款科技经费5.89亿元；科技产业和科研成果转化支持经费3.08亿元。获国家自然科学基金资助项目157项，资助经费8734.8万元，其中重点项目5项，重大计划重点支持项目1项，重大项目课题1项。主持国家重点研发计划项目4项，课题20项，资助经费12197万元。获江苏省自然科学基金34项，其中杰青项目2项，优青项目2项，获江苏省社科基金9项。

在科技奖励方面，参与获得国家科技进步二等奖1项，获省部级奖励84项，其中河海大学主持33项，主要有：高等学校科学研究优秀成果奖（科学技术）一等奖1项，二等奖3项；江苏省科学技术奖一等奖1项，二等奖1项，三等奖1项；江苏省第十五届哲学社会科学优秀成果奖一等奖2项，二等奖3项，三等奖5项；大禹水利科学技术奖特等奖1项，三等奖1项。

在科技成果及基地方面，发表SCI/SSCI1595篇，1区2区SCI论文占比33%。发明专利数量保持稳定，获中国专利优秀奖1项，授权国内发明专利762件。“江苏省城乡饮用水安全保障研究中心”获江苏省发展改革委批准立项建设；“水文水资源与水利工程科学国家重点实验室”通过5年评估，获得优秀。

（河海大学）

中国电力建设集团有限公司 2018年科技发展与创新情况

（一）强化顶层设计，统筹创新驱动战略部署

为深入贯彻“十九大”精神，落实国家科技部、国资委《关于进一步推进中央企业创新发展的意见》，切实有效的推动集团创新驱动战略实施，提出中国电建《关于进一步推进中央企业创新发展的意见》实施方案，确定了技术攻关、协同创新平台、成果转化应用、国际科技创新合作、研发投入、创新激励机制、创新人才队伍建设、双创工作推进、创新成果基金等各方面的工作要求和进度安排，进一步丰富细化了创新工作任务清单和责任主体，为公司创新驱动战略的持续纵深推进提供了可靠的依据。

（二）创新型企业建设

认真学习贯彻党的十九大创新理念及全国科技创新大会精神，积极落实集团公司“十三五”创新驱动发展战略，持续推动成员企业创新型企业、高新技术企业建设工作。年度新增5家省、市级创新型企业，14家企业分获省级、市级创新型企业认定，高新技术企业已增至86家；不断增加创新资金投入，2018年研发投入占营业收入3.04%。有力的促进了集团公司与成员企业发展方式转变和创新能力提升。

（三）研发平台体系建设

着力打造国家级高端研发平台。充分发挥协同创新优势，持续加大资源投入，新增国家级研发平台2个，国家级研发平台已达8个。依托企业技术中心、国家能源水电工程技术研发中心、垃圾焚烧技术与装备国家工程实验室等一批国家级研发平台，把脉水电、风电、太阳能等可再生能源领域科技创新的战略方向，深入开展中国风电、太阳能技术标准“走出去”、优化能源配置推动能源供给侧改革研究、垃圾焚烧烟气污染物超低排放处理技术研究等事关行业发展的政策性、战略性课题研究，做好相关领域标准化体系建设和管理工作，为国家可再生能源行业重点工程建设、行业可持续发展和科学监督评估提供支撑。

在稳步推进国家级创新技术平台的同时，所属企业根据自身发展需要及技术优势，积极推进省级创新技术平台建设。2018年集团新增省部级以上研发平台7家，省部级研发平台达83个。其中，以华东、成都、中南、贵州勘测设计研究院有限公司等为代表

的一批设计企业，加强了数字化经济和区域新能源业务打造，新增数字城市CIM技术浙江省工程研究中心、浙江省智慧轨道交通工程技术研究中心、贵州省分布式能源技术应用工程研究中心等专业研发平台，为集团转型升级创造了条件。

积极培育集团海外研发平台。有效引导并扶持有意愿、有能力的企业持续推进海外创新工作，结合集团海外发展战略，支持并资助山东电力建设第一工程有限公司、海外投资有限公司等分别组建巴西电网工程技术（美洲）研究院、老挝南欧江流域电力开发研究院等2家典型海外研发机构，围绕重点海外工程的技术研发、创新成果转化应用，以及属地化管理等方面持续开展工作，加快海外研发机构建设步伐，提升企业海外创新能力，促进集团属地化发展和海外品牌影响。

（四）科技项目管理情况

持续强化集团创新战略引领和成员企业创新主体作用，在做好传统优势业务领域关键共性技术研发工作的基础上，加大新兴产业技术攻关投入力度、强化现代信息技术融合应用，系统推进重点技术攻关和标准化建设，促进各业务领域核心关键技术研发和转化应用。积极整合集团内外创新资源，充分发挥成员企业技术优势，积极承担国家重大科技任务，牵头组织并参与了“堰塞坝险情处置与开发利用保障技术与装备研发”等12项新立国家重点研发计划、国家自然科学基金项目及课题；不断加大企业重大技术攻关组织管理力度，在持续有效推进国际标准应用、水环境治理、水电设计施工一体化、水文气象等重大专项的同时，全面开展“太阳能热发电设计、装备制造及施工建造系统集成技术研究”等光热发电、地铁信息化、核电领域3项重大专项，积极筹划推进军民融合、川藏铁路建设重大技术攻关，新增76项集团级重点项目和标准化建设项目，以及两千多项成员企业自立项目，强化新兴产业技术攻关和现代信息技术融合，有效推进了各业务领域现代技术体系的建设。较好地发挥了集团在技术创新方面的战略指引和带动作用。

（五）重大科技成果情况

2018年，持续推进集团及各成员企业科技项目研究，取得大批具有良好经济社会效益的科技创新成果。其中，由集团单位和个人同时牵头完成的“超深与复杂地质条件混凝土防渗墙关键技术”“300m级特高拱坝安全控制关键技术及工程应用”，参与完成的“超大型水电站用金属结构关键材料成套技术开发应用”“水力式升船机关键技术及应用”分别获国家科技进步、技术发明二等奖；“高混凝土面板堆石坝关键技术创新”成果获首届国际大坝委员会科技创新奖，“300m级高心墙堆石坝施工关键技术研究与应用”等一批创新成果先后获得298项省部级科学技术奖项。大批重大技术攻关的持续推动和优秀创新成果的广泛应用，不仅为提升公司发展质量、巩固市场优势、提高品牌影响力提供了有力的技术支持，也为各相关行业的技术进步、健康发展做出了积极贡献。

知识产权创造与管理能力稳步提升。组织开展知识产权核心竞争力专题研究，促进知识产权创造由量到质的转变。新授权专利2643项，其中发明专利420项，累计有效达到12136项，其中发明专利1890项。不断完善技术标准体系建设，年度制修订国家与行业标准415项，其中新立项134项，完成发布159项。组织开展水电、火电、地铁等工法体系研究，年度获行业和省部级工法340余项，集团级工法397项，促进了工法体系的科学完备有效性。

有序推进科技成果工程化。积极完善科技创新投入、研发、转化、应用机制，依托集团所属水环境公司、地铁公司等平台公司，集成集约集团现有的技术资源，全面推动水资源与水环境治理技术领域、地铁等领域业务技术体系建设。围绕解决重点业务领域重大技术难题，加强合作创新，实施联合攻关，积极推动产学研结合，利用内外科技资源，探索多种方式，实现集团公司各业务领域技术跨越发展，以现场观摩、技术咨询等多种形式交流推广科技成果，有效促进了科技成果的转化应用。

（六）科技创新体制机制建设

深入研究国资委、科技部和财政部等相关部委对于中央企业股权及分红激励最新政策和工作要求，结合集团所属企业现状和成员企业实施分红激励意愿，积极推进集团股权激励和分红激励方案实施；积极推进集团科技成果转化基金建设研究工作，促进科技成果资本化、产业化；开展集团科技创新项目低息贷款方案研究，并开展《中国电力建设股份有限公司科技项目优惠贷款管理办法》制定，争取拓宽成员企业创新资金来源；促进了集团科技体制机制创新。

在企业发展中，不断完善《中国电力建设股份有限公司科技进步考核暂行办法》。系统研究集团科技发展要求，完善相关创新要素，科学调整指标权重，较好引导各企业创新驱动发展功能定位和发展新要求。依据中国电建集团科学技术奖励办法，设立科技奖励专项资金，加大对科技人才的激励力度，表彰做出突出贡献的先进集体和个人。

（七）协同创新情况

积极整合集团内外优质科技创新资源，依托企业技术中心、国家工程实验室、工程技术中心、院士工作站、博士后工作站等各级研发平台，与行业权威科研机构、高校，以及产业链上下游相关企业，进行全方位、多层次科技合作，组织开展重大技术攻关、重大工程建设咨询、院士学术讲座和专项技术培训，为服务国家重大战略实施、重点工程建设提供有力支撑和保障。

（1）联合开展技术攻关，系统推进产学研用深度融合。在水电业务领域，携手河海大学、清华大学、武汉大学、中国水利水电科学研究院等权威高校和科研机构，积极推进“共建水安全与水科学协同创新中心”建设，结合老挝南欧江梯级流域、雅砻江锦屏一级、澜沧江如美、拉哇等国内外水利水电工程，系统开展“复杂条件下特高土石坝建设与长期安全保障关键技术”“大坝安全评估智能管理技术”“土石坝异常渗流探测及长期渗流安全分析评价关键技术研究”“混凝土数字化施工与精细化控制成套技术”等大批工程共性技术攻关，为强化国家水资源和水利水电工程安全，提高工程建设质量奠定坚实基础。在火电业务领域，先后与清华大学、同济大学、华北电力大学、中国电力科学研究院、上海电力学院等科研院所建立战略合作伙伴关系，广泛开展科技合作，持续推进变电站节能技术体系研究、地下变电站全寿命周期成本研究、脱硫废水蒸发处理技术研究等多项技术攻关，为推进火电高效节能环保创造良好条件。同时，积极与中船重工集团等大型企业组队出海，联合开展海上散货自动化转运设备与系统研制等研究工作，为孟加拉吉达港燃煤电厂工程建设物资设备物流管控提供解决方案。在新能源领域，与河海大学、天津大学、上海交通大学等高校联合开展分布式光伏与梯级小水电互补联合发电技术研究及应用示范、海上风电开发系统创新方法集成与示范应用、新能源发电技术研究等一批国家重点研发计划任务；与国家电网有限公司、上海市电力公司等企业，联合开展智能电网、电动车、储能电站等领域关键技术研究，以及上海市深远海域海上风电重大示范工程关键技术攻关等一批地方科技任务，为实现水光多能互补、新能源发电，特别是海上风电开发等技术的推广示范应用提供支撑。在战略新兴领域，分别与浙江大学、华北电力大学、清华大学等高校，联合开展垃圾焚烧烟气污染物超低排放处理技术研究、太阳能光热发电的应用研究、非补燃式压缩空气储能技术研究、空气储能技术应用研究等重点研究工作，努力做好垃圾焚烧、光热发电、高效储能等战略新兴业务关键技术与人才培育和储备。

（2）发挥创新主体作用，推动新兴产业技术创新联盟发展。凭借在水环境治理、太阳能发电、地下管廊等领域技术开发和成果转化优势，成为水环境产业技术创新战略联盟（简称水环境联盟）理事长单位、光伏发电产业技术创新战略联盟副理事长单位、中国城市地下综合管廊产业联盟副理事长单位，以及国家太阳能光热产业技术创新战略联盟、青海省太阳能产业技术创新战略联盟单位，为推动新兴业务快速发展创造良好条件。其中，牵头组织的水环境联盟，年度新增 31 家单位入盟，成员涵盖基础研究、技术、装备、施工等产业链上下游单位，共计达 119 家。同时，发起并联合深圳市深港产学研环保工程技术股份有限公司等 5 家联盟成员单位，共同出资成立“华浩淼水生态环境技术研究院”，围绕水环境领域科研和工程项目，先后组织联盟成员单位联合开展技术攻关，进行技术交流数十余次，及时推动 8 项水环境治理领域团体标准发布，为完善水环境治理技术体系，加快水环境行业技术标准体系建立创造了良好条件。因成效突出，水环境联盟顺利通过了 2018 年中国产业技术创新战略联盟协同发展网员单位审批，成为 152 家国家试点联盟之一。

（3）积极组织和参与国内外学术交流活动，扩大企业影响力。以重大创新需求与关键技术为导向，依托企业院士工作站、博士后工作站等平台，加强与行业权威专家、学协会的沟通联系，积极开展学术研讨与交流。积极承办 2018 非洲国家水资源开发与水环境治理研修班、缅甸水资源管理能力建设研修班、斐济水源分析和实验室实践海外培训班等高端技术培训；凭借与美国本特利公司联合组建的 ECIDI-Bentley 中国 BIM 工程研究院，面向行业协会、政府部门以及工程领域相关企业等开展多项 BIM 解决方案及产品的宣传推广，以及工程三维数字化技术人才的培养认证；组织参与全球能源互联网与大学创新发展论坛、“电力之光”中国电力科普日展览、改革开放 40 年中国水电纪念大会、水科院组建 60 周年学术活动周，通过主旨报告及专题报告宣讲等多种方式，进一步宣传企业在相关业务领域的技术创新成果，不断扩大集团在国内外相关行业影响力。

（中国电力建设集团有限公司）

中国葛洲坝集团股份有限公司 2018 年科技工作情况

（一）科学技术成果

中国葛洲坝集团股份有限公司拥有国家级企业技术中心和博士后科研工作站、院士专家工作站，在水利水电、环保、装备等领域拥有多项国际领先、国际先进的科技成果。截至 2018 年底，取得包括国家科技进步奖在内的重大科技成果 1900 多项，其中国家级科技奖 22 项，省部级科技奖 120 余项；3900 余项专利获得国家授权，其中发明专利 483 项；主参编的

100余项国家及行业标准已发布；51项工法被评为国家级工法，379项工法被评为省部（行业）级工法；获得100余件软件著作权登记证书，注册商标122件；多次荣获国家鲁班奖、詹天佑奖及优质金质奖等奖项。

近年来，随着公司院士专家工作站建立，技术创新体系不断得到完善，在一些新的技术领域取得了新的突破。超大型水电站用金属结构关键材料成套技术、高韧性纤维混凝土制备与应用技术、特大型水电站深埋洞室群爆破施工控制理论与关键技术、高压富水复杂地层盾构成洞技术、黑臭水体修复技术、道路基础设施智能管养关键技术、超大型垂直升船机金属结构埋件及设备安装技术、现场混装爆破技术、大埋深超长隧洞施工关键技术等达到国际领先水平。同时，压缩空气储能装备技术、冰（水）蓄冷空调技术、大型中高电压电极锅炉、再生资源利用、水环境治理、固废处置技术、土壤修复技术等也达到国内领先或国际先进水平。

（二）技术中心

2004年，中国葛洲坝集团股份有限公司技术中心被国家发展和改革委员会、财政部、海关总署、国家税务总局联合认定为国家级企业技术中心，成为水利水电行业首家国家级技术中心。2018年，公司加强技术中心建设，16家子公司技术中心被认定为省级及以上技术中心。加强技术中心建设情况如下：

一是发布了科技研发机构达标管理办法。明确科技研发机构建设和达标标准，通过宣贯、调研，摸清19家单位科技研发机构建设现状。督促各单位科研机构提升技术支持服务水平，加强研发能力和转化能力。

二是完成4项重大科研项目和24项一般科研项目立项工作。组织参加科技部专项“重大自然灾害检测预警与防范”的子课题“堰塞湖风险评估与应急抢险技术和装备研发”项目研究，获得300余万元资金支持；“岩石爆破中侧向起爆条件下的爆炸能力传输机制与效益”项目获得国家自然科学基金委员会21万元资助资金，基础科学研究实现新突破。

三是规范科研预算管理。召开重大科技项目经费预算专题会，加大新兴业务应用研发，跟踪检查各单位科研经费投入和使用情况，年度科技投入比率提高至2.6%，年度科技投入达到28.86亿元，较上一年度提高了28.1%。

四是葛洲坝集团股份技术中心通过国家发改委2017～2018年度国家企业技术中心评价，位列34名，评定为“优秀”，较上一评价年度有了极大提升。同时，葛洲坝一公司、葛洲坝五公司、葛洲坝勘测设计公司等9家单位企业技术中心顺利通过湖北省发改委年度评价，葛洲坝五公司技术中心评价为“优秀”。

（三）院士专家工作站

葛洲坝股份公司院士专家工作站（以下简称工作站）2017年6月挂牌成立，入站院士达8名。2018年度，工作站筑巢引凤，建章立制，深入推进工作站建设。

一是制度建设。发布院士专家工作站管理办法、院士专家工作站建设指南等3项办法（指南），明确院士专家工作站建设、管理和运行要求。

二是科研机构建设。推动装备公司与马伟明院士合作，成功申报武汉市大规模混合物理储能国家技术创新中心创建，一公司与钱七虎院士团队联合成立南京地下空间研究院，绿园公司与陈勇院士团队共建固废处理利用研究所。

三是武汉市科协给予公司院士专家工作站30万元专项资金补助，并给4名符合条件的入站院士成功申请近50万元工作津贴，相关单位也积极配发院士津贴，并投入专项研发经费500余万元，同时为院士团队配备研发人员近百人。

四是推动葛洲坝易普力公司、葛洲坝绿园公司、葛洲坝装备公司等与院士团队新签订5个研发合同，涉及民爆、电化学储能、水环境治理等，研发金额合计400余万元。

五是组织“创新引领发展，科技助力提质”为主题的2018年“科普活动周”活动，旨在进一步促进科技创新与企业发展质量的紧密结合，提升科技创新支撑企业发展的能力。

（四）科技创新

2018年，公司进一步解放思想，加大科技创新，高新技术企业达到26家。主要创新内容：

一是扎实开展公司高新技术企业维护工作，53个科技项目顺利通过武汉市科技局审查，为公司节省1.65亿元。

二是公司顺利入选2017年度武汉市“千企万人”支持计划入选企业范围。

三是葛洲坝水务运营公司所属塘沽水厂、葛洲坝水泥公司所属当阳公司和松滋公司认定为湖北省“高新技术企业”；葛洲坝六公司被认定为云南省第八批知识产权优势企业。

四是优化公司科学技术奖评审，增设科技成果推广奖，增设了专家提名推荐成果通道，进一步提升成果质量。

五是召开新兴业务领域专利管理专题会，增强新兴业务领域单位知识产权保护重视程度，注重专利质量，提升专利管理工作水平。

六是组织开展“总工行”系列活动，组织各单位科技信息分管领导共同参观葛洲坝绿园公司淮安循环经济产业园和葛洲坝装备公司高端装备产业园，深入园区，现场学习。

七是开展了公司2018年度科学技术奖的评选工作。公司对“海泥固化专用材料及滩涂软基地基处理关键技术与应用”等6项成果授予一等奖，对“深地下特大型水电洞室群爆破施工强扰动效应控制理论与关键技术”等13项成果授予二等奖，对“一种防渗墙成槽循环钻进施工方法”等24项成果授予三等奖，共计43项成果获公司科学技术奖。

（五）主要科技成果

中国葛洲坝集团股份有限公司2018年获行业及以上科学技术奖66项，获省部级及行业级工法44部，获国家授权发明专利70件。

（中国葛洲坝集团股份有限公司）

雅砻江流域水电开发有限公司 2018年度科技工作情况

（一）技术创新体系建设情况

1. 博士后科研工作站　2018年，第四批博士后顺利通过出站报告评审。8月，第四批和第五批博士后分别完成出站和进站手续办理，保证了雅砻江流域水电开发有限公司（简称雅砻江公司）博士后科研工作站持续有效运行。

2. 企业技术中心　根据四川省经济和信息化委员会对省级企业技术中心要求，2018年每月定期报送了雅砻江公司科技创新月报；6月完成省级企业技术中心年度考核报告的报送，目前中心运行维护情况良好。

3. 中国锦屏地下实验室　2018年4月，雅砻江公司与清华大学联合申报的国家重大科技基础设施项目“极深地下极低辐射本底前沿物理实验设施”立项及可行性研究报告顺利通过中国国际工程咨询公司评审，并报送至国家发展改革委。12月，项目可行性研究报告获得国家发展改革委批复。

稳步推进中国锦屏地下实验室（二期）建设，按计划开展实验室相关工作：完成中国锦屏地下实验室（二期）第一阶段配套工程高压输电工程招标，启动中国锦屏地下实验室E厅（深地中微子实验厅）初步开挖方案论证。

2018年，CDEX实验基于第二阶段CDEX-10实验系统，在世界著名物理学顶级学术周刊《物理评论快报》上发表正式研究成果，在4-5GeV范围内自旋无关暗物质直接探测灵敏度达到$8\times10^{-42}cm^2$，取得了世界最好结果。

4. 科技创新管理平台　2018年雅砻江公司正式启动了科技创新管理平台建设，借助信息化手段提升科研管理水平，实现科技创新成果的共享和利用。2018年完成科技创新管理平台项目招标工作以及平台需求调研，并开始平台设计和开发工作。

5. 雅砻江虚拟研究中心　2018年11月，由雅砻江公司主办的雅砻江虚拟研究中心2018年度学术交流会在成都召开。来自国家自然科学基金委员会、国内高等院校、科研机构及勘测设计单位等20余家单位参加本次大会。

会议特别邀请了6位院士和专家分别围绕深地科学研究、大坝工程建设智能监控、大坝安全研究、可再生能源发展趋势、增强地热系统、暗物质探测及地下实验室建设做了精彩主旨报告。下午分三个会场，分别以“水电站建设和运行”“风光水互补清洁能源开发和梯级电站调度”“深地基础科学”3个主题开展学术交流，共进行了35项学术报告，与会专家开展了热烈的研讨。

（二）合作创新有关情况

1. 雅砻江联合基金（第二期）　2018年，为推进雅砻江联合基金（第二期）2017年已批准项目的顺利开展，积极配合和推进各项目组到雅砻江公司及流域现场的调研工作，推进研究工作，督促课题牵头单位及时组织召开项目启动会。

2018年3月完成2018年度雅砻江联合基金项目组织申报工作。11月，召开雅砻江联合基金2018年度会议评审和管理委员会会议，审定了雅砻江联合基金2018年度资助项目及资助额度。2018年度共资助8个重点支持项目、4个培育项目。12月，2019年项目指南在国家自然科学基金委网站发布。

2. 国家重点研发计划课题和专题研究　雅砻江公司承担的国家“十三五”重点研发计划“深部围岩长期稳定性分析与控制”课题于2018年6月顺利通过科技部组织的中期验收评审，11月召开项目年度总结会议；“特高拱坝及近坝库岸长期安全稳定运行”课题于2018年5月召开项目中期研讨会，11月召开专题一、专题五中期成果检查会。

“西南水电能源基地水—能源—粮食资源特征及协调关系”专题于2018年1月签订专题任务书，6月开展西南水电基地技术交流和实地调研，9月参加课题第三次研讨会议，目前研究工作正在有序开展；“水电开发对下游水温情势影响模式研究”专题于2018年12月与项目承担单位中国石油集团科学技术研究院有限公司续签了项目组织实施协议，继续深入开展下一步研究工作。

（三）科技成果情况

（1）2018年，雅砻江锦屏一级水电站项目荣获具有国际工程咨询领域“诺贝尔奖”之称的“菲迪克

2018年工程项目杰出成就奖”，在全球所有获奖工程项目中排名第一。

(2)“300m级特高拱坝安全控制关键技术及工程应用”项目荣获2018年度国家科学技术进步二等奖，这是雅砻江公司第七次获得国家科技进步奖。

(3) 雅砻江公司2018年获得了各类省部级奖19项，其中包括PMI（中国）项目管理大奖1项、中国土木工程詹天佑奖1项、中国电力优质工程奖1项，省部级科技奖一等奖5项、二等奖8项、三等奖3项。

(4) 雅砻江公司董事长陈云华荣获第五届潘家铮奖；副总经理王继敏荣获中国大坝杰出工程师奖。

(5) 2018年，雅砻江公司启动7项专利的申报工作，并获得申请号。3项发明专利和3项实用新型专利获得授权。

(6) 2018年，雅砻江公司员工在国内外期刊发表科技论文共计303篇，其中核心期刊86篇，SCI收录1篇，EI收录1篇。

（雅砻江流域水电开发有限公司　杜成波）

黄河水利科学研究院 2018年科研工作情况

2018年，黄河水利科学研究院（简称黄科院）认真学习贯彻党的十九大精神，以习近平总书记新时期治水方针为指引，按照水利部、黄河水利委员会（简称黄委）党组决策部署，凝心聚力、开拓进取，实现治黄科研改革发展新跨越。总体工作得到黄委充分肯定，获黄委“2018年度绩效考核先进单位”称号。

（一）重要治水科技支撑取得新成绩

一是为水利行业强监管提供科技支撑。完成对宁夏回族自治区防汛工作督导检查；协助开展黄河流域“清四乱”专项行动，完成了陕西省10个地市暗访工作；完成甘肃省病险水库除险加固评估调研；完成新疆水库大坝安全隐患排查工作的重点抽查。选派专家5人次全程参加黄河流域（片）小型水库安全运行和山洪灾害防御、河道防洪专项督查，历时106天。选派专家50余人次，参加水利部、黄委组织的全国农村水利相关检查、督查、暗访等20余次。

二是按照水利部、黄委要求，做好重大专项工作。承担水利部交办的十大水利问题研究。作为组长单位，主持了焦作市等10个地市水生态文明城市建设技术评估与验收。

三是为治黄中心工作发挥决策参谋作用。做好黄河防汛调度、汛期防洪防凌调度等技术支撑。开展黄河河情及跟踪分析，完成年度咨询及跟踪研究报告。做好无定河“7·26”洪水总结，提出2018年桃汛洪水冲刷降低潼关高程方案，编制黄河口生态需水指标及生态调度方案。开展黄河下游河道综合治理模拟试验，黄委领导对模型试验作用给予充分肯定。

（二）重大科研项目获得新立项

10个国家自然科学基金项目获批立项。国家重点研发计划项目“黄河干流骨干枢纽群泥沙动态调控关键技术”“黄河凌汛监测与灾害防控关键技术研究与示范”获批立项。积极参与其他单位牵头申报项目，1个课题获批。目前，在研国家自然科学基金项目及重点研发计划课题、专题共计85项，达到了青年博士人均1项国家级项目。

争取到水利部2019年部门预算项目1237万元，在总体预算压减的大形势下，实现小幅增加。

（三）重大奖项申报取得新突破

作为牵头单位，一年内获得4个省部级科技进步奖（一等奖以上），在黄科院历史上尚属首次。“黄河下游宽滩区滞洪沉沙功能及滩区减灾技术研究”获中国大坝工程学会科技进步奖特等奖。“黄河水沙冰凌输移模型库和标准构建及模拟系统研发与应用”获大禹水利科学技术奖一等奖，“黄河流域砒砂岩区辨识与抗蚀促生关键技术及应用”获河南省科技进步奖一等奖，“黄河下游河道综合治理关键技术研究及推广应用”获2018年中国产学研合作创新成果奖一等奖。另有3项科研成果分获2018年黄委科技进步奖特等奖和一等奖。

（四）“产学研用”孕育新平台

一是科研平台升级。成功获批“湖库功能恢复与维持”“水电工程磨蚀测试与防护”“农村水环境治理”3个河南省工程技术研究中心，这是黄科院首次牵头获得河南省级平台资格。与多家优势单位成功申报“中原地区枣产业国家创新联盟”，这是第一批林业和草原国家创新联盟。大力推进“水利部堤防安全管理中心”申报；适应当前国家生态文明发展战略需要，聚焦当前四大水问题，积极筹建水利部黄河流域水生态水环境重点实验室。

二是资质标准升级。“工程咨询（水利水电）专业资质”完成从丙级到乙级的升级，“涉密信息系统集成资质”完成从无到有的突破。

三是学科建设升级。培育了水生态水环境、河口生态研究、水利信息化3个学科方向，新增技术服务项目合同近2000万元。

四是学术交流升级。先后主办和承办中国大坝工程学会、中国水利学会学术年会，第五届中国（国际）水生态安全战略论坛等学术会议，黄科院成果走进设计、地方及建设单位视野，扩大科技影响力。

“治黄科技讲坛”“青年科技论坛”特邀院士、国内顶尖专家开讲，师之技，效之法。

（五）服务市场开拓迈出新步伐

全年签订合同额2.1亿元，横向合同额1.5亿元，经济增长10%，创历史新高。“固结植生生态护坡技术”被《青海日报》等媒体专题报道，“黄河泥沙资源利用关键技术与应用”通过水利部评价，“自吸式管道水库清淤技术”在新疆的推广应用初显成效，“水利工程精准化管理系统”在黄藏寺水利枢纽等工程中的应用收获好评。

（六）2018年科技项目鉴定和验收情况

（1）“黄河泥沙资源利用关键技术与应用”成果通过水利部推广中心评价。2018年，“黄河泥沙资源利用关键技术与应用”成果通过水利部科技推广中心评价，专家组一致认为该项目成果意义重大，可以大规模推广应用。

自2007年开始，在科技部、水利部等多个项目的资助下，项目组针对泥沙资源利用方向和途径不明晰、开发利用无序可循、成套技术和设备缺乏、转型利用成本高、综合效益评价方法缺失等瓶颈问题，采用系统调研、理论研究、技术研发、精细设计、应用示范的研究思路，产学研用相结合，取得了泥沙处理与资源利用普适性强、理论创新突出、技术装备领先的“测—取—输—用—评”全链条技术。

（2）2个国家重点研发计划项目参加水利部督导取得优异成绩。2018年，黄科院两个重点研发计划项目，“黄河口演变与流路稳定综合治理研究”和“鄂尔多斯高原砒砂岩区生态综合治理技术”参加了水利部国际合作与科技司组织的督导工作。督导专家组认为两个项目管理规范，经费使用合理，整体进展符合任务书进度计划和成果指标要求，均给予“优”的评价。

（3）“水闸工程安全评价及除险加固关键技术研发”行业专项通过验收。2018年水利部国际合作与科技司验收黄科院牵头承担的水利部公益性行业科研专项项目“水闸工程安全评价及除险加固关键技术研发（编号：201501036）”。验收专家组听取了项目组的成果汇报，对提交的技术文件进行了认真审阅，经质询和讨论，认为该项目按期全面完成了任务书规定的工作内容，研究成果丰富，达到了预期目标，同意通过验收。

该项目作为水利行业共性问题列入行业专项，由黄科院牵头，南京水科院、河海大学、长江科学院等单位参加完成，华北水电大学等承担了部分实验工作。项目历时三年，围绕影响三、四类水闸判别的主要因素，对主要病害的形成与发展机理、检测与监测、评价与修复技术及配套政策等进行了系统研究，为提升我国水闸工程安全评价及除险加固工作的科学性提供了技术支撑。项目成果已在黄河下游涵闸、荆北长江干堤新滩口闸等工程中得到示范运用，取得了较好的经济效益和社会效益。

（黄河水利科学研究院　娄萱）

中国电建集团贵阳勘测设计研究院有限公司2018年科技工作情况

（一）创新平台及体系建设成绩突出

规划中期调整。中国电建集团贵阳勘测设计研究院有限公司（简称贵阳院）对《贵阳院“十三五”科技发展（创新）规划》进行了中期对照评估，适当地调整了有关指标，有利于今后若干年的科技创新工作开展。

获批国家级企业技术中心。2018年7月，国家发展改革委正式公布了2017～2018年（第24批）新认定及全部国家企业技术中心名单，贵阳院被认定为国家级企业技术中心。贵阳院是该年度贵州省唯一获此殊荣的企业，也是贵阳国家高新区自成立以来唯一一家获得国家认定企业技术中心的企业。该高新区一次性给予贵阳院500万元的创新资金支持。

各省级创新平台运行良好。贵阳院省级企业技术中心，完成了三年一次评价；贵阳院院士工作站完成2017年度总结和信息报送并提交了全国院士专家工作站认证，已通过贵州省审查待全国科协审批；向科技厅提交了创新型领军企业2017年度报告，对照任务指标已基本完成合同；完成了博士后工作站、技术先进型服务企业申报。

院级科技创新平台工作有序开展。2018年6月，召开了院级科技创新平台2018年度工作计划审定会，确定了各中心2018年度需重点完成的工作任务，实现对省级中心和国家级中心创新工作的实质性支撑。另外，新成立了贵阳院集成装配式建筑研究中心、院工程GIS研发中心，并撤销了院绿色建筑研究中心。

积极组织二级单位申报省级科技创新平台、团队。2018年8月，组织申报贵州省工程技术研究中心、科技创新人才团队、重点实验室、科普示范基地，并邀请贵州师范大学专家到院进行申报辅导。

组织工程科研院向贵州省工信厅申报完成贵阳院技术创新示范企业能力建设项目，获得以奖代补专项资助50万元；向贵州省科学仪器共享服务平台报送科学仪器共享信息，获得贵州省科技厅10万元经费后补助。

（二）创新团队及人才培养持续加强

贵阳院于2018年再次组建了贵州省BIM科技创新人才团队、集成装配式建筑及市政设施科技创新人才团队等2个院级科技创新团队并向贵州省科技厅进行了申报。

2018年11月，贵州省第四批高层次创新型人才公示，贵阳院湛正刚同志获"十"层次人才，邱焕峰、郑克勋获"千"层次人才。贵阳院共获得160万经费支持。

（三）各级科研立项斩获颇丰

2018年，贵阳院获得中国电建集团科研项目立项4项（其中承担2项，参与2项），获经费资助超过300万元；获得贵州省科技支撑计划项目立项5项，省科技基金一般项目1项，专利战略项目1项，参与贵州省重大专项1项，共获得经费资助270万元。

贵阳院承担的《水电工程建设征地移民安置补偿费用分析研究》《四级配水工碾压混凝土关键技术研究与应用》顺利通过集团公司验收；《绿色水电评价指标体系研究》《乌江干流（贵州段）人工增殖放流鱼类效果初步研究》《高砾石土心墙坝坝料特性及坝体变形控制关键技术研究》等5项集团公司科研项目顺利通过验收同时进行了成果鉴定。

贵阳院开展了2批院级科研项目验收工作。对10项院级科研项目、1项标准编制及4项主编专著、1项参编专著进行了验收评审，14项通过验收，2项同意终止。

（四）科研成果获奖丰硕

全年贵阳院组织报奖42项，获奖35项，其中，电力工程科学技术进步奖一等奖1项；中国电建科学技术奖二等奖2项、三等奖1项，作为参加单位一等奖1项；贵州省优秀工程勘察设计奖一等奖2项，二等奖4项，三等奖3项；中国电力规划设计协会"四优奖"一等奖2项，二等奖2项，三等奖2项；电力行业优秀工程咨询成果奖一等奖2项，二等奖1项，三等奖4项；中国水土保持学会优秀设计奖三等奖1项；中国电建优秀工程勘测设计奖一等奖2项、二等奖1项、三等奖1项。

开展了两年一度的贵阳院科学技术奖评审。共有42项成果参评。这次会议共评选出贵阳院2018年度科学技术奖29项，其中一等奖5项，二等奖6项，三等奖18项。

（五）技术标准示范作用凸显

年度贵阳院新获得2项能源行业标准和6项贵州省地方标准主编任务。新获得2项能源行业标准英文版翻译任务，还首次参编《高海拔型风力发电机组》1项国家标准。

贵阳院主编完成的《水电站油系统技术规范》NB/T 35118—2018，已于2018年4月13日发布，于2018年7月1日正式实施。主编完成的贵州省地方标准《贵州岩溶场地岩土工程勘察技术规程》，于2018年9月4日发布、2019年3月4日正式实施。

组织提交了贵阳院主编2016～2018年能源领域行业标准（9项）专项资金补助相关资料，并每项获水电水利规划设计总院专项资金补助5万元，共计45万元。

（六）知识产权管理行业引领

知识产权工作又上新台阶，2018年初贵阳院发布了第二版知识产权管理体系文件，而后完成了全院30个单位的知识产权体系的内审和管理评审工作。贵阳院知识产权管理体系2016年通过认证后，2018年接受了第二次监督审核，无不符合项出现。

2018年，通过调研、引进，建立了覆盖提案、专利、商标、版权等无形资产的信息化管理平台，提供从提案挖掘、提案评价、提出申请、公开、实质审查、授权、维持、许可、转让、诉讼等知识产权全生命周期管理，实现提案评价、审查答复等电子化流程管控。

贵阳院专利授权有效量已达1350件，全年完成专利申报498件（其中发明223件，实用新型274件，外观设计1件）；发明专利获得授权64件，实用新型专利获得授权183件；获得商标5件（19个类别）；申请计算机软件著作权44件，获得证书38件；评选出贵阳院工法10项，申请并获得中国电建工法4项，申请贵州省工法3项获得1项。知识产权类型逐步拓展全面。

开拓性的开展了专利申请权转让工作，贵阳院向贵州建工集团八公司转让4件发明专利共计100万元。

2018年，贵阳院承担了中国电建2个知识产权项目，共获得资助100万元；受邀参加了集团公司2018年知识产权管理工作经验交流培训，受到集团和兄弟企业的一致好评。

2018年贵阳院申请各类专利资助261.32万元，获得贵阳市研发费用补助62.5万元，高新区研发费用补助62.5万元。

（七）强化技术与质量管理

2018年，贵阳院发布了10项技术质量制度，持续健全了院级技术质量管理体系。

2018年3月，编制了《贵阳院质量工作要点》；4月，开展了与中国电建集团中南勘测设计研究院有限公司技术质量管理交流活动；同时，召开了技术协调会议并编制相应纪要，院跨专业和新领域的产品的技术要求得到有效协调。

积极开展各类质量抽查，不断提升院的产品质量水平。2018年9月，组织院副总工开展2017年度质量考核工作，检查了18个二级生产单位和22个项目部的质量执行情况，现场检查覆盖了三大板块，共计抽查产品、算稿和图纸1000余份。2018年10～11月，抽查了10个项目部的评审会议纪要，开展了评审意见落实情况检查工作 。

2018年10月，由贵阳院牵头，中国水利电力质量管理协会评审组专家一行5人莅临贵阳院进行了电力行业卓越绩效标杆企业的现场评价，推荐贵阳院评定为2018年全国电力行业卓越绩效标杆企业(AAAA)。贵阳院从卓越绩效AAA到AAAA。

响应集团的质量管理要求，2018年9月，组织院属各单位开展“大力提升质量，建设质量强企”为主题的“质量月”活动，参与质量知识竞赛答题934人次，开展质量主题演讲40余次，开展现场质量检查190余次。

（中国电建集团贵阳勘测设计研究院有限公司　杨桃萍）

中电建水电开发集团有限公司2018年科技工作简要情况

2018年，中电建水电开发集团有限公司按照“十三五”科技创新规划和2018年度科技工作计划开展科技工作，加大科技创新力度，促进科技成果转化，完成科技投入2265.84万元。

公司参与开展的“分布式光伏与梯级小水电互补联合发电技术研究及应用示范项目”列入国家重大研发计划（项目编号：2018YFB0905200），参与研究的“综合措施下多沙河流高水头水电站水轮机抗沙蚀关键技术研究及应用”获得湖南省重大水利科技项目立项（合同编号：湘水科计〔2017〕230-17）。

2018年，公司取得授权专利7项。

在科技成果方面，公司完成了“水电工程生态环境修复集成技术研究”六个子课题的审查、组织并通过了“高水头水电站多泥沙处理综合研究”课题的结题验收和科技鉴定。

公司控股的四川松林河流域开发有限公司和西昌飓源风电开发有限公司，按计划稳步推进高新技术企业申报工作。

公司工程项目管理系统（PRP）于2018年11月20日实现上线试运行，开始在夏特、巴拉项目建设中逐步应用与完善。突出公司主营业务特色的“职工创新工作室”“青年论坛”等双创活动开展的有声有色。

（中电建水电开发集团有限公司）

中国水利水电第四工程局有限公司2018年科技工作情况

中国水利水电第四工程局有限公司（简称水电四局）是国家认定的高新技术企业，2018年，核心业务稳中有进，企业产值已近200亿元；获“改革开放40年百项经典工程”1项，获2017～2018年度中国水利工程优质（大禹）奖1项，获2018年中国电力优质工程奖2项。

（一）体制机制建设

2018年，建立了“工程技术专家库”，筛选各专业领域的技术专家150余人，为公司提供技术支持、科技评审等专业服务，使公司在科技创新、项目策划等工作中拥有了更加灵活、更加强大的技术力量支撑，同时组织所属各单位相继建立了专家委员会。

公司被评为2018年青海省知识产权优势企业。

2018年，公司和青海大学联合成立坝道工程医院青海分院。依托企业自身和青海大学科研技术、施工实力，与总院联网，协同运作，为青藏高原地区基础设施工程打造一个体检、诊断、修复、抢险优质综合服务平台，实现互（物）联网时代基础设施工程“体检在现场、诊断在云端、专家在全球、服务在身边”的快速抢修模式。

青海省省级企业技术中心的评价考核，中国水利水电第四工程局有限公司技术中心以95分的成绩位列第2名。

（二）科技成果

中国水利水电第四工程局有限公司的“黄登水电站大坝综合施工技术研究”“三分裂大截面全铝合金导线张力放线关键技术”分别荣获2018年度电力建设科学技术进步奖二等奖、三等奖；“基于激光扫描数据的三维重建关键技术在水利水电工程中的研究应用”荣获中电建集团2018年度中国电建科学技术奖二等奖；“200m级高碾压混凝土坝全面智能温控关键技术研究及应用”荣获中国大坝工程学会科学技术奖二等奖；“高寒地区高拱坝冬季施工综合技术研究与应用”荣获青海省科学技术奖三等奖。

自主创新研发的“一种用于隧道施工的盾构机姿态复核方法”“一种精确控制水泥桥面铺装高程的方法”“一种混凝土伸缩缝的预填充施工工具”“一种综合管廊工作环境监控方法”获国家发明专利。

与中国电建集团国际工程有限公司、清华大学等单位合作完成的“国际工程技术标准应用研究（水电施工、路桥、港航部分）”荣获中电建集团2018年度中国电建科学技术奖一等奖；与青海大学、中国水电基础局有限公司等单位合作完成的“青藏地区土石坝综合防渗关键技术研究与应用”荣获2018年度青海省科学技术奖三等奖；与中国长江三峡集团有限公司、水利部长江水利委员会、长江勘测规划设计研究院等单位共同完成的“长江三峡枢纽工程”项目联合申报了2019年度国家科技进步奖。

2018年中国水利水电第四工程局有限公司共获省部级科技进步特等奖1项、二等奖3项、三等奖3项；省部级工法39项；获集团公司科技进步特等奖1项、一等奖1项、二等奖1项、三等奖1项。

2018年中国水利水电第四工程局有限公司共获授权专利102件，其中国家发明专利7件、实用新型专利93件，外观专利2项。

2018年中国水利水电第四工程局有限公司总经理席浩荣获第五届潘家铮奖、“青海省第十二批自然科学与工程技术学科带头人”评价为“优秀”。

（三）标准编写

公司主持编写的《水电水利工程仓储运行管理规程》（DL/T1903—2018）、《光伏发电土建工程施工质量评定标准》（NB/T 32047—2018）由国家能源局批准发布，分别自2019年5月1日和10月1日起实施。

（四）学术活动

2018年8月，中国水利水电第四工程局有限公司在青海西宁组织召开基础设施工程灾害防控学术报告会暨坝道工程医院青海分院成立大会，国内有关高校及科研院所专家学者，相关企事业单位代表共计200余人参加大会。

2018年10月，依托黄登水电站在丽江组织召开2018年专委会年会暨全国碾压混凝土筑坝技术和水电工程施工新技术学术交流会。来自全国各地水利水电建设、设计、监理、施工单位的专家学者150余人参加了这次交流会议。

2018年，为纪念中国水利水电第四工程局有限公司建局60周年，组织编撰了纪念系列丛书，丛书包括《砥砺奋进六十年》《科技引领 品臻致远》《我与四局共成长》《含英咀华 点墨春秋》《山川情怀 焕彩人生》五册，共计280余万字，从不同角度记录了水电四局人六十年激越奋进的创业历程，反映出水电四局60年发展波澜壮阔的时代脉络，展现了水电四局人一甲子筚路蓝缕的建设成果，勾画出一代代创业者为了水电四局发展奋斗和奉献的光辉形象，诠释了水电四局人自强不息、勇于超越的精神内涵。

（中国水利水电第四工程局有限公司）

中国水利水电第五工程局有限公司 2018年科技工作情况

2018年，中国水利水电第五工程局有限公司（简称水电五局）践行“创新驱动发展战略”，坚持围绕服务于在建工程项目，服务于企业发展和品牌战略，全面推进科技创新工作，创新体系不断完善，创新能力持续提高，科技工作取得良好的成绩。

（一）科技创新体系建设情况

近年来，水电五局坚持走企业自主创新的发展之路，将高新技术引入传统的施工领域，深入推进创新型企业建设，取得了良好的效果。2018年，水电五局荣膺“国家知识产权优势企业”，进一步完善和强化了水电五局的科技创新体系。同时，水电五局依托在建项目，进一步加强了与高校、科研院所、协会、兄弟单位的沟通学习交流，努力构建了开放式技术创新体系。

2018年11月，中国人民大学、中央财经大学、中国社会科学院联合发布的《中国企业创新能力百千万排行榜（2018）》中，水电五局与华为、腾讯、中兴、格力等知名企业同时入选。这是水电五局继2017年之后再次入选，充分彰显了企业的创新发展能力。2018年，四川地区共有31家企业强势入榜，其中多为计算机、通信和其他电子设备制造企业，上榜的建筑施工企业仅有4家。

2018年12月，四川省企业联合会、四川省企业家协会、四川省技术创新服务中心、四川经济日报社联合发布“2018年四川企业技术创新发展能力100强”榜单。水电五局位列百强榜第2位，同时还上榜了四川企业技术创新发展最具潜力20强、四川企业发明专利拥有量100强、四川企业技术创新发展能力研究与试验经费投入100强。

（二）科技项目实施情况

2018年，水电五局新立项科研立项163项，非水电项目所占比例明显增加，专业涉及水电工程、国际业务、基础设施、高速公路、桥梁工程、市政工程等多个领域，无论数量还是质量都创下了历史新高，基本实现了业务全覆盖。

2018年，水电五局新技术、新工艺研究开发项目认定备案、税前加计扣除工作取得新的进展。《超大异形断面调压井开挖施工技术研究》等152个研发项目通过了科技厅备案。

（三）科技创新成果

1. 科技成果鉴定　2018年，水电五局共有4项科技成果通过了中国电力建设集团有限公司组织的专家鉴定，其中《振水工高流速流道镜面混凝土施工关键技术》达到了“国际领先水平”，《薄层软弱围岩特长公路隧道精细施工关键技术研究》《连续钢箱梁步履式多点顶推控制技术》《城市河湖水系生态治理施工技术》3项达到了“国际先进水平”。

2. 国家专利和计算机软件著作权　水电五局在科技课题的开展过程中，坚持做好围绕核心业务的专利开发和布局工作，通过专利技术引领发展，提高企业竞争力，大幅度提升了公司自主创新能力。2018年水电五局新申请的专利中共有159项获得国家知识产权局授权，其中一种振动碾自动操作系统及其使用方法、一种竖井下弯段上部混凝土滑模施工方法等15件获得了发明专利授权，一种高流速大断面泄洪洞低坍落度砼入仓系统、一种有砟轨道快速多功能施工设备等140件获得了实用新型专利授权，混凝土面板浇筑表面保温材料铺设装置、一种轮式划线装置等4件获得了外观专利授权。

2018年，由水电五局自主研发和申报的《子企业科技创新管理系统》《ZSWJ高企管理系统》《项目成本管理手机APP系统软件》《临时试验室经营信息管理系统》《悬式水轮发电机组轴线调整系统》等16项信息化技术获得了国家版权局计算机软件著作权授权，科技管理信息化取得了新成绩。

3. 省部级工法　2018年，水电五局获得了107项省部级工法。其中《高瓦斯隧道二衬负压压浆施工工法》《高速公路大厚度高模量沥青混合料一次成型施工工法》等23项工法被评为四川省工程建设工法；《黄泛区粉质砂土路基填筑施工工法》《市政道路雨水管涵施工工法》等5项工法被评为河南省工程建设省级工法；《高土石坝智能摊铺、数字化碾压填筑施工工法》《无人驾驶振动碾自动碾压施工工法》等14项工法获评中国电力建设工法；《竖井进出水塔双曲线过流面混凝土施工工法》《大体积弧形倒坡混凝土快速施工工法》等5项工法获评为中国水利水电工程建设工法；《超低能耗建筑土建及气密性检测施工工法》《超大型沉井施工工法》等60项工法被评为中国电建集团工法。

4. 科技成果获奖情况　2018年，水电五局共有31项科技成果获得了省部级、行业及中国电建集团奖励，其中，中国施工企业管理协会科学技术奖特等奖1项、二等奖3项，中国电力科学技术奖一等奖1项，水力发电科学技术奖二等奖1项，中国大坝工程学会会科学技术奖一等奖、二等奖各1项，中国大坝工程学会技术发明奖三等奖2项，电力建设科学技术进步奖一等奖1项、二等奖2项、三等奖7项，中国电力创新奖二等奖1项，中国电力建设集团有限公司科学技术奖一等奖3项，河南省工程建设协会科技创新成果奖一等奖1项，全国电力职工技术成果奖三等奖6项。

（中国水利水电第五工程局有限公司　袁幸朝）

水电技术创新

300m级特高拱坝安全控制关键技术及工程应用研究

为满足国家西电东送战略、能源结构调整、环保与减排、防洪及水资源高效利用的需要，规划并建设了一批坝高超过200m至300m级特高拱坝工程。其中锦屏一级拱坝坝高305m，是世界第一高坝。

300m级特高拱坝面临诸多世界级难题：①水推力较200m级呈几何级数增长，突破千万吨级大关，对结构抗裂、基础承载、整体稳定等提出了严峻的挑战；②我国西部山高谷深，地质条件十分复杂，如锦屏坝址左右岸地形不对称，左岸中上部砂板岩倾倒变形，坝基受多条断层软弱带切割，基础深部强烈卸荷拉裂现象突出，在如此复杂的地质环境下建世界最高的拱坝，堪称世界级难题；③我国西部地震活动强烈，地震烈度高，如大岗山设计水平峰值加速度达0.557g，为当前世界高坝之最；④枢纽泄洪流量大，坝身孔口多，如溪洛渡拱坝坝身泄量达31000m^3/s，设有表、中、深、底共4层25个孔口，为世界结构最复杂的拱坝。特高拱坝安全控制不当，影响十分巨大。如奥地利Kolnbrein特高拱坝因结构抗力不够，蓄水后坝底出现贯穿性严重开裂事故；法国Malpasst拱坝因基础失稳溃坝。我国规范明确要求坝高超过200m需专门论证。论证的重点为大坝安全控制。

项目依托锦屏一级、溪洛渡、大岗山拱坝，组织优势科研团队，产学研用相结合，持续20多年攻关，系统分析已有特高拱坝安全控制方法的局限性，深入剖析已建拱坝出现破坏评价方法、坝—基变形协调、结构抗裂、整体稳定、抗震安全与措施、建设过程安全控制及运行状态安全评价，创建了特高拱坝安全控制理论方法标准及评价体系，确保了锦屏一级、溪洛渡、大岗山等特高拱坝的成功建设，实现了300m级特高拱坝建设关键技术的重大突破。

主要研究成果及创新点有：

(1) 建立了300m级特高拱坝安全控制的3K设计方法与标准，研发了提高特高拱坝坝基与坝体变形协调性的成套技术。建立了特高拱坝混凝土结构安全(KD)、基础抗滑安全(KF)和拱坝整体安全(KO)的3K设计方法与标准，创建了特高拱坝分坝高区段合理确定建基面的设计方法，发明了改善坝趾应力状态的贴脚结构，解决了300m级特高拱坝结构抗裂、基础抗滑和整体稳定的安全控制难题。

(2) 构建了特高拱坝防震抗震设计方法与安全评价体系。提出了以设计地震峰值加速度一致和主干断裂发生概率最大的设定地震确定原则，发展了基于设定地震并采用NGA反应谱衰减关系确定场地相关设计反应谱的方法；创建了特高拱坝基于设定地震、波动理论、材料及接触非线性的动力有限元仿真分析方法；发明了反映无限地基辐射阻尼影响的黏弹性材料和满足抗拉强度、弹性模量相似要求的模型坝体材料，提出了台面地震动确定方法，实现了特高拱坝大型振动台动力仿真模型试验研究；系统完善了特高拱坝的抗震措施体系，满足了特高拱坝极端地震不溃的控制要求。

(3) 创建了特高拱坝施工过程快速反馈设计技术和运行期安全评价体系。研发了施工地质信息快速精准采集、三维地质建模和工程地质校准技术；开发了以3K方法标准为核心的拱坝施工全过程动态仿真与实时反馈设计技术，设计施工联动的三维协同技术；实现了特高拱坝建设过程的安全控制；创建了特高拱坝运行期正常工作状态的弹性变形“四性”评价、应力评价及渗流渗压评价的多维安全评价准则，为特高拱坝长期运行安全提供了技术保障。

(中国电建集团成都勘测设计研究院有限公司　胡万雨)

大型地下厂房洞室群围岩稳定耗散能理论分析方法研究及应用

项目依托锦屏一级、猴子岩、黄金坪等水电工程，基于能量储存与耗散的观点对围岩变位、应力调整、破坏全过程、围岩时效变形特征开展分析。从开挖卸荷与能量耗散及释放的角度，对变形破坏机理、力学行为模拟、稳定评价标准等展开研究，建立基于能量耗散与释放理论的围岩稳定与支护分析体系，认识和理解地下洞室群围岩变形破坏现象、评价洞群围岩安全状况。

具体研究内容如下：

(1) 通过试验资料分析，发现峰值抗压强度、极限应力和极限应变均与围压存在较好的线性相关关系。提出了考虑围压时，围岩软化—硬化路径发生变化的应力应变关系。建立了岩体弹性＋软化、弹性＋硬化破坏全过程的本构关系模型。该本构关系模型所需参数少，且能够自然模拟不同围压岩体的力学行为和残余变形特征，即能够方便模拟不同围压下，岩体可能表现出的弹性、软化、塑性硬化等应力应变关系。解决了围岩加卸载计算中难以模拟破坏全过程的问题。

(2) 地下工程围岩不同部位由于处于不同围压状态，其遵循的应力路径各不相同。岩石的变形破坏过程是围岩能量的储存和耗散过程。岩石的强度和允许的极限变形均是能量存储能力和耗散特征的体现。项目提出围岩耗散能稳定分析模型(EDM)，推导了岩体抗能和耗散能计算公式。考虑了围岩释放力的时间效应，引入了与时间相关的指数形式的释放荷载，从而可以考虑围岩变形的时效作用，解决了传统弹塑性分析方法模拟时效变形、岩体破坏能量耗散定量评价的问题。

(3) 锚杆、锚索、灌浆措施可以有效加固围岩，提高围岩稳定性，但是其对应的能量关系还少有详细的研究。课题详细推导了锚杆、锚索、灌浆措施对单位体积岩体的能量贡献，推导了锚杆、锚索、灌浆支护结构措施的能量补给公式，以及支护措施对围压的附加作用。比以往的仅从受力、或仅从围岩参数变化研究加固机理的思路有新的发展。揭示了支护结构措施对围岩的补给抗能内在机理。提出了考虑支护措施的能量耗散比围岩稳定判据，从能量的角度解释了支护加固结构对围岩稳定的作用机理。岩石能量耗散比判据可以明确分辨围岩是处于弹性、软化或塑性硬化(部分破坏)、完全破坏状态。依据围岩能量耗散比分布与实测洞周松弛区的对应发育深度，给出了围岩分区耗散比指标，克服了以往弹塑性分析不能定量确定破坏区、强、弱松弛区的技术难题。

(4) 建立了围岩最优锚固时机、合理支护强度、锚索(锚杆)预紧系数等支护设计方法体系，定量解决了围岩适时、适度支护问题，提出了最优加固时间理论，改变了仅依靠经验和观测数据确定支护时机的不足。

项目研究成果已成功应用于锦屏一级、猴子岩、黄金坪等高地应力区地下工程，保障了地下洞室群施工及运行安全，促进了行业技术进步，对其他行业地下工程具有重要的推广应用价值。

(中国电建集团成都勘测设计研究院有限公司　胡万雨)

复杂地质条件下500m级深竖井关键技术研究

正在建设的一些抽水蓄能电站及高水头引水式电站，其压力竖井高度突破500m。对于大直径深竖井一般都采用传统的导井+钻爆法施工，利用大直径反井钻机一次成井施工尚未有类似的研究。厄瓜多尔美纳斯水电站两条竖井具有的大直径、高深度、复杂地质条件等多项参数为水电行业世界之最，尚无成功经验可供借鉴。因此，中国水利水电第八工程局有限公司受中国电力建设股份有限公司委托，开展了500m级深竖井大直径反井钻机一次成井施工技术研究。

（一）主要研究内容

（1）开展了深竖井开挖设备选型及钻机钻压、转速、钻孔精度控制等技术研究。

（2）开展了火山岩地层间不整合接触等不良地质条件，深井支护参数对大直径竖井一次扩挖成型影响研究。

（3）开展了深竖井人员材料运输、安全监视和控制系统研究。

（4）开展了反井钻机全断面一次开挖成型进度研究。

（二）主要创新点

（1）首次在水电工程领域使用500m级大直径（ϕ5.5m/ϕ6.0m）深竖井反井钻机全断面一次成型开挖施工技术；同时在施工过程采用定向钻机及稳定钻杆，配合高精度定向仪进行钻孔精度控制，钻孔精度达万分之一（0.01%），有效解决了深竖井钻机钻孔偏差控制难的问题。

项目采用南非Master Drilling公司71RM型定向钻机从竖井顶部向下钻进先导孔，然后更换RD5-550反井钻机从下向上一次将竖井扩挖至设计断面尺寸。在先导孔钻进过程中，使用GEROYE DATA高精度定向仪对先导孔进行定位，每50m检查一次，及时掌握钻头的三维空间位置，测出先导孔的偏斜数据，为先导孔纠偏提供依据；同时采用定向钻杆控制钻头顺开孔方向直线钻进。定向钻杆总长度10m，是从国外专业勘探设备厂家定制，自带钻头，定向钻杆的底部和上部设置有两处直径与钻头直径相同的稳定钻杆，中部设置六条弹性纵肋，确保钻杆紧贴岩面，控制先导孔钻进差值。通过在施工过程中采用定向钻机及稳定钻杆，配合高精度定向仪对先导孔钻孔精度进行了有效控制，钻孔精度达万分之一（0.01%），从而有效解决了深竖井钻机钻孔偏差控制难的问题。

先导孔施工完成后，从竖井顶部开始自上向下将先导孔扩挖至直径16″，为反挖钻杆施工提供空间；在先导孔扩孔完成之后，将先导孔钻机更换为RD5-550全断面反井钻机，在竖井底部安装设计直径5.5m（通风电缆竖井为6.0m）的反扩刀盘，从下向上一次将竖井扩挖至设计直径。全断面开挖完成的竖井井壁完整、光滑，最大程度上减小了对井壁围岩的扰动和破坏，保证了井壁围岩的整体稳定，大大提高了支护以及后续施工过程中人员和设备的安全性，同时避免传统的导井法（人工爆破扩挖溜渣）施工工艺存在的安全风险高、进度慢、人工劳动强度大、职业健康危害性高、井内环境条件不良等问题。

（2）研制了一种双绳系同步卷扬系统及一种竖井井口模块化封口装置，改进了竖井内部吊盘自动水平调节系统，保证深竖井施工安全。

深竖井施工使用的卷扬机由于下降深度大，绕绳长且冗余度大，任何细微偏差，都会造成卷扬机不同步，项目研制了一种双绳系同步卷扬系统有效解决了这个问题。针对竖井施工安全问题突出的特点，对竖井封口盘模块化设计以及竖井内部吊盘水平调节系统进行研究，研制出一套适合竖井施工的封口盘装置及竖井内部吊盘自动水平调节装置，制定了一套深井施工的安全技术措施和相应的安全规章制度，保障了竖井的安全施工。

（3）编制了大直径长竖井反井钻全断面施工工法，形成了大直径深竖井全断面开挖施工体系。

开挖过程中进行地质预判、不良地质段灌浆、回填及支护处理、渗水处理、钻孔精度控制及施工安全等进行研究，编制了大直径长竖井反井钻全断面施工工法，形成了一套大直径深竖井全断面开挖施工体系，实现竖井反井钻机全断面开挖的标准化和规范化。

（三）推广应用情况

所研究的关键技术在厄瓜多尔美纳斯水电站压力竖井和通风电缆井施工成功应用，取得的主要成果如下：

（1）形成了一套控制钻孔精度的一系列方法。

（2）成功处理了多达11次的水流失现象。

（3）在破碎带采用铁皮瓦及型钢支架构成防护筒，然后在空腔内回填混凝土，使其达到安全稳定的状态。

（4）在井壁布置纵向和横向塑料排水板，在井壁和衬砌混凝土之间形成排水系统，有效的避免了井壁渗水的影响。

（5）井壁围岩未受扰动、井壁光滑、整体性好、稳定性强，在Ⅰ类围岩区域可以不用任何支护；Ⅱ、Ⅲ类围岩采用系统锚杆、单层柔性防护网支护；Ⅳ、Ⅴ类围岩采用系统锚杆、双单层柔性防护网支护，支护方法简单、快捷。

（6）创造反井钻机全断面开挖的最高月成井记录

为 172m/月。

（7）研制出一套适合竖井施工的模块化封口盘装置及竖井内部吊盘水平调节装置，成功解决了井口防护和吊盘倾斜的问题。

（8）编制了有针对性的专项施工方案和措施，有效地规避了深竖井施工的安全风险。在施工中不断完善，形成了一整套深竖井施工的安全技术措施和相应的安全规章制度。

（中国水利水电第八工程局
有限公司　杨承志）

复杂地质条件下巨型尾水调压室断面形状选择研究

（一）工程概况

白鹤滩水电站地下厂房采用首部开发方式，总装机容量 16000MW，共 16 台机组，左右岸各布置 8 台 1000MW 机组。尾水系统采用一洞三机的布置型式，尾水调压室稳定断面面积超过 $2000m^2$，断面尺寸巨大。

尾水调压室区域总体为缓倾单斜岩层，倾角 15°～20°，岩性为玄武岩。左岸尾水调压室最大埋深约 300m，发育层间错动带 C_2，最大主应力 19～23MPa，方向 N30°～60°W，近水平；右岸尾水调压室最大埋深约 500m，发育层间错动带 C_3、C_{3-1}、C_4、C_5，最大主应力 22～26MPa，方向 N0°～20°E，近水平。尾水调压室所处区域地质条件复杂，围岩应力强度比在 0.15～0.5 之间，处于中高等初始应力水平。高地应力及层间错动带、断层、柱状节理等不利地质构造对大跨度调压室围岩稳定影响较大，现以右岸尾水调压室为代表，拟定长廊形方案和圆筒形方案进行毛洞条件下的围岩稳定计算分析，并最终选择合理的调压室断面形状。

长廊形尾水调压室与主厂房、主变压器洞平行布置，调压室下部由二道隔墙分隔为三室，三机或二机共用一室，隔墙以上三室连通，尾水调压室跨度 33m，总长度 365m，中隔墙厚度 45m，以改善中隔墙稳定性，典型断面见图 1。

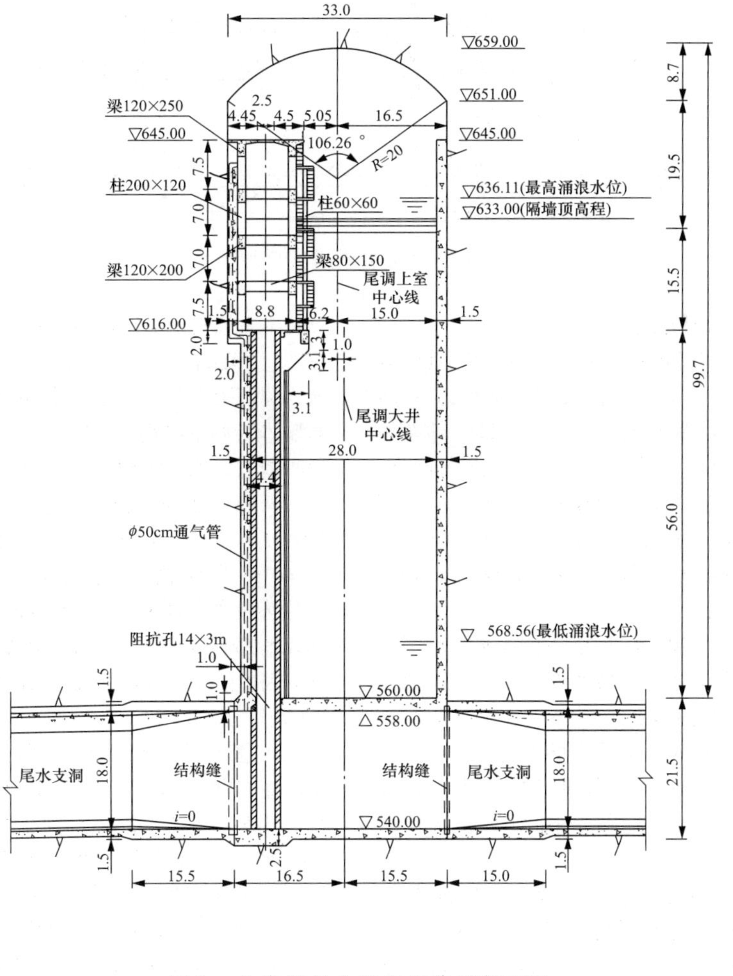

图 1　长廊形尾水调压室典型断面图

圆筒形调压室三机或二机共用一室，最大开挖直径 56～62m，井间岩柱厚度约 80m，按照 1.5 倍开挖平均直径控制，典型断面见图 2。

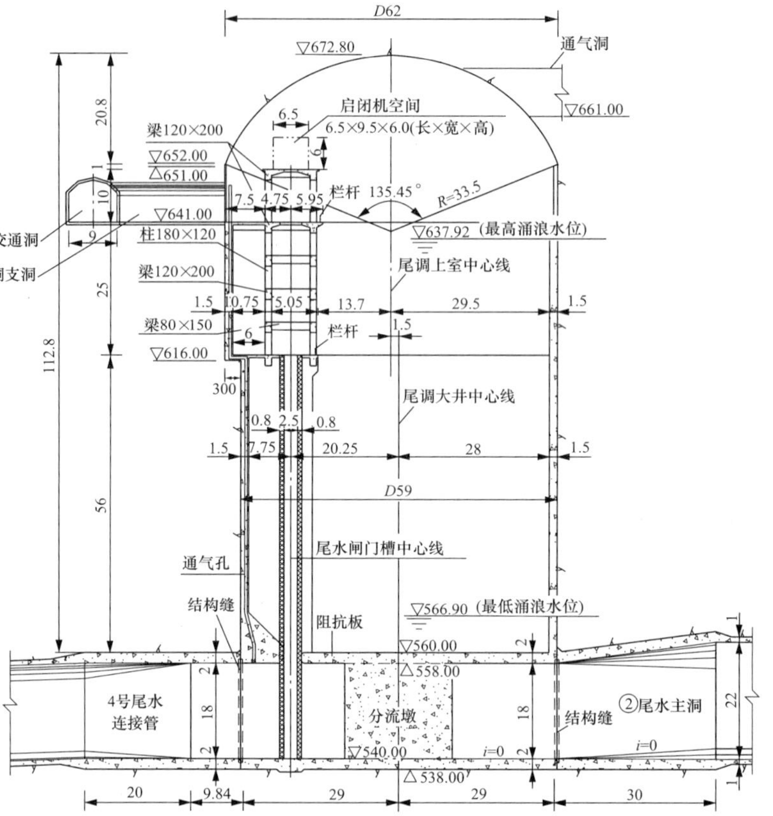

图 2 圆筒形尾水调压室典型断面图

（二）围岩稳定对比分析

1. 应力分析 长廊形调压室方案开挖后顶拱应力集中，层间错动带 C_4、C_5 下部浅层岩体出现应力松弛，中隔墙受高边墙变形挤压致使中心部位高应力集中，中隔墙最大应力值约为 40MPa，浅层为塑性变形后的松弛区域，尾水洞拱顶和底部出现明显的应力集中区域；圆筒形调压室方案开挖后穹顶应力集中，边墙基本不出现明显的应力松弛，EW 侧边墙表现为明显的应力集中区域。

长廊形调压室方案顶拱应力集中范围明显大于圆筒形；长廊形调压室方案在高边墙部位大范围出现应力松弛，圆筒形调压室方案边墙仍保持较高的应力水平，有利于维持边墙稳定。从围岩的应力分布状态、高应力集中程度与范围来看，圆筒形方案更利于控制顶拱的高应力集中和边墙的应力松弛问题，圆筒形方案优势较明显。

2. 变形分析 长廊形调压室方案开挖后顶拱变形量均不大于 20mm，层间错动带下方岩体变形较大；高边墙整体变形量级达 100～120mm，中部受层间错动带作用，中隔墙变形量级为 150mm；中隔墙浅层出现受层间带与小断层组合切割的大变形，同时在高应力屈服后出现塑性大变形，变形稳定问题较突出。圆筒形调压室方案开挖后穹顶变形量级较小；边墙整体变形量级约为 60mm，局部受断层切割变形量有所增大，变形量级小于 80mm。

长廊形方案中隔墙未能改变远离隔墙部位的高边墙大变形，尾水调压室高边墙变形量级达 100～120mm，局部受层间错动带影响变形超过 150mm，存在潜在的变形稳定问题；圆筒形尾水调压室的变形量基本都小于 80mm，不存在明显的整体变形稳定问题；因此，就控制变形稳定角度而言，圆筒形方案明显优于长廊形方案。

3. 塑性区分析 两方案的主要差别表现在中隔墙岩柱的塑性区分布，长廊形调压室方案开挖后中隔墙塑性区虽未贯通，但塑性区深度超过 10m，中心 20m 厚度范围保持弹性；圆筒形调压室方案开挖后洞周浅层岩体屈服，仅受小断层切割部位塑性区稍大，但仍小于 10m，尾水调压室间围岩大部分保持弹性。因此，从塑性区分布上来看，圆筒形尾水调压室方案占优。

4. 块体分析　长廊形方案开挖后边墙的大变形块体数量显著多于顶拱，受主要结构面分布特征制约，大变形块体沿线分布，形成规模较大的块体位移大于100mm的潜在不稳定区域，总方量约2.5万m^3；中隔墙顶部受C_4切割部分块体失稳，方量约为$270m^3$。

圆筒形方案开挖后大变形块体受主要结构面分布特征制约，形成沿线分布。受层间错动带C_4、C_5、f_{813}、f_{816}、f_{817}切割时形成的块体位移大于100mm的潜在不稳定区域方量约0.5万m^3。

因此，从块体稳定角度而言，圆筒形方案总体占优。

（三）结语

针对两种尾水调压室方案高应力、高边墙大变形、塑性区分布、块体稳定等主要围岩稳定问题进行综合比较，可得出如下结论：

（1）选择合理的调压室断面形状是调压室的设计重点，在高地应力、长大缓倾结构面发育等复杂地质条件下更应特别重视。

（2）围岩稳定性是尾水调压室形状选择考虑的首要因素。

（3）长廊形方案中顶拱的高应力集中和边墙的大范围松弛，中隔墙围岩稳定问题较突出，而圆筒形尾水调压室穹顶应力集中程度和范围均较小，圆筒形方案中边墙仍保持较高的初始应力水平。圆筒形方案在保障围岩稳定性方面具有明显的优势。

目前，该工程尾水调压室已进入底部分岔段开挖阶段，穹顶及井身均已顺利开挖完成，左岸尾水调压室穹顶最大变形约21mm，井身最大变形约53mm，右岸调压室穹顶最大变形约50mm，井身最大变形约41mm，变形量值总体处于平稳状态。实践证明在高应力条件下圆筒形方案围岩稳定性更优。

（中国电建集团华东勘测设计研究院有限公司
杨飞　倪绍虎　陈益民
孟江波　吕慷）

土石坝长效安全运行重大关键技术研究

“土石坝长效安全运行重大关键技术研究”为企事业单位委托科技项目，由河海大学与水利部交通运输部国家能源局南京水利科学研究院合作于2018年10月完成。

项目收集典型水库大坝勘测、施工和运行过程中的各种监测信息，并进行统计分析；研究地震、洪水等可能影响大坝安全的外部随机变量的统计特性；研究大坝物理力学参数的随机反馈分析方法，开发大坝应力场、位移场及渗流场反馈分析软件；研究基于监测资料的大坝风险因子识别理论和方法；通过模型试验与数值分析相结合的方法研究地震、特大洪水等小概率事件发生时大坝可能失效模式，并建立与破坏模式相对应的控制方程与风险分析方法；研究建立水库大坝正常使用极限状态和承载能力极限状态两级安全设防下的安全风险控制标准，进一步完善水库大坝风险评估和管理的理论与方法。具体研究内容：

（1）土石坝勘测、施工和运行过程中各种监测信息的收集和统计分析。

（2）研究地震、洪水等可能影响大坝安全的外部随机变量的统计特性。

（3）研究大坝物理力学参数的随机反馈分析方法。

（4）研究基于监测资料的大坝风险因子识别理论和方法。

（5）研究极端事件发生时大坝可能失效模式，并建立与破坏模式相对应的控制方程与风险分析方法。

（6）研究建立水库大坝正常使用极限状态和承载能力极限状态两级安全设防下的安全风险控制标准。

（河海大学）

面板堆石坝精细化模拟与动态控制关键技术研究

“面板堆石坝精细化模拟与动态控制关键技术研究”为河南省河口村水库工程建设管理局委托项目，中国水利水电科学研究院、河南省河口村水库工程建设管理局、南京水利科学研究院、中国地质大学（北京）合作完成。

随着混凝土面板堆石坝坝高的增加、坝基条件复杂程度的提升，其安全控制要求也越来越高，考虑渗流场及温度场的影响，建立堆石材料的尺度效应、时间效应、剪胀特性、湿化特性与渗流特性等模型，能显著提高其应力变形分析水平。建立水—热—力耦合数学模型，研究面板堆石坝动态控制精细化模拟中结构模拟、材料模型、加速算法等，开展大坝全生命周期应力变形性状预测方法研究，对提高面板坝变形控制水平、确保大坝成功建设与安全运行都具有极其重要的意义。

（一）主要研究内容

该项目综合采用理论分析、地质勘察、原位测试、室内试验与数值模拟等手段，重点研究了面板堆石坝精细化模拟与动态控制中的关键技术问题：①基于三场耦合的混凝土面板堆石坝理论构建与数值分析方法研究；②三维数字大坝模型一体化构建技术；③面板坝大规模精细化模拟GPU并行加速算法；④堆石材料的力学特性与本构模型；⑤安全监测与数据分析方法；⑥面板堆石坝动态控制与分析方法研究；⑦混凝土面板堆石坝精细化模拟与动态分析平台建设。

（二）主要创新点

（1）通过水-热-力全耦合理论架构的构建，建立了基于三场耦合理论的混凝土面板堆石坝安全分析数学模型，提出了耦合求解的有限元数值分析方法。

（2）提出了堆石材料E-B模型参数K与最大粒径的对数模型、流变幂函数模型、八参数湿化模型、多内在状态变量的剪胀方程，完善了粗粒料渗透试验的缩尺准则与方法，提出了面板坝垫层料和过渡料的设计准则。

（3）基于多源异构、非结构化数据特征，建立了融合地质-地形-坝体结构的一体化三维数字大坝构建体系，提出了模型网格离散优化方法；提出了基于GPU并行技术的网格与数值迭代求解的优化算法。

（4）设计研发了大坝分层沉降的分布式光纤监测新方法；提出了监测数据的贝叶斯不确定性反分析等模型；考虑应力变形、渗流稳定、温度控制等多指标控制，提出了基于数据可靠性、重要性权重的综合反演分析理论方法。

（三）推广应用情况

项目研究成果成功应用于河口村水库、吉林台一级、出山店水库、前坪水库等工程施工控制中，提高了工程的科技含量，确保了工程的正常建设，带来了极大的社会经济效益和生态效益。

（中国水利水电科学研究院）

荒沟抽水蓄能电站土石坝填筑料现场碾压工艺性试验研究

荒沟抽水蓄能电站上水库主坝及副坝分别为混凝土面板堆石坝和心墙土石坝，坝体填筑工程量约311万m^3；其填筑料料场位于坝址上游，地下厂房硐室开挖料直接运输至料场进行加工后再运至坝体碾压填筑。根据《碾压式土石坝施工规范》（DL/T 5129—2013）要求，堆石料应优先采用岩性单一，且数量与质量应有可靠保证，反滤料及过渡料可采用人工制备。因此，该工程需在碾压施工前对坝料进行碾压工艺性试验研究。

（一）工艺性试验目的

通过碾压工艺性试验，复核已堆存的洞挖石料质量是否满足设计要求，确定各种填筑料的施工压实机具和经济合理的压实工艺参数（铺料方法、铺层厚度、碾压遍数、加水量等），确定级配曲线、孔隙率、干容重及渗透系数等有关质量控制参数，制定有关的施工技术措施和检验方法。

（二）主要技术指标

1. 洞挖料物理、力学及化学性指标　洞挖料岩性为新鲜～微风化长白花岗岩，通过试验结果可知：相对密度为2.64～2.65，干密度值为2.60～2.62g/cm^3，饱和密度2.62～2.63g/cm^3，吸水率为0.26%～0.43%，饱和吸水率为0.30%～0.47%，孔隙率为0.76%～1.52%，变形模量11.4～17.1GPa，SO_3含量在0.06%～0.09%，其干抗压强度77.1～101.0MPa，饱和抗压强度为61.9～78.9MPa，属坚硬岩石；软化系数均大于0.75，属不软化岩石。

2. 垫层料设计指标　压实后最小干密度2.23g/cm^3，洞挖料块石最大粒径100mm，孔隙率不大于17%；压实后渗透系数$k \geqslant 1\times10^{-2}$cm/s，小于5mm颗粒含量15～30%，不均匀系数不小于15，曲率系数1～3。

3. 过渡料设计指标　压实后最小干密度2.17g/cm^3，洞挖料块石最大粒径300mm，孔隙率不大于19%；小于5mm颗粒含量10%～20%，不均匀系数不小于15，曲率系数1～3。

（三）碾压试验及过程控制

1. 试验方法及场地要求　采用以“全质量法”为主，“干密度”校核为辅的方法。选择一处基面平整坚实的宽阔地带作为试验场地，面积为50m×60m，并用填料在地基上先铺压一层达到设计压实标准，使作为基准面的表面平整度不超过±5cm。

2. 试验步骤（流程）　基面处理→填料运输、上料→人机结合摊铺整平→网格点布设、测松铺厚度→洒水→碾（振）压→测量碾（振）压后的沉降量→灌水法取样检测压实度及含水量→进入下一试验循环。

3. 碾压试验方案及组合　过渡料、垫层料试验采用后退法卸料，人工配合机械摊铺整平，铺料厚度误差不宜超过碾压试验确定层厚的10%。按照3种不同加水量和3个碾压遍数进行3场共计9个试验组合。每次试验以相同厚度、相同含水量为一场；其试验顺碾压方向分为3个小区分别对应不同碾压遍数。

4. 试验场地布置及碾压设备　碾压试验场地选择在上水库库盆上游备料场，面积50m×60m，一场试验布置3个试验组合，依次布置6场试验。试验段采用的振动碾为LSS2502型自行式25t震动平碾。

5. 碾压过程控制　统一先静压2遍后再开始振动碾压，垫层料、过渡料分别采用高、低频振动压实，所有填料均采用进退搭接法碾压，搭接宽度大于10cm；振动碾行进速度实测为2.5km/h，各细分小场之间最小搭接宽度不小于1.0m。

6. 试验场次组合与试验数据测定

(1) 试验场次组合：试验组合采用经验法和淘汰法进行，每一试验组合只变动一个试验参数。为避免摊铺后加水量不同而相互影响，不同含水量的同一填料同一铺筑厚度填料分开试验。

(2) 沉降量观测：先在碾压试验区域绘制1.5m×2.0m方格网并石灰标出，采用全站仪对方格网交点进行高程测量。试验后，各试验组合均在振压6、8、10遍前后，分别测出方格网交点高程进行沉降量计算。

(3) 室内外试验检测：颗粒级配试验，10mm以上部分在碾压现场进行筛分，10mm以下部分在室内烘干后筛分；渗透试验按有关规范在现场进行。

(四) 碾压试验成果分析

1. 碾压遍数与沉降量关系分析　从观测记录可知：垫层料和过渡料均随着碾压遍数的增加，其沉降量值呈递减趋势，符合正常规律。从沉降量和不同加水量横向对比关系上看，二者之间在含水率发生变化后，小于静2+振6几乎没有区别，但在大于静2+振8以上后则沉降量会有轻微改变。

2. 碾压遍数与干密度试验汇总分析　从试验结果可知，过渡料和垫层料在碾压遍数分别为6、8、10遍的干密度和孔隙率的实测值均满足设计指标要求；干密度实测值均随碾压遍数的增加而增加，但若加水量过大或碾压遍数过多都会对碾压密实度有一定影响，且干密度有随着碾压遍数的增加而出现逐渐降低的趋势。经过对比，碾压遍数以静2+振8、加水量为10%的试验结果更具经济合理性。

3. 级配筛分试验汇总分析　从试验结果可以看出，垫层料、过渡料采用岩性好硬度高的花岗岩，碾压前后的颗粒级配整体有着显著变化，碾压后表面细颗粒有明显增加，致使5mm以下部分颗粒含量有显著增加。另外，从不均匀系数和曲率系数上看，过渡料C_U和C_C值、垫层料C_U值均满足设计要求，垫层料碾压前后的曲率系数C_C不能满足设计指标要求，因此需做必要的级配调整。

(五) 结语

该电站堆石坝的垫层料、过渡料的施工松铺控制厚度均以45cm为宜，压实厚度为40cm；其含水率控制，以加水量（体积比）分别为10%和13%时最佳；进行洒水碾压施工时以静压2遍+振压8遍为宜；当无洒水时，则应以静压2遍+振10遍控制，其静压和振压时的行驶速度应控制在2～3km/h。

（中国水利水电第三工程局有限公司
贾高峰　陈书军
中国电建集团西北勘测设计研究院有限公司
王保欣　李志龙）

强震区深厚覆盖层 250m级特高土心墙堆石坝防渗系统关键技术研究与应用

该项目依托深厚覆盖层上世界最高的长河坝水电站大坝工程，针对强震区深厚覆盖层250m级特高土心墙堆石坝建设的关键技术和难点，从防渗系统结构、试验和计算方法、抗震性能及监测技术等方面开展研究。

(一) 研究内容

(1) 坝体—坝基材料静、动力特性研究。对心墙料静、动力特性进行了研究，采用不同尺寸三轴试验与平面应变试验相结合的方法，明确了级配缩尺等试验方法对心墙料特性的影响，心墙料在高应力下压缩后的渗透性，以及现场原位剪切强度等相关数据。并通过大量的原状样和钻孔取芯样试验成果对比研究，明确了钻孔取样和原状样的规律性。针对目前的反滤设计准则对冰碛土适应性差的现状，提出了抛填心墙料反滤试验和泥浆渗透试验方法，研究反滤料对心墙料的反滤效果。针对接触土料布置范围和厚度等缺少理论依据的不足，提出了高塑性接触黏土料性能特殊试验。研究了高塑性黏土在不同变形和应力状态下的渗透特性。通过室内配合比研究和现场实际成墙试验研究高强度、1.4m厚防渗墙墙体材料。并对覆盖层进行了室内和现场试验对比研究，建立了适用于粗粒土地基的考虑K_0固结初始各向异性并反映剪胀性的弹塑性本构模型；依据载荷试验采用遗传算法对覆盖层参数进行了优化反演。

(2) 坝体—坝基防渗系统结构布置研究。对已建防渗体位于深厚覆盖层上的多座100～200m之间的类似工程进行了资料收集和分析整理。对坝体心墙和反滤的结构尺寸、材料及联合防渗及反滤效果等进行了分析验证；对坝基防渗结构的选择、布置进行了系统梳理研究，采用了2道分开布置的防渗墙防渗结构体系，系统研究了坝基双防渗墙布置情况下的渗流规律性，找出影响副墙分担水头比例的关键因素，提出提高副墙分担水头比例的工程措施。采用有限元子结构方法系统研究了防渗墙与心墙采用的插入式或廊道式连接结构，通过研究比较廊道与两岸的自由式、简支式和半固端式等多种连接方式，提出廊道与岸坡应采用半固支方式连接的方案。对连接部位高塑性黏土区的布置范围和厚度开展了大量的计算分析和试验研究，对最后优选的防渗系统进行三维应力变形及防渗性能评价。

(3) 坝体—坝基应力变形模拟方法研究。采用不同本构模型的数值模拟和离心机模型试验对比结合的方法，研究坝体及坝基的应力变形状态。采用线弹性、非线性弹性及弹塑性模型防渗墙混凝土，对应直剪和单剪试验，采用不同的接触面模型模拟泥波和防渗墙底残渣。使用模型试验研究影响有限元数值模拟坝基防渗墙应力变形的敏感因素，探求更好的模拟方法，将大变形分析法（RITSS 法）用于研究土石坝工程中结构（防渗墙）与周围土的相互作用问题，以解决小变形分析方法不能准确描述结构体周围土体复杂应力和变形状态的问题和防渗墙应力高估等问题。采用离心机模型试验成果与数值分析成果对比的方法对比研究坝基防渗墙壁、廊道等的应力变形。采用应力与渗流真耦合的方法研究填筑顺序及蓄水速度对大坝应力变形带来的影响。

（4）坝体—坝基动力反应分析和抗震措施研究。同时采用有限元总应力和有效应力法、离心机振动台模型试验方法对坝体—坝基的动力反应进行研究，对其抗震安全性进行评估，研究坝体的地震破坏模式，采用离心机振动台试验与数值计算对比研究的方法，对抗 9 度强震的深厚覆盖层上 250m 级土心墙堆石坝坝体—坝基的抗震能力和加固措施进行预测分析。采用有限元子结构法研究防渗墙、廊道等的动力安全性；研究不同的坝顶抗震措施的加固效果。

（5）防渗系统监测技术研究。通过工程调研、计算分析的方法明确了监测重点部位及难点。通过对防渗墙上、下游侧土压力计进行研究，提出了支杆扩张器埋设方法；研发了用于观测深厚覆盖层变形的大量程电位器式位移计，该仪器量程可达 1200mm、耐水压可达 4MPa。采用在防渗墙上下游侧顶部安装埋设大量程位错计的方法对深厚覆盖层上 250m 级土心墙堆石坝坝基防渗墙与覆盖层之间的相对错动变形进行监测。并对强震监测、两岸高塑性黏土的剪切变形监测，心墙沉降及与反滤的沉降差监测等进行了研究。

（二）创新成果

（1）首次提出了基于弹性垫层和半固端方式的坝基廊道与岸坡连接的新型结构，解决了坝基廊道对强震沉陷和深厚覆盖层不均匀沉降的适应性难题；首次研究揭示了主副防渗墙按比例分担水头的渗流规律，提出了副墙合理分担水头的方法，解决了高水头下两道坝基防渗墙联合防渗的技术难题。

（2）改进完善了适用于坝基及其防渗结构、反映剪胀性的弹塑性本构模型和新型防渗墙与覆盖层接触面模型及其分析计算方法。揭示了覆盖层应力变形性态，进一步提高了坝基防渗墙应力计算成果的合理性。

（3）提出了适用于宽级配冰碛土的抛填心墙料反滤试验和泥浆渗透反滤试验以及接触黏土性能特殊试验方法，充实了反滤料、接触黏土设计方法和理论。首次采用数值分析和离心机振动台模型试验相结合的方法，综合评估了强震区深厚覆盖层土心墙堆石坝的极限抗震能力。

（4）研发了大量程电位器杆式位移监测仪器，解决了深厚覆盖层坝基超大沉降变形和耐高水压等监测技术难题。

（中国电建集团成都勘测设计研究院有限公司
胡万雨）

双江口水电站 300m 级心墙堆石坝可行性研究阶段筑坝关键技术研究

双江口水电站采用碎石土心墙堆石坝，最大坝高 314m，为目前世界在建的第一高坝；坝体填筑总量约 4400 万 m^3，河床覆盖层一般厚 48～57m、最大厚度达 67.8m，现行规范规定和已有经验已不能满足建设的需要。因此，在可行性研究阶段，开展了 300m 级心墙堆石坝筑坝关键技术研究。

该项目针对双江口大坝开展了 5 项专题、23 个子题的研究，现简介如下：

（一）筑坝材料特性研究

1. 防渗土料改性试验研究　推荐采用黏土掺合花岗岩破碎料，比例为 50%：50%；掺砾料的含水率约为 8.8%，与填筑最优含水率（7.7%）接近，有利于施工。

2. 防渗土料材料特性及试验方法研究　提出了掺砾料固结排水剪切快速试验方法，揭示了等应力比路径下心墙料的应力应变规律和各向异性等应力应变规律；进行相关试验，揭示了接触面等应力比路径下变形、强度特性；提出断裂区的大小和断裂韧度可作为描述其裂缝扩展行为的重要指标。

3. 堆石料材料特性及试验方法研究　进行了围压不变的平面应变试验，结果显示，破坏时的偏应力要比常规三轴试验大，且有更加明显的软化现象。单向加荷试验结果表明，堆石料应力诱导各向异性显著。研究表明，颗粒相对破碎率与塑性功基本符合双曲线关系。

4. 堆石料湿化特性试验及经验模型研究　“单线法”和“双线法”试验得到的湿化变形量差别较大，应以“单线法”为主。堆石料的湿化轴向变形随湿化应力水平的增大而增大，而湿化轴向应变与围压的相关性不大，湿化体积应变随湿化应力水平和围压的增加而增加。岩性对湿化量的大小有重要影响，岩性越硬，其湿化应变量越小。

5. 堆石料流变特性试验及经验模型研究　进行

堆石料的流变研究，宜采用三轴流变试验。双江口堆石料的流变量与时间关系仍可采用幂函数表达，其流变规律符合九参数模型。从流变试验成果看，上游坝壳料由于岩性较差，较之下游坝壳料表现出较大的流变变形。

（二）坝体及坝基变形与稳定分析理论和方法研究

1. 考虑接触特性的大坝数值分析　在设置接触面单元的局部部位会发生位移及应力的不连续现象，但这种差别的影响范围仅发生在接触界面附近一定范围之内，对坝体总体的位移和应力分布影响不大。采用不同的接触面模型，其计算结果均符合一般规律，且结果差别较小。

2. 黏性土抗裂机理及计算理论研究　构造了平面应变条件下考虑压实黏土脆性开裂过程的有限元算法和基于无单元法的裂缝弥散理论的计算模式和点插值无单元法与有限元法的耦合方法。分析表明，双江口心墙堆石坝设计方案坝肩不会发生横河向张拉裂缝。

3. 考虑湿化和流变效应的大坝数值分析　湿化变形主要发生在上游坝壳内，引起指向上游的变形增加，对心墙的影响较小，对沉降最大值影响甚微。流变效应主要导致大坝产生沉降，对坝体的应力状态影响很小。

4. 考虑流固耦合的大坝数值分析　提出了以有效小主应力为判断指标，全面考虑坝壳和心墙的拱效应、坝体与岸坡的拱效应的水力劈裂判定方法。分析结果表明，心墙的渗透稳定性可以得到保障，心墙、帷幕等渗控体系起到了很好的防渗作用。

5. 心墙水力劈裂数值分析　指出心墙中可能存在的渗水弱面以及在水库快速蓄水过程中所产生的弱面水压楔劈效应是心墙发生水力劈裂的另一个重要条件。推导和建立了用于描述水力劈裂发生和扩展过程的有限元—无单元数值仿真模型。分析表明，按照设计的蓄水方案，大坝心墙不会发生水力劈裂破坏。

6. 非线性指标坝坡稳定分析及可靠度研究　保证心墙堆石坝，尤其是建基于覆盖层上的高坝的坝坡稳定措施，尚需进一步研究。研究得出的各工况下坝坡稳定最小可靠指标均满足规范要求。

（三）心墙堆石坝结构及分区设计

1. 双江口心墙堆石坝布置型式比较　对比研究直心墙、斜心墙和弧形心墙3种方案，只在投资方面略有差异，直心墙方案投资最省。

2. 深厚覆盖层坝基防渗处理方案研究　经研究，采用直心墙坝方案，宜将心墙底部覆盖层全部挖除。

3. 坝体填筑技术指标对坝体应力和变形特性的影响　分析表明，大坝直心墙方案的坝体材料和分区设计从应力和位移的角度看是合理的；大坝上游堆石区在上部是否采用花岗岩料对大坝的应力及变形影响极小。

（四）心墙堆石坝坝体动力反应分析及抗震措施研究

1. 坝体材料及覆盖层坝基动力特性试验研究　首次成功进行了最高围压力3000kPa的大型高压力和复杂应力条件下的粗粒土动力特性试验。对大坝的反滤料Ⅰ、心墙掺砾料混合料、坝基砂、坝基砂砾料、主堆石料及过渡料等进行动力试验，提出相应的本构计算模型参数指标，为坝体抗震设计和动力分析工作提供依据。

2. 坝体及覆盖层地基动力本构关系及计算方法研究　对Hardin模型进行了改进，提出了PZ模型和改进的临界PZ模型以及由Hardin模型推导PZ参数的方法。

3. 高坝抗震安全评价方法研究　对计入地基、考虑边界为黏弹性、输入地震动波、采用基频与地震波主频确定阻尼系数等问题作了深入研究。计算成果表明，大坝在设计和校核地震情况下，抗震能力是有保障的，且还具有一定的承受超标准地震动荷载的能力。

4. 坝体与坝基振动台地震动力模型试验研究　开展了一般重力场下高土质心墙堆石坝大型振动台模型试验。试验得到不同幅值输入下的动力特性和动力反应性状等成果，可以作为验证和改进土石坝地震动力反应计算模式、分析方法和计算程序的基本资料。

5. 坝体与坝基三维动力响应分析及抗震措施研究　频谱分析和强度折减法分析表明，双江口大坝具有良好的抗震能力，坝坡是稳定的。首次采用基于已建土石坝实际震害的ANN模型对大坝震害进行预测表明，在设计地震情况下，震害等级为4级。

提出大坝抗震措施，主要包括：在坝顶坝高1/5范围采用加筋处理，坝顶预留较大超高裕度，对可能液化砂层大部分挖除或压重处理，提高坝料填筑标准，上、下游坝面设置干砌石及大块石护坡，分层分散设置枢纽泄水建筑物等。试验和计算表明，在设计地震情况下加筋后坝坡动力安全系数至少提高15%，在校核地震情况下动力安全系数提高得更多。

（五）心墙堆石坝渗流分析及渗控措施研究

1. 心墙堆石坝坝料渗透特性研究　试验得出掺砾料的渗透系数，验证了设计反滤Ⅰ料级配的合理性。实验还表明，心墙上游侧保护黏土有“上堵”垫板裂缝接触渗流的功能；如果混凝土垫板未形成上下游贯通性裂缝，心墙黏土仍具有较高接触冲刷抗渗强度。

2. 枢纽区渗流分析及渗控措施优化研究　通过

分析，坝体坝基的防渗系统（心墙＋防渗帷幕）能够有效控制地下水的分布和渗压。地下厂房区排水设计合理，考虑一定的安全储备，宜保留“人字顶”排水孔幕，加密上游侧和右侧的排水孔幕孔间距，F_1断层附近的帷幕应局部适当加厚。

3. 心墙堆石坝非稳定渗流研究　水库初次蓄水时，心墙上游侧出现较大的渗透力，河谷两岸心墙与混凝土基座之间发生接触渗透破坏的可能性较大。应针对水库初次蓄水非稳定渗流场的心墙土料最大渗透坡降与允许渗透坡降之间关系开展进一步研究。水库放空时，两岸坝肩和岸坡出现渗流逸出，对上游库区岸坡稳定不利，应予以重视。

4. 坝体坝基防渗系统随机缺陷对坝区渗流场影响研究　上部帷幕对渗流场的影响较大，应重视施工质量。心墙开裂和心墙混凝土垫板产生上下游贯通的裂缝，对坝区的渗流影响较大。若心墙某个高程上的局部施工缺陷所占比例过大，会使该高程其他部位的渗透梯度值增大很多，甚至会超过其允许梯度值，影响心墙的整体渗透稳定。

（国电大渡河流域水电开发有限公司
段斌　李善平　严锦江
中国电建集团成都勘测设计研究院有限公司
李永红　王观琪）

向家坝水电站机组跳闸应急补水策略研究

向家坝水电站所处金沙江河段为通航河段，下游2km处为水富港；由于所处河段为山区型河流，河道狭窄，出库流量的变化会引起下游河道水位的剧烈变化，严重时会影响航道、港口、通航设施的正常使用以及船舶的航行安全。金沙江下游航运要求向家坝水电站下泄流量应不低于1750m^3/s，且电站下游水位小时变幅不超过1m，日变幅不超过4.5m。为满足这一要求，在向家坝水库运用与电站运行调度时制定了相应的应急补水策略，当机组事故导致下泄流量突变时，通过及时开启泄洪闸门向下游补水，以防止电站下游水位变幅过大。

当前的应急补水策略是通过直接开启泄水闸门进行应急补水。因电站距离水富县城生活区较近，实际执行时为安全起见，运行人员要先开启定向广播通知下游民众远离江边沿岸，通过视频监控确认下游水域无人后才开启闸门补水。这种应急补水方式耗时较长，虽然可以满足电站水位变幅的要求，但造成了一定的弃水损失。

该研究分析了机组跳闸后电站出力损失、下泄流量变化与下游水位变幅之间的内在关系，研究在满足航运对水情要求的前提条件下，投入机组旋转备用容量、开启备用机组、开启泄洪闸门等不同方式应急补水策略的可行性，从而对比制定出最优的应急补水策略。这些策略有助于提高运行人员应急响应水平，优化应急补水响应时间，减小开启泄洪闸门造成的弃水损失，提高电站运行的经济性。

（一）技术创新点

（1）通过分析数据得出了向家坝出库流量与下游水位、向家坝下游水位变幅与电站出力损失之间的关系，采用数值拟合的方法得出了它们之间的经验关系式。

（2）通过分析研究，编制出在不同电站出力情况下，无需应急补水时的电站最大允许减少出力对应表（满足电站下游水位变幅要求）和需要应急补水时的补水策略表、闸门开启策略表。

（3）针对应急补水的时效性分析，提出在全厂失电情况下快速恢复泄洪设施电源的优化建议，完成监控系统一键启动柴油机恢复泄洪设施电源流程。

（二）实施效果及应用推广情况

该项目从理论上对向家坝电站的应急补水策略进行了研究和探讨，是对现有应急补水策略的延伸和发展，根据电站出力及机组故障台数进行下游应急补水时，在实施新的策略表后相比原有策略表预计可节水约62.7%～100%，计划后续将研究结果应用于向家坝水库运用和电站运行调度实践。项目成果目前已为电厂在制定应急补水预案时提供策略查询和数据支撑，同时也为深刻总结电站运行规律提供经验参考，提高应急处置能力。

（向家坝水力发电厂　陈保臻）

荒沟抽水蓄能电站混凝土抗溶出型侵蚀试验研究

荒沟抽水蓄能电站位于黑龙江省海林市境内，装机容量1200MW，为一等大（1）型工程。地质勘察资料显示，坝址区地下水、地表水的HCO_3^-含量分别为0.68、0.39mg/L，输水发电系统区地下水HCO_3^-含量为0.62mg/L，下水库进（出）水口地表水HCO_3^-含量为0.42mg/L。根据GB 50287—2006《水力发电工程地质勘察规范》规定，当HCO_3^-含量小于0.70mg/L时，环境水可判定为中等溶出型侵蚀。在这种环境水中，混凝土孔隙溶液中的钙离子向环境水中扩散，使得孔隙率有所增加，混凝土的耐久性能降低。因此，为针对溶出型侵蚀特性区域进行混凝土配合比设计提供依据，开展了荒沟抽水蓄能电站混凝土抗溶出型侵蚀试验研究。现将有关情况简介如下。

（一）试验概况

1. 试验材料　采用冀东普通 42.5 水泥，所用骨料均取自荒沟抽水蓄能电站下水库砂石加工系统，原材料各项指标均满足规范要求。

2. 试验方法

（1）试件制备：试验拌和二级配常态混凝土，水胶比分别选择 0.30、0.40、0.50、0.60，控制混凝土坍落度在 70～90mm，通过筛除将小石与中石剔除，成型 40mm×40mm×40mm 砂浆试件。试验过程中的混凝土成型与砂浆试件养护均按照《水工混凝土试验规程》进行。

（2）侵蚀试验设备：采用带定速搅拌圆筒形容器，试验期间间隔一定的周期更换软水（pH 值为 7.16，以 CaO 计的钙离子浓度为 1.8mg/L），每次更换的侵蚀溶液量保持恒定，在试验换水的同时采集侵蚀溶液样品，对侵蚀溶液中的离子浓度变化进行测定，分析在一定侵蚀试验周期内溶液中离子的变化情况。

3. 指标选取　对于混凝土的溶出型侵蚀来说，CaO 的溶出是溶蚀过程的具体体现，并且 CaO 的溶出量与混凝土受溶蚀的程度存在着正比例的关系，是反映混凝土溶蚀程度的一个较好的研究对象。CaO 累计溶出比例为混凝土在溶蚀的作用条件下累计溶出的钙离子总量（以 CaO 计）与未受侵蚀混凝土中钙离子（以 CaO 计）总量的比值，该参数能够在一定程度上反映出溶蚀作用的侵蚀程度。

（二）实验结果与分析

1. pH 值的变化分析　在试件浸泡过程中，pH 值的变化能够在一定程度上反映由于试件内部连通孔隙中溶出溶液所带出的碱的含量。在本次试验中采用 LIDA pHS-3C pH 计（精度为 0.01）对试样浸泡过程中侵蚀溶液的 pH 值进行监测。

由试验结果可知：试件浸泡过程中 pH 值的变化整体趋势分为三个阶段：①浸泡试验前期（0～4 天）pH 值增大速率很快，迅速升高至 11～12；②随着试验的进行（5～14 天），在 pH 迅速升高后，又呈现迅速下降趋势，曲线斜率为负值；③在浸泡试验进行到一定时间后（14 天后），pH 值的变化趋于平稳，维持在 8～9 之间。

前两个阶段 pH 值的变化主要与试件表层结晶的碱性物质有关。在浸泡初期，由于有较多的碱性物质［主要为水泥水化反应的生成物 $Ca(OH)_2$］进入水溶液中，使得浸泡溶液的 pH 值迅速升高；随后，溶液开始呈弱碱性，即 pH 值有所降低。在第三阶段中，试件内部孔隙中的碱性物质通过混凝土中的微细孔隙和毛细通道向表层扩散，使得碱性物质的扩散过程依然在进行，达到一个近似动态的平衡过程，所以，此阶段溶液的 pH 基本维持在一定范围内小振幅波动。

由于 pH 值测试自身特点的限制，pH 值监测数据只能用于过程的粗略监控和辅助分析。

2. CaO 累计溶出比例变化分析　钙离子浓度用 EDTA 滴定法测定。试验用 EDTA 溶液、钙指示剂，试验仪器有铁架台、滴定管、锥形瓶、烧杯、电子秤等。精确度为 ±0.04mmol/L，约相当于 ±2 滴 EDTA 溶液。

试验对不同浸泡时间的侵蚀溶液进行测定，并计算不同水胶比砂浆试件 CaO 累计溶出比例，试验结果如图 1 所示。

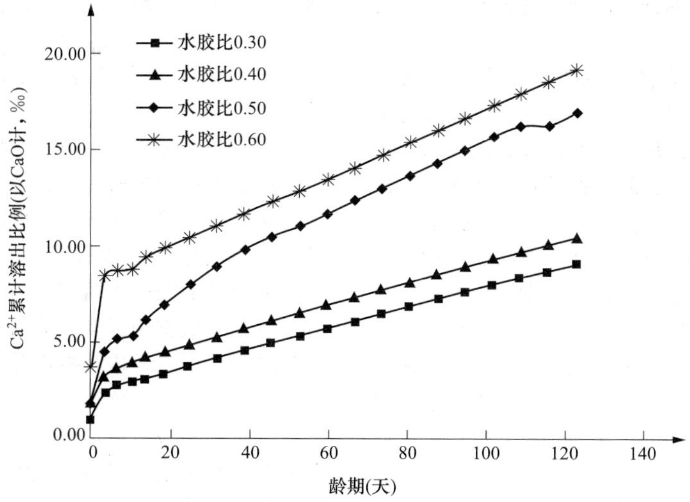

图 1　CaO 累计溶出比例随龄期的变化

由试验结果可知：

(1) 砂浆试件在软水中浸泡初期（0～4天），浸泡溶液中CaO的累计溶出比例曲线斜率较大，说明试件表层中的Ca^{2+}迅速溶出至溶液中。在侵蚀龄期为4～14天时，CaO累计溶出比例随龄期变化的曲线斜率迅速减小，并与在第14天左右降低至最小。在浸泡一段时间（14天）后，CaO的溶出速率（CaO累计溶出比例随龄期变化的曲线斜率）略有增加，并维持在一定的速率左右。

(2) 不同水胶比砂浆试件在软水浸泡的过程中，CaO累计溶出比例也有一定的差异，随着水胶比的增大，试件CaO累计溶出比例也越大，说明水胶比越大，试件中的Ca^{2+}向侵蚀溶液中扩散的速度越快，说明试件对于溶出型侵蚀的耐久性越差。

（黑龙江牡丹江抽水蓄能有限公司
崔志刚　鲁恩龙　赵兵
中国电建集团西北勘测设计研究院有限公司
孙宇飞）

强震区卸荷裂隙密集带复杂岩体边坡稳定性评价与加固关键技术

项目针对高坝水电工程中的高边坡不稳定和边坡永久加固等技术难题，开展了大岗山水电站右岸卸荷岩体形成机理、稳定分析方法、安全评价体系、加固处理措施、不同施工顺序对边坡安全系数的变化影响、多方法监测手段实施动态监测控制等研究，解决了卸荷裂隙密集发育边坡的稳定性评价与加固治理的难题，形成了一套完整的分析加固处理技术。主要研究内容如下。

(1) 右岸边坡卸荷岩体形成机理及失稳模式研究。深化边坡工程地质研究，分析控制右岸边坡稳定性的主要因素，并根据边坡岩体的岩性、结构面几何特征与空间组合关系、风化卸荷特征及水文地质条件等，对右岸边坡岩体进行岩体质量分类和稳定性分区；对不稳定边坡区域，分析边坡变形破坏机理；根据不同部位边坡岩体的地质特征，特别是根据优势节理、断层、卸荷裂隙密集带、岩脉等空间展布、组合关系，确定边坡潜在的失稳模式及组合；对结构面的物质组成进行深入研究，结合试验分析成果，采用综合方法研究岩体及结构面的力学参数；分析评价工程边坡的稳定性。

(2) 卸荷岩体地质结构分类及参数取值方法研究。通过总结研究高边坡坡体内部卸荷裂隙密集带的地质结构特征，具有“从外到里、拉张为主、成带展布”的总体特点、“每带带宽数米至十余米、每带数条至十余条、单条张开宽度数厘米至30cm、延伸长达350m、呈串珠状分布、尖灭后斜列再现”等特征，提出卸荷岩体的地质结构分类方法。针对该类非完全连通特殊的地质结构，采取平洞追踪调查连通率，并视带为面，考虑部分地段张开简化为结构面，部分地段闭合则作为岩体，提出基于改进的Jennings准则确定其综合抗剪强度参数的取值方法。

(3) 边坡稳定评价体系及评价标准的研究。通过对大岗山右岸边坡稳定的控制因素、破坏区域、破坏机理、滑动模式及稳定安全性进行系统分析，结合工程安全、经济及施工要求，确定了大岗山右岸边坡采用下三层抗剪洞加固期安全系数不低于1.05，边坡继续下挖施工期间施工期安全系数不低1.15，完建及运行期正常工况下安全系数不低于1.25的稳定控制标准，同时，结合现场施工条件，确定了“边评价、边施工”的动态评价体系。

(4) 稳定分析方法的运用及稳定性综合分析研究。结合大岗山工程地质特点，除采用规范规定的平面极限平衡法外，还采用三维极限平衡法、严格三维分析方法、边坡裂隙渗流分析、非线性有限元法 、多重网格法及变形加固理论等多种方法，综合分析论证了右岸边坡的稳定性，提出了大岗山右岸高边坡的加固治理措施，治理后的边坡满足边坡稳定控制标准。对右岸边坡工程施工进行动态稳定控制，提出施工期边坡的开挖程序要求，并根据边坡开挖、锚索及抗剪洞施工的动态分析成果，提出各阶段开挖控制高程、抗剪洞施工顺序、相应的加固措施及施工要求，为边坡工程施工安全提供了技术保障。

(5) 加固措施的作用机理及加固效果评价研究。根据大岗山工程地质特点，结合各加固措施的作用机理，借鉴国内外工程经验，提出右岸边坡“锚索加固、抗剪洞及斜井阻滑、立体排水”的综合治理措施。

(6) 施工爆破对边坡稳定影响分析，施工时序研究。按照大岗山缆机平台和坝肩槽边坡实际开挖程序和支护状况，采用时程法和拟静力法相结合的混合方法研究爆破振动荷载的组合作用对边坡的稳定性影响，研究抗剪洞施工时序对边坡稳定性的影响，从原始位移监测数据中提取相关信息，采用时间序列法对边坡关键点的位移进行模拟分析，以找出边坡变形与开挖、支护等工程施工活动的相关性进行分析，合理选择及优化边坡开挖时序、锚索和抗剪洞施工时序，使其对直线工期的影响降低到最低。抗剪洞施工顺序应保证在整个抗剪洞施工过程中，边坡施工期安全系数不低于1.05，同时使边坡安全系数达到1.15，以满足右岸坝肩继续下挖的安全要求。

（7）边坡动态监测体系的建立研究。边坡动态监测体系在全面或基本查清大岗山右岸边坡地质条件的基础上，特别是随着大岗山右岸边坡卸荷裂隙密集带的发育特点和展布特征的逐步揭示，根据右岸边坡的失稳和变形模式，结合水电工程岩石高边坡的监测布置原则、监测项目和监测仪器选型的要求，建立包括传统监测和微震监测相结合的岩石高边坡变形监测体系。

（8）通过边坡监测成果分析与反馈分析进行稳定性评价研究。根据边坡动态监测体系，结合大岗山右岸边坡的基本地质条件、卸荷裂性密集带的展布特征、边坡失稳和变形模式、边坡施工开挖过程等边界条件，对边坡浅部、深部变形、边坡支护荷载和微震监测成果进行分析。采用三种方法对边坡各类岩体的力学参数进行反演并对边坡变形进行预测、对边坡安全稳定进行评价。模拟岩石渐进破坏的边坡稳定方法是通过“基元”赋值和离心加载技术，对边坡渐进破坏进行模拟；裂隙岩体参数反馈分析的边坡稳定性研究是通过裂隙岩体 *REV* 值的确定，并考虑岩体的非线性屈服准则，对边坡各类岩体的变形模量包括主要断层结构面的强度参数进行反演；滚动预测反馈分析的边坡稳定性研究是运用滚动预测方法，对边坡分步开挖阶段及运行期的边坡安全稳定进行评价。

（中国电建集团成都勘测设计研究院有限公司　胡万雨）

去学水电站 170m 级高沥青混凝土心墙堆石坝设计关键技术研究

去学水电站位于定曲河（金沙江一级支流）最大支流硕曲河干流上，距四川省得荣县城约 50km，距云南省迪庆州香格里拉县约 126km，总装机容量 246MW。其大坝为沥青混凝土心墙堆石坝，坝顶高程为 2334.2m，坝顶宽度为 15m，坝顶轴线长度为 219.85m，最大坝高 173.2m，心墙高度 132m，大坝及心墙高度均位列已建同类工程之首。坝址为非对称陡峻狭窄河谷，宽高比 1.26，河床左岸发育基岩深槽；坝址区岩性为较软的大理岩化细晶灰岩，地层岩溶较发育；地震设防烈度较高，该超高沥青混凝土心墙堆石坝设计难度大。因此，承担设计任务的中国电建集团北京勘测设计研究院有限公司开展了设计关键技术研究。主要研究情况如下：

1. 河床基础深槽处理措施研究　根据大坝心墙基础开挖揭露的地质情况，河床底部为下切强烈的深槽，坝轴线方向宽 18m，深 32m。右岸上部开挖基础整体平顺，而河床底部深槽与右岸岸坡开挖基础之间存在 41m 宽的岩基平台，考虑到河床深窄基坑施工难度大，为确保施工进度，对岩基平台不再进行爆破开挖。深窄、不对称的基础体型，右岸 41m 宽平台的存在使基础开挖体型存在较大突变，对平台以及深槽附近心墙的受力极为不利，影响防渗安全。研究采用高混凝土基座布置方案对基础开挖体型进行修正，混凝土基座高度 32m。修正后的心墙基础体型平顺，改善了心墙的工作性态，同时，有效降低心墙高度至 132m。

2. 陡峻边坡心墙接头结构研究　坝址区属高陡不对称河谷地形，沥青混凝土心墙与混凝土基座接头型式直接关系到大坝防渗系统的安全，为此开展了心墙接头模型试验，对接头部位的沥青玛蹄脂、心墙与基座接触面的型式、心墙和基座是否设置铜止水等进行了试验研究，成果表明：在模拟运行工况中心墙接头部位可能的应力变形情况下，接头部位设置沥青玛蹄脂，并采用弧面基座设置铜止水，且心墙下部局部放大，接头部位均未发生渗漏。

3. 陡边坡沥青混凝土心墙变形协调性研究　去学水电站沥青混凝土心墙高度大，坝址处河谷狭窄，两岸边坡不对称，尤其左岸混凝土基座边坡设计为 1∶0.33。在大坝施工和运行过程中，心墙在陡边坡接头部位可能发生较大的剪切位移，影响心墙的防渗安全性，因此将左岸陡边坡心墙沥青混凝土的油石比调整为 7%，在不引起较大剪切应变情况下，提高靠近左岸陡边坡附近心墙沥青混凝土的变形能力。

4. 坝料分区原则研究　坝料分区按当地材料坝就地、就近取材和挖填平衡原则，达到确保坝体安全、节省工程投资和加快进度的目的。考虑到去学超高沥青混凝土心墙堆石坝的结构功能、坝坡稳定、坝料强度、坝体渗透性、压缩性等要求，上坝料利用枢纽区开挖和纽巴雪料场开采的玄武质熔结角砾岩，其饱和抗压强度 116～125MPa，软化系数 0.86，满足坝体填筑要求。

坝体各筑坝材料间应变形协调，尽可能减少坝体变形对沥青混凝土心墙的不利影响，同时兼顾坝料渗透反滤保护、结构功能要求。心墙为高 132m 的柔性传力结构，为控制其施工期、运行期的挠度变形，应特别注意心墙上下游过渡料、上下游堆石料填筑指标的设计。坝址左岸岸坡陡峻，为尽量减小该部位坝体变形量，改善心墙及其与基座接触面的工作条件，在左岸坝体陡于 1∶0.5 的岸坡接触部位设置碾压增模区，提高坝料填筑指标，减少左岸心墙附近坝体的不均匀变形量，使坝体堆石模量呈梯度过渡。左岸碾压增模区顶部高程 2305m，距混凝土基座宽 5m 以 1∶0.5 坡度向右岸放坡，上下游以 1∶0.5 坡度放坡至河床。上坝料填筑设计指标见表 1。

表1 坝体主要填料设计指标表

名称	设计干密度 (g/cm^3)	孔隙率 (%)	渗透系数 (cm/s)	最大粒径 (mm)	铺层厚度 (cm)	$<P_{10}$ (%)	$<P_5$ (%)	$<P_{0.075}$ (%)
上游堆石Ⅰ	≥2.32	≤21	$10^{-2}\sim10^{-3}$	800	80～100	10～25	<15	<5
下游堆石Ⅰ	≥2.32	≤21	$>10^{-1}$	800	80～100		<10	<5
下游堆石Ⅱ	≥2.35	≤20	$10^{-1}\sim10^{-2}$	800	80～100	10～20	<10	<5
过渡料Ⅰ	≥2.35	≤20	$\geq10^{-3}$	60	20～30	—	25～40	≤5
过渡料Ⅱ	≥2.32	≤21	$\geq10^{-2}$	150	40～60	—	15～25	3～5
碾压增模Ⅰ	≥2.35	≤20	$10^{-2}\sim10^{-3}$	800	80～100	10～25	<15	<5
碾压增模Ⅱ	≥2.38	≤19	$10^{-1}\sim10^{-2}$	800	80～100	10～20	<10	<5

5. 抗震措施研究 工程场地地震基本烈度为Ⅷ度。由于坝体高度大，河谷狭窄，两岸岸坡陡峻，为确保地震工况下坝体安全，减少震害影响，拦河坝采用了如下抗震措施：

（1）结合坝体应力变形及地形地质条件等特点，对坝体进行合理分区，采用级配和性能较好的石料填筑施工，并适当提高碾压标准。心墙为柔韧性好的沥青混凝土，适应振动和变形能力强，且具有裂缝自愈能力。

（2）考虑地震涌浪高度，并结合工程实际情况及工程经验预留地震沉降，使坝顶高程满足地震时的超高要求，不发生库水漫顶。

（3）对坝顶宽度适当加大，取15m；坝体高程2305m以上，铺设双向聚丙烯土工格栅；上游坝坡在死水位2305m以下5m至坝顶高程范围，以及下游坝坡，均采用厚80cm的干砌块石护坡。

（4）沥青混凝土墙与基座连接部位采用心墙厚度逐渐扩大的形式连接，接触面设沥青玛蹄脂和铜止水，以提高地震时的防渗性能。

（5）施工中严格控制填筑层厚、碾压遍数、加水量等施工参数，做好过程控制，确保坝体碾压密实，减少地震沉陷。

（中国电建集团北京勘测设计研究院有限公司
刘士佳 孔彩粉 杨健 刘海宇）

向家坝升船机过机船舶吃水自动检测研究

向家坝升船机采用的是“齿轮齿条爬升螺母保安式一级垂直全平衡升船机”，承船厢设计标准水深为3m，过机船舶吃水深度控制为2m。为快速、精准掌控船舶实际吃水数据，项目组开展了船舶吃水自动检测方案的研究，综合查阅了当前船舶吃水检测技术，最终确定采取单波速超声波检测技术，在上游趸船或浮堤布置仰扫式吃水检测系统，在辅助闸首处布置侧扫式吃水检测系统。项目研究的主要内容包括：①超声波仰扫检测吃水系统；②超声波侧扫检测吃水系统。

（一）技术创新点

（1）超声波仰扫检测吃水系统方案采用了基于顺序统计的粗差剔除算法、点云数据中值滤波算法、吃水点云数据的实时动态分割、时分复用技术、三维动态显示技术等多种关键技术，实现了通航船舶高精度离船检测。

（2）超声波侧扫检测吃水系统方案采用了时分复用技术、浮动式侧扫吃水检测补偿技术、水下声同步技术、高速数据处理技术、三维动态显示技术等多种关键技术，实现了通航船舶高精度离船检测。

（3）检测系统布置实现了事前检测要求，同时检测工装设计轻巧、安装简便、维护检修方便。

（二）实施效果及应用推广情况

该研究项目设计并建造了超声波仰扫检测船舶吃水样机、超声波侧扫检测船舶吃水样机，进行了向家坝升船机过机船舶吃水、航速自动检测系统研究，样机性能指标达到了设计要求，并通过了专家评审，取得了预期的研究成果，并计划于2019年在向家坝电站升船机投入工程应用。

船舶吃水检测系统的建立，对船舶“超吃水”过机违规行为起到了良好的控制作用，消除了因“超吃水”过机船舶搁浅引发的设备损坏、人员伤亡的重大安全隐患。

（向家坝水力发电厂 陈保臻）

水电水利工程地下水勘察评价及危害防治技术

近些年来，西南地区相继建成了雅砻江二滩、锦屏一级、官地，金沙江溪洛渡、向家坝，大渡河瀑布沟等巨型电站，正在建设大渡河大岗山、长河坝、猴子岩、两河口等一批巨型水利水电工程。尽管在这些大型或巨型水电水利工程的实践上取得了丰富的成果，但其建设过程中地下水的勘察评价及危害性防治等方面的研究尚未系统的总结与研究。水电水利工程本身是涉水工程，地下水对水电工程的影响比其他工程活动更为明显，地质体—地下水—工程结构的相互作用的范围更大、作用的强度更高、作用机理更复杂、致灾的危害更大，而目前工程地下水领域研究相对比较薄弱，勘察评价方法不够成熟，工程灾害事件时有发生，因此重视和加强工程的水文地质研究，具有重要理论和工程现实意义。为此，该项目在中国电建集团成都勘测设计研究院有限公司历年已建和在建水电水利工程的基础上，通过资料收集分析和补充调查试验，系统分析、研究总结水利水电工程中的地下水勘察评价及危害性防治技术，尤其是西南地区水电水利工程中重大地下水问题的调查、分析、评价这些问题的技术方法和危害防治技术。

项目以西部大型水电水利工程项目勘测设计实践为依托，通过系统研究和总结，取得以下创新性成果：

(1) 研发了一套涵盖地下水取样、测温、参数获取、渗流场模拟、非接触信息采集、污染物运移的水文地质参数原位测试及调查装置。这些装置适用于浅层及深层地下水取样，不同深度地下水温度测量，现场或室内获取水文地质参数，示踪剂投放及水动力场模拟以及地下水污染物运移过程调查等工作。

(2) 首创了基于模型试验及 GOCAD 软件的渗透张量及渗透系数综合测试原理及方法，提出了适用于水电水利工程获取水文地质参数的自由振荡式、注水、抽水及溢水等现场测试方法。

(3) 发展和完善了查明地下水补径排条件的环境同位素方法，结合基岩裂隙水控制结构、水库蓄水全过程斜坡地下水渗流演化规律等，对水库的渗漏源和库岸稳定提供了勘察评价及方法。

(4) 创新研发了防渗复合材料，基于所研发复合材料的防渗结构、地下水降水、截排水等技术，构建了水电水利工程枢纽建筑物区雾化降水的地下水防治技术体系。

研究成果已在溪洛渡、锦屏一级、大岗山、两河口、官地、猴子岩、米林、开茂等多个水电水利工程的地下水勘察评价及防渗设计工作中应用，显著提高了地下水勘察评价的准确度，节约了大量勘探成本和设计周期，降低了地下水对工程的危害性，取得了显著的经济社会效益。

（中国电建集团成都勘测设计研究院有限公司 胡万雨）

水利工程建设管理智能化关键技术研究与应用

“水利工程建设管理智能化关键技术研究与应用”为科技部“十二五”科技支撑项目以及水利部公益性行业经费项目，由中国水利水电科学研究院承担，于2012年1月开始研究，2018年10月结题。

（一）主要研究内容

项目针对水利工程建设管理智能化的关键问题开展了深入研究，形成了水利工程建设管理云平台，能够为水利工程建设管理提供标准化、数字化、实时化、精细化及协同化管理手段，并在此平台上形成了“1套标准、2套系统、3项物联网关键技术、1个数字档案中心”的综合水利工程建设与运行管理服务体系。

(1) 针对目前水利工程建设管理智能化水平低的现状，开展了水利工程建设管理云平台的建设与应用研究，为水利工程建设各单位的协同管理提供了重要的平台。包括：云平台结构建设、平台功能模块开发及用户协同管理应用实现。

(2) 结合水利工程建设管理云平台的建设，开展了水利工程建设过程中各类重要信息的采集、传输、分析及展示标准。

(3) 建立大坝碾压施工、灌浆施工过程实时监控系统，对关键施工过程进行实时精细化管理，开展了海量数据处理、大数据挖掘以及关键施工工序物联网技术等方面研究。

(4) 基于填筑施工机械无人驾驶技术，开发了大坝智能化填筑碾压系统，该系统具有很好的适应性与移植性。极大提高了施工效率，也有效提高了工程建设质量与进度。

(5) 开展水利工程重要建设文档的碎片化生成、签批流程的关键技术研究，并借助于文档编码系统，建立基于云平台的数字化标准化的水利工程建设数字档案中心。

（二）主要创新点

(1) 提出了水利工程建设信息管理架构标准，首次建立了实时共享的“设计－施工－监理－检测－业主”五位一体、以数据采集、传输与应用为主线的“感知层－网络层－中间层－应用层－目标层”水利工程建设单位群体协同的水利工程建设管理云平台。

(2) 结合水利工程文档管理现状，提出了水利工程建设信息文档编码体系，首次建立了基于云平台的数字化标准化的水利工程建设数字文档中心，实现了水利工程建设信息文档的实时化、精细化、体系化管理，极大地提高了文档管理与应用水平。

(3) 利用物联网技术，构建了基于填筑施工机械无人驾驶技术的大坝智能化填筑碾压系统。基于北斗高精度定位导航系统、物联网、云计算、图像识别及大数据挖掘等技术，实现大坝碾压、工程灌浆等重要施工环节的实时、真实、可靠有效控制；基于水利工程建设管理相关标准规范，建立了图像识别、传感器实时监测与便携式智能终端等多数据物联采集体系；实现了施工环境自动感知、碾压路径自动规划、人机操作便捷切换、坝料压实程度自动判别的大坝填筑智能碾压施工功能。

(4) 结合灌浆工程施工工序，构建了关键全过程信息实时采集与分析的灌浆工程实时智能化监控系统。基于钻孔过程实时感知技术、岩体无损检测技术以及灌浆过程记录仪等，实现灌浆前地层可灌性复合感知、灌浆过程实时监控、灌后检测信息分析及灌浆质量多维评价功能，为灌浆工程的信息透明、过程可控、质量可靠提供重要的技术手段。

(三) 推广应用情况

项目研究成果已经在河南出山店水库、新疆阿尔塔什水利枢纽、安徽江巷水库、老挝南俄 3 水电站、云南德厚水库等工程中得到了推广应用，取得了良好的应用效果，产生了重要的社会与经济效益。

(中国水利水电科学研究院)

特硬岩地层 TBM 施工高效掘进关键技术研究

MINAS-San Francisco 水电站位于南美洲厄瓜多尔，为小流量高水头引水式水电站，主要由拦河坝、引水隧洞、调压井、地下厂房洞室群等组成。引水隧洞是整个电站工程的重要组成部分，全长 13896.62m，最大埋深 610m；沿线地层主要由安山质凝灰岩、石英二长岩侵入、黑色闪长岩以及火山角砾岩等组成，岩性变化大，岩石比较致密，属于高磨蚀性岩石，部分地段岩石抗压强度大于 200MPa。引水隧洞的 75%为双护盾 TBM 施工，其余为钻爆法施工。TBM 施工急需解决岩石强度高、摩擦性高引起的刀具磨损和非正常磨损增加，滚刀更换频繁，整机维护力度大，岩石的可掘进性差，TBM 掘进效率低下问题。中国水利水电第八工程局有限公司受中国电力建设股份有限公司委托开展了特硬岩地层 TBM 掘进施工关键技术研究。

(一) 主要研究内容

(1) 开展了不同岩石强度段 TBM 运行参数精细化施工技术研究。

(2) 基于 TBM 破岩机理及刀具损耗原理，系统开展了 TBM 刀具选型研究。

(3) 开展了快速更换刀具、刀箱技术研究。

(二) 主要创新点

(1) 为提高特硬岩破岩效率，开展了室内和现场滚刀刀型比选试验，构建了特硬岩地层滚刀磨损预测模型，优化了 TBM 刀具参数，解决了特硬岩地层的 TBM 破岩难题。

(2) 研发了背装式滚刀限位装置、边刀支撑板快速更换装置，降低了刀具消耗，减少了特硬岩掘进对刀箱和边刀支撑板结构的损坏，大幅提高了施工效率。

(3) 构建了 TBM 施工掘进预测模型，提出了特硬岩 TBM 施工参数的优化方案，提高了 TBM 掘进参数与特硬岩掘进的匹配性。

(三) 推广应用情况

该项目成果已应用于 MINAS-San Francisco 水电站工程引水隧洞工程，实现了该水电站引水隧洞特硬岩地层条件下的精细化高效掘进施工。

(中国水利水电第八工程局有限公司
杨承志)

西部复杂地质环境区水电工程重大滑坡灾变演化过程及控制关键技术

西南地区是我国水力资源最为富集的地区，近十多年来西南水电资源开发也卓有成效。西南水电工程开发建设地区的地质环境有着其特殊性和复杂性：高陡地形、高地震烈度、高地应力、复杂的地质构造格局和软弱岩性，滑坡地质灾害尤为突出，极大地制约了水电工程的规划和建设。本项目以西部水电工程重大滑坡为依托，对滑坡灾变模式、灾变演化机理和灾变过程等开展了深入系统研究，取得以下主要创新性成果：

(1) 揭示了西部水电工程滑坡成生规律，总结并提出了西部水电工程中出现的 7 种主要滑坡灾变模式，揭示了相关灾变演化机理，并确定了其演化阶段的划分标准和宏观识别标志。

(2) 提出了基于灾变演化机理的牵引式、推移式和复合式滑坡的刚体极限稳定性计算方法和基于悬臂板理论及极限平衡理论的反倾岩质边坡弯曲倾倒模式的稳定性计算方法。

(3) 提出了滑坡失稳—涌浪—堵江—溃决全灾变过程分析方法。构建出堰塞坝渗透破坏至溃坝的数值模拟流程；标定出离散元数值模拟的细观参数，开展堰塞坝堆积形态反演分析。

（4）建立了基于演化全过程的西部重大滑坡灾变防控技术方法。构建多种滑坡演化过程预测模型；提出滑坡关键控制部位的确定方法；建立滑坡—抗滑桩体系多场信息综合监测新体系。

研究成果已在溪洛渡、锦屏一级、瀑布沟、官地、楞古、深溪沟、藏木等多个水电工程滑坡的勘察评价和防治工作中成功应用，取得了显著的经济社会效益。

（中国电建集团成都勘测设计研究院有限公司　胡万雨）

南水北调中线工程新型聚脲基防渗体系关键技术与实践

“南水北调中线工程新型聚脲基防渗体系关键技术与实践”为南水北调中线干线工程建设管理局委托项目，由中国水利水电科学研究院、南水北调中线干线工程建设管理局、北京化工大学合作完成。

南水北调中线工程，是缓解京、津、华北地区水资源危机的战略性工程，解决地区之间水分布的严重不平衡。在调水过程中要尽量减少由于渗漏造成的水资源损失，同时，减少由于渗漏产生的安全问题，项目组以穿黄隧洞防渗工程为背景，从理论模型、材料、检测手段、设备、施工工艺等方面进行系统研究，形成了系列聚脲基防渗体系成套关键技术，旨在填补防渗结构和材料性能指标设计的空白，突破防渗材料在复杂环境应用受限的壁垒，现实意义重大。

（一）主要研究内容

（1）防渗结构设计和材料性能指标设计的理论研究。

（2）适应南水北调中线水工建筑物的聚脲基防渗体系材料研究。

（3）聚脲防渗体系材料的质量评价和寿命预测体系的建立。

（4）聚脲基防渗体系的拓展应用，首创了止水效果快速检测方法。

（5）聚脲基防渗体系工法（EP _ DTEW）的改进和完善，并进行聚脲基防渗体系关键技术的实际工程应用和推广应用。

（二）主要创新点

（1）构建了多界面防渗体系剥离模型。

（2）研发了高性能聚脲基复合防渗体系材料。

（3）提出了聚脲基材料质量评价和体系寿命预测方法。

（4）首创了止水结构的止水效果快速检测方法。

（5）形成了聚脲基复合防渗体系工法。

（三）推广应用情况

项目成果成功应用于南水北调穿黄隧洞（110条）与天津箱涵（100条）的伸缩缝止水效果快速检测；以及穿黄隧洞（1100条及22000m^2）与天津箱涵（5764条）伸缩缝及接缝等部位的渗漏防治，有力保证了南水北调中线工程的按期通水及正常运行，满足京津冀地区人民生活用水需要，创造了巨大社会效益，产生直接经济效益分别为2.84亿元和1.92亿元，同时得到国务院南调办领导的肯定与赞扬。在武引渠道应急抢险工程中产生经济效益0.25亿元。

该项成果为水工建筑物防渗设计提供理论依据，引领了国内外复杂环境防渗体系新材料新工艺，填补了技术空白，提升了水利行业防渗处理的工作效率和实施效果，具有广阔的推广应用前景。

（中国水利水电科学研究院）

黄河水利科学研究院2018年科研创新平台建设情况

1. 创新引领型平台建设再创佳绩　2018年，黄河水利科学研究院（简称黄科院）牵头申报的“湖库功能恢复与维持”“水电工程磨蚀测试与防护”“农村水环境治理”3个河南省工程技术研究中心获批立项建设，这是黄科院首次牵头获得河南省工程技术研究中心。

湖库功能恢复与维持工程技术研究中心旨在围绕湖库功能恢复与维持技术研究领域，开展湖库功能恢复与维持技术应用基础研究和应用技术研究，搭建湖库库容长期维持调控技术与淤损库容恢复技术交流平台，研发湖库泥沙处理与资源利用技术和装置，提出不同类型湖库功能恢复与维持方案，为实现湖库水沙资源的高效利用提供坚实的科技支撑。

水电工程磨蚀测试与防护工程技术研究中心将围绕水电工程的水力机械和水工建筑物磨蚀测试和防护技术研究领域，开展材料磨蚀性能测试和以提高抗磨寿命为导向的技术开发和技术应用工作，建立磨蚀测试与分析平台，研发新型抗磨蚀材料和产品，提出磨蚀防护综合技术解决方案，为延长建筑物和机组设备使用寿命、保障水电工程长期稳定高效运用提供强有力技术保障。

农村水环境治理工程技术研究中心围绕农村水环境治理技术研究领域，开展农业非点源污染迁移机理、排放负荷核算与管控措施等研究工作，提出农业非点源污染负荷精准核算与生态拦截技术，研发农村生活污水治理技术、盐碱地改良技术，提出农业农村水环境治理的绿色模式，补齐我院生态环境平台建设的短板。

2. 与多家优势单位成功申报“中原地区枣产业国家创新联盟” 2018 年，黄科院与多家优势单位共同申报的“中原地区枣产业国家创新联盟”由国家林业和草原局批复成立，这是第一批成立的林业和草原国家创新联盟。该联盟由洛阳师范学院牵头，成员单位包括黄科院、中国农科院农业基因组研究所等十余家。该联盟理事长由洛阳师范学院梁留科校长兼任，黄科院教高姚文艺兼任副理事长。

（黄河水利科学研究院 娄萱）

“水安全与水科学协同创新中心”获教育部认定批准

教育部发布 2018 年度省部共建协同创新中心认定名单，河海大学牵头组建的“水安全与水科学协同创新中心”成为教育部首批认定的省部共建协同创新中心。

中心由河海大学牵头，联合清华大学、南京水利科学研究院、中国水利水电科学研究院、中国长江三峡集团有限公司、中国电力建设集团有限公司共同组建，依托水利工程学科开展了长达六年多的建设运行。中心于 2012 年 5 月正式组建；2013 年 4 月，被认定为首批“江苏省高校协同创新中心”；2014 年，在国家“2011 协同创新中心”认定工作中进入答辩；2016 年，在江苏高校协同创新中心绩效评估中获得 A 等，进入二期建设；2018 年，在教育部省部共建协同创新中心认定工作中，以江苏省内排名第一的成绩被推荐至教育部。中心持续有效地开展建设运行工作，为其获批省部共建协同创新中心奠定了坚实的基础。

教育部及江苏省将对省部共建协同创新中心在人才计划、招生指标、科研任务和分配政策等方面给予政策倾斜和优先支持；省部共建协同创新中心的协同创新成效，将作为高校“双一流”建设成效评价的重要参考。

（河海大学）

获奖项目简介

锦屏一级特高拱坝枢纽泄洪消能与减雾关键技术

“锦屏一级特高拱坝枢纽泄洪消能与减雾关键技术”获 2018 年度水力发电科学技术奖一等奖。

随着我国西部高山峡谷中水电工程的持续开发，工程规模巨大，大坝高度达到 300m 级，岸边隧洞的规模及流速不断增加，带来了枢纽泄洪消能及安全防护等难题。高拱坝常采用挑、跌流的泄洪消能方式，表、深孔分层出流，上、下水舌空中碰撞的消能方式能有效削弱入水射流的集中强度，减轻水垫塘的消能负担，具有水流冲击小、消能效果好的显著特点，在二滩、小湾、溪洛渡、构皮滩等高拱坝工程中被广泛应用，但近年来二滩等高拱坝工程运行实践表明，碰撞消能方式在很好地解决高拱坝坝泄洪消能问题的同时，泄洪雾化加剧，威胁电厂及机电设备的正常运行，影响大坝下游雾化区边坡的稳定安全性；鉴于高拱坝坝身表、深孔联合泄洪时雾化产生的严重性及危害性较大，开展窄河谷、复杂地质条件的高拱坝坝身泄洪消能方式研究，处理好泄洪、消能和雾化的相关关系，降低表、深孔联合泄洪时的雾化影响是非常必要的。岸边隧洞泄洪的工程不断增多，要求泄洪洞的泄流能力不断增加，超 50m/s 量级高速水流的泄洪控制、出口消能、空化空蚀问题直接影响工程的安全性和经济性，甚至成为工程成败的制约因素，深入研究高水头大流量泄洪洞的水力学问题对水电工程开发建设具有重要意义。

锦屏一级水电站枢纽泄洪设施由坝身 4 个表孔、5 个深孔、2 个放空底孔、坝后水垫塘以及右岸 1 条有压接无压泄洪洞组成，工程地处深山峡谷，地质条件复杂，左岸雾化区断层带及深部裂缝发育，河谷水面宽度仅 60m；大坝最大高度 305m，为世界第一高混凝土坝，校核洪水流量为 15400m^3/s；泄洪洞上下游水位差 240m、洞内最大流速达 51.55m/s；坝身泄洪消能、雾化防护、泄洪洞的空化空蚀、水流归槽等问题相当突出。依托该工程开展高水头、大流量、窄河谷、复杂地质条件下的特高拱坝枢纽泄洪消能与减雾关键技术的专题研究，取得丰富的研究成果，可为后续工程提供借鉴。

该项目取得授权专利 36 件，其中发明专利 2 件，实用新型专利34件，发表论文11篇，获四川省住房和城乡建设厅优秀工程设计奖一等奖2项、优秀工程设计专项工程奖1项，中国勘察设计协会数字化工厂设计大赛二等奖，电建集团科技进步一等奖。

（一）主要成果及创新点

（1）提出了特高拱坝坝身表、深孔水流空中交错泄洪消能及减雾综合技术，研发了特高拱坝坝身泄洪表孔出口非完全透空新体型，显著减轻了泄洪雾化的范围及强度，开创了超300m级特高拱坝坝身泄洪消能的新型式。针对高拱坝坝身泄洪消能及雾化防护的技术难题，提出了坝身孔口水流交错泄洪消能技术，表孔采用新型“I”形宽尾墩＋底板非完全透空体型、深孔出口闸墩平直出流体型，实现了表、深孔水流横向穿插、纵向拉伸、空中交错、分散入塘的消能目的，大大减轻了坝身泄洪雾化的范围及强度。并提出了坝后水垫塘运行维护配套技术，在二道坝内设置泵房，埋设永久管道，实现了水垫塘检修期抽排自动化，大幅降低了水垫塘运行维护成本。

（2）针对锦屏一级高陡边坡、地质条件复杂、深部裂缝发育等特点，提出了适用于泄洪雾化边坡的饱和一非饱和渗流分析方法，揭示了雾化边坡的控制性滑移模式；提出了“不开挖、立体排水、防排结合、分区保护、按需锚固”的雾化边坡综合加固成套技术，解决了特高拱坝泄洪雾化条件下超高陡边坡稳定分析和加固技术难题。针对泄洪雾化边坡地下水预测难的问题，研发了适用于泄洪雾化边坡的饱和一非饱和的渗流分析方法，揭示了雾化边坡入渗特征、范围，合理确定了泄洪雾化边坡渗流荷载，为边坡排水系统设计提供了依据。采用离散元揭示了雾化边坡的控制性滑移模式，评价了雾化边坡的稳定性，提出了雾化边坡综合加固技术，成功解决了泄洪雾化作用下复杂地质条件深部裂缝高陡边坡的稳定分析与加固设计的技术难题。

（3）提出了特高水头窄河谷有压接无压泄洪洞全程泄洪水流控制综合技术，包括进口消涡、有压段整流、龙落尾控压、燕尾挑坎水流归槽等技术，解决了240m世界最大水头泄洪洞的泄洪水流安全控制难题。进水口采用新型透水式导墙有效控制水流漩涡；有压洞内控制水流流速小于25m/s，高位明流无压洞控制水流流速小于30m/s，将75％的水头集中在25％的龙落尾段；提出了龙落尾渥奇曲线段和反弧段防空化的定量控压参数和计算方法；泄洪洞出口首次采用燕尾式挑流消能及防冲护岸技术，实现了狭窄河谷、复杂地质、特高水头泄洪洞的泄洪消能安全运行。

（4）提出了超高流速泄洪洞三维高效掺气减蚀成套技术和高水头大泄量长隧洞的补气技术，研发了过流面防空蚀涂层结构技术，解决了超50m/s高速水流泄洪洞空蚀防护问题。结合体型变化、水流流态和掺气效果，在易发生空化的洞段上游预先形成掺气水流，设置4道底板掺气和1道侧墙掺气设施，在不影响底部水流掺气效果的前提下促使侧面水流掺气，研发了适应50m/s流速量级高速反弧末端水流的凸型底坎新型三维掺气设施；提出了高水头大泄量长隧洞补气掺气系统定量设计方法；为进一步防止高流速集中段过水表面空蚀，提出了高速水流防空蚀涂层结构的技术。

（二）应用情况与推广前景

该成果成功应用于锦屏一级水电站枢纽泄洪消能工程，解决了狭窄河谷、复杂地质条件下高水头、大泄量高坝工程的泄洪消能与防护关键技术问题，提高了工程经济指标，为工程正常运行奠定了坚实的基础。成果已经在猴子岩水电站、长河坝水电站等工程中成功运用，已在双江口、两河口、叶巴滩、孟底沟等一大批高水头、大泄量的水电工程勘测设计中得到推广应用，并纳入即将颁布的《拱坝设计规范》《水工隧洞设计规范》水力设计的相关条文中，促进了我国相关规程规范的修编。

（三）获奖单位

中国电建集团成都勘测设计研究院有限公司、雅砻江流域水电开发有限公司、四川大学、南京水利科学研究院、中国水利水电科学研究院。

（四）获奖人

周钟、祁宁春、游湘、许唯临、饶宏玲、张公平、杨弘、唐忠敏、胡亚安、张东、曾勇、刘文潮、潘晓红、李旭东、蒙富强。

（水力发电科学技术奖励工作办公室）

各向异性岩石力学特性力学模型及工程应用

“各向异性岩石力学特性力学模型及工程应用”获2018年度水力发电科学技术奖一等奖。

各向异性岩体广泛分布于中国西南水电开发区域，对水电工程安全具有重要的影响。针对我国水电工程建设中涉及各向异性岩石力学的重大工程实践，在各向异性岩体变形特性、各向异性岩体强度特性、各向异性岩体力学本构模型、各向异性耦合力学模型、多尺度数值分析方法与工程应用研究等方面，开展自主创新，取得了重大进展。研究成果已在金沙江白鹤滩水电站坝线比选设计中得到应用在各向异性岩石力学领域形成了具有创新性的科学理论和技术方法，促进了水工结构工程学科和岩石力学学科的发展，为重大水电工程建设特别是白鹤滩水电站建设提供了科学依据和技术支撑。

研究成果在重要学术刊物上发表论文 156 篇，SCI /EI 收录 87 篇。成果多次参加国际学术交流，特邀报告 5 次，主题报告 6 次。授权和公告国家发明专利 11 件，获软件著作权登记证书 5 项。培养博士后 3 名，毕业博士 12 名，硕士 21 名，获江苏省优秀博士学位论文 2 篇，优秀硕士论文 1 篇，培养了一批高层次科技创新人才。

（一）主要成果及创新点

（1）各向异性岩体变形特性研究：推导了各向异性岩体 Boussinesq 解答，建立了基于承压板试验的节理刚度反分析方法，得到了各向异性岩体变形参数解析公式，建立了基于试验的变形参数区间确定，提出了各向异性岩体变形参数数值均匀化确定方法。研究表明，白鹤滩柱状节理岩体变形各向异性的主要控制因素是柱体倾斜、EDZ 区域，层内错动带和尺寸效应。

（2）各向异性岩体强度特性研究：提出了基于节理因子法的各向异性强度参数确定的经验公式；将声波波速引入到岩体质量评价体系，建立了各向异性岩体强度与波速之间的关系；建立了基于连续介质和非连续介质数值模拟的强度特性研究方法。

（3）各向异性岩体力学本构模型：通过组合强度参数的空间分布把经典的各向同性准则拓展到各向异性力学中，提出了基于微结构张量的各向异性屈服准则；采用微结构张量理论对建立了考虑微结构张量带抗拉的各向异性非线性模型；结合微结构张量的屈服函数和各向异性损伤建立了各向异性损伤力学模型。通过对 FLAC3D 二次开发，将上述模型应用于高坝工程各向异性岩石工程的力学分析。

（4）各向异性耦合力学模型：开展了正交节理岩体渗流应力耦合物理模型试验，研究了各向异岩体的变形渗透演化规律；确定各向异性岩石的渗透特性；基于节理空间分布推导了各向异性岩体的渗透张量；开展了各向异性岩石双重介质模型渗流模拟。

（5）多尺度数值分析方法：提出了改进限制重心 Voronoi 算法，建立了符合工程现场的各向异性岩体几何模型；基于内聚力单元方法，开发了各向异性岩体精细结构的连续-非连续数值模拟技术；基于数值均匀化理论和并行计算，建立了适用于大型水电工程的多尺度数值模拟方法，克服了连续介质本构模型和参数取值的难题。

（二）应用情况与推广前景

天然岩体由于地质成因不同造成了其独特的地质构造特征，各向异性岩石力学问题是岩体工程中普遍存在的重大关键技术问题。随着中国西南大型水电建设工程的深入，各向异性岩石力学问题已经成为工程安全的重要挑战之一，特别是白鹤滩水电站建设中，玄武岩柱状节理岩体力学特性和工程应用，成为决定工程成败的关键问题。研究成果紧密结合大型水电工程实践，在各向异性岩体变形特性、各向异性岩体强度特性、各向异性岩体力学本构模型、各向异性耦合力学模型、多尺度数值分析方法与工程应用研究等方面，开展自主创新，取得了重大进展，是研究团队近 10 余年的研究工作总结，对于水电工程建设具有重要的工程实践价值。

（三）获奖单位

河海大学、中国电建集团华东勘测设计研究院有限公司。

（四）获奖人

吴关叶、徐卫亚、孟庆祥、徐建荣、王环玲、石安池、闫龙、何明杰、赖道平、郑文棠、狄圣杰、宁宇、吉华、贾朝军、林志南。

（水力发电科学技术奖励工作办公室）

景洪水力式新型升船机建设关键技术研究与应用

“景洪水力式新型升船机建设关键技术研究与应用”获 2018 年度水力发电科学技术奖一等奖。

通航建筑物是世界各国综合运输体系和水资源综合利用的重要基础设施。升船机作为通航建筑物的两大类型之一，具有适应水头高、通过速度快等显著优点，尤其适用于高坝通航。升船机建设涉及水力学、机电、制造、控制等诸多学科技术问题，其运行的安全性和可靠性一直是阻碍其发展的重要技术难题。我国升船机大多应用于中西部高坝通航，提升高度大、上下游水位变幅大且变率快，受枢纽电站运行影响显著，传统的钢丝绳卷扬提升式和齿轮齿条爬升式升船机应用受到了较大限制。

水力式升船机是我国自主发明的一种全新的升船机型式，其利用水能作为提升动力和安全保障，通过开启充水阀或泄水阀对竖井充泄水，驱动竖井中的平衡重升降从而带动船厢升降运行。在任何条件下，平衡重均能自动调整淹没水深与船厢重量平衡，不仅能较好的解决传统升船机船厢漏水重大安全难题，同时特别适合船厢入水对接，能较好解决我国通航枢纽水位大幅快速变化的升船机对接难题。为此，在国家 863 计划、国家自然科学基金、交通部科技项目和重大工程科技专项的支持下，对这一新型升船机进行了长达 15 年的开拓性研究，形成了中国原创的水力式升船机建设成套技术，并将研究成果成功应用于景洪水力式升船机的建设，建成了世界首座水力式升船机，实现了水力式升船机从概念模型到工程应用的转化。

项目研究成果获得专利38件，其中发明专利10件，另有12件发明专利已被受理公开中；获科技成果推广1项、施工工法1项，发表专著3部、代表性论文48篇。

（一）主要成果及创新点

（1）基于“等惯性+等阻力”原理，研发了竖井群连通、“T”型管、竖井/平衡重最优间隙、竖井环型消能工、锥形体平衡重等多种流量均衡和液面稳定的水力驱动同步新技术；建立了基于主辅阀协同控制理论的水力式升船机运行控制系统，成功解决了非恒定、大流量、高流速条件下水力驱动系统多竖井水位同步及变速运行控制关键问题。

（2）揭示了水力式升船机“水—机—厢”多重耦合作用下的船厢倾斜机理，提出了船厢临界失稳判别标准；研发了集同步轴与联结装置、大型膜片联轴器、大型厚壁卷筒、低速重载锥齿轮箱于一体的微间隙封闭环形机械同步系统设计、制造与安装技术；发明了船厢自反馈抗倾覆导向系统。攻克了无电机纠偏下的船厢抗倾重大技术难题。

（3）创新了超高大直径钢衬竖井群及中空薄壁塔楼高精度一次成型施工技术，实现了全行程平衡重浮筒与竖井间隙的精准控制；提出了高地震烈度区塔柱在内外水激励下的结构型式，保障了塔柱结构安全。

（4）揭示了船厢出入水附加水动力荷载机理，提出了出入水过程阀门控制方式，研发了楔形底船厢结构，解决了船厢出入水运行稳定问题；发明了稳压减振箱和阀前环向强迫掺气技术，解决了高水头工业阀门空化与振动问题。

（5）通过一体化系统观测与调试，提出了基于以水力驱动系统同步为核心、机械同步系统主动抗倾为保障、沿程导向系统极限锁定为安全储备的三大系统工作机制，形成了水力式升船机设计、制造、安装、调试与运行标准。

（二）应用情况与推广前景

该项研究成果所形成的水力式升船机基础理论、设计、制造、安装、运行、管理等建设成套技术，已成功应用于澜沧江景洪水力式升船机工程，各项运行指标均满足设计要求，获得了全面成功。

该项研究成果所建立的水力式升船机理论和设计方法先后在西江那吉、澜沧江景洪、乌江一线沙坨、沅水拓口、清水江白市升船机方案比选中得到应用；相关的理论和设计方法作为交通运输部《交通运输重大技术方向和技术政策》中“解决1500～3000t级大水域高升程升船机建设关键技术”重点推荐高坝通航技术之一。

水力式升船机是完全具有我国自主知识产权的新型升船机型式，与钢丝绳卷扬、齿条爬升等传统升船机相比，水力式升船机在技术先进性、安全可靠性、经济合理性等方面具有较大优势，特别在应对下游水位变幅、船厢漏水和安全保障与运行维护方面具有明显的优越性，特别适合我国高坝通航需求，代表升船机未来发展方向，在金沙江高坝通航、乌江第二线通航设施、右江白色、红水河岩滩等工程具有广阔的应用前景。

（三）获奖单位

华能澜沧江水电股份有限公司、水利部交通运输部国家能源局南京水利科学研究院、中国葛洲坝集团机电建设有限公司、中信重工机械股份有限公司、中国电建集团昆明勘测设计研究院有限公司、西安航天自动化股份有限公司、中国水利水电第八工程局有限公司。

（四）获奖人

向泽江、胡晓林、胡亚安、邹锐、吉勇、张步斌、黄群、王处军、刘金山、陈兆新、梁秀华、王虎军、付云权、田智洪、刘同欣。

（水力发电科学技术奖励工作办公室）

喜马拉雅域大埋深超长隧洞施工关键技术研究与应用

“喜马拉雅域大埋深超长隧洞施工关键技术研究与应用”获2018年度水力发电科学技术奖一等奖。

该项目主要依托巴基斯坦NEELUM-JHELUM（以下简称NJ）水电站进行研究和应用。NJ水电站工程是“中巴经济走廊”的标志性工程，电站位于阿萨德.查谟和克什米尔州，总装机容量969MW，引水隧洞地处喜马拉雅域强烈构造区，轴线长28.58km，其中单洞段长8.95km，直径为11.40m，钻爆法施工；双洞段单长19.63km，采用TBM和钻爆法相结合的施工组织方案（其中TBM施工段长度2×11.52km，直径8.50m）。洞段最大埋深1900m，最大水平主应力108.80MPa。NJ水电站引水隧洞建设中面临沿线岩层软硬互层、高地应力、极强岩爆、软岩大变形和通风排烟等一系列技术挑战，在喜马拉雅域首次运用TBM施工是世界级难题，引水隧洞施工是NJ水电站工程建设成败的关键。

针对引水隧洞穿越区域地质条件的复杂性，由中国葛洲坝集团联合多家科研单位组成的项目组积极开展科技攻关，研发了大埋深高地应力隧洞中极强岩爆的预警和灾害防控的技术，提出了微震监测传感器布置策略，构建了岩体破裂定位分区式横观各向同性速度模型，实现了岩爆孕育过程中破裂源的精准定位和预警，改进了深孔地应力测试设备；研发了软岩高地应力隧洞TBM安全高效施工成套技术，发明了TBM安装间高低台阶制作及施工方法，对敞开式TBM进行了适用于软岩大变形可扩挖的技术改造，研发了一整套施工方法及TBM防卡脱困技术；研发了超长距离超前地质预报技术，提出了小口径钻机稳固性方法，对造孔设备进行了改造，实现了超长距离钻孔探测，并结合TST、CFC等物探方法实现了超长距离软岩、破碎带、涌水段的地质预测；发明了长距离隧洞施工期的快速通风排烟装置及方法，实现了大埋深超长隧洞的高效节能通风排烟。

该技术成果对促进行业科技进步起到了较大作用，获授权专利24件（发明专利9件），省部级工法3项。

（一）主要成果及创新点

（1）研发了大埋深高地应力隧洞中极强岩爆的预警和灾害防控的成套技术。改进了隧洞深孔地应力测试技术，解决了深孔空心包体推送、岩芯取芯等三维应力测量的关键技术难题，提出了隧洞施工过程中基于极限储存能的岩爆判据，实现了大埋深隧洞岩爆等级的中长期预测；研发了软硬互层条件下TBM隧洞岩爆微震监测技术，克服了软硬互层条件下TBM隧洞岩爆孕育过程中岩体微破裂难以精准定位的困难，提出了基于微震监测信息的软硬互层条件下TBM隧洞岩爆定量动态预警方法，实现了软硬互层条件下TBM隧洞掘进过程岩爆发生区域与等级的及时预警；提出了NJ-TBM岩爆等级微震判别方法，突破了传统人工判别的局限，创新了“锚、网、拱、喷”一体化的TBM极强岩爆吸能控制技术，实现了喜马拉雅域大埋深高地应力TBM隧洞高强度岩爆的动态安全控制。

（2）研发了高地应力隧洞TBM安全高效施工成套技术。系统论证了NJ工程采用TBM施工长引水隧洞的必要性及可行性，选择了适宜本工程地质特点的TBM。提出了TBM成套系统优化设计方法，发明了TBM安装间的高低台阶结构，实现了“短安装间长始发洞”重大创新设计突破，极大地压缩了安装间施工工期。采用超前地质预报系统及时探明前方围岩分布状况，指导操作人员动态调整TBM掘进参数；根据引水隧洞地应力高、易发生软岩收敛变形和硬岩岩爆的特点，借助地应力测试和岩爆监测预警信息，及时采取相应措施，调整支护方式：研发了自进式锚杆小管棚，有效改进了软岩断层带易卡机的难题；在高岩爆风险段，实施卸压孔以降低应力，水涨式和胀壳式锚杆快速锚固L1区出露破裂岩石，首创防爆钢筋网片和TH梁、钢纤维混凝土喷层的综合支护措施，构建了TBM安全高效施工的动态掘进和支护方法，有效规避了施工风险。创新性地提出TBM技术改造，发明了敞开式TBM的施工弃渣清理系统及方法，实现了快速弃渣。创新改造仰拱湿喷设备及工艺，加快了岩爆段掘进进度，在确保施工安全的前提下，施工效率逐步提高，实现了TBM在喜马拉雅域首次成功应用。

（3）研发了超长距离超前地质钻探技术。对轻型地质钻机的钻孔系统布置、岩芯取样设备和综合资料解释等提出了改进方法和措施，实现了以轻型地质钻机水平钻孔最远钻深280m的重大突破，扩展了轻型小口径钻孔地质预报的适用范围，准确的识别了TBM安装间和始发洞的地质条件；采用超前钻，结合TST、CFC等辅助性物探方法，获得高定位精度的三维空间围岩性态，建立不同地质界面的地球物理方法成像特征识别模式，使地质预报的科学性、可靠性和准确性得到了提高。

（4）发明了大埋深长隧洞施工期快速通风排烟装置与方法。发明了一种长距离隧洞施工期快速通风排烟装置及方法；创新布置通风系统，优化通风方式，维持通风效率，提供了安全的施工环境，实现了深长隧洞空气质量长期稳定符合OSHA标准。

（二）应用情况与推广前景

创新施工技术成果在巴基斯坦NJ工程成功应用，对喜马拉雅域及世界上类似地质环境的施工建设具有重大的借鉴意义。树立了良好的集团形象，增强了市场竞争力，并实现了在巴基斯坦约500亿元项目的滚动开发。

（三）获奖单位

中国葛洲坝集团第三工程有限公司、中国葛洲坝集团股份有限公司、中水北方勘测设计研究有限责任公司、中国科学院武汉力岩土力学研究所、西安科技大学、中国葛洲坝集团第五工程有限公司、中国科学院地质与地球物理研究所。

（四）获奖人

邓银启、冯兴龙、冯夏庭、王焕明、陈洪莲、胡泉光、张为明、汪文桥、王西奎、郑选荣、陈方明、陈卫忠、洪松、陈松 、吕高。

（水力发电科学技术奖励工作办公室）

流域梯级水电站协同调度关键技术与应用

“流域梯级水电站协同调度关键技术与应用”获2018年度水力发电科学技术奖一等奖。

流域梯级水电站群协同调度涉及防洪、发电、供水、航运、生态、电网安全等社会、经济可持续战略发展的诸多方面，是一类随机、动态、时变、离散、非线性复杂耦合优化决策问题。随着长江上游世界规模最大水电站群的建成和相继投运，防洪减灾、雨洪资源化利用、梯级补偿调节、水电站群协同调度和区域环境改善不仅潜力巨大，而且难度空前，引发了一系列亟待解决的国际学术前沿问题和工程技术难题，举世瞩目。

针对上述国家重大水利枢纽工程运行调度需求与基础理论和技术支撑之间的突出矛盾，经近十年的研究积累和技术攻关，坚持学研产用相结合，在100多项国家研究计划和重大工程应用项目支持下，开展了系统性的研究工作，以提升流域水电站群安全稳定高效利用水平为目标，以复杂系统分析、运筹优化技术和系统科学理论为基础，以大气—天气—陆面多维时空尺度非线性综合广域预报、大规模巨型库群联合防洪全景调度、多维时空尺度跨区协同优化发电调度和供水—发电—环境适应性调控为研究主线，以流域断面水量—能量转换为纽带，以调度运行过程物质流、能量流和信息流映射关系为载体，凝练工程问题，聚焦科学问题，解决关键技术，采用理论研究和工程检验分析相结合的方法，通过理论突破、技术攻关和应用创新，解决长江上游梯级水电站群协同调度研究的科学问题和关键技术，形成一套理论可靠、技术先进、适于应用推广的集成解决方案，建立流域梯级水电站群协同调度理论及技术体系。

（一）主要成果及创新点

(1) 创建了一套流域水文动力特性演化分析与多维时空广域综合预报建模的理论和方法体系。系统地提出了流域水文动力特性演化机理和水文过程耦合系统分析的理论与方法，发明了大气—海洋—陆地界面过程驱动的分布式陆气耦合中长期水文概率预报技术，建立了流域产流系统动力学模拟方法和Nash河道汇流理论与技术，创建了水文模型参数自适应优化及多模型耦合自寻优的实时校正一综合预报理论，解决了流域多维时空降雨—径流广域径流短期综合预报的技术难题。应用效果表明，长江上游中长期径流预报相对误差控制在±15%以内，短期洪水作业预报精度提高到90%以上，预见期由3～4天延长至7天。

(2) 首创了大规模混联水库群防洪兴利联合全景调度与多属性风险决策方法。率先提出了多区多标准防洪库容优化分配及联合防洪全景调度理论与方法，突破了长江上游控制性水库群联合防洪库容共用和优化建模的理论瓶颈；创建了水库群汛期防洪兴利多目标协同优化调度理论与关键技术，有效减小了常遇洪水时水库下游的防洪压力，极大提高了水库群汛末蓄满率；揭示了防洪调度过程“不确定性模拟—调洪演算—风险评估—决策响应”风险传递链的演化规律及水库群防洪调度对多重不确定性的响应机理，实现了流域干支流控制性水库群多维时空防洪兴利联合调度。成果的应用显著提高了长江中下游防洪能力和洪水资源利用率，水库群洪水资源利用效率提高到90%以上。

(3) 系统地提出了长江上游水电站群全周期多尺度自适应协同优化发电调度技术。发明了水电站水头—流量—出力全动力特性空间曲面建模及其梯级水电站群优化运行方法，建立了水电站群多维时空嵌套自适应优化调度模型；创造性地提出了大规模水电站群分区优化控制与跨网调峰响应多级协同调度技术，率先提出了水电站群多目标协同优化调度及适应性调控技术，定量揭示了多目标协同竞争关系及其互馈演化协变机理；创新性建立了不确定条件下水电站群效益—风险均衡调度及决策的理论与技术体系，攻克了随机扰动胁迫下长江流域水电站群短期实时发电优化调度的理论与技术难题，实现了长江上游巨型水电站群全周期多尺度自适应协同发电调度、跨网调峰和多属性风险决策。工程应用效果表明，长江中上游水电站群水量利用率显著提高，多年平均增发电量达3%。

(4) 研发了拥有自主知识产权和核心技术的流域水电站群分布式远程协同调度优化决策高级应用系统。提出了基于持续集成方法和松耦合模型驱动的分布式系统集成开发方法体系，攻克了水电站群协同优化调度海量异构数据融合、大数据深度挖掘与混合云模式下基础云平台建设等共性支撑技术，建立了业务模型远程调用与业务功能互操作协同机制，突破了综合调度模型方法库规范化构建与智能决策寻优互操作技术瓶颈，解决了系统开发集成部署和在长江上游水电站群应用的关键技术难题。

（二）应用情况与推广前景

项目研究成果在三峡梯级、金沙江中游和下游梯级、清江梯级、华中电网直调水电厂等长江中上游干支流26座大型关键性控制水电站群的运行与管理中发挥了关键作用，为高精度和长预见期降雨径流预报和水电站群多维时空尺度联合防洪、发电、供水、生态调度提供了技术保障，显著提高了水库群汛期防洪效益和枯期兴利效益，有效降低了洪水超标、供水不足、欠蓄、欠发、发电出力受阻、环境流量溢缺等风险。研究工作在复杂水电能源优化调度领域摆脱并跨越了西方的技术模式，形成了我国自主知识产权，在我国大规模水电站群联合预报调度方面，确立了优势地位。成果的应用具有很强的示范、带动和技术扩散能力，对产业结构优化升级有显著技术跨越的作用，解决了我国水电能源科学中的重大科学和关键技术问题，有力地推动了行业科技进步。

（三）获奖单位

华中科技大学、三峡水利枢纽梯级调度通信中心、长江勘测规划设计研究有限责任公司、国家电网公司华中分部、长江水利委员会水文局、长江水利委员会长江科学院。

（四）获奖人

周建中、陈璐、覃晖、丁毅、赵云发、莫莉、孙新德、戴明龙、曾小凡、周超、刘懿、张胜、严冬、王永强、闫宝伟。

（水力发电科学技术奖励工作办公室）

大型水泵水轮机稳定性与厂房减振关键技术及工程应用

“大型水泵水轮机稳定性与厂房减振关键技术及工程应用”获2018年度水力发电科学技术奖一等奖。

近年来随着我国水电事业的发展，机组单机容量不断增大，机组结构尺寸相应增大，水头和转速也不断提高，机械刚度相应降低，使得机组与厂房振动成为电站设计和运行管理的一个重要问题。与常规水电机组相比，抽水蓄能电站采用的可逆式水泵水轮机发电电动机机组多具有水头高、容量大、转速快、双向旋转、过渡过程复杂、多采用地下厂房等显著特点。由于其结构振动问题的复杂性以及运行工况复杂，这使得抽水蓄能电站机组与厂房结构振动问题更为复杂和难以处理。此外，抽水蓄能机组特有的“S”特性，使得机组存在低水头并网困难的问题。本项目依托张河湾抽水蓄能电站，系统地开展了大型水泵水轮机稳定性、厂房振动机理与结构动力特性及厂房振动测试研究，取得了一系列的技术创新成果，解决了张河湾电站厂房振动过大和低水头并网困难的技术难题。

（一）主要成果及创新点

1. 水泵水轮机方面

（1）发明了叶片进口边呈月牙形的新型转轮和进出口厚度相当的新型活动导叶。

（2）有效降低了机组振动和压力脉动，尤其是活动导叶与转轮之间动静干涉而产生的压力脉动（无叶区压力脉动）大幅降低，其通频脉动幅值降低了40%～60%，且100Hz的2倍叶片过流频率分量幅值也大幅降低，额定工况从之前的3.3%降到了0.5%；厂房振动幅值大幅减小，母线层楼板垂直振动由之前4.1mm/s降至0.5mm/s。

（3）“S”特性大幅改善，取消非同步导叶，水轮机工况同步并网水头裕度约25m。

（4）水泵工况空化性能改善，全水头运行范围内无空化。

2. 厂房振动方面

（1）国内外首次对抽蓄机组与厂房结构开展如此全面而系统的振动测试，测点分布广，测试结构多。例如各层楼板振动分布矩阵，楼梯与立柱各处振动等。

（2）首次揭示了厂房振动过大机理。通过变转速、变励磁、变负荷等工况下的测试分析，确定无叶区压力脉动中的2倍叶片过流频率成分是厂房振动过大的根源。

（3）首次揭示了局部结构高频共振诱发厂房整体结构振动的机理，为厂房减振设计提供了依据。中间层（母线层）立柱与水轮机层立柱有100Hz附近的自振频率，且此两处振动最为强烈，而前20阶厂房整体结构自振频率均小于35Hz，可见发生了局部结构共振继而诱发整体结构振动的现象。

（4）针对厂房结构动力特性计算分析涉及水力、机械、电磁和结构多种因素、结构部件多连接复杂、荷载和边界条件复杂以及传递路径难以识别的特点，本项目建立了水电站引水发电系统完善的水力—机械—电磁—厂房结构全耦联动力精细化三维有限元系统模型，首次应用有限元功率流理论识别了机组振动向厂房结构的传递路径。形成了厂房振动分析评价体系。

（二）应用情况与推广前景

该项目依托张河湾抽水蓄能电站，系统地开展了大型水泵水轮机稳定性、厂房振动机理与结构动力特性及厂房振动测试研究，取得了一系列的技术创新成果，解决了张河湾电站厂房振动过大和低水头并网困难的技术难题，并在蒲石河、黑麋峰、仙居、深圳和洪屏等抽水蓄能电站得到了推广应用。该项目成果具有极强的推广应用前景，并产生显著的经济效益和社会效益。

（三）获奖单位

国网新源控股有限公司技术中心、河北张河湾蓄能发电有限责任公司、通用电气水电设备（中国）有限公司、大连理工大学。

（四）获奖人

路建、宫奎、Jean-Bernard Houdeline、唐拥军、马震岳、张鑫、樊玉林、谷振富、桂中华、朱海峰、秦俊、王勇、王国柱、郭旭东、刘杰。

（水力发电科学技术奖励工作办公室）

长江上游重大水利工程影响下鱼类保护关键技术研究与应用

“长江上游重大水利工程影响下鱼类保护关键技术研究与应用”获 2018 年度水力发电科学技术奖一等奖。

该研究围绕长江上游重大水利工程对鱼类资源的影响，研究了鱼类行为学和水力学相互作用关系，建立了亲鱼产卵的物理模型实验技术与方法；构建了生态水力学模型，研究了大型水利工程生态调度方案和过鱼设施生态友好设计方法，形成了重大水利工程影响下鱼类保护关键技术。该成果在三峡工程、金沙江梯级等成功进行了检验和工程应用，产生了显著的生态效益和经济效益，具有广阔的应用前景。

研究成果获授权发明专利 10 件，其中国际专利 1 件，受理实审专利 8 件；获软件著作权登记证书 2 项；发表期刊论 140 余篇（其中 SCI 论文 50 余篇，EI 及中文核心 60 余篇），出版著作 4 部；荣获国际水利与环境工程学会（IAHR）A. T. 伊本奖。

（一）主要成果及创新点

（1）揭示了鱼类游泳行为与产卵行为水动力学驱动机制。结合物理模型和原位观测，开创性建立了四大家鱼产卵行为的水动力学机制实验方法，揭示了亲鱼产卵行为与流速之间定量关系，量化了亲鱼产卵的触发流速、喜好流速及流速涨率的范围；探明了水流速度对裂腹鱼类游泳能力和游泳过程生理耗能的影响，从流速、紊动和压力三个方面确立了引发鱼类偏好和感知的特定水力指标及范围，量化了不同水动力条件下多种鱼类上行和下行过程的行为学特征和水力学需求。

（2）构建了鱼类过障与产卵行为生态水力学模型。创建了兼顾计算效率与鱼类行为特征的欧拉—拉格朗日—刺激响应计算方法，突破了已有模型无法体现鱼类主动响应水流刺激的瓶颈，构建了考虑鱼类游泳行为和游泳姿态的轨迹模型，再现了鱼类通过鱼道的运动轨迹；建立了产卵场逆向推求方法，确定了监测断面鱼卵样本对应的产卵区域，结合水力学模型和四大家鱼产卵行为的水动力学机制，建立了四大家鱼产卵行为生态水力学模型。

（3）促进四大家鱼自然繁殖的生态流量过程调度。提出了促进四大家鱼自然繁殖的适宜流量范围，确定了三峡生态调度期间的生态流量过程，包括起始流量、流量日增长量、持续涨水时间，为促进长江中游四大家鱼自然繁殖生态调度提供科学依据。

（4）提出了窄深型仿自然鱼道结构。提出了窄深型仿自然鱼道的设计概念，通过将流场“纵向分层，横向分区”的研究思路，利用窄深型断面水深较大的特点，分层分区地满足不同鱼类上溯条件，有效解决了狭窄河道修建仿自然鱼道的问题；对同一鱼道中的竖缝式、仿生态式及两者连接段型式进行结合，实现了一条鱼道中两种水流条件的衔接与匹配，显著提升了过鱼效率。

（二）应用情况与推广前景

研究成果在面向四大家鱼产卵的三峡工程生态调度中进行了连续 7 年（2011～2017 年）的应用，产卵量有了显著的提升，创造经济效益 9 亿余元；在金沙江溪洛渡坝下气体过饱和灾害防治中进行了应用，有效降低了鱼类死亡率，再未发生 2014 年的大规模死鱼事件；在贵州北盘江马马崖一级水电站集运鱼系统中运行进行了应用，为马马崖一级水电站创造经济效益 1 亿余元。研究成果经济和生态效益显著。

（三）获奖单位

水利部交通运输部国家能源局南京水利科学研究院、三峡大学、长江水利委员会长江科学院。

（四）获奖人

陈求稳、陈进、石小涛、施文卿、林育青、陈端、李卫明、胡柳明、王丽、陈诚、黄明海、唐磊、曾晨军、王智娟、胡晓。

（水力发电科学技术奖励工作办公室）

适应复杂环境的水工建筑物聚脲基防渗防护体系关键技术研究与应用

“适应复杂环境的水工建筑物聚脲基防渗防护体系关键技术研究与应用”获 2018 年度水力发电科学技术奖二等奖。

防渗抗冲磨防护问题一直是水利水电工程中的一项技术难题，尤其是复杂环境下的防渗抗冲磨防护。虽然从 20 世纪开始，我国已逐步发展了一系列的高分子防渗抗冲磨防护材料，但因为材料性能和结构设计不适应于复杂环境，导致防渗抗冲磨防护涂层的破坏失效仍然是一个客观存在的事实。随着高分子材料学科发展，针对不同复杂环境，在理论模型指导下设计材料性能指标及结构尺寸，是保障水工建筑物防渗抗冲磨防护安全运行的新手段。

该项目以南水北调中线穿黄隧洞、天津箱涵、溪洛渡水电站等工程为依托，密切联系工程实践，以解决复杂环境下水工建筑物防渗抗冲磨防护为目的，通过理论研究、材料研制、模型构建、质量评价、工法制定及工程实践相结合的方式，解决了潮湿、低温、早龄期等施工环境及长期浸水、高速水流冲刷等运行环境下的关键技术难题，建立了适应复杂环境的水工建筑物聚脲基防渗抗冲磨防护体系，并已在工程实践中得到成功应用。

（一）主要成果及创新点

（1）在系统分析总结国内外现有技术的基础上，研发了适应复杂环境聚脲基复合防渗抗冲磨防护材料体系。基于分子结构设计和逐步加成聚合技术，将仿生多巴胺链节和纳米级水滑石接枝于分子结构中进行改性，得到聚脲基复合防渗膜材料；基于浸润理论和物理化学表面改性技术，研制了多界面黏结性的聚脲基复合防渗底漆材料。该系列材料可在潮湿、低温、高速水流等复杂环境下使用。

（2）基于内聚力、流固耦合、老化动力学、温度变形等理论，构建了复杂环境下水工建筑物防渗结构常见剥离破坏结构模型。仿真分析了界面黏接层的剥离破坏过程，提出了全寿命期剥离破坏模型计算参数取值方法，通过有限元计算揭示了渗漏和剥离破坏发生发展的变化规律，为复杂环境下防渗抗冲磨防护结构设计优化和材料指标设计提供了技术支撑。

（3）首次采用高分子材料基因工程研究方法，构建了聚脲基复合防渗抗冲磨防护体系的质量评价和寿命预测方法。根据材料光谱图像的基因归属和表征，建立了固、液聚脲基防渗材料的光谱图像指纹数据库，提出了基于光谱图像指纹数据库的聚脲类材料成分分析和质量评价体系。在全寿命期多界面防渗抗冲磨防护体系剥离模型的指导下，构建防渗抗冲磨防护体系的剩余寿命预测方法。

（4）通过室内试验、现场试验以及工程应用，建立了适应复杂环境的聚脲基防渗抗冲磨防护体系工法（EP_DTEW工法）。分析了高速水流冲磨对涂层剥离破坏过程和锚固作用机理，提出了提高水工建筑物抗冲磨性能的嵌入式锚固结构等措施，研发了集喷涂、灌填一体化的多功能灌填设备，制定了工程质量控制标准。

（二）应用情况与推广前景

该项目研究成果推动了我国水工建筑物防渗抗冲磨防护技术的发展；在新材料、新工艺、设计理论、质量控制和实施效果等方面得到全面提升；实现了水工建筑物在复杂环境下的防渗抗冲磨防护，填补了相关领域的技术空白。

该项目研发的适应复杂环境的水工建筑物聚脲基防渗抗冲磨防护体系关键技术，已在南水北调中线穿黄隧洞及天津箱涵工程、溪洛渡水电站工程、贵州道塘水库工程、永定桥浆砌石面板坝工程、四川武引水库工程中得到成功应用。该项目的研究成果也可用于水工建筑物的抗腐蚀、抗冻融、保温等防护领域，以及运行前的止水效果快速检测，应用前景广阔。

（三）获奖单位

中国水利水电科学研究院、中国三峡建设管理有限公司、北京化工大学。

（四）获奖人

李炳奇、张国新、廖建新、汪小刚、程德虎、刘有志、刘小楠、袁志刚、符昌胜、潘东。

（水力发电科学技术奖励工作办公室）

大型水电工程建设场地地质灾害监测预警与应急管理研究及应用

“大型水电工程建设场地地质灾害监测预警与应急管理研究及应用”获2018年度水力发电科学技术奖二等奖。

该项目围绕我国西南高山峡谷区大型水电工程建设面临的地质灾害频发及防灾减灾困难等实际问题，以金沙江乌东德、白鹤滩水电站建设场地内典型、重大的地质灾害体为研究对象，开展了系统的地质灾害监测预警与应急管理专项研究及应用工作。具体是在前期充分的地质查勘和技术研究的基础上，研发应用多种先进且适用性强的地质灾害监测传感设备，建立多项创新性、科学性的监测预警技术，开发了系统、全面的地质灾害监测预警与应急管理信息平台，实现对灾害体在时、空、域的灾变诱发因素和变形破坏信息进行动态监测和研判分析，构建了“全面感知、真实分析、实时控制”的闭环控制体系，有效降低大型水电工程的建设和运营风险。

（一）主要成果及创新点

（1）研究揭示了西南地区水电工程建设场地气候条件、地震工况、地质作用和建设活动等导致泥石流形成的致灾机理，首次建立了金沙江下游河段泥石流危险性动态预测模型和综合监测预警指标，通过降水、孔压、含水、振动、泥位、强震动、灾害体运动、临灾特征等参数的实时监测，创新形成以临界雨量分级预警和泥石流发生趋势预测模型分析为主，物源移动及全天候视频远程监控为辅，集自动警报、应急指挥于一体的水电工程泥石流灾害综合监测预警技术体系，实现了泥石流灾害的全面监测、动态感知、综合分析和应急处置。

（2）创新融合“蜘蛛人”立面调查、临空测绘及无人机遥感解译技术，实现对高陡边坡危岩体快速精细调查与监测安装施工，具有准确度高、调查系统全面、地形无限制等优点，有效解决了高陡边坡危岩体调查危险性大、数据采集难、施工困难等技术难题。针对复杂地形高陡边坡危岩体监测，首次研究提出了从初期位错应变到失稳位移形变的分级预警指标，创新研发了基于散射理论、物联网传输、微波电光调制、光相干检测的分布式光纤监测设备及配套计算分析系统，设计生产了适用于水电工程高陡边坡监测敷设的特种光纤，形成应力应变、相对位移等多种监测要素相互印证的高边坡危岩体综合监测预警技术。

(3) 结合高陡峡谷区构造地质条件、边坡形态及结构特征，研发了高陡边坡强震动响应实时监测系统，创新形成适用于峡谷区水电工程高陡边坡强震动加速度随高程放大系数的计算方法，结合实测结果及不同地形特点，提出了高陡边坡在强震作用下的动力响应特征及不同高程的变化规律，为峡谷区水电工程高陡边坡强震动稳定性评价提供了技术支撑。

(4) 构建了大型水电工程建设自然地质灾害防控体系，研发了集数据自动获取、实时处理分析、状态全面评判、精准预测预报、应急联动管理于一体、WEB端和移动终端双重控制的水电工程地质灾害监测预警与应急管理信息平台，实现了对水电工程枢纽区内地质灾害的高效管理，可精准、实时的掌握地质灾害隐患的发育动态和变化趋势，智能提供辅助决策支撑，实现多种方式发布预警信息和应急联动处置，提升了水电工程地质灾害监测预警的信息化、智能化及应急管理水平。

（二）应用情况与推广前景

该项目以金沙江乌东德、白鹤滩水电站建设场地内典型、重大的地质灾害体为研究对象，开展多项重大技术难题攻关和理论研究分析，并研发应用多种先进且适用性强的地质灾害监测传感设备，建立多项创新性、科学性的监测预警技术，构建了“全面感知、真实分析、实时控制”的闭环控制体系。

通过该项目的研究与应用，其成果为西南深切峡谷区水电工程枢纽区地质灾害防控提供了关键技术支撑、理论研究依据、新型设备应用，大力促进国内地质灾害监测自动化技术、预警平台信息化技术、应急管理一体化技术的长足进步与发展，可在其他水电工程地质灾害防治中推广应用。同时，该成果不仅适用于水利水电工程地质灾害防治，也可以在国土资源、地矿开采、市政交通等领域推广应用。

（三）获奖单位

中国三峡建设管理有限公司、中国水力发电工程学会风险管理专委会、中国科学院水利部成都山地灾害与环境研究所、中国地质科学院地质力学研究所、中国地质调查局水文地质环境地质调查中心。

（四）获奖人

樊启祥、殷跃平、时斌、陈宁生、杨宗立、汪志林、顾功开、丁长青、胡斌、於三大。

（水力发电科学技术奖励工作办公室）

特大型升船机施工安全控制关键技术

“特大型升船机施工安全控制关键技术”获2018年度水力发电科学技术奖二等奖。

随着我国西部大开发战略的实施和水利工程的大规模建设，解决高坝快速通航问题显得尤为迫切。升船机在过坝时具有不耗水、过闸时间短等优点，是通航建筑的一个重要组成部分。三峡升船机、向家坝升船机均为齿轮齿条垂直爬升式升船机，受进度及施工程序约束，金属结构施工与土建施工形成了多重立体交叉作业。由于现场施工点多面广、高差巨大、且存在交叉作业，给现场安全管理带来了严峻挑战，在模板施工安全、金属结构施工安全、顶部梁系施工安全、高空作业平台施工安全等方面体现得尤为明显，安全控制难度远超一般的水利工程。针对上述问题开展了专项技术研究，形成了特大型升船机施工安全控制关键技术，成功解决了上述问题。该项目形成了相关发明专利2件，实用新型专利6件，湖北省工法1项，获中国葛洲坝集团有限公司特等奖1项，一等奖1项。

（一）主要成果及创新点

(1) 高精度复杂结构塔柱群液压自升式模板安全施工技术。设计了液压自升式模板，研发了预埋承重锚锥（实用新型专利：ZL201220211813.1）及预埋锚锥精确定位装置（实用新型专利：ZL201120476692.9），采用了对拉＋锚固系统相结合的方式，解决了锚固系统及模板自身结构安全问题。

(2) 多功能高空作业平台安全施工技术。摒弃了传统的排架搭设方案，研发了专用的多功能高空作业平台，平台可自提升或自爬升，满足了作业空间、载荷、迫近要求。吊挂平台设置有多根连墙杆作为保险装置，自爬升平台设置有重在锁定装置，保证了平台的使用安全；平台上方设置有专用防护平台，防止物体打击，解决了常规排架方案安全风险大、施工干扰大等问题。

(3) 大跨度高位现浇混凝土贝雷架安全施工技术。设计了浇筑大跨度混凝土梁用组合式贝雷架承重排架（发明专利：ZL201210379226.8），解决了贝雷架体系的结构安全问题；设计了薄壁墙体大荷载贝雷架钢结构支座，解决了支座安全问题；研发了建塔抬吊技术、贝雷架空中拼接技术，解决了贝雷架的吊装安全问题；实施了全过程荷载仿真模拟试验，并在实际施工过程中对贝雷架受力情况进行了全过程监测，解决了浇筑过程中贝雷架的结构安全问题。

（4）升船机立体交叉作业风险控制技术。从立体交叉作业的危险源辨识、危险源评价、安全组织结构设计等方面全方位进行风险分析及控制，通过安全检查（SCL）和预先危险性分析（PHA）进行危险源辨识；引入管理抵消因子 M 进行危险源评价，强调管理因素在控制风险中的作用，使评价方法更加科学合理；从“一纵一横”两大管理层面进行安全组织结构构建，全面控制住了升船机的立体交叉作业安全风险。

（二）应用情况与推广前景

该技术成功应用于三峡升船机，并推广应用至向家坝升船机工程中，升船机建设做到了安全、优质、高效，达到了各项高标准指标要求。该技术的成功应用有效降低了大型升船机施工过程中的安全风险，提高了施工效率，其首次在大型升船机建设安全控制方面的成系统的摸索总结具有重大的现实意义，对于建设过程中需要重点关注的控制项目及方法进行了总结，为以后的大型升船机建设起到了很好的借鉴意义，目前国内大型、巨型水电站升船机建设处于高峰期，该成果具有广阔的推广应用前景。

（三）获奖单位

中国葛洲坝集团三峡建设工程有限公司。

（四）获奖人

李国建、李友华、汪文亮、张新宇、程雷梓、张俊霞、李晓萍、石莉。

（水力发电科学技术奖励工作办公室）

大型水电机组定子局部放电智能监测预警关键技术研究与应用

“大型水电机组定子局部放电智能监测预警关键技术研究与应用”获 2018 年度水力发电科学技术奖二等奖。

大型水轮发电机组定子局放智能监测预警系统从发电关键设备最关键但又最难解决的绝缘问题入手，在确保设备安全稳定的前提下，准确、智能、自动预判发电机组的定子绝缘隐患，提供具有极高参考价值的状态检修建议，提高了设备安全管理水平和检维修效率，给企业带来巨大的经济效益。同时，该系统是在发电机实际工作条件下，通过可靠技术手段实现对定子局放的实时监测、智能分析、准确预判，系统能够自行识别绝缘故障的早期征兆，对故障部位、严重程度、发展趋势做出分析判断，提出针对性维修建议，这些功能能够极大地提高设备的状态检修能力，有助于大渡河流域设备管理手段由预防性维修向状态检修的跨越式发展。

（一）主要成果及创新点

（1）首创了局放分类算法，研发了基于全球性局放大数据的智能分析系统，实现了机组局放状态的实时在线监测，智能判断绝缘故障类型、支路位置及严重程度，并进行趋势分析和分级预警。

（2）提出了基于环氧云母耦合器和隔支路安装耦合器的在线监测方案，在保障机组安全运行前提下，实现了高频局放信号的高效采集。

（3）研发了多耦合器的定时噪声分离技术，并首次应用于大型水电机组，有效排除发电机外部的高频噪声干扰，确保监测结果的准确性。

（二）应用情况与推广前景

国电大渡河流域各级电站的发电设备局放在线监测系统和状态检修工作正在积极稳步推进。继大渡河大岗山电厂 1 号机组局放在线监测取得显著成效后，陆续在大岗山 2、3、4 号发电机，铜街子 12 号发电机，深溪沟 3 号发电机上改造增补了同类型的发电机组局放在线监测系统，并在大岗山 3 号机深溪沟 3 号机，铜街子 12 号机的检修计划中，起到了关键性的技术指点作用。长远来看，定子局放智能监测预警系统的技术手段在检修计划的制订中会起到愈加明显的指导作用，并必将引领水力发电行业的设备管理方针由预防性检修向状态检修过渡。这一先进技术及其带来的设备状态检修的管理体制值得在全国水电行业得到全面推广和应用，为我国的电力行业的管理进步，效益提升提供更多更好的技术基础。

（三）获奖单位

国电大渡河流域水电开发有限公司、国电大渡河大岗山水电开发有限公司、国电科学技术研究院有限公司成都分公司、加拿大 IRIS Power 公司。

（四）获奖人

李林、杨忠伟、Greg C . Stone 、周业荣、孟宪宽、邓方雄、江建明、高伟、杨俊双、周洪宇。

（水力发电科学技术奖励工作办公室）

高重力坝地基深厚软弱破碎岩体处理技术研究与应用

“高重力坝地基深厚软弱破碎岩体处理技术研究与应用”获 2018 年度水力发电科学技术奖二等奖。

向家坝水电站混凝土重力坝坝高 162m，坝址地质条件复杂，坝基岩体为层状结构的沉积岩，岩层总体缓倾下游。岩层层面和层间软弱夹层、左岸挤压带和挠曲核部破碎带，均可成为潜在的深层滑移控制面。此类滑面物理力学参数低，对大坝深层抗滑稳定极为不利，坝基变形问题突出；部分坝段建基面以下挤压破碎带或挠曲核部破碎带埋藏较浅，破碎带岩体变模较低，承受坝体荷载后，会产生不同程度的不均匀变形，如未处理好，将会使混凝土大坝产生裂缝，而导致严重的后果。另外，坝基下覆的软弱夹层、左岸挤压带和挠曲核部破碎带内碎屑结构岩体的允许比降为4～5，碎块结构岩体的允许比降为2～3，抗渗透破坏能力低，坝基渗透稳定问题突出，而向家坝工程蓄水后，坝基及消力池排水孔总的出水量达17.2m^3/min，而且部分排水孔出水还携带碎屑状颗粒、细沙。如此大的排水量，对于容许比降较小的碎屑结构岩体、碎块结构岩体，会造成渗透破坏的风险。

该研究课题依托向家坝工程，针对向家坝工程特殊复杂的地质条件，创新提出了解决上述问题的理论，并在工程中予以实践。近6年的运行实践表明，依托向家坝工程提出的上述理论是合理的，在工程实践中被证明是可行的。上述研究成果和坝基综合处理的成功实践经验，可以作为后续规范修编的依据，也可以为同类其他高重力坝复杂坝基的处理提供参考。研究成果共取得国家发明专利5件，实用新型专利1件，工法1部，发表论文10多篇。

（一）主要成果及创新点

（1）采用先进的综合地质勘察手段和试验方法，查明了不良地质体的空间分布和特性；研究提出了坝基应力变形、抗滑和渗透稳定的综合分析方法、设计原则和安全控制标准；采用了“扩大坝基、开挖置换、三维传力、渗控调节、不良地质体针对性处理”等综合处理方法，统筹解决了渗控、抗滑和应力变形控制等技术难题，在齿槽坝踵部位保留有60m厚软弱破碎岩体的坝基上成功修建了162m高重力坝。

（2）针对高重力坝地基60m厚软弱破碎岩体的防渗处理，首次采用了防渗墙及墙下帷幕灌浆技术，研发了高压冲挤水泥灌浆的新工艺，取得了良好的效果。首次研究采用了坝基排水孔出水量可调节的抽排减压技术，解决了向家坝坝基抗滑、渗透稳定、基底应力控制三者的综合平衡问题。

（3）对大坝地基破碎带开挖回填的碾压混凝土，研发了设置灌浆系统的横缝诱导孔成缝新工艺，形成了横缝并缝施工全过程的新技术，实现了大仓面碾压混凝土连续施工，满足了置换混凝土整体受力的要求。

（4）开发了针对向家坝复杂坝基处理和监测信息的三维信息管理系统，提高了基础处理的针对性和效果，为工程安全运行监测和反馈分析提供了便捷直观的平台。

（二）应用情况与推广前景

该项目以金沙江向家坝水电工程为依托，研究中创新的方法、采用的先进技术、提出的科技成果、申请的一系列专利可以直接推广运用到相关的工程中，具有良好的应用推广前景。研究产生的相关设计准则及措施为高混凝土重力坝坝基综合处理技术提供了新的途径，具有重要的实践价值和普遍的学术意义，也可为重力坝规范的进一步修订提供重要参考依据，对于今后水利水电工程建设和科技水平的提高具有重要意义，具有较大的经济、社会效益。

（三）获奖单位

中国三峡建设管理有限公司、中国电建集团中南勘测设计研究院有限公司、清华大学、武汉大学。

（四）获奖人

樊启祥、冯树荣、潘江洋、王毅华、张永涛、王毅、曾祥喜、邹阳生、王恩志、周红波。

（水力发电科学技术奖励工作办公室）

水电水利工程水下大孔口浮体闸门封堵技术研究及应用

“水电水利工程水下大孔口浮体闸门封堵技术研究及应用”获2018年度水力发电科学技术奖二等奖。

水电工程中，引、泄水流道的混凝土及门槽埋件长期受水流和泥沙的磨蚀和冲刷，破坏严重且频繁，若得不到及时封堵或修复，将对工程的安全运行造成严重威胁。传统的方法是降低库水位或进行潜水员水下修复，大量弃水代价昂贵，且受流域流量的整体控制，实施困难，水下施工人员安全和施工质量难以保障。所以，水库大坝水下泄水孔首道闸门门槽及上游流道，由于常年在水下，在不放空水库的条件下是不具备检修和修复条件的，需要封堵流道进口创造旱地施工检修条件。对于泄水道因闸门事故、挡水失效，流道出现异常过流的应急抢险工程，失去调控的高速下泄水流严重危及大坝安全，要求短期内及时封堵且一次成功不留后患，此条件下传统封堵方法均无法实施。

浮体闸门封堵技术提供了一种在静水和动水条件下，封堵水库大坝泄水道进口的装置。其核心产品技术——浮体拍门成功解决了动水条件下封堵泄水道（孔）孔口的世界难题，是目前唯一成功应用并证实具有较高安全可靠性的动水封堵技术措施，填补了行业在该技术领域的空白，取得了专利15件（其中发明专利2件，实用新型专利13件）。

（一）主要成果及创新点

（1）首次系统地提出了利用浮体闸门实现无门

槽、无大型启闭设备，能够在静水及动水条件下封堵流道孔口的技术，可广泛应用于水下流道修复和应急抢险封堵。

（2）首次提出了无门槽、静水条件下大孔口浮体闸门封堵方法以及成套技术，研发了潜式、半潜式、自动潜行式等系列浮体闸门，解决了高、中、低水头等多种条件下，泄水道长期运行冲蚀破坏后，无旱地条件修复的难题。

（3）首创了浮体拍门动水封堵技术，取得了“一种泄水孔封堵装置及封堵方法”“一种浮体拍门”两项发明专利，解决了泄水道孔口高速水流、复杂流态下的封堵难题。

（4）首次采用了一种由多节密封箱体拼装而成的门叶结构，结合充排水系统，可控制潜浮闸 门体安装时在水中的沉浮稳定。

（5）首次采用了一种具有门枢的密封盖板，既解决了门槽顶部孔口和流道孔口需要同时封堵的问题，又解决了浮体拍门动水条件下支承、导向、就位等施工难题。

（6）创新性的提出了坝面不平整度水下测量、导向就位等关键技术，解决了静水条件下浮体闸门导向就位等安装难题。

（7）研发了专用的大体积橡胶水封，解决了浮体闸门在不太平整的混凝土面封水及支承难题。

（二）应用情况与推广前景

2000 年，浮体闸门封堵技术首次应用并顺利完成水下封堵，之后多次成功应用于国内、外多个大、中型水电站流道应急封堵和流道修复工程中，包括刘家峡水电站泄水道磨蚀破坏修复工程、刘家峡水电站溢洪道修复工程、龚嘴水电站冲砂底孔修复工程、福建水口水电站底孔修复工程、哈萨克斯坦 CHARDARA 水电站泄水底孔封堵、鲁地拉水电站临时生态孔封堵工程。研究成果提高了我国水电站修复、改造、应急抢险的技术水平，为水利水电工程的安全运行和流道修复提供可靠的技术储备，保障了水电水利工程本身和下游的生命财产安全，多项首创技术成果填补了行业空白，达到了国际领先水平，有助于中国水电技术走向世界。

（三）获奖单位

中国电建集团西北勘测设计研究院有限公司。

（四）获奖人

朱增兵、廖永平、姚栓喜、苑连军、谭大基、王海峰、丁晓利、李岗、赵春龙、郭富权。

（水力发电科学技术奖励工作办公室）

复杂多变条件下雅砻江梯级水库群精细化调度关键技术

“复杂多变条件下雅砻江梯级水库群精细化调度关键技术”获 2018 年度水力发电科学技术奖二等奖。

近年来，气象要素的改变打破了雅砻江流域水文循环平衡，直接引起了区域水资源量的改变。同时，以极端降水为代表的极端天气事件发生的强度、频率、历时等在全球范围均呈加剧趋势，特别超常规的洪水事件，对流域的防洪安全构成了严峻威胁。传统调度方式如何适应气候异常、电网建设、市场改革以及电站运行要求变化等变化条件，在保证流域安全的前提下，充分发挥新形势下雅砻江下游水库群联合调度的综合效益是关键难题。

该项目采用理论分析、数值模拟与优化求解相结合等研究方法，结合“十二五”期间国家科技支撑计划等国家重大科技项目需求，针对复杂变化条件下雅砻江流域水库群经济与安全运行所涉及的核心问题，以联合调度综合效益最大为核心，以高精度径流预测、洪水安全预警、年调度计划编制以及实时优化调度为研究对象，开展了系统性研究。

（一）主要成果及创新点

（1）首次建成了雅砻江流域空天地水雨情一体化自动测报体系，构建西南复杂环境下高精度降水预报模式，发展了基于数据挖掘的中长期径流预报模型以及考虑高寒融雪和梯级开发影响的短期径流预报模型，提高了西南复杂环境下全流域多尺度高精度降雨和径流预报的精度和遇见期。

（2）首次构建了多源地形数据融合的泄水过程数值模拟模型，研发了大河湾洪水分级率定与模拟技术，形成了基于公共安全风险评估的泄水决策技术体系，支撑了流域洪水风险评估与预警。

（3）首次提出了基于年径流丰枯转换分析的末蓄能组合期望效益量化方法，建立了基于双协同策略的梯级水库群中长期发电调度模型，提高了雅砻江梯级水库群中长期发电调度效益。

（4）创新性提出了基于负荷自动分配策略的梯级水电站短期精细化发电计划编制方法，首次提出了雅砻江梯级水电站短期发电计划的适应性调整策略，支撑了雅砻江梯级水电站的实时调度运行。

（5）开发了雅砻江流域梯级水库群精细化调度高级应用软件，由梯级风险调度与决策支持系统、公共安全信息管理与决策支持系统以及三维可视化展示平台三个子系统组成，在雅砻江流域水库群水情预报和联合调度实际工作中得到成功应用，有效提升了流域水库群联合调度的精细化水平。

（二）应用情况与推广前景

研发的雅砻江水库群联合调度系统平台部署在雅砻江流域水电开发有限公司集控中心，在雅砻江水库群长中短期预报调度、流域公共安全管理等业务中得到了广泛应用。协助雅砻江流域水电开发有限公司编制了一系列梯级水电站水库调度规程、发电计划管理制度，为雅砻江流域联合预报调度以及公共安全管理提供了有力的技术支撑。此外，研究成果涵盖了气象水文预报技术、洪水模拟与风险预警技术以及发电调度与控制技术等新技术，这些成果可广泛应用于长江干流、黄河流域等国内众多流域水库群联合调度中。该成果提高了雅砻江水库群的联合运行效益与适应变化条件的能力，提高了应对大河湾突发洪水事件的效率，有助于雅砻江流域水库群的经济与安全运行，取得的社会与经济效益显著。

（三）获奖单位

雅砻江流域水电开发有限公司、中国水利水电科学研究院、河海大学、长江水利委员会长江科学院。

（四）获奖人

陈云华、蒋云钟、聂强、王旭、缪益平、闻昕、战永胜、廖卫红、周永、王超。

（水力发电科学技术奖励工作办公室）

重大水利水电工程鱼类生境保护关键技术与应用

“重大水利水电工程鱼类生境保护关键技术与应用”获2018年度水力发电科学技术奖二等奖。

随着我国水电开发程度的提高，国家对河流（尤其是鱼类）生态保护的要求越来越高，水电开发中面临的河流生态保护问题也越来越突出。生态环保已成为制约我国水电可持续发展的重要因素之一。鱼类保护是当前水电开发生态环境保护的重点和热点。生境保护是鱼类保护的重要内容之一。支流生境保护和水库生态调度是水电开发中鱼类生境保护的重要措施。目前，大型水电开发中，在干流开发时如何筛选和规划适宜的支流进行重点保护，在干流电站运行时如何通过生态调度营造鱼类自然繁殖所需的水文条件，是实践中亟待解决的问题。

为了更好地解决水电开发和与鱼类保护为代表的河流生态保护之间的矛盾，促进我国水电的可持续发展，科技部于2012年启动了“十二五”国家科技支撑计划课题“重大水利水电工程生态保护技术及标准规范研究”。该研究依托该课题中的“筑坝河流生态需水调控技术研究”和“支流替代生境保护关键技术与应用研究”专题开展相关工作。

（一）主要成果及创新点

（1）提出了一套大型水电开发中支流生境保护的可行性及适宜性评估理论和技术：凝炼了河流鱼类生境保护的概念和内涵，提出基于模糊相似理论的干支流物种和生境相似性分析方法，构建了支流生境保护的可行性分析、适宜性评价的理论方法，形成了从保护生境选择到优化筛选的系统评估技术。

（2）提出了一套大型水电开发中针对鱼类保护需求的梯级水库生态调度理论和技术：凝炼了水库生态调度方案制定的基本步骤，建立了我国筑坝河流（段）的分类方法，提出了基于水文—近岸区涨落关系的生态流组分确定方法，以及水电开发中河流敏感生态水文过程识别方法，归纳了我国筑坝河流生态调度规则，建立了大型水电工程生态调度方案制定标准化流程，形成了《河流水电梯级生态流调控技术评估指南》。

（3）应用支流生境保护的可行性及适宜性评估理论和技术，首次对长江上游赤水河、澜沧江下游南腊河等重要支流生境进行了全面评估，并提出了保护和管理对策。应用针对鱼类保护需求的梯级水库生态调度理论和技术，计算了长江上游珍稀特有鱼类国家级自然保护区干流河段的生态基流以及鱼类敏感生态需水，制定了兼顾鱼类生态保护的溪洛渡—向家坝梯级水库生态调度方案。

（二）应用情况与推广前景

该项目研究成果解决了干流水电开发过程中如何筛选拟保护的支流生境，如何开展梯级水库生态调度等技术难题，推动了我国河流水电梯级开发过程中鱼类生境保护理论和技术的发展，提高了我国河流生态保护水平。

该项目研发的支流生境保护可行性及适宜性评估理论和技术，已在长江上游赤水河、大渡河、澜沧江下游南腊河等重要支流得到了应用；针对鱼类保护需求的梯级水库生态调度技术，在溪洛渡—向家坝梯级水库生态调度中得到了应用。

该项目研究成果可应用于重大水利水电工程鱼类生境保护规划、支流保护生境比选、生态流调控方案制定及优化等，推动了我国河流生态保护技术的标准化，应用前景广阔。

（三）获奖单位

水电水利规划设计总院、中国水利水电科学研究院、中国电建集团成都勘测设计研究院有限公司、中国电建集团华东勘测设计研究院有限公司。

（四）获奖人

顾洪宾、薛联芳、彭期冬、冯顺新、姜昊、张陆良、陆波、林俊强、董磊华、吴赛男。

（水力发电科学技术奖励工作办公室）

大粒径心墙砾石土填筑质量检测设备及快速测定技术

“大粒径心墙砾石土填筑质量检测设备及快速测定技术”获2018年度水力发电科学技术奖二等奖。

随着我国高土石坝技术的发展，砾石土心墙料被广泛使用。针对超大粒径砾石土料的击实试验及含水率快速检测问题，中国电力建设股份有限公司于2011年立项开展研究，课题由中国水利水电第五工程局有限公司承担，主要依托长河坝水电站大坝工程开展相关试验研究。长河坝水电站位于四川省甘孜藏族自治州康定县境内，坝址距成都362km。电站总装机容量260万kW。工程枢纽建筑物由砾石土直心墙堆石坝、左岸引水发电系统和右岸泄洪洞系统组成。电站水库总库容10.75亿m^3，调节库容4.15亿m^3。拦河大坝为砾石土直心墙堆石坝，坝顶高程1697m，最大坝高240.0m，总填筑量3417万m^3，其中砾石土心墙料填筑428.3万m^3。河床覆盖层深约80m，场区地震基本烈度为8度，大坝地震设防烈度为9度。

项目在国内外首次研制出击实筒直径达800mm的气动式全自动超大型击实仪，研制出大型红外微波干燥机和移动实验室，提出了砾石饱和面干含水率测定替代法，通过对细料含水率的测定与加权计算，快速获得砾石土心墙料的含水率，形成了超大粒径砾石土料的压实度试验及含水率快速测定专有装备和技术，取得了良好的工程应用效果。

项目研究获得发明专利2件，实用新型专利9件，省级工法1项，发表论文3篇。

（一）主要成果及创新点

（1）研制出击实筒直径达800mm的气动式全自动超大型击实仪，通过全料击实对比试验，揭示了颗粒尺寸效应的影响规律，为研究大粒径砾石土全料击实特性提供了重要的技术支撑。

（2）通过击实仪的设计和制作，研发了击实仪击锤提升及落距控制技术、击锤落点均匀分布技术和电气自动化控制技术。

（3）研制了用于砾石土快速烘干的大型红外微波设备，在不破坏土体本身结构的情况下，实现土样快速加热烘干，大幅度缩短了含水率检测时间。

（4）研发了由红外微波烘干设备、高精度流量计和其他测试计算设备组成的车载移动试验室，不仅使干密度的检测时间缩短了近7h，而且提高了试验检测的准确性。

（5）提出了砾石饱和面干含水率测定替代法，通过对细料含水率的测定与加权计算，快速获得砾石土心墙料的含水率，检测时间比传统方法缩短了6～8h，效率提高了4倍。

（二）应用情况与推广前景

研究成果在长河坝水电站和长河坝水电站等砾石土心墙坝施工中取得了良好的应用效果，保证了施工质量，同时大大加快了施工进度，产生了良好的经济效益与社会效益，在同类工程施工中具有较高的推广应用价值。

（三）获奖单位

中国水利水电第五工程局有限公司。

（四）获奖人

吴高见、张邯涛、江万红、张永春、杨建平、谭小军、李法海、薛凯、胡宗容、梁涛。

（水力发电科学技术奖励工作办公室）

乌东德水电站超深覆盖层超深基坑围堰施工关键技术

“乌东德水电站超深覆盖层超深基坑围堰施工关键技术”获2018年度水力发电科学技术奖三等奖。

在我国的水利水电大型围堰工程中，已建成数以万计常规深度的防渗墙工程，但墙厚达1.2m且孔深超过90m以上的防渗墙非常少见，尤其对于存在较多大直径漂石和大量陡岩的地段，尚无施工先例。在建中的我国第三座超千万千瓦级水电站——乌东德水电站，大坝围堰基础覆盖层深度55～77m，属于超深覆盖层、超深基坑综合防渗型高水头围堰，堰体设计为“复合土工膜＋塑性混凝土防渗墙＋墙下帷幕灌浆”的防渗结构体系，其中防渗墙为国内目前深度和厚度最大、承担水头最高的混凝土防渗墙（上游土石围堰最大堰高67m，复合土工膜防渗高度40m，防渗墙最大深度达97.54m，承受最大水头为150m；下游土石围堰最大堰高42m，复合土工膜防渗高度18m，防渗墙最大深度93.4m，承受最大水头为130m）。该围堰工程具有地质条件复杂、覆盖层深厚、工程量大、工期紧、防渗体系结构复杂、施工工艺要求高、工序多等特点，其施工难度之大、施工强度之高、施工任务之重世所罕见。该项目以乌东德水电站大坝防渗围堰工程为依托，针对围堰工程施工中急需解决的关键技术问题，开展立项科研活动。

该项目获得授权发明专利1件、实用新型专利2件，行业工法2项，发表论文1篇。

（一）主要成果及创新点

（1）研发的深厚防渗墙成槽施工技术，解决了厚度1.2m、深100m级的深厚防渗墙造孔成槽难题，达到了确保工程质量和提高施工工效的目的。

（2）研究采用的深厚防渗墙混凝土浇筑施工技术，提高了施工效率，确保了施工质量，开创了国内1.2m厚、深100m级的防渗墙接头孔拔管施工先例。

（3）发明了土石围堰综合防护技术。研发了土石围堰新型防渗斜墙施工技术、分期过流土石围堰防护方法等，改变了传统的土石围堰施工方法，解决了效率低、围堰抗冲刷能力较差，且占地面积大、安全隐患等难题，实现了土石围堰安全度汛。

（二）应用情况与推广前景

该项目研究成果成功应用于乌东德水电站大坝围堰防渗工程中，大大提高施工效率，工程整体被评为金沙江乌东德水电站优质样板工程。

乌东德水电站大坝围堰防渗从2014年11月开始实施，2016年6月底，全部施工完成，施工进度满足控制性工期要求，大坝围堰防渗经历了汛期考验，基坑渗漏量小于100L/min，防渗质量远高于国内外同类工程水平，达到了汛前完成围堰工程的工期目标，为后期基坑开挖等相关项目施工提供了进度及安全保障。该项技术在通过上述工程实践应用后证明，其技术领先，安全可靠，灵活高效，是一套行之有效、适用性很强的技术，为深厚覆盖层综合防渗型高水头围堰施工安全、优质、快速施工提供了典范，在今后深厚覆盖层综合防渗型高水头围堰施工工程特别是特大型水电站超深覆盖层超深基坑围堰施工工程施工中将有良好的应用前景。

（三）获奖单位

中国葛洲坝集团三峡建设工程有限公司、中国葛洲坝集团基础工程有限公司。

（四）获奖人

李国建、曹中升、周志远、袁瑞卿、李哲朋、常福远、黄家权。

（水力发电科学技术奖励工作办公室）

强溶蚀复杂地层防渗灌浆技术研究与应用

“强溶蚀复杂地层防渗灌浆技术研究与应用”获2018年度水力发电科学技术奖三等奖。

该项目依托托口水电站，针对强溶蚀复杂地层防渗灌浆技术进行研究。托口水电站大坝和厂房之间河湾地块长约9km，防渗帷幕沿线白垩系红层主要呈全～强风化状，全风化岩（土）体中胶结物多被溶蚀，结构松散，孔隙率较大，透水率10～100Lu，中等透水。红层底部与可溶和不可溶岩界线附近，以及地下水变幅区内，溶蚀现象较为突出，溶蚀沟槽、洞穴极为发育。

可行性研究阶段专门针对深厚白垩系红层特性进行过现场常规灌浆工艺水泥灌浆试验，但不能满足河湾地块基本防渗要求。施工设计阶段进一步研究表明，托口水电站河湾地块防渗工程技术问题主要有：①线路长、帷幕深，地层结构复杂，工程类比采用防渗墙加灌浆帷幕防渗体系，难度大、工期长、投资巨大；②上部红层钻灌成孔困难、分段封闭无法实施、劈裂跑浆压力受限，采用常规的灌浆工艺难以形成有效的防渗帷幕；③深部灰岩段上覆红层较厚，不便采用套管隔离，岩溶管道软弱充填物不能实施高压挤密灌注，抗渗强度无法确保。

对此，为解决托口水电站河湾地块防渗工程上述技术难题，本着技术进步、科技创新精神，积极开展强溶蚀复杂地层防渗灌浆技术研究与应用十分必要。同时，充分利用当地丰富优质黏土资源，结合托口水电站河湾地块复杂的地层结构，以及工程防渗灌浆要求，积极开展渗透型、充填型、封堵型等黏土水泥系列浆液，及其与地层结构相适应的创新、安全、经济、有效的灌浆工法，对于拓展我国水电行业应对各种复杂地层防渗工程的技术手段与方法具有重要的意义。

（一）主要成果及创新点

（1）首次提出了一种“脉冲式高压冲挤灌浆技术”。突破常规的稳压灌浆技术思想，提出一种变频、变量脉动式高压冲挤灌浆技术新思路，充分借助一种脉冲式瞬间冲挤高压，对松软地层实施一种有效可控的挤密、压渗与劈楔灌注。

（2）推出了一组“新型黏土水泥系列浆液”。响应国家提出的资源节约、绿色环保要求，充分利用当地优质的黏土资源，研究出了黏土水泥稳定浆液、黏土水泥膏状浆液、黏土水泥速凝膏状浆液系列组合浆液。组合浆液均以黏土水泥浆液为基础，通过添加适量的稳定组剂、膏浆组剂或速凝组剂，即可实现三种系列浆液的依次变换。系列浆液配置简单、性能良好、资源节约、绿色环保。

（3）发明了一种“封孔止浆材料与工艺”，以及一种“孔管封填、高压冲挤灌浆”施工工法，及其封孔止浆材料快凝可控、强度可调，混合泵送、工艺简单；孔管封填高压冲挤灌浆工法可实现对松软地层的三维封闭、小段原位、瞬间冲挤、挤劈灌注，且灌入量与冲挤压力双指标控制性灌注，灌浆强度有效可控。

（4）创新提出了“浆体自封、高压冲挤”灌浆工艺。采用螺旋管借助膏浆自封效应，可有效实现深厚覆盖层无套管隔离条件下，深部岩溶管道的充填与高压挤密灌浆。

（5）发明了一种松软地层“钻灌一体、高压冲挤灌浆”施工工法。钻孔、灌浆、固孔一体，钻灌安全、快捷；分段上下回转反复原位冲挤灌注；可变换采用分段孔口与孔底双压力控制高压冲挤灌注；可变换采用全孔先稳定浆液自上而下钻灌一体，后自下而上膏状浆液高压挤劈复合灌注。

（6）发明了一种高压冲挤灌浆工艺配套的成套系统。系统主要包括优选动力头式全液压钻机、混凝土泵式结构单杠往复脉冲泵、带有单向控制的高压冲挤灌浆钻具组等，新老兼顾、简单实用。

（7）发明了一种与高压冲挤灌浆工艺配套的高压冲挤灌浆头。采用一种N型特殊结构，依据钢球重力下垂自封原理，实现一种向上无弹簧复位单向控制，可有效地预防高压冲挤灌浆过程中脉冲反压泥沙倒灌堵管事故。

（二）应用情况与推广前景

项目研究成果较好解决了托口水电站河湾地块复杂地层灌浆防渗工程技术难题，确保了工程质量，加快了工程进度，促进了蓄水发电，有效的推动了当地经济的发展，同时带动了水库移民工作的顺利进行。推出的多项研究成果，极大提升了我国水电行业应对各种复杂地层防渗加固处理的综合技术水平。研究成果可广泛应用于水利、水电、市政、港口、交通、环境、地灾等领域的类似地层灌浆防渗工程。

（三）获奖单位

中国电建集团中南勘测设计研究院有限公司、五凌电力有限公司。

（四）获奖人

胡大可、曾再祥、李永丰、杨松林、王少华、樊勇、舒王强。

（水力发电科学技术奖励工作办公室）

金沙江下游梯级全寿命期绿色水电开发生态保护关键技术

“金沙江下游梯级全寿命期绿色水电开发生态保护关键技术”获2018年度水力发电科学技术奖三等奖。

水力资源作为清洁与可再生能源，发电成本低廉，运行调度灵活，具有资源、生态、社会、经济等综合效益，是我国能源供应的重要组成部分。当前中国水电建设已经突破技术制约和资金制约，但是面临着移民和环境保护的巨大压力。协调处理好水电建设与环境保护的关系，真正实现“在开发中保护，在保护中开发”是推动水电发展的必然选择。本项目依托国家自然科学基金重大项目与多项面上项目以及20余项重大工程委托科研项目，历时十余年，通过理论研究、技术研发与工程应用相结合，构建了全寿命期绿色水电开发生态保护技术体系。

（一）主要成果及创新点

（1）首次建立了维持生境空间尺度需求的栖息地保护规划技术和巨型深水库低温水控制关键技术。包括：创建了珍稀特有鱼类“三场”识别与保护技术；率先建立了鱼类栖息地生态功能可持续的梯级水电开发规划技术；系统揭示流域水电梯级开发下的低温水累积效应并建立了巨型深水库水温预测模型；形成了分层取水叠梁门低温水综合控制技术。为梯级水电开发的鱼类栖息地保护和水温过程控制提供了科学依据。

（2）首次创立了水电工程施工区生态扰动恢复技术。包括：揭示了生境基材活化机理；建立了考虑生态因子、种间互作相耦合的扰动陡边坡生态恢复物种遴选方法；建立了扰动陡边坡生态恢复工程AHP-模糊综合评价模型；创立了植被混凝土生境构筑系列技术和层片叠加法群落构建技术；研发了高强度骨料施工废水循环利用和零排放处理技术。为解决梯级水电开发建设实施阶段生态扰动恢复问题提供了依据与途径。

（3）首次创建了金沙江下游梯级全寿命期水电开发的生态环境维护与梯级动态联合管控技术。包括：形成了以生态监测系统为核心的维护与调控评价技术；构建了流域管理与项目管理协同的环境维护体系；建立了全面管控与精准管控相耦合的复式环境管理模式。为梯级水电开发环境保护的全过程控制提供了依据。

（二）应用情况与推广前景

该成果已成功应用于三峡、向家坝、溪洛渡、白鹤滩、乌东德等大型水利水电工程的生态保护，以及长江上游的生态修复，缓解了西南水电工程开发过程中带来的生态环保问题，有利于开发河段及工程施工区生物多样性的提升，一定程度上改善区域小环境，促进了生态友好型绿色水电工程的建设，有力服务于水利水电开发与生态环境保护可持续发展、中央绿色发展理念、河长制，具有非常显著的生态效益。

（三）获奖单位

中国三峡建设管理有限公司、四川大学、三峡大学。

（四）获奖人

樊启祥、王小明、邓云、刘大翔、杨少荣、魏凡、洪文浩。

（水力发电科学技术奖励工作办公室）

基于 HydroStation 平台的水电站全生命周期管理系统

“基于 HydroStation 平台的水电站全生命周期管理系统”获 2018 年度水力发电科学技术奖三等奖。

该项目以水电站全生命周期管理、建筑信息模型（BIM）和技术状态管理等国外先进的管理理论为主要依据，以 HydroStation® 水电水利工程三维数字化设计平台及相关应用成果为基础，采用 Bentley MicroStation 和 Assetwise（简称 eB）、Aecosim 等商用基础软件，引入国外相关先进的工程管理理论和数字化技术进行水电站全生命周期管理系统、技术和应用研究。针对我国水电行业的水工建筑、水电建设、运行管理的技术和管理特点，解决了设计施工一体化、三维数字化移交、行业级系统集成、集团业务流程整合、数字化运维管理，以及虚拟现实、大数据信息挖掘与专家决策等关键技术难题，实现水电站全生命周期过程中的工程数字化移交方法，完成了相关全生命周期技术管理标准和规范的制定，并开发完成基于全信息三维模型的“水电站工程信息模型（HEIM）”“工程数据中心”软件平台和一系列三维数字化应用系统，构建了具有行业特色和国际先进水平的水电站工程数据中心和水电站全生命周期管理系统。依托典型水电工程实现了水电站全生命周期信息跨地域、跨企业、跨系统的一体化高效管理和利用，帮助水电站的建设和管理组织优化业务流程、提高生产效率、缩短开发周期、节约建造成本、降低运营风险、扩大投资收益、培养科技人才、积累智力资产，从而发挥出水电站最大的经济和社会效益。项目取得丰富的研究成果，包括发明专利 2 件、软件著作权登记 7 项，近期发表论文 24 篇。

（一）主要成果及创新点

（1）首个提出基于 HydroStation 工程三维数字化协同设计平台和水电站三维全信息模型的工程全生命周期管理解决方案，围绕覆盖工程全过程的工程数据中心，建立工程全生命周期管理系统，创新实现统一编码服务的工程数据中心、设计施工管理一体化、智能三维数字化档案、三维全信息模型轻量化发布及虚拟现实三维展示等关键技术，核心解决工程数据信息跨阶段、跨单位、跨平台损失问题，实现集团型企业和设计施工总承包项目的数据共享利用，促进工程行业信息化发展。

（2）基于工程全生命周期管理系统，创导工程设计数字化生产管理模式，首次完成实施工程数字化移交、大数据云中心托管服务等新型业务，结合数据自动化采集业务，联通生产系统、监控系统、检修系统等信息系统的数据，提出了全生命周期、全业务过程的数据整合方法，以虚拟现实三维场景展现工程面貌、分析工程状态、监控施工资源等，使工程设计、施工、运营业务不断向数字化、自动化、智能化发展，为全面建设“智慧工程”提供基础。

（3）研究分析国内外各行业应用的 BIM 技术，以贯穿设计、施工、运营阶段为原则，初步建立与工程全生命周期管理系统相关的技术标准体系，行业内率先完成工程数字化设计、工程编码、工程数字化移交等新技术标准。始终坚持标准先行，以标准为导向，从顶层进行规划设计，确保项目执行有据可依。为后续其他水电项目及其他专业项目提供了技术指导，以引领行业发展为目标的统筹规划。水电站全生命周期管理系统标准体系涵盖三大类标准，包括通用标准、软硬件及信息安全标准、业务及应用标准。

（二）应用情况与推广前景

该项目研究成果目前已在或正在沙坪二级水电站、仙居抽水蓄能电站、彭水水电站、杨房沟水电站、成都地铁、上海堤防处等近百个项目/单位中获得推广应用。通过应用该项目，已产生直接经济效益 1.47 亿元，仅沙坪、仙居、彭水项目近三年应用本项目成果已累计产生经济效益 6750 万元。

通过在水电站勘测、设计、施工、运行全过程中运用三维数字化、网络远程化管理，为水电工程建造阶段的设计、施工、采购、运维等管理提供了全方位的数据服务，大幅提高了工程建设的进度管理、物资管理、采购管理、计划管理、决策管理等的综合信息化管理能力和效率，大大缩短“基建—运行”的过渡磨合期，有效减少了建设周期，降低了建设成本，降低了运行维护成本，全面提高了电站数字化管理水平和效率，提升了电站安全性、可靠性和智能化程度，使得我国水电站管理水平快速达到国际领先水平。

水电站通过应用水电站三维全生命周期远程管理系统应用每年可节省直接管理成本 15%，节省直接人力成本 20%，运行阶段每年直接节省运营成本 10%左右。十三五期间，全国水利水电、轨道交通、市政及综合管廊等投资规模预计超过 10 万亿元，按照项目 BIM 应用比率为 30%，BIM 应用费占项目总费用比率 0.6%计算，平台推广潜在市场及效益将达到 180 亿元。

（三）获奖单位

中国电建集团华东勘测设计研究院有限公司、浙江华东工程数字技术有限公司。

（四）获奖人

张春生、王国光、张业星、蒋海峰、王金锋、徐震、邓新星。

（水力发电科学技术奖励工作办公室）

非线性防晕材料自动检测及发电机防晕结构多参量检测系统的研发与应用

“非线性防晕材料自动检测及发电机防晕结构多参量检测系统的研发与应用”获 2018 年度水力发电科学技术奖三等奖。

大型发电机线棒端部防晕，对改善电位梯度、降低端部电场和抑制电晕放电有着非常重要的作用。随着电力行业的发展和大型发电机额定电压的迅猛提升，对发电机核心部件——定子线棒的绝缘性能提出了更高的要求。防晕技术是发电机定子线棒的两大关键技术之一，如何能够在保证经济性的前提下，全面提高发电机绕组起晕电压水平、解决电晕和放电问题成为业界关注的焦点。项目依托哈尔滨电机厂有限责任公司目前开发的全空冷巨型水轮发电机、火电和核电定子线棒等项目，根据科研开发和试验的需要，借鉴了多年的理论和试验研究经验，进行立项研究。

该项目开拓性的研究开发了非线性防晕材料自动检测仪器，系统研究了防晕结构电场热场的多参量无损检测方法。项目发表企业技术规范 1 篇，学术论文 5 篇，获得专利 2 件，研究成果广泛应用到生产实际中，有效地提升了哈尔滨电机厂有限责任公司在国内外市场上的竞争力，未来将创造更大的经济效益与社会效益。

（一）主要成果及创新点

（1）项目开拓性的研究开发了防晕材料自动检测装置，系统研究了防晕结构电场热场的多参量无损检测方法。结合防晕材料和结构试验非线性复杂特点，联合采用了 V-I 自动测量技术、可视化技术，紫外成像、红外热像和高速摄像技术，有限元防晕计算技术，系统建立了大型发电机定子线棒防晕材料自动可视化和防晕结构多参量检测装置和方法。项目全面提升了防晕检测方法和手段，大幅提高了防晕材料和结构的检测精度和效率，推动大型发电机行业防晕检测技术手段的更新，全面提升国内外线棒防晕技术的研究水平。

（2）采用电流防泄漏技术、高压保护技术、量程自动切换技术和可视化技术，首次开发了非线性高电阻防晕材料自动检测装置，能够实现防晕材料的自动升压、自动换挡、自动显示、自动判断、自动存储和自动保护等一系列全自动操作，检测精度高、反应速度快和稳定性好，实现了防晕材料阻值的自动检测和控制。通过该装置，可以提高检测的准确性和效率，并能够对多电压下的防晕材料伏安特性进行分析判断，提升了防晕材料的检测指标，保证了线棒防晕质量的稳定性。

（3）首次综合运用紫外成像、红外热像和高速摄像技术，进行防晕结构多参量无损检测试验，为大型电机定子线棒及绕组端部电场和热场提供试验方法和手段，提升防晕结构设计能力和可靠性。建立了防晕结构多参量检测的试验方法和准则，填补了防晕结构系统检测方法的空白。

（4）采用三维参数化建模与有限元计算相结合的方式，进行了 1000MW 水轮发电机定子线棒的防晕电场和热场的计算分析，并与防晕结构多参量检测结果进行真机对比验证，表明该方法具有世界先进水平，可以有效提升大型发电及防晕的设计优化能力，计算和分析技术达到国内外先进水平。

（二）应用情况与推广前景

该项目成果已成功应用到 700MW 小湾混流式水轮发电机、1000MW 白鹤滩巨型水轮发电机、1000MW 核电半速汽轮发电机等大容量发电机的防晕设计与检测中，确保了这些项目的防晕系统的安全稳定。项目中前瞻性的研究成果，为开发更大电压等级的定子线棒和绕组防晕材料和结构提供了技术储备，使线棒防晕材料和防晕结构的检测和设计能力达到并超过国内外先进水平。项目研究成果可推广应用于大型汽轮、水轮、燃机和核能等不同类型的发电机产品线棒防晕材料研发、防晕结构设计和事故分析处理等方面，应用前景广阔，有效提升了国内发电机产品的运行稳定性，提高大型发电机组绝缘在国内外市场上的竞争力。

（三）获奖单位

哈尔滨电机厂有限责任公司、哈尔滨理工大学、哈尔滨大电机研究所。

（四）获奖人

孙永鑫、潘延明、陈庆国、张大鹏、隋银德、满宇光、宋春辉。

（水力发电科学技术奖励工作办公室）

大型高流速常年泄流泄洪洞耐冲磨混凝土施工关键技术

“大型高流速常年泄流泄洪洞耐冲磨混凝土施工关键技术”获 2018 年度水力发电科学技术奖三等奖。

我国西部高山峡谷地区大型高流速常年泄流泄洪洞工程，均具有断面尺寸大、流量大、流速高，且泄洪洞边墙和底板为抗冲磨高标号混凝土，断面尺寸不一、底板坡陡多变，混凝土入仓难度大，温控防裂难度大等特点，普遍面临碉室平整度要求高、体型控制难、裂缝控制难等技术难题。项目依托大岗山水电站，在泄洪洞混凝土浇筑施工过程中，对高流速泄洪洞体型控制技术和$C_{90}50$硅粉混凝土温控防裂技术作了重点研究。项目研究取得了国家实用新型专利4件，形成省级工法3项，发表科技论文8篇；经中国电力建设集团有限公司鉴定，该项研究成果达到了国际先进水平。

（一）主要成果及创新点

（1）研制了液压轨道爬行式多向移动新型布料机，可实现变坡底板常态混凝土全方位浇筑布料，操作简单，运行方便，布料均匀，施工效率高。

（2）研制了多功能液压自行式新型钢模台车，爬坡能力强，可自行调节高度和自动输料，安全高效，改变了传统的边墙泵送混凝土施工工艺，实现了变高多变坡斜洞边墙常态混凝土衬砌施工，有利于混凝土的体型控制和温控防裂。

（3）针对进水口溢流堰复合曲面结构，研究采用了双向导轨滑模和“内拉内撑”翻模技术，保证了耐冲磨混凝土施工质量。

（4）研究采用了粉煤灰高强耐冲磨混凝土，通过施工过程温度及应力场的仿真分析和反馈优化，提出了“早通水、大流量、短历时”冷却方式，结合其他综合温控措施，有效控制了混凝土裂缝。

（二）应用情况与推广前景

该成果应用于大岗山水电站泄洪洞工程和长河坝水电站泄洪洞工程，降低了工程造价和施工成本，减少了施工工序以及设备和能源的消耗。该成果应用后，实现了大断面隧洞边墙常态混凝土入仓条件，大量节约水泥，节能减排，且可以满足不同断面混凝土衬砌施工。现场以数值仿真模拟为指导，采取大流量、早通水的温控措施，大大降低了高强硅粉混凝土开裂风险，泄洪洞浇筑质量优良，保证了泄洪洞在高流速频繁使用状态下的安全，确保了附近城镇居民的人生和财产安全，极具有推广应用价值，社会效益显著。

（三）获奖单位

中国水利水电第七工程局有限公司。

（四）获奖人

刘晓宁、雷文、魏平、甘露、彭志海、高军、朱家林。

（水力发电科学技术奖励工作办公室）

高水头大容量冲击式水轮机组安装技术

“高水头大容量冲击式水轮机组安装技术”获2018年度水力发电科学技术奖三等奖。

该项目依托的厄瓜多尔科卡科多辛克雷水电站，其冲击式水轮机运行中存在尾水支洞“有压”和“无压”两种工况、投运前期机组存在孤网运行等比较复杂的工况，而合同要求机组在复杂的工况条件下整个水头和功率范围内能够安全稳定运行，各项性能指标要求较高，机组安装工艺及质量控制难度大。因此，该项目通过技术分析、论证、实施验证，选择最优的工艺措施和新的施工材料，提高了技术水平及施工质量，成功解决了技术难题，确保机组长期连续安全、可靠、稳定运行。通过该课题研究，修订了9项施工工艺；发表专业技术论文10篇；获得国家知识产权局授权的发明专利1件、实用新型专利4项；形成云南省工法1项，中国电建集团工法2项。经专家评审，该项目研究成果在该领域达到了国际领先水平。

（一）主要成果及创新点

（1）针对水轮机配水环管安装精度要求高、Q500D钢材可焊性差、保压浇筑混凝土等难点，制定了一套合理的安装焊接工艺措施，保证了配水环管安装质量。

（2）发明了一种大型冲击式水轮发电机组机壳的安装方法，保证了上部机壳N面法兰安装精度，有效防止浇筑混凝土时机壳的变形和位移，以确保机组尾水有压运行时的气密封性。

（3）研制了一种结构简单、操作简便的多功能工装进行水轮机主轴安装调整，提高了工作效率。并且《一种多功能冲击式水轮机轴调整支撑工具》获得了国家实用新型专利授权。

（4）在利用模拟转轮安装调整喷嘴过程中，辅助使用了三角函数计算验证测量误差法，确保喷嘴安装精度。并且《大型冲击式水轮机组采用模拟转轮调整、安装喷嘴施工工法》获得公司级和电建集团施工工法。

（5）采用一种螺栓拉伸器专用吊具托装螺栓拉升器，使螺栓拉伸工具在空中可以任意旋转至所需要拉伸的螺栓位置，在操作过程中简便、安全、可靠、降低施工强度，提高工作效率、降低施工成本。并且《一种悬吊式转轮螺栓拉伸器吊具》获得了国家实用新型专利授权。

（6）对密闭、内循环双水冷二次冷却的技术供水系统安装工艺创新及技术改进，使该系统运行稳定、可靠，确保了机组推力瓦及各部位导瓦的温度完全满足设计及合同要求。

（7）针对机组尾水支洞存在“无压”和“有压”两种运行工况，采用密封性预检方法，确保主轴密封的气密封可靠。

（二）应用情况与推广前景

通过开展高水头大容量六喷嘴冲击式水轮机组安装技术研究，总结出高水头大容量六喷嘴冲击式水轮机组安装工艺技术，为同类型水电站冲击式水轮机组安装提供指导和借鉴，为水利水电行业冲击式水轮机组安装技术不断发展提高提供一份宝贵的资料。

目前厄瓜多尔 CCS 电站 8 台机组运行可靠、稳定，产生了良好的经济效益和社会效益，得到了厄瓜多尔 CCS 业主和墨西哥咨询公司的认可，为后续海外市场的开拓打下了良好的基础。另外，依据本电站冲击式水轮机的结构特点以及在“有压”和“无压”两种运行工况和前期存在孤网运行工况下运行的技术质量要求，截至 2016 年底具世界同类型机组首例。因此，该项工艺技术研究可应用于今后相关同类型水电站机组安装项目上，具有广阔的推广应用价值。

（三）获奖单位

中国水利水电第十四工程局有限公司、中国水电建设集团国际工程有限公司、哈尔滨电机厂有限责任公司。

（四）获奖人

彭贵军、周玉龙、王建利、尚志、陈婉 、刘和林 、张自敏。

（水力发电科学技术奖励工作办公室）

水电行业技术标准体系课题研究

“水电行业技术标准体系课题研究”获 2018 年度水力发电科学技术奖三等奖。

伴随着我国水电工程建设和技术的快速发展，我国水电行业技术标准建设也取得了巨大的成绩，水电行业现行技术标准基本涵盖了规划设计、工程建设施工、设备制造与安装、运行管理各方面，为我国水电工程建设和运行管理提供了有力的技术保障和支持。但长期以来，水电行业技术标准建设存在着明显的系统性不强、管理条块分割、部分标准间逻辑关系不清、内容交叉重复矛盾等问题。从水电工程全生命周期角度看，现有水电行业标准重点是在规划设计与建设领域，有关工程运行维护、高坝大库紧急放空、流域安全、溃坝风险、退役管理等方面标准较为薄弱，存在内容缺失。尚未形成水电行业技术标准体系的闭环管理，缺乏快速有效的标准建设反应机制。

为适应我国水电行业发展的新形势、新任务、新要求，系统解决我国水电行业技术标准建设中存在的主要问题，受国家能源局委托，水电水利规划设计总院于 2015 年启动了水电行业技术标准体系课题研究，组织我国能源水电行业的标准化技术委员会、设计院、工程局、科研院所等单位开展研究工作。课题研究成果为行业标准复审和整合精简等标准化工作奠定了坚实的基础。

（一）主要成果及创新点

（1）按水电工程全生命周期的理念系统地建立了水电行业技术标准体系框架。经对我国现有水电工程技术标准的全面系统梳理，提出我国的水电行业技术标准体系框架采用三层框架结构。第一层次是水电行业的通用及基础标准，是指导整个水电行业工程全阶段的技术标准；第二层次是按水电工程全生命周期不同阶段展开的技术标准；第三层次是水电工程不同阶段按专业门类或建筑物类别、设备类别展开的技术标准。此框架结构，层次清晰、结构合理、分类较为科学，具有一定的可分解性和可扩展空间，内容涵盖水电工程规划、工程勘察设计、设备制造调试及验收、工程施工与验收、工程运行维护、工程退役、工程管理、工程安全等环节。

（2）按水电工程全生命周期理念建立了《水电行业技术标准体系表》，补充了运行维护、退役方面的技术标准。通过对标国外水电行业以及国内其他行业技术标准体系建设情况，在对我国现有水电工程技术标准全面梳理和系统分析的基础上，按照水电行业技术标准体系框架，遵循以标准的“管理和维护”为主的原则，同时考虑标准的“使用和监管”，按照“增量严控，存量求精”的要求，以“标准族”的形式对现有标准进行梳理完善，在研究缺失的技术标准的同时，努力合并、归类相关技术标准，以水电工程全生命周期理念建立了《水电行业技术标准体系表》。针对我国水电行业技术标准“重建设、轻运维”的现状，补充了运行维护和退役方面的技术标准。完善了水电工程安全、流域安全、环境保护、运行调度、仪器检验检测和报废等方面的技术标准。

（3）提出将能源领域水电行业技术标准代号确定为 NB/SD。鉴于水电行业技术标准的特殊性和重要性，建议将能源领域水电行业技术标准的代号由 NB、DL、SD、SDJ 等统一调整为 NB/SD。

（4）理顺标准间的逻辑关系和相互关系，建立“标准族”概念。建立“标准族”，按照“标准族”的思路和方式，梳理标准间的逻辑关系，将具有内部联系的技术标准组织在一起，通过同时制（修）订，努力合并、归类相关技术标准，同时发布实施，实现向新体系的平稳过渡。

（二）应用情况与推广前景

健全和完善了水电行业技术标准体系，满足水电行业安全、健康发展的需要，进一步提升水电行业技术水平和标准管理能力。为我国水电工程建设和运行管理提供技术保障和支持，为简政放权后水电行业建设和政府管理提供技术支撑和监管依据，为今后水电行业技术标准的制（修）订和管理提供体系原则、依据和支持，促进水电行业技术标准科学有序发展。适应中国水电“走出去”的需要，推动中国水电技术标准国际化，提高中国水电技术的国际化水平。

水电行业技术标准体系课题研究提出的标准框架、体系表和制定、修订建议，在水电行业中得到广泛运用。2016 年开始，国家能源局在下达年度能源领域水电行业的技术标准时将课题成果的体系表作为立项依据，能源行业水电标准化技术委员会按研究成果进行标准的立项审核、复评审和审查；水电勘测设计院、水电工程局、科研院所等单位，均按体系表进行年度技术标准的立项申报，并按研究建议的相关标准拟编或修订内容开展编制工作。

（三）获奖单位

水电水利规划设计总院、中国电建集团北京勘测设计研究院有限公司、中国葛洲坝集团股份有限公司。

（四）获奖人

郑声安、李昇、彭土标、赵轶、党林才、李仕胜、刘荣丽。

（水力发电科学技术奖励工作办公室）

大型梯级水电站群负荷实时智能调度技术

“大型梯级水电站群负荷实时智能调度技术”获 2018 年度水力发电科学技术奖三等奖。

大渡河中下游紧邻的瀑布沟、深溪沟、枕头坝一级三座水电站总装机容量 498 万 kW，其组成的巨型水电站群是四川电网主力调峰调频基地。实际运行中，深溪沟、枕头坝水库库容小，水位受上游瀑布沟负荷影响大，传统电站级 AGC 难以协调、经济地控制水位，被迫处于停用状态，只能被动接受电网调度“带固定负荷”指令，导致两库极易出现水位大起大落、弃水以及水库拉空等现象，严重影响梯级电站安全、经济运行。

该项目以大渡河瀑、深、枕三站 AGC 实际控制工程问题为依托，针对高强度调峰调频需求下的巨型梯级水电站群联合运行所涉及的实时调度问题进行了深入研究，实现了瀑、深、枕三站梯级总负荷的实时智能分配、经济运行，取得了大型流域调度模式由单机组“直调”向多电站“一键调”的重大突破。大渡河成为国内第一家投入梯级水电站群负荷实时智能控制系统运行的大型流域，取得了良好的示范效益。

（一）主要成果及创新点

（1）发明了适应电网高强度调峰调频需求的梯级水电站群负荷实时智能调度方法。传统梯级水电站群优化调度技术难以适应电网调峰调频负荷频繁变化需求，导致绝大多数水电群优化调度成果难以实际应用，水电机组只能被动接受电网负荷固定指令，频繁地人工申请电网负荷调节，易产生水库水位大起大落、弃水、水库拉空等现象，严重影响梯级水电站安全、高效运行。针对高强度调峰调频需求下的巨型梯级水电站群实时优化调度问题，首次引入无监督学习方法对水电站群负荷分配的历史场景进行深度学习，发明了梯级水电站群负荷实时智能调度方法，实现了适应电网高强度调峰调频需求的负荷分配策略自主选取、模型智能匹配。

（2）创建了涵盖安全调度、经济调度全要素的大型梯级水电站群负荷实时分配模型簇。以梯级电站群中径流式电站水位安全控制为硬约束，融合出力平衡、水量平衡、流量平衡、水位、发电流量、出库流量、有功可调区间、电站出力变幅、避开振动区、站间负荷转移等 10 类约束，引入非高效水位区间惩罚函数，构建了水位异常控制、水位平稳等安全调度模型和蓄能最大、少调负荷、弃水总量最少、小负荷分配等经济调度模型，创建了涵盖安全调度、经济调度全要素的大型梯级水电站群负荷实时分配模型簇，解决了电网实时负荷平衡与流域经济运行耦合的建模难题。

（3）提出了适用于梯级水电站群负荷分配的双向逐次逼近耦合高效算法。梯级水电站群负荷实时智能调度需要实时追踪电网指令并进行分配计算，计算实时性要求非常高，针对当前梯级水电站群负荷分配求解算法计算速度慢、耗时长，难以满足电网对大型梯级水电站群负荷分配响应性要求的技术瓶颈，提出了适用于梯级水电站群负荷实时分配的双向逐次逼近耦合高效算法，通过正向、逆向同时求解确定双向最优决策子序列，并利用主线程进行双向耦合计算确定最优决策序列，梯级水电站群负荷分配计算时间少于 2s，实现了大型梯级水电站群负荷分配的实时快速响应。

（4）开发了大型梯级水电站群多场景自适应负荷实时智能控制系统。针对当前流域梯级水电站群负荷分配依赖人工调整、智能化水平低的调度难题，基于上述理论研究成果，开发了大型梯级水电站群负荷实时智能控制系统。通过实时感知调度约束条件的动态变化，自动选取最优控制策略，智能匹配负荷分配模型，实现了包含瀑布沟、深溪沟、枕头坝一级的大型梯级主力调峰调频水电站群的负荷实时智能分配，解决了大型梯级水电站群负荷实时调度存在的调度效率低、响应慢、安全风险大等技术难题，取得了大型流域调度模式由单机组“直调”向多电站“一键调”的重大突破。

（二）应用情况与推广前景

研究成果成功应用于大渡河瀑布沟、深溪沟、枕头坝3座大型水电站，电网调度机构向三站下达总负荷，实现了大型流域调度模式由单机组“直调”向多电站“一键调”的重大突破。

该成果适用于流域梯级水电站群负荷实时智能分配，特别是大型梯级水电站群负荷实时智能分配，在电力市场化改革不断深入的背景下，该研究成果的应用有利于实现流域梯级电站群市场交易合约电量的最佳配置，将产生巨大的经济、社会和环境效益，具有良好的推广应用前景。

（三）获奖单位

国电大渡河流域水电开发有限公司、四川大学、南瑞集团有限公司。

（四）获奖人

周业荣、李攀光、钟青祥、徐麟、陈仕军、贺玉彬、何红荣。

（水力发电科学技术奖励工作办公室）

复杂地形多种料源高面板堆石坝变形控制筑坝技术

“复杂地形多种料源高面板堆石坝变形控制筑坝技术”获2018年度水力发电科学技术奖三等奖。

抽水蓄能电站由于其良好的调峰填谷的发电作用以及占地范围较少、开发周期短的特点，在当今时代方兴未艾。在复杂地形条件下，用多样性料源填筑高面板堆石坝，如何控制坝体的不均匀沉降是工程成败的关键，因此，有必要对此方面的施工技术进行研究。

本课题的研究成果将进一步丰富我国抽水蓄能电站在复杂地形条件下、多样性料源修建高面板堆石坝的施工经验，并为国内外类似工程提供系统的经验和技术资料，具有较大的推广价值。

（一）主要成果及创新点

(1) 通过优化坝体堆石分区，修整坝轴线W地形，设置增模区，有效解决了复杂地形带来的不均匀沉降和坝顶挠曲变形；合理利用软岩堆石料和坝后压坡体，基本实现了挖填平衡，经济和环境效益显著。

(2) 采用数字化施工技术，对复杂料源、运输、加水实行全程监控；对大坝填筑碾压全过程实时在线监控，创新采用“堆饼”施工工法，有效控制填筑厚度，保证了大坝填筑质量，其中增模区的孔隙率平均值达16.8%。

(3) 坝后坡创新设置混凝土框格梁，覆土种植适应性强的小叶女贞灌木，形成生态护坡，对开挖岩质边坡采用客土喷播全面绿化，生产废水循环使用实现零排放，在5A级风景区及水源保护地实现了绿色施工。

（二）应用情况与推广前景

该课题研究成果应用于溧阳抽水蓄能电站上水库面板混凝土堆石坝主坝和下水库库盆开挖工程以及贵州省夹岩水利枢纽及黔西北供水工程。对复杂地形多种料源高面板堆石坝变形控制筑坝技术进行研究，将施工工艺和施工参数形成系统成果，促进新技术、新工艺在类似工程中推广应用。

（三）获奖单位

中国水利水电第十二工程局有限公司、江苏国信溧阳抽水蓄能发电有限公司、中国电建集团中南勘测设计研究院有限公司。

（四）获奖人

沈益源、沈仲涛、劳俭翁、龚家明、赵仲舒、石含鑫、练新军。

（水力发电科学技术奖励工作办公室）

大型竖井混凝土施工成套技术研究及应用

“大型竖井混凝土施工成套技术研究及应用”获2018年度水力发电科学技术奖三等奖。

在我国水利水电工程建设中，竖井作为水工建筑物中一种重要的结构，具有深度大、孔身成型精度要求高、外观质量要求高、质量控制指标严格等特点。竖井结构一般为矩形或圆形，混凝土施工中面临着施工条件差、干扰因素多、安全风险大等难题。

目前国内坝体竖井通常采用小钢模板组拼或整体提升模板，随着主体结构分层浇筑、逐层上升；地下工程竖井一般采用液压滑模衬砌成型。传统小钢模组拼、整体提升模板施工存在模板安拆需借助起吊设备、施工效率低下、精确调校定位难，井身形体质量难以保证需后期进行缺陷处理，安全隐患突出等技术难题。地下工程竖井深度大，滑模安拆困难、施工安全风险大；溜管供料易离析、易堵管，混凝土浇筑质量控制难度大；滑模滑升时，对滑模偏移监测要求极高，否则易产生结构扭曲，导致混凝土墙面倾斜。鉴于上述问题，项目研发了大型竖井混凝土施工成套技术，成功应用于三峡、向家坝、溪洛渡等工程。该研究成果已获得国家发明专利4件、实用新型专利3

件，获省级工法1项。

（一）主要成果及创新点

（1）发明了竖井液压自升模板及施工方法、液压爬升模板辅助调整方法、预埋锚锥精确定位方法，改变了坝体竖井混凝土长久以来采用小钢模现场组拼或整体提升模板施工的传统方式，解决了传统方法施工效率低下、借助起吊设备、孔身成型质量较差、安全隐患突出等难题，实现了深竖井混凝土优质安全高效施工。

（2）提出了竖井滑模偏移监测新技术，创新了竖井滑模测量方法。发明的竖井滑模偏移监测装置，解决了传统测量方法中控制点随滑模爬升多次传递而造成累积误差大、滑模偏移监测依赖人工测量导致数据失真等技术难题，实现了简单、准确、快速监测滑模偏移值，从而有利于控制滑模运行的质量。

（3）研制了竖井衬砌施工成套专用设施。研发的可拆卸辐条式新型滑模，降低了深竖井滑模安装及拆除安全风险；研制的大落差混凝土浇筑用缓冲器、深竖井混凝土浇筑用分料装置、旋转式混凝土溜槽等设施，解决了深竖井混凝土溜管供料易离析、易堵管的施工难题，实现了快捷、均匀供料及分料，保证了混凝土浇筑质量。

（二）应用情况与推广前景

项目成果已成功应用于三峡、向家坝、溪洛渡、乌东德等特大型水电工程，施工质量优良，产生经济效益约2060万元。该项目关键技术总体达到国际先进水平，显著提升了我国水电工程竖井混凝土总体技术水平，为大型竖井混凝土优质、安全、高效、绿色施工提供了有力的技术支撑。项目成果可实现标准化应用，具有广泛的推广应用价值，形成的多项发明专利技术在水电施工领域属独创性成果，具有很强的市场竞争力。可广泛推广应用于煤矿竖井、烟囱、高层建筑物电梯井、高大粮仓等类似工程，市场前景广阔。

（三）获奖单位

中国葛洲坝集团三峡建设工程有限公司。

（四）获奖人

李友华、詹剑霞、朱俊杰、周雄、方延洪、张欣、路佳欣。

（水力发电科学技术奖励工作办公室）

水工结构物软硬交界区域复合土工膜力学特性研究及工程应用

“水工结构物软硬交界区域复合土工膜力学特性研究及工程应用”获2018年度水力发电科学技术奖三等奖。

水电开发越来越深入西部深山峡谷地带，这些地区普遍面临“河谷狭窄深切、地质条件复杂、来流量大”等地形地质水文特征，多采用高围堰挡水、隧洞导流方式。作为水电开发先行技术的高水头围堰技术亟待创新提升，攻克降低围堰风险、节省围堰费用，实现经济快速开发的关键技术。该项目通过研究工程结构物软硬交界区域复合土工膜力学特性基础理论及工程应用，在复合土工膜关键部位的试验模型设计、应变集中预测、结构破坏细观机理推究、复合土工膜结构自适应变形能力扩展、高分子锚固抗渗结构研制等方面取得重大突破并实现了规模化应用，安全高效建成了国内最高的白鹤滩水电站斜墙式复合土工膜防渗土石围堰。项目研究已获得美国授权专利1件，中国发明专利5件、实用新型专利15件；发表论文17篇（SCI、EI检索10篇），参编专著1部。

（一）主要成果及创新点

（1）首次开展了涵盖复合土工膜斜墙、围堰填料及周边锚固相互作用的离心模型试验，全面揭示了高围堰复合土工膜整体及连接部位应变分布规律。

（2）建立了能反映复合土工膜应变集中的“周边膜”本构模型，改进了复合土工膜应变计算方法，从根本上提高了对土工膜工作性态的预测精度。

（3）率先采用PFC颗粒流程序开展了高水头作用下复合土工膜渐进破坏的细观数值模拟，追踪了受力变形过程中各材料颗粒间相互作用及细观组构的变化，解译了土工膜变形破坏机理，提出了关键连接部位设计的细观力学原则，拓展了复合土工膜研究手段。

（4）研制了能自动适应堰体变形的复合土工膜连接结构及高分子材料联合抗渗锚固技术，解决了白鹤滩水电站83m高围堰复合土工膜与防渗墙、趾板连接接头易发生撕裂破坏的问题，有效控制了基坑渗流。

（二）应用情况与推广前景

本项目成果已经全部应用于金沙江白鹤滩水电站围堰工程的设计与实施过程中，高水头复合土工膜防渗相关技术在白鹤滩水电站工程中得到充分应用与验证。相关框架体系、数值模拟技术、试验与计算方法等还部分应用于西部多个大型水电工程导流工程建设中，如澜沧江苗尾水电站及西藏大古水电站等工程中。此外，高水头复合土工膜防渗技术还在中国东部抽水蓄能电站（如浙江仙居抽蓄）、堤防防洪（珠海横琴新区天沐河防洪工程）、交通、垃圾填埋场及河道整治等环境岩土工程中推广运用。课题所做的基础性研究工作将对相关技术起到有益的推进与推广作用。

（三）获奖单位

中国电建集团华东勘测设计研究院有限公司、长江水利委员会长江科学院。

（四）获奖人

周垂一、王永明、任金明、邓渊、梁现培、邬志、蔡建国。

（水力发电科学技术奖励工作办公室）

45°缓倾斜井反导井开挖及复杂结构滑模衬砌技术

“45°缓倾斜井反导井开挖及复杂结构滑模衬砌技术”获2018年度水力发电科学技术奖三等奖。

随着我国工程建设的迅猛发展，斜井工程施工将会越来越多。国内外目前主要采用经济、快速、安全的反井法进行斜井掘进，此法适用倾角一般在60°～90°。猴子岩斜井距离长达185.1m且倾角为45°，加上城门洞型复杂断面和踏步及排水沟等结构等需同步浇筑，采用反井法施工尚无先例，在45°倾角下导孔轨迹到底会如何变化、精度控制方法、正向开挖轮廓线及块度控制、滑模受力以及如何快速、安全和优质进行衬砌浇筑均受到极大挑战。课题依托猴子岩水电站出线洞工程，通过对斜井倾角、溜渣模型、导井直径等一系列因素的研究和分析，确定了斜井全断面开挖的爆破参数，并经过爆破振动影响论证；通过对斜井开挖围岩稳定性分析，计算出循环进尺控制长度；通过一系列的研究分析，制定了全断面开挖的实施方案及控制措施。课题研究形成发明专利1件和实用新型专利3件，获省部级工法3项。

（一）主要成果及创新点

（1）开展了斜井导井溜渣规律理论分析和研究，为45°缓倾角斜井采用反导井法自上而下一次扩挖成型的施工方案提供了依据。

（2）基于反井法导孔钻进轨迹研究，提出了钻机开孔角度补偿的方法，提高了钻孔精度；研究采用倾斜机座及可伸缩式吊杆，提高了反井钻机对缓倾角斜井钻孔的适应性，保障了斜井反井法的顺利实施。

（3）通过理论分析和现场试验，研究采用环形密孔微差控制爆破技术，实现了开挖轮廓、爆破规模和爆块粒径的精确控制，避免了堵井现象发生。

（4）研发了45°复杂结构城门洞型斜井边顶拱、排水沟、踏步一体化“液压伸缩导梁自行式滑模”，形成了成套工法技术，实现了45°斜井带有踏步及沟槽的城门洞型复杂结构一次连续浇筑成型。

（二）应用情况与推广前景

为解决猴子岩水电站斜井导井开挖、全断面正向扩挖堵井高风险以及斜井衬砌断面极其复杂且衬砌施工困难等重大难题，通过多方面的施工技术措施研究，将反井钻机施工技术及“导梁自行式”滑模施工技术运用到45°城门洞型斜井中。既保证了斜井施工的人员与设备安全，同时在很大程度上促进了施工进度，将施工干扰降到了最低程度。不仅对依托工程确保施工安全及保证施工进度有重要意义，而且对水电工程领域其他类似施工有重要的参考价值。

（三）获奖单位

中国水利水电第七工程局有限公司、国电大渡河猴子岩水电建设有限公司。

（四）获奖人

向建、张学彬、王峻、郑正勤、王焕强、张登柱、袁平顺。

（水力发电科学技术奖励工作办公室）

水环境治理工程智能管控关键技术研发与集成应用

“水环境治理工程智能管控关键技术研发与集成应用”获2018年度水力发电科学技术奖三等奖。

我国水环境污染大、隐患多，水资源保障能力弱，水生态受损严重，国民的“水安全”受到了威胁。造成这些问题的主要原因是治理水平偏低、污染物排放总量巨大；此外，产业布局不合理、科技支撑和投入不足、法律法规标准和管理体制机制不完善、节水和环境意识不强等也是重要原因。

茅洲河流域内水体现状污染严重，水体黑臭，水生态环境亟待改善。为实现茅洲河流域水环境标本兼治，中电建水环境治理技术有限公司将非工程措施与工程措施相融合，以实现“信息采集自动化、传输网络化、管理数字化、决策科学化”的目标。为有效解决工程范围广，技术复杂，涉及单位多，工程的安全、质量、进度等综合管控难度大的难题，项目集成应用GIS技术、网格化管理、视频结构化分析、北斗定位等现代信息通信技术，研发了一套适合于复杂水环境治理工程管理的信息化体系，构建了适用于水环境治理工程要求的综合管控平台，实现工程的动态和智能化管理目标。

（一）主要成果及创新点

（1）首次提出水环境治理工程管控“1218”智能信息化系统架构，研发了一系列适合于复杂水环境治理工程的现场快速数据采集终端，综合应用窄带传输、物联网等现代通信网络技术，成功构建了适用于多工程水环境治理智能化综合管控平台。

（2）创新性地全面集成网格化管理、多源大数据融合、视频识别分析、水环境治理多场景动态感知物联网等技术，实现了工程多视角、多维度、多方位的立体可视化管控，填补了水环境治理全面智能化管控空白。

（3）提出“1+6+N”联合开发、快速实施的信息化建设模式，创造性地实现了工程建设和信息系统开发应用同步，破解了水环境工程建设周期短、参建单位多，信息管理复杂的难题。

（二）应用情况与推广前景

水环境治理智能管控平台通过茅洲河流域综合治理工程成功的验证应用，现已推广到广州车陂涌、棠下涌水质提升工程，白云区城中村管网改造项目以及福建光明港项目等水环境治理项目。项目研究成果坚持“两个开放”，在系统层面，采用的平台技术科学开放，具有良好的可扩展性，为水环境治理工程智能管控技术的可持续发展提供了保障；在应用层面，以服务工程，服务社会为目标，向政府的工程监管机构等开放应用，建立了完善的应用推广体系，在水环境治理行业具有广阔的应用前景。

水环境治理工程管控平台在运行期间，系统运行安全、稳定、可靠；为许多水环境治理工程项目管理提供了权威的、安全的、稳定的地图服务和专题应用服务，为将来系统应用推广起到了奠定了基础。

（三）获奖单位

中电建水环境治理技术有限公司、中国水利水电第三工程局有限公司、中国电建集团西北勘测设计研究院有限公司。

（四）获奖人

王民浩、陈惠明、陶明、杨立、段红波、周利雪、辜晓原。

（水力发电科学技术奖励工作办公室）

水库沥青混凝土面板智能喷淋冷却系统关键技术研究与应用

“水库沥青混凝土面板智能喷淋冷却系统关键技术研究与应用”获 2018 年度水力发电科学技术奖三等奖。

水库面板上的沥青混合料，夏天阳光直射时，其表面温度可达 70～80℃。在如此高的温度下，沥青软化，黏度减小，沥青在骨料之间起到润滑作用，沥青混凝土抗剪切能力大大减小，骨料之间有相互滑动的趋势。防渗层用的混合料，为了达到渗透性小的要求，沥青用量较多，这就容易引起斜坡流淌。国内外沥青混凝土面板工程大多发生过斜坡流淌现象，有的沥青混凝土面板工程斜坡流淌情况极为严重，以至于不得不铲除面板，重新修建。因此，为防止沥青混凝土面板在高温季节发生流淌，需设置夏季喷淋降温保护系统，利用水的流动及蒸发带走热量，降低面板表面温度。本项目依托河北张河湾抽水蓄能电站上水库沥青混凝土面板工程进行设计研究，系统解决了水库沥青混凝土面板夏季高温斜坡流淌的问题，提高沥青混凝土面板的热稳定性，保障面板安全。

（一）主要成果及创新点

（1）开展了太阳辐射下的面板温度测量与分析，根据沥青混凝土面板材料热稳定性能与不同区域温度分布的关联关系，首次提出了基于温度场的水库沥青混凝土面板喷淋降温方案。

（2）通过超长喷淋管路精细化的水力计算分析和多种喷淋方式的比较，优化了管路布置和设计参数，首次将间歇式调节喷头应用于沥青混凝土面板喷淋系统，解决了水库喷淋环管远端水压不足导致的喷淋效果不佳的问题，并实现节水节能。

（3）首先将红外测温技术应用于沥青混凝土面板喷淋系统，实现喷淋智能启闭，并根据温度设置分区喷淋，实现按需分区流量分配，建立了沥青混凝土面板喷淋智能控制系统。

（二）应用情况与推广前景

水库沥青混凝土面板喷淋冷却系统在内蒙古呼和浩特抽水蓄能电站上水库沥青混凝土面板工程中施工完成后，已经历了 5 年以上运行考验，目前无任何损坏及故障发生，应用效果良好。

河北张河湾抽水蓄能电站上水库沥青混凝土面板工程，后期改造中应用了智能喷淋冷却系统技术研究成果，已经历了 3 年运行考验，自动运行情况良好，大大减少了面板喷淋冷却系统的运行维护工作量。

这种水库沥青混凝土面板喷淋冷却系统技术可在水利水电工程中大力推广使用，也可为其他喷淋冷却、灌溉工程、混凝土养护工程等提供借鉴，具有很高的应用和推广价值。

（三）获奖单位

中国电建集团北京勘测设计研究院有限公司。

（四）获奖人

阳春树、赵铁、李仕宏、李振中、武媛、杨威、陈建华。

（水力发电科学技术奖励工作办公室）

澜沧江流域水电站群巨型分布式集控监控系统的构建及应用

“澜沧江流域水电站群巨型分布式集控监控系统

的构建及应用”获2018年度水力发电科学技术奖三等奖。

集控监控系统是实现流域水电站群远程集中控制和梯级优化调度的核心自动化系统，在水能利用和流域梯级水电站管理中的地位举足轻重。传统集控监控系统沿用电站级系统功能架构，存在结构紧耦合，扩展性、稳定性、维护性差，数据处理技术落后、丢失率高，处理能力、容载力弱，无定制、复杂工况处理能力差等问题，安全风险较大。项目依托国家“十二五”科技支撑计划（澜沧江流域水电开发安全与高效利用系统集成与示范）及企业科技攻关项目（集控监控系统改造），通过理论研究、技术攻关和试验验证，构建了一套真正适用于流域水电站群巨型集控中心的分布式监控系统，从系统架构、数据处理、功能模块等方面彻底解决了传统集控监控系统存在的问题，显著提升了系统的安全性、可靠性、适用性和智能性。项目研究获授权专利11件，其中发明专利6件，另有被受理发明专利6件；登记软件著作权3项，编写行业标准2项，发表论文70余篇，出版专著1部。项目成果得到专家评价委员会高度评价，一致认为达到国际先进水平。

（一）主要成果及创新点

（1）构建了澜沧江流域梯级水电站群远程集中控制的巨型分布式监控系统，通过以电站为单元的横向解耦，解决了传统监控系统的结构紧耦合问题，提高了系统可扩展性、稳定性和维护便利性。实现了澜沧江流域小湾、糯扎渡等十余座水电站的远程监视和控制，部分电厂已实现无人值班，控制容量超过2000万kW，设计机组台数超过百台，数据设计规模超过百万点。

（2）提出了冷热数据分级存储技术、专家知识库智能报警技术和可定制报表分析技术，扩展了数据存储能力，提升了海量数据综合分析效率。

（3）构建了逻辑强耦合和结构弱耦合的分布式数据架构，提出了分布式数据动态加载和自动同步技术，解决了巨型集控监控系统数据膨胀和控制可靠性问题。

（4）构建了多振动区巨型水电机组有功控制策略，提出了一二次调频的协调控制技术和基于多重回归建模方法的泄洪闸门控制技术，实现了机组有功的精准调整和闸门开度的智能控制。

（二）应用情况与推广前景

成果成功应用于澜沧江流域小湾、糯扎渡等十余座水电站，控制容量近2000万kW，机组近百台，设计数据规模超百万，部分电厂无人值班。通过优化调度提高水能利用率，近三年增发电量143.3亿kW·h，取得直接经济效益35.06亿元。在澜沧江湄公河流域防洪、抗旱、航运和生态安全等方面取得了巨大的社会效益。2016年澜沧江湄公河下游国家发生大范围旱灾时，向下游补水114.36亿m^3，受到了湄委会及各成员国的一致好评；在中国水利部与湄委会联合评估中得到高度认可，为实现澜湄合作国家战略发挥了重要作用。

（三）获奖单位

华能澜沧江水电股份有限公司、南瑞集团有限公司。

（四）获奖人

胡林、马月姣、徐麟、鲁铭、周星、唐睿高、万建强。

（水力发电科学技术奖励工作办公室）

大型水电机组高灵敏继电保护技术深化研究及应用

“大型水电机组高灵敏继电保护技术深化研究及应用”获2018年度水力发电科学技术奖三等奖。

大型水电机组造价昂贵、电机设计参数安全裕度小，对区域电网稳定运行具有重要影响，要求继电保护更灵敏快速切除故障。而现有保护技术仍存在一些瓶颈，运行中一旦暴露往往造成绕组、铁芯烧损等严重后果。项目通过深入研究高灵敏度继电保护技术，创新保护原理，改进保护方法，全面提升保护整体性能。项目研究获国内外授权专利28件，其中2项国际专利获美国、日本、俄罗斯授权；取得软件著作权登记证书5项，主导制定（或修订）GB/T 32898—2016《抽水蓄能发电电动机变压器组继电保护配置导则》、DL/T 684—2012《大型发电机变压器继电保护整定计算导则》等国家或行业标准15项，发表SCI论文2篇，EI论文24篇。

（一）主要成果及创新点

（1）研制成功发电机组专用光学电流互感器。大型发电机中性点侧电流互感器的配置仍在很大程度上受制于定子绕组型式和中性点侧铜环布置的要求，分支电流互感器装设和差动保护配置受到限制，内部故障仍存在保护死区，特别是小匝数匝间短路不能灵敏动作。项目研制了发电机专用光学电流互感器，可在所需的任意分支安装，实现由完全纵差、多个不完全纵差、多个裂相横差保护构成的多重差动保护系统，最大限度减少甚至完全消除保护死区，任一短路均有多种差动保护来反映，灵敏度显著提升。而且，光学电流互感器无饱和问题，可简化制动判据、降低定值门槛，提高了灵敏度和动作速度。

（2）建立了完整的转子匝间故障理论分析体系，

提出了基于分支谐波环流的转子匝间保护，全工况下均可灵敏检测3%匝比短路故障。以往转子匝间保护主要采用微分线圈动测法，需在定子槽内预埋感应线圈，已建机组无法应用，且该方法在重负荷下灵敏度不足。本项目基于多回路数学模型的构建及转子匝间故障独有特征的分析，提出了一种易于实现且高灵敏的保护方案，利用转子匝间短路时定子分支上感应出的谐波环流来反映故障，全工况下均可反映匝比3%轻微匝间短路。而且，该方法无需增加设备，实施简便。

(3) 提出了定子侧接地保护的参数动态补偿方法、比率制动防误技术和电压互感器一次断线闭锁新判据，全面彻底地解决了机组接地保护的难题。项目采用动态参数补偿方式，分段、分工况进行差异化参数补偿，全工况下误差均小于5%，同时保证可靠性和灵敏度。采用动作门槛经高压侧零序电压比率制动的方法，在本侧接地时灵敏动作，高压侧接地时可靠防止误动，兼具选择性和速动性。依据接地故障时不产生负序电压特点，在零序电压判据基础上增加负序电压低条件，可靠防止电压互感器一次断线时主变低压侧接地保护误动。

(4) 提出了发电机组变频启动系统差动保护方法，从原理上保证了选择性，且具有高灵敏度，输出变压器的内部故障切除时间由秒级缩短至毫秒级。

(二) 应用情况与推广前景

项目解决了机组保护存在的难题，首次实现光学互感器在发电机组上的应用，是机组保护技术革新的重要节点。项目成果奠定了国内机组保护的世界领先地位，引领了行业发展，对支撑我国电力发展有重要意义。成果适用于各类水力发电机组和抽水蓄能机组，现已在三峡电站、广州蓄能水电厂、观音岩水电站等数百台机组上应用，销售额逾4亿元。并在巴西、俄罗斯、印度等近100个海外国家使用，随着“一带一路”战略的深入推进，海外推广前景广阔。

(三) 获奖单位

南京南瑞继保电气有限公司、清华大学、北京交通大学。

(四) 获奖人

陈俊、王光、桂林、王凯、陈佳胜、张琦雪、郝亮亮。

(水力发电科学技术奖励工作办公室)

水工岩体损伤状态精细识别与安全预警关键技术

“水工岩体损伤状态精细识别与安全预警关键技术”获2018年度水力发电科学技术奖三等奖。

岩体是水工建筑物的重要组成部分和承载结构，其力学性能与安全状态直接关系到水电工程建设成败。近年来随着国民经济的发展，复杂地质条件下的工程建设不断增多，出现了大量高地应力地下工程，其突出特点是埋深大、地应力水平高，应力与岩体强度之间的矛盾非常尖锐，工程开挖过程中，由于开挖卸荷、爆破等原因，岩体不可避免地产生损伤，形成损伤区。损伤区的存在将导致围岩内部物质结构、力学行为和工程响应都发生根本性变化，降低围岩强度，增加岩体渗透能力，直接威胁到工程和环境安全。

为此，在国家自然科学基金、企业集团重大科研专项等项目的支持下，以国家重大工程建设为依托，组织骨干科研技术人员，以“产学研用”模式进行理论创新、技术攻关和工程应用，突破了一系列关键技术难题，取得多项重要创新性技术发明。项目研究获得授权发明专利19件、实用新型专利33件，取得软件著作权登记证书5项，SCI、EI收录论文53篇，纳入3部国家（行业）规程规范，出版专著3部，有力推动了我国地下工程防灾减灾技术的进步。

(一) 主要成果及创新点

(1) 发明了小尺度岩石损伤状态孕育演化系列试验与测试技术。提出了强卸荷条件下套孔取样技术与损伤破裂演化实时追踪技术，研发了卸荷速率和时间效应影响测试方法，突破了小尺度损伤岩石真实力学性能难以准确测定的技术瓶颈；开发了具有自主知识产权的图像增强与分割程序，有效提取了岩石变形劣化过程中细观结构动态信息与细观结构特征参数，揭示了岩石细观裂纹产生、扩展、积聚至破坏的内在机制，建立了岩石细观损伤力学本构模型与“宏观—细观”损伤渐进过程定量描述方法；提出了岩石细观尺度RVE的Monte Carlo重构方法，重现了岩石细观尺度RVE的损伤变化过程，实现了岩石细观尺度微结构RVE损伤过程的统计再现和量化损伤数据的可视化。解决了岩石损伤状态与演化过程难以定量描述的技术难题。

(2) 提出了大尺度岩体细部结构和损伤程度精细识别方法。提出了岩体结构均质区划分、结构面密度、结构面产状、结构面直径的函数回归数学方法，突破了有限尺寸岩体抽样、离散元接触本构、合成岩体模拟方法等关键技术瓶颈，研发了大尺度岩体结构特征数字近景摄影采集和三维结构网络重构技术；建立了能够真实反映掘进速率影响的消除瞬态卸载效应计算方法，发现了钻爆法开挖存在爆炸荷载和地应力高速卸载两个明显的激励源，TBM开挖仅存在单个明显的地应力瞬态高速卸载诱发的激励源；构建了基于膨胀边界伺服法、内部逐步填充法、连续网格控制法为基础的重叠、不重叠细观模型生成方法，首次揭示了损伤局部化现象及对围岩真实承载能力的影响，建立了破坏区、破损区、损伤区和扰动区的损伤分区新方法和力学判据。突破了损伤区测试精度难以满足工程建设需求的技术瓶颈。

（3）建立了损伤岩体力学性能评价方法与安全预警系统。发明了损伤区随时间和尺寸变化的测试方法，提出了地质构造粗糙度识别方法和分形数学描述方法，全面揭示了断面形态、尺寸、时间、地质构造等因素对损伤区的影响模式和影响机制；提出了多声波参数综合分析方法，揭示了入射条件和裂隙结构对声波波速、波幅及其衰减系数的影响规律，突破了波速对细小裂隙不敏感而无法准确识别的技术瓶颈；基于应变能理论建立了广义多轴应变能屈服准则，提出了扩容安全度指标 DSF 以描述围岩损伤破裂程度；发明了以声发射、空心包体应力计、光纤光栅和声波为主的岩体损伤原位综合测试技术，构建了以围岩破裂和应力扰动监测为主、变形监测为辅的损伤岩体安全性态实时监测系统。实现了岩体安全状态的实时监测和有效预警。

（二）应用情况与推广前景

该项目成果为白鹤滩水电站、锦屏二级水电站、中国锦屏暗物质地下实验室等国家重大工程建设提供了技术支撑，确保了人员和工程安全；有力推动了我国地下工程防灾减灾技术的进步，并为交通、矿山、跨流域长距离调水、地下实验室、核废料储置等领域的地下工程建设提供了技术借鉴。

（三）获奖单位

中国电建集团华东勘测设计研究院有限公司、中国科学院武汉岩土力学研究所、河海大学。

（四）获奖人

侯靖、单治钢、陈祥荣、徐建荣、陈建林、褚卫江、刘宁。

（水力发电科学技术奖励工作办公室）

岩石盖重固结灌浆施工工艺研究

“岩石盖重固结灌浆施工工艺研究”获 2018 年度水力发电科学技术奖三等奖。

固结灌浆作为一项改善破碎岩石力学性能措施，广泛应用于水电站大坝基础工程。有混凝土盖重固结灌浆方法与基础混凝土浇筑相伴，影响坝基混凝土连续浇筑，占用直线工期，且钻孔过程易损伤混凝土中的冷却水管，浆液从损伤处进入冷却管影响其畅通性和混凝土养护冷却，灌浆过程存在混凝土抬动变形的风险。找平混凝土无盖重固结灌浆、无盖重固结灌浆和“引管＋无盖重固结灌浆”方法是有盖重固结灌浆方法革新和发展，较好解决了坝基混凝土浇筑与固结灌浆施工相互干扰的矛盾，但存在细小裂隙因压力不足灌浆效果较差、裂隙发育岩体表面冒浆、串浆、漏浆多，建基面表层灌浆效果差等缺点。为解决以上问题，依托白鹤滩水电站左岸坝基固结灌浆工程进行了“岩石盖重固结灌浆工艺研究”。

（一）主要成果及创新点

研究成功岩石盖重固结灌浆工艺。在大坝基础开挖时，在建基面高程以上预留厚度 5m 的岩石层作为岩石盖重，进行固结灌浆，灌浆孔方向垂直建基面。岩石盖重固结灌浆工艺与混凝土盖重固结灌浆工艺进行对比分析优点如下：

（1）岩石盖重固结灌浆工艺将固结灌浆时间提前到坝基开挖阶段，使固结灌浆与混凝土浇筑完全脱离，实现了坝基混凝土的连续浇筑；岩石盖重开挖后建基面浅层灌浆质量检查不合格区域采用引管灌浆方式补强灌浆，亦不影响坝基混凝土浇筑，解决了坝基固结灌浆施工与混凝土浇筑相互影响、相互干扰的问题。

（2）盖重岩石层内无冷却水管，可使用高效钻孔设备，如液压钻机、潜孔钻机等，钻孔进度快，效率高，节省固结灌浆工期。

（3）岩石盖重固结灌浆是在预留岩石盖重面上进行灌浆作业，灌浆作业不损伤混凝土、不损坏混凝土中的冷却水管，有效保证了混凝土质量。

（4）混凝土盖重固结灌浆施工时，须安排专人通水、检查、维护盖重混凝土中的冷却水管，确保灌浆后冷却水管畅通。岩石盖重无冷却水管，不存在冷却水管维护问题，节省了冷却水管维护费。

（5）岩石盖重固结灌浆完成后即可进行盖重层岩石开挖，不需完全清理附着在岩石表面的浆液、岩粉等，节省工作面清理费用。

（6）相同的盖重厚度，岩石盖重使用的灌浆压力较混凝土盖重高，岩石盖重有利于浆液在裂隙、节理等通道中扩散、填充、凝固胶结，灌浆效果好。

（7）岩石盖重固结灌浆过程发现的地质缺陷处理手段不限于钻孔灌浆（包括灌注水泥砂浆），可采用多种手段处理，如开挖置换、旋喷等，不需考虑对混凝土的影响。

（二）应用情况与推广前景

研究成果在白鹤滩水电站左岸大坝成功应用，效果显著。岩石盖重固结灌浆施工弥补了混凝土盖重固结灌浆和无盖重固结灌浆施工工艺缺点，将固结灌浆工序与坝基开挖相结合，解决了固结灌浆与混凝土浇筑之间相互影响相互干扰的矛盾，缩短工程直线工期；施工不损坏混凝土和混凝土冷却水管，有利于坝基混凝土养护和连续浇筑；灌浆压力大，灌浆效果好；使用高效率钻孔设备，钻孔速度快，工期省；可应用于各类岩石坝基固结灌浆。

（三）获奖单位

中国水利水电第四工程局有限公司。

（四）获奖人

冯涛、吴涛、刘俊国、滕鸿煜、张兴、罗增录、郭长安。

（水力发电科学技术奖励工作办公室）

水电工程移民安置独立评估管理信息系统研发与应用

“水电工程移民安置独立评估管理信息系统研发与应用”获2018年度水力发电科学技术奖三等奖。

该项目结合金沙江下游的向家坝、溪洛渡、乌东德、白鹤滩4个大型电站建设征地移民安置独立评估工作实际需要，深入研究并首次创建了覆盖独立评估工作事前、事中、事后全过程的信息化管理模型；梳理了各评估单位的评估方法和指标体系，构建了一套覆盖面全、语义统一的指标库，研究并实现了适应于多工程、多阶段、多单位的易维护、可扩展信息模型和评估模型；借助移动互联网、云计算、大数据等现代化信息技术研发了水电工程移民安置独立评估管理信息系统，为独立评估单位、移民管理机构、工程业主等单位提供了信息化管理手段，促使向家坝、溪洛渡、乌东德、白鹤滩征地移民独立评估工作的规范、科学、有序、有效的管理。

（一）主要成果及创新点

（1）提出了内业外业有效协同全过程信息化调查评估模型。水电工程建设征地移民安置独立评估分为外业跟踪调查和内业分析评估等工作环节，整个跟踪调查与评估时间跨度长，对评估对象的信息一致性、延续性、继承性、协同性要求很高。系统创新性地提出了内业外业有效协同模型，实现了内外业信息的无缝对接和延续继承，有效避免了传统工作方式中信息的重复采集、前后不一致、难以回溯等问题，缩短了外业采集至内业评估的整体工作周期，极大地提高了工作效率。

（2）提出了评估对象深度参与的高保真信息采集模型。水电工程建设征地移民安置独立评估对象涉及众多移民个人群体，评估指标多样复杂，采用传统工作方式，评估数据与评估结果的误差性和真实性较难保证。系统创新性地提出了评估对象深度互动模型，让评估对象以真人语音、现场视频、触屏手写等输入形式，直接参与到信息采集过程中，大大提高了信息的保真度和置信度，极大地降低了篡改评估数据和评估结果的几率。

（3）以样本对象为核心的大数据体系，使得各类数据有机融合。建立了本底阶段、蓄水阶段、跟踪阶段、验收阶段等各阶段以样本对象为核心包含移民生产生活水平、区域社会经济发展、移民权益实现等指标的大数据体系，并与搬迁前的实物指标调查、搬迁前后的空间位置、多媒体影像资料相关联，构成了一套完整的移民搬迁前后的数据链，形象直观反映了移民搬迁安置的全过程。

（4）与不同工程、不同区域的独立评估工作相适应。目前国内水电工程建设征地移民安置独立评估刚起步，尚未有统一的独立评估工作规范，在不同的历史时期、不同的工程或同一工程不同的区域，对独立评估方法和要求都不尽相同，这对以标准统一、流程固化、业务规范著称的信息化管理方式带来了巨大的挑战和冲击。为此，在本系统的设计之初，开发设计人员充分考虑系统的可配置性和灵活性，在一库一策和区域性业务管理等方面作了大量的研究和实践，在确保程序实用性和稳定性的基础之上，使系统具有了较强的业务适应和功能扩展能力，降低了系统推广风险。

（二）应用情况与推广前景

该系统的研发填补了我国在水电工程移民安置独立评估管领域管理软件系统研发的空白，为独立评估信息化工作进行了统一规划设计、统一建设、集中存储管理，建设目标明确，功能完善合理，提高了独立评估工作效率，极大地减轻独立评估工作人员的工作量，带动了各独立评估单位工作方法的交流和融合，促进了独立评估方法的统一和标准的完善，为移民工作各方在移民群众面前树立了良好的形象。

该系统开创性的将信息化技术引入独立评估工作，提出了独立评估工作全生命周期的信息化模型；创建以调查样本为枢纽的时空大数据体系，实现了海量异构调查数据的统筹统建；首创多租户、多层级、多时空的独立评估智能计算模型。这些在理论和方法上的创新都为后来者开展类似工作和研究奠定了良好的基础。

（三）获奖单位

中国长江三峡集团有限公司、长江水利委员会网络与信息中心。

（四）获奖人

姚英平、金和平、姚元军、嵇培欢、周竞亮、张军、李岸昀。

（水力发电科学技术奖励工作办公室）

获得2018年度国家科学技术奖的水电科技项目

根据国家科学技术奖励办公室公布的2018年度国家技术发明奖、自然科学奖和科学技术进步奖的获奖项目，水电科技有2个项目获得国家技术发明奖，4个项目获得国家科学技术进步奖，有关情况见表1和表2。

表1　　获得2018年度国家技术发明奖的水电科技项目

序号	等级	项目名称	主要完成人	备注
1	二等奖	水力式升船机关键技术及应用	马洪琪（华能澜沧江水电股份有限公司） 曹以南（中国电建集团昆明勘测设计研究院有限公司） 胡亚安（南京水利科学研究院） 郑大迪（中国长江三峡集团公司） 袁湘华（华能澜沧江水电股份有限公司） 吴一红（中国水利水电科学研究院）	原序号为二等奖（通用项目）10，编号F-304-2-01，推荐单为云南省
2	二等奖	重大工程结构安全服役的高韧性纤维混凝土制备与应用关键技术	徐世烺（浙江大学） 李庆华（浙江大学） 谭恺炎（中国葛洲坝集团股份有限公司） 余江滔（同济大学） 陈志远（中国葛洲坝集团股份有限公司） 王振宇（浙江大学）	原序号为二等奖（通用项目）47，编号F-310-2-05，推荐单位为浙江省

表2　　获得2018年度国家科学技术进步奖的水电科技项目

序号	等级	项目名称	主要完成人	主要完成单位	备注
1	二等奖	超大型水电站用金属结构关键材料成套技术开发应用	周德光，张熹，邹扬，刘国权，余雪松，万天明，李谦，张建中，翟泳，白学军	首钢集团有限公司，秦皇岛首秦金属材料有限公司，北京科技大学，中国水利水电第七工程局有限公司，中国电建集团华东勘测设计研究院有限公司，中国葛洲坝集团机械船舶有限公司，天津大桥焊材集团有限公司	原序号为（通用项目）40，编号J-215-2-04，推荐单位为中国钢铁工业协会
2	二等奖	超深与复杂地质条件混凝土防渗墙关键技术	宗敦峰，刘建发，肖恩尚，王玉杰，孔祥生，韩伟，刘志明，张社荣，石峰，赵明华	中国水电基础局有限公司，中国水利水电科学研究院，水利部水利水电规划设计总院，天津大学	原序号为（通用项目）67，编号J-222-2-01，推荐单位为中国施工企业管理协会
3	二等奖	300m级特高拱坝安全控制关键技术及工程应用	王仁坤，祁宁春，洪文浩，李德玉，杨强，周钟，赵文光，杨建宏，张冲，邵敬东	中国电建集团成都勘测设计研究院有限公司，中国三峡建设管理有限公司，雅砻江流域水电开发有限公司，清华大学，中国水利水电科学研究院，四川大学，国电大渡河流域水电开发有限公司	原序号为（通用项目）68，编号J-222-2-02，推荐单位为中国大坝工程学会

续表

序号	等级	项目名称	主要完成人	主要完成单位	备注
4	二等奖	气候变化对区域水资源与旱涝的影响及风险应对关键技术	严登华，张建云，王国庆，鲍振鑫，杨志勇，王振龙，钟平安，秦天玲，关铁生，翁白莎	南京水利科学研究院，中国水利水电科学研究院，河海大学，安徽省（水利部淮河水利委员会）水利科学研究院	原序号为（通用项目）69，编号 J-222-2-03，推荐专家为王浩，周绪红，邓铭江

（本年鉴编辑部）

获得 2018 年度 中国电力科学技术奖的水电科技项目

根据中国电机工程学会和中国电力科学技术奖励工作办公室公布的《中国电力科学技术奖奖励通报（2018 年度）》，获得 2018 年度中国电力技术发明奖的水电科技项目有 1 项，有关情况见表 1；获得 2018 年度中国电力科学技术进步奖的水电科技项目有 13 项，有关情况见表 2。

表 1　获得 2018 年度中国电力技术发明奖获奖的水电科技项目

序号	等级	获奖项目	受奖人	备注
1	三等奖	大型竖井混凝土施工成套技术研究及应用	李友华、詹剑霞、汪文亮、唐明西、黄家权、马少甫	原序号为 7，推荐单位为中国能源建设集团有限公司

表 2　获得 2018 年度中国电力科学技术进步奖的水电科技项目

序号	等级	获奖项目	受奖单位	受奖人	备注
1	一等奖	300m 级高心墙堆石坝施工关键技术研究及应用	中国水利水电第五工程局有限公司、四川大学、河海大学、中国电建集团成都勘测设计研究院有限公司、四川二滩国际工程咨询有限责任公司、中国水电基础局有限公司	吴高见、李法海、薛凯、田中涛、樊鹏、韩兴、姚强、江万红、孙林智、杨建平、周家文、李洪涛、王嵛民、戴松贵、朱晟	原序号为 4，推荐单位为中国电力建设集团有限公司
2	一等奖	白鹤滩水电站施工导流与基坑渗流控制关键技术	中国电建集团华东勘测设计研究院有限公司、三峡金沙江云川水电开发有限公司宁南白鹤滩电厂	吴关叶、周垂一、徐建荣、樊义林、陈炜旻、石安池、王永明、郧志、蔡建国、任金明、徐剑、李军、王克祥、张志鹏、邓渊	原序号为 5，推荐单位为中国电力建设集团有限公司
3	二等奖	强溶蚀复杂地层防渗灌浆技术研究与应用	中国电建集团中南勘测设计研究院有限公司、五凌电力有限公司	胡大可、曾再祥、李永丰、杨松林、王少华、樊勇、舒王强、钟平、周运东、吴宏丽	原序号为 31，推荐单位为中国电力建设集团有限公司
4	二等奖	大渡河流域安全风险智能管控关键技术	国电大渡河流域水电开发有限公司、四川大学	涂扬举、周业荣、严军、令狐克海、陈建康、沈定斌、贺玉彬、向文平、李艳玲、王勇飞	原序号为 32，推荐单位为国家能源投资集团有限责任公司

续表

序号	等级	获奖项目	受奖单位	受奖人	备注
5	二等奖	复杂地质环境下水电工程大型滑坡灾变演化过程及控制关键技术	中国电建集团成都勘测设计研究院有限公司、中国地质大学（武汉）	张世殊、胡新丽、章广成、冉从彦、彭仕雄、谢剑明、王刚、吴建川、赵小平、石定国	原序号为33，推荐单位为中国电力建设集团有限公司
6	二等奖	爆破挤淤形成悬浮式海堤关键技术	中国电建集团华东勘测设计研究院有限公司、中国水利水电第十二工程局有限公司	单治钢、徐学勇、李洪林、孙淼军、汪明元、李炜、杜文博、王永明、王宽君、周力沛	原序号为34，推荐单位为中国电力建设集团有限公司
7	三等奖	百兆瓦级抽水蓄能机组静止变频器关键技术、设备研制及工程应用	国网新源控股有限公司、南京南瑞继保电气有限公司、安徽响水涧抽水蓄能有限公司、国网浙江省电力有限公司	刘为群、石祥建、陈俊、高苏杰、魏伟、衣传宝、周喜军	原序号为78，推荐单位为国家电网有限公司
8	三等奖	乌东德水电站超深覆盖层超深基坑围堰施工关键技术	中国葛洲坝集团三峡建设工程有限公司、中国葛洲坝集团基础工程有限公司	李国建、曹中升、周志远、袁瑞卿、李哲朋、常福远、黄家权	原序号为86，推荐单位为中国能源建设集团有限公司
9	三等奖	400MW级大型抽水蓄能机组关键技术与工程应用	国网新源控股有限公司、浙江仙居抽水蓄能有限公司、中国电建集团华东勘测设计研究院有限公司、哈尔滨电机厂有限责任公司、东方电气集团东方电机有限公司	郑小康、丁光、覃大清、姜成海、倪晋兵、孟贤、葛军强	原序号为87，推荐单位为国家电网有限公司
10	三等奖	强震区大岗山高拱坝复杂地层基础处理技术研究及应用	国电大渡河大岗山水电开发有限公司、中国葛洲坝集团基础工程有限公司、中国电建集团成都勘测设计研究院有限公司、中国水利水电科学研究院	杨忠伟、吕鹏飞、刘翔、邢占清、李桂林、赵连锐、吴楠	原序号为88，推荐单位为国家能源投资集团有限责任公司
11	三等奖	高土石坝复合土工膜面板防渗关键技术研究	中国电建集团海外投资有限公司、中国电建集团昆明勘测设计研究院有限公司、中国水电建设集团十五工程局有限公司	张国来、俞祥荣、喻建清、蔡斌、吴玉江、宁宇、李宜田	原序号为89，推荐单位为中国电力建设集团有限公司
12	三等奖	三叶片新型潮汐发电机组设计、制造及工程示范建设研究与应用	龙源电力集团股份有限公司、清华大学、龙源电力集团股份有限公司温岭江厦潮汐试验电站、中国电建集团华东勘测设计研究院有限公司	张宝全、王正伟、王浩平、何家兴、陈国海、肖业祥、罗永要	原序号为90，推荐单位为中国电机工程学会

续表

序号	等级	获奖项目	受奖单位	受奖人	备注
13	三等奖	西南地区水电工程泥石流综合治理关键技术	中国电建集团华东勘测设计研究院有限公司、三峡金沙江云川水电开发有限公司宁南白鹤滩电厂、中国科学院水利部成都山地灾害与环境研究所、昆明市东川区泥石流防治研究所	侯靖、彭育、陈宁生、汪志林、张开平、石安池、徐建荣	原序号为91，推荐单位为中国电力建设集团有限公司

（本年鉴编辑部）

中国电力建设集团有限公司 2018年重大科技项目成果简介

中国电力建设集团有限公司2018年重大科技成果主要有超深与复杂地质条件混凝土防渗墙关键技术、300m级特高拱坝安全控制关键技术及工程应用、水力式升船机关键技术及应用、超大型水电站用金属结构关键材料成套技术开发应用、复杂环境混合地层条件下地铁修建关键技术与应用、±800kV特高压直流输电线路设计及施工关键技术研究与应用、300m级高心墙堆石坝施工关键技术研究及应用等项目，现简介如下。

（一）超深与复杂地质条件混凝土防渗墙关键技术

完成单位：中国水电基础局有限公司。

该项目历经13年攻关，形成了超深与复杂地质条件混凝土防渗墙技术体系，首创复杂地质条件下200m级超深防渗墙造孔成槽施工工法体系和成套装备，解决了传统装备无法满足施工要求的难题。研发超深与复杂地质条件防渗墙槽孔固壁技术，开发了新型防渗墙正电胶固壁泥浆，研制了大体积泥浆自动搅拌系统。创新超深防渗墙混凝土浇筑成墙技术体系，首创“接头管法”防渗墙相邻墙段连接技术，研究形成超深混凝土防渗墙“气举法”槽孔清孔换浆、泥浆下混凝土浇筑和防渗墙内预埋灌浆管等技术。

该成果获2018年国家科技进步二等奖1项，省部级科学技术特等奖1项、一等奖3项，获授权专利35件，获国家级工法5项，主编行业规范2部，发表论文113篇、专著13部。项目成果成功应用于国内所有11项超深防渗墙工程，创造了防渗墙深201m的世界纪录，并推广应用于交通、市政、矿山、环保工程等多个领域，经济、社会和环境效益显著。

（二）300m级特高拱坝安全控制关键技术及工程应用

完成单位：中国电建集团成都勘测设计研究院有限公司。

项目依托锦屏一级、溪洛渡、大岗山拱坝的设计安全控制，组织优势科研技术团队，产学研用相结合，持续20多年科技攻关，创建了特高拱坝安全控制的3K方法体系与成套技术，形成了特高拱坝施工动态反馈设计技术和运行期安全评价体系。成果解决了工程重大技术难题，确保了工程成功建设与安全运行。同时，核心技术已推广应用到多座特高拱坝设计中，确立了我国特高拱坝设计位居国际领先地位。项目获得授权发明专利39件，软件著作权登记证书11项，发表论文101篇。成果已获得2018年国家科技进步二等奖1项，省部级科技进步一等奖3项，省部级优秀设计一等奖3项，溪洛渡获得世界FIDIC工程项目杰出奖，锦屏一级获得中国土木工程詹天佑奖。

（三）水力式升船机关键技术及应用

完成单位：中国电建集团昆明勘测设计研究院有限公司。

该项目依托国家863计划等20余项科技项目，历时十余年联合攻关，提出了水力式升船机设计、制造、施工、运行成套技术，建成了世界首座一种利用水能作为提升动力和安全保障措施的全新升船机——澜沧江景洪水力式升船机，实现了升船机发展史上真正意义的自适应“全平衡”，从原理上根本消除了传统升船机运行安全风险，解决了难以适应大水位变幅条件的困难，避开了制约升船机发展的制造安装运维难题，显著提升了升船机安全性、可靠性、适用性和经济性。

该项目获授权发明专利21件，在编规范6项，出版专著2部，发表论文100余篇，获2018年国家技术发明二等奖1项，省部级科技特等奖2项，中国专利奖1项。项目成果为世界首创、中国原创，是世界通航技术领域的重大创新，达到了国际领先水平。世界通航领域权威组织国际内河委员会已将水力式升船机确定为第三种垂直升船机类型，其突破了传统升船机的技术瓶颈，更具技术优势，为高坝通航领域提供了一种全新、先进、实用的技术选择。

（四）超大型水电站用金属结构关键材料成套技术开发应用

完成单位：中国水利水电第七工程局有限公司。

金属结构是水电站可靠运行的关键，压力管道是水电站的“主动脉”，是金属结构的核心。随着超大型水电站高水头（200m）、大型化（100 万 kW）的发展，对压力管道的强韧性和可焊性提出了极高的要求。针对影响世界上水电机组扩容的最大技术瓶颈，即缺乏高强、特厚钢板及配套焊材和焊接成套技术进行攻关，历经十余年，通过全产业链协同创新，首次开发了超大型水电站金属结构关键材料成套技术，包括高性能系列钢板、高强韧焊材、高效焊接技术。

该项目成果获得 2018 年国家科技进步二等奖、北京市科学技术一等奖、冶金科学技术一等奖、中国电力科学技术一等奖，获授权发明专利 8 件，制定国家标准 3 项，发表论文 51 篇，企业级技术秘密 14 项。开发的水电用钢系列产品稳居市场占有率第一，其中 150mm 特厚板占有率 100%。该项目成果已应用在 31 个重大水电工程，其中国内 23 个，总装机 6774 万 kW，占“十一五”以来国内新增水电装机的 50%以上，其中包括已投产单机容量最大的向家坝水电站、单机容量最大的仙居抽水蓄能电站、巴基斯坦塔贝拉电站、非洲最大的吉布Ⅲ水电站等超大型水电工程。

（五）复杂环境混合地层条件下地铁修建关键技术与应用

完成单位：中国电建集团铁路建设有限公司。

深圳地铁 7 号线具有现场环境条件复杂、施工难度大、技术要求高、工期紧、对环境影响控制要求高等特点，线路建设过程中需大量穿越建（构）筑物、繁华商业区、河流、桥梁、地下管线、既有地铁与铁路等一系列国际难题，核心技术突破与安全应用已成为制约地铁建设、创新驱动的命门所在，国内外可供借鉴的经验极其有限，多未形成系统性的解决方案。

为确保深圳地铁 7 号线安全、高效完成建设目标，中国电建所属中国电建集团铁路建设有限公司开展了复杂环境混合地层条件下地铁修建关键技术与应用研究。创立了繁华商业区地铁车站与超大地下空间同步施工技术，创建了地下运营车站竖向增层拓建技术，研发了小净距重叠盾构隧道下穿高铁轨道群施工技术。

该项目获得发明专利 19 件、实用新型 59 件，国家级工法 1 项、省部级工法 56 项，出版专著 9 部，发表论文 219 篇，获得中国施工企业管理协会科学技术特等奖。经国内知名专家鉴定，成果水平达到国际领先水平。研究成果依托深圳地铁 7 号线，直接产生经济效益 7.58 亿元。

（六）±800kV 特高压直流输电线路设计及施工关键技术研究与应用

完成单位：中国电建集团山东电力建设第一工程有限公司。

项目依托巴西美丽山直流特高压输电一期工程，针对工程实际，系统规划、科学研究，在工程设计、装备制造、工程施工等方面全面开展集成创新和自主创新，掌握关键技术，形成完全自主和系统性的知识产权。主要技术创新有：首次设计出“拉线塔无混凝土螺旋桩基础”和“自立塔复合螺旋桩基础”；创新研制了“轻型螺旋桩安装设备”，首次创新设计了特高压输电线路拉线塔“全预制装配式基础”，首次提出了单柱拉线塔。科技成果的研究与应用，促使巴西美丽山特高压项目一期工程提前 2 个月投入商业运行，工程建设创造了 5 项“世界第一”和 3 项“海外第一”

该成果共取得各类科技成果 35 项，其中省（部）级工法 6 项，发明专利 2 件，实用新型专利 13 件，申报国际 PCT 专利 6 项，论文 6 篇。

（七）300m 级高心墙堆石坝施工关键技术研究及应用

完成单位：中国水利水电第五工程局有限公司。

项目依托长河坝水电站砾石土心墙堆石坝工程（大坝建于深厚覆盖层上，坝体高 240m，覆盖层和坝体的总高度 293m，坝体高度大，地震设防烈度高达 9 度），根据工程特点、难点，开展复杂地质条件下高堆石坝施工技术研究，形成了系统的复杂地质条件高心墙堆石坝施工关键技术，提出了心墙土料改性的成套施工新工艺；研制了土石坝精细化施工的系列新设备；研发了基于信息技术的质量检测和控制新方法。解决了深厚覆盖层上 300m 级堆石坝建设的一系列工程技术难题。

项目形成了 3 项行业标准；获得了 53 件发明及实用新型专利，获得 8 项软件著作权登记证书；研制和应用了 15 套软硬件新装备，形成了 40 项国家级及省部级施工工法；培养了一大批站在行业技术前沿、勇于创新的高素质人才。项目还获得省部级科进步特等奖 1 项，一等奖 2 项。研究成果在长河坝、两河口、双江口、苏丹上阿特巴拉等国内外大型水电工程应用，并为澜沧江古水、如美，金沙江其宗等高心墙堆石坝工程的设计和施工提供了技术支撑和实践经验，经济社会与环境效益显著，有力地推动了行业科技进步，具有广泛的推广应用前景。

（中国电力建设集团有限公司）

中国电建集团北京勘测设计研究院有限公司 2018 年科技成果获奖情况

中国电建集团北京勘测设计研究院有限公司 2018年科技成果获奖情况见表1。

表1 中国电建集团北京勘测设计研究院有限公司2018年科技成果获奖情况

序号	项目名称	获奖情况
1	水电行业技术标准体系课题研究	水力发电科学技术奖三等奖
2	水库沥青混凝土面板智能喷淋冷却系统关键技术研究与应用	水力发电科学技术奖三等奖
3	沥青混凝土面板智能喷淋系统技术研究	电力建设科学技术进步奖二等奖
4	沂蒙电站地下厂房 BIM 技术设计研究与应用	电力建设科学技术进步奖三等奖
5	一种大流量高水头新型胶凝砂砾石过水围堰研究与应用	云南省人民政府科学技术进步奖三等奖
6	基于物联网的中小流域暴雨洪水预报系统关键技术与应用	大禹水利科学技术奖三等奖
7	无黏性土渗透变形类型判别及相关性研究	电力工程科学技术进步奖二等奖
8	脱贫攻坚能源政策研究	电力工程科学技术进步奖二等奖
9	物探数据综合分析系统研发与应用	电力工程科学技术进步奖三等奖
10	狭窄河谷高陡坝肩缆机系统布置新结构及应用	电力工程科学技术进步奖三等奖
11	内蒙古呼和浩特抽水蓄能电站工程设计	水电行业优秀工程设计一等奖
12	去学水电站工程勘测	水电行业优秀工程勘测一等奖
13	白俄罗斯维捷布斯克水电站工程设计	水电行业优秀工程设计三等奖
14	埃塞俄比亚 ADAMA 二期风电场工程设计	电力行业优秀工程设计一等奖
15	华润新能源海原西华山风电场（宁夏海原 01、02、03）300MW 风电工程设计	电力行业优秀工程设计二等奖
16	碧江区锦江石林（特色山茶小镇）项目工程测量	北京市优秀测绘地理信息工程一等奖
17	辽宁清原抽水蓄能电站施工控制网	北京市优秀测绘地理信息工程二等奖
18	华润海原西华山 300MW 风电项目	中国电力优质工程奖
19	四川大渡河大岗山 4×650MW 水电站	中国电力优质工程奖

（中国电建集团北京勘测设计研究院有限公司 海显丽）

中国电建集团成都勘测设计研究院有限公司2018年科技成果获奖情况

中国电建集团成都勘测设计研究院有限公司　2018年科技成果获奖情况见表1。

表1　中国电建集团成都勘测设计研究院有限公司2018年科技成果获奖情况

序号	成果名称	获奖情况
1	300m级特高拱坝安全控制关键技术及工程应用	国家科技进步奖二等奖
2	特高坝枢纽泄洪消能运行安全监测控制技术	天津市科学技术进步奖一等奖
3	大型地下厂房洞室群围岩稳定耗散能理论分析方法及应用	四川省科技进步奖三等奖
4	城市河湖水系生态重构与保障关键技术	四川省科技进步奖三等奖
5	锦屏一级特高拱坝枢纽泄洪消能与减雾关键技术	水力发电科学技术奖一等奖
6	重大水利水电工程鱼类生境保护关键技术与应用	水力发电科学技术奖二等奖
7	西部复杂地质环境区水电工程重大滑坡灾变演化过程及控制关键技术	中国岩石力学与工程学会科学技术奖一等奖
8	强震区卸荷裂隙密集带复杂岩体边坡稳定性评价与加固关键技术	大禹水利科学技术奖二等奖
9	300m级高心墙堆石坝施工关键技术研究与应用	中国施工企业管理协会科学技术进步奖一等奖
10	300m级高心墙堆石坝施工关键技术研究与应用	中国电力科学技术进步奖一等奖
11	复杂地质环境下水电工程大型滑坡灾变演化过程及控制关键技术	中国电力科学技术进步奖二等奖
12	强震区大岗山高拱坝复杂地层基础护理技术研究及应用	中国电力科学技术进步奖三等奖
13	复杂水工结构的钢筋数字化设计和数字交付一体化	全国电力职工技术成果奖二等奖
14	基于数据中心的水电工程地质勘察与分析一体化系统研究与开发	全国电力职工技术成果奖三等奖
15	水电水利项目水土保持监测近景摄影测量技术及应用研究	全国电力职工技术成果奖三等奖
16	多滑面深层抗滑稳定分析方法研究及程序开发	全国电力职工技术成果奖三等奖
17	水电工程岩体多尺度动态响应机理与变形协同控制技术	教育部科技进步奖一等奖
18	轴流转桨式水轮机组事故状态下电站安全保护技术及应用研究	电力工程科学技术进步奖二等奖
19	强震区深厚覆盖层特高土石坝建设关键技术及工程应用	中国大坝工程学会科技进步奖一等奖

（中国电建集团成都勘测设计研究院有限公司　吉华伟）

中国电建集团贵阳勘测设计研究院有限公司 2018 年度科技成果获奖情况

中国电建集团贵阳勘测设计研究院有限公司 2018 年科技成果获奖情况见表 1。

表 1 中国电建集团贵阳勘测设计研究院有限公司 2018 年科技成果获奖情况

序号	项目名称	获奖情况
1	复杂地质条件岩体力学参数取值与应用系统研究	电力工程科学技术进步奖一等奖
2	北盘江董箐水电站工程水土保持设计	中国水土保持学会优秀设计奖三等奖
3	北盘江马马崖一级水电站工程地质勘察	中国电力规划设计协会“四优奖”一等奖
4	贵州省北盘江善泥坡水电站工程勘察	中国电力规划设计协会“四优奖”三等奖
5	贵州北盘江善泥坡水电站工程设计	中国电力规划设计协会“四优奖”二等奖
6	贵州毛家河水电站工程设计	中国电力规划设计协会“四优奖”二等奖
7	贵州晴隆苏家屯风电场工程	中国电力规划设计协会“四优奖”一等奖
8	贵州遵义太阳坪风电场工程	中国电力规划设计协会“四优奖”三等奖
9	北盘江马马崖一级水电站工程地质勘察	2018 年度贵州省优秀工程勘察设计奖一等奖
10	大渡河大岗山水电站水库区滑坡体自动化监测	2018 年度贵州省优秀工程勘察设计奖一等奖
11	贵州北盘江善泥坡水电站工程设计	2018 年度贵州省优秀工程勘察设计奖二等奖
12	北盘江善泥坡水电站工程地质勘察	2018 年度贵州省优秀工程勘察设计奖二等奖
13	红河州建水（个旧）至元阳高速公路项目个旧至元阳段初步设计阶段 1：2000 地形图	2018 年度贵州省优秀工程勘察设计奖二等奖
14	贵州省威宁县草海综合治理工程 1：500 地形图成果	2018 年度贵州省优秀工程勘察设计奖二等奖
15	贵州省黔南州石龙水库工程可研阶段 1：2000 地形图	2018 年度贵州省优秀工程勘察设计奖三等奖
16	重庆市奉节县城市市政地下管线基础信息普查与更新	2018 年度贵州省优秀工程勘察设计奖三等奖
17	贵州毛家河水电站工程设计	2018 年度贵州省优秀工程勘察设计奖三等奖
18	岷江龙溪口航电枢纽工程初步设计报告	2018 年电力行业优秀工程咨询成果奖一等奖
19	岷江龙溪口航电枢纽工程环境影响报告书	2018 年电力行业优秀工程咨询成果奖一等奖
20	贵州织金县铁厂坝风电场工程可行性研究报告	2018 年电力行业优秀工程咨询成果奖二等奖
21	中广核太阳能西藏谢通门 30MWp 并网光伏电站项目	2018 年电力行业优秀工程咨询成果奖三等奖
22	藏中和昌都电网联网工程水土保持方案报告书	2018 年电力行业优秀工程咨询成果奖三等奖
23	贵州清水河格里桥水电站调整概算报告	2018 年电力行业优秀工程咨询成果奖三等奖
24	西藏澜沧江如美水电站可行性研究阶段库岸稳定评价工程地质专题报告	2018 年电力行业优秀工程咨询成果奖三等奖
25	贵州乌江沙沱水电站四级碾压混凝土筑坝关键技术研究及工程应用	电力创新奖一等奖

（中国电建集团贵阳勘测设计研究院有限公司　王芳）

中国葛洲坝集团股份有限公司 2018年科技成果获奖情况

中国葛洲坝集团股份有限公司2018年科技成果 获奖情况见表1。

表1 中国葛洲坝集团股份有限公司2018年获行业及以上科学技术奖统计

序号	项目名称	获奖情况
1	重大结构安全服役的高韧性纤维混凝土制备与应用关键技术	国家技术发明奖二等奖
2	超大型水电站用金属结构关键材料成套技术开发应用	国家科学技术进步奖二等奖
3	特大型水电站深埋洞室群爆破施工控制理论与关键技术	湖北省科学技术进步奖一等奖
4	道路基础设施智能管养关键技术及应用	湖北省科学技术进步奖一等奖
5	高压富水复杂地层盾构成洞技术理论研究及应用	湖北省科学技术进步奖二等奖
6	黑臭水体精准诊断及强化减负修复关键技术与应用	湖北省科学技术进步奖二等奖
7	超大型垂直升船机金结埋件及设备精准安装技术创新与实践	四川省科学技术进步奖三等奖
8	安全高效现场混装爆破关键技术研究与应用	重庆市科学技术进步奖三等奖
9	数码电子雷管精细化爆破在改造陈旧海堤应用	电力建设科技进步奖二等奖
10	复杂条件大规模高密集锚索快速施工技术研究	电力建设科技进步奖二等奖
11	大型抽水蓄能电站机电管路标准化施工工艺研究	电力建设科技进步奖二等奖
12	特大型升船机施工安全控制关键技术	电力建设科技进步奖二等奖
13	大断面深竖井安全高效开挖施工关键技术	电力建设科技进步奖二等奖
14	大型竖井混凝土施工成套技术研究及应用	电力建设科技进步奖二等奖
15	大型地下洞室群异形混凝土结构施工成套装备	电力建设科技进步奖二等奖
16	硬岩长隧道TBM高效施工关键技术研究与应用	电力建设科技进步奖二等奖
17	平原地区输水建筑物底板高效施工关键技术	电力建设科技进步奖三等奖
18	大型水工建筑物深孔门槽快速施工技术研究暨获奖证书	电力建设科技进步奖三等奖
19	隧洞渐变段顶拱快速施工模板技术研究	电力建设科技进步奖三等奖
20	复杂地形地貌条件坝肩地质缺陷处理关键技术	电力建设科技进步奖三等奖
21	双曲拱坝坝肩槽开挖形体控制测量技术	电力建设科技进步奖三等奖
22	超大管径压力钢管立装制造自动焊接技术研究	电力建设科技进步奖三等奖
23	液压滑模技术在超长竖井砼浇筑施工中的应用	电力建设科技进步奖三等奖
24	高埋深TBM隧洞快速施工技术	电力建设科技进步奖三等奖
25	长斜井混凝土施工技术研究	电力建设科技进步奖三等奖
26	地下厂房桥式布料机浇筑系统研究与应用	电力建设科技进步奖三等奖
27	风电塔筒“移动工厂”制造技术研究与应用	电力建设科技进步奖三等奖

续表

序号	项目名称	获奖情况
28	光伏支架钢管立柱现场钻孔施工技术	电力建设科技进步奖三等奖
29	瓦房屋顶光伏安装技术	电力建设科技进步奖三等奖
30	藏中联网 500kV 输电线路施工技术研究	电力建设科技进步奖三等奖
31	光伏组件支架安装施工技术研究与应用	电力建设科技进步奖三等奖
32	马熊沟二级电站压力钢管混凝土施工技术研究	电力建设科技进步奖三等奖
33	软土地基高架桥施工支撑结构研究与应用	电力建设科技进步奖三等奖
34	预应力锚栓笼扩展式风机基础研究与应用	电力建设科技进步奖三等奖
35	砂石层接地斜井护管技术开发应用	电力建设科技进步奖三等奖
36	变电站防沙尘技术研究及应用	电力建设科技进步奖三等奖
37	导线弛度及间隔棒位置计算 APP 开发和应用	电力建设科技进步奖三等奖
38	宜昌市庙嘴长江大桥	中国施工企业管理协会科学技术奖一等奖
39	大型竖井混凝土施工成套技术研究及应用	中国施工企业管理协会科学技术奖一等奖
40	钢渣沥青混凝土在公路中的规模化应用关键技术研究	中国施工企业管理协会科学技术奖一等奖
41	堤防超深塑性混凝土防渗墙施工技术研究与应用	中国施工企业管理协会科学技术奖二等奖
42	深厚含砾石粉细砂层钻孔灌注桩施工关键技术研究与应用	中国施工企业管理协会科学技术奖二等奖
43	双塔双索面结合梁自锚式悬索桥施工关键技术	中国施工企业管理协会科学技术奖二等奖
44	复杂地质条件长隧洞 TBM 施工关键技术研究及应用	中国施工企业管理协会科学技术奖二等奖
45	超大桁距特大型钢桁拱桥架设及深水基础施工关键技术	中国施工企业管理协会科学技术奖二等奖
46	绩溪抽水蓄能电站超长斜井施工关键技术研究	中国施工企业管理协会科学技术奖二等奖
47	热带季风地区超长土坝高效优质施工关键技术研究与应用	中国施工企业管理协会科学技术奖二等奖
48	高大承重排架高效施工关键技术研究与应用	中国施工企业管理协会科学技术奖二等奖
49	岩石锚索内置挤压套锚固技术研究与应用	中国施工企业管理协会科学技术奖二等奖
50	乌东德水电站超深覆盖层超深基坑围堰施工关键技术	中国施工企业管理协会科学技术奖二等奖
51	复杂海洋环境下桥梁施工关键技术及应用	中国施工企业管理协会科学技术奖二等奖
52	大尺寸水轮发电机组安装精密测量技术	中国施工企业管理协会科学技术奖二等奖
53	向下送料连续浇筑竖井混凝土关键技术研究与应用	中国施工企业管理协会科学技术奖二等奖
54	景洪水力式新型升船机建设关键技术研究与应用	水力发电科学技术奖一等奖
55	喜马拉雅区域大埋深超长隧洞施工关键技术研究与应用	水力发电科学技术奖一等奖
56	特大型升船机施工安全控制关键技术	水力发电科学技术奖二等奖
57	乌东德水电站超深覆盖层超深基坑围堰施工关键技术	水力发电科学技术奖三等奖
58	大型竖井混凝土施工成套技术研究及应用	水力发电科学技术奖三等奖
59	环保科技创新实用成果	中国环境科学学会科技创新成果

续表

序号	项目名称	获奖情况
60	台阶爆破设计系统软件开发及应用	中国爆破行业协会科学技术奖一等奖
61	地下矿山智能采矿爆破技术与装备	中国爆破行业协会科学技术奖二等奖
62	emc-1便携式装药器研制与应用技术	中国爆破行业协会科学技术奖二等奖
63	大型竖井混凝土施工成套技术研究及应用	中国电力科学技术进步奖三等奖
64	乌东德水电站超深覆盖层超深基坑围堰施工关键技术	中国电力科学技术进步奖三等奖
65	强震区大岗山高拱坝复杂地层基础处理技术研究及应用	中国电力科学技术进步奖三等奖
66	山区大跨度特小半径曲线桥双导梁架桥机T梁架设技术	中国公路学会科学技术奖三等奖

（中国葛洲坝集团股份有限公司）

中国水利水电第五工程局有限公司 2018年科技成果获奖情况

中国水利水电第五工程局有限公司2018年科技成果获奖见表1。

表1 中国水利水电第五工程局有限公司2018年科技成果获奖情况

序号	项目名称	获奖情况
1	300m级高心墙堆石坝施工关键技术研究与应用	中国施工企业管理协会科学技术奖特等奖
2	门槽二期混凝土悬挂式自适应滑模研发与应用	中国施工企业管理协会科学技术奖二等奖
3	百米级特大整流锥式竖井进出水塔关键施工技术	中国施工企业管理协会科学技术奖二等奖
4	尾水隧洞开挖体型控制综合技术研究	中国施工企业管理协会科学技术奖二等奖
5	300m级高心墙堆石坝施工关键技术研究及应用	中国电力科学技术奖一等奖
6	强震区深厚覆盖层特高土石坝建设关键技术及工程应用	中国大坝工程学会科学技术奖一等奖
7	百米级特大整流锥式竖井进出水塔关键施工技术	中国大坝工程学会科学技术奖二等奖
8	高土石坝跨心墙道路减压板的研制与快速拆连方法	中国大坝工程学会技术发明奖三等奖
9	水工铜止水新型可调式成型与熔焊技术	中国大坝工程学会技术发明奖三等奖
10	大粒径心墙砾石土填筑质量检测设备及快速测定技术	水力发电科学技术奖二等奖
11	深厚覆盖层300m级砾石土坝关键技术研究	电力建设科学技术奖一等奖
12	“三心圆”异形超大型压力钢管制作安装技术	电力建设科学技术奖二等奖
13	冲击式水轮机配水环管安装施工技术	电力建设科学技术奖二等奖
14	混凝土大板试件取芯装置研制	电力建设科学技术奖三等奖
15	水电站厂房网架式钢屋架施工研究	电力建设科学技术奖三等奖
16	长坡面大面积无砂混凝土垫层施工技术研究	电力建设科学技术奖三等奖
17	复杂地质条件大型洞室开挖施工技术研究	电力建设科学技术奖三等奖
18	孔底加柔性垫层连同保护层一次爆除施工研究	电力建设科学技术奖三等奖

续表

序号	项目名称	获奖情况
19	大型抽水蓄能电站水轮发电机组轴线调整技术	电力建设科学技术奖三等奖
20	高级配混凝土布料机上料系统研发与应用	电力建设科学技术奖三等奖
21	百米级特大整流锥式竖井进出水塔关键施工技术	中国电力创新奖二等奖

（中国水利水电第五工程局有限公司　袁幸朝）

中国水利水电第八工程局有限公司 2018 年科技成果获奖情况

中国水利水电第八工程局有限公司 2018 年科技　成果获奖情况见表 1。

表 1　中国水利水电第八工程局有限公司 2018 年科技成果获奖情况

序号	项目名称	获奖情况
1	水泥灌浆智能控制系统关键技术和成套设备	中国大坝工程学会技术发明奖一等奖
2	构皮滩水电站垂直升船机特高塔体施工关键技术	中国大坝工程学会科技进步奖二等奖
3	500m 级深竖井大直径反井钻机一次成井施工关键技术	中国大坝工程学会科技进步奖二等奖
4	盾构侧穿 350km/h 高速铁路桥梁桩基综合技术研究	中国市政工程协会科学技术奖二等奖
5	景洪水力式新型升船机建设关键技术研究与应用	水力发电科学技术奖一等奖
6	基于岩体动力损伤仿真技术的角砾熔岩控制爆破	中国爆破行业协会科学技术奖二等奖
7	岩石基础垂直孔复合消能爆破开挖技术	中国爆破行业协会技术发明奖一等奖
8	复杂环境混合地层条件下地铁修建关键技术与应用	中国施工企业管理协会科学技术进步奖特等奖
9	软弱地层运营地铁隧道综合纠偏技术研究	中国施工企业管理协会科学技术进步奖二等奖
10	铁路桥梁静载试验自动控制装置的研制	中国铁道学会科学技术奖三等奖

（中国水利水电第八工程局有限公司　杨承志）

黄河水利科学研究院 2018 年科技成果获奖情况

黄河水利科学研究院 2018 年科技成果获奖情况　见表 1。

表 1　黄河水利科学研究院 2018 年科技成果获奖情况

序号	项目名称	获奖情况
1	黄河下游宽滩区滞洪沉沙功能及滩区减灾技术研究	中国大坝工程学会科学技术奖特等奖
2	黄河水沙冰凌输移模型库和标准构建及模拟系统研发与应用	大禹水利科学技术奖一等奖
3	黄河流域砒砂岩区辨识与抗蚀促生关键技术及应用	河南省科技进步奖一等奖
4	黄河下游河道综合治理关键技术研究及推广应用	中国产学研合作创新成果一等奖

（黄河水利科学研究院）

专利项目简介

河海大学 2018 年获得国家水利水电类专利情况

河海大学 2018 年度获得水利水电类国家授权专利情况见表 1。

表 1 河海大学 2018 年度获得水利水电类国家授权专利清单

序号	专利名称	专利类别	专利号	授权时间
1	一种柔性张拉的土工膜与土双面接触循环剪切试验装置及试验方法	发明专利	ZL201810089241.6	2018 年 12 月 7 日
2	一种水产养殖池塘底泥重金属稳定剂、其制作方法及其应用	发明专利	ZL201711018874.X	2018 年 9 月 21 日
3	一种厚度可调的西瓜瓜瓤切割专用刀具及其拆卸装置	发明专利	ZL201710579044.8	2018 年 10 月 30 日
4	一种提高城市泵站斜向进流箱涵流量分配均匀性的方法	发明专利	ZL201710799727.4	2018 年 11 月 30 日
5	表层床沙污染物吸附/解吸特性测量装置及其使用方法	发明专利	ZL201710438454.0	2018 年 4 月 3 日
6	一种用于水产养殖水体净化的微生态浮床及其使用方法	发明专利	ZL201710299350.6	2018 年 4 月 3 日
7	一种河塘底泥改性制备生态化填料的方法及其应用	发明专利	ZL201710440923.2	2018 年 9 月 25 日
8	清洗植物根部土壤的洗根机	发明专利	ZL201710233266.4	2018 年 3 月 6 日
9	风速-温度-湿度三场可调控的混凝土养护系统及方法	发明专利	ZL201710264278.3	2018 年 3 月 20 日
10	一种压电式波浪能发电装置及海上灯塔供电系统	发明专利	ZL201710181513.0	2018 年 10 月 9 日
11	一种压电传感器	发明专利	ZL201710106748.3	2018 年 8 月 28 日
12	一种带圆弧螺旋形叶片的冷却塔用双转轮水轮机	发明专利	ZL201611243298.4	2018 年 11 月 27 日
13	一种带阿基米德螺旋形叶片的冷却塔用双转轮水轮机	发明专利	ZL201611243331.3	2018 年 12 月 7 日
14	一种带对数螺旋形叶片的冷却塔用双转轮水轮机	发明专利	ZL201611243131.8	2018 年 12 月 7 日
15	一种增设分流装置的泵站虹吸式出水管	发明专利	ZL201611143984.4	2018 年 7 月 20 日
16	一种改善城市雨水泵站进水流态的组合式整流装置	发明专利	ZL201610993941.9	2018 年 12 月 25 日
17	梯级水库泄洪溶解气体过饱和预警系统和方法	发明专利	ZL201610865702.5	2018 年 1 月 16 日
18	一种计算拱坝裂缝宽度及确定防渗材料厚度的方法	发明专利	ZL201610933955.1	2018 年 7 月 6 日
19	一种分布式光纤测斜装置及测斜方法	发明专利	ZL201610683629.X	2018 年 8 月 21 日
20	一种制作不同几何形态沙坡的装置系统及制作方法	发明专利	ZL201610841540.1	2018 年 11 月 9 日

续表

序号	专利名称	专利类别	专利号	授权时间
21	一种感官水温记忆式自动回旋节水水龙头	发明专利	ZL201610835089.2	2018年8月21日
22	长距离供水管道事故快速关阀装置及方法	发明专利	ZL201610817616.7	2018年12月14日
23	研究水体温度在周期光照条件下变化规律的实验装置	发明专利	ZL201610804729.3	2018年5月11日
24	湖库浅水域藻种群生物量一体化量测装置与方法	发明专利	ZL201610808571.7	2018年7月24日
25	面向产粘沉性卵鱼类繁殖需求的梯级水库调控系统及方法	发明专利	ZL201610808570.2	2018年4月20日
26	一种室内潜流带区域地下水生成循环系统及操作方法	发明专利	ZL201610779356.9	2018年10月23日
27	一种基于天气预报描述性数据量化日照时数的方法	发明专利	ZL201610749607.9	2018年9月21日
28	一种集漩涡消涡和发电于一体的实验模拟装置	发明专利	ZL201610815096.6	2018年4月3日
29	一种省水船闸及其船舶过闸方法	发明专利	ZL201610829284.4	2018年8月17日
30	考虑软基固结和混凝土徐变的闸首施工仿真方法	发明专利	ZL201610499037.2	2018年9月25日
31	一种地下厂房多块体围岩变形的数值模拟方法	发明专利	ZL201610503822.0	2018年8月7日
32	一种新型建筑物隔震基础	发明专利	ZL201610389036.2	2018年4月10日
33	一种离心式提取土壤溶液的离心套管装置	发明专利	ZL201610310382.7	2018年12月18日
34	一种雨水收集与利用装置	发明专利	ZL201610328027.2	2018年1月19日
35	一种稻田渗滤液提取装置	发明专利	ZL201610541869.6	2018年9月25日
36	野外河床演变情况下测量潜流带实验装置及其实验方法	发明专利	ZL201610536369.3	2018年3月20日
37	一种监测洪水过程底泥中污染物释放的实验系统及其实验方法	发明专利	ZL201610538491.4	2018年6月19日
38	一种河流不同粒径泥沙就地分选系统及其使用方法	发明专利	ZL201610538492.9	2018年5月11日
39	监测水工程安全性态的分布式传感光纤声发射装置及方法	发明专利	ZL201610483276.9	2018年1月19日
40	分布式传感光纤声发射融合感知系统及运行方法	发明专利	ZL201610481845.6	2018年4月20日
41	水工混凝土结构服役性态光纤声发射感知装置及方法	发明专利	ZL201610481035.0	2018年6月19日
42	一种去温度干扰的传感光纤监测装置及使用方法	发明专利	ZL201610461443.X	2018年7月24日
43	混凝土坝应力应变多模块互校正式光纤监测装置	发明专利	ZL201610458038.2	2018年8月21日
44	集成声发射源扩张装置的水工程施工性态光纤感知设备	发明专利	ZL201610460606.2	2018年7月24日
45	一种堤坝渗流性状时空监控装置及监测方法	发明专利	ZL201610305697.2	2018年8月21日
46	一种传感光纤测渗增敏装置及使用方法	发明专利	ZL201610304115.9	2018年10月23日
47	一种渗流性态监测用传感光缆及使用方法	发明专利	ZL201610304598.2	2018年6月19日
48	一种基于体积法的泵站流量测法	发明专利	ZL201610271889.6	2018年11月23日
49	一种带生态池的灌溉渠道	发明专利	ZL201610388241.7	2018年12月14日
50	一种用于野外充电的便携式微型水力发电设备	发明专利	ZL201610279716.9	2018年5月29日

续表

序号	专利名称	专利类别	专利号	授权时间
51	一种带有可折叠类椭圆导流罩的便携式水力发电装置	发明专利	ZL201610281063.8	2018年9月4日
52	一种水工程渗流性态融合感知系统及方法	发明专利	ZL201610294922.7	2018年3月20日
53	一种基于距离势函数任意凸多边形块体离散单元法	发明专利	ZL201610218708.3	2018年6月8日
54	一种预制混凝土箱型结构与现浇混凝土结合式水闸闸墩结构及其施工工艺	发明专利	ZL201610093966.3	2018年4月3日
55	模型试验中桥墩冲刷坑实时动态超声测量方法	发明专利	ZL201610027199.6	2018年2月6日
56	一种空间预应力索杆体系整体安全性评价方法	发明专利	ZL201511026320.5	2018年5月8日
57	一种堤坝浸润线在线诊断装置及方法	发明专利	ZL201610091992.2	2018年12月14日
58	堤防快速堵漏设备	发明专利	ZL201610089486.X	2018年3月20日
59	涉水结构物及其基础渗流性态光纤自适应辨识系统及方法	发明专利	ZL201610088196.3	2018年1月19日
60	一种水利工程渗漏隐患光纤定位系统及定位方法	发明专利	ZL201610085986.6	2018年1月16日
61	一种恒压式田间土壤透气速率测定仪	发明专利	ZL201510890233.8	2018年4月20日
62	一种重塑土样制备装置	发明专利	ZL201510961444.6	2018年1月16日
63	一种低造价生态混凝土及其制备方法	发明专利	ZL201610086346.7	2018年3月9日
64	一种利用海洋能发电的能量搜集装置	发明专利	ZL201511016786.7	2018年2月23日
65	一种多功能无土栽培装置	发明专利	ZL201610068665.5	2018年5月11日
66	一种复合纳米生物质炭材料的制备方法及其应用	发明专利	ZL201610070845.7	2018年7月31日
67	非恒定流模拟试验中水深自动跟踪装置及方法	发明专利	ZL201610066184.0	2018年5月11日
68	非均匀颗粒离散单元快速线性接触检测方法	发明专利	ZL201610025242.5	2018年10月23日
69	一种水工模型用的雾化降雨强度测量装置及测量方法	发明专利	ZL201610013022.0	2018年9月21日
70	一种野外测量潜流交换量的实验装置及其实施方法	发明专利	ZL201610005840.6	2018年6月19日
71	期刊信息管理系统	发明专利	ZL201511017588.2	2018年8月21日
72	一种地震作用下高耸升船机塔柱结构动态分布系数分析方法	发明专利	ZL201510981346.9	2018年12月14日
73	一种干湿调控促转化-太阳能电动驱动定向运移-套作富集植物的镉污染稻田土壤联合修复方法	发明专利	ZL201510881965.0	2018年4月20日
74	一种计算不同状态挺水植被水流阻力的方法	发明专利	ZL201510524660.4	2018年3月27日
75	管道内水-气耦合瞬变流的模拟方法	发明专利	ZL201510819625.5	2018年8月17日
76	一种设施土壤抗蒸发剂及其制备方法	发明专利	ZL201510852987.4	2018年8月17日
77	一种微生物-电动联合修复设施连作酸化土壤的方法	发明专利	ZL201510812771.5	2018年8月21日
78	基于Godunov格式的有压管道中水柱分离的模拟方法	发明专利	ZL201510833139.9	2018年10月23日
79	一种基于三维CFD的液柱分离-弥合水锤的模拟方法	发明专利	ZL201510827880.4	2018年10月23日
80	一种褐煤微波干燥炉流场数值模拟方法	发明专利	ZL201510463785.0	2018年4月3日
81	一种生物活性钙及其制备方法和应用	发明专利	ZL201510330598.5	2018年10月23日

续表

序号	专利名称	专利类别	专利号	授权时间
82	基于云技术平台的混凝土施工质量智能可视化监控系统	发明专利	ZL201510263153.X	2018年8月31日
83	一种研究混凝土断裂过程区材料力学行为方法	发明专利	ZL201510226960.4	2018年3月9日
84	一种冷却水管管壁热交换系数测试装置及测试方法	发明专利	ZL201510252349.9	2018年4月3日
85	用于小型灌区的水田灌溉水利用系数测试系统及测试方法	发明专利	ZL201510138091.X	2018年7月24日
86	混凝土振捣质量监控反馈数据实时图形数字化通信方法	发明专利	ZL201410190266.7	2018年1月16日
87	一种大体积混凝土导温系数现场测定装置及测定方法	发明专利	ZL201310187117.0	2018年6月1日

（河海大学）

中国葛洲坝集团股份有限公司 2018年获得国家发明专利情况

中国葛洲坝集团股份有限公司2018年获得国家　　发明专利情况见表1。

表1　　中国葛洲坝集团股份有限公司2018年获得国家发明专利情况

序号	专利名称	专利类型	专利号	授权日期
1	一种隧洞洞挖及衬砌混凝土平行作业的施工方法	发明专利	ZL201510329584.1	2018年6月15日
2	一种小断面隧洞边墙衬砌立模施工装置	发明专利	ZL201610399564.6	2018年7月20日
3	闸坝溢流面混凝土免顶模快速施工方法	发明专利	ZL201610295544.4	2018年1月23日
4	多层施工吊篮	发明专利	ZL201610019015.1	2018年2月27日
5	闸墩牛腿钢筋施工方法	发明专利	ZL201610335602.1	2018年3月23日
6	跨河沉管整体安装的施工方法	发明专利	ZL201610413761.9	2018年3月23日
7	双连拱隧道中导洞拱顶回填施工方法	发明专利	ZL201610036578.1	2018年5月1日
8	一种大型结构钢筋无变形吊具及吊装方法	发明专利	ZL201710114355.7	2018年5月4日
9	挡流板截流装置及方法	发明专利	ZL201610376237.9	2018年6月26日
10	湿喷混凝土衬砌工作台车	发明专利	ZL201610736476.0	2018年7月27日
11	湿喷混凝土衬砌设备组合台车	发明专利	ZL201610736519.5	2018年11月9日
12	一种便于现场指挥的测量放样方法	发明专利	ZL201610958731.6	2018年11月9日
13	混凝土面板坝止水铜片碾压成型机	发明专利	ZL200510018571.9	2018年6月4日
14	有可伸缩及移动通道的大型管道系统	发明专利	ZL201610595076.2	2018年2月2日
15	适用于转弯段施工的钢筋台车	发明专利	ZL201610737658.X	2018年8月31日
16	一种变截面异型结构支墩清水混凝土一次成型的施工方法	发明专利	ZL201710221426.3	2018年11月2日
17	一种堆石坝垫层料的制备系统及方法	发明专利	ZL201610456226.1	2018年1月5日
18	深水钢护筒配接装置及方法	发明专利	ZL201610593169.1	2018年6月29日
19	圆角矩形截面隧洞混凝土衬砌用钢模台车	发明专利	ZL201610641616.6	2018年11月20日

续表

序号	专利名称	专利类型	专利号	授权日期
20	一种大坝冷却水换向及分水装置	发明专利	ZL201410266047.2	2018年4月10日
21	一种灌浆廊道永久伸缩缝渗水处理方法	发明专利	ZL201511016143.2	2018年4月10日
22	一种混凝土布料机浇筑系统	发明专利	ZL201511005419.7	2018年4月10日
23	一种模板止浆器	发明专利	ZL201610824188.0	2018年4月10日
24	一种可快速拆装悬挂梭式可逆供料线	发明专利	ZL201610938709.5	2018年4月10日
25	自动定位垂直转向变轨钢模台车	发明专利	ZL201610138421.X	2018年4月10日
26	一种适用于直线型隧洞轴线定位测量的装置及方法	发明专利	ZL201710374749.6	2018年9月11日
27	一种适用于大型地下洞室快速放样锚杆孔位的测量方法	发明专利	ZL201710378196.1	2018年9月11日
28	可适应变位的大齿轮周期性喷雾润滑装置	发明专利	ZL201610045659.8	2018年9月21日
29	一种升船机主机房钢格构柱施工方法及安装精度控制方法	发明专利	ZL201710284690.1	2018年12月7日
30	一种水力式升船机提升系统施工方法及安装精度控制方法	发明专利	ZL201710296884.3	2018年10月9日
31	一种水力浮动式升船机卷筒和同步轴系的装配方法	发明专利	ZL201710295878.6	2018年10月9日
32	分块式大型减震水箱钢结构突扩体	发明专利	ZL201710448748.1	2018年1月16日
33	一种用于水力浮动式垂直升船机竖井钢衬安装的同轴度测量装置及检测方法	发明专利	ZL201610739219.2	2018年7月31日
34	一种用于电缆敷设的制动系统及制动方法	发明专利	ZL201610697030.1	2018年7月6日
35	水力式升船机浮筒平衡重施工系统及方法	发明专利	ZL201610921680.X	2018年7月3日
36	一种松散覆盖层中顶管外壁触变泥浆润滑套成形的施工方法和检测设备	发明专利	ZL201610141265.2	2018年4月10日
37	一种自凝自稳复合土形成工艺及装置	发明专利	ZL201610137543.7	2018年6月29日
38	砂砾石层灌浆模拟装置以及利用该装置进行试验的方法	发明专利	ZL201610968472.5	2018年10月9日
39	可拆式混凝土变形缝止水型腔模的施工方法	发明专利	ZL201510918830.7	2018年5月18日
40	一种水工混凝土磷渣复合胶凝材料的制备方法	发明专利	ZL201610784292.1	2018年9月28日
41	一种水泥窑协同处置生活垃圾产生窑灰的处理装置及方法	发明专利	ZL201610762329.0	2018年9月28日
42	一种G级油井水泥及其加工工艺	发明专利	ZL201510338948.2	2018年10月12日
43	一种硅酸盐水泥熟料	发明专利	ZL201610668137.3	2018年5月18日
44	一种基于全站仪的空间目标的位置和朝向标定方法	发明专利	ZL201510737776.6	2018年5月29日
45	适合于上向孔爆破装药的高分子乳化剂及其制备方法	发明专利	ZL201510737153.9	2018年3月16日
46	耐热型多孔粒状铵油炸药及其制备方法	发明专利	ZL201510225125.9	2018年5月29日
47	精确控制结构面开挖倾斜向下光面爆破孔方向的方法	发明专利	ZL201611051482.9	2018年8月31日
48	高温乳化炸药冷却物料管系统	发明专利	ZL201610197311.0	2018年10月30日
49	低剪切乳化用高分子乳化剂及其制备方法	发明专利	ZL201510737987.X	2018年3月20日

续表

序号	专利名称	专利类型	专利号	授权日期
50	用于超宽船舶纵向移动的装置及方法	发明专利	ZL201610260880.5	2018年3月2日
51	一种支撑圆筒的安装方法	发明专利	ZL201610579544.7	2018年3月2日
52	一种适用于钢管与钢管斜交组合成形的焊接处理方法	发明专利	ZL201610482877.8	2018年7月3日
53	一种用于外圆磨削的装置	发明专利	ZL201310114821.3	2018年8月28日
54	一种升船机承船厢安装方法	发明专利	ZL201610596559.4	2018年10月9日
55	一种悬浮式重锤测斜仪及测量方法	发明专利	ZL201610176001.0	2018年5月8日
56	一种堆石体密度测试系统	发明专利	ZL201310343169.2	2018年4月10日
57	一种超高掺粉煤灰混凝土	发明专利	ZL201610003070.1	2018年3月6日
58	一种用于水电站地下厂房混凝土快速入仓的装置和方法	发明专利	ZL201610359062.0	2018年4月10日
59	一种恢复热脱附后土壤耕作性的方法	发明专利	ZL201610345651.3	2018年3月23日
60	高流动度吹填海泥防渗固化材料及其制备方法	发明专利	ZL201610633127.6	2018年8月24日
61	一种矿山充填用硅铝基尾砂胶结剂及其制备方法	发明专利	ZL201510278303.4	2018年3月23日
62	一种沥青混合料温拌剂的制备方法和应用	发明专利	ZL201710611042.2	2018年6月19日
63	漂浮式刮吸泥系统及刮吸泥的操作法	发明专利	ZL201510838865.X	2018年10月16日
64	大型设备旋转施工方法	发明专利	ZL201710048960.9	2018年10月9日
65	预埋式承重螺栓变形监测预警装置	发明专利	ZL201310229454.1	2018年4月10日
66	船用晶闸管可逆直流调速控制系统	发明专利	ZL201310118838.6	2018年4月10日
67	垂直向上钻孔用可调支撑架	发明专利	ZL201310232959.3	2018年9月28日
68	一种电气盘车控制装置及其方法	发明专利	ZL201610119498.2	2018年9月28日

（中国葛洲坝集团股份有限公司）

中国电建集团北京勘测设计研究院有限公司 2018年获得国家专利授权情况

中国电建集团北京勘测设计研究院有限公司 2018年获得国家专利授权情况见表1。

表1 中国电建集团北京勘测设计研究院有限公司2018年获得国家专利授权清单

序号	专利名称	专利类型	专利号	授权公告日
1	基于多源数据的地质结构面三维模型自动建模方法和系统	发明专利	ZL201510532062.1	2018年4月20日
2	一种工程地质内外业一体化的信息化系统	发明专利	ZL201510532049.6	2018年5月18日
3	用于重力坝岸边度汛缺口过流的挑、跌流消能结构	发明专利	ZL201610994532.0	2018年8月17日
4	一种赶鱼系统及赶鱼方法	发明专利	ZL201710018508.8	2018年9月28日
5	内加强月牙肋型钢岔管水压试验监测系统	发明专利	ZL201610140422.8	2018年12月21日

续表

序号	专利名称	专利类型	专利号	授权公告日
6	用于石质文物保护的高透气性水平防渗排水复合材料	实用新型	ZL201720232798.1	2018年1月23日
7	抽水蓄能电站过渡过程机组尾水管正压保证系统	实用新型	ZL201720537870.1	2018年2月9日
8	一种地震勘探无线三分量姿态采集器	实用新型	ZL201721112199.2	2018年5月4日
9	一种井下探测用抗压换能器	实用新型	ZL201721105957.8	2018年5月4日
10	洞室堵头周边止水结构	实用新型	ZL201721106013.2	2018年5月4日
11	一种狭窄陡峻河谷岸边全洞式溢洪道的布置结构	实用新型	ZL201721155732.3	2018年5月4日
12	一种狭窄陡峻河谷沥青混凝土心墙堆石坝的坝内防渗结构	实用新型	ZL201721162377.2	2018年5月4日
13	一种水利水电工程岸边泄洪洞的布置结构	实用新型	ZL201721155731.9	2018年5月4日
14	带有预埋压浆管的基础环型式的风力发电机基础结构	实用新型	ZL201721169026.4	2018年5月4日
15	一种河湖淤积泥沙生态清淤设备	实用新型	ZL201721177185.9	2018年5月4日
16	一种适用于海上风电低桩承台基础的抗冰结构	实用新型	ZL201721464105.8	2018年8月3日
17	一种治理浅层地下水污染的系统	实用新型	ZL201721468001.4	2018年8月3日
18	一种地下水污染的治理系统	实用新型	ZL201721462690.8	2018年8月3日
19	一种河湖珍稀种质资源迁移保护设备	实用新型	ZL201721566516.8	2018年8月3日
20	一种种质资源原位保护的清淤装置	实用新型	ZL201721566503.0	2018年8月3日
21	一种河湖污染底泥生态清淤一体化设备	实用新型	ZL201721559301.3	2018年8月3日
22	一种潜水平推式清淤系统	实用新型	ZL201721719031.8	2018年8月3日
23	一种潜泥滚吸式清淤系统	实用新型	ZL201721715316.4	2018年8月3日
24	水电站高压厂用电接地系统	实用新型	ZL201820082489.5	2018年10月19日
25	大孔径预应力锚固工程的推送锚固剂的工具	实用新型	ZL201820712267.7	2018年12月4日
26	一种油水分离式集水井	实用新型	ZL201820340484.8	2018年12月4日
27	一种井间电火花震源的发射电极头	实用新型	ZL201820341310.3	2018年12月4日
28	一种用于电法勘探电极的无线定位夹子	实用新型	ZL201820711647.9	2018年12月4日
29	灯泡贯流式水电站的轴承供油管路系统	实用新型	ZL201820340491.8	2018年12月4日
30	用于管道取水的可拆卸式取水口	实用新型	ZL201820340943.2	2018年12月4日
31	一种分区电热融冰弧形闸门的门槽结构	实用新型	ZL201820340485.2	2018年12月4日
32	一种适用于单母线分段接线的差动保护连接系统	实用新型	ZL201820341340.4	2018年11月30日
33	一种冲刷牵引式井下探测器	实用新型	ZL201721105958.2	2018年5月4日

（中国电建集团北京勘测设计研究院有限公司　吉乐琳）

中国电建集团成都勘测设计研究院有限公司 2018年获得国家专利授权情况

中国电建集团成都勘测设计研究院有限公司2018年获得国家专利授权256件，其中发明专利授权67件，见表1。

表 1 中国电建集团成都勘测设计研究院有限公司 2018 年获得国家授权发明专利清单

序号	专利名称	专利类型	专利号	授权日期
1	高土石不过水围堰边坡失稳风险率检测方法	发明专利	ZL201510170871.2	2018 年 4 月 3 日
2	用于沟水处理及泥石流防护的拦挡组合结构以及方法	发明专利	ZL201510337331.9	2018 年 11 月 13 日
3	企业网络安全事件管理系统及其方法	发明专利	ZL201510346924.1	2018 年 3 月 6 日
4	用于多引导线的三维定数布筋方法	发明专利	ZL201510420916.7	2018 年 6 月 21 日
5	三维钢筋模型隐藏和显示的处理方法	发明专利	ZL201510423840.3	2018 年 2 月 1 日
6	沥青心墙基座及其施工方法	发明专利	ZL201510650774.3	2018 年 2 月 8 日
7	边坡用植物钉	发明专利	ZL201510824757.7	2018 年 2 月 11 日
8	渗水管、植被恢复区节水灌溉系统及其施工方法	发明专利	ZL201510822117.2	2018 年 6 月 26 日
9	风力发电机组用浅埋基础结构	发明专利	ZL201510837180.3	2018 年 7 月 3 日
10	沟水处理排水洞结构和沟水处理排水方法	发明专利	ZL201510851901.6	2018 年 4 月 26 日
11	一种基于 DSI 插值的三维地质趋势面的生成方法	发明专利	ZL201510848538.2	2018 年 6 月 15 日
12	一种基于信息互通的专业间三维设计协同方法	发明专利	ZL201510846865.4	2018 年 6 月 5 日
13	一种生成原型水轮机运转综合特性曲线的方法	发明专利	ZL201511002955.1	2018 年 7 月 3 日
14	大坝下游管涌出口保护结构	发明专利	ZL201610103763.8	2018 年 9 月 18 日
15	一种导流隧洞封堵结构	发明专利	ZL201610137579.5	2018 年 10 月 12 日
16	一种适用于山区河流的流水景观需水量计算方法	发明专利	ZL201610159098.4	2018 年 5 月 4 日
17	迂回型鱼道回旋上升段休息池	发明专利	ZL201610162694.8	2018 年 5 月 29 日
18	软岩试样用饱水装置以及饱水方法	发明专利	ZL201610188819.4	2018 年 9 月 3 日
19	一种特定复合型蚀变岩/带综合抗压强度指标获取方法	发明专利	ZL201610223774.X	2018 年 3 月 27 日
20	隧道初期支护的加固方法	发明专利	ZL201610225659.6	2018 年 9 月 21 日
21	携剪试验制样装置以及制样方法	发明专利	ZL201610273892.1	2018 年 6 月 5 日
22	岩芯柜	发明专利	ZL201610291012.3	2018 年 2 月 6 日
23	水电中闸室补气结构	发明专利	ZL201610321703.3	2018 年 11 月 5 日
24	导流洞快速封堵结构及其封堵方法	发明专利	ZL201610334502.7	2018 年 1 月 22 日
25	用于水工围堰工程的复合防渗墙及其施工方法	发明专利	ZL201610494890.5	2018 年 4 月 4 日
26	用于山区河道导流明渠的消能结构	发明专利	ZL201610480547.5	2018 年 1 月 31 日
27	止浆防渗管片及隧道管片衬砌结构	发明专利	ZL201610474526.2	2018 年 5 月 3 日
28	用于沟水处理的排水洞漩流竖井消能结构及排水方法	发明专利	ZL201610606320.0	2018 年 5 月 4 日
29	岸坡防冲抗滑结构	发明专利	ZL201610605908.4	2018 年 7 月 31 日
30	山区复杂地质条件地区用引水渠道结构	发明专利	ZL201610615800.3	2018 年 6 月 28 日
31	升降箱体溢流坝	发明专利	ZL201610664463.7	2018 年 2 月 24 日
32	高烈度地区框架结构楼梯防震结构	发明专利	ZL201610664432.1	2018 年 10 月 10 日
33	一种复合型蚀变岩/带的工程地质分类方法	发明专利	ZL201610663338.4	2018 年 10 月 25 日
34	碾压式土石坝碾压次数的实验确定方法	发明专利	ZL201610670720.8	2018 年 7 月 4 日
35	适用于高地应力条件下的地下洞室群结构及其施工工艺	发明专利	ZL201610801715.6	2018 年 7 月 6 日

续表

序号	专利名称	专利类型	专利号	授权日期
36	深厚覆盖层地基防渗墙结构	发明专利	ZL201610802341.X	2018年5月3日
37	一种确定掺气设施通气孔断面面积的方法	发明专利	ZL201610802362.1	2018年7月5日
38	坝体防渗用层状复合材料、坝体防渗结构及其施工方法	发明专利	ZL201610802911.5	2018年11月6日
39	预警式双护盾TBM	发明专利	ZL201610881112.1	2018年5月4日
40	钢管混凝土拱桥的弦管组装结构	发明专利	ZL201610943935.2	2018年3月8日
41	TBM刀盘卡机时破碎岩体反扭矩模拟试验装置	发明专利	ZL201610944038.3	2018年12月21日
42	新建洞室的初期支护方法	发明专利	ZL201610976838.3	2018年8月6日
43	建于土料匮乏区深覆盖层上的高坝结构	发明专利	ZL201610979458.5	2018年11月6日
44	倒挂顶推式闸门	发明专利	ZL201610994469.0	2018年12月13日
45	双吊点拉杆闸门	发明专利	ZL201611002044.3	2018年8月2日
46	高心墙堆石坝坝底微拱型廊道结构	发明专利	ZL201610997779.8	2018年5月4日
47	过鱼设施的进鱼口结构	发明专利	ZL201611016295.7	2018年7月26日
48	一种土石坝坝体裂缝的修复方法	发明专利	ZL201611018999.8	2018年11月13日
49	设置在挡水坝内的鱼道系统	发明专利	ZL201611018834.0	2018年8月24日
50	用于混凝土坝接缝灌浆的悬臂键槽模板结构	发明专利	ZL201611018753.0	2018年5月4日
51	干旱地区高陡喷混边坡生态护坡结构	发明专利	ZL201611015911.7	2018年12月18日
52	取水口冲沙结构	发明专利	ZL201611018783.1	2018年12月13日
53	上游水位变幅较大工程用的鱼道系统	发明专利	ZL201611035350.7	2018年9月18日
54	挑梁式挡土墙结构	发明专利	ZL201611037365.7	2018年8月2日
55	一种混凝土重力坝横缝漏水处理结构	发明专利	ZL201611041088.7	2018年8月28日
56	基于迹线确定岩体结构面产状的方法	发明专利	ZL201611037229.8	2018年12月26日
57	混凝土坝横缝灌浆的方法	发明专利	ZL201611052962.7	2018年6月19日
58	水库浸没区砖混建筑地坪提升结构及工艺	发明专利	ZL201611070917.4	2018年3月27日
59	新增挑梁框架包钢锚拉法结构及工艺	发明专利	ZL201611067384.4	2018年7月25日
60	基于GOCAD的TRT测试成果解译方法	发明专利	ZL201710072916.1	2018年11月27日
61	覆盖层边坡过流保护结构	发明专利	ZL201710137814.3	2018年12月4日
62	双层主索索道桥	发明专利	ZL201710240483.6	2018年4月3日
63	索道桥桥台	发明专利	ZL201710344642.7	2018年6月27日
64	一种拱坝结构安全性的分析处理方法	发明专利	ZL201710373521.5	2018年11月5日
65	一种拱坝结构的安全评价方法	发明专利	ZL201710374587.6	2018年11月5日
66	一种硬岩隧道岩爆的主动防治方法	发明专利	ZL201710481115.0	2018年4月18日
67	贯流式水轮机基本参数计算方法	发明专利	ZL201710724349.3	2018年12月18日

（中国电建集团成都勘测设计研究院有限公司　吉华伟）

中国电建集团贵阳勘测设计研究院有限公司 2018 年获得国家专利授权情况

中国电建集团贵阳勘测设计研究院有限公司 2018 年获得国家授权专利情况见表 1。

表 1 中国电建集团贵阳勘测设计研究院有限公司 2018 年获得国家授权专利清单

序号	专利名称	专利类别	专利号	授权公告日
1	一种拱坝径向贯穿裂缝处理结构	实用新型	ZL201621445542.0	2018 年 1 月 2 日
2	一种挡土墙结构	实用新型	ZL201720589227.3	2018 年 1 月 2 日
3	一种坝内廊道荧光栏杆	实用新型	ZL201720663245.1	2018 年 1 月 2 日
4	一种隧洞勘探用仪器支架	实用新型	ZL201720663306.4	2018 年 1 月 2 日
5	一种混凝土压应力计安装方法	发明专利	ZL201610614106.X	2018 年 1 月 30 日
6	一种污水净化装置	实用新型	ZL201720655723.4	2018 年 1 月 30 日
7	一种用于新老混凝土层面结合的结构	实用新型	ZL201720676841.3	2018 年 1 月 30 日
8	一种坝顶轻型防护结构	实用新型	ZL201720703762.7	2018 年 1 月 30 日
9	一种覆盖层护坡排水结构	实用新型	ZL201720704146.3	2018 年 1 月 30 日
10	一种具有识别水位功能的水龙头装置	实用新型	ZL201720704539.4	2018 年 1 月 30 日
11	一种河道治理用多功能船	实用新型	ZL201720710300.8	2018 年 1 月 30 日
12	一种海绵城市社区生态型蓄水装置	实用新型	ZL201720710375.6	2018 年 1 月 30 日
13	一种城市内涝排水结构	实用新型	ZL201720710564.3	2018 年 1 月 30 日
14	一种高压条件下页岩气水锁效应评价装置	实用新型	ZL201720737984.0	2018 年 1 月 30 日
15	一种堆石坝面板变形监测装置	实用新型	ZL201720738194.4	2018 年 1 月 30 日
16	一种预制箱梁模板	实用新型	ZL201720765739.0	2018 年 1 月 30 日
17	一种边坡坡脚种植槽集排水结构	实用新型	ZL201720765789.9	2018 年 1 月 30 日
18	一种隧道进洞结构	实用新型	ZL201720766650.6	2018 年 1 月 30 日
19	一种可变介质孔中雷达试验装置	实用新型	ZL201720774007.8	2018 年 1 月 30 日
20	一种用于位移传感器检验的通用夹具	实用新型	ZL201720787249.0	2018 年 1 月 30 日
21	一种可变介电常数表面雷达试验装置	实用新型	ZL201720789812.8	2018 年 1 月 30 日
22	一种水垫塘结构	实用新型	ZL201720788022.8	2018 年 2 月 2 日
23	一种预应力锚索隔离支架安装结构	发明专利	ZL201510551104.6	2018 年 2 月 6 日
24	一种拦污排的架设方法及格栅可伸缩的拦污排浮筒	发明专利	ZL201610413787.3	2018 年 2 月 6 日
25	一种挡土斜墙的加固方法及结构	发明专利	ZL201610526777.0	2018 年 2 月 6 日
26	一种置于卸荷岩体上的混凝土趾板基础加固结构	实用新型	ZL201720714337.8	2018 年 2 月 6 日
27	一种小孔口整体铸造潜孔弧门	实用新型	ZL201720714338.2	2018 年 2 月 6 日
28	一种短桩梁锚联合支护结构	实用新型	ZL201720757540.3	2018 年 2 月 6 日
29	一种与引水渠相交的导流洞出口结构	实用新型	ZL201720781485.1	2018 年 2 月 6 日
30	一种岸基位置的土工膜系统	实用新型	ZL201720262109.1	2018 年 2 月 9 日
31	一种水电工程压力管道洞室群布置结构	实用新型	ZL201720930623.8	2018 年 2 月 9 日

续表

序号	专利名称	专利类别	专利号	授权公告日
32	一种风车式驱鸟器	实用新型	ZL201720756095.9	2018年2月13日
33	野外斜坡地表入渗性能与渗透系数测量方法与装置	发明专利	ZL201410613641.4	2018年2月23日
34	一种提高水电站高耸混凝土结构抗震性能的装置	实用新型	ZL201720978085.X	2018年2月23日
35	一种山区风电场高陡弃渣边坡加筋锚固生态修复系统	发明专利	ZL201610017762.1	2018年2月27日
36	一种表孔弧形闸门V型底止水的改进方法及结构	发明专利	ZL201610021693.1	2018年2月27日
37	一种集防渗膜锚固、截洪和通行为一体的结构	发明专利	ZL201610036729.3	2018年2月27日
38	一种水土流失监测设备	实用新型	ZL201720710596.3	2018年2月27日
39	一种水利胶水管的收放运输装置	实用新型	ZL201720774730.6	2018年2月27日
40	一种水利工程闸门区域水质水量检测设备	实用新型	ZL201720906338.2	2018年2月27日
41	一种带辅助测量装置的回弹仪	发明专利	ZL201510185364.6	2018年3月13日
42	一种用于结构混凝土施工的标准化预埋组件及其施工方法	发明专利	ZL201510474228.9	2018年3月13日
43	一种应用于高土石坝抗震加筋的坝面点式防护结构	实用新型	ZL201720503381.4	2018年3月16日
44	一种引水隧洞结构	实用新型	ZL201720978055.9	2018年3月16日
45	一种桩基成孔钻遇岩溶的处理方法及封堵结构	发明专利	ZL201610335653.4	2018年3月27日
46	一种利用泄水洞拦挡树木的方法及装置	发明专利	ZL201610526813.3	2018年3月27日
47	一种特高水头定轮闸门的改进方法及定轮闸门	发明专利	ZL201610573328.1	2018年3月27日
48	溢洪道下游施工滞后时的临时发电方法及堆石自溃坝	发明专利	ZL201610612233.6	2018年3月27日
49	一种拦污栅槽的改进结构	实用新型	ZL201721107873.8	2018年3月27日
50	一种优化的水工隧洞结构	实用新型	ZL201721107903.5	2018年3月27日
51	一种可将弯曲钢筋伸直的简易工具	实用新型	ZL201721107927.0	2018年3月27日
52	一种生态式框架宾格护岸结构	实用新型	ZL201721109979.1	2018年3月27日
53	一种工程地震勘探聚能震源弹	实用新型	ZL201621323273.0	2018年4月3日
54	一种用于锚喷支护引水隧洞的新型集石坑结构	实用新型	ZL201720710398.7	2018年4月3日
55	一种位移传感器立式智能检验仪	实用新型	ZL201720787291.2	2018年4月3日
56	一种排水洞结构	实用新型	ZL201721026999.2	2018年4月3日
57	一种倒垂固定装置及其固定方法	发明专利	ZL201510988501.X	2018年4月6日
58	一种超宽水域横断面垂向水温日变化规律观测方法及系统	发明专利	ZL201610110695.8	2018年4月6日
59	一种水库坝前拦鱼警示缆索结构	发明专利	ZL201610194765.2	2018年4月6日
60	一种水库上下游及干支流鱼类栖息地综合保护系统	发明专利	ZL201610446965.2	2018年4月6日
61	一种尾矿库分隔坝结构及其施工工艺	发明专利	ZL201610584515.X	2018年4月6日
62	一种岩心结构面倾角测量尺	实用新型	ZL201721037494.6	2018年4月6日
63	一种海绵城市雨水收集净化装置	实用新型	ZL201721261191.2	2018年4月17日
64	一种自来水厂生产废水的处理方法及装置	发明专利	ZL201510997167.4	2018年4月20日
65	一种特细砂水工大体积常态混凝土	发明专利	ZL201610413406.1	2018年4月20日
66	一种地下空洞三维结构探测装置	实用新型	ZL201721084909.5	2018年4月27日

续表

序号	专利名称	专利类别	专利号	授权公告日
67	一种悬挂漂浮式拦污装置	实用新型	ZL201721309538.6	2018年5月1日
68	一种潜孔平面全水柱钢闸门门叶结构	实用新型	ZL201721300023.X	2018年5月4日
69	一种平面定轮闸门主轨道的改进结构	实用新型	ZL201721301300.9	2018年5月4日
70	一种高窄潜孔平面滑动事故闸门结构	实用新型	ZL201721309110.1	2018年5月4日
71	一种潜孔弧门侧轨的结构	实用新型	ZL201721309539.0	2018年5月4日
72	一种用于表孔弧门的双向止水装置	实用新型	ZL201721309141.7	2018年5月8日
73	一种高窄孔口表孔弧门与液压机的连接结构	实用新型	ZL201721309144.0	2018年5月8日
74	一种潜孔平面闸门喇叭口式通气结构	实用新型	ZL201721309145.5	2018年5月8日
75	一种城市排水用的排浸结构	实用新型	ZL201721350020.7	2018年5月8日
76	一种改善护坦受力条件的结构	实用新型	ZL201721351248.8	2018年5月8日
77	用于重力坝接触灌浆的止浆座结构	实用新型	ZL201721367945.2	2018年5月8日
78	一种光伏支架	实用新型	ZL201720769632.3	2018年5月11日
79	对风力电场临时施工道路的改造方法及植草路面结构	发明专利	ZL201510622515.X	2018年5月15日
80	一种管廊内外结合的排水系统结构	实用新型	ZL201720994358.X	2018年5月15日
81	一种表孔弧门底水封装置	实用新型	ZL201721306836.X	2018年5月15日
82	一种新型复合挡墙	实用新型	ZL201720464740.X	2018年5月29日
83	一种水池的集沙结构	实用新型	ZL201721132407.5	2018年5月29日
84	一种升船机自动过鱼装置	实用新型	ZL201721248913.0	2018年5月29日
85	一种诱鱼丁坝	实用新型	ZL201721248924.9	2018年5月29日
86	一种金属蜗壳钢衬底部接触灌浆布置结构	实用新型	ZL201721248966.2	2018年5月29日
87	一种轨道槽的排水孔结构	实用新型	ZL201721251634.X	2018年5月29日
88	一种水电站室内开关站	实用新型	ZL201721251641.X	2018年5月29日
89	一种设置过鱼通道的生态型升船机	实用新型	ZL201721260997.X	2018年5月29日
90	一种水电站厂房楼板的排水沟结构	实用新型	ZL201721261783.4	2018年5月29日
91	一种墙体中部的暗柱结构	实用新型	ZL201721261785.3	2018年5月29日
92	一种水库施工期临时供水结构	实用新型	ZL201721297809.0	2018年5月29日
93	一种独立鱼箱过鱼式升船机	实用新型	ZL201721298473.X	2018年5月29日
94	一种人工鱼巢	实用新型	ZL201721300192.3	2018年5月29日
95	一种船闸消防管过鱼结构	实用新型	ZL201721304484.4	2018年5月29日
96	一种表面观测墩模板	实用新型	ZL201721369130.8	2018年5月29日
97	一种涵洞式钢坝闸门顶止水结构	实用新型	ZL201721439307.7	2018年5月29日
98	压力钢管接触灌浆预埋管布置结构	实用新型	ZL201721453856.X	2018年5月29日
99	一种排架柱与墙体的连接结构	实用新型	ZL201721464950.5	2018年5月29日
100	一种浮动式发电机组泄流水温观测装置及其安装方法	发明专利	ZL201510650488.7	2018年6月01日
101	一种基于地形地貌条件的鱼类栖息地划分方法	发明专利	ZL201610412188.X	2018年6月01日

（中国电建集团贵阳勘测设计研究院有限公司　汪飞）

中国水利水电第五工程局有限公司 2018年获得国家专利授权和软件著作权登记证书情况

中国水利水电第五工程局有限公司2018年获得国家专利授权159件，其中发明专利15件，实用新型专利140件，外观设计专利4件。专利授权情况见表1。

表1 中国水利水电第五工程局有限公司2018年获得的专利授权情况

序号	专利名称	专利类型	申请号	授权公告日
1	一种竖井下弯段上部混凝土滑模施工方法	发明专利	ZL201610033890.5	2018年1月26日
2	一种变截面桥墩的支撑装置	发明专利	ZL201610188881.3	2018年1月26日
3	一种用于混凝土面层施工的一体化设备	发明专利	ZL201610451624.4	2018年1月26日
4	一种振动碾自动操作系统及其使用方法	发明专利	ZL201610063981.3	2018年3月27日
5	一种高塑性混凝土及控制其拌合性能的方法	发明专利	ZL201610514380.X	2018年4月17日
6	一种用于边坡混凝土防护的一体设备	发明专利	ZL201610789261.5	2018年5月4日
7	一种自动控制轨道测量小车及轨道测量方法	发明专利	ZL201610973430.0	2018年5月4日
8	一种用于排水沟槽的衬砌装置	发明专利	ZL201610793722.6	2018年6月5日
9	一种可变弧桥梁落地支架装置	发明专利	ZL201611202998.9	2018年7月20日
10	一种用于陡坡定向爆破的布炮机器人	发明专利	ZL201610573841.0	2018年8月21日
11	一种砂浆空心砖预制机	发明专利	ZL201610664234.5	2018年9月21日
12	一种陡坡定向爆破掩体防护装置	发明专利	ZL201610575309.2	2018年10月19日
13	泥炭土坝基的处理方法	发明专利	ZL201610791951.4	2018年10月19日
14	一种振动平碾循环碾压施工方法	发明专利	ZL201611241578.1	2018年11月9日
15	用于爆破孔的聚能槽切割装置	发明专利	ZL201710327507.1	2018年12月28日
16	一种水利水电工程防沉没浮体	实用新型	ZL201720516335.8	2018年1月26日
17	一种双曲面椎体的固定装置	实用新型	ZL201720214412.4	2018年1月26日
18	一种脱模器	实用新型	ZL201720512962.4	2018年1月26日
19	一种深孔平面闸门门槽埋件安装装置	实用新型	ZL201720473182.3	2018年1月26日
20	一种用于回填注浆的装置	实用新型	ZL201720513882.0	2018年1月26日
21	一种用于T梁负弯矩张拉千斤顶定位的托架装置	实用新型	ZL201720584277.2	2018年1月26日
22	用于爆破孔的聚能槽切割装置	实用新型	ZL201720512931.9	2018年1月26日
23	一种铲斗斗唇	实用新型	ZL201720356560.X	2018年2月9日
24	一种钢筋预弯工装	实用新型	ZL201720372836.3	2018年2月9日
25	一种有砟轨道快速多功能施工设备	实用新型	ZL201710593919.X	2018年2月9日
26	一种上坝料可移动式自动加水系统	实用新型	ZL201720601509.0	2018年2月9日
27	一种切割圆板固定割枪支架	实用新型	ZL201720376800.2	2018年2月9日
28	一种砾石土洗筛装置	实用新型	ZL201720356573.7	2018年2月9日
29	一种高强钢压力钢管组圆装置	实用新型	ZL201720513112.6	2018年2月9日
30	一种坡面铜止水定位装置	实用新型	ZL201720421938.X	2018年2月9日

续表

序号	专利名称	专利类型	申请号	授权公告日
31	一种步履式多点同步顶推工作平台	实用新型	ZL201720659659.7	2018年2月9日
32	一种便携气压式模板脱模剂刷涂装置	实用新型	ZL201720600272.4	2018年2月9日
33	一种用于桥梁斜腹板振捣的装置	实用新型	ZL201720632228.1	2018年2月9日
34	一种钢绞线解盘简易架	实用新型	ZL201720583819.4	2018年2月9日
35	一种用于定向预裂爆破的装药装置	实用新型	ZL201720584019.4	2018年2月9日
36	一种桥面防撞墙钢筋定位安装装置	实用新型	ZL201720513049.6	2018年2月9日
37	一种边墙衬砌台车混凝土浇筑旋转可伸缩快速输料装置	实用新型	ZL201720810943.X	2018年2月9日
38	一种墩柱施工作业平台	实用新型	ZL201720695344.8	2018年2月9日
39	一种环保型高速压浆料搅拌机	实用新型	ZL201720792323.8	2018年2月9日
40	一种地下综合管廊深基坑降水管井水泵限位自动启停装置	实用新型	ZL201720793135.7	2018年2月9日
41	一种固定橡胶支座的夹具	实用新型	ZL201720840153.6	2018年2月9日
42	一种牵引移动式趾板灌浆系统	实用新型	ZL201720793112.6	2018年2月9日
43	一种无机结合料试件的制作和脱模装置	实用新型	ZL201720889559.3	2018年2月9日
44	一种预制板运输小车	实用新型	ZL201720814918.9	2018年2月9日
45	一种异形混凝土自动洒水养护装置	实用新型	ZL201720795649.6	2018年2月9日
46	一种发电机定子铁损实验装置	实用新型	ZL201720811078.0	2018年2月9日
47	一种放炮后尘土及炮烟有害物质清除装置	实用新型	ZL201720863426.9	2018年2月9日
48	一种防渗土工膜垫层中混凝土与土石回填区的过渡结构	实用新型	ZL201720585171.4	2018年2月9日
49	一种边坡潜孔钻机钻孔操作平台	实用新型	ZL201720695371.5	2018年2月9日
50	绿色环保型油桶存放平台	实用新型	ZL201720963408.8	2018年2月13日
51	一种截水、防雨保护心墙接触黏土的装置	实用新型	ZL201720928374.9	2018年2月27日
52	一种砂砾石分段预埋阻塞灌浆装置	实用新型	ZL201710599430.3	2018年2月27日
53	一种现浇箱梁组合侧模支撑系统	实用新型	ZL201720928373.4	2018年2月27日
54	一种水电工程中锈蚀螺帽拆除装置	实用新型	ZL201710629223.8	2018年2月27日
55	一种原状土取样试模	实用新型	ZL201720562912.7	2018年3月16日
56	一种轻型动力触探仪	实用新型	ZL201710686269.3	2018年3月16日
57	一种针梁台车混凝土分料装置	实用新型	ZL201721004037.7	2018年3月16日
58	一种针梁台车上预埋灌浆钻孔的导向定位装置	实用新型	ZL201721016921.2	2018年3月16日
59	一种斜坡面泥浆涂刷装置	实用新型	ZL201720928372.X	2018年3月16日
60	一种水轮机筒阀同步调整装置	实用新型	ZL201721036120.2	2018年3月16日
61	一种带伸缩软管的针梁台车混凝土分料装置	实用新型	ZL201721003990.X	2018年3月16日
62	一种钢筋弯曲机	实用新型	ZL201721003513.3	2018年3月16日
63	一种用于公路陡坡地形的截水沟结构	实用新型	ZL201721036121.7	2018年3月16日
64	一种用于隧道爆破粉尘除尘的布墙台车	实用新型	ZL201720965962.X	2018年4月10日
65	一种长杆液压启闭机竖立、吊装装置	实用新型	ZL201721082438.4	2018年4月10日

续表

序号	专利名称	专利类型	申请号	授权公告日
66	一种油罐运输、安装一体化装置	实用新型	ZL201710887895.9	2018年4月10日
67	一种拐臂止推压板轴向间隙测量装置	实用新型	ZL201721176403.7	2018年4月10日
68	一种可折叠的超径料筛选剔除装置	实用新型	ZL201721004023.5	2018年4月10日
69	一种路面垫层填料超径料车载移动式剔除装置	实用新型	ZL201721082183.1	2018年4月10日
70	一种多级边坡截污沉淀箱	实用新型	ZL201721082534.9	2018年4月10日
71	一种井筒模板支撑装置	实用新型	ZL201710826380.8	2018年4月10日
72	一种无支架可拆卸伸缩式缓降装置	实用新型	ZL201721208308.0	2018年4月10日
73	一种可拆卸式三脚架装置	实用新型	ZL201721204920.0	2018年4月10日
74	一种混凝土垫块预制装置	实用新型	ZL201721248311.5	2018年4月10日
75	一种水利水电工程混凝土检测用骨料快速烘干箱	实用新型	ZL201721204899.4	2018年4月10日
76	振动碾液压油缺油报警保护装置	实用新型	ZL201710854030.2	2018年4月10日
77	一种道路结构层摊铺施工钢模板支撑体系	实用新型	ZL201721263427.6	2018年5月1日
78	一种用于高瓦斯隧道施工的多功能托架装置	实用新型	ZL201721263457.7	2018年5月1日
79	一种隧道台车定时自动水雾帘幕装置	实用新型	ZL201721263577.7	2018年5月1日
80	一种拌和系统自动控制多用出料口	实用新型	ZL201721007865.6	2018年5月4日
81	一种防止碰撞开裂的蓄能式吊罐	实用新型	ZL201720966021.8	2018年5月4日
82	一种清理雨污水井杂物的工具	实用新型	ZL201721297125.0	2018年5月4日
83	一种用于锚杆的自锚装置	实用新型	ZL201721297385.8	2018年5月4日
84	一种砖砌体简易搭设支架	实用新型	ZL201721248225.4	2018年5月4日
85	一种钢管焊接地线装置	实用新型	ZL201711135361.7	2018年6月1日
86	一种高流速大断面泄洪洞低坍落度混凝土入仓系统	实用新型	ZL201721531143.0	2018年6月1日
87	一种气压平衡式宽广起伏场地保温防雨材料快速收放机	实用新型	ZL201721248227.3	2018年6月1日
88	一种用于风动钻机钻孔孔口的除尘装置	实用新型	ZL201721566314.3	2018年6月1日
89	一种扰动土试样制备系统	实用新型	ZL201721561319.7	2018年6月1日
90	一种防扬尘混凝土搅拌系统	实用新型	ZL201721566277.6	2018年6月1日
91	一种排水用报警装置	实用新型	ZL201721561365.7	2018年6月1日
92	一种便携式道路结构层厚度检测装置	实用新型	ZL201721611194.4	2018年6月1日
93	一种建筑施工用钢筋校直机	实用新型	ZL201711187814.0	2018年7月6日
94	一种盾构机加固型刀盘	实用新型	ZL201721651175.4	2018年7月6日
95	一种用于开凿山体沟渠的一体化破碎装置的清理装置	实用新型	ZL201721561296.X	2018年7月6日
96	一种用于斜面岩壁的炮孔打孔装置	实用新型	ZL201721528409.6	2018年7月6日
97	一种二衬堵头钢端模	实用新型	ZL201721610935.7	2018年7月6日
98	一种双台车式隧道压浆机	实用新型	ZL201721611193.X	2018年7月6日
99	一种用于隧道二衬的带模负压压浆系统及压浆方法	实用新型	ZL201721669035.X	2018年7月6日
100	一种平石安装工具	实用新型	ZL201720513374.2	2018年7月6日
101	一种利用半自动切割机自动切割坡口的工装	实用新型	ZL201721803330.X	2018年7月6日

续表

序号	专利名称	专利类型	申请号	授权公告日
102	一种盾构机刀盘	实用新型	ZL201721712465.5	2018年7月6日
103	一种高速公路防风防眩板	实用新型	ZL201721738449.3	2018年7月6日
104	一种用于隧道爆破后局部循环降尘的装置	实用新型	ZL201721713207.9	2018年7月6日
105	一种坝体料斜坡摊铺装置	实用新型	ZL201721717503.6	2018年7月6日
106	一种水轮机水导油盆负压消除装置	实用新型	ZL201721670287.4	2018年7月17日
107	一种施工用道渣清筛机	实用新型	ZL2017217430608	2018年8月7日
108	一种水电站超大型压力钢管翻转、焊接一体化装置	实用新型	ZL201820027825.6	2018年8月7日
109	一种折叠式吊篮	实用新型	ZL201721776001.0	2018年8月7日
110	一种预制梁张拉施工升降作业平台	实用新型	ZL201721803366.8	2018年8月7日
111	一种挤压边墙定型模板	实用新型	ZL201721775764.3	2018年8月7日
112	一种混凝土材料层间黏结强度检测装置	实用新型	ZL201820051356.1	2018年8月7日
113	一种双通道电加热水管	实用新型	ZL201721829539.3	2018年9月7日
114	一种水泥石灰土摊铺装置	实用新型	ZL201721827133.1	2018年9月7日
115	一种锚杆拉拔力检测装置	实用新型	ZL201820098836.3	2018年9月7日
116	一种夹尺器装置	实用新型	ZL201820299328.1	2018年9月7日
117	一种简易的活动导叶安拆装置	实用新型	ZL201820098825.5	2018年9月7日
118	一种渗滤节水循环系统	实用新型	ZL201820115705.1	2018年9月7日
119	一种边坡六棱块压缝装置	实用新型	ZL201820052023.0	2018年9月7日
120	一种压力钢管弧度测量装置	实用新型	ZL201820299288.0	2018年9月7日
121	一种具有夹持体的防滑直螺纹连接套筒	实用新型	ZL201820049973.8	2018年9月7日
122	一种混凝土时控自动喷水养护装置	实用新型	ZL201820209766.4	2018年10月2日
123	一种自撑式竖井压力钢管安装平台	实用新型	ZL201820151188.3	2018年10月2日
124	一种轴流转浆式转轮翻身装置	实用新型	ZL201820238140.6	2018年10月2日
125	一种下机架拼装工装	实用新型	ZL201820143017.6	2018年10月2日
126	一种桥墩翻模法模板拆除装置	实用新型	ZL201820098779.9	2018年10月2日
127	一种洪水和泥石流实时检测报警装置	实用新型	ZL201820337588.3	2018年10月2日
128	一种坝料自动加水系统报警装置	实用新型	ZL2018203231124	2018年10月2日
129	轴流转浆式转轮翻转回转轴吊耳装置	外观设计	ZL201830200939.1	2018年10月2日
130	一种用于混凝土养护的电加热水管	实用新型	ZL201820238158.6	2018年10月2日
131	一种路拌法一体化智能施工装置	实用新型	ZL201721827106.4	2018年10月26日
132	一种用于隧道二衬空腔检测的便携式自导向成像装置	实用新型	ZL201820098877.2	2018年10月26日
133	一种可移独脚桅杆吊装装置	实用新型	ZL201820279163.1	2018年10月26日
134	一种组合工字钢梁安装装置	实用新型	ZL201820280412.9	2018年10月26日
135	一种城门洞型小断面衬砌模板支撑系统	实用新型	ZL201820323106.9	2018年10月26日
136	一种可拆卸链式压重体	实用新型	ZL201820323246.6	2018年10月26日
137	一种洪水检测传感器	实用新型	ZL201820337578X	2018年10月26日
138	一种激光式干砌石夜间砌筑控制装置	实用新型	ZL201820280404.4	2018年10月26日

续表

序号	专利名称	专利类型	申请号	授权公告日
139	一种干砌石砌筑控制装置	实用新型	ZL201820280402.5	2018年10月26日
140	一种公路用隔音板	实用新型	ZL201820279164.6	2018年10月26日
141	一种泥石流检测传感装置	实用新型	ZL201820337657.0	2018年11月20日
142	一种充气式防风反光路锥	实用新型	ZL201820279129.4	2018年11月20日
143	一种预制梁混凝土蓄水养生装置	实用新型	ZL201820323276.7	2018年11月20日
144	一种水下填料抛填系统	实用新型	ZL201820375111.4	2018年11月20日
145	一种高圆柱墩分节施工辅助设施	实用新型	ZL201820345349.2	2018年11月20日
146	混凝土面板浇筑表面保温材料铺设装置	外观设计	ZL201830168987.7	2018年11月20日
147	一种组合式水轮发电机转子吊装辅助平台	实用新型	ZL201820345392.9	2018年11月20日
148	一种接地铜排半自动弯折装置	实用新型	ZL201820345666.4	2018年11月20日
149	一种接触黏土快速补水装置	实用新型	ZL201820345466.9	2018年11月20日
150	一种制动器严密性耐压试验辅助测试装置	实用新型	ZL201820666454.6	2018年12月7日
151	一种路基边坡作业台车	实用新型	ZL201820299507.5	2018年12月7日
152	一种液压平移卸车装置	实用新型	ZL201820151246.2	2018年12月7日
153	一种编织袋提袋架	实用新型	ZL201820311774.X	2018年12月7日
154	一种用于隧道施工逃生管道的连接弯头	实用新型	ZL201820450424.1	2018年12月7日
155	一种混凝土面板浇筑表面保温材料铺设装置	实用新型	ZL201820577277.4	2018年12月7日
156	一种混凝土溜送缓冲装置	实用新型	ZL201820451811.7	2018年12月7日
157	一种保证刷握与集电环间隙一致的装置	实用新型	ZL201820625303.6	2018年12月7日
158	混凝土试块钳	外观设计	ZL201830344096.2	2018年12月7日
159	一种轮式划线装置	外观设计	ZL201830331624.0	2018年12月7日

由中国水利水电第五工程局有限公司完成的16项软件成果，2018年获得中华人民共和国国家版权局颁发的计算机软件著作权登记证书，有关情况见表2。

表2 中国水利水电第五工程局有限公司2018年获得的计算机软件著作权证书情况

序号	软件著作权名称	登记号	登记日期	登记证书号
1	CAD对象属性批量导出程序软件	2018SR057135	2018年1月24日	软著登字第2386230
2	多格式电子水准数据后处理软件	2018SR057135	2018年1月24日	软著登字第2386236
3	基础支护土压力计算程序系统	2018SR119738	2018年2月23日	软著登字第2448833
4	CAD边界面积自动导入Excel表宏系统	2018SR119526	2018年2月23日	软著登字第2448621
5	悬式水轮发电机组轴线调整系统	2018SR158038	2018年3月9日	软著登字第2487133
6	水轮发电机定子铁损试验数据分析软件	2018SR480045	2018年6月28日	软著登字第2819140
7	立式水轮发电机组各部件同心度计算与调整系统	2018SR480057	2018年6月28日	软著登字第2809152
8	抽水蓄能电站座环打磨量计算软件	2018SR458574	2018年6月28日	软著登字第2787669
9	立式水轮发电机组导轴承轴瓦间隙计算软件	2018SR535601	2018年7月18日	软著登字第2864696
10	ZSWJ高企管理系统	2018SR535597	2018年7月18日	软著登字第2864692
11	过磅大数据统计处理软件	2018SR734188	2018年9月11日	软著登字第3063283
12	临时试验室经营信息管理系统	2018SR734196	2018年9月11日	软著登字第3063291

续表

序号	软件著作权名称	登记号	登记日期	登记证书号
13	水轮发电机组转子配重量及方位计算软件	2018SR736119	2018 年 9 月 11 日	软著登字第 3065214
14	子企业科技创新管理系统	2018SR781042	2018 年 9 月 26 日	软著登字第 3110137
15	项目成本管理手机 App 系统软件	2018SR906009	2018 年 11 月 13 日	软著登字第 3235104
16	气瓶信息化管理系统	2018SR915291	2018 年 11 月 15 日	软著登字第 3244386

（中国水利水电第五工程局有限公司　袁幸朝）

中国水利水电第八工程局有限公司 2018 年获得国家专利授权和软件著作权登记证书情况

中国水利水电第八工程局有限公司 2018 年获国家专利授权 119 件，其中发明专利 13 件，实用新型专利 106 件。专利授权情况见下表 1。

表 1　　中国水利水电第八工程局有限公司 2018 年获得国家专利授权情况

序号	专利名称	专利类型	专利号	授权公告日
1	一种简支混凝土下料装置	实用新型	ZL201720681143.2	2018 年 1 月 5 日
2	一种旋转喷雾机平台	实用新型	ZL201720731802.9	2018 年 1 月 5 日
3	一种碾压混凝土铜止水固定架	实用新型	ZL201720729109.8	2018 年 1 月 5 日
4	一种预制墙板及其连接结构	实用新型	ZL201720492873.8	2018 年 2 月 2 日
5	一种预制构件模具	发明专利	ZL201610351449.1	2018 年 2 月 2 日
6	门槽混凝土垂直送料机	发明专利	ZL201610490194.7	2018 年 2 月 2 日
7	一种堆石混凝土专用预制模板系统	实用新型	ZL201720803474.9	2018 年 2 月 2 日
8	楼梯间预制隔墙	实用新型	ZL201720834177.0	2018 年 2 月 2 日
9	一种预设吊装孔的深基坑混凝土支撑结构	实用新型	ZL201720761115.1	2018 年 2 月 2 日
10	一种模板结构及其对拉螺杆张拉封堵装置	实用新型	ZL201720641169.4	2018 年 2 月 9 日
11	隧道掘进机背装式盘形滚刀紧固装置	发明专利	ZL201610783587.7	2018 年 2 月 9 日
12	一种强透水松散地层快速堵漏装置	实用新型	ZL201720923105.3	2018 年 2 月 16 日
13	一种骨料运输防破碎装置	实用新型	ZL201720921706.0	2018 年 2 月 16 日
14	一种用于带式输送机的卸料装置	实用新型	ZL201720922752.2	2018 年 2 月 16 日
15	一种用于控制混凝土坝温度的智能通水管路系统	实用新型	ZL201720957041.9	2018 年 2 月 27 日
16	一种接缝灌浆预埋管路装置	实用新型	ZL201720892427.6	2018 年 2 月 27 日
17	预制剪力墙纵向连接钢筋的校正装置	实用新型	ZL201720339917.3	2018 年 2 月 27 日
18	带预制外挂板的装配式建筑体	实用新型	ZL201720518959.3	2018 年 2 月 27 日
19	带预制隔墙的卫生间装配式建筑体	实用新型	ZL201720834600.7	2018 年 2 月 27 日
20	节能燃气锅炉	实用新型	ZL201720855850.9	2018 年 3 月 9 日
21	一种钻机断裂钻杆捕捞器	实用新型	ZL201721082842.1	2018 年 3 月 16 日
22	一种多层重叠空区并段台阶中深孔崩落处理方法	发明专利	ZL201510985526.4	2018 年 3 月 20 日
23	一种灌浆抬动装置	实用新型	ZL201721073415.7	2018 年 4 月 10 日

续表

序号	专利名称	专利类型	专利号	授权公告日
24	桥面系施工轨道吊运装置	实用新型	ZL201721107490.0	2018年4月10日
25	膺架现浇梁支架整体自动拆除装置	实用新型	ZL201721108365.1	2018年4月10日
26	一种用于胶带机输送带的保护装置	实用新型	ZL201721097941.7	2018年4月10日
27	一种用于止水埋设的卷筒装置	实用新型	ZL201720956567.5	2018年4月10日
28	棒磨机骨料输送器	实用新型	ZL201721045426.4	2018年4月10日
29	用于T梁钢筋绑扎的胎架结构	实用新型	ZL201721058800.4	2018年4月10日
30	桥面系施工轨道转运装置	实用新型	ZL201721108230.5	2018年4月10日
31	竖井井口模块化封口装置	实用新型	ZL201721192586.1	2018年4月10日
32	一种带式输送机的桁架提升装置	实用新型	ZL201720982991.7	2018年4月10日
33	S型双向旋转楼梯	实用新型	ZL201721193621.1	2018年4月10日
34	一种桥墩墩身钢筋的施工方法及钢筋骨架	发明专利	ZL201610163800.4	2018年4月13日
35	用于厂房的多功能皮带机混凝土输送系统	实用新型	ZL201721238985.7	2018年4月13日
36	砂浆铺设装置	实用新型	ZL201720892413.4	2018年4月13日
37	一种多跨高架桥梁的连续倾倒式拆除方法	发明专利	ZL201610909747.8	2018年4月17日
38	一种用于大体积碾压混凝土入仓的可提升钢栈桥装置	实用新型	ZL201721238983.8	2018年4月20日
39	一种防护架及防护结构	实用新型	ZL201721258062.8	2018年4月27日
40	跨线连续梁整跨拆除用组合支架	实用新型	ZL201721268946.1	2018年5月1日
41	弧形铜止水连续加工设备	实用新型	ZL201721271860.4	2018年5月1日
42	皮带拉力可调装置	实用新型	ZL201721184898.8	2018年5月1日
43	一种混凝土预冷及预热一体化装置	实用新型	ZL201721348754.1	2018年5月8日
44	一种污水处理系统中的泥浆位置检测装置	实用新型	ZL201721223601.4	2018年5月10日
45	一种土体沉降测试仪自定位沉降环	实用新型	ZL201721537995.0	2018年5月11日
46	用于钢栈桥钢管桩的多用途导向架	实用新型	ZL201721356215.2	2018年5月15日
47	一种旋转构件焊机地线连接装置	实用新型	ZL201721494682.1	2018年5月15日
48	一种测斜管	实用新型	ZL201721538011.0	2018年5月29日
49	一种消能预制件结构	实用新型	ZL201721453655.X	2018年5月29日
50	一种大体积混凝土冷水供应装置	实用新型	ZL201721462495.5	2018年5月29日
51	灌浆孔口快速连接器	实用新型	ZL201721477666.1	2018年6月8日
52	TBM内循环水系统	实用新型	ZL201721505497.8	2018年6月8日
53	一种隧洞混凝土养护修补台车	实用新型	ZL201721622213.3	2018年6月8日
54	一种地铁车站施工场地内便捷照明灯架	实用新型	ZL201721640237.1	2018年6月8日
55	一种通气孔免拆模板	实用新型	ZL201721571769.4	2018年6月8日
56	一种用于地铁运营隧道的地面纠偏回调方法	发明专利	ZL201510896063.4	2018年6月15日
57	焊机固定装置	实用新型	ZL201721638862.2	2018年6月15日
58	一种钢绞线穿线装置	发明专利	ZL201610647337.0	2018年6月22日
59	鄂破进料口堵石处理装置	实用新型	ZL201721097285.0	2018年6月22日
60	转子磁轭键槽拉刀的导向装置	实用新型	ZL201721579083.X	2018年6月22日

续表

序号	专利名称	专利类型	专利号	授权公告日
61	自升式液压止水模板	实用新型	ZL201721628638.5	2018年6月22日
62	一种大跨度洞室顶拱支护系统	实用新型	ZL201721690906.6	2018年6月22日
63	一种TBM边刀刀箱定位测量工具	实用新型	ZL201721629025.3	2018年7月3日
64	移动式脚手架	实用新型	ZL201721638806.9	2018年7月3日
65	可拆卸式预制混凝土围墙	实用新型	ZL201720324278.3	2018年7月6日
66	一种隧洞弧形底板混凝土拖模装置	实用新型	ZL201721731847.2	2018年7月6日
67	一种倒悬体预制混凝土模板装置	实用新型	ZL201721486637.1	2018年7月13日
68	一种预埋件堵浆装置及楼板预制结构	实用新型	ZL201721065973.9	2018年7月17日
69	一种预制保温外墙板	实用新型	ZL201721065647.8	2018年7月20日
70	高土石坝复合土工膜表面柔性应变计的安装结构及方法	发明专利	ZL201710018440.3	2018年8月7日
71	跨线连续梁拆除方法及拆除用支架	发明专利	ZL201610918643.3	2018年8月10日
72	一种可被翻越的错车平台	实用新型	ZL201820001954.8	2018年8月10日
73	一种大跨度多连拱拱式渡槽或桥梁的支撑系统	实用新型	ZL201820007214.5	2018年8月10日
74	一种灌注桩桩头的凿除装置	实用新型	ZL201820001875.7	2018年8月17日
75	一种埋弧焊机	实用新型	ZL201820055661.8	2018年8月17日
76	一种用于山地密林的测量棱镜头	实用新型	ZL201820151911.8	2018年8月17日
77	综合管廊	发明专利	ZL201610993530.X	2018年8月21日
78	用于公路面层的补缝条	实用新型	ZL201820058563.X	2018年8月24日
79	一种适用于水利施工的起重扒杆	实用新型	ZL201820041901.9	2018年8月24日
80	硫磺砂浆自动搅拌机	实用新型	ZL201820091569.7	2018年8月31日
81	用于轮轨式移梁机大车行走机构千斤顶的防脱落装置	实用新型	ZL201820131881.4	2018年9月7日
82	一种混凝土布料机重量限制器及混凝土布料机	实用新型	ZL201820135470.2	2018年9月7日
83	一种输送皮带接头胶接面的剥层装置	实用新型	ZL201820152135.3	2018年9月7日
84	一种用于检查孔封堵的吊封装置	实用新型	ZL201820109754.4	2018年9月14日
85	一种钢结构抹面平台	实用新型	ZL201820169374.X	2018年9月14日
86	一种土石围堰与混凝土围堰的交接面防渗装置	实用新型	ZL201820177649.4	2018年9月21日
87	一种防汛挡水装置	实用新型	ZL201820198959.4	2018年9月21日
88	布料机桁架伸缩驱动总成的支撑套架	实用新型	ZL201820232764.7	2018年9月21日
89	一种混凝土生产细骨料预冷装置	发明专利	ZL201510947954.8	2018年10月12日
90	一种预制构件灌浆缝密封装置	实用新型	ZL201820321609.2	2018年10月12日
91	一种预制集成储能墙板	实用新型	ZL201820321646.3	2018年10月12日
92	一种隧洞内简易起吊装置	实用新型	ZL201820347148.6	2018年10月16日
93	一种大风天气下大坝水平仓面保温被固定结构	实用新型	ZL201820354972.4	2018年10月26日
94	适用于混凝土廊道的保温门	实用新型	ZL201820377443.6	2018年10月26日
95	一种钢筋混凝土叠梁门挡水结构	实用新型	ZL201820377489.8	2018年10月26日
96	适用于冷却水管敷设的弧形间距定位卡	实用新型	ZL201820393714.7	2018年10月26日

续表

序号	专利名称	专利类型	专利号	授权公告日
97	一种预制构件斜支撑底部埋件及其预埋结构	实用新型	ZL201820390222.2	2018年10月26日
98	一种预制构件斜支撑及其安装结构	实用新型	ZL201820390906.2	2018年10月26日
99	一种预制构件存储、运输架	实用新型	ZL201820401648.3	2018年10月26日
100	一种预制构件堆放、运输架	实用新型	ZL201820401038.3	2018年10月26日
101	适用于混凝土坝的坝后装配式防护栈桥	实用新型	ZL201820392688.6	2018年11月9日
102	一种装配式预制构件的立体生产系统	实用新型	ZL201820492132.4	2018年11月9日
103	一种大风天气下混凝土廊道侧墙及底板的保温固定结构	实用新型	ZL201820442798.9	2018年11月16日
104	侧墙模板台车	实用新型	ZL201820570251.7	2018年11月16日
105	适用于岩质边坡的悬挑钢平台	实用新型	ZL201820393318.4	2018年11月16日
106	铁路箱型梁架桥机的绞座式前支腿	实用新型	ZL201820052110.6	2018年11月23日
107	一种土工CBR试件养护及收纳装置	实用新型	ZL201820545005.6	2018年11月23日
108	一种混凝土廊道预制件的定型模板	实用新型	ZL201820581427.9	2018年11月23日
109	适用于混凝土坝缓坡面的防护装置	实用新型	ZL201820392848.7	2018年11月23日
110	用于中顶板施工的模板台车	实用新型	ZL201820598775.7	2018年11月23日
111	收放式中顶板施工用模板台车	实用新型	ZL201820598878.3	2018年11月23日
112	覆盖层下溶洞发育地层的防渗施工方法	发明专利	ZL201610705475.X	2018年11月30日
113	一种装配式建筑现浇模板及封堵结构	实用新型	ZL201820492109.5	2018年12月7日
114	一种方管桁架连接结构	实用新型	ZL201820699167.5	2018年12月7日
115	一种施工现场用气瓶运输车	实用新型	ZL201820693552.9	2018年12月7日
116	一种易于卸渣的旋挖钻机钻头	实用新型	ZL201820771631.7	2018年12月18日
117	用于江边取水的悬挑式取水装置	实用新型	ZL201820801260.2	2018年12月18日
118	一种用于钻孔灌注桩钢筋笼的可拆卸吊筋系统	实用新型	ZL201820830885.1	2018年12月28日
119	TBM后配套设备轨道	实用新型	ZL201820823316.4	2018年12月28日

由中国水利水电第八工程局有限公司完成的3项软件成果，2018年获得中华人民共和国国家版权局颁发的计算机软件著作权登记证书，有关情况见表2。

表2 中国水利水电第八工程局有限公司2018年获得的计算机软件著作权证书情况

序号	软件名称	登记号	登记日期	登记证书号
1	BIM标准化云平台V1.00.11	2018SR238421	2018年4月9日	软著登字第2567516号
2	地铁车站施工监测数据管理与分析系统V1.0	2018SR239006	2018年4月10日	软著登字第2568101号
3	基于Matlab隧道近接施工影响分区的计算软件V1.0	2018SR412645	2018年6月4日	软著登字第2741740号

（中国水利水电第八工程局有限公司　杨承志）

哈尔滨电机厂有限责任公司 2018年获得国家专利授权情况

2018年，哈尔滨电机厂有限责任公司通过一系列管理举措，专利工作取得了优异的成绩，主要有：

（1）突出专利质量导向，引导技术部门从关注专利数量到关注专利质量和结构的转变。2018年共申报专利180件，其中发明专利60件；组织申报中国专利奖1项。

（2）对公司知识产权管理办法及工作流程进行修订和宣贯。举办专利培训达100余次。

（3）全面梳理和清查生产、经营过程中知识产权侵权风险较高的重点环节和重点领域，甄选有价值专利140件并建档。

（4）对白鹤滩机组等公司重点产品组织申报专利50件。

（5）对公司的专利逐项进行筛选和甄别，选取公司的配套产品、公司的通用型装置、工具类、已废业的热加工业务专利、保护期很长，技术已处于成熟期或下降期的专利形成双创项目转移转化清单，助力助推公司建立并实施的双创项目成果多渠道转移转化机制。

（6）对公司的核心产品的自由运作权进行认定，对其法律状态和权利归属进行分析论证，对已经发生的和即将发生的知识产权纠纷的相关技术进行鉴定，通过对侵权风险的专项分析和产品自由运作权的分析制定预警方案，应对知识产权风险，增加知识产权收益。

（7）做好国家级知识产权优势企业的复核和总结上报工作。

（8）“大型水电机组顶盖的修复方法”发明专利进入第二十届中国专利优秀奖预获奖项目。

公司2018年在水电方面共获得专利授权105件，其中发明专利10件，详见表1。

表1　　2018年水力发电设备获得国家专利授权情况

序号	专利名称	专利类别	专利号	授权时间
1	一种带稳流功能的液位计套筒安装结构	实用新型	ZL2018205226296	2018年10月12日
2	控制环耳孔用抗磨瓦的简易压装工具	实用新型	ZL2017206044248	2018年1月30日
3	悬式水轮发电机推力头热套固定结构	实用新型	ZL2017205519146	2018年1月30日
4	一种带有自平衡浮球及减震装置的浮球阀	实用新型	ZL201820374237.X	2018年10月12日
5	一种两用轴孔加工辅助工具	实用新型	ZL2018203768280	2018年10月12日
6	一种静止励磁系统的新型整流柜阻容保护装置	实用新型	ZL2018203772680	2018年10月12日
7	一种发电机定子端部整体刚度加强将结构	实用新型	ZL201820377502X	2018年9月21日
8	大型电机铂热电阻的直流电阻数据自动采集设备	实用新型	ZL2018204084813	2018年9月21日
9	一种立式水轮发电机铜环引线铜排间隔固定装置	实用新型	ZL201820485094X	2018年10月12日
10	大型水轮电机定子线圈斜边间隔块拆解钳	实用新型	ZL2018204911638	2018年10月12日
11	可变速抽水蓄能发电电动机转子铁心压紧结构	实用新型	ZL2018204973583	2018年10月12日
12	垫片式转轮静平衡工具	实用新型	ZL2018204973672	2018年10月12日
13	水轮发电机轴承用多点排油雾结构	实用新型	ZL2017205901959	2018年1月30日
14	水轮发电机推力轴承瓦中高压油阻尼结构	实用新型	ZL2017205901408	2018年1月30日
15	一种发电电动机滑转子结构	实用新型	ZL2017205891162	2018年5月11日
16	一种灯泡式水轮发电机推力轴承瓦温度检测结构	实用新型	ZL2017205896325	2018年1月30日
17	一种立式水轮发电机定子铁心测温单元	实用新型	ZL2017205896310	2018年1月30日
18	用于斜支臂上机架水轮发电机的基础连接机构	实用新型	ZL201720546997X	2018年6月1日
19	水电站进水阀接力器控制液动阀	实用新型	ZL2017205587942	2018年1月30日

续表

序号	专利名称	专利类别	专利号	授权时间
20	适用于水电站工程的机组轴承润滑油外循环冷却装置	实用新型	ZL2017205513614	2018 年 5 月 8 日
21	流道式三电极电解池	实用新型	ZL2017206471452	2018 年 1 月 30 日
22	水轮机大型阀体两端盲阀轴孔同轴度测量工艺方法	发明专利	ZL2016103174381	2018 年 1 月 30 日
23	水轮机活动导叶上下端面处过渡结构	实用新型	ZL2017205512541	2018 年 5 月 11 日
24	水轮机导叶打分半键工具	实用新型	ZL2017205775388	2018 年 5 月 8 日
25	转子引线定位工具	实用新型	ZL2017205774991	2018 年 1 月 30 日
26	机座人孔防护工具	实用新型	ZL2017205772322	2018 年 1 月 30 日
27	整圆冲片调角划线工具	实用新型	ZL2017205828027	2018 年 1 月 30 日
28	一种大型水电机组转轮静平衡的配重工具	实用新型	ZL2018205092075	2018 年 10 月 12 日
29	一种在气压变化大的环境下测量水位的压力变送器	实用新型	ZL2018205126207	2018 年 10 月 12 日
30	水轮机活动导叶带平压孔的密封结构	实用新型	ZL2017205511426	2018 年 1 月 30 日
31	大型可变速发电电动机转子交流励磁线棒槽部固定结构	实用新型	ZL2017205906331	2018 年 1 月 30 日
32	可变速发电电动机转子三相交流励磁线棒光纤测温装置	实用新型	ZL2017205901997	2018 年 1 月 30 日
33	发电机定子铜环引线处的光纤温度传感结构	实用新型	ZL2017205908182	2018 年 1 月 30 日
34	三相大容量交流励磁绕组端部防变形结构	实用新型	ZL2017205976014	2018 年 1 月 30 日
35	新型油混水监测装置	实用新型	ZL2017206042149	2018 年 1 月 30 日
36	切向倾斜布置的顶盖均压管	实用新型	ZL2017206042153	2018 年 5 月 8 日
37	可调节式焊角测量器	实用新型	ZL2017206044869	2018 年 5 月 8 日
38	波纹板裁剪工具	实用新型	ZL201720604621X	2018 年 2 月 2 日
39	分瓣式定子铁心翻身工具	实用新型	ZL2017206047689	2018 年 1 月 30 日
40	一种特定预紧力下的单个螺栓疲劳试验装置	实用新型	ZL2017205898104	2018 年 1 月 30 日
41	水轮发电机机坑内定子安装平台结构	实用新型	ZL2017205833472	2018 年 1 月 30 日
42	可变速发电电动机故障工况顺泰态转子位置测量仪	实用新型	ZL2017205898087	2018 年 5 月 8 日
43	一种适用于抽水蓄能机组的转轮室压力测量装置	实用新型	ZL2017205898138	2018 年 1 月 30 日
44	活动导叶模型数控加工夹具装置	实用新型	ZL2017205826695	2018 年 1 月 30 日
45	水轮发电机定子铁芯单段夹紧工具	实用新型	ZL2017205891177	2018 年 5 月 8 日
46	一种水轮发电机转子引线双向限位的线夹结构	实用新型	ZL2018205126298	2018 年 10 月 12 日
47	水轮发电机定子线圈压紧换位工具	实用新型	ZL2018203784781	2018 年 9 月 21 日
48	仿锤形流道的混流式水轮机	实用新型	ZL2017205515499	2018 年 5 月 8 日
49	带漏油收集装置的水轮机油压装置回油箱	实用新型	ZL2017209765169	2018 年 4 月 13 日
50	水轮机转动部件起吊翻身架	实用新型	ZL2017209769475	2018 年 4 月 13 日
51	一种具有磨损量反馈功能的导轴承润滑油防飞溅装置	实用新型	ZL201721044566X	2018 年 4 月 13 日
52	大型水轮发电机磁极交流阻抗试验防电弧电极杆	实用新型	ZL2017213238587	2018 年 5 月 4 日
53	一种水轮发电机线棒包装结构	实用新型	ZL2017210446183	2018 年 5 月 25 日

续表

序号	专利名称	专利类别	专利号	授权时间
54	球头成型工具	实用新型	ZL2017210445693	2018年4月13日
55	多槽型定子模具卸料装置	实用新型	ZL2017211278664	2018年4月13日
56	一种水轮发电机的转子磁轭	实用新型	ZL2017211545241	2018年7月13日
57	水发定子线圈屏蔽层阻值测量方法	发明专利	ZL2015108693313	2017年12月19日
58	安装于转闭上的球阀位置液压锁锭装置	实用新型	ZL2017215128505	2018年5月25日
59	大型发电机定子线圈绝缘现场修复方法	发明专利	ZL2016108807215	2018年8月21日
60	大型水轮发电机测温元件交流耐压试验平台	实用新型	ZL2017212393532	2018年4月13日
61	水轮发电机碳刷磨损在线监测装置	实用新型	ZL2017209401139	2018年4月13日
62	水轮发电机组气体灭火防止误投入系统	实用新型	ZL2017209409677	2018年4月13日
63	水轮发电机转子支架托筋式结构	实用新型	ZL201720940922X	2018年5月8日
64	适用于水轮发电机定子槽底的测温元件的防护结构	实用新型	ZL2017209401092	2018年6月15日
65	大型水轮机转轮静平衡实验装置	实用新型	ZL2017209504775	2018年4月13日
66	一种水轮机用剪断销状态在线监测元件	实用新型	ZL201720623959X	2018年1月30日
67	弹性油箱毛毡砂轮抛光装置	实用新型	ZL201720623941X	2018年5月8日
68	一种大型立式水轮发电机推力轴承瓦组合式拆卸装置	实用新型	ZL2017206239674	2018年5月11日
69	一种立式水轮发电机上挡风板压力自释放装置	实用新型	ZL2017206239689	2018年5月8日
70	一种大型立式水轮发电机坑温度自平衡控制装置	实用新型	ZL2017206239585	2018年1月30日
71	剔除压力脉动干扰信号的方法	发明专利	ZL2015105058836	2018年5月11日
72	大高尺寸单上环板分瓣式座环工地加工方法	发明专利	ZL2016106696862	2018年7月13日
73	主轴工作密封快磨损的远程反馈结构	实用新型	ZL2017206507428	2018年5月25日
74	一种用于水轮发电机定子的新型光纤信号温度测量装置	实用新型	ZL2017206507432	2018年5月8日
75	顶盖减压排水管结构	实用新型	ZL2017205507324	2018年5月8日
76	大型抽水蓄能机组双工况调速器主配压阀	发明专利	ZL2016104381726	2018年8月21日
77	水轮发电机磁极线圈径向支撑结构	实用新型	ZL2017209765173	2018年5月8日
78	大型立式水轮发电机定子全绝缘压紧结构	实用新型	ZL2017206239513	2018年5月11日
79	一种确定混流式水轮机尾水管压力脉动幅值的方法	发明专利	ZL2015108284788	2018年7月13日
80	一种发电机定子线圈焊接支撑装置	实用新型	ZL2018206236079	2018年11月20日
81	一种小型水电机组的离心开关	实用新型	ZL2018205132640	2018年11月13日
82	大型电机定子线棒槽电位测量防高压触碰数显杆	实用新型	ZL2018204911642	2018年11月6日
83	大型电机定子铁心槽内过盈配合线棒无损拆除机	实用新型	ZL2018204084743	2018年11月13日
84	定子线圈端部感应钎焊的柔性连接中频感应器	实用新型	ZL2018203763342	2018年11月6日
85	一种线圈转角接头铣胎	实用新型	ZL2018205092200	2018年11月6日
86	水轮发电机整块的圆弧铣胎工具	实用新型	ZL2018204973687	2018年11月6日
87	适用于蓄能机组的锯齿槽密封	实用新型	ZL2018204855002	2018年11月6日
88	一种大型开口环类零件矫形装置	实用新型	ZL2018205132937	2018年11月13日
89	适用于水轮发电机的带拖块的弹性支撑	实用新型	ZL2018205331983	2018年11月13日

续表

序号	专利名称	专利类别	专利号	授权时间
90	一种筒形阀沉余控制装置	实用新型	ZL2018206464997	2018年11月13日
91	一种巨型立式水轮发电机铁心端部温度测量结构	实用新型	ZL2018206460943	2018年11月3日
92	一种用于高压油顶起装置的新型安全阀组	实用新型	ZL2018205125806	2018年11月6日
93	一种水轮发电机磁极铁心拉杆结构	实用新型	ZL2018206464234	2018年11月6日
94	一种水轮发电机组磁轭的径向鸽尾组合健结构	实用新型	ZL2018206460981	2018年11月6日
95	一种带时间记录功能的剪断销报警装置	实用新型	ZL201820646097.7	2018年11月6日
96	垫圈弯型装置	实用新型	ZL201820381205.2	2018年11月6日
97	弯路偏心连接装置	实用新型	ZL201820497357.9	2018年11月13日
98	一种机械过速装置液动阀用安装支架	实用新型	ZL201820522628.1	2018年11月20日
99	采用三坐标测量臂检查转轮叶片装配角度的方法	发明专利	ZL201610927497.0	2018年11月23日
100	一种水电定子线圈通用一模多压直化模	实用新型	ZL2017206672868	2018年5月11日
101	发电机定子线圈包带机支撑装置	实用新型	ZL2017206739730	2018年5月8日
102	一种定子线圈压换位装置	实用新型	ZL2017206672783	2018年5月8日
103	一种巨型水轮发电机励磁铜排新型固定结构	实用新型	ZL2018206464978	2018年12月11日
104	大型水电机组用四瓣不等径轴成体的加工方法	发明专利	ZL2016109413795	2018年12月11日
105	水轮机活动导叶钝边出水边卡门涡频率预估方法	发明专利	ZL2016103216647	2018年12月11日

（哈尔滨电机厂有限责任公司　刘保生）

国电大渡河流域水电开发有限公司 2018年度获国家专利授权和软件著作权登记证书情况

国电大渡河流域水电开发有限公司2018年获得　　的国家专利授权40件，有关情况见表1。

表1　　国电大渡河流域水电开发有限公司2018年度获国家专利授权情况

序号	专利名称	专利类型	专利号	授权日期
1	大跨度混凝土顶板可移动承重排架	实用新型	ZL201720580506.3	2018年1月30日
2	一种可分散消能的多通道坎消力池	实用新型	ZL201720488061.6	2018年2月6日
3	野外遥测站自适应多功能调节太阳能板支架	实用新型	ZL201721068448.2	2018年3月27日
4	一种新型气动复位制动器	实用新型	ZL201720937876.8	2018年3月27日
5	一种针对高速旋转部件宏观性态的实时监测系统	实用新型	ZL201721321115.6	2018年4月17日
6	非接触式发电机组气隙异物在线检测报警结构	实用新型	ZL201721321713.3	2018年5月8日
7	一种立式水轮机主轴的挡水圈结构	实用新型	ZL201720843543.9	2018年4月17日
8	智能安全梯及安全梯监测系统	实用新型	ZL201820004546.8	2018年7月31日
9	智能安全带及安全带监测系统	实用新型	ZL201721825346.0	2018年7月31日
10	测量机器人观测站智能控制系统	实用新型	ZL201721262851.9	2018年6月5日
11	多类型测量仪器同轴调整装置	实用新型	ZL201721763477.0	2018年6月29日

续表

序号	专利名称	专利类型	专利号	授权日期
12	一种解决低压直流系统设备屏柜工作环境温度高的散热顶板	实用新型	ZL201721400971.0	2018年5月11日
13	一种水电站综合数据处理系统	实用新型	ZL201721274404.5	2018年5月11日
14	一种基于水电站洞式厂房结构的500kV断路器闪络保护装置	实用新型	ZL201721402538.0	2018年5月11日
15	一种新型弧形闸门开度测量装置	实用新型	ZL201720875613.9	2018年6月5日
16	基于解决电力系统通信设备屏柜温度高的散热柜门	实用新型	ZL201721400975.9	2018年7月24日
17	一种混流式水轮机水导轴承冷却装置	实用新型	ZL201721605186.9	2018年6月19日
18	一种出口断路器合闸回路结构	实用新型	ZL201720662403.1	2018年8月7日
19	一种发电机出口断路器无压合闸装置	实用新型	ZL201621241845.0	2018年1月16日
20	一种可调节切割装置	实用新型	ZL201721740991.2	2018年7月10日
21	一种便于穿戴的安全装置	实用新型	ZL201721740935.9	2018年8月14日
22	继电器校验底座	实用新型	ZL201820379568.2	2018年9月25日
23	循环式灌浆施工系统	实用新型	ZL201820524207.2	2018年11月6日
24	一种防渗体灌浆抬动测量系统	实用新型	ZL201820769337.2	2018年11月27日
25	一种超声波水泥细度检测系统	实用新型	ZL201820882883.7	2018年12月4日
26	一种用于混凝土坝基排水孔毛细透排水管	实用新型	ZL201820753572.0	2018年12月11日
27	一种缆索起重机	实用新型	ZL201820752296.6	2018年11月8日
28	一种水工建筑抗震缝结构	实用新型	ZL201820882882.2	2018年12月25日
29	一种灌浆记录仪	实用新型	ZL201820771980.9	2018年12月25日
30	大体积混凝土温控保护装置	实用新型	ZL201820769598.4	2018年12月11日
31	一种屏柜编码锁	实用新型	ZL201820483287.1	2018年12月11日
32	一种用于变截面隧洞施工的钢模台车	实用新型	ZL201820577939.8	2018年11月13日
33	户外测站自密封结构	实用新型	ZL201721492051.6	2018年7月27日
34	一种水轮发电机组上机架进人孔安全围栏	实用新型	ZL201820657020.X	2018年12月21日
35	一种实现平稳并网的同期合闸系统	实用新型	ZL201820971170.8	2018年12月18日
36	一种覆盖层基础泄水槽结构	实用新型	ZL201820762555.3	2018年12月11日
37	一种能自动脱钩的装置	实用新型	ZL201820674704.0	2018年11月27日
38	水电站鱼道系统	实用新型	ZL201820393670.8	2018年12月01日
39	户外工程测量雨感结构	外观设计	ZL201730463856.7	2018年4月17日
40	户外测站自动启闭保护罩	外观设计	ZL201730552075.5	2018年10月19日

由国电大渡河流域水电开发有限公司开发的7项软件，2018年取得中华人民共和国国家版权局颁发的计算机软件著作权登记证书，有关情况见表2。

表2 国电大渡河流域水电开发有限公司2018年获得国家计算机软件著作权登记证书情况

序号	软件名称	登记号	登记日期	登记证书号
1	双江口水电站海量三维实景展示平台V1.0	2018SR055618	2018年1月24日	软著登字第2263741号
2	双江口水电站地下空间安全监测软件V1.0	2018SR047055	2018年1月22日	软著登字第2376150号

续表

序号	软件名称	登记号	登记日期	登记证书号
3	大渡河水调自动化闸门命令票系统	2018SR012471	2018年1月5日	软著登字第2341566号
4	大渡河水调自动化发电调度系统1.0	2018SR119422	2018年2月23日	软著登字第2448517号
5	日常工作考核评价管理系统V1.0	2018SR513838	2018年7月4日	软著登字第2842933号
6	大渡河工程数据管控中心平台V1.0	2018SR566364	2018年7月19日	软著登字第2895459号
7	大渡河监控计划曲线跟踪系统1.0	2018SR717783	2018年9月6日	软著登字第3046878号

（国电大渡河流域水电开发有限公司）

黄河勘测规划设计有限公司 2018年获得国家专利授权情况

黄河勘测规划设计有限公司2018年度获得国家专利授权情况见表1。

表1 黄河勘测规划设计有限公司2018年度获得国家专利授权清单

序号	专利名称	专利类别	专利号	授权日期
1	TBM刀盘	发明专利	ZL201610646233.8	2018年1月30日
2	具有深厚砂砾石层深切河谷的黏土心墙坝基础防渗方法	发明专利	ZL201610558383.3	2018年4月20日
3	用于起吊闸门的自锁式拉杆	发明专利	ZL201610563596.5	2018年5月11日
4	泥石流拦挡重力坝体结构	发明专利	ZL201610581441.4	2018年5月11日
5	适于山洪沟的泥石流拦挡格栅坝	发明专利	ZL201610581794.4	2018年5月11日
6	长距离、多负荷节点线状供电无功补偿方法	发明专利	ZL201610366684.6	2018年5月22日
7	适于短隧洞开挖的敞开式硬岩掘进机刀头	发明专利	ZL201610622522.4	2018年7月6日
8	多泥沙河流综合利用水库分期汛限水位优化方法及其系统	发明专利	ZL201610683944.2	2018年7月6日
9	水电站门机行走全行程精确定位系统	发明专利	ZL201610287525.7	2018年8月10日
10	一种快速闸门起吊系统及闸门起吊方法	发明专利	ZL201710311619.8	2018年8月10日
11	隧洞管片回填灌浆质量无损检测的工程B超方法	发明专利	ZL201610661015.1	2018年9月18日
12	用于三维SH波或多波地震勘探的智能检波器	发明专利	ZL201710519284.9	2018年11月23日
13	豆砾石回填灌浆封闭环的施工方法	发明专利	ZL201710271992.5	2018年12月4日
14	分裂式止水带的施工方法	发明专利	ZL201610699728.7	2018年12月11日
15	适于双护盾TBM施工的豆砾石回填灌浆预制管片	发明专利	ZL201710271991.0	2018年12月28日
16	提高三维地形生成精度的方法	发明专利	ZL201610299917.5	2018年12月28日
17	用于水渠渠坡衬砌快速修复的渠道钢围堰系统	实用新型	ZL201720639417.1	2018年1月2日
18	用于水渠渠坡衬砌快速修复的渠道钢围堰	实用新型	ZL201720639409.7	2018年1月2日
19	用于渠道检修的增流装置	实用新型	ZL201720639413.3	2018年1月2日

续表

序号	专利名称	专利类别	专利号	授权日期
20	一种明塔式分水井	实用新型	ZL201720155508.8	2018年1月2日
21	软弱颗粒测定装置	实用新型	ZL201720762409.6	2018年1月5日
22	一种管片钢筋笼快速、高精度成型装置	实用新型	ZL201720155832.X	2018年1月12日
23	新型多孔斜交圆管涵结构	实用新型	ZL201720849472.3	2018年1月30日
24	自动化双恒温空间的岩石冻融试验系统	实用新型	ZL201720896732.2	2018年1月30日
25	自清洁式岩石冻融自动化试验装置	实用新型	ZL201720896760.4	2018年1月30日
26	一种供水工程检修阀门井结构	实用新型	ZL201720514338.8	2018年2月2日
27	配重可调式光伏电站支架基础结构	实用新型	ZL201721035730.0	2018年3月2日
28	承力等分式光伏电站支架基础结构	实用新型	ZL201721035729.8	2018年3月2日
29	适于输水管道的回转式水过滤装置	实用新型	ZL201721106054.1	2018年3月20日
30	适于敞开式掘进机的破岩刀盘	实用新型	ZL201720560306.1	2018年4月17日
31	降水井井口综合保护装置	实用新型	ZL201721302937.X	2018年4月17日
32	门式启闭机小行程多工位起升小车行走驱动装置	实用新型	ZL201721359890.0	2018年4月27日
33	适于狭窄河床的溢洪道联合消能结构	实用新型	ZL201721359891.5	2018年5月25日
34	适于多泥沙河流过滤、分水的水闸结构	实用新型	ZL201721489647.0	2018年5月25日
35	一种管道供水工程进水池结构	实用新型	ZL201721531941.3	2018年5月29日
36	便携冲击式微水试验测试仪	实用新型	ZL201721651215.5	2018年5月29日
37	钻孔微水试验测试系统	实用新型	ZL201721650482.0	2018年6月5日
38	多功能渗透和湿度扩散试验装置	实用新型	ZL201721508668.2	2018年6月15日
39	多孔介质含水层参数测试物理试验平台	实用新型	ZL201820035416.0	2018年7月24日
40	农村生活污水检查井	实用新型	ZL201820035417.5	2018年8月14日
41	适于城市合流管涵的溢流式防倒灌导流三通井	实用新型	ZL201820134988.4	2018年8月28日
42	新型锚篮式抗拔桩静载荷试验装置	实用新型	ZL201820134589.8	2018年9月4日
43	适于小流量污水管道的防堵防臭型检查井	实用新型	ZL201820247523.X	2018年9月18日
44	具有围岩收敛变形监测系统的护盾式 TBM	实用新型	ZL201820265924.8	2018年9月18日
45	贴面式多翼缘止水带弯头	实用新型	ZL201820281499.1	2018年9月25日
46	基坑地下连续墙支护用钢支撑结构	实用新型	ZL201820431849.8	2018年10月30日
47	江河边岸仿土毯式立体消能护坡	实用新型	ZL201820389770.3	2018年10月30日
48	江河边岸孔管式消能护坡	实用新型	ZL201820389796.8	2018年10月30日
49	贴面式多翼缘止水带连接件	实用新型	ZL201820473956.7	2018年11月6日
50	用于水工钢闸门平压的旁通管道系统	实用新型	ZL201820452400.X	2018年11月6日
51	水电站地下式厂房机组出口闸门的布置结构	实用新型	ZL201820452985.5	2018年11月6日
52	弧形挡墙式水平弯管镇墩	实用新型	ZL201820507945.6	2018年11月6日
53	悬浮过滤潜流湿地系统	实用新型	ZL201820373965.9	2018年12月4日
54	悬浮过滤垂直流湿地系统	实用新型	ZL201820373971.4	2018年12月4日
55	悬浮过滤湿地系统	实用新型	ZL201820374173.3	2018年12月4日

续表

序号	专利名称	专利类别	专利号	授权日期
56	脉冲式水质净化系统	实用新型	ZL201820450125.8	2018 年 12 月 4 日
57	一种河道型悬浮过滤水质净化系统	实用新型	ZL201820473837.1	2018 年 12 月 4 日
58	水质净化用水力清渣系统	实用新型	ZL201820502218.0	2018 年 12 月 4 日
59	砾堆氧化废水处理系统	实用新型	ZL201820525730.7	2018 年 12 月 4 日

（黄河勘测规划设计有限公司 李冠成）

黄河水利科学研究院 2018 年获得国家专利授权和软件著作权登记证书情况

黄河水利科学研究院 2018 年获得国家专利授权 11 件，有关情况见表 1。

表 1 黄河水利科学研究院 2018 年获得国家专利授权项目情况

序号	专利名称	专利类别	专利号	授权日期
1	一种黄河下游宽滩区避水村台	发明专利	ZL201720945878.1	2018 年 3 月 9 日
2	基于垂向自适应的水库极细颗粒泥沙提取系统搭载装置	发明专利	ZL201710040393.2	2018 年 12 月 4 日
3	一种钢塑复合聚氨酯活动导叶立面密封装置	发明专利	ZL201610149320.2	2018 年 8 月 21 日
4	一种堤坝漏洞封堵装置	发明专利	ZL201710016929.7	2018 年 9 月
5	一种浮萍式堤坝漏洞封堵方法	发明专利	ZL201710016930.X	2018 年 9 月
6	一种水库抽沙方法	发明专利	ZL201610259827.3	2018 年 1 月 2 日
7	一种水库抽沙系统	发明专利	ZL201610259826.9	2018 年 4 月 10 日
8	一种组合式混凝土钢模具	实用新型	ZL201720764100.0	2018 年 1 月 16 日
9	一种组合式圆柱体试件制作模具	实用新型	ZL201720764136.9	2018 年 1 月 16 日
10	一种组合式塑性混凝土模具	实用新型	ZL201720763606.X	2018 年 1 月 16 日
11	一种自动化控制雨污径流的弃除装置	实用新型	ZL201721179546.3	2018 年 5 月 18 日

由黄河水利科学研究院完成的 9 项软件成果，2018 年获得中华人民共和国国家版权局颁发的计算机软件著作权登记证书，有关情况见表 2。

表 2 黄河水利科学研究院 2018 年获得国家计算机软件著作权登记证书情况

序号	软件名称	开发完成日期	登记号	登记证书号
1	多沙河流一维非恒定水沙数学模型软件	2016 年 12 月 31 日	2018SR072645	软著登字第 2401704 号
2	黄河下游水污染应急调度模型软件	2015 年 5 月 31 日	2018SR072623	软著登字第 2401718 号
3	一维河道水流泥沙输移的数据同化系统	2017 年 5 月 1 日	2018SR029561	软著登字第 2358656 号
4	水利工程精准化管理系统 V1.0	2018 年 5 月 30 日	2018SR438972	软著登字第 2768067 号

续表

序号	软件名称	开发完成日期	登记号	登记证书号
5	雷达冰凌监测软件	2018年5月1日	2018SR438972	软著登字第2912622号
6	区域供水工程调节计算系统V1.0	2017年4月1日	2018SR515940	软著登字第2845035号
7	数字地理高程（DEM）数据源调整软件	2017年2月1日	2018SR518132	软著登字第2847227号
8	水资源监控系统运行维护经费测算软件	2017年11月29日	2018SR515950	软著登字第2845045号
9	防汛系统运行维护经费测算软件	2017年11月29日	2018SR515807	软著登字第2844902号

（黄河水利科学研究院　娄萱）

9

国际合作与技术交流

国际技术交流

高坝大库抗震安全国际学术研讨会在成都召开

2018年5月12～13日，在纪念汶川地震10周年之际，为总结高坝大库抗震领域的最新研究成果，探讨高坝大库抗震面临的新问题，由中国大坝工程学会和中国水力发电工程学会主办的“高坝大库抗震安全国际学术研讨会”在四川成都举行。大会的主题是“高坝大库抗震安全”。来自中国、巴西、瑞士、韩国、日本、菲律宾和伊拉克等多个国家的与会代表共计260余人。会议开幕式由中国电力建设集团有限公司总工程师、国际大坝委员会副主席、中国大坝工程学会副秘书长周建平主持。

（一）领导致辞

（1）中国大坝工程学会理事长矫勇在致辞中说，十年之前，汶川发生了强烈地震，造成了严重的人员伤亡，经济社会发展受到了重大的灾难，我们的高坝大库在那场地震当中也同样遭受了破坏。在党中央的全面领导下，我们取得了汶川地震抗震工作的全面胜利，取得了灾后重建的全面胜利。我们在取得胜利之后，在地震10周年纪念之日，要痛定思痛，认真回顾和反思那场地震带给高坝大库和我们的灾害。由此产生以下几个方面的反思：一是强震对高坝大库的灾害非常重大。汶川地震仅四川一个省就有1997座水库遭到毁坏，其中67座面临溃决，310座面临高危险。高坝大库遭受结构性破坏。二是地震灾害是一个综合的复杂事件，我们面临的是气象、水文等一系列不确定性。水库大坝的抗震救灾工作，既要考虑结构性问题，也要考虑复杂事件的综合性问题。三是在高坝大库抗震设计上应深入研究，充分考虑抗震因素的不确定性。以紫坪铺大坝为例，所在地区是8度的地震区，以9度设防，但“5·12”汶川地震面对的地震烈度是11度，距离震中只有17km。这说明在大坝设计时很难预见许多突发的因素，这些预见不到的事件一旦发生会产生不可预见的后果。四是要以更谨慎、更深入、更持之以恒的态度对高坝大库进行研究。西南大坝水库的高坝、高边坡、高烈度像人的“三高”一样存在高风险，我们要让高坝大库更加坚固，让地震灾害发生时不给人类带来更大的次生灾害。

（2）中国水力发电工程学会副理事长兼秘书长袁柏松在致辞中表示，高坝大库对保障我国的水安全、人员安全、生态和气候方面和高坝大库抗震安全、自身安全都有极大的重要性，提高水利水电建设安全意识具有重要意义。汶川地震当中高坝大库经受住了考验，4座百米以上的大坝都完好无损，充分地显示了中国水利水电抗震基础设施水平的高超，以及建筑质量的稳妥和可靠。经过多年开发实践，中国的水电已经形成了规划、设计、施工、制造、运行、管理一套完整的产业链。水利水电已成为中国推动“一带一路”、建设科技强国的重要力量。而科学可靠的防灾技术是推动水电事业持续发展的重要保障。

（3）国电大渡河流域水电开发有限公司总经理涂扬举在致辞中说，世界水电看中国，中国水电主战场在四川。水库大坝作为绿色可持续发展的重要基础设施，承担着保障国家防洪安全、能源安全等的重要功能，是实现“绿水青山”美丽中国梦的重要依托。大渡河公司牢固树立“生态优先、安全发展”理念，坚持“高标准开工、高水平建设、高质量投产、高效率收尾”目标，与建设各方一道，密切合作、创新引领，攻克了复杂地质条件、深厚覆盖层及高烈度地震带筑坝等系列技术难题，实现了瀑布沟、深溪沟、大岗山、猴子岩、枕头坝一级等水电站高质量投产。研发了高精度自动监测技术，建立了包括抗震安全在内的安全风险预警体系，大幅度提升地震灾害易发、多发条件下的流域安全智能感知、预警与管控能力，成功预警并治理重大、特大地震灾害十余处。

（4）瑞士专家、国际大坝委员会地震与大坝专委会主席Martin Wieland在致辞中表示，今年是国际大坝委员会设立地震与大坝专业委员会六十周年，同时也是中国汶川地震十周年纪念。自专委会设立以来，各国专家一直密切关注国际上地震造成的大坝事故，并总结各方经验。2009年，曾经与中国大坝工程学会合作举办过地震与大坝安全专题国际研讨会。他认为，如今多数专家在研究地震对大坝的影响时，都十分关注地震地表运动对大坝造成的破坏，而低估了地震带来的泥石流、滑坡等次生灾害对大坝的破坏。建议在今后的工作中，加强这些方面的研究。

（二）大会报告

（1）会议特邀中国工程院院士陈厚群、中国科学院院士张楚汉、中国工程院院士孔宪京与国际大坝委员会地震与大坝专委会主席 Martin Wieland 分别作了题为“汶川地震中沙牌拱坝的震情验证”“高坝水库蓄水河谷-库坝变形机理研究”“高土石坝抗震研究最新进展”和“水库诱发地震的抗震设计标准及大坝工程设计 Effect of reservoir-triggered seismicity on seismic design criteria and design of large dam projects”的大会主旨报告。

（2）大会共收到 64 篇论文，邀请 18 位专家做了为期 2 天的大会报告。报告围绕高坝大库场地地震动输入，高坝大库抗震设计标准，高坝大库抗震分析理论与方法，高坝大库抗震试验研究方法和技术，高坝坝体与地基材料动态特性、高坝大库现场测试与动力性态检测、健康诊断与鉴定，强震震后大坝震损调查、震害分析、灾害评估以及次生灾害影响，震后大坝安全度评价与修复加固技术，水库地震的预测、监测及其影响研究，边坡与地下结构动力分析理论、方法、抗震设计及地质灾害防治等 10 个议题展开研讨。

（三）大会调研

为增强技术交流效果，2018 年 5 月 14 日，会议安排了会后工程技术调研。78 名中外代表调研了紫坪铺、沙牌、都江堰工程和唐家山堰塞湖。

该会议也是“汶川地震 10 周年国际研讨会暨第 4 届大陆地震研讨会”的专题会场之一，会议的召开将对促进国内外坝工学术交流与合作，推动大坝安全、绿色、智能化发展，以及有效应对地震等自然灾害的风险和不确定性发挥积极作用。

（本年鉴编辑部摘编）

中国大坝工程学会参加国际大坝委员会第 86 届年会和第 26 届大会情况

国际大坝委员会第 86 届年会和第 26 届大会于 2018 年 7 月 1～7 日在奥地利维也纳召开，来自 80 多个国家的 1500 多名代表参加了会议。会议由奥地利大坝委员会承办。会议举办了“水利水电工程国际研讨会”、各专业委员会议、第 86 届执行会议、第 26 届大会和技术展览等。

中国大坝工程学会组织了 70 多人的代表团参加了此次会议。

（一）参会情况

1. 第 86 届年会暨“水利水电工程国际研讨会” 该研讨会于 2018 年 7 月 2 日召开。会议就气候变换导致水库运行的改变（蓄水、冻土、冰川融化、侵蚀和淤积）、许可和安全评估（水利结构建设和运行、操作设备的检测与评估）、大坝和坝基止水（长效性能及扬压力分布评估）、硐室和发电引水通道（设计、施工和监测、发电引水通道与压力钢管）、库岸边坡的稳定性（水库运行、雪崩、脉冲波、溃坝等的影响）等议题进行了研讨。长江科学院黄国兵所长、段文刚总工、闫霞工程师、清华大学金峰教授、南京水利科学研究院王士军教高、水电水利规划设计总王富强高工、中国水利水电科学研究院张龑博士在会上作了交流报告；中国水利水电科学研究院柳春娜高工、黄河水利科学研究院张雷高工、南京水利科学研究院庞琼工程师等在论文展示区进行了论文展示。中国代表参加会议并与各国专家进行了交流。

2. 国际大坝委员会各专业委员会会议 2018 年 6 月 30 日，国际大坝委员会 26 业委员会会议相继召开。国际大坝委员会专委会主席，贾金生、陈国庆和望西炯出席了国际大坝委员会各专业委员会议，并于 7 月 1 日主持召开了胶结颗粒料坝专委会、水电站与水库联合运行专委会、水库大坝移民专委会会议。

国际大坝委员会水库移民专委会由中国提议、于 2017 年 7 月在第 85 届执行会议通过设立，具体工作由中国三峡集团公司组织开展，主席由中国三峡集团移民工作局副局长望西炯担任。本次会议期间召开了专委会成立仪式及第一次工作会议，并召开了专题研讨会。国际大坝委员会主席安东·斯莱斯（Anton Schleiss）、荣誉主席贾金生、副主席杰拉尔德·赞思（Gerald Zenz）、秘书长米歇尔·迪·维奥（M. De Vivo）等嘉宾出席会议并讲话，祝贺水库移民专委会成立，强调了移民工作在水电工程建设中的重要性以及成立水库移民专委会的必要性，希望通过专委会促进国际交流和经验分享，使国际社会了解到移民工作的最新实践及进展，为相关问题提供解决方案。会议期间，中国、巴西、哥伦比亚、德国、日本、印尼等国家代表围绕移民工作政策、组织架构、专业人才培养、危机应对、移民返迁、安置地发展等内容进行了深入交流研讨。水库移民工作是水利水电工程建设的重要组成部分，水库移民专委会的成立和持续性工作将加强各方交流、分享移民案例，促进水库移民工作更好开展。

四川大学副校长许唯临、黄河水利科学研究院副院长江恩慧、长江勘测规划设计研究院副总工黄艳、中国水利水电科学研究院张国新所长、郑璀莹教高、徐耀教高、徐泽平教高、王海波教高、卢正超教高、李曙光高工、南京水利科学研究院王士军教高、郦能惠教高等代表团专家作为专委会委员分别参加了相关专委会的会议，围绕专委会工作进行研讨，并与专委会各国专家就相关领域的技术进展进行了深入交流。

3. 国际大坝委员会第 26 届大会 2018 年 7 月 4 日，国际大坝委员会第 26 届大会召开。大会开幕式上颁发了国际大坝委员会首届科技创新奖，由中国水利水电科学研究院、南京水利科学研究院、中国电建集团等单位的贾金生、郦能惠、徐泽平、向建等共同完成的《高混凝土面板堆石坝关键技术创新》成果荣获国际大坝委员会科技创新奖。

大会共设四个议题，分别是：水库淤积和可持续发展、大坝安全和风险分析、大坝与地质，以及小坝与堤防。大会共收录了来自 36 个国家的 227 篇论文，其中中国专家论文 20 篇，论文数居第二。中国水利水电科学研究院徐泽平教高作为“小坝与堤防”议题的副主席主持了会议，中国水利水电科学研究院王玉杰教高、郑璀莹教高、南京水利科学研究院李宏恩教高、张士辰高工、厉丹丹高工等专家围绕相关议题作大会报告。

4. 国际大坝委员会第 86 届执行会议　会议于 2018 年 7 月 3 日召开，由国际大坝委员会主席安东·斯莱斯（Anton Schleiss）主持。在国际大坝委员会第 86 届执行会议上，国际大坝委员会副主席、美国大坝学会前主席麦克·罗杰斯（Michael Rogers）当选为国际大坝委员会新一届主席，任期为 2018～2021 年。埃塞俄比亚 Michael Abebe、伊朗 Ali Noorzad 分别当选为非洲区和第六位副主席。F. Lemperiere（法国）、Larry Stephens（美国）、Patrick Le Delliou（法国）荣获国际大坝委员会终身成就奖。会议表决通过 2022 年国际大坝委员会第 90 届年会在伊朗设拉子（Shiraz）召开。同时加拿大、印度和法国大坝委员会分别报告了 2019、2020、2021 年国际大坝会议的筹备情况。

（二）有关活动

1. 国际大坝委员会亚太地区分会（ICOLD-APG）会议　2018 年 7 月 1 日下午，国际大坝委员会亚太地区分会（ICOLD-APG）会议召开。来自亚太地区 16 个国家大坝委员会的 45 位代表参加了会议，中国作为亚太分会主席和秘书长国家，承办了此次会议。该次会议是我国专家周建平担任国际大坝委员会亚太区分会主席的第一次会议，会议由亚太分会秘书长徐泽平博士主持。国际大坝委员会主席安东·斯莱斯（Anton Schleiss）、荣誉主席贾金生、秘书长米歇尔·迪·维奥（Micheal De Vivo）、等出席了会议并讲话。会上亚太地区各国代表介绍了各国家委员会近一年来的工作进展，对近年各国水库大坝建设、技术进展和关注问题进行了研讨，并对下一年的工作进行了讨论。会议还就开展“亚太地区国家大坝安全调查研究”的建议进行了讨论，根据讨论意见，此项工作将纳入亚太地区的工作计划。中国水利水电科学研究院结构所所长、中国大坝工程学会副秘书长张国新、综合部主任郑璀莹参加了会议，并围绕中国大坝工程学会过去一年的活动和中国坝工领域关注的技术问题，以及第九届中日韩坝工技术研讨会的筹备进展做报告。周建平主席、徐泽平秘书长在会议中强调了未来两年的工作重点，即进一步围绕大坝安全强化各国合作。

2. 大会技术展览　中国大坝工程学会参加了本次会议的技术展览，展示了中国大坝建设总体情况、沥青混凝土施工技术、胶结颗粒料坝筑坝技术和水下渗漏检测和深水清淤等技术。

3. 未来大坝安全合作　会议期间，中国大坝工程学会与美国大坝学会、西班牙大坝委员会、巴西大坝委员会、加拿大大坝学会就未来在大坝安全方面的合作进行了商谈，并分别与埃及大坝委员会和伊朗大坝委员签订了合作框架协议，协议双方将在坝工技术领域，尤其是围绕新技术，进行深入的合作交流并开展技术培训。中国大坝工程学会副理事长兼秘书长贾金生受理事长矫勇委托，在协议上签字。

此次会议的主要成果：①中国专家活跃在国际大坝会议舞台上，作为荣誉主席、现任副主席、专委会主席、专委会委员、大会主持人，以及参会代表深度参与会议各个环节，全方位展示中国的成就和进展，得到了各方好评；②通过交流进一步巩固了与美国、巴西、西班牙、日本、韩国等国家的合作机制，加强了与加拿大、法国、埃及、伊朗等国的沟通交流，就未来进一步推进大坝安全领域的合作交流与多国达成了共识；③中国专家参加了国际大坝委员 27 个专委会中的 23 个专委会的活动，本次会议在大会的投稿数仅次于法国居第二，通过专委会和国际研讨会、大会交流，充分宣传了中国在水利水电相关领域的新理念、新技术和工程实践进展，包括泥沙淤积治理、超深复杂基础的防渗墙施工、高水头大流量泄洪消能、胶结颗粒料筑坝技术等，获得了广泛的关注；④中国在水利水电工程领域的进展和对国际坝工技术发展的推动作用得到了广泛认可，获得了国际大坝委员会首届科技创新奖。

（中国大坝工程学会秘书处　郑璀莹　袁玉兰）

几内亚苏阿皮蒂水利枢纽项目业主人员培训班结业典礼在河海大学举行

2018 年 12 月 18 日，河海大学举行几内亚苏阿皮蒂水利枢纽项目业主人员培训班结业典礼。几内亚驻华使馆经济参赞卡巴·依帕依马·索利，中国长江三峡集团公司副总经理张定明，中国水利电力对外有限公司（CWE）执行董事、党委书记李丽，中国华电集团公司四川宝珠寺水力发电厂总经理张德智，四川省岷源水利水电工程设计有限公司总经理乐成军，河海大学校长徐辉、副校长徐卫亚、校党委副书记郭继超出席结业典礼。结业典礼由徐卫亚副校长主持。

苏阿皮蒂水利枢纽工程被称为几内亚“三峡工程”。该枢纽工程业主人员培训项目由三峡集团中水电公司委托我校实施，为期一年半。几内亚政府对此次培训项目高度重视，阿尔法·孔戴总统于今年“中非合作论坛北京峰会”结束后，专程前往三峡坝区看望学员。该培训项目的圆满完成是校企合作模式下服务国家“一带一路”倡议、落实“中非合作论坛北京峰会”成果、实施国际化水电开发属地化人才培养的典型案例。

近年来，河海大学紧密围绕“一带一路”倡议，充分发挥学科特色优势，发起成立“一带一路”水战略联盟，设立“一带一路”水与可持续发展基金，全面提升服务“一带一路”的能力和水平。学校大力推进对外教育合作交流，深化政产学研合作创新，聚力构建“一带一路”教育共同体，与政府部门、“走出去”企业等密切合作，为“一带一路”沿线国家培养水利水电本土化人才，积极服务中国水利水电“走出去”战略，取得了明显成效。

（河海大学）

雅砻江流域水电开发有限公司 2018 年国际合作与交流情况

2018 年 5 月 29 日，雅砻江流域水电开发有限公司（以下简称雅砻江公司）副总经理王继敏出席 SNEC（2018）第 12 届国际太阳能光伏与智慧能源（上海）展览会，并分别与华为、特变电工、乐叶高层进行了沟通交流。

2018 年 6 月 5 日，雅砻江公司副总经理吴世勇出席中美清洁能源联合研究中心 CERC 能源与水联盟在成都举办的 2018 年度工作会议，中国科技部、美国能源部以及联盟中美双方负责人等出席了会议。

2018 年 6 月 25～30 日，雅砻江公司副总经理吴世勇出席第 3 届岩石动力学及应用在挪威科技大学举办的国际会议，并受邀作为会议专家小组成员进行了技术交流。会议邀请有关领域国际专家围绕岩爆、矿震、塌方等动力学灾害及措施展开研讨。

2018 年 6 月 28 日，雅砻江公司派员参加了成都国检联合德国莱茵集团举办的“携手推动风能产业持续发展”公益论坛。

2018 年 7 月 12 日，第 5 届地质力学与硬岩国际研讨会（The 5th International Symposium on Fracturing Geomechanics & Hard Rock Forum）在大连召开。大会由大连理工大学、澳大利亚联邦科学与工业研究组织（CSIRO）和山东科技大学共同主办，会议议题包括地质力学、岩爆模拟与检测、增强型地热系统等领域的新进展，与会专家学者来自中国、德国、英国、美国、韩国、澳大利亚等。雅砻江公司副总经理吴世勇出席会议并受邀做了题为《锦屏二级水电站深埋长大水工隧洞群岩爆综合防治关键技术》的主题报告。

2018 年 9 月 4 日、9 月 25～30 日、9 月 29 日，雅砻江公司派员分别参加了非洲能源互联网发展暨中非企业家论坛、赴德国参加了欧洲国际风能展会及参加非洲能源互联网研究成果宣介会。

2018 年 9 月 23～24 日，第 2 届地质力学、地下能源、地下资源国际会议在成都召开，会议由四川大学和澳大利亚莫纳什大学主办，四川大学水利水电学院承办，中南大学、雅砻江流域水电开发有限公司、中国矿业大学、中国矿业大学（北京）、北京科技大学、中国科学院武汉岩土力学研究所、太原理工大学、河南理工大学、北京矿冶科技集团有限公司、神华集团、大同煤矿集团公司、中国平煤神马集团等单位协办。雅砻江公司副总经理吴世勇出席会议并作题为《锦屏二级水电站深埋长大水工隧洞群岩石力学关键问题研究与实践》的特邀英文报告。

2018 年 10 月 25～26 日，雅砻江公司派员参加了中国自然科学基金委、美国自然科学基金委、南京大学等组织召开的中美食物、能源和水系统关联环境学术研讨会。

2018 年 10 月 15～17 日，雅砻江公司组织并参加中国大坝工程学会 2018 学术年会暨第 10 届中日韩坝工学术交流会。雅砻江公司董事长陈云华出席大会。雅砻江公司副总经理吴世勇受邀在第 10 届中日韩坝工技术交流会上作题为“二滩大坝长期运行性态分析研究”特邀报告，同时受邀主持了下半场交流会。雅砻江公司副总经理王继敏荣获第 2 届大坝杰出工程师奖。雅砻江公司相关部门和单位代表参加了会议。

2018 年 10 月 17～19 日，雅砻江公司参加水资源高效利用与土木工程新技术国际研讨会。雅砻江公司董事长陈云华受邀出席现代水电国际论坛，并作题为“雅砻江流域数字化管理实践与智能化探索”的特邀报告。雅砻江公司副总经理吴世勇在水系统调度国际研讨会上作题为“雅砻江流域风光水互补清洁能源基地建设进展”的特邀报告，雅砻江公司战略发展部和信息管理部参加了相关会议。会议期间，雅砻江公司董事长陈云华与国际水电协会执行长 Richard TAYLOR、国际水电协会发展部主任 Greg TRACZ、国际水电协会运营部主任 Kate STEEL 一行进行了座谈交流。

2018 年 11 月 10 日，岩石力学与工程创新 2025 高端论坛暨武汉岩土所建所 60 周年纪念活动在武汉举行，雅砻江公司副总经理吴世勇出席了会议。会议由中国科学院武汉岩土力学研究所主办。中国科学院院士陈祖煜、陈云敏、魏悦广，中国工程院院士钱七虎、葛修润、郑颖人、顾金才、谢和平、张铁岗、蔡美峰、钮新强、丁烈云、王复明、康红普、陈湘生、张建民、谢先启，美国工程院院士 Derek Elsworth，国际地质工程联合会主席冯夏庭教授等院士专家出席了会议。来自国内外数十家高校、科研机构及企业的有关领导和代表参加了会议。

2018 年 11 月 19～21 日，由中国岩石力学与工程学会主办、以“展示中国岩石力学与工程进展，服务‘一带一路’建设与发展”为主题的 CHINA ROCK 2018-第 15 届中国岩石力学与工程学术年会在北京隆重举行。雅砻江公司副总经理吴世勇作为学会常务理事出席了会议。中国科协党组成员宋军、中国工程院院士钱七虎、顾金才、蔡美峰、康红普、金智新、徐寿波，中国科学院院士张楚汉、何满潮，中国岩石力学与工程学会理事长、国际地质工程联合会主席冯夏庭、俄罗斯科学院院士 Mikhail Guzev、国际岩石力学与岩石工程学会副主席 Seokwon Jeon(Korea)、Stuart Read(New Zealand)、Norikazu Shimizu (Japan)、联合国教科文组织教席“地球环境灾害与减灾”首席科学家、日本岛根大学教授汪发武、国际地下物流学会主席 Johan Visser(Netherland)、越南岩石力学学会副理事长 Dac Manh Phung(Vietnam) 等院士专家出席了会议，来自全国高校、科研机构及企业的有关领导和代表 4000 余人参加了会议。

2018 年 11 月 21～22 日，工程能力国际论坛在北京召开。雅砻江公司副总经理吴世勇受邀出席了会议。此次论坛由中国科协主办，世界工程组织联合会 (WFEO)、亚太工程学会联合会（FEIAP）支持举办。中国科协党组成员、书记处书记束为，WFEO 候任主席龚克，联合国教科文组织亚太科学局主任沙赫巴兹·汗在开幕式上致辞，8 个国际科技组织、20 个国家的工程师组织代表和联合国教科文组织的代表 160 余人出席会议。

2018 年 12 月 7 日，中国锦屏地下实验室（CJPL）国际咨询委员会第 3 次会议在北京召开。雅砻江公司副总经理、中国锦屏地下实验室管委会委员兼实验室副主任何胜明出席会议。来自美国、加拿大、意大利等国的知名物理及岩石力学专家出席了会议，会议对锦屏地下实验室二期建设、本底控制、低本底设施情况、各物理实验及拟申请开展物理实验情况进行了交流和讨论，提出了针对性的专家咨询意见。

（雅砻江流域水电开发有限公司　杜成波）

哈尔滨电机厂有限责任公司 2018 年国际学术交流情况

2018 年 3 月，“同步水轮发电机（含发电电动机）技术要求”国际标准工作组（IEC/TC2/WG33）第 4 次工作会议在巴西圣保罗成功召开，会议由哈尔滨大电机研究所孙玉田（标准研制工作组召集人）组织，巴西福伊特公司承办。与会专家基本同意标准结构顺序调整及增加附录的方案，并逐条对标准草案内容进行了讨论。

2018 年 4 月，国际电工委员会/水轮机技术委员会第 33 工作组（IEC/TC4/WG33）“模型到原型压力脉动换算”第 9 次国际工作组会议在瑞士召开，会议讨论将该国际标准制定工作推进到委员会阶段(CD)，此国际标准由我国牵头制定，哈尔滨大电机研究所专家覃大清担任标准工作组召集人。

2018 年 5 月，国际电工委员会/旋转电机标准化技术委员会（IEC/TC2）2018 年年会在中国上海召开，哈尔滨大电机研究所孙玉田作为中国代表团代表，参加了此次会议。孙玉田作为 IEC/TC2/WG33“同步水轮发电机（含发电电动机）技术要求”国际标准工作组召集人，对正在制定中的 IEC 60034-33 国际标准工作情况进行了汇报，该报告得到各国代表的肯定。

（哈尔滨电机厂有限责任公司　刘保生）

2018 年农村水电国际交流与合作有关情况

（一）举办第八届今日水电论坛

水利部、联合国工业发展组织、赞比亚能源部和赞比亚水利卫生和环保部于 2018 年 11 月 6～7 日在赞比亚卢萨卡联合举办第八届今日水电论坛。论坛由东南部非洲共同市场和国际小水电中心承办，主题为水电促进非洲工业发展。论坛通过了《卢萨卡宣言》，倡议进一步通过南南合作推进非洲水电开发，强调绿色发展理念，提出创新投融资体制，为非洲水电及工业发展作出更大贡献。今日水电论坛已成为各国小水电交流合作的重要平台，为推进“一带一路”建设和全球包容可持续工业发展，推动实现联合国 2030 年可持续发展议程涉水目标及非盟 2063 年议程愿景创造了有利条件。

（二）开展小水电技术标准国际化工作

2018年，中国政府和联合国工发组织共同签署文件，正式启动小水电国际标准技术导则项目。国际小水电联合会与联合国工业发展组织合作完成了标准体系设计和小水电技术导则共5大类26项内容的中英文编写工作，为推动小水电“走出去”，在“一带一路”倡议下开展国际产能合作，促进国际小水电发展，推动国际合作创造有利条件。

（三）编写《2019世界小水电发展报告》

2018年，国际小水电中心与联合国工发组织合作开展《2019世界小水电发展报告》编制，邀请141个国家186名专家参与编撰，完成了165个国家和区域报告的整理编辑及中国绿色小水电研究与实践等案例部分的征集和编辑工作。2013年，国际小水电中心与联合国工发组织共同完成的全球首部英文版《2013世界小水电发展报告》正式发布，2016年再版，系统、全面地介绍了全球160个国家的小水电开发状况、潜力、政策和挑战。

（四）联合国机构项目框架下开展全球小水电合作

2018年国际小水电中心完成了“全球环境基金（GEF）中国小水电增效扩容改造增值项目”启动报告，递交联合国工发组织，启动了22个试点电站与工发组织项目合同文件的签署工作。该项目由水利部与联合国工业发展组织共同申请，旨在巩固和提高中国已有小水电增效扩容改造成果，通过修复河道生态，提升安全生产管理和自动化控制水平，带动减排技术推广应用，促进中国小水电可持续发展。在联合国工发组织包容与可持续工业发展理念框架下，向埃塞俄比亚、尼日利亚、吉尔吉斯斯坦、缅甸和秘鲁5个国家提供技术帮助，支持小水电在上述国家的成片开发，2018年完成有关站点的测绘、地勘和设计工作，完成选址技术评估报告及现场考察报告。

（五）促进中非可再生能源技术转移南南合作

国际小水电中心参与联合国开发计划署中国—加纳、中国—赞比亚南南合作可再生能源技术转移项目，牵头实施小水电技术转移示范项目及有关活动，该项目于2014年12月启动，项目执行期为4年，通过与赞比亚、加纳开展可再生能源南南合作，提高有关国家可再生能源利用率、技术水平、电气化率，改善人民生活条件。2018年，国际小水电中心派专家赴赞比亚，为赞方进行小水电政策、技术、管理培训，访问赞比亚能源部门并启动小水电站示范项目建设。

（六）为发展中国家提供技术培训和科技合作

国际小水电中心和水利部农村电气化研究所为发展中国家提供技术培训、技术情报交流和科技合作，2018年，共举办13期援外培训/研修班，为40个国家439名政府官员和技术人员提供了技术培训，培训区域覆盖东南亚、南亚、中亚、西亚、非洲等发展中国家，内容涉及小水电开发、清洁能源、水资源管理、水资源调查与规划、农村电气化、水电站与大坝安全、水利工程建设与管理、减贫与可持续发展、气候变化等。开展与巴基斯坦、尼泊尔、印度尼西亚、塞尔维亚、墨西哥小水电与农村电气化技术联合研究，与东盟可再生能源技术转移、非洲能力建设合作，建设国家级联合研究中心（实验室）、区域技术转移与培训中心等海外合作平台，积极参与中欧水资源交流平台框架下各项活动，通过项目合作和联合研究，形成区域辐射效应，提升与南亚、东盟、中东欧、非洲、拉美地区的小水电技术合作能力，拓展产能国际合作，助力小水电“走出去”。

（国际小水电中心　常方圆
水利部农村电气化研究所　王林军）

黄河水利科学研究院2018年国际学术交流情况

2018年10月15～16日，中国大坝工程学会2018学术年会暨第10届中日韩坝工学术交流会在郑州召开，来自18个国家和地区的700余名专家学者齐聚黄河迎宾馆，共襄坝工学科盛宴。黄河水利科学研究院（以下简称黄科院）作为本次会议承办单位之一，高度重视会议组织工作。由科研处统筹协调，从各业务所及相关部门抽调近40名青年骨干组成大会工作组，超前谋划，全力筹备，严密对接，圆满完成了会议安排的综合协调组、接待和服务保障组、技术资料组、宣传报道组、资源配备组等各项工作，确保大会有序进行。会议期间，挂靠黄科院黄河小浪底研究中心的水库泥沙处理与资源利用专委会承办了“水库泥沙淤积控制与可持续管理专题研讨会”并召开专业委员会2018年度工作会议。

在该次会议上黄科院论文23篇被录用。黄科院副院长、总工程师江恩慧应邀在“水库大坝青年论坛”做“治黄战略研究与实践”的报告；黄科院副院长部国明在“水库泥沙淤积控制与可持续管理专题研讨会”做“多沙水库支流拦门沙坎综合治理技术—以小浪底畛水为例”报告。黄科院多名专家也分别在分会场作主题报告，并就相关问题和与会代表进行了讨论交流。黄科院近期在水工建筑物修复、堤防监测、黄河下游滩区治理水库淤积防治、人工防汛石材研发、生态护坡施工技术等领域取得的科研技术成果得到了充分宣传和推广。

会上，黄科院主持并申报的“黄河下游宽滩区滞洪沉沙功能及滩区减灾技术研究”获得大会颁发的中国大坝工程学会科技进步特等奖，张向萍博士发表的论文《过去1000年黄河下游河道变迁与河患变化》获得第八届汪闻韶院士青年优秀论文奖。

2018年4月12～14日，黄科院应邀作为主办单位之一参加了第5届中国（国际）水生态安全战略论坛。该论坛由北京大学发起，围绕水生态环境前沿科技研究、生态治理技术以及理念、制度、热点焦点问题等，开展学术研讨交流，积极推进水生态文明建设。

黄科院院长王道席应邀主持了特邀报告会。论坛期间共有约40位专家现场作学术报告。黄科院多名专家在论坛做了专题报告。通过参与主办“水生态安全战略论坛”，充分展示了黄科院近年在水生态环境领域研究的最新成果，加强了与业内“学界、政界、商界”的学术交流与技术合作。

2018年4月，印度比哈尔邦水利部部长辛格希率7人代表团来黄科院访问，就河流泥沙管理、堤防安全监测、物理模型试验技术等与黄科院科研人员开展技术交流。黄科院多名专家介绍了黄科院核心科研成果，针对代表团关心的泥沙治理、堤防安全管理等技术，双方还进行了深入交流讨论。印度代表团认为，中国黄河与印度恒河有许多相似之处，黄河治理的许多成功经验非常值得学习，并表示下一步希望能有机会邀请黄河治理专家赴印度恒河考察并提供治理技术。代表团一行还参观了“模型黄河”试验基地，并听取了“模型黄河”总体建设及模型试验情况介绍。

（黄河水利科学研究院）

对外经营与国外工程

中国电力建设集团有限公司2018年国际合作与经营情况

2018年，中国电力建设集团公司（以下简称集团）对外承包工程业务完成营业收入同比增长11.44%，占集团年度完成营业额的24.14%；新签合同额同比增长12.39%，占集团年度境内外新签合同额的34.13%。公司68家子企业在125个国家执行工程总承包或施工承包类项目合同2776项，在建项目合同总金额同比增长6.77%，占集团总体38.86%。集团公司国际业务从业人数合计98305人。

（一）国际管控

2018年，通过集团化建设，集团内国际资源得到整合，集团国际业务得以统筹与协调，成员企业参与国际经营的积极性得以保护和提高，在全球形成了集团化竞争优势。在116个国家设有373个当地机构，在125个国家有在建项目；联合营销、分层营销和授权营销构成了集团化立体营销体系；“一母多子”品牌体系形成；建立了较为完善的组织和工作制度体系；行业布局渐趋合理，竞标、融资和投资三驾马车成为主要营销方式，大中小项目齐头并进，中国电建国际业务的全球化布局基本形成。为更好适应集团国际业务发展的新情况，进一步加强履约监管工作，设立项目履约监管中心，在不改变项目履约单位应承担的履约主体责任和直接责任、不改变区域总部应承担的风险防范和履约监管中心职责、不改变专业部门应承担的项目履约专业技术支持职责的基础上，通过整合公司资源、统筹集团内外资源，健全海外项目履约监管体系，牵头组织海外重大风险项目、重点关注项目、痛点难点事项的监管和处置。

（二）国际经营

2018年，集团签约并生效的竞标项目达340个同比增长23.39%，集团中标的海外现汇EPC项目——沙特港务设施项目，合同额超过206.04亿元。集团海外新能源共签约302.18亿元，总装机容量350万kW，创历史新高，在集团国际业务新签合同中的占比排名首次取代公路，成为仅次于火电、水电之后排名第三的行业。在越南、阿根廷、南非和乌克兰等新能源市场业绩优异；联合中信保、华为等多家新能源企业，成立国际新能源解决方案平台（INES）。

签署的印尼TAS镍矿开采和泰国猜也蓬钾盐矿项目合同总额超过75亿元。中标了菲律宾国家电网公司棉兰老岛-维萨亚斯电网直流联网换流站项目、巴林和阿布扎比海水淡化项目、南非红石光热项目等。全年中标13个援助项目，合同额6.13亿元。塞尔维亚贝尔格莱德绕城公路成为第一个在欧洲实现优惠贷款融资关闭的项目。首次在安提瓜和巴布达、巴拿马、吉布提、圣多美和普林西比、乌克兰、俄罗斯、南非、罗马尼亚、阿尔巴尼亚、智利等10多个国别签订工程合同。

在债权卖断条件下，帮助加纳政府实现表外融资；伊拉克鲁迈拉燃气电站以卖方信贷方式实现融资关闭；越南油汀光伏电站以远期跟单信用证福费廷及特险项下应收账款无追索卖断实现融资关闭；老挝世贸中心等4个项目以“建信通”（出口信用特险融资）完成融资；采用承包商贴息和支付部分保费方式推进玻利维亚庞贝欧公路项目；在香港成功发行3亿美元永续债。2018年，集团与日本东芝、软银、法国NEOEN等多家国际知名企业建立战略合作关系。在拉美，与欧洲企业紧密合作已成为主流商业模式；在中东，与国际著名开发商开展多层次合作。2018年与西方企业在第三方市场合作中标及在建项目11个。

（三）国际履约

强化项目履约管理，履约能力持续提高。沙特延布三期5×66万kW燃油电站项目进度与质量良好，获得“一带一路”联合工作组赞扬；津巴布韦卡里巴南岸水电站扩机项目投产发电；塔吉克斯坦格拉夫纳亚水电站技改项目首台机组提前发电；斯里兰卡莫洛嘎哈堪达大坝项目（M坝）实现竣工；科特迪瓦苏布雷水电站全部机组完成验收；赤道几内亚吉布洛上游调蓄水库工程实现竣工；刚果（金）宗果Ⅱ水电站项目竣工移交；阿尔及利亚23.3万kW光伏电站项目全部并网发电；玻利维亚圣何塞水电站一级电站实现提前并网发电；巴基斯坦特里肯波顿15万kW风电项目进入商业运行；沙特MGS一期项目正式点火运行；摩洛哥努奥二、三期光热电站项目荣获该国“社会贡献奖”和“经济就业促进奖”；新加坡T217地铁项目荣获新加坡陆路交通管理局颁发的“施工环境优秀奖”；马里古伊那水电站等13个境外项目荣获中国对外承包工程商会颁发的“中国海外工程杰出营地”和“中国海外工程优秀营地”奖；巴基斯坦萨希瓦尔2×66万kW燃煤电站项目荣获国家优质工程金质奖；印度古德洛尔电厂一期2×60万kW工程、安哥拉索约-卡帕瑞输变电工程和几内亚凯乐塔水利枢纽工程荣获中国建设工程鲁班奖（境外工程）。

首次完成成员企业国际工程履约评价。组织完成了2017年度成员企业国际工程履约能力评价工作，共有36家成员企业和337个海外在建项目参评，对在质量管理、职业健康安全管理、施工进度管理等项目履约方面表现优异的8家获评A级企业和17个获评优秀项目经理部进行了表彰，同时要求成员企业对排名后5%的项目经理部进行约谈和督导，有效保障集团国际工程履约能力和国际业务竞争力不断提升。

开展海外重大经营风险项目管控处置专项工作。针对海外重大经营风险项目进一步分类梳理项目的风险点，通过专题会议、点对点督导、现场巡查、专家支持、现场督办等措施，指导和帮助项目实施单位找准问题、制定措施，贯彻落实并持续跟踪改进，对重点项目派出督导工作组常驻现场，协调集团内外资源推动重大经营风险化解，海外重大风险项目管控处置工作总体取得积极进展，个别风险已减弱到可控范围内或已实质性完工。

（四）国际商务

海外事业部加强与相关国家部委、主管单位和各行业协会的对接，代表集团公司积极组织并参加了2018年中非合作论坛北京峰会、第九届国际基础设施投资与建设高峰论坛、中央企业国际合作与业务交流工作座谈会、第四届连云港论坛、第三届香港“一带一路”高峰论坛、国际商会中国国家委员会环境与能源委员会2018年下半年工作会议暨能源行业国际化经营的机遇与挑战座谈会。

发挥集团外事局职能，创“中国电建”外事管理品牌。2018年“集团外事管理系统”新增、优化23项功能。新上线“公证认证工作管理”模块。外事局组织编写了15万字的《外事文件汇编》和《外事工作指导手册》，发布了《中国电力建设股份有限公司APEC商务旅行卡管理办法（2018年版）》，组织召开了股份公司外事工作培训会，共有64家成员企业122人参加学习。2018年外事局全年共审批和办理出国（境）团组12598批次，29677人次；新办证照8144本；邀请外国人来华团组741批次，1758人次；办理公证及认证11096本。在外交部领事司全国因公出国（境）签证排名中位列第三、央企第一。

（五）国际重大投融资项目

截至2018年底，电建集团在境外12个国家实施投资项目共计23个，其中正式投产运营项目12个，在建的投资项目11个，项目大多分布在亚洲地区。2018年电建集团境外运营及在建投资项目年度完成投资总额78.28亿元。其中已投产运营项目本年度完成投资额为17.54亿元；在建项目本年度完成投资额60.74亿元。

（中国电力建设集团有限公司）

中国电力建设集团有限公司国际重大工程承包项目2018年进展情况

1. 老挝南欧江梯级水电站项目　该项目是电建集团通过对老挝南欧江全流域整体规划获得全流域开发权，以BOT模式投资建设的水电站项目。该项目总装机容量为127.2万kW，年平均发电量约50.64亿kW·h，特许经营期为29年。2018年12月23日，南欧江二期全面完成年度11个关键节点目标。

2. 巴基斯坦卡西姆燃煤电站项目　该项目由电建集团和卡塔尔AMC公司共同投资开发的2×66万kW卡西姆港燃煤电站，是中巴经济走廊排在首位的“优先实施项目”。2018年4月25日项目正式完工，提前67天进入商业运营，2018年累计发电75.59亿kW·h。该项目荣获2018年度巴基斯坦环境保护优秀大奖。

3. 津巴布韦旺吉燃煤电站三期扩机项目　该项目装机规模为2台33.5万kW的亚临界燃煤发电机组，由中国电建集团与津巴布韦电力公司（ZPC）以BOO模式共同投资开发，该项目是中资企业目前在津巴布韦的最大火电项目，也是津巴布韦独立以来最大的能源基础设施建设项目。2018年6月27日，该项目正式开工。

4. 科特迪瓦苏布雷水电站项目　该项目是科特迪瓦国家能源平衡战略的核心项目，总装机容量为27.5万kW，预计年发电量11.9亿kW·h，由中国电建以EPC模式承建。2018年5月22日，该项目所有机组通过验收，进入质保期。

5. 摩洛哥努奥光热电站项目　该项目是全球单机容量最大的光热电站工程，包括二期20万kW槽式光热电站和三期15万kW塔式光热电站，由中国电建集团与SENER组成联营体以“EPC＋OM”模式承建。2018年1月10日，努奥二期项目并网一次成功。2018年8月15日，努奥三期项目首次并网一次成功。2018年10月22日，努奥二期和三期项目荣获摩洛哥瓦尔扎扎特省政府颁发的“社会贡献奖”和“经济就业促进奖”。

6. 巴基斯坦萨希瓦尔燃煤电站项目　该项目是“中巴经济走廊”优先实施项目，电站总装机容量132万kW，年发电量超过90亿kW·h。2018年8月17日，项目通过竣工验收，实现全面竣工。该项目荣获巴基斯坦能源部颁发的设计金奖、巴基斯坦总理阿巴西亲自签发的“杰出成就奖”和中国施工企业管理协会组织评选的“国家优质工程金质奖”。

7. 津巴布韦卡里巴南岸水电站扩机工程项目　该项目扩机工程设计安装2台单机容量15万kW的混流式水轮发电机组，总装机容量30万kW，公司以“EPC＋F”模式签约。2018年3月28日，举行项目竣工仪式。

8. 阿尔及利亚23.3万kW光伏电站项目　该23.3万kW光伏电站项目是中阿首个光伏电站合作项目，公司以EPC模式签约。2018年1月18日，项目电站全部并网发电。

9. 沙特阿美MGS一期项目　该项目MGS（燃气增压站）一期项目属于沙特东气西输主管线扩建项目，包括建设两座大型天然气压缩站，使日输气能力从84亿立方英尺提升至96亿立方英尺，是沙特国王亲自关注的重点项目，由中国电建集团以EPC模式承建。2018年1月2日，项目首台燃机完成全部调试工作，正式点火运行。

10. 赞比亚下凯富峡水电站项目　该项目总装机容量为75万kW，是赞比亚40年来投资开发的第一个大型水电站项目，公司以“EPC＋F”模式签约。2018年6月21日，项目完成首笔融资放款。

11. 巴基斯坦特里肯波顿15万kW风电项目　该项目总装机容量15万kW，共安装87台0.1715万kW的风力发电机组，公司以EPC模式签约。2018年9月13日，该项目全线投产发电，工期累计提前96天完工。

（中国电力建设集团有限公司）

中国电建集团北京勘测设计研究院有限公司2018年国际业务开展情况

2018年，中国电建集团北京勘测设计研究院有限公司（以下简称“北京院”）立足于水电、风电、太阳能、房建和路桥的勘测设计与工程总承包项目，重点开拓非洲、东南亚市场，综合内外部资源的协调与培养，提升海外项目跟踪执行能力，大力发展国际市场。

2018年北京院国际业务成功签订了合同额约12.77亿元，包括印尼巴丹托鲁水电站中国电力建设集团（股份）有限公司境外工程承包项目内部委托实施协议、埃塞俄比亚哈雷雷—维尔巴萨水电项目可行性研究报告评审咨询服务委托合同书、援阿塞拜疆移动式电站项目等10个援外物资项目可行性研究合同、阿根廷4个风电场（18.5万kW）调查及技术评判咨询服务采购合同、几内亚共和国林桑3.3万kW AC光伏项目勘察测量服务合同、非洲佛得角电力公司项目顾问咨询服务合同等16项合同。

2018年北京院国际项目的履约能力进一步增加，积极配合集团和其他窗口公司，先后完成了水电、风电多个项目的收购尽职调查和可研报告审查等技术咨询工作；印度尼西亚巴丹托鲁水电站总承包项目与水电十局的紧密联营体正式组建，并与集团签署了内部委托实施协议，正式以联营体的形式开展项目履约工作，设计项目完成了基本设计的大部分工作；尼泊尔上崔树里3A水电站完成大坝及主要水工建筑物震后整体修复方案设计及全厂机电设计工作，并获得业主和工程师的批准。

北京院将进一步加大国际市场开拓力度。巩固传统国际水电市场，稳步推进国际转型业务，加强技术服务和商务协调，做好相关合同商签，力争实现国际水电项目快速增长；同时，继续加强与集团内平台公司、海外区域总部及外部窗口单位的联系，通过优质的技术服务、快速响应配合，争取新的项目合作机会。根据国际项目的合同要求和项目特点，探索项目管理模式，配套相应的责权利考核，通过强化过程监督，充分调动和发挥各层级人员效能。

（中国电建集团北京勘测设计研究院有限公司 王珊珊）

中国电力建设集团有限公司承建的海外水电工程 2018 年进展情况

（一）巴基斯坦塔贝拉四期扩建工程

中国电力建设集团有限公司（以下简称中国电建）所属的中国水利水电第七工程局有限公司（以下简称水电七局）承建的巴基斯坦塔贝拉四期扩建工程首台机组成功并网发电。工程于 2013 年 10 月 29 日开工，先后克服深水区蜂窝状直腹式钢板桩围堰的设计与施工、百米级深水下叠梁门安装与拆除、复杂结构混凝土快速拆除等多项工程技术难题，完成世界最大压力钢管岔管群的安装建设。2018 年，塔贝拉四期扩建项目成功获得 Section 1 项下 T4 低位取水口拦污栅安装和 Section 3 项下压力钢管相关施工等两个移交证书。

该电站是目前巴基斯坦最大的水力发电站，其发电量占巴基斯坦全国发电量的 1/3，具有灌溉、发电、防洪等效益。电站整体装机容量将从原有的 3478MW 扩增至 4888MW，能够大大缓解巴基斯坦目前电力供应紧张的情况。

2018 年，项目继续围绕已完成的科研成果进行奖项申报，其中百米级深水无导轨下闸技术在中国大坝工程学会、中施企协会及中电力建设科学技术进步奖项评选中获奖。钢板桩围堰施工工法获批中国水利工程协会工法。

（二）白俄罗斯维捷布斯克水电站工程

由中国电建所属的北京院设计、水电九局承建的白俄罗斯维捷布斯克水电站竣工。白俄罗斯维捷布斯克水电站是白俄罗斯境内最大的水电站，以发电为主，兼顾航运，素有“白俄三峡”的美誉，装机总容量 40MW。水电九局经过 3 年时间建设，电站首台机组于 2016 年 12 月底并网发电，2017 年 7 月船闸具备通航条件，年均发电量 1.38 亿 kW·h。2018 年 7 月 31 日维保期结束，举行电站竣工移交仪式，并进行 EPC 交钥匙。该电站是中国与白俄罗斯经济技术合作的重点项目，也是中白两国“一带一路”战略合作成果的重要标志。

（三）科特迪瓦苏布雷水电站项目

苏布雷水电站位于萨桑德拉河上纳瓦瀑布处，是科特迪瓦国家能源平衡战略的核心项目，总装机容量为 275MW，年发电量 11.9 亿 kW·h，由中国电建以 EPC 模式承建。项目于 2013 年 9 月 24 日开工，总工期 56.5 个月，原计划 2018 年 5 月竣工，在中科双方的共同努力下，比合同工期提前 8 个月建成投入使用，成为中科合作的又一标志性、典范性工程。

2017 年 11 月 2 日，苏布雷水电站举行了隆重的竣工典礼。2018 年 5 月 22 日，该项目全部机组顺利通过验收，标志着该项目全面进入质保期。

中国电建荣获了“中科合作奖”。

（四）柬埔寨桑河二级水电站

桑河二级水电站是柬埔寨已建的最大水电工程，位于柬埔寨王国东北部上丁省西山区境内的桑河干流上，由中国所属的水电八局承建。该电站大坝全长 6500m，是亚洲第一长坝；共安装 8 台中国制造的 50MW 灯泡贯流式机组，总装机容量 400MW，占柬埔寨全国总装机容量的近 20%。电站于 2013 年 10 月开工，2017 年 12 月 9 日首台机组投产发电；2018 年 10 月 21 日，8 台机组全部投产发电；12 月 17 日，电站正式投产竣工。

（五）赞比亚下凯富峡水电站项目

下凯富峡水电站项目位于赞比亚首都卢萨卡西南 90km 的凯富埃河上，总装机容量为 750MW，是赞比亚 40 年来投资开发的第一个大型水电站项目，由中国电建集团以“EPC＋F”模式承建。2015 年 11 月 28 日，该项目隆重举行开工仪式。

2018 年 6 月 6 日，项目首仓大坝碾压混凝土开盘浇筑；6 月 21 日，项目完成首笔融资放款；8 月 21 日，水电站引水系统主体混凝土首仓浇筑。

（六）津巴布韦卡里巴南岸水电站扩机工程

卡里巴南岸水电站扩机工程是津巴布韦独立以来开工建设的规模第二大能源项目，是在原有电站基础上进行扩机建设，设计安装 2 台单机容量 150MW 的混流式水轮发电机组，总装机容量 300MW，由中国电建集团以“EPC＋F”模式承建，由中国进出口银行提供优惠贷款。

2014 年 9 月 4 日，时任津巴布韦总统穆加贝为卡里巴南岸水电站扩机工程开工剪彩，标志着项目正式启动。2017 年 12 月 25 日，项目首台机组成功并网发电。

2018 年 2 月 26 日，项目第 2 台机组成功并网发电；3 月 28 日，津巴布韦总统埃默森·姆南加古瓦出席该工程竣工仪式，为电站进行揭牌剪彩，标志着津巴布韦独立以来最大的水电项目全面建成投产。

（中国电力建设集团有限公司）

津巴布韦卡里巴南岸扩机工程科技创新及社会效益

里巴水电站位于非洲赞比亚和津巴布韦两国交界的赞比西河中游卡里巴峡谷内，工程为在南岸岸坡山体内布置单独的引水发电系统，主要建筑物包括进水口、2条引水隧洞、地下厂房、尾水调压室、尾水隧洞、尾水出口、以及地面主变和330kV开关站。

（一）技术创新及科技成果

工程开工建设以来，工程建设项目高度重视工程建设中的每一项技术创新，取得了较好技术创新效益：

(1) 施工中积极进行技术创新，采用了建筑业十大项中的20项新技术、2项新材料、10项新设备，为创精品工程奠定了基础。

(2) 2项科技项目成果获得省部级科技进步奖，《扩机工程深水围堰爆破拆除及防护技术》荣获2018年度中国爆破协会科技进步二等奖，《大直径埋藏式调压井施工关键技术》荣获中国电建集团科技进步二等奖；《大直径地下调压井多仓体滑模施工工法》获得省部级工法；《提高无黏结锚索张拉一次验收合格率》荣获中国电力协会QC三等奖。

（二）社会效益

通过采取属地化管理，聘用当地优秀劳工管理人员、律师，有效解决了劳务纠纷，按时发放工资，保证劳务的积极工作，前后为当地提供了3000多个就业岗位；与当地军队、警察、劳工部、安全管理局、海关等保持友好协作关系，资助当地交通设施、教育文化、民生工程等基础设施建设100余万美元，认真履行央企的社会责任，树立了良好企业品牌！

（中国水利水电第十一工程局有限公司　张昆）

印尼 Poso-1 水电站工程建设进展情况

（一）工程概况

Poso-1水电站位于印度尼西亚东部苏拉维西岛中央中苏拉维西省 Poso 湖下游 Poso 河上，整个 Poso 河流域共规划了3级，分别为 Poso-1(4×3万kW)、Poso-2(3×6.5万kW＋4×6.5万kW) 和 Poso-3。Poso-1水电站距中苏拉维西省省会帕卢 (Palu) 约235km。Poso-1水电站利用 Poso 湖形成水库，闸址距 Poso 湖出口约14km，闸址处的集水面积为1920.70km^2，多年平均流量139.96m^3/s，正常蓄水位511.70m，最低运行水位507.00m。电站总引用流量300m^3/s，利用水头约50m。Poso-1水电站采用低闸引水式开发，主要建筑物包括闸坝、右岸取水口、引水钢管、钢制调压塔、压力钢管、地面厂房等。该工程业主、主体施工单位为印尼 PT Poso Energi Satu Pamona 公司（以下简称业主），设计单位为中国电建集团成都勘测设计研究院有限公司（以下简称成都院）。

（二）工程进展情况

1. 项目勘测设计过程

(1) 项目前期设计情况。Poso 河三个梯级的可研报告均由日本咨询公司在20世纪80年代完成，Poso-2由业主在可研报告的基础上进行了基础设计和详细设计。成都院于2010年开始介入 Poso 河流域水电设计咨询工作，于2010年完成了 Poso-2水电站的相关咨询工作。

(2) 项目基础设计情况。2013年7月，业主项目经理阿里（Ali）先生和商务经理拉赫曼（Rahman）在成都与成都院签署了关于 Poso 河流域开发合作的 MOU（谅解备忘录）。2014年9月，业主与成都院在雅加达签订了 Poso-1水电站闸坝及取水口基础设计合同，按照合同要求，成都院于2014年11月底提交了《印度尼西亚共和国中苏拉威西省 Poso-1水电站首部枢纽闸坝及取水口基础设计报告》，并通过了业主组织的评审。2014年11月26日，业主又在雅加达与成都院签订了 Poso-1水电站引水发电建筑物基础设计复核咨询合同，成都院于2015年4月底提交了《印度尼西亚共和国中苏拉威西省 Poso-1水电站引水发电建筑物基础设计复核报告》，于2015年5月通过了业主组织的评审。

(3) 项目详细设计情况。2016年6月4日，业主在雅加达与成都院签订了 Poso-1水电站闸坝及取水口详细设计合同，合同内容包括了闸坝及取水口详细设计，引水发电建筑物详细设计复核，闸坝及取水口详细设计印尼大坝安全委员会审查配合，及现场设计咨询等4个部分。①闸坝及取水口详细设计。2015年9月，在接收并确认业主提供的全套闸坝及取水口设计输入资料后，成都院随即正式开展 Poso-1水电站闸坝及取水口详细设计工作，至2016年底已全部完成合同规定的闸坝及取水口详细设计工作。②引水发电建筑物详细设计复核。2015年9月，在接收并确认业主提供的全套引水发电建筑物设计资料后，成都院随即正式开展 Poso-1水电站引水发电建筑物详细设计复核工作，于2016年7月完成并提交了《印度尼西亚共和国中苏拉威西省 Poso-1水电站引水发电建筑物详细设计复核报告》，并于同月通过了业主的评审。③闸坝及取水口详细设计印尼大坝安全委员会审查配合。为了配合印尼大坝安全委员会Poso-1水电站审查工作，在Poso-1水电站闸坝及取水口详细设计成果的基础上，成都院完成并提交了相关设计报告、计算报告、技术要求共27份，并派遣水工处张公平、机电处陈相楠多次赴印尼配合业主准备会议材料，参加会议，并作项目汇报。经过三次会议，Poso-1水电站最终于2016年8月通过了印尼大坝安全委员会的审查，项目获得了设计许可和施工许可。④现场设计咨询。在开展Poso-1水电站详细设计的同时，为了配合Poso-1水电站现场施工进展，积极解决现场施工过程中的技术问题，成都院从2015年12月起开始开展现场咨询工作，至2018年12月底累计已完成15人·月现场咨询任务。

2. 项目现场实施进展

（1）闸坝及取水口。闸址区导流明渠于2015年8月开始进行开挖施工，2016年3月底开挖、衬砌完成，并开始过流；2016年8月，Poso-1水电站闸坝及取水口基础及详细设计通过印尼大坝安全委员会评审，正式获得设计和施工许可，并开始一期工程（包括左岸重力坝、1～3号泄洪闸、冲沙闸、消力池及海漫）土建施工；2017年11月，Poso-1水电站闸坝及取水口一期工程土建施工和金属结构安装调试完成，并实现一期工程过流和二期工程（包括1～2号取水口和右岸重力坝）截流；截至2018年12月，Poso-1水电站闸坝及取水口二期工程已完成全部混凝土施工和闸门安装调试及蓄水前准备工作。

（2）引水发电建筑物。截至2018年12月，Poso-1水电站引水发电建筑物（包括引水钢管、调压塔、压力钢管和地面厂房）已经完成全部开挖、支护、混凝土和机电设备安装调试工作，电站计划于2019年6月底实现首台机发电。

（中国电建集团成都勘测设计研究院有限公司 张公平）

巴西圣西芒水电站特许经营权转让2018年进展情况

（一）电站概况

圣西芒（SãoSimão）电站位于巴西戈亚斯州和米纳斯吉拉斯州交界的巴拉那伊巴河干流，工程开发任务为发电和防洪。该电站1978年6月完成土建工程，原装机容量26.8万kW×6台，2000年进行增容改造，增容后的装机容量28.5万kW×6台。同时在现发电机右侧预留4个安装机位，最终装机可达268万kW。根据我国有关技术标准规定，该工程为一等大（1）型工程，相应主要水工建筑物级别为1级，次要水工建筑物级别为3级。

该电站枢纽采用河床混凝土坝、坝后式厂房、溢洪道、两岸土石坝布置型式。坝轴线为折线，坝顶总长约3680.00m，最大坝高约127.00m。其中左岸、右岸土石坝分别长约1664 m、1440m，河床重力坝长约576m。电站正常蓄水位401.00m，调节库容为55.4亿m^3，具有季调节能力。下游正常尾水位339.30m，电站坝址控制流域面积171370km^2，多年平均流量2380m^3/s。溢洪道布置在右岸为9孔开敞式泄洪闸，最大泄量24100m^3/s。电站进水口布置于溢洪道左侧，单机引用流量425.0m^3/s。主厂房尺寸为167m×23m（长×宽）。

（二）特许经营权转让

2017年5月，巴西联邦政府宣布对圣西芒等4个水电项目的特许经营权招标。2017年9月27日国家电投海外公司以最低溢价中标圣西芒电站30年特许经营权。随后按照巴西电力监管局ANEEL要求，提交各种法律、技术、财务和合规资格文件，11月10日，正式签署项目特许经营权协议，并确定圣西芒交割过渡期为6个月。

（三）电站运营顺利接管

为平稳顺利交割，海外公司组建圣西芒公司境外管理团队和提出管理方案，借鉴三峡巴西公司良好管理经验，派出国内骨干任董事会、CCO等重要管理职位，明确了公司“双VP”、关键部门负责人“双配制”管理架构等措施，有力保障电站稳定过渡和顺利接管。经过6个月过渡期，2018年5月10日，海外公司正式接管圣西芒电站，顺利实现自主运营。

（四）电站运营模式

电站采取车间式管理，主要负责全厂的日常运维工作。电站经理是电站日常运营维护的主要负责人，负责电站运行、维护及安全管理等方面的工作。

（1）运行管理。电站设发电计划工程师1名、发电运行主管1名，统计分析专责1名，发电计划专责1名，值班运行人员18人，值班运行人员分三班倒班开展运行工作（五值三倒）。电厂接管前，所有运行人员跟随Cemig运行班组进行为期半年的倒班实习，所有前台倒班运行人员经过系统培训，并取得ONS调度上岗资格证。

（2）维护管理。电站设维护工程师1名，维护计划工程师和维护主管各1名，下辖6名电气技术员，6名机械技术员，负责电厂日常性维护消缺保养等工作。

（3）检修技改管理。圣西芒公司在圣保罗设有检修管理经理1名、技改管理经理1名，共9人组成电站技术团队，不属于电站人员配置。电站重大缺陷及检修技改等均外委第三方专业公司。技术团队作为电站安全技术保障体系，对电站检修技改规划、生产技术、工作流程、资源组织等方面进行指导，强化技术指导、技术研发对安全生产的支撑作用。一般情况，每台机组每年进行一次7天左右的定期预防性维护（有大修的除外）；机组大约在运行32000h后，安排一次40～60天左右的大型检修。维护计划由维护计划工程师负责修订，再经电站运维管理团队和圣保罗技术团队商定上报ONS批准后实施。

（4）安全管理。圣西芒公司在圣保罗设置HSE经理1名，在电站配置2名HSE专责，分别为健康安全专责和环境专责，接受圣西芒公司HSE经理的工作指导和管理。HSE管理部门主要负责电站工作人员安全培训、承包商HSE合规性检查、生产现场人、物、环境的安全管理、PPE管理、危险化学品管控、安全管理制度完善等安全监督管理工作。

（5）组织机构。电厂主要设经理1人，IT专员1人，运维工程师1人等，直属员工46人，第三方员工24人。

（五）运营管理成果

2018年是圣西芒公司组建第一年，公司所有人员克服电站设备老化严重、人员少、工作任务重等困难，全面完成电站年度生产任务。

（1）加强设备巡视和维护。针对电站设备老旧的现状，加强设备巡检与维护管理。成功处理2号主变低压侧套管漏油、500kV短线路绝缘子破损等重大设备缺陷和隐患，有效保证了等效可利用率目标的实现。2018年全年机组不可利用小时数仅2708h（含计划检修时间），与2017年相比下降近50%；年强迫不可利用小时数332.51h，仅为2017年非停时间的1/3左右。

（2）合理规范组织检修。按照巴西电力监管相关规定和技术规范要求，分别完成3、4、5、6号机组的7天预防性检修和2号机组的60日大修。自接管后完成发电量60.76亿kW·h，全年实现发电量92.20亿kW·h。

（3）安全可控在控。巴西公司始终坚持中西安全文化结合，做到人员落实、制度落实、责任落实；中方外派团队不定期向巴方运行团队传达SPIC相关安全文件要求，结合季节特点定期提示电站运营团队加强防火、防汛工作，强化各项工作质量管理等要求；制定年度HSE的KPI指标，坚持员工安全教育，全年共组织填报风险预控卡395份，安全观察卡1708份。截至2018年12月31日，电站连续安全生产236天，未发生人身伤害事故和未遂事件、未发生责任性较大及以上设备事故、未发生重大环境污染事故及环保减排未达标问题。

（六）设备现状及技改规划

由于圣西芒电站运行年限长，同时原特许经营商CEMIG很早就停止了对电厂的技改投入，电站的电气一次、二次设备已严重超期服役。在电站接管之初，就考虑对电站设备进行升级改造。技改规划的总体思路是：鉴于大坝、厂房等水工建筑物状况良好，不考虑进行技改；水力机械及金属结构总体不错，只进行局部改造，重点是对其电气控制及机械液压控制系统等进行更新。初步计划在2019年完成技改前期的设计、招标、采购等准备工作，并优先完成优先对厂房桥机、坝顶门机、尾水门机等起重设备的技术改造，发变电主设备的正式技改工作计划从2021年4月1日开始到2027年12月31日结束，以每年一台机的速度完成电站整体技改。

（国家电力投资集团公司海外投资有限公司 陈晓祥）

玻利维亚圣何塞水电站工程建设情况

圣何塞（San Jose）水电站工程位于玻利维亚科恰班巴省哈帕雷区，距离科恰班巴市115km。该水电站采用2级引水发电，毛水头约684m，2级水电站的总装机容量12.4万kW。1级水电站已于2018年1月17日顺利实现提前并网发电，2级水电站计划2019年2月28日完工。

圣何塞1级水电站为引水式开发，收集了原有San Isabel水电站的尾水以及其他7条河流的水量，通过库容130000m^3的一级调节水库以及引水竖井进入引水隧洞，主引水隧洞长度约4876m，副引水洞长度3950m，最大净水头307m，设计净水头294m，设计引用流量21.4m^3/s，2台机组总装机容量5.5万kW，年发电量3.47亿kW·h；圣何塞2级水电站，最大净水头360m，设计净水头342m，设计引用流量23m^3/s，2台机组总装机容量6.9万kW，年发电量4.07亿kW·h。

圣何塞1级水电站的尾水进入容量为35000m^3的二级调节水库，从该调节水库通过长度约6692m的隧洞引水到圣何塞2级水电站调压井。

该项目合同金额约为1.25亿美元。

（一）工程特点

该工程项目的主要施工内容为地下工程，即18.6km长的引水隧洞开挖与衬砌施工，引水竖井和调压井数量较多。主要存在以下施工特点：

（1）18.6km的超长深埋小断面引水隧洞施工，洞径3.7m。主要地质条件为两种类型的岩石，即石英砂岩以及泥质页岩。

(2) 5座竖井及调压井施工，洞径从2.7～7.5m不等，深度40～120m。主要地质条件为堆积层、石英砂岩以及泥质页岩。

(3) 引水隧洞开挖与衬砌施工共布置了7个支洞，分12个作业面进行，地下开挖工作面多。单头最大掘进长度为1.8km，需要根据各个掘进面的地质条件、掘进长度、地下水条件等确定合适的出渣运输方式和设备、供电方式、通风方式、支护方式来确保施工安全及施工工期。

(4) 鉴于竖井和调压井数量多，需根据不同竖井或调压井的深度、直径、地质条件等确定合适的开挖方式（正井或反井）。

(5) 该水电站属于引水式发电方式，圣何塞1级电站收集了原有San Isabel电站的尾水以及其他另外7条河流的水量来进行发电，圣何塞2级电站收集了1级电站的尾水进行发电，工程施工范围大，地上与地下工作面高峰时多达22处。

（二）工程进展及科技创新

该水电站由中电建所属水电十一局参建，项目自2014年7月开工以来，员工克服了地质条件差、道路塌方、施工环境恶劣等难题，一方面加大技术创新力度，保证施工质量与进度，另一方面积极克服语言障碍，严格遵守玻利维亚法律法规，坚持提升属地化管理水平，增强HSE管理能力，稳定劳务队伍。

2018年工程进展情况：①完成了圣何塞1级水电站地上工程以及地下工程的试运行，圣何塞1级电站于2018年1月17日投入运行；②完成了2级电站引水洞砼衬砌以及灌浆施工，2级电站1号支洞封堵，1A号支洞封堵以及2号支洞封堵施工；③完成了2号调压井的开挖和支护施工，预计2019年1月底完成2号调压井的混凝土衬砌施工。

工程建设施工单位根据该工程特点及需要，积极研究新工艺、新方法，有针对性地开展、并完成了“超长深埋富水条件下小断面隧洞工程开挖施工技术研究及应用”“复杂地质条件下经济高效开挖竖井的技术研究及应用”“页岩地质条件下穿有水河道隧洞开挖防坍塌技术研究”“小断面引水隧洞异形模板砼快速衬砌施工技术研究”等4个项目课题研究，累计科研投入3465万元；《自进式锚杆施工工法》获2017年电建工法。

该工程建设以来，受到玻利维亚国家和主流媒体的广泛关注和报道，以及业主的多次信函表扬。中国企业形象和品牌美誉度进一步提升；同时，良好的履约能力，为继续开展玻利维亚能源建设项目奠定了良好的基础。

（中国水利水电第十一工程局有限公司　刘金明）

科特迪瓦格西波-波波里水电站工程2018年建设情况

（一）工程概况

格西波-波波里水电站位于科特迪瓦境内的萨桑德拉河上，为干流“一库六级”水电梯级开发的第3级，工程场址位于苏布雷市，电站坝址距上游苏布雷水电站坝址约15km。该水电站也是中国企业继成功建设苏布雷水电站之后，成功中标的又一水电项目，是国家“一带一路”项目建设的进一步延伸。该工程主体建筑物的布置方案充分利用坝址区河段瀑布形成的天然落差，通过修建高度不大的挡大坝，选择合适的发电厂房和尾水渠位置，对厂房和尾水渠进行深开挖，以获得较大的发电水头和电站装机容量，经济效益显著。

为充分利用两岸地形，大坝轴线拱向下游。大坝坝型主要为均质土坝，在溢洪道和厂房两侧布置心墙土坝，均质土坝和心墙土坝之间采用过渡坝连接。坝顶高程108.50m，坝顶宽度9.0m，全长约4.2m，最大坝高约17m，全线采用灌浆帷幕进行防渗。电站库容8200万m^3，为日调节电站，电站采用坝式开发，正常蓄水位106.00m，设计洪水位为106.00m，非常洪水位为107.00m。坝顶高程108.50m，电站装机容量11.29万kW，最大引用流量为774m^3/s。

溢洪道布置在萨桑德拉河原河道左岸支流上，由6孔溢洪道组成，单孔闸门净宽12.0m，总净宽72.0m，闸室均采用开敞式，均装有弧形闸门对水流进行控制。溢洪道闸室后设长40.5m、宽92.0m的消力池进行消能。同时，为保证下游居民生活用水，在溢洪道闸墩上布置一生态流量管。电站厂房位于主河道右侧，距溢洪道约810m。厂房为河床式贯流机组厂房，厂区枢纽建筑物主要由主机间坝段、安装间、副厂房、引水渠、尾水渠、主变场、回车场等组成。

根据施工进度安排，该工程采用两期施工。一期为全年导流，通过左岸河道泄流，修建河道右侧的大坝、混凝土溢流坝段和厂房坝段，导流期3年。二期为枯期导流，通过溢流坝段泄流，修建左岸大坝，导流期为6个月。

该项目的EPC合同由科特迪瓦能源公司与中国水电国际建设集团国际工程有限公司（以下简称中国水电）2017年11月签订，设计单位为成都勘测设计研究院，主体施工为中国水电第五工程局。合同额3.36亿美元。其中，合同额15%的资金由业主自筹，其余向中国进出口银行贷款。根据EPC合同约定，工程建设总工期为40个月，首台机组将于开工后的第34个月投产运行。

（二）工程进展情况

1. 勘测设计过程

（1）2015年9月～2016年初，中国水电完成了该项目可研阶段的地质勘察、测绘工作。现场完成的勘探试验项目主要包括：钻孔51.4m/3孔，浅井24.3m/10个；土体检测10组，岩石强度试验2组，骨料碱活性试验2组；常水头注水试验6段，压水试验10段。

（2）2017年7～10月，中国水电开展了该项目的补充地质勘察工作，进一步探明工程区的地质情况。勘察工作包括工程区及料场的测量、地表地质测绘、钻探、浅井、地球物理勘探和岩土体物理力学性质试验等。

（3）EPC合同签订后，总包方启动详细初步阶段勘测设计工作，包括该阶段的勘察和详细初步设计报告的编制，该阶段的设计成果于2018年初正式提交业主，经过多次修编后，报告于2018年底通过咨询工程师审查。该报告的审查通过，也为后续施工图设计工作的顺利开展奠定了良好的基础。

（4）总包方委托设计分包方编制该项目的融资可研报告《格西波—波波里项目融资可研报告》，并于2018年6月提交中国进出口银行评审，截至2018年底，银行基本认可该报告的融资方案和设计方案，受中美贸易摩擦影响，项目融资工作受到一定的影响，也对后续的设计和施工工作的开展带来了一定困难。

（5）根据工程建设需要，枢纽建筑物的开挖施工图于2018年初提交业主，也标志着项目进入了施工图设计阶段。2018年主要完成的设计产品包括溢洪道、厂房、大坝的结构图、开挖图、基础处理图和部分底板钢筋图等。但受融资进度影响，勘测设计工作较为缓慢。

2. 项目进展　根据业主对工程建设的要求，一期围堰于2018年3月开始填筑，同年8月围堰填筑结束。2018年6月厂房和尾水渠开始开挖，同年9月溢洪道开始开挖。受项目融资影响，现场施工进度缓慢，截至2018年底主要施工项目形象面貌如下：

（1）临建工程。现已完成机修车间、现场油库、现场试验室、筛分、拌和站、钢筋加工厂，以及33kv临时供电设施的建设，目前正在进行拌和站、筛分系统运行调试工作。

（2）主体工程。①大坝：完成PK1＋600和PK3＋650全部坝基范围清障，以及PK2＋811至PK2＋971的帷幕灌浆生产试验。②溢洪道：基坑大面已基本成型，除上游齿槽未开挖外，其余部位均已挖至设计高程。③厂房：主要进行基坑石方开挖工作，基坑已开挖至EL86m高程。④尾水渠：主要进行桩号0＋000～0＋150之间的石方开挖工作，基坑大面已开挖至EL87m高程。

（中国电建集团成都勘测设计研究院有限公司
商开卫）

几内亚凯乐塔水利枢纽工程建设进展情况

目前，几内亚运行最大的水利枢纽——凯乐塔水利枢纽（Kaleta）工程是一座完全采用中国标准，由中几两国共同出资、三峡集团中国水利电力对外公司（CWE）EPC总承包（中国水利水电第三工程局有限公司施工承包）承建的水利枢纽。该水利枢纽不仅解决了几内亚电力短缺问题，也成为中几合作的新见证。

凯乐塔水利枢纽位于西非几内亚共和国，项目位于孔库雷河下游一段河道较为宽阔处。大坝采用碾压混凝土重力坝，由挡水坝段、引水坝段、溢流坝段、泄洪底孔坝段组成，坝顶高程114.00m，最大坝高31m，坝顶宽5m，坝轴线长1150m。正常蓄水位110m，死水位109m，坝址多年平均流量346m^3/s，水库库容2300万m^3。发电厂房为压力钢管引水式地面厂房，总长117.60m，总宽51.85m，总高度63.00m，主要建筑物包括主厂房、安装间、GIS楼及出线、副厂房、压力管道等。电站装有3台立式轴流转桨式水轮发电机组，采用“一机一管”布置，每条长度约84.347m。水轮机安装高程52m，机组的中心间距为22m，单机额定容量为7.82万kW，总装机容量为23.46万kW，多年平均发电量为9.65亿kW·h。

项目于2012年4月18日正式开工，2012年5月25日一期截流完成，2014年11月12日二期截流完成，2015年4月15日大坝混凝土浇筑完成，2015年5月28日首台（3号）机组、6月20日第二台（2号）机组、8月28日第三台（1号）机组顺利通过72小时试运行投产发电，实现一年三投的建设目标，2015年9月20日主体工程通过完工验收。

在工程建设过程中，由于几内亚经济发展落后、基础设施欠完善、物资紧缺、环境恶劣，尤其是2014年年初埃博拉疫情暴发，凯乐塔项目的推进遇到了很大困难。在中几双方人员的共同努力下，项目团队克服重重困难，采取一切能采取的措施，确保施工人员安全，施工得以继续，进度也有了保障。埃博拉疫情爆发期间，在几内亚很多项目陷入停滞情况下，中方员工继续坚守阵地，确保项目按期发电。项目投产之际，吸引各大媒体高度关注，彭博新闻社等多家海外媒体给予高度赞扬。

2015年9月28日，几内亚总统孔戴、刚果（布）总统、尼日尔总统，以及尼日利亚、加纳、塞拉利昂、阿联酋等10余国家领导人和使节，乘坐直升机飞抵现场，共同出席凯乐塔水利枢纽现场发电庆典活动。据悉，多国首脑共同出席水利枢纽发电仪式在全世界尚属首次，充分显示出该项目对于几内亚国家发展的非凡意义。凯乐塔电站的投运对改善几内亚电力紧缺局面、满足国民经济发展对能源的需求、改善人民的生活水平，具有十分重要的作用。同时，凯乐塔水利枢纽也将带动几内亚其他水利枢纽项目的进一步执行。庆典中，中国中央电视台、新华社非洲分社、几内亚多家主流媒体进行了现场采访报道。

凯乐塔水利枢纽工程的建成改善了几内亚电力严重短缺的状况，使几内亚国家的总装机容量翻番，促使几内亚进入能源自给自足的时代，为经济、社会发展提供电力支撑，并为几内亚矿业发展提供能源保障。

凯乐塔水利枢纽工程的建成投产，实现了中国标准“走出去”，高标准建立精品工程，彰显中国品牌形象，践行国家“一带一路”发展倡议。

工程建成投产为几内亚社会发展做出了突出贡献，且设计效果艺术性与观赏性强，成为几内亚工程建设的里程碑，为纪念其重大意义，几内亚政府发行了以凯乐塔水利枢纽为背景最大面值货币。

截至2018年底，凯乐塔水利枢纽已累计发电约27.08亿kW·h。“几内亚凯乐塔水利枢纽工程”是非洲大陆能源项目的成功典范，被誉为“西非水电能源领域一颗闪耀的明珠”。也被中国建筑业协会评为2018年度中国建设工程鲁班奖（境外工程）。

（中国水利水电第三工程局有限公司
许泾川　方涛）

赞比亚下凯富峡水电站工程 2018年建设进展情况

下凯富峡水电站位于赞比亚首都卢萨卡东南约90km的Kafue河上，工程枢纽建筑物包括碾压混凝土大坝、坝身泄洪系统、右岸引水系统、调压井和地面式厂房。项目总工期，1549天（51个月）；首台机组发电，1437天（48个月）；业主营地（Township），730天。合同金额15.66亿美元。

（一）2018年工程进展情况

2018年，下凯富峡项目生产进入高峰期，各部位工作全面展开，现场积极组织设备高效运行、保障材料供应，项目总体进度可控。

（1）大坝混凝土浇筑。大坝RCC浇筑至497.5m高程，浇筑高度47m（总高130.5m），累积浇筑51.7万m^3（总方量130万m^3）。

（2）厂房、尾水渠及开关站浇筑。厂房主体一期混凝土全部完成，累计浇筑93540m^3；二期混凝土紧跟机电安装进行浇筑，目前1～5号机尾水管层混凝土已浇筑完成，累积浇筑5540m^3（总计18940m^3）。尾水渠左岸边坡混凝土浇筑至367.2m高程，右岸已完成浇筑至387.0m高程。开关站电缆沟及控制楼基础开挖完成，垫层浇筑完成。

（3）引水系统。引水洞、发电洞、调压井开挖已全部完成，混凝土工作全面展开，其中进水塔浇筑12.5m（509～521.5m高程），发电洞衬砌完成108m，调压井底板浇筑完成（488.5m高程以下）。

（4）永久道路。目前已完成永久道路路床开挖185万m^3，回填43.8万m^3，路床开挖回填全部完成；subbase料填筑完成40km，道路填筑施工满足进度计划，永久道路排水沟砌筑基本完成，满足雨季材料进场运输及防洪度汛要求。

（5）业主运营村。业主运营村总建筑面积51045㎡，目前累计完成建筑面积26310㎡，总体完成51%。其中15栋A型房施工完成，93栋B型房完成42栋，剩余51栋B型房及49栋C型房主体基本完成，中学、宾馆施工全部完成。

（6）砂石系统供应。砂石拌和系统全面投入生产，月生产14万t砂石骨料，自投产以来，累积生产140万t砂石骨料，全面保障了现场大坝RCC施工。

（二）科技创新

2018年项目部科技立项共计20项，结题9项，科研投入费用累计6250万元。项目在施工过程中积极研究新工艺、新方法，其中《围堰填筑施工中CSG+喷混凝土联合防渗施工》《大坝碾压混凝土施工中底部加浆振捣（GEVR）施工》已申报电建工法，《一种用于固定铜止水的工具》已申请实用新型专利。同时项目积极开展QC质量控制活动，2018年4月份发布的QC活动《提高块石区高喷防护质量》被评为公司QC小组成果发布三等奖。

（三）社会影响与效益

（1）2018年，该项目5次登上国内央视舞台，11次登上赞比亚国家电视台，《新华非洲》和《非洲华侨周报》采稿25篇，当地主流媒体报纸报道20多次，企业形象和品牌美誉度进一步提升。

（2）响应国家“一带一路”，成立技工培训学校，同时2018年7月黄河水院以培训学校为依托，与项目共建大禹学院，培养赞比亚国际和下凯富峡项目急需的焊接、机械维修、测量等专业本土技术技能型人才。

（3）2018年，项目部积极履行社会责任，捐赠10万元物资与当地并肩抗击霍乱；为当地村民义务打17口水井，解决当地村民吃水问题；修缮社区小学，捐赠建筑材料和文具用品；参加属地齐坎卡塔尔区卫生部门举行的儿童健康周活动，协助进行健康筛查工作，发放疫苗、杀虫药和维生素等活动，受到当地政府及社会各界高度评价。

（4）2018年11月，项目业主单位对2018年下凯富峡水电站建设施工单位合理利用资源，组织现场施工，克服重重挑战，良好履约，保障现场施工进度，顺利按时保质保量完成了一系列重大节点任务给予高度赞扬。

（中国水利水电第十一工程局有限公司　甄潜）

尼日利亚KAINJI水电站改造项目全面竣工

2018年8月31日，尼日利亚KAINJI水电站改造项目全面竣工。此前，项目于2016年6月取得完工验收证书，项目进入消缺和质保期。该项目业主为尼日利亚国家电力公司（PHCN），项目资金来源为世行贷款。

该水电站为尼日利亚已建最大水电站，位于尼日尔河流域的尼日尔州纽布萨镇。建于1963～1969年间，为坝后式电站，目前共装有8台机组，单机容量8～12万kW，总装机容量76万kW，电站以330kV电压等级接入系统。项目改造前，该水电站总发电能力仅只有22.5万kW左右，其中5号机组已停运多年，6号和12号机组不能满负荷运行、经常故障停机、发电效率低下，严重影响当地的电力供应。为提升该电站发电能力，PHCN采用世行贷款，于2011年与中国电建集团华东勘测设计研究院有限公司正式签订电站改造EPC合同。该项目的主要合作伙伴为哈尔滨电机厂有限责任公司和中国水利水电第八工程局有限公司。哈电为水轮机发电机组供应商，负责3台机组改造所需设备的供货及安装指导；水电八局为安装分包商，负责现场设备安装施工。

该水电站改造项目范围包括5号、6号、12号3个机组单元设备以及电站公用设备，涵盖了水轮机发电机组、调速器、励磁系统、发电机电压设备、主变压器、监控保护设备、厂用电设备、厂房桥机、进水口及尾水金属结构设备、大坝电梯等电站主要机电设备的改造设计、供货、安装和调试，要求改造后恢复各机组的额定发电能力。

由于该水电站建成年代久远、各机组单元主要设备及公用系统设备规格型号差异较大、改造涉及范围广、原始图纸资料匮乏等等，给电站改造工作带来很大难度。在整个电站改造修复过程中，如何将原定桨式机组改造为转桨式机组、实现埋入部分与新供部件完美衔接，如何对2台运行近40年的主变压器进行现场检测、预期寿命的研判以及修复，如何对多种操作控制模式并存的计算机监控系统（DCS）进行改造以及如何实现深水区域水下检测及修复等，是改造的重点难点和关键所在。

该水电站升级改造完成后，机组发电能力和发电效率得到了极大的提升。5、6、12号3台机组均恢复了额定出力，各项运行指标明显提高，整个电站拥有34万kW稳定可靠的出力保证，机组效率也得到了显著提高，其中5号和6号机组水轮机加权平均效率超过了94.5%，发电机额定工况下的效率超过了98.5%。该水电站改造项目的成功实施具有重要意义：

（1）该项目自签约以来，一直备受国内外媒体关注，中国中央电视台、中国国际广播电台、尼日利亚当地媒体等均对项目进行过采访和报道。世界银行代表、尼日尔流域管理局、尼日利亚电力部部长等多次视察项目现场，密切关注项目进展。项目的执行及管理，得到了世行和业主的高度评价，树立了中国企业良好的形象，展现了我国“一带一路”和“水电技术走出去”的中国建设者风采和技术水平。

（2）由于电站历史久远，原始资料严重缺失，改造难度巨大，这是本改造工程区别于其他改造或新建工程的一个重大的特点。项目团队经多次现场考察与现场实测，采用现场实测反向建模技术，“无中生有”，成功实现了机组再造，解决了新老设备接口方面的问题，确保了项目成功实施，形成了水电站改造整体解决方案，为非洲等欠发达国家类似情况的水电站改造积累了宝贵的实施经验。

（3）该项目所涉及的设备和材料绝大部分是从中国国内采购出口到尼日利亚的，特别是哈电水轮发电机组的出口，极大地促进了中国水电品牌的推广。另外，对于主机制造和现场安装等相关的20余个标准，说服业主和监理采用了中国标准（GB/T、DL/T等），促进了中国技术标准的输出。

（4）电站改造后，不但在很大程度上提升了当地电网的电力供应能力、改善了民生，而且通过实施过程中的技术培训，提高了电厂的运维能力和当地人员的技术、管理水平。

（5）该项目的成功实施，为后水电时代水电“再制造”发展方向树立了品牌、铸造了形象、修炼了内功，为世界水电再制造提供了发展和实施的典型案例，为落实我国国家能源局关于水电站延寿改造的要求提供了实践经验和标杆。

（中国电建集团华东勘测设计研究院有限公司
沙滨　嵇建飞）

10

技术标准与图书

标准化管理工作情况

2018 年电力标准化管理工作情况

2018 年，电力标准化工作的主要任务是围绕全面实施电力标准化战略，贯彻落实《标准化法》、国家质量提升行动指导意见，突出电力标准制修订、企业标准化、标准国际化三个重点领域，加强电力标准化体制机制、新一代能源体系标准、标准支撑科技成果转化机制、中国电力企业联合会（简称中电联）标准四项建设，努力实现电力标准化工作再上新台阶。

（一）电力标准化工作取得新进展

贯彻新标准化法精神，中电联标准化会议召开。会议总结 30 年来标准化工作所取得的丰硕成果，向行业发出了《电力企业实施标准化战略倡议书》，并就电力行业贯彻落实《标准联通共建“一带一路”行动计划（2018～2020 年）》实施方案征求意见。

加快电力标准项目制修订工作。2018 年下达计划共 647 项，其中，住房和城乡建设部工程建设国家标准计划 11 项，国家标准委国家标准计划 46 项，国家能源局行业标准计划 356 项，中电联标准计划 234 项。完成标准报批 481 项，其中，国家标准 76 项，行业标准 266 项，中电联标准 74 项，英文标准 46 项。2018 年经有关部门批准发布标准共 492 项，其中，国家标准 49 项，包括国家标准委批准发布 43 项，住房和城乡建设部批准发布工程建设国家标准 6 项；能源局批准发布行业标准 337 项，行业标准英文版 46 项，中国电力企业联合会发布中电联标准 74 项。截至 2018 年底，电力标准共有 3595 项，其中，电力国家标准 515 项，电力行业标准 2589 项，中电联标准 134 项。

不断完善电力标准化组织机构。2018 年，全国电力需求侧管理标准化技术委员会获得国家标准委批准筹建；能源行业电力机器人标准化技术委员会获得国家能源局批准成立。截至 2018 年底，中电联负责管理 43 个电力（能源）行业标准化技术委员会、21 个全国标准化技术委员会、16 个国际电工技术委员会的中国业务以及 23 个中电联标准化技术委员会。承担国家能源局主管的全国电力监管标准化技术委员会秘书处工作，承担能源行业风电标准化技术委员会秘书处支撑单位工作，继续承担能源行业风电标准化技术委员会风电场运行维护及并网管理两个分技术委员会工作。

国际标准化工作取得新突破。为支持电动汽车产业发展，推动充电技术进步，促进相关国际标准化工作，2018 年 8 月 28 日，中电联与日本电动汽车用快速充电器协会（CHAdeMO）达成了在电动汽车充电设施领域加强技术和标准合作意愿；10 月 26 日，第一届中日第三方市场合作论坛期间，李克强总理、日本安倍晋三首相共同会见了包括中电联、日本电动汽车用快速充电器协会（CHAdeMO）等企业在内的中日合作换文代表。

组织申报《虚拟发电厂的架构与功能要求》《变电站通信网络智能电子设备（IEDs）物理资源配置语言》两项国际标准提案。提交 IEC《电动汽车充电漫游服务的信息交换》第 2～4 部分国际标准提案材料。继续开展电力标准英文版建设与推广应用，截至 2018 年底，共完成 321 项电力标准英文版翻译工作，初步形成了工程建设标准英文版体系。

（二）重点领域标准化取得丰硕成果

（1）电力标准有效推动电力技术进步，保证电力安全经济运行。在火电领域重点围绕提高施工和检修质量，完善检测技术，加快自动控制网络化运行、推进燃料管理智能化，规范环保材料的选用和指标的检测，机组可靠性评价等方面开展标准化工作。GB/T 36293—2018《火力发电厂分散控制系统技术条件》规定了火力发电厂分散控制系统（DCS）的硬件、系统软件、应用功能、资料、包装储存和验收测试的技术要求。DL/T 5210《电力建设施工质量验收规程》第 2～5 部分系列标准注重新技术、新工艺、新材料、新装备、新流程的应用。T/CEC 156《火力发电企业智能燃煤系统》系列标准规范了火力发电企业智能燃煤系统结构及各组成部分的功能要求和技术指标。DL/T 1828—2018《火电厂烟气脱硝再生催化剂》规定了火电厂烟气脱硝再生催化剂的术语和定义、失活催化剂可再生判断规则、再生催化剂性能、试验方法和检验规则。

在水电领域重点开展了水电基础和通用、施工安全、施工安装、设备和试验、运行维护等领域的标准化工作。GB/T 36550—2018《抽水蓄能电站基本名词术语》规定了抽水蓄能电站、水工建筑物、水力机械、金属结构、电气设备、调试试验和运行等方面的基本名词术语。DL/T 5773—2018《水电水利工程施工机械安全操作规程 混凝土运输车》规定了水电水利工程中混凝土搅拌运输车、自卸车、机车及其他混凝土运输车在作业运行、维护保养方面的安全操作等内容。GB/T 51320—2018《建设工程化学灌浆材料应用技术标准》规定了建设工程化学灌浆材料应用设计、材料应用施工、质量检查、职业健康安全与环境保护等。DL/T 710—2018《水轮机运行规程》规定了水轮机运行一般要求、运行操作、稳定及经济运行、监视检查和维护、异常运行及事故处理。

核电常规岛和BOP领域标准体系得到进一步完善，形成涵盖通用和基础、前期工作、工程设计、设备、建造、调试、运行、退役等8个部分、201项标准组成的标准体系表，新立项23项标准，发布14项标准。

在新能源领域重点开展了垃圾发电、风力发电、太阳能发电、微电网及储能等标准化工作。DL/T 1842—2018《垃圾发电厂运行指标评价规范》规定了垃圾发电厂运行指标统计的内容与方法，以及垃圾发电厂运行评价原则、评价指标、评价与要求方法和评价指标。GB/T 36569—2018《海上风电场风力发电机组基础技术要求》规定了单桩基础、多桩承台基础、导管架群桩基础、重力式基础、筒型基础与浮式基础等各类风力发电机组基础选型、使用工况、技术要求、运维要求。GB/T 51311—2018《风光储联合发电站调试及验收标准》规定了风光储联合发电站调试和验收的基本规定、设备调试、分系统调试、风光储联合发电站调试、工程启动验收和试运行、工程移交生产验收和竣工验收等。NB/T 10113—2018《光伏发电站技术监督导则》规定了光伏发电站技术监督的原则、内容及管理要求。GB/T 36119—2018《精准扶贫 村级光伏电站管理与评价导则》规定了村级光伏扶贫电站规划设计、施工、验收、运行维护、信息监测、收益分配等方面管理与评价要求。GB/T 36270—2018《微电网监控系统技术规范》规定了微电网监控系统的工作环境、结构及配置、系统功能、性能指标等技术要求。GB/T 36276—2018《电力储能用锂离子电池》规定了电力储能用锂离子电池的规格、技术要求和检验规则等内容。

在电网领域重点开展了特高压交直流混联大电网、柔性直流输电、输变电设备状态检修和在线监测、电动汽车充电设施、配用电等领域的标准化工作。DL/T 1798—2018《换流变压器交接及预防性试验规程》规定了换流变压器交接及预防性试验的项目、周期和要求。DL/T 1870—2018《电力系统网源协调技术规范》规定了电力系统网源协调基本技术要求及应遵循的基本原则。GB/T 37008—2018《柔性直流输电用电抗器技术规范》在总结现有柔性直流输电用电抗器特点的基础上，规定了相关的术语、使用条件、技术参数、试验项目等。GB/T 18039.10—2018《电磁兼容 环境 HEMP环境描述 辐射骚扰》（IEC 61000-2-9：1996，IDT）规定了高空核电磁脉冲的早期、中期以及晚期的辐射环境，以及电场强度、波形宽度、上升时间、能量等电磁场波形参数。GB/T 36117—2018《村镇光伏发电站集群接入电网规划设计导则》规定了村镇光伏发电站集群接入配电网规划设计的基本原则、接入系统分析和接入系统规划等技术要求。

电动汽车充电设施领域。为了适应换电技术路线的新变化以及大功率充电、无线充电和电动汽车充电设施与智能电网的互动等技术的发展，充电设施标准体系也随之进行完善，现已形成传导充电、换电、无线充电三大技术标准体系。GB/T 51313—2018《电动汽车分散充电设施工程技术标准》、GB/T 36278—2018《电动汽车充换电设施接入配电网技术规范》、NB/T 33029—2018《电动汽车充电与间歇性电源协同调度规范》规范了电动汽车分散充电设施的规划、设计、施工和验收，统一了技术要求。对电动汽车充换电设施接入配电网、电动汽车充电与间歇性电源协同调度的技术架构和技术要求进行了规范。

（2）首个中电联标准上升为国际标准。由中国牵头编制的电动汽车充电漫游信息交互系列国际标准第一部分：通用要求（IEC 63119-1）经过2年时间起草，2018年底经过IEC TC69全体17个正式成员国的投票，一致同意通过了表决，这意味着由中国主导的世界上第一个电动汽车充电服务领域国际标准完成了标准编制程序。该标准同步也在欧盟标准投票通过，经15个欧盟国家投票全票通过，成为欧盟标准。

（3）企业标准化工作力度进一步加大。2018年，越来越多的电力企业从自身的发展出发，制定切实可行的标准化行动方案，促进了标准化普及应用和专业工作的深度融合。国家电网公司修订并发布《国家电网公司技术标准战略纲要（修订版）》（国家电网科〔2018〕623号）；中国南方电网有限责任公司组织制定了公司技术标准战略发展纲要，成立了公司技术标准化委员会、技术标准化委员会办公室等机构。实现了“全专业、全过程、全方位、全层次”覆盖的技术标准体系建设。浙江省能源集团有限公司发布《打造“新浙能”五年发展规划（2018～2022）》，重塑企业核心竞争力，努力推动企业朝着技术型、协同型和服务型现代能源企业高质量发展。2018年，共有53家电力企业通过了标准化良好行为企业确认。

（4）多项电力标准获国家及行业荣誉。2018年10月14日，世界标准日主题活动公布了2018年中国标准创新贡献奖获奖名单。GB/T 30149—2013《电网通用模型描述规范》等42项标准、Q/GDW 11040—2013《电力需求侧管理项目节约电力电量测量与验证通则》等20项标准获一等奖，GB/T 30155—2013《智能变电站技术导则》等36项标准、IEEE 1860—2014《1000kV及以上特高压交流系统电压调节及无功补偿技术导则》等3项标准以及GB/T 18916.1—2012《取水定额　第1部分：火力发电》等取水定额标准获二等奖。电力标准获奖数量和层次在各个行业中领先。

（中国电力企业联合会　周丽波）

2018年农村水电技术标准制修订情况

2018年，水利部农村水利水电司主持编写农村水电技术标准共13项，其中《小水电电网技术管理规程》(SL 528—2018) 为当年新发布的1项标准。截至2018年底，农村水电现行有效标准达56项，其中国家技术标准16项、行业技术标准40项。2018年农村水电技术标准制修订情况见表1。

根据《水利标准化工作管理办法》要求和2018年水利技术标准制修订计划安排，2018年共组织对《小型水电站下游河道减脱水防治技术导则》等5项标准发文征求意见，组织召开了《小型水电站技术改造规范》等9项标准的送审稿审查会，完成了《小型水电站安全检测与评价规范》等10项标准的报批稿审核送审，其中，《小水电建设项目经济评价规程》等4项标准通过报批稿审定会审查，《小型水轮发电机励磁系统技术条件》等3项目标准完成报批工作。组织开展农村水电强制性标准研编，并完成了研编报告。

按新《标准化法》要求，2018年组织相关部门、科研院所和企业对农村水电已颁技术标准应用情况和应用效果、存在问题等开展了调查，回收调查表1万多份，对农村水电技术标准体系分类和完善进行了深入研究，为体系表修订奠定了基础。

2018年，国际小水电中心与联合国工发组织合作“小水电国际标准技术导则项目”文件签署，项目正式启动。截至2018年底，已完成小水电国际标准体系设计和小水电技术导则5大类26项内容的中英文编写工作，完成了征求意见稿。制定有利于全球小水电发展并与大多数发展中国家经济社会发展和需求相适应的相关技术标准，对促进世界小水电的健康绿色发展具有重大意义，是“一带一路”倡议下，为世界小水电发展作出的中国贡献。

表1　2018年农村水电在编技术标准情况

序号	标准名称	编制	性质	已完成
1	小型水轮发电机励磁系统技术条件	制定	行业标准	办文会签
2	小型水电站下游河道减脱水防治技术导则	制定	行业标准	送审稿审查会
3	中小河流水能开发规划编制规程	修订	行业标准	办文会签
4	小型水电站技术改造规范	修订	国家标准	送审稿审查会
5	小水电建设项目经济评价规程	修订	行业标准	报批稿审定会
6	小型水电站安全检测与评价规范	修订	国家标准	送审稿审查会
7	小水电环境影响评价规程（合并修订《农村水电站工程环境影响评价》《小水电规划环境影响评价》）	修订	行业标准	送审稿审查会
8	小型水电站初步设计报告编制规程	修订	行业标准	办文会签
9	小型水电站施工技术规范	修订	国家标准	送审稿审查会
10	小型水电站建设工程验收规程	修订	行业标准	送审稿审查会
11	小型水轮机基本技术条件	修订	行业标准	送审稿审查会
12	农村水电数据库表结构与标识符	制定	行业标准	送审稿审查会

（水利部农村水电及电气化发展局　赵虹）

中国电建集团成都勘测设计研究院有限公司 2018 年标准化工作情况

中国电建集团成都勘测设计研究院有限公司（简称成都院）2018 年共承担国家、行业、团体技术标准制定、修订项目 159 项，其中主编技术标准 57 项，在编企业技术标准项目 52 项，翻译技术标准英文版 22 项；发布主编行业标准 5 项、参编行业标准 8 项（见表 1）。2018 年新立项国家及行业技术标准 31 项，其中主编行业标准 9 项，参编 22 项，新立项企业标准 12 项。完成中国电力建设集团有限公司“国际水电工程勘测设计技术标准应用研究”专题（五）研究工作，完成水电水利规划设计总院“中国水电技术标准‘走出去’研究”课题研究工作。

表 1　　2018 年成都院主编、参编行业技术标准发布情况

序号	属性	标准编号	标准名称	制定/修订	主编/参编
1	行业标准	NB/T 35109—2018	水电工程三维激光扫描测量规程	制定	主编
2	行业标准	NB/T 35115—2018	水电工程钻探规程	修订	主编
3	行业标准	NB/T 35116—2018	水电工程全球导航卫星系统（GNSS）测量规程	制定	主编
4	行业标准	NB/T 35117—2018	水电工程钻孔振荡式渗透试验规程	制定	主编
5	行业标准	NB/T 35121—2018	水电工程沟水治理设计规范	制定	主编
6	行业标准	NB/T 35111—2018	水电工程渣场设计规范	制定	参编
7	行业标准	NB/T 35112—2018	水电工程层析成像技术规程	制定	参编
8	行业标准	NB/T 35118—2018	水电站油系统技术规范	制定	参编
9	行业标准	DL/T 1803—2018	水电厂辅助设备控制装置技术条件	制定	参编
10	行业标准	NB/T 32043—2018	光伏发电工程可行性研究报告编制规程	制定	参编
11	行业标准	NB/T 10080—2018	水电工程陆生生态调查与评价技术规范	制定	参编
12	行业标准	NB/T 10084—2018	水电工程运行调度规程编制导则	制定	参编
13	行业标准	NB/T 10085—2018	水电工程水文预报规范	制定	参编

（中国电建集团成都勘测设计研究院有限公司　鞠琳）

哈尔滨电机厂有限责任公司 2018 年标准化工作有关情况

（一）标准工作会议情况

2018 年 5 月，全国大型发电机标准化技术委员会 2018 年第一次标准起草工作组会议在陕西省西安市召开，会议进行了 3 项国家标准与 2 项行业标准的制、修订讨论工作。哈尔滨大电机研究所选派主要起草人，对其前期所做的调研、试验和分析分别进行了详细的阐述，并与参会专家进行充分的研讨，完成了标准的草稿。

2018 年 5 月，中国电机工程学会电机专业委员会 2018 年第一次标准起草工作组会议在陕西省西安市召开，会议进行了 2 项学会标准制定工作的讨论，其中哈尔滨大电机研究所专家参与了该标准制定工作。

2018 年 7 月，中国电工技术学会大电机专业委员会 2018 年学术年会在青海省西宁市召开，来自全国各地的委员及专家学者共 45 位代表参加了会议。哈尔滨电机厂有限责任公司派专家代表主任委员致欢迎词，哈尔滨大电机研究所作为标委会秘书处主持了会议。

2018 年 8 月，全国大型发电机标准化技术委员会 2018 年第二次标准起草工作组会议在山西省大同市召开，会议对 2 项国家标准的制、修订进行了讨论。哈尔滨大电机研究所专家参加此次会议并参与 2 项标准的起草。会议经过充分研讨，形成 2 项标准征求意见稿及编制说明等文件。

2018 年 8 月，国际大电网 2018 年会议在法国巴黎举办，哈尔滨大电机研究所孙玉田作为国际大电网会议 SC A1 旋转电机专业委员会的中国委员参加了此次会议。作为 SC A1.55 专题研究项目《分瓣铁心定子的研究》的工作组组长，孙玉田向委员会及工作组成员介绍了该项目的进展情况，获得与会人员的肯定。同时，他在 SC A1 旋转电机专业委员会的学术研讨会议上发表了一篇论文，并与会专家进行了充分

交流。

2018 年 8 月，中国电机工程学会电机专业委员会学术年会暨在役汽轮发电机的新运行技术研讨会在山西省大同市召开。哈尔滨大电机研究所孙玉田作为专委会秘书长参加并主持了会议。会议重点安排了“在役汽轮发电机的新运行”学术报告 4 篇。哈尔滨大电机研究所张宏撰写的《水轮发电机推力轴承长宽比对性能的影响》入选本次会议优秀论文。

2018 年 8 月，全国海洋能转换设备标委会第一次工作组会议在广东省广州市召开，会议进行了 3 项国家标准初稿的讨论工作，确定了标准名称、标准结构、组内成员工作分工等事项。哈尔滨大电机研究所王晓航参与了国家标准《潮流能源评估及定性描述》的制定工作。

（二）标准制修订情况

2018 年，在国家标准化管理委员会、中国机械工业联合会、中国电器工业协会等指导下，在秘书处挂靠单位哈尔滨大电机研究所大力支持下，经过全体委员及委员单位共同努力，全国大型发电机标准化技术委员会、全国水轮机标准化技术委员会和全国海洋能转换设备标准化技术委员会秘书处组织行业单位开展了 19 项国家标准及行业标准的制定与修订工作。其中，6 项标准已发布，13 项标准在编。在编标准情况见表 1。

表 1　大电机、水轮机、海洋能转换设备 2018 年在编标准情况

序号	标准名称	工作要求	当前状态
1	电机用埋置式热电阻　第 1 部分：一般规定、测量方法和检验规则	修订 JB/T	报批阶段
2	电机用埋置式热电阻　第 2 部分：铂热电阻技术要求	修订 JB/T	报批阶段
3	电机用埋置式热电阻　第 3 部分：铜热电阻技术要求	修订 JB/T	报批阶段
4	发电机液体内冷空心导线　第 2 部分：不锈钢空心导线	修订 JB/T	报批阶段
5	YXKK 系列高效率高压三相异步电动机技术条件（机座号 710～1120）	制定 JB/T	报批阶段
6	YXKS 系列高效率高压三相异步电动机技术条件（机座号 710～1120）	制定 JB/T	报批阶段
7	氢冷电机气密封性检验方法及评定	修订 JB/T	报批阶段
8	汽轮发电机状态在线监测系统应用导则	修订 GB/Z	报批阶段
9	小容量节能环保隐极同步发电机技术要求	修订 GB/T	报批阶段
10	水轮机基本技术条件	制定 GB/T	报批阶段
11	海洋能、波浪能、潮流能和其他水流能转换装置术语	制定 GB/T	报批阶段
12	潮流能源评估及定性描述	制定 GB/T	起草阶段
13	波浪能和潮流能转换装置产品研发基本程序	制定 NB/T	起草阶段

（哈尔滨电机厂有限责任公司　刘保生）

南方电网调峰调频发电有限公司 2018 年标准化工作情况

南方电网调峰调频发电有限公司 2018 年主持或参与《智能水电厂技术导则》等 1 项国际标准、《抽水蓄能电站计算机监控系统验收试验规程》等 5 项行业标准、《抽水蓄能电站机电设备配置导则》等 6 项中国电力企业联合会团体标准和《抽水蓄能电站机组启动调试技术导则》等 6 项企业标准的编制工作，见表 1。

表 1　南方电网调峰调频发电公司水电在编技术标准情况

序号	标准名称	编制	性质	当前状态
1	智能水电厂技术导则	制定	国际标准	初稿
2	抽水蓄能电站计算机监控系统验收试验规程	制定	行业标准	送审稿
3	抽水蓄能电站自动发电控制自动电压控制技术规范	制定	行业标准	送审稿
4	水电厂非电量保护技术规范	制定	行业标准	大纲审查
5	抽水蓄能电站生产准备导则（英文版）	制定	行业标准	大纲审查

续表

序号	标准名称	编制	性质	当前状态
6	抽水蓄能电站无人值班技术规范（英文版）	制定	行业标准	大纲审查
7	抽水蓄能电站机电设备配置导则	制定	团体标准	大纲审查
8	水电站用水下机器人控制系统功能导则	制定	团体标准	报批稿
9	抽水蓄能电站设计质量控制管理导则	制定	团体标准	报批稿
10	抽水蓄能电站机组断路器试验规程	制定	团体标准	报批稿
11	发电电动机空冷器技术规范	制定	团体标准	报批稿
12	水电厂应急预案编制导则	制定	团体标准	初稿
13	抽水蓄能电站机组启动调试技术导则	制定	企业标准	送审稿
14	抽水蓄能电站计算机监控系统技术规范	制定	企业标准	送审稿
15	抽水蓄能电站励磁系统技术规范	制定	企业标准	送审稿
16	抽水蓄能电站调速器系统技术规范	制定	企业标准	送审稿
17	抽水蓄能电站机变保护技术规范	制定	企业标准	送审稿
18	新建抽水蓄能电站（机组）投运导则	制定	企业标准	送审稿

（南方电网调峰调频发电有限公司）

技术标准制修订情况

2018年国家标准化管理委员会下达的电力国家标准制定或修订计划项目

2018年，国家标准化管理委员会下达的电力国家标准制定或修订计划项目46项，见表1。

表1 2018年国家标准化管理委员会下达的电力国家标准制定或修订计划项目

序号	项目名称	制定/修订	主编单位	采用国际标准
1	火力发电厂汽轮机安全保护系统技术条件	制定	国网湖南省电力公司电力科学研究院	
2	电力系统站域死区（失灵）保护技术导则	制定	国家电网有限公司国家电力调度控制中心、中国电力科学研究院有限公司、中国南方电网电力调度控制中心、国家电网公司华东分部、国网上海市电力有限公司等	
3	继电保护在线监视与分析技术规范	制定	国家电网有限公司国家电力调度控制中心、中国电力科学研究院有限公司、中国南方电网电力调度控制中心、国网浙江省电力有限公司、国网冀北电力有限公司、国网江苏省电力有限公司等	
4	同步发电机组涉网保护技术要求	制定	中国电力科学研究院有限公司、国家电网有限公司国家电力调度控制中心、中国南方电网电力调度控制中心、南瑞集团有限公司、清华大学、内蒙古电力（集团）有限责任公司等	

续表

序号	项目名称	制定/修订	主编单位	采用国际标准
5	继电保护整定计算数据及软件技术规范	制定	中国电力科学研究院有限公司、国家电网有限公司国家电力调度控制中心、中国南方电网电力调度控制中心、国家电网公司华中分部、国家电网公司西北分部、国家电网公司东北分部、国家电网公司华北分部等	
6	太阳能热发电站接入电力系统技术规定	制定	中国电力企业联合会、中国电力科学研究院有限公司	
7	太阳能热发电站接入电力系统检测规程	制定	中国电力企业联合会、中国电力科学研究院有限公司	
8	电站流程图第一部分：制图规范	制定	中国电力工程顾问集团西南电力设计院有限公司	
9	能源互联网规划技术导则	制定	中国电力科学研究院有限公司	
10	用户接入电网供电方案技术导则	制定	国家电网有限公司、中国电力科学研究院有限公司等	
11	统一潮流控制器技术规范	制定	全球能源互联网研究院有限公司	
12	智能水电厂技术导则	制定	南瑞集团有限公司、中国长江三峡集团公司、国网新源控股有限公司、南方电网调峰调频公司、五凌电力有限公司、广州健新自动化科技有限公司	
13	智能水电厂经济运行系统技术条件	制定	南瑞集团有限公司、中国长江三峡集团公司、国网新源控股有限公司、南方电网调峰调频公司、五凌电力有限公司、广州健新自动化科技有限公司	
14	智能水电厂大坝安全分析评估系统技术规范	制定	南瑞集团公司、中国长江三峡集团公司、国网新源控股有限公司、南方电网调峰调频公司、五凌电力有限公司、广州健新自动化科技有限公司等	
15	同步发电机调速系统参数实测及建模导则	制定	中国电力科学研究院有限公司、国家电网有限公司国家电力调度控制中心、中国南方电网电力调度控制中心、南方电网科学研究院有限公司等	
16	同步发电机励磁系统建模导则	制定	国家电网有限公司国家电力调度控制中心、中国电力科学研究院有限公司、中国南方电网电力调度控制中心、国家电网公司西南分部等	
17	电网安全稳定控制装置技术规范	制定	中国南方电网电力调度控制中心、国家电网有限公司国家电力调度控制中心、中国电力科学研究院有限公司、国家电网公司华北分部、国家电网公司华东分部、广东电网有限责任公司等	
18	电网设备模型参数和运行方式数据规范	制定	国家电网有限公司国家电力调度控制中心、中国电力科学研究院有限公司、中国南方电网电力调度控制中心、国家电网公司华中分部等	
19	电力系统实时数字仿真技术规范	制定	国家电网有限公司国家电力调度控制中心、中国电力科学研究院有限公司、中国南方电网电力调度控制中心、南方电网科学研究院有限公司、国家电网公司华东分部	
20	直流输电系统机电暂态仿真建模技术导则	制定	国家电网有限公司国家电力调度控制中心、中国电力科学研究院有限公司、中国南方电网电力调度控制中心、南方电网科学研究院有限公司、国家电网有限公司发展策划部、国家电网公司华中分部等	

续表

序号	项目名称	制定/修订	主编单位	采用国际标准
21	电力系统自动高频切除发电机组技术规定	制定	国家电网有限公司国家电力调度控制中心、中国电力科学研究院有限公司、中国南方电网电力调度控制中心、国家电网公司华中分部等	
22	电力系统电压稳定评价导则	制定	国家电网有限公司国家电力调度控制中心、中国电力科学研究院有限公司、中国南方电网电力调度控制中心、国家电网公司华北分部等	
23	电力系统安全稳定计算规范	制定	国家电网有限公司、国家电网有限公司国家电力调度控制中心、中国电力科学研究院有限公司、中国南方电网电力调度控制中心、南方电网科学研究院有限公司、北京电力交易中心有限公司等	
24	电力系统电压和无功电力技术导则	制定	国家电网有限公司国家电力调度控制中心、中国电力科学研究院有限公司、中国南方电网电力调度控制中心、国家电网公司华东分部、国家电网公司华中分部、国家电网公司西北分部等	
25	电力系统自动低频减负荷技术规定	制定	国家电网有限公司国家电力调度控制中心、中国电力科学研究院有限公司、中国南方电网电力调度控制中心、国家电网公司华东分部等	
26	直流工程数模混合仿真建模及试验规范	制定	国家电网有限公司国家电力调度控制中心、中国电力科学研究院有限公司、国网湖北省电力有限公司、中国南方电网电力调度控制中心等	
27	电力系统自动低压减负荷技术规定	制定	国家电网有限公司国家电力调度控制中心、中国电力科学研究院有限公司、南瑞集团有限公司、国家电网公司华东分部、中国南方电网电力调度控制中心、深圳供电局有限公司等	
28	电力系统在线潮流数据二进制描述及交换规范	制定	国家电网有限公司国家电力调度控制中心、中国电力科学研究院有限公司、中国南方电网电力调度控制中心、国网江苏省电力有限公司、国网浙江省电力有限公司、深圳供电局有限公司等	
29	电力系统大面积停电恢复技术导则	制定	国家电网有限公司国家电力调度控制中心、中国电力科学研究院有限公司、中国南方电网电力调度控制中心、国网北京市电力公司等	
30	电网运行风险监测、评估及可视化技术规范	制定	国家电网有限公司国家电力调度控制中心、中国电力科学研究院有限公司、中国南方电网电力调度控制中心、北京科东电力控制系统有限责任公司、国家电网公司华北分部等	
31	电力系统网源协调技术要求	制定	国家电网有限公司国家电力调度控制中心、中国电力科学研究院有限公司、中国南方电网电力调度控制中心、中国长江电力股份有限公司三峡水力发电厂、中国广核集团有限公司等	
32	电网运行安全校核技术规范	制定	国家电网有限公司国家电力调度控制中心、中国电力科学研究院有限公司、中国南方电网电力调度控制中心、国家电网公司华东分部等	
33	风电场受限电量评估导则	制定	中国电力科学研究院有限公司、国家电网有限公司国家电力调度控制中心、中国南方电网电力调度控制中心、国家电网公司西南分部等	
34	电网在线安全分析与控制辅助决策技术规范	制定	国家电网有限公司国家电力调度控制中心、中国电力科学研究院有限公司、北京科东电力控制系统有限责任公司、中国南方电网电力调度控制中心、南瑞集团有限公司、国网福建省电力有限公司等	

续表

序号	项目名称	制定/修订	主编单位	采用国际标准
35	电力系统稳定器整定试验导则	制定	国家电网有限公司国家电力调度控制中心、中国电力科学研究院有限公司、中国南方电网电力调度控制中心、浙能技术研究院有限公司、国网浙江省电力有限公司、国家电网公司华东分部等	
36	并网电源一次调频技术规定及试验导则	制定	国家电网有限公司国家电力调度控制中心、中国电力科学研究院有限公司、中国南方电网电力调度控制中心、国网陕西省电力公司、国网冀北电力有限公司等	
37	电力系统安全稳定控制策略描述规范	制定	国家电网有限公司国家电力调度控制中心、中国电力科学研究院有限公司、中国南方电网电力调度控制中心、国家电网公司华东分部等	
38	调度侧风电光伏功率预测系统技术要求	制定	中国电力科学研究院有限公司、国家电网有限公司国家电力调度控制中心、中国南方电网电力调度控制中心、国网北京市电力公司、国网山东省电力公司、国网山西省电力公司等	
39	新能源场站调度运行信息交换规范	制定	中国电力科学研究院有限公司、国家电网有限公司国家电力调度控制中心、中国南方电网电力调度控制中心、国家电网公司西南分部等	
40	风电场功率控制系统调度功能技术规范	制定	中国电力科学研究院有限公司、国家电网有限公司国家电力调度控制中心、国网吉林省电力有限公司、中国南方电网电力调度控制中心等	
41	电动客车顶部接触式充电系统　第1部分：通用要求	制定	中国电力企业联合会、青岛特来电新能源有限公司、国家电网有限公司、中国汽车技术研究中心、青岛海汇德电气有限公司等	
42	电动汽车无线充电系统商用车应用特殊要求	制定	中国电力科学研究院有限公司	
43	电动汽车无线充电系统互操作性要求及测试　第1部分：地面端	制定	国家电网有限公司、中国电力科学研究院有限公司、中兴集团	
44	电网气象信息交换技术规范	制定	国网电力科学研究院、国家电网有限公司国家调度控制中心、中国气象局公共气象服务中心	
45	立体停车库无线供电系统技术要求及测试规范	制定	中国电力科学研究院有限公司	
46	交流1kV及直流1.5kV以上电力设施　第2部分：直流	制定	中国电力科学研究院有限公司	

（中国电力企业联合会　许松林　刘永东）

2018年住房和城乡建设部下达的电力工程建设国家标准制定或修订计划项目

2018年，住房和城乡建设部下达的电力工程建设国家标准制定或修订计划项目11项，见表1。

表 1　2018 年住房和城乡建设部下达的电力工程建设国家标准制定或修订计划项目

序号	项目名称	制定/修订	主编单位	采用国际标准
1	火力发电工程项目规范	制定	电力规划设计总院等	
2	变电工程项目规范	制定	电力规划设计总院等	
3	输电工程项目规范	制定	中国电力工程顾问集团中南电力设计院有限公司等	
4	配电工程项目规范	制定	国网经济技术研究院有限公司等	
5	核电工程常规岛项目规范	制定	中广核工程有限公司等	
6	风力发电工程项目规范	制定	水电水利规划设计总院等	
7	太阳能发电工程项目规范	制定	水电水利规划设计总院等	
8	电力接地通用规范	制定	中国电力科学研究院有限公司等	
9	电力工程电气装置施工安装及验收通用规范	制定	中国电力企业联合会、中国电力科学研究院有限公司等	
10	电力系统规划通用规范	制定	电力规划设计总院等	
11	工程建设国家标准复审（电力工程部分，2018 年度）	制定	中国电力企业联合会	

（中国电力企业联合会　许松林　刘永东）

2018 年国家能源局下达的电力行业标准制定或修订计划项目

2018 年，国家能源局下达的电力行业标准制定或修订计划项目 356 项，其中水电、新能源及电气等部分（即未含火电、核电）计划项目 253 项，见表 1。

表 1　2018 年国家能源局下达的电力行业标准制定或修订计划项目

序号	标准名称	制定/修订	主要起草单位	代替标准
1	差动电阻式孔隙压力计	制定	国电南京自动化股份有限公司	
2	混凝土面板堆石坝移动边墙施工规范	制定	中国水利水电第十二工程局有限公司	
3	水电水利工程混凝土表面环氧树脂类材料修补施工技术规范	制定	中国葛洲坝集团股份有限公司、厦门鹭恒达建筑工程有限公司、葛洲坝集团试验检测有限公司、长江水利委员会长江科学院	
4	水电水利工程环氧树脂类表面修补材料试验规程	制定	中国葛洲坝集团股份有限公司、厦门鹭恒达建筑工程有限公司、葛洲坝集团试验检测有限公司、长江水利委员会长江科学院	
5	水电水利工程混凝土结构表面涂层防护技术规范	制定	珠江水利委员会珠江水利科学研究院、厦门鹭恒达建筑工程有限公司、西京学院、陕西省混凝土结构安全与耐久性重点实验室、南京水利科学研究院、长江水利委员会长江科学院	
6	水工碾压混凝土现场碾压试验规程	制定	中国葛洲坝集团股份有限公司、葛洲坝集团试验检测有限公司	

续表

序号	标准名称	制定/修订	主要起草单位	代替标准
7	水工碾压式沥青混凝土心墙现场碾压试验规程	制定	中国葛洲坝集团股份有限公司、葛洲坝集团试验检测有限公司	
8	水利水电工程液压深搅铣防渗墙施工技术规范	制定	中国水电基础局有限公司	
9	流域梯级水电站经济调度控制技术导则	制定	国电大渡河流域水电开发有限公司、中国长江电力股份有限公司	
10	水电厂机组自动化元件及系统运行维护与检验试验规程	修订	中国水科院天津机电研究所、中国长江三峡集团公司	DL/T 619—2012
11	水电厂励磁系统技术监督规程	制定	中国长江电力股份有限公司	
12	水电厂时钟同步系统技术条件	制定	中国长江电力股份有限公司、中国水利水电科学研究院、中国电建集团北京勘测设计研究院有限公司、中国电建集团昆明勘测设计研究院有限公司	
13	水电厂直流系统技术监督规程	制定	中国长江电力股份有限公司、国网四川省电力公司电力科学研究院	
14	水轮机筒形阀控制系统运行与检修规程	制定	中国长江电力股份有限公司	
15	水电站库容超声波法测量规程	制定	国网甘肃省电力公司电力科学研究院、国网甘肃省电力公司刘家峡水电厂、龙羊峡水电站、中国长江三峡集团公司、大唐岩滩水力发电有限责任公司等	
16	抽水蓄能电站水库运行管理规范	制定	国网新源控股有限公司、中国南方电网调峰调频发电公司	
17	户用光伏并网箱技术规范	制定	中国质量认证中心	
18	抽水蓄能电站静止变频启动设备安装调试规程	制定	水电水利规划设计总院、中国长江三峡集团有限公司、中国电建集团北京勘测设计研究院有限公司、中国电建集团华东勘测设计研究院有限公司	
19	柔性变电站技术导则	制定	全球能源互联网研究院有限公司等	
20	静止同步串联补偿器功能规范	制定	国网天津市电力公司电力科学研究院、全球能源互联网研究院有限公司等	
21	混合式高压直流断路器应用性能术语	制定	全球能源互联网研究院有限公司	
22	配电网柔性切换装置技术规范	制定	国网浙江省电力有限公司电力科学研究院、丽水供电公司	
23	并联型电网侧风电次同步振荡抑制装置技术规范	制定	全球能源互联网研究院有限公司、国网冀北电力有限公司	
24	低压变频器电压暂降及短时中断穿越能力测试技术规范	制定	全球能源互联网研究院有限公司等	
25	低压配电线路补偿装置检测技术规范	制定	国网福建省电力有限公司电力科学研究院、福建工程学院、国网福建省电力有限公司福州供电公司	

续表

序号	标准名称	制定/修订	主要起草单位	代替标准
26	交流采样远动终端技术条件	修订	中国电力科学研究院	DL/T 630—1997
27	公共电网信息模型交换规范	制定	中国电力科学研究院、南瑞集团有限公司、国家电网有限公司国家电力调度控制中心、中国南方电网电力调度控制中心	
28	变电站自动化远程运行维护系统技术规范	制定	国网江苏省电力公司电力科学研究院、国网江苏省电力公司、国电南瑞科技股份有限公司	
29	变电站监控系统图形界面规范	制定	国网浙江省电力有限公司、中国南方电网有限责任公司、中国电力科学研究院有限公司、国网电力科学研究院、国网浙江省电力有限公司绍兴供电公司、国网吉林省电力有限公司等	
30	变电站自动化系统及设备检测规范 第1部分：概论	制定	中国电力科学研究院有限公司、国家电网有限公司国家电力调度控制中心、中国南方电网电力调度控制中心、国网电力科学研究院、国网浙江省电力有限公司、国网安徽省电力有限公司等	
31	调度自动化主站智能告警技术规范	制定	中国南方电网电力调度控制中心、国家电网有限公司国家电力调度控制中心、南方电网科学研究院有限公司、南瑞集团有限公司、中国电力科学研究院有限公司	
32	电力无线宽带接入网设备测试规范	制定	国网电力科学研究院、国网信通部、南方电网公司系统运行部、国电南瑞科技股份有限公司、国网信通产业集团	
33	电力用智能换相装置技术规范	制定	国网电力科学研究院	
34	六氟化硫气体回收装置技术条件 第1部分：六氟化硫气体回收装置	修订	广州供电局有限公司电力试验研究院	DL/T 662—2009
35	六氟化硫气体回收装置技术条件 第2部分：SF_6/N_2混合气体回收装置	修订	国网安徽省电力公司电力科学研究院、国家电网公司运检部、中国电力科学研究院有限公司、国网陕西省电力公司电力科学研究院、国网河北省电力公司电力科学研究院等	DL/T 662—2009
36	智能变电站继电保护及相关二次设备检修调试技术规范	制定	国网浙江省电力公司调控中心、中国南方电网电力调度控制中心、武汉凯默电气有限公司、北京四方继保电气股份有限公司、南京南瑞继保电气有限公司等	
37	同步调相机二次系统技术导则	制定	国网经济技术研究院有限公司、国家电网公司基建部、中国南方电网电力调度控制中心、南京南瑞继保电气有限公司、国电南瑞科技股份有限公司、河南电力设计院等	
38	变电站继电保护综合记录与智能运维装置通用技术条件	制定	中国南方电网电力调度控制中心、国家电网有限公司国家电力调度控制中心、国网浙江省电力公司调控中心、武汉中元华电有限责任公司、武汉凯默电气有限公司、北京四方继保电气股份有限公司等	

续表

序号	标准名称	制定/修订	主要起草单位	代替标准
39	就地化保护装置检测规范　第1部分：智能管理单元	制定	中国电力科学研究院有限公司、国家电网有限公司国家电力调度控制中心、国网浙江省电力公司、国网江苏省电力公司、国网山东省电力公司、国电南瑞科技股份有限公司、许继电气股份有限公司等	
40	就地化保护装置检测规范　第2部分：线路保护	制定	中国电力科学研究院有限公司、国家电网有限公司国家电力调度控制中心、国网浙江省电力公司、国网江苏省电力公司、国网山东省电力公司、国电南瑞科技股份有限公司、许继电气股份有限公司等	
41	就地化保护装置检测规范　第3部分：变压器保护	制定	中国电力科学研究院有限公司、国家电网有限公司国家电力调度控制中心、国网浙江省电力公司、国网江苏省电力公司、国网山东省电力公司、国电南瑞科技股份有限公司、许继电气股份有限公司等	
42	就地化保护装置检测规范　第4部分：母线保护	制定	中国电力科学研究院有限公司、国家电网有限公司国家电力调度控制中心、国网浙江省电力公司、国网江苏省电力公司、国网山东省电力公司、国电南瑞科技股份有限公司、许继电气股份有限公司等	
43	发电厂继电保护及安全自动装置技术监督导则	制定	西安热工研究院有限公司、国家电网有限公司国家电力调度控制中心、中国南方电网电力调度控制中心、中国华能集团有限公司、大唐东营发电厂、南京南瑞继保电气有限公司等	
44	抽水蓄能电站发电电动机变压器组继电保护整定计算技术规范	制定	国家电网公司西北分部、保护设备制造厂家、抽水蓄能电站等	
45	变电站站域失灵（死区）保护装置技术规范	制定	湖南电科院、河南电科院、华东分中心、国家电网有限公司国家电力调度控制中心、浙江电科院、江苏电科院、南京南瑞继保电气有限公司、北京四方继保电气股份有限公司等	
46	智能变电站网络性能测试装置技术规范	制定	国网江西省电力有限公司电力科学研究院、中国南方电网公司电力调度控制中心、广东电网有限责任公司电力科学研究院等	
47	配电继电保护装置检验规程	制定	广州供电局有限公司、国网上海电科院、南方电网科学研究院有限责任公司、南京南瑞继保电气有限公司、珠海许继电气有限公司	
48	交流架空输电线路绝缘子并联间隙使用导则	修订	中国电力科学研究院有限公司、南瑞集团有限公司、国网浙江省电力有限公司、国网冀北电力有限公司、国网湖南省电力有限公司、国网辽宁省电力有限公司等	DL/T 1293—2013
49	交流输电线路用复合外套金属氧化物避雷器	修订	中国电力科学电科院有限公司	DL/T 815—2012
50	10kV台架变压器防雷技术导则	制定	南方电网科学研究院有限责任公司	
51	电力系统雷电侵入波监测导则	制定	深圳供电局有限公司	

续表

序号	标准名称	制定/修订	主要起草单位	代替标准
52	电力需求响应系统通信一致性测试规范	制定	中国电力科学研究有限公司、南方电网科学研究院有限责任公司、上海电器科学研究所（集团）有限公司、杭州赫智电子科技有限公司、成都云数环能科技有限公司等	
53	电力需求响应系统检验规范	制定	中国电力科学研究有限公司、南方电网科学研究院有限责任公司、上海电器科学研究所（集团）有限公司、杭州赫智电子科技有限公司、成都云数环能科技有限公司等	
54	电力需求响应信息交换规范与OpenADR适配器技术要求	制定	中国电力科学研究有限公司、南方电网科学研究院有限责任公司、上海电器科学研究所（集团）有限公司、杭州赫智电子科技有限公司、成都云数环能科技有限公司等	
55	变电设备在线监测装置现场测试技术应用导则　第2部分：电容型设备与金属氧化物避雷器绝缘在线监测装置	制定	国网福建省电力有限公司电力科学研究院、中国电力科学研究院有限公司、国网冀北电力科学研究院、广东电网有限责任公司电力科学研究院等	
56	变电站直流系统状态评价导则	制定	国网安徽省电力有限公司电力科学研究院、中国电力科学研究院有限公司、国网陕西省电力有限公司、国网湖南省电力有限公司	
57	变电站直流系统状态检修导则	制定	国网安徽省电力有限公司电力科学研究院、中国电力科学研究院有限公司、国网陕西省电力有限公司、国网湖南省电力有限公司	
58	高压电缆高频局部放电带电检测技术导则	制定	广州供电局有限公司、中国电力科学研究院有限公司、绍兴大明电力设计院	
59	电力安全工作规程　高压试验室部分	修订	中国电力科学研究院有限公司、国家电网有限公司	DL 560—1995
60	电力安全工作规程　电力线路部分	修订	国家电网有限公司、中国电力科学研究院有限	DL 409—1991
61	电力安全工作规程　发电厂和变电站电气部分	修订	国家电网有限公司、中国电力科学研究院有限公司	DL 408—1991
62	油纸绝缘电力设备频域介电谱测试导则	制定	中国南方电网有限责任公司超高压输电公司检修试验中心、中国电力科学研究院有限公司、重庆大学、四川电力科学研究院	
63	农村电网低压电气安全工作规程	修订	国网山东省电力公司淄博供电公司、中国电力科学研究院有限公司	DL/T 477—2010
64	配电变压器运行规程	修订	中国电力科学研究院有限公司、中国南方电网有限公司、国网江苏省电力公司、杭州钱江电气股份有限公司、上海置信电气股份有限公司等	DL/T 1102—2009
65	农村电网剩余电流动作保护器安装运行规程	修订	中国电力科学研究院有限公司、国网浙江省电力有限公司、南京鼎牌电器有限公司等	DL/T 736—2010
66	农村无人值班变电站运行规定	修订	中国电力科学研究院有限公司、国家电网有限公司、国网河北省电力公司等	DL/T 737—2010

续表

序号	标准名称	制定/修订	主要起草单位	代替标准
67	三相负荷不平衡自动调节装置选型与检测技术规范	制定	中国电力科学研究院有限公司、国家电网有限公司、国网安徽省电力公司、国网山东省电力公司、国网江苏省电力公司等	
68	剩余电流动作保护器检测规程	制定	中国电力科学研究院有限公司、国网福建省电力有限公司电力科学研究院、南京鼎牌电器有限公司等	
69	10kV配网一次电力设备交接试验规程	制定	广州供电局电力试验研究院、重庆大学、国网电力科学研究院	
70	综合管廊电力舱技术导则	制定	国网北京市电力公司、北京电力经济技术研究院、国网上海市电力公司、国网浙江省电力公司、国网北京经济技术研究院、中国电力建设集团上海电力设计院有限公司等	
71	海底电缆通道监控预警系统技术规范	制定	国网福建省电力有限公司	
72	输电电缆故障测寻技术规范	制定	广州供电局有限公司电力试验研究院、中国电力科学研究院有限公司	
73	海底电缆系统预鉴定试验规范	制定	中国电力科学研究院有限公司	
74	费控断路器可靠性试验规程	制定	中国电力科学研究院有限公司、中国南方电网有限责任公司、国网重庆市电力公司、国网湖南省电力公司、国网山东省电力公司、国网山西省电力公司等	
75	电厂上网关口电能计量屏柜技术规范	制定	国网江苏省电力有限公司电力科学研究院	
76	电能计量设备用元器件技术规范　第1部分：总则	制定	中国电力科学研究院有限公司、中国南方电网有限责任公司、国网湖南省电力公司、国网冀北电力有限公司、许继集团、河北申科、上海复旦微等	
77	电能计量设备用元器件技术规范　第2部分：液晶显示器	制定	中国电力科学研究院有限公司、南方电网广东电科院、中国电子技术标准化研究院、河北冀雅电子有限公司、国网湖南省电力公司等	
78	电能信息采集与管理系统　第6-1部分：终端升级技术要求	制定	国网浙江省电力公司、中国电力科学研究院有限公司	
79	配电自动化终端设备调试验收规程	制定	广州供电局有限公司电力试验研究院、广东电网公司、深圳供电局有限公司、国网天津市电力公司、南京金智科技股份有限公司等	
80	配电自动化终端测试仪技术条件	制定	广州供电局有限公司电力试验研究院、广东电网公司、深圳供电局有限公司、国网天津市电力公司、南京金智科技股份有限公司等	
81	非入户式居民用户负荷监测终端技术规范	制定	天津大学、国网江苏省电力有限公司、天津求实有限公司	
82	电力源网荷友好互动终端技术规范	制定	国网江苏省电力有限公司	
83	配电自动化系统终端运维技术规范	制定	国网电力科学研究院	
84	配电自动化系统终端即插即用技术规范	制定	中国电力科学研究院有限公司	

续表

序号	标准名称	制定/修订	主要起草单位	代替标准
85	电网风区分布图绘制技术导则	制定	南方电网科学研究院有限责任公司、中国电力科学研究院、广东电力设计院	
86	带电作业绝缘配合导则	修订	中国电力科学研究院有限公司	DL/T 876—2004
87	带电作业虚拟现实实操平台	制定	中国电力科学研究院有限公司	
88	带电作业用导线软质遮蔽罩	修订	中国电力科学研究院有限公司	DL/T 880—2004
89	配电线路带电作业用线夹技术条件	制定	国网江苏省电力公司常州供电公司、中国电力科学研究院有限公司	
90	带电作业用绝缘操作杆工具附件	制定	中国电力科学研究院有限公司	
91	光纤复合绝缘子技术条件	制定	中国电力科学研究院有限公司	
92	电力系统用棒形支柱复合绝缘子-定义、试验方法及验收规则	修订	中国电力科学研究院有限公司	DL/T 1048—2007
93	35kV 及以下架空线路用针式复合绝缘子技术规范	制定	中国电力科学研究院有限公司	
94	架空线路用柱式复合绝缘子技术条件	制定	中国电力科学研究院有限公司	
95	电力系统现场污秽度测量及评定　第 4 部分：自然污秽的试验盐密修正方法	制定	清华大学深圳研究生院	
96	覆冰地区绝缘子选型导则	制定	重庆大学	
97	盘形悬式瓷绝缘子红外检测技术规范	制定	国网江西省电力公司电力科学研究院、湖南湖大华龙电气与信息技术有限公司	
98	配电网线损一体化测量装置通用技术条件	制定	中国电力科学研究院有限公司	
99	高压费控装置通用技术条件	制定	国网四川电力公司计量中心、中国电力科学研究院有限公司	
100	直流互感器用合并单元通用技术条件	制定	中国电力科学研究院有限公司	
101	电力试验检测车　第 4 部分：开关电器交流耐压试验车	制定	苏州华电电气股份有限公司	
102	工频电压互感器现场校验成套装置技术条件	制定	中国电力科学研究院有限公司	
103	工频电流互感器现场校验成套装置技术条件	制定	中国电力科学研究院有限公司	
104	直流互感器校验仪通用技术条件	制定	中国电力科学研究院有限公司	
105	电气装置安装工程　电力变压器、油浸电抗器、互感器施工及验收规范	制定	安徽送变电工程有限公司、中国电力科学研究院有限公司	
106	电气装置安装工程　母线装置施工及验收规范	制定	中国电力科学研究院有限公司、安徽送变电工程有限公司	
107	110kV～750kV 架空输电线路铁塔基础施工工艺导则	制定	安徽送变电工程有限公司、国网交流建设公司	
108	变电（换流）站土建工程验收规程施工记录等统一表式	制定	江苏省送变电有限公司	
109	接地装置短路暂态特性参数测试导则	制定	云南电网有限责任公司电力科学研究院、陕西电科院、清华大学、南方电网科学研究院有限公司等	

续表

序号	标准名称	制定/修订	主要起草单位	代替标准
110	电力接地系统土壤电阻率、接地阻抗和地表电位测量技术导则	制定	国网辽宁省电力有限公司电力科学研究院、国网陕西省电力公司电力科学研究院、广东电网有限责任公司电力科学研究院、中国电力科学研究院有限公司	
111	电压监测仪检定装置技术规范	制定	国网河南省电力公司电力科学研究院	
112	电压监测装置运维规程	制定	国网河南省电力公司电力科学研究院	
113	高压并联电容器补偿装置使用技术条件	修订	国网浙江省电力公司绍兴供电公司	DL/T 604—2009
114	油浸式电力变压器绕组光纤测温装置技术规范	制定	国网辽宁省电力有限公司电力科学研究院、中国电力科学研究院有限公司、南方电网科学研究院有限责任公司等	
115	油浸式电力变压器绕组光纤测温装置试验方法	制定	国网辽宁省电力有限公司电力科学研究院、中国电力科学研究院有限公司、南方电网科学研究院有限责任公司等	
116	消弧线圈并联低电阻接地装置	制定	南方电网科学研究院有限责任公司、广东电网公司、中国电力科学研究院有限公司、绍兴大明电力设计院	
117	发电机出口侧电压互感器技术导则	制定	中国大唐集团科学技术研究院有限公司火力发电技术研究所、中国大唐集团科学技术研究院有限公司华中分公司、中国电力科学研究院有限公司等	
118	天然酯绝缘油电力变压器选用导则	制定	中国电力科学研究院有限公司、国网河南省电力公司电力科学研究院、中国南方电网有限责任公司等	
119	大型油浸式变压器（电抗器）充气存放技术要求及评价方法	制定	山东电工电气集团有限公司、山东电力设备有限公司、山东输变电设备有限公司、南瑞集团有限公司、国网江苏省电力公司	
120	电力直流电源系统用测试设备通用技术条件　第8部分：绝缘监测装置校验仪	制定	国网四川电力科学研究院、中国电力科学研究院有限公司等	
121	电力用高频开关整流模块	修订	中国电力科学研究院有限公司、深圳奥特迅电力设备股份有限公司、许继电源有限公司	DL/T 781—2001
122	电力企业应急演练评价标准	制定	北京宽信安泰信息技术有限公司、全球能源互联网研究院有限公司	
123	电力应急电源装备测试导则	制定	广州供电局有限公司电力试验研究院、广东产品质量监督检验研究院、工业和信息化部电子第五研究所、上海科泰电源股份有限公司、深圳市盈九州实业有限公司等	
124	电力行业反恐怖防范标准电网部分	制定	全球能源互联网研究院有限公司、国家电网有限公司、中国南方电网有限责任公司、内蒙古电力公司	
125	电力行业反恐怖防范标准火电、风电部分	制定	中国华能集团有限公司、中国大唐集团有限公司、水电水利规划设计总院、中国电建集团中南勘测设计研究院有限公司	

续表

序号	标准名称	制定/修订	主要起草单位	代替标准
126	电力行业反恐怖防范标准水电工程部分	制定	中国长江三峡集团公司、水电水利规划设计总院、中国电建集团北京勘测设计研究院有限公司、中国电建集团成都勘测设计研究院有限公司	
127	额定电压10kV及以下架空绝缘导线金具	修订	中国电力科学研究院有限公司	DL/T 765.3—2004
128	防振锤技术条件和试验方法	修订	中国电力科学研究院有限公司	DL/T 1099—2009
129	输电线路杆塔用热浸镀锌螺栓与螺母	修订	全球能源互联网研究院有限公司	DL/T 284—2012
130	输电杆塔用地脚螺栓与螺母	修订	山东电工电气集团有限公司	DL/T 1236—2013
131	复合芯导线用碳纤维技术规范	制定	全球能源互联网研究院有限公司	
132	GIS变电站开关操作瞬态电磁骚扰抗扰度试验	制定	中国电力科学研究院有限公司	
133	港口岸电系统总则	制定	南瑞集团有限公司、国家电网有限公司、交通运输部水运科学研究院、中国船级社	
134	港口综合能源管控系统设计规范	制定	南瑞集团有限公司、国家电网有限公司、上海国际港务（集团）股份有限公司、中国南方电网有限责任公司	
135	岸基供电系统　第1部分：通用要求	制定	南瑞集团有限公司、国家电网有限公司、上海电动工具研究所（集团）有限公司、上海国际港务（集团）股份有限公司	
136	岸基供电系统　第3部分：变频电源	制定	南瑞集团有限公司、国家电网有限公司、上海电动工具研究所（集团）有限公司、上海国际港务（集团）股份有限公司	
137	电力光纤通信运行管理规程	修订	国家电网公司信息通信分公司、国家电网公司信息通信部、中国南方电网调度控制中心、国家电网公司华中分部、国网江苏省电力有限公司等	DL/T 547—2010
138	中长期电力交易安全校核技术规范	制定	中国南方电网电力调度控制中心、国家电网有限公司国家电力调度控制中心、清华大学、国电南瑞股份有限公司	
139	配电网调度图形模型规范	制定	国家电网有限公司国家电力调度控制中心、国网福建省电力有限公司、国网江苏省电力公司、南瑞集团有限公司	
140	水轮机调速器涉网性能检测技术规范	制定	国家电网有限公司国家电力调度控制中心、中国电力科学研究院有限公司等	
141	并网厂站电力监控系统安全防护设备调试验收标准	制定	国家电网有限公司国家电力调度控制中心、国网吉林省电力有限公司	
142	电力系统旋转事故备用容量配置标准	制定	中国电力科学研究院有限公司	
143	水力发电机组一次调频试验导则	制定	中国电力科学研究院有限公司、国家电网有限公司国家电力调度控制中心、中国南方电网调度控制中心、国网福建省电力调度控制中心、国网四川省电力调度控制中心、国网陕西省电力调度控制中心	

续表

序号	标准名称	制定/修订	主要起草单位	代替标准
144	新能源和小水电供电系统频率稳定计算导则	制定	国网四川省电力公司	
145	变电站巡检机器人检测技术规范	制定	中国电力科学研究院有限公司	
146	智能电网　术语	制定	国网浙江省电力有限公司、中国电力科学研究院有限公司、全球能源互联网研究院有限公司、北京智中能源科技有限公司、机械科学研究总院等	
147	输变电钢管结构制造技术条件	修订	电力工业电力设备及线路器材质量检验测试中心	DL/T 646—2012
148	配网复合材料电杆及其配套横担技术条件	制定	国网电力科学研究院武汉南瑞有限责任公司	
149	工业园区综合能源系统规划技术导则	制定	中国电力科学研究院有限公司、国网北京经济技术研究院有限公司、南方电网科学研究院有限公司、广东电网公司电力科学研究院等	
150	区域能源互联网综合评价导则	制定	中国电力科学研究院有限公司、国网北京经济技术研究院有限公司、南方电网科学研究院有限公司、广东电网公司电力科学研究院等	
151	能源互联网能量交换装置功能规范	制定	中国电力科学研究院有限公司	
152	能源互联网与分布式发电系统互动功能规范	制定	中国电力科学研究院有限公司	
153	能源互联网与分布式储能系统互动功能规范	制定	中国电力科学研究院有限公司	
154	需求侧电力辅助服务导则	制定	工业领域电力需求侧管理促进中心、中国电力科学研究院有限公司、国网电力科学研究院、南方电网科学研究院有限公司等	
155	电力工程信息模型应用统一标准	制定	中电联电力发展研究院有限公司	
156	变电站室内轨道式巡检机器人系统通用技术条件	制定	国网江西省电力公司检修分公司、国网山东省电力公司	
157	发电厂用风机泵类电机变频器节能评估试验导则	制定	中国大唐集团科学技术研究院有限公司华东分公司、国家电网安徽省电力公司电力科学研究院	
158	电站阀门分类导则	制定	西安热工研究院有限公司	
159	电站阀门检修导则　第3部分：止回阀	制定	国家电投集团河南电力检修工程有限公司	
160	管道焊接接头超声波检验技术规程　第1部分：通用技术要求	制定	中国电力科学研究院有限公司	
161	管道焊接接头超声波检验技术规程　第3部分：衍射时差法	制定	中国电力科学研究院有限公司	
162	管道焊接接头超声波检验技术规程　第4部分：在役检测	制定	中国电力科学研究院有限公司	
163	气体绝缘金属封闭设备用外壳材料及焊接评价导则	制定	中国电力科学研究院有限公司、平高电气股份有限公司	

续表

序号	标准名称	制定/修订	主要起草单位	代替标准
164	输变电工程电磁环境监测技术规范	修订	国网电力科学研究院、国电环境保护研究院、湖北省电力试验研究院	DL/T 334—2010
165	发电厂监控系统信息安全防护技术要求	制定	中国电力企业联合会科技开发服务中心、国网河南省电力公司电力科学研究院、华能电力股份有限公司长兴发电厂司等	
166	发电厂监控系统信息安全管理技术导则	制定	中国电力企业联合会科技开发服务中心、国网浙江省电力公司电力科学研究院、杭州安恒信息技术有限公司等	
167	变压器油中含气量的现场检测方法	制定	国网江苏省电力公司电力科学研究院、国电电科院、国网浙江省电力公司电力科学研究院、国网安徽省电力公司电力科学研究院、山东中惠仪器	
168	变压器油中金属元素的测定方法	修订	国网湖南省电力公司电力科学研究院、国网河北省电力公司电力科学研究院、国网浙江省电力公司电力科学研究院等	DL/T 263—2012
169	电力用矿物绝缘油现场处理及换油规范	制定	国网湖北省电力公司检修公司、国网湖南省电力公司电力科学研究院、西安热工研究院有限公司、国网湖北省电力公司电力科学研究院等	
170	六氟化硫混合绝缘气体充补气技术规范	制定	国网安徽省电力公司电力科学研究院、中国电力科学研究院有限公司、国网山东省电力公司电力科学研究院、国网江苏省电力公司电力科学研究院、国网湖南省电力公司电力科学研究院、国网福建省电力公司电力科学研究院等	
171	运行变压器油中甲醇含量的测定气相色谱法	制定	广东电网有限责任公司电力科学研究院、国网湖南省电力科学研究院、国网福建省电力公司电力科学研究院等	
172	电力设备仓储系统安全标识技术规范	制定	国网浙江省电力有限公司嘉兴供电公司、国网浙江平湖市供电有限公司、广州易能互联网服务有限公司	
173	差动电阻式锚杆应力计	修订	国电南京自动化股份有限公司	DL/T 1065—2007
174	差动电阻式锚索测力计	修订	国电南京自动化股份有限公司	DL/T 1064—2007
175	差动电阻式位移计	修订	国电南京自动化股份有限公司	DL/T 1063—2007
176	水电站防水淹厂房安全检查技术规程	制定	国家能源局大坝安全监察中心、中国电建集团华东勘测设计研究院有限公司、中国长江电力股份有限公司	
177	陶瓷电容式压力传感器	制定	南瑞集团有限公司	
178	水电水利工程施工用电安全技术规范	制定	中国水利水电第十二工程局有限公司	
179	水利水电工程缆机施工技术规程	制定	中国水利水电第四工程局有限公司、中国三峡建设管理有限公司	
180	水电水利工程施工机械安全操作规程 爬罐	制定	中国葛洲坝集团股份有限公司、中国葛洲坝集团第六工程有限公司	
181	水电水利工程施工机械安全操作规程 桥式布料机	制定	中国葛洲坝集团股份有限公司、中国葛洲坝集团第六工程有限公司	

续表

序号	标准名称	制定/修订	主要起草单位	代替标准
182	水电厂计算机监控系统试验验收规程	修订	南瑞集团有限公司、中国水利水电科学研究院、中国电建集团成都勘测设计研究院有限公司、中国长江电力股份有限公司等	DL/T 822—2012
183	水工建筑物水泥灌浆施工技术规范	修订	中国水电基础局有限公司、中国长江三峡集团有限公司	DL/T 5148—2012
184	水工混凝土建筑物缺陷检测和评估技术规程	修订	中国水利水电科学研究院	DL/T 5251—2010
185	抽水蓄能机组自动控制系统技术条件	修订	南瑞集团有限公司、国网新源控股有限公司、中国水利水电科学研究院、中国电建集团华东勘测设计研究院有限公司	DL/T 295—2011
186	水电站泄洪预警广播系统技术规范	制定	国电大渡河水电开发有限公司	
187	水力发电厂计算机监控系统与厂内设备及系统通信技术规定	修订	南瑞集团有限公司、中国水利水电科学研究院、中国电建集团成都勘测设计研究院有限公司、中国长江电力股份有限公司	DL/T 321—2012
188	水力发电厂水轮机技术监督导则	制定	西安热工研究院有限公司、中国长江电力股份有限公司	
189	电化学储能电站接入电网设计规范	制定	国网上海市电力公司电力科学研究院	
190	电力储能用梯次利用锂离子电池系统技术导则	制定	武汉蔚来能源有限公司、中国电力科学研究院有限公司、上海蔚来汽车有限公司、国网河南省电力公司电力科学研究院等	
191	分布式储能系统接入配电网设计规范	制定	国网江苏省电力有限公司电力科学研究院、中国电力科学研究院有限公司、国网北京经济技术研究院	
192	电力储能用超级电容器	制定	广东电网有限责任公司电力科学研究院	
193	电力储能用超级电容器试验规程	制定	广东电网有限责任公司电力科学研究院	
194	电化学储能系统溯源编码规范	制定	协鑫能源研究院、云南电网电力科学研究院	
195	分布式电源接入电网承载力评估导则	制定	国家电网有限公司、中国电力科学研究院有限公司、国网浙江省电力公司等	
196	光伏发电站电势诱导衰减治理技术规范	制定	北京群菱能源科技有限公司、南方电网综合能源有限公司、常州中海电力科技有限公司	
197	光伏电站生产准备导则	制定	上海电力新能源发展有限公司、中国三峡新能源有限公司	
198	新能源场站智能化建设基本技术规范	制定	国家电力投资集团公司、中国水利水电科学研究院、国家电投北京电力有限公司、国家电投五凌电力有限公司、北京中水科水电科技开发有限公司等	
199	发电厂和变电站照明集中式供电系统技术规范	制定	南方电网综合能源有限公司	
200	发电企业生产运营中心光伏发电数据接入系统技术规范	制定	国家电力投资集团有限公司、中国三峡新能源有限公司	
201	光伏发电站支架技术要求	制定	国家电力投资集团有限公司、上海摩昆新能源科技有限公司、衡水神龙实业有限公司、中国三峡新能源有限公司	

续表

序号	标准名称	制定/修订	主要起草单位	代替标准
202	光热发电工程项目质量管理规程	制定	中国长江三峡集团有限公司、中国电力工程顾问集团西北电力设计院有限公司、中国大唐集团新能源股份有限公司、龙源电力团股份有限公司、内蒙古电力勘测设计院有限责任公司、首航节能光热技术股份有限公司、中控太阳能技术有限公司	
203	光伏发电工程项目质量管理规程	制定	中国长江三峡集团有限公司、中国电建集团中南勘测设计研究院有限公司、中国大唐集团新能源股份有限公司等	
204	多能互补分布式能源能效评估技术导则	制定	中国电力科学研究院有限公司等	
205	配电网电线电缆节能评价技术规范	制定	国网（北京）节能设计研究院有限公司	
206	电力地理信息系统图形符号分类与代码	修订	国网黑龙江省电力有限公司、国网信通产业集团亿力吉奥有限公司、国网湖北省电力公司、国网河南省电力公司	DL/Z 397—2010
207	电力行业信息化标准体系	修订	国网信息通信产业集团有限公司、国家电网公司信息通信分公司、中国南方电网有限责任公司、中国华能集团有限公司	DL/Z 398—2010
208	全国电网名称代码	修订	国家电网公司信息通信分公司、国网信息通信产业集团有限公司、中国南方电网有限责任公司、国家电网有限公司国家电力调度通信中心、国家能源局信息中心	DL/T 510—2010
209	电力无线虚拟专网技术规范	制定	中国电力科学研究院有限公司、中国南方电网电力调度控制中心、国网浙江省电力公司、国网四川省电力公司	
210	电力移动应用App安全防护标准	制定	全球能源互联网研究院有限公司、国家电网有限公司、中国电力科学研究院有限公司、国网江苏省电力有限公司、国网浙江省电力有限公司、国网福建省电力有限公司等	
211	电力数据脱敏实施规范	制定	全球能源互联网研究院、国家电网有限公司、中国南方电网有限责任公司、中国国电集团公司	
212	电力信息系统软件外部信息交互接口测试规范	制定	中国电力科学研究院有限公司、国网江苏省电力有限公司、远光软件、中国软件测评中心	
213	电力行业电子标签通用技术要求与测试规范	制定	中国电力科学研究院有限公司、国网信息通信产业集团有限公司、中国南方电网有限责任公司	
214	电力行业云服务设计与技术要求	制定	国网上海市电力公司、国网江苏省电力有限公司、中国电力科学研究院有限公司、国网浙江省电力有限公司、国网安徽省电力有限公司、国网四川省电力有限公司、国网信息通信产业集团有限公司	

续表

序号	标准名称	制定/修订	主要起草单位	代替标准
215	电力行业移动互联应用基础支撑平台技术规范	制定	江苏电力信息技术有限公司、南京南瑞集团公司信息通信技术分公司、北京中电普华信息技术有限公司	
216	电力云基础设施安全技术要求	制定	国网辽宁省电力有限公司、中国电力科学研究院有限公司、国家电网公司信息通信分公司、国网信息通信产业集团有限公司、南瑞集团有限公司	
217	电力量子保密通信系统密钥交互接口技术规范	制定	国网信息通信产业集团有限公司、中国电力科学研究院有限公司	
218	电网信息通信应急能力评估标准规范	制定	国家电网有限公司	
219	电力地理信息系统地图数据产品与服务	制定	国网冀北电力有限公司、厦门亿力吉奥信息科技有限公司、国网福建省电力有限公司	
220	电力行业元数据管理技术标准	制定	中国南方电网有限责任公司、鼎信信息科技有限责任公司	
221	输变电设施可靠性评价规程	修订	中国电力企业联合会可靠性管理中心、国家电网有限公司、国网宁夏电力公司	DL/T 837—2012
222	电力可靠性基本名词术语	修订	中国电力企业联合会可靠性管理中心、重庆大学	DL/T 861—2004
223	电力设施高空警示球	制定	国家电力器材产品安全性能质量监督检验中心、浙江省高处作业防护技术重点实验室、国网河南省电力公司	
224	海底电缆退扭装置通用技术条件	制定	国网浙江省电力公司舟山供电公司、国家电力器材产品安全性能质量监督检验中心、浙江启明电力集团有限公司、浙江舟山海洋输电研究院有限公司等	
225	架空输电线路施工卡线器	制定	中国电力科学研究院有限公司、国家电力器材产品安全性能质量监督检验中心	
226	架空输电线路接续管保护装置	修订	中国电力科学研究院有限公司、国家电力器材产品安全性能质量监督检验中心	DL/T 1192—2012
227	低温下电容型验电器的使用导则	制定	国网黑龙江省电力有限公司电力科学研究院	
228	低温下电容型验电器预防性试验规程	制定	国网黑龙江省电力有限公司电力科学研究院	
229	电力用个人保安线通用技术条件	制定	浙江上检电力检测有限公司	
230	电力用安全帽动态性能测试装置	制定	杭州紫阳电气安全设备厂	
231	电力用便携式电动绞磨	制定	宁波天弘电力器具有限公司	
232	电力用可塑性绝缘遮蔽带通用技术条件	制定	3M（中国）有限公司、乐源万创科技发展（北京）有限公司	
233	电缆牵引报警装置技术条件	制定	杭州自效科技有限公司	
234	电力行业劳动环境监测技术规范	修订	国网山东省电力公司电力科学研究院、全国电力劳动环境检测监督总站、国网职业病防治院、国网重庆市电力公司电力科学研究院等	DL/T 799.1～DL/T 799.7—2010

续表

序号	标准名称	制定/修订	主要起草单位	代替标准
235	电力技术转移服务规范	制定	中国电力企业联合会科技开发服务中心、全球能源互联网研究院有限公司、中能国研（北京）电力科学研究院	
236	电力专利价值评价规范	制定	中国电力企业联合会科技开发服务中心、中国电力科学研究院有限公司、全球能源互联网研究院有限公司、中能国研（北京）电力科学研究院	
237	发电企业安全生产标准化实施指南	制定	中国电力企业联合会、中国电力技术市场协会	
238	多雷区风电场集电线路防雷改造技术规范	制定	中节能风力发电（张北）运维有限公司、北京乾源风电科技有限公司、大唐新能源试验研究院	
239	风电场监控系统信息安全防护技术规范	制定	中能电力科技开发有限公司、龙源电力集团股份有限公司、国家电投集团电站运营技术（北京）有限公司、中国三峡新能源公司	
240	风电场雷电预警系统技术规范	制定	北京乾源风电科技有限公司、大唐新能源研究院、粤电阳江海上风电有限公司	
241	风电场无人机集电线路安全巡检技术规范	制定	江西大唐国际新能源有限公司、龙源电力集团股份有限公司、中能电力科技开发有限公司、深圳市大疆创新科技有限公司等	
242	风电场无人机叶片检测技术规范	制定	大唐定边风电有限公司、龙源电力集团股份有限公司、中能电力科技开发有限公司、深圳市大疆创新科技有限公司、	
243	风力发电机组免爬器安全管理技术规范	制定	航风智维（北京）科技有限公司	
244	风力发电机组升降机安全管理技术规范	制定	龙源（北京）风电工程技术有限公司、龙源电力集团股份有限公司、中国三峡新能源公司	
245	海上风电场生产准备导则	制定	龙源（北京）风电工程技术有限公司、龙源电力集团股份有限公司、中国三峡新能源公司	
246	海上风电场运行风险管理规程	制定	中国三峡新能源有限公司、龙源电力集团股份有限公司、中国大唐集团新能源股份有限公司	
247	海上风力发电场基本术语	制定	中国三峡新能源有限公司、龙源电力集团股份有限公司、中国大唐集团新能源股份有限公司	
248	风电场无人机巡检作业技术规范	制定	中国三峡新能源有限公司、龙源电力集团股份有限公司、中国大唐集团新能源股份有限公司、中国电建集团华东勘测设计院有限公司等	
249	风电机组电气仿真模型验证方法	修订	龙源电力集团股份有限公司、中能电力科技开发有限公司、中国大唐集团新能源股份有限公司、北京鉴衡认证中心、深圳市大疆创新科技有限公司	NB/T 31053—2014
250	风电场并网性能监测评估方法	制定	中国电力科学研究院有限公司	

续表

序号	标准名称	制定/修订	主要起草单位	代替标准
251	风电场阻抗特性评估技术规范	制定	中国电力科学研究院有限公司	
252	分散式风电接入配电网技术规定	制定	中国电力科学研究院有限公司、国家电网有限公司国家电力调度控制中心、国网新疆电力公司、国网冀北电力有限公司、国网吉林省电力有限公司	
253	风电资源与运行能效评价规范	制定	中国电力科学研究院有限公司、南方电网科学研究院有限责任公司、南瑞集团有限公司、湖北省电力勘测设计院、远景能源科技有限公司	

（中国电力企业联合会　许松林　刘永东）

2018年国家能源局下达的电力行业标准英文版翻译计划项目

2018年，国家能源局下达的电力行业标准英文　　版翻译计划项目16项，见表1。

表1　　2018年国家能源局下达的电力行业标准英文版翻译计划项目

序号	标准项目名称（英文）	标准项目名称（中文）	标准编号	归口单位
1	Technical requirements for computer supervision and control systems communication with intelligent electronic	水力发电厂计算机监控系统与厂内设备及系统通信技术规定	DL/T 321—2012	电力行业水电站自动化标准化技术委员会
2	Requirements for internal cooling water quality and it ′ s system in large generators	大型发电机内冷却水质及系统技术要求	DL/T 801—2010	电力行业电机标准化技术委员会
3	Data acquisition and management system for electrical energy part4-5: communication protocol - object oriented data exchange protocol	电能信息采集与管理系统　第4-5部分：通信协议-面向对象的数据交换协议	DL/T 698.45—2017	电力行业电测量标准化技术委员会
4	Test methods for proximate analysis of coal by automatic instrumental procedures	煤的工业分析　自动仪器法	DL/T 1030-2006	电力行业电厂化学标准化技术委员会
5	Guide for power frequency parameters measurement of 1000kV AC overhead transmission lines	1000kV交流架空输电线路工频参数测量导则	DL/T 1179—2012	全国特高压交流输电标准化技术委员会
6	Technical specification for magnetically controlled shunt reactor	磁控型可控并联电抗器技术规范	DL/T 1217—2013	电力行业电能质量及柔性输电标委会
7	The technical specification for prefabricated optical cable in smart substation	智能变电站预制光缆技术规范	DL/T 1623—2016	中国电力企业联合会
8	Calibration specification for high voltage testing instruments Part2: Power transformer tap-changers tester	高压测试仪器及设备校准规范　第2部分：电力变电压器分接开关测试仪	DL/T 1694.2—2017	全国高电压试验技术和绝缘配合标准化技术委员会高电压试验技术标准化分技术委员会

续表

序号	标准项目名称（英文）	标准项目名称（中文）	标准编号	归口单位
9	X-ray digital radiography guideline for electrical power equipment	电力设备X射线数字成像检测技术导则	DL/T 1785-2017	全国高电压试验技术和绝缘配合标准化技术委员会高电压试验技术标准化分技术委员会
10	Technical guideline for the synchronous monitoring of DC bias current distribution	电网直流偏磁电流分布的同步监测技术导则	DL/T 1786—2017	全国高电压试验技术和绝缘配合标准化技术委员会高电压试验技术标准化分技术委员会
11	Calibration specification of Relative dissipation factor and capacitance tester	相对介损及电容检测仪校准规范	DL/T 1787—2017	全国高电压试验技术和绝缘配合标准化技术委员会高电压试验技术标准化分技术委员会
12	Field calibrating specifications for HVDC instrument transformers	高压直流互感器现场校验规范	DL/T 1788—2017	全国高电压试验技术和绝缘配合标准化技术委员会高电压试验技术标准化分技术委员会
13	General specifications conditions of supply apparatus for partial discharge measuring of power transformers	变压器现场局部放电测量用电源装置通用技术条件	DL/T 1790—2017	全国高电压试验技术和绝缘配合标准化技术委员会高电压试验技术标准化分技术委员会
14	Code for model test of river diversion and closure during construction for hydropower & hydraulic engineering	水电水利工程施工导截流模型试验规程	DL/T 5361—2006	电力行业水电施工标准化技术委员会
15	Technical specification for surface thermal insulation construction of hydraulic concrete	水工混凝土表面保温施工技术规范	DL/T 5750—2017	电力行业水电施工标准化技术委员会
16	Code for manufacture, installation, acceptance and acceptance of bellows expansion joints of pressure pipe in hydropower and water conservancy projects	水电水利工程压力钢管波纹管伸缩节制造安装及验收规范	DL/T 5751—2017	电力行业水电施工标准化技术委员会

（中国电力企业联合会　许松林　刘永东）

2018 年由水电水利规划设计总院归口管理的技术标准制修订计划项目

2018 年，由水电水利规划设计总院归口管理的　技术标准制修订计划项目 42 项，见表 1。

表 1　2018 年由水电水利规划设计总院归口管理的技术标准制修订计划项目

序号	标准项目名称	修订/制定	主要起草单位	代替标准
1	水力发电工程项目规范	制定	水电水利规划设计总院、中国电建集团北京勘测设计研究院有限公司、中国电建集团西北勘测设计研究院有限公司等	
2	水电工程标识系统编码标准	制定	水电水利规划设计总院、中国长江三峡集团有限公司、中国电建集团华东勘测设计研究院有限公司、中国电建集团中南勘测设计研究院有限公司、中国电建集团成都勘测设计研究院有限公司、中国电建集团北京勘测设计研究院有限公司	

续表

序号	标准项目名称	修订/制定	主要起草单位	代替标准
3	水电工程安全标识规定	制定	水电水利规划设计总院、中国电建集团中南勘测设计研究院有限公司、中国长江三峡集团有限公司、中国电建集团贵阳勘测设计研究院有限公司	
4	水电工程节能技术通则	制定	水电水利规划设计总院、中国电建集团北京勘测设计研究院有限公司等	
5	水电工程信息分类与编码 第4部分：水工建筑物	制定	中国电建集团华东勘测设计研究院有限公司、中国电建集团成都勘测设计研究院有限公司、浙江华东工程数字技术有限公司	
6	水电工程招标设计报告编制规程	修订	水电水利规划设计总院、中国电建集团华东勘测设计研究院有限公司	DL/T 5212—2005
7	水电工程水文测验及资料整编规范	制定	中国电建集团贵阳勘测设计研究院有限公司、中国电建集团华东勘测设计研究院有限公司、中国电建集团中南勘测设计研究院有限公司、中国长江三峡集团有限公司	
8	水电工程泥沙监测系统技术规范	制定	中国电建集团成都勘测设计研究院有限公司、中国电建集团中南勘测设计研究院有限公司、中国电建集团贵阳勘测设计研究院有限公司、中国电建集团昆明勘测设计研究院有限公司、中国电建集团华东勘测设计研究院有限公司、中国长江三峡集团有限公司	
9	水电工程水情自动测报系统技术规范	修订	水电水利规划设计总院、中国电建集团中南勘测设计研究院有限公司、中国电建集团西北勘测设计研究院有限公司、中国电建集团成都勘测设计研究院有限公司	NB/T 35003—2013
10	水工混凝土技术性能规定	制定	水电水利规划设计总院、中国长江三峡集团有限公司、中国电建集团中南勘测设计研究院有限公司、武汉大学	
11	水工沥青技术性能规定	制定	中国电建集团北京勘测设计研究院有限公司等	
12	水电工程钢闸门及辅助装置系列标准	制定	中国电建集团成都勘测设计研究院有限公司、中国电建集团华东勘测设计研究院有限公司	
13	水电工程清污机设计规范	制定	中国电建集团中南勘测设计研究院有限公司、中国电建集团华东勘测设计研究院有限公司 、中国电建集团成都勘测设研究院有限公司、中国电建集团昆明勘测设计研究院有限公司	
14	水电站桥式起重机基本技术条件	制定	中国电建集团华东勘测设计研究院有限公司	
15	水电工程清污机技术条件	制定	中国电建华东勘测设计研究院有限公司、浙江华东机电工程有限公司	
16	水电工程后评价技术导则	制定	中国电建集团北京勘测设计研究院有限公司等	
17	水电工程劳动安全与工业卫生后评价规程	制定	水电水利规划设计总院、中国电建集团中南勘测设计研究院有限公司、中国电建集团西北勘测设计研究院有限公司、中国水利水电建设工程咨询有限公司、国网新源控股有限公司、华能澜沧江水电股份有限公司	

续表

序号	标准项目名称	修订/制定	主要起草单位	代替标准
18	水电工程金属结构设备状态在线监测系统技术条件	制定	国电大渡河流域水电开发有限公司、成都众柴科技有限公司	
19	水电工程铁磁性钢丝绳在线监测技术规程	制定	国电大渡河流域水电开发有限公司、成都众柴科技有限公司	
20	水电工程质量监督管理规程	制定	水电水利规划设计总院	
21	水电工程信息分类与编码 第12部分：运行维护	制定	中国长江三峡集团有限公司、中国长江电力股份有限公司	
22	水电工程数据库表结构及标识符	制定	中国长江三峡集团有限公司、中国电建集团北京勘测设计研究院有限公司、中国电建集团华东勘测设计研究院有限公司、中国电建集团成都勘测设计研究院有限公司、中国电建集团贵阳勘测设计研究院有限公司、中国电建集团中南勘测设计研究院有限公司、中国电建集团昆明勘测设计研究院有限公司、中国电建集团西北勘测设计研究院有限公司	
23	水电工程档案分类导则	制定	中国电建集团中南勘测设计研究院有限公司、中国电建集团成都勘测设计研究院有限公司、中国电建集团北京勘测设计研究院有限公司、中国电建集团华东勘测设计研究院有限公司、雅砻江流域水电开发有限公司	
24	水电工程生产运行文件收集与档案整理规范	制定	雅砻江流域水电开发有限公司 、中国长江三峡集团有限公司、中国电建集团昆明勘测设计研究院有限公司、中国电建集团华东勘测设计研究院有限公司、国电大渡河流域水电开发有限公司	
25	水电工程档案信息化导则	制定	中国电建集团昆明勘测设计研究院有限公司	
26	水电工程档案鉴定销毁管理规程	制定	中国电建集团中南勘测设计研究院有限公司、中国电建集团成都勘测设计研究院有限公司、中国电建集团华东勘测设计研究院有限公司、雅砻江流域水电开发有限公司	
27	水力发电厂劳动定员标准	制定	中国长江三峡集团有限公司、中国长江电力股份有限公司、水电水利规划设计总院	
28	水电工程岩土试验仪器设备校验规程	制定	中国电建集团北京勘测设计研究院有限公司等	
29	混凝土重力坝设计规范	修订	中国电建集团华东勘测设计研究院有限公司、水电水利规划设计总院等	NB/T 35026—2014
30	抽水蓄能电站静止变频启动设备安装调试规程	制定	水电水利规划设计总院、中国长江三峡集团有限公司、中国电建集团北京勘测设计研究院有限公司、中国电建集团华东勘测设计研究院有限公司	
31	水电工程清污机制造安装及验收规范	制定	中国电建集团华东勘测设计研究院有限公司、浙江华东机电工程有限公司	
32	水电工程设计概算编制规定	制定	水电水利规划设计总院（可再生能源定额站）、中国电建集团北京勘测设计研究院有限公司	

续表

序号	标准项目名称	修订/制定	主要起草单位	代替标准
33	水电工程费用构成及概（估）算费用标准	制定	水电水利规划设计总院（可再生能源定额站）、中国电建集团北京勘测设计研究院有限公司、中国电建集团成都勘测设计研究院有限公司	
34	水电工程对外投资项目造价编制导则	制定	水电水利规划设计总院（可再生能源定额站）、中国电建集团北京勘测设计研究院有限公司	
35	水电工程水力机械抗泥沙磨蚀技术导则	制定	中国电建集团成都勘测设计研究院有限公司	
36	水电站工程安全防护保护管理规定	制定	水电水利规划设计总院、中国电建集团西北勘测设计研究院有限公司、国网新源控股有限公司、华能澜沧江水电股份有限公司、雅砻江流域水电开发有限公司、黄河上游水电开发有限责任公司、五凌电力有限公司、中国长江三峡集团有限公司	
37	水电工程隐患判定标准	制定	水电水利规划设计总院、中国电建集团中南勘测设计研究院有限公司、中国电建集团西北勘测设计研究院有限公司、中国电建集团昆明勘测设计研究院有限公司、中国电建集团华东勘测设计研究院有限公司、中国电建集团北京勘测设计研究院有限公司、中国电建集团成都勘测设计研究院有限公司、中国电建集团贵阳勘测设计研究院有限公司、国网新源控股有限公司、华能澜沧江水电股份有限公司、雅砻江流域水电开发有限公司、黄河上游水电开发有限责任公司、五凌电力有限公司、中国长江三峡集团有限公司、国家能源局大坝安全监察中心、四川能源监管办、贵州能源监管办、云南能源监管办	
38	土工动三轴试验仪校验规程	制定	中国水利水电科学研究院	
39	土工共振柱试验仪校验规程	制定	中国水利水电科学研究院、三峡大学	
40	光伏发电工程工程量清单计价规范	制定	水电水利规划设计总院（可再生能源定额站）、中国电建集团北京勘测设计研究院有限公司、中国电建集团西北勘测设计研究院有限公司	
41	生物质气化多联产系统技术导则	制定	水电水利规划设计总院、湖北省电力勘测设计院、南京林业大学等	
42	生物天然气工程等级划分及设计安全标准	制定	水电水利规划设计总院、中国电建集团西北勘测设计研究院有限公司	

（水电水利规划设计总院　杜刚）

水电水利规划设计总院 2018 年标准送审稿审查项目情况

2018 年，水电水利规划设计总院组织标委会委员和有关专家对《水电工程环境影响后评价技术规范》等 86 项在编的能源领域行业标准开展了审查工作，同时，根据审查会意见和建议，要求编制组做进一步修改完善，形成报批稿，尽早报国家能源局批准发布实施。水电水利规划设计总院 2018 年标准送审稿审查项目，见表 1。

表1 水电水利规划设计总院2018年标准送审稿审查项目

序号	项目编号	项目名称	备注
1	能源20160565	水电工程环境影响后评价技术规范	
2	能源20140822	水电工程水温实时监测系统技术规范	
3	能源20140850	水电工程环境保护总体设计报告编制规程	
4	能源20140451	水电工程水土保持设计规范	
5	能源20110005	水力资源调查评价规范	
6	能源20110159	水电工程建设征地企业处理规划设计规范	
7	能源20150584	水电工程水库库底清理设计规范	
8	能源20150574	大中型水轮机选用导则	
9	能源20150603	水电工程预可行性研究报告编制规程	
10	能源20150583	水电工程生态制图规范	
11	能源20110160	水电工程移民安置综合设计规范	
12	能源20150594	水电工程建设征地处理范围界定规范	
13	能源20150585	水电工程建设征地实物指标调查规范	
14	能源20150578	水电工程建设征地移民实物指标分类编码规范	
15	能源20140846	水电工程通信设计内容和深度规定	
16	能源20140854	水电工程水文预报规范	
17	能源20120418	水电工程运行调度规程编制规范	
18	能源20140857	潮汐电站资源调查规范	
19	能源20140856	潮汐电站水能规划设计规范	
20	能源20160571	少数民族地区水电工程建设征地移民安置规划设计规定	
21	能源20120118	水电工程阶段性蓄水移民安置实施方案专题报告编制规程	
22	能源20150580	梯级水电站运行方式编制导则	
23	国能综通科技〔2017〕52号	《水电工程小流域水文计算规范》英文版	英文
24	国能综科技〔2016〕876号	水力发电厂供暖通风与空气调节设计规范	英文
25	国能综科技〔2016〕876号	河流水电开发环境影响后评价规范	英文
26	国能综通科技〔2017〕52号	高海拔风力发电机组技术导则	英文
27	国能综科技〔2016〕876号	水电站分层取水进水口设计规范	英文
28	国能综科技〔2016〕876号	水电工程水情自动测报系统技术规范	英文
29	国能综科技〔2016〕876号	水电工程建设征地移民安置验收规程	英文
30	国能综科技〔2016〕876号	水电工程设计洪水计算规范	英文
31	国能综科技〔2016〕876号	抽水蓄能电站选点规划编制规范	英文
32	国能综科技〔2016〕876号	水电工程环境监理规范	英文
33	国能综科技〔2016〕876号	抽水蓄能电站水能规划设计规范	英文
34	国能综科技〔2016〕876号	水电工程泥沙设计规范	英文
35	国能综科技〔2016〕876号	水电工程钢闸门设计规范	英文

续表

序号	项目编号	项目名称	备注
36	国能综科技〔2016〕876号	QPG型卷扬式高扬程启闭机系列参数	英文
37	国能综科技〔2016〕876号	水力发电厂照明设计规范	英文
38	国能综科技〔2016〕876号	水电工程钢闸门设计规范	英文
39	国能综科技〔2016〕876号	水电工程岩体质量检测技术规程	英文
40	国能综科技〔2016〕876号	水电工程地震勘探技术规程	英文
41	国能综科技〔2016〕876号	水电工程覆盖层钻探技术规程	英文
42	国能综科技〔2016〕876号	水电工程地质勘察水质分析规程	英文
43	能源20140805	水电工程地质测绘规程	
44	能源20140819	水电工程水库库岸防护工程勘察规程	
45	能源20120412	水电工程泥石流勘察与防治设计规程	
46	能源20140821	水电工程水库专业项目工程勘察规程	
47	能源20140436	水电工程施工机械选择设计规范	
48	能源20140838	水电工程水文地质勘察规程	
49	能源20140437	潮汐发电工程地质勘察规范	
50	20150603	水电工程预可行性研究报告编制规程	
51	发改办工业〔2008〕1242号，计划编号：电力行业43	碾压混凝土重力坝设计规范	
52	能源20140440	碾压混凝土拱坝设计规范	
53	20130841	水电工程探地雷达探测技术规程	
54	能源20150564	水电工程岩芯档案收集与整理规范	
55	能源20140837	水电工程物探规范	
56	能源20130842	水电工程电法勘探技术规程	
57	能源20150557	水电水利工程沉沙池设计规范	
58	能源20150552	水电工程放射性探测技术规程	
59	能源20140804	水电工程水库区工程地质勘察技术规程	
60	能源20170123	水电工程防恐防暴设计规范	
61	能源20150540	水电工程岩爆风险评估技术规范	
62	能源20090158	水电工程泄水建筑物消能防冲设计导则	
63	能源20150598	水库蓄水应急预案编制规程	
64	能源20090186	风电机组塔筒设计制造安装及验收规范	
65	能源20140827	光伏发电站直流发电系统设计标准	
66	能源20150659	海上风电场工程设计概算编制规定及费用标准	
67	能源20150660	海上风电场工程概算定额	
68	能源20140828	生物质发电工程地质勘察规范	
69	能源20140868	海上风电场岩土试验与测试规程	
70	能源20130840	光伏发电工程地质勘查规范	

续表

序号	项目编号	项目名称	备注
71	能源20090183	风电场工程节能评估技术规范	
72	能源20150657	陆上风电场工程设计概算编制规定及费用标准	
73	能源20150658	陆上风电场工程概算定额	
74	能源20140871	风电场工程竣工图文件编制规程	
75	能源20100380	光伏发电工程电气设计规范	
76	能源20150568	水电工程竣工决算报告编制规定	
77	能源20150569	水电工程竣工决算专项验收规程	
78	能源20140472	风电机组地基基础设计规定	
79	能源20150665	风电场项目后评价规程	
80	能源20160631	风电场工程劳动安全与工业卫生设计规范	
81	能源20140870	风电机组招标文件编制导则	
82	能源20160629	风电场工程道路设计规范	
83	能源20170833	海上风电场工程预可行性研究报告编制规程	
84	能源20150671	陆上风电场施工安全技术规范	
85	能源20170830	海上风电场风能资源测量及海洋水文观测规范	

（水电水利规划设计总院　杜刚）

中国葛洲坝集团股份有限公司 2018年主编和参编技术标准情况

2018年，中国葛洲坝集团股份有限公司主编和参编，并发布的国家技术标准和行业技术标准共5项，其中，电力国家技术标准1项，电力行业技术标准4项，见表1。

表1　中国葛洲坝集团股份有限公司2018年主编和参编并发布的标准情况

序号	标准名称	标准编号	参编情况	发布时间	实施时间	备注
1	电气装置安装电缆线路施工及验收标准	GB 50168—2018	主编	2018年11月8日	2019年5月1日	葛洲坝电力公司
2	水工混凝土界面处理剂施工技术规范	DL/T 5761—2018	主编	2018年4月3日	2018年7月1日	葛洲坝勘测设计公司
3	水电水利水泥改性膨胀土施工技术规范	DL/T 5775—2018	主编	2018年12月25日	2019年5月1日	葛洲坝公司、葛洲坝基础公司
4	气体绝缘金属封闭输电线路施工及验收规范	DL/T 5779—2018	主编	2018年12月25日	2019年5月1日	葛洲坝集团公司、葛洲坝机电公司、葛洲坝国际公司
5	水电水利基础处理竣工资料整编及验收规范	DL/T 5774　2018	参编	2018年12月25日	2019年5月1日	葛洲坝试验检测公司

（中国葛洲坝集团股份有限公司）

新 颁 标 准

2018年国家标准化管理委员会发布的电力国家标准

2018年，国家标准化管理委员会发布的电力国家标准43项，见表1。

表1 2018年国家标准化管理委员会发布的电力国家标准

序号	标准编号	标准名称	归口标委会
1	GB/T 24836—2018	1100kV气体绝缘金属封闭开关设备	全国特高压交流输电标准化技术委员会
2	GB/T 24837—2018	1100kV高压交流隔离开关和接地开关	全国特高压交流输电标准化技术委员会
3	GB/T 24838—2018	1100kV高压交流断路器	全国特高压交流输电标准化技术委员会
4	GB/T 24839—2018	1000kV交流系统用支柱绝缘子技术规范	全国特高压交流输电标准化技术委员会
5	GB/T 24840—2018	1000kV交流系统用套管技术规范	全国特高压交流输电标准化技术委员会
6	GB/T 24841—2018	1000kV交流系统用电容式电压互感器技术规范	全国特高压交流输电标准化技术委员会
7	GB/T 24842—2018	1000kV特高压交流输变电工程过电压和绝缘配合	全国特高压交流输电标准化技术委员会
8	GB/T 24843—2018	1000kV单相油浸式自耦电力变压器技术规范	全国特高压交流输电标准化技术委员会
9	GB/T 24844—2018	1000kV交流系统用油浸式并联电抗器技术规范	全国特高压交流输电标准化技术委员会
10	GB/T 24845—2018	1000kV交流系统用无间隙金属氧化物避雷器技术规范	全国特高压交流输电标准化技术委员会
11	GB/T 24846—2018	1000kV交流电气设备预防性试验规程	全国特高压交流输电标准化技术委员会
12	GB/T 2694—2018	输电线路铁塔制造技术条件	中电联标准化中心
13	GB/T 36115—2018	精准扶贫 村级光伏电站技术导则	中电联标准化中心
14	GB/T 36116—2018	村镇光伏发电站集群控制系统功能要求	中电联标准化中心
15	GB/T 36117—2018	村镇光伏发电站集群接入电网规划设计导则	中电联标准化中心
16	GB/T 36119—2018	精准扶贫 村级光伏电站管理与评价导则	中电联标准化中心
17	GB/T 36270—2018	微电网监控系统技术规范	全国微电网与分布式电源并网标准化技术委员会
18	GB/T 36271.1—2018	交流1kV以上电力设施 第1部分：通则	全国高压电气安全标准化技术委员会
19	GB/T 36273—2018	智能变电站继电保护和安全自动装置数字化接口技术规范	中电联标准化中心
20	GB/T 36274—2018	微电网能量管理系统技术规范	全国微电网与分布式电源并网标准化技术委员会

续表

序号	标准编号	标准名称	归口标委会
21	GB/T 36276—2018	电力储能用锂离子电池	全国电力储能标准化技术委员会
22	GB/T 36277—2018	电动汽车车载静止式直流电能表技术条件	能源行业电动汽车充电设施标准化技术委员会
23	GB/T 36278—2018	电动汽车充换电设施接入配电网技术规范	能源行业电动汽车充电设施标准化技术委员会
24	GB/T 36280—2018	电力储能用铅炭电池	全国电力储能标准化技术委员会
25	GB/T 36283—2018	智能变电站二次舱通用技术条件	电力行业继电保护标准化技术委员会
26	GB/T 36285—2018	火力发电厂汽轮机电液控制系统技术条件	全国电站过程监控及信息标准化技术委员会
27	GB/T 36290.2—2018	电站流程图　第2部分：图形符号	全国电站过程监控及信息标准化技术委员会
28	GB/T 36291.1—2018	电力安全设施配置技术规范　第1部分：变电站	全国高压电气安全标准化技术委员会
29	GB/T 36291.2—2018	电力安全设施配置技术规范　第2部分：线路	全国高压电气安全标准化技术委员会
30	GB/T 36293—2018	火力发电厂分散控制系统技术条件	全国电站过程监控及信息标准化技术委员会
31	GB/T 36294—2018	抽水蓄能发电企业档案分类导则	中电联标准化中心
32	GB/T 36545—2018	移动式电化学储能系统技术要求	中电联标准化中心
33	GB/T 36547—2018	电化学储能系统接入电网技术规定	全国电力储能标准化技术委员会
34	GB/T 36548—2018	电化学储能系统接入电网测试规范	全国电力储能标准化技术委员会
35	GB/T 36549—2018	电化学储能电站运行指标及评价	全国电力储能标准化技术委员会
36	GB/T 36550—2018	抽水蓄能电站基本名词术语	中电联标准化中心
37	GB/T 36558—2018	电力系统电化学储能系统通用技术条件	全国电力储能标准化技术委员会
38	GB/T 36567—2018	光伏组件检修规程	中电联标准化中心
39	GB/T 36568—2018	光伏方阵检修规程	中电联标准化中心
40	GB/T 36569—2018	海上风电场风力发电机组基础技术要求	能源行业风电标准化技术委员会风电运行维护分技术委员会
41	GB/T 36570—2018	水力发电厂消防设施运行维护规程	中电联标准化中心
42	GB/T 36571—2018	并联无功补偿节约电力电量测量和验证技术规范	中电联标准化中心
43	GB/T 36573—2018	电力线路升压运行节约电力电量测量和验证技术规范	中电联标准化中心

（中国电力企业联合会　许松林　刘永东）

2018年住房和城乡建设部发布的电力工程建设国家标准

2018年，住房和城乡建设部发布的电力工程建设国家标准6项，见表1。

表 1　2018 年住房和城乡建设部发布的电力工程建设国家标准

序号	标准编号	标准名称	归口标委会
1	GB 50217—2018	电力工程电缆设计标准	中电联标准化中心
2	GB/T 50548—2018	330kV～750kV 架空输电线路勘测标准	中电联标准化中心
3	GB/T 51307—2018	塔式太阳能光热发电站设计标准	中电联标准化中心
4	GB/T 51311—2018	风光储联合发电站调试及验收标准	中电联标准化中心
5	GB/T 51313—2018	电动汽车分散充电设施工程技术标准	能源行业电动汽车充电设施标准化技术委员会
6	GB/T 51320—2018	建设工程化学灌浆材料应用技术标准	中电联标准化中心

（中国电力企业联合会　许松林　刘永东）

2018 年国家能源局发布的电力行业标准

2018 年，国家能源局发布的电力行业标准 337 项，其中，水电、新能源及电气等部分 226 项，见表 1。

表 1　2018 年国家能源局发布的电力行业标准

序号	标准编号	标准名称	代替标准	实施日期
1	NB/T 31129—2018	风力发电机组振动状态评价导则		2018 年 7 月 1 日
2	NB/T 31130—2018	风力发电场设备润滑技术监督规程		2018 年 7 月 1 日
3	NB/T 31131—2018	风力发电场测量技术监督规程		2018 年 7 月 1 日
4	NB/T 31132—2018	风力发电场电能质量技术监督规程		2018 年 7 月 1 日
5	NB/T 31133—2018	海上风电场风力发电机组混凝土基础防腐蚀技术规范		2018 年 7 月 1 日
6	NB/T 32041—2018	光伏发电站设备后评价规程		2018 年 7 月 1 日
7	NB/T 32042—2018	光伏发电工程建设监理规范		2018 年 7 月 1 日
8	DL/T 1013—2018	大中型水轮发电机微机励磁调节器试验导则	DL/T 1013—2006	2018 年 7 月 1 日
9	DL/T 1093—2018	电力变压器绕组变形的电抗法检测判断导则	DL/T 1093—2008	2018 年 7 月 1 日
10	DL/T 1094—2018	电力变压器用绝缘油选用导则	DL/T 1094—2008	2018 年 7 月 1 日
11	DL/T 1095—2018	变压器油带电度现场测试方法	DL/T 1095—2008	2018 年 7 月 1 日
12	DL/T 1096—2018	变压器油中颗粒度限值	DL/T 1096—2008	2018 年 7 月 1 日
13	DL/T 1147—2018	电力高处作业防坠器	DL/T 1147—2009	2018 年 7 月 1 日
14	DL/T 1799—2018	电力变压器直流偏磁耐受能力试验方法		2018 年 7 月 1 日
15	DL/T 1800—2018	水轮机调节系统建模及参数实测技术导则		2018 年 7 月 1 日
16	DL/T 1801—2018	水电金属结构及设备焊接接头相控阵超声检测		2018 年 7 月 1 日
17	DL/T 1802—2018	水电厂自动发电控制及自动电压控制系统技术规范		2018 年 7 月 1 日
18	DL/T 1803—2018	水电厂辅助设备控制装置技术条件		2018 年 7 月 1 日
19	DL/T 1804—2018	水轮发电机组振动摆度装置技术条件		2018 年 7 月 1 日
20	DL/T 1805—2018	电力变压器用有载分接开关选用导则		2018 年 7 月 1 日
21	DL/T 1806—2018	油浸式电力变压器用绝缘纸板及绝缘件选用导则		2018 年 7 月 1 日

续表

序号	标准编号	标准名称	代替标准	实施日期
22	DL/T 1807—2018	油浸式电力变压器、电抗器局部放电超声波检测与定位导则		2018年7月1日
23	DL/T 1808—2018	干式空心电抗器匝间过电压现场试验导则		2018年7月1日
24	DL/T 1809—2018	水电厂设备状态检修决策支持系统技术导则		2018年7月1日
25	DL/T 1810—2018	110(66)kV六氟化硫气体绝缘电力变压器使用技术条件		2018年7月1日
26	DL/T 1811—2018	电力变压器用天然酯绝缘油选用导则		2018年7月1日
27	DL/T 1813—2018	油浸式非晶合金铁心配电变压器选用导则		2018年7月1日
28	DL/T 1814—2018	油浸式电力变压器工厂试验油中溶解气体分析判断导则		2018年7月1日
29	DL/T 1815—2018	电化学储能电站设备可靠性评价规程		2018年7月1日
30	DL/T 1816—2018	电化学储能电站标识系统编码导则		2018年7月1日
31	DL/T 1817—2018	变压器低压侧用绝缘铜管母使用技术条件		2018年7月1日
32	DL/T 1818—2018	可逆式水泵水轮机调节系统试验规程		2018年7月1日
33	DL/T 1819—2018	抽水蓄能电站静止变频装置技术条件		2018年7月1日
34	DL/T 1823—2018	六氟化硫气体中矿物油、可水解氟化物、酸度的现场检测方法		2018年7月1日
35	DL/T 1824—2018	运行变压器油中丙酮含量的测量方法　顶空气相色谱法		2018年7月1日
36	DL/T 1825—2018	六氟化硫在线湿度测量装置校验　静态法		2018年7月1日
37	DL/T 1832—2018	配电网串联电容器补偿装置技术规范		2018年7月1日
38	DL/T 1836—2018	矿物绝缘油与变压器材料相容性测定方法		2018年7月1日
39	DL/T 1837—2018	电力用矿物绝缘油换油指标		2018年7月1日
40	DL/T 1838—2018	电力用圆形及异形绝缘管		2018年7月1日
41	DL/T 1839.1—2018	电力可靠性管理信息系统数据接口规范　第1部分：通用要求		2018年7月1日
42	DL/T 1839.2—2018	电力可靠性管理信息系统数据接口规范　第2部分：输变电设施		2018年7月1日
43	DL/T 1839.4—2018	电力可靠性管理信息系统数据接口规范　第4部分：供电系统用户供电		2018年7月1日
44	DL/T 1840—2018	交流高压架空输电线路对短波无线电测向台（站）保护间距要求		2018年7月1日
45	DL/T 1841—2018	交流高压架空输电线路与对空情报雷达站防护距离要求		2018年7月1日
46	DL/T 1845—2018	电力设备高合金钢里氏硬度试验方法		2018年7月1日
47	DL/T 1846—2018	变电站机器人巡检系统验收规范		2018年7月1日
48	DL/T 1848—2018	220kV和110kV变压器中性点过电压保护技术规范		2018年7月1日
49	DL/T 1851—2018	发电厂钢制衬胶管道和管件		2018年7月1日
50	DL/T 319—2018	架空输电线路施工抱杆通用技术条件及试验方法	DL/T 319—2010	2018年7月1日

续表

序号	标准编号	标准名称	代替标准	实施日期
51	DL/T 363—2018	超、特高压电力变压器（电抗器）设备监造导则	DL/T 363—2010	2018年7月1日
52	DL/T 432—2018	电力用油中颗粒度测定方法	DL/T 432—2007	2018年7月1日
53	DL/T 474.1—2018	现场绝缘试验实施导则 绝缘电阻、吸收比和极化指数试验	DL/T 474.1—2006	2018年7月1日
54	DL/T 474.3—2018	现场绝缘试验实施导则 介质损耗因数 $\tan\delta$ 试验	DL/T 474.3—2006	2018年7月1日
55	DL/T 474.4—2018	现场绝缘试验实施导则 交流耐压试验	DL/T 474.4—2006	2018年7月1日
56	DL/T 474.5—2018	现场绝缘试验导则 避雷器试验	DL/T 474.5—2006	2018年7月1日
57	DL/T 485—2018	电力企业标准体系表编制导则	DL/T 485—2012	2018年7月1日
58	DL/T 489—2018	大中型水轮发电机静止整流励磁系统试验规程	DL/T 489—2006	2018年7月1日
59	DL/T 515—2018	电站弯管	DL/T 515—2004	2018年7月1日
60	DL/T 521—2018	真空净油机验收及使用维护导则	DL/T 521—2004	2018年7月1日
61	DL/T 5285—2018	输变电工程架空导线（800mm^{2}以下）及地线液压压接工艺规程	DL/T 5285—2013	2018年7月1日
62	DL/T 5313.9—2018	水电水利基本建设工程单元工程质量等级评定标准 第9部分：土工合成材料应用工程		2018年7月1日
63	DL/T 5313.14—2018	水电水利基本建设工程单元工程质量等级评定标准 第14部分：混凝土面板堆石坝工程		2018年7月1日
64	DL/T 5342—2018	110kV～750kV架空输电线路铁塔组立施工工艺导则	DL/T 5342—2006	2018年7月1日
65	DL/T 5343—2018	110kV～750kV架空输电线路张力架线施工工艺导则	SDJJS2—1987、DL/T 5343—2006	2018年7月1日
66	DL/T 5761—2018	水工混凝土界面处理剂施工技术规范		2018年7月1日
67	DL/T 5762—2018	梯级水电厂集中监控系统安装及验收规程		2018年7月1日
68	DL/T 5765—2018	20kV及以下配电网工程工程量清单计价规范		2018年7月1日
69	DL/T 5766—2018	20kV及以下配电网工程工程量清单计算规范		2018年7月1日
70	DL/T 5767—2018	电网技术改造工程工程量清单计价规范		2018年7月1日
71	DL/T 5768—2018	电网技术改造工程工程量清单计算规范		2018年7月1日
72	DL/T 5769—2018	电网检修工程工程量清单计价规范		2018年7月1日
73	DL/T 5770—2018	电网检修工程工程量清单计算规范		2018年7月1日
74	DL/T 583—2018	大中型水轮发电机静止整流励磁系统技术条件	DL/T 583—2006	2018年7月1日
75	DL/T 692—2018	电力行业紧急救护技术规范	DL/T 692—2008	2018年7月1日
76	DL/T 710—2018	水轮机运行规程	DL/T 710—1999	2018年7月1日
77	DL/T 800—2018	电力企业标准编写导则	DL/T 800—2012	2018年7月1日
78	DL/T 929—2018	矿物绝缘油、润滑油结构族组成的测定 红外光谱法	DL/T 929—2005	2018年7月1日
79	DL/T 984—2018	油浸式变压器绝缘老化判断导则	DL/T 984—2005	2018年7月1日
80	DL/Z 1812—2018	低功耗电容式电压互感器选用导则		2018年7月1日
81	NB/T 31148—2018	风力发电机组钢制筒形塔架监造导则		2018年10月1日
82	NB/T 32047—2018	光伏发电站土建施工单元工程质量评定标准		2018年10月1日

续表

序号	标准编号	标准名称	代替标准	实施日期
83	DL/T 1004—2018	电力企业管理体系整合导则	DL/T 1004—2006	2018年10月1日
84	DL/T 1120—2018	水轮机调节系统测试与实时仿真装置技术规程	DL/T 1120—2009	2018年10月1日
85	DL/T 1231—2018	电力系统稳定器整定试验导则	DL/T 1231—2013	2018年10月1日
86	DL/T 1852—2018	工频接地电阻测量设备检测规程		2018年10月1日
87	DL/T 1853—2018	10kV有载调容调压变压器技术导则		2018年10月1日
88	DL/T 1858—2018	水电厂自动滤水器技术条件		2018年10月1日
89	DL/T 1859—2018	水电厂转速监测装置技术条件		2018年10月1日
90	DL/T 1860—2018	自动电压控制试验技术导则		2018年10月1日
91	DL/T 1861—2018	高过载能力配电变压器技术导则		2018年10月1日
92	DL/T 1863—2018	独立型微电网运行管理规范		2018年10月1日
93	DL/T 1864—2018	独立型微电网监控系统技术规范		2018年10月1日
94	DL/T 1867—2018	电力需求响应信息交换规范		2018年10月1日
95	DL/T 1868—2018	电力资产全寿命周期管理体系规范		2018年10月1日
96	DL/T 1869—2018	梯级水电厂集中监控系统运行维护规程		2018年10月1日
97	DL/T 1870—2018	电力系统网源协调技术规范		2018年10月1日
98	DL/T 1871—2018	智能电网调度控制系统与变电站即插即用框架规范		2018年10月1日
99	DL/T 1872—2018	电力系统即时消息传输规范		2018年10月1日
100	DL/T 1873—2018	智能变电站系统配置描述（SCD）文件技术规范		2018年10月1日
101	DL/T 1874—2018	智能变电站系统规格描述（SSD）建模工程实施技术规范		2018年10月1日
102	DL/T 1875—2018	智能变电站即插即用接口规范		2018年10月1日
103	DL/T 506—2018	六氟化硫电气设备中绝缘气体湿度测量方法	DL/T 506—2007	2018年10月1日
104	DL/T 5771—2018	农村电网35kV配电化技术导则		2018年10月1日
105	NB/T 10110—2018	风力发电场技术监督导则		2019年5月1日
106	NB/T 10111—2018	风力发电机组润滑剂运行检测规程		2019年5月1日
107	NB/T 10112—2018	风力发电机组设备监造导则		2019年5月1日
108	NB/T 10113—2018	光伏发电站技术监督导则		2019年5月1日
109	NB/T 10114—2018	光伏发电站绝缘技术监督规程		2019年5月1日
110	DL/T 282—2018	合并单元技术条件	DL/T 282—2012	2019年5月1日
111	DL/T 283.1—2018	电力视频监控系统及接口　第1部分：技术要求	DL/T 283.1—2012	2019年5月1日
112	DL/T 283.2—2018	电力视频监控系统及接口　第2部分：测试方法	DL/T 283.2—2012	2019年5月1日
113	DL/T 283.3—2018	电力视频监控系统及接口　第3部分：工程验收		2019年5月1日
114	DL/T 404—2018	3.6kV～40.5kV交流金属封闭开关设备和控制设备	DL/T 404—2007	2019年5月1日
115	DL/T 411—2018	电力大屏幕显示系统通用技术条件	DL/T 411—1991、DL/T 631—1997、DL/T 632—1997	2019年5月1日
116	DL/T 537—2018	高压/低压预装式变电站	DL/T 537—2002	2019年5月1日

续表

序号	标准编号	标准名称	代替标准	实施日期
117	DL/T 559—2018	220kV～750kV电网继电保护装置运行整定规程	DL/T 559—2007	2019年5月1日
118	DL/T 627—2018	绝缘子用常温固化硅橡胶防污闪涂料	DL/T 627—2012	2019年5月1日
119	DL/T 802.9—2018	电力电缆用导管技术条件　第9部分：高强度聚氯乙烯塑料电缆导管		2019年5月1日
120	DL/T 846.5—2018	高电压测试设备通用技术条件　第5部分：六氟化硫气体湿度仪	DL/T 846.5—2004	2019年5月1日
121	DL/T 846.6—2018	高电压测试设备通用技术条件　第6部分：六氟化硫气体检漏仪	DL/T 846.6—2004	2019年5月1日
122	DL/T 848.2—2018	高压试验装置通用技术条件　第2部分：工频高压试验装置	DL/T 848.2—2004	2019年5月1日
123	DL/T 856—2018	电力用直流电源和一体化电源监控装置	DL/T 856—2004	2019年5月1日
124	DL/Z 860.1—2018	电力自动化通信网络和系统　第1部分：概论	DL/Z 860.1—2004	2019年5月1日
125	DL/T 860.4—2018	电力自动化通信网络和系统　第4部分：系统和项目管理	DL/T 860.4—2004	2019年5月1日
126	DL/T 860.10—2018	电力自动化通信网络和系统　第10部分：一致性测试	DL/T 860.10—2006	2019年5月1日
127	DL/T 860.904—2018	电力自动化通信网络和系统　第90-4部分：网络工程指南		2019年5月1日
128	DL/T 890.452—2018	能量管理系统应用程序接口（EMS-API）　第452部分：CIM稳态输电网络模型子集		2019年5月1日
129	DL/T 890.453—2018	能量管理系统应用程序接口（EMS-API）　第453部分：图形布局子集	DL/T 890.453—2012	2019年5月1日
130	DL/T 974—2018	带电作业用工具库房	DL/T 974—2005	2019年5月1日
131	DL/T 978—2018	气体绝缘金属封闭输电线路技术条件	DL/T 978—2005	2019年5月1日
132	DL/Z 1080.2—2018	电力企业应用集成 配电管理系统接口　第2部分：术语	DL/Z 1080.2—2007	2019年5月1日
133	DL/T 1080.100—2018	电力企业应用集成 配电管理系统接口　第100部分：实现框架		2019年5月1日
134	DL/T 1100.1—2018	电力系统的时间同步系统　第1部分：技术规范	DL/T 1100.1—2009	2019年5月1日
135	DL/T 1100.3—2018	电力系统的时间同步系统　第3部分：基于数字同步网的时间同步技术规范		2019年5月1日
136	DL/T 1100.4—2018	电力系统的时间同步系统　第4部分：测试仪技术规范		2019年5月1日
137	DL/T 1100.6—2018	电力系统的时间同步系统　第6部分：监测规范		2019年5月1日
138	DL/T 1405.2—2018	智能变电站的同步相量测量装置　第2部分：技术规范		2019年5月1日
139	DL/T 1405.3—2018	智能变电站的同步相量测量装置　第3部分：检测规范		2019年5月1日
140	DL/T 1876.1—2018	六氟化硫检测仪技术条件—分解产物检测仪		2019年5月1日
141	DL/T 1879—2018	智能变电站监控系统验收规范		2019年5月1日
142	DL/T 1880—2018	智能用电电力线宽带通信技术要求		2019年5月1日

续表

序号	标准编号	标准名称	代替标准	实施日期
143	DL/T 1881—2018	智能变电站智能控制柜技术规范		2019年5月1日
144	DL/T 1882—2018	验电器用工频高压发生器		2019年5月1日
145	DL/T 1883—2018	配电网运行控制技术导则		2019年5月1日
146	DL/T 1886—2018	水电水利工程砂石筛分机械安全操作规程		2019年5月1日
147	DL/T 1887—2018	水电水利工程砂石破碎机械安全操作规程		2019年5月1日
148	DL/T 1888—2018	160kV～500kV挤包绝缘直流电缆使用技术规范		2019年5月1日
149	DL/T 1889—2018	输电杆塔用紧固件横向振动试验方法		2019年5月1日
150	DL/T 1890—2018	智能变电站状态监测系统站内接口规范		2019年5月1日
151	DL/T 1893—2018	变电站辅助监控系统技术及接口规范		2019年5月1日
152	DL/T 1894—2018	电力光纤传感器通用规范		2019年5月1日
153	DL/T 1898—2018	智能变电站监控系统测试规范		2019年5月1日
154	DL/T 1899.1—2018	电力架空光缆接头盒　第1部分：光纤复合架空地线接头盒		2019年5月1日
155	DL/T 1899.2—2018	电力架空光缆接头盒　第2部分：全介质自承式光缆接头盒		2019年5月1日
156	DL/T 1899.3—2018	电力架空光缆接头盒　第3部分：光纤复合架空相线接头盒		2019年5月1日
157	DL/T 1900—2018	智能变电站网络记录分析装置技术规范		2019年5月1日
158	DL/T 1901—2018	水电站大坝运行安全应急预案编制导则		2019年5月1日
159	DL/T 1903—2018	水电水利工程仓储运行管理规程		2019年5月1日
160	DL/T 1904—2018	可逆式抽水蓄能机组振动保护技术导则		2019年5月1日
161	DL/T 1907.1—2018	变电站视频监控图像质量评价　第1部分：技术要求		2019年5月1日
162	DL/T 1907.2—2018	变电站视频监控图像质量评价　第2部分：测试规范		2019年5月1日
163	DL/T 1908.907—2018	电力自动化通信网络和系统　第90-7部分：分布式能源（DER）系统功率变换器对象模型		2019年5月1日
164	DL/T 1909—2018	－48V电力通信直流电源系统技术规范		2019年5月1日
165	DL/T 1910—2018	配电网分布式馈线自动化技术规范		2019年5月1日
166	DL/T 1911—2018	智能变电站监控系统试验装置技术规范		2019年5月1日
167	DL/T 1912—2018	智能变电站以太网交换机技术规范		2019年5月1日
168	DL/T 1913—2018	DL/T 860变电站配置工具技术规范		2019年5月1日
169	DL/T 1914—2018	DL/T 698.45至DL/T 860的数据模型映射规范		2019年5月1日
170	DL/T 1917—2018	电力用户业扩报装技术规范		2019年5月1日
171	DL/T 1918—2018	电力工程接地用铝铜合金技术条件		2019年5月1日
172	DL/T 1919—2018	发电企业应急能力建设评估规范		2019年5月1日
173	DL/T 1920—2018	电网企业应急能力建设评估规范		2019年5月1日
174	DL/T 1921—2018	电力建设企业应急能力建设评估规范		2019年5月1日
175	DL/T 1931—2018	电力LTE无线通信网络安全防护要求		2019年5月1日

续表

序号	标准编号	标准名称	代替标准	实施日期
176	DL/T 1932—2018	6kV～35kV 电缆振荡波局部放电测量系统检定方法		2019年5月1日
177	DL/T 1933.4—2018	塑料光纤信息传输技术实施规范　第4部分：塑料光缆		2019年5月1日
178	DL/T 1933.5—2018	塑料光纤信息传输技术实施规范　第5部分：光缆布线要求		2019年5月1日
179	DL/T 1940—2018	智能变电站以太网交换机测试规范		2019年5月1日
180	DL/T 1941—2018	可再生能源发电站电力监控系统网络安全防护技术规范		2019年5月1日
181	DL/T 1943—2018	合并单元现场检验规范		2019年5月1日
182	DL/T 1944—2018	智能变电站手持式光数字信号试验装置技术规范		2019年5月1日
183	DL/T 1946—2018	气体绝缘金属封闭开关设备X射线透视成像现场检测技术导则		2019年5月1日
184	DL/T 1948—2018	架空导体能耗试验方法		2019年5月1日
185	DL/T 1950—2018	变电站数据通信网关机检测规范		2019年5月1日
186	DL/T 1951—2018	变压器绕组变形测试仪通用技术条件		2019年5月1日
187	DL/T 1952—2018	变压器绕组变形测试仪校准规范		2019年5月1日
188	DL/T 1953—2018	电容电流测试仪通用技术条件		2019年5月1日
189	DL/T 1954—2018	基于暂态地电压法局部放电检测仪校准规范		2019年5月1日
190	DL/T 1956—2018	绝缘管型母线运行监测系统通用技术条件		2019年5月1日
191	DL/T 1957—2018	电网直流偏磁风险评估与防御导则		2019年5月1日
192	DL/T 1958—2018	电子式电压互感器状态检修导则		2019年5月1日
193	DL/T 1959—2018	电子式电压互感器状态评价导则		2019年5月1日
194	DL/T 1960—2018	变电站电气设备抗震试验技术规程		2019年5月1日
195	DL/T 5161.1—2018	电气装置安装工程质量检验及评定规程　第1部分：通则	DL/T 5161.1—2002	2019年5月1日
196	DL/T 5161.2—2018	电气装置安装工程质量检验及评定规程　第2部分：高压电器施工质量检验	DL/T 5161.2—2002	2019年5月1日
197	DL/T 5161.3—2018	电气装置安装工程质量检验及评定规程　第3部分：电力变压器、油浸电抗器、互感器施工质量检验	DL/T 5161.3—2002	2019年5月1日
198	DL/T 5161.4—2018	电气装置安装工程质量检验及评定规程　第4部分：母线装置施工质量检验	DL/T 5161.4—2002	2019年5月1日
199	DL/T 5161.5—2018	电气装置安装工程质量检验及评定规程　第5部分：电缆线路施工质量检验	DL/T 5161.5—2002	2019年5月1日
200	DL/T 5161.6—2018	电气装置安装工程质量检验及评定规程　第6部分：接地装置施工质量检验	DL/T 5161.6—2002	2019年5月1日
201	DL/T 5161.7—2018	电气装置安装工程质量检验及评定规程　第7部分：旋转电机施工质量检验	DL/T 5161.7—2002	2019年5月1日
202	DL/T 5161.8—2018	电气装置安装工程质量检验及评定规程　第8部分：盘、柜及二次回路接线施工质量检验	DL/T 5161.8—2002	2019年5月1日

续表

序号	标准编号	标准名称	代替标准	实施日期
203	DL/T 5161.9—2018	电气装置安装工程质量检验及评定规程　第9部分：蓄电池施工质量检验	DL/T 5161.9—2002	2019年5月1日
204	DL/T 5161.10—2018	电气装置安装工程质量检验及评定规程　第10部分：66kV及以下架空电力线路施工质量检验	DL/T 5161.10—2002	2019年5月1日
205	DL/T 5161.11—2018	电气装置安装工程质量检验及评定规程　第11部分：通信工程施工质量检验	DL/T 5161.11—2002	2019年5月1日
206	DL/T 5161.12—2018	电气装置安装工程质量检验及评定规程　第12部分：低压电器施工质量检验	DL/T 5161.12—2002	2019年5月1日
207	DL/T 5161.13—2018	电气装置安装工程质量检验及评定规程　第13部分：电力变流设备施工质量检验	DL/T 5161.13—2002	2019年5月1日
208	DL/T 5161.14—2018	电气装置安装工程质量检验及评定规程　第14部分：起重机电气装置施工质量检验	DL/T 5161.14—2002	2019年5月1日
209	DL/T 5161.15—2018	电气装置安装工程质量检验及评定规程　第15部分：爆炸及火灾危险环境电气装置施工质量检验	DL/T 5161.15—2002	2019年5月1日
210	DL/T 5161.16—2018	电气装置安装工程质量检验及评定规程　第16部分：1kV及以下配线工程施工质量检验	DL/T 5161.16—2002	2019年5月1日
211	DL/T 5161.17—2018	电气装置安装工程质量检验及评定规程　第17部分：电气照明装置施工质量检验	DL/T 5161.17—2002	2019年5月1日
212	DL/T 5210.5—2018	电力建设施工质量验收规程　第5部分：焊接	DL/T 5210.7—2010	2019年5月1日
213	DL/T 5344—2018	电力光纤通信工程验收规范	DL/T 5344—2006	2019年5月1日
214	DL/T 5362—2018	水工沥青混凝土试验规程	DL/T 5362—2006	2019年5月1日
215	DL/T 5425—2018	深层搅拌法地基处理技术规范	DL/T 5425—2009	2019年5月1日
216	DL/T 5772—2018	水电水利工程水力学安全监测规程		2019年5月1日
217	DL/T 5773—2018	水电水利工程施工机械安全操作规程 混凝土运输车		2019年5月1日
218	DL/T 5774—2018	水电水利基础处理工程竣工资料整编及验收规范		2019年5月1日
219	DL/T 5775—2018	水电水利工程水泥改性膨胀土施工技术规范		2019年5月1日
220	DL/T 5776—2018	水平定向钻敷设电力管线技术规定		2019年5月1日
221	DL/T 5777—2018	水工混凝土掺用硅粉技术规范		2019年5月1日
222	DL/T 5778—2018	水工混凝土用速凝剂技术规范		2019年5月1日
223	DL/T 5779—2018	气体绝缘金属封闭输电线路施工及验收规范		2019年5月1日
224	DL/T 5780—2018	智能变电站监控系统建设规范		2019年5月1日
225	DL/T 5781—2018	配电自动化系统验收技术规范		2019年5月1日
226	DL/T 5782—2018	20kV及以下配电网工程后评价导则		2019年5月1日

（中国电力企业联合会　许松林　刘永东）

2018年发布的由水电水利规划设计总院归口管理的技术标准

2018年，由水电水利规划设计总院归口管理的水电勘察设计技术标准和风电规划、设计、施工、安装技术标准，共发布42项，见表1。

表1 2018年发布的由水电水利规划设计总院归口管理的技术标准

序号	标准名称	标准编号	实施日期	代替标准
1	生物质锅炉供热成型燃料产品贮运技术规范	NB/T 34061—2018	2018年7月1日	
2	生物质锅炉供热成型燃料工程设计规范	NB/T 34062—2018	2018年7月1日	
3	生物质锅炉供热成型燃料术语	NB/T 34063—2018	2018年7月1日	
4	生物质锅炉供热成型燃料工程运行管理规范	NB/T 34064—2018	2018年7月1日	
5	生物质锅炉供热成型燃料试验方法通则	NB/T 34065—2018	2018年7月1日	
6	气体绝缘金属封闭开关设备配电装置设计规范	NB/T 35108—2018	2018年7月1日	DL/T 5139—2001
7	水电工程三维激光扫描测量规程	NB/T 35109—2018	2018年7月1日	
8	水电站地下埋藏式月牙肋钢岔管设计规范	NB/T 35110—2018	2018年7月1日	
9	水电工程渣场设计规范	NB/T 35111—2018	2018年7月1日	
10	水电工程层析成像技术规程	NB/T 35112—2018	2018年7月1日	
11	水电工程钻孔压水试验规程	NB/T 35113—2018	2018年7月1日	DL/T 5331—2005
12	水电岩土工程及岩体测试造孔规程	NB/T 35114—2018	2018年7月1日	DL/T 5125—2009
13	水电工程钻探规程	NB/T 35115—2018	2018年7月1日	DL/T 5013—2005
14	水电工程全球导航卫星系统（GNSS）测量规程	NB/T 35116—2018	2018年7月1日	
15	水电工程钻孔振荡式渗透试验规程	NB/T 35117—2018	2018年7月1日	
16	水电站油系统技术规范	NB/T 35118—2018	2018年7月1日	
17	风电场标识系统编码规范	NB/T 31145—2018	2018年10月1日	
18	风电机组检修提升机技术规范	NB/T 31146—2018	2018年10月1日	
19	风电场工程风能资源测量与评估技术规范	NB/T 31147—2018	2018年10月1日	
20	光伏发电工程可行性研究报告编制规程	NB/T 32043—2018	2018年10月1日	
21	光伏发电工程预可行性研究报告编制规程	NB/T 32044—2018	2018年10月1日	
22	光伏发电站直流发电系统设计规范	NB/T 32045—2018	2018年10月1日	
23	光伏发电工程规划报告编制规程	NB/T 32046—2018	2018年10月1日	
24	水电工程水土保持设施验收规程	NB/T 35119—2018	2018年10月1日	
25	水电工程施工总布置设计规范	NB/T 35120—2018	2018年10月1日	DL/T 5192—2004
26	水电工程沟水治理设计规范	NB/T 35121—2018	2018年10月1日	
27	抽水蓄能电站设计规范	NB/T 10072—2018	2019年3月1日	DL/T 5208—2005
28	抽水蓄能电站工程地质勘察规程	NB/T 10073—2018	2019年3月1日	
29	水电工程地质测绘规程	NB/T 10074—2018	2019年3月1日	DL/T 5185—2004
30	水电工程岩溶工程地质勘察规程	NB/T 10075—2018	2019年3月1日	DL/T 5338—2006
31	水电工程项目档案验收工作导则	NB/T 10076—2018	2019年3月1日	

续表

序号	标准名称	标准编号	实施日期	代替标准
32	堆石混凝土筑坝技术导则	NB/T 10077—2018	2019年3月1日	
33	水轮机进水球阀选用、试验及验收规范	NB/T 10078—2018	2019年3月1日	
34	水电工程水生生态调查与评价技术规范	NB/T 10079—2018	2019年3月1日	
35	水电工程陆生生态调查与评价技术规范	NB/T 10080—2018	2019年3月1日	
36	潮汐电站水能设计规范	NB/T 10081—2018	2019年3月1日	
37	潮汐电站资源调查评价规范	NB/T 10082—2018	2019年3月1日	
38	水电工程水利计算规范	NB/T 10083—2018	2019年3月1日	DL/T 5105—1999
39	水电工程运行调度规程编制导则	NB/T 10084—2018	2019年3月1日	
40	水电工程水文预报规范	NB/T 10085—2018	2019年3月1日	
41	风电场工程节能报告编制规程	NB/T 10086—2018	2019年3月1日	
42	陆上风电场工程施工安装技术规程	NB/T 10087—2018	2019年3月1日	

（水电水利规划设计总院）

2018年大电机、水轮机新颁标准

2018年，由哈尔滨大电机研究所归口管理的大电机、水轮机技术标准，新发布标准6项，见表1。

表1 2018年哈尔滨大电机研究所发布的大电机、水轮机标准

序号	标准编号	标准名称
1	JB/T 1473—2018	矿山磨机用大型三相同步电动机 技术条件
2	JB/T 2224—2018	大型三相四极同步电动机技术条件
3	JB/T 13371—2018	空内冷发电机转子不等壁厚矩形含银铜导线技术条件
4	JB/T 6517—2018	大型发电机氢油水控制系统技术条件
5	JB/T 13370—2018	大型空冷隐极同步发电机转子热运转试验导则
6	JB/T 13372—2018	水轮发电机制动器用微型吸尘器

（哈尔滨电机厂有限责任公司 刘保生）

2018年发布的水利技术标准

2018年，水利技术标准共发布29项，其中国家标准10项，水利行业标准19项，见表1。

表1 2018年发布的水利技术标准

序号	标准名称	标准编号	实施日期
1	工程泥沙设计标准	GB/T 51280—2018	2018年9月1日
2	灌溉与排水工程设计标准	GB 50288—2018	2018年11月1日
3	水工建筑物抗震设计标准	GB 51247—2018	2018年11月1日
4	节水灌溉工程技术标准	GB/T 50363—2018	2018年11月1日

续表

序号	标准名称	标准编号	实施日期
5	小型水轮机现场验收试验规程	GB/T 22140—2018	2018年12月1日
6	小型水电站施工安全标准	GB 51304—2018	2019年4月1日
7	生产建设项目水土保持技术标准	GB 50433—2018	2019年4月1日
8	生产建设项目水土保持监测与评价标准	GB/T 51240—2018	2019年4月1日
9	水土保持工程调查与勘测标准	GB/T 51297—2018	2019年4月1日
10	生产建设项目水土流失防治标准	GB/T 50434—2018	2019年4月1日
11	水质　阿特拉津的测定　固相萃取—高效液相色谱法	SL 761—2018	2018年4月25日
12	山洪灾害预警设备技术条件	SL 762—2018	2018年4月25日
13	火电建设项目水资源论证导则	SL 763—2018	2018年6月20日
14	水利水电建设项目安全验收评价导则	SL 765—2018	2018年6月20日
15	水情预警信号	SL 758—2018	2018年9月1日
16	径流实验观察规范	SL 759—2018	2018年9月1日
17	城镇再生水利用规划编制指南	SL 760—2018	2018年9月1日
18	混凝土重力坝设计规范	SL 319—2018	2018年10月17日
19	混凝土拱坝设计规范	SL 282—2018	2018年10月17日
20	碾压混凝土坝设计规范	SL 314—2018	2018年10月17日
21	溢洪道设计规范	SL 253—2018	2018年10月17日
22	生产建设项目水土流失量测算规范	SL 773—2018	2019年1月23日
23	水利水电工程启闭机设计规范	SL 41—2018	2019年1月23日
24	小水电电网技术管理规程	SL 528—2018	2019年1月23日
25	水工隧洞安全监测技术规范	SL764—2018	2019年3月5日
26	大坝安全监测系统鉴定技术规范	SL 766—2018	2019年3月5日
27	山洪灾害调查与评价技术规范	SL 767—2018	2019年3月5日
28	水闸安全监测技术规范	SL 768—2018	2019年3月5日
29	水工混凝土结构耐久性评定规范	SL775—2018	2019年3月5日

（水利部国际合作与科技司　曾向辉　荆诚然
中国水利学会　李建国）

截至 2018 年已完成电力标准英文翻译

截至 2018 年，已完成电力标准英文翻译 320 项，　　项，见表 1。
其中，水电、光伏、输变电（不含火电、核电）228

表 1　　已完成电力标准英文翻译

水电、光伏			
序号	标准编号	标准名称	英文名称
1	GB 50794—2012	光伏发电站施工规范	Code for construction of PV power station
2	GB 50796—2012	光伏发电工程验收规范	Code for acceptance of photovoltaic power project
3	GB 50797—2012	光伏发电站设计规范	Code for design of photovoltaic power station

续表

水电、光伏			
序号	标准编号	标准名称	英文名称
4	DL 5270—2012	核子法密度及含水量测试规程	Test code for density and moisture by nuclear methods
5	DL 5016—1999	混凝土面板堆石坝设计规范	Design specifications for concrete face rockfill dams
6	DL 5108—1999	混凝土重力坝设计规范	Design specification for concrete gravity dams
7	DL 5180—2003	水电枢纽工程等级划分及设计安全标准	Classification & design safety standard of hydropower projects
8	DL/T 507—2014	水轮发电机组启动试验规程	Start-up test code for hydro-generating units
9	DL/T 563—2016	水轮机电液调节系统及装置技术规程	Technical code for electro-hydraulic regulating system and unit used in hydraulic turbines
10	DL/T 578—2008	水电厂计算机监控系统基本技术条件	Specification of computer supervision and control system for hydraulic power plants
11	DL/T 583—2006	大中型水轮发电机静止整流励磁系统及装置技术条件	Specification for static rectified excitation systems and devices for large and medium hydraulic generators
12	DL/T 751—2014	水轮发电机运行规程	Specification of operation for hydraulic generators
13	DL/T 827—2002	灯泡贯流式水轮发电机组启动试验规程	Start-up test code for bulb hydro-generating units
14	DL/T 817—2014	立式水轮发电机检修技术规程	Technical code for maintenance of vertical hydro-generators
15	DL/T 1067—2007	蒸发冷却水轮发电机（发电/电动机）基本技术条件	Fundamental technical specifications for evaporative cooling hydrogenerator (generator/motor)
16	DL/T 1085—2008	水情自动测报系统技术条件	Specification for automatic hydrological telemetry system
17	DL/T 1107—2009	水电厂自动化元件基本技术条件	Specification of automatic components for hydraulic power plants
18	DL/T 1197—2012	水轮发电机组状态在线监测系统技术条件	Specifications of on-line condition monitoring system for hydraulic turbine-generator units
19	DL/T 5018—2004	水电水利工程钢闸门制造安装及验收规范	Specification for manufacture installation and acceptance of steel gate in hydraulic and hydroelectric engineering
20	DL/T 5042—1995	河流水电规划编制规范	Specification on compiling hydropower planning of river
21	DL/T 5055—2007	水工混凝土掺用粉煤灰技术规范	Technical specification of fly ash for use in hydraulic concrete
22	DL/T 5070—2012	水轮机金属蜗壳现场制造安装及焊接工艺导则	Technological guide for manufacturing, assembling and welding of metal spiral case of turbine in site
23	DL/T 5083—2010	水电水利工程预应力锚索施工技术规范	Specification of prestressing tendon construction for hydropower and water conservancy project
24	DL/T 5100—1999	水工混凝土外加剂技术规程	Technical code for hydraulic concrete admixtures
25	DL/T 5102—1999	土工离心模型试验规程	Code of geotechnical centrifuge model tests
26	DL/T 5110—2000	水电水利工程模板施工规范	Construction specifications for formwork of hydropower and water conservancy engineering
27	DL/T 5110—2013	水电水利工程模板施工规范	Construction specifications for formwork of hydropower and water conservancy projects

续表

水电、光伏			
序号	标准编号	标准名称	英文名称
28	DL/T 5112—2009	水工碾压混凝土施工规范	Construction specification for hydraulic roller compacted concrete
29	DL/T 5113.1—2005	水电水利基本建设工程单元工程质量等级评定标准　第1部分：土建工程	Quality degree evaluate standard of unit engineering for hydropower and water conservancy construction engineering Part 1：Civil department
30	DL/T 5113.3—2012	水电水利基本建设工程单元工程质量等级评定标准　第3部分：水轮发电机组安装工程	Quality degree evaluate standard of unit engineering for hydropower and water conservancy construction engineering Part 3：Turbine and generator units installation engineering
31	DL/T 5113.4—2012	水电水利基本建设工程单元工程质量等级评定标准　第4部分：水力机械辅助设备安装工程	Quality degree evaluate standard of unit engineering for hydropower and water conservancy construction engineering Part 4：Auxiliary equipment of hydraulic machinery installation engineering
32	DL/T 5113.5—2012	水电水利基本建设工程单元工程质量等级评定标准　第5部分：发电电气设备安装工程	Quality degree evaluation standard of unit engineering for hydropower and water conservancy construction engineering Part 5：Electric generation equipment installation engineering
33	DL/T 5113.10—2012	水电水利基本建设工程单元工程质量等级评定标准　第10部分：沥青混凝土工程	Quality degree evaluate standard of unit engineering for hydropower and water conservancy construction engineering Part 10：Bituminous concrete engineering
34	DL/T 5113.11—2005	水电水利基本建设工程单元工程质量等级评定标准　第11部分：灯泡贯流式水轮发电机组安装工程	Quality degree evaluate standard of unit engineering for hydropower and water conservancy construction engineering Part 11：Bulb turbine and generator units installation engineering
35	DL/T 5115—2008	混凝土面板堆石坝接缝止水技术规范	Technical specifications for joint seal of concrete face rockfill dam
36	DL/T 5117—2000	水下不分散混凝土试验规程	Test code on non-dispersible underwater concrete
37	DL/T 5128—2009	混凝土面板堆石坝施工规范	Specifications for concrete face rockfill dam construction
38	DL/T 5129—2013	碾压式土石坝施工规范	Specification for Rolled Earth-rockfill dam Construction
39	DL/T 5135—2013	水电水利工程爆破施工技术规范	Specifications of excavation blasting for hydropower and water resources projects
40	DL/T 5141—2001	水电站压力钢管设计规范	Specifications for design of steel penstocks of hydroelectric stations
41	DL/T 5144—2001	水工混凝土施工规范	Specifications for hydraulic concrete construction
42	DL/T 5148—2001	水工建筑物水泥灌浆施工技术规范	Technical specification for cement grouting construction of hydraulic structures
43	DL/T 5150—2001	水工混凝土试验规程	Specifications for hydraulic concrete
44	DL/T 5151—2001	水工混凝土砂石骨料试验规程	Code for testing aggregates of hydraulic concrete
45	DL/T 5152—2001	水工混凝土水质分析试验规程	Test code of water analysis for hydraulic concrete
46	DL/T 5162—2002	水电水利工程安全防护设施技术规范	Technical specification of safety and protection facility for hydropower and water resources construction

续表

水电、光伏			
序号	标准编号	标准名称	英文名称
47	DL/T 5166—2002	溢洪道设计规范	Design specification for river-bank spillway
48	DL/T 5169—2002	水工混凝土钢筋施工规范	Specification for construction of hydraulic concrete reinforcement
49	DL/T 5173—2003	水电水利工程施工测量规范	Specification of construction survey in hydroelectric and hydraulic engineering
50	DL/T 5178—2003	混凝土坝安全监测施工规范	Technical specification for concrete dam safety monitoring
51	DL/T 5181—2003	水电水利工程锚喷支护施工规范	Construction specifications for anchor and shotcrete support of hydropower and water conservancy engineering
52	DL/T 5193—2004	环氧树脂砂浆技术规程	Technical code of epoxy resin mortar
53	DL/T 5195—2004	水工隧洞设计规范	Specification for design of hydraulic tunnel
54	DL/T 5198—2013	水电水利工程岩壁梁施工规程	Code for the construction of crane girders anchored to rock mass for hydropower and water resources projects
55	DL/T 5199—2004	水电水利混凝土防渗墙施工规范	Specification of concrete cut-off wall used for hydropower and water conservancy project
56	DL/T 5200—2004	水电水利工程高压喷射灌浆技术规范	Technical specification of jet grouting For hydropower and water resources projects
57	DL/T 5207—2005	水工混凝土抗冲磨防空蚀技术规范	Technical specification for abrasion and cavitation resistance of concrete in hydraulic structures
58	DL/T 5209—2005	混凝土坝安全监测资料整编规程	Data compilation code for concrete dam safety monitoring
59	DL/T 5214—2005	水电水利工程振冲法地基处理技术规范	Technical specification for vibroflotation ground treatment of hydroelectric and water resources projects
60	DL/T 5215—2005	水工建筑物止水带技术规范	Specification for waterstop for hydraulic structures
61	DL/T 5238—2010	土坝灌浆技术规范	Technical specification of grouting for earth dam
62	DL/T 5241—2010	水工混凝土耐久性技术规范	Technical specifications for durability of hydraulic concrete
63	DL/T 5251—2010	水工混凝土建筑物缺陷检测和评估技术规程	Technical code for defect detection and evaluation of hydraulic concrete structures
64	DL/T 5255—2010	水电水利工程边坡施工技术规范	Technical specification of slope construction for hydropower and water resources project
65	DL/T 5259—2010	土石坝安全监测技术规范	Technical specification for earth rockfill dam safety monitoring
66	DL/T 5296—2013	水工混凝土掺用氧化镁技术规范	Technical specification for use of magnesium oxide in hydraulic concrete
67	DL/T 5297—2013	混凝土面板堆石坝挤压边墙技术规范	Technical specification for extruded curb in the concrete-faced rockfill dam
68	DL/T 5303—2013	水工塑性混凝土试验规程	Test code for hydraulic plastic concrete

续表

水电、光伏			
序号	标准编号	标准名称	英文名称
69	DL/T 5307—2013	水电水利工程施工度汛风险评估规程	Risk assessment code for flood control on construction of hydropower and water resources project
70	DL/T 5308—2013	水电水利工程施工安全监测技术规范	Technical specification for construction safety monitoring of hydropower and water resources projects
71	DL/T 5310—2013	沥青混凝土面板堆石坝及库盆施工规范	Specifications for asphalt concrete face rockfill dam and reservoir basin construction
72	DL/T 5311—2013	水电水利工程砂石料开采及加工系统运行规范	Specification for aggregate quarrying and processing plant of the hydroelectric and water conservancy projects
73	DL/T 5313—2014	水电站大坝运行安全评价导则	Guide for safety assessment of large dams for hydropower station in operation
74	DL/T 5314—2014	水电水利工程施工安全生产应急能力评估导则	Guide of emergency capability assessment for construction safety in hydropower and water resources projects
75	DL/T 5315—2014	水工混凝土建筑物修补加固技术规程	Technical code for repair and reinforcement of hydraulic concrete structures
76	DL/T 5317—2014	水电水利工程聚脲涂层施工技术规程	Technical code for construction of polyurea coating in hydropower and water resources project
77	DL/T 5330—2005	水工混凝土配合比设计规程	Code for mix design of hydraulic concrete
78	DL/T 5332—2005	水工混凝土断裂试验规程	Norm for fracture test of hydraulic concrete
79	DL/T 5333—2005	水电水利工程爆破安全监测规程	Code for blasting safety monitoring of hydropower and water resources engineering
80	DL/T 5362—2006	水工沥青混凝土试验规程	Test code for hydraulic bitumen concrete
81	DL/T 5363—2006	水工碾压式沥青混凝土施工规范	Specifications for construction of hydraulic roller compacted bituminous concrete
82	DL/T 5370—2007	水电水利工程施工通用安全技术规程	General technical specification for safety of hydroelectric and hydraulic engineering construction
83	DL/T 5371—2007	水电水利工程土建施工安全技术规程	Technical code of safety for hydroelectric and hydraulic civil construction engineering
84	DL/T 5372—2007	水电水利工程金属结构与机电设备安装安全技术规程	Technical specification for safety of installation of metal structure and mechanical & electrical equipment of hydroelectric and hydraulic engineering
85	DL/T 5373—2007	水电水利工程施工作业人员安全技术操作规程	Technical operation code of safety for workmen of hydroelectric and hydraulic construction engineering
86	DL/T 5387—2007	水工混凝土掺用磷渣粉技术规范	Technical specification for phosphorous slag powder use in hydraulic concrete
87	DL/T 5389—2007	水工建筑物岩石基础开挖施工技术规范	Construction technical specifications on rock-foundation excavating engineering of hydraulic structures
88	DL/T 5400—2016	水工建筑物滑动模板施工技术规范	Construction technical specification for hydraulic structure sliding formwork
89	DL/T 5406—2010	水工建筑物化学灌浆施工规范	Specification for chemical grouting construction of hydraulic structures
90	DL/T 5420—2009	水轮发电机定子现场装配工艺导则	Technological guide for stator assembly in site of hydraulic generators

续表

水电、光伏			
序号	标准编号	标准名称	英文名称
91	DL/T 5432—2009	水电水利工程项目建设管理规范	Specification of project management for hydropower and water resources engineering
92	DL/T 5702—2014	水电水利工程沉井施工技术规范	Technology code for construction of open caisson of hydropower and water resources project
93	DL/T 5703—2014	水电水利工程预应力锚杆用水泥锚固剂技术规程	Technical specification for cement anchoring agent for prestressed anchor of hydropower and water resources projects
94	DL/T 5719—2015	水电水利工程施工基坑排水技术规范	Technical specification of foundation pit drainage for hydropower and water conservancy engineering construction
95	DL/T 5724—2015	水电水利工程砂石系统废水处理技术规范	Technical specifications for wastewater treating about aggregate system of hydropower project
96	DL/T 5728—2016	水电水利工程控制性灌浆施工规范	Specification of controlled grouting for hydropower and water resources projects
97	DL/T 5742—2016	水电水利地下工程施工测量规范	Specification of construction survey for hydroelectric and hydraulic underground works
98	DL/T 5743—2016	水电水利工程土工合成材料施工规范	Construction specification of the geosynthetics for hydropower and water conservancy project
99	SD 335—1989	水电站厂房设计规范	Design code for hydropower house

输变电			
序号	标准编号	标准名称	英文名称
100	GB 50052—2009	供配电系统设计规范	Code for design electric power supply systems
101	GB 50059—2011	35kV～110kV 变电站设计规范	Design code for substation (35kV～110kV)
102	GB 50060—2008	3kV～110kV 高压配电装置设计规范	Code for design of high voltage electrical installation (3kV～110kV)
103	GB 50062—2008	电力装置的继电保护和自动装置设计规范	Code for design of relaying protection and automatic device of electric power installations
104	GB 50147—2010	电气装置安装工程　高压电器施工及验收规范	Code for construction and acceptance of high-voltage electric equipment installation engineering
105	GB 50148—2010	电气装置安装工程　电力变压器、油浸电抗器、互感器施工及验收规范	Code for construction and acceptance of power transformers oil reactor and mutual inductor installation engineering
106	GB 50149—2010	电气装置安装工程　母线装置施工及验收规范	Code for construction and acceptance of busbar equipments installation engineering
107	GB 50150—2006	电气装置安装工程　电气设备交接试验标准	Standard for hand-over test of electric equipment electric equipment installation engineering
108	GB 50168—2006	电气装置安装工程　电缆线路施工及验收规范	Code for construction and acceptance of cable system electric equipment installation engineering
109	GB 50169—2006	电气装置安装工程　接地装置施工及验收规范	Code for construction and acceptance of grounding connection electric equipment installation engineering
110	GB 50170—2006	电气装置安装工程　旋转电机施工及验收规范	Code for construction and acceptance of rotating electrical machines electric equipment installation engineering

续表

输变电

序号	标准编号	标准名称	英文名称
111	GB 50171—2012	电气装置安装工程　盘、柜及二次回路结线施工及验收规范	Code for construction and acceptance of switchboard outfit, complete cubicle and secondary circuit installation engineering
112	GB 50172—2012	电气装置安装工程　蓄电池施工及验收规范	Code for construction and acceptance of battery installation engineering
113	GB 50173—2014	电气装置安装工程　66kV 及以下架空电力线路施工及验收规范	Code for construction and acceptance of 66kV or under overhead electric power transmission line installation engineering
114	GB 50194—2014	建设工程施工现场供用电安全规范	Safety code of power supply and consumption for construction site
115	GB 50217—2008	电力工程电缆设计规范	Code for design of cables of electric engineering
116	GB 50227—2008	并联电容器装置设计规范	Code for design of installation of shunt capacitors
117	GB 50233—2005	110～500kV 架空送电线路施工及验收规范	Code for construction and acceptance of 110～500kV overhead transmission line
118	GB 50254—1996	电气装置安装工程　低压电器施工及验收规范	Code for construction and acceptance of low-voltage apparatus installation engineering
119	GB 50255—2014	电气装置安装工程　电力变流设备施工及验收规范	Code for construction and acceptance of power conversion equipment installation engineering
120	GB 50256—2014	电气装置安装工程　起重机电气装置施工及验收规范	Code for construction and acceptance of electrical device of crane installation engineering
121	GB 50257—2014	电气装置安装工程　爆炸和火灾危险环境电气装置施工及验收规范	Code for construction and acceptance of electric equipment on fire and explosion hazard electric equipment installation engineering
122	GB 50545—2010	11kV～750kV 架空输电线路设计规范	Code for design of 110kV～750kV overhead transmission line
123	GB 50548—2010	330kV～750kV 架空输电线路勘察规范	Code for investigation and surveying of 330kV～750kV overhead transmission line
124	GB 50665—2011	1000kV 架空送电线路设计规范	Code for design of 1000kV overhead transmission line
125	GB/T 14285—2006	继电保护和安全自动装置技术规程	Technical code for relaying protection and security automatic equipment
126	GB/T 19963—2011	风电场接入电力系统技术规定	Technical rule for connecting wind farm to power system
127	GB/T 26399—2011	电力系统安全稳定控制技术导则	Technical guide for electric power system security and stability control
128	GB/T 50063—2008	电力装置的电气测量仪表装置设计规范	Code for design of electrical measuring device of power system
129	GB/T 50613—2010	城市配电网技术规范	Code for planning and design of urban distribution network
130	GB/T 50789—2012	±800kV 直流换流站设计规范	Code for design of ±800kV DC converter station
131	GB/T 50832—2013	1000kV 系统电气装置安装工程电气设备交接试验标准	Standard for acceptance test of electric equipment of 1000kV system electric equipment installation engineering

续表

输变电			
序号	标准编号	标准名称	英文名称
132	DL 5002—2006	地区电网调度自动化设计技术规程	Specifications for the design of dispatch automation in district power networks
133	DL/T 385—2010	变压器油带电倾向性检测方法	Determination of electrostatic charging tendency of transformer oil
134	DL/T 478—2013	继电保护和安全自动装置通用技术条件	General specification for relaying protection and security automation equipment
135	DL/T 559—2007	220kV～750kV 电网继电保护装置运行整定规程	Setting guide for 220kV～750kV power system protection equipment
136	DL/T 598—2010	电力系统自动交换电话网技术规范	Technical specifications for automatic exchange telephone network of electric power system
137	DL/T 664—2016	带电设备红外诊断应用规范	Application rules of infrared diagnosis for live electrical equipment
138	DL/T 846.1—2016	高电压测试设备通用技术条件 第1部分：高电压分压器测量系统	General technical specifications for gigh voltage test equipment Part 1: High voltage divider measuring system
139	DL/T 846.4—2016	高电压测试设备通用技术条件 第4部分：脉冲电流法局部放电测量仪	General technical specifications for high voltage test equipment Part 4: Pulse current based partial discharge detector
140	DL/T 846.7—2016	高电压测试设备通用技术条件 第7部分：绝缘油介电强度测试仪	General technical specifications for high voltage test equipment Part 7: Dielectric strength detector of insulating oil
141	DL/T 846.10—2016	高电压测试设备通用技术条件 第10部分：暂态地电压局部放电检测仪	General technical specifications for high voltage test equipment Part 10: Transient earth voltage based partial discharge tester
142	DL/T 846.11—2016	高电压测试设备通用技术条件 第11部分：特高频局部放电检测仪	General technical specifications for high voltage test equipment Part 11: Ultra high frequency based partial discharge tester
143	DL/T 846.12—2016	高电压测试设备通用技术条件 第12部分：电力电容测试仪	General technical specifications for high voltage test equipment Part 12: Power capacitor tester
144	DL/T 849.6—2016	电力设备专用测试仪器通用技术条件 第6部分：高压谐振试验装置	General specifications for special test instruments used for power equipment Part 6: High voltage resonant test device
145	DL/T 866—2004	电流互感器和电压互感器选择及计算导则	The guide for selection and calculation of current transformers and voltage transformers
146	DL/T 1124—2009	数字电力线载波机	Digital power-line carrier terminals
147	DL/T 1147—2009	电力高处作业防坠器	Mobile fall arrester on power altitude working
148	DL/T 1209.4—2014	变电站登高作业及防护器材技术要求 第4部分：复合材料快装脚手架	Specification for substation ascending operation and protective device Part 4: Composite quick-installed scaffold
149	DL/T 1241—2013	电力工业以太网交换机技术规范	Technical specifications for electric power industrial ethernet switch

续表

输变电			
序号	标准编号	标准名称	英文名称
150	DL/T 1254—2013	差动电阻式监测仪器鉴定技术规程	Specification for appraisal of elastic wire resistance type sensor
151	DL/T 1298—2013	静止无功补偿装置运行规程	Code of operation for static var compensator
152	DL/T 1391—2014	数字式自动电压调节器涉网性能检测导则	Test guidelines of digital automatic voltage regulator performance relate to power grid
153	DL/T 1400—2015	油浸式变压器测温装置现场校准规范	Calibration specifications for on-site temperature measuring equipment of oil-immersed transformer
154	DL/T 1517—2016	二次压降及二次负荷现场测试技术规范	Technical specification for field testing of secondary voltage drop and secondary loads
155	DL/T 1518—2016	变电站噪声控制技术导则	Technical guide for noise control of substation
156	DL/T 1620—2016	架空输电线路山火风险预报技术导则	Technical guide of wildfire risk forecast for overhead transmission lines
157	DL/T 5003—2005	电力系统调度自动化设计技术规程	Specifications for the design of dispatch automation in electric power systems
158	DL/T 5013—2012	35kV～220kV 无人值班变电站设计规程	Technical code for the design of 35220kV unattended substation
159	DL/T 5033—2006	输电线路对电信线路危险和干扰影响防护设计规程	The design rules of telecommunication lines against danger and interference effects from power transmission lines
160	DL/T 5040—2006	输电线路对无线电台影响防护设计规程	Code for designing of radio stations against effects from power transmission lines
161	DL/T 5044—2004	电力工程直流系统设计技术规定	Technical code for designing DC system of power projects
162	DL/T 5049—2006	架空送电线路大跨越工程勘测技术规程	Technical code for exploration and surveying of large crossing overhead transmission line
163	DL/T 5056—2007	变电站总布置设计技术规程	Technical code of general plan design for substation
164	DL/T 5076—2008	220kV 及以下架空送电线路勘测技术规程	Technical code of exploration and surveying for 220kV and lower level overhead transmission line
165	DL/T 5092—1999	110kV～500kV 架空送电线路设计技术规程	Technical code for designing 110kV～500kV overhead transmission line
166	DL/T 5130—2000	架空送电线路钢管杆设计技术规定	Technical regulation for design of steel transmission pole
167	DL/T 5138—2001	架空送电线路航空摄影测量技术规定	Technical specifications for aerial photographing and surveying of overhead transmission line
168	DL/T 5143—2002	变电所给水排水设计规程	Design code of water supply and drainage for substation
169	DL/T 5147—2001	电力系统安全自动装置设计技术规定	Designing technical rules for security and automaticity equipment of power system
170	DL/T 5154—2012	架空输电线路杆塔结构设计技术规定	Technical regulation of design for tower
171	DL/T 5155—2002	220kV～500kV 变电所所用电设计技术规程	Technical code for designing auxiliary power system of 220kV～500kV substation

续表

输变电			
序号	标准编号	标准名称	英文名称
172	DL/T 5161.1—2002	电气装置安装工程质量检验及评定规程 第1部分：通则	Specification for construction quality checkout and evaluation of electric equipment installation Part 1：General rules
173	DL/T 5161.2—2002	电气装置安装工程 质量检验及评定规程 第2部分：高压电器施工质量检验	Specification for construction quality checkout and evaluation of electric equipment installation Part 2：High voltage electric power equipment
174	DL/T 5161.3—2002	电气装置安装工程质量检验及评定规程 第3部分：电力变压器、油浸电抗器、互感器施工质量检验	Specification for construction quality checkout and evaluation of electric equipment installation Part 3：Power transformer，oil immersed reactor and mutual inductor
175	DL/T 5161.4—2002	电气装置安装工程质量检验及评定规程 第4部分：母线装置施工质量检验	Specification for construction quality checkout and evaluation of electric equipment installation Part 4：Bus bar installation
176	DL/T 5161.5—2002	电气装置安装工程质量检验及评定规程 第5部分：电缆线路施工质量检验	Specification for construction quality checkout and evaluation of electric equipment installation Part 5：Cable ling
177	DL/T 5161.6—2002	电气装置安装工程质量检验及评定规程 第6部分：接地装置施工质量检验	Specification for construction quality checkout and evaluation of electric equipment installation Part 6：Ear thing device
178	DL/T 5161.7—2002	电气装置安装工程质量检验及评定规程 第7部分：旋转电机施工质量检验	Specification for construction quality checkout and evaluation of electric equipment installation Part 7：Electrical rotating machines
179	DL/T 5161.8—2002	电气装置安装工程质量检验及评定规程 第8部分：盘、柜及二次回路结线施工质量检验	Specification for construction quality checkout and evaluation of electric equipment installation Part 8：Switchboard outfit complete cubicle and secondary circuit
180	DL/T 5161.9—2002	电气装置安装工程质量检验及评定规程 第9部分：蓄电池施工质量检验	Specification for construction quality checkout and evaluation of electric equipment installation Part 9：Battery
181	DL/T 5161.10—2002	电气装置安装工程质量检验及评定规程 第10部分：35kV及以下架空电力线路施工质量检验	Specification for construction quality checkout and evaluation of electric equipment installation Part 10：35kV and under over-head power levels
182	DL/T 5161.11—2002	电气装置安装工程质量检验及评定规程 第11部分：电梯电气装置施工质量检验	Specification for construction quality checkout and evaluation of electric equipment installation Part 11：Elevato
183	DL/T 5161.12—2002	电气装置安装工程质量检验及评定规程 第12部分：低压电器施工质量检验	Specification for construction quality checkout and evaluation of electric equipment installation Part 12：Low-voltage apparatus
184	DL/T 5161.13—2002	电气装置安装工程质量检验及评定规程 第13部分：电力交流设备施工质量检验	Specification for construction quality checkout and evaluation of electric equipment installation Part 13：Power converter equipment
185	DL/T 5161.14—2002	电气装置安装工程质量检验及评定规程 第14部分：起重机电气装置施工质量检验	Specification for construction quality checkout and evaluation of electric equipment installation Part 14：Crane

续表

输变电			
序号	标准编号	标准名称	英文名称
186	DL/T 5161.15—2002	电气装置安装工程质量检验及评定规程 第15部分：爆炸及火灾危险环境电气装置施工质量检验	Specification for construction quality checkout and evaluation of electric equipment installation Part 15: Electric device of explosion atmospheres
187	DL/T 5161.16—2002	电气装置安装工程质量检验及评定规程 第16部分：1kV及以下配线工程施工质量检验	Specification for construction quality checkout and evaluation of electric equipment installation Part 16: 1kV and under feeder cable engineering
188	DL/T 5161.17—2002	电气装置安装工程质量检验及评定规程 第17部分：电气照明装置施工质量检验	Specification for construction quality checkout and evaluation of electric equipment installation Part 17: Electric lighting device
189	DL/T 5168—2002	110kV～500kV架空电力线路工程施工质量及评定规程	Code for construction quality checkout and evaluation of 110kV～500kV overhead transmission lines
190	DL/T 5216—2005	35kV～220kV城市地下变电站设计规定	Design Rules of 35kV～20kV Urban under ground substation
191	DL/T 5217—2013	220kV～500kV紧凑型架空输电线路设计技术规程	Technical code for design of 220kV～500kV compact overhead transmission line
192	DL/T 5218—2012	220kV～750kV变电站设计技术规程	Technical code for designing 220kV～750kV Substation
193	DL/T 5219—2005	架空送电线路基础设计技术规定	Technical regulation for designing foundation of overhead transmission line
194	DL/T 5220—2005	10kV及以下架空配电线路设计技术规程	Code for designing over-head distribution transmission line up to 10kV
195	DL/T 5221—2005	城市电力电缆线路设计技术规定	Technical rule for design of urban power cables
196	DL/T 5222—2005	导体和电器选择设计技术规定	Design technical rule for selecting conductor and electrical equipment
197	DL/T 5223—2005	高压直流换流站设计技术规定	Technical rule for designing HVDC converter station
198	DL/T 5224—2005	高压直流输电大地返回运行系统设计技术规定	Technical rule for the design of HVDC earth return operation system
199	DL/T 5225—2005	220kV～500kV变电所通信设计技术规定	Technical rule of communication design for 220kV ～ 500kV substation
200	DL/T 5231—2010	±800kV及以下直流输电接地极施工及验收规程	Specification for construction and acceptance of earthing pole in ±800kV & under DC transmission
201	DL/T 5232—2010	±800kV及以下直流换流站电气装置安装工程施工及验收规程	Specification for construction and acceptance of electric equipments in ±800kV & under converter station
202	DL/T 5233—2010	±800kV及以下直流换流站电气装置施工质量检验及评定规程	Specification for construction quality checkout and acceptance of electric equipments in ±800kV & under DC converter station
203	DL/T 5235—2010	±800kV及以下直流架空输电线路工程施工及验收规程	Code for construction and acceptance of ±800kV and under DC overhead transmission line

续表

输变电			
序号	标准编号	标准名称	英文名称
204	DL/T 5236—2010	±800kV及以下直流架空输电线路工程施工质量检验及评定规程	Specification for construction quality checkout and evaluation of ±800kV and under DC overhead transmission line
205	DL/T 5242—2010	35kV～220kV变电站无功补偿装置设计技术规定	Technical rules for designing of reactive power compensation equipment in 35kV～220kV substations
206	DL/T 5254—2010	架空输电线路钢管塔设计技术规定	Technical regulation of design for steel tubular tower structures of overhead transmission line
207	DL/T 5320—2014	架空输电线路大跨越工程架线施工工艺导则	Construction technology guideline for tension stringing of large crossing overhead transmission line
208	DL/T 5340—2006	直流输电线路对电信线路危险影响设计技术规程	Technical code for designing of telecommunication lines against danger effects from DC power transmission lines
209	DL/T 5342—2006	750kV架空送电线路铁塔组立施工工艺导则	Construction technology guidance for the assembling and erection of the steel towers of 750kV overhead transmission line
210	DL/T 5343—2006	750kV架空送电线路张力架线施工工艺导则	Construction technology guidance for tension stringing of 750kV overhead transmission line
211	DL/T 5352—2006	高压配电装置设计技术规定	Technical code for designing high voltage electrical switchgear
212	DL/T 5391—2007	电力系统通信设计技术规定	Design technical code of dispatching communication of electric power system
213	DL/T 5392—2007	电力系统数字同步网工程设计规程	Specifications of engineering design for digital synchronization network of electric power system
214	DL/T 5404—2007	电力系统同步数字系列（SDH）光缆通信工程设计技术规定	Technical rule of electric power system engineering design for SDH optical fiber cable communication project
215	DL/T 5405—2008	城市电力电缆线路初步设计内容深度规程	Code for content depth on preliminary design of urban power cables
216	DL/T 5426—2009	±800kV高压直流输电系统成套设计规程	System design standard for ±800kV HVDC system
217	DL/T 5429—2009	电力系统设计技术规定	Technical code of design for the electric power system
218	DL/T 5430—2009	无人值班变电所远方监控中心设计规程	Technical code for designing of remote monitoring and control center about unattended substation
219	DL/T 5439—2009	大型水、火电厂接入系统设计内容深度规定	Design regulation of content and profundity for hydro and fossil fuel plant connecting to the system
220	DL/T 5440—2009	重覆冰架空输电线路设计技术规程	Technical code for designing of overhead transmission line in medium & heavy icing area
221	DL/T 5453—2012	串补站设计技术规程	Technical code for the design of series compensator station
222	DL/T 5457—2012	变电站建筑结构设计技术规定	Technical code for the design of substation buildings and structures
223	DL/T 5459—2012	换流站建筑结构设计技术规程	Technical code of architectural & structural design for converter station
224	DL/T 5460—2012	换流站站用电设计技术规定	Technical code for the design of auxiliary power system of converter station

续表

输变电			
序号	标准编号	标准名称	英文名称
225	DL/T 5484—2013	电力电缆隧道设计规程	Code for design of power cables tunnel
226	DL/T 5485—2013	110kV～750kV 架空输电线路大跨越设计技术规程	Technical code for design of long span crossing of 110kV～750kV overhead transmission line
227	DL/T 5486—2013	特高压架空输电线路杆塔结构设计技术规程	Technical code for design of tower structures of UHV overhead transmission line
228	DL/T 5732—2016	架空输电线路大跨越工程施工质量检验及评定规程	Specification for construction quality inspection and evaluation of large crossing overhead transmission line

（中国电力企业联合会　许松林　刘永东）

水 电 新 书

中国电力出版社 2018 年水电新书

中国电力出版社 2018 年水电新书见表 1。

表 1　中国电力出版社 2018 年水电新书

序号	书号	项目名称	作者	定价（元）
1	978-7-5198-2827-1	改革开放四十年——中国水电（上卷）	中国水力发电工程学会	150
2	978-7-5198-2956-8	改革开放四十年——中国水电（下卷）	中国水力发电工程学会	180
3	978-7-5198-2572-0	抽水蓄能电站工程建设文集 2018	中国水力发电工程学会电网调峰与抽水蓄能专业委员会	200
4	978-7-5198-2665-9	大型水电工程建设总承包论文集	中国水力发电工程学会	190
5	978-7-5198-2678-9	全球能源分析与展望 2018	国网能源研究院有限公司	188
6	978-7-5198-2895-0	全球能源分析与展望 2018（英文版）	国网能源研究院有限公司	188
7	978-7-5198-2677-2	中国能源电力发展展望 2018	国网能源研究院有限公司	98
8	978-7-5198-2861-5	中国能源电力发展展望 2018（英文版）	国网能源研究院有限公司	108
9	978-7-5198-2573-7	水力发电厂金属结构技术监督	李文波、陈红冬等	58
10	978-7-5198-2349-8	抽水蓄能电站 TBM 施工技术	李富春、吴朝月等	90
11	978-7-5198-2282-8	水利水电工程压力管道技术——第九届全国水利水电工程压力管道学术会议论文集	中国电建集团昆明勘测设计研究院有限公司	180
12	978-7-5198-2212-5	中国电力标准化年度发展报告 2018	中国电力企业联合会	398
13	978-7-5198-3087-8	漫画安全——电力生产人身事故案例集（第二版）	李小勤	28

续表

序号	书号	项目名称	作者	定价（元）
14	978-7-5198-2239-2	电力安全应急知识题库	中国华电集团有限公司	32
15	978-7-5198-3057-1	可再生能源发电企业安全事件案例分析　抽水蓄能分册	国家电网有限公司安全监察质量部	98
16	978-7-5198-2651-2	可再生能源发电企业典型安全事件案例分析　常规水力发电分册	国家电网有限公司安全监察质量部	120
17	978-7-5198-2000-8	电力安全生产系列画册（口袋书）现场应急处置	本书编写组	16
18	978-7-5198-1999-6	电力安全生产系列画册（口袋书）职业健康	本书编写组	16
19	155198.786	电力企业现场作业安全常识　外用人员	本书编写组	15
20	978-7-5198-2083-1	《防止电力生产事故的二十五项重点要求》案例警示教材（彩图本）	国家能源局电力安全监管司、中国电机工程学会	128
21	978-7-5198-2191-3	中国华电集团有限公司电力建设数据手册	中国华电集团有限公司基建工程部	280
22	155198.721	中国水力发电信息（2017 年报）	中国水力发电工程学会	30
23	978-7-5198-1920-0	中国能源建设（2017 年合订本）	中国能源建设集团有限公司工程研究院	150
24	978-7-5198-2637-6	常规变电站继电保护现场检验标准化作业	国网辽宁省电力有限公司电力调度控制中心、国网辽宁省电力有限公司技能培训中心	198
25	978-7-5198-1960-6	水电站典型作业危险点分析及控制措施	本书编委会	75
26	978-7-5198-1666-7	土石坝技术　2017 年论文集	水电水利规划设计总院、中国水力发电工程学会混凝土面板堆石坝专业委员会、中国电建集团昆明勘测设计研究院有限公司、水利水电土石坝工程信息网、国家能源水电工程技术研发中心高土石坝分中心	130
27	978-7-5198-1661-2	水电水利建设工程项目划分实用手册	四川大唐国际甘孜水电开发有限公司	120
28	978-7-5198-1588-2	中国水力发电年鉴　第二十一卷	中国水力发电工程学会	350
29	978-7-5198-1728-2	灯泡贯流式水轮发电机组运行与检修	五凌电力有限公司	85
30	978-7-5198-2768-7	天荒坪电站运行 20 周年总结	华东天荒坪抽水蓄能有限责任公司	180
31	978-7-5198-2828-8	抽水蓄能电站工器具使用与管理	华东天荒坪抽水蓄能有限责任公司	45
32	978-7-5198-2769-4	抽水蓄能电站设备巡定检管理	华东天荒坪抽水蓄能有限责任公司	128
33	978-7-5198-2810-3	抽水蓄能运维技术文集（第三辑）	华东天荒坪抽水蓄能有限责任公司	248
34	978-7-5198-1529-5	抽水蓄能电站基建工程管理岗位培训教材　水工综合管理	国网新源控股有限公司	65
35	978-7-5198-1521-9	抽水蓄能电站基建工程管理岗位培训教材　工程质量管理	国网新源控股有限公司	55

续表

序号	书号	项目名称	作者	定价（元）
36	978-7-5198-1523-3	抽水蓄能电站基建工程管理岗位培训教材　工程机电管理	国网新源控股有限公司	52
37	978-7-5198-1524-0	抽水蓄能电站基建工程管理岗位培训教材　工程安全管理	国网新源控股有限公司	50
38	978-7-5198-1537-0	抽水蓄能电站基建工程管理岗位培训教材　工程技经管理	国网新源控股有限公司	48
39	978-7-5198-1803-6	朱伯芳院士传	鲁顺民	150
40	978-7-5198-0292-9	大体积混凝土裂缝防治及诊断关键技术	李松辉	55

（中国电力出版社）

《水电站典型作业危险点分析及控制措施》出版发行

2018年5月1日，由国网新源控股有限公司组织编写，中国电力出版社出版发行的《水电站典型作业危险点分析及控制措施》面世。水电站危险点分析预控，是对电力生产中的每项工作根据作业内容、工作方法、工作环境、人员状况等进行关联分析，对可能引发事故的各种不安全因素进行分析判断、预测，并依据安全规程、制度制定针对性的防范措施，使之程序化、规范化地落实于生产现场。

为明确安全生产风险评估预控管理要求，坚持“安全第一，预防为主，综合治理”，运用有效评估方法，对各类运检业务进行风险评估，确定风险等级，落实风险管控措施，从而有效控制安全事故的发生，国网新源控股有限公司在总结多年来运检实践经验的基础上，组织编写了该书。

该书主要内容涵盖值守操作、主设备系统、电气一次系统、电气二次系统、水工金属结构、现场试验与检验、水电站典型重大安全风险作业，详细、完整地阐述了值守业务、操作业务、安全工器具（工具）使用，发电电动机及其辅助设备、水泵水轮机及其辅助设备、开关站设备、高压电缆设备、主变压器系统、发电电动机电压设备、SFC及启动母线系统、厂用电设备、计算机监控系统、机组励磁系统、线路保护及自动装置设备、主变压器保护系统、机组继电保护、直流系统、机组状态检测系统、水工设施、闸门系统检修，机组检修后整机启动试验、高压试验、金属检测、电测热工危险点及预控措施。

（中国电力出版社）

《灯泡贯流式水轮发电机组运行与检修》出版发行

2018年3月1日，五凌电力有限公司组织编写《灯泡贯流式水轮发电机组运行与检修》，由中国电力出版社出版发行。贯流式水轮发电设备从1982年开始研制到现在，已有一百多年的历史，机组设计水平日益成熟，灯泡贯流式机组在水电工程中得到了广泛的应用。为使水电厂生产管理人员了解并掌握灯泡贯流式水轮发电机组的基本理论、基本结构、检修工艺流程、运维技术及故障处理，保证电网及水电厂安全稳定运行，五凌电力有限公司在总结多年运行与检修经验的基础上，组织编写了该书。

该书共分八章。主要内容为概述部分、水轮机结构、发电机结构、水轮机检修、发电机检修、机组检修试验、运行与维护、故障处理。

（中国电力出版社）

中國水力發電年鑒

11

水电建设管理

工 程 管 理

杨房沟水电站 EPC 工程总承包管理实践

杨房沟水电站是国内首个百万千瓦级水电站采用 EPC 工程总承包模式进行建设的水电工程。经过参建各方两年半的共同努力，工程进度、质量、安全及文明施工、环保水保等建设目标有序推进，已累计完成合同产值约 20 亿元。在合同履约过程中，参建各方能够齐心协力，解决工程具体问题，合同节点普遍提前实现。但也存在不少具体问题，需要各方发挥各自智慧加以研究解决。该合同总工期 108 个月，2016 年 1 月 1 日工程开工，2021 年 11 月 30 日首台机组投产发电，2024 年 12 月 31 日工程竣工。

（一）EPC 工程总承包实施模式

杨房沟水电站 EPC 工程总承包模式是建立在“商业化契约精神”及“信托责任理念”基础上的一种项目管理模式。工程总承包企业按合同约定，对工程项目的质量、工期、造价等向业主负责。中国水利水电第七工程局有限公司与中国电建集团华东勘测设计研究院有限公司按 60%∶40%比例成立杨房沟水电站总承包联合体，按“统一领导、统一组织、统一规则、统一管理，两级核算”的基本运营规则进行管理。总承包联合体由董事会、监事会、总承包项目部、安全生产委员会、风险管理委员会、工程技术委员会组成。总承包部是董事会领导下的项目经理负责制。双方派员进入联合体总承包部各个职能部门，项目经理由责任方法人出任。总承包部现场分为现场经营层、生产管理层及生产实施层。

（二）EPC 工程总承包管理实践

实践证明，传统 DBB 模式下，由于大中型水电工程参建单位众多，建设管理协调难度较大，工程进度与投资往往难以受控，确定以施工为主体、以设计为龙头、设计施工高度融合的 EPC 工程总承包模式，把设计、采购、施工和试运行等作为一个整体全部委托给一个管理主体组织实施，把出资人从传统项目管理中解放出来。

1. 实施手段与措施　正确处理设计、采购和施工三者之间的关系是工程总承包项目成功与否的关键因素之一。摸索建立起符合杨房沟水电工程实际的管理体系，主要有以下手段与措施。①自律管理。该工程总承包部自律管理体系是“管理层的自律＋作业班组层的他律”相结合的管理体系。②一体化。一体化就是将设计、采购、施工深度整合，让相互交叉各方在总承包部的统一引领下，相互配合成为一个有机整体，管理效率进一步加强。③信息化。总承包部根据工程实际，开发并建立了 BIM 管理信息系统，将设计管理、质量验评、进度管理、投资管理、安全监测、水情测报、视频监控、智能温控、智能灌浆、施工仿真等功能深度整合。有效加快了信息流转速度，同时也增加了 EPC 总承包管理的透明度。④标准化。考虑到 EPC 工程总承包项目的复杂性和多样性，在工程实施中引入标准化。在工程质量方面，出台标准化文件 23 份，并定期开展宣贯与培训。在安全方面，制定了《安全文明施工标准化手册》，不断强化培训与检查考核，规范现场操作行为。

2. 现场实践情况　目前总承包部工程安全形势受控，实体质量稳步提升，施工进度均有超前。①安全生态管理。以“六化管理”为抓手，强化“一个手册”“两个规划”“七个台账”为管理重心。未发生安全事故，安全生产形势有序、受控。连续两年顺利通过电力工程建设项目安全生产标准化一级达标考核，也成为凉山州安全风险管理体系建设首个试点单位。②质量管理。建立起“四体系”（保证体系、责任体系、检查体系、评价体系），运用“四化”（制度化、标准化、表单化、信息化）手段，全过程跟踪质量管理人员履职情况，并循环完成闭合。2016 年度评定 776 个单元工程，优良单元 731 个，综合优良率 94.2%；2017 年度评定 3075 个单元工程，优良单元 2994 个，综合优良率 97.4%。③进度管理。实行三级管理：一级为总承包部施工生产管理系统，由总承包部施工管理部及机电部具体负责执行；二级为工区施工生产管理系统，由工区施工部具体负责执行；三级为工区作业层施工生产管理系统，由作业班组级具体负责执行。根据关键线路进度计划偏差严重程度，分三级预警。目前大坝及泄洪系统工期满足合同要求，地下厂房土建开挖提前 6 个月。④成本管理。目前杨房沟总承包部采取的结算方式分为对外对内分序进行，业主对总承包部采用季度节点结算；总承包部对内部作业工区采用的是“背靠背”结算。目前主要成本风险均出现在与地质相关的项目，比如危岩体处理、地质缺陷工程量与投标阶段预估工程量有较大差异。⑤综合管理。EPC工程总承包管理将原大多属业主管理的事项也转交到总承包单位，无论是对设计单位，还是对施工单位而言，都是一项极为严峻的挑战。

（三）现阶段实践模式总结

杨房沟水电站EPC工程总承包模式经历了两年多的探索与实践，参建各方也经历了一定时间的磨合，对工程的总体认知与管理理念也趋于一致，积累了许多宝贵的经验，也遇到一些具体的棘手问题需要反思与解决。

1. EPC总承包管理优势　毋庸置疑，EPC工程总承包，相对于传统的管理模式，切实表现出了特殊优越性。①简化管理环节，统一协调，资源整合能力得到显著提升。采用EPC管理模式，所有管理环节都要服从统一指挥，设计、采购与施工三者成为利益共同体，各环节实现统一管理和协调，所有施工资源容易实现统一调度与调配，提高了资源使用效率，并合理有效地进行进度深度交叉，能使工程建设总周期缩短。②充分发挥设计与施工各自优势，有利于提高工程质量。通过联合体方式，促进设计与施工单位以工程项目为聚焦点，各自发挥专业特长，既有利于提高工程实体质量，又利于提升双方企业的核心竞争力。③项目管理专业化程度高。为实现全面整体管理，总承包单位需要派出比传统模式更多、更强的专业技术人员与中高级管理人员，发挥自身技术优势与管理优势，为总承包管理提供强大的技术与管理支撑，从而促进项目目标的顺利实现。④方便开展系统、并行与综合整体管理。系统管理是EPC管理模式在实施过程中区别DBB模式的最鲜明的特征，用综合总体管理的思路，寻求最佳管理方案，用经济高效的手段达到工程质量、安全与进度要求。⑤降低业主风险。实施EPC工程总承包，对业主而言，工程管理的风险大大降低，对于总承包商来说，必须承担更多责任，责任更多意味着风险加大。⑥成本导向作用更加突出。EPC总承包，有效加强各环节各要素间的联系，以设计为中心，以目标成本管理为手段，从而推动设计优化，推行限额设计，促进技术创新，动态核算各项成本支出，及时解决工程建设过程中所出现的问题，最终实现预期的造价控制。

2. EPC工程总承包模式建议与反思　项目实施以来，虽然工程总体处在稳定推进的状态，但仍有许多值得反思与总结的地方。①总承包方合同风险、费用承担过于集中。EPC模式下，工程总承包商拥有更多盈利机会，也承担着更多责任和风险。若发包人愿意承担一些工程风险，承包商就可以减少风险费用，这样项目最终总成本才会最低。②合同工期长，如何有效分担风险值得思考。项目实施风险的大小，取决于报价阶段对风险分析和估计，类似于杨房沟这类大型水电工程实施EPC总承包管理，因前期勘察无法完全准确查明所有地质缺陷，采用总价固定承包方式是否适当需待商榷。现阶段，危岩体清理合同清单列示为8万m^2，现场实施已经超过48万m^2（含清坡），左岸边坡f27、f37断层均在招标阶段未能预测等情况出现。如何化解和突破EPC总承包固定总价的难题，依然考验各方智慧。③出资人如何避免过度管理的问题。在总承包管理中，业主只关心工程质量和工程安全，对进度尤其是工程成本不再关心，经常组织到大型工程进行调研，力求把其他工程优秀的质量和安全文明施工展现在杨房沟，因此在现场管理过程中容易陷入片面强调质量和安全文明施工，双方在具体问题上的认同产生差异，对工程推进有一定影响。④法律与审计风险。因采用EPC工程总承包模式，建设周期长、地质条件复杂，同时大部分合同风险责任由总承包商承担，显然也增大了承包人的法律风险。又是固定总价合同，因此工程完工审计重点将由传统的业主单位转移到总承包单位，这就对总承包单位在工程建设中各类工程合同签证、清理与归档提出更高要求，审计风险也大幅增加。

（中国水利水电第七工程局有限公司　中国电建集团华东勘测设计研究院有限公司　申茂夏　张春生　李东林　侯靖　陈雁高　徐建军　刘军）

基于RFID的抽水蓄能电站智慧物资管理系统研究及应用

基于RFID技术，构建了抽水蓄能电站智慧物资管理系统，成功应用于天荒坪抽水蓄能电站，极大减轻了物资管理人员工作量，消除了物资管理过程中的遗失、遗漏以及由此引起的财产安全隐患，提高了物资管理的效率和效果。

（一）RFID技术简介

1. RFID系统构成　完整的RFID系统包括硬件系统和软件系统。硬件包括读写器、电子标签和天线。读写器是RFID系统最重要的部分，它可以单独具有读写、显示、数据处理等功能，也可以与计算机或其他系统进行联合，完成对射频标签的操作。电子标签由耦合元件、芯片及微型天线组成。天线主要用来在标签和读写器之间传递射频信号。软件主要包括相应的数据管理系统和桌面端、手机端等信息管理系统，配合硬件使用。

2. RFID 系统工作原理　RFID 工作原理如图 1 所示，阅读器将要发送的信号经天线向外发送，进入阅读器工作区域的电子标签接收此脉冲信号，卡内芯片中的有关电路对此信号进行调制、解码、解密，然后对命令请求、密码、权限等进行判断。若为读命令，控制逻辑电路则从存储器中读取有关信息，经加密、编码、调制后通过卡内天线再发送给阅读器，阅读器对接收到的信号进行解调、解码、解密后送至中央信息系统进行有关数据处理；若为修改信息的写命令，有关控制逻辑引起的内部电荷泵提升工作电压，提供擦写 EEPROM 中的内容进行改写，若经判断其对应的密码和权限不符，则返回出错信息。

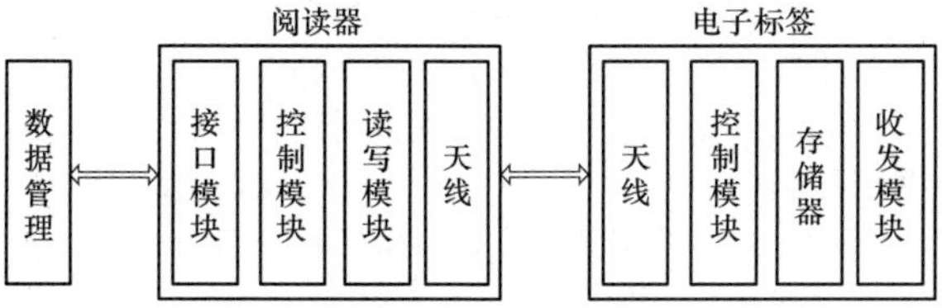

图 1　RFID 系统工作原理

（二）管理系统关键技术

1. 系统架构　智慧物资管理系统由云服务器、电脑桌面系统、手机 APP、手持机和 RFID 标签组成。云服务器是智慧工具管理系统的数据中心，将桌面系统、手机 APP、手持机和 RFID 关联起来，保存、接受、处理、分析物资管理过程中的各种静态及动态数据。桌面客户端，通过简洁明确的人机交互界面，实现物资入库、出库、盘点、台账、理货、备品备件定额管理等主要管理功能。手机 APP，主要用于 Android 终端或者 IOS 终端，方便物资管理人员随时对库存物资进行查询。手持机体积小，方便携带，主要用来办理物资的入库及出库。RFID 标签，主要用来记录物资的出入库相关信息，粘贴于物资表面，通过桌面式读写器、手持机等终端的识别实现物资的出入库管理和盘点管理等。

2. RFID 电子标签　抽水蓄能电站的物资种类繁多，物资盘点任务量大，对 RFID 识别距离、速度及群读识别有很高的要求。因此，电子标签需要根据物资的形状、大小、材质、使用方式和应用环境等进行设计和制造。对金属类工具，选用柔性基材的 RFID 抗金属标签，阅读距离控制在 20cm 内，保证工器具借还时不产生误读和干扰；对于金属类易耗品，选用箱体式 RFID 标签进行集中管理；对于非金属类物资选用对称偶极子 RFID 标签，易于调节标签的阅读距离和信息采集灵敏度；对远程货仓，选用带有高频 RFID 阅读器和高频 RFID 标签的锁止器，通过刷卡方式控制存储仓位的开关，并在每一个远程货仓内布置一个中转站，将存储仓位的开关信息和物资出入库信息上传至云服务器中。

3. 远程控制及管理　在综合分析的基础上，采用“集中管理，独立控制”模式，通过 5G 和 WiFi 无线网络技术实现信息的通信，通过嵌入式技术完成系统控制。远程控制包括中心系统和存储仓位系统。存储仓位系统与中心系统的连接采用广域网，默认采用无线通信连接，使存储仓位管理不受网络条件限制；存储仓位管理采用以太网方式，扩容方便，维护简单。利用网络间的协议转换，实现存储仓位远程控制及管理。

（三）智慧物资管理系统功能实现

1. 电脑终端基本功能　①物资入库。物资入库是仓储作业的首要环节。系统依据入库单信息以及用户为入库单选择的存放仓位，验收无误后，按照编码规则为入库物资打印 RFID 标签并生成物资台账，将标签粘贴到物资上，手持设备就可以读取 RFID 电子标签信息，当 RFID 标签采集完成后，会与入库单和物资台账进行比对，核对货物数量及型号，如有错漏需人工处理，最后将货物运送到指定位置，按照规则进行摆放。②物资出库。物资出库是指根据出库单信息，将所需物资发放到需用单位的业务活动。使用 RFID 手持设备进行扫描下架出库物资 RFID 标签，最后把数据发送到智慧物资管理平台更新数据库完成出库。③物资盘点。物资盘点是通过 RFID 读取设备，对仓位上的物资进行自动扫描，读取实物数量，并传输到仓储管理系统盘点凭证中进行对比，对于其中出现的差异需要由仓储管理人员说明差异原因并生成盘点报告。④物资台账。对库存物资信息进行查询，智慧展示库存物资名称、存储位置、用途、数量、等信息；可基于关键字、模糊字段等多方位进行智慧查询。⑤物资理货。用户可根据库存管理需要，创建理货任务根据理货任务内容，实现对物资理货的闭环管理。⑥备品备件定额管理。对备品备件的库存数量进行监测，数量低于预警阈值时通过智慧平台进行提示。

2. 手机终端基本功能　包括入库单查询、出库单查询、物资盘点和物资理货功能。用户可在手机端入库单、出库单、盘点及理货信息进行查询，管理员与物资部领导可查看所有入库单、出库单、盘点及理货的执行情况，各仓库管理员只能查看自己负责仓库的入库单、出库单、盘点及理货信息。

3. 手持机终端基本功能 ①物资入库。仓库管理员用手持设备扫描货架 RFID 标签，再扫描上架物资 RFID 标签，确认物质入库。②物资出库。仓库管理员用手持设备扫描下架物资 RFID 标签，确认物资出库。③物资盘点。仓库管理员用手持设备扫描货物 RFID 标签，进行盘点，盘点数据通过手持设备上传智慧物资子系统。

（华东天荒坪抽水蓄能有限责任公司
中国电建集团西北勘测设计研究院有限公司
王春明 徐汉坤 郑凯 危伟 马晓晨 游光华
赵毅峰 郑小刚 吴燕飞 朱中山 范建强 沈浩）

水电工程成本管理和成本控制研究

目前，水利水电建设市场竞争激烈，施工企业的利润空间越来越小，这就要求施工企业不断加强成本管理和成本控制，以提高项目盈利水平。从施工企业项目管理角度出发，有必要对成本管理和成本控制做一些研究。

（一）开源节流，增收节支

项目成本控制，一是要认真履行已签施工承包合同，完成各项工作内容，在此基础上争取最大收益，此为开源；二是要强化物资设备管理和劳务分包管理，提高施工质量，降低物资消耗，节约开支，是为节流。

1. 开源、增收 开源、增收措施的业务对象是业主，要以承包合同、优势单价、技术与经营有效结合为重点。①合理利用合同有利条款。任何项目实施，都必须以合同为依据。但合同一旦签订，就是一成不变的，但在复杂的施工条件下往往存在着变化。这就需要仔细研究合同条款和具体施工条件及施工工序的差异，只要依据充分，进行有效的变更和索赔，成为项目赢利的关键。②合理利用优势单价。合理利用优势单价，就要求施工企业在实际施工中，尽量利用设计变更等条件，增加优势单价的工程数量，从而谋取更大的利润。也可以利用一些较为模糊的边界条件，将一些单价较低的项目按单价较高的项目来进行施工结算。例如基础工程，可以采用浆砌块石、浆砌片石、干砌块石、片石混凝土浇筑等多种方式施工，均可以达到设计的要求。上述方案施工企业应尽量选择利润空间大的方案，充分利用优势单价，增加企业经济效益。③技术、经营紧密结合。其应体现在项目实施的各个阶段，技术人员应首先提出能够达到设计意图的几套方案，该方案应在便于施工的情况下实现利益最大化。然而在实际施工过程中，由于一味地追求施工速度，忽视了技术与经营的结合，浪费了大量成本，也就错过了显著提高企业效益的机会。

2. 节流、节支 水利水电工程施工承包合同中，成本可分为施工成本（包括直接费、其他直接费和现场经费）和经营管理成本（包括企业管理费、财务费和其他费用），其中施工成本一般占合同总价的 70% 以上，所以施工成本是成本控制的主要内容。施工企业要做到节流、节支，主要有以下几点：①从人、财、物配置入手，结合行业统一定额，制定出合理的、可操作性强的内部成本核算定额，逐级进行部分成本核算和全成本核算。②对主要工程材料费、人工费、机械费和管理费进行核算与分析，人工费管理实行基本工资和效益工资相结合；材料费管理实行以内部核算定额消耗为基准，严格控制采购库存量。③机械费管理实行以设备运行保养费为基准，充分发挥设备效率。④把主辅材料消耗水平和费用支出与完成工程量挂钩，严格进行考核奖罚。⑤逐步建立成本分析的核算反馈制度。由成本控制部门对工程各分部分项工程进行成本核算，分析各分部分项工程经济效益和利润状况，以保证成本核算的准确度。

节流节支的重点是加强项目材料费用和劳务分包费用控制：

（1）材料费用控制。材料费用在项目成本中往往占有很高比例，通常情况下不低于 50%。材料费用控制应从以下着手：①凡材料物资收发、领退以及不同核算主体间的内部转移，都要经过清点和填制必要的凭证，并经一定的审批手续，以防止乱领、乱用，坚决杜绝因使用不合格材料而造成返工和增加补救措施费用。②施工企业根据分阶段控制材料消耗数量，确定材料消耗额度。这项工作应该在技术部门进行施工设计的时候将相关材料消耗数量提交物资管理部门来实现消耗控制。③重视材料价格控制。要以工程合同中规定的材料价格为准绳，多方询价比价，选择最优的采购方案进行材料采购，以达到节约成本的要求。

（2）劳务分包费用的控制。纯粹的劳务分包费用在项目成本中的比例比较低，通常情况不超过 15%。但实际操作过程中，劳务分包费用通常会包含一部分施工企业不易进行控制的小型机具和易耗材料费用，增加了一定的费用控制难度。劳务分包队伍的优劣，直接影响项目的施工进度、施工质量，进而影响项目的施工成本。施工企业进行劳务分包的时候，除了劳务谈判确定分包队伍外，经常采用招标方式确定劳务队伍，这样对项目部以合理低价选择优秀的劳务队伍是有利的。

（二）过程控制，成本管理

过程是输入转化为输出的一组彼此相关的资源（人员、资金、设施、设备、技术和方法）和活动。

过程管理，主要是侧重于对动态形势的活动的认识、控制和优化。充分利用资源，最有效地发挥各方面积极性，及时准确克服不利因素，求得相对高质管理效果是过程管理追求的目标。

严格过程控制，可以有力地避免或克服传统管理中“反复抓”的管理弊端，使整体管理水平不断地提高。当施工单位中标承建一个工程项目，就必须从人、财、物的有效组合和使用过程中狠下功夫。诸如对施工组织机构的设立和人员、机械设备的配备，在满足施工需要的前提下，机构要精简，人员要精干高效，设备要充分有效利用。对材料消耗、配件的更换及施工工序控制，都要按规范化、制度化、科学化进行，这样既可以避免或减少不可预见因素对施工的干扰，也使自身生产经营状况在影响工程成本构成因素中的比例降低或控制在合理范围，从而有效控制成本，提高效益。过程控制要全员参与、全过程控制，这与施工人员的素质、施工组织水平有很大关系。

当然，施工项目成本控制，牵扯到工程施工的方方面面。如：①一个完整的项目成本控制方案，还应该包括与业主单位、设计单位、监理单位的业务关系协调，项目管理费用的控制，机械使用费用的控制，甚至包括与地方的关系处理；②对于施工企业来说，安全生产应该是重中之重的头等大事，一个施工项目的赢亏很大程度上会受到安全事故赔偿的影响；③实际施工过程中，推广新产品、新工艺、新技术的应用，能减少投入，降低成本。随着国际市场的不断变化，水电行业施工企业间的竞争力亦随之不断增强，施工企业尤其要切实搞好施工项目成本管理，此为提高项目管理水平及增加企业效益的关键所在。

（中国水利水电第七工程局有限公司
国际工程公司　刘波）

基于BIM的水利水电工程全生命周期管理平台建设与应用

（一）现状分析

水利水电工程的全生命周期包括工程规划、设计、建造、运行、维护与废止等生命过程。工程建设期间参与单位众多，涉及设计、施工、监理、管理等诸多方面，管理的人、机、材复杂且存在大量不确定性因素，加之工程施工期长、季节性强、技术复杂，需要协调的关系多，项目的进度、质量、安全、投资等管控复杂。在传统的多部门多层级的工程信息共享与决策模式下，信息的碎片化及孤岛化问题将随着项目建设的推进、信息的积累与更新逐步显现，巨大的信息管理重复工作量和高昂的人力成本将给工程建设管理带来挑战。从建设阶段转向投产运行阶段的过程中，工程业主需要从参建各方接收大量数据，但目前数据移交接收的技术和手段还停留在旧有模式下，所移交的数据还需要经过大量的人工筛查处理以及手工录入，数据的完整度和可用性得不到有效保障，还远不能满足集约化、标准化、流程化管理的需求。因此，需要采取先进、高效、合理的方法对水利水电工程各个阶段进行科学管理。

（二）平台建设

基于建筑信息模型（BIM）的水利水电工程全生命周期管理三维数字化应用系统的开发以水利水电工程全生命周期管理和技术状态管理等国外先进的管理理论为主要依据，以 HydroStation® 水电水利工程三维数字化设计平台及相关应用成果为基础，采用了 Bentley MicroStation 和 Assetwise、Aecosim、iDAM 等商用基础软件，并针对我国水利水电工程全生命周期中的技术和管理特点，引入了国外相关先进的工程管理理论和数字化技术进行水利水电工程全生命周期管理系统、技术和应用研究。

1. 系统设计原则　该系统在开发过程中主要遵循以下几项原则：①符合水利水电工程现有工作模式；②信息及时采集、传递和集中管理；③系统功能完备；④专业化数据处理和分析；⑤使用简单、操作便捷；⑥便于升级与维护；⑦系统安全可靠。

2. 系统逻辑架构　基于 BIM 的水利水电工程全生命周期管理系统需覆盖勘察设计阶段、施工阶段以及运营阶段全过程。主要由工程数据中心和若干业务子系统构成，工程数据中心是全生命周期系统的基础平台，为全过程的工程内容提供统一的存储管理机制，同时建立起网状的、能记录历史状态的信息模型，将工程内容有机关联起来，并向子系统提供统一的数据服务；业务子系统包括数字化档案管理子系统、虚拟现实三维展示子系统、大坝安全监测信息管理子系统、三维数字化设计与施工管理子系统、枢纽建筑物全生命周期管理子系统和电厂设备全生命周期管理子系统等，业务子系统均按需求独立开发，各自构建自己的服务，基于企业服务总线（ESB）将所有的服务整合到一起，实现工程数据中心与业务子系统间、子系统与子系统间的数据交换。

3. 系统功能架构　基于上述的逻辑架构，水利水电工程全生命周期系统功能框架设计如下：系统由两大部分构成，即工程数据中心和业务应用及在线服务。工程数据中心是实现数据存储、共享和流转的基石，用于管理、存储和控制项目的相关信息，为业务系统提供工程信息服务。同时，工程数据中心也是系统的基础框架，通过相关技术确立系统集成的规范和接口，为业务系统的集成奠定基础。业务应用及在线服务是构建在基础框架之上的结合水电工程项目实际需要提供的业务应用和信息服务。

4. 标准体系　从信息化角度建立的水利水电工程全生命周期管理系统标准体系，包括通用标准、软硬件及信息安全标准和业务及应用标准等三类。

（三）应用实例

仙居抽水蓄能电站枢纽由上水库、下水库、输水系统、地下厂房洞室群和开关站组成。结合勘察、设计、施工和运维管理全方位需求，利用三维 BIM 技术建立了地形、地质、水工、建筑、电气、水机、暖通、给排水等专业的主要对象、建/构筑物、构件、设备等，开发了工程数据中心和全生命周期业务应用系统，系统包括工程三维数字化系统设计平台、设计施工一体化 BIM 应用平台、数字化运维管理平台。全生命周期业务应用系统的具体建设内容如下：

（1）数字化勘察设计子系统。按工程专业领域划分，勘察设计子系统包括三大模块：地质模块、枢纽模块和工厂模块。各模块之间具有密切的关联关系，设计成果需要相互参考。三大模块涵盖的子专业如下：①勘测三维勘察模块，涵盖测绘、勘探、试验、物探、观测、地质、岩土等专业；②枢纽三维设计模块，涵盖坝工、引水、施工、厂房、建筑等专业；③工厂三维设计模块，涵盖厂房、建筑、水机、电气、暖通、金结等专业。全生命周期管理系统不仅覆盖三大模块的专业应用环境以提高设计的单点效率，还以 Projectwise+Microstation 软件构建了以“协作”为中心的协同平台，使三大模块能够高效地进行协作，同步提高企业整体设计效率。

（2）施工管理子系统。基于施工 BIM 模型，结合工程现场需要，开发了工程进度、质量、安全、投资管理模块，施工期安全监测、视频监控模块，水雨情报信息查询模块，混凝土智能温控信息查询模块。

（3）数字化运维管理子系统。对电站运行维护管理需求进行分析，利用工程三维数字化、数字化移交、网络通信、实时监控等技术手段，开发了以水电站运维 BIM 模型为基础、集合运行维护所需数据的数字化运维子系统。该系统以三维场景、三维模型、设备与构件目录树为入口，进行大坝安全监测管理、电站枢纽管理、设备资产管理、设备状态管理等工作，展示电站三维面貌、台账管理、实现对象的空间定位管理、对象的关系管理、档案的关系管理、移动应用等，形成统一的工程运维管理平台，为电站运行维护服务。

（中国电建集团华东勘测设计研究院有限公司
熊保锋　张帅　岳超）

二维码技术在丰宁抽水蓄能电站施工管理中的应用

河北丰宁抽水蓄能电站一期、二期共计 6 条引水隧洞，12 条尾水隧洞，均采用压力钢管衬砌，压力钢管制造安装工程量共计约 4.5 万 t，约 1753 节个制作单元，由于一、二期钢管制作工程量较大，标识牌制作量较大，投入成本较大，且标识牌容易丢失。

为便于施工现场各类信息的有效查询，采用二维码技术对各类设备及产品进行标识，通过手机扫取二维码能够及时了解各类信息。

钢管制作完成防腐工作后，在管外壁粘贴二维码，检查人员或安装人员用手机扫取钢管上粘贴的二维码后可获取到此单元钢管的诸多信息，如管节号、钢管安装部位、钢管壁厚、材质、内径、管长、加劲环参数、管重、焊缝数量、出厂日期、验收情况、制作负责人及质量负责人等详细信息，方便快捷。

施工现场每台套设备上编制专用二维码，手机扫取二维码后，设备名称、型号、原值、生产厂家、检验有效期、相关责任人、使用状况等相关信息会立刻弹出，设备从出厂到使用过程中各环节信息跃然眼前。

丰宁抽水蓄能电站手机网络已基本覆盖整个工程，通过二维码技术的应用，在施工现场可以第一时间获取各类设备及产品的信息，利用二维码技术展现工程信息，可以替代原始的标识标牌，节约施工成本，促使项目管理实现深度信息化，切实提升施工信息管理水平及工作效率。

（中国水利水电第三工程局有限公司　杨联东）

厄瓜多尔水电站总承包项目劳工管理研究

随着中资企业在厄瓜多尔不断开发、拓展，如何做好当地用工成本及风险控制一直是被关注的重点。通过德尔西项目的实践，探索出一些劳工管理的经验和措施，取得了较好的效果，规避了较大的劳工风险，避免了劳工成本的增加。

（一）项目概况

德尔西水电站为长引水式电站，位于厄瓜多尔萨莫拉—钦奇佩（Zamora Chinchipe）省境内的萨莫拉（Zamora）河上。总承包项目部成立时，设置了劳工管理机构，配有中方专业劳工管理人员，聘用当地劳工律师、劳工高管、专业管理人员。各分包项目部也配有专门劳工管理机构和人员。项目履约过程中，项目部严格执行当地劳工法律规定，按照中方与属地员工1∶4的比例招聘属地员工，按照属地员工25∶1的比例招聘属地残疾员工，高峰期聘用当地劳工超过1000人。项目部每月按期发放员工工资、缴纳员工社保。

（二）合同类型

根据厄瓜多尔《劳动法》，劳工雇佣合同可以是：①固定劳工合同；②业务范围内以履约项目或提供服务为目的的合同；③基于特定项目而签署的合同；④专业服务合同；⑤短期临时合同；⑥按劳动任务的用工合同；⑦偶然合同；⑧按工作量计量的合同；⑨季节性合同；⑩明示和默认的合同。根据劳动合同类型和德尔西项目的用工性质，只有前5项合同型式适合在该项目劳工雇佣时采用。

（三）劳工成本

在厄瓜多尔进行工程建设时，人工成本和用工风险已成为困扰中资企业“走出去”的一个重要因素，突显在劳工、工会两大难题上，加之税务、环保、劳工相关法律经过多次修改，经营环境已变得十分苛刻，给工程生产及成本控制带来巨大挑战。

1. 劳工额外权益　2015年12月16日修改生效的厄《劳动法》规定，员工月最低工资为366美元，员工除享有正常月工资以外还享有其他额外权益，主要条款有：①员工分红。在厄注册成立的公司每年须将利润的15%用于员工分红，其中10%直接发放给公司员工，另外5%则依据员工的家属负担，直接发给该公司的员工。新法案规定，每个员工所得分红不得超过厄每年基本工资的24倍（8496美元），超过部分须上缴国家。②第13项工资。雇主在每年12月24日前向员工支付一份报酬，此报酬应为全年12个月工资总额的平均数，用于感谢员工一年以来对公司的贡献。③第14项工资。雇主在每年8月15日前向员工支付一份报酬，此报酬金额为366美元，用于帮助员工家庭在开学前为子女购买学习用品和校服等。④储备基金（FONDOS）。为企业提供超过1年以上服务的员工，有权利接受雇主给予每月支付其工资总额的8.33%的金额作为储备基金。⑤年公休及未公休补偿。在公司工作满1年的员工每年可以享受15天的带薪休假时间，如由于工作原因无法正常休假的，经公司批准可给予在当月工资基础上增加15天工资作为补偿。

2. 社会保险成本　①厄瓜多尔《社会保障法》规定，公司对正式及试用员工均需缴纳社会保险。社保费用占工资总额的21.6%，其中9.45%由个人承担（直接从工资中扣除，公司代缴），12.15%由公司承担，且缴费比例逐年提高。德尔西项目2016年每月平均支出社保成本近6万美元。另外，企业还需向厄全国职业教育培训委员会、教育信贷与奖学金委员会分别缴纳雇员工资额的0.50%，作为员工的培训基金。②厄社保费用主要用于医疗保险和养老保险。中方员工虽可享受当地医疗保险，在公立医院就诊无需再花费任何费用，但厄公立医院设施条件简陋，就诊患者众多，候诊往往需要等待多天，加之语言沟通不畅，中方员工往往选择自行购买药品或者私立医院就诊，医疗保险对中方员工来说形同虚设。养老保险必须是在厄工作满35年退休后的厄公民才能享受，中方员工根本无法满足。

（四）用工风险

厄瓜多尔保护劳动者权利的规定非常严苛。包括工人可享受的最低工资权、健康工作条件权、无歧视权、工会权、集体协商权、罢工权、享受利润分配权、无理被辞补偿权、安全和劳动医疗权等。各项规定严重加大了中资企业在厄用工风险。

1. 新法案加大了企业用工风险　因厄瓜多尔有关法律改革，进一步加大了企业用工风险。①新法案规定，无固定期限劳动合同不再设试用期，直接签订合同。此法案使得企业人力资源管理更加被动，并造成工程后期辞退员工时增加大量成本。②新法案规定，试用期满后如员工主动申请辞职，公司除结清员工工资及13、14项工资等外，可按照正常手续辞退；如公司强制辞退员工，应提前1个月告知员工，根据工作年限向员工额外支付3个月以上工资。此项法案进一步增加了企业辞退员工的成本和风险。③厄劳工部规定，根据企业规模和员工人数须雇佣一定比例（25∶1）的残疾人，否则每年予以3000美元左右的罚款。德尔西项目2016年起年平均用工人数约1250人，需雇佣50名厄残疾人。而一旦解聘残疾员工，需一次性支付相当于其月工资18倍的离职补偿金。④禁止解雇的主要情况：怀孕期间，哺乳期，工会领导人，员工请病假时或者需要社保局临时抚恤金帮助时。

2. 工会带来的用工风险　30名以上员工的企业，同一公司可组建一个以上工会，加入工会与否由员工自行决定。工会的成立本无可厚非，然而由于厄瓜多尔局势变化多端，社会问题尖锐，很多工会诞生之日起就以反政府、抵制法律、抵制中资企业为目的。①集体合同。《劳动法》规定，50%的员工组成的工会可与雇主谈判、签订集体合同，争取的利益（如增加工资）惠及企业全体员工。以德尔西项目为例，工会于2015年5月成立，于2015年11月向公司提交集体合同，该合同中的不合理要求及条件所增加费用达到1千多万美元。该工会会员未超过规定比例，且工会成立时部分会员系伪造签字，经多次听证调解，判定该合同无效。若合同通过，将对公司造成重大损失。②工会挑拨员工带来损失。工会应着力于维护员工正当利益。但厄瓜多尔部分工会煽动员工游行、罢工等，从而达到谋取私利的目的。以德尔西项目为例，2016年期间工会教唆工人在签认考勤时向中方管理人员挑衅，发生肢体冲突并暗中录像上传至社交网站，毁坏中资企业声誉。③工会会费成本。根据《劳动法》规定，工会成立后企业所有在职员工都应缴纳会费，企业要给予工会提供必要的办公场地及设备。以德尔西项目为例，每月每名在职员工都需缴纳10美元工会会费，但大部分工人及中方员工并未加入工会却仍要承担会费，造成部分员工对公司不满，容易造成矛盾。

（五）应对措施及办法

1. 积极成立工会，争取主动权　海外项目公司可积极成立工会，将中方和当地员工吸纳入会，推举诚实可信人员组建委员会，争取主动权，避免当地人员非法利用工会造成项目损失。在争取工会管理主动权的同时，还应聘请当地劳工律师主动分析应对工会集体合同，协助劳工管理，解决和应对劳工突发事件。

2. 成立专门劳工管理部门　德尔西项目成立了专门劳工管理部门，一名中方负责人管理日常工作，聘请一名或多名当地劳工高管、劳工律师负责合同、管理及纠纷等。设专人负责劳工考勤，建立劳工个人档案，对员工请假、休假、工作表现等进行记录和统计。取得了较好效果。

3. 密切与工会的关系　南美在建项目80%的劳资矛盾源于项目劳工工会。若与工会关系僵持，会严重制约雇主与劳工之间的关系，影响正常生产，甚至可能危及人身和财产安全。积极加强与工会的关系，主动协调出现的矛盾和风险，是保证项目顺利实施的重要前提。

4. 加强员工培训教育　需主动加强当地员工培训教育，促其提高技能和获得知识，增强企业归属感和凝聚力；同时对中方员工不合理行为及时批评和教育，在“尊重、平等”的原则下开展外籍员工管理，和谐的劳资关系能明显促进项目经济效益和社会效益。

5. 积极承担社会责任　海外项目离不开当地社会的支持，所以必须积极承担力所能及的社会责任。①根据当地政府需求，捐赠市政所需设备、设施及物质。②根据施工区域周边居民需求，捐赠水管、水桶等生活用品。③关注当地弱势群体，向孤儿院捐赠衣物，向残疾儿童捐赠轮椅等。④在当地重大节日，如圣诞、元旦等，向当地政府、学校、生活福利机构、项目员工等赠送节日礼品。⑤在遭遇地震、泥石流等自然灾害后，及时捐赠应急物资，调动设备开展抢险救援。⑥响应当地政府号召，积极参与舞蹈节、庆典游行等活动。⑦对进入施工区域的地方道路，项目部义务完善防护等。⑧加强与当地政府部门的沟通，在紧急情况下，确保相关部门能及时提供帮助和保护。在当地政府、居民中树立良好企业形象，让其确信一个具有良好社会责任意识的大型企业必能建成优良的工程项目。

（中国电建集团西北勘测设计研究院有限公司　姚安华）

国际EPC项目分包商结算的精细化管理

国际EPC模式下的工程结算，涉及成本控制、成本核算及风险控制的诸多方面，是合同管理中的重要环节之一，基于精细化管理要求，对国际工程中的分包商结算实行全要素、全过程、无缝隙的管理，不但能使项目设计、采购和施工各过程默契衔接，“环环相扣”，而且能够保证合同实施主体的利润最大化。

（一）国际EPC项目中分包商结算特点及影响

1. 结算的两个极端　在国际EPC项目中，在对分包商的结算上走向两个极端，造成结算管理混乱不清。①对中方严格、对外方松散。以国外某水电站项目为例，在中方分包商结算时，模式套用国内分包商结算模式，其结算资料自行提交，结算步骤和程序略微复杂。在对当地分包商结算时，多数资料由EPC项目部的合同部代为收集提供，结算的某些工作由工程部与合同部代劳，结算步骤和程序较为简单；在结算程序中，工程部、财务部、主管领导及项目经理的签字审批以平行、非逐级的顺序进行。②对中方松散、对外方严格。以国外某风电项目为例，与前面提到的某水电站项目分包商结算相反。分包商结算时，当地分包商的结算资料由其自行准备，甚为严格；而中方分包商结算时略微粗宽泛，多数资料由EPC项目部的合同部门负责收集提供，而此时合同部只根据工程部已签认工程量进行审核。反映在结算程序中，工程部、财务部、主管领导及项目经理的签字审批按顺序进行，不可平行进行，审批采取逐级负责制。③两个极端影响成本控制。国际项目结算宽严不一的情况，弱化了合同管理对项目顺利实施、对项目能否盈利的管控力度。

2. 结算格式多样化　在国际EPC项目分包商结算管理中，没有形成分包商结算管理程序，出现多种结算格式、程序和制度。①中国特色。主要表现在两个方面：一是在格式上仍然采用国内申报表格格式。

二是出于“与人方便”考虑，对国内分包队伍，合同模式采取“模拟的”内部队伍管理模式。即共用总（发）包方公司名称进行商业活动和经营，结算采用内部循环报账。此时，总（发）包方被动承担法律风险、税务风险，而分包商可以独善其身。与此同时，给分包商用总（发）包方的资金干别人的项目打开了方便之门。②国际特色。在分包商结算时，货币支付一般采用美元或者当地货币，因此汇率变化是非常重要的。在中东某国市政工程实施中，分包合同签订时，汇率固定为6.2。3年后合同中期结算时，市场汇率已经飙升至6.8，导致分包商损失惨重。③多样化导致成本核算复杂化。结算格式既有中国特色，又有变通的折中格式，还有以发包方名义进行经营活动和结算的分包商特点；既有项目所在国的支付货币、汇率影响，又有不同的税务政策，势必引发成本核算复杂化。因此，国际EPC项目分包商结算，不能简单套用国内结算程序。

3．结算管理不规范　①同一合同的补充或变更的单独结算。对于工期较长的国际项目，由于参与合同管理的人员流动性强，遇到分包商签订补充合同或工程变更时，往往容易出现单独结算而非原合同项下结算。②同一分包商不同标段的累计结算。对于当地分包商管理难度较大，以及项目管理人员流动性大，为了便于管理，往往出现同一分包商的不同标段累计结算。③大融合不利于风险控制。若同一合同的补充或变更单独结算，就无法形成一份完整的结算资料，难以迅速反映此合同结算状态，不利于风险控制。相反，针对同一分包商的新增工作，不加以区分，均采用同一合同的补充协议模式无原则累计结算，会出现无数次支付预付款，无数次让分包商提交预付款保函事件。这样很容易出现预付款递减不清楚或保函金额不对等事件。甚至于不同合同，有时也采用累积结算，导致合同结算混乱。某一个合同结算或者管理出现了问题，就牵扯到其他合同的正常执行和管理，会影响整个项目的顺利履约。合同管理的基本要素由合同内容约定，无论各分包商与发包方签订多少合同，对于分包商管理和结算都应根据对应的具体合同进行，有效把控结算风险。

（二）完善分包商结算的对策

1．反映要素的统一格式　分包商结算必须采用能反映结算要素的统一格式，既可追溯结算过程又可反映结算内容。①时间横轴管理。从时间横轴管理角度来看，一张完善的分包商结算单或支付凭证应能清楚、明了地反映某一事项的截止上次结算、本次结算及截至目前的结算状态。每个合同通过连续的多次支付凭证，完整地反映此合同的整个结算过程。②事项纵轴管理。根据事项纵轴管理，一张完善的分包商结算单或支付凭证，从上到下简单、明了地反映分包商本次结算（变更）、扣减（预付款支付、扣回和未扣回）；质保金扣除、返还和未返还；罚款；税款及实际支付金额以及未支付金额的所有明细。

2．统一结算程序　①结算过程中的各部门负责制。结算由合同部发起，工程部对现场“工程量”负责；合同部对“量”复核，对“价”负责；财务部复核“价”，对“财务和税务”政策负责。随后提交至主管领导及项目经理进行审批。②结算过程中一票否决制。在结算过程中，各部门对不符合的结算内容，一票否决，经修改审批通过后，完成结算。

3．各部门应增强成本概念　凡涉及变更、索赔、扣罚款有关文件，各部门应及时通知合同部及财务部。合同管理人员应有责任心和职业操守，财务部对此应进行监督。例如，项目实施中某部门协助分包商代购材料，协议此项金额在分包商结算中扣除，但代购部门在工作完成后，并未通知合同部，造成合同部不知情而漏扣。又如，中东某国政府规定在该国注册的公司可免收合同金额5%的增值税。虽经严格审核，但未在该国注册的公司5%的增值税屡屡漏扣，税金自然由总（发）包方承担。因此，项目各部门主观能动性的发挥，对项目成本控制影响甚大。

4．实行单个合同负责制　可避免同一分包商的不同标段结算、成本和风险混合，堵塞合同结算管理漏洞。①“一合同”“一管理”。无论某分包商在此项目上有几个标段，均应实施一个合同一项管理工作。对每个合同的往来文件单独编号，提交如预付款保函和履约保函等相应的合同资料；实施单个合同过程管理，保证扣罚款等一一对应，最大程度上降低合同履约风险等。②“一合同”“一结算”。一是同一合同项下的变更、索赔和反索赔等结算，均应在同一个合同的结算过程中不断累积，而不是单独进行变更或索赔结算。二是同一分包商的不同合同结算，不能机械地在同一合同基础上进行补充，无法清晰反映每个合同执行状态。若出现人员流动，易导致各种风险漏洞不断涌现。

（中国电建集团西北勘测设计研究院有限公司
张星　安科强）

国际工程造价文件编制方法研究

随着全球经济不断发展和一体化，国内各企业的国际工程业务比重日益增加。准确地编制工程造价文件，有利于投资决策、行业影响及项目盈利。目前，国内尚未发布统一的国际工程造价文件编制规范，国际工程因国别不同，其政治、经济和文化迥异，编制造价文件的相关政策要求不一致，人工工资和效率及技术能力、施工机械的进口程度、国内工业化程度、地方税收等差别较大，根据参与若干国际工程造价文件编制工作实际，结合印度尼西亚苏拉威西省拉苏洛水电站工程设计概算（简称拉苏洛概算）对国际工程造价文件的编制方法进行一些研究。

（一）工程造价差异

国际工程大多分布在发展中国家和不发达国家，部分国家尚未形成完善的行业标准和规范，大多依靠其他国家的技术支持。我国各行业标准和规范已建立完善的体系，也基本被当地政府和业主所认可，但因其政治、经济和文化方面与国内相差较大，虽然采用的标准和规范基本与国内一致，造价文件编制却有一定的差异，现分析如下：①人工费。当地人工工资一般较低，但其效率及技术能力也偏低，需要花费较长的时间和较多的指导；中方人工在国外需要支付较高的工地补贴，工资水平与国内相比较高；当地劳务法对当地劳务的占比有一定的要求，需通过分析综合确定人工预算单价。②材料费。部分主要建筑材料（如水泥、钢筋等）在当地不具备生产条件，需通过进口采购，运杂费高昂；部分主要建筑材料（如炸药、雷管等）对公共安全隐患较大，所在国管制较严，采购基本被指定公司垄断，价格高昂。③机械费。大型施工机械基本需要进口，其折旧、修理、安拆的条件均较复杂。受到当地进口机械出入境政策影响或由于退场费用异常高昂，大部分进口机械在项目完工后无法转移回国，若无后续项目基本处于闲置状态，而在闲置期间需要大量的保养费用，部分企业不得已任其报废，无法采用国内机械折旧费标准计算其费用。④其他直接费。包括冬雨季施工、夜间施工增加费，小型临时设施摊销费，安全文明施工措施费及其他费用。该项目相关措施和临时设施一般与国内相似，其费用可采用国内类似地区的相应标准编制。⑤间接费。受当地税收制度、物价和汇率影响，承包人管理人员工资和差旅交通费用与国内相比较高，施工人员和机械进退场较复杂且费用较高，导致承包人组织施工生产和经营管理所需要的企业管理费一般有所增加；受当地税收制度影响，中方和当地人员需缴纳的社会保险费用一般较高，部分国家的工会组织也会提出比较严苛的规定，导致承包人用于生产工人及管理人员的规费一般有所增加；受国际工程风险较大的影响，承包人为筹集资金而发生的各项费用一般有所增加，如金融机构手续费、保函手续费等。⑥税费。当地税收制度一般与国内相差较大，对中方企业的财务要求较高，多数国家无论建安施工或设备采购均缴纳增值税，其税率远高于国内建安工程税率，部分国家除了缴纳增值税外，还需缴纳交易税、消费税等不同明目的税费。在国际工程实施前期，须对当地的税收制度做充分调研。

（二）编制方法概述

根据上述分析，材料费和税费可通过前期的充分调研准确把握，人工费、机械费、间接费可结合工程实际具体分析确定，若能准确把握这些费用的重大差异，国际工程造价文件的质量就能得以保证。因此，在国际工程造价文件编制中加入人工费、机械费、间接费等投资分析复核的内容十分必要。现参考国内工程造价文件编制，结合拉苏洛概算编制经验，在充分收集当地政策法规、行业标准、建材来源、材料价格、运费和税费等基础资料的基础上，对人工费、机械费和间接费等重点费用的编制方法进行研究。

（三）编制方法研究

1. 人工费　①人工预算单价。在工程实施过程中，人工预算单价编制应遵守当地劳务法中关于保证当地劳务用工比例的规定。结合中方和当地劳务的技术能力水平，综合考虑高级熟练工、熟练工、半熟练工、普工的中外用工比例。对中方人工，可参考国内企业境外补贴标准在费用标准规定的人工预算单价基础上进行调整；对于当地人工，可针对显著的工效降低和加班补贴、奖金等因素就当地人工预算单价进行适当调整。如拉苏洛概算人工预算价格中，高级熟练工的中国人工比例为100%，熟练工的中印人工比为2∶8，半熟练工的中印人工比为1∶9，普工的印尼人工比例为100%。②人工费分析复核。国际工程造价文件编制完成后，应重点分析复核中外人工比例、人工费比例、人工总费用的合理性。经对拉苏洛概算人工费统计分析：中外人工比复核，中方人工定额耗量约681人·年，当地人工约6603人·年，当地劳务用工占比约90%，满足当地劳务法规定；人工费比例复核，建筑安装工程直接费约105957.96万元，人工费占比约18%，根据类似国际工程实施经验，人工费所占比重基本合适；人工总费用复核，根据施工组织设计报告，本工程平均人数约为1000人，工期7年，人工总耗量约7000人·年。经统计分析，人工定额总耗量约7283人·年，基本与施工组织设计人工总耗量相当；中方人工工资约88341元/(人·年)，当地人工工资约19273元/(人·年)，与市场价格相当。经分析，人工总费用基本合适。

2. 机械费　根据拉苏洛水电站施工组织设计配置的施工机械种类和数量，经初步估算，该工程施工机械购置费共计约11768万元。若根据国内《水电工程施工机械台时费定额》计算，该工程施工机械折旧费约3400万元，约占购置费的30%。因当地主要施工机械需进口，进退场较复杂，根据当地进口机械出入境相关规定，该工程机械难以转移回国，考虑加速折旧，施工机械折旧费统一在定额标准基础上扩大1.6倍，调整后的机械折旧费约为5477.86万元，约占购置费的47%，与国内折旧过半的施工机械购置费相当，基本合适。

3. 间接费　根据工程实际，经初步估算，该工程间接费共计17287.89万元，经分析测算，若按国内《水电工程费用构成及概（估）算费用标准（2013年版）》计算，该工程间接费约为15000万元，与实际费用相比略有不足。因此，间接费费率按实际费用统一进行调整。

国际工程造价文件编制是一个极其复杂的过程，拉苏洛概算编制表明，材料预算单价和税费可通过前期调研准确把握，人工预算单价、施工机械折旧费、间接费可结合工程实际具体分析确定；各行业间造价文件编制有一定相通性，可根据工程实际研究借鉴。

（中国电建集团中南勘测设计研究院有限公司
张庆　柳娜）

企 业 管 理

中国长江三峡集团有限公司水电工程建设创新管理情况

中国长江三峡集团有限公司（简称三峡集团）认真贯彻国家关于加快建设创新型国家的号召，结合自身实际提出主动服务“六大战略”、积极打造“五大平台”、努力实现“三大引领”、努力完成“三大转变”的发展战略。充分发挥创新是引领发展的第一动力作用，经过数十年的不断发展，取得了一系列水电工程建设与运行核心关键技术的突破，在水电规划设计、施工、初期运行管理等方面已建立健全较为完备的技术管理体系，形成了大型水电工程建设成套关键技术，全面提升了水电事业发展的科技含量。已成为世界上水电装机规模最大、在建规模最大、发展速度最快的清洁能源公司之一，水电科技水平已跻身国际先进行列，成为引领世界水电技术发展的重要力量。

（一）水电创新世界引领

历经三峡工程和金沙江下游水电开发建设，三峡集团在百米级江河深厚覆盖层防渗结构、大坝复杂基础无盖重固结灌浆、复合散能爆破快速施工等方面取得重大突破，创造了高水头大流量泄洪消能、全坝应用低热水泥混凝土、超大型地下洞室群开挖与支护等一系列世界纪录，以核心科技筑就5座世界装机规模排名前10位的超级水电工程。

三峡集团建设运行的葛洲坝、三峡、向家坝、溪洛渡、白鹤滩和乌东德这6座水电站，总装机容量超过7000万kW，是长江上重要的水电站群和骨干电源点。三峡集团充分发挥牵头组织和系统集成的核心作用，带动全产业链在新技术、新材料、新工艺、新装备等方面升级换代，使中国水电装备用20年时间走过了发达国家100年的发展历程，实现了从三峡工程70万kW机组技术的追赶，到向家坝80万kW机组的整体超越，再到现在白鹤滩正待安装的100万kW机组的全面引领这三大跨越，通过实现巨型水电机组自主创新，让中国水电装备逐渐成为全球水电行业的响亮品牌。

三峡集团成功建造了世界上技术难度最高、规模最大、承载力最强、安全性更好的三峡升船机，攻克了大型设备研制和高精度安装等一系列技术难题，齿条螺母柱等大型部件制造达到国际领先水平，实现了从中国制造到中国创造的飞跃。三峡集团坚持自主创新、集成创新，推进管理、设计、技术、工艺全方位创新，广泛应用世界前沿科技，确定将乌东德工程建成“精品工程、创新工程、绿色工程、和谐工程、廉洁工程”、将白鹤滩工程建成“精品工程、创新工程、绿色工程、民生工程、廉洁工程”，全面提升工程智能建造水平。立足中国水电技术保持世界引领、面向国家重大科研专项和乌东德、白鹤滩水电站工程建设需求，在大坝智能建造、百万千瓦机组制造安装、库区地质灾害防治等世界级重大技术问题进行攻关，始终保持全球水电开发领跑地位。

（二）环保创新绿色发展

三峡集团除国内大水电是节能减排、保护生态环境的绿色能源主力军，国际业务与新能源业务的迅速发展也为三峡集团建设国际一流清洁能源增添了更多活力。依托福建三峡海上风电产业园，通过自主创新和协同创新，实现从跟跑到引领。同时积极引领中国水电全产业链走出去，建好管好南亚、非洲、欧洲、巴西等重点工程项目，成为“一带一路”建设水电开发的领跑者。

三峡集团对长江干流葛洲坝至溪洛渡梯级水库群实行统一联合调度，建设了国内水电企业规模最大、功能最齐全的流域水雨情遥测系统和智慧调度决策支持体系，研发巨型电站群远方“调控一体化”控制系统，梯级电站水能利用提高率超过4%，有力促进长江“黄金水道”发挥黄金效益。同时，在水电站运行管理中持续开展抗旱补水调度、长江口压咸应急调度和促进鱼类自然繁殖等调度研究。2011～2017年，三峡水库累积实施10次针对“四大家鱼”繁殖的生态调度，促进宜昌江段四大家鱼繁殖规模达到17.6亿颗，繁殖贡献率达40%。三峡集团坚持绿色环保优先，建设工程的同时也积极开展珍稀特有动植物保护工作，多年来也取得了可喜的成绩。三峡集团中华鲟研究所突破了中华鲟淡水全人工繁殖技术难关，实现了中华鲟子二代幼鱼规模化培育。30多年来，累计投放中华鲟500多万尾，运用声呐等追踪标记技术成功追踪幼鱼下行入海。此外，针对三峡地区特有珍稀植物如珙桐、荷叶铁线蕨等研发掌握了一套拥有自主知识产权的引种驯化和移栽技术，迁地保护的1.7万余株三峡特有珍稀植物移栽成活率达到90%以上，数项繁殖技术达到国内领先水平。三峡坝区施工迹地恢复良好，已建成为具有区域影响的三峡珍稀植物保护基地和科普基地。当前，三峡集团正在抓紧筹划投身共抓长江大保护的伟大使命，要在长江珍稀动植物保护、污水处理和水质保护、园林建设等方面深耕细作，为国家科技创新规划的实施做出新的、更大的贡献。

（三）智能创新国之重器

随着市场经济的深入发展，金沙江水电开发面临新形势、新问题。通过开展识别与定位跟踪、物联网、移动互联、云计算等关键技术研究，先后开发应用了建筑市场信息系统、人员设备定位跟踪系统、基于标准业务和工艺流程的质量管控移动应用系统、计量签证系统、物资核销系统、造价信息系统，实现了资源投入、业务过程、真实成本的实时、实地、实物、实人、实据管理，满足工程建设规范化、标准化、流程化、精细化的发展要求，保证大型水电工程安全优质高效地建设和投运。

随着溪洛渡工程在大型水电工程建设全过程数字化动态管控关键技术取得突破性进展，三峡集团根据“全面感知、真实分析、实时控制”的特高拱坝智能化建设理论，决定在乌东德、白鹤滩实施大坝工程智能建造重大科研项目。深入开展大坝混凝土施工全过程监控、大坝混凝土温控全过程监控、多维多场多要素工程全生命周期性态仿真分析与工作性态评价、全坝应用低热水泥混凝土全性能复核和规律研究、大坝智能建造协同与信息管理平台等的研究。切实解决复杂环境下300m级特高拱坝温控防裂、变形协调、抗震安全等三大关键技术难题，建成无缝大坝，保障长江流域国家重大工程的长期安全稳定运行，形成中国坝工智能建造标准和规范，引领水电技术发展，培养数字化人才。确保工程规范、有序、协调、健康、高效建设，升级打造国际一流三峡品牌。

目前，信息平台已初步升级上线混凝土施工、混凝土温控等模块：混凝土施工全过程监控已投入运行，对全仓混凝土数据进行实时采集和分析；混凝土温控全过程监控已初步投入运行，多维多场多要素安全与进度仿真研究取得阶段性进展。实现大坝浇筑无裂缝及一条龙施工全过程、精细化、数字化及科学化管理。围绕长江流域巨型梯级电站群，开展联合智慧调度技术攻关，掌握核心技术和主动权，努力实现由行业并行者向领跑者的转变。

（四）制度创新管理争优

三峡集团按照“业务全覆盖、项目全生命周期”的原则和“分类分级、分层分步管理”程序，完善集团科技管理体系。新编修编科技管理制度13项、废止2项，发布《关于深入开展大众创业万众创新工作的指导意见》，设立员工科研项目，鼓励自主创新。同时，增设科技进步奖和技术发明奖，加大科技创新奖励范围和力度，产生了良好的效果。下一步，三峡集团将不断完善科技创新管理机制，进一步激发员工科技创新活力。①推进科技成果转化和激励。鼓励员工积极申请专利，牵头参与制定技术标准；对具备条件的知识产权，大力推动其科技成果的转化和产业化；加大科技创新资金投入和科技创新支持力度；大力推进科技型企业股权激励政策研究和岗位分红试点，增强核心技术能力；用好用活科技创新投资基金。②培育科研团队和科技人才。以生态环境中心和海上风电产业园等为重点，打造一批国家级科创平台；以重大工程项目为依托，培养一批专业化科研团队；推动建立院士工作站，带动培育一批专家型科技人才；推动建立产业技术创新战略联盟，增强行业引领能力和主导权；积极承担参与国家重点研发计划和课题，提升员工技术水平；做好总结和凝练，形成一批重大科技创新成果。③着力推动大众创业万众创新。用活科技创新投资基金。利用集团资本投资平台优势，设立清洁能源技术创新创业投资基金，以氢能及燃料电池创新技术、先进储能创新技术等能源行业战略性新兴产业投资为主题，加快孵化和培育面向未来的新兴产业，加快推进中小微企业自主创新和成果产业化。④联合工会、共青团委扎实创建职工（劳模）创新工作室和青年创新创效工作室，为广大职工搭建施展才华、岗位成才平台，培育和造就一支知识型、技术型、创新型高素质科技人才队伍。

（摘自2018年《中国三峡工程报》）

黄河上游水电开发有限责任公司2018年经营管理情况

2018年，黄河上游水电开发有限责任公司（简称黄河公司）稳步推进清洁能源高质量发展，扎实推动改革创新，各项工作再创佳绩。首次获得国家电投集团公司（简称集团公司）综合业绩考核第一名。利润总额完成下达目标的134%；年内投产新能源197万kW。截至2018年底，黄河公司总装机容量达1792万kW，其中：水电1083万kW、光伏388万kW、风电189万kW、火电132万kW。资产总额突破千亿元大关。科技引领、绿色发展及经济社会贡献等方面取得丰硕成果。黄河公司荣登“2018全球新能源企业500强”榜单，获得首届青海省“文明企业”称号。黄河公司董事长当选“2018十大新能源年度人物”。太阳能电力公司西宁分公司荣获“全国五一劳动奖状”。

（一）安全环保

狠抓责任落实和体系推进，实现安全目标“零死亡”。健全完善三个责任体系，开展班组安全管理评价，加强安全培训和制度规程调考，建立违章积分下岗和主要负责人连带处罚机制，推进承包商安全等同管理，安全基础进一步夯实。扎实推进安健环体系建设，强化风险预控措施落实，安健环体系“二钻”以上单位超过90%，生产单位HSE管理工具应用率和固化率达到100%。认真落实防汛责任和各项措施，经受住大流量、长历时泄洪考验。防控结合，开展各类专项检查和隐患排查治理，对排查的1363项隐患，整改率99.6%。制定生态环境保护提升方案并扎实推进。中央环保督查问题全部整改完成。持续提升环保设施设备水平，完成鑫业公司生阳极烟气治理等5项环保技改工作。黄河公司西宁火电废水零排放项目荣获“2018年发电行业水处理技术创新成果”一等奖。

（二）生产经营

联合黄河水利委员会（简称黄委会）开展洪水资源化利用和龙羊峡水库汛期限制水位提升研究。加强水情预报与防洪调度相结合，研判黄河上游来水趋势，向黄委会提出龙羊峡小流量泄洪运行方式，及时调整龙羊峡以下各水电站水库运行方式，多年调节水库和梯级水库群协调运行作用得到充分发挥。经积极协调，并取得黄委会和地方政府支持，龙羊峡电站投产31年来，首次达到2600m设计正常蓄水位，水库运用取得重大突破。紧紧抓住黄河来水偏丰机遇，统筹谋划，全年发电量同比增加49%。正确处理安全生产与发电效益关系，加大汛前龙羊峡出库，加强设备巡查与维护，及时消除设备缺陷，全年完成水电机组检修70台·次，提高了电站持续生产能力。加强市场分析和统筹谋划，创新实施水、火发电权置换，水电新能源送山东、宁夏、陕西、江苏等10省区，外送电量同比增加45%。完善对标工作机制，扎实开展“两金”压控，存货同比降低2744万元；收回各类陈欠账款6.01亿元，占应收陈欠账款的61%（不含补贴）。按期完成集团公司物资采购管理系统推广应用。除大宗原材料外，物资集中采购比例达到97%，降低采购成本约5%。主动加强议价谈判，融资成本处于市场最低水平。完成15亿元的债转股工作，资产负债率降至70.76%。强化税收筹划，加强政策争取，每年减免土地使用税3947万元，全年所得税税负比集团公司平均值低19%。

（三）机制改革

组建资产管理中心、电力运营公司、维检公司等单位并试运行。持续深化内部分配制度改革，风电公司、电力检修公司、中型水电公司等单位陆续实行市场化薪酬分配机制，项目部经理负责制、标准成本控制等配套制度同步运行。因地制宜开展“三供一业”移交，23个项目全部按期签订移交协议。

（四）企业管理

在持续强化经济责任审计和工程审计的基础上，对6家单位创新开展履职专项内控评价。全面优化提升内控合规体系，决策、招标、合同、资金4个领域实现线上合规审查。提高依法治企和法律风险防范能力。深入开展制度评估、修编及宣贯工作，全年修编制度124部。黄河公司本部通过“三标体系”认证；生产型单位质量管理体系贯标率达到100%。优化财务共享系统，资金计划在共享平台全流程管理，新增两家财务集中管控单位。加强全过程合规管理，加快前期手续办理和后期竣工验收，有效降低政策风险。18个项目完成土地证、房产证办理。羊曲水电站河段环评和移民安置规划报告获得批复。拉西瓦、积石峡、班多水电站完成竣工结算和部分专项验收。拉西瓦水电站完成移民安置专项验收，为其他电站移民验收积累了宝贵经验。巨亭水电站提升至正常高水位，完成工程竣工验收。加快信息化建设，加强网络信息安全管理，ERP系统拓展了综合统计和合同管理模块。

强化“三基建设”，紧紧围绕“6·30”发电目标、防洪度汛等重点工作，开展“亮身份、见行动、作表率”主题实践活动，成立巡察工作机构，制定五年规划，全面启动内部巡察。驰而不息纠正“四风”，加大监督检查力度，强化制度约束，作风建设在巩固中不断深化。总结完善派驻、联点单位垂直监督机制，不断提升监督质量和效果。加大企业文化宣贯力度，推进文化理念与公司战略、管理、行为全面融合。新闻宣传多维度展示公司发展成果，在多媒体发表报道995篇，荣获中国电力新闻特等奖和一等奖。扎实开展安全生产民主监督、技能竞赛等专项工作，全面提升员工安全意识和技能水平。获得青海省安全知识竞赛第一名。深入开展“安全生产·青年争先”等主题实践活动和青年创新论坛，激发青工队伍生机与活力。2名青年获评“全国青年岗位能手”，1个集体荣获“全国青年安全生产示范岗”荣誉称号。

（五）扶贫工作

协助青海省政府成功化解省投集团外债到期兑付风险，稳定地区经济发展。承办“国家电投远方助学”研修班，系统培训了100名边远贫困地区骨干教师。成立扶贫工作机构，制定精准脱贫行动方案，大力开展脱贫攻坚。建成羊旗村清洁能源供暖示范项目，援建畜牧养殖合作社，购进并培育藏羊1100余只。广大员工捐款118.4万元建立了扶贫专项资金。定点帮扶的尕布村已实现脱贫摘帽。黄河公司获得“省级定点扶贫先进单位”“成效显著的省级结对共建单位”荣誉称号。

（黄河上游水电开发有限责任公司　许为宁）

湖北清江水电开发有限责任公司2018年经营管理情况

（一）经济社会效益

清江梯级电站运行方式灵活，在发电的同时，承担了华中电网大部分调峰调频任务，在防洪、航运和旅游方面发挥了巨大的经济效益和社会效益。

1. 发电效益明显　2018年清江流域梯级电厂完成发电量73.63亿kW·h，上缴各项税费近10亿余元。2018年梯级电厂通过优化水库调度和运行方式，累计节水增发电量4.09亿kW·h，增发率5.3%。

2. 防洪效益突出　2018年清江流域总降水接近常年略偏少，降水时空分布不均，具有强降水发生早、冬春季降水偏多、夏秋季降水偏少、极端性强、旱涝交替等特点，通过梯级水库调度，保障了流域全年下泄流量均衡，未发生重大洪涝灾害；汛期水布垭水库与隔河岩水库共为长江中下游防洪预留10亿m^3防洪库容，使清江干流梯级的防洪能力大为提高，也为长江中下游防汛提供有力支持。2018年4月22日，隔河岩～高坝洲区间出现平均日雨量达132.9mm的强降水，其中高坝洲单站日雨量达到301mm，为有资料记载以来同期最大值，高坝洲站最大6h雨量频率超50年一遇，最大24h雨量接近50年一遇。清江梯级水库调度中提前预控将高坝洲库水位降至78.5m附近运行；在实际调度根据降雨强度实时调整发电安排，将部分发电负荷转移至水布垭水库减小隔河岩下泄流量，有效遏制高坝洲库水位的快速上涨，成功避免高坝洲弃水，洪水调度过程中库区未出现因泄洪原因引起的各类安全事件。

3. 生态效益显著　2018年梯级水库在长期调度策略和实时调度中统筹兼顾生态基流需求，同时多次应地方政府要求对高坝洲库区水体进行置换，切实履行社会责任，做好生态环境保护工作。

4. 促进旅游经济　在隔河岩水库建成后，形成了高坝大库，风景优美，长阳县旅游经济继续保持较好的增长态势，除国家5A级景区隔河岩库区清江画廊外，清江方山景区获评国家4A旅游景区，乡村旅游快速发展。截至2018年底，长阳县乡村旅游示范点达30多个；长阳第三届廪君文化旅游节、“清江画廊杯”2018年全国马拉松游泳锦标赛等大型综合性节庆赛事和榔坪木瓜花节、渔峡口椪柑展销、清江方山万人年猪宴等系列乡村旅游受人瞩目，“大美清江、梦幻长阳”的品牌影响不断扩大。2018年长阳县累计接待游客超过950万人次，实现旅游收入92.3亿元，旅游业固定资产投资完成5.3亿元。

（二）水布垭工程通过国家竣工验收

2018年12月26日，湖北清江水布垭水电站工程竣工验收会在宜昌召开。会议通过了湖北清江水布垭水电站工程竣工验收鉴定书。该电站位于清江中游河段湖北恩施土家族苗族自治州巴东县境内，是清江流域梯级滚动开发的最上一级龙头工程，总装机容量184万kW，设计年发电39.84亿kW·h，是清江干流上最大的梯级电站，是华中电网骨干调峰调频电站。233m水布垭大坝是世界最高混凝土面板堆石坝。截至2018年底，水布垭电站已累计发电405.3亿kW·h。在2016年清江流域100年一遇特大洪水和2017年50年一遇特大秋汛中，水布垭枢纽工程发挥了显著的防洪效益。电站的建成还极大带动了地方经济发展。

水布垭水电站工程2002年1月获国家开工批准，同年10月实现截流。2007年7月首台机组发电，2008年8月4台机组全部投产。自2010年2月～2018年11月，先后通过了消防、枢纽工程、工程档案、劳动安全与工业卫生、建设征地移民安置、水土保持、环境保护、工程决算等8个专项验收。

水布垭水电站工程竣工验收，标志着清江流域水电开发建设使命圆满完成，工程进入正常运行管理、全面发挥效益的新阶段。

（三）安全管理

2018年，清江公司认真贯彻落实湖北能源关于加强安全工作的要求，以防人身事故、防设备事故为重点，克服流域电厂设备老化、高危项目密集开工、清江流域隔—高区间遭遇历史罕见暴雨等不利安全因素，圆满完成湖北能源下发的年度安全生产目标，连续保持清江公司安全生产良好态势。

1. 流域 22 台机组连续 2 年实现“双零”目标 清江公司流域电厂 22 台机组连续 2 年全部实现“零障碍、零非停”的“双零”目标。其中，隔河岩电厂连续 8 年实现机组“双零”目标，高坝洲电厂连续 5 年实现机组“双零”目标，清能公司 11 台机组连续 3 年实现“双零”目标，水布垭电厂连续 2 年实现“双零”目标。

2. 连续 8 年保持安全生产形势稳定向好 2018 年，清江公司 24 个高危项目密集开工，通过安全风险分级管控和隐患排查治理双重机制的有效运行，全年未发生各类安全事件，安全生产连续 2 年全口径实现“零障碍、零事故”的“双零”目标。安全管理水平得到行业主管部门、地方安全监督管理部门、三峡集团、湖北能源认可。

3. 成功应对隔—高区间 50 年一遇罕见暴雨 2018 年 4 月 22 日，隔—高区间遭遇 50 年一遇历史罕见暴雨，给高坝洲电厂生产运行和高坝洲日调节的水库安全运行均带来极大危害。通过对以往大洪水应急管理经验总结和积累、通过超前预控水位和开展梯级电站间负荷转移，成功应对了这场历史罕见暴雨，未发生洪涝灾害造成财产损失、水库弃水、水淹厂房事件。

4. 质量监督管理规范有序 2018 年，是清江公司质量监督管理工作全面开展的第一年，清江公司从建章立制起步，起草了《清江公司质量监督管理标准》《质量、安全责任追究管理标准》，以检修现场、晒谷坪电站增效改造项目日常质量巡视、开展丰富多彩的质量安全月活动作为工作的切入点，以一般质量问题、质量缺陷的调查、分析、处理为抓手，质量监督管理态势初步树立，各单位、员工质量意识明显提高。

（湖北清江水电开发有限责任公司）

国网新源控股有限公司 2018 年经营管理情况

国网新源控股有限公司（简称国网新源公司）成立于 2005 年 3 月 31 日，是国家电网有限公司直属单位之一。截至 2018 年末，国网新源公司管理单位 60 家，分布在 20 个省（自治区、直辖市），管理装机容量 6020.4 万 kW。

（一）人力资源

坚持党管干部原则，健全选拔、培养、任用、激励、考核、监督六位一体的管理体系。坚持正确用人导向，以党建综合考核为抓手，落实“一报告、两评议”制度，全面从严加强干部队伍建设。加大专家人才培养力度，构建生产准备人员和基建人才培训体系，形成机电、技经和水工 3 个专业，新手、熟手和熟手、能手两个层级的共 6 张学习地图和 6 个培养体系。优化党校、一中心三基地发展规划，构建“企业大学”培训体系，一机多模仿真培训系统、心理实训室等实训场室试运行，完成 12 门管理类内训课程和 78 个水电运维类培训课件开发，强化人才培养，员工队伍素质持续提升。

（二）发展规划

主动适应外部政策环境变化，组织开展抽水蓄能服务电网、新能源消纳、储能技术等研究，及时研判关联行业和市场发展态势。成功引入国内上市公司和地方能源企业资本，在衢江项目完成抽水蓄能混合所有制改革试点。跟进和参与选点规划调整，浙江等 4 省份选点规划取得批复，从源头控制项目投资风险，巩固了良好开发格局。深入践行“两山”理论，严格贯彻落实生态环保要求，推行项目前期“两个机制”，系统排查疏导制约因素，开展可研阶段专题内审，依法合规推进项目开发。完成浙江衢江、山东潍坊、吉林蛟河、河北抚宁、新疆哈密等 5 个项目核准开工任务，桐城等 13 个项目可研、栗子湾等 17 个项目预可研有序推进，公司管理装机容量突破 6000 万 kW。

（三）经营管理

面对融资趋紧情况，探索资金信托运作方式，落实融资租赁 21.35 亿元，完成公司发债 20 亿元，资金保障能力进一步增强。历年陈欠增值税退税额全部收回。加强抽水蓄能电价政策研究，推动建立合理价格机制，丰满大坝重建工程电价测算、新投产项目电价申报等工作稳步推进，已投产电站实现电费全额结算。解决历史遗留问题，亏损企业治理工作取得重大突破，国投公司完成改制，小孤山清算工作有序推进。推进信息化智慧型企业建设，完成公司数据资产管理体系顶层设计，开展公司级全业务数据中心技术架构和技术选型设计，明确电站级数据中心总体要求，信息化建设取得阶段性成果。加强“三全五依”法治企业建设，注重发挥法律审核保障作用，成立在京单位法律服务中心，开展丰宁法务经理制试点工作。推进技术创新，形成科技创新成果 111 项、管理创新成果 88 项、QC 成果 85 项，取得专利授权 258 项，完成国家、行业及国网技术标准报批 21 项，获得中国电力、水力发电等省部级科技进步奖 15 项。聚焦工程安全质量，发挥大党建价值创造力。国网新源公司获评全国“安康杯”竞赛活动示范单位，16

家基层单位获评优胜集体，4个班组获评优胜班组。

（四）生产运行

编制全员岗位安全责任清单，组织安全述职，完善安全奖惩制度，安全责任体系更加严密。创新建立区域安全稽查机制，试点开展东北区域安全稽查。召开建设项目施工单位、设计单位、监理单位座谈会，实施安全质量履约分级约谈，保障工程建设质量。组织主机设备缺陷通报会，开展发电电动机、主变压器、球阀、水轮机等主设备健康状态评价方法研究，从源头探索设备质量提升方式方法。加强缺陷隐患防治，开展“六查六防”、危化品治理、电气火灾治理等专项行动，针对家族性、典型性缺陷组织专项反措排查，全年排查治理隐患298项，消除缺陷7652项。加强设备运检管理，完成机组检修198台·次，机组启动成功率继续保持99.95%以上。注重安全领域科技创新，“五系统一中心”研究与应用项目获得国家能源局电力建设领域安全管理一级成果。圆满完成上合青岛峰会、中非北京峰会、上海进博会等重大保电任务。

（五）工程建设

组织召开设计、施工、设备数字化专题座谈会，开展设备智能化研发，推进数字化智能型电站研究和建设。深化“五系统一中心”建设，完成基建智能管控系统的研发和应用。加强“三通一标”建设，完成通用设备7个分册、通用设计5个分册、通用造价1个分册的编制工作，修订18项标准化施工工艺示范手册。推行区片制、架子队、安全文明施工“5S”管控、第三方安全质量巡查等管控手段。开展无爆破切割等24项施工技术、装备研究及应用，工作效率、工程质量和工艺水平大幅提高。江西洪屏抽水蓄能电站获得国家优质工程“金奖”，浙江仙居抽水蓄能电站获得中国安装优质工程奖（中国安装之星）。2018年12月12日上午，丰满水电站旧坝拆除工程成功实施首次爆破，这座运行了80年之久的大坝结束了历史使命，进入坝体混凝土拆除阶段。

（国网新源控股有限公司　韩冰）

南方电网调峰调频发电有限公司 2018年企业管理有关情况

截至2018年底，南方电网调峰调频发电有限公司（简称调峰调频公司）已建成投运的电厂有7座，总装机容量980万kW，包括：天生桥二级水电站132万kW（6×22万kW）、鲁布革水力发电厂60万kW（4×15万kW）、广州蓄能水电厂240万kW（8×30万kW）、惠州蓄能水电厂240万kW（8×30万kW）、清远蓄能水电厂128万kW（4×32万kW）、海南琼中抽水蓄能电站60万kW（3×20万kW）、深圳抽水蓄能电站120万kW（4×30万kW）。在建抽水蓄能电站有2座，总装机容量240万kW，其中，梅州抽水蓄能电站120万kW（4×30万kW）、阳江抽水蓄能电站120万kW（3×40万kW）。正在建设海南文昌2×46万kW级燃气—蒸汽联合循环电厂。拥有国内首个兆瓦级电池储能站——深圳宝清电池储能站，目前已投运0.6万kW。

（一）项目前期工作

积极推动海南后续天然气电源规划，提出海南后续气电开发建议，完成琼海气电项目选址工作并得到地方政府认可，琼海市政府已向海南省发展改革委报送了启动琼海气电项目前期工作的请示报告。

密切跟进广西抽水蓄能选点规划、贵州抽水蓄能选点规划审查，以及广东调峰电源发展规划专题（2017～2030年）、抽水蓄能选点规划研究专题（2017～2030年）开展情况，编制南方五省区抽水蓄能规划选点报告，启动了南宁项目前期工作。

（二）水电科技发展

推进科技项目成果应用，大力推进水下机器人在水电厂的应用，完成天厂、广蓄以及南网系统外锦屏电厂水道检测工作；按计划推进国家重点研发专项“海水抽水蓄能电站前瞻技术研究”项目，新增了国家重点研发专项“梯次利用动力电池规模化工程应用关键技术”项目；举办第三届调峰调频技术论坛，评选了58篇优秀论文，其中，一等奖8篇，二等奖16篇，三等奖34篇。

2018年，获得中国南方电网有限责任公司专利奖（三等奖）1项，职工技术创新奖（三等奖）1项；完成专利申请63项，授权50项。

（三）标准化工作方面

2018年，加强规范性文件文本审核，重点关注关联文件的管理要求，增加部门会签流程及集中评审环节，全年共召开17期制度集中评审会，印发管理制度55项，作业指导书2项，业务指导书17项。

优化法人治理结构，制定《公司法人治理结构优化方案》，理顺公司治理关系，对各子公司章程进行全面修订，明确分公司治理结构。公司管理制度体系目前涵盖安全管理、生产管理、调度管理、规划建设、营销服务、人力资源、财务管理、物资管理、信息管理、监审内控、党群工作、行政办公、基础管理等13个领域。截至2018年底，调峰调频公司有效管理制度164项，典型作业标准250项。

（南方电网调峰调频发电有限公司　曹娅）

华能澜沧江水电股份有限公司 2018年经营管理情况

2018年，华能澜沧江水电股份有限公司（简称澜沧江公司）紧紧围绕中国华能集团有限公司（简称集团公司）发展战略和工作部署，实现了发展规模、质量和效益同步提升，在集团公司年度绩效考核中排名第一。截至2018年底，澜沧江公司投产装机容量达2120.88万kW，占云南省统调装机容量的28%，占统调水电装机容量的41%。全年完成发电量817.22亿kW·h，占云南省调发电量的31.12%，占云南省调水电总发电量的37.62%。继续保持云南省装机规模第一、发电量第一。按照“一级法人、两级管理”体制，本部设置20个职能部门，下设31个二级单位，并代管滇东能源公司及其下属3家基层企业，共有员工3100余人。

（一）安全管理

安全管理责任进一步加强。各单位狠抓隐患排查、违章整治，强化风险管控，“全员安全生产责任制落实年”等专项活动取得实效，继续保持全年零事故良好态势。防洪度汛、应急处置扎实开展，各项目实现安全度汛；金沙江上游两次堰塞湖险情、苗尾库区沿江公路滑坡等得到妥善处置，瑞丽江一级电站进水口边坡塌滑治理顺利完成。“生态攻坚”取得新突破，大华桥、里底、乌弄龙水电站蓄水阶段环保验收顺利通过，黄登水电站建成国内首个升鱼机过鱼系统。安全文化建设成效显著，苗尾·功果桥和糯扎渡水电站荣获“全国安全文化示范企业”称号，小湾电厂运维四班荣获“全国安全管理标准化示范班组”称号。

（二）市场营销

深挖潜力，紧抓政策、抢发电量、提升电价、开拓市场，获得西电东送协议内电量336亿kW·h；促成云电送桂汛枯比调整，增送汛期电量21亿kW·h；实现云贵水火置换交易价格提高2.8分/(kW·h)；探索梯级运行方式，小湾、糯扎渡两库首次消落至死水位，增发枯期电量约20亿kW·h；构建“日分析、周总结”电量协调机制，完成汛期省内交易合约、西电东送增量95亿kW·h；澜上电价攻坚战取得阶段性胜利，澜上电站2018年130亿kW·h电量实现全额消纳；能源销售公司实现独立运作，代理用户电量同比翻了5番，创建三方合作机制，有效增加了瑞丽江一级电站枯期发电收益；一系列举措实现关键指标同比大幅提升、量价协同进一步优化，发电量连续两年实现两位数增长。

（三）生产经营

机组动态检修在全流域推广实施，缩短检修工期81天，增发电量3亿kW·h；功果桥、漫湾电厂先后实现“无人值班”运行，生产领域改革发展带来的活力日益凸显。小湾、龙开口等一批机组设备缺陷问题得到有效解决，大修全优率同比提高1.2个百分点，景洪等6个电厂实现全年“零非停”。18台新投机组实现无缝交接、稳定运行，创造了突出的经济效益。累计厂用电率、供电煤耗同比下降。合理压降成本费用支出，切实降低融资成本，持续优化资产结构，按期完成金中公司股权转让。全年实现营业收入155.16亿元，同比增长20.78%，发电量同比增长11.62%。

（四）项目发展

机组投产再创纪录，苗尾、黄登、大华桥电站全部投产，里底两台、乌弄龙首台机组发电，托巴开关站按期投运，发挥了电站投产最大效益。融入“一带一路”取得重要成果，柬埔寨桑河二级电站全部投产并顺利转入商业运行，得到柬埔寨国家高度肯定。“一年十八投”任务高质量超额完成，基建信息网、数字大坝技术深入推广，工程实物质量进一步提升，桑河7号、大华桥4号及乌弄龙1号等机组投产达到“精品机组”要求。项目前期有序推进，缅甸瑞丽江二级项目已与亚洲世界公司签署合作协议；柬埔寨上丁、松博项目预可研立项获得集团公司同意；托巴项目投资、市场消纳、电价问题研究进一步深化，工程开工建设指日可待。

（五）创优创新

成功申报4项“十三五”国家重点研发计划项目，获得授权专利34项，成功入选云南科技创新智库第一批成员单位。检修分公司自主完成7个电站和托巴500kV开关站检修和调试工作，检修核心技术攻关取得突破。景洪水力式升船机科技创新成果荣获国家技术发明二等奖，高碾压混凝土坝成果获大坝工程学会科技进步特等奖。糯扎渡水电站获詹天佑奖，小湾水电站申报詹天佑奖通过评审，滇东胜境、一把伞风电获电力优质工程奖。全年共获国家级科技奖励1项，省部级科技奖励17项。

（六）企业管理

持续深化体制机制改革，实现“需求、采购、决策”三分离；全面修订公司本部内控手册，废止、新建、修订制度134个，管理流程和制度运转更加贴合，工作效率和执行力大幅提升；初步建立以业绩为引领的正向激励机制，绩效奖励在完成难点、重点工作方面的激励作用得到充分发挥。法律和决策事项管理进一步优化，全年984份签报均从法律、内控、审计、业务角度分别进行了审核，管理风险得到有效防控；东升矿业诉讼案最终取得全面胜诉，规避了重大损失。

各项宣贯活动扎实开展；巡视组反馈的8个方面39类77个问题已全部整改完成；作风建设成效明显，大力开展“机关作风建设年”、形势任务教育等活动，设置“慵懒散”曝光台，公司上下干事创业热情更加聚集，促进了管理与责任、监督的有效融合；群团优势得到有效发挥，工会活力不断增强，“送医下基层”等活动深获职工好评，职工道德讲坛扎实开展，模范引领，凝聚合力。小湾电厂运维部获得“全国工人先锋号”称号，糯扎渡电厂生技部、苗尾·功果桥电厂机电物资部分别获得“云南省工人先锋号”称号。

（七）和谐水电

澜沧江公司累计投入15亿元，帮扶澜沧、沧源、双江、耿马四县拉祜族、佤族聚居区，实施精准扶贫。同时投入1663万元实施“百千万工程”，着力解决澜沧江周边群众“看病难、吃水难、行路难、发展难”等问题，实施“素质提高、民生保障、民族文化和生态保护”四项主题工程53项，惠及云南、西藏10州（市）25个县（区），荣获“云南省扶贫先进集体”称号。扎实推进环保制度建设、环保“三同时”管理、环保风险管控、环保验收、环保科研和水土保持等项工作，修编《环境保护水土保持工作规定》，印发《污染防治攻坚实施方案（2018～2020年）》，在建工程和电厂环境保护未发生环境污染事件。

（华能澜沧江水电股份有限公司）

国电大渡河流域水电开发有限公司2018年经营管理情况

大渡河流域水电开发有限公司（简称大渡河公司）是集水电开发建设与运营管理于一体的大型流域水电开发公司，为国家能源投资集团有限责任公司（简称国家能源集团）下属大一型企业、四川省工业企业最大规模50强企业和最佳经济效益10强企业。大渡河公司股东分别为国家能源集团（原中国国电集团公司）、国电电力发展股份有限公司、四川川投能源股份有限公司。

2018年，在国家能源集团的坚强领导下，大渡河公司坚定不移贯彻落实国家能源集团年度工作部署，围绕“四个认真、四个坚持”年度工作主线，推进智慧企业建设，主动作为、奋发进取，各项工作全面完成，各项指标再创新高，公司安全生产保持连续13年无事故纪录；日发电量、月发电量、年发电量均创历史最好水平；再次获得国家能源集团考核A级。

（一）工程建设情况

大渡河公司依托龚嘴、铜街子两座母体电站，对四川大渡河和西藏帕隆藏布流域水电资源实施“流域、梯级、滚动、综合”开发，拥有水电资源约3000万kW。截至2018年底，大渡河公司投产装机容量2340万kW，年发电量415亿kW·h，在川投运装机容量占四川统调水电总装机容量的1/4，承担了四川电网主要调峰调频任务。目前，大渡河公司所属大渡河干流龚嘴、铜街子、枕头坝一级、沙坪二级、深溪沟、瀑布沟、大岗山、猴子岩等水电站已投产发电，金川水电站、参股并代管的双江口水电站正在建设，沙坪一级、枕头坝二级、老鹰岩、丹巴、巴底和安宁等水电站正在积极开展前期研究工作。

（二）安全生产管理

严格落实安全风险管控责任，动态管控重大危险源，安全风险可控在控。扎实推进安全文明生产标准化建设，制定并落实三年达标计划，大岗山、枕头坝、革什扎通过国家能源集团达标验评。落实“安全隐患排查深化年”要求，印发《安全生产诚信承诺和诚信报告制度》，开展“重细节、找问题、强管理”专题活动，高质量完成流域七厂九站检修改造任务，设备健康水平持续提升。加强防汛安全管理，开展实战应急演练，成功应对了“5·21”乐山沙湾突发山洪险情和“7·12”瀑布沟建库以来最大洪水。全面建成安全风险管控数据中心，有效防控了猴子岩开顶、大岗山黄草坪滑坡体变形加剧风险，大渡河公司安全风险管控数据中心获第三届中国设备管理创新成果一等奖。大渡河公司连续9年获中央在川及省属重点企业安全生产先进单位，被评为四川省唯一的电力企业安全监管同业对标综合标杆企业，实现连续安全生产4872天。

（三）生产经营情况

坚持以效益为中心，提前谋划，多渠道争取有利政策，促成瀑深枕三站联调补偿等优惠政策落地。科学研判市场，动态调整合同谈判策略和节奏，实现年度保价增量目标。强化财务集中管控，认真落实“两压双控”措施，度电可控成本同比降低22.06%，资金归集率达到99.5%。

（四）智慧企业建设

加快推进智慧企业建设项目落地，主导编写《智慧企业指引》，在2018中国智慧企业论坛上成功发布，成为首个智慧企业建设行业标准。大渡河公司决策指挥中心初步建成，采购与合同数据中心、智慧物资管控中心等21个专业数据中心投入使用，财务共享数据中心稳步提升，智慧工程、智慧电厂、智慧调度、智慧检修四大单元脑试点全面推广，建成水电大数据平台和企业级数据仓库。举办了科技创新大会、首届智慧企业大数据建模竞赛，大渡河公司智慧企业成果在全国企业管理创新大会、第二届中国企业改革发展论坛等平台上作经验交流，代表国家能源集团在北京科博会和第二届“一带一路”科博会等高级别大型展会上展示，大型水电机组定子局放智能监测预警关键技术在大岗山、铜街子、深溪沟水电站成功应用。

（五）科技创新情况

积极响应国家“双创”号召，依托智慧企业建设，积极布局电能替代市场，发挥好成都清洁综合能源公司平台作用。主动拓展碳交易市场，完成了国家能源集团39家企业碳盘查。落实与成都市政府签订的战略合作框架协议，积极参与成都低碳经济新模式建设，成为成都低碳城市试点建设的第三方专业服务机构。统筹推进氢能发展研究，与东方电气等燃料电池研发机构签订战略合作协议，成为成都市氢能联盟副理事长单位。整合成立大汇科技平台公司，大力拓展技术研发、产品推广、咨询服务等新产业。

（国电大渡河流域水电开发有限公司）

12

水电站生产运行

电力生产及管理

中国长江电力股份有限公司 2018 年生产管理情况

2018 年，中国长江电力股份有限公司（简称长江电力）全面完成了年度各项工作任务，全年发电量 2154.82 亿 kW·h，生产经营指标均创历史新纪录，改革发展取得新进展。

（一）水库来水及水位情况

2018 年，三峡水库来水总量为 4569.75 亿 m^3，平均流量 14500m^3/s，最大流量 60000m^3/s，出现在 7 月 14 日；最小流量 3850m^3/s，出现在 2 月 28 日；来水与历史同期多年均值相比偏多 1.3%；与上年同期相比偏多 8.4%。2018 年三峡水库平均库水位 162.56m，比上年同期高 0.34m；最高库水位 175.00m，出现在 10 月 31 日；最低水位 145.05m，出现在 6 月 11 日。

葛洲坝水库主要对三峡下泄的非恒定流过程进行航运反调节，基本按照径流式运行，库水位主要依据三峡电站调峰、两坝间及葛洲坝下游航运要求进行控制。2018 年，葛洲坝水库平均库水位为 64.64m，与上年同期低 0.11m。

2018 年，溪洛渡水库来水总量为 1574.08 亿 m^3，平均入库流量 4990m^3/s，最大流量 16300m^3/s，出现在 7 月 16 日；最小流量 1400m^3/s，出现在 4 月 13 日；来水与历史同期多年均值相比偏多 7.8%，与上年同期相比偏多 13.2%。2018 年溪洛渡水库平均库水位 579.27m，比上年同期低 1.88m；最高水库水位 599.89m，出现在 10 月 17 日；最低水库水位 547.90m，出现在 5 月 30 日。

2018 年，向家坝水库平均库水位 375.48m，比上年同期低 0.86m；最高水库水位 379.92m，出现在 10 月 17 日；最低水库水位 370.27m，出现在 6 月 30 日。

（二）电力生产情况

梯级电站 2018 年总发电量 2154.82 亿 kW·h，较上年同期多发电量 45.89 亿 kW·h，增加 2.18%。其中，三峡电站完成发电量 1016.15 亿 kW·h，较上年同期增加 4.11%；葛洲坝电站完成发电量 183.18 亿 kW·h，较上年同期减少 3.85%；溪洛渡电站完成发电量 624.69 亿 kW·h，较上年同期增加 1.76%；向家坝电站完成发电量 330.80 亿 kW·h，较上年同期增加 0.72%。

梯级电站单日、单月和全年发电量，以及三峡、溪洛渡年发电量均刷新历史纪录。三峡电站发电量首次突破千亿大关，再次刷新国内单座水电站年发电量纪录。

（三）安全生产情况

长江电力继续以“五大安全风险”管控为抓手，深入推进双重预防机制建设。扎实开展承包商安全施工能力评估和二十五项反事故重点要求实施情况评价，安全风险管控关口进一步前移。大力推进科技兴安，运用“互联网＋”、大数据等信息化、智能化手段提升本质安全型企业建设水平，设备关键性管理指标保持行业领先水平，梯级电站安全生产实现“零人身伤亡、零设备事故”目标。

（四）年度岁修情况

2017～2018 年度岁修共安排机组 A 级检修 5 台·次、C/D 级检修 70 台·次，输变电设备检修 84 项。该年度岁修工作 2017 年 11 月 1 日开工，长江电力科学谋划，克服工期紧、任务重等不利因素，严把安全、质量、进度关，于 2018 年 6 月 2 日高质量完成。

2018～2019 年度梯级电站检修从 2018 年 10 月 14 日开始，计划 2019 年 6 月 10 日结束。共安排 A 级检修 8 台·次、B 级检修 2 台·次、C/D 级检修 73 台·次；安排输变电设备检修 94 项。

三峡电站 2018～2019 年度岁修工作从 2018 年 10 月 14 日开始，计划 2019 年 5 月 26 日结束；截至 2018 年 12 月底，完成 B 级检修 1 台·次、C/D 级检修 11 台·次、8 项输变电设备检修。

葛洲坝电站 2018～2019 年度岁修工作从 2018 年 10 月 22 日开始，计划 2019 年 6 月 1 日结束；截至 2018 年 12 月底，完成机组 C/D 级检修 6 台·次、输变电设备检修 11 项。

溪洛渡电站 2018～2019 年度岁修工作从 2018 年 10 月 25 日开始，计划 2019 年 6 月 10 日结束；截至 2018 年 12 月底，完成机组 C/D 检修 3 台·次、输变电设备检修 6 项。

向家坝电站 2018～2019 年度岁修工作从 2018 年 11 月 16 日开始，计划 2019 年 4 月 29 日结束；截至

2018年12月底，完成机组C/D级检修2台·次、3项输变电设备检修。

（五）梯级枢纽效益

深入贯彻“三精”理念，通过优化联合调度，梯级电站累计节水增发电量99.3亿kW·h，为梯级电站发电量再创新高、三峡电站发电量首次突破千亿大关做出突出贡献。三峡工程汛期成功应对4场超44000m^3/s洪水，梯级水库累计拦洪150亿m^3，防洪减灾成效显著；三峡水库连续第9年实现175m试验性蓄水目标，枯水期累计为下游补水227亿m^3；积极开展梯级枢纽联合生态调度试验。梯级枢纽巨大社会效益得到国家防总和社会各界高度评价。

（六）科技创新成果

长江电力坚持科技引领、创新驱动，通过科技创新解决实际难题、提升管理效率。规划推进公司智能化建设，开展电站设备在线监测系统整合及智能决策支持系统研究。成功研制水电站水下检查检修专用机器人，激光技术在水电行业应用取得新成果；葛洲坝智能电站数据信息平台成功上线运行；全年国家授权专利211件，共获得约50项行业、集团公司技术创新成果奖，全年Ⅰ类自主科研项目申报数量大幅提升，创历年新高。科技创新呈现量、质双提升的良好发展态势，科技创新成果得到了行业和中国长江三峡集团有限公司的高度肯定，其中“流域梯级水电站协同调度关键技术与应用”获得2018年度水力发电科学技术奖一等奖、“三峡电站调速器冗余结构建模及故障反演仿真研究”获得第六届全国电力行业设备管理创新成果特等奖，长江电力获得中国长江三峡集团有限公司“2018年度科技管理先进单位”等称号。

（中国长江电力股份有限公司　王军）

三峡水力发电厂 2018年生产管理情况

（一）电力生产情况

2018年，三峡水力发电厂机电设备运行安全稳定，实现年度“双零”目标；32台单机容量为700MW的机组连续两年实现“零非停”，截至2018年12月31日，电厂连续安全生产4520天；年发电量1016.15亿kW·h，创历史最高纪录，成为全国首个单座年发电量突破1000亿kW·h的电厂，连续第二年年发电量居世界第一。

全年发电设备（不含电源电站）利用小时台平均为4521.87h，同比增加179.65h；机组平均可用小时（运行小时与备用小时之和）为8169.19h，同比减少28.32h；机组平均等效可用系数为93.66%，同比下降1.14个百分点。三峡电源电站发电设备利用小时台平均为4824.64h，同比减少53.85h；机组平均可用小时为8421.18h，同比减少200.86h；机组平均等效可用系数为96.13%，同比减少2.3个百分点。

全电站机组自动开停机4087台·次，成功4082次，成功率99.88%，其中开机成功率为99.76%。

2018年7月3日，三峡电厂34台机组实现当年全部并网运行，7月19日，出力达到满负荷22500MW。全年34台机组全开运行累计1184.27h，其中，22500MW设计额定出力累计运行352.38h。

2018年三峡电站500kV输电设备保持安全运行，未发生非自然因素导致的计划外停运；500kV母线电压合格率100%；自动装置投入率100%。

（二）防洪及试验性蓄水情况

2018年汛期，三峡水库来水相对丰富，最大洪峰流量达60000m^3/s，出现在2018年7月11日。汛期，三峡电厂共收到长江防总8条调度令、三峡梯调44条操作令。三峡电厂严格按照调度要求执行：泄洪深孔23孔先后开启运行，启闭88扇次，累计运行2031.19h；排漂孔共开启1孔运行，启闭6扇次，累计运行15.5h，泄洪设备设施操作正确率100%，泄洪设施运行正常。

（三）检修情况

1. 泄洪设备设施　2017～2018年度岁修期间，三峡电厂完成了23个深孔、3个排漂孔、8个排沙孔的全面检查和检修，完成了3个泄洪深孔弧门水封更换。2018～2019年度岁修中，三峡电站水工金属结构设备主要是常规检修，涉及6个深孔泵站、23个深孔、3个排漂孔、1个冲沙闸和8个排沙孔。

2. 发变电设备　三峡电站2017～2018年度岁修自2017年11月1日开始，至2018年5月20日结束，历时201天，主要完成1台机组A级检修，17台次机组C级检修，8台次机组D级检修；主要实施完成了左岸电站6台机组调速器系统和励磁调节器的换型改造，地下电站机组调速器一次调频程序改进，3号发电机GCB开关加装，保护精益化查评整改，以及32号机组移动备励接入试验等重点项目；新发现并处理了1号机组定子铁芯压紧螺杆断裂、7号机组推力瓦表面存在气孔、圆斑缺陷等问题。

三峡电站2018～2019年度岁修于2018年10月14日开工，计划于2019年5月26日完工，总工期控制在225天。发变电设备方面，计划完成2台机组A级检修、1台机组B级检修、19台机组C级检修、12台机组D级检修。

3. 输电设备　三峡电站母线及出线设备自投运以来，按计划实施GIS预防性试验、出线断复引及清扫等例行维护检修项目，设备运行正常。2017～

2018年度岁修，完成了三峡左、右岸电站和地下电站500kV开关站6条母线、22回进出线检修。

（四）科技创新情况

2018年，三峡电厂共申报获得水力发电科学技术奖1项，第十届全国电力职工技术成果奖3项，湖北省第六届职工技术创新成果奖6项，中国长江三峡集团有限公司职工技术创新成果奖23项，中国长江三峡集团有限公司优秀创新团队2个，长江电力科技创新成果奖43项，实用新型专利14件，Ⅰ类自主科研项目11项，以及第七届全国电力行业设备调控运维优秀班组推荐申报工作，获得中国长江三峡集团有限公司职工技术创新成果一等奖1项和中国长江三峡集团有限公司、中国长江电力股份有限公司40余项创新成果奖。

（五）2018年电站效益

1. 社会效益　2018年汛期，长江上游流域降水总体偏多，尤其是7月份，长江上游岷沱江、嘉陵江及上游其他区域发生多轮次强降雨。三峡水库汛期共迎来5次洪峰。在5次洪峰中，形成两场编号洪水，“长江2018年第1号洪水”（峰值53000m^3/s）和“长江2018年第2号洪水”（峰值6000053000m^3/s）。三峡电厂严格落实上级调度指令，精准控制三峡出库流量，充分利用三峡调洪能力，有效降低了荆江河段超警戒水位，保证了长江中下游防洪安全。

为满足三峡—葛洲坝枢纽下游航运、工农业供水及生态补水需求，三峡电站上游水位从2017年11月26日的174.74m降至2018年6月10日10时的145.24m，累计向下游补水226.7亿m^3。

2. 发电效益　2018年，三峡水库总入库水量为4569.71m^3，同比上年增加355.61亿m^3。三峡电厂积极采取节水增发、节能降耗措施，通过合理安排运行方式、根据水位变化精准调节机组出力、及时清漂、降低厂用电率与变损率（2018年，厂用电率为0.076%，变损率为0.393%）等方式，进一步提高发电效益。2018年，三峡电站发电量1016.15亿kW·h（其中，电源电站发电量为4.8246亿kW·h），完成全年计划发电量的110.09%，较上年同期多发电量40.1亿kW·h，年发电量创历史最高纪录。

（三峡水力发电厂）

向家坝水力发电厂 2018年生产管理情况

（一）电力生产情况

2018年，向家坝水力发电厂（简称向家坝电厂）累计发电330.8亿kW·h，机组等效可用系数96%，年利用小时数5520.96h，单机年最大发电量48.4亿kW·h，设备关键指标继续保持行业领先水平。

2018年，实行“诊断运行”＋“预防性状态检修”的精益生产管理方式，依托在线监测及趋势分析系统，健全各层级、各周期的诊断分析体系。依托年度设备评估结果，统筹规划岁修重点检修项目、非标项目，发扬“一次把事情做好”的理念，及时消除设备隐患1539项，全年自动开停机成功率首次达到100%，8台机组全开并网运行时间长达2847.5h。探索形成了较为成熟的闸门运行方案，全年累计启闭闸门2460次，泄洪设备累计运行2658.36h，闸门动作次数和泄洪设施累计运行时间均创历史之最；下泄洪水362亿m^3，闸门最大泄洪流量达9544m^3/s，泄洪设施经受了长周期、持续泄洪考验。

（二）安全管理情况

截至2018年12月31日，向家坝电厂连续安全生产达2500天，实现“零人身伤亡事故、零设备质量事故、零环保事件”的“三零”目标，未发生责任性弃水及非计划停运事件，连续两年实现“零非停”目标，安全生产创历史最好水平。本质安全建设、重大风险管控、应急能力建设等工作均取得重大进展，优质高效完成了国调继电保护精益化查评，以95.26高分通过“防止电力生产事故的二十五项重点要求”复查评。

持续加强重大风险管控与隐患排查治理双重预防机制，全面落实重大风险管控措施，制定《向家坝电站有害气体廊道风险管控措施》，大力实施大坝廊道通风系统及有害气体在线监测系统整治。强化危险源动态辨识，全年共辨识危险源540项、环境因素60项，通过147次专项安全检查行动，发现并整改隐患300余项，重大风险始终可控、在控，保障设备良好运行状态。

持续提升应急能力建设，完善全厂应急预案体系，新增隧道火灾应急演练、坝区反恐应急演练等全电站管理项目，深入推进“双盲”应急演练方式，全年共开展应急演练55次，高效应对暴雨、雷电等极端恶劣天气35次，应急处置能力得到大幅提升。

（三）工程建设情况

向家坝电厂坚持贯彻“建管结合，无缝交接”的管理理念，全面接管升船机运维管理。精心组织试通航调度工作，建立通航协调机制，健全管理制度和业务流程，发布规程29部、现场操作指南34部、应急预案6部，研究并提出升船机生产管理模式优化建议方案。全力运行管理好升船机通航配套设施、供配电系统等已接管设备，及时发现和治理隐患90余项，完成通航配套设施、下闸首检修门及门机、上下闸首排水系统、10kV/400V 供配电系统、通航建筑物等设备接管运行和首次维护。

2018 年 1 月、9 月，先后完成两个阶段的实船试航试验，测试了在 1600～8250m^3/s 下泄流量时不同船型、不同工况下升船机通航条件和船舶航行特性，为开展通航工作提供了有利的技术支持。2018 年 5 月 26 日，升船机正式投入试通航运行。升船机全年安全通航 105 天，累计运行 591 厢·次、过船 491 艘、通过货物 17 万吨，进一步拉动了金沙江航运事业发展，拓展长江“黄金水道”功能，推动了长江经济带发展。

（四）科技创新情况

进一步健全科技创新机制，规范科研工作流程。推进研究智能预警系统、水电厂工作票办理支持系统，有序实施“智慧电站”建设，初步完成“智慧电站”规划方案，完善“两地办公”方式下的远方应急会商机制。管理创新能力实现新提升，在 2018 年湖北省企业管理现代化创新成果中取得优异成绩，“以智慧电厂为目标，推进水电厂运行工作‘两化’融合”荣获一等奖，“巨型水电站生产部门多专业边界管理探索与实践”荣获三等奖。

2018 年共开展 37 项自主科研项目、19 个 QC 活动课题，申报知识产权 86 项，获得专利 97 项，获批专利数量和质量均创新纪录，荣获中国水利水电质量管理协会“QC 小组先进单位”称号，获得一等奖 1 项、二等奖 1 项、三等奖 2 项。

（五）内部管理情况

打造全枢纽运行管理模式，初步形成三项制度改革常态化建设，有序完成“新三定”人岗对应收尾工作，完善以业绩价值贡献为导向的业绩考核评价体系，形成差异化薪酬激励的长效机制。深化人事管理改革，通过岗位平级调整和选拔补充等工作，推动建立了“干部及管理人员能上能下”周期化、常态化长效机制，提振了广大干部员工干事创业的精气神。

建立以技术委员会、专业委员会及专业工作组为构成的三级技术管理体系，充分发挥技术优势，促进各专业融合，全面提升设备管理水平和技术创新能力。全面落实新体系下三标一体化管理要求，完成体系文件换版和认证工作。运用族标准思路，提出水电行业公用辅助设备 8 部标准编制建议，共主编或修编、翻译 14 部公司级、行业级技术标准，大幅提升了电厂技术竞争力和行业影响力。

坝区管理、升船机运维及通航管理新业务蓬勃开展。不断健全完善坝区管理制度体系，成立向家坝电站社会治安综合治理等组织机构，强化坝区消防安全监督，实现全年坝区管理“六不发生”目标；加快推进向家坝电站安全保卫立法及专用公路移交等重点项目，完成坝区永久规划方案招标，实现坝区环境新跨越。以建立“大系统全覆盖、运维合一”的升船机生产管理体系为目标，围绕设备性能完善、通航效率提升、设备智能化维护、船舶安检自动化建设、升船机运维一体化管理等开展研究，持续优化完善管理流程，总结运维调度经验，提高通航管理水平和应急处理能力，促进通航管理提质增效，着力打造行业标杆。

（向家坝水力发电厂　陈保臻）

黄河上游水电开发有限责任公司所属大中型水电站 2018 年生产管理情况

（一）班多水电站

2018 年，完成发电量 16.32 亿 kW·h，综合厂用电率 0.69%，耗水率 10.52 m^3/（kW·h），故障弃水 0 次；实现安全生产“八不发生”，全年安全生产 365 天，累计安全运行 2635 天。

建立了安全生产三大责任体系；组织开展涵盖 62 个岗位安全生产责任制修编工作。修订安全生产管理制度 86 部、技术标准 77 部，对健康安全环境（HSE）管理工具应用相关管理要求进行融入、固化；识别、获取安全生产、环保、职业健康、质量相关法律法规、规章制度及国家、行业标准 62 部，上传至 OA 系统，补充、完善了法律法规数据库。

制定并落实 2018 年应急管理重点工作计划，完善应急管理机构，修订完善应急预案 24 部，编制发布应急处置卡 115 张，组织开展各类应急演练 19 次，应急能力建设自评估得分 708.5 分，得分率 74.6%（合格）。

深入开展隐患排查治理。按类别建立检查表库，编制标准检查表 34 张；全年共排查出各类不符合项 152 项，完成整改 138 项，整改率 90.78%；未整改项已制定整改计划，并采取临时防范措施。

认真落实年度安全教育培训计划，拓宽思路，提升培训效果。修订承包商安全管理规定，有效防范和遏制承包商安全生产事故。

组织实施 330kV 出线电气设备改造工程、厂内桥式起重机电气控制系统改造、电站污水处理系统设备改造、大坝防汛电源改造、电站安全设施专项治理、后方供电电源改造，委托天津大学进行机组进水口事故闸门动水落门试验，不断提升设备健康、经济运行水平。

汛前完成了班唐线出线设备改造，积极开展“防汛及电网大面积停电”以及“防汛及水淹厂房”双盲实战应急演练，提高全员应急能力。2018 年，电站遭遇 10 年一遇的洪水，最大入库流量达 3330m^3/s。全厂上下合力，积极应对，累计清除漂浮物及拦污栅杂物 7348.6m^3，确保电站安全度汛。

每月定期召开生产工程项目专题会，完善招标工作流程，做好成本控制工作，全年共签订合同 72 份，各项经济活动运转良好。

加强车辆管理，完善交通危险点路线图，确定了安全协理员职责，截至 2018 年 12 月底，安全行车 29.3 万 km。

开展班组建设自评价及整改工作，召开班组建设经验交流观摩会，成立创新工作室；开发领先指标卡 13 张，推行领先指标卡线上运行，降低班组人员负担。认真开展 QC 小组活动及成果发布，海洋王 QC 小组的“降低运行电量报表计算耗时及错误率”课题获黄河上游水电开发有限责任公司（简称黄河公司）三等奖；组织班组长到广西长洲水电站、广州抽水蓄能电站开展班组建设调研，交流学习经验，逐步规范班组建设。

（二）龙羊峡水电站

2018 年，完成发电量 76.88 亿 kW·h，完成年计划的 112.62%；综合厂用电率 0.72 %，发电耗水率 2.96m^3/(kW·h)，运行负荷率为 82.63%。

调整安全生产委员会及安全生产监督体系、保证体系、应急管理体系的成员及职责，修订安全生产责任制有关规定。编制了 HSE 管理工具的应用实施导则和应用固化提升整改任务分解表，补充完善了作业现场、设备、工器具的目视化管理标示。针对辨识出的 16 个中高风险制定控制措施计划，明确年度重点管控风险。深入开展各种安全大检查活动，针对发现的隐患制定整改措施。

完善防汛制度 8 部、应急预案 8 部。组织开展了库岸边坡大规模滑塌的专项应急实战演练，完善水情测报系统，增加观测设施，增设泄水雾化区的安全警示和防护隔离，确保电站安全度汛。汛期共提落闸门 196 次，55 天泄洪期间保证了电站设备设施的安全运行。11 月 5 日，水库水位首次蓄至设计水位 2600m，及时采集大坝运行性态数据。

完成机组 C 级检修 5 台·次、D 级检修 2 台·次，线路检修 4 条次；处理了 4、2 号机组励磁滑环碳刷打火、2 号机组顶盖真空破坏阀底座焊缝开裂、3 号机组尾水人孔门漏水等重大缺陷；针对年内机组长期大负荷运行工况下主变压器温升居高不下，特别是 3 号主变压器总烃超标等问题，采取管路隔磁、法兰处加装短接线、强迫风冷等措施，确保主设备持续安全稳定运行。

落实技术监督年度计划，2018 年共计完成技术监督项目 3600 项。开展了基于电站监控系统数据的大数据分析应用，实时掌握设备运行性能和安全健康水平。

2018 年，共排查隐患 107 条，整改率达 100%。严格执行“两票三制”，共执行开停机 653 次，办理工作票 1200 张，操作票 1062 张，“两票”合格率 100%，有力推动了安全生产局面持续稳定。

成立质量管理体系工作领导小组，开展了质量管理体系建立、贯标工作。经过评审，质量管理体系建设工作被准予注册，按期通过了质量管理体系贯标认证。

合理安排机组运行方式，优化负荷分配，耗水率同比降低 15%，运行负荷率达 80%以上，超计划完成年发电任务。

加强预算管理，提高资金使用效率。2018 年，共签订各类合同 156 份，合同金额 8913.81 万元，合同履约率达 100%。全年压控金额 22.43 万元，压控总库存的 6.10%；同时，及时对淘汰、废旧物资进行处置，处置物资占固定资产总额的 0.8%，提高了资产使用效率。

组织开展环境污染因素辨识工作，编制了突发环境污染专项应急预案。按照当地政府的批复和实施方案，办公区域生活污水管网于 9 月份接入龙羊峡镇市政污水管网。全年未发生“三废”污染事件。

2018 年，修订发布管理标准 169 部、技术标准 131 部、工作标准 68 部，并及时组织制度宣贯培训。

修订完善中层干部管理规定、员工岗位动态管理规定，调整岗位 25 人次，占全体员工总数的 20%。开展重点岗位人员的专项取证培训，共 44 人次参加了专业培训。

依托职工创新工作室，规范有序开展职工创新工作，结合设备检修和技改开展“五小”“QC”成果发布，积极鼓励员工创新创造，共取得创新成果 13 项。

（三）拉西瓦水电站

2018 年，完成发电量 130.04 亿 kW·h，完成计划的 113.23%；综合厂用电率 0.44%，较计划值降低 0.13%；发电耗水率 1.87m^3/(kW·h)，较计划值降低 0.06m^3/(kW·h)。实现全年安全生产 365 天，长周期安全生产记录 3521 天。

健全安全生产保证、监督、支持三大责任体系。加大反违章查处力度，2018 年，查处严重违章 2 起；发出各类处罚单 24 份，考核金额 5.36 万元；发出嘉奖单 5 份，奖励金额 0.98 万元。持续完善安健环体系建设，HSE 管理工具的应用率和固化率达到 100%。2018 年，通过了第二方评估，达到了安健环“三钻”水平。

年内按计划完成应急预案演练 13 次，其中果卜岸坡变形体塌滑专项应急预案演练采取实战演练方式进行，得到黄河公司相关部门和州县安监局等有关部门的好评。

增强外委工程安全管控能力，2018年共完成修理项目32项、技改项目3项、零购项目4项。

全年累计出车10275次，车辆安全行驶39万km。

汛期，加强枢纽工程和果卜岸坡变形体观测数据的跟踪，面对黄河多年一遇的洪水，电站累计泄水47天，总泄水量22.91亿m^3，3个表孔累计操作263次，创电站投运以来泄流时间最长、单孔操作次数最多纪录。

强化技术监督问题整改，规范技术监督管理。全年完成电气设备绝缘监督项目共405台次、金属监督84件、化学监督286次，热工、电测表计检定425块。先后发现1B A相乙炔含量异常、750kV GIS 14B气室异常放电、6号水轮机转轮叶片裂纹等重大设备隐患，为检修策划提供了技术支撑。

全年共排查出隐患284项，发现缺陷133项，已处理缺陷123项，消缺率为92.48%，针对暂不能整改的隐患均制定了整改计划，并采取了防范措施；办理工作票2195张，执行操作票420张，两票合格率100%。

为提高“两个细则”管理水平，对AGC、AVC功能进一步完善，有效降低了考核分值，全年考核9985.7分、补偿44511.9分。

全年共修订发布管理标准115部、技术标准62部、工作标准59部。启动“三标一体”管理体系贯标认证工作，制定管理体系建设方案，注重与安健环体系有机融合，2018年底，企业“三标一体”管理体系顺利通过中国船级社认证审核，取得认证。2018年，举办内部培训24次，累计525人·次参加；参加高培中心培训9人·次，累计592学时；参加黄河公司、西北网调等举办的各类培训86人次，累计1792学时。

2018年，企业生产成本各项资金费用完成率均为100%；累计完成公开招标项目4项、询比价项目54项、签订各类合同111份，未发生违规情况，经营行为规范有效。按期完成了企业“两金”压控目标。组织开展班组安全管理评价工作，细化班组建设管理，规范班组“三会一活动”；每月开展专业班组小指标竞赛，激发班组活力。

（四）李家峡水电站

全年发电量71.12亿kW·h，完成年计划的112.06%，创历史新高；综合厂用电率0.443%，较计划值降低0.14个百分点；发电耗水率3.28 m^3/(kW·h)，较计划值低0.07 m^3/(kW·h)。全年实现了“八个不发生”“三个一百天”“零事故、零死亡”，未发生人身轻伤、设备异常及以上安全事件，安全生产365天，长周期安全记录6782天。

进一步优化三大体系的工作界面和管理职责。扎实推进安健环、“三标一体”管理体系建设。25项HSE管理工具全部得到应用。组织完成了安健环年度内审及管理评审工作，得分58.08分。2018年10月，中国安全科学研究院对企业进行“三标一体”监督评审，认定体系运行符合认证要求，并保持认证注册。

年内开展各类专项检查和隐患排查治理19次，共发现隐患235项，已闭环整改228项，整改完成率为97.02%。全年安全行车约24万km无事故。较出色地完成了电站周边的消防救援任务，被地方政府授予荣誉锦旗2面。

组织开展李家峡水电站地质灾害隐患排查，共排查出10个地质灾害隐患，编制完成李坎公路滑坡群勘测及稳定性评价综合试验报告及物探报告。开展了水淹厂房双盲式实战演练、夜间水淹厂房应急演练等10项防汛专项应急演练。2018年7月12日～10月11日，3孔泄水道分3个时段进行泄水，历时47.58天，总泄水量33.41亿m^3，闸门操作172次，水道修复抢修7次。水电站经受住流量大、历时长的泄洪考验，确保了大坝安全度汛。

全年共完成机组检修6台·次，跨年度B、C修各1台·次，D修3台·次，B修1台·次；完成全厂公、辅助设备检修项目；完成厂内、坝内电梯及11台起重设备年检；完成11台压力容器外观检查；计划监督项目完成率、合格率均100%；完成修理项目36项，技改、零购项目21项，信息化项目5项。

加强设备缺陷、两票及开停机管理。全年共发现缺陷101条，消除92条，主要完成了转轮裂纹处理35条，处理了2号机组上导摆度超标、水导甩油、导叶漏水量大、尾水人孔门母材裂纹等安全隐患；完成了1、2号主变压器油气套管，第一、二串开关，GIS大修及隔离刀操作机构更换，以及1、2号机组在线监测安装等工作。执行操作票846张、办理工作票2699张；执行开机539次、停机539次，开停机成功率均为100%。

全年“两个细则”共发生考核7352.913分，补偿32812.05分，综合补偿25459.137分，在黄河公司所属电站综合补偿分排名第一。

修订了24部应急预案，补充完善了应急物资及其台账记录，开展了年计划专项预案演练，提高了企业应急管理水平和防范、处置应急事件的能力。及时完成政府督办的李坎公路滑坡群隐患、生产区域污水系统改造，以及电站前后方油、水、噪声检测工作等

26 项环境保护重点工作。

全年主动向调度申请停机或调整负荷 910 次，其中同意 583 次；担任系统第一调频厂 1000.64h，未发生系统频率越限情况；全年系统电压、频率合格率为 100%。

2018 年，废止 12 部不适用的管理标准和规定，发布并备案 209 部管理标准、31 部规章制度、24 部应急预案、176 部法律法规，合并修订 77 部技术规程，新增 19 部管理标准、2 部职业健康管理制度、7 部党群管理制度、10 部职业健康相关法律规章、15 部环境保护相关法律规章及标准，确保制度建设情况符合企业管控实际，满足正常工作需要。

强化合同管理，最大限度规避经营风险。全年共签订合同 137 份，电商采购 7 批次，合计金额 12091.37 万元，其中公开招标采购金额 6471.34 万元、询价采购金额 564.54 万元、直接采购金额 4954.23 万元，材料费用、可控成本、存货余额等均未突破考核指标。

全年举办及参加各类培训班 97 个，累计培训人数 1425 人次；年内，11 名安全管理人员、2 名高空操作人员经培训取证，14 名员工取得救护员培训合格证，19 名员工取得进网电工许可证，企业主要负责人与职业卫生管理人员均取得职业卫生健康培训合格证，2 名员工完成了电焊工培训取证及复证，5 名员工进行了压力容器培训取证。

（五）公伯峡水电站及苏只水电站

公伯峡水电站：全年完成发电量 64.19 亿 kW·h，完成年计划的 111.18%；综合厂用电率 0.26%，较计划值低 0.24 个百分点；发电平均耗水率 3.86 m^3/(kW·h)，较计划值高 0.06 m^3/(kW·h)。苏只水电站：全年完成发电量 11.02 亿 kW·h，完成年计划的 105.60%；综合厂用电率 0.57%，较计划值低 0.15 个百分点；发电平均耗水率 22.71m^3/(kW·h)，较计划值高 1.86m^3/(kW·h)。

安全生产局面总体稳定，环保工作有序开展，实现“八不发生”，安全督察问题可整改项整改率 100%，年内安全生产记录 365 天，长周期安全记录 2113 天。

组织编制发布了《HSE 工具与分公司管理制度融入对照表》，年内共完成了 18 部安全生产管理标准的修编工作。加大现场安全监督检查力度，年内通过各类安全检查共发现问题 145 项，整改完成 140 项，整改率达 96.55%。共考核两票违章人员 25 人·次，离岗培训 1 人·次，考核管理人员 12 人·次。严肃承包商考核管理，年内发现并纠正违章 3 次，停工整改 2 次，考核金额 3000 元。完成“三标一体”监督评审和换版工作，评审组一致同意企业三标体系保持认证。

完成了应急预案的修订、外部评审、备案和发布工作，完成了相应演练工作。开展应急能力评估，评估得分为 75.1 分。

修订了水淹厂房、局地暴雨、超标准洪水、地质灾害等应急预案，并有组织地开展了水电站防汛应急抢险实战演练，取得了良好的防范效果。

组织完成了公伯峡水电站 1 号机组 A 级检修，2、3、5 号机组 C 级检修，4 号机组 D 级检修；组织完成了苏只水电站 1、3 号机组 C 级检修，1、2 号机组 D 级检修工作；消除了公伯峡水电站 3 号机组推力油冷器漏水、4 号机组主轴密封漏水量过大和苏只水电站 3 号机组主轴密封漏水量过大等重大缺陷。完成强震系统改造、水情自动化系统安装、监控网络安全检测装置安装、起重设备维修、消防控制系统维修、直流系统换型、工业电视改造、苏只水电站检修动力盘更换等项目。实施公、苏两站监控系统物理整合，顺利实现了两站在公伯峡中控室的集约化控制。

年内通过隐患排查共发现隐患 28 条，治理 26 条，整改治理率达 93 %，未整改的 2 项已按要求建立了隐患排查治理档案。加强“两票三制”管理，年内两票合格率均为 100%。加强运行人员业务培训，年底顺利实现了公伯峡、苏只水电站运行人员的合并和两站的集中控制。

提高了经济合同履约能力，全年签订经济合同共计 148 份，没有发生合同纠纷、无效合同等事件。开展“两金”压降工作，公伯峡水电站“两金”压降 40.65 万元；有计划地开展了废旧物资技术鉴定、报废、处置工作，全年共报废处置废旧物资 414 项。将依法治企要求纳入部门综合业绩考核责任书，经济合同法律审查率达 100%。

全年共计制定、修订三大标准 174 部。

（六）积石峡水电站

2018 年，完成发电量 42.25 亿 kW·h，完成年调整计划的 115.37%，同比增加 17.80 亿 kW·h，发电量创历史新高；综合厂用电量 2897.03 万 kW·h，同比增加了 911.55 万 kW·h，综合厂用电率为 0.69%；机组年均耗水率 6.24m^3/(kW·h)，同比减少 0.02 m^3/(kW·h)；保护、自动装置投入率及正确动作率 100%；年累计发现缺陷 235 条，缺陷消除率 100%；技术监督完成率 100%。年内实现“八不发生”“三个一百天”和“全年无异常”的安全生产目标，年度安全运行 365 天，累计安全运行 2947 天。

加强设备缺陷管理，消除了孟清线、孟官Ⅱ线管母漏气等重大缺陷；扎实开展隐患排查治理工作，查出隐患 17 项，治理完成 16 项。深入推进安健环质体系建设，对HSE管理工具应用进行了固化，更新完善了风险数据库。推进和规范环保管理，编制环境保护三年提升计划，实现了站区污水零排放。进一步完善应急管理体系，作为黄河公司试点单位开展应急处置卡编制工作，发布、实施应急处置卡79部、应急操作卡26部。

按计划组织开展各类培训，共21人取得培训证书，举办各类培训班25期，参加606人·次。加强外包工程安全管理，年度内未发生安全事件，外包工程安全管理成效显著。组织各种形式的车辆安全检查24次、车辆检查456台·次，查出并消除车辆存在的安全隐患12项，全年安全行驶27.61万km。

认真开展防汛工程项目的策划、跟踪、落实，5项防汛工程项目均按期完成。汛期及时组织人员对机组进水口拦污栅及坝前漂浮物清理，共清理杂物4000m^3，清理方量较往年增加近10倍。通过合理安排，少泄洪水4.5亿m^3，抢发电量7200万kW·h。

积极开展机组AGC、一次调频控制策略优化，持续提高电能质量，“两个细则”全年补偿20554分。

规范企业经营活动，全年共完成10项招标工作，签订各类经济合同130份，未出现合同纠纷、无效合同等事件。持续开展“两金”压降工作，存货余额较上年减少6万元。加强制度建设，制定企业“三标”修订计划，并明确融入HSE管理工具，年内发布标准268部。强化企业风险管理，查找工程项目管理、健康安全环保等7类风险并制定应对举措。提升内控合规体系建设，结合工作实际，将决策领域表单由原来的4种类型细分优化为12种类型，合同领域表单由原来的4种类型细分优化为6种类型。内控合规表单全部实现线上运行。档案信息化系统顺利投运，实现原有档案系统数据迁移。

组织开展班组安全建设提升工作，提升了班组7S管理水平。黄河公司2018年度班组安全管理经验交流会在积石峡水电站召开，电气班作为代表在会上进行了工作成果交流发言。成立“大禹”职工创新工作室，“发电厂干式励磁变压器散热方式优化研究”项目顺利通过黄河公司专家评审并推进实施，实现了员工自主创新的新突破。

（七）盐锅峡水电站及八盘峡水电站

发电量：全年共完成发电量38.08亿kW·h，完成年度目标的100.51%，全年应发电量完成率达到99.30%，其中：盐锅峡水电站（以下简称盐站）完成27.65亿kW·h，完成年度目标的103.73%；八盘峡水电站（以下简称八站）完成10.44亿kW·h，完成年度目标的92.87%。综合厂用电率：盐站为1.12%，低于指标值0.27个百分点；八站为1.43%，低于指标值0.17个百分点。发电耗水率：盐站为10.76 m^3/(kW·h)，高于指标值0.64m^3/(kW·h)；八站为29.3m^3/(kW·h)，高于指标值2.3m^3/(kW·h)。技术监督完成率：100%。交通安全情况：未发生各类交通事故，全年车辆累计安全行驶43.35万km。实现全年“八不发生”的安全目标。截至2018年12月31日，企业实现长周期安全生产2779天，其中：盐站安全生产6467天，八站安全生产2779天。

加强安全制度建设，修订完善了生产管理类制度37部、安全监督类制度30部、各类技术规程标准280部，并发布了2018年度现行有效的安全生产管理制度目录清单。强化安健环管理提升，狠抓HSE管理工具应用，使企业HSE管理工具全部固化到相关规章制度中，固化率达到100%。配合黄河公司完成了对企业的安全生产尽职督查工作，共完成了各项整改113项。共完成安全技术劳动保护措施计划23项，完成反事故措施计划3项。同时，强化应急管理，编制1部综合应急预案和25部专项应急预案并通过甘肃能监办评审备案；组织完成了盐站、八站电力设备事故桌面演练及防汛实战演练。

强化机组检修、工程项目安全监督管理，开展了工程项目施工安全和承包商安全管理专项治理工作，进一步落实了安全生产主体责任；全年共完成盐站10号机组A级检修和4台机组C级检修，完成了八站2号机组A级检修和3台机组C级检修。

2018年，电站接连遭遇“7·19”“7·23”“8·2”“8·20”4次重大汛情，特别是面对“7·23”历史上最大汛情、两站机组全部被迫停机局面，企业及时应对，迅速启动相应的应急预案，经过13个昼夜的连续奋战，将两站16台机组恢复运行，取得了抗洪抢险最后胜利。据统计，在整个汛期，盐站实测最大出库流量3207m^3/s，最大含沙量151kg/m^3，轻便栅拦污栅清污124栅·次，固定拦污栅清污4栅·次，库区漂浮物清理12次，累计清理污物4500多立方米；八站实测最大出库流量4000m^3/s，最大含沙量216kg/m^3，拦污栅清理85栅·次，门槽漂浮物清理59栅·次，机组蜗壳内杂物清理8台·次，工业取水口拦污栅清理8栅·次，库区漂浮物清理6次，累计清理污物4700多立方米。

强化安全隐患排查治理，全年共治理两站各类隐患39项，消除两站设备缺陷959项。编制实施了《质量、环境、职业健康安全管理体系综合管理手册（2018年版）》，顺利通过了安全管理体系认证。

针对设备陈旧老化、安全可靠性差、生产效率低下、检修任务繁重的现状，开展全面技术改造的可行性研究，委托中国电建集团西北勘测设计研究院有限公司编制完成了《八盘峡水电站全面技术改造可行性研究报告》和《盐锅峡电站1～8号发电机改造工程可研报告》，并通过了黄河公司内部审查和外部专家审查，两站全面技术改造工作取得积极进展。

完成了166部制度的制定、修订工作，充分发挥规章制度对规范生产经营和内控管理的积极作用。扎扎实实推进两大体系建设，已编制完成管理标准144部，发布实施的管理标准7部、技术标准262部，有效提升了企业现代化管理水平。

全年举办各类内部培训班21期，培训职工1186人·次；组织参加黄河公司、集团公司等外部培训班30期，培训职工69人·次；组织参加相关专业技术人员取证、复证等资格培训班6期，共有88人完成了取证复证。

将创新课题与开展QC小组活动相结合，全年共取得“八站机组受油器小缸体结构优化改进”“盐站8号机组AGC调节模式革新”等4项QC成果和10项职工创新成果，并进行了表彰奖励。制定了两站拦污栅优化方案，盐站轻便拦污栅清污时间由原来的4h缩短至2h，固定拦污栅清污时间由原来的3天缩短至25h完成，八站一扇拦污栅清污时间由原来的6h缩短至4h，为主汛期少泄水、多发电提供了保障。

（八）青铜峡水电站

全年完成发电量14.46亿kW·h，完成年计划的102.54%，实发电量完成率100.33%，发电量创历史新高；综合厂用电率1.31%，低于计划值0.24个百分点；发电耗水率21.55m^3/(kW·h)，高于计划值0.95m^3/(kW·h)。11月发生一起起重伤害事故，未实现“八个不发生”安全目标；安全生产标准化达标整改项目完成率100%。

全面推进“三标一体”建设工作，质量管理体系取得中国船级社质量认证公司颁发的认证证书，HSE管理工具应用固化率达到100%，安健环体系内评估57.1%，保持“二钻”评级。安全生产标准化达标整改项目完成率100%，安全生产管控能力不断强化。结合专项安全检查，安排安全监督整改113项，整改完成率100%。专业化安全监督队伍不断壮大，20人完成安全管理资质的复证、换证及取证工作。强化外包工程等同化管理要求，进一步规范作业流程，逐项消除安全死角。

加强隐患排查和缺陷治理，在高温天气、大负荷情况下，加密电气设备红外测温检测和巡回检查，消除2号主变压器低压套管渗油、26T自用变压器绝缘击穿、6号机组事故油系统管路刺油、4号和5号主变压器低压侧进线连接点温度偏高等缺陷，全年消除设备缺陷147项（含光伏电站），治理设备隐患29项（含光伏电站）。主设备预试完成率80.05%；主要仪表校验率91.39%；继电保护及自动装置投入率100%。

全年组织完成6台机组等级检修和4台机组状态检查及检修，主要消除了4号机组水轮机过流部件磨蚀破坏、受油器操作油管和铜瓦磨损，9号机组导水叶卡阻，1、3、5号机组主轴密封磨损严重，1号机组转轮渗油以及机组蜗壳进入树根杂物等缺陷和隐患，保证了机组的安全稳定运行。2018年度下达修理项目51项，投资完成率99.82%，项目完成率98.04%；技改项目13项，投资完成率82.27%，项目完成率76.92%；零购4项，完成率100%。技术监督主要完成预试主设备333台·套，预试完成率80.05%，校验主要仪表276块，校验率91.39%。信息管理工作，电站各项模块完成功能升级、完善及扩展工作；电站局域网完成了网络与信息安全风险评估、调度数据网边界设备的安全漏洞自查与整改。

汛期共计清理拦污栅426孔，清理污物17000多立方米。电站经受住了5个多月持续大流量运行考验。

2018年，共计制定发布技术标准144部、管理标准236部、工作标准183部。修订发布《宁电分公司内控合规管理规定》《宁电分公司内控合规手册（A版）》等规章制度。强化成本管控，持续推进“两金”压降。落实电费回收工作，2018年，电费回收率100%，2017年陈欠电费全部收回。2018年，共组织开展各类培训班40期，参培人数478人·次；12人完成特种作业取证复证。

（黄河上游水电开发有限责任公司　许为宁）

雅砻江流域水电开发有限公司2018年电力生产情况

2018年，雅砻江流域水电开发有限公司（简称雅砻江公司）无新投产机组。截至2018年12月31日，雅砻江公司总装机容量达到1470万kW，分别为桐子林水电站60万kW，二滩水电站330万kW，官地水电站240万kW，锦屏二级水电站480万kW，锦屏一级水电站360万kW。

（一）安全生产情况

2018年，雅砻江公司不断深化“流域化、集团化、科学化”的发展与管理理念，认真组织开展电力生产“严细务实年”活动，通过持续强化风险预控和隐患排查双重预防机制建设、积极推动流域电站与主要设备厂家技术合作、持续加强网源关系协调、持续推动流域电站运行管理模式优化升级等一系列举措，巩固“创新突破”成果，有效保障流域梯级电站稳定发电能力。同时，通过合理控制水库水位消落、深挖梯级电站群经济运行潜力，全面完成年度电量目标。

截至2018年12月31日，雅砻江公司全年电力安全生产情况总体良好，未发生直接责任性一般及以上人身伤亡事故、直接责任性较大及以上事故，安全生产态势持续稳定，各电力生产单位电力生产长周期安全运行天数分别为：二滩水力发电厂4113天、官地水力发电厂1511天、锦屏水力发电厂2195天、集控中心2565天。

（二）水库运行情况

2018年，雅砻江流域来水属偏丰水系列，其中两大控制性水库：二滩水库为季调节水库，天然来水频率为28.4%，全年平均天然入库流量为1828m^3/s，比多年平均来水偏多11.4%，比2017年同期来水偏多19.7%，全年最大入库洪峰流量为6500m^3/s，入库总水量为578.052亿m^3；锦屏一级水库为年调节水库，来水频率为17.9%，全年平均天然入库流量为1449m^3/s，比多年平均来水偏多17.7%，比2017年同期来水偏多19.3%，全年最大入库洪峰流量为5460m^3/s，入库总水量为460.784亿m^3。

2018年，二滩水库年初水位为1199.66m，1～4月水位逐步消落，4月末消落至最低水位1155.70m；此后水位逐步回蓄，10月末蓄至1199.88m，年末降至1198.72m。锦屏一级水库年初水位为1876.01m，1～5月水位逐步消落，5月末消落至最低水位1801.01m；此后水位逐步回蓄，10月末蓄至1879.83m，年末降至1878.14m。

（三）发电情况

2018年，雅砻江公司完成发电量741.13亿kW·h。其中，桐子林水电站完成发电量23.44亿kW·h，比2017年增加4.49亿kW·h；二滩水电站完成发电量159.75亿kW·h，比2017年增加11.39亿kW·h；官地水电站完成发电量121.80亿kW·h，比2017年增加2.44亿kW·h；锦屏二级水电站完成发电量248.87亿kW·h，比2017年减少3.10亿kW·h；锦屏一级水电站完成发电量187.29亿kW·h，比2017年增加1.92亿kW·h。

（四）技术指标

1. 主设备完好率　2018年，桐子林、二滩、官地、锦屏二级、锦屏一级水电站主设备完好率、水工建筑物完好率均为100%。

2. 机组等效可用系数　2018年，桐子林水电站机组等效可用系数为94.58%，比2017年提高5.69%；二滩水电站机组等效可用系数为91.68%，比2017年提高6.06%；官地水电站机组等效可用系数为91.42%，比2017年降低2.24%；锦屏二级水电站机组等效可用系数为88.90%，比2017年提高0.75%；锦屏一级水电站机组等效可用系数为92.76%，比2017年降低1.69%。

3. 发电设备平均利用小时数　2018年，桐子林水电站发电设备平均利用小时数为3905.79h，比2017年增加747.94h；二滩水电站发电设备平均利用小时数为4840.99h，比2017年增加344.981h；官地水电站发电设备平均利用小时数为5074.80h，比2017年增加101.55h；锦屏二级水电站发电设备平均利用小时数为5184.70h，比2017年减少64.68h；锦屏一级水电站发电设备平均利用小时数为5202.35h，比2017年增加53.43h。

4. 发电耗水率　2018年，桐子林水电站发电耗水率为18.34$m^3/(kW·h)$，比2017年增加0.55%；二滩水电站发电耗水率为2.35$m^3/(kW·h)$，比2017年降低1.26%；官地水电站发电耗水率3.34$m^3/(kW·h)$，比2017年降低0.89%；锦屏二级水电站发电耗水率为1.33$m^3/(kW·h)$，与2017年持平；锦屏一级水电站发电耗水率为1.85$m^3/(kW·h)$，比2017年降低1.07%。

5. 生产用厂用电　2018年，桐子林水电站生产用厂用电量为676.9140万kW·h，生产厂用电率为0.289%，比2017年减少0.033%；二滩水电站生产用厂用电量为2593.496万kW·h，生产厂用电率为0.162%，比2017年减少0.013%；官地水电站生产用厂用电量为1486.816万kW·h，生产厂用电率为0.122%，与2017年基本持平；锦屏二级水电站生产用厂用电量为3106.380万kW·h，生产厂用电率为0.125%，比2017年增加0.012%；锦屏一级水电站生产用厂用电量为2714.185万kW·h，生产厂用电率为0.145%，与2017年基本持平。

（五）检修情况

1. 机组检修　2018年，雅砻江公司完成桐子林、二滩、官地、锦屏二级、锦屏一级5座电站共计35台次机组C级检修工作，1台次机组A级检修工作。

2. 技术改造　2018年，雅砻江公司完成桐子林水电站通信设备UPS电源系统改造，二滩水电站二普一线保护装置、500kV电缆斜井防火报警系统、1～6号主变压器绝缘油中气体色谱在线监测系统、工业电视系统、6kV厂用电保护及备自投装置、500kV GIS开关控制系统、大坝电梯等改造，官地水电站1～4号发电机变压器组保护系统、现地控制单元LCU改造。

（雅砻江流域水电开发有限公司　周琪）

中国水电顾问集团所属的3个水电厂2018年生产管理情况

（一）桃源水电厂

2018年，完成发电量8.58亿kW·h，机组利用小时数 4767h（超设计值 363h），耗水率 55.18m^3/(kW·h)，年内实现“零非停”，累计安全运行 1888 天。

1. 安全管理　对接修编完成了 23 项安全管理标准；开展了 13 次安全检查，共发现问题或隐患 101 项，按时整改完成率 100％；组织参加外部安全员培训 2 人·次，组织全体员工进行了新版安规培训、交通安全知识培训、应急培训、防汛专项等 6 次培训；开展部门级应急演练活动 31 次，开展船闸事故应急演练活动 6 次和 2018 年防洪度汛实战演练；对全厂 15 台（套）承压类和 10 台（套）机电类特种设备进行了全面的排查，对检查发现的问题进行整改，6 月底已全部整改完成，整改率 100％；对现有 614 套各类灭火设备，由生产运行部负责日常巡查和登记。

2. 防洪度汛　调整了电站防汛指挥部的成员，编制了 2018 年度防洪度汛方案和防洪度汛应急预案。汛前组织水库库岸和水工建筑物专项检查、泄洪闸系统专项检查和泄洪闸门启闭试验；组织开展了 2018 年度防汛应急演练。全年共泄洪 9 次，泄洪总时长 195h，调度操作泄洪闸门 89 次，总泄洪水量 4.413 亿 m^3，确保了防汛、发电、通航三不误。

3. 发电情况　2018 年，电站累计入库水量 478.15 亿 m^3，较 2017 年同期少 252.03 亿 m^3，减少 34.52％；水量利用率 99.04％，较 2017 年同期 73.66％高 25.38 百分点；平均水头为 8.32 m，较 2017 年同期提高 0.74m；平均耗水率为 55.18m^3/(kW·h)，较 2017 年同期降低 4.34m^3/(kW·h)；发电 8.58 亿 kW·h，在来水同比 2017 年减少 34.52％的情况下电量仅减少 5.04％，在来水比多年平均值减少 26.37％的情况下超同期发电量设计值 8.25％。

4. 通航情况　2018 年，电站船闸通航继续保持“安全通航零事故”纪录，实现安全通航 260 天，通过各类船舶 4851 艘，较 2017 年同期 4507 艘增加 7.6％；通航 2371 闸，通航总吨位 400.99 万 t。

5. 检修情况　主要完成船闸设备 C 级检修、25 孔泄洪闸门及控制系统 C 级检修、机组进尾水口和船闸上闸首门机等金属结构设备常规检修，完成 8 台·次机组及全厂公用设备等机电设备的 C 级检修。右河槽泄洪闸支铰更换大修工作历经 2 个枯水年度，于 2018 年 2 月竣工，右岸泄洪闸液压启闭机运行过程中产生的异响问题基本得到解决。

6. 水工管理　开展了汛前水工安全专项检查，4 月和 6 月先后与设计院就船闸上游引航道右侧岸坡滑坡问题、右槽下游冲坑及格宾石笼护坦整体冲刷问题、厂房 8～9 号机组尾水反坡段冲坑问题以及左槽闸坝与双洲副坝接触部位下游漏水问题 4 项问题进行了方案设计讨论，设计院已提出了初步修复方案。

（二）沙阡水电厂

完成发电量 11783.94 万 kW·h，上网电量 11664.62 万 kW·h，完成全年任务的 84.6％。

全年开展了 10 次安全检查，6 次专项检查，共查出隐患问题 57 项，整改率 100％。共开展班组安全活动 24 次、技术问答 55 次、反事故预想 55 次、专题安全教育培训 15 次、外包单位人员培训 5 次、劳务派遣人员安全教育培训 3 次、新员工三级安全教育 1 次，安全管理人员取证培训 3 人，安全管理人员复训 4 人。开展应急演练 4 次。

开展防汛专项检查，共检查出问题缺陷 17 项。全年总入库 18.15 亿 m^3，共弃水 0.96 亿 m^3，最大洪峰 1980m^3/s 流量一次。实现安全度汛。

完成电站计划性检修项目 233 项，其中包括 1、2 号水轮发电机组检修 164 项，电气预防性试验 35 项，大坝金属机构检修 29 项，引水隧洞检查 1 项和特殊项目 4 项。

（三）大湾水电厂

2018 年，完成发电量为 13018.39 万 kW·h，耗水率 6.16m^3/(kW·h)，年内实现“零非停”，保持了“零事故”的良好态势，累计安全运行 1430 天。

重新修编印发了生产管理标准 58 部、工作标准 31 部、安全技术规范 15 部、运行规程 31 部、检修规程 64 部；抓各项工作的精细化管理，对必须掌握的知识和技能采取了定期抽查考试，取得了很好的效果。

积极推进安全生产标准化建设，进一步提高电厂标准化管理水平。更换了全厂盘柜、开关柜、配电箱、阀门等设备的标识牌共 622 块，墙面新增安装禁止、警告、指令、提示标志牌共 759 块。大力开展水库经济优化调度，如：洪峰期间在满足机组安全运行规范的前提下满发超发；在洪峰过后合理拦蓄洪尾以增加水库蓄水量；上游来水较小时抬高水库水位以提高发电运行水头来提高发电效益。

开展了 1、2 号机组 C 级检修，对全站一次设备和辅助设备进行了维护、清污，消除了大部分缺陷。11 月 18 日，组织开展了 1 号机组甩负荷试验，对调速器控制参数进行了优化调整，解决 1 号机组甩满负荷停机问题，确保机组安全稳定运行。

（中国水电顾问集团桃源水电厂
中国水电顾问集团沙阡水电厂
中国水电顾问集团大湾水电厂）

五凌电力有限公司 2018年生产管理情况

五凌电力有限公司（简称五凌电力）全面负责沅水流域梯级电站的开发、建设与运营，与国家电投湖南分公司实行“两块牌子、一套人马”的管理模式。截至2018年12月底，五凌电力装机容量752.9万kW，其中水电486.07万kW，火电120万kW，风电76.75万kW，光伏70.08万kW；在建项目73.2万kW。2018年，五凌电力坚持稳中求进，聚焦经营发展，着力提质增效，各方面工作取得积极成效。

（一）着力稳定效益水平，生产经营在艰难中持续盈利

完成发电量203.8亿kW·h。五强溪、凌津滩、新能源分公司等16家单位实现盈利，黔东公司等3家单位同比减亏。

全年水量利用率达96.6%，同比提高21%，创历史新高，增发电量2.46亿kW·h。积极协调，水电降价幅度好于预期。湘西水电群窝电问题得到有效改善。全年12家直管水电厂累计完成发电量132.64亿kW·h，继续发挥公司基础支撑作用。

全年回收新能源补贴3468万元。新能源板块弃风弃光率同比下降7.7%；全年实现盈利2.2亿元，同比增长3.6倍，成为公司重要利润增长极。

黔东火电机组全年利用小时3976h，全年完成发电量49.08亿kW·h，创历史新高，同比减亏1.63亿元，超额完成年度减亏目标。

工程公司取得电力设施“承装类二级、承修类一级、承试类一级”资质，新拓展金安桥水电检修等外部市场，第一次承修60万kW级大机组，全年产值超过6000万元。科技公司首次应用机载激光雷达、无人测量船等新技术新装备，提高了工作效率和管理水平；获得高新企业所得税退税115万元。

完成沅江公司30亿元债转股工作，公司资产负债率降至71.57%，连续7年降低。完成龙家山小水电等低效无效资产处置。压降法人层级，注销燃料公司等8家单位。开展税收筹划，落实增值税下调政策，年度综合税负率同比降低5.22%。

（二）着力推动高质量发展，持续优化产业布局

全年新增装机容量31.9万kW，其中新能源装机容量25.2万kW。落水洞、麻窝水电站投产发电。荆竹山、涟源龙山、紫云山风电项目实现全投。内蒙古乌海光伏项目仅用80天实现投产，创造了公司光伏工程建设新标杆。朝晖项目首批28万kW光伏项目具备并购条件。安徽金寨20万kW可再生能源基地示范项目签订合作框架协议。中俄界河黑龙江水电国际项目前期工作取得进展。参与长沙高新区国家第二批增量配电试点项目，签约蓝思科技等3家特大优质客户，全年签约电量超过80亿kW·h，在湖南发电企业中排名第一。

五强溪扩机项目上网电价得到函复、航道通航条件影响评价手续获得批复。三板溪电厂完成环保专项验收。托口电厂调概工作通过水电水利规划设计总院审查，枢纽工程、水保通过专项验收。白市电站湖南库区通过移民安置竣工验收。窑坡山风电等新能源场站通过工程专项验收。新疆布尔津风机遗留问题和青河土地问题得到解决。黔东、白市、托口和挂治、东坪、株溪口送出线路完成移交。

（三）着力夯实安全基础，安全生产局面持续稳定

实现安全事件、违章人次双下降，五凌电力首度荣获湖南省安委会安全生产考核评价“优秀单位”。创建安全示范班组，近尾洲水电厂荣获集团公司班组安全建设示范单位，电厂运维分部同时获得集团公司安全建设示范班组。公司本部、五强溪电厂通过集团公司年度安健环体系评审。三板溪、挂治、洪江、碗米坡、近尾洲等5家单位全部通过职业健康与安全、质量、环境管理三标体系认证。

全年组织安全生产督查30余次，排查问题513项，通过落实整改措施，有效防范不安全事件的发生。严格落实重大缺陷隐患“一单四制”管理要求，创新开展全员生产安全事故隐患排查清单试点研究工作，凌津滩主轴换型、洪江操作油管断裂、株溪口轮叶连杆窜出等重大设备问题得到有效治理，常规水电板块4年来首次无一类障碍。积极应对甘肃古浪和四川河口、麻窝电站山洪、滑坡等地质灾害影响，实现安全度汛。强化交通安全管理标准化建设和日常监管，安全行车620万km无事故。

（四）着力推进管控改革，企业管理水平持续提升

公司“四集三化”和水电厂“12345”管控模式成为企业管理特色和亮点。推动“平台公司＋事业部”管控模式落地，新能源板块薪酬激励体系基本形成；新疆、云南事业部机构调整完成，新疆区域新能源场站生产运维实现外委；湖南等区域22个场站接入长沙新能源生产运营中心。集团公司法律事务管理系统在公司试点运行。16起法律诉讼案胜诉，白市网箱诉讼案通过法院调解结案。

实施“干部能上能下”动态管理，全年提拔重用7名奋斗者，对外输送干部、骨干6人，3名处级、科级干部降职使用。推进“三通道”建设，32名技术技能人才全部通过集团公司胜任能力认证。公司8名同志参加集团公司秋季干部培训班，7人获优秀学员称号。

大、中型水电站“基于专家评估的定期检修”模式在集团公司系统推广，状态检修体系规划初步成

形。完成5项国家标准、2项行业标准、1项集团公司标准编写。获24项实用新型专利、4项软件著作权证书。公司ERP建设获中国电力企业联合会管理创新一等奖；4项成果获集团公司管理创新成果奖；8项成果获得集团公司科学技术进步奖。刘强同志荣获“2018中国电力科技先进工作者”称号。

（五凌电力有限公司）

中电建水电开发集团有限公司 2018年电力生产管理情况

中电建水电开发集团有限公司（简称水电开发公司）是中国电力建设股份有限公司的控股公司，2018年结合电力体制深化改革与四川电力市场实际情况，向管理和创新要效益，推进电力生产管理集约化模式；深化标准化管理，狠抓精益运行；加强标杆电站提炼成果的推广转化运用，电力生产取得了较好的成效。

（一）发电情况

2018年，水电开发公司新增装机容量6万kW，总装机容量达328.4万kW，其中：水电293.4万kW，风电30万kW，光伏5万kW；全年实际完成发电量108亿kW·h，完成年度计划的102%。

2018年6月20日，四川电网开始全网弃水，水电开发公司所属多个水电站均在受限通道内，弃水电量也相应增加。到11月16日，川电外送结束，水电按不弃水方式运行，水库电站蓄水。水电开发公司全年弃水电量超过30亿kW·h，比2017年多超过4亿kW·h。

（二）设备检修

2018年，水电开发公司所属子公司根据实际情况安排了机组检修，完成了大金坪水电站1号机组、圣达水电站2号机组、柳洪水电站3号机组、坪头水电站3号机组、五一桥水电站2号机组等6台机组A级检修工作。美姑河公司在汛期不影响发电量的情况下开展了坪头水电站3号机组A级检修。同时，还开展B级检修机组1台、C级检修机组25台，保障了机组安全稳定运行。

（三）主要工作及举措

1. 推进电力生产管理集约化模式　2018年，继续坚持做好“电力生产远程监控（应急）中心”值班工作，收集、记录、整理各电站生产营销基础数据，查看生产情况及重要工作和发生事件，跟踪、监督各电站日生产工作计划完成情况，并及时反馈各电站生产信息，通过快报的形式发布。通过集中管理，各级人员均能准确掌握生产状况，共享电力生产信息，做到了电力生产心中有数。

根据国家能源局和四川省能源局要求，为下一步国家制定解决弃水问题的相关政策提供准确依据，水电开发公司于2018年2月组织召开了水电流域综合监测平台对接工作会，配合国家可再生能源信息中心做好水电流域综合监测平台数据对接工作，制定了对接工作方案，并在4月底前完成了大金坪等9个电站的数据对接工作。

四川盐源公司于2018年6月4日开始在大德风电场变电站内远程监控甲米河一、二级水电站。克州新隆能源开发有限公司集控中心设计单位已确定，2018年8月13日发布“克州新隆公司克孜勒苏河流域集控中心设备安装工程施工招标公告”，按计划开展设备采购安装等工作。同年11月21日开始安谷水电站远控沙湾水电站试运行。推进集控中心建设工作，将不断加强集约化管理，提高工作效率和效益。

2. 深化标准化管理，狠抓精益运行　水电开发公司自开展电力企业标准化良好行为确认工作以来，现已有6家控股子公司先后通过中国电力企业联合会标准化良好行为“AAAA”级确认。为贯彻落实股份公司通用管理标准，2018年4月25～27日隆重召开“水电板块标准贯标暨标准化建设研讨会议”，宣贯了水电板块通用管理标准，讨论标准化建设工作。为实施中国电力建设股份有限公司通用管理标准，编制并印发了贯彻通用管理标准实施方案，在年终安全检查考核时进行了检查，各子公司均按进度要求开展并完成了相应工作，以遵循股份公司业务“走出去”的战略导向，推进标准统一，实施优化精细化管理，打造中国电建品牌。

2018年，在安全生产管理上，加强了精细化管理，坚持“生命至上，安全发展”的理念，认真按标准落实各项生产工作，通过电力生产管理信息、工业电视等系统，及时掌握电站安全生产状况，确保了安全经济运行。

（四）加强标杆电站提炼成果的转化运用

2018年，在赞拉水电站建设过程中，积极运用标杆水电站提炼成果，提前部署，多次现场协调，以标杆水电站为标准，对工程项目一一对应，结合现场实际施工进度有序落实。2018年8月，3台机组全部投运，9月顺利投入商业运行。

美姑河水电开发有限公司和圣达水电有限公司在获得2017年“中国电力建设股份有限公司发电企业运营指标优秀管理单位”称号基础上，前者推行《设备自主检修，探索院企合作模式》，后者推行《营销模式创新助推利润增长》，两公司的典型经验在中国电力建设股份有限公司范围内进行了广泛推广。

（中电建水电开发集团有限公司）

三门峡水力发电厂 2018年生产管理情况

（一）电力生产情况

三门峡水力发电厂（简称三门峡电厂）是三门峡黄河明珠（集团）有限公司的分公司。该发电厂为坝后式水电站。共有7台水轮发电机组，5台单机容量为6万kW的轴流转桨式机组，2台单机容量为7.5万kW的混流式机组，总容量45万kW。

2018年，三门峡水库入库水量414.14亿m^3，较2017年多215.25亿m^3。虽然来水大幅增加，但是电力生产遇到前所未有的困难。受上网空间进一步缩小、调峰任务增多、出力受限及电网检修等的影响，发电上网和经济运行困难重重。面对巨大的压力和困难，三门峡水电厂迎难而上，积极应对，加强与防办沟通，提高水情预测分析精度，根据实际情况采取不同策略，科学安排机组运行方式；采用多渠道多层次的方式加强与省调沟通，在保证开机成功率和开机速度的情况下，努力争取省调的理解和支持。针对电网运行方式标准更改，积极研究制定应对之策，通过更改稳控装置功能、3号机组倒至虢都变电站并网、充分利用线路性能等方式，成功化解了出力受限压力，提高水能利用率。

2018年，三门峡水电厂发变电设备运行情况良好，全厂平均利用小时数4128.17h，较2017年增加3373.56h（平均增加754.62h）；厂用电率为0.35%，损耗率为0.74%。厂年累计发电18.58亿kW·h，比2017年增加18.27%。受来水大幅变化，以及发电水头降低等因素影响，非汛期发电耗水率为10.82m^3/(kW·h)，较2017年有所增加。

（二）汛期发电情况

2018年汛期发电期间，三门峡水库入库水量221.53亿m^3，较2017年同期（65.46亿m^3）增加238.42%；发电用水量69.71亿m^3，较2017年同期（56.15亿m^3）增加24.15%；汛期发电量32280万kW·h，较2017年（35268.4万kW·h）减少2988.4万kW·h，同比减少8.47%。

2018年汛期，三门峡水力发电厂机组平均负荷率57.42%，与2017年（78.34%）降低20.92%。汛期发电耗水率为21.59m^3/kW·h，较2017年同期（15.92m^3/kW·h）增加5.67m^3/kW·h。整个汛期机组全停6次，累计约481.5h。累计弃水量141.16亿m^3，累计弃水天数36天。

（三）机组检修情况

2018年，水电厂持续加强设备的精细维护工作，精益求精，设备健康水平得到进一步提升。通过加大对设备的巡回检查力度，成立操作巡回班、安全隐患排查、月度值长集中检查、设备特巡等手段，把设备巡检工作提升到新高度，及时发现解决了1F、4F顶盖上水增大，5F拦污栅片进入蜗壳后振动大，技术供水系统17、18号泵电源隔离开关过热等安全隐患；认真开展技术监督及设备检修，完成了室外避雷器带电测试、三22旁开关保护及母联充电保护定检等，保证设备在正常状态运行。

2018年是机组改造全部完成后首个汛期，首次在汛前不进行水下部分检查，为了确保机组设备良好，根据水情专门安排每台机进行了为期一周的设备技术监督检查维护，为汛期发电运用积累了经验；积极进行设备技术改造，先后完成7号水轮发电机组扩大性大修，水电厂排水系统改造更新，机组网源协调有关涉网试验，监控系统安全等级保护测评备案以及厂房289.5m高程层环境治理等重点项目；强化缺陷管理，严格执行缺陷管理考核办法，加强缺陷记录、处理过程以及消缺程序的监督检查，提升缺陷管理质量。在机组运行工况差和机组长时间满发等特殊时期，加强电气一次设备过热、二次端子松动发热、监控盘励磁盘电源模块、顶盖系统等重要部位的特巡和维护工作，及早发现问题并处理。自行研制了更换剪断销的专用工具，提高了消缺效率，减轻了劳动强度。加强对疑难缺陷、典型缺陷的分析工作，进一步提高分析质量，完成了《6号机组出口软连接过热缺陷分析》等5项分析报告。全年自动开停机2329次，自动开停机成功率达到97.7%，其中6月份达到100%。在开停机次数较2017年增加29%的基础上，自动开停机成功率提高了1.4个百分点。

（四）科技创新情况

2018年，水电厂积极开展科技攻关，水电厂变压器状态检修项目已通过集团公司验收；明珠大厦远方控制项目研究报告已初步完成。加强科技理论研究和技术总结，集团公司《科技与管理》杂志发表论文10篇。进行了水电厂科技成果评审，评出6项科技成果，上报集团公司4项，其中1项获奖。积极参与机组增容改造项目大禹奖材料编制和电站运行40周年重大技改修编。王好锋、肖魁荣获集团公司先进科技工作者称号。

（五）安全生产情况

2018年，三门峡电厂狠抓安全生产基础管理，持续推行安全生产网格化责任体系建设和全面深化管理责任体系，连续20年未发生五级及以上电力安全生产事故。结合工作实际，不断将安全生产网格化管理关口前移、重心下移。开展了“安全生产月”主题活动、“规范工作流程，强化文明生产”专项活动和“今天我是安全员”等常态化安全活动；组织全厂职工安规考试、交通安全知识培训、安全知识答题，全面提升职工安全意识。坚持按月开展安全检查和隐患排查治理工作，并开展了季节性、节假日及特殊天气等专项安全检查，认真落实隐患整改110余项，发放安全缺陷奖励169项，营造了良好的安全生产氛围。2018年全年未发生重大交通、设备、火灾和人身重伤、死亡事故，实现了3个连续安全生产100天，创造了连续安全生产7505天的新纪录。

[三门峡黄河明珠（集团）有限公司　孙淑兰]

黄河万家寨水利枢纽有限公司 2018年生产管理情况

黄河万家寨水利枢纽有限公司（简称万家寨公

司）是随着国家“九五”重点工程——万家寨水利枢纽的建设而组建的，先后开发兴建了万家寨水利枢纽和龙口水利枢纽两座大型水利枢纽工程。万家寨水利枢纽以供水、发电为主，兼有防洪、防凌等综合功能，水库总库容 8.96 亿 m^3，调节库容 4.45 亿 m^3；大坝为混凝土重力坝，最大坝高 105m；电站装机容量 108 万 kW，设计每年可向山西供水 12 亿 m^3，向内蒙古自治区供水 2 亿 m^3。龙口水利枢纽是万家寨水利枢纽工程的反调节配套工程，水库总库容 1.96 亿 m^3，调节库容 7100 万 m^3；大坝为混凝土重力坝，最大坝高 51m，电站装机容量 42 万 kW。

2018 年，万家寨公司圆满完成了各项工作目标和重点工作任务，取得了良好的经济效益、社会效益和生态效益，为山西、内蒙古两地经济社会发展、民生改善做出了突出贡献。

（一）抓生产，增效益，枢纽功能充分发挥

服从流域统一调度，统筹安排防洪、防凌、发电、排沙、供水、应急调度等工作，继续加大机电设备更新改造力度，加强水工建筑物的维修管护，重点开展泄水建筑物、泄水设施和机电设备检查维护，努力发挥工程的综合效益。着眼打基础利长远，年内利用上游大流量来水持续稳定的有利时机，成功组织万家寨、龙口两座水库联合排沙工作，经实测，排沙后万家寨水库库容增加了 1.56 亿 m^3，龙口水库库容增加了 0.25 亿 m^3，为万家寨公司今后可持续发展奠定良好基础，同时也为黄河流域水库泥沙调度积累了宝贵经验。成功进行了万家寨大坝设计最高蓄水位运行试验，大坝各项监测数据均无异常，各项设施设备通过全面检验。万家寨水电站远程控制龙口水电站系统投入试运行，提高了两站水能利用率和调度效率。积极推进库区管理工作，与黄河水利委员会山西河务局签署联合执法协议，开启了库区管理合作新模式，配合完成准朔铁路征地和供水管路改建工作，加大枢纽区域绿化工作力度。积极协调两网调度，圆满完成年度电力生产任务，2018 年完成发电 48.47 亿 kW·h，供水 3.2 亿 m^3。此外，2018 年 10 月，万家寨水电站月发电 5.12 亿 kW·h、龙口水电站月发电 2.58 亿 kW·h，创造了自首台机组投产发电以来的单月发电量最高纪录。

（二）抓管理，提质量，经营管理规范有序

不断规范内部管理，优化办事流程，提高工作效率，各项工作取得实效。2018 年 12 月，电站管理局顺利通过国家一级水利工程管理单位现场复核验收。水利档案工作规范化管理通过综合评估，被水利部办公厅批准为一级单位。启动了协同办公平台项目建设并顺利上线试运行。按期完成公司公务用车制度改革；策划实施了万家寨水利枢纽首台机组投产发电 20 周年和万家寨水电站连续安全生产 5000 天专题宣传。积极推进支持子公司发展工作，进一步细化了实施办法，完善对外承揽项目激励机制。继续做好援藏和扶贫工作，派出两名工程建设管理经验丰富的同志继续支援西藏拉洛水利枢纽工程建设。成立了对口帮扶工作领导小组，全力做好水利部和山西省委安排的精准扶贫工作任务。

（三）抓安全，守红线，安全生产稳定向好

认真贯彻“党政同责、一岗双责、失职追责”的安全生产责任制，全面落实全员安全生产责任，进一步修订完善了安全生产管理制度，形成了“层层负责、人人有责、各负其责”的安全生产责任体系。深入推进水利安全生产标准化建设，2018 年 3 月，万家寨公司被水利部安全生产标准化评审委员会授予“第四批水利安全生产标准化一级单位”称号。持续加大隐患排查治理和风险管控力度，万家寨水电站 1、2、3、5 号发电机定子铁芯溢出Ⅱ级重大隐患治理完毕，并在国家能源局山西监管办公室和水利部安监司顺利销号，安全生产管理基础进一步夯实。2018 年 6 月，经水利部专家组综合评定，万家寨水利枢纽大坝顺利通过鉴定并再次被确定为“一类坝”。大力弘扬“生命至上、安全发展”理念，认真开展“安全生产月”活动，形成了多部门合作、职工广泛参与的安全文化氛围。2018 年，万家寨水电站创造连续安全生产 5000 天新纪录，全年未发生生产安全事故。截至 2018 年底，万家寨水电站实现连续安全生产 5013 天，龙口水电站实现连续安全生产 3392 天。

（黄河万家寨水利枢纽有限公司　赵欢欢）

国家电投集团广西长洲水电公司 2018 年生产管理情况

国家电投集团广西长洲水电开发有限公司（简称长洲水电公司）为国家电投集团广西电力有限公司下属企业，主要负责长洲水利枢纽工程的建设和运营管理及新能源项目的开发建设工作。长洲水利枢纽工程位于广西梧州市，工程于 2003 年 12 月开工，2007 年 3 月船闸通航，2007 年 10 月首台机组（1 号）投产发电，2009 年 10 月最后一台机组（15 号）投产发电，是一座以发电为主，兼有航运、养殖、环保、供水灌溉等综合利用效益的大型水利枢纽。电站共安装 15 台单机容量为 42MW 的灯泡贯流式机组，总装机容量 630MW，年设计发电量约 30.14 亿 kW·h。

2018 年，长洲水电公司紧密围绕集团公司年度重点工作部署及广西公司“主动作为谋发展，七力并重增效益”要求，创造了安全生产双提升，经营效益“结硕果”的良好局面。截至 2018 年 12 月 31 日，长洲水电公司连续安全生产 4081 天，实现了“零事故、零伤亡”的安全目标；实现了“零弃水”，水电年发电量达 37.76 亿 kW·h，超设计发电量 7.62 亿 kW·h，刷新投产以来历史发电量纪录。机组年累计利用小时数达 5993h，部分机组运行小时数超过 7000h。

保安全，久久为功。全力打牢安全基础，保持了"零事故、零伤亡"安全纪录，以集团公司安全示范班组建设为契机，狠抓"三基"，班组安全建设树立标杆；明确职责，安全生产责任覆盖全员；策划修正，防洪度汛方案持续优化；预案先行，应急管理体系有效运行。实现了集团公司及广西公司年初下达的各项安全指标。

增发电，勇创新高。全公司上下一心挖潜提质增效，精细操控，保证机组经济稳定运行；密切沟通，努力争取负荷超计划电量曲线运行；勤于清污，确保垃圾"不过夜"，保障机组汛期高效稳定运行。全年实现增发电量 2.67 亿 kW·h。

围绕生产，开展"长洲工匠"技术比武和"安康杯"劳动竞赛，形成你追我赶、人人争先的良好氛围。

（国家电投集团广西长洲水电开发有限公司）

故县水力发电厂 2018 年生产管理情况

（一）电力生产情况

故县水力发电厂（简称故县水电厂）为三门峡黄河明珠（集团）有限公司子公司河南明珠洛河水力发电有限公司管理的水电厂。该电厂属坝后式水电站。共有 3 台单机容量为 2 万 kW 的水轮发电机组。2018 年，该电厂水库来水量总计 5.931 亿 m^3，同比减少 26.7%。面对洛河来水偏枯和库水位较低等不利因素，故县水力发电厂始终把节水发电贯穿于整个发电过程中，在不同阶段，根据来水量的变化情况，严格按故县水利枢纽管理局防办下达的指令，适时对发电计划进行调整。同时，在充分利用水资源上狠下功夫，积极开展挖潜增效，节约利用好每一滴水，最大限度增加发电量。2018 年，该电厂年累计发电量 9880 万 kW·h，年均耗水率 5.42m^3/(kW·h)。

（二）设备改造与检修情况

2018 年，故县水电厂扎实开展设备改造、检修及消缺工作，先后完成亮寻线保护装置改造、寻 111 断路器更新改造，对 2 号机组转动油盆进行了更换，对备用轴承瓦进行了修复。完成高压电气设备预防性试验和 3 台机组的水下部分检查工作，对变压器油及机组透平油、压力容器安全阀、起重设备进行了检验。一年来，该电厂组织安全大检查 12 次，完成整改项目 26 项，处理各类缺陷 87 项。通过一系列有效工作，确保了全厂设备安全稳定运行。

（三）安全生产情况

2018 年，故县水电厂坚持贯彻"安全第一，预防为主，综合治理"的安全工作方针，树立"安全是最大效益"的安全发展理念，进一步落实全员安全责任，持续构建安全生产网格化管理和班前会制度等长效机制，强化安全保障措施，杜绝生产安全责任事故的发生，全方位打造文明安全的生产工作氛围。在汛期到来之前，组织开展"汛期保厂用电""防汛演习""人员逃生"等演练，进一步锻炼了突发事故处理的应变能力。2018 年 5 月 1 日～9 月 31 日，开展"隐患排查治理竞赛"活动，进一步增强了职工隐患排查治理工作的责任心和积极性。组织参加水利部组织的安全知识网络答题活动，职工答题率达到 91.1%。结合实际开展了安全对话谈心活动。通过各种措施，进一步夯实了以安全为中心的基础管理工作，最大限度地消除了各类不安全因素，杜绝了各类不安全事件的发生，实现了全年无事故的安全目标，保持了安全生产的良好形势。截至 2018 年底，故县水电厂实现连续安全生产 8376 天。

[三门峡黄河明珠（集团）有限公司　孙淑兰]

技术改造

白莲河抽水蓄能电站钢管鼓包原因分析与处理措施

白莲河抽水蓄能电站总装机容量 4×30 万 kW，额定水头 195m，单机额定流量 176.1m^3/s。尾水系统采用两机一洞布置，尾水支洞长 128.755m，洞径 7.4m，尾水管至尾水闸门门槽中心下游侧 20m 采用钢板衬砌，尾水系统其余洞段均采用钢筋混凝土衬砌。

（一）钢管设计参数

尾水系统①、②机组与③、④机组分别共 1 个输水单元。③尾水支洞钢衬范围总长 74.63m，共 39

节。钢衬标准管节长2m，内径7.4m，壁厚22mm，材质16MnR，回填厚0.7mC20混凝土。钢衬抗外压稳定采用加劲环，标准管节加劲环间距1m，材质16MnR，断面尺寸30mm×250mm（厚×高）。为满足机组技术供水要求，在③机组尾水支洞正底部开槽埋设了机组技术供水排水管。

③尾水支洞钢衬段全长全断面进行固结灌浆，灌浆孔间排距3m×2m，孔径ϕ50，入岩5m，灌浆压力1.2MPa。钢衬顶部120°范围内利用管壁预留固结灌浆孔进行回填灌浆，灌浆压力0.4MPa。钢衬底部90°范围内进行接触灌浆，灌浆压力0.2MPa。

（二）钢管鼓包情况及现场查勘

白莲河抽水蓄能电站4台机组自2010年12月全部投产，总体运行情况良好。2015年9月7～22日，在电站组织开展③机组C级检修中，首次发现在紧挨尾水管下游侧③尾水支洞钢衬段第2、3号管节存在鼓包。此后，原设计、施工单位等相关专业技术人员进行了3次现场查勘。

1. 第一次查勘　发现紧挨尾水管下游侧的③尾水支洞钢衬段2、3号管节共10个鼓包，其中明显的6个集中在2号管节两加劲环间，及2、3号管节间环缝附近。断面上均分布在钢管两侧腰线以下，最大鼓包直径约1.2m，高4～5cm，最小鼓包直径约0.7m，高2cm。锤击鼓包及相邻区域无空鼓声。其余管段均未发现异常，钢管焊缝及灌浆孔也未发现明显渗水。

2. 第二次查勘　对地下厂房系统渗控廊道全面巡查，发现地下水不发育，除⑤渗控廊道F8断层带内洞顶有较大线状滴水外，其余部位洞壁均干燥，局部偶见潮湿。各排水和厂房检查廊道排水沟侧排水孔内均无反水，个别排水孔甚至出现无水现象。所有排水孔的测压表读数全部为零，打开阀门均无排气排水。可排除因地下水产生外水压力导致钢衬鼓包的可能性。

3. 第三次查勘　经详查，鼓包主要出现在2号管节两加劲环间共16个，2号管节末端与3号两管节环缝间有7个，最大直径0.96～1m，高4.7～5cm；最小直径0.4～0.5m，高2cm。

此外，自首次发现鼓包并经充水运行约3个半月后，③尾水支洞鼓包尺寸无明显变化，但数量有增加（与检查方法有关）。其发展趋势与程度看，底部鼓包较大，腰线及洞顶较小，横断面上鼓包从底部逐渐向腰线及洞顶蔓延扩展；从压力钢管轴线（发电水流方向）看，因受两侧加劲环限制，该方向上游无扩展，无鼓包，范围主要限制在2号管节两加劲环间及2号与3号管节环缝附近，发展规模与程度自2号管节向3号逐渐减弱，并有向下游发展趋势。

（三）钢管鼓包原因初析

1. 钢管抗外压能力复核　稳定分析采用解析法复核，其结果见表1、表2。地下水安全监测及厂房排水系统现场巡视结果表明，地下厂区围岩透水性弱，地下水较不发育，钢衬设计外水压力取值合理，钢衬具有一定的抗外压稳定安全裕度，鼓包的产生非设计原因所致。

表1　尾水钢管管壁厚度计算成果

计算截面管道桩号	钢管内径（mm）	设计内水压力（MPa）	单位围岩弹性抗力（MPa/cm）	计算壁厚（含锈蚀厚度）（mm）
③尾支0+003.000	7400	138.2	0	22

表2　尾水钢管抗外压稳定计算复核成果

计算截面管道桩号	钢管内径（mm）	管壁厚度（mm）	综合外水折减系数	设计外压（MPa）	加劲环环间管壁抗外压稳定安全系数	加劲环自身抗外压稳定安全系数
③尾支0+003.000	7400	22	0.40	0.80	2.35 [1.8]	1.81 [1.8]

2. 地下水监测成果分析　监测资料表明，2015年三季度③尾水支洞监测断面外水压力实测最大值约0.15MPa，发生部位为③尾水支洞Pb4-1测点，远小于钢衬设计外水压力。

由Pb4-1测点外水压力变化过程可见，电站运行后外水压力一直维持在较稳定状态。外水压力与流道充水和上水库蓄水没有相关性，且没有随流道充水的影响而明显增加或减少。

3. 钢管鼓包原因初析　初步分析基本上排除设计、施工、管理、钢板质量、管道内水外渗、尾水系统地下水位过高，及隧洞围岩失稳等方面原因。

为满足机组技术供水要求，在③机组尾水支洞正底部开槽（800mm宽×700mm深）埋有1根DN400机组技术供水排水管，供排水管安装完后回填C20素混凝土。第三次查勘时，利用③、④机组放空检修机会，对该供排水管进行压水试验。结果表明，钢衬鼓包钻孔处外水流量及压力变化与③机组技术供排水管内压变化有直接的水力联系，可确定造成钢衬鼓包的原因是供排水管在③尾水支洞钢衬段2、3号管节处存在破裂（渗漏）点。

（四）钢管鼓包处理方案

钢管鼓包的处理方案如下：

（1）选取若干横断面实测确定鼓包范围，将变形区域位置和拟切割范围划线，并切除。

（2）凿除钢衬鼓包洞段范围内底部③机组技术供水排水管管槽回填的素混凝土，找出该供排水管在③尾水支洞钢衬段2、3号管节处破损（渗漏）点，予以修复，并对修复焊缝探伤，对整个管道压水试验。

（3）在2号管节底部靠近上游加劲环侧加焊ϕ50排水支管，并接入③尾水支洞钢衬底部ϕ50外排水主管内，回填C25自密实混凝土至钢衬底部高程以下约5cm处。

（4）凿除钢衬周边混凝土，径向凿深3cm，钢板纵缝、横缝及灌浆孔补强板部位局部深5cm，环向及轴向应超出钢衬未切除端至少5cm，以便瓦片的安装和焊接。

（5）钢衬瓦片采用Q345R，厚22mm，瓦片上设预留灌浆孔。

（6）钢衬焊接完毕后，利用钢衬预留孔进行回填灌浆，以填充钢衬与混凝土间空腔，灌浆压力0.2MPa。经现场锤击后，接触灌浆采用化学灌浆，灌浆压力0.2MPa。

（7）灌浆结束后对灌浆孔进行封堵，并沿钢衬内壁布置1圈套管以增加钢衬抗外压稳定能力。套管材质与钢衬一致，厚22mm，宽400mm。

（8）除锈及防腐处理。

（中国电建集团中南勘测设计研究院有限公司
李冲　张战午　王化龙　王健姣）

石泉水电厂引水管道钢衬脱空原因分析及处理

石泉水电厂安装3台单机容量为45MW的水轮发电机组，坝后式厂房。其引水管道布置在坝内，每台机组一管，每条管全长55.4m，圆管内径为5.5m；斜直段及以上部分，不设钢板衬砌；下弯段及其以下部分采用钢板衬砌，衬砌段长度为20.2m，圆管段内衬钢板厚度为14mm，下渐变段内衬钢板厚度为12mm。3台机组于1974年6月投产运行。之后，机组每3年大修一次，每次大修对机组压力引水管道、蜗壳、尾水管锥管段进行外观检查，用铁榔头敲击钢衬板表面确定是否存在脱空现象。检查发现，引水管道钢衬脱空且呈逐年递增的趋势，2005年各机组空穴面积已达检查总面积的20%～30%，且有渗水。因此，进行了原因分析和处理方法研究，从2008年开始陆续对3台机组空穴进行灌浆处理，6年后复检灌浆覆盖率达到94%。现将该电站引水管道钢衬脱空处理情况简介如下。

（一）处理方案

经研究，为填补空穴和缝隙，阻断渗水通道，采用灌浆方法处理。选择灌浆材料主要考虑其可灌性、水中凝固性以及适应钢衬板因温度变化和水压力作用而产生的微变形等几方面的特性。电厂拟定的灌浆原则为：①面积小于0.3m^2、深度小于3mm的空穴可以不进行灌浆处理；②对于脱空深度大于20mm的脱空区域，采用水泥砂浆进行灌浆；③脱空深度为5～20mm的区域采用纯水泥浆灌注；④脱空深度小于5mm的细小裂缝采用化学灌浆。

化学灌浆材料，结合工程的具体情况，施工选用两种水溶性聚氨酯浆材，即HW水溶性聚氨酯化学灌浆材料和LW水溶性聚氨酯化学灌浆材料，配合比为1∶1。这是经过改性的新型聚氨酯材料，其突出特点之一是易分散于水中，遇水自乳化，立即进行聚合反应，固结物具有良好的弹性、抗渗性、耐低温性，对岩石、混凝土、土粒等具有良好的黏接性能，浆液及其固结体无害、无毒，对水质无污染；特点之二是固结物具有弹性止水和膨胀止水的双重作用，能适应钢衬板的微变形情况。

（二）施工技术要点

施工流程为：搭设脚手架→检查脱空区域→布孔→打孔→连接灌浆嘴→灌浆→去掉灌浆嘴→扩孔塞焊→抛光磨平。

1. 脱空区域确定　现场脱空区域检查方式主要为敲击检查，但敲击只能判断出有无明显脱空，对脱空的深度、微小空穴的检查有难度。因此，采用敲击法普查、振动法复核和钻孔法测量空穴深度相结合的方式进行脱空区域确定。

2. 布孔　在敲击检查完成后进行，从起灌段开始，按尽量少的原则，最低处设灌浆孔，上部设通气孔（又作为第二层的灌浆孔）布置。布孔应充分考虑脱空深度及在该位置开孔的可灌性，充分考虑浆液排气的范围，尽量避免浆液因无法排气造成的死角，影响灌浆效果。开孔位置还要避开钢衬的接头、加筋环等部位。

3. 通风和压水检查　钻孔后，采用通风和压水方法来检查脱空区域的串通情况。根据记录来预估灌浆量，还可检查外漏点。通风压水的压力一定要小，控制在 0.1MPa，压力过大容易形成新的脱空甚至造成钢衬板变形。

4. 灌前资料分析　通风压水检查后，对已做工序作业记录进行分析，根据脱空深度的不同，配比不同浓度的浆液分区灌浆，避免脱空区域浆液无法进入，二次灌浆。如在灌浆中发现，下渐变段以上至下弯管段存在大面积的脱空区域，当化灌材料配比 LW：HW＝3：4 的情况下，采用一侧钻孔灌浆，在化学灌浆液还未到达另一侧最远端时，早起浆液已经凝结，阻碍灌液行进；经现场反复试验，化灌材料配比调整为 LW：HW＝1：4 并两侧同时进行灌浆处理，则能较好的解决该问题。

5. 灌浆　灌浆施工前，要做好准备工作，根据脱空范围估算耗浆量，配备相应的灌浆设备、材料，杜绝灌浆过程中出现中断，造成进浆孔、送浆管堵塞。灌浆压力可根据钢衬的壁厚、脱空面积的大小等实际情况确定，一般压力控制在 0.1～0.2MPa。除控制好压力外，还应加强抬动观测，钢板的变形控制在 0.05mm 以内，一旦有异常变化，即停止灌浆，防止钢衬发生变形。灌注时自下而上分层进行，用锤子敲击震动钢衬保证浆液流通。待各高处孔分别排出浓浆后，依次将其孔口阀门关闭，同时记录各孔排出的浆量和浓度。以灌浆孔停止吸浆延续 5min 结束。灌浆完毕后，拆卸灌浆嘴时的会造成压力的损失，这点也是关系到灌浆效果，通常采用扎管，待浆液凝固后拆除。

6. 质量检查　对钢衬脱空首轮灌浆后的情况进行检测，为快速高效，以振动法检测为首选。在灌浆部位安装振动传感器，用锤子敲击衬砌表面，通过振动信号传到振动测试分析仪，分别记录振动历时和频谱分析信号，通过波形判定检测区域钢衬板是否存在微小间隙，以评定浆液的充填情况。对未填充密实的区域，在钢衬上重新开孔进行二轮灌浆。

（三）灌浆效果

2014 年再次对 2008 年处理过的 3 号机组蜗壳进行检查，钢衬表面光滑，未见鼓包、开裂现象，检查脱空面积为 7.325m^2，较灌浆前脱空面积 118.09m^2 降低 94%，其中 0.3m^2 以上范围集中的空穴面积只有 1.45m^2，表明施工质量优良，效果较好。

（大唐石泉水力发电厂　樊锐）

万家寨水电厂 1～4 号机组接力器锁锭漏油分析及升级改造

万家寨水电厂装有 6 台混流式水轮发电机组，单机容量 180MW。其 1～4 号机组接力器锁锭为销轴活塞式结构，见图 1；锁锭的投入和拔出均靠调速器液压系统驱动，液压系统额定压力 6.4MPa。该电厂 1998 年 11 月首台机组发电，2000 年 6 月机组全部投产；运行至 2010 年后，1～4 号机组相继发现接力器锁锭漏油。为解决此问题，电厂对接力器锁锭进行了技术改造。

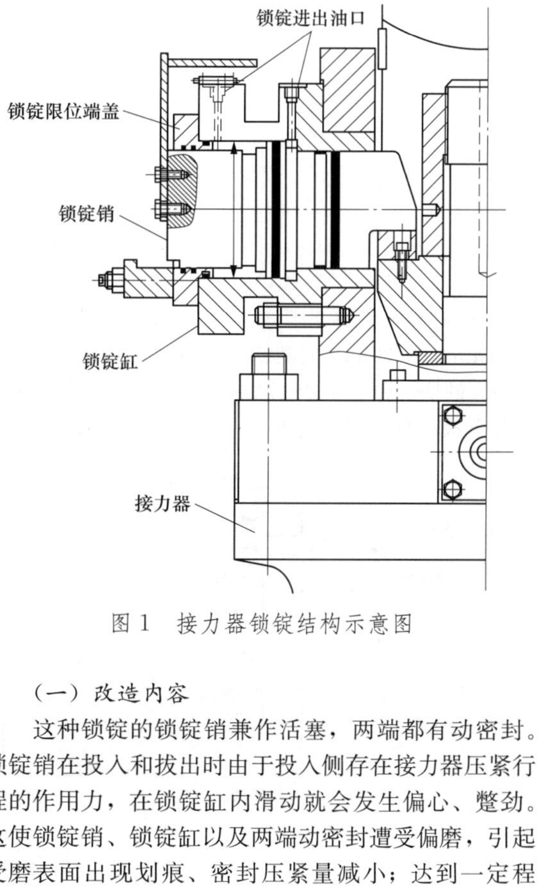

图 1　接力器锁锭结构示意图

（一）改造内容

这种锁锭的锁锭销兼作活塞，两端都有动密封。锁锭销在投入和拔出时由于投入侧存在接力器压紧行程的作用力，在锁锭缸内滑动就会发生偏心、蹩劲。这使锁锭销、锁锭缸以及两端动密封遭受偏磨，引起受磨表面出现划痕、密封压紧量减小；达到一定程度，导致漏油。因此，对锁锭驱动部分进行了改造，锁锭销取消活塞功能，仅作为销轴使用，锁锭的投入和拔出由外置的液压缸来完成。

1. 外置液压缸及其附件设计　为了确保改造后的锁锭销在外置锁锭液压缸的驱动下的投入和拔出功能且行程不变，将外置锁锭液压缸的行程和原锁锭行程设计一样；且外置锁锭液压缸的连接法兰与原锁锭限位端盖的外形尺寸一样，以便将外置的锁锭液压缸安装到原锁锭缸上。另外，设计了一个活套法兰与外置液压缸活塞杆进行连接，然后将活套法兰固定在改造后的锁锭销上，以实现锁锭销的投、拔功能。为了防止活塞杆和活套法兰之间的连接出现松动或脱落，在外置液压缸活塞杆的端部螺杆上设计了锁紧螺母和背帽。外置液压缸及其附件见图 2。

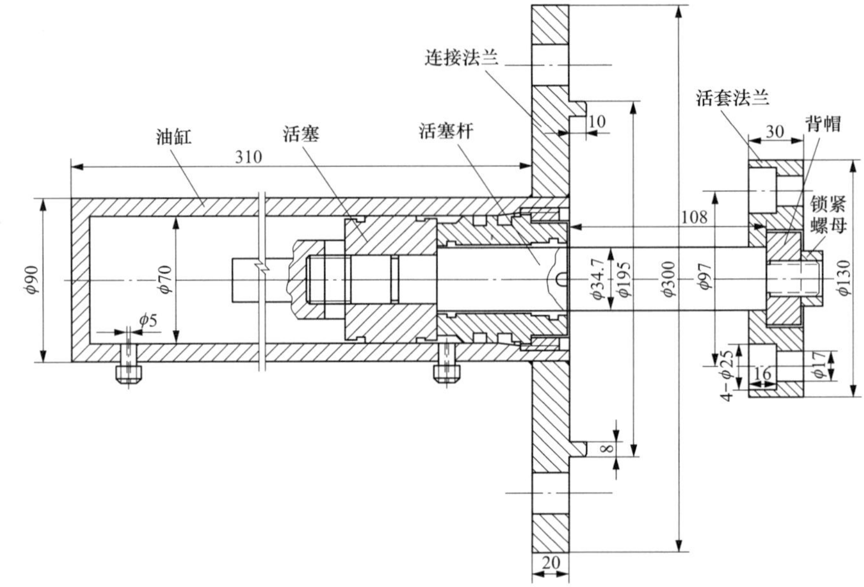

图 2　外置锁锭液压缸及其附件（单位：mm）

2. 对原锁锭销的改造　主要是上端加工一个 ϕ131mm、深 30mm 的圆槽（中间还有 ϕ35mm、深 12mm 的槽）和 4 个 M16 螺孔，以便通过活套法兰与外置液压缸活塞杆连接，见图 3。根据安装位置，在改造后的锁锭销圆周方向上确定 M18 的导向杆螺栓孔，该导向杆具有防止锁锭销转动和触碰锁锭行程开关推杆的作用。

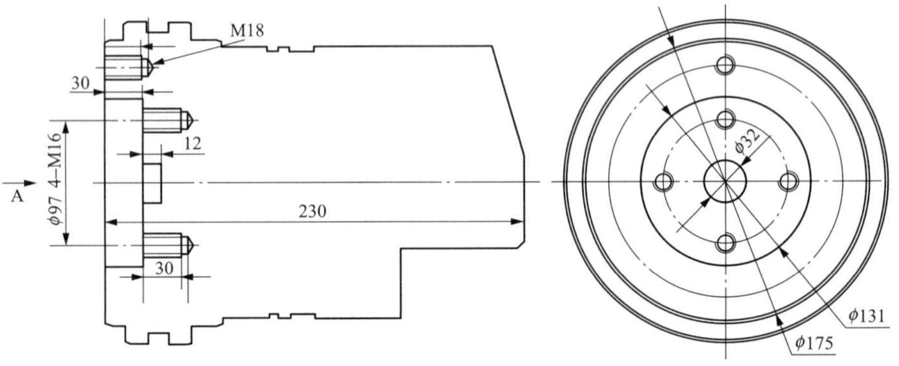

图 3　改造后的锁锭销（单位：mm）

3. 进出油管　改为定制的高压软管，便于安装和拆卸。

（二）施工要点

（1）外置锁锭液压缸应按图纸要求加工，并按有关规定进行出厂试验，应动作灵活、无渗漏。

（2）拆除原锁锭限位端盖，安装改造后的锁锭。安装后先连接油泵进行投入和拔出试验，检查改造后的锁锭动作是否灵活、行程是否合适。

（3）检查试验合格后，连接锁锭的进出油管、行程开关等辅助部件，用调速系统压力油驱动锁锭，全面检查锁锭动作是否灵活、反馈信号是否正确以及有无渗漏等。

（4）经上述安装调试合格后，锁锭即可投入正常运行。

万家寨水电厂于 2014 年开始，陆续对 1～4 号机组接力器锁锭进行改造。改造后，运行良好，解决了漏油的问题，确保了机组安全、可靠、高效运行。

（万家寨水电厂　黄永华　郭小鹏）

宝珠寺电厂水轮发电机组增设纯机械过速保护装置

宝珠寺电厂安装4台水轮发电机组。由于历史原因，仅有2号机组设置了纯机械过速保护，其余3台机组过速保护均为电气控制的保护，不满足相关反措和安全标准化的要求。针对该隐患，电厂技术人员多方咨询设计厂商，根据调速器液压设计回路及调速器各部件的现场布置，在现有的调速器结构不大幅度调整的情况下，增设了纯机械过速装置，满足了电厂在失去电源的情况下，能够自动关闭机组导水机构的功能。

（一）原有过速保护系统介绍

宝珠寺电厂原过速保护系统由调速器、SP事故配压阀、测压接头、测速元件、外接管路接头、液压元器件、机组LCU及相关逻辑和相关控制回路组成，设有115%额定转速＋主配压阀拒动或停机过程中＋剪断销剪断＋转速大于115%额定转速构成的一级保护，140%额定转速为二级保护。机组的转速测量方式主要是永磁机测频和磁盘测频两种方式。当转速超过115%额定转速时，一级过速继电器动作，驱动调速器事故停机电磁阀动作，快速关闭导叶，从而实现停机；当转速超过140%额定转速时，二级过速继电器动作，驱动调速器事故配压阀电磁阀动作，快速关闭导叶的同时，关闭快速闸门。

显然，原过速保护系统快速关闭导叶的指令执行，必须在有电的前提下才能完成。当机组甩负荷过程中又有全厂失电事故发生，此时机组过速将无法控制，事故的后果是难以想象的。

（二）增设纯机械过速保护装置

1. 总体方案　保留原有的电气二级过速保护，增设一套纯机械过速保护装置，转速动作值为150%的额定转速。该装置能保证在全厂失电的情况下，转速到达150%的额定转速时，依然可以动作事故配压阀，迅速切换油路操作导叶关闭导叶，从而使机组的过速得到控制。

2. 纯机械过速装置部件安装　宝珠寺电厂采用了ALSTOM公司DEVSS系列纯机械液压过速保护装置，由离心探测器、脱扣器、配压阀、过速保护切换阀、安装附件组成。离心探测器器选择在便于安装及维护的发电机下端轴上，此安装部位方便安装且不影响其他部位的工作；脱扣器和换向阀通过安装支架固定在下机架的上平面上，方便拆卸。在安装离心探测器过程中，调整离心探测器与脱扣器的距离为1.5mm，检查转环把合间隙调整到位，支架与脱扣器安装牢固，各油管路连接正确、无渗漏现象。

3. 液压系统的改造　图1示出纯机械过速保护装置液压原理。在原液压图上增设一个二位三通的方向阀，此液控单向阀受事故电磁阀和机械过速保护阀的控制，无论是过速电磁阀还是机械过速保护阀的动作，都可以使得事故配压阀动作，作用于事故停机。改造后，原一级、二级过速流程保持不变，依然通过电磁配压阀动作，油路切换，事故配压阀动作，压力油直接进入导叶关闭腔，将导叶关闭。当一级、二级过速失效，转速继续升高，探测器柱塞克服预紧力向外运动，当向外的运动量达到或大于飞摆与脱扣器触发机构的间隙时，触动触发机构，进而带动液压阀组切换工作油路，机械过速行程阀阀芯左移，液压阀上部与排油接通，液压阀在下端压力的作用下，向上移动，此时无论原一级、二级过速保护系统电磁阀处于何种状态，压力油作用事故配压阀动作，关闭导叶接力器，实现机组停机。机组停机后，脱扣器仍然保持动作后状态，需要手动复归。

4. 装置调试试验　在管路和设备安装完毕后，将机械过速保护信号动作事故停机流程节点解除；将压油装置建压到油压可以操作接力器动作即可，操作接力器完成两次以上的全行程动作，确认各液压管路无渗漏；将油压建至额定油压，操作接力器至全开位置，手动动作机械过速保护脱扣器，事故配压阀动作，关闭时间为7.1s，满足调保计算要求。同时对调速器开机时间、调速器零点漂移进行校验，均应满足要求。然后将动作事故停机流程接点恢复，进行机械过速保护启动事故停机流程试验。

第一台机组调试时，发现在复归电磁阀过程中，有部分压力油通过回油管上窜至调速器机械柜处，严重影响调速器的安全生产运行。经分析研究，发现实际施工将单项阀的回油管与漏油箱管路接通，在复归过程中，液压阀与事故配压阀处的高压油通过单向阀排至漏油管，因漏油管直径较小，无法及时排油，导致漏油管暂时带压，致使部分压力油调速器机械柜漏油孔“喷出”。

为了处理该异常现象，同时便于过速限制器装置的检修，分别在保护装置P口管路上装设一个进油阀1，在A出口处增设阀门2，在卸载阀排油管至调速器漏油管处增设阀门3，根据实际运行情况调整阀门开度，达到了过速保护装置切除检修又不影响机组正常运行的目的，同时也有效地杜绝了电磁阀复归后的喷油状况。

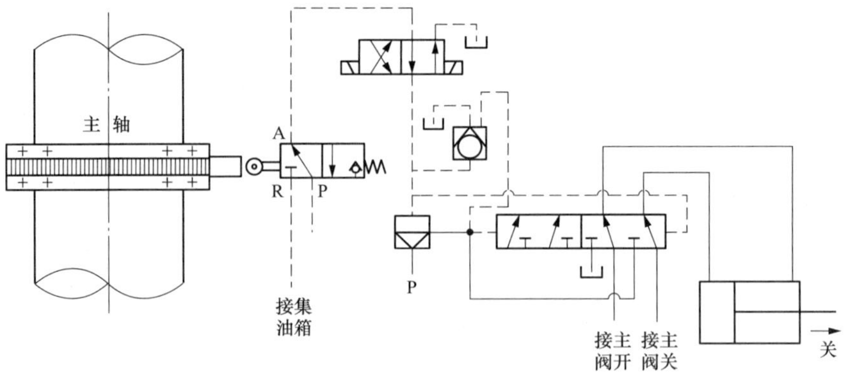

图1　纯机械液压过速保护原理图

受到现场条件的限制，未能进行厂内原型过速试验，只是人为动作液压换向阀的触动臂验证事故配压阀的动作情况。纯机械过速保护是原有两级过速保护的后备保护，在机组实际运行过程中尚未发生失效导致纯机械过速保护动作的情况，因此该装置的实际动作情况，有待进一步来验证。

（宝珠寺水力发电厂　方仲超　杨继承）

三板溪水电厂3号发电机定子接地故障处理

三板溪水电厂安装4台单机容量为25万kW的水轮发电机组，2006年投产发电。机组由哈尔滨电机厂有限责任公司生产，发电机型号是SF250-36/10200。2016年8月22日，电厂3号机组带25万kW负荷运行，定子A相发生接地故障，引起非计划停运。现场检查发现定子U4支路、第39槽下层线棒发生接地故障。将线棒拆除后，发现铁芯最下层扇形冲片（简称冲片）移位突出8mm，切入第39槽下层线棒，导致其发生金属性接地。

（一）原因分析

三板溪水电厂3号机组定子，冲片与鸽尾筋配合开的是平行四边形槽，铁芯鸽尾槽靠冲片交替叠装形成；端部的冲片，为提高整体性采用黏结技术。造成该定子铁芯下层端部冲片（简称端片）滑移逸出的原因可能有下列三方面：

（1）铁芯下层端片黏结不牢。这导致冲片间的抗剪切力低，当片间抗剪切力小于端片与压指间摩擦力时，冲片就可能发生滑移。造成端片黏结不牢的原因主要是胶的使用方法不当、质量控制不严，如涂刷的胶在压紧前已固化，黏结后的端片间的黏结强度就不够。

（2）铁芯压紧度不够。这导致压力无法传递到下端，使小压齿板侧紧、大压齿板侧松，铁芯整体度不好，尤其是大压齿板侧端片的整体性差。大压齿板侧铁芯整体性松动，将引起铁芯翘曲、振动及噪声。严重的翘曲会使黏结端片层间分离，造成冲片间的摩擦力减小。当冲片间的摩擦力小于端片与压指间摩擦力并相差较大时，靠叠片形成的鸽尾就变形而无法限制冲片间出现滑移。

（3）机组运行状态。机组长时间运行，定子铁芯较最初发电时已发生松动，整体性下降，端片整体黏结效果下降；机组频繁启停，在一定程度上会增加端片滑移的几率。

三板溪电厂机组投产发电已过10年，机组参与电网调峰任务，启停次数频繁。本次发生定子接地的3号机组，为该厂运行时间最长（33765h）、启停次数最多（2200次）的机组；但该机组未发现严重铁心翘曲，端片滑移逸出与铁芯压紧度不够无直接关系。3号机组定子铁芯端片滑移逸出的直接原因是：定子端部阶梯段冲片的结构有缺陷，端片黏结不牢。

（二）处理情况

为了彻底解决定子铁芯端片滑移问题，经研究，决定对3号机组定子铁芯冲片进行拆除，更换新的冲片重新叠装，并优化铁芯端片结构与安装工艺流程。主要措施如下：

（1）改进工艺流程。定子铁芯冲片叠装前，在压指与第一层端部冲片之间均匀涂一层二硫化钼，以降低两者间的摩擦系数，进而减小摩擦力。在定子装配完成后，喷红瓷漆9130之前采取防护措施，防止压指与第一片端片间渗入9130漆。

（2）更换定子穿心螺杆。新的M36螺杆，上端使用圆螺母＋碟形弹簧压紧结构，并增加薄螺母锁紧和戴上绝缘螺帽；螺杆下端也增加薄螺母锁紧，防止机组长期运行后定子铁芯松动。

（3）优化定子端部阶梯段冲片的结构。一是将定子端部阶梯段冲片及上、下第一段的基本冲片不开平行四边形槽，而开鸽尾槽。这部分铁芯鸽尾槽由冲片本身自带，不再靠叠片形成，虽然叠片效率较低，但是限位能力明显提高。二是将端片在制造厂内黏结成3mm厚的整体形式，黏结质量得到较好控制，端片整体性也更优，几乎与厚钢板等效。

三板溪水电厂3号机组经A级检修，对定子扇形片进行拆除及重新叠装，并优化铁芯端片结构与安装工艺流程，修后机组运行安全稳定。

（五凌电力三板溪水电厂
袁德雄　张强　张志勇）

沙沱发电厂设置发电机集电环及碳刷热成像在线监测系统

2013年6月26日，沙沱发电厂2号机组在运行中，因发电机集电环及碳刷发生温度过高故障而停机。其余机组也有频发碳刷温度偏高和打火现象。为保证机组安全运行，电厂增派人员加密开展巡查及温度测量，但这不但耗工、耗时，而且还不能保证对设备运行状况的实时监控制和预警，存在严重的安全隐患。为避免此类事件再次发生，经研究决定，应用红外线热成像技术，设置集电环和碳刷运行温度在线监测系统，以便及时处理。

所设置的红外线热成像在线监测系统主要由前端设备和后台服务器组成。在发电机集电环及碳刷圆周上布置4个热成像摄像头，通过光纤将数据传输至后台服务器，搭建软件平台，实现实时监测。该系统的功能特点如下：

（1）分区监控和自动报警功能。分4个扇区对发电机碳刷和集电环温度进行实时监视，能自动追踪、显示温度最高点，能准确测量出集电环、碳刷运行温度情况。任一碳刷最高温度超标，则发出报警信息，系统自动记录下扇区编号和碳刷编号，维护人员根据信息记录，即可快速确定发热点位置。

（2）一键切换功能和分析功能。当常规监视发现机组异常时，系统可以实现自动巡检模式一键切换现场分析模式功能。也可以基于报警信息的快速定位切换到报警位置点和自动回复到自动监视状态。系统可以对热像图进行区域分析，点分析和线分析，实时显示所选区域最高、最低和平均温度。

（3）报表功能和自我诊断功能。系统可以根据时间区间选择数值生成报告，并可以导出Word/Excel格式；系统具有自我诊断功能以及供断电自动保存与恢复功能。

通过查新，未见针对碳刷运行温度实时监视的文献报道，沙沱发电厂对碳刷采用的热成像在线监测技术属于首创。

实施前，2号机组因集电环及碳刷发生故障停机，事故处理花了近7天时间；后安排专业人员每两个小时对运行碳刷、集电环开展巡视检查和温度测量工作，每天至少4人；运行碳刷、集电环属于大电流裸露、高速转动部件，手动测量存在较大人员和设备安全风险。

应用实施后，多次及时发现集电环、碳刷温度异常升高和打火情况，避免事故发生。据统计，2014年5月12日～10月15日，通过红外热成像在线监测，电厂及时发现集电环、碳刷温度异常升高和打火情况103次，其中1号机组45次，2号机组19次，3号机组17次，4号机组22次，为打磨处理赢取最佳时间。同时，消除巡视、测量的安全隐患，每日节约4人次的人力资源。

（沙沱发电厂　赵梅）

柘溪水力发电厂220kV母线保护改造的二次安全措施

柘溪水力发电厂根据检修工作安排计划，对220kVⅠ、Ⅱ段母线RCS-915AB母差保护装置进行换型，原有的南瑞RCS-915AB型微机保护装置将更换成深圳南瑞继保电气有限公司生产的BP-2CA-G型微机母差保护装置；对220kV WMZ-41B母差保护装置进行换型，原有的南自WMZ-41B型微机保护装置将更换成南京南瑞继保电气有限公司生产的PCS-915A-G型微机保护装置。220kV母线保护改造是一项涉及范围广、技术复杂的工作，尤其是二次安全措施的执行和恢复，在一次设备不停电的状态下执行起来就更加要慎之又慎。现将柘溪水力发电厂220kV母线保护改造采取二次安全措施的情况简介如下。

（一）二次安全措施

（1）二次安全措施的执行为：①在母差保护屏对侧解开母差跳闸出口、联跳主变压器、启动母联失灵、远切/联切回路全部二次线；②在室内端子箱处对母差保护屏各间隔电流进行隔离；③母差保护屏接入交流电压安全隔离；④在直流馈线屏上解开母差保护屏直流电源；⑤在母差保护屏对侧解开交流电源；⑥在母差保护屏对侧解开遥信、中央信号、故障录波等全部二次线。

（2）二次安全措施的恢复为：①在母线失灵保护屏检查直流电源、交流电源、遥信、中央信号、信息子站、故障录波等全部二次线已恢复；②母线失灵保护屏交流电压恢复；③在室内端子箱处恢复母线失灵保护屏各间隔电流；④在母线失灵保护屏对侧恢复母线失灵保护跳闸出口、联跳主变压器、远切/联切回路。

（3）工作票上的安全措施见表1，二次措施票上的主要内容见表2。

表1 工作票上的安全措施

检修工作应执行的安全措施	
1	退出母差保护柜上所有保护连接片
2	在上位机上投入“220kV 母差事故试验按钮”
3	拉开母差保护的装置直流电源快分开关
应设遮栏、应挂标示牌	
1	在开关站线保室母差保护柜悬挂“在此工作”标示牌
2	在开关站线保室母差保护柜相邻的运行柜柜上装设“运行设备”红布幔

表2 二次措施票上的主要内容

序号	应拆开回路	执行	恢复
1	母差保护跳母线上各断路器的跳闸回路		
2	失灵启动回路		
3	变压器高压侧断路器失灵联跳开出回路		
4	交流电流回路在电缆侧短接并确认短接可靠后再打开连接片		
5	各段母线电压回路可靠断开		
6	LCU 信号回路公共端拆开		
7	录波及信息子站公共端拆开		

（二）注意事项

本次改造试验只校验改造后的母线失灵保护本屏装置开入及开出回路的正确性。

（1）主变压器、线路、母联、旁路保护装置中红黄牌产品及5年未进行检修的保护装置，应通过整组试验或进行装置开出传动试验验证主变压器、线路、母联、旁路间隔启动失灵回路及主变解除失灵复压闭锁回路的正确性。需要进行的回路验证工作应在母线失灵保护更换开工以前完成，待母线失灵保护更换时所有相关回路直接接入。

（2）母线保护改造前，还需申请母联断路器停电，对母线保护用的母联断路器操作箱的 SHJ 手合接点进行检查验证；在母线保护改造期间，如果1号变压器一直处于停电检修状态，两套母线保护带负荷时都无法对1号变压器电流进行检测，1号变压器送电时，两套母线保护应同时退出。

（3）220kV 双套母线失灵保护换型工作检修申请应纳入月度检修计划管理。主变压器、线路、母联和旁路间隔失灵启动回路的改动，退出单套保护屏的对应的全套保护申请应纳入检修计划管理。

（4）母线失灵保护 A、B套改造检修卡中检修影响内容应注明施工中将短时、分别退出的保护。

（5）母线失灵保护 A 套改造检修卡中应注明：在母线失灵保护 A 套改造开始后退出 220kV 失灵保护屏全套保护；母线失灵保护 A 套投运后拆除 220kV 失灵保护屏。现场实施时屏柜内压板投退应提前申请。

（6）检修卡中保护型号应填写正确，屏号、第 X 套保护等无需填写。

（7）改造过程涉及自动信息规范化流程，应提前提交信息点表。

（8）各间隔启动失灵回路、主变压器失灵联跳回路将涉及定值调整，应提早向继电保护定值整定部门申请并提供相应资料和说明。

（9）断路器失灵启动回路、失灵联跳出口回路、母差保护跳闸回路及交流电流、交流电压回路等二次回路全部在带电状态下进行二次安全措施布置，为了更慎重起见，在二次措施布置完成后，还应该用万用表的直流电压档检查直流开入及开出回路是否确已解开。总之，要确保二次安全措施的万无一失。

（柘溪水力发电厂　何文）

三板溪水电厂定子铁芯改造采用修复的硅钢片

三板溪水电厂安装4台单机容量为25万kW的混流式水轮发电机组，2006年投产发电。机组由哈尔滨电机厂有限责任公司生产，发电机型号是SF250-36/10200。2017年3月，2号机组定子改造，铁芯硅钢片要全部拆除重新叠装，如果全部购买新的，将要花费近900万元；而之前3号机组定子铁芯改造拆出有近13万张旧硅钢片，如能修复后继续使用，则可大大节约改造成本。因此，电厂开展了相关研究工作，决定采用旧硅钢片修复后继续使用的办法。

大型发电机定子铁芯对硅钢片间绝缘的要求很高，绝缘涂层不但要有适当电阻率，还要有较高表面附着力，在高温和压力的作用下不发生塑性变形，且厚度要均匀。如果修复工艺不到位，易出现油漆膜脱落，片间短路，铁芯松动和铁芯发热等一系列问题。因此，三板溪水电厂根据拆下硅钢片实际情况及硅钢片使用性能要求，制定了严格的修复质量要求，见表1，并强调修复过程中所用材料、器件和所进行的检测工作，必须符合国家和电力行业现行技术标准的要求。

表1　硅钢片修复质量要求

类型	项目	要求
机械	外观	冲孔及边缘无毛刺，扇形片平整无弯曲痕迹
	漆膜柔性	试样沿直径为10mm的圆棒弯曲90°，漆膜无开裂和剥落
	附着力	使用百格刀将试样涂层划出100个正方形，在划痕处贴透明胶带，然后撕下胶带，划痕范围无剥离
	硬度试验	用2H硬度铅笔以45°用力划试验片的双面涂层，漆膜无破损
化学	耐溶剂性	使用丙酮溶剂擦拭表面，漆膜未露出低材
电气	击穿强度	满足GB/T 1408.1—2006《绝缘材料电气强度试验方法》要求
	富兰克林试验	RTD-1表面电阻测试仪，试验压力为5.2MPa、试验电压为0.5V，电流稳定后记录电流值，电流值不超过0.05A

三板溪水电厂旧硅钢片修复，委托德阳远东机电责任有限公司进行。该公司针对电厂所提出硅钢片修复要求，制定了硅钢片修复工艺，步骤如下：

（1）对拆下硅钢片进行挑选和堆垛，检查冲片额部、鸽尾、孔径、槽部、尺端变形和缺角少边，对缺角少边的必须作报废处理，对变形的冲片挑选出来，进行修复后达到平整要求的进入下道工序，未达到的报废。

（2）对堆垛的定子冲片边缘进行初步处理，将冲片边缘原有半导体绝缘浮漆去除。

（3）全部冲片进行去油、去污并进行清洗。

（4）冲片清洗后通过烤漆炉进行烘干。

（5）用毛刺机对冲片进行双面打磨处理，经打磨后的冲片必须表面光滑平整，冲片槽口边缘无毛刺。

（6）将打磨后的全部冲片的双面粉尘处理干净。

（7）将冲片通过烤漆线进行涂漆，选用西安绝缘材料厂生产的133C型硅钢片绝缘漆，并按照133C漆涂刷技术要求进行涂漆，所修复的扇形硅钢片整体厚度（含双面漆膜）控制在0.521～0.525mm，局部高点不超过0.535mm。

（8）每千片抽一片检查漆膜附着力、漆膜厚度和绝缘情况，应符合要求。

（9）将修复完工后的冲片装箱，待冷却后进行防潮和防水包装。

三板溪水电厂2号机组定子铁芯采用修复的硅钢片进行改造获得成功。改造后的机组运行稳定，节约成本约400万元，经济效益显著。

（五凌电力三板溪水电厂
袁德雄　张志勇　张强）

安康联营电站水轮机主轴密封水压异常波动处理

安康联营电站是安康水电站为了保障下游18km处安康城市生产生活需要，利用坝体右岸排沙洞设计建设的电站，安装一台混流式水轮发电机组，容量为52.5MW。该机组水轮机主轴密封采用的是水压端面密封形式，如图1所示；采用两路水源提供压力水，一路取自机组技术供水系统，一路取自电站消防水系统。

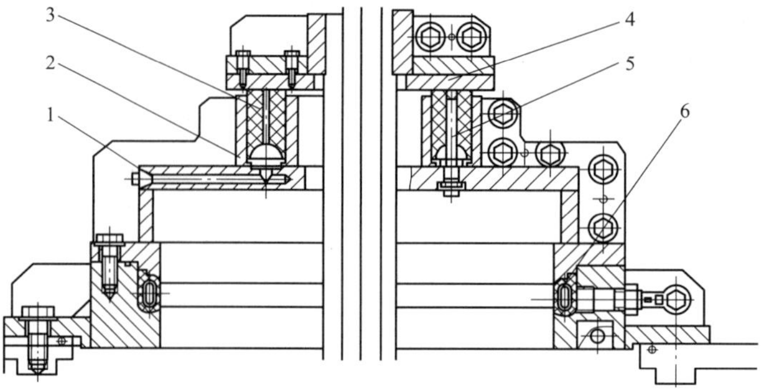

图1 主轴密封结构示意图

1—供水管；2—密封底座；3—密封橡胶块；4—转环；5—密封块定位销；6—检修密封

该电站实际运行表明，水轮机主轴密封块下腔水压，开停机过程中在0～0.5MPa范围内波动，有时0.3MPa以上水压持续1min，严重超出主轴密封橡胶块工作水压要求范围。按设计，当主轴密封橡胶块下腔水压低于设定值，密封橡胶块没有足够的升力，密封不住顶盖与主轴之间的水，会造成顶盖水位过高；超过设定值，升力过大，会使主轴密封橡胶块与转环摩擦力过大，并且造成润滑冷却水量不足，橡胶块易磨损，甚至烧毁，机组被迫停机检修。该主轴密封水压异常波动，成为该电站运行的一大安全隐患。

（一）原因分析

安康水电站和安康联营电站两个电站的水轮机主轴密封都是采用水压端面密封形式。通过对这两电站运行过程各部位水压观测、分析后发现，两个电站机组在开停机过程中，各部水压受水锤影响比较明显，主轴密封水压都不稳定，但安康水电站在0.05～0.2MPa之间，安康联营电站在0.00～0.5MPa之间。经研究，造成安康联营电站主轴密封水压异常波动的原因如下：

(1) 机组开停机水锤影响较大。主轴密封水源通常由技术供水系统供给，会受电站工作水头变化以及机组开停机水锤影响。由于联营电站技术供水取水单一、只有1台、供水系统较简单、系统水容量也小，而安康水电站供水系统母管接有6个取水口，4个取自机组引水钢管、2个取自坝前，供水系统母管管路也长，相对容量大；因此，前者对机组开停机引起的水锤消纳能力比后者弱，即安康联营电站主轴密封水压受机组开机水锤的影响要比安康电站的大。

(2) 顶盖运行水压影响。当顶盖压力水小于密封橡胶块下端水压时，密封橡胶块正常工作，但顶盖水压大于密封水压，就会推动密封橡胶块裙边内陷，进入密封橡胶块下端，增高密封水压。顶盖水可窜入主轴密封橡胶块下端这事，曾通过关闭主轴密封进水阀，看到主轴密封管路压力表有压力指示、排水管路有大量水流出的试验得到证实。安康水电站机组顶盖水压开停机过程在0～0.2MPa之间，正常运行在0.08MPa左右；而安康联营电站机组顶盖水压在开停机过程在0～0.59MPa，正常运行在0.25MPa左右，其主轴密封水压异常波动与顶盖水窜入应有关联。

（二）解决方法

解决主轴密封水压异常波动问题，应从消除机组开机水锤对主轴密封供水系统的影响和降低顶盖运行水压着手。为了给主轴密封提供一个稳定可靠的水源水压，提出了采用开启式水箱解决方案，即在电站适当高程和合适地方设置一个开启式水箱作为水源，利用高程差，给主轴密封提供水压相对稳定的水源。但这涉及方面多，有难度。而降低顶盖运行水压，要同设计、制造单位沟通，一时也难办到。比较现实的办法，是在现系统上作些改进。为此，2016年10月，为了消除其他水源因素对主轴密封水压的影响，安康联营电站对主轴密封管路进行改造，将原有的预埋管路封闭，重新用明管铺设。为了消除顶盖水倒灌引起主轴密封水压超高，电站在供水管路上加装了一套排水装置，安装了安全阀，当管路中水压超过0.2MPa就自动泄压，以满足主轴密封对水压运行要求。经此改造，安康联营电站水轮机主轴密封一直安全运行。此方法管路改造小，费用低，但难消除水锤影响，安全阀需要及时调整维护。

（安康水力发电厂　李军　朱晓东
王申　徐东升　成安　宋红丽）

水情预报与调度

2018年清江梯级水电站调度运行情况

（一）2018年清江梯级总体运行情况

2018年，水布垭以上流域降雨量为1384.3mm，较多年同期偏多0.3%。1～5月降雨整体偏多，较多年同期偏多34.6%；6～12月整体偏枯，降雨量较多年同期偏少15.6%。汛期降水量898.1mm，占全年降水量的64.9%，较多年平均偏少2.7%。

2018年，水布垭入库水量为76.57亿m^3，较多年同期偏少14.9%。1～5月入库水量为36.22亿m^3，较多年同期偏多26.5%；6～11月水布垭来水持续偏枯，12月份来水偏多30.3%，6～12月水布垭入库水量为40.34亿m^3，较多年同期偏少34.2%。

2018年，清江梯级三电厂发电72.80亿kW·h，较2017年减少30.8%。其中：水布垭电厂发电36.01亿kW·h，较2017年同期减少31.4%；隔河岩电厂发电27.29亿kW·h，较2017年同期减少31.1%；高坝洲电厂发电9.50亿kW·h，较2017年同期减少27.1%。

（二）经济调度

2018年，清江梯级三电厂累计节水增发电量4.09亿kW·h，累计增发率5.3%，其中水布垭、隔河岩、高坝洲水能利用提高率分别为0.4%、8.3%、14.9%。

促进梯级及三厂水能利用提高率较高的主要因素有：

（1）梯级水库长期调度方式优化、科学。2018年初编制《2018年清江梯级水库调度策略》《2018年清江梯级汛期电厂运行方式安排》等长期指导方案，对月末、汛前等关键水位进行确定，做到水头和水量的合理利用。

（2）中短期调度在长期调度策略的框架下，重点做好以下工作：一是分析目前水库入库水量情况、土壤含水情况、上游水库蓄水情况，根据气象预报预测流域未来来水情况；二是掌握梯级水库水位情况、流域电厂机组及线路检修计划、电网线路检修计划以及与梯级水库有关的项目施工或试验情况；三是结合气象状况、气温预测、周边电厂发电情况以及三峡水库水位及消落计划等情况分析电力市场。综合考虑以上内容制定中短期发电计划及机组运行方式安排，做到中短期调度统筹化、精细化、合理化。

（3）实时调度中深入践行“用好每方水，调好每度电”的调度理念，优化日96点发电计划、优化机组开机方式、减少机组不合理运行工况，提高流域机组运行的经济性、安全性。

（4）与电网构建有效的沟通机制，在流域遭遇暴雨时，能在电网的支持下快速有效地增加发电计划或开展站间负荷转移，减少弃水风险，充分利用雨洪资源。

（三）防洪调度

2018年清江梯级未发生大洪水过程，水布垭全年最大洪峰流量2730m^3/s。清江公司精心备汛，成功应对隔—高区间突发强降雨。2018年4月22日，隔—高区间遭遇历史罕见暴雨，日平均雨量达132.9mm，其中高坝洲单站日累计降雨量301mm，为有水文记录以来的最大单日降水。此次过程高坝洲站最大6h雨量频率超50年一遇，最大24h雨量接近50年一遇。此次降雨来临前，根据当地气象部门的预警，高坝洲水库提前着手降低水位，及时开展电站间负荷转移，将隔河岩计划转移至水布垭，减少高坝洲入库水量，通过提前预控水位和开展站间负荷转移，为高坝洲多腾出约3028万m^3库容，有效避免高坝洲发生弃水。

（四）提高服务公益意识，积极做好水库综合利用

（1）配合洞坪水电站下游左岸护坡处理项目部分修复施工。为配合洞坪下游左岸护坡水毁部分修复施工，清江公司提前谋划，于2018年1月编制了《配合洞坪尾水下游左岸护坡施工调度预案》，提出了施工期间水位控制方案以及相应调度措施。并将施工各阶段对水布垭水位的要求体现在《清江梯级水库2018年调度策略》和《2018年度清江梯级水库汛期调度运用计划》中。

在实际调度中，综合考虑梯级水库腾库迎汛、梯级电站机组检修、电网渔兴线路检修等诸多因素，精心调度，为洞坪施工创造有利条件，保证了施工的顺利进行。

（2）配合地方政府建设项目施工。为配合长阳水

利水电局清江护岸工程（长阳永和坪段）建设项目施工及兼顾高坝洲取水需求，2018年2月3～8日高坝洲库水位按76.7～77.3m，9～10日按77.2～77.7m控制运行。为配合长阳县高坝洲贫困地区旅游渡运码头工程永和坪、叹溪沟两个点进行水上平台施工，2018年9月15～25日高坝洲库水位控制在76.7～77.2m之间运行。为配合长阳县清江护岸工程施工，2018年11月3～18日高坝洲库水位按77～77.5m控制运行。为配合长阳防洪治理工程（朱津滩段）施工，高坝洲于2018年12月18日开始加大发电降水位，20～28日库水位按76.7～77.2m控制运行，29日至次年1月1日按78.2m控制运行。

（3）配合长阳县成功举办全国马拉松游泳锦标赛。2018年8月27～29日，全国马拉松游泳锦标赛在高坝洲库区的长阳县城附近水域举办，应长阳县政府要求，需要控制高坝洲水质及水位等，于8月21～24日对高坝洲水体进行置换；27～29日隔河岩、高坝洲控制发电流量运行，库水位控制在79m附近，使得比赛顺利进行。

（4）积极开展科研工作，开拓创新，提升优化调度水平。历时5年研发的清江梯级智能对象化水电调平台系统于2018年9月30日正式上线运行。该系统实现了对象化智能分级报警、对象化界面、自动对点、数据冻结、AGC非推荐运行区等创新功能，使系统运行监视、维护管理和数据传输等工作更加智能、安全、高效、便捷。

（湖北清江水电开发有限责任公司）

丰满水电站全面治理工程施工期水库调度情况

丰满水电站全面治理（重建）工程（简称丰满重建工程）是在原丰满水电站大坝下游120m处新建一座碾压混凝土重力坝，工程已于2012年10月29日正式开工，预计2020年末竣工，是世界首例原址重建大坝工程。在新坝施工期要求原水库的发电、防洪、供水、灌溉、航运、养殖、旅游等综合利用功能不变，同时国家电网公司要求发生100年一遇洪水时争取老坝不泄洪、保证工程具备旱地施工条件。因此，水库调度工作面临着安全度汛、保证下游用水和保障工程干地施工的三重压力。

面对水库调度工作中层出不穷的问题，调度边界条件的巨变，调度复杂程度的激增，国家电网东北电力调控分中心采取丰满白山梯级水库联合调度的策略，根据丰满重建工程每年施工项目对水库调度的要求，综合考虑施工安全、防洪安全、供水安全，制定各年度的水库调度实施方案，成功化解了防洪、供水和施工之间的矛盾，满足了各方需求，确保了丰满重建工程的顺利实施。

（一）施工准备期（2013～2014年）的水库调度

根据2013年流域来水特丰的预报，春汛前主动降丰满水位4.2m、腾库容14亿m^3，夏汛主汛前主动降丰满水位3m、腾库容11亿m^3，成功应对丰满水库春汛历史第一来水、夏汛70年一遇特大洪水，将70年一遇洪水洪峰流量由17300m^3/s削减为2100m^3/s，并为嫩江和松花江洪水错峰135h，避免了洪水叠加形成更大灾害，创造了巨大防洪减灾效益。同时，将丰满坝下交通桥施工围堰设防流量由500m^3/s提高到1000m^3/s，避免了江桥围堰被冲毁，直接减少损失450万元，间接减少损失15000万元（丰满重建工程晚开工一年的损失）。将新建泄洪兼导流洞下游围堰施工时间推至主汛期后，避免了围堰被冲毁，直接减少损失100万元。

（二）主体施工期（2015～2018年）的水库调度

2015年，丰满重建工程主体施工全面开始，工程有了旱地施工要求。为了争取100年一遇洪水时老坝不泄洪，化解防洪、供水和旱地施工的矛盾，2014年7月国家电力调度控制中心组织编制了《丰满水电站全面治理（重建）工程施工期水库调度实施方案》，用以指导施工期的水库调度。

2015年，通过积极开展长期来水预测工作，成功应对了流域年来水较历年同期少37%的不利局面，确保了下游用水要求。丰满水库农业灌溉期外又先后5次加大出流，共计多出库水量3.75亿m^3，保证了水库下游吉林省100万亩水田的抗旱用水，受到了吉林省的肯定和表扬。

2016年，春汛丰满水库来水特丰，为保证工程干地施工，丰满水库首次启用泄洪兼导流洞进行了施工导流，年导流水量34.95亿m^3。另外，通过精心调控丰满水库水位，保证了泄洪兼导流洞岩坎拆除工程的旱地施工条件，节约工程投资150万元。

2017年，丰满流域春汛来水特丰、夏汛连续发生成灾洪水。为了确保工程旱地施工，进行了施工导流，历时93天，年导流水量46.68亿m^3，成功应对了3次成灾洪水，将丰满水库最大入库流量由10400m^3/s削减至出库623m^3/s，防洪减灾效益十分显著。另外，通过制定科学合理的导流方案，成功化解了丰满机组检修、导流洞缺陷处理、下游河道施工与施工导流的矛盾，成功避免了下泄水流对丰满下游左岸护岸及公路的大面积冲刷，直接减少损失800万元。

2018年，成功应对了台风摩羯、温比亚、苏力、飞燕外围云系带来的强降雨，进行了30天施工导流，年导流水量 16.71 亿 m^3，保证了丰满重建工程的旱地施工。同时采取蓄白山、降丰满的策略，8 月全力开展白山水库蓄水工作，白山水库拦蓄水量达 18.21 亿 m^3，汛末蓄满白山水库，解决了丰满老坝拆除施工丰满水库水位控制要求与保证丰满水库下游工农业及城市用水需求的矛盾，有效保障了后期丰满水库下游综合用水安全。汛后精准控制丰满水库水位，保证了丰满老坝拆除工作顺利进行。

（三）结语

2013～2018 年，国家电网东北电力调控分中心每年 3 月和 6 月都召开来水会商会，开展长期来水预测工作，成功预测了 2013、2017 年的丰水和 2015、2018 年的枯水。在准确的长期来水预测基础上，通过超前谋划，提前控制，枯水年保证了丰满水库下游供水需要，丰水年保证了丰满重建工程干地施工，实现了施工安全、防洪安全、供水安全，获得了发电、防洪、供水、灌溉、航运以及施工等各方的好评。

（国家电网东北电力调控分中心　郭希海）

刘家峡水库汛限水位动态控制研究

（一）龙羊峡、刘家峡水库的运行实践

1. 龙羊峡水库运行实践　龙羊峡水库具有多年调节能力，死水位 2530m，设计汛期限制水位 2594m，黄委会允许的汛限水位 2588m，正常蓄水位 2600m，校核洪水位 2607m。

1988 年正常运行以来，由于 2005 年前黄河上游来水持续偏枯，龙羊峡水库运行水位长期偏低，在汛限水位以下尚有较多库容可存蓄洪水。尽管 2005 年底水位接近正常蓄水位，但 2006～2015 年 10 年间，7、8、9 月 3 个月初平均水位分别为 2575.86、2581.39、2583.33m，低于汛限水位 2588m。另外，龙羊峡水库属多年调节水库，即使今后上游来水正常，从运行和水库特性分析，每年汛期运行水位不可能均达到汛限水位，从实施调度的角度来说，龙羊峡水库有一定空闲库容为刘家峡水库超汛期限制水位运行所用。

2. 刘家峡水库的运行实践　刘家峡水库具有年调节性能，死水位 1694m，设计汛期限制水位 1726m，黄委会允许的汛限水位 1727m，正常蓄水位 1735m，校核洪水位 1738m。

刘家峡水库在龙羊峡水库投产后汛期 7、8、9 月平均水位分别为 1719.95、1721.77、1724.27m，较汛限水位 1727m 分别低 7.05、5.23、2.73m；汛期 7、8、9 月最高水位分别为 1729.45、1731.36、1733.39m，汛期有超汛限水位 1727m 运行记录。因此，刘家峡水库在龙羊峡水库投入运行后已有多次超汛期限制水位运行的经验。

综上所述，综合两库运行实践，黄委会允许龙羊峡水库汛限水位 2588m，比原设计汛限水位低 6m，增加防洪库容 21.56 亿 m^3，允许刘家峡水库汛限水位 1727m，比原设计汛限水位高 1m，减少防洪 1.58 亿 m^3，但龙刘两库净增防洪库容 19.98 亿 m^3，总防洪库容比原设计防洪库容增加约 30%，为研究抬高刘家峡水库汛限水位提供了有利条件。

（二）龙羊峡—刘家峡水库的原洪水联合运行设计

1. 防洪对象　龙刘两库联合防洪的保护对象是龙羊峡水电站设计确定的防洪对象，即龙刘区间已建梯级电站、盐锅峡、八盘峡及兰州市。

2. 洪水与地区组成　黄河上游洪水采用原龙羊峡设计的 1964 年、1967 年两种典型，洪水地区组成采用 1964 年、1967 年典型比例分配放大和按照上、下游同频、区间相应两种地区组成，黄河上游典型洪水和地区洪水共组成 4 种洪水过程。

3. 控制泄量及泄量判别方式

(1) 刘家峡水库承担下游 3 个防护对象的防洪，其标准分为 2000 年、1000 年、100 年一遇，为保证达到预定防洪标准，在不考虑洪水预报情况下，只能控制下泄流量调洪（见表 1）。另外，西北院专家研制了一套安全可靠的判别图，用此图做泄量判别时，同时考虑流量和洪量，二者同时超标才加大泄量，这大大提高了对下游防护对象的防洪安全程度。

表 1　刘家峡水库各级控制流量

项目	洪水重现期（年）			
	$N\leqslant100$	$100<N\leqslant1000$	$1000<N\leqslant2000$	$N>2000$
控制最大泄量（m^3/s）	4290	4510	7260	敞泄

(2) 1983 年黄河上游河段防洪规划后确定的龙羊峡各级控泄流量：1000 年一遇及以下洪水时，控制最大下泄流量不超过 4000m^3/s；超过 1000 年一遇洪水直至可能最大洪水，均控制最大下泄流量不超过 6000m^3/s。

龙羊峡采用入库流量作为判别指标。天然入库流量超过1000年一遇洪峰流量7040m³/s时，则认为洪水已超过1000年一遇标准，允许最大下泄流量由4000m³/s跳级至6000m³/s。

4. 龙刘水库联合防洪调度规则　两库联合防洪调度，既要保证刘家峡水库下游各防护对象达到预定防洪要求，又要保证两库自身防洪安全。在此前提下，尽可能使两库防洪库容之和较小，且调洪库容都得到较充分利用，以减少龙羊峡预留调洪库容。

（三）刘家峡水库汛期超汛限水位的计算与分析

在设定条件下，调洪计算得到的刘家峡最高水位均在其校核洪水位1738m以下，但刘家峡在起调水位1731m下，计算的最高水位1738.9m，超过水库校核洪水位。故认为刘家峡可抬高汛限运行水位最高1730m。另外，龙羊峡起调水位2588m、刘家峡起调水位在1728～1730m时，龙羊峡调洪计算得出最高水位差异较小，但刘家峡汛期可提高水位最高为1730m，说明龙羊峡防洪库容再大，也无法控制龙刘区间洪水，刘家峡水库为调节龙刘区间洪水，必须留有一定的防洪库容。

因此，龙羊峡汛限水位2588m，为刘家峡水库汛期超汛限水位运行提供了条件。龙羊峡水库防洪库容大，且运行水位低于汛限水位，运行水位至汛限水位间的空闲库容可拦蓄部分小洪水，减少龙羊峡下泄流量，亦为刘家峡水库汛期超汛限水位运行提供条件。

（四）刘家峡水库汛期超汛限水位运行效益

根据1919年～2000年径流系列，分别计算得刘家峡水库主汛期运行水位抬高1、2、3m时的年发电量，并按现行上网电价0.15元/(kW·h)计算，刘家峡水电站可增加发电量0.173、0.346、0.471亿kW·h，分别增加年收入达260万、519万、707万元，且不需要另外增加投入，其效益显著。

（国网甘肃省电力公司刘家峡水电厂
沈利平　贾怀森　高承众
中国电建集团西北勘测设计研究院有限公司
姬生才　王进学）

宝珠寺电站洪水调度优化方案研究

（一）原汛期洪水调度的优化潜力

宝珠寺电站为大（1）型工程，正常蓄水位588m，汛期限制水位583m，死水位558m，调节库容为13.40亿m³。水库汛期防洪调度基本原则是：确保安全、减轻淤积、多发电量。泄洪建筑物开启顺序：对称开启2右底孔、2左底孔、2中孔、外表孔、内表孔。

原调度运行方式规定，汛期水库水位达到汛限水位583m，且入库洪峰流量不超过8750m³/s时，控制水位在583m运行，即对洪峰流量在8750m³/s以下的洪水基本不调蓄，存在较大的弃水现象，汛期洪水调度方案有优化潜力。

（二）汛期洪水调度优化方案及其效益

近年宝珠寺汛期未发生洪水时，库水位大多低于汛限水位，可临时适当抬高运行水位。宝珠寺以上干支流电站相继建成，拦蓄了部分泥沙，入库泥沙呈现减少趋势。为此，在满足大坝防洪安全、下游和库区防洪要求下，宝珠寺汛期洪水调度可优化。具体方案如下。

1. 洪水预报　宝珠寺、碧口水电站水雨情信息采集已实现自动测报，洪水预报精度达到了甲级水平，但预见期短。在此基础上，通过水文气象耦合应用、短中长期预报结合及水文气象新技术新方法等，延长预见期，争取到24～120h预报预泄时间。

2. 预报调度　优化调度结合气象、降雨及洪水预报，先判别洪水类型（区间型、全流域型、上游型），再根据相应类型洪水预报调度的启用条件，实施洪水预报调度。

（1）区间型洪水峰量小，过程陡涨陡落，历时短。优化方案如下：①满足区间型洪水预报调度启用条件时，水库才允许蓄水；②预报入库洪峰流量（Q）小于全厂满发流量（Q_f）956m³/s时，电站平均发电流量等于入库流量，维持水位不超过汛限水位；③当5000m³/s≥Q>Q_f时，电站按Q_f发电，剩余水量蓄在水库里，控制水库最高水位587m；④当5500m³/s≥Q>5000m³/s时，电站按Q_f发电，剩余水量弃水下泄，维持汛限水位运行；洪峰流量过后、洪水处于退势时，关闭泄洪设施，电站按Q_f发电，剩余水量蓄在库里，控制水库最高蓄水位586m；⑤当6000m³/s≥Q>5500m³/s时，电站按Q_f发电，剩余水量弃水下泄，维持汛限水位运行，洪峰流量过后、洪水处于退势、且入库流量小于5500m³/s后，关闭泄洪设施，电站按Q_f发电，剩余水量蓄在库里，控制水库最高水位585m；⑥当Q>6000m³/s时，原则上恢复正常防洪调度，提前将水位降到汛限水位，但在洪峰过后，洪水处于退势、且入库洪水流量小于5500m³/s后，满足区间型洪水预报调度启用条件时拦蓄洪尾水量。

（2）全流域型洪水洪水量较大，峰有大有小，总体上较区间型小，洪峰流量多在2000m³/s以上，整体呈“区间洪水造峰，上游洪水造量”的组合，洪水过程较长。优化方案如下：①满足全流域型洪水预报调度启用条件时，水库才允许蓄水；②当Q<Q_f时，电站平均发电流量等于入库流量，维持水库水位不超

过汛限水位；③当 $2500m^3/s \geqslant Q > Q_f$ 时，电站按 Q_f 发电，剩余水量蓄在库里，控制水库最高水位 587m；④当 $3000m^3/s \geqslant Q > 2500m^3/s$ 时，洪峰流量过后、洪水处于退势时，电站按 Q_f 发电，剩余水量蓄在库里，控制水库最高蓄水位 587m；⑤当 $3500m^3/s \geqslant Q > 3000m^3/s$ 时，电站按 Q_f 发电，剩余水量弃水下泄，维持汛限水位运行，洪峰流量过后、洪水处于退势、且入库流量小于 $3000m^3/s$ 后，关闭泄洪设施，电站按 Q_f 发电，剩余水量蓄在库里，控制水库最高水位 587m；⑥当 $5000m^3/s \geqslant Q > 3500m^3/s$ 时，电站按 Q_f 发电，剩余水量弃水下泄，维持汛限水位运行，洪峰流量过后、洪水处于退势、且入库流量小于 $3000m^3/s$ 后，关闭泄洪设施，电站按 Q_f 发电，剩余水量蓄在水库里，控制水库最高位 587m；⑦当 $Q > 5000m^3/s$ 时，原则上恢复正常防洪调度，提前将库水位降到汛限水位，但等到洪峰过后，洪水处于退势、且入库洪水流量小于 $3000m^3/s$ 后，满足全流域型洪水预报调度启用条件时拦蓄洪尾水量。

（3）上游型洪水峰小量大，洪峰流量为 $1000 \sim 2500m^3/s$，缓涨缓落历时长。优化方案如下：①满足上游型洪水预报调度启用条件时，水库才允许蓄水；②当 $Q < Q_f$ 时，电站平均发电流量等于入库流量，维持水库水位不超过汛限水位；③当 $1500m^3/s \geqslant Q > Q_f$ 时，电站按 Q_f 发电，剩余水量蓄在水库里，控制水库最高水位 587m；④当 $2500m^3/s \geqslant Q > 1500m^3/s$ 时，电站按 Q_f 发电，剩余水量弃水下泄，维持汛限水位运行，洪峰流量过后、洪水处于退势时，关闭泄洪设施，电站按 Q_f 发电，剩余水量蓄在库里，控制水库最高水位 587m；⑤当 $Q > 2500m^3/s$ 时，恢复正常防洪调度，水位提前降到汛限水位，但等洪峰过后，洪水处于退势、且入库洪水流量小于 $2000m^3/s$ 时，满足上游型洪水预报调度启用条件时拦蓄洪尾水量。

3. 实测洪水验证　按《水文情报预报规范》要求，对宝珠寺汛期洪水调度优化方案进行检验。根据不同类型实测洪水过程验证计算结果，上述优化方案均满足控制水位要求，也满足上下游及宝珠寺防洪安全要求，表明优化方案合理可行，符合本流域洪水特性。

4. 优化方案效益　优化方案实施后，可增加多年平均发电量约 3835 万 kW·h，占设计多年平均发电量 1.74%。按目前电价计算，可增加收入 1428 万元。此外，增发水电可节约煤耗、减少废气排放，按燃煤火电煤耗 320g/(kW·h) 计算，每年可节约煤炭 1.23 万 t，减少废气排放的环境效益明显。同时，汛期多拦蓄洪水，将减轻下游洪水损失和防洪压力，具有一定的防洪效益。

（中国电建集团西北勘测设计研究院有限公司
卢锟明　赵文发　程龙　袁超）

大坝安全管理

2018 年度水电站大坝注册与备案进展情况

2018 年，国家能源局大坝安全监察中心（简称大坝中心）严格按照年度计划开展水电站安全注册，并及时安排新申请大坝的注册工作；明确了各注册、备案水电站大坝责任人；与各派出机构加强联系、沟通与反馈。在开展注册工作时，对于发现的大坝安全信息化、监控和监测管理等问题及时反馈给内部相关部门。

大坝中心在一季度积极配合国家能源局安全司梳理、核实已注册和备案水电站大坝运行和主管单位的大坝安全责任人，并于 4 月初报安全司，其后又根据安全司的反馈意见进行了修改完善，国家能源局于 5 月正式公布；5 月，完成了大坝注册现场检查业务培训授课工作，并完成《水电站大坝安全注册登记工作标准》《水电站大坝安全注册登记管理实绩考核评价标准》修订。

2018 年，受理注册申请 150 座，其中首次注册登记的 45 座，注册登记换证的 104 座，变更注册登记的 1 座；完成现场检查 154 座，对 154 座大坝进行了注册登记等级评审和上报，共发证 144 座大坝（其中，呼蓄上库坝等 17 座大坝为 2017 年评审，2018 年批复；高砂等 3 座为注册信息变更换发注册证）。

2018 年已经国家能源局批复同意在大坝中心注册的大坝有 517 座，比上年末（473 座）增加了 44 座（新注册 51 座，注销 7 座，总数增加 44 座），其中注册等级为甲级的有 476 座，乙级 40 座，丙级 1 座（响水）。办理了福建古田溪三级、古田溪四级、万安溪、丰海、后垄溪二级，新疆哈巴河山口和吉林原丰满大坝共7座大坝的注册登记注销工作。2018年办理了14座大坝首次登记备案和15座大坝的延续备案，目前备案大坝总数为77座。详细情况见附表1。

国家能源局2013年发文通报和督办以及2016年2月新梳理出的150座已投运未注册大坝中（白云和录巴寺装机容量核准到5万kW以下，不再统计在内），有131座大坝完成注册（备案），2座尚未完成安全鉴定等前期工作，1座尚未投运，16座不在监管范围内。

表1　2018年大坝安全注册情况统计表

类型	大坝名称	备注
受理申请（共150座）	初始45座：晴朗、桥巩、那邦、洪屏上库坝、洪屏下库坝、仙居上库坝、甲岩、竹格多、舟坝、昭化、大河家、枕头坝一级、野三河、飞仙关、烟岗、东水峡、乡城、旺村、官帽舟、南极洛河、白龙江沙湾、善泥坡、马马崖一级、铜钟、九龙峡、三岔河、沙沱、巴郎口、洞松、娘拥、古学、沙尔布拉克、哈德布特、萨里克特、尼勒克一级、塔勒德萨依、梨园、鲁地拉、花园、普西桥、黄金坪、金平、金元、清蓄上库坝、清蓄下库坝 换证104座：六郎洞、雷打滩、珠窝、落坡岭、蓬辣滩、长潭、青溪、枫树坝、新丰江、长湖、陈村、纪村、富春江、惠蓄上库坝、惠蓄下库坝、铅厂、鲁基厂、南桠河三级、刘家峡、泉水、柘林、照口、鱼剑口、庙林、紫兰坝、乐滩、福堂、百龙滩、大化、沙湾、湖南镇、黄坛口、天荒坪上库坝、天荒坪下库坝、别迭里、铁门关、托海、龚嘴、良浅、孔头、柳坪、色尔古、上犹江、沙溪口、五一桥、小湾、洪坝、湾坝、天生桥一级、大山口、阴坪、公伯峡、新安江、池潭、竹洲、凤滩、柘溪、沙县城关、古田溪一级、古田溪二级、格里桥、洪家渡、凌津滩、毛尖山、三道湾、龙首二级、宝兴、构皮滩、滩坑、水泊峡、狮泉河、查龙、金河、金鸡滩、下桥、汉坪嘴、云峰、石龙、双沟、松山、小山、东西关、金牛坪、察汗乌苏、金银台、罗湾、索风营、华安、街面、水东、雍口、老江底、石泉、天生桥、东津、安康、万安、西龙池上库坝、西龙池下库坝、龙桥、白沙河、拉气、龙头石、白莲河上库坝 变更1座：哈巴河山口	
注册检查（共154座）	初始46座：宁朗、撒多、那邦、苗家坝、桥巩、晴朗、洪屏上库坝、洪屏下库坝、仙居上库坝、甲岩、舟坝、昭化、竹格多、野三河、大河家、烟岗、东水峡、飞仙关、枕头坝一级、乡城、旺村、南极洛河、官帽舟、白龙江沙湾、善泥坡、马马崖一级、铜钟、九龙峡、三岔河、沙沱、巴郎口、洞松、娘拥、古学、沙尔布拉克、哈德布特、萨里克特、尼勒克一级、塔勒德萨依、梨园、鲁地拉、金平、金元、黄金坪、普西桥、花园 换证107座：阿鸠田、碧口、麒麟寺、六郎洞、雷打滩、珠窝、落坡岭、柘林、青溪、蓬辣滩、长潭、富春江、南桠河三级、惠蓄上库坝、惠蓄下库坝、陈村、纪村、铅厂、鲁基厂、照口、刘家峡、龚嘴、泉水、新丰江、沙湾、鱼剑口、庙林、长湖、枫树坝、湖南镇、黄坛口、乐滩、紫兰坝、托海、福堂、沙溪口、天荒坪上库坝、天荒坪下库坝、上犹江、大化、阴坪、别迭里、百龙滩、小湾、良浅、孔头、洪坝、湾坝、五一桥、铁门关、大山口、新安江、天生桥一级、柳坪、色尔古、公伯峡、沙县城关、凌津滩、竹洲、格里桥、柘溪、凤滩、古田溪一级、古田溪二级、毛尖山、池潭、洪家渡、三道湾、龙首二级、宝兴、构皮滩、滩坑、金河、水泊峡、狮泉河、金鸡滩、查龙、下桥、石龙、双沟、松山、小山、汉坪嘴、东西关、云峰、金牛坪、察汗乌苏、金银台、罗湾、索风营、华安、街面、水东、雍口、老江底、东津、安康、白莲河上库坝、龙头石、白沙河、龙桥、西龙池上库坝、西龙池下库坝、万安、石泉、拉气、天生桥 变更1座：哈巴河山口	

续表

类型	大 坝 名 称	备注
注册评审（共 154 座）	初始 44 座：苗家坝、青羊沟、桥巩、那邦、宁朗、撒多、南山一级、晴朗、洪屏上库坝、洪屏下库坝、仙居上库坝、甲岩、舟坝、昭化、野三河、大河家、竹格多、枕头坝一级、飞仙关、乡城、烟岗、东水峡、九龙峡、善泥坡、马马崖一级、铜钟、官帽舟、白龙江沙湾、旺村、南极洛河、鲁地拉、哈德布特、沙尔布拉克、古学、巴郎口、沙沱、娘拥、洞松、尼勒克一级、三岔河、萨里克特、塔勒德萨依、花园、梨园 换证 110 座：珠窝、落坡岭、白山、红石、洪口、牛头山、过渡湾、黑麋峰上库坝、黑麋峰下库坝、宝泉上库坝、宝泉下库坝、碧口、麒麟寺、阿鸠田、弄另、六郎洞、董箐、雷打滩、柘林、青溪、蓬辣滩、长潭、富春江、南桠河三级、惠蓄上库坝、惠蓄下库坝、陈村、纪村、铅厂、鲁基厂、照口、刘家峡、龚嘴、泉水、新丰江、沙湾、鱼剑口、庙林、长湖、枫树坝、湖南镇、黄坛口、乐滩、紫兰坝、托海、福堂、沙溪口、天荒坪上库坝、天荒坪下库坝、上犹江、大化、阴坪、别迭里、百龙滩、小湾、良浅、孔头、洪坝、湾坝、五一桥、铁门关、大山口、新安江、天生桥一级、柳坪、色尔古、公伯峡、沙县城关、凌津滩、竹洲、柘溪、凤滩、古田溪一级、古田溪二级、毛尖山、池潭、小山、松山、双沟、石龙、云峰、滩坑、宝兴、水泊峡、汉坪嘴、三道湾、龙首二级、金河、金鸡滩、下桥、构皮滩、格里桥、洪家渡、查龙、东津、华安、金银台、街面、安康、天生桥、老江底、东西关、水东、雍口、察汗乌苏、罗湾、索风营、石泉、金牛坪、狮泉河	
注册证发放情况	能源局批复：517 座 已发证：503 座 待发证：14 座	
大坝备案（共 14 座）	红岩子、达克曲克、去学、齐热哈塔尔、上通坝、浩口、角木塘、固滴、象鼻岭、杨家湾、达阿果、龙洞、汗牛河、万家口子	
注册注销（共 7 座）	丰满、古田溪三级、古田溪四级、万安溪、丰海、后垄溪二级、哈巴河山口	

（国家能源局大坝安全监察中心　郭玉嵘）

2018 年水电站大坝安全定期检查工作情况

2018 年，国家能源局大坝安全监察中心（简称大坝中心）继续动态排查和发布大坝重点关注问题报告，加强治理情况督查和跟踪。在开展水电站大坝安全定检工作时，对于发现的大坝安全信息化、监控和监测管理等问题及时反馈给内部相关部门。

2018 年严格按照年度计划开展定检工作，各区域主管和总监结合定检排查大坝缺陷，跟踪定检意见落实情况。持续跟踪 2017 年专委会梳理出的第一批存在安全缺陷和隐患的水电站大坝的缺陷和隐患治理情况。

四轮定检总结已完成初稿，正在进行补充修改工作。

截至 2018 年 12 月 31 日，启动了 75 座大坝定检工作（按启动通知已发统计，2018 年计划启动的 75 座中，哈巴河山口大坝因注册注销不再开展定检工作，此外新增规划外的红岩子大坝），召开了 75 座大坝定检专家组首次会议、4 座大坝定检专家组第二次会议、63 座大坝定检专家组末次会议，完成了 51 座大坝定检评审会，完成了 52 座大坝审查意见备案及转发。详细情况见表 1。

表1 2018年定期检查情况统计表
（截至2018年12月31日）

类型	大坝名称
2018年12月31日前 启动（发启动函并召开首次会）大坝 （共75座）	五轮定检75座：张窝、撒鱼沱、响水、大勐统大坝、赛珠、小岩头、安康、龙羊峡、刘家峡、大山口、班多、别迭里、宝瓶河、龙首二级、金家坝、百花滩、沙溪、苍溪、凤仪、红岩子、龙凤、大盈江四级、龙开口、杨柳滩、土卡河、石门坎、公伯峡、功果桥、金鸡滩、金牛坪、叶茂、金沙峡、莲麓、松树岭、老虎嘴、苏只、挂治、老江底、普定、索风营、鱼塘、沙溪口、照口、高砂、大兴、青龙、杂谷脑古城、水津关、瓦屋山、石垭子、锁儿头、腾龙桥二级、藤子沟、沙河上库、响水涧上库坝、响水涧下库坝、小石峡、金安桥、洪家渡、仙游上库坝、仙游下库坝、张河湾上库坝、张河湾下库坝、糯扎渡、新丰江、枫树坝、芹山、周宁、白沙河、马堵山、寺坪、富春江、百丈漈一级、木里河沙湾、拉气
2018年12月31日前 召开二次会的大坝 （共4座）	五轮定检4座：乐滩、景洪、构皮滩、葛洲坝
2018年12月31日前 完成专家组工作（召开末次会） （共63座）	四轮定检6座：十三陵上池、池潭、凤滩、朝阳寺、大洑潭、沙湾 五轮定检57座：偏桥、久隆洪坝、五一桥、大盈江二级、大盈江三级、铁门关、蒲石河上库坝、蒲石河下库坝、江边、石板水、克田、滩坑、倮马、苏家河口、山秀、雷打滩、巴山、大勐统、青居、响水、下六甲、平班、赛珠、董箐、天花板、下桥、团坡、黑麋峰上库坝、黑麋峰下库坝、格里桥、小岩头、景洪、库什塔依、溪口上库坝、溪口下库坝、撒鱼沱、张窝、联补、洛古、地洛、石泉、拉气、乐滩、庙林、西龙池上库坝、西龙池下库坝、大埔、古顶、小山、黄花寨、毛尖山、蓬辣滩、耿达、构皮滩、白莲河上库坝、沙溪、苍溪
2018年12月31日前 完成审查意见评审 （共51座）	四轮定检30座：三板溪、引子渡、弄另、达开、凤凰谷、漫湾、湾坝、洪坝、金溪、沙湾、东津、洪门、白山、红石、筱溪、羊湖、龙滩、宝泉上库坝、宝泉下库坝、大洑潭、朝阳寺、隔河岩、十三陵、池潭、东风、凤滩、江西江口、重庆江口、映秀湾、洛东 五轮定检21座：宝兴、华光潭一级、华光潭二级、蒲石河上库坝、蒲石河下库坝、孔头、铁门关、五一桥、大盈江二级、江边、倮马、山秀、巴山、响水、赛珠、撒鱼沱、张窝、石板水、克田、滩坑、库什塔依
2018年12月31日前 完成审查意见转发 （共52座）	四轮定检42座：三板溪、引子渡、弄另、达开、凤凰谷、漫湾、湾坝、洪坝、金溪、沙湾、东津、洪门、白山、红石、筱溪、羊湖、龙滩、宝泉上库坝、宝泉下库坝、大洑潭、朝阳寺、隔河岩、十三陵、池潭、东风、凤滩、江西江口、重庆江口、映秀湾、洛东、吉林台一级、三道湾、糯租、居甫渡、惠州蓄能上、下库坝、太平驿、鱼跳、修文、窄巷口、铜头、水东 五轮定检10座：宝兴、华光潭一级、华光潭二级、蒲石河上库坝、蒲石河下库坝、孔头、铁门关、水泊峡、河口、腊寨

第四轮定检于2011年开始，截至2018年12月31日，303座大坝定检工作已全部启动，其中302座大坝已完成定检审查意见的备案和转发工作，柘溪大坝定检专家组工作已完成，因大坝防洪标准和防洪能力不足，需要对坝顶进行加高处理，待加高方案审查后，才能完成大坝定检报告和审查意见。详细情况见表2。

表 2 第四轮定期检查完成情况统计表

（截至 2018 年 12 月 31 日） 单位：座

启动年份	启动定检	已全部完成	审查意见在编	定检报告在编	尚未完成专家组工作
2011 年	36	36	0	0	0
2012 年	35	35	0	0	0
2013 年	52	52	0	0	0
2014 年	62	62	0	0	0
2015 年	58	57	0	1①	0
2016 年	60	60	0	0	0
合计	303②	302	0	1	0

① 柘溪。

② 第四轮定检总数：303 座。

第五轮定检自 2017 年开始以来，截至 2018 年 12 月 31 日，已启动 152 座大坝定检工作，其中 10 座大坝已完成定检审查意见的备案和转发工作，14 座大坝定检审查意见已评审、但尚未转发，40 座大坝已完成专家组工作，88 座大坝尚未完成专家组工作。详细情况见表 3。

表 3 第五轮定检开展情况（152 个）

（截至 2018 年 12 月 31 日）

类型	大 坝 名 称	数量
审查意见已转发	规划内 10 座：水泊峡、河口、腊寨、宝兴、华光潭一级、华光潭二级、孔头、铁门关、蒲石河上库、蒲石河下库	10
审查意见已评审	规划内 14 座：山秀、倮马、巴山、滩坑、大盈江二级、江边、五一桥、赛珠、响水、撒鱼沱、张窝、克田、石板水、库什塔依	14
末次会已开	规划内 36 座：拉气、小岩头、大勐统、沙溪、苍溪、蓬辣滩、石泉、黄花寨、耿达、古顶、大埔、团坡、平班、青居、天花板、下六甲、溪口上库、溪口下库、西龙池上库、西龙池下库、洛古、联补、地洛、格里桥、黑麋峰上库坝、黑麋峰下库坝、雷打滩、下桥、董箐、大盈江三级、庙林、苏家河口、小山、毛尖山、白莲河上库、构皮滩、乐滩、景洪 规划外 2 座：偏桥、久隆洪坝	40
二次会已开	规划内 2 座：葛洲坝、双沟	2
首次会已开	规划内 85 座：挂治、老江底、龙开口、水津关、瓦屋山、安康、金安桥、青龙、金沙峡、索风营、金鸡滩、杨柳滩、锁儿头、响水涧上、下库、大山口、金家坝、龙羊峡、金牛坪、苏只、班多、松树岭、藤子沟、莲麓、公伯峡、大兴、石垭子、小石峡、老虎嘴、鱼塘、凤仪、杂谷脑古城、百花滩、别迭里、沙河上库、仙游上库坝、仙游下库坝、宝瓶河、龙首二级、洪家渡、大盈江四级、普定、叶茂、龙凤、石门坎、土卡河、沙溪口、照口、刘家峡、张河湾上库坝、张河湾下库坝、高砂、功果桥、腾龙桥二级、高滩、马迹塘、凌津滩、陡岭子、蔺河口、马鹿塘（二期）、小湾、仁宗海、深溪沟、瀑布沟、上犹江、察汗乌苏、温泉、铜湾、清水塘、汉坪嘴、石龙、陇或、坡甲、潘家口下池、糯扎渡、百丈漈一级、木里河沙湾、寺坪、白沙河、新丰江、枫树坝、马堵山、富春江、芹山、周宁 规划外 1 座：红岩子	86
已取消	规划内 6 座：茄子山、芒里、蹇家湾、后垄溪一级、后垄溪二级、哈巴河山口	6

（国家能源局大坝安全监察中心 杜雪珍）

2018年水电站大坝安全应急管理概述

2018年地震、台风等各类自然灾害频发，给水电站大坝运行安全带来严峻挑战。为确保运行水电站大坝运行安全，国家能源局大坝安全监察中心（简称大坝中心）积极配合水电站运行管理单位，做好应急准备和预警，及时指导电力企业开展相关突发事件的应急响应，为保障水电站大坝运行安全保驾护航。

一是严格按照国家能源局和大坝中心的规定，落实专人按照有关制度进行值班。二是及时收集、掌握大坝安全突发事件信息，按大坝中心的《大坝安全突发事件应急响应工作制度》快速响应，配合开展现场应急处置。2018年全年超过5级且影响范围内有距离较近大坝的地震共有12次，针对这些地震，及时进行了跟踪，开展应急响应、了解震损情况和对大坝的影响。对“5·28”吉林松原5.7级地震、“8·3”青海玉树5.1级地震、“8·13”云南玉溪5.0级地震、“9·4”新疆喀什5.5级地震、“9·8”云南普洱5.9级地震、“9·12”陕西汉中5.3级地震、“9·28”西藏阿里5.1级地震、“10·16”新疆精河5.4级地震、“10·31”四川西昌5.1级地震等9场地震编写了应急简报，及时向国家能源局报告地震对水电站大坝运行安全的影响情况。三是跟踪了8号、9号、10号、12号、14号、15号、16号、18号、22号等9场台风的影响；对10号台风“安比”、14号台风“摩羯”、18号台风“温比亚”启动了Ⅳ级应急响应，编写应急简报及时报告台风影响和水电站大坝运行情况。四是针对7月发生的“7·20”四川福堂坝沟、舟曲桃关沟泥石流灾害事件提供应急处置技术支持，指导企业及时开展应急响应和处置。五是积极参与国家能源局应对“10·11”金沙江白格堰塞湖事件应急处置相关工作；11月3日原金沙江白格堰塞体处河道再次堵江后，大坝中心按照国家能源局的统一部署，领导带班组织多次会商、分析堰塞体湖的发展趋势和可能风险，及时提出了梨园大坝的应急调度方案，同时派出专家参与现场应急响应和处置，派出专业人员在北京国家能源局本部参与应急会商和处置工作，每日数次开展险情研判和信息报送，为白格堰塞体的应急处置发挥了技术支撑作用。

（国家能源局大坝安全监察中心　王小清）

国家电力投资集团有限公司大坝管理中心成立

国家电力投资集团有限公司（简称国家电投）拥有国内运行水电站（水库）大坝134座，对应电站131座，装机容量2092.67万kW，分布在全国15个省区，在国内已形成黄河、沅水一北一南两大流域基地。在新时代面临新的发展阶段，国家电投以“建设具有全球竞争力的世界一流清洁能源企业”为发展战略，致力于通过加强水电存量资产的高质量管理提高水电产业核心竞争力。2018年4月，国家电投在西安挂牌成立国家电投集团大坝管理中心（简称国家电投大坝中心），这是国家电投加强水电存量资产高质量管理的专业化、集约化创新举措。

国家电投大坝中心以大坝管理信息化和小水电站大坝定检为抓手，实现对大坝安全管理全覆盖的监督和监控。率先提出打造国内领先的大坝安全管理工作统一信息平台，将大坝安全管理专业化业务与信息化深度融合。将应用GIS、BIM、大数据等多项先进技术搭建大坝安全管理工作平台、监测工作平台、性态分析诊断平台、工作监督平台和信息共享交流平台，利用移动巡检、微信小程序实现业务应用的“触手可及”。依托平台，通过“无盲区”开展集团公司所有大坝定检和巡查，全面摸清大坝存在的安全风险与隐患，科学合理设定不同大坝重点监管项目，实现所有项目自动化实时监测，实现风险管控与隐患治理分级管控、全程监督、闭环管理，最终实现“一坝一策略”的监管模式。

国家电投大坝中心的成立，将对有效控制大坝安全风险、强化落实大坝安全主体责任起到积极作用。

（国家电力投资集团有限公司大坝管理中心　刘涵）

大坝安全监测与分析

2018年水电站大坝安全监控管理情况

2018年，国家能源局大坝安全监察中心（简称大坝中心）承担的水电站大坝安全监控管理，主要工作情况如下：

（一）大坝安全监控

按照有关规定，继续对水电站大坝运行管理单位报送的大坝安全信息进行安全监控，每日对报警情况进行检查和处理，跟踪、反馈结构性问题，对监测管理问题及时反馈，对结构安全疑点及时联系运行单位检查和关注。大坝中心每月编写大坝安全监控工作月报表，对接入、监控等总体情况、月度变化情况进行检查，对发现的问题提出明确的整改要求。

与此同时，组织完成新注册（备案）大坝的监测信息接入工作，督促接入进度滞后大坝的运行管理单位及时进行整改，完成了所有已接入大坝的重点关注测点的设置工作。

2018年对监控方法（如模型、规则等）继续研究完善，引入了时间序列特征值的计算方法等性方法；全年共完成了31座大坝的精细化监控，新接入的大坝均已及时完成了初步监控，完成80余座的一般性监控。截至2018年底，已对完成接入的561座大坝实施监控，其中48座为精细化监控，80座为一般性监控，433座为初步监控。

（二）汛期大坝度汛安全监控

按照《国家能源局综合司关于切实做好2018年电力行业防汛抗旱工作的通知》（国能综通安全〔2018〕59号）要求，2018年进一步加强对度汛安全监控工作的组织领导，成立汛情监控领导小组，制定大坝度汛安全监控工作要求；健全完善汛期值班制度，落实专人负责汛期值班。3月发文各有关电力企业要求开展汛情报送工作；全面检查了所有注册、备案大坝的汛限水位、各频率洪峰流量等水情信息，修订完善了监察数据库；开通了微信报送功能，并对汛情统计等软件进行了升级。为了加强水电站大坝运行安全风险预控，有效实施分类监控、重点监察，根据2018年气象、水情预测及大坝定检安全评判结果，调整并明确了汛期重点监控的大坝名单。对已有的汛情监控软件进行了升级，增加了汛情监控GIS功能，并添置了全国72小时降雨预报动态数据，每日更新两次。进入汛期后，落实专人每天跟踪气象变化，每日进行汛情会商，对500多座大坝报送的汛情进行监控分析，每周编写《水电站大坝汛期运行安全周报》，报能源局安全司及各派出机构；对监控发现的水库水位未经防汛主管理部门同意的超汛限运行情况，及时提醒电力企业控制安全风险。

此外，还于4月参加吉林丰满、白山大坝防洪度汛安全督查和江苏能源监管办组织的宜兴抽水蓄能和溧阳抽水蓄能电站防汛工作督查；5月参加清原抽水蓄能电站工程防洪度汛应急演练现场观摩，并作为评估专家对应急演练现场点评；6月参加云南能源监管办组织的乌东德水电站防汛工作督查；结合大坝注册现场检查，对江西洪屏、柘林，福建池潭、沙溪口、良浅、孔头，湖南凤滩、柘溪，广西大化、乐滩，云南小湾、梨园，四川柳坪、色尔古、龚嘴，甘肃水泊峡、东水峡等多座水电站大坝开展防汛工作检查。

（国家能源局大坝安全监察中心　沈静　杜德进）

2018年水电站大坝安全监测管理工作情况

2018年，国家能源局大坝安全监察中心（简称大坝中心）担负的水电站大坝安全监测管理工作，主要情况如下：

（一）日常监测监管工作

为充分掌握电力企业监测系统组成、运行和工作开展情况，汇总、总结各运行单位年报、监测工作开展情况、注册和定期检查等各种渠道的信息，全面掌握各大坝安全监测系统的现状和存在问题，编制完成2017年电力行业大坝安全监测情况通报，提出监测工作改进的意见和要求，并向电力行业发布。

根据电力企业监测工作开展情况的检查和考核结果，每月编制监测管理月报，汇总统计监测管理中所发现的问题，并记录处理情况，实行闭环管理。

为加强水电站大坝安全监督管理，及时进行大坝安全信息接入和确认工作，累计完成24座接入电力企业自查报告审查，完成10座信息接入确认和监测指标的设置。

为提高大坝安全监测人员的业务素质，提升监测工作质量和大坝安全管理水平，大坝中心通过在线监测管理平台，对监测管理中发现的监测系统或监测工作存在问题反馈电力企业，向电力企业累计反馈了290条监测问题，指导和督促电力企业规范、高效的开展监测系统更新维护和工作改进。

（二）监测管理信息化工作

为进一步加强技术监督管理手段的创新，对监测管理平台进行了升级完善。开发了新的监测管理的界面，重点展示监测系统状态、监测工作评分和评级、监测问题及异常数据处理等监测管理指标，同时对监测管理的各项功能进一步升级和完善，加强反馈问题的封闭管理，完善了监测系统状态、监测频次等网上流程管理机制。为方便大坝监测信息查阅及处理，同步开发了手机端数据缺报、异常数据等重要提示功能。

（三）大坝安全监测信息诊断分析辅助系统研发

为提高大坝安全监督管理技术水平，提升对大坝中心主系统监测信息实时分析的能力和效率，大坝中心组织研发了大坝安全监测信息诊断分析辅助系统。该系统根据电力企业上报的监测数据，综合坝型、监测类别、分析要求等，快速生成相关监测整编分析成果，发现大坝运行中存在的异常现象，辅助大坝中心技术人员快速分析评判大坝安全状况。

（国家能源局大坝安全监察中心　吴伟）

大坝安全监察信息共享平台上线运行应用

在国家“互联网＋”战略引领下，国家能源局大坝安全监察中心（简称大坝中心）创新开拓了“互联网＋大坝安全监察”新模式，推进监管模式的智慧化转变，2018年初步完成水电站大坝安全监察信息共享平台的建设开发并上线试运行，于9月底向国家能源局及其派出机构介绍并开放了该平台。

共享平台对各项大坝安全监察业务重新进行定义和关联，更好地体现业务间的逻辑关系，使得系统功能的扩展方便、快速，业务间衔接平滑无缝、路径缩短、效率提高。通过共享平台可开展在线监督、日常监控、安全状况研判、远程技术支持等工作，并逐步实现了国家能源局、各派出机构与大坝中心之间大坝安全信息全面、实时共享，提高了各方传递大坝安全信息的效率和大坝中心为国家能源局及其派出机构提供技术支撑的质量，进一步提升了大坝安全管理和监督工作水平，并为今后向电力企业与行业提供高水平、高质量的技术监督和服务夯实根基。

（国家能源局大坝安全监察中心　陈铿）

柔性测斜仪在去学水电站高土石坝中的应用

（一）柔性测斜仪简介

柔性测斜仪是基于微电子机械系统（MEMS）测试原理测试加速度和位移的传感器，具有3D测量、精度高、可重复利用、自动实时采集等特点，在国内外的边坡、地铁线路中已有较多应用。

目前国内常见的柔性测斜仪有北京博安达代理的阵列式位移计（SAA，加拿大）、北京盛科瑞代理的三维地面变形监测仪（3D-GBMS Continuous Deformation System，韩国）、北京基康的多维度变形测量系统（BGK6150SI，国产）等。

柔性测斜仪工作原理：以北京博安达SAA为例，如图1所示，通过检测各部分的重力场，可以计算出各段轴之间的弯曲角度θ，利用计算得到的弯曲角度和已知各段轴长度L（即测点间距），每段SAA的变形$\Delta\chi$便可以完全确定出来，即$\Delta\chi=\theta\cdot L$，再对各段算术求和$\sum\Delta\chi$，可得到距固定端点任意长度的变形量χ。

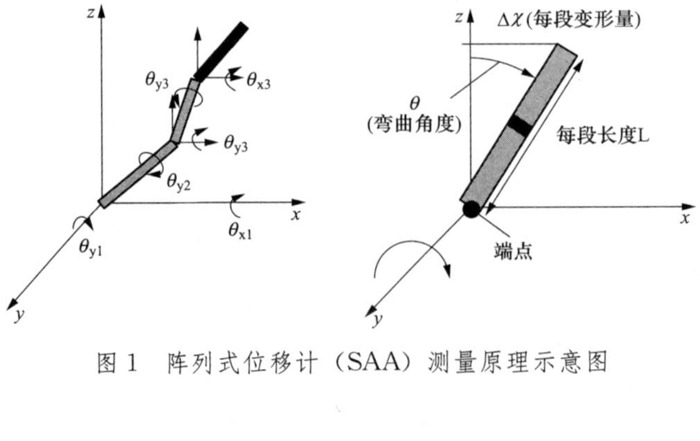

图1　阵列式位移计（SAA）测量原理示意图

（二）工程应用情况

1. 概况　去学水电站拦河坝为沥青混凝土心墙堆石坝，坝顶总长 219.85m，坝顶宽 15.00m，最大坝高 164.20m，心墙最大高度 132.00m，水库总库容 1.33 亿 m^3。工程于 2014 年 2 月正式开工，填筑过程连续，2017 年 7 月开始正式发电。

在心墙下游侧约 30cm 共布设 3 条柔性测斜仪，均采用北京博安达 SAA，分别位于（坝横）0+040.00、（坝横）0+070.00 和（坝横）0+140.00 桩号处，以掌握心墙变形情况。仪器为竖向垂直安装，安装深度分别为 108、132、96m。仪器所用的预埋管采用活动式测斜仪专用管材，每隔 5m 安装一个电磁沉降环，可保证在施工期采用活动式测斜仪获取大坝在施工期的水平和沉降变形物理量，待填筑接近坝顶后安装柔性测斜仪，活动式测斜仪及电磁沉降环同步作废。

2. 运行情况　去学水电站应用的 3 条柔性测斜仪均于 2017 年 1 月安装完成，运行已满一年，尚未出现测点损坏现象，状况良好。

竖直安装的柔性测斜仪可对坝体水平位移进行监测。取 X 向为上下游方向（正值代表向下游变形），Y 向为坝轴线方向（正值代表向左岸变形）。图 2 是所应用的单根长 132m 的柔性测斜仪各深度测点部位水平向累计位移分布图。可以看出，最大监测断面心墙部位呈现向下游偏右岸方向变形趋势，X 向最大位移约 90mm，Y 向最大位移约 −15mm，监测成果符合沥青混凝土心墙堆石坝蓄水后一般变性规律。

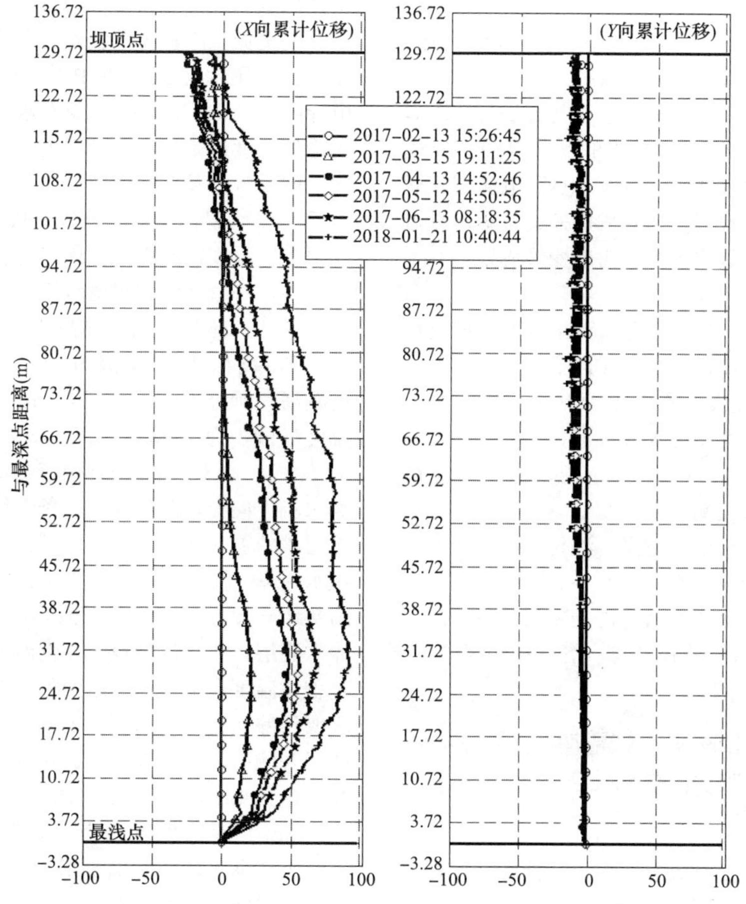

图 2　去学水电站柔性测斜仪各深度测点部位水平累计位移分布图

3. 安装要点　该水电站柔性测斜仪主要的安装方法如下：

（1）预埋测斜管。与大坝填筑施工同步进行，需做好相应的保护措施。

（2）测斜孔检查。采用孔内摄像头查看测斜孔内壁状况，并用测深仪测量孔深实际值（精确到 0.1m）。

（3）固定架搭设。在管口一侧搭设固定架，安装爬梯，供人员作业。

（4）PE 管准备及入管。采用整根无接头的方式用PE管（外径40mm，壁厚约2mm）对柔性测斜仪进行保护。将PE管前端削成锥形，将PE管塞入预埋管内。

（5）SAA入管。将SAA卷轮抬放在固定架上，在SAA表面涂抹润滑油，由一人负责SAA下放，其余人员负责卷轮转动，将SAA下放至孔底后；再缓慢拉起20～30cm，上下往复移动数次，并使其下端也能保持自然顺直的状态。

（6）回填。将提前准备好的干细过筛河砂，从PE管与预埋管之间孔隙放入，提拉SAA＋PE管组合，使其尽量保持顺直状态，直至细砂填充满PE管与预埋管之间的整个孔隙。灌满之后先用无纺布缠绕保护好孔口处，待孔内砂料自然沉降，隔日再进行补灌；直至孔口被整个集料覆盖无法进行补灌时再停止砂料回填。

（7）孔口保护。采用厚度不小于6mm的钢板，加工保护箱，对测斜管孔口进行保护。

4. 数据采集　将便携式笔记本电脑连接SAA，用笔记本安装的SAASuite软件中的SAARecorder模块完成SAA的运行状况诊断测试。电压/电流测试通过后，即可连续采集数据。现场数据采集完毕，点击保存即可回室内进行数据转换，输出变形成果。

（三）结语

在该水电站柔性测斜仪应用过程中，发现该类仪器在土石坝工程中推广使用尚存在以下问题：

（1）SAA目前埋设单根长度通常不超过150m，在定制加长后的稳定性缺乏工程考证。

（2）仪器外部电缆牵引长度越长信号衰减越严重，牵引过长会导致监测成果失真。

（3）预埋孔越深出错率越高，深孔段存在变形较大及落石堵孔等不确定因素。

（中国电建集团中南勘测设计研究院有限公司　肖亚子　谭坚）

苗家坝水电站采用温度示踪法探测水库渗漏

苗家坝水电站位于甘肃省境内，其挡水建筑物为建基于深厚覆盖层上的混凝土面板堆石坝（坝高为111m、覆盖层最大厚度为48m），水库正常蓄水位800m，相应库容2.68亿m^3。2016年10月，该电站采用温度示踪法探测水库渗漏，现简介如下。

（一）测试布置

在其大坝坝底布置一系列水位观测孔，并对这些观测孔以及库水和尾水进行温度、电导测试。观测孔位置见图1。坝底水位观测孔Up2、Up4、Up6、Up8～Up16基本位于一条直线上，是判断该大坝坝体渗漏状况的最佳位置；Up1、Up3和Up5位于这条直线上方马道中部，能够观测坝体内水流情况；坝肩绕坝孔分别为Oh2、Oh6、Oh7、Oh8、Oh11、Oh12、Oh16、Oh19，其中由于坝左岸山体滑坡，导致了最靠近左岸的观测孔Up7被碎石掩埋，所以取靠近Up7的Oh19代替。对库水采样分为3个点，分别位于库水1、库水2、库水3。

（二）测试分析

1. 库区温度、电导分析　从库水测试结果可以看出，测试点库水1处的温度随深度逐渐下降，电导在0～6m之间变化较小，但在7m以下变化较大。库水2的分层性得到明显的体现，深度0～24m和25m以下明显是两种水体，这里需要注意的是25m以下出现低温水，温度降到10℃以下，估测更深层的库水温度更低。库水3所表现出来的规律和库水2规律相似。从尾水测试结果来看，尾水温度约为21℃，电导约为383μS/cm；结合库水测试结果可以看出，无论从温度还是从电导，都表明尾水是来自于库水上部，即库水2及库水3中0～25m区段的库水。

2. 孔内温度、电导分析　从观测结果可以看出，孔内空气温度随高程降低而降低，两者具有一定的线性关系，一直持续到接触水为止。坝底一条直线上的观测孔（大部分观测孔在高程702m以下时接触水）在702m高程处中间观测孔的温度低，越靠近两岸温度越高。所有观测孔中Up13观测孔内接触到水时的温度最低，为7.5℃，比Up13稍高的是Up5，水温为7.9℃，并且Up5正好位于Up13上方马道上，顺着水流方向看，两者位于一条直线上。同一时期的发电尾水的温度较高，约为21℃，所以可以据此排除尾水影响。由于底层库水水温较低（低于7.5℃），由热传导原理可以明确Up13中的异常低温水来源于库水底层，并且流量较大，低温的库水在往下游渗漏过程中温度会上升，下游测得的温度越接近库水温度表明渗漏通道中的库水补给越快，即为主要渗漏区。两岸观测孔的水温较高，其中左岸的Oh19孔水温最高，达到14.3℃，右岸也未测到低温，但是计算得到702m高程空气温度为12.9℃，也比其他观测孔高。该数据表明两岸属于低渗漏区，渗漏水流速慢，持续的时间长，温度就会高于主要渗漏区。

3. 坝脚水位观测孔温度、电导分析　Up13中水温较为稳定，约为7.5℃，远低于尾水温度21℃，更接近于底层库水的温度，因此可以断定其水体受到地层底部低温热源影响，而与尾水无关。虽然随着发电，尾水位上升，也会导致Up13中水位的上升，但是由于渗漏梯度的存在，使得尾水回灌的距离并不能抵达Up13。正是这种现象的出现才导致Up13中水体滞留时间较长，电导值变得较高，明显高于尾水和库水的电导值。现场测试期间 Up13 电导值相差较大值，9 月 6、7 日的低电导值，判断是由于受到现场注水试验的影响，注入钻孔内的水电导值约为 280μS/cm，大大降低了 Up13 中的水体的电导；而 9 月 10 日的高电导值，则是受到人工示踪试验的影响。两次对 Oh19 的温度、电导测量都反映出相类似的规律，曲线形状相似，尤其是温度曲线，在 14.4～15.2℃之间变化，大幅度大于 Up13 中的温度；两次测量的电导曲线都表现出上层水体电导偏小，深部电导偏大。

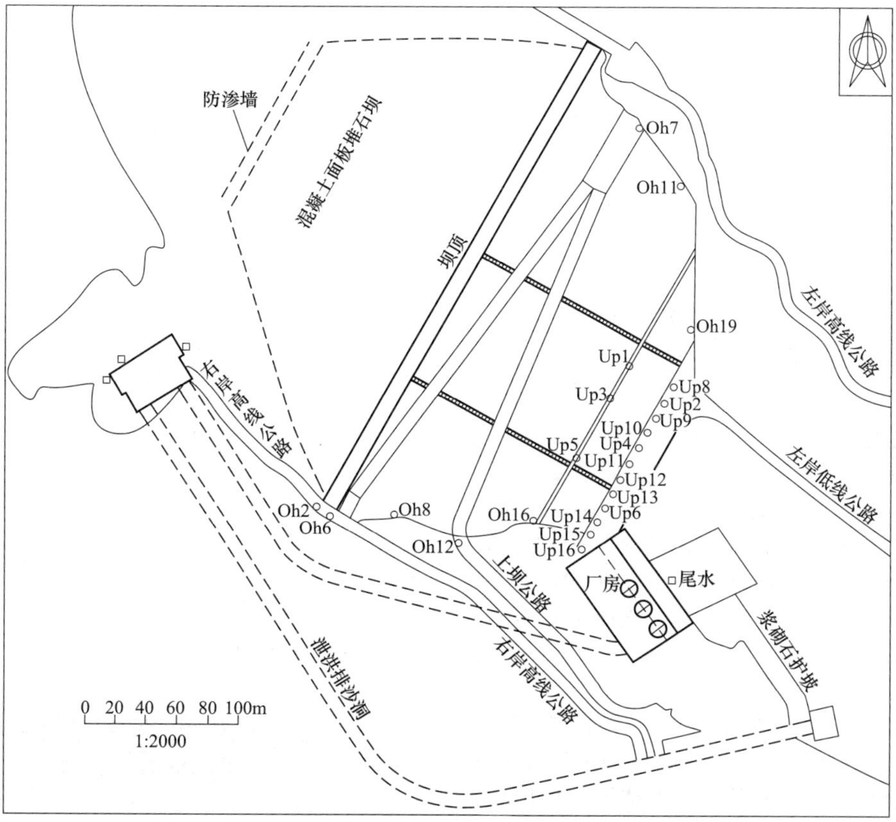

图 1 观测孔及采样点分布图

综合分析可以确定：地层深部存在集中渗漏通道，渗漏通道中心位于 Up13 钻孔所在地层下部，致使 Up13 中水体温度最低，而 Up6、Up14 距 Up13 较远，其钻孔内水体温度也随之逐渐增大。

4. 绕坝观测孔温度、电导分析　左坝肩 Oh7 钻孔内的水体温度和电导基本上都处于一个非常稳定不变的数值，温度稳定在 17.1℃，而电导则稳定在 540～560μS/cm 之间，可见受库水影响较小。左坝肩 Oh11 中水体温度变化较小，在 15.9～16.2℃之间变化，电导值在 734m 高程以上差异较大，但是在该高程以下则稳定在 300μS/cm 左右，电导值低于坝后库区，推测受到下降泉的干扰。总的来说，左坝肩渗流状况良好。

右坝肩 Oh2 中温度差异较大，752m 高程以上温度较高，约为 19.3℃，而 750m 高程以下区段温度约为 15.4℃，最低达到 15.0℃；电导值相对较为稳定，在 410～440μS/cm 之间变化，Oh2 中水体主要来源于库区，但是在 752m 高程以上区段受到边坡水影响，致使该区段水体温度较大。Oh16 孔水体存在臭味，底部的电导非常大，约有 560μS/cm，说明水体滞留时间较长。

总的来说，该大坝右坝肩所存在的库水渗漏量较小，右坝肩处于较为安全的运营状态，但是从长期的安全运营角度出发，应对大坝右坝肩的绕渗孔继续观测。

5. 综合分析　从前述分析可知，该水库大坝主要存在一条主要渗漏通道，该渗漏通道致使 Up5 和 Up13 中测得低温区段，其中 Up5 和 Up13 都处于该渗漏通道附近。从温度示踪来看，该渗漏通道的渗漏量较大。至于该渗漏通道所处高程，推断处于 690m 高程以下更低高程处，应该是防渗墙底部存在的弱风化破碎带局部存在集中渗漏。左右坝肩存在微弱渗漏，相比主渗漏通道来说，渗漏量非常小。

（三）结语

本次渗流探测采用温度示踪法，结合坝体构造和工程地质情况，进行渗流场以及渗漏通道的研究，采用现场温度、电导测定，根据温度场，最终确定出了地下水渗流场分布。

本次探测中未发现较强的绕坝渗流，坝基的渗漏量也较小。但由于观测孔的管径较小，很多孔内可能存在挤压变形，致使探测仪器无法探测较深部位的渗流状况，因此在今后大坝的运行过程中，仍应继续维持各项观测，及时发现渗流异常状况，以保证大坝安全。

（大唐四川电力检修运营有限公司　陈容）

南瑞沉降环定位传感器的研制与应用

沉降监测是土石坝安全监测最主要的监测项目之一。常规沉降监测一般采用沉降环监测，即在土体里竖直埋设一根沉降管，沉降管外套沉降环（磁环），沉降环埋设安装在设计的沉降监测高程。测量时，人工将电磁沉降探头由沉降管孔口放下，根据反馈信号记录每个沉降环相对于孔口的距离。该种方法采用人工测量方式，工作量大，监测密度低，精度不高且无法做到实时自动测量。

南瑞集团有限公司研制了沉降环定位传感器来解决这一问题。该传感器是基于常规沉降环监测方法研制而成，完全解决了常规沉降环监测依赖人工测量的缺点，适用于土石坝、边坡、填筑体及路基的沉降自动化监测，尤其适合常规沉降环监测的自动化改造。

该传感器基于磁致伸缩的原理，外形为细长杆结构，采用485总线实现传感器间的串联，可以串接多达16支传感器。如图1所示，将传感器固定在沉降管内沉降环的安装高程，沉降环随土地沉降时，传感器固定不动，即可测出沉降环相对于传感器的位移量。

有两种安装方式可选：一种是传感器从沉降管管口用钢丝绳串联悬挂固定，以孔口为相对基准，测量各沉降环的相对沉降量，辅以孔口高程校准即可测量各沉降环的绝对沉降量。这种安装方式一般应用于已有沉降测量管自动化改造项目。另一种是传感器固定在沉降管管底基座上，传感器之间用钢管连接固定，随土体填筑依次向上连接。这种安装方式一般应用于新建工程，可以随土体填筑同步测量沉降，不会造成沉降量的丢失。

该产品已在镇安抽水蓄能电站和葛山水库投入应

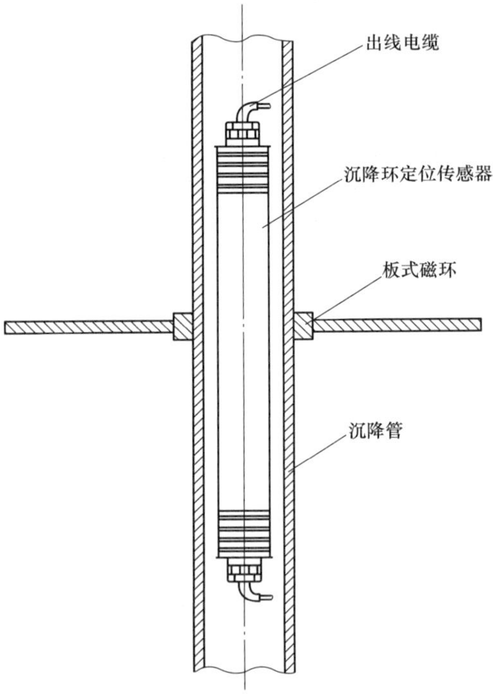

图1　沉降环定位传感器安装示意图

用。它的投入使用实现了土石坝沉降高精度自动化测量，具有良好的工程推广使用价值。

（南瑞集团有限公司　郑水华　沈慧　李学胜）

高坝洲大坝安全监测自动化改造

高坝洲大坝主要监测项目有：变形监测、渗流监测和环境量监测等，大坝自建成以来一直采用人工监测，无安全监测自动化系统。2018年，湖北清江水电开发有限责任公司（简称清江公司）对大坝4条倒垂、4条正垂8个测点，升船机4条倒垂10个测点，大坝引张线4条20个测点，大坝基础廊道及灌浆平洞53个测压管、5个量水堰实施了安全监测自动化改造。

（一）仪器选型

本次改造将引张线装置由有原来的浮托式改为无浮托式，采用碳纤维丝代替原铟钢丝测线，以避免浮托装置对自动化监测精度的影响；垂线及引张线自动化监测仪器采用光电CCD式自动化监测仪，其优点是无传统电学仪器存在的飘移现象，缺点是其观测精度对环境要求较高，观测环境需保持干净、无水雾；渗流渗压则采用业内稳定性良好的基康传感器。

CCD类仪器的工作原理是：当一束平行光垂直

照向CCD时，线体在CCD光敏面上产生一个投影，CCD的光敏源将光强转换成电荷量存储。CCD驱动器产生相应逻辑时序将电荷信息移出，移出信号经过整形处理后，算出线体的准确坐标，据此得到测点的位移值。由于CCD输出为数字信号，故无“零飘”问题，被测线体上无须附着任何感应物，不影响线体自由变化，是真正的非接触式测量。

（二）项目改造内容

本次改造于2017年12月～2018年6月进行，主要内容有：①垂线、引张线原有旧设备拆除，观测基墩改造及观测站（房）环境改造；②高坝洲大坝自动化安全监测系统的系统组网建设，包括供电通信网络布设、设备安装部位相关土建改造以及整个系统的防雷接地等工作；③高坝洲大坝垂线、引张线、升船机垂线及大坝渗流监测项目测点的自动化设施更新改造安装；④高坝洲大坝所有本次改造自动化测点监测采集子系统的建设，以及与清江公司目前使用的数据采集分析系统（南瑞DSIMS4.0系统）数据库成功对接；⑤系统调试。

（三）项目重难点及解决方案

该项目变形监测自动化系统均选用光电CCD式仪器，要确保设备运行稳定可靠，必须改造其设备安装环境，确保观测站（房）内无积水、无掉渣、无滴水，环境湿度常年在80%以下，此为该项目重难点。解决方案如下：

1. 坝顶引张线

（1）安装槽排水方案。安装槽两边打入膨胀螺钉，混凝土立模现浇3cm左右槽沿，所有盖板采用内扣式，确保外部无渗水；每两测点中心点处均设置一个直径约5cm的排水孔，排水孔左右两端测点以减坡方式向其推进，确保安装槽内无积水。

（2）坝顶引张线测点测站处观测墩瓷砖贴面，确保光滑平整。测站顶端保护罩设置不锈钢安装座，安装座完全覆盖整个测站。安装座安装时底部垫入防渗橡胶垫后打入膨胀螺钉，表面再用水泥砂浆覆盖；保护罩为外扣式，材质为不锈钢框架加铝制表面，提手环焊制在左右两侧，确保防水可靠，提手及重量便于操作。

2. 基础廊道垂线房

（1）改造垂线房排水沟，所有排水沟自室内到室外均采用减坡方式，确保沟内水流及时排出。

（2）在垂线井口周围打入膨胀螺钉立模现浇一圈3cm宽左右的井沿，根据井沿大小制安一个外扣其外的不锈钢防渣防水保护罩，在防水防渣保护罩上开两个直径ϕ20cm的孔，一个置于保护罩坡底，外接PVC管，用于防水、防渣，一个位于垂线钢丝处，确保垂线处于开孔中央，确保钢丝处于自由状态。

（3）在防水防渣管道下方放置过滤桶，接住落渣，将落水排入排水沟流出观测房。

（4）观测房墙面涂抹防水涂料，房间内安装除湿烘干机，降低观测房内湿度。

（四）改造效果

（1）坝顶引张线安装槽无积水，线体达到防风要求，测站清爽干燥，运行近一年以来，CCD仪器未出现因镜面起雾模糊造成的测值异常。

（2）观测房内地面不再有积水和锈渣，垂线井内的落渣和滴水准确的引到了排水沟和过滤桶内。

经过在汛期内湿度最大的2个月的跟踪测试，高坝洲大坝廊道垂线观测房内的湿度从改善前的99%，下降到了稳定的60%左右，除了能保证垂线监测自动化设备的正常运行，还使大坝垂线人工观测环境得到了改善。

观测站（房）夏季湿度高是行业内存在的普遍问题，光电CCD式、电容式等自动化监测仪器，都会因环境湿度大影响其运行可靠性。完备的观测站（房）防潮除湿措施能有效降低其湿度，提高了自动化监测仪器运行可靠性，降低设备故障率。

（湖北清江水电开发有限责任公司　饶浩芳　孟竞）

老挝南立1-2水电站外部变形监测网设计与实施

老挝南立1-2水电站装机容量2×50MW，为一等大（1）型工程；枢纽建筑物主要由混凝土面板堆石坝、2座黏土心墙坝、左岸岸边溢洪洞、右岸泄洪兼导流洞、右岸引水系统、地面发电主厂房、地面GIS开关站及尾水渠组成。电站外部变形监测控制网的设计与实施情况如下。

（一）外部变形监测设计

1. 水平位移监测控制网　由基准点、工作基点和其他网点构成，采用边角网组网。基准网点由J01、J02、J03、J04共计4个点构成，布设在大坝下游通视条件较好、高差较小、地质条件良好、基础稳固、能长久保存的地方；工作基点由NC01～NC06共计6个点构成，布设在靠近大坝左右岸边坡及公路区域、基础相对稳定、相互通视、方便监测的位置。水平位移监测网采用边角网一等精度观测，采用图形强度较高的大地四边形、三角形等图形构成边角网。

2. 垂直位移监测控制网　由二等水准网、二等水准支线和三角高程导线网构成；二等垂直位移监测控制网由9个点组成，在坝址下游1.3km处布置3个水准基准点，在监测区域布置6个工作基点。由于水准基准点处于近似相同的环境中，稳定性基本一致，符合拟稳平差的基本要求；三等电磁波测距三角高程测量路线与平面监测网观测方向一致；部分监测网点采用二等水准支线联测高程。

（二）外部变形监测实施

1. 垂直位移监测控制网

（1）观测仪器：二等水准测量采用高精度电子水准仪及数码水准标尺。

（2）外业观测：独立观测两次，平均值作为观测初始基准值。

（3）观测技术要求：均按照我国 GB/T 12897—2006《国家一、二等水准测量规范》的要求进行，各种观测限差由程序进行自动检查，超限部分按规范进行了重测。水准测量测站观测限差：视线长度不小于 3m 且不大于 50m，前后视距差不大于 1.5m，任一测站上前后视距差累积不大于 6.0m，视线高度不小于 0.55m 且不大于 2.80m，数字水准仪重复设站次数不少于 2 次。

2. 水平位移监测控制网

（1）观测仪器：水平角测量和边长测量均使用带自动目标识别功能的全站仪测量机器人和圆棱镜，仪器标称测角精度±0.5″，边长测量精度±（0.6mm+1ppm×D）。

（2）方向观测：按规范及设计要求进行。

（3）各项观测限差：方向观测中误差（测角中误差）为±0.5″（±0.7″），边长测量中误差为±（1.0+1.0ppm×D）mm，三角形最大闭合差为 3.5″，同方向值各测回较差为 5″，边长往返测较差为±2（$a+b\times D$）mm，边长往返测二时段较差为$\pm 2\sqrt{2}(a+b\times D)$ mm。

3. 监测控制网的平差计算

（1）垂直位移监测控制网平差计算：根据设计要求，确定稳定点，并将高程联测至水准网基准点（BM01～BM03）上，再以 BM03 的高程成果作为起算高程进行平差计算；高程联测以原水准点 S03 起算，高程传递至垂直位移基准网点，再进行整网平差计算；根据最小二乘法原理，采用间接观测平差法进行严密平差计算，其水准路线权的确定为 $P_i=1/S_i$；三角高程权的确定为 $P_i=1/S_i^2$。式中 S_i 为测段长度，单位为 km。

二等水准观测：第一次观测，每千米水准测量的全中误差 M_W=±1.06mm，最弱点高程中误差 M_{S06}=±1.17mm；第二次观测，每千米水准测量的全中误差 M_W=±1.65mm，最弱点高程中误差 M_{S06}=±1.83mm。

三等三角高程观测：第一次观测，最弱点高程中误差 NC05 为±1.68mm；第二次观测，最弱点高程中误差 NC05 为±1.18mm。

二等、三等垂直位移监测网的两次外业观测数据，经过检验和平差计算，每千米水准测量偶然中误差、全中误差均小于规范的要求，最弱高程点位中误差优于设计书中规定的±2mm 的设计要求。

（2）水平位移监测控制网平差计算：以 NC06 为起算点、NC06→NC03 的坐标方位角为起算方位角，以赫尔默特方差分量估计结果作为观测权，按最小二乘法原理，采用经典自由网平差模型，进行整体严密平差计算。

第一、二次观测，测角中误差 m_γ 分别为±0.63″、±0.53″，小于 0.7″的要求；平差后测边中误差 m_S 分别为±（0.33+0.33ppm×D）、±（0.40+0.40ppm×D）mm，优于测距精度±（1.0+1.0ppm×D）的要求；最弱方向中误差均为±0.4″，最弱相邻点边长相对中误差分别为 1/496000、1/409000。

平差后的点位精度：水平位移监测控制点点位精度评定结果见表 3，第一次观测最弱点点位中误差 M_{J01}=±1.0mm；第二次观测最弱点点位中误差 M_{J01}=±1.1mm。总体优于设计点位中误差不超过±2mm（坝前不超过±2.5mm）要求。

老挝南立 1-2 水电站平面监测控制网点位误差精度评定见表 1。

表 1 平面监测控制网点位误差精度评定表 单位：mm

序号	J01	J02	J03	J04	NC01	NC02	NC03	NC04	NC05	NC06
第一次	1.0	0.8	0.7	0.5	0.4	0.6	0.3	0.7	0.7	0
第二次	1.1	0.9	0.8	0.6	0.5	0.8	0.4	0.8	0.9	0

（三）结语

两次观测的测角中误差均小于规范±0.7″的精度要求；边长相对中误差小于规范 1/30 万的精度要求；最弱点点位中误差不大于±2mm（坝前≤±2.5mm）的设计要求，监测控制网的观测精度满足规范和设计技术要求，为电站运行期间的大坝安全提供了可靠的基准数据保障。

（中国电建集团昆明勘测设计研究院有限公司 周坤）

柬埔寨额勒赛下游水电站初蓄期面板堆石坝监测资料分析

"柬埔寨额勒赛下游水电站初蓄期面板堆石坝监测资料分析"项目为企事业单位委托科技项目，由河海大学与中国华电额勒赛下游水电项目（柬埔寨）有限公司合作，于2018年7月完成。

柬埔寨额勒赛下游水电站由相距约8km的上、下电站两个梯级组成，即额勒赛下游上电站和额勒赛下游下电站。根据上电站混凝土面板堆石坝初蓄期（2013～2016年）的原型观测资料，采用比较法、作图法、特征值统计法、数学模型法、混合法等多种方法，对额勒赛下游水电站大坝初蓄期的环境量、变形、渗流、应力应变、面板接缝等资料进行分析，得到了各监测量的统计特征量，重点分析了各监测量的收敛性及变化趋势，并与国内外类似工程监测资料进行比对，综合评价了大坝的安全状态。完成的具体研究工作如下：

（1）变形监测资料分析包括大坝内部水平位移、垂直位移及面板挠度等监测资料的误差分析、时空分析、模型分析、综合分析和监控预报模型等内容，综合评估大坝变形状态，重点分析收敛性及趋势性变化和可能存在的异常现象。

（2）渗流监测资料分析包括渗透压力、绕坝渗流、地下水位等监测资料的误差分析、时空分析、模型分析、综合分析和监控预报模型等内容，综合分析评价大坝的渗流状态，重点分析渗流量和绕坝渗流地下水位渗流趋势性变化以及可能存在的异常现象，并评估大坝防渗与排水设施的运行情况。

（3）应力和应变监测分析包括面板混凝土内埋设的应变计、无应力计和压应力计等观测资料的误差分析、时空分析、模型分析、综合分析和监控预报模型等内容。

（4）接缝监测分析对开合度监测资料的误差分析、时空分析、模型分析、综合分析和监控预报模型等内容。

（5）大坝安全状态评价根据有关规范要求，以上述各个观测项目的观测资料误差分析、定性和定量分析成果为依据，类比国内外相关工程监测资料，对大坝安全工作性态进行综合评价。

（河海大学）

折线型大坝水平位移监测

曲线型坝的坝轴线为非直线，各部位位移测点所处的坝轴线方向或所要监测的位移方向不同。折线型坝一般需监测各位移测点所处的垂直于和平行于该处坝轴线的方向位移。

对于折线型或曲线型坝，也可按照拱坝在不同坐标系中计算径切向位移量的方法，将主坝轴线坐标系旋转至各段不同坝轴线方向的坐标系，再计算在旋转后相应坐标系中的坐标位移量。

（一）折线型大坝水平位移监测工程实例

图1所示为浙江龙游社阳水库黏土心墙坝，坝顶轴线为由三段直线组成的折线，坝顶总长487m，坝体共设5个横向断面水平垂直位移测点，大坝两岸山体基岩各设置1个水平位移工作基点基左、基右，采用Leica TM50全站仪按四测回边角测量法及极坐标法监测坝体各位移测点水平位移。

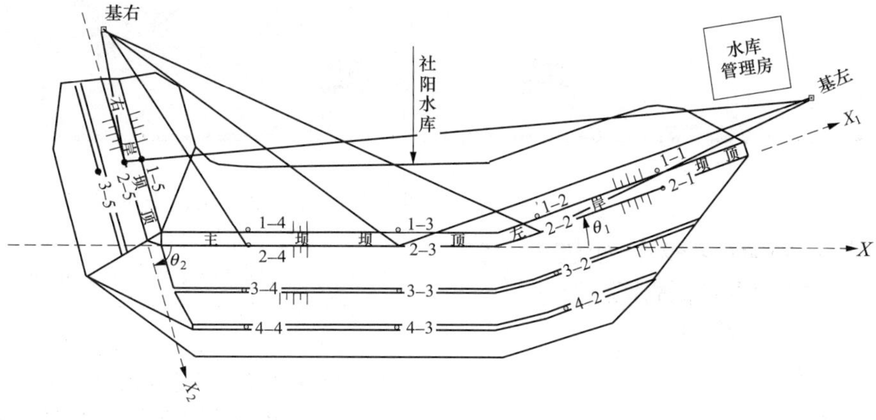

图1　折线型坝水平位移观测计算

（二）折线段大坝各测点水平位移观测计算

（1）主坝轴线方向确定的主坝坐标系中水平位移计算。在主坝轴线 X 方向确定的主坝坐标系中（为使得所有测点 X、Y 坐标全为正，可将该坐标系适当平移）解算第3、第4横断面位移测点坐标及其位移量，即将工作基点基左、基右及第3、第4横断面中相关的位移测点坐标全部在该坐标系中解算。

在本工程中，在主坝坝顶 2-3 测点安置全站仪，以基左（740.2586，245.4892）、基右（200.0000，200.0000）作为已知点进行水平方向、垂直角（观测 EDM 三角高程用）、平距观测。为得到坝顶其他位移测点的坐标，同时观测其他位移测点的水平方向、垂直角、平距。在平差计算中，以方向中误差，测边固定误差，测边比例误差分别为 0.7、0.6、1.0，按先验方差进行平差计算得到 2-3 测点在主坝坐标系中的坐标及中误差分别为（471.6271，341.2497）；（$m_X=\pm0.37$mm，$m_Y=\pm0.57$mm）。在主坝坝顶 2-3 测点安置全站仪同时（极坐标法）观测得到了坝顶 2-4 测点的坐标及中误差分别为（354.0467，341.2217）；（$m_X=\pm0.61$mm，$m_Y=\pm0.56$mm）。在主坝坝顶 2-4 测点安置全站仪以基右（200.0000，200.0000）作后视点按极坐标法观测得到了本测站最弱点 4—4 测点的坐标及中误差分别为（356.0495，385.2777）；（$m_X=\pm0.21$mm，$m_Y=\pm0.60$mm）。考虑到工作基点本身的误差传播导致最弱点 4—4 测点的坐标位移量全中误差为：

$$\begin{cases}m_{\Delta X}=\sqrt{2}\times\sqrt{0.37^2+0.61^2+0.21^2}=\pm1.05\\ m_{\Delta Y}=\sqrt{2}\times\sqrt{0.57^2+0.56^2+0.60^2}=\pm1.40\end{cases}$$

均满足规范规定的 3.0mm 的精度要求。

（2）X_1 方向确定的左岸大坝坐标系中水平位移计算。在 X_1 方向确定的左岸大坝坐标系中（将主坝坐标系旋转 θ_1 角，$\theta_1=-15°57'16''$ 或 $\theta_1=344°02'44''$，并适当平移）解算第 1、第 2 横断面位移测点坐标及其位移量，即将工作基点基左、基右及第 1、第 2 横断面中相关的位移测点坐标全部变换到该坐标系中解算。

在本工程中，在左岸坝顶 2-2 测点安置全站仪，以旋转后坐标系中的基左（644.2659，439.5102）、基右（137.3215，247.2707）作为已知点进行水平方向、垂直角（观测 EDM 三角高程用）、平距观测。为得到坝顶其他位移测点的坐标，同时观测其他位移测点的水平方向、垂直角、平距。平差计算中以方向中误差，测边固定误差，测边比例误差分别为 0.7、0.6、1.0，按先验方差进行平差计算得到 2-2 测点在左岸大坝坐标系中的坐标及中误差分别为（450.0387，469.5626）；（$m_X=\pm0.52$mm，$m_Y=\pm0.59$mm）。在左岸坝顶 2-2 测点安置全站仪以基左（644.2659，439.5102）作后视点按极坐标法观测得到了本测站最弱点 4-2 测点的坐标及中误差分别为（453.5897，513.5689）；（$m_X=\pm0.22$mm，$m_Y=\pm0.60$mm）。考虑到工作基点本身的误差传播导致最弱点 4-2 测点的坐标位移量全中误差为：

$$\begin{cases}m_{\Delta X}=\sqrt{2}\times\sqrt{0.52^2+0.21^2}=\pm0.79\\ m_{\Delta Y}=\sqrt{2}\times\sqrt{0.59^2+0.60^2}=\pm1.19\end{cases}$$

均满足规范规定的 3.0mm 的精度要求。

（3）X_2 方向确定的右岸大坝坐标系中水平位移计算。在 X_2 方向确定的右岸大坝坐标系中（将主坝坐标系旋转 θ_2 角，$\theta_2=74°00'10''$，并适当平移）解算右岸大坝第 5 横断面位移测点坐标及其位移量，即将工作基点基左、基右及第 5 横断面中相关的位移测点坐标全部变换到该坐标系中解算。

（浙江华电乌溪江水力发电有限公司
珺海荣　濮久武）

其　他

金安桥水电站顺利完成金沙江干流“11·3”白格堰塞湖险情的应急处置

（一）事件背景

2018 年 11 月 3 日，西藏自治区昌都市江达县波罗乡白格村境内金沙江右岸“10·11”山体滑坡点发生二次滑坡，滑坡堵塞金沙江干流河道再次形成堰塞湖。据长江防总分析，如堰塞湖水位约 2966m 时溃决，届时石鼓水文站以上洪峰流量均超 10000 年一遇，梨园水库入库洪峰流量 16000m^3/s、过程洪量近 8 亿 m^3，将对堰塞湖下游沿江造成重大险情。

（二）监视到位汇报及时

11 月 3 日 23 时，金安桥水电站水调中心值班人员发现白格堰塞湖下游叶巴滩电站流量数据异常下降，随后立即联系长江防总，得知金沙江白格村境内再次滑坡形成堰塞湖的消息后，及时将相关情况汇报金安桥公司领导，并立即汇报上级相关单位及部门，严密监视金安桥水电站上游金沙江干流各水文站水位流量数据。

（三）切实落实防汛主体责任

险情发生后，金安桥水电站切实落实防汛主体责任，恢复防汛值班，停止一切防汛设备检修，共5次严格执行长江防总有关水位控制的调度令，提前腾库，密切跟踪堰塞体的处置进展，按要求及时向政府及防汛主管部门上报相关情况，配合政府部门的现场检查。

（四）勠力同心，实现应急处置期间零弃水

在险情发生伊始，金安桥水电站就与国家能源局云南监管办、长江防总及金沙江中游各梯级电站等相关单位建立了沟通联络机制，实现相关信息实时共享，内、外部勠力同心、共同应对突发险情。对堰塞湖水量进行滚动测算，制定应对“11·3”白格堰塞湖险情水库调度方案，最大限度避免弃水风险、减少灾害损失。11月5日13时，金安桥库水位1417.51m，至11月13日1时最低消落至1402.64m，累计腾库2.70亿m^3，为后续堰塞湖处置期间金安桥水电站实现零弃水打下坚实基础。

（五）堰塞湖洪峰经过情况

“11·3”金沙江白格堰塞湖通过人工干预，于11月12日10时50分开始溃堰过流，13日18时溃堰洪峰流量达到31000m^3/s；14日1时40分，洪峰到达巴塘水文站，峰值20900m^3/s；14日13时15分，洪峰到达奔子栏水文站，峰值15700m^3/s；15日8时40分，洪峰到达石鼓水文站，峰值7170m^3/s。经金沙江中游梨园、阿海水电站拦蓄，金安桥水电站未发生较大洪水。经现场检查，本次险情未对金安桥库区、大坝和设备设施造成影响。11月16日前后，各级政府、防汛部门陆续解除了应急响应，此次应急处置取得阶段性胜利。

经过金安桥水电站有限公司前期积极有序的组织、安排和应对，认真落实防汛主体责任，顺利完成金沙江干流“11·3”白格堰塞湖险情的应急处置，保证了金安桥水电站的安全和利益。

（金安桥水电站有限公司　官文丰）

拉哇水电站工程科学应对金沙江白格堰塞湖险情

拉哇水电站工程位于金沙江上游，左岸为四川省甘孜藏族自治州巴塘县拉哇乡，右岸为西藏昌都自治州芒康县竹巴笼乡，上游为叶巴滩水电站，下游为巴塘水电站。2018年拉哇水电站正进行前期准备工程建设，华电金沙江上游水电开发有限公司拉哇分公司（简称拉哇分公司）为建设单位，四川二滩国际工程咨询有限责任公司（简称二滩国际）为监理单位。

（一）白格堰塞湖险情及拉哇前期工程应急处置工作

1. 第一次白格堰塞湖　2018年10月10日22时6分，西藏江达县波罗乡以下约10km处金沙江岸坡发生大面积垮塌，导致金沙江主河道断流快速形成大库容堰塞湖，堰塞体存在溃坝风险。拉哇水电站坝址位于堰塞体下游约180km（河道），堰塞湖泄流时洪水到达拉哇工区时间短、洪峰衰减小，电站前期工程在此次堰塞湖危及范围内。

鉴于灾害情况紧急，拉哇分公司立即启动应急响应，成立白格堰塞湖灾害业主应急指挥部（以下简称业主应急指挥部）。二滩国际迅速启动应急预案，立即进入应急工作状态赶赴现场全力协助、配合开展工区低洼施工点人员安全撤离、安置以及设备安全转移工作。

11日10～19时，二滩国际按业主应急指挥部要求组织各标段施工人员有条不紊将拉哇工区内人员全部撤离至巴塘县城内安置点。截至12日晚8时，各施工单位工区内大部分材料、固定式设备以及所有废弃、有用油料移至指定安全地带。

13日13时30分左右，受上游堰塞湖自然泄流影响，拉哇电站坝址区出现洪峰，洪峰流量达到7400m^3/s，坝址水位到达2555.24m，超过100年一遇洪水标准。13日14时后水位开始回落，流量开始减小；14日上午8时流量趋于稳定，险情基本解除。

10月18日，在各方的共同努力下，绝大部分工作面恢复现场施工。

2. 第二次白格堰塞湖　2018年11月3日下午5时，原金沙江白格堰塞湖垮塌处再次发生塌方阻断河流形成堰塞湖。堰体加高，本次险情更加严峻。晚7时，监理人员赶赴现场，按照业主应急指挥部的抢险要求，协助工区人员撤离以及2570m高程以下设备、材料转移工作，4日下午7时左右，工区内所有人员全部转移至县城内安置。

受“11·3”白格堰塞湖断流影响，5日凌晨5时左右，拉哇水电站坝址区流量趋于稳定，流量为150m^3/s；至下午18时，工区内抢险人员全部撤离出工区，抢险设备、物资转移至安全点存放。

6日上午10时，为保障下游索桥主索安全，经对堰塞湖泄流洪水的科学研判、分析，业主应急指挥部决策拆除上游索桥桥面，当日工区低高程隧道洞口的封堵施工基本完成。

8日，考虑到工区内度洪安全以及灾后恢复工作的道路保障，工区内继续全力抢修通往右岸交通工程标砂混系统的道路以及左岸炸药库通往拉英通乡的公路。11日，通往右岸交通工程道路基本形成，并对相关设备进行转移，对灰罐拆除、切割、转移处理；

12日凌晨4点，工区内人员全部撤离，工区进行了全面封闭。

"11·3"白格堰塞湖采取堰塞体开挖导流槽人为干预。12日8时，堰塞湖库区水位到达人工开挖导流槽最低点，开始漫流。13日下午6时，堰塞湖溃决泄流洪峰出现为31000m^3/s；晚9时15分，洪水抵达拉哇水电站坝址；晚11时15分，洪峰达到拉哇水电站坝址，推算洪峰最大流量达到22000m^3/s，坝址水位到达2566.87m，远远超过工程10000年一遇洪水11100m^3/s；晚11时20分后水位开始回落，流量开始减少。至11月15日上午8时，流量趋于稳定，险情基本解除。

（二）白格堰塞湖对拉哇水电站工程造成危害

白格堰塞湖事发突然，堰塞湖体量大、危害大，第二次堰塞湖泄流洪水远远超出电站水文资料10000年一遇洪水历史记录。该堰塞湖人工干预风险高、抢险难度大，溃坝风险高，大江大河堰塞湖相关记录少，可借鉴、指导资料少。

白格堰塞湖地灾事件导致拉哇水电站前期工程工区低线公路路基严重毁坏，低线交通洞室倒灌积水，左右岸交通连接索道桥冲毁，场内交通几乎处于中断状态，工程损毁严重。处于关键线路的3个关键隧道工作面（②、④、⑫号隧道等）因道路中断而处于停工状态；处于关键线路上的金沙江大桥右岸桥台施工和拱座施工因道路中断处于停工状态；右岸交通工程标的砂混系统和临建平台全部冲毁，需异地选择重建；右岸炸药库因道路和临建场地冲毁成为孤岛，无法恢复施工等。受两次白格堰塞湖影响，各工作面工期直接影响1～5个月。

（三）结语

拉哇水电站前期工程在业主应急指挥部的科学研判、正确指挥下，在监理单位的全力协助以及施工单位的通力配合下，两次堰塞湖险情均未发生人员伤亡事件，并将损失降到最低。

（四川二滩国际工程咨询有限责任公司
刘通通）

清江梯级水电站水毁修复项目全部完工

2016年7月、2017年10月，清江水布垭、隔河岩、高坝洲3座梯级水电站均发生不同程度的险情和灾情，直接经济损失达6000多万元。业主湖北清江水电开发有限责任公司（简称清江公司）对水毁工程的修复工作分轻重缓急陆续启动，2018年10月结束，历时27个月。

（一）暴雨及洪水情况

2016年7月19日，水布垭水电站以上流域48h面平均降雨160mm，是有水文资料以来的最大值；水布垭最大入库流量13100m^3/s，库水位最高涨至397.17m（正常蓄水位400m），最大泄洪流量4520m^3/s，泄洪历时59h，总泄量5.6亿m^3；隔河岩最大入库流量9742m^3/s，最大泄洪流量5378m^3/s，泄洪历时215h，总泄量11.2亿m^3；高坝洲最大入库流量8470m^3/s，最大泄洪流量7635m^3/s，总泄量31.3亿m^3。

2017年10月1～2日，清江流域出现强降水，水布垭以上流域面雨量达82.3mm；水布垭最大入库流量6710m^3/s，库水位最高涨至399.91m，最大泄洪流量2580m^3/s，泄洪历时110h，总泄量3.1亿m^3；隔河岩最大入库流量6000m^3/s，最大泄洪流量4770m^3/s，泄洪历时261h，总泄量7.6亿m^3；高坝洲最大入库流量6420m^3/s，最大泄洪流量5460m^3/s，总泄量14.7亿m^3。

（二）水毁情况

1. 水布垭水电站　2016年，受"7·19"强降雨及泄洪影响，坝区多个排洪沟发生山洪泥石流，主要公路边坡多处坍塌，严重堵塞交通，大小两个地下厂房对外交通短时中断；物资仓库围墙和库房玻璃被丛家湾滑坡体泥石流冲坏，一楼库房物资遭雨水浸泡；强雾化区工程边坡和护岸遭受不同程度的破坏，泄洪影响区观测设施多处损毁；地下厂房多处渗水，雾雨危及小电站抽水电源可能引发水淹厂房风险；左右岸边坡、滑坡、公路局部排水系统严重损毁、几乎瘫痪，水布垭大桥左岸桥头护岸也被山洪水冲垮；正常电力生产和枢纽运行安全均受到严重威胁。受2017年秋汛泄洪影响，地下厂房及周边排水洞新发现局部积渣、积水、渗水现象。

2. 隔河岩水电站　2016年汛后检查发现，隔河岩下游左右岸混凝土护坡和河床二级消力池混凝土护坦、左右岸混凝土护坡结构缝和左岸下游护坡坡脚护坦板均存在一定程度的水毁破坏。2017年1月，水垫池抽干后检查发现，底板护坦有一处面积862m^2的冲蚀磨损区，靠近左侧边墙处钢筋裸露，最大深度为25cm；护坦底板与左侧边墙连接部位有一处堆积物，直径约5m、高度约2m，由钢筋和混凝土块缠绕形成团状；另有局部蜂窝麻面、钢筋裸露等缺陷。受2017年秋汛暴雨影响，隔河岩右坝头工程边坡发生局部垮塌。

3. 高坝洲水电站　2016年"7·19"洪峰过后，重约5万t的网箱及其附属物所形成的长约300m、最宽处达150m的巨型垃圾堆积物，积压在高坝洲坝前，严重危及人身安全、坝体安全、行洪安全和发电安全。下游左右岸浆砌石护坡均发生不同程度损毁，左岸损毁长约345m，面积约3200m²；右岸损毁长约200m，面积约为2200m²。受2017年秋汛泄洪影响，下游左岸局部又出现新的浆砌石护坡损毁。

（三）修复情况

本次清江水毁工程修复项目多达17大项、39小项，实际结算金额约3600万元，修复面积近8.9万m²，混凝土浇筑量约1.8万m³，浆砌石砌筑1.2万m³，新增和修复排水沟约2575m。主要修复情况如下：

（1）水毁工程修复，较大项目委托长江勘测规划设计研究有限责任公司进行专项设计，公开招标；一般项目由清江公司库坝中心自己设计，发包方式采取竞争性谈判。陆续签订了大小38个合同，涉及26家施工单位。针对水毁修复项目中高空临边、施工用电、物体打击等高危作业风险，推行“领导带班、旁站监管、反复交底、日查日改”等管理手段，最终打赢了水毁修复攻坚战。

（2）水布垭右岸坝子沟区域整治过程中，受2017年特大秋汛及2018年3月初强降雨影响，1号集石坑右侧边坡移民路外侧土质边坡出现沉降及开裂变形，局部路面混凝土断裂，内侧两处百姓房屋出现裂缝险情。清江公司果断委托设计单位进行抢险变更设计，确定采取增加锚筋桩、衡重式钢筋混凝土挡墙、贴坡混凝土及格构支护等多种工程措施对坝子沟区域进行抢险处理。该修复工程最终于2018年10月完成。

（3）隔河岩大坝水垫池C50一级配环氧混凝土修补面积达862m²，浇筑方量153m³，无论修补面积、体积均为国内罕见，且在高温、多雨的季节实施，2017年主汛前完成。10月份经历泄洪考验后，进行全面水下检查，对修补部位进行重点详查，未见异常。

（4）高坝洲水电站坝前巨型堆积物的复杂程度、打捞难度、打捞工作量在国内水电站都属罕见，可供借鉴的排险打捞经验比较缺乏。清漂打捞工作又关系到当地民生和水利枢纽的安全稳定运行，清江公司主动担负起国有企业应承担的社会责任，将抢救渔民生命财产放在了第一位，及时启动突发事件应急程序，大胆探索，妥善处置，自2016年7月20日至8月16日，奋战28个日夜，顺利完成了清漂抢险任务。通过清漂抢险，锻炼了一批队伍，填补了国内坝前巨型堆积物在清漂打捞技术上的空白。

（5）开展“电力建设工程施工安全年”活动，做好安全、质量、进度、投资四大控制。主汛前完成隔河岩大坝水垫池修补、充水，战胜坝子沟治理工程突发险情，消除梯级水电站39处重大工程缺陷和隐患，包括水淹厂房、泄洪消能、边坡稳定、厂房渗漏、人身安全等6类安全隐患；同时实现所有外包工程的安全、质量目标，确保了三大枢纽工程两个年度的安全度汛。在水毁修复完成后，全面检查、梳理水毁修复资料，将所有资料分类录入库坝中心文档库。

（6）以隔河岩右坝头垮塌区域岩性分析、隔河岩4号机组引水洞渗水分析、水布垭地下厂房1号施工支洞积水抽排、隔河岩消力池充水、水布垭左岸240平洞渗压分析等实战工作有针对性地解决问题，提升员工的综合分析能力。以隔河岩消力池、隔河岩下游护坡、水布垭地下厂房吊车梁、水布垭厂房后边坡排水沟等部位实施的抗冲耐磨、密封、防渗、高弹性等特征的不同类型的环氧施工实践，提升员工对特种修补材料的选型、配比、试验的认识。依托边坡治理、洞室支护等水毁实践，培养了一批能够应对施工队伍管理及技术水平参差不齐、多工作面、高风险、长工期等不利条件的项目管理队伍。

（湖北清江水电开发有限责任公司　贡建兵）

万家寨水利枢纽排沙洞淤堵原因分析及疏通处理

万家寨水利枢纽排沙洞布置在13～17坝段电站进水口左下侧，共5条，由现浇混凝土进口段及排沙钢管两部分组成，采用虹吸式接驼峰堰的进口型式。排沙钢管轴线长130m，直径为2.7m，出口设在尾水平台下部，在坝前水位952.00m时单管泄量57.00m³/s，管内流速9.86m/s。每条排沙洞在进口沿上游坝面设置进口检修门一道，底坎高程912.00m；在坝内下0+009.40m处设有事故门一道，底坎高程917.00m；在出口设平板工作闸门。

2014年8月主汛排沙期间，上游水位在955m左右，2号排沙出口工作门提至全开后，发现无过流现象。随后保持闸门全开状态，持续约3天时间后将2号排沙工作门落至全关。判断确认2号排沙洞发生淤堵。

（一）淤堵情况

2号排沙洞发生淤堵后，先后尝试利用水头压力挤压、通入低压气扰动洞内淤泥等方法进行疏通，但均未取得满意效果。2015年9月组织潜水员进行了水下检查。检查发现，主要淤积物为淤泥，还有少量杂草，淤积方量大概为700m³左右。事故闸门底坎处淤积厚约为1.2m，两侧厚约为1.5m；事故闸门上游侧由1.5m厚一直倾斜向下，直到淤泥高度距管顶部20cm左右，淤堵处距事故闸门约为9m；事故闸门再往下游方向平均淤积厚度约为1.2m，一直延伸到拐弯处。倾斜管段内淤泥完全淤堵住的位置距水平段淤积高度约为6m。出口工作闸门底坎处有一层较薄淤泥，往上游淤泥逐渐变高，潜水员由工作闸门槽向上游2.5m左右就因高度不足而不能前进，用钢板尺向内测量发现，完全淤堵住的位置距离工作闸门槽4m左右。2号排沙洞整体淤积情况如图1所示。

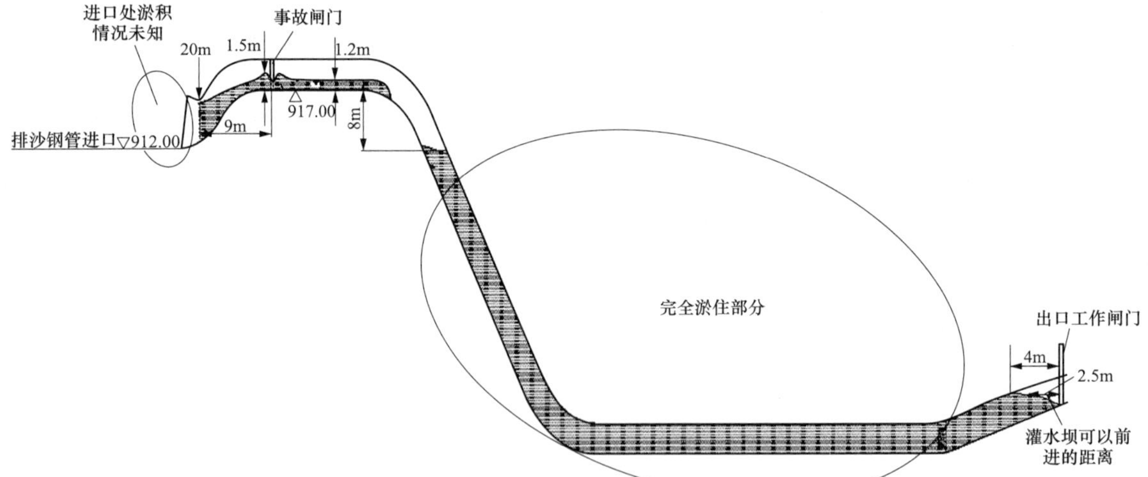

图1 2号排沙洞整体淤积情况

（二）淤堵原因分析

（1）2013年主汛期近坝区域排沙效果不佳，形成淤积。2013年8、9两月上游实际来水比较均匀，平均库水位955.72m，期间头道拐来沙2609.4万t，万家寨出库沙量4795.6万t，汛后最大库容比汛前增加0.143亿m^3。但坝前4km范围内冲刷效果欠佳，发生泥沙淤积，汛后实测坝前淤积高程为920m，比排沙洞进口检修门底坎高程912m高出8m，此时排沙洞进口处已经形成了泥沙淤积。

（2）2014年凌汛期排沙洞未泄水排沙，导致坝前泥沙板结。2014年黄河封河槽蓄水增量释放早且均匀，致凌峰较小，本年度冲刷潼关高程试验泄流指标结合万家寨机组实际出流能力制定，试验期间万家寨无非发电用水。同时为保证山西引黄工程用水，万家寨库水位仅降至960m左右，未达到排沙运用正常运行最高水位957m，故2014年度凌汛期万家寨电站排沙洞没有进行泄水排沙。由于此次凌汛期排沙洞没有运行，自2013年主汛排沙至下个排沙运行周期时间将达到12个月，期间只有发电机组运行取水，对坝前区域淤积的泥沙产生扰动有限，导致该区域泥沙板结，流动性变差。

（3）排沙洞运行方式有待优化。排沙洞原运行方式闸门操作均按设计运行方式进行，即启门操作过程为：先静水提进口事故门至全开后，再动水提出口工作门；闭门操作过程则为：先动水将出口工作门落至全关后，再静水将进口事故门落至全关，然后再将出口工作门提到全开，以期排除钢管内部分泥水，最后将出口工作门落至全关。执行落门程序时，出口工作门动水关闭后，排沙钢管内高含沙水流会突然停滞，所挟泥沙在静水中迅速沉淀，进口事故门关闭后，再打开出口工作门以期排出管内泥沙时，由于排沙钢管内为静水，不具备初始动能，裹挟泥沙能力以及对沉淀的泥沙冲刷效果十分有限，导致有部分泥沙沉淀或堆积在管内，不能全部排出至尾水。

（4）进口事故闸门密封不严存在漏水。在低水位运行过程中，水流含沙量很大，进口事故闸门底坎会存留淤泥，导致闸门落至全关时闸门底角附近存在漏水缝隙，加上闸门水封在启闭过程中也会发生挤压变形和破损，存在封水不严的情况。夹沙水流漏进排沙钢管，水流在管内积存淤泥的阻滞作用下流速缓慢，裹挟的泥沙逐渐沉淀淤积，导致排沙钢管内过水通道日渐窄小，最终整条排沙钢管发生淤堵。

（三）排沙钢管淤堵水下疏通

查明排沙钢管内泥沙淤堵情况后，决定对其分段进行水下清理。

（1）将进口事故门门槽底坎及该区域上下游半米区域清理干净，保证事故门能落至全关。现场配置潜水泵进行事故门门槽内抽水减压。使水位下降并保持在918.00m附近，以减小作用在钢管中部淤泥上的静水压力，保证排沙洞下游安全作业。

（2）在下游尾水作业平台布设施工作业场地，采用高压水冲泥结合吸排泥系统的方式清理出口段。使用吸排泥系统从冲散的淤积物坡脚开始吸泥，完成后拉动吸泥管及管头不断向上游前进，通过硬质的吸泥管道排出至下游尾水，清理至排沙洞中部斜坡段底部886.00m处。

(3) 配置潜水泵先将顶部积水排出，再采用清水置换淤泥的方式清理至斜坡段894.00m附近。在斜坡段底部区域894.00～886.00m之间存在一段固结严重的淤积层，清水置换法不管用，采用对接钢管加压击穿板结淤泥层的方法。在板结淤泥层顶部使用多根2m长的DN40钢管对接推入到淤积物中，高压潜水泵向钢管内注水加压，配合推进钢管直到穿透板结淤泥层，然后反复上下拉拽搅动，形成过水通道并将其逐步扩大。

(4) 过水通道形成后，先后3次在进口事故门槽充灌清水至排沙运用最高水位957m，再开启排沙洞出口工作门模拟过流并对钢管内残留淤泥进行冲刷，结果均显示2号排沙洞正常过水。为确保洞内清淤效果，打开排沙钢管放空阀排空管内积水后，进入排沙洞内检查，发现钢管内仅管底存在薄层稀泥，排沙钢管内整体清淤效果良好，2号排沙洞进口事故门以下淤堵物已全部疏通完毕。

（四）结语

万家寨2号排沙洞淤堵水下疏通施工历时3个多月，从发现不能过流到检查判断淤堵情况到尝试自然疏通到最终确定水下清理方案并实施完成经历了漫长的两年时间，耗费了大量的人力、物力。因此，水库泥沙问题应引起高度重视，应吸取教训，加强对泥沙问题的研究，统筹规划、综合治理、运维兼顾，将泥沙淤积对泄水建筑物的不利影响降到最低。

（黄河万家寨水利枢纽有限公司　吴凌丞）

13

环境保护与水库移民

环　境　保　护

乌东德水电站工程2018年生态环境保护工作情况

2018年，乌东德工程建设部按照《金沙江乌东德水电站环境影响报告书》《金沙江乌东德水电站水土保持方案报告书》及其批复意见的要求，开展环保、水保相关工作，各项环保、水保设施正常运行，运行效果整体满足要求。年度未发生环保责任事件，未受到行政或刑事处罚。

1. 环境保护体系　按照环评、水保报告及其批复意见的要求，乌东德工程建设部与长江水资源保护科学研究所签订环境监理和水土保持监理备忘录，完善了施工区环境监理和水土保持监理机构。环境监理与水土保持监理于2015年10月正式进场开展监理工作，2018年工作正常开展，重点对施工区古树移栽养护、生活垃圾清运、生活污水处理设施运行以及危险废物管理等进行了监理。

2. 环境保护工程　2018年3月，成功开展了齐口裂腹鱼人工繁育工作，并在鱼苗开口饵料培养与小瓜虫病防治方面取得了研究突破。2018年9月27日，组织开展年度增殖放流活动，放流珍稀鱼苗7.2万余尾，其中近4万尾齐口裂腹鱼全部为站内自繁育鱼苗。绿化二期工程继续实施，逐步改善施工区环境，发挥降尘、减缓水土流失的效用；为进一步打造美丽工区，创建绿色工程，组织开展了三期绿化规划设计工作。

（中国三峡建设管理有限公司　孟友瑞　李华）

向家坝与溪洛渡水电站工程2018年环境保护工作情况

2018年，向家坝与溪洛渡两电站各项已建环保水保设施的运行和管护到位，较好地发挥了环保、水保效益，同时开展了施工区水、气、声环境监测、水土保持监测工作，并配合完成了川滇两省环境保护行政主管部门对两电站开展的环境保护监察活动。年度未发生环保责任事件，未受到行政处罚。

全年开展2次珍稀特有鱼苗放流活动，放流达氏鲟、胭脂鱼、长薄鳅、长鳍吻鮈等6种鱼苗共计18万余尾，完成了年度计划，历年累计放流数量达到158万余尾。此外，向家坝水电站新滩坝翻坝转运码头工程顺利通过了竣工环境保护验收。

2018年，中国三峡建设管理有限公司向家坝与溪洛渡工程建设部完成两电站施工迹地生态恢复专项设计报告技术审查工作，同时对两电站施工迹地生态恢复的招标采购方案进行深入研究，提出了建议方案并上报审批，有效保障了后续工作的有序开展；9月，组织完成施工迹地恢复项目招标工作，两电站项目分别分3个标段实施，内容包括场地清理、渣场治理、迹地恢复、表土管理等。

为确保在质量、安全、环保达标的情况下，落实各项水土保持措施，制定了水保周例会、日巡查、现场协调机制等管理措施，及时解决施工过程中遇到的各种困难。经努力，工程防护及迹地恢复施工已全部完成，为现场验收工作创造了有利条件；按照规程规范要求，组织开展了两电站弃渣场稳定性评估工作，结合地质勘探、室内试验等相关工作，编制了弃渣场稳定性评估报告，评估结果为弃渣场专项防护设计提供了技术支撑。此外，还编制了表土综合利用设计报告、溪洛渡水电站水土保持设计（弃渣场）变更报告等专题报告，并组织了专项审查；过程中组织对各单位的水保相关总结报告进行内部审查并及时督促修改完善，为两电站水土保持设施专项验收提供了翔实的基础材料。

2018年12月15～17日，两电站开展了水土保持设施技术预验收工作；在此基础上，12月19日，两电站顺利通过了水土保持设施（枢纽工程）自主验收，验收委员会认为向家坝、溪洛渡水电站水土流失防治指标达到水土保持方案确定的目标值，并满足现行的建设类项目一级水土流失防治标准，水土保持设施运行良好，符合水土保持设施验收的条件，同意两电站水土保持设施通过验收。

（中国三峡建设管理有限公司）

中电建水电开发集团有限公司2018年环境保护工作情况

中电建水电开发集团有限公司严格遵守环保法律

法规，在环境保护工作中制定计划目标，落实责任制；将计划目标和工作任与年度考核直接挂钩，通过激励约束措施力求有效推进相关工作并取得实质成果。通过有效管控，2018年度未发生一般及以上突发环境事件，环保工作进度、质量整体受控。环境保护主要工作情况如下：

（一）制度建设情况

为进一步提升公司环境保护管理水平，有序开展环境保护工作，修订完善了环境保护管理制度，同时依据国家和行业有关标准、规程和规范，分别编制了《水力发电厂建设期环境保护管理示范文本》等管理标准。做到管理工作有规可依，严格执行。

（二）工作完成情况

（1）编制完成筹建项目四川省阿坝州巴拉水电站的环境保护总体设计及“三同时”实施方案，委托水电水利规划设计总院召开四川省大渡河沙湾电站生态机组专题会明确可适时建设意见，全面完成了四川省大渡河安谷电站6个环保科研课题研究报告审查。

（2）在建工程新疆克州乌恰县克孜河夏特水电站、四川省阿坝州杨家湾水电站严格落实了施工期的水环境、大气环境、声环境保护措施和固体废弃物处置措施；先后建成安谷水电站生态试验场和沙湾水电站鱼道等环保专项工程，启动了四川省黑水河毛尔盖电站鱼类增殖站扩建工程；协调落实了沙湾水电站生态机组建设事项；全面启动了毛尔盖水电站环保措施整改工作。

（3）严格按照建设项目水保、环保自主验收程序，积极推进项目环水保验收，完成四川省西昌市黄联关风电场水土保持和环境保护竣工自主验收。沙湾水电站、安谷水电站竣工环保验收准备工作基本就绪，拟对竣工验收调查报告进行技术评审后开展验收。

（三）生态流量执行情况

中电建水电开发集团有限公司指导督促各子公司完成投产电站下泄生态流量“一站一策”实施方案编制、评审工作，按要求实施生态流量泄放、满足下游生产、生活和生态用水。

（四）鱼类增殖放流情况

按计划开展各投产水电站鱼类增殖放流工作，共增殖放流各类鱼苗60万尾。其中，安谷水电站、沙湾水电站增殖放流胭脂鱼、长薄鳅、唇鲻、黄颡鱼、长吻鮠、白甲鱼、中华倒刺鲃、岩原鲤、圆口铜鱼等优质鱼苗30余万尾，毛尔盖水电增殖放流齐口裂腹鱼、重口裂腹鱼和松潘裸鲤优质鱼苗30万尾。

（五）宣传培训情况

2018年年初，印发了《关于贯彻学习新修订〈建设项目环境保护管理条例及配套法规〉的通知》，对国家新修订的《建设项目环境保护管理条例》及配套法规进行了宣贯和解读；在国家“环境日”，以展板的形式举办了环境保护宣传活动；2018年8月，组织了覆盖两级公司全部环境保护管理人员专项培训，公司领导、行业专家对国家环保法规政策、建设项目环境保护管理以及公司对环境保护工作要求进行了讲解，进一步提高了环保管理人员的专业水平和认识。

（六）资金投入情况

2018年，安谷水电站滨水湿地及生态试验场、沙湾水电站鱼道工程、毛尔盖水电站鱼类增殖站二期扩建工程等环保专项工程，累计投入环境保护专项费用13000多万元。

（中电建水电开发集团有限公司）

雅砻江流域水电开发有限公司 2018年生态环境保护工作情况

2018年，雅砻江流域水电开发有限公司（简称雅砻江公司）凝心聚力，强力推动流域生态环境保护工作，健全完善生态环境保护管理体系，完美收官流域下游各水电站竣工环保水保验收，创新实施流域鱼类增殖放流站自主运行，各项生态环境保护工作有序开展，雅砻江流域生态环境保护管理再上新台阶。

（一）完善管理体系

雅砻江公司加强环保管理体系的顶层设计，成立了雅砻江公司环境保护管理委员会，将环境保护上升到安全生产的同等高度，并组成了以环委会统筹协调、环境保护管理中心监督执行、各单位具体落实的管理架构，开创了流域环保工作的新局面。根据国家、政府修订出台的环保水保相关法律法规、制度指南，雅砻江公司结合流域环境保护管理实际，修编了《环境保护与水土保持管理办法》，并在流域各二级单位进行了宣贯执行。梳理总结多年鱼类增殖放流站运行管理经验，融合其他鱼类增殖放流站先进管理理念、方法和制度，编制了《鱼类增殖放流站运行管理办法（试行）》，加强流域鱼类增殖放流站自主运行管理。

（二）环保水保工作情况

1. 环保水保管理　2018年3月，雅砻江公司召开年度环保水保工作会，会上安排布置了流域各单位环保水保工作，并在会后印发了公司环保水保年度工作计划；8月，组织流域环保水保自查自纠活动，督导流域各单位对各自区域内环保水保进行自查自纠，建立环保风险管控清单制和销号制，并开展实施交账制和追责制。2018年，雅砻江公司每季度组织全流域环保水保专项巡检，严格遵照环评批复及要求，按照“三同时”管理制度，对照环保水保年度工作计划，对现场各项环保水保措施设计、施工、验收及运行进行全方位检查，将现场环保水保问题和隐患梳理总结成通报发布，及时督查整改。雅砻江公司在积极迎接水利部长江水利委员会、中央环保督察“回头看”巡视组等环保水保主管单位的多次现场检查中未受到批评和处罚。

2. 环保水保验收　在雅砻江公司督导开展的自查自纠活动中，流域各单位积极梳理了各项配套工程环保水保行政手续，有效推动了手续补齐，并完成了官地水电站对外交通公路（经久转运站至金河段）改造工程等项目竣工水土保持验收。2018 年 1、3 月，桐子林水电站、锦屏一级水电站先后通过竣工环境保护自主验收。2018 年 1 月，锦屏一级水电站完成水土保持设施自主验收报备，这是水土保持验收行政许可取消后，第一个在水利部完成报备的自主验收项目；9 月，锦屏一级水电站水土保持设施通过水利部长江水利委员会现场核查。至此，雅砻江下游桐子林、二滩、官地、锦屏一级和二级等 5 座水电站竣工环保水保验收全部完成。

3. 环保水保奖项　2018 年 1 月，经四川省水土保持局严格考核，雅砻江公司（排名第一）和两河口建设管理局（排名第四）均荣获四川省水土保持局通报表扬，并分别荣获“四川省 2017 年度生产建设项目水土保持工作先进单位”。2 月，锦屏二级水电站、官地水电站分别荣获水利部“2017 年度生产建设项目国家水土保持生态文明工程”称号。5 月，锦屏一级水电站、桐子林水电站工程分别荣获“四川省 2017 年度生产建设项目水土保持生态文明工程”称号，并在此基础上向水利部申报“国家级水土保持生态文明工程”。至此，雅砻江下游的桐子林、二滩（环境友好工程，2006 年）、官地、锦屏一级和锦屏二级 5 座水电站全部荣获省级或部级水电行业生态环境保护相关奖项。

（三）流域鱼类保护

1. 工程措施保护　2018 年，雅砻江公司开展两河口鱼类保护措施专题优化设计，组织到大华桥、黄登等水电站开展了过鱼设施调研工作，在广泛调研基础上优化了两河口水电站过鱼方案，并通过了四川省水产局的审查。2018 年 10 月，雅砻江中游鱼类增殖放流站建成投运。该站投资 1.1 亿元，占地约 4.33 万 m^2；包括鱼种培育池 18 口，亲鱼池 43 口，防疫隔离池 4 口，生物饵料培育池 9 口，蓄水池 2 座，仿生态养殖池 3 口；已驯化养殖长丝裂腹鱼、长薄鳅、细鳞裂腹鱼、鲈鲤等 5 种近期放流鱼类，未来可保护杨房沟、卡拉、孟底沟和楞古 4 座水电站河段的鱼类资源。

2. 栖息地保护　雅砻江公司各单位严格按照相应环评批复及要求，严格落实生态流量泄放，保障减水河段保持中大型河流生境，以满足水生生物繁衍生息；继续采取叠梁门分层取水，以减缓下泄低温水对鱼类的影响。2018 年初，雅砻江公司启动了锦屏大河湾减水河段水生生物栖息地生态保护效果评估工作，初步数据表明大河湾栖息地水文、水质、水生生物等方面生态保护效果良好；同时还启动了减水河段生境修复与再造技术研究工作，为各栖息地生境提供了多种有针对性的修复方案。4 月，启动了雅砻江流域上游水电开发的环境保护管理研究，旨在辨识雅砻江上游水电开发过程中环境保护的重点和难点，并提出针对性保护管理和解决方案，坚决执行在保护中开发，在开发中保护。

3. 鱼类增殖放流　2018 年 4 月，两河口水电站鱼类增殖放流站放流 1 龄鱼苗 12 万尾；5 月，二滩·桐子林水电站鱼类增殖放流站放流鱼苗 23 万尾；6 月，锦屏·官地水电站鱼类增殖放流站放流鱼苗 205 万尾，首次达到并超过最大设计放流规模 200 万尾；中游鱼类增殖放流站在锦屏·官地水电站鱼类增殖放流站督导下放流鱼苗 10 余万尾。至此，雅砻江公司顺利完成年度放流任务，全年放流鱼苗 250 余万尾，多年累计放流鱼苗共计 900 余万尾。

雅砻江公司通过对比鱼类增殖放流站自主运行和外委运行两种管理模式的综合效益，发现自主运行的成本远低于外委运行，同时放流效果和科研成果也更为丰硕，还可为公司掌握繁育核心技术和积累养殖管理人才。基于以上优势，雅砻江公司以公司员工为基础，以锦屏·官地水电站鱼类增殖放流站为中心站，统筹运行管理流域 4 座鱼类增殖放流站，充分发挥“一个主体开发一条江”的优势，切实养护一条江的鱼类资源。

（雅砻江流域水电开发有限公司　李天才）

羊曲水电站项目表土资源利用与土壤改良措施研究

羊曲水电站位于青海省海南州兴海县与贵南县交界处，是黄河干流龙羊峡水电站上游“茨哈、班多和羊曲”3 个规划梯级电站的最下一级，装机容量 1200MW。工程主要开发任务为发电，主要由枢纽建筑物、施工生产生活设施及其辅助设施、料场、交通道路工程、弃渣场及表土堆存场、移民安置工程、水库淹没影响区等部分组成。项目区处于青藏高原，气候属大陆性高原干旱气候，区域多年平均气温

2.3℃，多年平均降雨量403.8mm，多年年均蒸发量1378.5mm；降雨主要集中在每年的5～9月。区域土壤类型属于青藏高原高山草甸土壤带，土壤分布规律呈较明显的垂直地带性和地域性，从高海拔至低海拔依次为为高山草原土、山地草甸土、灰褐土、黑钙土、栗钙土，石砾质冲积土和沙质冲积土、新积土。栗钙土和新积土在电站所在的河谷地带分布较多。植被类型为青藏高原高山草甸植被，植被盖度为20%～50%。

（一）表土及可用土壤资料情况

工程施工征占用的耕地、林地、草地数量较多，总面积3059.33hm²。施工后期需迹地恢复、耕地复垦的面积较大。经分析，工程需要复垦的耕地面积约26.0hm²，需要恢复的植被面积约116.31hm²，需覆土总量约为54.23万m³。

工程前期完成表土剥离量8.13万m³，剥离区域为左岸业主营地及承包商营地征占用的耕地范围及右岸混凝土拌合系统占用的草地范围，分别集中堆存于左、右岸表土堆存场。前期三通一平工程结束后，对可恢复区域进行植被恢复建设，其中场内外交通工程边坡框格及部分路肩已覆土，覆土量约1.19万m³；业主营地及承包商营地绿化工程覆土量约5.90万m³。施工后期，本工程尚有128.59hm²的施工扰动面积需要回覆表土，还需覆土47.14万m³，除去已经剥离堆存的1.04万m³的表土外，尚有46.10万m³的表土缺失量。

电站建设区内原地貌形态绝大部分已消失殆尽。工程区表土主要富集在水库库区左岸待淹没的耕地上，表层土厚度为45～60cm；枢纽工程建设区范围内除前期剥离的少量表层土集中堆存在右岸表土堆存场内外，右岸弃渣场堆渣范围内尚有少量原状表层腐殖土，左岸表土堆存场周边及右岸弃渣场周边尚有一定量由表土及沙砾石混合堆积的、可供利用的混合土。

根据工程现场表土及可利用土壤资源现状分布调查情况及后续覆土需求量，结合水土保持法律法规及水土保持技术规范要求，枢纽工程建设区内分布有可利用土壤资源的区域均应作为表土收集区域，表土缺口量从库区左岸待淹没的耕地表层剥离。表土及可利用土壤剥离厚度根据调查点土壤耕植层或腐殖层厚度并考虑后期绿化、土地复垦覆土所需的表土回覆量来确定。经过计算，本工程施工后期在枢纽工程建设区内需剥离可利用土壤量约24.94万m³；覆土需求量缺口部分从库区左岸待淹没部分耕地表层剥离，剥离表土总量约22.20万m³。

（二）土壤改良措施

分析结果表明，枢纽工程建设区域内表土资源均发育于黄土母质，区域土壤为栗钙土，且绝大部分为栗钙土的耕作层、腐殖层、犁底层和心土层，均为土壤熟化层和半熟化层。由于受地形、气候条件及成土过程的影响，枢纽区土壤绝大部分砾石含量≥10%，局部区域砾石含量≥20%，砾石含量远远高于质量控制标准要求；土壤pH介于8.1～9.5之间，属于碱性或强碱性土壤；有机质含量在0.116%～0.954%之间，含量较低；土壤全氮含量在0.24～0.80g/kg、全磷含量在0.43～0.72g/kg、全钾含量在18.28～27.69g/kg之间，氮磷钾等养分含量较低；电导率介于0.154～3.050dS/cm之间，基本满足质量控制标准要求。总体评价，枢纽工程建设区土壤砾石含量大，pH值较高，有机质及养分含量低，整体质量差，土壤需经过改良或改造方可利用于耕地复垦和植被恢复。而库区耕地剥离表土整体质量较好，稍加培肥、改良后可直接用于耕地复垦及林草地植被恢复覆土。综合考虑土壤改良费用，改良周期等因素，推荐耕地复垦采用库区土壤进行改良，林地和草地植被恢复采用枢纽区土壤改良。

1. 耕地复垦及土壤改良方案　场区平整土地后，利用库区剥离的表土覆土60cm，用土壤改良剂每亩3kg稀释100倍后进行地面播洒；亩施优质有机肥料（粪尿肥）800kg，或商品有机肥80kg，撒施在地面；每亩再施用尿素30kg，过磷酸钙100kg，氯化钾10kg用作基肥，撒施均匀；用机械深翻18～25cm，耙耱2～3次，达到地面平整，土块细碎，土肥相融。次年春季3月中下旬，每亩追施尿素10kg，即可用于作物种植。

2. 林地和草地土壤改良方案　pH高于8.5的土壤，需通过施加硫磺粉改良酸碱性。在土壤pH满足要求的基础上，场区平整土地、覆土30cm后，用土壤改良剂每亩2kg稀释100倍后进行地面播洒；每亩再施用尿素20kg，过磷酸钙50kg，有机肥料（粪尿肥）500kg，或商品有机肥40kg，撒施均匀；施肥后，用机械深翻18～25cm，耙耱2～3次，达到地面平整，土块细碎，土肥相融。改良后的土壤即可进行植物绿化。

3. 土壤改良剂选用　选用“如金菌”土壤改良剂（种植专用），其作为用于农业生产的一种绿色环保型多功能调节剂，内含放线菌、光合细菌、酵母菌、乳酸菌、枯草芽孢杆菌等几十种有益微生物以及各种有机酸、植物生长调节剂等代谢产物。有效活菌数200亿/mL。其主要功能为改善土壤结构与黏性，促进团粒结构形成，活化土壤；增强土壤保水保肥能力，降低灌溉频率，抑制土壤水分蒸发与养分流失；增加土壤有益菌群数量，抑制有害杂菌生长繁殖，减少植物根部疾病以及农药施用量；增加土壤疏松程度，有效防止土壤板结，便于作物根部扩张，促进根部发育进而提高作物产量；改善土壤 pH 及其他理化性质，使重金属在土壤中发生沉淀、螯合等反应，消除农作物对重金属的吸收。

（三）结语

表土资源不仅是人类的生存之本，而且再生周期漫长，因此对表土的剥离保护和利用应进行科学的规划和分配。本水电站工程位于青藏高原，对其表土资源的供需平衡分析及改良措施的应用，不仅可保护将被废弃或淹没的土壤资源，而且解决了施工后期土地复垦、生态恢复的覆土需求，避免了因绿化缺土、选择新的土料厂进行开采时对生态环境的破坏。而质量、数量均满足植物生长的表土储量，大大缩短了土地复垦质量控制的周期，对保护和改善项目建设区生态环境、防止水土流失起到了重要作用。

（中国电建集团西北勘测设计研究院有限公司
李百凤 赵鸿 夏朝辉）

安谷水电站生态试验场建设情况

安谷水电站是大渡河干流梯级开发的最后一级，坝址位于四川省乐山市沙湾区，总装机容量 772MW，多年平均年发电量为 31.44 亿 kW·h。电站开发任务为发电、防洪、航运、灌溉和供水，兼顾湿地与水生生态保护。安谷水电站于 2015 年 8 月全部投产发电。

安谷水电站左侧河网水流条件复杂，原始生境多样，物种资源丰富，生态系统结构十分复杂。根据环保要求，需依托本区域资源环境优势，规划建立国内第一座具有原型尺度的人工生态试验场，开展水生态保护与修复的理论和技术研究。2018 年初，安谷水电站生态试验场开工建设。

（一）建设的重要意义

针对大渡河水电梯级开发所产生的生态环境问题，重点研究水电工程的生态效应及水生态修复技术，将天然河流长期观测与人工可控试验相结合，使安谷水电站河流生态监测站、鱼道工程监测站、鱼类增殖放流站、天然河流试验场与人工生态试验场相互促进，推动学科交叉、学术交流和合作研究，为创建绿色水电开发的代表性工程打下基础，最终将安谷水电站生态试验场建设成为我国水利水电行业一流的水生态基础研究与应用研究基地，并逐步将科技支撑区域由大渡河流域推向全国，支撑我国绿色水电建设，推动我国水生态保护相关学科发展。

（二）生态试验场的科研支撑功能

根据安谷水电站影响区的水生态现状、水电开发的生态影响以及我国河湖水生态保护工作的相关科研需求，生态试验场可提供如下科研功能：

（1）库区生态系统演变过程与机制研究。通过长时间的监测，研究库区生态系统演变过程，辨析不同时期库区生境时空分布特征，揭示库区生态系统演变的主要驱动机制。

（2）水利工程的生态效应研究。研究水文情势对污染物输移、转化和降解特性的影响；研究浮游生物与底栖生物种群结构及优势类群、沉水植被分布对水文情势的响应，揭示人类胁迫对水域生态系统的影响。

（3）生物多样性保育机制研究。研究生境特征与生物多样性之间的关系，建立生物多样性与生境因子间的相互关系模型，揭示影响生物多样性保育的关键生境因子，辨识生物多样性保育的关键生态过程，为制定相应的生态修复措施提供理论基础。

（4）河道生态修复技术研究。在 20km 的分汊河网中选择试验河段，将露天生态试验场的河流生态修复研究成果应用其上，通过长期跟踪调查，分析生态修复技术的应用效果，在此基础上重点研究河道地形（深潭、浅滩）、河床底质条件、滨岸带植被与底栖动物和鱼类栖息环境之间的关系，研究水文情势与植物、鱼类种群的相互关系，研究河床环境与生境要素的相互关系，研究护岸工程对鱼类栖息环境的影响等，进一步丰富和推广我国河道生态修复技术。

（5）鱼类保护和恢复技术与效果评价。在安谷水电站左岸天然河道中，现有天然鱼类产卵场和索饵场，针对天然河道鱼类栖息环境的底质、水流条件和食物链环境等进行现场跟踪调查，并通过控制水流、地质条件，在人工试验河道内开展定量研究，揭示鱼类栖息环境的关键参数。

（中电建水电开发集团有限公司）

岩泊渡水电站建设对湖南张家界大鲵国家级自然保护区的影响评价

（一）工程概况

岩泊渡水电站位于湖南省慈利县岩泊渡镇境内之澧水干流中游，下距慈利县城 20km；水库正常蓄水位 105.50m（相应库容 1514 万 m^3），死水位 104.50m（死库容 1274 万 m^3），消落深度 1.0m（占最大水头比例约为 10.1%），调节库容 240 万 m^3；电站装机容量 25MW，满发流量 343.4m^3/s，年发电量 9272 万 kW·h，保证出力 2.51MW，装机利用小时 3709h；坝址河段规划为Ⅵ级航道，建设 100t 级升船机。该电站工程涉及湖南张家界大鲵国家级自然保护区（简称保护区）实验区（澧水干流岩泊渡库区及坝下至茶庵电站大坝）、2年一遇洪水淹没涉及保护区——澧水支流宜冲桥（九龙溪）及渔米渡。

（二）保护区概况

1996年11月，国务院以国函〔1996〕113号批准建立湖南张家界大鲵国家级自然保护区。该保护区是我国第一个以大鲵为保护对象的国家级自然保护区，位于张家界市永定区、武陵源区、慈利县、桑植县，常德市石门县和怀化市辰溪县境内；据调查统计和估算，其野生大鲵资源总量约2000尾，呈不连续点状分布；每年可采集到野生大鲵苗约1500尾，大鲵资源呈衰减趋势。野生大鲵多栖息在地下溶洞内，溪河中分布较少，受胁迫形势严峻。大鲵人工养殖有一定成效，达3万多尾。张家界大鲵保护工作起步较早，取得一定成绩，建立了个9大鲵保护站，组织了10次野生大鲵放流活动，取得一定效果，大鲵在慈利县主要分布在象市、三官寺、江垭、赵家岗、龙潭湾、高桥、金坪、金岩等乡镇。

（三）工程涉及区域内大鲵调查结果

对电站库首和库尾之间及坝下大鲵活动进行实地勘探调查，与此同时在岩泊渡镇进行实地调查，结果如下：

（1）工程涉及区域生境与大鲵适宜生境比较调查，结果表明：岩泊渡水电站涉及工程区域本身不具备适宜大鲵的栖息与繁衍的环境条件。

（2）工程涉及区域饵料与大鲵适宜饵料比较调查，结果表明：蟹类几乎没有在渔获物组成中出现，可见大鲵的最佳饵料生物未在岩泊渡工程涉及区域内大量而广泛的存在，不能为大鲵提供足够优质的蟹类饵料资源。

（3）工程涉及区域内大鲵栖息地环境适合度评价表明，论证区域内环境因子不适合大鲵的生存、摄食和繁殖，从某种程度上佐证了上述实地调查勘探结果。

综合结论：根据调查大鲵的生活习性，大鲵常栖息于山区性的急流中，在水质清澈、含沙量不大，水流湍急的洞穴中生活。成鲵常栖息在深潭内的岩洞、石穴之中。以前在索溪峪、龙潭湾、象市、三官寺、赵家岗、高桥、金坪等地的溪河岩溶洞及澧水干流上游高山激流中、水质好的地方有分布。而岩泊渡水电站工程库区河段主要为澧水干流河段，水流平缓，受人类开发利用程度较高。另外，根据调查，大鲵生境主要分布在澧水上游河段两岸的高山性激流中，不在库区范围内。因此，岩泊渡水电站工程建设对大鲵生境的影响程度有限，对大鲵的生存及分布无重大影响。

（四）工程建设对大鲵的影响评价

1. 施工期对大鲵的影响分析　岩泊渡大坝坝下河段虽未发现野生大鲵资源，但不能完全排除大鲵出现的可能，施工挖掘点应选择在距离河道较远的区域，以免对大鲵繁殖、摄食、迁徙等行为产生影响。工程施工期所产生的废水、废渣、噪声、振动和夜间照明设施对大鲵的繁殖、摄食、迁徙等行为有显著的影响，因此在工程施工阶段必须采取相应的措施，尽可能降低工程施工对野生大鲵资源的影响程度。

工程施工的噪声会影响大鲵推沙、繁殖等行为。因此，在大鲵繁殖和孵化期间，对于野生大鲵分布集中区应避免强噪音和强光照施工，夜间应停止施工。

大鲵出洞活动的数量与水温、光照强度的相关性较强；当光照强度在 y＝685－1431Lx 相对光照强度3%时，大鲵开始出洞活动或回洞隐藏；而当光照强度降至0Lx后约2h、水温在17.1～18.4℃时，大鲵出洞活动达到高峰期。因此，最好晚上要停止强光照施工。

2. 运营期对大鲵的影响分析　电站的正常调度运行对澧水干流的年径流及月径流影响不大。工程建设对大鲵没有明显影响，但不能排除大鲵误入的可能性，仍需对误入的大鲵及其饵料生物环境进行保护。

项目蓄水期间坝址下游自然水位变幅减小致河流生境层次简化，但是库区及各支流周边湿地会有小幅度增加，这将有利于库区及支流区域一些植物种类和植被的生长。随着这些物质种类的增多，原本偏干的生境可能逐渐向大鲵喜好的湿润生境转化，这将一定程度上改善库区及支流大鲵生境环境。大鲵喜栖息于安静的环境中，平常隐匿在山溪河流附近的洞穴中，不易被人类所发现，当环境中噪声、光线和水质酸碱性发生较大的改变后，基于物种对恶劣环境的躲避效应，大鲵会迁徙出原有的洞穴。

3. 对库区支流保护区缓冲区的影响分析　湖南张家界大鲵国家级自然保护区管理处以《关于拟建岩泊渡电站工程涉及湖南张家界大鲵国家级自然保护区关系的函》（湘鲵保函〔2016〕30号），明确该电站主体工程建设地点属于保护区实验区。岩泊渡水电站洪水期间库区可能受工程影响的支流主要为库尾的九龙溪（宜冲桥）、鱼米渡2条支流，现场勘查情况如下：

（1）九龙溪：该河段上游为宜冲桥村民聚居地，常张高速在该淹没区上方横跨而过，沿该河段两岸多为农田及村民自留地，水量较少，人类活动较为频繁，淹没区土地多为百姓开荒耕种用地。

（2）渔米渡：该区域河段跟宜冲桥情况大致类同，常张高速公路在该河段上方横跨而过，该支流上游多为居民生活生产区域，人类活动频繁，沿河两岸多为群众耕种用地，河内水量较少，几近干涸。

上述两条支流上游区域属于张家界大鲵国家级自然保护区的缓冲区，不涉及保护区核心区，支流无大鲵野生种群栖息地和大鲵分布点。

岩泊渡水电站属于日调节（径流式）电站，调蓄功能较弱，运行期基本上来多少水泄多少水。根据坝址上游断面流量与水位关系可知，建库（开闸）后来水各频率洪水时，支流九龙溪和渔米渡处的水位上升仅为 0.15～0.25m（其中 100 年一遇的洪水时水位上升 0.25m），项目建成后对支流水位影响很小；项目建成后库区及各支流周边湿地有小幅度增加，这将有利于改善张家界大鲵国家级自然保护区的缓冲区大鲵生境环境。

（五）结论

岩泊渡水电站工程附近 10km 内无大鲵自然保护点分布。施工期产生的噪声、生产生活废水、悬浮物、固体废弃物等，以及工程建成后的运行将改变大坝下游河段径流的时空格局并可能产生季节性断流，对保护区主要保护对象及其生境产生永久性的不利影响，但不会对保护区的结构和功能产生影响。为避免电站设计回水影响大鲵自然保护区的缓冲区，使岩泊渡水电站各频率回水在支流渔米渡、九龙溪处水位达到天然水位，建设单位与设计单位协商，提出将电站坝址位置下移及扩大坝址泄洪能力两个措施。通过以上两种措施，可使岩泊渡水电站各频率回水在支流渔米渡、九龙溪处水位保持天然状态，不影响缓冲区。

（湖南省水利水电勘测设计研究总院　凌尚）

水　库　移　民

新的土地政策及产业结构下水电移民生产安置方式研究

在我国水库移民实践中，大农业安置一直是最重要的生产安置方式。从大农业安置的土地来源来看，一是开发一定数量的耕地后备资源即开发土地安置，二是对移民安置区现有土地的内部调整即调整土地安置。由于受耕地后备资源有限性及自然条件等因素的制约，前者在移民安置实践中，往往仅占很小一部分，大部分是通过政府干预下的移民安置区土地调整来实现。但随着我国土地政策的变化，在行政干预下采用土地调整的生产安置方式已日益与当前的土地政策不协调。因此，中国电建集团中南勘测设计研究院有限公司组织开展了研究，通过解读新的土地政策，并结合对水电工程移民土地流转意愿的分析，探讨新形式下的生产安置方式。

（一）水电工程移民土地流转特殊性

相对于一般意义上的农村土地流转，水电工程移民安置过程中的土地流转具有其特殊性，移民土地流转意愿也因此跟随国家政策在一直发生着变化。

第一，主体特定。水电工程移民安置的转出方是承担移民安置的集体和农户，而转入方则是移民，主体是特定事物涉及的特定群体。第二，多重土地权益转移。移民在安置区获取土地使用权的同时，还获得了集体成员身份以及长久的生存和发展权，即享有和原居民同等的权利和义务。第三，流转目的不同。一般意义的土地流转是由分散走向集中的行为，是在公平基础上对土地利用效率的改进，其目的是为了发展适度规模经营；而水电工程移民安置土地流转是在国家行政干预下的由集中走向分散的行为，其目的是为了保证移民的生产生活，更多强调的是公平而非效率。第四，政府参与程度不同。一般意义上的土地流转主要是流转双方在平等自愿基础上的主动流转，政府在流转过程中只具有信息公开、监督管理等功能；移民安置区的土地流转是国家为了解决水利水电工程产生的非自愿移民而进行的行政干预下的土地流转，政府参与程度相对较高。

（二）新的土地政策及产业结构解读及分析

1. 新的土地政策解读

（1）土地流转政策：2012 年中央 1 号文件，提出按照依法自愿有偿原则，引导土地承包经营权流转，发展多种形式的适度规模经营，促进农业生产规模式创新。2013 年中央 1 文件，指出要坚持依法自愿有偿原则，引导农村土地承包经营权有序流转，鼓励和支持承包土地向专业大户、家庭农场、农民合作社流转，发展多少种形式的适度规模经营，集合农田基本建设，鼓励农民采取互利互换方式，解决承包地块细碎化问题。2014 年中央 1 号文件，强调鼓励有条件的农户流转承包土地的经营权，加快健全土地经营权流转市场，完善县乡村三级服务和管理网络，探索建立工商企业流转农业用地风险保障金机制，严禁农用地非农化。有条件的地方，可对流转给予奖补，土地流转和适度规模经营要尊重农民意愿，不能强制推动。2015年中央1号文件，强调要加快构建新型农业经营体系，坚持和完善农村基本经营制度，引导土地经营权规范有序流转，创新土地流转和规模经营方式，积极发展多种形式适度规模经营，提高农民组织化程度。

2014年11月20日，中共中央、国务院印发了《关于引导农村土地经营权有序流转发展农业适度规模经营的意见》（中办发〔2014〕61号），提出总体要求坚持农村土地集体所有，实现所有权、承包区、经营权三权分置，引导土地承包经营权有序流转，坚持家庭经营的基础性地位，积极培育新型经营主体，发展多种形式的适度规模经营，巩固和完善农村基本经营制度。

（2）三权分置政策：2016年10月30日，中共中央办公厅、国务院办公厅印发了《关于完善农村土地所有权承包权经营权分置办法的意见》。总的来说，三权分置政策一是明确严格保护承包权，强调维护好承包农户使用、流转承包地的各项权益，任何组织和个人都不能取代农民家庭的土地承包地位，任何组织和个人都不得强迫或者限制其流转土地；二是要求加快放活土地经营权，赋予新的经营主体在流转土地上享有占有、耕作并取得相应收益的权利，稳定经营预期，使其放心投入、培肥地力、完善农业基础设施，这样才能推动现代农业的发展。

（3）国务院679号令：2017年4月14日，国务院公布了《关于修改〈大中型水利水电工程建设征地补偿和移民安置条例〉的决定》（国务院令第679号），提出大中型水利水电工程建设征收土地的土地补偿费和安置补助费，实行与铁路等基础设施项目用地同等补偿标准，按照被征收土地所在省、自治区、直辖市规定的标准执行。679号令明确大中型水利水电工程采用征地区片综合地价，统一了征地补偿标准，维护了被征地农民的合法权益，减少了由土地补偿问题产生的种种纠纷，促进了社会和谐发展。

2. 新的产业结构分析

（1）三大产业结构变化分析：第一产业在GDP中的比重呈现持续下降的态势，同时内部结构逐步得到改善；第二产业的比重经历了不断波动的过程，但长期稳定保持在40%～55%之间，工业内部结构得到升级，制造业增加值稳步提高；第三产业在国民经济中的比重处于不断上升的过程之中，增加值比重由2000年的33%大幅上升至2015年的50.2%。

（2）家庭经济情况及受教育程度变化分析：随着我国第二、三产业以及城镇化的快速发展，农村中劳动力越来越容易在城镇中找到一份满意的工作，农村中劳动力外出打工的比重也在不断增加。其次，由社会经济的发展带来了农村家庭成员文化程度的提高，其外出打工获取劳动机会的几率也在增高。由于具有稳定的非农收入，土地已不再是生活的主要保障，农民对土地的依赖也越来越小。

（三）新形势下生产安置方式的转变

1. 托巴水电站移民生产安置方式　该电站规划设计基准年生产安置人口为8837人，推算至规划设计水平年，生产安置人口为9746人。

（1）调地安置环境容量分析：电站建设征收耕地的各集体经济组织人均耕地面积约为1.7亩，其中水田占23%，旱地占50%，陡坡地占27%；电站建设征地征收了涉及组耕地水田面积占总面积66%，旱地征收27%，陡坡地征收41%。在环境容量分析时配置耕地的主要考虑采用调整耕地的方式，且仅考虑在本组内调整耕地，确定分析安置标准为耕地面积0.8亩/人。经分析，至规划水平年涉及生产安置人口为9842人，有8659人无法在本组以土地资源进行安置，需考虑其他方式安置或远迁安置。

（2）移民生产安置意愿调查结果分析：大多数移民多表示不接受从其他组调整土地安置，因此在移民安置意愿调查过程中基本上选择了“长效补偿”的生产安置方式。

（3）背景政策分析：2007年，云南省人民政府办公厅印发了云政办发〔2007〕159号文，明确金沙江中游水电开发移民安置采用长效补偿政策。此后，澜沧江流域的黄登水电站、里底水电站等电站参照该文件有关规定，执行了逐年补偿的政策。2015年3月，云南省人民政府印发了云政发〔2015〕12号文，规范了云南省移民安置逐年补偿安置方式；2015年7月，云南省移民开发局印发了云移发〔2015〕100号文，进一步完善了全省大中型水电工程建设移民逐年补偿安置方式政策，明确了逐年补偿标准的计算方法和调整机制。

因此，托巴水电站工程建设移民采取以“长效补偿”为基础的安置方式进行安置，生产安置方式确定为以“长效补偿”为主的生产安置方案。

2. 五岳抽水蓄能电站移民生产安置方式　该电站位于河南省，是河南电网500kV骨干网架和鄂豫联络线的东通道关口，上水库正常蓄水位347.50m，下水库正常蓄水位89.184m，电站装机容量1000MW。电站建设征地涉及搬迁移民207人，土地3889.93亩。规划设计基准年为2016年，规划设计水平年为2019年。至规划设计水平年，搬迁安置人口为211人，生产安置人口383人。

(1) 安置区居民调整土地意愿分析：该电站建设征地共涉及12个村，81个村民小组。其中，涉及永久征收耕园地的有15个村民小组。建设征地永久征收耕地面积242.61亩，其中水田194.21亩，旱地48.4亩，征收园地面积69.37亩。耕园地征收面积占该15个村民组总耕园地面积的14.47%；征收的耕园地大多位于地形较平缓的地带，是当地居民从事农业生产的主要用地。经分析建设征地对涉及区域及移民的社会经济和农业生产整体影响较小，但是对个别组的影响较大。根据走访调查，大多数村民小组不愿意将本村组耕地调整给外组移民，这主要是因为随着国家对稳定家庭承包权经营权的重视，农民对自己土地私有意识和产权意识也在逐渐加强。

(2) 水电移民调整土地意愿分析：约32%的移民选择传统的调整土地安置，希望搬迁后获得适当数量的耕地；约68%的移民选择复合安置和其他安置方式（自谋职业和自谋出路安置）。当地政府及移民主管部门也主张尊重移民个人意愿，减少因调整土地不当引起的矛盾。

因此，五岳抽水蓄能电站工程建设采取复合安置和其他安置方式为主、调整土地安置为辅的生产安置方案：至规划设计水平年383人生产安置人口中，调整土地安置124人，复合安置172人，自谋职业、自谋出路安置87人。该规划方案与移民生产安置意愿高度吻合，也得到了当地人民政府及移民主管部门的认可，为以后的顺利实施打下良好基础。

(中国电建集团中南勘测设计研究院有限公司　王天一　王頔)

“同地同价同税”对水电移民征地补偿的影响分析

中国电建集团中南勘测设计研究院有限公司针对“同地同价同税”对水电移民征地补偿的影响进行了研究，现简介如下。

(一) 案例分析测算

托口水电站正常蓄水位方案建设征地涉及湖南省、贵州省4个县(市)10个乡(镇)，征收土地总面积79020亩，临时征用土地面积1523亩。现以该电站为例，测算实行16倍补偿、“同地同价”和“同地同价”且税费优惠情况下的移民投资，并根据不同的测算方案进行组合，提出水电工程实行“同地同价同税”给征地补偿带来的影响，并提出解决问题的对策和建议，为移民条例的修订提供参考。

测算结果见表1。

表1　托口水电站建设征地投资分析测算成果表

方案名称	方案组合内容	征地补偿补助费（万元）	耕地占用税（万元）	移民投资（亿元）
方案一	同地不同价不同税方案，即现行移民概算方案：征地补偿（16倍）＋耕地占用税（5～50元/m^2）	87487.82	65510.42	52.99
方案二	同地同价不同税方案1：征地补偿（区片地价）＋耕地占用税（5～50元/m^2）	95214.77	65510.42	53.76
方案三	同地同价不同税方案2：征地补偿（区片地价就高不就低）＋耕地占用税（5～50元/m^2）	97880.49	65510.42	54.07
方案四	同地同价同税方案：征地补偿（区片地价就高不就低）＋耕地占用税（2元/m^2）	97880.49	5951.46	48.11

从表1可以看出，在相同的税费标准条件下，按照同地同价（区片地价就高不就低）计算出的征地补偿费用最高，相比按照移民条例16倍计算出的征地补偿费用提高了11.9%，移民总投资也最高。在同地同价（区片地价就高不就低）政策下，按照公路、铁路工程耕地占用税收费标准，即2元/m^2的税费减免政策，移民总投资减少了5.96亿元，减小幅度为11.02%。

若水电项目移民征地能做到同地同价，则移民获得的土地补偿费用将大幅度提高，同时若能同公路、铁路项目一样享受国家税收减免的优惠政策，那么项目业主在这部分减少的资金完全可以抵消因同地同价政策执行带来的征地补偿款的增加，从而减少项目业主投资风险。当然，这仅仅是资金方面的静态计算，应该客观地看到，若实行同地同价同税可能会带来正反两方面的影响。

(二) 实行“同地同价同税”政策的正面影响

1. 有利于移民获得更多收益，促进生计恢复长期以来在水电工程建设中，一次性征用的土地较多，对移民的影响非常大，但是征地的补偿标准往往显著低于经济发展水平，也显著低于国内其他一般建设项目，严重损害了本行业移民的利益。若实行同地同价同税政策，移民的收益有了显著提高，能够更好地利用补偿款进行生计恢复。合理充分的货币补偿能确保被征地农民生活不下降，并且能随着当地社会经济的发展自主选择继续从事农业生产或是转向二、三产业安置。

2. 保护移民根本利益，有利于促进水电事业的发展　近年来，我国水电事业发展如火如荼，但“重工程、轻移民、重搬迁、轻安置”的做法时有发生，移民安置工作的不到位俨然已经成为外界为本行业贴上的一张“标签”，成为遏制水电发展的瓶颈。若水电工程移民能够真正做到“搬得出、稳得住、能致富”，解决好移民安置工作，将更加有利于促进水电事业的发展。

3. 减轻政府工作压力，有利于构建和谐社会　在全国的征地补偿执行同地同价政策的大背景下，水电项目坚持“16倍”的补偿标准已经在移民中形成了较强的抵触情绪，移民普遍觉得这是不公平待遇，自身利益受到了侵犯，征地工作在实施过程中常遇到移民阻挠，工作难度较大，群体事件时有发生，给社会发展带来了很多不稳定因素。从对托口水电站工程补偿标准的资金分析来看，实行同地同价同税后补偿标准明显提高，无疑使移民在获得公平补偿且获得更多利益后，能够减少因不公平待遇引起的群体性事件，更有利于减轻政府工作压力，构建和谐社会。

（三）实行“同地同价同税”政策的负面影响

1. 同地同价同税可能带来同库不同策　由于区片综合地价是以省为单位进行发布的，各省各地方公布的价格标准差异较大，很多大型的水电工程会跨市或跨省建设，若实行同地同价政策，则需要分别按照省级公布的征地标准执行，会带来同一工程不同标准，即同库不同策问题，带来移民的攀比心理，为项目带来风险。

可解决此问题的办法是在相邻的边界地区采取的标准为就高不就低，在不搭界的地区依然严格按照地方制定的综合区片价进行补偿，保证当地政策的执行，避免带来其他移民的不满。

2. 后扶政策与同地同价同税政策共同实行可能会引起其他项目移民的攀比　水电工程属于国家重点扶持的项目，是为了“公共利益的需要”，按照“前期补偿补助、后期扶持”的政策要求，符合条件的受影响移民将有资格享受国家专门的后期扶持政策，可选择现金直补，也可采取项目扶持，还可以实行两者相结合。若实行同地同价同税后，本行业内移民在征地补偿标准提高的同时又能享受后扶政策，可能会引起其他项目移民的攀比心理，引发其他项目移民的不满情绪。

我国水电工程建设周期长、淹没损失大、占地范围广，很多大型项目涉及移民所有的生产资料甚至社会网络均被破坏，给他们的生活带来了极大的影响，不仅仅影响当代的人口，甚至对子孙后代也产生了深远的影响，同时，公路、铁路工程多采用的是社会保障安置方式，而水电工程建设征地移民安置方式首先为解决移民生活保障为前提，因此，国家需要对水电工程移民有政策上的长期帮扶，保证他们的长远生计。

（四）结语

水电工程建设是关系到国计民生的大事，对水电项目征地补偿标准的改革也是在长期实践基础上提出的，从目前的形势来看，实行同地同价同税政策已是发展的必然趋势，是保证移民利益，维护社会和谐稳定，促进水利水电事业发展的必要条件。但是水电工程建设的情况较铁路、公路建设要复杂得多，不仅行业之间、地区之间存在差异，被征地人群的受教育程度和综合素质也存在着很大的差异，如果都用同一个标准去对待不同的人群，其得到的结果也会是各不相同。因此，在经济发展不平衡的现阶段，在水电工程中实行同地同价同税政策的过程中，仍然需要坚持“前期补偿、补助与后期扶持相结合的办法”，并积极探索多种安置方式相结合的安置途径，既要保证移民的当前利益，又要确保移民的长远生计。

（中国电建集团中南勘测设计研究院
有限公司　陈翠云）

城乡一体化下水库移民政策创新研究

“城乡一体化下水库移民政策创新研究”为教育部人文社科研究项目，由河海大学承担，于2018年9月完成。

该项目针对水库移民出现的问题以及问题演变、深化过程，分析了我国水库移民政策演变特征、动力以及现行政策的缺陷，旨在揭示解决水库移民问题的政策。

选取贵州、河南、江苏三省水利水电工程为例，通过调查和总结水库移民实践，进一步揭示：水库移民政策的属性；从政策实施的底层角度，如何看待实践中出现的问题；揭示了影响水库移民长期稳定安置的因素。城乡一体化发展过程中，从考察土地制度和公共资源配置制度的变革、农村生产方式变革、城乡相互促进、农村社会变革的角度，分析对水库移民活动的影响，阐述新形势下水库移民活动的特征、性质、要素流动等变化，水库移民活动利益主体、利益关系和利益诉求的变化；从水库移民活动内部客观要求，提出水库移民政策改革的因素和方向，重新调整政策目标、原则、方针。政府部门采纳成果1部，国有企业单位采纳成果1部。

（河海大学）

南方电网调峰调频发电有限公司 2018年水库移民情况

（一）梅州抽水蓄能电站项目

1. 电站建设征地　电站永久征地6743.63亩（不含进场公路），临时用地623.74亩，截至2018年12月31日全部完成土地丈量、分解到户，累计已办理征地补偿手续4436.98亩，完成应办理补偿手续面积总量（6923.56亩）的64.1%，工程用地满足现场施工需要。上水库区域茶园、果园等农作物土地完成清表。

2. 移民安置区建设　截至2018年12月31日，三坑安置区安置房总户数420户，其中320户移民房完成内外部装修，可交付使用，100户正在进行室内外装修。断掌凹安置区房屋及公共设施已进入架施工，127套安置房中，46户完成二层框架，27户完成一层框架，37户处于首层框架施工，17户处于基础处理。断掌凹对外连接道路已全部完工，两个安置区供水、供电、通信工程正在抓紧推进。

3. 移民安置实施方案　2018年7月19日，五华县人民政府办公室正式印发《广东梅州抽水蓄能电站建设征地补偿和移民安置实施方案（修订稿）》（华府办函〔2018〕128号），移民资格认定及分户12月底完成两榜公示，为下一步移民实施搬迁奠定坚实基础。

4. 临时搬迁情况　下库进出水口、下水库大坝施工影响区需提前临时搬迁的124户74座房屋已拆除70座，确保了下库坝和下库进出水口工程顺利施工。同时，上库区总共需拆除房屋29座，已拆除26座。

（二）阳江抽水蓄能电站项目

1. 电站建设征地　电站永久征地6308.78亩（不含进场公路），截至2018年12月31日，4179.63亩林地完成丈量补偿并提交工程施工，1300亩耕地完成丈量统计。由于地方政府和村民就补偿相关事宜存在分歧，导致砂石加工系统、下库坝导流洞等部分标段施工受阻，目前地方政府已成立工作组进村入户进行政策宣传和移民安置补偿方案的解读及其他相关协调工作。

2. 移民安置区建设　镇南堡移民安置区（设计安置232户）已完成房屋基础工程、区内道路及附属设施建设并于2018年12月3日完成验收移交。2018年12月11日完成安置区首层房屋工程施工招标并签订施工合同，12月28日首层房屋施工单位进场施工。

3. 移民安置实施方案　2018年11月28日，阳春市蓄能办制定《关于解决受阳江抽水蓄能电站项目“封库令”影响村民生产生活补助、生产安置、房屋征收补偿及安置房建设方案（征求意见稿）》，12月10日涉及的5个村民小组联合反馈了意见。村民提交的反馈意见与地方政府的补偿方案分歧较大。12月23日，地方政府组织召开村民代表座谈会，就补偿方案进行宣贯，就村民提出的诉求进行答复。

4. 报批报建工作　2018年11月5日，公司就阳蓄项目水田指标预购费缴纳标准和省政府、省国土厅达成一致意见并完成费用缴纳，同时与阳江市国土局签订水田指标预购协议。12月11日，国土报批材料报送至国家自然资源部，目前正在根据国家自然资源部要求补充完善相关资料。

（南方电网调峰调频发电有限公司　曹娅）

水电水利规划设计总院组织开展水库移民专业学术交流情况

2018年，水电水利规划设计总院积极牵头开展多次水库移民专业的技术交流。

1月10～13日，中国水力发电工程学会水库专业委员会、水电水利规划设计总院、水利部水利水电规划设计总院联合在广州成功举办了“2018年水库移民政策、技术、管理论坛暨水利水电工程征地移民规划设计技术交流会”。会议由中水珠江规划勘测设计有限公司、广东省水利电力勘测设计研究院具体承办。副主任委员单位和委员单位共81家240余人参加了论坛。水库移民政策技术管理论坛作为一年一度的全国水利水电工程移民行业的业界盛会，该次论坛的主题是“土地改革惠民，开发利益共享”。开幕式环节由水库专业委员会副主任委员、水利部水利水电规划设计总院书记陈伟主持会议，广东省水库移民工作局王胜端副局长、中水珠江规划勘测设计有限公司蒋翼总经理和广东省水利电力勘测设计研究院王伟理事长（书记）分别致辞。经会务对上交的100多篇论文进行筛选后推荐22篇论文上会交流，并推选10篇作为优秀论文。这些论文主要围绕“三权分置”“利益共享”在移民工作中的影响和应用为中心议题。会议邀请中国土地勘测规划院总工办副主任、研究员卢艳霞博士做了“土地政策、产权制度改革”的专题讲座，分享了当前的有关土地政策。会议分两个小组交流，各组人员各抒己见，讨论现场非常热烈。随后水利总院陈伟书记和水电总院龚和平副院长向获得优秀论文的作者颁奖，并分别进行了总结讲话。

7月12～13日，“推动移民竣工验收，促进移民后续发展”研讨会暨中国水力发电工程学会水库专业委员会2018年年会在西宁市成功召开。会议由中国水力发电工程学会水库专业委员会、青海省移民安置局、中国水利水电工程勘测设计协会、中国电力规划设计学会征地移民专业委员会共同主办，中国电建集团西北勘测设计研究院有限公司协办。共有65家单位应邀参加会议，其中包括青海省国土资源厅、云南省移民开发局等34家政府部门，中国长江三峡集团有限公司、中国华电集团有限公司等11家项目业主单位，长江勘测规划设计研究有限责任公司、中国电建集团成都勘测设计研究院有限公司等15家规划设计单位，华北电力大学、同济大学等5家高等院校，参会领导、专家和代表共计170余人。会议研讨的主题是“推动移民竣工验收，促进移民后续发展”，以习近平新时代中国特色社会主义思想为指导，牢固树立以人民为中心的发展思想，保障移民安居乐业、社会安定有序，重点围绕水利水电工程移民竣工验收管理、移民后续发展途径和措施进行研讨。会议受到了各有关方面的高度重视和大力支持。该次会议共计收集到论文45篇，已编撰成册，其中收录移民竣工验收方面的论文14篇，移民后续发展方面的论文11篇，其他方面的论文20篇。会议共安排交流论文18篇，论文观点新颖、论证充分、紧扣实践，指导性强，能够引起与会专家和代表的共鸣，取得了较好的效果。会议要求在今后的工作中深入贯彻习近平新时代社会主义思想，贯彻五大发展理念，坚持不懈地做好水库移民工作。

8月14～19日，苏丹共和国水电部社会事务司司长 Abdel rahman Abdalla Mohamed、水电部社会事务司农业部项目经理 Sulieman Hajar Yagoub 及中国水利电力对外公司苏丹分公司经理王洪强先生等一行3人，来水电总院进行工作访问并赴河南、青海等地进行考察。双方围绕水电水利工程征地及社会评价工作等内容进行了友好交谈。顾洪宾代表水电总院对苏丹代表团一行来访表示欢迎，并介绍了水电总院的总体情况。苏丹水电部社会事务司 Mohamed 司长回顾了2017年中方代表团到苏丹期间考察情况，对我国征地及社会评价工作方面的先进经验表达了充分肯定。随后双方就征地移民及社会评价工作方面关注的问题进行了友好座谈，表示今后要进一步加强技术交流和合作。水电总院国际业务部、中国电建北京、华东、西北、中南等设计院相关专业负责人参加座谈。8月15～19日，在水电总院的安排下，苏丹代表团一行先后考察调研了南水北调新郑部分集中安置点及穿越黄河倒虹吸工程，黄河上游龙羊峡、积石峡水电工程移民安置情况，并与河南省政府移民办公室、青海省移民安置局等政府官员进行了友好交谈。

2018年11月7～9日，中国电力规划设计协会征地移民专家委员会在浙江杭州组织召开了2018年委员会工作会议。来自中国电力规划设计协会、水电水利规划设计总院、中国电建集团华东、北京、中南、昆明、成都、贵阳、西北以及中国能源建设集团广西电力设计研究院有限公司的23位代表参加了会议。中国电力规划设计协会副理事长兼秘书长李爱民到会指导，并就中国电力规划设计协会的组建、职能、工作目的等作了介绍。中国电建集团华东勘测设计研究院有限公司总工程师吴关叶出席了会议并致辞。郭万侦主任委员作了征地移民专委会2018年工作总结，对2019年工作提出了设想。会议明确了征地移民专委会的发展、行业评奖、团体技术标准、征地移民勘测设计费等，对征地移民专委会的职能和发展方向以及2019年度工作计划作了深入探讨。会议对提交的技术论文进行了交流，与会代表一致认为应充分发挥好协会的平台作用，助推征地移民专业发展。

（水电水利规划设计总院　文良友）

董箐水电站顺利完成建设征地移民安置竣工验收有关情况

董箐水电站坝址位于贵州省安顺市镇宁县良田乡和黔西南州贞丰县白层镇境内的北盘江干流上，水库正常蓄水位为490m，总库容9.55亿m^3，电站装机容量为88万kW。国家发展改革委核准工程总投资69.63亿元，其中，建设征地移民安置补偿投资11.96亿元。该电站项目于2006年11月截流，2009年2月获得核准，2010年6月4台机组全部投产发电，2010年6月工程基本完工。2005年施工准备期启动移民搬迁工作，2009年7月移民基本完成搬迁。

（一）主要过程

董箐水电站建设征地移民安置工作由安顺市人民政府、黔西南布依族苗族自治州人民政府监督管理，镇宁县、关岭县、贞丰县人民政府组织实施，项目业主贵州北盘江电力股份有限公司参与；移民安置规划设计单位、移民综合监理单位、移民独立评估单位皆为中国电建集团贵阳勘测设计研究院有限公司（简称贵阳院）。

移民安置实施阶段，由于移民意愿变化、集镇和集中居民点建设条件变化等原因，董箐水电站建设征地处理范围、实物指标、移民安置方式、规划方案、补偿补助标准及补偿费用较可行性研究阶段成果均发生了较大的调整。2017年7月5日，贵州省水库和生态移民局、贵州北盘江电力股份有限公司（简称北盘江公司）以《关于委托开展贵州北盘江董箐水电站建设征地移民安置竣工验收相关工作的函》（黔移函〔2017〕72号），委托水电水利规划设计总院（简称水电总院）开展贵州北盘江董箐水电站建设征地移民安置竣工验收技术服务和技术验收工作。接受此任务后，水电总院高度重视，组织成立了验收专家组，启动了验收工作。

2007年8月，贵州省人民政府以《贵州省人民政府关于北盘江董箐水电站建设征地移民安置规划大纲的批复》（黔府函〔2007〕149号）批复了《北盘江董箐水电站建设征地移民安置规划大纲》；同月原贵州省移民办审核通过了《北盘江董箐水电站建设征地移民安置规划报告》。

2017年7月16～18日，水电总院会同有关单位对董箐水电站移民安置实施情况进行了初步现场查验，形成了《董箐水电站移民安置竣工验收专家组现场查验情况报告》，提出了开展移民安置规划调整及资金审计等工作要求，并拟定了初步的工作计划安排。随后，贵阳院开展了移民安置规划调整报告的编制工作。

2017年8月27～28日、2017年10月25～26日，水电总院先后两次会同贵州省水库和生态移民局主持召开了《北盘江董箐水电站建设征地移民安置规划调整报告》的审查会议，对规划调整报告的编制思路、编制方法、移民安置方案及规划设计、单项工程设计、补偿费用概算等提出了具体的修改意见。设计单位按照修改意见对规划调整报告进行了完善，于2018年5月编制提交了修改成果。

2018年7月6日，水电总院会同贵州省水库和生态移民局组织项目业主、设计单位再次对规划调整报告中移民安置补偿费用概算相关问题进行沟通、协调。其后，设计单位对移民安置补偿费用概算进行了调整，提交了规划调整报告最终成果。2018年7月，贵州省水库和生态移民局以《省水库和生态移民局关于〈北盘江董箐水电站建设征地移民安置规划调整报告〉的审核意见》（黔移函〔2018〕76号）审核通过了规划调整报告，为北盘江董箐水电站建设征地移民安置竣工验收提供了依据。

为进一步落实董箐水电站建设征地移民安置竣工验收各方责任，明确时间安排及相关事宜，2018年10月26日，水电总院会同贵州省水库和生态移民局在贵阳主持召开了北盘江董箐水电站建设征地移民安置竣工验收准备会议，会议听取了北盘江公司关于董箐水电站移民安置工作的介绍，镇宁县、关岭县、贞丰县关于董箐水电站建设征地移民安置实施工作的报告，综合设计、综合监理、独立评估单位的工作报告，以及审计单位对资金审计情况的汇报。会议就建设征地移民安置实施情况及存在的问题进行了讨论，对移民安置竣工验收工作进行了总体部署，对下步工作计划进行了统一安排。

2018年11月下旬，镇宁县、关岭县、贞丰县完成了县级自验工作。2018年12月初，安顺市、黔西南州完成了市级自验工作。2018年12月10日，安顺市水库和生态移民局、黔西南州水库和生态移民局分别以安移呈〔2018〕27号、州移呈〔2018〕31号向贵州省移民局报送了开展董箐水电站建设征地移民安置竣工验收的请示。

2018年12月13日，贵州省生态移民局（原贵州省水库和生态移民局）以黔移呈〔2018〕3号文件呈报贵州省人民政府。贵州省人民政府批示同意贵州省移民局开展董箐水电站竣工阶段移民专项验收工作安排。

2018年12月21日，贵州省生态移民局（原贵州省水库和生态移民局）在贵阳主持召开北盘江董箐水电站竣工阶段建设征地移民安置专项省级验收会议，验收委员会同意通过北盘江董箐水电站竣工阶段建设征地移民安置专项验收。

（二）方式及内容

通过现场查验、资料分析、座谈讨论等方式，对农村移民生产安置、移民搬迁安置、集镇迁建、临时用地复垦、专业项目复（改）建、移民档案管理、移民资金使用和审计、移民实施机构设置及运作、移民工作管理、移民政策管理、移民后期扶持、土地手续办理等情况进行查验。经过查验，董箐水电站移民安置基本满足竣工验收条件。

（三）几点经验

（1）打好“感情牌”。一是和各级政府部门建立长期、良好、可靠的协作关系，通过沟通交流，对各项创新工作能及时达成共识（如长补、返包等如何实施、如何配合），投产后一致认同移民安置竣工验收是维护移民合法权益的需要，并最终实现了政企合作共赢的目标。二是加强与设计监理等单位沟通合作，使业主意见能通过设计监理得以实现。

（2）争取“政策牌”。一是“耕地长期补偿”政策。2009年国家审定的董箐移民安置方式是“一次性补偿”，核准后贵州省人民政府要求实施“耕地长期补偿”，尽管实施结果仅少部分自愿选择“耕地长期补偿”，但减少了搬迁人口、结余了安置资金。结余资金由地方政府用于后续发展项目。二是库区专项“返包代建”政策。在2007年开展可行性研究时即争取将库区交通及集镇场平返包业主实施，加快了进度、保证了质量、节省了投资，将代建结余资金交还地方政府。

(3) 落实“实施牌”。一是对内使劲，在当前地方政府主要精力投入脱贫攻坚的情况下，业主深度参与，和设计监理人员一起，帮助地方移民部门开展项目和资金清理、移民档案整理、有关报告编制等工作。二是对外借力，及时确定技术服务和验收专家单位、资金审计单位，借助这些单位的技术力量和节点要求，有效推动了验收工作进展。

（水电水利规划设计总院　吴立恒
贵州黔源电力股份有限公司　张琼）

行业标准《水电工程建设征地实物指标分类编码规范》制定有关情况

根据国家能源局《关于下达2015年能源领域行业标准制（修）订计划的通知》（国能科技〔2015〕283号）的要求，由中国长江三峡集团有限公司、水电水利规划设计总院等单位承担《水电工程建设征地实物指标分类编码规范》（简称《规范》）的制定工作，标准计划编号为“能源20150578”，标准主管机构为水电水利规划设计总院，技术归口单位为能源行业水电规划水库环保标准化技术委员会。

2015年9月，由中国长江三峡集团有限公司、水电水利规划设计总院等单位成立规范编制组，规范编制工作正式启动。2015年11月，形成《规范》编制工作大纲；2016年6月，编制组形成《规范》（初稿）。在此基础上，规范编制组经过广泛调研，多次组织研讨，于2016年12月提出了《规范》（征求意见稿），2017年1月发函向水利部水利水电规划设计总院等22家单位征求意见。2017年4月，收到有关单位反馈的修改意见和建议，共25条。

2017年4月17日，根据反馈的修改意见和建议，编制组在成都组织召开会议，进行了认真审议，采纳17条，部分采纳7条，未采纳1条，对《规范》（征求意见稿）进行修改、补充和完善，2017年6月形成《规范》（送审稿），并报送水电水利规划设计总院申请审查。

2018年4月16日和12月26日，水电水利规划设计总院分别在北京和成都组织召开了《规范》送审稿审查会以及报批稿审定会。会议听取了编制组对本规范编制情况和主要内容的汇报，与会专家对本规范逐章逐条进行了认真审查。审查认为，编制组提交审查的技术文件齐全，编制依据充分，格式规范，逻辑严谨，结构清晰，用词准确，规定明确，与国内相关标准相协调，具有可操作性，同意通过审查，提交国家发展改革委审批发布。

《规范》目的主要是为满足水电工程建设征地移民实物指标数据采集、存储、交换、共享和利用工作要求，规范水电工程建设征地移民实物指标分类编码工作，提高移民实物指标信息化管理水平。《规范》适用于大中型水电工程规划及设计、建造调试及验收、运行维护等阶段建设征地移民实物指标成果管理以及相关信息系统开发、应用。

《规范》主要对实物指标代码的定义及所包含的内容进行了说明，规定了应分类、分级进行赋码；强调了编码的唯一性、适用性、规范性和简明性等原则；对实物指标代码结构、权属人代码结构、指标分类代码结构、顺序代码分别进行了说明，并附上了代码结构示意图。

《规范》明确了赋码规则，详细说明了权属人关键特征码；规定了16个指标大类赋码规则，并罗列了各类指标核心属性分类码表和具体的分类代码表供参考。

（中国长江三峡集团有限公司　嵇培欢）

行业标准《水电工程建设征地实物指标调查规范》修订有关情况

为贯彻落实国务院于2006年7月以第471号令发布《大中型水利水电工程建设征地补偿和移民安置条例》的相关要求，适应水电工程项目核准和水电工程建设需要，2007年国家发展改革委发布了《水电工程建设征地实物指标调查规范》（DL/T 5378—2007）（简称《实物调查规范》）等8项规范，并于2007年12月1日起实施。2007系列移民规范的发布实施，进一步系统地规范了水电工程建设征地移民安置规划设计工作，对提高水电工程规划设计质量，促进移民安置工作顺利实施和水电开发健康发展起到了重要的作用。

实物指标调查是移民安置规划设计的基础性工作，因其项目多、涉及面广、程序复杂、政策性强，是涉及相关方切身利益的一项工作，关注度高。通过十几年的水电建设和移民安置工作实践，以及近年来国家法制化建设进程的深入，对移民法规及水电工程标准体系提出了新的要求，需在总结十几年水电建设和移民工作实践经验基础上，针对实践中出现的新问题、新需求和推广应用新技术、新方法，衔接行业技术标准编制新的要求，对规范进一步完善和修订。2015年7月，国家能源局印发了《关于下达2015年能源领域行业标准制（修）订计划的通知》（国能科技〔2015〕283号），将《实物调查规范》列入修订范围，主编单位为水电水利规划设计总院和中国电建集团昆明勘测设计研究院有限公司，参编单位为中国电建集团中南勘测设计研究院有限公司、中国电建集团贵阳勘测设计研究院有限公司、国电大渡河流域水电开发有限公司。据此，成立编制组，开展编制工作。

实物指标调查是移民安置规划的基础性工作，涉及移民的切身利益，是移民关注的焦点之一，如何规范、准确地准确查清实物指标意义重大。2007年国家发展改革委发布了《实物调查规范》，并于2007年12月1日起实施。《实物调查规范》的发布实施，很好地规范了水电工程建设征地实物指标调查工作，为移民安置规划设计提供了良好的基础，有效保障移民合法权益，促进移民安置工作顺利实施和移民社会的稳定。

近年来，人口、房屋及附属设施、零星树木、民风民俗及宗教实施、土地、专业设施、企事业单位等的分类、调查要求等随着各行业规定的修订有了一些新的变化；同时随着我国水电开发向纵深发展，逐步向三江上游推进，涉及移民的民族、生产生活习俗、实物指标项目和种类发生了一些的变化，移民安置规划深度的不断深化也对实物指标调查提出了新的要求，另外为满足移民管理工作数字化、信息化的需要，对实物调查的工具、方法和精度也提出了新的要求，现行《实物调查规范》已不能完全适应和满足发展及变革的要求，迫切需要进行修订和完善，满足实物指标调查的需要，促进新技术、新方法的推广、应用，提高工作质量和效率，准确查清实物指标为目的。

随着近十年来水电开发高峰期的建设实践，对移民安置规划设计提出了新要求，为了给水电开发决策提供支持，不仅要求缩短设计周期，而且要求更深入、细致、准确地设计成果，以提高决策的效率，避免投资风险。实物指标调查是移民安置规划设计的基础性工作，因其项目多、涉及面广、程序复杂，用传统的调查方法，整个调查工作在水电工程前期工作流程中往往占用较多的时间。在实物调查实践中，人口调查属性随户籍制度改革发生较大变化，房屋的结构、功能混合性强，区位价值突出，土地、企业、公路等分类需与新的行业标准相衔接。

因此，结合目前水电工程开发建设及移民安置规划设计的特点，从全面反映实物指标内容，完善其调查方法，充分与相关行业的法规和技术标准进行衔接，推广新技术的运用，为移民信息管理提供便利，对原有的实物指标调查规范进行修订和完善非常必要。

为较好地完成好修编工作，编制组于2015年11月编制了《水电工程建设征地实物指标调查规范修订大纲》，并由水电水利规划设计总院在昆明组织召开了修订大纲评审会议。随后，编制组根据评审后的修订大纲开展《水电工程建设征地实物指标调查规范》的修订工作，经过2016～2018年长达3年的修编、多次的讨论和审查，以及征求相关单位的意见，国家能源局于2018年12月25日以2018年第16号公告批准了该项行业标准。

《水电工程建设征地实物指标调查规范》的主要技术内容包括基本规定、农村调查、城市集镇调查、专业项目调查、企事业单位调查、经济社会调查、阶段工作要求及成果。本规范修订的主要技术内容有：①增加了“企事业单位调查”一章；②增加了“经济社会调查”一章；③增加了“阶段工作要求及成果”一章；④删除了实物指标调查的组织和程序相关内容；⑤补充完善了搬迁人口、土地调查相关内容；⑥补充完善了英雄烈士纪念设施调查的相关内容。

（中国电建集团昆明勘测设计研究院有限公司　唐良霁）

《云南省大中型水利水电工程移民安置方式实践与创新研究》通过验收

云南省作为水利水电工程移民大省之一，随着移民数量不断增多，可利用的土地资源不断减少，尤其是库区所在市（州）耕地资源十分有限，人地矛盾突出，用于安置移民的土地资源容量有限，难以仅靠以土安置方式安置移民，且库区多为少数民族聚居区，移民外迁安置难度大，移民安置成为水利水电工程建设中的关键问题之一。因此，对移民安置方式的探索和研究也一直是云南省移民安置中的热点和重点。

云南省委、省政府高度重视水利水电移民安置工作，多年来省领导一直高度关注、指导移民工作。面对云南省移民安置难题，2006年，云南省人民政府指出，在不断总结现行移民安置经验教训的基础上，探索创新移民补偿方式、安置方式和后期扶持方式，进一步调动地方政府和广大移民群众支持水电工程建设的积极性，是新时期移民安置亟待解决的重大课题。长期以来，经过不断的总结和完善，云南省建立了较为完善的水利水电工程移民工作管理体制和机制，并结合本省省情和工程实际，先后印发了《云南省人民政府办公厅关于印发向家坝水电站云南库区农业移民安置实施意见的通知》（云政办发〔2007〕157号）、《云南省人民政府办公厅关于印发云南金沙江中游水电开发移民安置补偿补助意见的通知》（云政办发〔2007〕159号）、《云南省人民政府关于进一步做好大中型水电工程移民工作的意见》（云政发〔2015〕12号）等一系列政策及管理文件，为全省大中型水利水电工程移民安置实施工作提供了政策依据，保障了移民搬迁安置工作得到顺利实施和工程顺利建设。云南省搬迁安置办公室（原云南省移民开发局）作为省人民政府的移民主管部门，主要负责全省大中型水利水电工程移民工作，多年来按照云南省委、省政府的部署和安排，组织开展了大量的调查研究工作，先后出台了包括前期管理、安置实施、移民验收、后期扶持等全过程的一系列管理规定，并针对不同流域、不同电站的特点出台了相应移民安置的措施和办法，为大中型水利水电工程移民安置顺利实施奠定了基础。

经过数十年的探索与实践，云南省广大水利水电工程移民工作者积累了大量水利水电工程移民安置方式的实践经验和成果，对移民安置方式和安置措施上进行了不断的创新，尤其是在逐年补偿安置方式方面取得了较为明显的成效。全省90余万水利水电工程移民总体得到了妥善安置，有效地促进了移民脱贫致富，库区和移民安置区社会总体稳定。为认真总结云南省水利水电工程建设中移民安置方式的实践经验和创新成果，指导今后的移民安置工作，2017年9月，云南省移民开发局通过招投标程序，委托水电水利规划设计总院开展“云南省大中型水利水电工程移民安置方式实践与创新研究”课题。根据要求，水电水利规划设计总院牵头组织了长期从事水利水电工程移民规划设计工作、熟悉云南省水利水电工程移民工作的中国电建集团昆明、华东、中南、西北勘测设计研究院有限公司等单位，组成了课题研究工作组，通过对金沙江、澜沧江流域水电移民安置典型案例分析，采取现场调研、工作座谈和集中讨论等方式，对全省水利水电工程移民安置方式的创新与实践，以及现行的国家有关政策规定进行了全面的分析研究、归纳总结，编制了《云南省大中型水利水电工程移民安置方式实践与创新研究》。2018年1月初，《云南省大中型水利水电工程移民安置方式实践与创新研究》通过云南省移民开发局组织的验收，并于2018年转为专著正式出版。

《云南省大中型水利水电工程移民安置方式实践与创新研究》着眼于云南省在大中型水利水电工程移民安置方式的实践和创新，收集分析了云南省水能资源、土地资源和水利水电工程移民安置相关资料，回顾了不同时期国家和云南省移民安置方式的政策沿革，分析研究了典型案例，阐述了以土安置方式、逐年补偿安置方式、其他安置方式的发展背景、历史演变、内涵及特点、实践情况，归纳总结了移民生产安置方式的创新点，提出了生产安置方式存在的问题，探索提出了云南省水利水电工程移民安置方式在今后可能的探索方向，对于今后水利水电工程移民安置工作有一定的参考借鉴价值。

（水电水利规划设计总院　文良友）

14

农村水电及电气化

农村水电建设

2018 年全国农村水电总体情况

2018 年，农村水电牢固树立新发展理念，积极践行中央新时期水利工作方针，以绿色小水电建设为主线，以扶持贫困地区农村水电开发为重点，以农村水电安全生产和水库水电站安全度汛为核心，大力推进农村水电增效扩容改造和农村小水电扶贫工程建设，积极开展绿色小水电创建，切实强化安全生产“双主体”责任和标准化建设，全面推进民生、平安、绿色、和谐水电建设，努力实现农村水电助力乡村振兴和改善河流生态双赢局面。农村水电全年完成投资 100.1 亿元。新增加发电设备容量 164.3 万 kW，总装机容量达到 8043.5 万 kW，年发电量 2345.6 亿 kW·h，农村水电各项工作取得明显成效。

（一）农村水电电源建设

1. 装机容量　2018 年，农村水电新增电站 194 座，投产发电设备容量 164.3 万 kW，其中新投产装机容量 116.1 万 kW，技改净增发电设备容量 48.2 万 kW。新增装机主要集中在我国西南地区。2018 年农村水电新增装机按规模划分，1 万（含）～5 万 kW（含）占新增装机总量的 58.7%；0.1 万（含）～1 万 kW 占总量的 34.2%；0.1 万 kW 以下占总量的 7.1%。截至 2018 年底，全国共有农村水电站 46515 座，农村水电装机容量达到 8043.5 万 kW，占全国水电总装机容量的 22.8%，占全国电力总装机容量的 4.2%。

2. 发电量　2018 年，全国农村水电发电量达 2345.6 亿 kW·h，较 2017 年减少 131.6 亿 kW·h，同比下降 5.3%。农村水电年平均利用小时数为 2916h，较 2017 年减少 209h，减少 6.7%。按照最新供电标准煤耗 308g/(kW·h) 计算，农村水电 2018 年全年发电量相当于节约了 7200 万 t 标准煤，减少二氧化碳排放 1.8 亿 t，减少二氧化硫排放 94 多万吨。

2018 年，全国农村水电发电量占全口径水电发电量的 19.0%，占全国总发电量的 3.3%，比 2017 年下降 0.5 个百分点。中国电力企业联合会电力工业统计快报显示，2018 年全国水电年发电量同比增长 3.2%，占全国总发电量的 17.6%。全国发电量中火电发电量同比增长 7.3 个百分点，占总发电量的 70.4%。水电设备年平均利用小时数 3613h，同比增长 16h。

3. 开发率　截至 2018 年末，农村水电装机容量占全国农村水能资源技术可开发量的 62.8%，较 2017 年增长了 0.8 个百分点；农村水电年发电量占农村水能资源技术可开发量的 43.8%。开发率较高的省份主要集中在我国东部、东南沿海和中部地区。

（二）供用电情况

截至 2018 年末，全国有农村水电的县共 1519 个，比 2017 年减少 39 个。农村水电县主要集中在我国西南大部、中部和南部地区。四川省最多，有 162 个，云南省 116 个，湖南省 96 个。

2018 年，农村水电上网电量为 2149.5 亿 kW·h，就近供电电量 38.1 亿 kW·h。全国农村水电上网平均电价为 0.294 元/(kW·h)，较 2017 年下降 0.022 元/(kW·h)；就近直接供电电价为 0.330 元/(kW·h)，较 2017 年下降 0.010 元/(kW·h)。

（三）完成投资

2018 年，全国农村水电建设完成投资 100.1 亿元，农村水电站完成投资按区域分布：东部 15.1 亿元，占 15.1%；中部 21.7 亿元，占 21.6%；西部 63.3 亿元，占 63.3%。从各省农村水电建设完成投资看，云南省完成投资 18.3 亿元，贵州省完成投资 12.8 亿元，四川省完成投资 11.7 亿元，位列全国前 3 名。陕西、湖北、广西、湖南、重庆等地都超过了 5 亿元。在完成的总投资中，财政资金为 19.4 亿元，占 19.4%。从完成投资的财政资金构成看，中央资金 15.7 亿元，占 81.1%；地方财政资金 3.7 亿元，占 18.9%。

（四）经营情况

2018 年，全国农村水电全年发售电总收入 687.2 亿元，上交税金 53.0 亿元。截至 2018 年底，农村水电站固定资产达 5094.9 亿元。

截至 2018 年底，全国农村水电独立核算单位共有 29959 个，其中国有企业占 9.7%；集体企业占 10.0%；事业单位占 7.9%；私营、国有参股和外资等其他企业占 72.4%。农村水电 2018 年末从业人数达 56.9 万人，其中，技术人员 17.7 万人。

（水利部农水水电司　曲鹏）

2018 年农村小水电扶贫工程建设情况

2016 年，水利部和国家发展改革委联合启动了农村小水电扶贫工程，重点在水能资源丰富的贫困地区，以保护生态环境为前提，以增加贫困地区建档立卡贫困户收入、增强贫困地区电力保障、促进贫困地区发展为重点建设农村水电扶贫项目，助力建档立卡贫困村、贫困户脱贫。

2016～2018 年累计安排中央预算内投资 13 亿元，在江西、湖北、湖南、广西、重庆、贵州、陕西 7 省（自治区、直辖市）建设农村水电扶贫工程，各省份按年度将资金分解至 100 个项目，其中 2016 年试点项目 27 个，2017 年建设项目 35 个，2018 年建设项目 36 个，建设扶贫装机容量 53.3 万 kW，项目总投资 49.4 亿元。2018 年中央下达 5 亿元预算内投资用于湖北、湖南、重庆、广西、贵州、陕西 6 省（直辖市）农村小水电扶贫工程建设，各省份安排建设装机容量共 20.1 万 kW，计划帮扶贫困户约 2 万户。截至 2018 年底，农村水电扶贫工程已建成项目 60 个，投产装机容量 31.8 万 kW，累计已兑现扶贫收益 7000 多万元，3 万多建档立卡贫困户受益。

农村水电扶贫工程项目建设多渠道增加了贫困农民收入，有效改善了贫困地区基础设施条件，增加了贫困群众自我发展能力，建立了脱贫解困新机制，得到了地方党委政府、项目业主、贫困村组和建档立卡贫困户的欢迎。

为规范项目建设管理，国家发展改革委和水利部于 2016 年制定《农村小水电扶贫工程试点实施方案》并于 2017 年修订形成了《农村小水电扶贫工程实施方案（修订）》，明确规定了农村水电扶贫工程项目选择条件、中央补助政策、项目计划管理、建设管理、投资管理、投资回报、扶贫对象范围、机制等。2017 年水利部出台《农村小水电扶贫建设方案（2018～2020 年）》（水规计〔2017〕293 号），计划用 3 年的时间，在湖北、湖南、重庆、贵州、陕西、广西和西藏 7 省（自治区、直辖市）开展农村小水电扶贫工程建设，新增装机容量 38 万 kW。按照“国家补助、市场运作、贫困户持续受益”的要求，各地在项目选择、建设管理、收益金管理、探索长效扶贫机制等方面总结形成了“五明确五确保”经验。

为确保农村小水电扶贫工程建设质量、进度和成效，2018 年，水利部委托第三方机构对已实施的农村小水电扶贫工程建设项目开展了检查评价，根据评价结论，督促各地加强整改，目前，工程整体进展顺利。

（水利部农水水电司　赵虹）

2018 年绿色小水电站创建情况

2018 年，共创建绿色小水电站 121 座，全国累计创建绿色小水电站 165 座。2018 年，水利部继续组织开展绿色小水电站创建工作，重点结合农村水电增效扩容改造和河流生态修复实施创建。组织开发了绿色水电管理信息系统，完善了电站可视化申报要求，提高了申报质量和初验、审核效率。根据水利部新“三定”规定，调整组建了由总工程师任主任委员，部有关司局负责同志任委员的水利部绿色小水电站评定委员会，进一步完善评定委员会评定办法，增加了评定委员会办公室复核抽查程序。建立了涉及水文水资源、水生态、水利水电工程等专业的绿色小水电建设技术评估专家组，为创建工作提供了组织保障和技术支撑。

各地积极开展创建，完成了业主申报、省级初验和公示等创建程序。评定委员会办公室组织技术支撑单位严格按照《绿色小水电评价标准》，对所有通过省级初验的电站逐一进行材料复核和必要的现场检查，并组织对部分电站进行评定委员会办公室复核抽查。2018 年 12 月 28 日，评定委员会会议审议同意河北省石家庄市土贤庄水电站等 121 座水电站为 2018 年度绿色小水电站。

2017 年以来，全国已有 19 个省份创建了 165 座绿色小水电站，在生态改善、惠及民生和标准化建设等方面发挥了典型示范作用。浙江成功创建了 38 座绿色小水电站，居全国之首，目前正在创新举措，创建流域型“绿色小水电”。山西省对 7 座绿色小水电站给予每座 50 万元的奖励，给予 32 座完成生态流量泄放和监测设施的水电站每座 10 万元的奖励，以沁河流域为单元补助农村水电站绿色改造 50 万元。陕西省要求增效扩容改造、小水电扶贫等项目率先达到“绿色小水电”标准。浙江、福建、湖北、广东、广西、重庆、云南、陕西等 8 个省（自治区、直辖市）利用全球环境基金，实施白云峡等 24 个小水电绿色改造项目，提升绿色小水电的国际影响力。

（水利部农水水电司　张学进）

农 村 水 电 管 理

2018 年农村水电行业安全监管工作情况

2018 年农村水电行业安全生产总体情况保持稳定，安全生产形势持续向好，主要工作情况如下：

（1）明确监管思路。水利部机构改革到位后，及时印发《水利部关于全面加强农村水电安全监管工作的通知》（水电〔2018〕245 号），对农村水电安全监管工作做了全面安排和部署，要求夯实安全生产责任，以农村水电站水库大坝为重点强化安全监管，加快推进安全生产标准化建设，夯实监管基础，强化监管能力和手段，提升监管信息化水平。

（2）夯实监管基础。将安全生产相关信息纳入了新修订的农村水电统计报表制度，增设“汛限水位”“安全标准化达标评级”“生产主体联系人及信息”等相关指标，逐步建立农村水电安全监管信息台账。根据水利部网信工作部署，把农村水电安全监管工作信息化、智慧化需求纳入水利部九大信息系统一并建设。

（3）强化重点环节监管。2018 年 4 月在北京召开农村水电安全生产工作座谈会，传达学习 2018 年水利安全监督工作会议精神，部署 2018 年工作。指导做好度汛安全工作，及时下发《水利部办公厅关于做好农村水电站安全度汛工作的通知》，部署农村水电站防汛度汛工作，开展安全隐患自查和排查治理。组成 3 个工作组对河北等 6 省安全度汛情况进行了督导检查，并就发现问题通过“一省一单”进行了反馈并要求及时整改到位。

（4）强化重点领域监管。落实农村水电站水库大坝安全责任，做好农村水电站水库大坝防汛保安工作。2018 年 5 月下发了《国家防汛抗旱总指挥部关于进一步加强农村水电站水库大坝安全度汛工作的通知》，对农村水电站水库大坝情况进行全面排查，全面落实水库大坝安全责任。

（5）推动安全生产标准化。持续推进安全生产达标评级。完成 2018 年度农村水电站安全生产标准化一级审定，新增一级电站 6 个。指导各地以达标评级为抓手推动标准化建设。截至 2018 年底，全国已建成标准化电站 2500 多座，其中一级 74 个，二级 1000 多个，三级 1500 多个。

（6）深入开展教育培训。2018 年，水利部在江西南昌举办了全国农村水电安全生产培训班，培训班采取专题讲座和案例教学的方式进行。内容包括当前安全生产面临的形势和问题、安全监管工作重点和要求、小型水库大坝安全管理智能化、《农村水电安全生产监督检查导则（修订）》解读、《农村水电安全生产标准化评审办法》修订变化及建设重点、《农村水电站技术管理规程》应用，以及标准化达标电站典型经验分享。

（水利部农水水电司　张翔）

2018 年长江经济带小水电站清理整改工作情况

2018 年 6 月，国务院领导对小水电无序开发、违规建设造成的生态环境突出问题作出重要批示，水利部与国家发展改革委、国家能源局联合开展小水电生态环境突出问题排查，并单独派出 10 个工作组专项检查调研，邀请专家专题研讨，会同相关部门联合向国务院上报了有关情况报告。为切实纠正小水电开发中存在的生态环境突出问题，保护和修复河流生态系统，促进长江经济带走出一条生态优先、绿色发展的新路子，水利部联合国家发展改革委、生态环境部、国家能源局于 2018 年 12 月 6 日联合印发了《关于开展长江经济带小水电清理整改工作的意见》要求长江经济带 10 省提高政治站位，省级水利、发展改革、生态环境、能源等相关部门组成联合工作组，将小水电清理整改工作纳入河长制湖长制工作内容和考核体系，以此为契机全面梳理小水电建设管理的各项制度；计划 2019 年 1 月底前，各省编制完成小水电清理整改工作省级实施方案；以河流或县级区域为单位开展小水电问题核查评估工作，于 2019 年 7 月底前提出退出、整改或保留的评估意见，2019 年 10 月底前制定“一站一策”实施方案；按照“一站一策”要求限期退出涉及自然保护区核心区或缓冲区、严重破坏生态环境的违规水电站，全面整改审批手续不全、影响生态环境的水电站，2020 年底前完成清理整改。

（水利部农水水电司　王亮）

水利部关于全面加强农村水电安全监管工作的通知

2018年10月10日，水利部以水电〔2018〕245号文印发《关于全面加强农村水电安全监管工作的通知》，全文如下。

农村水电点多、面广，关乎公共安全。一段时间以来，一些地方由于监管责任不落实，监管基础薄弱、能力不足、手段不够等原因，导致安全事故时有发生。为贯彻落实党中央、国务院关于加强安全生产工作的要求，根据水利部“三定”规定，现就加强农村水电安全监管有关工作通知如下：

（一）总体要求

深入贯彻落实《中共中央、国务院关于推进安全生产领域改革发展的意见》，牢固树立安全发展理念，以严格农村水电安全生产责任制为体制保障，压实安全监管责任；以农村水电站水库大坝安全监管为重点，防范化解安全风险；以农村水电安全生产标准化为抓手，提升安全生产水平；以农村水电安全监管能力建设为引领，提升安全生产监管信息化水平，加快构建完备的监管体系，推动农村水电安全生产水平再上新台阶。

（二）进一步夯实安全生产工作责任

明确地方政府属地监管、行业主管部门专业监管的农村水电安全生产监管责任，全面落实农村水电企业安全生产主体责任。

（1）明确安全生产领导责任。按照党政同责、一岗双责的原则，明确领导责任，建立权责明确、尽职免责、失职追责的安全生产责任体系。

（2）明确安全生产监管责任。按照管行业必须管安全、管业务必须管安全、管生产经营必须管安全和谁主管谁负责的原则，进一步落实水行政主管部门农村水电安全生产监督管理职责，依法依规开展农村水电监督管理，将安全生产工作作为行业管理的重要内容，完善法规、标准和政策，加强对行业安全生产工作的指导监督。

（3）落实安全生产主体责任。农村水电企业法人对安全生产负主体责任。应遵循“安全第一，预防为主，综合治理”的方针，严格履行安全生产法律法规规定的主体责任。要督促企业以应急管理、隐患排查治理等风险防控为基础，以建立健全安全生产责任制为核心，完善安全生产规章制度，建立安全生产标准化管理体系，全面提升安全生产管理水平，做到安全责任、管理、投入、培训和应急救援“五到位”，切实夯实农村水电安全生产基础，预防和减少安全事故发生。

（三）努力提高安全生产管理水平

各级水行政主管部门要定期组织开展农村水电站隐患排查，立查立改。对不能立即整改的，要做到治理责任、资金、措施、期限和应急预案“五落实”，尽早消除安全生产隐患。

（1）以农村水电站水库大坝为重点，加强对已建农村水电站的安全监管。要按规定严格落实大坝安全鉴定、注册登记制度。要确保水电站大坝安全监测系统和泄洪闸门、启闭设备、动力电源等泄洪设施正常，确保能够按照防洪调度原则和设计规定安全运行。汛期要对水电站大坝近坝库岸和下游近坝边坡进行巡视检查，发现险情及时报告并妥善处理。要保证厂坝间通信设施畅通，应急备用电源靠得住、用得上。严格执行防汛调度命令和经批准的调度运用计划，严肃防汛纪律，不得违规超汛限水位运行。加强农村水电站水库的预测预警能力建设，完善报汛设施，并全面接入防汛指挥系统。

（2）以风险防控为重点，加强对在建农村水电站安全监管。严禁违反规划、未经审批擅自开工建设农村水电站，未经验收不得擅自蓄水或投运。在建农村水电站要落实工程施工与安全生产监督“三同时”制度，安全监管的重点是大坝、围堰、隧洞、泄洪建筑物及高边坡、深基坑等的安全保障措施和落实，易燃易爆等危险化学品的登记、保管、放置和使用，特种设备日常管理维护、运行及检测检验等。对跨汛期施工的新建和改扩建农村水电站，要对工地和宿营区的安全隐患进行排查，指导落实施工安全度汛措施。

要特别关注报废停运农村水电站的安全监管。全面开展安全影响评估，对于可能存在安全隐患的，要及时采取有效措施予以处置，不留隐患死角。

（四）全面加强安全生产监督管理

（1）夯实监管基础。结合行业特点和各地实际，推进农村水电安全生产监管权力清单和责任清单制定工作，建立监督考核机制，尽职照单免责、失职照单问责。完善以国家强制性标准为主体的农村水电安全生产技术标准体系。建立农村水电安全监管信息台账，包括“三个责任人”情况、电站和水库相关基础数据、隐患排查治理等信息，同步建立信息报送制度。注重与其他相关部门监管信息的对接。指导农村水电企业严格落实安全教育培训，切实做到先培训、后上岗。

（2）强化监管手段。通过开展“智慧水利”等信息化建设工作，充分利用互联网技术建立农村水电安全监管平台，实现农村水电安全监管信息化，有效开展安全监管全过程的动态监管。利用水利大数据分析当前农村水电安全生产总体态势，分析共性问题和薄弱环节，为不断改进安全监管工作提供基础。要采取"四不两直"等形式，及时发现问题，不断提高安全生产监督检查的效果。对违规水电站和安全隐患突出的水电站，应及时向当地人民政府汇报，按规定下达停产或关闭决定，提高监督检查效力，确保农村水电站生产安全和下游人民群众生命财产安全。

(3) 提升监管能力。要完善农村水电安全监管设施设备，将监管费用纳入财政预算。充分发挥农村水电行业相关科研院所、高校和企业的作用，通过购买服务的方式参与监督检查工作。鼓励推广应用保障安全生产的新设备、新技术、新材料和新工艺，推进农村水电安全生产技术进步。加强与市场监督管理、发改能源、应急管理、生态环境等部门的密切配合，推动联合执法。

(4) 强化社会和舆论监督。要在农村水电站厂区外设立农村水电安全生产和监管责任人公示牌，通过新闻媒体或新媒体等向社会公告农村水电安全监管和生产责任人名单，公布监督电话等内容，接受社会监督。可聘用电站周边群众担任社会监督员等形式，对违规违法建设运行等情况进行社会监督。

各级水行政主管部门要按照本通知精神，切实加强农村水电建设管理。今年汛期刚刚结束，各地要在做好水毁工程修复的同时，针对防汛度汛和安全生产情况进行全面总结，对发现的问题要求限期整改。请各地于12月底前将整改情况、本通知精神的贯彻落实意见及农村水电站"三个责任人"落实情况报送水利部农水水电司。水利部将采取"四不两直"的方式适时开展农村水电安全生产情况抽查，请各地做好配合工作。

（水利部农水水电司）

水利部、国家发展改革委、生态环境部、国家能源局关于开展长江经济带小水电清理整改工作的意见

2018年12月6日，水利部、国家发展改革委、生态环境部、国家能源局以水电〔2018〕312号文印发《关于开展长江经济带小水电清理整改工作的意见》，全文如下。

推动长江经济带发展是党中央作出的重大决策，是关系国家发展全局的重大战略。为全面贯彻落实习近平生态文明思想，坚决纠正中央环境保护督察、长江经济带生态环境保护情况审计等发现的小水电违规建设、影响生态环境等突出问题，决定开展长江经济带小水电生态环境突出问题清理整改工作。现提出如下意见：

一、总体要求

（一）指导思想

认真学习贯彻习近平生态文明思想和党的十九大精神，按照党中央、国务院关于长江经济带发展的决策部署，坚持共抓大保护、不搞大开发，正确把握生态环境保护、经济社会发展、社会稳定之间的关系，切实纠正小水电开发中存在的生态环境突出问题，保护和修复河流生态系统，促进长江经济带走出一条生态优先、绿色发展的新路子。

（二）基本原则

(1) 问题导向，分类处置。全面核查、科学评估存在的问题，按照退出、整改、保留三类，逐站提出处置意见，明确退出或整改措施。

(2) 依法依规，稳步推进。严格按照有关法律法规和技术标准，积极稳妥推进整改，尊重历史，务求实效，避免出现新的环境破坏和社会风险。

(3) 完善制度，规范发展。完善小水电建管制度，建立长效发展机制，健全监管体系，加强监督管理，既管好存量，又严控新建项目。

(4) 明确责任，形成合力。省负总责，市县抓落实，相关部门加强协调配合，建立上下联动、部门协作、责任清晰、高效有力的工作机制。

（三）总体目标

限期退出涉及自然保护区核心区或缓冲区、严重破坏生态环境的违规水电站，全面整改审批手续不全、影响生态环境的水电站，完善建设管理制度和监管体系，有效解决长江经济带小水电生态环境突出问题，促进小水电科学有序可持续发展。2020年底前完成清理整改。

二、主要任务

（一）问题核查评估

在有关部门前期组织开展的排查摸底基础上，重点核查项目是否涉及生态保护红线情况，是否履行了立项审批（核准）、环境影响评价、水资源论证（取水许可）、土地预审、林地征（占）用等手续。统筹考虑经济社会发展、能源需求、社会稳定、生态环境影响、电站布局优化、整改修复可行性等，以河流或县级区域为单元组织开展综合评估，提出退出、整改或保留的评估意见，报省级人民政府同意，建立台账。

（二）分类整改落实

1. 退出类

位于自然保护区核心区或缓冲区内的（未分区的

自然保护区视为核心区和缓冲区)；自2003年9月1日《环境影响评价法》实施后未办理环评手续违法开工建设且生态环境破坏严重的；自2013年以来未发电且生态环境破坏严重的；大坝已鉴定为危坝，严重影响防洪安全，重新整改又不经济的；县级以上人民政府及其部门文件明确要求退出而未执行到位的，列入退出类，原则上应立即退出。其中，位于自然保护区核心区或缓冲区内但在其批准设立前合法合规建设、不涉及自然保护区核心区和缓冲区且具有防洪、灌溉、供水等综合利用功能又对生态环境影响小的，可以限期（原则上不得超过2022年）退出。

退出类电站应部分或全部拆除，要避免造成新的生态环境破坏和安全隐患。除仍然需要发挥防洪、灌溉、供水等综合效应的电站外，其他的均应拆除拦河闸坝，封堵取水口，消除对流量下泄、河流阻隔等影响；未拆除的，应对其进行生态修复，通过修建生态流量泄放设施、监测设施以及必要的过鱼设施等，减轻其对流量下泄、河流阻隔等的不利影响。要逐站明确退出时间，制定退出方案，明确是否补偿以及补偿标准、补偿方式等，必要时应进行社会风险评估。

2. 保留类

同时满足以下条件的可以保留：一是依法依规履行了行政许可手续；二是不涉及自然保护区核心区、缓冲区和其他依法依规应禁止开发区域；三是满足生态流量下泄要求。

3. 整改类

未列入退出类、保留类的，列入整改类。对审批手续不全的，由相关主管部门根据综合评估意见以及整改措施落实情况等，指导小水电业主完善有关手续。依法依规应处罚的，应在办理手续前依法处罚到位。对不满足生态流量要求的，主要采取修建生态流量泄放设施、安装生态流量监测设施、生态调度运行等工程和非工程措施，保障生态流量。对存在水环境污染或水生生态破坏的，采取对应有效的水污染治理、增殖放流以及必要的过鱼等生态修复措施。要逐站制定整改方案，明确整改目标、措施。小水电业主要按照经批准的整改方案严格整改，整改一座，销号一座。

（三）严控新建项目

各地要依法依规编制或修订流域综合规划及专项规划，并同步开展规划环评，合理确定开发与保护边界。除与生态环境保护相协调的且是国务院及其相关部门、省级人民政府认可的脱贫攻坚项目外，严控新建商业开发的小水电项目。坚持规划、规划环评和项目联动，对小水电新建项目严格把关，不符合规划及规划环评、审批手续不全的一律不得开工建设。对已审批但未开工建设的项目，全部进行重新评估。

三、保障措施

（一）高度重视，精心组织

各地要认真贯彻落实习近平总书记关于长江经济带发展的重要讲话精神和国务院领导批示要求，切实提高政治站位，主动扛起长江经济带生态环境保护的政治责任，增强落实“把修复长江生态环境摆在压倒性位置”指示要求的思想自觉和行动自觉，加强组织领导，周密安排部署，把小水电清理整改工作抓实抓好。

（二）明确责任，加强指导

小水电数量多、情况复杂，水利、发展改革、生态环境、能源等相关部门要组成联合工作组，进一步明确各部门责任，逐级压实责任，层层传到压力。要指导市县将省级实施方案确定的目标任务分解落实，按照“一站一策”要求明确整改措施、时限、责任人和资金，确保整改到位。

（三）强化监督检查，严格考核问责

各地要将清理整改纳入河长制、湖长制工作内容和考核体系。加强对小水电清理整改工作的指导，发现问题及时处理。对整改难度大、问题突出的要挂牌督办。对责任不落实、监管不到位、进展缓慢或敷衍塞责、弄虚作假等问题，要通报批评、公开约谈；对情节严重的，要严肃问责追责。要主动向社会公开清理整改工作情况，接受人民群众监督。

（四）完善相关政策，建立长效机制

各地要以此次清理整改为契机，制定小水电相关监督管理政策，完善全过程监督管理制度，加强生态环境保护的事中事后监管，建立监测监督体系。健全小水电绿色可持续评价管理制度，研究制定充分反映生态保护和修复治理成本的小水电优先上网及电价政策，鼓励打造绿色可持续电站。要安排专项资金，用于小水电综合评估、合法退出，以及生态流量监测平台、建设管理监管信息平台等。

各地要按照本意见要求，认真组织实施，及时通报清理整改情况。请于2019年1月底前编制完成小水电清理整改工作省级实施方案，经省（直辖市）人民政府同意后报水利部、发展改革委、生态环境部、国家能源局备案。有关部门将在2019、2020年联合组织开展清理整改回头看活动，对各地整改情况进行调研指导。

（水利部农水水电司）

农村水电改造

2018年农村水电增效扩容改造情况

（一）下达中央财政奖励资金

2018年，水利部商财政部预拨2018年农村水电增效扩容改造中央财政奖励资金10.6亿元，已累计预拨中央资金40.5亿元，占“十三五”各地申请中央资金的86%。

（二）完成项目调整工作

2018年，水利部指导广东等14个省份对“十三五”增效扩容改造项目进行了调整备案，将部分位于自然保护区内、无法取得环评手续、无法正常实施的项目调整出了实施范围，并将一批手续完备、改造潜力较大的项目递补进实施范围。调整后共有1340条河流纳入实施范围，其中生态改造项目1993个，计划修复减脱水河段3059km；电站增效扩容改造项目2194个，改造后装机容量达468万kW、年发电量178亿kW·h，分别比改造前增加26.3%和43.8%。

（三）开展项目督查调研

2018年，水利部组织对6个存在问题较多的省份和2个河流生态改造工作成效明显的省份开展督查调研，实地查看36个农村水电增效扩容改造项目。通过现场查看、文件资料查阅、与业主座谈交流等方式开展工作，重点查看了项目工程进展情况、资金管理与使用情况、项目环评情况、项目实施的初步成效、已完工项目验收及绩效评价开展情况、存在的主要问题及下一步工作安排等。督查后将发现的问题与有关省份交换了意见，并要求及时整改到位。同时对收集到的先进经验做法进行了总结，通过行业会议与各地进行推广交流。

（四）解决环评制约问题

2018年长江经济带生态审计后，及时与被冻结小水电环评手续的相关省份联系，掌握各省环评工作的具体进展［包括已完成环评情况，未编制报告(表)，正在编制，编制完成已提交环保部门，环保部门受理情况、已审待批等详尽资料］，分析存在问题，研究推动工作。2018年底再次对22个省和新疆生产建设兵团的项目环评进行全面摸底，掌握各地环评开展情况和存在问题。

（五）项目进展超过预期

截至2018年底，纳入“十三五”增效扩容改造实施范围的1340条河流中，已有571条河流完成改造任务；1191个生态改造项目和1368个电站增效扩容改造项目建设完工，完工率分别为60%和62%，项目单位共到位资金103.93亿元，完成投资96.5亿元。项目实施进展顺利，整体进度超过目标进度。

（水利部农水水电司　张丽）

普定水电站增容改造工程电气一次设计

（一）电站概况

普定水电站位于乌江上游南源贵州省普定县三岔河中游，距贵阳市125km。水库正常蓄水位1145m，总库容4.21亿m^3，为不完全年调节水库。原总装机容量7.5万kW，共装设3台2.5万kW立轴混流式水轮发电机组，年平均发电量3.16亿kW·h。电站于1989年12月开工建设，1993年11月开始蓄水，1994年5月第一台机组发电。投产至今已运行24年，多数设备已到经济运行年限。同时，受当时设计、制造条件限制，设备及其配套设施较差，电站运行过程中出现一系列问题。为此，2015年6月19日业主对电站机组进行了增容改造，改造后总装机容量为8.7万kW，共装设3台单机容量2.9万kW的立轴混流水轮发电机组。截至2018年，电站首台改造机组已顺利投产，第二台改造机组已完成充水前的准备工作，较好地达到了改造前的预期目标。

（二）电气主接线

该水电站发电机电压侧接线采用发变组单元接线，110kV侧采用单母线分段接线，35kV侧采用单母线分段接线；1、3号三绕组变压器35kV中压出线经两段35kV母线、通过四回35kV出线引出，在发电机出口装设专用真空型发电机出口断路器。发电机中性点采用经避雷器接地方式。双绕组变压器110kV侧中性点设置有放电间隙和避雷器，三绕组变压器高压中性点设置有放电间隙和避雷器，中压侧中性点采用经避雷器接地方式。

（三）增容改造的必要性与目标

1. 改造的必要性　该水电站主要机电设备运行

现状及存在问题如下：①发电机定子绕组绝缘等级低，为B级绝缘。②发电机出口断路器及开关柜故障多，备品备件难以采购。③发电机出口母线为铝母排套热缩管，投运至今未进行更换，接头温度高、绝缘老化严重。④主变压器损耗大，绝缘老化严重，存在不同程度渗漏；主变压器设计方案不合理，气体继电器、压力释放阀预防性试验时不能按规程规定校验，通风冷却效果差。⑤厂用变压器损耗大，不符合当下国家节能降耗要求。⑥电缆桥架多处由于老化及电缆布置较多损坏严重。

2. 改造的目标　工程电气一次主要改造范围为：水轮发电机、发电机母线、主变压器、干式变压器、坝区0.4kV开关柜、电缆桥架等。

（四）改造内容

1. 发电机的改造　该水电站机组技术改造的主要目的除了技术更新，消除老化设备、提高机组运行稳定性外，另一个目的是增加机组的额定出力，提高电站发电效益。根据论证分析，确定该水电站全厂3台水轮发电机组以技术改造为主，适当增容，水轮机额定出力由2.564万kW增大到2.978万kW，发电机额定容量由2.5万kW增容到2.9万kW，机组额定转速由原来的187.5r/min增加到200r/min。根据该电站现有发电机参数，结合目前新建电站参数水平，确定该电站发电机额定电压仍为10.5kV，发电机原绝缘等级为B/B级，等级太低，不符合目前发电机技术水平，改造后绝缘等级为F/F级。

2. 主变压器　主变压器更换或改造原因：①机组改造增容的需要。水轮发电机已增容，发电机额定容量为2.9万kW，在主接线不变的情况下，相匹配的主变压器额定容量为35000kVA（原主变压器容量31500kVA）。②主变压器安全运行的需要。该电站主变压器已运行23年，已接近主变压器25年的安全运行年限。③节能降耗的需要。该电站主变压器型号为8系列产品，根据国家节能降耗相关规程规范和贵州省2010年版《110kV变电站标准化设计》均要求新建或改造项目的主变压器型号采用节能产品，主变压器型号要求10系列以上。主变压器能耗的高低直接影响生产成本，且长时间运行下由于损耗导致的能量浪费非常庞大。所以，在响应国家节能政策和为了电站长期发展利益下，采用新型低能耗变压器势在必行，见表1。

3. 厂用变压器　厂用变压器更换或改造原因：为了满足变压器安全运行需要，该电站厂用变压器已运行23年，原变压器采用的是油浸式变压器，为了响应国家节能降耗的要求，改造后的厂用变压器采用新型低能耗非晶合金变压器。

表1　改造前后主变压器的主要技术参数对比

	改造前	改造后	
型号	SFLF-31500/110	SS35000/110	S35000/110
额定容量（MV·A）	31.5	35	35
额定电压	121±2×2.5%/10.5kV	121±2×2.5%/38.5±2×2.5%/10.5kV	121±2×2.5%/10.5kV
联结组标号	YN，d11	YNyn0d11	Ynd11
冷却方式	油浸水冷	自冷	自冷
空载损耗（kW）	34.5	≤24.1	≤143.1
负载损耗（kW）	145	≤147.1	≤122.8

（五）电缆桥架改造

根据该水电站原电缆桥架存在安装不规范、电缆线外露、电缆桥架设计偏小、无防火隔板等现象，电缆桥架改造采用钢制电缆桥架（钢制外壳内装无机防火槽盒、防火护罩）；电缆吊架的设计应充分考虑电缆检修、维护及电缆串层要求；垂直靠墙安装的电缆桥架采用复合托盘式竖井桥架（钢制外壳内装无机防火槽盒、防火护罩）；电缆沟内壁架采用装配型托臂。电缆桥架内的无机防火槽盒为一次成型，防火槽盒与电缆桥架嵌装，其规格与电缆桥架配套并在制造厂与电缆桥架一起装配。对原来在安装过程没有设置防火隔板的部分桥架进行了增设防火隔板措施；电缆有外露的地方增加了电缆桥架宽度及深度，并且对现场凌乱的电缆进行了规整。对之前支吊架设置不合理的地方重新规划并且补装；改造后的电缆桥架采用热镀锌表面处理，较原来更美观耐用。

（普定水电站　黎家海
中国电建集团贵阳勘测设计研究院
有限公司　陈丹燕）

石头河坝后水电站主变压器增容更新改造

（一）工程概况

石头河坝后水电站位于陕西省岐山、眉县、太白三县交界处的斜峪关，属石头河水库水能梯级开发中第一级水能利用工程。该水电站共安装 4 台混流式机组，总装机容量 1.85 万 kW，其中 1G、2G、3G 机组为一期工程，容量为 1×0.65 万 kW+2×0.5 万 kW，1G 机组为容量是 0.65 万 kW 的低水头大流量机组，2G、3G 为同型号高水头机组，3 台机组出线电压均为 6.3kV，电气主接线为“三机一变”，35kV 电压侧单母线接线，安装 1 台容量为 16000kV·A，35kV 的升压变压器，3 台发电机组生产的电量经此台主变压器升压后再经一条 10.8km、35kV 输电线路并网于宝鸡供电局五丈塬变电站。1990～1991 年 3 台机组相继并网发电，设计年发电量 5600 万kW·h，年利用小时数 3400h。二期工程 4G 机组，容量为 1×0.2 万kW，为低水头小流量机组，10kV 出线，直接并网于枢纽变电站 10kV 母线，于 1998 年并网发电，设计年发电量 1005 万 kW·h，年利用小时数 4100h。

该水电站经过增效扩容改造，从新主变压器投入 3 年运行情况来看，各项性能指标均在正常范围内。主变压器的增容更新改造从根本上消除了安全隐患，确保了设备的安全稳定运行。同时满足了 3 台机组改造后最大出力的变压器容量需求，对该水电站的安全发供电起到重大作用，同时大大降低了损耗，提高了经济效益。

（二）主变压器改造的必要性

该水电站主变压器为 SFL-16000/35/6.3kV 油浸风冷式三相无载调压变压器。该变压器为 1976 年 5 月出厂产品，1989 年由上级调拨而来，至 2015 年已投运 39 年，主要存在以下问题：①变压器出厂距当时已投运 39 年，超过报废期限，在近几年电站进行的电气设备定期校试中，校试单位因担心在主变压器绝缘试验时发生绝缘击穿，而不愿意对变压器外施高压。近 6 年来变压器一直未曾进行大修，变压器具体健康状况很难预计，施工单位考虑到变压器绝缘老化程度，也不愿承担该变压器的大修。②该主变压器现属淘汰类高损耗型变压器。变压器铭牌标识的空载损耗为 19.6kW，短路损耗为 105kW，而相同容量、电压比的低损耗变压器一般空载损耗为 15.2kW，短路损耗为 69.3kW，若按照变压器负荷 12900kVA 运行 3600h（每年 6～10 月）计算，现运行的高损耗变压器比同容量的一台低损耗变压器多损耗电能 10 万 kW·h，若变压器一年运行 8040h 计算，主变压器年运行损耗电能与低损耗变压器相比，将多达 14.6 万 kW·h。③变压器顶盖，器身与冷却器、干燥器联结法兰处渗漏油严重，冷却风扇易出现故障，由于配件购置困难，常在发电高峰期因主变风冷却装置不能全部投入，而影响主变压器运行。④考虑到 1G 机组因“引红济石”工程而进行改造，即改造后水头提高，容量不变，则 3 台机组最大出力将达到 16500kW，视在功率达 20625kV·A（目前最大视在功率 16375kV·A），主变压器容量不能满足 3 台机组出力需求。

（三）改造方案比较

（1）方案一。更换 1 台 SFZ_{11}-16000kVA/35/6.3kV 同容量新型节能变压器，以满足目前运行方式。考虑到该水电站 1G 机组如进行改造，待改造完成后再新增 1 台 SZ_{11}-8000kVA/35/6.3kV 主变压器，2 台并联运行，总容量达 24000kV·A，在满足 3 台机组最大出力同时且有容量富裕。该方案优点：①对以后 1G 机组是否改造具有较大灵活性；②运行灵活，可靠性高；③容量有较大富裕，相对较安全。缺点：①全部完工后，总投资较大，达 275 万元（一期 125 万元，二期 150 万元）；②运行操作频繁，发生差错率相对增加。

（2）方案二。购置 1 台 SZ_{11}-25000kVA/38.5/6.3kV 变压器，更换现有主变压器，这样不但可满足目前的需要，且可满足以后 1G 机组改造后出力增加的需要。该方案优点：①相对 2 台主变压器总投资少，共 148 万元；②主接线简单，运行维护方便。缺点：①相对两台并联变压器而言运行不灵活；②空载损耗相对 2 台主变压器稍大。

（3）方案三。一次购置 2 台新变压器，分别为 SF_{11}-8000kVA/35/6.3kV、 SZ_{11}-12500kVA/35/6.3kV 更换现有主变压器。这样，既可满足目前之需要，也可满足以后 1G 机组改造后的需要。该方案优点：同方案一。缺点：同方案一，且一次性投资大。

从上述 3 个方案比较看，应从方案一、方案二中选取，方案三不可选。当时的意见是：如该站 1G 机组改造完全可行，则选方案二；如 1G 机组改造一时不能确定，则应选方案一。

（四）改造效果

2012 年，上级批复，同意实施该水电站增效扩容改造工程。其中，包含对该水电站 1G 机组的改造，鉴于各方案的技术性和经济性，方案二被最终确定。该工程从 2015 年 3 月开始，2016 年 3 月相继完成。特别是 1G 机组改造后的设计水头由原来的 52m 提高到 70m（适用水头范围 50～90m），确保丰水期具备与 2G、3G 机组高水头满负荷同时运行，3 台机组最大出力 16500kW，大大提高了年发电量。达到了本次主变压器增容改造的主要目的（见表 1）。

其次，通过对该水电站主变压器的增容更新改造，从根本上解决了丰水期上网无功负荷欠缺问题：因为在 3 台机组运行过程中，充分利用新主变压器有载调压方式不需停电就可通过调节分接开关来调低母线电压，保证了3台机组无功负荷满发问题。另外，新主变压器在机组满负荷情况下，较旧主变压器温度大大降低，以前即便开启冷却风机强迫油循环（ONAF）主变压器温度也达到85℃左右，而现在只需油浸自冷（ONAN）温度也最大才达到63℃左右。

表1 机组—主变压器最大负荷对照表

项目 年份	有功功率（万kW）			合计功率（kW）	主变压器			
	1G	2G	3G		电流（A）	有功功率（kW）	温度（℃）	运行时间（h）
2016年	6500	5000	4995	16495	277	16492	59.1	288
2017年	6500	5000	4993	16493	276	16490	58.9	334
2018年	6505	5000	5000	16505	290	16500	62.9	截至7月31日，756（止）

（石头河水库灌溉管理局 王希）

岩屋潭Ⅰ级水电站增效扩容改造工程

（一）电站概况

岩屋潭Ⅰ级水电站地处湖南省沅陵县凉水井镇境内，是沅水一级支流兰溪流域中下游一级电站，始建于1977年，1979年投产发电，至2018年已运行发电近39年。电站总库容1.2亿m^3，调节库容6700万m^3，属年调节水库。主要建筑物有空腹重力坝、有压引水隧洞、压力钢管、主副厂房、升压站等。电站总容量为：2×3000kW+1×3200kW=9200kW。2台主变压器：SJL1-8000/35kV及SJL1-4000/35kV。原设计年平均发电量为3055万kW·h，年利用小时为3320h。而改造前近5年发电量统计，年平均发电量为2326万kW·h，年利用小时为2528h。通过增效扩容改造，提高了水能资源利用，增加了发电效益，提高了电站可靠性与自动化水平。

（二）增效扩容改造原因

1. 电站现状与存在问题 该水电站1～2号水轮机为PO263-BM-134，发电机为TS325-44/22，为1959年产品，从其他水电站拆迁而来，3号水轮机为HL123-LJ-140，发电机为TS325-36/20，1978年产品。①该水轮机为20世纪50年代仿苏模型，由于当时设计、制造水平、生产工艺等条件限制，通过蜗壳测流法测定：1～2号水轮机额定效率约为67%；3号水轮机额定效率约为78%。②3台发电机经过多年运行，绝缘已严重老化，绝缘等级为B级，易受潮，严重影响电站安全运行。③3台机组金属蜗壳为半埋式，壁厚为10mm。经测量蜗壳外壁锈蚀厚度约为1mm，蜗壳内壁锈蚀厚度约为1.5mm。④3台调速器为CT-40，额定油压为2.5MPa。灵敏度较低，操作不可靠，经常出现卡阻现象。不能满足“无人值班（少人值守）”的现代自动化要求。⑤3台进水蝶阀为手电两用型式。进水蝶阀锈蚀严重，经常采用关闭进水检修闸门进行检修，运行维护极为不便，且具有很大安全隐患。

2. 电站增效扩容改造必要性 ①该水电站运行年久，主要机电设备产品性能与现阶段差别较大。②根据电站多年运行实际，目前装机容量与来水量相比存在装机容量偏小，特别是丰水期（4～8月降雨量占全年80%以上）存在大量弃水。③该水电站水库属年调节水库，充分利用水能资源可给整个流域梯级电站带来较好效益。

（三）增效扩容改造方案

1. 增效扩容改造内容 根据该水电站运行管理实际，经对电站多年水文、水能复核以及运行情况综合分析比较，该增效扩容改造主要内容是对引水压力隧洞进行抹面降糙，对水轮机、发电机、调速器、变电设备、电气控制设备及相应辅助设备进行更新改造，对进口蝶阀及附属设施进行更换，对厂房进行维修改造，完善管理设施，增设必要的工情及水力监测设施。

2. 增效扩容改造设计方案 ①3台水轮机全部更换。根据国内现有水轮机型谱以及多数厂家推荐，适合该水电站水轮机转轮型号为HLA551，最大水头50m，最小水头30m，加权平均水头41.5m，原为2台转轮直径1.34m、额定水头35.3m和1台转轮直径1.4m、额定水头30.5m。原水轮机额定水头与电站实际运行水头范围等参数不完全相适应。最后选定2台转轮直径1.34m、额定水头38m、额定流量11.9m^3/s、额定转速375r/min；1台转轮直径1.4m、额定水头35m、额定流量12.9m^3/s、额定转速333.3r/min。总装机容量为3×4000kW，设计年保证出力（保证率$P=90\%$）1760kW，多年平均发电量为3650万kW·h，年利用小时为3040h。根据选定的模型综合特性曲线，水轮机最大允许吸出高度分别为+4.41m和+4.61m。新选定的水轮发电机组安装高程经复核为129.615m和129.82m，按原实际安装高程更有利于机组抗空蚀，且不因机组安装高程变化影响厂房结构，确定增容改造后机组安装高程维持原高程 126.1m 不变。转轮定为不锈钢材料。②3 台发电机全部更换，发电机绝缘等级由 B 级改为 F 级；发电机的冷却方式由风冷改为采用空气冷却器水冷方式；适当增加发电机转动部分重量，使转动惯量能满足调保计算要求；尽量利用原定子基础螺栓，防止破坏原发电机机墩结构。2 台水轮发电机组选定为 SF4000-16/3250，额定电压 6.3kV，额定电流 458.2A；1 台 SF4000-18/3250，额定电压 6.3kV，额定电流 458.2A。③3 台套调速器及油压装置采用高油压蓄能式组合式结构，型号为 YWT-PLC-2500-16，油压为 16MPa。该调速器灵敏度以及可靠性较高，占地小，整体美观且操作方便。④3 台套进口蝶阀更换为 1750HD741H-10VK-YYZ，油压为 16MPa。该蝶阀采用双偏心自关闭结构，关阀可靠性高。蝶阀主密封采用金属硬密封结构，可减少维护和检修工作量。⑤变电设备、电气控制设备及相应附属设备全面更新改造。电气设备的选择本着节能降耗以及满足“五防”要求，实现电站增效扩容改造后“无人值班（少人值守）”的运行模式。⑥其他附属设施。取消原中压气机室所有设施；增设取至蝶阀前压力引水管冷却水管及相应过滤设备和减压阀等，发电机机坑增设 2 根冷却水环管；起吊设施满足起重要求，只需简单维护即可用。

（四）增效扩容改造及效果

①为在增效扩容改造实施中不影响正常发电，尽可能利用该水电站年调节水库，根据改造工程量和工期需要，跨两个年度枯水季节完成。从 2013 年 7 月设备招标，到 2015 年 3 月改造工程全部实施完成。②2015 年 3 月 2 日，3 台机组做三机一管甩负荷试验。试验结果表明，甩负荷试验均在规范要求范围内且结果远远小于改造前甩负荷试验结果。③改造完成后该水电站实现了“无人值班，少人值守”的运行模式，原每班 8 个人值班，现由 2 个人值守。④电站装机容量由 0.92 万 kW 增至 1.2 万 kW，且 3 台机组均能超负荷运行。2015～2017 年，3 年平均年发电量达到 3790 万 kW·h，年利用小时为 3158h。相比改造前装机容量增加 30%，年均发电量增加 50%以上，电站效益得到明显提高。

（怀化市水利电力勘测设计研究院 张灵锋）

15

机构与学术团体

机　　构

水电建设单位情况一览表

单位名称	地　　址	邮政编码
国家电网有限公司	北京市西城区西长安街86号	100031
国网新源控股有限公司	北京市西城区白广路二条1号	100761
中国南方电网有限责任公司	广东省广州市黄埔区科学城科翔路11号	510663
南方电网调峰调频发电有限公司	广东省广州市龙口东路32号	510630
中国华能集团有限公司	北京市西城区复兴门内大街6号	100031
中国大唐集团有限公司	北京市西城区广宁伯街1号	100033
中国华电集团有限公司	北京市西城区宣武门内大街2号	100031
国家能源投资集团有限责任公司	北京市西城区阜成门北大街6-8号	100034
国家电力投资集团有限公司	北京市西城区金融大街28号院3号楼	100033
中国长江三峡集团有限公司	北京市海淀区玉渊潭南路1号	100038
中国长江电力股份有限公司	湖北宜昌市西坝建设路1号	443002
国投电力控股股份有限公司	北京市西城区西直门南小街147号	100034
大唐国际发电股份有限公司	北京市西城区广宁伯街9号	100033
汉能控股集团有限公司	北京市朝阳区水岸南街1号	100107
新华水力发电有限公司	北京市丰台区海鹰路1号院7号楼万润大厦	100070
中国三峡建设管理有限公司	四川省成都市高新区府城大道东段288号	610041
雅砻江流域水电开发有限公司	四川省成都市双林路288号	610051
华能四川水电有限公司	四川省成都市人民南路四段47号华能大厦	610041
大唐四川发电有限公司	四川省成都市蜀金路1号	610091
国电大渡河流域水电开发有限公司	四川省成都市高新区天韵路7号	610041
华电四川发电有限公司	四川省成都市高新区蜀绣西路100号	610041
华电金沙江上游水电开发有限公司	四川省成都市高新区蜀绣西路100号	610041
国电四川发电有限公司	四川省成都市天晖北路9号	610041
四川华电杂谷脑水电开发有限公司	四川省成都青羊工业园区（东区）同城路8号	610009
国电四川发电有限公司南椏河水电分公司	四川省成都市高新区天晖北街9号	610041
中电建水电开发集团有限公司	四川省成都市高新区天府二街139号	610041
四川美姑河水电开发有限公司	四川省成都市温江区人和路368号	611130
国投云南大朝山水电开发公司	云南昆明市官渡区新昆洛路新亚洲城星都国际63栋	650213
华能澜沧江水电股份有限公司	云南省昆明市官渡区世纪城中路1号	650214
华能澜沧江上游水电有限公司	云南省昆明市官渡区世纪城中路1号	650214

续表

单位名称	地　址	邮政编码
华电云南发电有限公司	云南省昆明市西山区红塔东路6号	650228
国家电投云南国际电力投资有限公司	云南省昆明市西山区滇池路1302号	650228
国电金沙江旭龙（奔子栏）水电开发有限公司	云南省迪庆藏族自治州德钦县升平镇南坪街70号	674500
贵州乌江水电开发有限责任公司	贵州省贵阳市南明区新华路9号	550002
贵州黔源电力股份有限公司	贵州省贵阳市南明区都司高架路46号	550002
龙滩水电开发有限公司	广西南宁市民族大道126号	530022
广西桂冠电力股份有限公司	广西南宁市民族大道126号	530022
五凌电力有限公司	湖南省长沙市天心区五凌路188号	410004
湖南澧水流域水利水电开发有限责任公司	湖南省长沙市香樟路393号	410014
湖北清江水电开发有限责任公司	湖北省宜昌市东山大道95号清江大厦	443000
福建水口发电集团有限公司	福建省福州市台江区白马南路333号	350004
汉江水利水电集团有限责任公司	湖北省丹江口市环形路3号	442700
陕西汉江投资开发有限公司	陕西省西安市高新区沣惠南路32号	710065
国投甘肃小三峡发电有限责任公司	甘肃省兰州市七里河区敦煌路353号	730050
黄河上游水电开发有限责任公司	青海省西宁市五四西路43号	810008
青海省水利水电集团有限责任公司	青海省西宁市西关大街57号	810001
国电新疆吉林台水电开发有限公司	新疆伊犁州尼勒克县	835716
国电新疆开都河流域水电开发有限公司	新疆库尔勒市人民东路华誉商务大厦14楼	841000
国电阿克苏河流域水电开发有限公司	新疆阿克苏市塔中路7号金地美居大厦4楼	843000
中国水电顾问集团投资有限公司	北京朝阳区北湖渠路15号京环大厦主楼10楼	100101
华能西藏雅鲁藏布江水电开发投资有限公司	四川省成都市武侯区科园二路10号航利研发中心1栋二单元	610093
广东省粤电集团有限公司	广东省广州市天河东路2号粤电广场	510630

（本年鉴编辑部）

水电设计单位情况一览表

序号	单位名称	主要领导及总工程师	职工人数	地　址	邮　编	电　话	传　真	网　址
1	水电水利规划设计总院	院长：郑声安 总工程师：彭才德	280	北京市西城区六铺炕北小街2号	100120	010-51973283	010-62356230	http://www.creei.cn/
2	中国电建集团北京勘测设计研究院有限公司	董事长：郝荣国 总工程师：吕明治	1135	北京市定福庄西街一号	100024	010-51972599	010-65728792	http://www.bhidi.com/
3	中国电建集团华东勘测设计研究院有限公司	董事长：张春生 总工程师：侯　靖、吴关叶	4250	浙江省杭州市高教路201号	311122	0571-56628888	0571-88076606	http://www.ecidi.com/

续表

序号	单位名称	主要领导及总工程师	职工人数	地 址	邮 编	电 话	传 真	网 址
4	中国电建集团西北勘测设计研究院有限公司	董事长、总经理：廖元庆 总工程师：周 恒	2332	陕西省西安市雁塔区丈八东路18号	710065	029-88290001	029-88290000	http://www.nwh.cn/
5	中国电建集团中南勘测设计研究院有限公司	董事长：冯树荣 总工程师：潘江洋	2420	湖南省长沙市雨花区圭塘香樟东路16号	410014	0731-85072055	0731-85584080	http://www.msdi.cn/
6	中国电建集团成都勘测设计研究院有限公司	董事长：黄 河 总工程师：余 挺	2105	四川省成都市温江区政和街8号	61130	028-87329997	028-87329997	http://www.chidi.com.cn/
7	中国电建集团贵阳勘测设计研究院有限公司	董事长：潘继录 总工程师：范福平	1533	贵州省贵阳市观山湖区兴黔路16号	550081	0851-85388101	0851-85388999	http://www.ghidri.com.cn/
8	中国电建集团昆明勘测设计研究院有限公司	董事长：冯峻林 总工程师：张宗亮	1809	云南省昆明市人民东路115号	650051	0871-63062050	0871-63138701	http://www.khidi.com/

（中国水力发电工程学会 殷利利）

水利设计单位情况一览表

序号	单位名称	主要领导及总工程师	在职职工人数	地 址	邮 编	电 话	传 真	网 址
1	水利部水利水电规划设计总院	院长：沈凤生 总工程师：温续余	193	北京市西城区六铺炕北小街2-1号	100120	010-63206688	010-62070508	http://www.giwp.org.cn
2	长江勘测规划设计研究院	院长：钮新强 总工程师：杨启贵	2929	湖北省武汉市解放大道1863号	430010	027-82927792	027-82829202	http://www.cjwsjy.com.cn
3	黄河勘测规划设计研究院有限责任公司	董事长：张金良 总工程师：景来红	1783	河南省郑州市金水路109号	450003	0371-66026449 0371-66023501	0371-65959236	http://www.yrec.cn
4	中水淮河规划设计研究有限责任公司	董事长：周 虹 总工程师：马东亮	230	安徽省合肥市滨湖新区云谷路2588号	230601	0551-65707505 0551-65707515	0551-65707500	http://www.cwhh.com.cn
5	中水珠江规划勘测设计有限责任公司	董事长：凌耀忠 总工程师：刘元勋	1000	广东省广州市天河区天寿路沾益直街19号	510610	020-38810724	020-87117050	http://www.prpsdc.com

续表

序号	单位名称	主要领导及总工程师	在职职工人数	地址	邮编	电话	传真	网址
6	中水东北勘测设计研究有限责任公司	董事长：金正浩 总工程师：苏加林	1060	吉林省长春市朝阳区工农大路888号	130021	0431-85092001	0431-85092000	http://www.neidri.com
7	中水北方勘测设计研究有限责任公司	董事长：李孝振 总工程师：杜雷功	1100	天津市河西区洞庭路60号	300222	022-28702840 022-28702222	022-28343991	http://www.tidi.ac.cn

（中国水利水电勘测设计协会）

水利水电施工单位情况一览表

序号	单位名称	主要领导及总工程师	地址	邮编	电话	传真	网址
一	中国电力建设股份有限公司	董事长：晏志勇 总工程师：宗敦峰、周建平	北京市海淀区车公庄西路22号	100048	010-58368693	010-58382888	http://www.powerchina.cn
1	中国水利水电第一工程局有限公司	董事长、党委书记：徐银林	吉林省长春市经济技术开发区东南湖大路3799号	130033	0431-87987316	0431-87991536	http://www.zsyj.com/
2	中电建建筑集团有限公司	执行董事、总经理：常满祥 总工程师：梁宏生	北京市西城区六铺炕南小街1号	100120	010-58689270	010-62018014	http://www.sdej.com
3	中国水利水电第三工程局有限公司	执行董事、总经理：张育林 总工程师：王鹏禹	陕西省西安市浐灞区世博大道4069号	710024	029-86178686	029-86267407	http://3j.sinohydro.com
4	中国水利水电第四工程局有限公司	党委书记、董事长：高建民 副总经理、总工程师：张文山	青海省西宁市昆仑东路77号	810007	0971-8088057	0971-8088058	http://www.csdsj.com
5	中国水利水电第五工程局有限公司	董事长、党委书记：贺鹏程 副总经理兼总工程师：吴高见	四川省成都市一环路东四段8号	610066	028-84461307	028-84422633	http://5j.powerchina.cn/
6	中国水利水电第六工程局有限公司	执行董事、总经理：刘　宝 总工程师：杨成文	辽宁省沈阳市浑南新区新隆街2号	110179	024-83899766	024-83899888	http://6j.powerchina.cn
7	中国水利水电第七工程局有限公司	执行董事、总经理：申茂夏 总工程师：向　建	四川成都市解放路二段329号	610081	028-83370023	028-83383888	http://7j.sinohydro.com

续表

序号	单位名称	主要领导及总工程师	地　址	邮　编	电　话	传　真	网　址
8	中国水利水电第八工程局有限公司	党委书记、董事长：朱素华 总工程师：涂怀健	湖南省长沙市天心区常青路8号	410004	0731-82822169	0731-85563353	http://www.baju.com.cn/web/
9	中国水利水电第九工程局有限公司	执行董事、总经理：徐鹏程 党委书记：王忠禄 总工程师：王　军	贵州省贵阳市观山湖区诚信南路501号（国际企业大厦）	550081	0851-87980581	0851-87980582	http://www.zgsdjj.com/
10	中国水利水电第十工程局有限公司	党委书记、董事长（执行董事）：何其刚 党委副书记、总经理：陈　勇 总工程师：陈　茂	四川省成都市十二桥路七号	610072	028-87772278	028-87716129	http://10j.powerchina.cn
11	中国水利水电第十一工程局有限公司	党委书记、董事长（执行董事）：张玉峰 副总经理兼总工程师：杨和明	河南省郑州市高新技术开发区莲花街59号	450001	0371-86019001	0371-86019003	http://www.cwb11.com
12	中国水利水电第十二工程局有限公司	董事长、党委书记：刘光华 总工程师：沈仲涛	浙江省杭州市环城北路141号	310004	0571-86829018	0571-86829008	http://www.water12.com
13	中国电建市政建设集团有限公司	党委书记、董事长（执行董事）、法定代表人：何占颂 副总经理兼总工程师：杨　涛	天津市华苑产业区榕苑路2号	300384	022-58569000	022-58569002	http://www.stecol.cn
14	中国水利水电第十四工程局有限公司	党委书记、董事长（执行董事）：洪　坤 总经理：王曙平 总工程师：和孙文	云南省昆明市环城东路192号	650041	0871-63335216	0871-63333460	http://14j.powerchina.cn/
15	中国水电建设集团十五工程局有限公司	董事长：梁向峰 总工程师：何小雄	陕西省西安市雁塔区科技路16号	710065	029-88758206	029-88758100	http://15j.powerchina.cn/
16	中国水利水电第十六工程局有限公司	执行董事、总经理：林文进 总工程师：吴秀荣	福建省福州市湖东路82号	350003	0591-87821294	0591-87853663	http://16j.sinohydro.com
17	中国水利水电基础局有限公司	执行董事、总经理：刘建发 总工程师：肖恩尚	天津市武清区雍阳西道86号	301700	022-29341551	022-29345523	http://jc.sinohydro.com
二	中国葛洲坝集团有限公司	董事长、法人代表、总经理：陈晓华 总工程师：郭光文	湖北省武汉市硚口区解放大道558号	430033	027-59270253	027-59270256	http://www.cggc..cn
1	中国葛洲坝集团第一工程有限公司	党委书记、董事长：陈　刚 副总经理（分管科技）：张晓瑞	湖北省宜昌市东山大道54号	443002	0717-6719353	0717-6851598	http://www.cggc1.cn/

续表

序号	单位名称	主要领导及总工程师	地址	邮编	电话	传真	网址
2	中国葛洲坝集团第二工程有限公司	党委书记、董事长：陈立新 总工程师：林本华	四川成都青羊工业发展区广富路8号C7	610091	028-68253777	028-68338401	http://www.cggc2.cn/
3	中国葛洲坝集团第三工程有限公司	集团股份公司副总经理、公司党委书记、董事长：冯兴龙 总工程师：黄河江	陕西省西安市雁塔区锦业路36号	710061	029-89678611		http://www.cggc3.cn/
4	中国葛洲坝集团三峡建设工程有限公司	董事长、党委书记：周建华 总工程师：李友华	湖北省宜昌市东山大道11号三峡大厦	443002	0717-6791338		http://www.gzbsx.cn/

（中国电力建设股份有限公司　中国葛洲坝集团有限公司）

学术团体

中国水力发电工程学会2018年工作情况

2018年，中国水力发电工程学会（简称水电学会）围绕“传承、创新、发展”的主题，积极为水电科技工作者服务、为党和政府科学决策服务、为水电企业和会员服务、为水电事业创新发展服务，团结引领广大会员和专业委员会促进科技创新，推动学术繁荣，培育创新人才，联系指导省级学会协同发展，各项工作迈上新台阶。

（一）召开八届三次理事会和3次常务理事会议，全体理事积极履职共谋发展

2018年9月26日，水电学会八届三次理事会议在北京召开，八届理事和授权代表、监事、学会专委会和省级水电学会代表约150人出席大会。张野理事长作题为《凝聚合力激发活力增添动力，竭诚服务水电清洁能源事业可持续发展》的工作报告；审议通过了学会章程增加党的建设和社会主义核心价值观内容、八届理事会部分成员变更增补、成立监事会、2017年度财务收支及2018年度预算和1～8月财务收支情况等事项。

全年根据议事需要共召开常务理事会议3次，其中2次为通信方式。审议通过的事项有：推荐科协优秀科技工作者代表、水电学会2017年度财务收支情况和2018年度预算报告、水力发电科学技术奖第二届奖励委员会组成方案、设立水电英才奖、组建清洁能源装备冷却技术专业委员会、监事会监事推荐、修订印章管理规定、财务管理办法、分支机构管理办法、分支机构经费收支管理办法、制定会计档案管理办法、八届三次理事会审议事项等。

（二）推进深化改革强化内部治理，学会发展动能不断增强

（1）社团评估和能力评估获得较高评价。积极参与民政部“社会组织评估”并获评4A等级，进一步增强了承接政府转移职能和参与政府购买社会服务的能力，提升了规范化管理水平。积极参与中国科协“综合能力评估”、申报“世界一流学会建设”项目，水电学会综合能力进入全国学会前列，并获连续3年每年100万元经费资助。

（2）继续稳步推进深化改革工作。成立了监事会，加强对理事会（常务理事会）履职、学会财务运行管理和内部治理的监督检查，促进学会健康发展。对印章管理、分支机构及其财务管理、会计档案管理、科技项目及合同管理、成果鉴定程序、秘书处人员考核等9个管理制度进行了修订、制定，进一步增强依法依规依章程办会的能力和水平。加强财务预算和决算管理，发挥监事的财务监管作用，有效防范财务风险保障学会健康发展，2012年以来连年获评中国科协全国学会财务决算工作先进单位。编制发布《学会2018年年报》，持续推进开放型学会建设，不

断扩大学会社会影响力和公信力。

（3）持续加强对分支机构的管理和加大对省级学会的联系指导。召开一年一度的水电学会专业委员会和省级水电学会秘书长工作会议，共同研究进一步加强能力建设和提高服务水平。加强对分支机构的管理指导，完善相关规章制度以提高规范化管理水平。组建清洁能源装备冷却技术专业委员会，进一步扩大专业学科覆盖面和提升学术交流水平。组织开展中国科协“学会分支机构发展现状和管理情况研究”，促进新时代社团组织分支机构创新发展。进一步密切与省级水电学会的沟通和联系，推进资源共享，共促学会工作取得新突破。不定期到专委会和省级学会调研了解情况和诉求，共促自身和行业健康发展。

（三）成功策划举办改革开放40年中国水电系列纪念活动

水电学会党委牵头研究策划了系列纪念活动，重点举办了1场改革开放40年中国水电纪念大会，召开大中型水电工程总承包论坛、风光水能互补开发研讨会、西藏水电发展论坛等3场高端学术会议，组织出版1本纪念文集和制作1部宣传片。活动共吸引400多名行业新老领导、院士专家和水电科技工作者代表积极参与，分享水电建设成就经验和未来设想，围绕当前国家政策导向和行业热点难点深入展开学术研讨，积极探寻新时代下促进行业健康发展的新思路、新途径、新突破，成果显著，极大鼓舞了广大水电工作者竭诚服务中国和“一带一路”沿线各国水电清洁能源可持续发展的信心与决心。

纪念文集征稿得到了行业新老领导和各单位的大力支持，收到投稿200多篇，经评审录用150余篇，分上、下册公开出版发行。联合水电水利规划设计总院、中央新影制作的《江河作歌　水电筑梦》宣传片，展现了改革开放40年来中国水电的巨大成就，网络传播广泛，得到了行业内外的认可。开展完成了国内大中型水电站、我国建设的国外水电站数据统计工作，以此为基础资料在今后每年滚动更新。

（四）继续搭好学术交流平台，推动学术繁荣和技术创新

（1）与国家电网共同成功举办一年一度的中国水电发展论坛暨水力发电科学技术奖颁奖典礼。300余名新老领导、院士专家和代表共同回顾过去一年我国水电事业取得的新成绩、新进展，分享行业各单位在水电科研和工程实践中取得的新成果、新经验。会上进行了2017年度水力发电科学技术奖、《水力发电学报》优秀论文奖颁奖仪式；举行了《潘家铮全集》和《谭靖夷纪念文集》赠书仪式，寄送学会全体会员单位。

（2）加强横向资源融合共促学术创新发展。与兄弟学会共同主办蒸发冷却技术在抽水蓄能机组应用评估暨推介会、2018高坝大库抗震安全国际学术研讨会，协办国际水电协会（IHA）“水电与未来能源系统北京论坛”，研讨推动蒸发冷却技术的成果转化和推广应用，论道促进水工抗震防灾关键技术创新发展，探讨加快能源转型步伐、推动实现《巴黎协定》目标承诺。会议层次高、规模大、影响广、效果好，共有400余名中外专家踊跃报名积极参会，征集中外专家学者优秀研究论文60余篇并形成论文集。

（3）大力营造各专业学科学术协同繁荣发展局面。水电学会32个分支机构积极发挥专业特色和学科带头作用，灵活组织召开大型学术年会或小型高端学术研讨，内容涉及水库移民政策研究、大中型水电站安全生产管控及应急管理、水电工程垂直升船机技术、继电保护与励磁系统运行维检修技术、水电厂智能化应用、贯流式机电设备新技术应用、新时期大坝安全监测监控与监管创新等，广泛交流探讨本专业的技术难题和发展方向，根据行业和各单位需求积极组织专家传道授业解惑，对创新技术理念、交流科技成果、促进学术繁荣等起到了积极推动作用。经统计，全年学会及分支机构共开展学术交流活动40余场·次，参会人数5200余人·次，出版论文集24部共6700册、论文1600多篇，会议交流论文480余篇。同时也存在各分支机构活跃程度不一的情况，有的全年组织2～3场学术活动，有的一场没有开展，需要进一步加强对分支机构的管理和督导，促进各专业学科协同发展。

（4）省级水电学会成为推动行业学术进步和科技创新的坚实力量。各省级学会作为我国水电行业科技社团的重要组成部分，坚持发挥学术交流基础作用，持续拓展学术进步和科技创新服务领域，新时代下群团组织在推进创新驱动发展中的优势和作用愈加显现。甘肃、福建、湖南、湖北、四川、北京、陕西、广东、青海、云南等省（市）水电学会积极转观念、抓创新、强服务、谋发展，在学术交流科技咨询、技术讲座专业培训、青年托举人才培养、水电知识技能竞赛、科技服务精准扶贫等方面积极探索发展，不断取得新成绩打开新局面。

（5）进一步加强国际科技学术交流与合作。水电学会秘书处设立国际部，聘用国际事务专员，以更好地服务中国水电走出国门、引领国际。先后接待IHA、日本三菱综合研究所等国际机构专家来访，就共同促进水电与新能源可持续发展等进行交流。组织翻译IHA《2018水电现状报告—行业趋势及思考》，收集整理形成年度电力能源国际会议指南2期，一并上传学会网站供会员单位下载使用。推进2019世界水电大会（巴黎）组团工作，申报科协民间科技组织

事务专项和青年科学家参与国际组织专项，积极促进中国工程师参与国际水电事务和国际组织任职。高坝通航专委会主任委员李云出任国际航运协会内河委员会委员，同时该专委会牵头组织成立国际航运协会升船机工作组，副主任委员胡亚安担任工作组主席，为协会成立以来首次由非欧美国家专家担任，彰显了中国水电的国际影响和实力。

（五）加强科普传播正确引导舆情，促进行业良性发展

（1）有序推进中国水电科技博物馆筹建工作。在中国长江三峡集团等单位大力支持下，完成了博物馆主体场馆建设，开展了展陈方案设计；组织召开中国水电史料及科技博物馆藏品征集研讨会，为藏品收集等博物馆筹建相关事项建言献策或提供有益线索；召开大中型水电站建设成就研讨会，加快行业信息化智能化建设管理。同时依托科协平台积极推进网上会史馆建设工作，对学会成立以来的历史资料和重大事件等系统梳理和上网，努力打造成为学会重要资料存续和对外宣传推广的新窗口，取得了排名前3的建馆成绩。

（2）挂牌水电科普教育基地。在全国科技工作者日联合常务理事单位汉能集团举行“水电与新能源科普论坛暨科普教育基地授牌仪式”，将汉能集团的清洁能源展示中心作为水电与新能源科普教育基地，为水电行业弘扬科技、宣传环保、倡导绿色增添了新平台。8月，组织接待大连理工大学“走进爱心企业传递公益能量”暑期社会实践团队参观基地并座谈。

（3）支持四川水电学会举办第五届李冰杯水利水电知识竞赛。水电学会专家出席活动并做“如何科学全面认识水电”的科普知识讲座，延续了近年来坚持开展科普进校园活动的传统。期间联合水利水电出版社，为地处全国连片深度贫困地区凉山州的西昌学院捐赠了一批水利水电专业书籍共计400余册、价值5万余元，积极支持开展教育扶贫工作；联合有关参赛院校在西昌市开展了“爱惜生命之源，关注点点滴滴”保护水资源、节约用水的宣传活动，受到了当地市民的肯定和称赞。

（4）继续多渠道推进日常宣传工作。充分发挥院士领衔的科普传播专家团队作用，及时组织召开科普论坛或撰写文章引导舆情。加强与新华网、能源报、电力报等主流传媒的合作，合力扩大水电宣传。专人管理官网“中国水电网”和微信公众号，加强日常更新和维护。重新编制纸质版《学会简讯》并发送会员单位。

（5）注重做好学术期刊和专著出版管理。学会及各分支机构依托大型学术交流研讨活动，积极组织征集出版论文集共24部。在各单位大力支持下推进编纂出版《中国水力发电年鉴　第二十二卷》（2017），持续做好行业技术管理总结积累打造科技品牌。继续加强会刊《水力发电学报》管理，努力提升学报影响力，评定好学报年度优秀论文奖。联合主办协办好《水电能源科学》等6种期刊，编辑出版《水力发电信息年报》（2018）。

（六）做好科技评奖评价和人才举荐，服务行业创新发展

（1）有序推进完成水力发电科学技术奖励委员会换届至第二届。根据奖励办法规定和国家奖励办对委员组成中院士和知名专家的比例要求，进一步充实了委员会专家力量，促进奖励工作更加规范和可持续发展。

（2）认真组织2018年水力发电科学技术奖申报和评审。共接收申报项目135项，经形式审查合格参评项目126项，成果内容涵盖了水电设计、制造、施工、运行、管理和科研等各方面。经严格有序的专业组专家网评、专家会评和奖励委员会终审，最终授奖36项成果，其中一等奖7项、二等奖9项、三等奖20项。重视和参与国家奖励办开展的社会力量设奖第三方评价，“水力发电科学技术奖”在奖励办备案的200多个奖项中位列第23，规范化运作和管理水平有了较大提升。组织做好2019年度国家科学技术奖评选申报工作，历年已有7项水力发电科学技术奖优秀成果经进一步推荐获国家科学技术奖。

（3）重视做好科技人才培养举荐工作。经学会组织专家评审，中国电建集团昆明勘测设计院有限公司张宗亮、中国水利水电第四工程局有限公司席浩、雅砻江流域水电开发有限公司陈云华获第五届潘家铮奖，中国电建集团华东勘测设计院有限公司刘宁、中国水利水电第七工程局有限公司李正兵、西南理工大学畅建霞获第五届张光斗优秀青年科技奖。应广大会员单位和工程技术人员的诉求，水电学会新设立面向水利水电工程基层一线工程师和科技人员的“水电英才奖”，将于2019年开始评奖，每年一评、每次奖励10人。做好有关奖项向国家奖励办备案以及奖励办法修制定完善工作，科学规范指导各项奖励评定工作开展。在中国科协领导下积极组织推荐亚太工程组织联合会工程师奖、联合国可持续发展目标青年工程师奖、宣传“展风采，树楷模”全国学会优秀党员科技工作者、第三届中国科协优秀科技论文，开展“引领世界科学的前沿科学问题、建设世界科技强国的工程技术难题”征集，申报青年人才托举工程、人社部专业技术人才知识更新工程、创新驱动助力工程示范项目等。

（4）科学管理运作好潘家铮水电科技基金。继续采用科学稳健的理财策略，保障本金安全，实现合理

收益，为有关奖励评定颁发等水电公益事业提供有力支撑。组织召开好一年一度的基金理事会议和秘书长工作会议，报告工作、研究不断加强和推进完善基金运作管理。继续开展大学生暑期水电社会实践教育活动，地点在大渡河流域瀑布沟、深溪沟、大岗山等水电工程，14 所高校的 24 名优秀学生参加，大力培育水电事业后备力量。开展 2018 年水电奖学金评定，并于青海大学举行了颁奖典礼。

(5) 积极推进水电专家库的更新和充实。为更加有效地发挥水电科技专家的作用，使水电科技成果评价和奖励评定等工作更具规范性、科学性和公正性，有力促进水电科技创新、科技成果转化和创新人才培养，组织对水电专家库现有专家进行了梳理、核查和确认，同时各单位推荐新专家进一步充实了专家库。

(6) 大力服务会员企业科技评价成果鉴定。制定《科学技术成果评价管理程序》进一步规范相关工作。全年组织院士专家完成来自各单位不同专业领域的技术成果鉴定 43 项，为行业企业开展科技成果评价鉴定方面的作用越来越突出，影响越来越广泛，越来越得到大家的认可和支持。

(七) 积极开展研究咨询和科技合作，为各方提供智力支持

(1) 积极开展行业发展研究和政策建言服务。加强与国家能源局等部门的联络沟通，助力推进水电发展"十三五"规划和能源技术创新规划实施。积极开展学科发展工程项目——我国应对气候变化清洁能源发展现状研究，促进水风光清洁能源互补协调发展，推进供给侧结构性改革，助力国家实现节能减排目标和《巴黎协定》国际承诺。有序推进雅砻江流域风光水能互补相关政策研究，为有关部门决策提供智力支持。

(2) 积极为企业创新发展提供科研咨询服务。发挥专委会的专家技术力量作用，围绕大中型水电工程设计施工总承包监理技术、水污染检测与防控及取水口突发事件快速处理、水电工程枢纽区地质灾害监测预警与应急管理、地质灾害隐患排查和风险评估及治理技术等大力开展咨询服务，促进企业科研创新和行业可持续发展。

(八) 加强党的建设，不断增强党组织政治核心思想引领作用

(1) 精心组织安排学习宣传贯彻十九大精神。制定十九大精神宣贯实施方案并全力推进，学会理事长、党委书记等负责人带头宣讲。在水电学会《章程》中增加党的建设和社会主义核心价值观有关内容，从源头上确保社会组织管理的正确政治方向和鲜明价值导向。

(2) 务实推进"三重一大"事项前置审议。水电学会党委积极发挥政治核心、思想引领和组织保障作用，全年共召开党委工作会议 5 次，就参与脱贫攻坚工作规划、规章制度制修订、设立水电英才奖、奖励委员会换届、水电科技博物馆筹建、成立监事会、组建新专委会、规范有关工作费用等 40 余事项进行了前置审议，有力保障了学会日常运作和健康发展。

(3) 积极组织开展好各项党建活动。水电学会党委和秘书处党支部作为试点单位积极推进中国科协"星级党组织"创建工作，并作为典型在总结会上进行交流。在分支机构中开展成立党小组试点并完成 7 家，积极推动党建工作逐步实现全覆盖。继续申报中国科协"党建强会"活动项目并获资助。组织会员参加科协第九届全国学会乒乓球赛并获团体组织奖、男单第三名的好成绩；参加"我与科协同成长"征文演讲比赛并分获一、二等奖和优秀组织奖。党支部积极推进活动常态化制度化；根据党员增加及时增补支部委员以更好地开展工作；组织召开好民主生活会，支部书记带头、全体党员轮流讲党课，使每位党员都得以锻炼和提升党性修养及担当意识。组织秘书处全体党员群众到红色传统教育基地红旗渠参观学习，弘扬先辈精神，砥砺创新发展。

(中国水力发电工程学会秘书处)

中国水力发电工程学会分支机构情况表

专委会名称	主任委员	秘书长	专业内容	挂靠单位
水能规划及动能经济专业委员会	彭才德	王海政	水能规划及动能经济	水电水利规划设计总院
水库专业委员会	彭 程	郭万侦	组织移民政策、管理、技术交流活动，开展水库经济政策研究，水库移民的调研、咨询、评估，为国家制定水库移民政策献计献策	水电水利规划设计总院

续表

专委会名称	主任委员	秘书长	专业内容	挂靠单位
环境保护专业委员会	顾洪宾	崔　磊	环境影响评价、咨询，环境保护设计，水土保持方案设计	水电水利规划设计总院
水文泥沙专业委员会	万文功	杨百银	水文、泥沙专业的学术交流和技术总结	水电水利规划设计总院
地质及勘探专业委员会	袁建新	张东升	水电水利工程地质、测绘、物探、钻探、岩土试验专业的学术交流	水电水利规划设计总院
水工及水电站建筑物专业委员会	李　昇	孙保平	水工	水电水利规划设计总院
水工水力学专业委员会	刘之平	章晋雄	水工水力学	中国水利水电科学研究院
高坝通航工程专业委员会	李　云	宣国祥	通航技术交流、通航科技发展战略及政策咨询、委托项目论证	南京水利科学研究院
碾压混凝土筑坝专业委员会	宗敦峰	郑桂斌	碾压混凝土筑坝技术（坝工、材料、运行、建设管理等）	中国安能建设总公司
混凝土面板堆石坝专业委员会	杨泽艳	王富强	混凝土面板堆石坝设计、施工、材料、变形观测、运行管理等技术交流、咨询	水电水利规划设计总院
水工金属结构专业委员会	龚建新	林朝晖	水利水电工程闸门及其启闭设备、通航设备的设计、制造、安装及验收	水电水利规划设计总院
水力机械专业委员会	赵　琨	戴康俊	水力机械设计、试验、安装、运行、改造	水电水利规划设计总院
电气专业委员会	于庆贵	郑　琳	电气一次专业	水电水利规划设计总院
自动化专业委员会	吴维宁	刘观标	水电新能源自动化及信息化相关内容	南瑞集团有限公司（国网电力科学研究院有限公司）
继电保护专业委员会	毕亚雄	张　舸	发电机、变压器和高压线路的继电保护	中国长江电力股份有限公司溪洛渡水力发电厂
施工专业委员会	宗敦峰	楚跃先	水利水电施工	中国电力建设股份有限公司
工程造价专业委员会	王忠耀	郭建欣	工程造价、工程经济技术管理	水电水利规划设计总院
信息化专业委员会	胡春宏	袁　宏	计算机及自动化技术在水电工程规划、设计、施工及电站运行中的应用	中国水利水电科学研究院
水电站运行管理专业委员会	裴哲义	李晓斌	水电站运行管理、水库经济运行	国家电网有限公司国家电力调度控制中心
电网调峰与抽水蓄能专业委员会	林铭山	郝荣国	开展抽水蓄能电站建设必要性、经济合理性及优化布局的研讨，介绍先进技术，组织学术交流，承接站点规划和技术咨询服务	中国电建集团北京勘测设计研究院有限公司

续表

专委会名称	主任委员	秘书长	专业内容	挂靠单位
大坝安全专业委员会	张秀丽	许传桂	涉及运行维护、安全监测、安全评价、补强加固、缺陷处理、应急管理等相关业务领域	国家能源局大坝安全监察中心
水电控制设备专业委员会	王德宽	刘同安	水轮机调节系统、发电机励磁系统、水轮发电机组自动化元件（装置）及其系统、智能仪表等	中国水利水电科学研究院
抗震防灾专业委员会	李德玉	欧阳金惠	大型水利水电工程、大电网的抗震防灾科学技术、预案及对策研究，大型水利水电工程振动安全与减振技术研究	中国水利水电科学研究院
电力系统自动化专业委员会	程永权	谢秋华	水电厂自动化系统，自动调压、调频装置，水电长距离输电稳定装置	中国长江三峡集团公司
梯级调度控制专业委员会	肖　舸	王玉华	流域梯级调度控制、流域水资源运用	中国长江电力股份有限公司
机械疏浚专业委员会	詹敏利	范志强	机械疏浚与吹填工程、水环境综合治理工程技术交流，在业内推广新技术、新工艺及新材料，向学会推荐行业内先进科学技术成果和人才等	长江水利委员会湖北长江清淤疏浚工程有限公司
小水电专业委员会	黄建平	舒　静	小水电方面学术交流、技术咨询、继续教育	水利部农村电气化研究所
水电监理专业委员会	陈东平	孙玉生	水电监理经验与技术交流，监理技术与理论研究	中国水利水电建设工程咨询北京有限公司
风险管理专业委员会	陈东平	时　斌	风险管理研究与实践，水电企业专项服务与培训及行业规范、标准的制定与推动	北京中颐允能科技有限公司
国际河流水电开发生态环境研究工作委员会	顾洪宾	周世春	组织开展澜沧江-湄公河等国际河流水电开发生态环境影响的研究工作，特别是对国际河流下游国家重点关注的问题进行长期跟踪和研究，同时组织开展或参与相关国际交流活动；为政府部门提供国际河流水电开发与环境保护的技术支持和技术服务，为水电开发业主提供技术咨询和建议	水电水利规划设计总院
贯流式水电站专业委员会	黄顺明	夏红梅	贯流式水电站运行管理、设计、制造、安装及科研	广东省水力发电工程学会
清洁能源装备冷却技术专业委员会	罗　安	阮　琳	组织开展清洁能源装备冷却技术领域的学科发展研究；围绕清洁能源装备冷却技术及配套设备，组织学术交流、产品发布、科普活动、技术咨询和技术培训等活动；架设技术与产品、技术与产业应用的桥梁；传播科学方法、推广先进技术、促进技术交流与企业合作	中国科学院电工研究所

（中国水力发电工程学会秘书处　殷利利）

各省、直辖市、自治区水力发电工程学会组织情况表

名称	会员总数	理事长	秘书长	办事机构地点	邮编	学术专业设置	会刊学报
北京水力发电工程学会	1563	郝荣国	徐力波	北京市朝阳区定福庄西街1号	100024	无	无
天津市水力发电工程学会	1353	杜雷功	邵月顺	天津市河西区洞庭路60号	300222	施工及基础处理专委会 水电成套设备专委会 水工专委会 机电专委会 大坝安全监测与管理专委会 动能经济及抽水蓄能专委会 勘测专委会	《水利水电工程设计》
河北省水力发电工程学会	220	杨立波	徐学章	河北省石家庄市富强大街3号	050011	无	无
山西省水力发电工程学会	722	孙万功	程天立	山西省太原市新建北路45号	030002	水电电气自动化专委会 水工建筑及水力机械专委会 水电站运行管理专委会 农村水电电气化专委会 抽水蓄能电站专委会	《电力学报》（双月刊）
江苏省水力发电工程学会	970	朱跃龙	顾圣平	江苏省南京市西康路1号河海大学水电馆314室	210098	水工结构专委会 水工水力学专委会 仪器仪表专委会 水电站运行调度专委会 自动化专委会 水力机械与系统专委会 青年工作委员会 科普工作委员会	无
上海市水力发电工程学会	292	李　巍	李健英	上海市临新路65弄	200335	无	《上海水利水电技术》
浙江省水力发电工程学会	1800	施俊跃	郑雄伟	浙江省杭州市上城区抚宁巷66号	310002	绿色水电专委会 大坝安全监测专委会 水电站运行管理专委会 机电设备专委会	《浙江水利水电》（内刊，学会通讯）
安徽省水力发电工程学会	764	杜贵和	谢　辉	安徽省合肥市黄山路9号	230022	水工专委会 小水电专委会 水电站运行专委会	无

续表

名称	会员总数	理事长	秘书长	办事机构地点	邮编	学术专业设置	会刊学报
福建省水力和清洁能源发电工程学会	1045	杜将武	陈瑞兴	福建省福州市湖东路231号前田大厦22楼	350013	水能及新能源规划专业委员会 工程勘查专委会 水工及水电站建筑物专委会 水力机械及金属结构专委会 水电站电气及自动化专委会 水电建设管理专委会 水电站运行管理专委会 施工机械及施工管理专委会 水库经济专委会 水电厂防汛及水库调度专委会 清洁能源专委会 《福建水力发电》编委会 《福建水力发电》编辑部 学术工委会 科普工委会 组织工委会	《福建水力发电》
河南省水力发电工程学会	1360	张金良	景来红	河南省郑州市金水路109号	450003	水能规划及动能经济专委会 水工及水电站建筑物专委会 水电站电气及自动化专委会 施工机械及施工管理专委会 水电站运行管理专委会 水工金属结构专委会 中小型水电专委会 地质专委会 青年工作委员会 泥沙专业委员会	无
湖北省水力发电工程学会	5014	常晓林	何金平	湖北省武汉市东湖南路8号武汉大学工学部第八教学楼	430072	水能规划及动能经济专委会 水工及水电站建筑物专委会 水工水力学专委会 水利水电工程施工专委会 水电站电气及自动化专委会 水电站运行管理专委会 水力机械专委会 中小水电专委会	《水电与新能源》
湖南省水力发电工程学会	2459	傅　胜	李蓓蓉	湖南省长沙市雨花区香樟东路16号	410014	水电站运行管理专委会 施工专委会 小水电及农村电气化专委会 水能规划与动能经济专委会 库区经济专委会 水工及水电站建筑专业委员会 勘测专业委员会 水电水利信息技术专业委员会 环境保护专委会 新能源专业委员会	《中南水力发电》
广东省水力发电工程学会	1760	李承军	夏红梅	广东省广州市天河区天河东路2号	510630	水能利用专委会 水工及水电站建筑专委会 水电建设管理及施工专委会 水电站运行与自动化专委会 风电及新能源专委会 光伏及再生能源专委会	无

续表

名称	会员总数	理事长	秘书长	办事机构地点	邮编	学术专业设置	会刊学报
广西水力发电工程学会	2766	陶先文	黄庭文	广西南宁市民主路6号	530023	水能规划及动能经济专委会 地质勘测专委会 水工及水电站建筑物专委会 水力机械专委会 金属结构专委会 水电站电气及自动化专委会 施工专委会 水电站运行管理专委会 小水电及农村电气化专委会 风险管理专委会 水电厂防汛及水库调度专委会 信息化专委会 工程造价专委会 电气及自动化专委会	《红水河》
四川省水力发电工程学会	3016	涂扬举	朱永国	四川省成都市天韵路7号	610041	地质勘测与灾害治理专委会 环境保护与移民专委会 电力市场专委会 施工与建设专委会 水电站运行与检修专委会 水工及水电站建筑物专委会	《四川水力发电》
贵州省水力发电工程学会	2292	张志强	谌　波	贵州省贵阳市新华路9号	550002	水库专委会 水电站管理专委会 学术工作委员会 水资源及水能规划专委会 水工与水电站建筑专委会 环境与资源专委会 地质及勘察专业委员会 小水电技术专业委员会 科普工作委员会 梯级调度控制专业委员会 水电站自动化专业委员会	《贵州水力发电》
云南省水力发电工程学会	2176	张　虹	李静涛	云南省昆明市拓东路73号	650011	水工及水电站建筑物专委会 水能规划及动能经济专委会 水电站电气及自动化专委会 水力机械及金属结构专委会 施工机械及施工管理专委会 水电站运行管理专委会 工程经济定额预算专委会 地质及勘测专委会	《云南水力发电》 《云南省水力发电工程学会简报》
陕西省水力发电工程学会	2074	马海晨	沈兴正	陕西省西安市丈八东路18号	710065	水工专委会 规划动能经济专委会 工程地质勘测专委会 机电运行专委会 水电站施工专委会 工程造价专委会 水电站自动化专委会 水库及环保专委会 新能源专委会 青年科技工作委员会 咨询工作委员会 科普工作委员会	内部期刊《学会简讯》、学会为《西北水电》支持办刊单位

续表

名称	会员总数	理事长	秘书长	办事机构地点	邮编	学术专业设置	会刊学报
甘肃省水力发电工程学会	1729	李永清	秦　睿	甘肃省兰州市安宁区万新北路249号	730000	水电站建筑与施工管理专委会 地质及勘探专委会 动能经济及水库调度专委会 水力机械及金属结构专委会 水电站运行管理专委会 风力发电专委会	内部期刊《西部可再生能源与微电网》
宁夏水力发电工程学会	350	田军仓	王红雨	宁夏银川市贺兰山西路539号宁夏大学土木与水利工程学院	750021	水电站运行专委会 水力机械气蚀磨损专委会 电气自动化专委会 工程地质与水工专委会 风力发电及新能源专委会	无
青海省水力发电工程学会	2018	王思德	曹光明	青海省西宁市五四西路43号	810008	小水电专委会 水工专委会 工程造价专委会 水能专委会	《青海水力发电》

（中国水力发电工程学会秘书处　殷利利）

中国水力发电工程学会成功举办改革开放40年中国水电系列纪念活动

为总结回顾改革开放以来我国水电事业取得的成就和经验，传承弘扬中国水电的改革创新和拼搏奋斗精神，谋划中国水电和新能源事业迈向更好更高质量发展，中国水力发电工程学会党委牵头研究策划了系列纪念活动，重点举办了1场改革开放40年中国水电纪念大会，召开了大中型水电工程总承包论坛、风光水能互补开发研讨会、西藏水电发展论坛等3场高端学术会议，组织出版了1本纪念文集和制作了1部宣传片。活动共吸引400多名行业新老领导、院士专家和水电科技工作者代表积极参与，分享水电建设成就经验和未来设想，围绕当前国家政策导向和行业热点难点深入展开学术研讨，积极探寻新时代下促进行业健康发展的新思路、新途径、新突破，成果显著，极大鼓舞了广大水电工作者竭诚服务中国和“一带一路”沿线各国水电清洁能源可持续发展的信心与决心。

纪念文集征稿得到了行业新老领导和各单位的大力支持，收到投稿200多篇，经评审录用150余篇，分上、下册公开出版发行。联合水电水利规划设计总院、中央新影制作的《江河作歌　水电筑梦》宣传片，展现了改革开放40年来中国水电的巨大成就，网络传播广泛，得到了行业内外的认可。

开展完成了国内大中型水电站、我国建设的国外水电站数据统计工作，以此为基础资料在今后每年滚动更新。

（中国水力发电工程学会）

中国水力发电工程学会大型水电工程建设总承包论坛在北京召开

2018年7月26日，大型水电工程建设总承包论坛在北京召开，会议由中国水力发电工程学会主办，雅砻江流域水电开发有限公司承办，中国水利水电第七工程局有限公司、中国电建集团华东勘测设计研究院有限公司、中国水力发电工程学会施工专委会协办。来自水电开发、设计、施工、运行管理、行业中介机构和媒体等40余家单位的100多名领导、专家和代表，交流分享改革开放40年来我国水电体制和建设管理模式改革发展的实践经验，深入探讨展望如何促进工程总承包这一国际通行的建设项目组织实施方式的推广应用，更好地发挥总承包企业的技术和管理优势，推动产业转型升级，竭诚服务于中国及“一带一路”沿线各国大型水电工程建设健康发展。

水电学会理事长张野、中国电建股份副总经理姚强、原中国水电顾问集团总经理李菊根分别作讲话。张野指出，改革开放40年来，中国水电体制机制改革释放科技创新的巨大活力，水电开发建设管理模式变迁见证水电事业的科学发展。水电规模和发电量从改革开放初期1978年的装机容量1727万kW、年发电量446亿kW·h，发展为2017年底装机容量34119万kW、年发电量11945亿kW·h，分别增长了近19倍和26倍，约占全球水电总装机容量的1/3、水电总发电量的29%。水电作为社会综合效益巨大的清洁能源，为国家节能减排、防洪抗旱、供水灌溉、航运旅游、地方经济社会发展做出了重要贡献。2016年国家发布《关于进一步推进工程总承包发展的若干意见》，对深化改革工程建设管理模式和推广工程总承包制具有积极指导意见，而杨房沟水电站开创了国内百万千瓦级大型水电工程实施总承包的先河，是我国大型水电工程建设管理模式的大胆创新和尝试。

大会共邀请9个主题报告，包括杨房沟水电站EPC建设管理、做大做优承包模式实现项目价值最大化、阻碍工程总承包发展的突出问题即对策建议、大型水电站工程EPC总承包管理实践、践行“一带一路”倡议推动中国电建海外水电投资业务持续健康快速发展、水电工程建设总承包实践经验与思考、海外EPC总承包工程实践等。报告内容丰富精彩，提出的问题直面未来发展难点，抛出的思考建议引发强烈共鸣。

讨论交流环节，与会专家代表展开热烈讨论和广泛交流，围绕水电工程总承包现状及未来发展，从体制机制变革、技术创新、管理心得、价值实现等多个方面碰撞出智慧的火花。

论坛还广泛开展了论文征集工作，共收到并录用论文103篇，将交由出版社正式出版发行。

（中国水力发电工程学会）

中国大坝工程学会 2018年工作情况

（一）党建领航，协同争先，积极开创社团改革发展新局面

（1）强化理论学习，发挥党组织“领头雁”作用。学会功能型党委按照“党委委员带头讲、会员代表广泛讲、学会平台落地讲、专题座谈深入讲、基层组织系列讲、媒体联动合力讲”的总体布局，开展了十九大精神宣传教育活动。通过微信公众号平台，及时向会员单位和个人会员推送《宪法》修正案学习资料。与北京师范大学联合主办第一期“水科学名人大讲堂”，特邀生态环境部副部长、九三学社中央副主席、第十三届全国政协常委黄润秋，围绕“学习贯彻习近平生态文明思想，以防范流域生态风险促进国家生态安全”做主题讲座。传达学习习近平总书记在深入推动长江经济带发展座谈会、考察三峡工程、庆祝改革开放40周年大会等的重要讲话精神；组织党员参观“真理的力量——纪念马克思诞辰200周年主题展览”；在北京宋庆龄故居开展“不忘初心，重温入党志愿书”主题党日活动。

（2）着力机构建设，发挥党组织战斗堡垒作用。通过建立党委工作机制，进一步推动了学会党委工作的制度化、规范化，促进了学会党委作用的充分发挥；通过认真执行“三会一课”制度，不断强化学会基层党组织建设。

（3）激发党组织活力，发挥“党建强会”作用。学会通过自媒体平台开设“致敬前辈”专栏，组织开展老一辈坝工专家典型事迹宣讲活动；结合“展风采，树楷模”活动，宣传水利水电专家在涉水领域方面的科技创新成就。赴贵州雷山县，开展主题为“成长路上，与你同行”的教育扶贫关爱活动；派代表赴广西河池市金城江区实地慰问通过中国少年儿童基金会的“春蕾计划”资助的10名广西女童。此外，学会成为水利部重庆市丰都县“八大工程”的帮扶单位；多次组织专家对贵州雷山县采用胶结坝的猫猫河山塘工程的设计、施工进行指导，并派人长期驻扎工程现场进行技术把关和施工质量控制。广泛开展“建家交友”活动，举办第二届全国大坝工程师乒乓球大赛，举办在线桥牌锦标赛并建立微信交流群，不断搭建会员交流平台。

（二）搭建平台，促进创新，推动水库大坝高质量发展

（1）2018年10月15～16日，中国大坝工程学会2018学术年会暨第十届中日韩坝工学术交流会在郑州召开，会议主题是“绿色和高质量的建设管理推动大坝安全和河流健康”，共有820名中外专家、学者参加，会议设有3个技术分会和5个专题研讨会。大会期间成立了中国大坝工程学会大坝数值模拟专业委员会，并举办“数值模拟进展与展望专题研讨会”。此次会议共收到中外论文208篇，共邀请到学术报告160多个；23家单位参加会间技术展览。

（2）5月10～11日，学会主办的第七届水库大坝新技术推广研讨会在成都召开，340余人参加。会议收集论文89篇，共邀请36位专家做了报告。报告围绕水利水电工程数字化、智能化建设与运行，大坝的检测、安全评估与修补加固，水库的清淤疏浚、污染治理与资源化利用，胶结颗粒料坝筑坝技术进展等议题展开研讨。

（3）5月12日，在第十个全国“防灾减灾日”之际，学会在四川成都共同发起举办“汶川地震十周年国际研讨会暨第四届大陆地震研讨会”。国务委员王勇出席研讨会开幕式，宣读了国家主席习近平的致

信并致辞。本次会议以“与地震风险共处”为主题，共计5个专题，35个分会场。与会代表和专家围绕地震科学研究热点、地震安全服务、应急救援等领域开展深入交流和研讨。

（4）5月12～13日，学会与中国水力发电工程学会主办的“高坝大库抗震安全国际学术研讨会”在四川成都举行。此会议也是“汶川地震十周年国际研讨会暨第四届大陆地震研讨会”的专题会场之一。共收集论文64篇，邀请18位专家作了为期两天的大会报告。

（5）10月18～19日，中国工程院主办、学会承办的“水资源高效利用与土木工程新技术国际研讨会”和“流域水循环调控工程安全与防灾减灾国际研讨会”在北京召开。来自17个国家和地区的200余名专家、学者参加会议。8位中外院院士及国际组织领导人作主旨报告，9位国内外知名专家学者作特邀学术报告，分享了在水资源高效利用与工程防灾方面的新理念、新技术和新方法。

（三）评选奖项，凝练成果，促进科技创新和人才发展

（1）学会推荐的由中国水利水电科学研究院、南京水利科学研究院、中国电建集团等单位共同完成的《高混凝土面板堆石坝关键技术创新》荣获首届国际大坝委员会科技创新奖。本次各国推荐共29个项目参评，4个项目获此殊荣。

（2）2018年度，学会向国家奖励委员会办公室提名的“三峡水库与下游河道泥沙调控关键技术及应用”“300m级特高拱坝安全控制关键技术及工程应用”项目获得国家科技进步奖二等奖。

（3）学会推荐的中国华能集团有限公司副总经理樊启祥，成为2018年“杰出工程师奖”获奖人。

（4）学会推荐的糯扎渡水电站、锦屏一级水电站成功获得第十五届中国土木工程詹天佑奖。学会推荐小湾、锦屏二级参加第十六届中国土木工程詹天佑奖评选，已确定为入选获奖工程并通过公示。

（5）2018年，经由学会推荐的“黄河下游河道综合治理关键技术研究及推广应用”获第十二届产学研合作创新成果一等奖。

（6）2018年，中国大坝工程学会开展了科技进步和技术发明奖的评选。共有42个项目参加评选。经评审，分别有3、5、17个项目获得学会科技进步奖特等奖和一、二等奖；并分别有1、3个项目获得技术发明奖一、三等奖。

（7）组织评选第二届大坝杰出工程师奖，最终中国电力建设集团有限公司宗敦峰、南京水利科学研究院蔡跃波、水利水电规划设计总院刘志明、雅砻江流域水电开发有限公司王继敏和中国电建集团昆明勘测设计研究院有限公司张宗亮获此殊荣。

（8）组织评选第八届汪闻韶院士青年优秀论文奖，最终评选出优秀论文3篇。

（四）拓宽渠道，强化宣传，为行业发展营造良好舆论氛围

（1）2018年，学会主办的微信公众号继续保持每周1～2期资讯推送频率，至2018年底已连续发布455期资讯。组织编印《大坝新闻》纸质参刊，寄送有关政府部门和会员单位领导、专家。

（2）打造网上会史馆，大力宣传学会在推动学科发展、学术交流、科技创新、成果转化、科技咨询、科学普及、人才成长、科技奖励、国际交往等方面作出的历史性突出贡献。学会网上会史馆在全国211家学会当中排名第24位。

（3）加强与主流媒体合作，加大对学会开展的相关活动的报道，开展专访或专题活动。

（4）围绕社会热点科学引导舆论。2018年7月23日，老挝Xe Pian-Xe Namnoy水电站桑南内水库副坝溃坝产生约6亿m^3洪水。学会密切关注，专业分析，并通过微信公众号发布文章，正确引领舆论导向。

（5）设立首批水库大坝科普教育基地。分别为：“三峡工程展览馆”、糯扎渡水电站“两站一园”“澎湃雅砻江展厅”和“大渡河智慧企业展厅”。以此为窗口，让更多的公众走进工程，实现与水库大坝的亲密接触。

（6）积极利用《学会名片》（中、英文版）小视频、会场展览、会议材料广告插页等多种宣传方式，开展学会自身宣传推广。

（7）开展水库大坝专题科普活动。3月，开展“知名学者看三峡”活动；4月，开展学会公众认知论坛策划和推广长江三峡中华鲟放流活动；5月，举行“中国工程院院士三峡行”活动。开展60余名师生“三峡娃娃行——童心圆梦溪洛渡”及35名青少年“三峡娃娃行”宜昌水电夏令营扶贫、扶智、扶志活动，组织清华大学30位学子分批前往老挝、厄瓜多尔及乌干达等开展水电基地参观实习活动，均被评选为2018年全国科普日优秀活动。

（五）凝聚力量，积极拓展，不断深化多双边交流合作

（1）支持中国专家国际任职，积极发挥在国际坝工领域的作用。学会副秘书长周建平担任国际大坝委员会副主席以来，积极履职。学会主导承办的国际大坝委员会亚太地区分会会议在奥地利召开，提议的“亚太地区国家大坝安全调查研究”，被纳入未来2年的工作计划。国际大坝委员会设置26个专委会，学会推荐我国专家参加了23个，其中胶结坝、水电站

与水库联合运行、水库大坝移民3个专委会主席由我国专家担任。

（2）积极组织和参与国际会议，搭建多边交流合作平台。主要有：①国际大坝委员会第26届大会暨第86届年会于2018年7月1～7日在奥地利维也纳召开，学会副理事长兼秘书长贾金生率中国70多名专家、代表参加；大会共收录了来自36个国家的227篇论文，其中中国专家论文20篇，论文数居第二；大会4个议题之一的小坝与堤防会议，由中国专家徐泽平主持，并有5位中国专家作报告；在水利水电工程国际研讨会上，有7位中国专家作了交流报告。②12月，国际大坝委员会举办了纪念成立90周年的大坝可持续发展论坛，学会组团参加，并制作了庆贺国际大坝委员会成立90周年、反映中国水库大坝成就的专题视频，在大会播放，反响良好。③组团参加突尼斯梅莱格大坝工程筑坝技术交流咨询会，经现场勘察，深入沟通和研讨，就相关技术问题达成了一致意见，推动了我国承建的梅莱格大坝建设项目的顺利进行。④10月16～17日，学会主办的第十届中日韩坝工学术交流会在河南郑州举行，30多位专家分别就水库大坝建设技术创新、运行管理和修补加固、抽水蓄能电站建设和运行、生态环保与可持续发展等议题在会上了交流报告。⑤10月16日，学会主办的第十一届“非洲水库大坝与水电可持续发展圆桌会议”在河南郑州召开，会议聚焦高质量发展中的水库大坝建设新理念、新技术。

（3）加强长期合作机制建设，推动人才培训和交流互访。主要有：①在国际大坝委员会第26届大会期间，与美国大坝学会、西班牙大坝委员会、巴西大坝委员会、加拿大大坝委员会就未来在大坝安全方面的合作进行了商谈，进一步巩固了合作交流机制，明确了未来合作的重点领域。②10月22日，西班牙大坝委员会董事会董事CifresGimenez Enrique来访，与学会就续签双方合作协议进行了商谈。③7月3日，分别与埃及大坝委员会和伊朗大坝委员签订了合作框架协议，将在坝工技术领域进行深入的合作交流并开展年轻工程师的技术培训。

（六）服务科技，团结奋斗，荣获多项中国科协荣誉

（1）经过项目申报、资格审查、专家评审和结果公示，学会获得第三期全国学会能力提升专项“世界一流学会建设项目”第三类项目支持，进入中国科协所属210家全国学会中排名前20%学会行列。

（2）2018年度，学会再接再厉，成为第四届中国科协青年人才托举工程的实施单位。中国水利水电科学研究院韩瑞和南京水利科学研究院的王智源两位博士经学会推选获得资助。

（3）由学会推荐的中国电力建设股份有限公司总工程师、学会副秘书长周建平，经过中国科协遴选当选为全国百名科技工作者的杰出代表之一，应邀出席5月30日召开的“纪念改革开放40周年、中国科协成立60周年暨百名科学家、百名基层科技工作者座谈会”。

（4）为纪念中国科协成立60周年，2018年9月，由中国科协科技社团党委主办的“我与科协同成长”征文演讲比赛在北京举办。经多轮选拔和激烈角逐，学会对外联络部主任周虹以《聆听智者》为题，荣获演讲比赛一等奖和优秀征文奖。

（5）2018年1月，经中国科协评审，学会被评为“2017年度全国学会科普工作优秀单位”。12月，学会荣获2018年全国科普日活动优秀组织单位。

（6）学会积极参与中国科协活动，如“不忘初心牢记使命——党的十九大精神知识竞答”“第七届中国科普摄影大赛”等主题活动，以及公众科学传播专题班、科协社团学术沙龙、年鉴培训班和科学家精神座谈会等活动。9月，组织参加中国科协全国学会乒乓球赛（第九届），取得较好成绩，并再次被授予“团体组织奖”。12月，经层层选拔，学会对外联络部主任周虹担任中国科协会史陈列馆讲解员，并在中国科协成立60年文艺汇演和弘扬新时代科学家精神座谈会上，分别进行了配乐诗朗诵《致敬》和《六十年光辉岁月》。

（七）建言献策，强化支撑，为水利水电科学发展服务

（1）承担完成了《水利工程质量检测管理规定》修订项目。完成了《〈水利工程质量检测管理规定〉修订研究报告》。提交的相关修订意见被《水利部关于发布水利工程质量检测单位资质等级标准的公告》（水利部公告〔2018〕3号）采用。

（2）参与《安全生产监管信息化工程（一期）水利部建设项目》的决策支持、安全检查等7个子系统的设计开发工作，提出水利安全生产评估与预警指标体系与核心评估模型。2018年，参与开发的系统已通过初步验收并投入试运行。

（3）承担全国病险水库水闸除险加固项目管理平台的开发维护。2018年，开展了全国各地病险水库、水闸除险加固摸底数据统计汇总、数据校核工作。

（4）推动了高坝抗震、高边坡安全、胶结坝、水下清淤及检测修补加固、高坝结构与材料、堰塞坝、堰塞湖、江河治理等项目立项，为行业科技发展提供了有力支持。在贵阳、重庆、拉萨、成都等地组织召开了多次新技术推广、培训会，得到各方好评。

（八）分支机构活跃，学术交流活动丰富多彩

（1）2018年5月5～6日，中国大坝工程学会流

域水循环与调度专委会和沈阳市科技局在沈阳组织召开了“第一届水资源调度系统研发及应用技术研讨会”，20余位业内专家做了主旨报告。10月17日，该专委会在北京组织召开了“水系统调度国际研讨会暨中国大坝工程学会流域水循环与调度专委会2018年学术年会”，来自国内外的相关专家、学者从陆地水循环遥感与模拟、气象水文预报、风光水多能互补、提高清洁能源转化效率、城市水系统调度与管理、水库泥沙调控与生态调度等角度作了主旨报告。

(2) 6月5～7日，学会水库泥沙处理与资源利用技术专业委员会在新疆和田举办2018年学术研讨会，围绕“水库安全运行与淤积防治”开展现场调研和学术研讨。6位专家作了专题报告，介绍了目前最新工程进展和研究探索。

(3) 7月12～13日，重大水利水电工程智能建设与管理关键技术交流会在天津召开。会上宣读了智能建设与管理专业委员会成立公函。技术交流会围绕智慧大坝、流域工程智慧建设、大坝智能化监控及大坝建设智能仿真技术开展交流。

(4) 10月15日，中国大坝工程学会水库大坝公众认知论坛在郑州举行。共30余名专家出席会议，围绕开展水库大坝公众沟通、维护公共关系、维护企业品牌的经验交流发言。

(5) 10月16日，学会数值模拟进展与展望专题研讨会在郑州召开。80余位委员代表出席会议。会上，3位专家作了特邀报告，16位专家学者作了交流报告，介绍了各自在数值模拟技术及应用方面、水库泥沙处理与资源利用方向的最新进展和思考。

(6) 10月16日，学会水库泥沙处理与资源利用技术专委会2018学术年会在郑州召开。来自10余家单位的代表围绕“水库淤积控制与可持续管理”这一主题作了14场精彩的学术报告。

(7) 11月19日，学会生态环境工程专委会学术会议在郑州召开。2位专家分别作了题为《高坝大库的河流生态环境效应》和《黄河下游宽滩空间生态廊道建设关键科技支撑》的报告。

(8) 12月3日，由学会大坝管理新技术产学研分会举办的首届水库大坝管理新技术研讨会在四川省成都市召开。43家单位的120余名代表出席了会议。15名专家作大会主旨及专题学术报告。

（九）完善组织机构，强化社团能力建设

1. 机构建设　2018年，学会新增设立了监事会；新增设立了大坝数值模拟、智能建设与管理、环境生态工程、大坝管理新技术产学研分会、水工混凝土建筑物检测与修补加固等5个专业委员会，学会分支机构达11个。同时，加大会员发展，至12月底，新增单位会员10家（共计225家），新增个人会员6432人（共计10022人）。

2. 制度建设　2018年，制定并经理事会通过了中国大坝工程学会分支机构管理评价办法、分支机构财务管理办法、监事会工作规则、科技进步奖奖励办法、技术发明奖奖励办法、固定资产管理办法、对外投资管理制度、财务信息监督、公开制度、项目管理办法、合同管理办法等规章制度。

3. 能力建设　2018年，通过强化学会制度化建设和进一步完善学会秘书处管理机制，通过工作实践和交流培训，逐步形成分工明确、精诚合作的团队，提升了为会员单位服务的力度和水平。同时，加强信息化建设，完成了基于互联网＋的水利水电技术服务平台一期建设，形成了“学会动态”“工程智库”“工程医院”“科技奖励”“会议管理”5大服务系统。

4. 数据库建设　学会建立和不断完善的世界大坝数据库已达13万座。

（中国大坝工程学会秘书处）

中国水利学会2018年工作情况

（一）服务创新型国家和社会建设

受水利部委托，承担水利技术标准日常管理工作，共完成152项在编标准管理和30项标准报批稿审定等工作，发布10项国家标准和19项水利行业标准，报批9项国家标准；开展《水利标准化工作管理办法》修订工作，完成报批稿。在团体标准研制方面，根据市场需求和团体会员实际情况，组织开展《生态护坡预制混凝土装配式护岸技术规程》等11项团体标准的立项论证，发布6项团体标准；与中国工程建设标准化协会签订团体标准战略合作协议，并联合发布《预制混凝土板桩式挡土墙技术规程》；中国水利学会团体标准《农村饮水安全评价准则》被水利部、国家扶贫办、国家卫健委三部委发文采信，作为全国脱贫攻坚成效考核的评价标准。

组织完成了2018年度水利职称考试工作，共有3845人参加了考试。

10月10～12日，2018年中国水博览会暨第十三届中国水务高峰论坛在北京展览馆成功举办。展会设置水务设备与技术、节水设施与饮水安全、水生态建设与水环境治理、智慧水利、防灾减灾设施与技术五大展区。展览面积15000m^2，参展企业108家，约11000人·次参观了展览。

（二）能力提升

成功申请中国科协世界一流学会项目。按照《项目合同书》要求，认真开展了各项工作：一是加强学会党建工作。修改完善《中国水利学会章程》，强化党的工作对学会的有效覆盖。结合中国科协和水利部重点工作任务，开展“重温入党志愿书”、知识竞赛等多次党建活动。二是提供精准多元的会员服务产品，修订了《中国水利学会会员管理办法》。资助该会举办的“水利青年科技论文（英文）竞赛”一等奖获得者赴巴拿马参加世界水大会。三是打造世界知名学术活动品牌。邀请重要涉水国际组织领导人出席学会年会并作学术报告。邀请外籍青年科技工作者和学生参加年会“水利科技青年论文（英文）竞赛”。四是推进科技期刊建设。开发涉水期刊门户网站，建立涉水期刊数据库和期刊群。五是设立具有国际影响力的科技奖项。邀请台港澳地区涉水科技成果完成单位申报大禹奖。六是建设国际权威的智库品牌。与国际水利与环境工程学会签订战略合作备忘录。成功竞选世界水理事会董事。启动修订学会团体标准管理办法。七是提供优质普惠的科普服务。9月18日，顺利承办“世界公众科学素质促进大会水利分会场”。开展了3次“中国水之行”大型公益科普活动。八是构建开放共享的产学融合服务平台。

（三）学会建设

召开十届七次、八次、九次常务理事会通讯会议，决定增补4名理事、2名常务理事，变更3名理事、2名常务理事、1名兼职副秘书长，新增51个单位会员，确认恢复2个专委会，审议通过有关制度办法等。召开十届十次理事会暨2018年党委会现场会，审议通过了2018年度学会工作总结和年度财务报告、2019年度计划等事项。

加强了分支机构管理。印发《中国水利学会分支机构管理办法》《中国水利学会分支机构财务管理细则》。接收8个新增专委会的申请，批复5个专委会的换届方案。建立分支机构、地方学会、单位会员联络员制度。在广西南宁举办分支机构和地方水利学会专兼职人员培训班。

5月18日，在重庆召开了分支机构和地方水利学会秘书长工作座谈会。中国水利学会秘书长汤鑫华作关于习近平治水兴水思想的专题报告。会议向参会代表介绍了学会一年来的工作情况、面临的新形势和新要求、今后一个时期的工作思路和主要任务等，围绕学会党建工作及会员服务、建立激励约束机制等进行了讨论。150余名代表参加会议。

（四）承担有关工作

1. 青年人才托举工程　在中国科协第一届青年人才托举工程项目测评中荣获第一届中国科协青年人才托举工程优秀项目实施单位称号。7月，学会启动了第四届青年人才托举工程（2018～2020）申报，并获得7个名额免答辩成绩。此外，学会还举办了青年人才学术交流会，申办了中国科协青年科学家论坛项目，全面助力青年人才的成长。

2. 主办期刊　学会主办的科技期刊共6种。2018年《水利学报》再次获得“2018年度中文科技期刊精品建设计划”资助。期刊工作委员会首次组团精彩亮相刊博会，并设立水利科技期刊专区。学会按照世界一流学会建设要求，着手准备建设中国水利学会英文期刊，赴相关单位进行多次走访调研。

3. 学科发展研究　学会承担学科发展报告（2018～2019）水利学科发展报告的编写工作，成立了学科发展报告编写工作组，在《水利学科发展报告（2016～2017）》基础上，组织原编写单位进行修订、审查其中的32个专题报告和1个综合报告。新版《水利学科发展报告（2018～2019）》预计2020年出版。

4. 决策咨询　结合“中国水之行”活动，针对临清市水环境水污染方面存在的问题，组织专家给出了建议和解决办法。一是要做好总体策划和顶层设计，宏观规划和微观项目一起抓，社会、经济、环境、生态、人文协调发展，整体推进，分步实施。二是要以运河文化为龙头，做好运河文化园＋国学园＋红色（英雄）园＋专业特色文化（轴承、皇砖、国画、武术、美食等）园，在传承历史的基础上创新发展。

5. 表彰举荐优秀科技工作者　完成了2018年度大禹水利科学技术奖的评审，获奖成果共62项。开展了2018年度“刘光文水文科技教育基金”奖励组织推荐工作。会同水利部水文局和河海大学联合发文，请有关高校推荐候选人并进行评选，完成此奖项年度奖励工作。按照张光斗基金会要求，完成了2018年度张光斗优秀青年科技奖的评审工作。

（五）国际交流

1. 国际学术会议　2018年10月20～21日，在南昌举办2018学术年会国际分会场。国际分会场兼具开放、高端、创新特色，来自南京水利科学研究院、河海大学、清华大学、中国水利学会青托人才代表等国内专家以及国际水利与环境工程学会（IAHR）、日本、韩国、美国等国外水利专家学者共60余人，共同就水资源、水生态、绿色发展等国际水科学问题展开交流研讨。

9月1～5日，中国水利学会秘书长汤鑫华赴印尼日惹市参加“第21届国际水利与环境工程学会亚太大会”，在会上作题为“中国的水问题及应对策略”的主旨报告。

9月18日，由中国科协主办、学会承办的“世界公众科学素质促进大会水利专题论坛”在国家会议中心成功举办。论坛主题为“科学素质促进水利可持续发展”，邀请了加拿大国家工程院院士 Abdul Ghani

Razaqpur教授和芬兰科学与人文院院士John Moore教授等分别作水利科普专题报告，向公众普及水科学知识、提升公众水科学素质。

2. 国际组织任职　中国水利学会秘书长汤鑫华在2018年世界水理事会成功当选世界水理事会董事（董事会成员单位代表），副秘书长刘咏峰当选副董事。

3. 国际交往　2018年1月，学会在北京与IAHR签署合作备忘录。根据备忘录精神，双方将在期刊发展、人才举荐、学术交流、人才培养等多领域展开合作。2018年5月23～27日，学会组团一行3人（学会副秘书长吴剑任团长）赴韩国参加韩国水资源协会2018年会，团组成员在会上作了专题报告，并参加了技术调研。9月12～16日，学会组团一行5人（学会副秘书长刘咏峰任团长）赴日本参加日本水文水资源学会2018年会，团组成员在会上与日韩等国专家互相交流。

（六）国内交流

1. 国内主要学术会议　2018年，学会及下属专业委员会共举办国内会议50余项，共计参会人数1万余人·次，交流论文4000余篇。

10月20～22日，中国水利学会2018学术年会在南昌举行，主题为“创新助力新时代人水和谐”。会议特邀中国工程院院士、南京水利科学研究院院长张建云，中国水利水电科学研究院水资源所所长王建华等10名专家学者作主旨报告。年会将“会”“展”“赛”“服”相结合，设节水、河湖长制等19个分会场，突出多学科、多领域的交叉融合；首次举办国际化的“水利青年科技论文（英文）竞赛”及其颁奖仪式；吸引3000余名中外学者学生参会，被中国科协列为2018年学术交流重点项目和示范品牌。本次年会共收到论文1000余篇，亦创历史新高。经组织专家评审，502篇水平较高的论文入选中国水利学会2018年学术年会论文集并正式出版。年会还颁发了2018年度大禹水利科技奖。

10月10日下午，学会在中国水博览会同期举办了第十三届中国水务高峰论坛。本届论坛共设8场活动，包括1个主论坛、5个分论坛和两场技术研讨会。主论坛围绕“推动绿色发展 守护绿水青山”的主题，安排了6个特邀报告，共吸引了1500余人·次参会交流研讨，取得了良好效果。

2. 两岸交流　学会海峡两岸水利科技交流促进工作委员会为海峡两岸水利科技工作者加强合作、加深了解、共同发展搭建了重要平台。10月17日，由学会海峡两岸水利科技交流促进工作委员会承办的“传承水利 放飞梦想——第6届海峡两岸青年工程交流营”在北京召开，交流会以水科技和水工程为主线，以水文化为载体，开展专题课堂授课、讨论、实验室和试验基地参观、水利工程参访、文化参访、成果交流与总结等具体活动，突出水文化的传承和青年在水利建设中的时代责任。

（七）科普活动

2018年，中国水利学会注重创新科普手段、培训科普队伍，组织开展了一系列兼具群众性、社会性、经常性的科普活动，取得显著成绩。一是承办世界公众科学素质促进大会水利专题论坛。论坛邀请了中国工程院院士王浩等5位国内外专家作精彩报告，并交流互动。二是精心组织大型水利公益科普活动“中国水之行”。2018年分别在山东临清、山西大同和广东深圳共组织3次活动。活动将“智库建设、学术交流、科普活动”融为一体，通过邀请专家与地方政府座谈交流、实地调研、建立水科普兴趣小组、开展科普讲座等形式，向城市党政领导和群众普及水生态文明知识理念，提升水科学素养。三是积极开展形式多样、丰富多彩的活动日活动。在“世界水日”“中国水周”“全国科技周”“全国科普日”之际，组织开展各类科普活动。四是编写科普图书。组织编写了《美丽长江——长江流域水生态科普读本》，本书为“中国水之行”丛书的分册之一。五是推荐优秀科普作品。推荐的《山洪灾害防御知识读本》入选科技部2018年“全国优秀科普作品”。

（八）党建强会

2018年，学会党支部在水利部直属机关党委领导下扎实开展党建工作，始终坚持以党建促发展。一是突出两个“维护”，加强党的政治建设。二是加强党员干部的理论学习和思想武装。三是加强支部的组织制度建设。2018年，在中国科协全国学会星级党组织创建活动中获得七星级党组织荣誉。在制度建设方面，修订了支部工作规则；在完善组织体系方面，结合业务分工，把党支部全体党员划分为3个党小组。同时，按照中国科协科技社团党委的要求，协助学会党委在学会所属数10个专委会、工委会层面启动党的工作小组建设，当年已经建成6个。在丰富组织活动方面，组织各分支机构、地方学会和单位会员参加中国科协主办的“不忘初心牢记使命”——党的十九大精神知识竞答活动，获得二等奖。组织秘书处全体职工赴上海、嘉兴参观中共一大会址，赴瑞金市、赣州市联合开展党建活动，赴巫溪县开展水利定点扶贫调研，赴“一·二九”运动纪念地集体宣誓，增强党员意识。四是强化正风肃纪，加强党员日常教育管理监督。五是健全落实党建工作责任制。

按照《党政机关干部选拔任用工作条例》的精神制定实施学会在新形势下的干部职工选拔任用办法，制定实施学会秘书处绩效工资分配办法、职工年度考评办法，形成奖优罚劣、优胜劣汰、能上能下、能进能出的用人局面和激励约束机制，激发学会秘书处干部职工的积极性和创造力。

结合中国科协创新驱动工程示范项目，发挥全国性学会作用，举办主题为“创新智造·砼艺生辉”大学生水利水运装配式技术设计大赛，推广装配化技术理念，培养行业技术人才。

针对不同人群设定不同层级与服务标准，分析不同人群的需求，拓宽服务渠道，丰富会员服务手段。2018年学会走访长江水利委员会、湖北省水利厅、河海大学、南京水利科学研究院等近20余家单位会员。

（中国水利学会秘书处　李志平）

中国电机工程学会 2018年工作情况

2018年，中国电机工程学会以习近平新时代中国特色社会主义思想为指引，认真贯彻中国科协工作部署，各项工作取得显著成效。

（一）学术影响力不断提升

以“新时代，新能源，新电力”为主题召开2018年学术年会，同期举办院士专家论坛、学术建设发布会、首届两岸四地电机工程学术研讨会、女工程师论坛等30项学术活动，吸引了包括20位院士在内的2000余位科技人员参加。承办清洁高效发电技术协作网2018年年会、第二十届中国科协年会分会场——清洁低碳重大技术研讨会、2018中国遂宁绿色发展科技创新大会——清洁能源与储能分论坛、2018年电气工程学院院（校）长论坛、第十五届青年学术会议等专题学术活动。主办第八届中国国际供电会议、第十一届电力系统技术国际会议；共同主办2018“紫金论电”——智能电网保护和运行控制国际学术研讨会、第二届能源互联网与能源系统集成国际会议、美中绿色能源高峰论坛。持续打造学术报告发布常态机制，面向社会发布电力行业环境保护、水电建设等8个专业发展报告和新能源功率预测、配电网触电保护等7份专题技术报告。扎实推进科技人员职业资格认定，组织开展高校能源动力类专业工程教育认证，稳步推进电气工程专业能力评价工作。

（二）咨询服务能力不断加强

深入开展课题研究、技术咨询、成果评价、团体标准、成果登记和科技查新管理等工作。2018年承担国家发展改革委、国家能源局、中国科学院、中国科协、国家电网有限公司等单位委托的“构建我国新一代电力系统研究”“雄安新区智慧能源系统战略研究”“多种新能源发电技术路线发展研究”等项目研究。首次开展“2035、2050电力科技重大发展方向研究”“新能源消纳状况与前景”和“面向综合能源系统的节能新技术研究”3项学会重点自立课题研究。受国家能源局委托，组织开展“660MW超超临界CFB机组示范项目技术装备评估”和“燃气轮机关键部件自主化制造项目技术评审”。完成科技成果评价224项、科技成果登记474项。认真履行电力行业科技查新管理服务职能，确认电力科技查新资质机构38家。团体标准工作有序推进，2018年发布CSEE标准71项，批准立项183项，并首次启动成套系列标准编制工作。

（三）科技奖励与人才举荐成果突出

完成2018年度中国电力科学技术奖评审工作，受理推荐项目379项，授奖项目134项，其中一等奖14项、二等奖42项、三等奖78项。推荐2018年度国家科技奖，获得国家科技进步奖4项。组织完成2018年顾毓琇电机工程奖评审，西安热工研究院有限公司原副总工程师危师让获此殊荣。推荐舒印彪董事长荣获中国工程院第十二届“光华工程科技奖”，推荐郭剑波院士荣获亚太工程组织联合会2018年“年度工程师奖”。完成2018年度中国电力科学技术人物奖评审，评选出中国电力科学技术杰出贡献奖10名、中国电力优秀科技工作者奖50名、中国电力优秀青年科技人才奖50名。组织开展第四届“青年人才托举工程”（2018～2020年度），入选中国科协项目资助3人，学会项目资助21人。积极组织国家“中青年科技创新领军人才”“第十五届中国青年女科学家”和“2018年度未来女科学家计划人才”推荐工作。

（四）科普工作成效显著

组织参加中国科协2018年全国科普日北京主场活动和北京科学嘉年华活动。以“新时代、新能源、新电力、共建美好生活”为主题成功举办首届“电力之光”中国电力科普日活动，北京主会场吸引了近5000名社会公众参与，10余个省市的省学会、专委会及电力企业在全国各地开展了形式多样的科普活动。组织开展2018年中国电机工程学会“电力之光”甘肃科普下乡暨扶贫活动。组织电力科普教育基地评选，2018年“山东电力电能计量馆”等29家单位被评为“电力科普教育基地”并获授牌。组织编撰出版《国家风光储输示范工程　储存风光输送梦想》科普丛书和《电气化小分队科普故事：蓝天保卫战》科普图书。积极组织首席科学传播专家申报工作，向中国科协推荐李立浧院士、刘建明主任为首席科学传播专家并协助组建团队。

（五）期刊质量持续提高

首次开展中国电机工程学会期刊优秀论文评选，承担中国科技期刊能源、化工与环境学科年度优秀论文遴选推介工作，启动能源电力领域发布高质量科技期刊分级目录工作。《中国电机工程学报》首次荣获“中国政府出版奖期刊奖”，连续16年荣获“中国百种杰出学术期刊”称号，并入选第三届全国“百强报刊”。《中国电机工程学会电力与能源系统学报》（英文刊）成功被科学引文索引（SCI）数据库收录，并入选“2018中国最具国际影响力学术期刊”。《高电压技术》《中国电力》《热力发电》《农村电气化》《农电管理》《动力与电气工程师》和《电信息》等办刊质量持续提高，国内外影响力显著增强。

（六）国际合作深入推进

与英国工程技术学会（IET）、国际大电网委员会（CIGRE）、国际供电会议组织（CIRED）、电气与电子工程师学会电力和能源分会（IEEE PES）等国际组织广泛交流，拓展合作。全面提升中日韩年会互访合作机制，开展中日可再生能源发电技术研讨会、中韩高压直流国际会议（HVDC）等双边学术交流活动。搭建国际交流平台，组织国内科技工作者参加电气电子工程师学会电力与能源分会（IEEE PES）2018年年会、国际大电网委员会（CIGRE）2018年大会、国际供电会议组织（CIRED）2018年技术会议等国际会议，全年组织和派员出境参加国际学术活动200余人·次。与英国工程技术学会（IET）签订《国际工程师资质认证项目合作协议》，共同开展工程师资质国际认证。与巴西联邦工程和农业委员会（CONFEA）探索开展工程师资格互认。扎实做好国际大电网委员会（CIGRE）、国际供电会议组织（CIRED）中国国家委员会工作。CIGRE中国国家委员会会员数位居全球第一，全年推荐40名专家加入CIGRE工作组，CIGRE 16个专委会均在中国国家委员会设立了专委会并每年举办工作会议及研讨会。积极参加CIRED战略规划研究组并在CIRED机构改革中发挥作用，成功申办2020年首届在欧洲以外召开的CIRED技术会议。

（七）学会系统组织管理不断加强

学会组织系统进一步完善，已初步形成专委会、省学会、海外分会/会员中心、高校会员中心的基本格局。通过组织召开“省级学会、专委会负责人培训班”“高校会员中心调研座谈会”“海外分会/会员中心工作会”等一系列专项会议，促进学会系统组织管理工作持续加强。深入开展创优评先工作，2018年共有17家专委会和12家省学会被评为先进集体。

专委会管理工作持续规范。组建能源互联网、清洁低碳发电和人工智能3个专委会，完成火力发电、输电线路、智慧用能与节能等18个专委会委员调整或更名工作。电力信息化、电力系统、火力发电、新能源并网与运行、能源系统、电力系统自动化、继电保护、直流输电与电力电子、核能发电分会、电力储能、电工数学、电力建设、智慧用能与节能、分布式发电及智能配电、燃气轮机发电、人工智能、能源互联网等多个专委会积极组织学术交流活动，各专委会全年共开展学术活动70余项。电力系统、新能源并网与运行、继电保护专委会联合主办的“清洁能源发展与消纳专题研讨会”反响很好。电力系统、分布式发电及智能配电、电力环境保护、水电设备、电力建设、城市供电、电工数学、超导与新材料应用技术等专委会积极组织撰写学会专业发展报告和专题技术报告。电力系统、智慧用能与节能、新能源并网与运行、燃气轮机发电、太阳能热发电、热工自动化、能源系统等专委会参与或承担学会咨询课题研究工作。各专委会学术影响力显著增强。

省级学会工作日益活跃。学会积极与国家电网有限公司、中国南方电网有限责任公司沟通协商，研究解决制约省级学会发展的共性问题，得到多方面大力支持。国家电网有限公司已下发《关于支持省级电机工程学会（电力学会）发展有关措施的通知》，为省级学会发展创造有利条件。江苏、广东、浙江、内蒙古、福建、重庆、云南、河南、江西、贵州等省级学会主动作为，积极组织开展省内学术交流、成果评价、职业培训等工作，学术影响力显著提升。北京、天津、广东、广西、甘肃、四川、福建、上海等省级学会充分发挥地域优势，积极参与并协助学会开展学术研讨会、科普活动、咨询评价等工作。各省级学会自我发展能力有效提升。

海外分会/会员中心运作初见成效。制定下发《中国电机工程学会海外会员中心/分会管理办法》。各海外分会/会员中心积极开展学术交流活动和发展海外会员。英国分会组织“中英未来能源论坛”，欧洲会员中心召开“能源转型战略及综合能源先进技术研讨会”，北美会员中心举办了“北加华人能源工作者技术交流联谊会”和“储能技术和应用研讨会”。

高校会员中心建设持续推进。目前学会已与清华大学等11所高校建立战略合作关系并设立会员中心。各会员中心充分发挥高校在学科建设和新技术成果研究方面的优势，开展多种形式的学术活动，其中，浙江大学会员中心举办的“玉泉论坛”，清华大学会员中心举办的系列学术报告会以及山东大学会员中心举办的专业学术讲座都取得了良好的示范效果，较好地发挥了学会与高校师生的纽带作用。

会员结构持续优化，深入推进会员规范登记，2018年新增个人会员12430人，累计完成个人会员信息规范登记81400人。完成高级会员和会士评选工作，评选出高级会员113人、会士和外籍会士27人。密切联系资深会员和老科技工作者，组织开展全国科技工作者日赠书活动、老科技工作者座谈会等活动。

（八）加强学会本部建设

坚持把党的政治建设摆在首位，持续推进“两学一做”学习教育常态化制度化。定期召开党委会议，认真落实“三重一大”决策制度。健全学会党建工作体系和制度，实施党建工作量化计划管理。坚持党建与学会业务工作相融合，积极开展中国科协党建强会活动和党建调研课题研究，被评为中国科协创建星级学会党组织优秀单位。优化人员结构，充实员工队伍。开展职业技能培训，提升员工职业素养。规范员工职级管理，完善薪酬与考核评价机制。推进财务规范化管理，制定学会财务管理制度20余项，出版《现代科技社团财务规范管理研究》专著并由科协向全国学会推广。完成学会办公自动化（OA）系统、移动应用APP等新系统建设，完善学会会员管理、财务规范化管理、数字化图书馆等信息系统，推动信息系统与学会业务协调发展。

（中国电机工程学会秘书处）

河海大学2018年举办水电学术活动情况

（一）第二届水利水电工程安全学术研讨会在河海大学召开

2018年10月6日，第二届水利水电工程安全学术研讨会在河海大学召开。中国工程院院士吴中如、王景全，河海大学党委书记唐洪武、校长徐辉等出席会议。会议开幕式由河海大学水利水电学院院长顾冲时主持。

唐洪武在致辞中表示，水利水电工程是调控水资源时空分布、优化水资源配置最重要的工程措施，其安全运行对于保障国家经济社会可持续发展具有重大意义。河海大学作为我国水利高等教育的发源地，始终秉承治水兴邦的历史使命，坚持面向国家重大需求，在水利水电工程安全监控、健康诊断、风险评定等方面广泛开展科技攻关，形成以吴中如院士领衔的高水平学术队伍，取得了一系列创新性研究成果，培养了一大批活跃在工程建设、工程管理以及科学研究第一线的高素质创新人才，为保障国家水利水电工程安全作出了突出贡献。立足新时代，学校将以习近平新时代中国特色社会主义思想为指导，继续坚持围绕行业办学的发展思路，聚焦一流学科建设，聚力内涵式发展，着力构筑“中国特色，世界一流”的水利学科高地，培养造就更多具有全球视野和国际水平的科技人才和创新团队，为行业提供强有力的人才保障和科技支撑。

徐辉校长宣读会议优秀论文获奖名单。会议还对优秀论文进行了表彰。

会议组委会代表、南瑞集团企协副会长刘观标代表组委会致辞。

会上，顾冲时、李季、沈振中、何勇军、蔡新、马福恒分别作“重大水工程安全保障理论和技术”“李家峡高拱坝长期运行反馈分析”“水库大坝除险加固效果的量化评价”“长距离调水工程安全运行保障关键技术研究进展”“农村小水电新型水工结构及降损技术研究”“典型发达国家大坝安全监管机制分析及启示”主旨报告。

（二）全国结构试验技术研讨会暨河海大学模拟地震水下振动台落成仪式在南京举行

2018年11月10日，全国结构试验技术研讨会暨河海大学模拟地震水下振动台落成仪式在南京举行。河海大学副校长郑金海，北京市水科学技术研究院副院长王理许，中国水力发电工程学会抗震防灾专业委员会主任李德玉，江苏省力学学会副理事长钱向东，防灾科技学院、同济大学、东南大学、山东大学等高校和科研院所有关专家出席活动。

郑金海副校长介绍了河海大学的办学发展历史和水利水工专业学科特色，并指出，河海大学模拟地震水下振动台的落成，为学校水利工程、环境科学与工程、土木工程、力学与材料工程等学科建设提供了新型试验平台，也为发展相关领域高层次人才提供了孕育摇篮，将为推动学校“双一流”建设迈上新台阶提供有力支撑。河海大学将把模拟地震振动试验台打造成一个面向国内外的开放共享平台，同时设立开放共享基金，在水下振动台共享使用和功能开发等方面，探索更多合作渠道，创新合作发展模式，实现彼此合作共赢。

中国水力发电工程学会抗震防灾专业委员会李德玉主任表示，利用振动台进行模型试验是研究震损机理及抗震措施的重要手段，河海大学水下振动台将为研究结构与流体动力相互作用这一方向的课题研究提供新的思路和方法。

河海大学实验室及设备管理处处长冯建刚主持落成仪式。模拟地震水下振动台位于河海大学江宁校区189试验基地结构试验大厅，是国内首个三向六自由度模拟地震水下振动台，其各项性能指标均达到国内领先水平，是河海大学面向国内外研究模拟地震领域水下振动试验技术的校级大型仪器设备共享平台。

在学术研讨会上，来自模拟地震领域的专家学者就振动台试验研究、水下振动台建设关键技术，以及振动台在抗震防灾和地震风险评估中的重要作用等方面作出了精彩报告。与会人员共同探讨了水下振动试验技术、模拟地震振动台实际应用技术、拟动力混合试验技术等结构试验技术以及试验技术未来的发展方向。

（河海大学）

黄河水利科学研究院2018年几项学术活动情况

（一）水库泥沙处理与资源利用技术专业委员会2018年学术研讨会

中国大坝工程学会水库泥沙处理与资源利用技术专业委员会（简称水库泥沙专委会）在新疆和田举办2018年学术研讨会，会议围绕“水库安全运行与淤积防治”开展技术调研和学术研讨。水利部科技推广中心副主任许平参加研讨会并致辞，来自全国各地的20余家科研、设计、施工单位的代表参加了本次会议。

本次会议是水库泥沙专委会组织的具有针对性的学术交流活动，以现场调研黄河水利科学研究院的“磨蚀防护技术”和“吸盘式水库管道排沙环保清淤技术与装备”为主题，促进了科研、设计、施工单位需求的对接。会议期间，黄河水利科学研究院与有关单位就中小型水库运行方案、水库调度规程编制，病险水库、病险水闸除险加固工程等方面的合作展开了深入探讨，并达成了初步合作意向。

（二）抗蚀促生边坡防护技术培训班

2018年8月29～30日，黄河水利科学研究院在内蒙古准格尔旗举办“抗蚀促生边坡防护技术”暨“鄂尔多斯高原砒砂岩区生态综合治理技术”专题培训班。来自水利部科技推广中心、东南大学、郑州大学、华北水利水电大学、黄河水利科学研究院、准格尔旗水保局、亿利资源集团、黄委会晋陕蒙监督局、北京林业大学、湘潭大学、榆林学院、青海省水利水电研究院、中国林科院荒漠化所、准格尔旗交通局执法局、准格尔旗水保监测站、准格尔旗砒砂岩生态治理研究中心、内蒙古同力建筑工程有限公司、鄂尔多斯市泰宝公司、伊东新园林绿化有限公司等30多家单位近百名代表参加了此次会议。

培训会采用“大会报告＋现场教学”的方式，由东南大学赵艳兵博士、华北水利水电大学李长明博士、郑州大学李晓龙副教授、亿利资源集团沙漠研究院张立欣副院长和黄河水利科学研究院刘慧博士分别进行了专题讲座。培训班成员冒雨对抗蚀促生边坡防护技术示范园区进行了实地考察，准格尔旗水保站刘军站长进行了现场教学。

为期3天的培训，得到了水利部推广中心领导及与会学员的高度认可，并引起《科学网》等媒体的关注，也对黄河水利科学研究院抗蚀促生边坡防护技术的推广起到了良好的推动作用。

（黄河水利科学研究院）

西藏水电发展论坛在北京召开

2018年9月27日，西藏水电发展论坛在北京召开，会议由中国水力发电工程学会主办，西藏开发投资集团有限公司承办，水电水利规划设计总院协办。来自与西藏水电开发相关的规划、设计、施工、运行管理、金融机构和媒体等40余家单位的100多名领导、专家和代表，深入交流我国西藏水电开发的实践经验，积极探讨并展望如何促进西藏水电的合理有序开发，将西藏的水电资源优势转变成现实的生产力，为西藏的经济发展和改善农牧民的生活作出贡献。

中国水力发电工程学会理事长张野、西藏自治区人民政府原副主席杨海滨、中国华能集团有限公司副总经理樊启祥、西藏开发投资集团有限公司总裁谭继文、中国人民武装警察部队水电指挥部原主任陈方枢、中国水电工程顾问集团公司原总经理李菊根、国家开发银行评审总监郑旭东、中国电力投资集团公司原副总经理石成梁等领导专家分别发表讲话。

大会邀请的9个专题报告，从西藏水电发展历程和发展展望、履行央企责任助力西藏发展、建设西藏水电服务国家能源、西藏水电开发与生态环境保护、高海拔深切高山峡谷地区一些关键技术问题的思考研究、加快西藏水电开发促进西藏经济发展、提高西藏水电市场竞争力的支持效应分析、西藏水电发展与理性思考等方面，阐述了西藏水电开发面临的问题并对其中一些难点提出了可行的解决方案，所分享的经验获得与会代表的赞许，提出的问题直接面向西藏水电未来发展大计，给出的建议引发了强烈的思考共鸣。

与会专家与代表展开热烈讨论和广泛交流，围绕西藏水电开发的现状及未来发展，从体制机制变革、技术创新、政策分析、投资评价等多个方面提出了多项建设性的解决思路。

（中国水力发电工程学会）

风光水能互补开发研讨会在青海西宁召开

2018年8月29日，由中国水力发电工程学会、青海省科学技术协会主办，青海水力发电工程学会承办，黄河上游水电开发有限责任公司协办的“风光水能互补开发研讨会”在西宁召开，60余名领导专家代表和新闻媒体记者参加了会议。

会上，黄河水电公司董事长谢小平作了《黄河公司水光互补开发的历程与经验》的主旨报告，介绍了黄河水电公司总体发展情况，结合水光互补光伏电站开发的历程与经验，围绕黄河上游水电规划及开发、光伏规划及开发、水光互补研究与应用、风光水储能互补研究等方面作了交流发言。有关专家还就《水风光互补研究思考》《雅砻江风光水互补基地规划》《华润电力黑水扎窝光伏扶贫项目案例分析》《风光水能互补与能源革命》等进行了专题交流。与会代表畅所欲言，围绕风光水能资源互补、技术互补、投资互补、电网调度、政策支持等内容展开交流探讨。会间，代表们到龙羊峡水电站、“水光互补”光伏电站及共和百兆瓦太阳能发电实证基地进行了实地考察。

通过此次研讨会，达到了风光水能互补技术分享交流的目的，为推动能源革命和消费转型，实现清洁能源可持续发展作了有益的探索。

（中国水力发电工程学会）

中國水力發電年鑒

16

统 计 资 料

2018 年全国水电增长情况表

全国及各省、自治区、直辖市	年底装机容量（万 kW）			发电量（亿 kW·h）		
	2018 年	2017 年	同比变化	2018 年	2017 年	同比变化
全　国	35259	34411	2.46	12321	11947	3.13
北　京	98	98		10	11	−11.84
天　津	1	1		0.2	0.07	114.29
河　北	182	182	0.02	17	20	−18.57
山　西	223	244	−8.79	43	42	1.88
内蒙古	242	242	−0.02	45	24	91.42
辽　宁	299	295	1.41	46	45	1.94
吉　林	385	380	1.24	79	77	1.88
黑龙江	104	103	0.86	26	25	4.08
上　海						
江　苏	265	265	−0.02	34	29	14.10
浙　江	1161	1160	0.08	192	212	−9.71
安　徽	312	310	0.54	53	57	−5.85
福　建	1322	1307	1.14	325	416	−21.80
江　西	627	615	1.89	116	157	−26.20
山　东	108	108	0.25	5	7	−27.29
河　南	401	399	0.48	144	100	44.34
湖　北	3675	3671	0.10	1471	1494	−1.50
湖　南	1598	1570	1.73	432	498	−13.30
广　东	1576	1486	6.06	292	301	−2.96
广　西	1677	1669	0.44	609	614	−0.82
海　南	154	114	35.70	27	26	4.04
重　庆	756	736	2.69	242	253	−4.21
四　川	7824	7714	1.42	3249	3164	2.70
贵　州	2212	2119	4.39	770	733	5.03
云　南	6649	6281	5.86	2699	2502	7.86
西　藏	160	158	1.12	57	51	12.67
陕　西	385	379	1.63	102	109	−6.90
甘　肃	927	868	6.86	444	374	18.65
青　海	1192	1191	0.09	517	332	55.83
宁　夏	43	43		20	16	26.65
新　疆	702	702		254	256	−0.80

（中国电力企业联合会）

2018年农村水电装机容量及发电量基本情况表

行政区划	2018年年末农村水电装机容量（kW）	装机容量占全国比重（%）	2018年年末农村水电年发电量（万kW·h）	发电量占全国比重（%）
全 国	80435263	100	23456083	100
北 京	42920	0.05	2430	0.01
天 津	5800	0.01	1469	0.01
河 北	403748	0.50	67103	0.29
山 西	206626	0.26	42452	0.18
内蒙古	95020	0.12	19325	0.08
辽 宁	454299	0.56	81074	0.35
吉 林	603410	0.75	179867	0.77
黑龙江	384460	0.48	93647	0.40
江 苏	40191	0.05	8915	0.04
浙 江	4099507	5.10	834464	3.56
安 徽	1112456	1.38	249476	1.06
福 建	7390664	9.19	1861904	7.94
江 西	3449893	4.29	732371	3.12
山 东	88899	0.11	5158	0.02
河 南	509490	0.63	105334	0.45
湖 北	3861738	4.80	935802	3.99
湖 南	6379772	7.93	1738922	7.41
广 东	7602484	9.45	1675262	7.14
广 西	4579711	5.69	1309217	5.58
海 南	493725	0.61	153719	0.66
重 庆	2874133	3.57	725152	3.09
四 川	12011238	14.93	4347891	18.54
贵 州	3507621	4.36	1055652	4.50
云 南	12128479	15.08	4305958	18.36
西 藏	375619	0.47	86225	0.37
陕 西	1578291	1.96	422839	1.80
甘 肃	2791778	3.47	1094117	4.66
青 海	1097135	1.36	521638	2.22
宁 夏	6240	0.01	690	0.00
新 疆	1731241	2.15	638557	2.72
新疆兵团	406975	0.51	127842	0.55
部直属	121700	0.15	31608	0.13

（水利部农水水电司 曲鹏）

2018 年全国电源建设投资完成情况表

单位：万元

地区	本年计划投资	本年完成投资	其中				
			水电	火电	核电	风电	太阳能发电
全 国	28590936	27871417	7002561	7864177	4471618	6461876	2071185
北 京	88457	85208		59433		25707	68
天 津	277470	226504		163165		59639	3700
河 北	1932006	1594888	191940	493900		801832	107216
山 西	434162	524306		39981		403300	81025
内蒙古	1133846	973722	23178	556814		82996	310734
辽 宁	1584477	1197817	71500	281774	493577	331786	19180
吉 林	470554	452644	271774	78037			102833
黑龙江	304490	259515	50008	97788		67214	44505
上 海	332595	355004		178004		177000	
江 苏	2787692	3023094	67012	645129	902508	1148111	260334
浙 江	1293649	1195878	207109	172376	513702	199072	103619
安 徽	924113	842611	185409	493365		74624	89213
福 建	1743297	1588946	127643	227976	806210	427117	
江 西	388814	356486	15426	103948		217734	19378
山 东	1187077	1493591	152230	540894	376255	326143	98069
河 南	770027	1141922	96635	649472		392496	3319
湖 北	695990	703048	128426	262518		257103	55000
湖 南	253211	251228	40155	26533		183502	1038
广 东	2601232	2612636	170032	1197612	822891	195817	226283
广 西	898786	839525	2999		556475	280051	
海 南	176400	159529	24762	45982			88785
重 庆	138833	142628	62050			48793	31785
四 川	4130565	3838915	3685850			148570	4496
贵 州	214737	217548	6350	7937		148316	54945
云 南	793838	827287	784609			38645	4033
西 藏	165238	158814	145293				13521
陕 西	721209	710747	107317	310773		242277	50380
甘 肃	273515	311015	11885	299130			
青 海	412152	389913				124806	265107
宁 夏	513747	442925		415910		27015	
新 疆	948755	953524	372971	515725		32212	32616

（中国电力企业联合会）

2018年大中型水电厂生产运行情况表

一、抽水蓄能电厂

	电厂名称	总装机容量（万kW）	机组台数（台）	年发电量（亿kW·h）	年抽水电量（亿kW·h）	等效可用系数（%）	各类工况运行总时间（h）	各工况启动次数（次）	启动成功率（%）
1	十三陵蓄能电厂	80.00	4	9.56	12.69	86.63	11841.47	2912	99.97
2	潘家口蓄能电厂	27.00	3	1.96	2.24	55.65	4822.69	1083	99.91
3	张河湾蓄能电厂	100.00	4	5.81	7.26	82.44	5453.69	1604	99.94
4	西龙池蓄能电厂	120.00	4	6.64	9.11	87.39	5705.33	1720	99.88
5	蒲石河抽水蓄能电厂	120.00	4	16.43	20.11	89.69	13044.2	3606	99.92
6	白山抽水蓄能电站	30.00	2	0.03	4.75	85.77	2907.81	662	100.00
7	宜兴抽水蓄能电厂	100.00	4	11.73	14.47	86.24	10803.32	3175	99.97
8	天荒坪抽水蓄能电厂	180.00	6	26.01	32.45	88.03	19972.53	4594	100.00
9	桐柏抽水蓄能电厂	120.00	4	17.14	20.74	88.24	12734.22	3350	99.94
10	仙居抽水蓄能电厂	150.00	4	19.08	23.45	80.95	11752.38	3293	99.91
11	仙游抽水蓄能电厂	120.00	4	24.71	30.75	89.58	21238.93	4082	100.00
12	洪屏抽水蓄能电厂	120.00	4	15.10	18.01	91.54	11317.41	2328	100
13	琅琊山抽水蓄能电厂	60.00	4	7.92	9.90	93.62	11345.90	3100	99.97
14	响水涧抽水蓄能电厂	100.00	4	15.27	18.91	88.54	13909.43	3111	99.87
15	响洪甸蓄能电厂	8.00	2	0.78	1.10	67.95	3930.06	935	100.00
16	泰山抽水蓄能电厂	100.00	4	4.30	5.33	87.83	4370.56	2270	100.00
17	宝泉蓄能电厂	120.00	4	17.71	21.99	85.06	13272.37	2822	99.96
18	回龙抽水蓄能电厂	12.00	2	1.03	1.31	67.92	4120.36	1310	100.00
19	白莲河蓄能电厂	120.00	4	10.22	12.64	88.85	7877.48	1682	100.00
20	黑麋峰抽水蓄能电厂	120.00	4	13.69	16.52	81.85	10388.89	2355	99.87
21	广州蓄能水电厂	240.00	8	24.52	31.1	80.99	2892.41	6942	99.93
22	惠州蓄能水电厂	240.00	8	22.85	28.42	93.1	2631.58	6580	99.98
23	清远抽水蓄能电站	128.00	4	17.92	22.46	93.06	3571.19	4477	99.93
24	深圳蓄能水电厂	120.00	4	6.43	8.02	91.3	1622.77	1575	98.67
25	海南蓄能水电厂	60.00	3	1.73	2	95.27	1264.66	713	98.88

续表

二、常规水电厂

水电厂名称			发电运行情况				水库运行情况			
			总装机容量（万 kW）	年发电量（亿 kW・h）	平均耗水率［m^3/（kW・h）］	等效可用系数（%）	年入库总水量（亿 m^3）	发电用水量（亿 m^3）	年末水位（m）	年末库容（亿 m^3）
26	北京华电水电		5.20	0.0936	7.60	99.36	3.95	0.71	148.95	25.71
27	河北华电混合蓄能		5.70	1.0312	6.83	97.76	6.46	7.04	196.94	7.02
28	万家寨电站		108.00	32.17	6.5	83.21	327.0	209.1	967.87	3.05
29	龙口电站		42.00	16.3	13.03	91.43	323.9	212.4	897.96	1.33
30	海勃湾水利枢纽电厂		9.00.	5.7483	43.98	98.7	256.25	252.78	1074.5	3.19
31	白山发电厂	白山站	150.00	21.81	3.71	81.99	77.96	80.81	412.83	49.4561
		红石站	20.00	4.40	16.80		73.76	73.92	289.68	1.58
32	丰满发电厂		28.90	14.12	7.53	84.42	127.81	106.38	247.48	37.3205
33	松江河水力发电公司	小山站	16.00	3.07	4.17	91.07	13.44	12.79	680.91	0.89432
		双沟站	28.00	3.97	3.99		17.55	15.84	580.38	3.10
		石龙站	7.00	1.36	12.34		17.79	16.79	478.79	0.30
34	桓仁水电厂		22.25	3.97	8.10	98.28	36.31	32.17	297.05	5.43
35	回龙山水电站		7.20	1.61	16.39	97.98	30.06	26.37	220.39	0.12
36	太平哨发电厂		16.10	2.66	11.57	93.38	32.25	30.82	191.39	0.18
37	尼尔基发电厂		25.00	8.19	15.94		149.25	130.55	213.63	53.358
38	新安江水力发电厂		85.00	13.22	5.35	94.85	91.63	70.77	101.16	139.88
39	富春江水力发电厂		36.00	7.96	27.23	93.08	218.78	216.78	23.24	4.5492
40	乌溪江水力发电厂		37.20	4.4238	3.77	94.31	14.56	16.68	201.17	6.69
41	陈村水电厂		15.00	1.8383	7.64	98.25	25.1316	14.0446	113.33	14.0972
42	沙溪口水力发电厂		30.00	7.461437	18.63	90.38	148.33	139.02	86.12	1.24
43	牛头山一级水电站		10.00	2.3894	2.14	95.04	5.4791	5.1153	324.80	0.5107
44	古田溪水力发电厂		32.00	6.6775	1.25	85.17	9.26	8.32	371.91	2.65
45	闽东水电厂		32.00	6.2669	0.65	93.53	4.41	4.06	729.72	0.95
46	华安水力发电厂		14.00	4.9588	8.27	90.85	43.77	40.99	93.21	0.04
47	安砂水力发电厂		12.83	4.3839	6.43	95.85	33.73	28.20	256.82	4.13
48	池潭水力发电厂		20.00	2.7361	9.15	92.79	29.02	25.05	265.89	4.14
49	棉花滩水电厂		60.00	8.4749	4.83	85.69	36.88	40.92	146.16	5.80
50	界竹口水电站		6.00	1.38	13.19	100.00	19.29	18.15	77.46	0.26
51	水口电厂		140.00	38.42	7.65	92.03	302.66	294.04	59.59	18.36
52	街面电厂		30.00	2.28	4.23	95.44	12.25	9.65	283.32	14.74

续表

水电厂名称			发电运行情况				水库运行情况			
			总装机容量（万 kW）	年发电量（亿 kW·h）	平均耗水率［m³/(kW·h)］	等效可用系数（%）	年入库总水量（亿 m³）	发电用水量（亿 m³）	年末水位（m）	年末库容（亿 m³）
53	白沙水电厂		7.00	1.1336	8.02	82.32	9.21	9.09	255.70	1.11
54	高砂水电公司		5.00	1.6501	39.14	84.43	70.17	64.58	102.93	0.24
55	照口水电厂		6.00	1.7843	43.43	94.40	80.80	77.49	97.55	0.26
56	万安水力发电厂		53.30	11.16	16.37	89.59	189.86	182.74	94.26	6.28
57	上犹江水电厂		7.20	2.0016	8.31	94.37	19.36	16.63	190.87	4.68
58	峡江水利枢纽		36.00	7.7045	37.88	92.87	309.46	291.85	43.78	4.44
59	小浪底水电厂	小浪底站	180.00	88.23	3.83	91.46	392.96	332.0	266.51	71.07
		西霞院站	14.00	7.01	36.42	94.13	392.96	255.0	133.82	1.0426
60	三门峡水电厂		45.00	18.57	12.68	—	414.14	235.58	317.35	4.45
61	故县水电厂		6.00	0.988	5.42	—	5.931	5.356	521.71	4.11
62	三峡水力发电厂		2250.00	1016.15	4.34	93.66	4569.75	4412.58	174.58	388.75
63	葛洲坝水力发电厂		273.50	183.18	21.78	94.79	4731.36	3989.45	65.60	6.98
64	水布垭电厂		184.00	36.01	2.26	90.45	76.56	81.27	388.66	36.34
65	隔河岩电厂		121.20	27.29	3.73	94.00	105.22	101.72	196.21	27.71
66	高坝洲电厂		27.00	9.50	11.33	92.04	109.57	107.59	78.52	3.63
67	松树岭水电站		5.00	1.23	10.23	98.00	12.51	12.62	383.36	—
68	老渡口水电站		9.00	3.50	5.26	97.35	18.71	18.41	473.23	0.68
69	吉牛水电站		24.00	10.28	0.935	95.54	20.72	9.61	2376	0.0179
70	猴子岩水电站		170.00	44.38	3.136	95.42	310.44	135.99	1832.76	5.51
71	鄂坪水电站		11.40	2.17	4.38	91.57	8.39	9.52	527.26	0.30
72	白沙河水电站		5.00	0.79	5.49	91.62	3.45	4.32	427	0.19
73	陡岭子水电站		7.05	1.13	7.06	96.90	6.58	7.99	243.72	0.12
74	野三河水电站		5.00	2.65	1.55	97.89	4.11	4.12	652.82	0.07
75	龙桥电站		6.00	4.71	3.50	100.00	17.13	16.49	579.24	0.06
76	五强溪水电厂		120.00	48.31	8.77	96.23	433.739	420.22	103.90	24.238
77	凌津滩水电厂		27.00	10.92	41.49	92.69	461.602	451.125	50.79	1.425
78	白云水电站		5.40	0.43	4.89	91.96	3.16	2.09	535.86	1.84
79	三江口水电站		9.90	3.39	7.46	91.37	25.33	25.27	612	0.09
80	桃源水电站		18.00	8.58	55.18	95.59	478	474	39.5	1.28
81	碗米坡水电厂		24.00	7.19	11.28	93.07	95.283	81.452	244.82	2.101
82	近尾洲水电站		6.32	2.87	59.95	89.38	193.832	171.462	66.00	1.543
83	洪江水力发电厂		27.00	8.24	18.06	93.69	151.67	148.35	188.85	1.736
84	三板溪水电厂		100.00	20.05	3.10	92.06	63.75	62.374	465.68	30.748
85	托口水电站		83.00	15.78	7.94	94.76	126.197	125.581	246.28	10.635

续表

水电厂名称		发电运行情况				水库运行情况			
		总装机容量（万 kW）	年发电量（亿 kW·h）	平均耗水率［m³/(kW·h)］	等效可用系数（%）	年入库总水量（亿 m³）	发电用水量（亿 m³）	年末水位（m）	年末库容（亿 m³）
86	挂治水电厂	15.00	3.38	18.98	95.00	64.198	64.203	320.88	0.374
87	白市水电站	42.00	10.22	8.18	92.17	83.292	83.565	296.11	5.089
88	马迹塘水电厂	5.55	1.86	67.80	94.17	138.545	125.94	55.62	0.124
89	东坪水电站	7.20	1.81	60.82	93.65	111.429	110.045	96.09	0.139
90	株溪口水力发电厂	7.40	2.01	55.95	94.28	112.873	112.257	87.17	0.315
91	江垭水电站	30.00	6.13	5.29		32.23	32.42	204.23	6.8966
92	皂市水电站	12.00	2.73	8.86		23.16	24.20	125.95	6.3585
93	鱼潭水电站	7.00	2.6551	10.17	97.10	32.9227	26.9918	242.82	0.7637
94	新丰江电厂	35.50	9.375	5.78		34.69	54.15	102.44	65.263
95	枫树坝电厂	17.60	3.002	7.46		20.49	22.39	138.29	5.040
96	南水电厂	8.70	1.791	3.60		7.629	6.454	205.08	5.533
97	长湖电厂	8.20	1.925	12.73		31.10	24.51	205.08	5.533
98	长潭电厂	6.40	0.481	10.49		8.177	5.048	146.03	1.034
99	青溪电厂	14.40	2.224	18.90		42.76	42.04	70.62	0.493
100	白石窑水电厂	9.20	2.66	36.90	90.00	104.80	99.97	36.50	1.084
101	飞来峡水利枢纽	14.00	5.42	32.78	83.95	268.70	183.10	23.84	4.11
102	濛里水电厂	5.00	1.70（出口） 1.55（销售）	54.04	0.97	96.11	91.65	45.00	0.675
103	平班水电厂	40.50	16.10	11.91	92.83	192.58	191.78	438.01	1.89
104	龙滩水电厂	490.00	146.54	3.31	93.41	473.33	485.06	356.37	104.36
105	岩滩水电厂	181.00	79.06	6.67	93.52	527.02	527.29	220.41	23.33
106	大化水电厂	56.60	29.43	18.15	93.86	543.02	542.87	153.86	3.71
107	百龙滩水电厂	19.20	9.67	46.18	93.48	556.02	446.64	127.09	0.75
108	乐滩水电厂	60.00	32.51	18.19	94.03	601.57	600.03	110.13	3.59
109	西津水电站	24.20	12.21	25.85	81.06	419.85	325.41	60.05	9.28
110	山秀水电站	7.80	3.03	39.36	89.65	199.95	119.25	85.57	2.61
111	金鸡滩水电站	7.20	3.65	37.87	90.34	178.74	138.23	88.37	0.96
112	金牛坪水电站	6.00	2.29	38.99	91.22	106.77	89.29	41.71	0.70
113	广西长洲水电厂	63.00	37.7614	31.9140	91.90	1504.0319	1205.1199	20.22	17.98
114	大广坝水电厂	24.20	6.89	5.70	96.95	45.01	39.32	138.17	11.43
115	彭水水电厂	175.00	57.7511	5.69	95.15	331.8249	328.9204	290.84	11.1712
116	银盘水电厂	64.50	27.7838	13.3	96.41	386.0006	369.4947	213.18	1.6376
117	马岩洞水电厂	6.60	2.3686	6.48	97.67	18.0124	15.3478	349.42	0.2206
118	藤子沟水电厂	7.00	1.7308	2.56	91.95	3.7846	4.4378	737.49	0.6455
119	鱼剑口水电厂	6.00	1.9578	5.14	95.75	10.5116	10.0653	247.82	0.0315
120	重庆江口水电厂	40.00	11.31	3.67	96.00	44.35	41.44	292.85	4.69

续表

序号	水电厂名称	发电运行情况				水库运行情况			
		总装机容量（万 kW）	年发电量（亿 kW·h）	平均耗水率[m^3/(kW·h)]	等效可用系数（%）	年入库总水量（亿 m^3）	发电用水量（亿 m^3）	年末水位（m）	年末库容（亿 m^3）
121	狮子滩电站	5.42	1.72	7.15	97.06	11.39	12.29	339.15	4.56
122	重庆渡口坝水电站	12.90	2.2713	1.2	92.84	2.5812	2.7356	546.10	0.34
123	旺村水电站	6.00	2.60	34.35	92.54	104.34	89.42	16.86	0.82
124	龟都府水电站	6.30	3.0524	35.00	94.98	172.91	106.83	545.00	0.559
125	晴朗水电站	18.00	7.5499	1.15	89.56	12.73	8.68	2656.50	0.002045
126	可河水电站	7.20	2.391	1.07	99.98	4.18	2.56	1412.00	0.0026
127	二滩水电站	330.00	159.7527	2.35	91.68	578.0524	378.6297	1198.72	56.6310
128	官地水电站	240.00	121.7952	3.34	91.42	518.2031	409.9794	1328.83	7.1230
129	锦屏一级水电站	360.00	187.2846	1.85	92.76	460.7836	349.8016	1878.14	76.1230
130	锦屏二级水电站	480.00	248.8656	1.33	88.90	471.5521	331.8059	1644.11	0.1239
131	桐子林水电站	60.00	23.4347	18.34	94.58	670.1309	428.7973	1012.95	0.6177
132	溪洛渡水力发电厂	1386.00	624.69	2.02	94.03	1574.08	1261.98	597.00	111.77
133	向家坝水力发电厂	640.00	330.80	3.70	96.00	1587.36	1223.93	376.07	46.09
134	大岗山水电站	260.00	93.15	2.44	95.1	393.88	227.29	1121.29	6.40
135	瀑布沟水电站	360.00	128.80	2.67	95.51	459.79	343.89	842.4	43.78
136	深溪沟水电站	66.00	26.80	12.28	88.01	483.44	329.88	655.96	0.25
137	枕头坝一级电站	72.00	27.02	13.41	94.59	510.57	362.34	620	0.44
138	沙坪二级电站（沙南）	34.80	16.10	27.20	90.00	416.90	409.5	552.5	1850.5
139	龚嘴水电站	77.00	38.65	8.90	92.03	547.02	343.90	522.26	0.44
140	铜街子水电站	70.00	35.6945	12.11	93.98	567.36	432.14	469.06	0.5232
141	冶勒水电站	24.00	6.87	0.70	97.02	4.96	4.82	2645.86	2.35
142	姚河坝电站	13.20	5.29	1.46	97.85	9.92	7.74	1674.25	—
143	南桠河发电厂	12.00	5.78	1.64	94.46	11.06	9.48	1367.30	—
144	栗子坪水电站	13.20	3.61	1.35	97.02	4.99	4.88	1999.35	0.00
145	太平驿电站	26.00	14.48	3.52	96.25	102.70	51.00	1080.10	0.004
146	龙安（古城）电站	10.00	3.29	10.00	0.98	52.40	38.69	844.04	0.0101
147	东西关电站	21.00	8.8954	34.3344	89.42	314.1086	164.6653	247.86	1.9641
148	青居电站	13.60	4.7027	18.4272	87.60	291.3039	162.2342	261.79	0.6924
149	雨城电站	6.00	2.3294	27.00	91.10	116.00	84.00	598.00	0.10
150	铜头电站	8.00	3.4997	5.40	92.59	31.09	25.50	760.00	0.11
151	小关子电站	16.00	7.0430	2.90	91.17	27.20	23.40	990.00	0.005
152	硗碛电站	24.00	9.2781	0.83	97.21	7.54	6.18	2132.00	1.621
153	宝兴电站	19.50	8.0987	1.30	96.79	12.30	11.36	1352.00	0.005
154	飞仙关电站	10.00	2.8422	20.00	86.10	113.00	83.00	623.00	0.27
155	民治电站	10.50	4.4437	1.85	96.92	10.31	8.50	1587.00	0.009
156	冷竹关电站	18.00	8.57	1.10	0.98	15.64	9.43	1760.92	0.0027
157	小天都电站	24.00	6.71	1.10	0.98	14.58	7.52	2153.23	0.0035

续表

水电厂名称		发电运行情况				水库运行情况			
		总装机容量（万 kW）	年发电量（亿 kW·h）	平均耗水率［m^3/(kW·h)］	等效可用系数（%）	年入库总水量（亿 m^3）	发电用水量（亿 m^3）	年末水位（m）	年末库容（亿 m^3）
158	拉拉山电站	9.60	3.22	1.80	0.98	10.25	5.80	3001.57	0.0073
159	自一里电站	13.00	7.17	0.90	1.00	6.94	6.14	2030.55	0.0026
160	水牛家电站	7.00	2.97	1.90	0.98	5.79	5.67	2255.41	0.90
161	木座电站	10.00	4.24	1.50	0.99	8.74	6.99	1543.50	0.0026
162	阴坪电站	10.00	4.41	1.90	0.98	11.07	9.01	1244.70	0.0083
163	亭子口水电站	110.00	28.5681	5.83	96.8	250.7943	167.0457	449.26	26.0247
164	宝珠寺水力发电厂	70.00	21.6363	4.50	91.47	118.83	97.26	583.00	17.91
165	紫兰坝水电开发公司	10.20	3.6580	22.68	98.27	126.01	82.95	488.00	0.31
166	红叶二级水电站	9.00	4.3764	2.92	95.85	16.47	12.77	2085.90	0.00
167	薛城水电站	13.80	6.1634	2.87	94.87	21.93	17.70	1708.56	0.01
168	狮子坪水电站	19.50	8.8269	1.02	97.76	10.73	8.99	2524.49	0.99
169	古城水电站	16.80	7.7564	3.06	97.90	33.20	23.72	1553.75	0.01
170	瓦屋山水电站	26.00	9.0302	1.52	96.84	14.04	13.69	1068.84	4.10
171	水津关水电站	6.30	2.3546	33.20	95.80	147.99	78.18	547.10	0.05
172	洛古水电站	11.00	4.2651	1.19	85.15	11.42	5.07	2040.24	0.17
173	联补水电站	13.00	5.2394	0.97	93.28	11.44	5.11	1672.08	0.02
174	地洛水电站	10.00	4.1054	1.36	97.43	11.84	5.59	1215.14	0.02
175	泸定水电站	92.00	25.3979	6.52	88.23	309.58	165.57	1369.44	1.63
176	楼方水电站	5.60	1.7743	7.77	96.82	17.46	13.79	701.30	0.07
177	宁郎水电站	11.40	3.7212	4.52	96.99	49.97	16.81	1853.58	0.01
178	撒多水电站	21.00	7.0070	2.55	99.41	51.43	17.86	1754.52	0.03
179	固滴水电站	13.8	0.9822	3.83	46.30	35.98	3.76	2311.00	0.01
180	俄公堡电站	13.20	5.4770	4.54	92.95	35.28	24.86	2315.15	0.01
181	卡基娃电站	45.24	14.6883	1.74	96.29	30.63	25.57	2849.56	3.55
182	立洲电站	35.50	11.1898	2.28	95.62	41.14	25.50	2086.86	1.74
183	上通坝电厂	24.00	8.4835	1.55	94.04	26.23	13.15	3135.90	0.01
184	毛尔盖水电站	42.60	17.7009	1.80	47.40	38.23	31.87	2123.09	4.412
185	圣达水电站	48.00	15.99	17.14	84.83	503.302	272.0459	429.73	0.1985
186	安谷水电站	77.20	23.71	11.79	94.53	538.8669	281.9112	397.52	0.6019
187	大金坪水电站	12.90	4.4781	2.21	100.00	16.17	9.90	1208.5	0.0025
188	洪一水电站	8.00	2.2068	1.35	100.00	6.71	2.98	1528.9	0.0002
189	五一桥水电站	13.70	4.8921	2.05	91.00	16.2855	10.0570	2424.18	0.00694
190	柳坪水电站	12.00	5.2395	5.85	49.80	43.76	31.08	1778.91	0.0084
191	雅都水电站	15.00	6.4782	4.76	49.30	38.02	30.84	1872.32	0.0374
192	柳洪水电站	18.00	6.452	1.00	89.07	15.24	6.49	1299.5	0.0028
193	坪头水电站	18.00	18.00	5.156	1.38	85.57	16.40	7.12	911.00
194	春厂坝水电站	5.40	1.857	2.95	80.97	12.42	5.47	2448.0	0.0062

续表

	水电厂名称	发电运行情况				水库运行情况			
		总装机容量（万 kW）	年发电量（亿 kW・h）	平均耗水率［m^3/（kW・h）］	等效可用系数（%）	年入库总水量（亿 m^3）	发电用水量（亿 m^3）	年末水位（m）	年末库容（亿 m^3）
195	赞拉水电站	6.00	1.047	3.3	88.42	4.05	3.46	2573.5	0.0091
196	黄金坪水电站	85.00	24.3869	6.06	91.47	361.60	147.18	1474.84	1.1335
197	长河坝水电站	260.00	72.0799	1.96	97.72	318.81	140.9	1674.65	8.3539
198	城东水电厂	8.40	3.7655	26.88	96.39	180.55	101.2165	449.06	0.1077
199	大兴水电站	7.50	3.3616	24.29	96.13	155.37	81.6533	568.5	0.162
200	汇溪水电站	7.50	2.4532	5.71	87.90	26.20	14.018	886.3	0.0013
201	虎头寺水电站	6.00	2.218	34.97	95.07	125.69	77.58	465.50	0.12
202	古学水电站	9.00	3.616	2.96	92.86	21.99	10.71	2269.97	0.000428
203	去学水电站	24.60	8.4077	2.12	96.03	37.9364	17.7925	2321.16	1.0845
204	娘拥水电站	9.30	3.689	3.04	96.07	24.03	11.20	3083.74	0.00486
205	硕中水电站	12.00	4.3596	2.49	95.89	26.00	10.86	2931.77	0.0062
206	硕渠水电站	18.00	7.060302	1.82	97.17	28.57	12.88	2753.55	0.0033
207	金康水电站	15.00	6.7179	0.88	97.68	9.54166	5.89064	1972.71	0.0053
208	金元水电站	10.80	4.0981	0.99	93.97	5.81429	4.070295	2607.12	0.0009
209	金平水电站	8.10	2.7501	0.95	98.00	3.728953	2.622456	3072.27	0.1310
210	天龙湖电厂	18.00	9.956	1.88	94.46	21.76	18.72	2145.00	0.24
211	沙阡水电站	5.00	1.178	15.00	95.10	18.15	17.18	500.00	0.344
212	仙女堡水电站	7.60	3.8014	3.99	95.00	21.47	15.17	1116.50	0.01
213	毛滩水电站	10.50	4.26	24.34	98.28	189.99	103.63	404.10	0.12
214	贵州乌江渡发电厂	128.00	37.95	3.42	92.03	127.48	129.94	744.93	15.1748
215	东风发电厂	69.50	29.38	3.28	93.68	96.5798	96.2630	969.32	8.5176
216	万家口子水电站	18.00	1.77	3.21	37.26	17.61	5.69	1419.29	1.14
217	天生桥一级水电厂	120.00	53.40	3.42	85.21	183.29	182.74	772.58	71.81
218	洪家渡电站	60.00	12.981	3.16	89.35	34.29	41.05	1114.57	27.67
219	索风营电站	60.00	21.4768	5.21	92.14	111.75	111.84	833.60	1.50
220	构皮滩水电站	300.00	73.62	2.39	100.00	174.79	176.18	607.88	37.54
221	思林水电站	105.00	35.9238	5.63	91.72	201.84	202.14	438.00	11.29
222	沙沱水电站	112.00	39.31	5.79	88.23	227.13	227.77	361.30	6.67
223	窄巷口水电站	5.40	1.11	7.65	97.11	9.68	8.45	1087.18	—
224	红林水电站	13.50	2.93	3.03	99.23	9.71	8.86	1016.09	0.00
225	大花水水电站	20.00	7.3307	2.97	94.79	23.21	21.76	857.98	1.83
226	格里桥水电站	15.00	5.6904	4.23	84.51	25.62	24.05	715.29	0.62
227	光照发电厂	104.00	22.48	2.83	92.25	71.16	63.63	728.76	23.75
228	普定发电公司	8.40	3.78	8.56	82.69	37.05	32.37	1136.32	2.08

续表

水电厂名称		发电运行情况				水库运行情况			
		总装机容量（万 kW）	年发电量（亿 kW·h）	平均耗水率［m^3/(kW·h)］	等效可用系数（%）	年入库总水量（亿 m^3）	发电用水量（亿 m^3）	年末水位（m）	年末库容（亿 m^3）
229	引子渡水电站	36.00	9.92	4.05	90.63	40.19	40.15	1065.52	2.29
230	贵州鱼塘电站	7.50	2.87	7.88	95.94	25.13	22.62	458.77	0.71
231	董箐发电厂	88.00	29.66	3.33	93.38	98.81	98.69	489.01	8.61
232	天生桥水力发电总厂（二级）	132.00	84.08	2.17	89.70	182.74	182.76	641.43	0.101
233	石垭子水电站	14.00	3.45	3.95	98.29	14.82	13.65	539.41	2.86
234	双河口水电站	12.00	5.06	5.31	93.43	33.24	26.89	558.99	0.94
235	冗各水电站	9.00	3.09	9.32	95.24	33.38	28.81	492.52	0.27
236	团坡水电站	8.00	2.71	3.30	88.89	11.66	8.94	804.81	0.0054
237	黄花寨水电站	6.00	2.2155	4.79	100.00	11.88	10.61	792.20	1.50
238	大田河水电站	10.00	4.08	1.28	89.86	6.70	5.22	779.60	0.026
239	马马崖电站	55.80	14.14	5.72	90.19	80.83	80.88	580.62	1.09
240	善泥坡发电厂	18.55	6.97	4.24	94.41	32.33	29.51	872.67	0.48
241	毛家河水电站	18.00	4.96	2.94	91.85	15.40	14.59	1294.84	0.11
242	灰洞水电站	5.00	1.94	6.49	98.48	14.04	12.56	645.48	0.0069
243	象鼻岭水电厂	24.00	6.66	3.93	89.72	28.26	26.15	1396.31	1.93
244	上尖坡水电站	6.00	2.29	4.43	97.08	16.19	10.16	665.05	0.10
245	金安桥水力发电厂	240.00	106.46	3.59	89.28	643.71	382.32	1416.48	8.16
246	大湾水电站	4.98	1.3018	6.16	96.71	8.1406	8.0223	745.12	0.20
247	观音岩水电站	300.00	124.16	3.85	93.63	682.83	487.59	1132.29	20.08
248	阿海水电站	200.00	84.6823	5.00	96.17	646.83	423.19	1502.46	7.73
249	鲁地拉水电站	216.00	86.0833	5.05	93.72	669.98	434.85	1221.32	15.43
250	梨园水电站	240.00	97.7403	3.74	92.14	547.40	365.46	1616.27	7.03
251	漫湾水电厂	167.00	72.11	4.65	91.68	340.3457	335.5692	991.57	3.1844
252	景洪水电厂	175.00	74.81	6.68	89.58	500.0611	499.4834	599.58	7.9753
253	小湾水电厂	420.00	162.95	1.83	96.66	355.8937	297.9693	1239.28	144.2326
254	糯扎渡水电厂	585.00	228.29	2.10	90.74	501.1831	478.5851	809.68	210.3182
255	功果桥水电厂	90.00	29.06	7.17	95.64	310.1948	208.3089	1306.05	3.0365
256	苗尾水电厂	140.00	59.93	4.18	97.73	302.3882	250.3017	1405.62	6.4756
257	龙开口水电厂	180.00	61.89	5.90	92.74	652.1240	369.3453	1295.69	4.7261
258	里底水电站	14.00	1.84	12.16	100.00	276.3574	21.0837	1815.34	0.6113
259	黄登水电站	142.50	42.52	2.87	100.00	304.3250	121.9538	1614.10	13.9723
260	大华桥水电站	69.00	25.36	6.06	100.00	296.4424	152.5751	1473.79	2.3508

续表

水电厂名称		发电运行情况				水库运行情况			
		总装机容量（万kW）	年发电量（亿kW·h）	平均耗水率[m³/(kW·h)]	等效可用系数（%）	年入库总水量（亿m³）	发电用水量（亿m³）	年末水位（m）	年末库容（亿m³）
261	徐村水电厂	8.58	3.4578	8.17	97.39	34.1539	28.2350	1304.66	0.6556
262	普西桥水电站	19.00	11.53	3.67	95.26	46.91	42.37	730.98	2.36
263	大盈江水电站	10.80	4.42	8.09	97.41	61.38	35.73	788.00	0.01
264	大寨水力发电厂	6.00	2.50	2.38	98.02	7.21	5.95	1481.41	0.00
265	螺丝湾水电站	6.00	6.02	2.37	95.40	16.04	14.25	2257.55	0.00
266	鲁布革水力发电厂	60.00	25.40	1.31	93.39	41.98	33.23	1127.89	0.7897
267	以礼河发电厂	32.15	12.9906	0.34	93.44	4.28	4.44	2218.71	3.05
268	崖羊山水电站	12.00	4.48	6.40	94.67	34.72	28.72	825.00	1.50
269	石门坎水电站	13.00	5.43	5.31	96.58	37.07	28.84	754.21	1.85
270	龙马水电站	28.50	11.86	3.66	92.01	61.28	43.43	615.10	2.49
271	居甫渡水电站	28.50	13.19	6.92	93.96	103.98	91.24	520.22	1.60
272	戈兰滩水电站	45.00	20.04	4.97	95.93	128.23	99.63	455.60	3.90
273	土卡河水电站	16.50	6.96	17.26	96.02	142.81	120.07	365.50	0.59
274	吉沙水电站	12.00	11.00	0.78	98.31	9.62	8.55	3130.75	0.01
275	冲江河水电站	7.03	6.66	2.04	94.24	15.05	13.56	2468.40	0.00
276	那兰水电站	15.00	7.03	4.28	96.07	40.37	30.11	424.07	1.83
277	马鹿塘水电站	30.00	13.80	1.18	94.24	28.53	16.29	620.76	4.22
278	勐野江水电站	6.80	3.33	3.22	96.71	16.87	10.66	760.66	0.29
279	岗曲河一级水电站	6.00	1.9529	3.28	99.65	11.4394	6.4058	2578.30	0.0527
280	泗南江水电站	20.10	10.42225	0.96	87.177	18.238	12.73522	899.20	2.40052
281	庙林水电站	7.15	3.03318	86.15	94.66	20.1211	13.5925	811.05	0.077
282	天花板水电站	18.00	7.296248	0.922	95.66	41.5191	30.8889	1062.78	0.49306
283	小岩头水电站	12.99	4.430496	1.00	98.267	28.2228	25.6969	1277.21	0.012
284	柴石滩水电站	6.00	1.335764	1.04	94.60	11.5629	10.4915	1626.02	2.0814
285	赛珠水电站	10.20	3.160361	0.94	85.39	2.6365	1.857	1814.16	0.012
286	普渡河六级水电站	9.60	4.970128	1.00	91.823	32.5711	23.7743	1087.58	0.0765
287	铅厂水电站	11.40	5.69295	0.75	97.085	26.9801	17.9897	1223.40	0.1636
288	甲岩水电站	24.00	10.223247	1.00	88.003	34.0378	27.2206	980.80	1.1045
289	石泉水力发电厂	22.50	7.12	10.00	88.64	87.44	71.24	400.24	1.10
290	喜河水力发电厂	18.00	5.54	13.81	93.05	92.83	76.55	361.75	1.64
291	蜀河水力发电厂	27.00	8.98	18.33	87.71	173.90	164.70	216.57	1.72
292	碧口水力发电厂	33.00	14.6827	5.022	99.23	93.2494	73.7295	702.81	1.3781
293	苗家坝水电站	27.00	10.7375	4.281	97.78	51.4128	45.9713	796.53	2.4382

续表

	水电厂名称	发电运行情况				水库运行情况			
		总装机容量（万 kW）	年发电量（亿 kW·h）	平均耗水率［m³/(kW·h)］	等效可用系数（%）	年入库总水量（亿 m³）	发电用水量（亿 m³）	年末水位（m）	年末库容（亿 m³）
294	麒麟寺水电站	11.10	4.4131	18.288	95.29	100.1817	80.7091	612.04	0.2245
295	青铜峡水电厂	32.70	14.46	21.54	94.72	389.24	311.44	1156.04	0.38
296	班多水电厂	36.00	16.32	10.52	93.59	261.18	171.71	2758.70	0.07
297	龙羊峡水电厂	128.00	76.88	2.96	94.52	292.64	227.30	2597.95	239.24
298	拉西瓦水电厂	350.00	130.04	1.87	96.57	266.16	243.67	2450.20	9.80
299	李家峡水电厂	160.00	71.12	3.28	89.59	266.70	233.54	2178.71	16.08
300	公伯峡水电厂	150.00	64.19	3.86	92.18	273.54	247.88	2003.90	5.28
301	苏只水电厂	22.50	11.02	22.71	95.91	272.41	250.15	1898.55	0.37
302	积石峡水电站	102.00	42.25	6.24	95.98	286.19	263.56	1850.55	1.82
303	盐锅峡水电厂	50.96	27.65	10.76	95.56	366.47	297.44	1619.22	0.42
304	八盘峡水电厂	22.00	10.44	29.30	92.19	407.83	305.86	1577.83	0.27
305	直岗拉卡水电公司	19.00	7.9558	30.72	95.62	256.55	244.39	2050	0.14
306	纳子峡水电站	8.70	3.94	3.67	91.59	16.40	14.44	3196.34	6.21
307	金沙峡水电站	7.00	3.07	6.01	90.05	19.59	18.46	2166.20	0.023
308	达拉河水电站	5.25	2.01	2.06	100.00	7.94	4.14	2264.01	0.10
309	代古寺水电站	8.70	3.34	5.22	100.00	19.46	17.43	1708	—
310	凉风壳水电站	5.25	2.26	8.29	87.63	20.55	18.75	1468.8	—
311	沙尔布拉克水电站	5.00	1.3046	9.01	96.26	18.02	11.75	799.18	0.74
312	和田水电厂	7.00	1.6726	5.17	76.30	23.49	8.65	1772.90	0.08
313	库什塔依水电站	10.00	3.35	6.00	96.00	20.72	20.32	1304.00	1.42
314	塔日勒嘎水电站	5.00	1.8306	8.40	41.79	16.8004	15.377	2249.5	0.3159
315	新疆呼图壁水电站	9.50	2.0012	2.02	100.00	4.0893	4.0488	1216.31	0.3363
316	萨里克特水电站	8.00	2.78	5.34	93.63	14.84	14.84	1908.8	—
317	温泉水电站	18.00	7.37	5.01	96.09	36.90	36.95	952.84	0.97
318	塔勒德萨依水电站	8.00	2.54	7.10	98.22	18.05	18.05	1774.74	—
319	察汗乌苏水电站	33.00	22.05	2.98	92.97	68.21	65.77	1641.89	0.60
320	吉林台一级水电站	50.00	10.47	3.36	95.30	35.07	35.18	1400.5	6.73
321	尼勒克水电站	24.00	13.30	2.28	97.92	35.26	30.35	1223.53	0.00
322	柳树沟水电站	18.00	7.51	4.87	97.81	37.23	36.56	1494.39	0.00
323	小石峡水电站	13.75	4.03	9.17	94.32	50.59	36.97	1480.11	—
324	多布水电站	12.00	4.09	20.49	89.48	156.41	83.83	3075.7	0.12

（各发电公司、各水电厂提供资料）

2018年全国电力统计基本数据一览表

项　　目	单位	2018年	2017年	比上年增长（±、%）
一、发电量	亿kW·h	69947	64529	8.40
水电	亿kW·h	12321	11947	3.13
其中：抽水蓄能	亿kW·h	329	328	0.44
火电	亿kW·h	49249	45877	7.35
其中：燃煤	亿kW·h	44829	41782	7.29
燃气	亿kW·h	2155	2032	6.04
燃油	亿kW·h	15	27	−42.53
其中：生物质发电	亿kW·h	936	813	15.23
核电	亿kW·h	2950	2481	18.87
风电	亿kW·h	3658	3046	20.09
太阳能发电	亿kW·h	1769	1178	50.24
其他	亿kW·h	1	1	−4.15
6000kW及以上火电厂发电量	亿kW·h	49167	45762	7.44
燃煤	亿kW·h	44821	41772	7.30
其中：煤矸石发电	亿kW·h	1286	1423	−9.58
燃气	亿kW·h	2134	2016	5.86
其中：常规燃气	亿kW·h	2053	1957	4.93
煤层气发电	亿kW·h	70	52	35.94
燃油	亿kW·h	15	27	−42.45
其他	亿kW·h	2143	1920	11.62
其中：余温、余气、余压发电	亿kW·h	1230	1129	8.96
垃圾焚烧发电	亿kW·h	481	376	28.08
秸秆、蔗渣、林木质发电	亿kW·h	427	413	3.40
二、全社会用电量	亿kW·h	69002	63636	8.43
A. 全行业用电合计	亿kW·h	59310	54849	8.13
第一产业	亿kW·h	746	684	8.99
第二产业	亿kW·h	47733	44571	7.09
其中：工业	亿kW·h	46954	43874	7.02
第三产业	亿kW·h	10831	9593	12.90
B. 城乡居民生活用电合计	亿kW·h	9692	8788	10.29
城镇居民	亿kW·h	5531	5010	10.40
乡村居民	亿kW·h	4162	3778	10.15
三、发电装机容量	万kW	190012	178451	6.48
水电	万kW	35259	34411	2.46

续表

项 目	单位	2018年	2017年	比上年增长（±、%）
其中：抽水蓄能	万kW	2999	2869	4.52
火电	万kW	114408	111009	3.06
其中：燃煤	万kW	100835	98562	2.31
燃气	万kW	8375	7580	10.49
燃油	万kW	173	197	−11.94
其中：生物质发电	万kW	10.47	1657	17.93
核电	万kW	4466	3582	24.68
风电	万kW	18427	16400	12.35
太阳能发电	万kW	17433	13042	33.66
其他	万kW	20	7	200.35
6000kW及以上火电厂装机容量	万kW	114100	110506	3.25
燃煤	万kW	100794	98517	2.31
其中：煤矸石发电	万kW	3240	3518	−7.90
燃气	万kW	8313	7532	10.37
其中：常规燃气发电	万kW	8139	7400	9.98
煤层气发电	万kW	151	113	33.32
燃油	万kW	170	193	−12.11
其他	万kW	4755	4199	13.24
其中：余温、余气、余发电	万kW	2854	2626	8.68
垃圾焚烧发电	万kW	889	722	23.08
秸秆、蔗渣、林木质发电	万kW	969	850	13.97
四、35kV及以上输电线路回路长度	km	1892018	1825611	3.64
1. 交流	km	1850631	1788212	3.49
其中：1000kV	km	11005	10073	9.25
750kV	km	20543	18830	9.10
500kV	km	187158	173772	7.70
330kV	km	30477	30183	0.97
220kV	km	434493	415311	4.62
110kV	km	652891	631361	3.41
35kV	km	514066	508682	1.06
2. 直流	km	41995	37399	12.29
其中：±1100kV	km	608		
±800kV	km	21723	20874	4.07
±660kV	km	2091	1334	56.75
±500kV	km	15428	13552	13.84
±400kV	km	1640	1640	

续表

项 目	单位	2018年	2017年	比上年增长（±、%）
五、35kV及以上变电设备容量	万kVA	699219	662928	5.47
1. 交流	万kVA	666622	630730	5.69
其中：1000kV	万kVA	14700	13800	6.52
750kV	万kVA	17030	14540	17.13
500kV	万kVA	136494	125508	8.75
330kV	万kVA	13125	13029	0.74
220kV	万kVA	213127	203352	4.81
110kV	万kVA	219379	209847	4.54
35kV	万kVA	52767	50654	4.17
2. 直流	万kVA	33196	32198	3.10
其中：±1100kV	万kVA	600		
±800kV	万kVA	17361	17841	−2.69
±660kV	万kVA	947	947	
±500kV	万kVA	13353	13410	−0.43
±400kV	万kVA	141		
六、新增发电装机容量	万kW	12785	13019	−1.80
水电	万kW	859	1287	−33.27
其中：抽水蓄能	万kW	130	200	−35.00
火电	万kW	4380	4453	−1.65
其中：燃煤	万kW	3056	3504	−12.79
燃气	万kW	884	571	54.87
其中：常规燃气	万kW	881	571	54.42
煤层气发电		2		
燃油	万kW			
其他	万kW	440	379	16.26
其中：余温、余气、余压	万kW	198	175	13.13
垃圾焚烧发电	万kW	148	123	20.53
秸秆、蔗渣、林木质发电	万kW	94	81	16.51
核电	万kW	884	218	306.44
风电	万kW	2127	1720	23.64
太阳能发电	万kW	4525	5341	−15.26
其他	万kW	10		
七、火电机组退役和关停容量	万kW	1197	929	28.79
八、年底主要发电企业电源项目在建规模	万kW	17890	20804	−14.01
水电	万kW	7940	7887	0.68
火电	万kW	6936	8637	−19.70
核电	万kW	1345	2289	−41.23
风电	万kW	1564	1909	−18.07

续表

项　　目	单位	2018年	2017年	比上年增长（±、%）
九、新增直流输电线路长度及换流容量				
1. 线路长度	km	3325	8339	−60.13
其中：±1100kV	km	3325		
±800kV	km		8339	−100.00
±660kV	km			
±500kV	km			
±400kV	km			
2. 换流容量	万kW	3200	7900	−59.49
其中：±1100kV	万kW	1200		
±800kV	万kW	2000	7700	−74.03
±660kV	万kW			
±500kV	万kW		200	−100.00
±400kV	万kW			
十、新增交流110kV及以上输电线路长度及变电设备容量				
1. 线路长度	km	56973	58084	−1.91
其中：1000kV	km	129	2846	−95.47
750kV	km	1573	899	74.97
500kV	km	14540	7999	81.77
330kV	km	828	2521	−67.16
220kV	km	20697	18810	10.03
110kV（含66kV）	km	19206	25010	−23.21
2. 变电设备容量	万kVA	31024	32595	−4.82
其中：1000kV	万kVA	900	3000	−70.00
750kV	万kVA	1140	1740	−34.48
500kV	万kVA	11160	8275	34.86
330kV	万kVA	612	783	−21.84
220kV	万kVA	8402	10433	−19.47
110kV（含66kV）	万kVA	8810	8364	5.33
十一、本年完成电力投资	亿元	8161	8239	−0.94
1. 电源投资	亿元	2787	2900	−3.89
水电	亿元	700	622	12.65
火电	亿元	786	858	−8.31
核电	亿元	447	454	−1.55
风电	亿元	646	681	−5.12
太阳能发电	亿元	207	285	−27.38
其他	亿元			
2. 电网投资	亿元	5374	5339	0.65
送变电	亿元	5133	5135	−0.04

续表

项 目	单位	2018年	2017年	比上年增长（±、%）
其中：直流	亿元	520	859	−39.41
交流	亿元	4613	4276	7.87
其他	亿元	241	204	18.10
十二、单机6000kW及以上机组平均单机容量				
水电：单机容量	万kW/台	6.10	6.07	0.02
机组台数	台	4894	4816	1.62
机组容量	万kW	29830	29252	1.98
火电：单机容量	万kW/台	13.38	13.15	0.23
机组台数	台	8070	7796	3.51
机组容量	万kW	107969	102501	5.33
十三、6000kW及以上电厂供热量	万GJ	480625	421084	14.14
十四、6000kW及以上电厂发电标准煤耗	g/(kW·h)	289.9	291.3	−1.3
十五、6000kW及以上电厂供电标准煤耗	g/(kW·h)	307.6	309.4	−1.8
十六、6000kW及以上电厂厂用电率	%	4.69	4.80	−0.11
水电	%	0.25	0.27	−0.02
火电	%	5.95	6.04	−0.09
十七、6000kW及以上电厂发电设备利用小时	h	3880	3790	90h
水电	h	3607	3597	10h
其中：抽水蓄能	h	1102	1176	−74h
火电	h	4378	4219	159h
核电	h	7543	7089	454h
风电	h	2103	1949	155h
太阳能发电	h	1230	1205	25h
十八、6000kW及以上电厂燃料消耗				
发电消耗标煤量	万吨	130805	121811	7.38
发电消耗原煤量	万吨	195719	177592	10.21
供热消耗标煤量	万吨	18104	16519	9.60
供热消耗原煤量	万吨	27523	24248	13.51
十九、供、售电量及线损				
供电量	亿kW·h	59508	54357	9.48
售电量	亿kW·h	55777	50835	9.72
线损电量	亿kW·h	3731	3522	5.93
线路损失率	%	6.27	6.48	−0.21
二十、发用电设备比				

注 1. 电源投资完成额口径为全国主要发电企业。

2. 从2018年5月份开始，三次产业划分按照《国家统计局关于修订〈三次产业划分规定（2012）〉的通知》（国统设管函〔2018〕74号）调整，为保证数据可比，同期数据根据新标准重新进行了分类。

（中国电力企业联合会）

2018年全国水电40MW及以上容量机组运行可靠性综合指标

机组分类	机组容量（MW）	台数	台年数	平均容量（MW/台）	利用小时 UTH	可用小时		不可用小时及次数						降低出力等效停运小时	等效可用系数 EAF（%）	等效强迫停运率 EFOR（%）
						运行 SH	备用 RH	计划停运		非计划停运		强迫停运				
								次数	小时	次数	小时	次数	小时			
抽水蓄能机组	全部	103	103	263.92	2585.83	2806.2	4816.88	7.76	1113.8	1.06	23.13	0.84	7.28	0	87.02	0.26
	40～99MW	7	7	67.14	1806.63	1783.97	3549.04	6.14	3418.2	1.00	8.79	0.86	4.45	0	60.88	0.25
	100～199MW	6	6	150	2506.47	2375.58	5596.27	8.50	788.09	0.17	0.05	0.17	0.05	0	91.00	0.00
	200～299MW	27	27	240.74	2298.06	2413.71	5217.87	7.30	1121.16	0.56	7.26	0.52	4.81	0	87.12	0.20
	300MW及以上	63	63	306.57	2705.33	2983.23	4676.46	8.06	1070.42	1.37	29.90	1.05	8.51	0	87.44	0.28
水电轴流机组	全部	158	156.07	103.46	4344.52	5520.6	2589.49	1.65	644.99	0.15	4.92	0.09	4.24	0	92.58	0.08
	40～99MW	74	73.75	57.78	3844.71	4822.25	3218.29	1.99	703.09	0.26	16.38	0.15	13.94	0	91.79	0.29
	100～199MW	75	73.31	136.35	4872.07	6140.48	2031.66	1.16	587.19	0.05	0.68	0.03	0.62	0	93.29	0.01
	200～299MW	9	9	204.94	2635.35	3769.05	4164.88	2.89	824.61	0.11	1.46	0.11	1.46	0	90.57	0.04
水电混流机组	全部	754	749.92	235.23	3986.98	5138.39	3022.9	1.32	587.75	0.11	10.96	0.06	4.66	6.31	93.09	0.09
	40～99MW	316	313.62	61.06	3488.24	4724.56	3527.74	1.22	505.47	0.06	2.24	0.05	1.31	58.06	93.54	0.03
	100～199MW	135	135	134.96	3332.65	4317.59	3754.12	1.38	661.36	0.07	26.94	0.04	26.63	0	92.14	0.61
	200～299MW	84	83.85	236.36	3359.92	4232.57	3901.01	1.35	623.85	0.11	2.57	0.02	0.60	0	92.85	0.01
	300MW及以上	219	217.45	547.93	4272.05	5481.73	2683.24	1.4	583.71	0.19	11.31	0.11	2.51	0	93.21	0.05
全部	全部	1015	1008.98	217.63	3839.66	4877.52	3213.32	2.03	657.13	0.21	12.02	0.14	4.95	5.07	92.30	0.10

（中国电力企业联合会）

中國水力發電年鑒

17

大 事 记

2018年大事记

一月

1月5日 三峡集团讯，2017年，长江电力积极践行“为长江提供防洪保障、为社会奉献清洁能源”的企业使命，科学运营管理长江干流溪洛渡、向家坝、三峡、葛洲坝4座梯级水电站。截至2017年12月31日，2017年发电量达到2108.9亿kW·h，首次突破2100亿kW·h，再次刷新2016年创造的发电量历史纪录。

1月7日 白鹤滩电站高低线拌和系统混凝土生产量突破90万m^3，累计达到909139.3万m^3。此次大坝混凝土生产量突破90万m^3，其中低线拌和系统生产混凝土786684.3m^3，高线拌和系统生产混凝土122455m^3。低线拌和系统当班最高产量4149m^3，日最高产量6597m^3。两系统班产量最高达到4149m^3，单楼最高班产量达到2340m^3，单楼最高日产量达到3672m^3。

1月8日 2017年度国家科学技术奖励大会在北京人民大会堂隆重举行。水电科技共有3个项目获奖，其中，“堆石混凝土坝”“水库高坝/大坝安全精准监测与高效加固关键技术”获国家技术发明奖二等奖（通用项目），“锦屏二级超深埋特大引水隧洞发电工程关键技术”获国家科学技术进步奖二等奖（通用项目）。

1月8日 《中国能源报》讯，截至2017年12月26日，四川省全年全口径外送水电（含国调机组）1389.87亿kW·h，同比增长7.99%，川电外送电量357.04亿kW·h，同比增长35.03%，均创历史新高。1389亿kW·h清洁水电外送，相当于节约标准煤4800多万t，减少二氧化碳排放超过1.28亿t、二氧化硫约120万t。

1月12日 由中国水力发电工程学会与国家电网公司联合主办的2018中国水电发展论坛暨水力发电科学技术奖颁奖典礼在北京举行。来自全国水力发电战线80多个单位的300余名新老水电工作者代表以及来自有关水电国际组织的专家出席了会议，共同见证过去一年我国水电科技事业取得的新进展，分享行业各单位在水电科技研究和工程实践中取得的新成果，共谋水电可持续发展。会议对2017年评选出的45项“水力发电科学技术奖”进行了颁奖，还对获得2017年度《水力发电学报》优秀论文奖的10篇获奖论文作者进行了表彰。

1月17日 世界首台百万千瓦水电机组转轮在东方电气集团东方电机有限公司白鹤滩转轮加工厂率先开焊。白鹤滩转轮厂房长149.78m，宽28.52m，高26.343m，最大起吊能力500t，于2017年8月正式移交给东方电机。白鹤滩水轮机转轮直径8.62m，高度3.92m，重量超过350t，转轮有15片叶片，每片叶片重达11t。转轮的上冠、下环、叶片单件分别铸造进行精加工后，运输至工地厂房焊接成为整体。由于运输条件的限制，转轮上冠分为大小不同的两瓣、下环分为相同大小的两瓣进行运输。

1月18～19日 中国华能集团有限公司一届四次职工代表大会暨2018年工作会议在北京召开。会议回顾总结了2017年及过去5年来工作取得的成绩，分析当前面临的形势，部署2018年工作。总经理黄永达作题为《以新思想引领公司高质量发展，加快创建具有全球竞争力的世界一流企业》的工作报告。2017年，中国华能集团有限公司累计完成发电量6608亿kW·h，其中，国内发电量6496亿kW·h，同比增长6.4%；实现合并营业收入2586亿元，同比增长5.1%；全年实现利润10.2亿元。截至2017年底，中国华能集团有限公司境内外全资及控股电厂装机容量17182万kW，同比增长3.8%；低碳清洁能源装机比重达到31%，同比提高2个百分点。

1月19日 农村水电与水库移民司召开2018年工作会议。2017年，水利部以人与自然和谐共生理念为引领，协调推进农村水电绿色发展，完成全国首批44个绿色小水电站创建，建成33座扶贫农村小水电站，对2300多座小水电站进行增效扩容改造。

1月19～22日 国家电网公司第三届职工代表大会第三次会议暨2018年工作会议在北京召开。会议总结2017年工作，分析形势，明确新时代战略目标和思路，部署2018年重点任务。董事长舒印彪作了题为《以习近平新时代中国特色社会主义思想为指导，为建设世界一流能源互联网企业不懈奋斗》的工作报告。2017年，国家电网实现售电量3.87万亿kW·h，同比增长7.47%；省间交易电量8735亿kW·h，同比增长10.6%；营业收入同比增长10.97%，实现利润同比增长5.10%。全年电网投资4853.6亿元，同比减少2.23%。农网投资1474亿元。全年110（66）kV及以上输电线路新增5.5万km，变电（换流）容量增加3.5亿kW。

1月22日 国家能源局发布2017年全社会用电量等数据。2017年，全社会用电量63077亿kW·h，同比增长6.6%。2017年，全国6000kW及以上电厂发电设备累计平均利用小时为3786h，同比减少11h。其中，水电设备平均利用小时为3579h，同比减少40h；火电设备平均利用小时为4209h，同比增加23h。2017年，全国电源新增生产能力（正式投产）

13372 万 kW，其中，水电 1287 万 kW，火电 4578 万 kW。

1 月 22 日 在国家发展改革委主办的 2018 年首场新闻发布会获悉，2017 年，我国发电量同比增长 6.5%，其中，火电发电量同比增长 5.2%。清洁能源发电量同比增长 10%，增速高于火电 4.8 个百分点，其中，水电、核电、风电、太阳能发电量同比分别增长 1.7%、16.5%、26.3%和 75.4%。

1 月 22～23 日 中国南方电网有限责任公司第三届职工代表大会第一次会议暨 2018 年工作会议在广州召开。会议总结 2017 年工作，分析形势，部署 2018 年和今后一段时期的重点任务。总经理曹志安作了题为《锐意进取，埋头苦干，扎实做好贯彻党的十九大精神开局之年的各项工作》的工作报告。2017 年，南方电网完成售电量 8902 亿 kW·h，增长 7.3%；营业收入 4946 亿元，增长 4.5%；资产总额 7445 亿元，增长 8%；完成固定资产投资 1151 亿元，同比增长 12.6%。全年完成西电东送电量 2028 亿 kW·h，创历史新高。

1 月 22～24 日 中国大唐集团有限公司 2018 年工作会议在北京召开。会议总结 2017 年工作，研究部署新时代新阶段奋斗目标和 2018 年重点工作。总经理陈飞虎作了题为《坚持以习近平新时代中国特色社会主义思想为指导，努力实现"一五八"战略逐步赶超阶段良好开局》的工作报告。2017 年，中国大唐集团有限公司资产总额达到 7266 亿元，营业收入达到 1710 亿元，装机规模达到 1.38 亿 kW，全年完成发电量 5169 亿 kW·h，实现利润 64.68 亿元，资产负债率降至 79.96%。

1 月 23～24 日 中国华电集团有限公司 2018 年度工作会议在北京召开。会议总结 2017 年工作，分析形势和任务，部署 2018 年重点工作。2017 年，中国华电集团有限公司实现销售收入 2006 亿元，同比增长 7.6%；资产负债率 80.8%，同比降低 0.73 个百分点；完成实发电量 5123 亿 kW·h，同比增长 4.1%；供热量 2.53 亿 GJ，同比增长 14.1%；清洁能源装机容量占 38.6%，同比提高 1.3 个百分点。

1 月 24 日 "国际能源网"报道，我国各种电力基地渐渐成形，包括 13 大水电基地、9 大煤电基地、7 大风电基地，以及光伏领跑者基地。其中，13 大水电基地的规划总装机容量超过 28576 万 kW，已建成装机容量为 12599 万 kW，在建装机容量为 5444 万 kW，筹建项目装机容量为 2378 万 kW，取消或停建项目为 236.4 万 kW（浙、闽、赣规划的 1417 万 kW 暂无具体数据）；7 大风电基地，规划预计到 2020 年，7 大千万级风电基地总装机容量将达 12600 万 kW，其中，河北 1080 万 kW，甘肃（酒泉）1270 万 kW，新疆（哈密）1080 万 kW，吉林 2300 万 kW，内蒙古 5780 万 kW，江苏 1000 万 kW；10 大光伏基地，再加上 2017 年之前的 10 大领跑者基地的 1720 万 kW，规划装机总量也随之达到了 4920 万 kW。

1 月 24 日 从国家能源局新闻发布会获悉，截至 2017 年底，我国可再生能源发电装机容量达到 6.5 亿 kW，同比增长 14%；其中，水电装机容量 3.41 亿 kW、风电装机容量 1.64 亿 kW、光伏发电装机容量 1.3 亿 kW、生物质发电装机容量 1488 万 kW，分别同比增长 2.7%、10.5%，68.7% 和 22.6%。可再生能源发电装机容量约占全部电力装机容量的 36.6%，同比上升 2.1 个百分点。

1 月 25 日 由中国电力建设集团有限公司承担设计施工的老挝南俄 4 水电工程举行开工典礼。南俄 4 水电项目位于老挝北部川矿省，为引水式开发，工程永久建筑物主要由首部枢纽、引水工程和厂区枢纽 3 部分组成。首部枢纽布置由碾压混凝土重力坝、溢流表孔、左岸冲沙底孔及消力池组成；右岸引水发电系统由进水口、引水隧洞、调压井、压力钢管及地面厂房组成。设计安装 3 台 8 万 kW 混流式机组，总装机容量 24 万 kW，计划建设工期 66 个月。

1 月 25 日 广州电力交易中心 2018 年工作会议召开。会议介绍，2017 年，南方区域全年西电东送电量达到 2028 亿 kW·h，首次突破 2000 亿 kW·h，同比增长 3.8%。其中，全年市场化方式增送云南富余水电 268 亿 kW·h，超额完成国家发展改革委下达的增送任务。2017 年各省累计交易电量 2680 亿 kW·h，达到全社会用电量的近 30%。

1 月 25～26 日 水电水利规划设计总院在秦皇岛市主持召开了河北抚宁抽水蓄能电站可行性研究阶段施工总布置规划专题报告审查会议。审查认为，报告的设计内容和工作深度满足《水电工程可行性研究阶段施工总布置规划专题报告编制暂行规定》要求，基本同意报告推荐的施工总布置规划方案和枢纽工程建设区施工用地范围，经补充和修改完善后，可作为河北省人民政府发布禁止在工程占地区新增建设项目和迁入人口通告，以及部署开展实物指标调查和移民安置规划设计的依据。该电站位于河北省秦皇岛市区境内，枢纽工程主要由上水库、输水系统、地下厂房及开关站、下水库等建筑物组成。装机容量 120 万 kW，初拟首台机组发电工期为 66 个月，施工总工期为 78 个月。

1 月 27 日 由中国科协调宣部主办，中国科协创新战略研究院、中国城市规划学会承办的"中国工业遗产保护名录"（第一批）发布会在中国科技会堂举行。在首批名录中，石龙坝水电站、丰满水电站、水丰水电站、佛子岭水库大坝、三门峡水利枢纽等 5

座水利水电工程入选。这些“遗产”最大的特点就是“还在使用”，而且，在可预见的未来还将继续使用下去。这足以证明，水利水电工程的可持续性、经济性和环保性。

1月28日 从四川省两会上获悉，四川省2017年水电装机容量达7564万kW，稳居全国第一，清洁能源发电量占总发电量的88%，初步建成国家重要的清洁能源基地。近年来，四川省依托省内丰富的水力资源，初步建成了全国最大的水电生产和外送基地。2017年四川省外送水电1389.52亿kW·h，相当于为受电地区节约标准煤5000多万吨，减少二氧化碳、二氧化硫排放分别超过1.3亿t、125万t。

1月28～29日 中国电力建设集团（股份）有限公司2018年工作会议在北京召开。会议总结2017年工作，分析面临的形势，部署2018年工作。总经理孙洪水作了题为《深化改革促转型，精益管理创效益，高质量稳步建设新时代世界一流企业集团》的工作报告。2017年，中国电建集团紧紧围绕加强党建、深化改革、精益管理、提质增效等中心工作，因势利导，攻坚克难，较好地完成了全年改革发展党建的各项任务目标。实现营业收入3635.18亿元，利润总额126.21亿元。资产负债率78.26%。

1月29～30日 水电水利规划设计总院在合肥市主持召开了安徽桐城抽水蓄能电站可行性研究阶段施工总布置规划专题报告审查会议。与会专家针对报告目前存在的问题提出了14条建议，待设计单位修改补充完善报告后将继续下一步审查工作。该电站位于安徽省桐城市境内，枢纽工程主要由上水库、输水系统、地下厂房及下水库等建筑物组成。装机容量128万kW，初拟首台机组发电工期为58个月，施工总工期为70个月。

1月29～30日 中国能源建设集团（股份）有限公司2018年工作会议在北京召开。会议总结2017年工作，分析形势，部署2018年各项工作。2017年，中国能建集团面对严峻复杂的经营环境和艰巨繁重的改革发展任务，加快转型、提质增效，经受住了严峻市场形势、激烈市场竞争和繁重改革发展任务的考验，实现了主要经营目标，内部改革深入推进，管理水平不断提高。新签合同金额同比增长7.13%、营业收入同比增长5.09%、实现利润总额同比增长18.20%。

1月31日 国家电力投资集团有限公司2018年工作会议在北京召开。会议总结2017年工作，分析形势，研究新时期战略定位，部署2018年工作。总经理孟振平作了题为《深入学习贯彻党的十九大精神，为建设世界一流综合能源集团而努力奋斗》的工作报告。2017年，国家电投集团营业收入突破2000亿元。电力总装机容量达到1.26亿kW，其中清洁能源占比为45.14%，光伏发电总装机容量突破千万千瓦。全年发电量4226亿kW·h。建成新能源生产运营中心28个、水电集控中心8个。

二月

2月1日 由中国电建集团西北勘测设计研究院有限公司设计的宝鸡市金陵河流域综合治理工程首座液压坝建成并成功蓄水。该工程位于宝鸡市金台区，工程通过人工修复措施促进河道水生态系统恢复，构建健康、完整、稳定的河流生态系统；金陵河下游金河尚居段液压坝，长度78m，坝高2.5m，回水长度约1km，形成景观水面约7万m^2。工程治理长度为9.8km，工程投资约1亿元。

2月1日 乌东德水电站二道坝工程建基面开挖正式通过验收。验收意见认为，该项工程建基面开挖爆破方案合理，施工工艺控制严格，已按设计要求完成开挖，且开挖质量满足设计及规范要求；同时，开挖揭示的岩体质量满足设计要求，验收资料齐备，项目施工内容均已完成，可正式通过验收。乌东德水电站二道坝工程为碾压混凝土重力坝，距大坝坝址约288m，其作用在于配合大坝主体形成水垫塘，使泄洪水流落在水垫塘内达到消能作用，减少泄洪水流对下游河床和两岸边坡的冲刷。

2月5～6日 中国长江三峡集团有限公司2018年工作会议暨二届五次职代会在三峡坝区召开。会议回顾总结2017年主要工作，分析面临形势，部署2018年重点工作。总经理王琳作题为《坚持高质量发展，培育全球竞争力，为加快建设世界一流清洁能源集团而不懈奋斗》的工作报告。2017年，三峡集团完成发电量2845.6亿kW·h，可控装机规模达到7001.7万kW，总装机规模达到1.24亿kW，资产规模超过7000亿元。营业收入同比增长率14.93%，净利润环比增长率7.88%，净资产收益率9.51%。

2月6日 从黑龙江省水利厅获悉，2017年，全省11个电站增效扩容改造项目和6个河流生态项目全部开工建设。新增水电装机容量320kW，新增年发电量832万kW·h；4个河流生态改造项目完工并通过完工验收，恢复了12900m减（脱）水河段河流生态流量。截至2017年末，累计完成投资1.5542亿元。

2月6～8日 中国葛洲坝集团（股份）有限公司四届一次职代会暨2018年工作会在宜昌召开。会议总结过去5年工作，明确未来3年的发展战略、发展目标和发展举措。总经理聂凯作《巩固转型成果，加快升级步伐，为开启公司跨越式发展新征程而努力奋斗》的工作报告。2017年，葛洲坝集团加快转型升级步伐、全面提升发展质量，实现了改革发展新突破。实现营业收入1068.07亿元，同比增长6.54%，其中，环保业务实现营收266.82亿元，同比增长60.13%。

2月26日 由中国电力建设集团有限公司所属企业设计施工的巴基斯坦塔贝拉4期扩建工程首台机组成功并网发电。该工程位于巴基斯坦西北开伯尔—普赫图赫瓦省境内印度河干流上。该4期扩建工程是将4号灌溉隧洞改为引水发电隧洞，并由压力钢管一分为3岔管，连接3台单机容量为47万kW的混流式机组，扩容141万kW。电站建成之后，电站整体装机容量将从原有的347.8万kW扩增至488.8万kW。

2月26日 国家能源局以国能发规划〔2018〕22号文发布《2018年能源工作指导意见》，确定2018年能源工作指导方针和主要目标。《意见》中有多处涉及水电的重要内容：积极推进已开工水电项目建设，年内计划新增装机规模约600万kW；年内计划开工建设金沙江拉哇等水电站；年内力争开工建设张北柔性直流试验示范工程、乌东德送电广东广西柔性直流、四川水电外送第四回直流等输电通道；扎实推进陕西、青海、新疆、陇彬、白鹤滩水电、金沙江上游水电电力外送输电通道，以及闽、粤联网工程前期论证；积极推进已开工项目建设，年内计划建成投产广东深圳、海南琼中等抽水蓄能电站。

2月28日 国家发展改革委、国家能源局以发改能源〔2018〕364号文发布《关于提升电力系统调节能力的指导意见》。《意见》强调，“十三五”期间，开工建设6000万kW抽水蓄能电站和金沙江中游龙头水库电站。到2020年，抽水蓄能电站装机规模达到4000万kW（其中，“三北”地区1140万kW），有效提升电力系统调节能力。

三月

3月1日 中共中央印发《深化党和国家机构改革方案》，武警水电部队组建为国有企业，由国务院国有资产监督管理委员会管理。1952年2月18日，中央军委根据毛主席的指示，选中解放军华东野战军步兵第90师改编为中国人民解放军水利工程第一师；1966年8月1日，为适应经济建设需要，根据周恩来签发、毛泽东圈阅的国防部命令，成立组建基建工程兵水电部队；1985年1月1日，水电部队由基建工程兵序列转入武警序列，1999年2月，水电部队划归武警总部统一管理，2009年6月，水电部队纳入国家应急救援力量体系。移交国务院国有资产监督管理委员会后，将以中国安能建设集团有限公司命名，继续承担水利水电工程建设任务。

3月13日 第十三届全国人民代表大会第一次会议举行第四次全体会议听取了国务委员王勇关于国务院机构改革方案的说明。根据此次国务院机构改革的具体方案，水利部职责将进一步优化。国务院三峡工程建设委员会及其办公室、国务院南水北调工程建设委员会及其办公室将并入水利部，不再保留这两个机构。

3月14日 水电水利规划设计总院在北京组织召开了《浙江磐安抽水蓄能电站工程安全预评价报告》审查会议。审查认为：预评价报告的内容和深度满足《水电工程安全预评价报告编制规程》要求，评价单元的划分合理，评价方法选用较为适当，危险、有害因素分析基本符合工程实际，评价结论客观、可信。该电站位于浙江省金华市磐安县境内，枢纽工程主要建筑物由上水库、下水库、输水系统、地下厂房和开关站等组成。装机容量为120万kW，共安装4台单机容量为30万kW的发电机组。

3月19日 国家统计局公布数据显示：2017年水电仅增长0.5%。从年均增速来看，水电发电量已经连续3年下滑。数据显示，2017年水力发电量11898亿kW·h，比上年增长0.5%；与2012年相比，水力发电量增加3177亿kW·h，年均增长6.4%。分地区看，四川、云南、湖北水力发电量分列前3位，均超过1000亿kW·h，分别为3041、2493、1499亿kW·h，比上年分别增长6.6%、9.4%和6.3%，3个地区约占全国水力发电量的6成。梳理发现，2015年水力发电量下滑11.3%，2016年下滑0.5%，2017年下滑4.3%。国家统计局认为，2017年水力发电量增速放缓，主要是受降水量大幅下降、来水差影响，2016年全国平均降水量730mm，为历史最多，2017年仅为641mm，创3年来新低。

3月20日 新疆“疆电外送”工程累计输送电量达1506.6亿kW·h，其中新能源340亿kW·h，共相当于输送标准煤4821万t。2010年，750kV新疆与西北联网第一通道建成投运，结束了新疆电网孤网运行历史，新疆电力资源首次实现外送。2013年6月，750kV新疆与西北主网联网第二通道建成投运，“疆电外送”能力提升到200万kW。2014年1月，±800kV哈密南—郑州直流输电工程投运，成为连接西部边疆和中原大地的“电力丝绸之路”。目前，“疆电外送”范围已经覆盖北京、上海、广东等16个省市，惠及人口超过2.5亿。

3月21日 由中国长江三峡集团有限公司与中国华能集团有限公司共同举办的“大型水电工程智能建造技术”专题研讨会在北京召开，来自水电企业、大专院校、科研等相关单位120余人分别在北京主会场、上海、成都、卡洛特、科哈拉等视频分会场参加了本次研讨会。美国马里兰州立大学土木与环境工程系斯奇尼艾文斯基教授、三峡集团乌东德、白鹤滩水电站工程建设部智能建造团队及相关企业代表围绕工程建设领域前沿创新科技、智能化建设理论、全生命周期拱坝全景信息模型（DIM）作了专题报告；为实现特高拱坝建设设计标准化，建设过程信息化、大数据化、施工技术自动化，工程性态仿真精细化、可视化，工程性态控制的智能化和工程管理科学化等目标，专家结合具体工程开展情况作了详细讲解，并与参会人员进行了深入交流。

3月28日 2018全球能源互联网大会在北京举行，全球能源互联网发展合作组织主席、中国电力企业联合会理事长、瑞典皇家工程科学院院士刘振亚发表了题为“全球能源互联网改变世界”的主旨演讲。大会首次发布了全球能源互联网“九横九纵”骨干网架规划。会议指出，建设全球能源互联网骨干网架，总体分3个阶段实施。到2035年，完成洲内互联，亚、欧、非率先实现跨洲联网，全球形成“五横五纵”格局，跨洲跨区电力流达2.8亿kW。到2050年，建成亚、欧、非和美洲主要联网通道，全球形成“七横七纵”格局，跨洲跨区电力流达7.2亿kW。到2070年，建设北极能源通道，全球形成“九横九纵”格局，跨洲跨区电力流达12.5亿kW。

四月

4月14日 由中国长江三峡集团有限公司和农业农村部长江流域渔政监督管理办公室、湖北省农业厅、宜昌市政府共同主办的“2018年长江三峡中华鲟放流活动”在宜昌市长江珍稀鱼类放流点举行，500尾中华鲟放归长江。除了中华鲟保护以外，三峡集团在长江上游及金沙江流域鱼类保护、生态调度、库区水生态系统修复等方面也开展了卓有成效的工作。截至目前，已先后掌握圆口铜鱼、长鳍吻鮈、齐口裂腹鱼等10余种长江珍稀特有鱼类人工繁殖技术并实施增殖放流，已累计放流达氏鲟、胭脂鱼等珍稀特有鱼类近150万尾。

4月18日 财政部以财税〔2018〕39号文发布《关于降低部分政府性基金征收标准的通知》称，自2018年7月1日起，将国家重大水利工程建设基金征收标准，在按照《财政部关于降低国家重大水利工程建设基金和大中型水库移民后期扶持基金征收标准的通知》（财税〔2017〕51号）降低25%的基础上，再统一降低25%。调整后的征收标准＝按照《财政部、国家发展改革委、水利部关于印发〈国家重大水利工程建设基金征收使用管理暂行办法〉的通知》（财综〔2009〕90号）规定的征收标准×（1－25%）×（1－25%）。《通知》指出，征收标准降低后南水北调、三峡后续规划等中央支出缺口，在适度压减支出、统筹现有资金渠道予以支持的基础上，由中央财政通过其他方式予以适当弥补。地方支出缺口，由地方财政统筹解决。

4月20日 中国华电福新周宁抽水蓄能电站下水库成功截流，标志着电站下水库工程建设全面铺开，进入大坝主体工程施工阶段。该电站位于宁德市周宁县境内，为日调节纯抽水蓄能电站，设计装机4台机组，装机容量共计120万kW，年发电量12亿kW·h，年抽水电量16亿kW·h。电站投产后，每年可减少电网煤炭消耗量约20.79万t，减少排放二氧化碳约41.58万t、氮氧化合物约1040t、二氧化硫约2765t。

4月24日 习近平总书记视察三峡工程并发表重要讲话。习近平强调指出，三峡工程成为改革开放以来我国发展的重要标志，是我国社会主义制度能够集中力量办大事优越性的典范，是中国人民富于智慧和创造性的典范，是中华民族日益走向繁荣强盛的典范。

4月24日 水电水利规划设计总院在北京组织召开了《安徽桐城抽水蓄能电站工程安全预评价报告》审查会议。审查认为：预评价报告的内容和深度满足《水电工程安全预评价报告编制规程》要求，评价单元的划分合理，评价方法选用较为适当，危险、有害因素分析基本符合工程实际，评价结论客观、可信。该电站位于安徽省桐城市境内，枢纽工程由上水库、下水库、输水系统、地下厂房及开关站等组成。装机容量为128万kW，共安装4台单机容量为32万kW的发电机组。

4月24日 水电水利规划设计总院在北京组织召开了《吉林蛟河抽水蓄能电站工程安全预评价报告》审查会议。审查认为：预评价报告的内容和深度满足《水电工程安全预评价报告编制规程》要求，评价单元的划分合理，评价方法选用较为适当，危险、有害因素分析基本符合工程实际，评价结论客观、可信。该电站位于吉林蛟河市境内，枢纽工程由上水库、下水库、输水系统、地下厂房系统等建筑物组成。装机容量为120万kW，共安装4台单机容量为30万kW的发电机组。

4月26日 罗闸河一级水电站按期实现下闸蓄水目标。该电站位于澜沧江右岸一级支流罗闸河下游峡谷段，工程以发电为主，主要建筑物包括拦河坝、引水建筑物和发电厂房等。水电站坝型为混凝土抛物线型双曲拱坝，最大坝高59m，坝长160.5m。发电引水口为塔墙式结构，隧洞总长约993m。发电厂位于坝址下游850m的左岸，由主厂房、副厂房、升压站等组成。电站装机容量 2×1.5 万 kW，年发电量 1.35 亿 kW·h，水库总库容 1396 万 m^3。

4 月 26 日 中国葛洲坝集团（股份）有限公司承建的江苏句容抽水蓄能电站土建及金属结构安装工程举行开工仪式，标志着该工程全面进入施工阶段。该电站总装机容量 135 万 kW，安装 6 台单机容量 22.5 万 kW 的可逆式水泵水轮发电机组。电站建成后，将具有近双倍容量功能，能有效增强电网用电峰谷的调控能力，缓解苏南供电紧缺的矛盾。

4 月 27 日 国家能源局以国能发监管〔2018〕36 号文发布《关于进一步促进发电权交易有关工作的通知》。《通知》要求，发电企业应在保障自身发、用电安全的基础上，按照《电力中长期交易基本规则》等有关规定自主、自愿参与发电权交易。在水电、风电、光伏发电、核电等清洁能源消纳空间有限的地区，鼓励清洁能源发电机组间相互替代发电，通过进一步促进跨省跨区发电权交易等方式，加大清洁能源消纳力度。

4 月 30 日 《中国能源报》讯，近年来，云南电力建设如火如荼，境内金沙江、澜沧江等流域投产了大量水力发电项目，并建成了近千万千瓦的新能源发电项目，目前，清洁能源发电量占比 94%。截至 2018 年 4 月 3 日，云南省西电东送电量累计突破 7000 亿 kW·h，达到 7002.66 亿 kW·h。云南最大限度消纳了水电，广东、广西减少了煤耗污染，减少标准煤消耗 2.2 亿 t、二氧化碳排放 5.8 亿 t、二氧化硫 28.7 万 t。

4 月 30 日 《中国能源报》讯，山东省政府针对山东能源消费中煤炭比重高的问题，启动“外电入鲁”大转型，不仅正在研究论证四川白鹤滩水电送山东特高压直流接入方案，还将积极支持海上风电发展，科学规划山东省海上风电基地接入电网总体方案并纳入电网规划。近年来，接纳省外来电 1150 万 kW，实现了与内蒙古、天津、河北、宁夏、陕西等省（市）电网的互联互通。截至目前，山东累计接纳省外来电 4000 亿 kW·h，相当于减少了省内煤炭消费约 1.8 亿 t。规划到“十三五”末全省接纳省外来电能力提高到 3000 万 kW 以上。

五月

5 月 3 日 《中国能源报》报道，国家电投黄河上游水电开发有限责任公司将建全球单体最大水光风多能互补集成优化示范工程。该工程包括 416 万 kW 水电、400 万 kW 光伏、200 万 kW 风电，建成后 3 种电源将通过多能互补 750kV 汇集站打捆送出，实现水光风电协调控制，多能互补后送入电网。目前，该项水光风多能互补工程所属的 750kV 多能互补汇集站、330kV 升压站、100 万 kW 并网光伏电站、40 万 kW 风电场工程建设正在快速推进。

5 月 5 日 由中国葛洲坝集团（股份）有限公司承建的河北丰宁抽水蓄能电站上水库大坝混凝土面板施工正式启动。该电站总装机容量 360 万 kW，是目前世界上在建装机容量最大的抽水蓄能电站项目。电站分两期开发建设，于 2016 年实现同步建设，工程总投资 192.37 亿元，计划于 2021 年首台机组发电，2023 年 12 台机组全部投产运行。

5 月 12～13 日 “2018 高坝大库抗震安全国际学术研讨会”在四川成都举行，主题是“高坝大库抗震安全”。会议由中国大坝工程学会和中国水力发电工程学会主办，来自国内工程抗震领域的企业、研究院所和大专院校 80 余家单位的 220 多名专家代表，以及来自国际组织和瑞士、巴西、日本、韩国、菲律宾、伊拉克等的 20 多名国际同行参加了会议。会议征集到中外研究者优秀研究论文 60 余篇，并形成了论文集。

5 月 16 日 国家能源局以国能发新能〔2018〕45 号文公布《关于修改水电领域 6 件规范性文件的通知》，对《国家能源局关于加强水电建设管理的通知》（国能新能〔2011〕156 号）等 6 件规范性文件的部分条款予以修改。

5 月 21 日 由国际水电协会（IHA）主办，中国水力发电工程学会、中国长江三峡集团有限公司、全球能源互联网发展合作组织、中国水利水电科学研究院协办的“水电与未来能源系统北京论坛”在三峡集团召开。论坛主要议题为：加快能源转型步伐，提高绿色低碳能源在能源结构中的占比，探讨水电科技创新，分享各国水电项目经验，推动实现巴黎协定的既定目标。来自规划和开发小型和大型能源系统经验的国际决策者和学者、专家共 100 多人参加了论坛。

5 月 23 日 水电水利规划设计总院在北京组织召开了《山东潍坊抽水蓄能电站工程安全预评价报告》审查会议。审查认为：预评价报告的内容和深度满足《水电工程安全预评价报告编制规程》要求，评价单元的划分合理，评价方法选用较为适当，危险、有害因素分析基本符合工程实际，评价结论客观、可信。该电站位于山东省潍坊市临朐县五井镇嵩山乡境内，枢纽主要建筑物由上水库、输水系统、地下厂房系统和下水库组成。装机容量为 120 万 kW。

5 月 23 日 水电水利规划设计总院在北京组织召开了《山西垣曲抽水蓄能电站工程安全预评价报告》审查会议。审查认为：预评价报告的内容和深度满足《水电工程安全预评价报告编制规程》要求，评价单元的划分合理，评价方法选用较为适当，危险、有害因素分析基本符合工程实际，评价结论客观、可信。该电站位于运城市垣曲县境内，枢纽工程由上水库、下水库、输水系统、地下厂房系统及地面开关站等组成。总装机容量 120 万 kW。

5 月 25 日国家发展改革委以发改投资规〔2018〕795 号文下发《水电前期工作中央预算内投资专项管理办法》的通知。通知根据国家有关要求，旨在加强水电前期工作管理，建立健全水电前期工作管理机制，促进水电持续健康有序发展，提高中央预算内投资使用效益和效率。《通知》明确，所属政府行为的水电前期工作由水电水利规划设计总院组织项目实施。

六月

6 月 1 日　华能澜沧江公司苗尾水电站 4 号机组顺利完成 72 小时满负荷试运行后正式投入商业运行。至此，苗尾水电站 4 台机组全部投产发电。该电站是澜沧江流域上游河段梯级规划中最下游一级电站，为砾质土心墙堆石坝，最大坝高 139.8m，水库正常蓄水位 1408.00m，相应库容 6.6 亿 m^3，安装 4 台单机容量为 35 万 kW 的水轮发电机组，多年平均发电量 64.68 亿 kW·h。2017 年 10 月 14 日、11 月 18 日、12 月 31 日，1、2、3 号机组已相继完成 72 小时试运行并正式投入商业运营。

6 月 3 日　第 15 届"中国土木工程詹天佑奖"颁奖大会在北京举行，雅砻江锦屏一级水电站工程、糯扎渡水电站工程荣获"詹天佑奖"。锦屏一级水电站位于四川省凉山彝族自治州盐源县和木里县境内，总装机容量 360 万 kW，2013 年正式投产发电。该电站被国内外公认为是建设管理难度最大、施工布置难度最大、工程技术难度最大、施工环境危险最大的巨型水电站。糯扎渡水电站工程位于云南思茅市境内，总装机容量 585 万 kW，2014 年 6 月投产发电。该工程针对"高水头、大体积、大变形"条件下超高心墙堆石坝建造难题，全面开展了 10 余年研究及实践，系统提出了采用人工碎石掺砾土料和软岩堆石料筑坝成套技术及超高心墙堆石坝成套设计准则。

6 月 9 日　湖南涔天河水库扩建工程 2 号机组完成 72 小时试运行并正式投入商业运行。至此，湖南涔天河水库扩建工程全部 4 台机组并网发电。涔天河水库扩建工程是以灌溉、防洪、长株潭河段补水为主，兼顾发电、航运等综合利用的大型水利枢纽工程。电站厂房布置在大坝下游河道转弯处右侧河漫滩，装机容量为 4×5 万 kW。2017 年 9 月 24 日、2018 年 2 月 1 日、2018 年 4 月 9 日，首台（4 号）、3 号、1 号机组相继完成 72 小时试运行后正式投入商业运营。

6 月 14 日　中国电力企业联合会在北京发布《中国电力行业年度发展报告 2018》，报告指出，截至 2017 年底，全国全口径发电装机容量达 177708 万 kW，比上年增长 7.7%，增速比上年回落 0.5 个百分点。其中，水电 34359 万 kW（抽水蓄能发电 2869 万 kW，增长 7.5%），增长 3.5%；火电 110495 万 kW（煤电 98130 万 kW，增长 3.7%），增长 4.1%；核电 3582 万 kW，增长 6.5%；并网风电 16325 万 kW，增长 10.7%；并网太阳能发电 12942 万 kW（分布式光伏发电 2966 万 kW），增长 69.6%。全国人均装机规模 1.28kW，比上年增加 0.09kW，略超世界平均水平。分区域看，华北、华东、华中和南方区域发电装机容量已超过 3 亿 kW；华中、南方区域水电装机占比分别为 42.6%和 37.9%；西北地区新能源装机占比为 32.8%；东北地区风电装机占比为 19.8%；华北、华东火电装机占比分别为 77.1%、74.5%。

6 月 14 日　中国电力企业联合会在北京发布《中国电力行业年度发展报告 2018》。报告指出，水电投资与上年基本持平、抽水蓄能投资创历史新高；受西南水电开发难度和成本上升、弃水问题突出等因素影响，全国水电新开工项目明显减少，导致2013～2016 年水电投资连续 4 年连续减少。2017 年，水电完成投资 622 亿元，主要是 2016 年、2017 年分别新开工 24 台和 26 台抽水蓄能机组。2017 年抽水蓄能机组完成投资达到 142 亿元，同比增长 68.6%，是历年抽水蓄能投资最多的一年。

6 月 15 日　河北丰宁抽水蓄能电站机电安装工程正式开工。该电站地处河北省承德市丰宁满族自治县境内。电站总装机容量 360 万 kW，电站分两期开发，一、二期工程装机容量分别为 180 万 kW，其中一期工程安装 6 台单机容量 30 万 kW 定速水泵水轮发电机组，二期工程安装 4 台单机容量 30 万 kW 定速水泵水轮发电机组和 2 台单机容量 30 万 kW 的变速水泵水轮发电机组。

6 月 20～28 日　青海开启"绿电 9 日"，连续 216 小时全部以水、风、光等清洁能源供电，再创新纪录。期间累计供电量 17.6 亿 kW·h，相当于减少燃煤 80 万 t，减排二氧化碳 144 万 t。风光水能互补技术作用初步显现。

6 月 27 日　《中国能源报》讯，水利部农村水电与水库移民司近日发布的《全国农村水电统计公报》数据显示，2017 年全年，农村水电完成投资 200 亿元，新增加发电设备容量 135.3 万 kW。全国共有农村水电站 47498 座，其中 2017 年，农村水电新增电站 161 座，总装机容量达到 7927.0 万 kW，占全国水电总装机容量的 23.2%，占全国电力总装机容量的 4.5%。年发电量 2477.2 亿 kW·h。

6月27～29日 水电水利规划设计总院在新疆哈密主持召开了新疆哈密抽水蓄能电站可行性研究报告审查会议。审查认为，报告达到了可行性研究阶段勘测设计工作内容和深度的要求，基本同意该报告。该电站位于新疆维吾尔自治区哈密市伊州区天山乡境内，枢纽工程主要由上水库、下水库、输水系统、地下厂房和地面开关站等建筑物组成。电站装机容量120万kW。

七月

7月1日 陕西省泾河东庄水利枢纽工程全面建设推进会在礼泉县举行。该工程位于泾河下游峡谷末端礼泉县叱干镇东庄村、淳化县车坞乡河段处，该水库工程属大（1）型工程，其开发任务为“以防洪、减淤为主，兼顾供水、发电及生态环境”。拱坝坝高230m，总库容32.76亿m^3，占陕西省1098座水库总库容的36%，为陕西最大水库。建设工期95个月，工程建成后，该工程集防洪减淤、供水、发电、生态改善于一身。电站装机容量11万kW，年平均发电量3亿kW·h，工程预计总投资154.34亿元。

7月5日 广州电力交易中心开展了2018年首次云贵水火置换交易，通过市场化交易方式，增送云南水电，减送贵州火电，交易规模达10.1亿kW·h。本次交易按照贵州省提出的出让意愿价格组织，其中贵州在广东侧交易关口出让价格为0.32599元/(kW·h)，折算到云南发电企业代发电价为0.13元/(kW·h)，即云南月度集中撮合交易最低限价，置换前后广东落地侧电量和价格保持不变。折算下来，贵州作为出让方，每度电可以获得0.12365元的补偿，弥补贵州火电企业让出发电空间的经济损失。

7月17日 受国家能源局委托，水电水利规划设计总院牵头组织开展的《中国水电技术标准“走出去”研究》在北京召开验收发布会。与会专家普遍认为，此项课题研究成果达到了国际领先水平，课题研究成果为今后推动与主要贸易国之间的标准互认，打造中国水电标准品牌，以水电标准质量提升支撑引领中国水电质量提升具有重要的指导意义，有利于提高中国水电技术的国际竞争力。

7月18日 国务院新闻办公室发表《青藏高原生态文明建设状况》白皮书显示，青藏高原多条大江大河流经高山峡谷，蕴藏着丰富的水能资源。西藏水能资源技术可开发量为1.74亿kW，位居全国第一。近年建成多布、金河、直孔等中型水电站，截至2017年底，全区水电装机容量达到177万kW，占全区总装机容量的56.54%。青海水能资源技术可开发量为2400万kW，建成了龙羊峡、拉西瓦、李家峡等一批大型水电工程，截至2016年底，青海省水电装机容量达1192万kW。四川省甘孜州和阿坝州水能技术可开发量约5663万kW，已建成水电总装机容量达1708万kW。

7月23日 当晚，老挝南部阿速坡省由韩国公司承建的桑边桑南内水电站发生严重溃坝事故，引发严重洪灾。泄出的近50亿m^3洪水，袭击了下游村庄的1300户家庭，已造成32人遇难、49人失踪，受灾群众近7000人。中国电力建设集团有限公司作为在老最大的中资企业，第一时间成立了紧急救援小组，组织距离事故现场最近的项目部人员携救援物资赶往灾区。按照统一部署，中国电建所属电建国际、电建海投、水电十局、水电三局、水电十五局、水电基础局、昆明院、成都院等多家成员企组织有关力量投入到此次救援工作当中。

7月27日 水电水利规划设计总院在北京组织召开了《山西浑源抽水蓄能电站工程安全预评价报告》审查会议。审查认为：预评价报告的内容和深度满足《水电工程安全预评价报告编制规程》要求，评价单元的划分合理，评价方法选用较为适当，危险、有害因素分析基本符合工程实际，评价结论客观、可信。该电站位于山西省大同市浑源县境内，枢纽工程主要建筑物由上水库、水道系统、地下厂房及开关站、下水库等部分组成。总装机容量150万kW，安装4台单机容量为37.5万kW的发电机组。

7月28日 由中国电力建设集团有限公司设计施工的海南琼中抽水蓄能电站最后一台机组通过15天的在网试运行考核，并正式投入商业运行，标志着海南岛第一座抽水蓄能电站全面投产发电。该电站位于海南省琼中县南渡江南源黎田河上游，属二等大(2)型水电工程，由上水库、下水库、输水系统、发电厂房和地面开关站等部分组成，总装机容量60万kW（3×20万kW），设计年发电量为10.02亿kW·h，电站以4回220kV交流出线接入海南电网。该电站的投产，预计每年可节省标准煤耗16.31万t，减少二氧化碳排放约42.7万t，减少二氧化硫及粉尘排放约0.14万t。2017年10月31日首台（1号）、2018年2月6日2号机组相继通过15天在网试运行考核，正式投入商业运行。

7月29日 著名水电专家、原电力工业部科学技术司副司长、中国水力发电工程学会原秘书长邴凤山同志因病与世长辞，享年82岁。邴凤山同志1961年毕业于华东水利学院（今河海大学），他主持编写了《现代工程数学手册》（共5卷）、《抽水蓄能电站》《现代管理科学手册》《随机水文学及系统分析》等技术专著，发表了《2020年中国水力发电科学和技术发展研究》等论文20余篇，参加研究的项目《最优化理论及其应用》获中国科学院科技成果一等奖。

八月

8月3日 国家发展改革委以发改能源规〔2018〕1144号文下发《关于修改〈关于调整水电建设管理主要河流划分的通知〉引用规范性文件的通知》。通知对《国家发展改革委关于调整水电建设管理主要河流划分的通知》(发改能源〔2016〕1346号)的部分条款予以修改。

8月8日 甘肃舟曲县插岗水电站采用互联网、物联网、大数据、云计算、智能控制、多传感器融合识别等先进技术实现智能化管理，并通过"博瑞云集中监管平台"在甘肃兰州市的集控中心实现远程操作和成功并网，标志着甘肃在"互联网+"智能水电站技术研发和组装使用率先取得突破性成果。

8月13日 水电水利规划设计总院在北京组织召开了《河北抚宁抽水蓄能电站工程安全预评价报告》审查会议。审查认为：预评价报告的内容和深度满足《水电工程安全预评价报告编制规程》要求，评价单元的划分合理，评价方法选用较为适当，危险、有害因素分析基本符合工程实际，评价结论客观、可信。

8月13～14日 水电水利规划设计总院在北京主持召开了《河北抚宁抽水蓄能电站工程防震抗震研究设计专题报告》审查会议。审查认为，报告的内容和工作深度满足现行规程规范的要求，基本同意该报告。该工程位于河北省秦皇岛市抚宁区境内，枢纽建筑物主要由上水库、下水库、输水系统、地下厂房和开关站等组成。电站总装机容量120万kW，安装4台单机容量为30万kW机组。

8月15日 著名水电专家、教育家、湖北省水力发电工程学会创始人、原武汉水利电力学院常务副院长王宏硕教授因病与世长辞，享年98岁。王宏硕同志1942年毕业于北京大学，同年赴日本东京大学进修；1944年回国，之后踏入教育界。先后发表了40多篇极具学术价值的论文，其中6篇获部级优秀论文奖，多项科技成果获省部级科技进步奖。他主编了《水工建筑物》通用教材，主持编撰了《中国水利百科全书》(水工建筑物分册)、《日汉水利水电工程词典》；作为首位学会理事长，创办学术刊物《湖北水力发电》(即现在的《水电与新能源》)，组建专委会，成立科技咨询服务部。

8月24日 国网华东分部与国网西南分部正式签订了西南水电送华东电能交易合作框架协议。根据协议，国网华东、西南分部将在西南水电送华东方面开展更加紧密和深入的合作，充分挖掘西南清洁能源输出能力和华东地区消纳能力，实现互惠共赢。根据协议，国网华东、西南分部还将充分利用柴拉直流和灵绍直流剩余通道能力，全力推进藏电送华东消纳，力争在2019年实现交易规模达2亿kW·h。

8月27日 巴基斯坦NJ水电站2号机组720小时考核试运行完成，这是继该电站3、4号机组完成720小时考核运行后的又一重要节点。该电站1号机组已于27日完成了72小时试运行，即将进入720小时试运行。该水电工程为高水头(420m)、长隧洞(68km)引水式电站，由水库、大坝、沉砂池、引水系统、地下发电厂房、尾水建筑物、开关站及附属设施等组成，主要任务为发电。电站安装4台混流式机组，总装机容量96.9万kW，投产后年发电量约51.5亿kW·h。

8月28日 经报国务院批准，中国国电集团公司与神华集团有限责任公司合并重组为国家能源集团。中国神华集团更名为国家能源投资集团有限责任公司，作为重组后的母公司，吸收合并中国国电集团公司。中国神华集团公司持有合资公司42.53%股权，中国国电集团公司持有合资公司57.47%股权。

8月29日 国家能源局以国能函新能〔2018〕98号文复函《关于广西抽水蓄能电站选点规划有关事项的复函》，同意在初选南宁、武鸣、钦州、来宾、桂林、灌阳作为比选站点的基础上，确定南宁(拟装机容量120万kW)站点为广西电网2025年新建抽水蓄能电站推荐站点。

8月29日 长江防汛抗旱总指挥部批复了溪洛渡水库和向家坝水库2018年联合蓄水方案。根据批复，在确保防洪安全的前提下，溪洛渡水库、向家坝水库分别自9月1日、9月5日起正式开展蓄水工作。溪洛渡水库9月1日可承接前期运行水位开始蓄水，逐步抬升水位，9月底可蓄至600m；向家坝水库从9月5日承接前期运行水位开始蓄水，9月中旬至正常蓄水位380m。

8月29～30日 由中国水力发电工程学会、青海省科学技术协会主办，青海省水力发电工程学会承办，黄河上游水电开发有限责任公司协办，主题为"传承 创新 发展"的"风光水能互补开发研讨会"在青海省西宁市召开。来自全国水力发电战线60余名专家代表齐聚一堂，参加研讨，共商新时代能源大计。此活动也是中国水力发电工程学会组织开展"改革开放40年：中国水电"纪念系列活动之一。

8月31日 国家防汛抗旱总指挥部下达《三峡水库2018年试验性蓄水实施计划的批复》，三峡水库第11次175m试验性蓄水将于9月10日启动。根据国家防总批复，在确保防洪安全和充分考虑中下游用水需求的前提下，三峡水库9月上旬可承接前期运行水位逐渐上浮水位。与往年一样，9月10日正式开始蓄水，起蓄水位按150～155m控制，9月30日蓄水位按162～165m控制，10月底或11月份争取蓄至175m。

九月

9月1日 西南—华东电网跨区水火发电权交易全面启动，计划9月底，实现西南水电送华东区域成交电量1.3亿kW·h。该交易是西南电网首例跨区发电权交易，也是全国范围内首次达成的跨区水火发电权交易，将助力华东地区减少标准煤消耗3.9万t、二氧化碳排放13.0万t、二氧化硫排放0.39万t，有效促进华东区域省份节能减排、绿色低碳经济发展，促进西南富余水电外送消纳和清洁能源发展。

9月7日 大渡河沙坪二级水电站6号机组通过72小时试运行投产发电。至此，沙坪二级水电站6台机组全部并网发电。沙坪二级水电站采用河床式开发，水库正常蓄水位554.00m，总库容为2084万m^3，最大坝高63.0m，安装6台单机容量为5.8万kW的灯泡贯流式机组，装机容量34.8万kW，与双江口、瀑布沟联合运行，保证出力12.45万kW，多年平均发电量为16.10亿kW·h。2017年6月30日首台（1号）、9月25日2号、12月1日3号、2018年4月4日4号、6月30日5号机组已相继完成72小时试运行正式投入商业运营。

9月9日 北盘江干流第四个梯级电站万家口子水电站1号机组顺利通过72小时试运行投产发电，至此，万家口子水电站2台机组全部并网发电。该电站为北盘江上游龙头电站，安装2台9万kW混流式水轮发电机组，属碾压混凝土双曲拱坝水电站，电站正常蓄水位1450m，最大坝高为167.5m，水库具有不完全年调节能力。电站保证出力3.33万kW，多年平均发电量71038.5万kW·h。8月20日，2号机组已顺利完成72小时试运行正式投入商业运行。

9月10～11日 在德国柏林召开的国际咨询工程师联合会2018年年会上，世界第一高坝锦屏一级水电站获“菲迪克2018年工程项目杰出成就奖”。锦屏一级水电站拥有305m的世界第一高坝，被国内外公认为是建设管理难度最大、施工布置难度最大、工程技术难度最大、施工环境危险最大的巨型水电站。电站在建设过程中，攻克了复杂地形地质条件下超高边坡稳定安全控制、复杂地质条件地基处理、特高拱坝高强度快速施工等一系列世界技术难题。

9月17日 中国葛洲坝集团有限公司与印尼PT. Lentera Damar Amerta签署了印尼拉里昂彼力30万kW水电站EPC合同。该电站位于印尼中苏拉威西省西吉县境内，规划装机容量30万kW，多年平均发电量约为16亿kW·h，电站主要建筑物包括拦河坝、引水系统、开关站、发电厂房等。项目建成后，不仅会大幅改善当地电力短缺的现状，还将为当地提供大量就业机会。

9月18日 大平田水电站首台机组顺利通过72小时试运行，正式投入运行。大平田水电站位于腾冲市五合乡、芒棒镇境内，电站枢纽工程主要由挡水建筑物（混凝土重力坝）、泄水建筑物（溢洪道及冲砂底孔）和发电建筑物（坝式取水口、压力钢管、发电厂房、GIS楼等）组成。电站总装机容量9.6万kW，年发电量4.09亿kW·h，工程总投资8.7亿元。电站投产发电可减少薪柴消耗量37.5万t，保护森林3.75万亩，替代标准煤1.32万t，减少二氧化碳排放32.72万t，减少二氧化硫排放0.47万t。

9月21日 广东惠州抽水蓄能电站工程竣工决算验收会议在工程现场召开。验收委员会认为，广东惠州抽水蓄能电站建设符合国家基建项目管理要求，实际工程投资控制在核准概算之内并有节余，财务管理规范有效，交付使用资产653329万元，电站运行情况良好，经济效益显著，具备验收条件，同意通过工程竣工决算验收。该电站位于广东省惠州市，总装机容量240万kW，安装8台30万kW可逆式抽水蓄能发电机组，设计年发电量45.63亿kW·h。

9月22日 中巴经济走廊首座水电站——卡洛特水电站顺利实现大江截流，标志着巴基斯坦首个完全使用中国技术和中国标准建设的水电项目进入全面施工阶段，也标志着“一带一路”沿线国家水电建设实现了新突破。卡洛特水电站位于巴基斯坦吉拉姆河上，装机容量72万kW，年发电量32亿kW·h，总投资约17.4亿美元。该电站采用BOOT方式开发，由中国企业投资、设计和施工，为中国企业和装备“走出去”提供了有利平台。

9月23日 杨家湾水电站（调度名为赞拉水电站）2号机组完成72小时试运行，正式并网发电，至此，该电站3台机组全部投产发电。该电站为四川阿坝小金县内抚边河水电梯级规划中的第四级电站，为引水式开发，引水隧洞长11.366km。装机3台，总装机容量6万kW，设计年发电量2.59亿kW·h。8月27日，该电站首批机组（1号、3号）完成72小时试运行后并网运行。

9月25日 深圳抽水蓄能电站4号机组顺利完成15天考核试运行，投产运行。至此，我国首座建于城市中的大型抽水蓄能电站全面投产。该电站位于深圳市盐田区和龙岗区之间，距深圳市中心直线距离仅20km，是南方电网首座全面国产化蓄能电站，电站地下厂房安装4台30万kW机组，总装机容量120万kW，设计年均发电量15.11亿kW·h。2017年12月27日首台（1号）、2018年3月27日2号、7

月12日3号机组已相继顺利完成15天考核试运行，正式投产运行。投产后，年平均发电量15.11亿kW·h，每年可节约标准煤15.8万t、节省天然气1.83万t、减排温室气体总量约2717.28t。

9月26日 由中国水力发电工程学会和水电水利规划设计总院联合主办的“改革开放40年中国水电”纪念大会在北京隆重召开。亲历见证了我国水电行业改革发展的汪恕诚、陆佑楣、周大兵、矫勇等老领导老专家，对我国水电发展和科技进步作出了巨大贡献的陈厚群、张楚汉、马洪琪、张建民等院士，以及来自政府有关部门、水电企事业单位、高校科研机构和有关行业社团组织的领导专家和水电工作者代表230余人参加了大会。

9月26日 在“改革开放40年中国水电”纪念大会上，中国水力发电工程学会理事长张野代表主办单位作了“改革开放40年水电建设发展成就与展望”的大会主题报告。张野指出，40年来，在国家改革开放总方针、路线的指引下，中国水电从小到大、从弱到强、从学习跟跑并跑到领跑直至全面超越，装机容量和年发电量均位居世界第一。改革开放初期，中国水电的总装机容量和发电量分别仅为1727万kW和446亿kW·h，截至2017年底这一数字已分别达到了3.41亿kW和1.19万亿kW·h，分别增长了约20倍和26倍，均已超过了全球水电开发量和发电量的1/4。改革开放40年来，我国水电累计发电量超过14万亿kW·h，约相当于替代标准煤43亿t，减排二氧化碳113亿t、二氧化硫0.37亿t、氮氧化物0.32亿t，为“保卫蓝天碧水”作出了重要贡献。

9月26日 由中国水利水电第八工程局有限公司承建的厄瓜多尔美纳斯水电站首台机组并网发电。该电站位于厄瓜多尔第三大城市昆卡西南方向90km处，是胡邦河流域重要的水利枢纽工程，电站以发电为主，同时兼具水土保持、旅游等综合功能。电站总装机容量为27.5万kW，年平均发电量为13亿kW·h。该电站是一座小流量高水头引水式电站，主要由大坝、引水隧洞、调压井、压力竖井、地下厂房洞室群、地面开关站、尾水工程组成。

9月28日 国家能源局以国能函新能〔2018〕116号文复函《关于浙江抽水蓄能电站选点规划调整有关事项的复函》，同意在初选衢江、磐安、泰顺、天台、建德、桐庐作为比选站点的基础上，确定衢江（120万kW）、磐安（120万kW）、泰顺（120万kW）、天台（170万kW）站点为浙江2025水平年抽水蓄能选点规划调整推荐站点。考虑电网需求与其他调峰能力建设存在一定不确定性，原则同意建德（240万kW）和桐庐（120万kW）站点作为推荐站点，两站点应在相关环境问题协调落实后，根据华东电网电力系统发展需要适时开发建设。

十月

10月8日 由中国葛洲坝集团有限公司承建的缅甸亚沙角水电站2号机组完成72小时试运行。至此，该项目所有试验项目全部完成，具备全面投产条件。该电站位于缅甸西北部Sagaing省Neyinzaya河上，工程主要由大坝、副坝、溢洪道、进水口、压力管道、发电厂房、尾水渠和开关站等建筑物组成。

10月12日 《中国能源报》讯，湖南能源监管办发布的《湖南省2017年水电企业成本专项监管报告》显示，2017年，湖南省水电企业发电总成本小幅降低，为60.39亿元，较上年减少3.14亿元，减幅4.94%，财务费用及税费成本大幅减少，检修费用大幅增加。报告汇总分析了全省25家企业共40个水电厂基础数据，总装机容量1095.61万kW，占统调水电装机容量的94.4%。报告从资产负债率、发电量、设备利用小时、上网电价、销售收入、利润总额、发电成本等方面分析了湖南省水电企业成本状况和生产经营情况。

10月15日 改革开放40周年电力成就展暨第17届中国国际电力设备及技术展览会在北京开幕。经过40年发展，到2017年中国水电装机容量3.4亿kW，是1978年的20倍，水电装机容量、发电量均居世界第一位。1986年中国建成第一座并网风电场，2010年风电装机容量突破4000万kW，超越美国成为世界第一，到2017年风电装机容量达1.6亿kW。1983年中国建成第一座光伏电站，2015年光伏电站装机容量突破4000万kW，超越德国成为世界第一，到2017年光伏电站装机容量达1.3亿kW。1991年中国第一座核电站并网发电，2017年核电装机容量3582万kW，在建容量2100万kW，分列世界第四和世界第一。

10月17日 《中国能源报》讯，国家能源局日前发布的《关于2017年度全国电力价格情况监管通报》显示，2017年，全国发电企业平均上网电价为376.28元/(千kW·h)，同比增长1.93%。其中，光伏发电最高，为939.90元/(千kW·h)，水力发电最低，为258.93元/(千kW·h)。风电、燃气发电、核电平均上网电价分别为562.30元/(千kW·h)、664.94元/(千kW·h)和402.95元/(千kW·h)。

10月19日 由中国水利水电科学研究院、国际水电协会、中国电力建设集团有限公司、中国长江三峡集团有限公司联合举办的“现代水电国际论坛”在北京举行。来自国际水电协会、水电开发企业、水电建设单位、研究机构、能源行政主管部门等30多家单位的近80名中外专家代表出席了会议。该论坛的主题为“数字化管理、可持续性和气候变化”，论坛分享了全球在可持续性、数字化和气候变化领域的成功举措和案例。

10月21日 由华能澜沧江水电股份有限公司控股开发的柬埔寨桑河二级水电站8号机组顺利通过72小时试运行，正式投产发电，至此，桑河二级水电站8台机组全部投产发电。该电站大坝全长6.5km，总装机容量40万kW，采用8台中国制造的5万kW灯泡贯流式机组。电站建成投产后，年发电量约19.7亿kW·h。2017年12月9日首台（1号）、12月30日2号、2018年4月9日3号、5月13日4号、6月17日5号、7月22日6号、9月13日7号机组已相继完成72小时试运行正式投入商业运营。2018年内实现“一年六投”的业绩。

10月22日，由中国电力建设集团有限公司承建的巴基斯坦塔贝拉4期水电站最后一台（15号）机组，完成全部有水调试并顺利移交业主，进入商业运行。至此，塔贝拉4期水电站的3台机组全部按期完成移交。巴基斯坦塔贝拉大坝是一座集灌溉、发电、防洪、调水等综合效益的工程；控制流域面积17万km^2，总库容137亿m^3，原总装机容量为347.8万kW，每年调水300亿m^3，灌溉农田40万hm^2。2018年3月2日首台（17号）、6月30日16号机组已相继完成有水调试顺利移交业主进入商业运行。

10月22～26日 国际电工委员会（IEC）第82届大会在韩国釜山召开。会议期间，IEC各国家委员会一致提名选举现任IEC副主席、中国国家电网有限公司董事长舒印彪为IEC第36届主席，任期为2020～2022年。这是该组织成立112年来，首次由我国专家担任最高领导职务，是我国参与国际标准工作的重要里程碑，是国家电网落实人类命运共同体理念，积极推进“一带一路”建设取得的又一重要成果。

10月25日 受青海省能源局的委托，水电水利规划设计总院在青海省西宁市组织召开黄河班多水电站枢纽工程专项验收会议。会议形成了《黄河班多水电站枢纽工程专项验收鉴定书》，验收委员会同意黄河班多水电站通过枢纽工程专项验收。该电站位于青海省兴海县与同德县交界处的黄河班多峡谷下游出口处，工程以发电为主。枢纽工程主要由河床式厂房、左岸泄洪闸和混凝土重力坝等建筑物组成，最大坝高78.72m，装机3台，总容量36万kW，多年平均发电量14.12亿kW·h。

10月25日 以“保护水生动物，共建生态环境”为主题的“中国华电，度度关爱：华电西藏公司2018年度鱼类增殖放流活动”正式举行，分装在400个鱼苗袋的7.3万尾鱼苗在放流人员的帮助下，顺着放流滑槽奔向雅鲁藏布江，此次放流品种主要为高原藏区珍稀鱼种，其中异齿裂腹鱼1.7万尾，拉萨裂腹鱼1.5万尾，巨须裂腹鱼1.5万尾，双须叶须鱼1.1万尾，尖裸鲤1.5万尾。

10月25～26日 陕西汉江投资开发有限公司所属水电厂开展了以“保护汉江，造福子孙后代”为主题的鱼类增殖放流生态修复保护活动。25日，汉江喜河水电厂向汉江投放草鱼和鲢鱼鱼苗各5万尾；26日，汉江蜀河水电厂将精心培育的黄颡鱼、大鳍鳠、蒙古鲌等9种类型，共计25万尾鱼苗放入库区中。

10月26日 丰满水电站原大坝拆除工程正式开工，计划于2019年4月30日完成拆除，2019年6月末首台机组发电、工程度汛具备良好的工程条件，标志着丰满水电站原大坝结束了运行长达80年之久的历史使命。丰满大坝位于吉林省吉林市境内松花江上的丰满峡谷谷口，始建于1937年日伪时期，当时乃亚洲第一高坝，为混凝土重力坝，长1080m，高91.7m。1942年大坝蓄水，1943年3月25日首台机组投产发电。

10月26日 由中国南方电网有限责任公司投建并负责电站运维的老挝南塔河1号水电站3台机组全部通过72小时试运行，正式投产发电。工程以发电为主，兼有防洪、灌溉等综合效益，设计正常蓄水位455.00m，相应库容17.55亿m^3。枢纽建筑物由混凝土面板堆石坝、溢洪道、发电引水系统、引水式发电厂房组成，最大坝高87.35m，安装3台单机容量5.6万kW的混流式水轮发电机组，总装机容量16.8万kW。该电站地处老挝博胶省和琅南塔省，电站建成后，发电量预计7.21亿kW·h，可让200多万人用上绿色电能。10月18日首台（1号）、10月22日2号、10月26日3号机组分别顺利完成72小时试运行，正式投产发电。

10月28～29日 第七届水利水电生态保护研讨会暨中国水力发电工程学会环境保护专委会学术年会在昆明召开。会议主题是“水利水电工程环境保护全过程管理中的高新技术研究与实践”，来自政府部门、行业部门、设计院、水产、森林及海洋等领域的研究院所、建设单位、环评单位、高校及行业协会等40余家单位的120多位领导和代表出席会议。会议收到44篇高水平论文，会上20位学者围绕会议主题作了精彩报告，对国内外水利水电全过程管理现状进行了系统分析并提出了政策建议。

10月29日 里底水电站首台（1号）机组完成72小时试运行，正式投入商业运营。该电站位于云南省迪庆州维西县巴迪乡境内，是澜沧江上游河段梯级规划开发的第三级电站。电站枢纽由拦河坝、溢洪道、河床式厂房等组成，拦河坝为混凝土重力坝，最大坝高76.6m，总库容0.725亿m^3。电站安装3台容量为14万kW的轴流转桨式机组，机组转子直径11.19m，多年平均发电量17.53亿kW·h。

10月30日　我国首个百万kW级EPC水电项目——杨房沟大坝首仓混凝土正式浇筑，表明大坝工程施工由基础开挖全面转入主体混凝土浇筑阶段。该电站位于凉山州木里县境内的雅砻江流域中游河段上，装机容量150万kW，多年平均年发电量68.7亿kW·h，最大坝高155m。本次大坝首仓浇筑混凝土1750m^3，浇筑时长约24h。电站建成后，每年可节约标准煤约230万t，减少二氧化碳排放475万t，减少二氧化硫约3.4万t。

10月31日　中国电力建设集团有限公司与印尼卡扬水电能源公司、印尼卡米组公司正式签署卡扬一级90万kW水电站、印尼44.3万kW泰普一级水电站项目EPC合同。卡扬梯级水电站位于印尼北加里曼丹省，将分5级电站开发，总装机容量900万kW。此次签约的项目为卡扬一级水电站。泰普一级水电站项目位于印尼苏门答腊岛北部的亚奇省，电站工程内容主要由混凝土双曲拱坝、左岸泄水道、右岸导流洞、电站引水系统、坝后厂房等组成，开发方式为BOT模式。

10月31日　《中国能源报》讯，在近日召开的“现代水电国际论坛”上获悉，国家能源局已组织编制能源行业标准《可持续水电评价导则》，水电运行期管理将进一步加强。2017年8月，国家水电可持续发展研究中心会同水电水利规划设计总院和其他设计院，启动能源行业标准《可持续水电评价导则》的编制工作，目前已形成《可持续水电评价导则（草稿）》，涵盖我国装机容量1万kW以上的常规水电和抽水蓄能电站，以运行期水电站为主，旨在通过加强水电开发与运行的事中事后监管，针对薄弱环节提出预警和改进措施，促进水电在社会和谐、环境友好、管理高效、经济合理方面持续改善，实现水电与流域/区域社会、经济、环境的协调发展，并指导未来我国水电建设与运行管理。

十一月

11月5日　黄河上游“龙头电站”龙羊峡水电站首次成功蓄水至2600m水位，标志着该电站主要运行参数达到设计值，将有效提高水库的发电效益和水资源利用效率。此次蓄水是龙羊峡水电站自1987年首台机组投产发电以来首次达到正常蓄水位。

11月5～6日　国网黑龙江牡丹江水力发电总厂所属莲花发电厂、镜泊湖发电厂相继完成了黑龙江省电网“黑启动”试验。莲花发电厂在预定的运行方式下，使电厂失去全部外部电源，利用厂用逆变电源为1号机组保流组提供机旁自用电源，带厂用电负荷恢复厂用电运行。镜泊湖发电厂失去全部外部电源，利用调配的应急电源车为镜新厂洞下400VⅡ段母线提供4号水轮发电机组机房电源，随后启动4号机组发电。黑龙江电力将试验获得的数据从理论上进行对比分析，进一步优化试验方案，把试验成果固化到现场运行规程和应急预案中，确保在系统一旦出现大面积停电时，尽快恢复电网供电。

11月6日　牛从直流（±500kV溪洛渡右岸电站送电广东同塔双回直流）2018年送电量突破300亿kW·h，送电量同比上年增长12%。溪洛渡直流工程西起云南省昭通市，东至广东省广州市，线路全长1223km，双回直流输电容量640万kW。自2014年投运4年来，工程已累计向广东输送清洁水电1415亿kW·h，相当于减少标准煤消耗4529万t，减排二氧化碳11312万t、二氧化硫84万t。

11月7日　塔吉克斯坦格拉夫纳亚水电站技改建设项目，首台机组提前并网发电。格拉夫纳亚水电站位于塔吉克南部哈特隆州境内，是瓦赫什河流域上9个梯级水电站的第七级，最大坝高51.8m，装机容量24万kW。该电站于1964年由苏联建成投运，至今已逾50载，机组、电气、闸门、起重等设备以及土建、监测等设施已大量老化、损坏，运行极不稳定，局部功能失效，亟需整体全面的技术改造。2016年，中国电建集团成都勘测设计研究院有限公司与中国水利水电第十六工程局有限公司联营体在国外多家投标人竞标中胜出。该电站技改范围主要包括更换部分机组及其附属设备，更换部分主变压器，厂内桥机改造，尾水渠和灌溉渠边坡、厂内混凝土等土建工程以及金属结构修复，计划于2021年2月完成技改。

11月7日　青海—河南±800kV特高压直流工程在青海海南州和河南驻马店市同时举行开工仪式。青海—河南工程完全靠清洁能源自身互补能力独立供电，将是全国乃至全世界第一条专为清洁能源外送而建设的特高压通道。该工程起于青海海南州，止于河南驻马店市，途经青海、甘肃、陕西、河南等4省，线路全长1587km，总投资约226亿元，计划2020年建成投运。

11月13日　“伟大的变革——庆祝改革开放40周年大型展览”在国家博物馆开幕。改革开放40年来，水利建设投入力度不断加大。1978～2017年累计投资5.02万亿元，占新中国成立以来水利建设投资的98%。1978～2017年，全国水库由75669座增加至98795座，水库总库容9963亿m^3，新增库容6393亿m^3，相当于16个三峡水库库容。全国堤防总长由13.0万km增加至30.6万km。

11月14日 云南金沙江中游电站送电广西直流输电工程担负着确保云电安全外送和持续满足广西中北部地区用电增长需求的重任。该工程的受端±500kV桂中换流站安全运行天数达到1027天，2018年送电量突破100亿kW·h。该工程自2016年5月28日投产以来，直流累计送电量已达到342.17亿kW·h。

11月15日 乌东德水电站二道坝4～7号坝段第12仓混凝土浇筑完成，标志着乌东德水电站二道坝混凝土浇筑高度整体过半，各项检测数据满足设计要求。乌东德水电站二道坝为梯形断面，建基面高程735m，坝高90.5m，坝顶长163m，宽9m，底宽59.08m，位于大坝坝轴线下游约363m。二道坝共分7个坝段进行混凝土浇筑，全坝采用低热水泥，总浇筑量约46.6万m^3。自2018年4月11日二道坝首仓垫层混凝土浇筑以来，截至目前已累计浇筑混凝土约31万m^3，约占总浇筑方量的2/3，已浇筑至高程783.7m。根据计划安排，二道坝计划于2019年2月浇筑到顶。

11月15日 中共中央组织部副部长张建春宣布了关于中国华能集团有限公司董事长、党组书记调整的决定：舒印彪同志任中国华能集团有限公司董事长、党组书记，免去其国家电网有限公司董事长、党组书记职务；免去曹培玺同志中国华能集团有限公司董事长、党组书记职务。

11月16日 从中国水力发电工程学会网站获悉，改革开放40年，农村小水电促进了农村初级电气化。1978年，乡办小水电站82387个，发电能力228.4万kW。到2007年底，乡村办小水电站27664个，发电能力为1366.6万kW，得到了较快发展。1978年后，为适应形势需要，1982年，中央领导同志提出要充分利用小水电资源，首批建设100个具有中国特色的初级农村电气化县。经过近10年的建设工作，在全国建成了109个农村初级电气化县。在这个基础上，1991年和1996年，国务院又批准了建设第二批200个和第三批300个农村水电初级电气化县。这样，到2000年，全国在小水电资源丰富地区共建成初级农村电气化县653个，实现了小水电事业和农村电气化事业相互促进、共同发展的新局面。

11月16日 湖北清江水布垭水电站工程竣工决算验收会议在湖北省宜昌市召开。验收委员会认为，湖北清江水布垭水电站建设符合国家基建项目管理要求，项目合同（协议）执行及结算情况总体良好，实际完成投资控制在批复的调整概算范围内并有节余，其财务账目清楚，财务管理比较规范，交付使用资产真实、准确；电站运行情况良好，经济效益和防洪效益显著，满足验收要求，同意通过工程竣工决算验收。该电站位于湖北省巴东县境内，电站总装机容量184万kW（4×46万kW）。

11月23日 藏中电力联网工程竣工投运。该工程是继青藏电力联网、川藏电力联网工程之后，国家电网有限公司建成的又一项突破生命禁区、挑战生存极限的高原超高压输变电工程。藏中电力联网工程由西藏藏中和昌都电网联网工程、川藏铁路拉萨至林芝段供电工程组成，起于西藏昌都市芒康县，止于山南市桑日县，跨越西藏3地市10区县。该工程总投资约162亿元，新建、扩建500kV及配套工程变电站16座，新建500kV及配套工程线路2738km。该工程于2017年3月获国家发展改革委可行性研究批复。

11月23日 潘家铮水电科技基金三届三次理事会议在青海大学召开。来自国家电网有限公司、中国华能集团有限公司、中国大唐集团有限公司、国家能源投资集团有限责任公司、中国电力建设集团有限公司等40余家理事单位的理事和代表及个人理事近50人参加了会议。会议由中国水力发电工程学会常务副秘书长、潘家铮基金秘书长吴义航主持。会议审议并通过了潘家铮基金三届三次理事会工作报告、基金2018年财务报告和2019年财务预算；按照民主程序完成了理事会部分理事变更事项；审议并同意《潘家铮水电科技基金章程（条文修改草案）》《潘家铮水电科技基金实施细则（条文修改草案）》。

11月23日 由中国水力发电工程学会和潘家铮水电科技基金管理委员会主办、青海大学承办的“第10届潘家铮水电奖学金颁奖典礼”在青海大学图书馆举行。来自青海省水利厅、青海省教育厅以及水电规划设计、建设施工、电网经营、大学、科研院等单位的领导和来宾，获奖单位的老师和学生，青海大学师生，共200余人出席了典礼。青海大学党委书记俞红贤致辞。中国水力发电工程学会理事长张野发表讲话。本届共有18所高校和科研院的60名优秀学生获得奖学金，两位获奖学生代表分别发表了感言。

11月27日 民政部发布《2017年度全国性社会组织评估等级结果公告》（第445号），中国水力发电工程学会获评“社会组织评估”AAAA级单位。本次评估是根据《社会组织评估管理办法》和《关于开展2017年度全国性社会组织评估工作的通知》的要求，自2017年11月开始，先后经过了自评申报、资格审查、第三方机构组织专家实地考察初评、全国性社会组织评估委员会终评、网站公示等程序，最终产生评估结果。

11月29日 广西壮族自治区发展改革委、工业和信息化厅以桂发改价格〔2018〕1398号文发布《关于暂缓降低部分水电丰水期上网电价有关事项的通知》，通知指出，自治区主电网统调水电及龙滩水电站、天生桥一级、二级水电站继续按桂政办发〔2018〕22号规定的“水电上网电价按已批复的上网电价96%调至90%”执行，其余水电企业2018年暂缓执行，电网企业应退还已扣除的电费。

11月29日　中共中央组织部有关负责同志宣布了中央关于中国华电集团有限公司董事长、党组书记任职的决定：温枢刚同志任中国华电集团有限公司董事长、党组书记，免去其中国华电集团有限公司总经理职务。

11月30日　水电水利规划设计总院在北京组织召开了《云南金沙江金安桥水电站扩机工程安全预评价报告》审查会议。审查认为：该电站扩机工程安全预评价报告的编制内容和深度满足《水电工程安全预评价报告编制规程》要求，评价单元的划分合理，评价方法选用较为适当，危险、有害因素分析基本符合工程实际，评价结论客观、可信。该电站扩机工程主要建筑物由右岸岸塔式进水口、引水隧洞、地下厂房、尾水调压室、尾水洞等组成。初选扩机容量为60万kW（2×30万kW），多年平均增发电量8.63/3.31亿kW·h（龙盘水库投产前/后）。扩机后，该电站总装机容量为300万kW，多年平均年发电量117.83/136.93亿kW·h（龙盘投产前/后）。

十二月

12月3日　中国水力发电工程学会、水力发电科学技术奖励委员会发布奖励通报，决定对2018年度水力发电科学技术奖获奖项目（共36项）给予奖励并通报表扬。由中国电建成都勘测设计院有限公司等单位组织完成的《锦屏一级特高拱坝枢纽泄洪消能与减雾关键技术》等7项科研成果获得一等奖，由中国水利水电科学研究院等单位完成的《适应复杂环境的水工建筑物聚脲基防渗防护体系关键技术研究与应用》等9个项目获得了二等奖，由中国能源建设股份有限公司等单位承担的《乌东德水电站超深覆盖层超深基坑围堰施工关键技术》等20项成果获得三等奖。

12月3日　中国水力发电工程学会、水力发电科学技术奖励委员会发布奖励通报，决定对第五届潘家铮奖获奖人（共3人）给予奖励并通报表扬。获奖者为中国电建集团昆明勘测设计研究院有限公司张宗亮、中国水利水电第四工程局有限公司席浩、雅砻江流域水电开发有限公司陈云华。

12月4日　浙江省发展改革委就衢江抽水蓄能电站项目核准事项作出批复，同意建设浙江衢江抽水蓄能电站项目。衢江抽水蓄能电站项目总投资73亿元，电站总装机容量120万kW。工程建成后将承担华东电网的调峰、填谷、调频、调相及紧急事故备用等任务，发电收入可达10亿元，年创税收超1亿元。

12月10～12日　水电水利规划设计总院在湖南省长沙市主持召开了湖南沅水托口水电站工程调整概算审查会议。会议基本同意该报告，同时对调整概算报告提出了修改完善意见，并要求持续推进相关问题的落实，尽快完成调整概算工作。该电站位于湖南省洪江市境内，枢纽建筑物由东游祠主坝（含泄水建筑物）、白土冲副坝、王麻溪副坝及坝后式电站厂房、引水系统、通航建筑物和河湾地块防渗工程等组成。电站装机容量83万kW（4×20万kW+2×1.5万kW生态放水小机组），多年平均电量为21.31亿kW·h，年利用小时2664h。

12月11日　乌东德电站送电广东广西特高压多端直流示范工程全面开工建设。该工程为世界首个特高压多端混合直流输电工程，工程建成后直接将云南清洁水电输送到两广地区。该工程西起云南昆明，落点分别为广西柳州、广东惠州，采用±800kV三端混合直流技术，送电规模达800万kW，直流线路全长1489km，计划于2020年投产送电，2021年全部建成投产。工程建成后，每年可送电320亿kW·h，相当于减少燃煤消耗920万t，减排二氧化碳2450万t。

12月12日　中国葛洲坝集团有限公司与哈萨克斯坦阿拉伊—奥伊尔有限公司签订了哈萨克斯坦腾太科河上游5座梯级水电站项目合同协议。腾太科河上游5座梯级水电站装机容量约48万kW，该项目内容包括5座梯级水电站的大坝、引水隧洞、厂房、机组、辅助设施和220kV输变电线路等。项目合同金额为15.01亿美元，总工期60个月。

12月13日　中共中央组织部有关负责同志宣布了中央关于中国大唐集团有限公司董事长、党组书记任职的决定：陈飞虎同志任中国大唐集团有限公司董事长、党组书记，免去其中国大唐集团有限公司总经理职务。

12月13日　中共中央组织部有关负责同志宣布了中央关于国家电网有限公司董事长、党组书记任职的决定：寇伟同志任国家电网有限公司董事长、党组书记，免去其国家电网有限公司总经理职务。

12月14～22日　中国水利水电建设工程咨询有限公司组织安全鉴定专家组，在成都顺利完成猴子岩枢纽工程竣工安全鉴定第三次现场活动。专家组综合分析认为：猴子岩水电站枢纽工程布置合理，工程设计符合国家和行业规程规范要求。工程建设程序和建设管理规范，枢纽工程已按审批的设计标准、规模与方案全部建成，枢纽土建工程、安全监测工程、金属结构和机电工程的施工、制造与安装质量满足设计、合同文件以及有关技术标准要求。目前，工程已全部完建，各建筑物及相应设备处于安全状态，具备枢纽工程专项竣工验收条件。该电站位于四川省甘孜藏族自治州康定市境内，水库正常蓄水位 1842.00m，总库容 7.06 亿 m^3，电站装机容量 170 万 kW（42.5 万 kW×4 台）。枢纽建筑物主要由拦河坝、两岸泄洪及放空建筑物、右岸地下引水发电系统等组成。

12 月 21 日 继 12 月 12 日白鹤滩水电站工程左岸首台（1 号）百万千瓦机组座环成功吊装后，右岸首台（14 号）百万千瓦机组座环也成功“迁入新居”。至此，白鹤滩水电站工程左右两岸机组安装工作均已全面铺开。

12 月 21 日 受贵州省发展改革委委托，水电水利规划设计总院在贵阳市组织召开乌江思林水电站枢纽工程专项验收工作会议。经会议讨论审议，形成了《贵州乌江思林水电站枢纽工程专项验收鉴定书》，验收委员会同意乌江思林水电站通过枢纽工程专项验收。该电站位于贵州省铜仁市思南县境内，工程以发电为主，其次为航运，兼顾防洪、灌溉等。水库正常蓄水位 440.00m，相应库容 12.05 亿 m^3，调节库容 3.17 亿 m^3，具有日调节性能，在和上游构皮滩水电站联合调度下，具备周调节性能。电站装机容量 105 万 kW（4×26.25 万 kW），保证出力 30.36 万 kW，多年平均发电量 40.72 亿 kW·h。

12 月 24～26 日 水电水利规划设计总院会同云南省搬迁安置办公室在昆明主持召开了金沙江向家坝水电站移民安置实施阶段建设征地移民安置实施规划设计调整报告评审会议。会议认为：因各种原因，实施规划调整报告反映的内容还不全面。会议要求相关单位按照本次会议的评审意见对实施规划调整报告和相关项目的专题设计报告进行修改完善，加快向家坝水电站云南库区移民安置收口工作。

12 月 26 日 乌东德水电站工程 2018 年“双百”目标圆满完成（全年实现大坝升高超过 100m，混凝土浇筑突破 100 万 m^3）。大坝全面进入了泄洪孔口复杂部位施工阶段，检测数据表明各项指标均满足设计要求，大坝工程质量优良。该电站大坝为混凝土双曲拱坝，最大坝高 270m，大坝共 15 个坝段，混凝土总量超过 270 万 m^3，采用 3 台平移式缆机浇筑，计划 2020 年 6 月浇筑到顶。

12 月 26 日 受湖北省能源局委托，水电水利规划设计总院在隔河岩组织召开水布垭水电站工程竣工验收会。验收鉴定书认为：湖北清江水布垭水电站枢纽工程已按批准的设计规模、设计方案全部建成，电站功能已实现。8 个专项验收已完成，收委员会同意湖北清江水布垭水电站通过工程竣工验收。该工程位于清江中游河段湖北恩施土家族苗族自治州巴东县境内，总装机容量 184 万 kW，设计年发电 39.84 亿 kW·h，混凝土面板堆石坝高 233m，截至目前，电站已累计发电 405 亿 kW·h。

12 月 27 日 2019 年全国能源工作会议在北京召开。会议总结 2018 年工作成绩，分析当前面临形势，部署 2019 年重点任务。国家发展改革委党组书记、主任何立峰，国家能源局党组书记、局长章建华出席会议并讲话。2018 年，能源发展主要目标任务顺利完成，进一步巩固发展了稳中向好、稳中提质的良好态势，可再生能源装机容量突破 7 亿 kW。其中，水电、风电、光伏发电装机容量分别达到 3.5 亿 kW、1.8 亿 kW 和 1.7 亿 kW。“三弃”状况好转，预计全年弃风率、弃光率同比分别下降 4.3 个和 3 个百分点，水能利用率 95%左右。

12 月 28 日 西藏昌都瓦托水电站首台（3 号）机组进入 72 小时运行。该电站是澜沧江支流金河水电规划中的第五个梯级电站，坝址位于西藏昌都市卡若镇乃帕村下游约 2.5km 处。电站装机容量为 5 万 kW，共安装 3 台混流式水轮发电机组，是一座以发电为主的中型水电工程。工程建设者克服气候干燥、高原缺氧等不适，针对重点及难点，确保机组顺利进入 72 小时运行。

12 月 28 日 黑水河鱼类栖息地生态修复工程开工仪式在四川省凉山彝族自治州宁南县老木河电站闸坝现场举行。黑水河流域面积 3591km^2，是 47 种鱼类的栖息地，其中 16 种为长江上游特有鱼类。工程建成后将作为鱼类栖息地保护生态试验场，为白鹤滩水电站库区鱼类提供适宜的水生生境，生态修复工程分为两个阶段进行建设。目前开工的第一阶段将持续至 2020 年，以重点保护区和试验区作为重点工作区段；第二阶段将以观察区的方案优化和建设为主，预计于 2021 年启动，并于 2025 年全部完工。

12 月 31 日 截至当日 24 时，三峡集团长江电力 2018 年度发电量达 2154.8 亿 kW·h，创造了长江干流梯级电站发电量新纪录。长江电力已连续 3 年年发电量超过 2000 亿 kW·h。其中，三峡电站年发电量达 1016.2 亿 kW·h；溪洛渡电站年发电量达 624.7 亿 kW·h；向家坝电站年发电量达 330.8 亿 kW·h；葛洲坝电站年发电量达 183.2 亿 kW·h。

12 月 31 日 由三峡集团中水电公司以 EPC 模式承建的乌干达伊辛巴水电站首台机组正式并网发电。该项目主要包括发电厂房、溢洪道、2 座重力连接坝、左右岸堆石坝以及输变电线路工程，安装 4 台轴流转桨式机组，总装机容量 18.32 万 kW，完建后年平均发电量 10.39 亿 kW·h。

12 月 31 日 在新疆准东经济技术开发区辖区内的±1100kV 昌吉换流站第二个高端换流器成功解锁，标志着昌吉—古泉±1100kV 特高压直流输电工程双极全压送电成功，我国自主设计建设的世界首个±1100kV 特高压直流输电工程实现工程应用。该工程于2015年12月获国家核准，2016年1月开工建设，起于新疆昌吉回族自治州昌吉换流站，止于安徽宣城市古泉换流站，途经甘肃、宁夏、陕西、河南；线路全长3293km，额定电压±1100kV，输电容量1200万kW，是目前世界上电压等级最高、输送容量最大、输电距离最远、技术水平最先进的输电工程。

12月31日 当日24时，云南澜沧江黄登水电站4号机组顺利通过72小时试运行，正式投产发电。至此，黄登水电站4台机组全部投产发电。该电站位于怒江州兰坪县营盘镇境内，共安装4台47.5万kW混流式水轮发电机组，总装机容量190万kW，多年平均发电量85.7亿kW·h。电站枢纽主要由碾压混凝土重力坝、坝身泄洪表孔、左/右岸泄洪放空底孔、左岸折线坝坝身进水口、左岸地下引水发电系统等组成，其中，碾压混凝土重力坝高203m。7月5日首台（1号）、7月12日2号、8月16日3号机组相继完成72小时试运行正式投入商业运营。2018年高水平完成了4台机组投产发电目标。

12月31日 当日24时，云南澜沧江大华桥水电站4号机组一次性通过72小时运行，正式投入商业运营。至此，大华桥水电站4台机组全部投产发电。该电站位于云南省怒江州兰坪县兔峨乡境内，安装4台23万kW混流式水轮发电机组，总装机容量92万kW，多年平均发电量39.18亿kW·h。电站主要枢纽建筑物由碾压混凝土重力坝、左岸地下引水发电系统等组成，其中，碾压混凝土坝坝高106m。6月9日首台（1号）、6月25日2号、7月12日3号机组相继完成72小时试运行正式投入商业运营。2018年内实现“一年四投”的业绩。

12月31日 当日24时，澜沧江乌弄龙水电站首台（1号）机组通过72小时试运行，正式投入商业运行。该电站位于云南省迪庆州维西县巴迪乡境内的澜沧江上游河段上，是澜沧江上游河段规划7个梯级电站中的第二级电站，安装4台混流式水轮发电机组，总装机容量99万kW，多年平均发电量44.51亿kW·h。水库正常蓄水位1906.00m。电站枢纽主要建筑物由碾压混凝土重力坝、坝身泄洪建筑物、右岸地下引水发电厂房系统等组成。

12月31日 当日24时，云南澜沧江里底水电站2号机组经过72小时试运行，正式投产发电。至此，里底水电站已有2台机组投产发电。该电站位于云南省迪庆藏族自治州维西傈僳族自治县巴迪乡境内，安装3台14万kW轴流转桨式水轮发电机组，总装机容量42万kW，多年平均发电量17.53亿kW·h。该工程枢纽由电站厂房、溢洪道、泄洪底孔、左、右岸非溢流坝段、中控楼及开关站等建筑物组成。10月29日首台（1号）机组顺利通过72小时试运行，提前投入商业运行。